# The Cambridge History of Seventeenth-Century Philosophy

## Volume II

EDITED BY

DANIEL GARBER

*University of Chicago*

MICHAEL AYERS

*Wadham College, University of Oxford*

with the assistance of Roger Ariew and Alan Gabbey

CAMBRIDGE
UNIVERSITY PRESS

PUBLISHED BY THE PRESS SYNDICATE OF THE UNIVERSITY OF CAMBRIDGE
The Pitt Building, Trumpington Street, Cambridge CB2 1RP, United Kingdom

CAMBRIDGE UNIVERSITY PRESS
The Edinburgh Building, Cambridge CB2 2RU, United Kingdom
40 West 20th Street, New York, NY 10011-4211, USA
10 Stamford Road, Oakleigh, Melbourne 3166, Australia

First published 1998

Printed in the United States of America

Typeset in Bembo

*A catalog record for this book is available from the British Library.*

*Library of Congress Cataloging-in-Publication Data*
The Cambridge history of seventeenth-century philosophy / edited by
Daniel Garber, Michael Ayers, with the assistance of Roger Ariew and
Alan Gabbey.
p.   cm.
Includes bibliographical references and indexes.
ISBN 0-521-58864-2
1. Philosophy, Modern – 17th century. I.  Garber, Daniel, 1949–
II. Ayers, Michael, 1935–
B801.C35   1997                    96-25475
190'.9'032–dc20                    CIP

Volume II ISBN 0-521-57233-9 hardback
Available only as a set: ISBN 0-521-58864-2 hardback

# CONTENTS

## VOLUME I

## III God

## IV Body and the Physical World

## VII Will, Action, and Moral Philosophy

# VI

# THE UNDERSTANDING

# THE COGNITIVE FACULTIES

## GARY HATFIELD

During the seventeenth century the major cognitive faculties – sense, imagination, memory, and understanding (or intellect)[1] – became the focus of argument in metaphysics and epistemology to an extent not seen before. The theory of the intellect, long an important auxiliary to metaphysics, moved to the centre of metaphysical dispute, especially concerning the scope and powers of the intellect and the existence of a 'pure' intellect. Rationalist metaphysicians such as Descartes, Spinoza, and Malebranche claimed that intellectual knowledge, gained independently of the senses, provides the framework for constructing a new theory of nature. Other writers, including Hobbes and Gassendi, denied the existence of a distinct intellectual faculty, and so challenged the metaphysicians' abilities to perceive the essences of substances directly. The theory of the senses, which had long been a part of philosophical discussion, took on a new urgency, for adherents of the new corpuscularian philosophy needed to replace the dominant Aristotelian theory of real sensory qualities and sensible species. The revival of scepticism and a renewed interest in method also brought the faculties into prominence, for sceptical challenges typically were directed towards the faculties of sense and understanding, and the theory of method was conceived as providing instructions for the proper use of one's cognitive equipment.

The theory of the faculties, then, is an important key to theories of knowledge in the seventeenth century. Indeed, rather than speak of seventeenth-century epistemology, it would be less anachronistic and more informative to speak of theories of cognition. The familiar (and over-stated) point that epistemology became fundamental to metaphysics during that century[2] can then be recast as the point that the theory of faculties became central in metaphysical dispute. Evidence for this change includes several works of general philosophical scope that contain 'understanding' in the title[3] or in which the theory of the faculties provides an organising principle.[4]

Following a survey of Renaissance and late scholastic theories of the faculties, succeeding sections of this chapter examine the cognitive faculties in connexion with scepticism, the search for new methods, the new corpuscularian philosophy, rationalist metaphysics, Cambridge Platonism, Locke and Berkeley, and the theory of cognition considered generally.

## I. THE FACULTIES IN RENAISSANCE AND LATE SCHOLASTIC PHILOSOPHY

The seventeenth century inherited a general classification of the cognitive faculties or powers. In the common scholastic Aristotelian terminology, the intellectual powers were separated from the sensory, and the latter were divided into internal and external senses. The external senses are the familiar five: vision, hearing, smell, taste, and touch. There was disagreement over the number of internal senses, but a basic list would include memory, imagination, common sense, and estimation (or cogitation).[5] Memory was ascribed both to internal sense and to the intellectual faculty; it was ascribed to the latter to account for memory of concepts and to allow for personal immortality. The faculty of imagination was said to receive images from the senses and produce images of objects that are not actually present, as when one imagines the face or voice of a friend ('image' suggests sight, but imagination extends to other senses). The common sense was viewed as the Aristotelian *koine*; it cognises and compares the deliverances of the individual external senses. The 'estimative' or 'cogitative' power was ascribed to animals – to whom intellection was denied – in order to account for discriminative powers extending beyond the proper and common sensibles, and for the ability to act appropriately in novel circumstances; it was included among the sensory powers of the human soul.

### 1. *Platonist versus Aristotelian theories*

The most general division in sixteenth- and early seventeenth-century writings on the faculties falls along Platonic and Aristotelian lines. The Platonist tradition includes Augustine and Renaissance Platonists such as Ficino and Giovanni Pico della Mirandola, while the Aristotelian includes Thomas Aquinas, Duns Scotus, and the authors of the late scholastic revival, notably, Toletus, Suárez, the Coimbran commentators, and Rubius. The two traditions, examined from the perspective of this discussion, differ primarily over the ontology of sense and intellect and the respective rôles of these faculties in the acquisition of knowledge.

Platonist authors maintained that the intellect can operate independently of the senses. By this they meant not merely that we can think without using the sensory faculties at the same time, but, more fundamentally, that the intellect can contemplate intelligible objects which are unavailable to the senses. The primary objects of such intellectual knowledge are spiritual or immaterial beings: God, souls, and immaterial Forms or archetypes. According to Ficino, universal Forms inhabit four worlds, including the human intellect and the prime intellect; he designates the latter as the seat of 'the first, intelligible, and ideal species', these being 'the preeminent objects for the intellectual eyes of all minds'.[6] He and other Platonists also held that reason and intellect reside in a separate rational soul, which is joined to the fleshly body through an intermediate body, a 'delicate and airy body which physicians and philosophers call spirit'. Between this 'intervening spirit' and the rational soul humans have a sensitive soul, shared with the beasts, which is the seat of sense and imagination. The sensitive soul causes error by diverting the rational soul from its intelligible objects.[7] The Platonist thinkers also held that the rational soul is 'impassible' (not susceptible to change) and thus cannot be affected by the body. This tenet flirted with the unorthodox position that the body is the mere instrument of the soul in the sense that the soul resides in it as does a captain in a ship.[8] Although Aristotelians, too, believed that a 'higher' being such as the human intellect cannot be causally affected by corporeal things acting alone (including the bodily states), they did not agree, as the Platonists maintained, that the intellect can operate independently of the body even in the acquisition of natural knowledge, by apprehending Forms or archetypes in the mind of God or ectypes residing in human minds.

Aristotelian authors denied that the soul is a separate substance joined to bodily substance and operating independently of the senses. Ontologically, they maintained that the soul of a living human being is the 'form' (see Chapter 23) of the body (although it can exist as a separate form after death), and they denied that the rational and sensory souls are distinct (a position attributed to Plato). They assigned intellection and sentience to a unitary human soul simply as powers.[9] Epistemologically, they held that all knowledge arises through the senses, including the knowledge of both nature and God. Orthodox Aristotelians argued that (in this life) every act of thought, including intellection, requires a material phantasm. At the same time, the intellect was not unimportant in the Aristotelian account of cognition, for it was uniquely responsible for abstracting 'intelligible species' (which are universals or common natures; see Chapter 8) from the sensible forms or species of particular bodies as received by the senses.[10]

Scholastic Aristotelian discussions of the faculties occupied a large literature full of lively and often incisive argumentation. Perhaps because Aristotelian theory asserted that all human knowledge (or at least all 'natural' knowledge) derives from the senses, the entire chain of cognition from the external senses through the internal senses to the intellect was the object of extensive scrutiny and debate.

These discussions are found primarily in the *De anima* commentaries and associated disputations.[11] As did textbook treatments of Aristotelian philosophy, these
works discussed the soul and its powers under the rubric of physics, the rationale
being that the soul is the form of a corporeal being, the human animal; even the
soul considered as a separable, immaterial substance was treated as a subject of
physics, though many contended that the separable soul was properly the subject
of metaphysics.[12] The faculty of the intellect and its various operations, together
with the rôles of the senses, imagination, and intellect in the abstraction of
intelligible species, were also discussed (albeit briefly) in commentaries on Aristotle's logical works.[13]

Leaving aside their subtle differences, the *De anima* writings of Suárez, the
Coimbrans, Toletus, Rubius, and the textbooks of Eustachius a Sancto Paulo and
Keckermann, among others, suggest the following generalised Aristotelian account of the chain of cognition. Cognition is a process by which the knower
comes to be in a way like the known thing. The process begins when the form of
a sensible quality of an object alters the sense organ, as in taste and touch, or an
intervening medium, as in vision, hearing, and smell.[14] Eventually, whether in the
medium or in the senses, the sensible quality produces an 'intentional species',[15]
or 'sensible species',[16] or just 'species',[17] which was said to 'represent' the quality
in the object. The species is received by the sensory power without literally
rendering the power coloured or warm or odorous; following Aristotle, its reception was described as that of a 'form' or 'species' 'without matter'.[18] Upon
receiving a species (passively), the sensory power is actualised to its characteristic
sensory activity (and it is to that extent active); in the act of sensing, a kind of
identity arises between the sensory power and the object sensed, which identity
permits the power to be 'directed toward' or 'attentive of' the object, and so to
cognise it. Each sense discriminates its 'proper sensible' – colour in the case of
vision, odour in olfaction, and so on – and some, including touch and vision,
discriminate common sensibles such as shape, size, and number. The 'common
sense' discriminates among the objects of the special senses (e.g., it discriminates
white from sweet). The species received by the external senses are retained as
'phantasms' in the internal senses. These phantasms are corporeal in nature; that
is, they are states of the corporeal organs informed by the sensitive power of the
soul. The cognitive acts of the sensitive power of the soul are adequate for the
perception (by the 'estimative power') of potential benefits and harms afforded by
the external bodies represented through the phantasms. Cognition of the natures
or essences of bodies requires intellection. The immaterial intellect 'illuminates'
the phantasm and abstracts the essence or 'common nature' of the represented

thing. The intellect knows by means of the phantasm present in a bodily organ, but, being immaterial, and not being the form of any bodily organ (even while remaining a power of the form of the human body), it does not receive the corporeal phantasm into itself. Rather, the 'agent intellect', 'together with the phantasm', produces an (immaterial) intelligible species in the 'patient' or 'possible' intellect. Reception of the phantasm by the patient intellect completes the act of understanding.[19] Finally, intellectual operations can be divided into three types: simple apprehension (of a form or forms), judgement (which entails predication), and discursive reasoning (as in a syllogism). Aristotelians ascribed these acts to the intellect alone, restricting the will primarily to sensory and intellectual desire.[20]

## 2. The senses: Intentional species and the visual pyramid

The notions of sensible and intentional species generated extensive discussion in the scholastic literature. Stringent theoretical demands were placed on these notions by the broader Aristotelian theory within which they functioned. The positing of species was driven by the Aristotelian theory that, in knowing, the soul must become 'like' the object known. This posit was constrained by the belief that the sensory soul does not unite with objects themselves nor take on, in the ordinary way, the qualities of things (such as heat or colour). An intentional species, in order to mediate cognition of an object, must be 'like' or 'similar to' a quality in the object without, as received by the sensory power, itself being a perceivable instance of that quality. Furthermore, it must mediate cognition of the object without violating the principle that species are that 'by which' objects are cognised, but not that which is itself cognised.[21]

Intentional species establish contact between the cogniser and the cognised by *representing* external objects; the representative relation arises from a *similitude* between species and object.[22] Although textbook authors such as Eustachius and Keckermann expressed this relation by calling species 'images' of objects, Toletus, Suárez, and Rubius were careful to observe that species could not be 'formal images', 'pictures', or 'formal similitudes' of objects; they argued that, so understood, species would displace external objects as the objects of perception.[23] In either case, it is difficult to understand how something can have a similitude with a quality, without itself being a perceivable instance of that quality. It might appear that the designation of species as 'intentional' solves this problem by rendering them mind-dependent and thereby placing the similitude in the eye of the beholder. But among scholastic Aristotelian authors the term 'intentional' did not always suggest mind dependence. Intentional species, in particular, were accorded mind-independent reality, as was their similitude with qualities. Further, intentional species, in the medium as well as in the external and internal sense organs, were said never to be without conditions of materiality, even while being forms 'without matter' (that is, forms that are not conjoined to matter in the usual way).[24] The being of such species, although denominated as 'intentional' by Toletus, Suárez, and Rubius, was considered by them to be a species of *real being* (rather than merely *rational being*).[25] Intentional species of colour are really there in the air or in some other medium, and they have a kind of similitude with the colours of objects, even if they do not instantiate those colours in the usual way and so cannot themselves be sensed (effecting no sensible species of their own). As a modifier of 'species', the term 'intentional' suggested two things: that such species serve to represent a distal object so that, when received by the sensory power, they direct that power towards the object; and that their corporeal being in the medium and organs is attenuated by comparison with qualities in objects.[26]

The denomination of intentional species as images was subsequently ridiculed by Descartes, who boasted that his optical theory dispensed with 'all those little images flitting through the air, called *intentional species,* which so worry the imagination of Philosophers'.[27] This criticism distorts the late scholastic understanding of optical theory and intentional species. The commentators who called species 'images' were not positing coherent images that fly through the air, like Epicurean *eidola*; rather, they adopted the perspectivist analysis of the transmission of colour through the medium. According to perspectivist theory, which was worked out in the technical optical literature[28] and summarised in the *De anima* tracts,[29] from each point on an illuminated object, rays of light are transmitted in all directions. Because the rays proceed from each point on the object in right lines to all points in the medium (barring opaque obstructions), all points of the object are represented at any point in the medium. At the eye – or at the crystalline humour – only rays normal to the surface are sensed; this selective receptivity establishes a point-for-point mapping between points on the object and points on the surface of the crystalline. This means that a cross-section of a 'visual pyramid' – a pyramid with its base on a distant object and its apex inside the crystalline – is received and sensed by the eye. This cross-section is transmitted along the optic nerve into the brain and to the common sense. It has the characteristics of a two-dimensional picture or image of the object at the base of the pyramid. It is to this extent geometrically equivalent to the retinal image as described by Kepler and Descartes (but without being inverted). It thus was accurate for Descartes to say that the scholastics were committed to images being conveyed into the brain, in the sense that a two-dimensional pattern is so conveyed; but Descartes, too, was committed to such a transmission.[30] Descartes's criticism of the imagistic character of intentional species, to the extent that it reflects a proper understanding of previous optical theory, over-generalises from the legitimate differences between his sensory theory and the scholastics' regarding colour as a 'real quality', the scholastic theory having the implication, rejected by Descartes, that there is something in the object 'similar to' the colour we experience phenomenally.

### 3. The intellect and its immateriality

The immateriality of the rational soul and of its intellectual power received special attention in the *De anima* commentaries and related treatises.[31] Much was at stake in these discussions, including the intelligibility of the Aristotelian account of the chain of cognition, the plausibility of personal immortality, and the possibility of natural cognition of God and other immaterial entities.

The notion that intelligible species are received into the intellect raised difficult questions concerning the interaction between the states of the sensory faculties (which are corporeal) and the immaterial intellect. According to standard Aristotelian theory, the act of intellection is completed when an intelligible species is received by the possible intellect, having been 'abstracted' from the corporeal phantasm. The language of abstraction may suggest that the sensible species (or at least the universal form or common nature found in it), having been 'purified' by the light of the agent intellect, is simply absorbed into the possible intellect. And yet it cannot be so. The sensible species (and any form found in it) is always bound up with material conditions. Aristotelian authors generally agreed that a phantasm, because it is corporeal, cannot by itself act on the possible intellect (an immaterial power of the soul), let alone be absorbed by it. The agent intellect, being immaterial itself, can so act, but not on its own accord; it must be determined in its action by a phantasm. Consequently, the agent intellect was considered the primary cause, and the phantasm was variously designated a 'material', 'instrumental', or 'partial' cause of the formation of intelligible species.[32] The coming into being of intelligible species is an act of the agent intellect, which was said to be capable of 'making all things'; the species is created in the patient intellect, which is capable of 'becoming all things'. The 'making' of the agent intellect, while dependent on a material phantasm, also requires a disposition on the part of the intellect. Aquinas had asserted that the light of the human intellect is a 'participated likeness' of the 'uncreated' (divine) light that contains the eternal types.[33] Later authors agreed that the intellect cannot literally receive phantasms, and indeed that it must 'make' the intelligible species. They nonetheless maintained that the intellect is a 'tabula rasa' (containing no innate species) and that phantasms derived from sense play an essential rôle in the creation of intelligible species.[34]

No question was more widely disputed in the *De anima* commentaries and the attendant literature than the ontology of the agent and patient intellects. That is to say, is the individual human soul, considered as the form of the human body, adequate by itself to perform the acts of understanding that humans do perform? The orthodox position – which had been held by Thomas and Scotus, and was affirmed by the Coimbrans, Toletus, Suárez, and Rubius – was that the individual human soul can function on its own and requires no help from a separate intellectual substance or from direct divine illumination.[35] Others disagreed. Augustinians maintained that the human soul by itself is incapable of grasping the forms or ideas of things without illumination from God.[36] Avicenna and Averroes had held that the agent intellect, or both the agent and possible intellect, exist separately from the individual human soul; according to their doctrine, individual sensitive souls inform individual human bodies, but all humans share a single intellect.[37] Zabarella repudiated Averroes while contending that the agent intellect is none other than God. In common with the Alexandrist tradition, he maintained that the 'organic soul' – the vegetative and sensitive soul – is the form of the material body, arising naturally from the potentiality of the matter of the body in humans just as it does in beasts; furthermore, an agent intellect must be posited to explain the act of abstraction, and it must be identified with the 'most intelligible' substance, namely, God, a position Zabarella attributed to Plato and Aristotle.[38] Earlier in the century, Pomponazzi reasoned that when the nature of the human soul is examined from the point of view of the philosopher who uses 'natural' arguments (arguments based upon natural reason, apart from faith and revelation), the most important arguments pertain to the 'mode of operation' of intellect and specifically to whether the immaterial objects of intellection demand an immaterial agent. In his view, the soul considered as subject is immaterial and independent of the body, but it requires the body as its object of thought; because of the latter requirement, he concluded that 'the human intellect in all its operations is the act of an organic body.' This led him to the further conclusion that the soul considered absolutely is material and mortal.[39] His position was perceived as one to be avoided.

These disagreements over the ontology of the intellect reveal a deeper common assumption, that an immaterial agency is required for the apprehension of universals, or of immaterial beings such as God and the soul. Corporeally based faculties – including the individual soul when considered as a form actualising the

potentiality of bodily organs, as in the case of the sensitive and imaginal powers –
were judged inadequate to such cognitive tasks. While the orthodox Aristotelian
position that the intellect is a power of the form of the human body and
always operates with a corporeal phantasm may seem contrary to this common
assumption, it is not; orthodox Aristotelians held that the intellect is not itself
the form of any bodily organ and that it operates as an immaterial intellectual
power.[40]

Those who posited an immaterial human intellect disagreed over its adequacy
for cognising wholly immaterial substances, such as God and the soul. Aristotelians
commonly held that human beings do not have direct natural cognition of such
substances. The Aristotelian dictum that all thought requires a phantasm, combined with the position that there are no phantasms of God and the soul, entailed
that in this life God and the soul are known only by their effects – God through
created things, the soul through its cognitive acts as directed towards the body –
and only confusedly, at that. As Toletus expressed it, an embodied intellect 'cannot
naturally possess clear and distinct cognition of immaterial substance'. Aquinas,
the Coimbrans, Rubius, and Eustachius expressed similar positions.[41] Platonists of
course turned the Aristotelian account on its head, contending that knowledge
arises in the first instance from the intellect, which directly perceives immaterial
Forms or Ideas.[42] Others combined an Aristotelian account of sensory and intellectual cognition of nature with a Platonic or Augustinian account of knowledge
of God and the soul. Albert the Great was known to have ascribed knowledge of
nature to abstraction from sensibles and knowledge of God and the soul to
intellectual intuition without a phantasm.[43] The question of whether human
beings enjoy immediate cognition of immaterial substance through the intellect
remained a central problem of metaphysics through the time of Kant.

## II. THE COGNITIVE FACULTIES AND SCEPTICISM

The sixteenth century saw increased interest in ancient sceptical arguments, both
Academic and Pyrrhonian, as vetted in Cicero's *Academia*, Diogenes Laertius's
*Lives*, and the writings of Sextus Empiricus (see Chapter 32). Among the various
arguments, some proceeded by attacking human knowledge at its sources, in the
faculties of sense and intellect.

Seventeenth-century philosophers used scepticism primarily to curb the pretensions of metaphysics. Montaigne's follower Charron used sceptical arguments
to undermine confidence in theoretical knowledge in order to direct readers to
the 'proper' study of humankind, humankind itself. Charron adopted a modified

version of the Aristotelian conception of the soul and its faculties, recognising vegetative, sensitive, apprehensive or imaginative, appetitive, and intellectual faculties; he then further subdivided the faculties of the human mind to include imagination or apprehension, reason, ratiocination, wit, judgement, understanding, and volition.[44] He observed that human beings, although naturally desiring knowledge, cannot reach genuine first principles because of deficient cognitive faculties.[45] Charron decried the 'faultiness and incertitude' of the senses, alluding to standard arguments, including cases of illness, in which things appear 'other than they are'; failures of sight at great distance, as when the sun appears much smaller than reason considers it to be; contradictions between senses which must be adjudicated by reason, as in the case of the infamous half-submerged stick; and examples in which animals surpass humans in sensory acuity.[46] While affirming the immateriality and immortality of the rational soul, he observed that it must operate by means of a bodily instrument, and that variations in this instrument dispose individuals to be better or worse reasoners. Because of bodily conditions, one cannot simultaneously achieve excellence of understanding, imagination, and memory. The understanding, he reasoned, operates best when the brain is dry, imagination when it is hot, and memory when it is wet; but wet is directly contrary to dry, while heat dries the brain and agitates the animal spirits excessively, thereby harming memory and disrupting the operation of the understanding.[47] Furthermore, humans should be humble about their rational powers, for beasts do reason, and there is greater distance between the rational ability of the best and worst human thinker than there is between humans and beasts – although humans are separated from beasts by their immaterial intellectual power, which is distinct from the merely discursive rational power shared with beasts.[48] Alluding to the great diversity in human opinions, Charron concluded that first principles cannot be found by humans on their own and are known only to God (who sometimes reveals them). Human beings should use their faulty cognitive faculties to cultivate such instrumental knowledge as they can glean and should spend the larger part of their study time in pursuit of moral wisdom.[49]

Other authors, including Sanchez, Mersenne, Gassendi, and Glanvill, used sceptical arguments to attack Aristotelian metaphysics in order to replace it with a more epistemically modest attitude towards natural human knowledge of nature. Sanchez, whose *Quod nihil scitur* appeared in 1581 and was reprinted in 1618 and after, argued that the Aristotelian quest for 'scientific' knowledge should be replaced by a search for empirical learning derived from actual experience with things.[50] He divided all knowledge into two kinds:

One kind is perfect, the kind by which a thing examined from all sides, both inside and outside, is understood [*intelligitur*]. And this is scientific knowledge [*scientia*], such as we should now like to acquire for Man – but science itself wishes otherwise. The other kind is imperfect, the kind by which a thing is apprehended by any means at all and after any fashion whatever. This is the kind with which we are familiar.[51]

'Scientific knowledge', or cognition properly so called, is beyond the limited intellectual and sensory capacities of humankind. The intellect must rely on the senses for its information; all cognition of external objects is sense-based. But the senses perceive 'only the outward appearances of things'; the natures of things 'can by no means be grasped by the senses', which cognise only 'accidents' such as colour, size, and shape, and even those imperfectly.[52] Further, the understanding depends on the instrument of the body for all acts of cognition. But in order to achieve the perfect cognition that constitutes science, this instrument would need itself to be perfect, which it never is, or, if it were for an instant, could not remain.[53] Sanchez finally commends the investigator to the investigation of nature under the guidance of 'experience' and 'judgement'. This investigation is tempered by realisation that 'nothing is known', but it nonetheless can result in the acquisition of a body of experience that guides one's interactions with things.[54]

Several seventeenth-century promoters of the new philosophy used sceptical arguments to challenge the adequacy of the faculties for achieving metaphysical knowledge. To this end, Mersenne, Gassendi, and Glanvill present sceptical critiques of the senses and intellect (and, to lesser extent, the imagination). Gassendi and Glanvill, harsh critics of Aristotelian philosophy, placed metaphysical knowledge in general beyond the pale of human faculties. The senses received the greatest attention, perhaps because, as Gassendi put it, 'the mind reasons only from those things that have appeared to the senses', or, as Glanvill had it, 'the knowledge we have comes from our senses.'[55] Though each contended that the understanding is incapable of achieving metaphysical knowledge (of the essences of things), they agreed in recommending the careful use of the understanding to sort through sensory appearances in order to frame useful (and possibly true) hypotheses for explaining those appearances; Gassendi preferred atomistic hypotheses, and Glanvill commended the aetherial philosophy of Descartes, endorsing a corpuscular account of sensory qualities.[56] Gassendi thereby rejected the position of his early *Exercitationes*, according to which only appearances can be known, now affirming that the intellect brings its own criterion to judgement and that it may indeed come to know things beyond the appearances, by inferring from 'indicative' sensory 'signs' to 'hidden' natural causes.[57]

Previously, Mersenne, in his *La verité des sciences* of 1625, had defended Aristotelian and other types of philosophy against sceptical attack. His defence was measured, and his examples of metaphysical and physical knowledge were modest, including the principle of contradiction and the maxim that natural bodies are moveable; but he also defended a common-sense version of the law of cause.[58] He classified the ten modes and other standard sceptical arguments by their relations to a cognitive faculty: the sceptic uses sensory phenomena to question sensory phenomena, intellectual to question intellectual, or sensory intellectual.[59] In 1625 Mersenne asserted that the senses are not deceived when used under proper conditions; and he held that although 'the understanding receives nothing except by the senses', nonetheless it is possessed of an indigenous 'spiritual and universal' or 'natural' light, which is undeceived in its proper operations, and by which it goes beyond the senses.[60] He conceded in effect that current knowledge consists largely of mere phenomenal regularities and does not penetrate to essences but contended that such knowledge suffices for 'science'; moreover, the understanding, when used properly, might attain knowledge of essences.[61] In the *Questions* of 1634 he expressed the more circumspect opinion that human knowledge will be limited to surface effects until God chooses to reveal the rational principles and modes of action of things.[62] As Gassendi and Glanvill later would assert, he held that mathematical knowledge is most resistant to sceptical challenge, appealing to the examples not only of arithmetic and geometry but also of 'subalternate' (or mixed-mathematical) sciences such as optics and astronomy.[63]

In contrast to these authors, Descartes employed sceptical arguments in the *Meditationes* to make evident the intellect's ability to grasp the essences of things. Like Mersenne and Gassendi, he was interested in establishing that some knowledge exists despite the sceptic's challenge, but unlike them, he claimed that the intellect can know the essences of things by direct intuition (independent of the senses). Furthermore, he used sceptical arguments to reveal this pure use of the intellect. As he repeated often, a chief use of the sceptical doubt in the *Meditationes* was to lead the mind 'away from the senses' and so prepare it for the contemplation of intelligible things.[64] Indeed, the process of doubting carried out in the First Meditation may be seen as an exercise intended to allow the reader to discover that, contrary to Aristotelian doctrine, there can be thought without a sense-based image, thought that arises through use of the intellect alone.[65] Once discovered, the pure faculty of the intellect is put to use in contemplating God, the soul, and the essence of matter considered as pure extension or pure continuous quantity. Here scepticism is used not to curb the pretensions of metaphysics, but to reveal an underutilised route to metaphysical knowledge through proper use of the intellectual faculty.

## III. THE COGNITIVE FACULTIES AND THE QUEST FOR NEW METHODS

Among those seeking a new philosophy, many proposed that a new logic, new organon, or new method was needed to properly direct the cognitive faculties of the investigator.[66] Aristotelian logic commonly was understood by late scholastic commentators to be an aid or instrument to the natural power of the human understanding; its study was not considered a necessary condition of right understanding and correct discursive reasoning, these being natural acts of the human intellect. But the study of logic was considered the surest means to the proper and effective use of the natural cognitive powers, which otherwise easily fall into error.[67] Several of the new philosophers accepted this conception of the rôle of logic or method, while finding one or another defect with Aristotle's *Organon* as an instrument of cognition. Among those who made method a central issue, their largest differences concerned the natural power of the human faculties and the need for an elaborate method, or set of logical precepts, for guiding the understanding.

Francis Bacon was pessimistic about the natural powers of the human faculties and believed that an assisting method was needed to attain truth. He signaled his intention to provide a new lesson in the proper direction of the faculties by entitling his major work on 'method' (his term) a *Novum Organum*. Of the four 'Idols' that hinder truth and promote error, those of the tribe have their foundation 'in human nature itself', including the false 'measure' provided by the human senses and the false and distorting 'mirror' of the human understanding. Bacon further characterised the unguided senses as dull, incompetent, and deceitful,[68] but his most extensive criticism was reserved for the understanding, which, he said, even in a 'sober, patient, and grave mind' is, when left on its own, 'a thing unequal, and quite unfit to contend with the obscurity of things'.[69] Indeed, he characterised the unguided understanding as prone to hasty generalisation, mistaken impositions of order and regularity on nature, unreasonably intransigent opinions, excessive influence from present instances, an unwillingness to let explanations end, infection by affections and desires, and flights of abstraction.[70] Nonetheless, Bacon maintained that, by means of a previously unseen synthesis between experience and understanding, his method could lead the cogniser to a knowledge of true natures or forms of things.[71] To counteract defects of sense, he proposed the collection of systematic natural histories drawn from every conceivable source; as an aid to memory, these histories must be carefully arranged in tabular form; to curb the natural proclivities of the understanding, they must be examined under the firm control of Bacon's inductive method. Only through such 'ministrations' to the faculties can scientific knowledge of nature be attained.[72]

In contrast, Descartes and other rationalist metaphysicians devised methods that played to their conception of the natural strength of the human intellect. Descartes's new method for directing the mind was largely inspired by geometrical and mathematical reasoning; it enjoined the investigator to break problems into small steps, proceed from the simple to the complex, make thorough reviews, and build certain and evident cognition by 'intuition and deduction' (in the language of the *Regulae ad directionem ingenii*) or by 'clear and distinct' mental perception. In the *Regulae,* Descartes contends that an important step in comprehending a method is to survey the 'instruments of knowledge', the most basic of which is the intellect, to which may be added imagination and sense-perception.[73] He returns to this theme of testing the instruments of cognition in the *Meditationes,*[74] where through careful scrutiny the intellect is established not only as the arbiter of sensory cognition but as a faculty capable of attaining truth independent of the senses. With respect to metaphysical knowledge, at least, the key to Descartes's method of discovery is the preparation of the intellect to perceive the 'primary notions' of metaphysics, which are by nature as evident or more evident than geometrical notions, but which will not be perceived by the intellect unless the mind has been properly withdrawn from the senses. There is no need for an elaborate method once the primary notions have been found, although inattentive minds may require a methodical presentation of the first truths, by the 'method of synthesis'. The operations of the intellect in perceiving such truths are natural to it and cannot be taught; if chained together in small steps, they cannot lead to error.[75]

Later rationalist metaphysicians, despite differences with Descartes on the ontology of the intellect and its ideas, followed him in seeking simple methodological precepts that aid the natural strength of the knowing power. Spinoza, whose few sustained remarks on method come in his *Tractatus de intellectus emendatione,* maintained that the intellect must look to its own operations to discover the 'way and method' of finding the truth. The key to this 'method' is the true idea itself, which is the criterion or 'standard' for all knowledge; the mind must first discover the true idea – the idea of God or Nature – and then 'deduce' all of its other knowledge from this idea.[76] Malebranche devoted one of six books of *De la recherche de la verité* to method, the previous five having covered sense, imagination, intellect, and will. The central rule of this method is to follow clear and distinct perceptions: 'We must give full consent only to those propositions that appear so evidently true that we cannot withhold our consent without feeling inner pain and the secret reproaches of reason.'[77] He offered tips on how the senses, imagination, and passions may be employed to aid rather than hinder the intellect, but he expected little from formal rules of method:

> We should not expect anything very extraordinary here, or anything that surprises and taxes the mind very much. On the contrary, in order for these rules to be good, they must be simple and natural, few in number, very intelligible, and interdependent. In a word, they should only guide our minds and regulate our attention without dividing it, for experience shows clearly enough that Aristotle's logic is not very useful because it occupies the mind too much and diverts attention that it should have brought to bear upon the subjects it is examining.[78]

His proffered rules emphasise clarity of reasoning, distinctness of conception, and simplicity and clarity of ideas. Arnauld and Nicole, in *La logique, ou L'Art de penser,* also charge errors largely to 'hastiness of thought and lack of attention'; these are to be remedied by reflecting on the mind's natural operations. Logic consists of such reflections. It is useful because it ensures right reasoning by drawing attention to the mind's proper use, provides a systematic analysis of error, and leads to knowledge of the mind's true nature.[79] Rules of reasoning are not, however, what Arnauld and Nicole considered most useful in their logic. They maintained that 'most human errors derive not from being misled by wrong inferences but rather from slipping into false judgements from which one draws bad conclusions.' To remedy this failing, they offered some gleanings from Descartes's and Pascal's unpublished papers.[80]

Among sense-oriented philosophers, Gassendi and Hobbes produced their own logical tracts as guides to correct thinking, whereas Locke repudiated logic but did not forsake the goal of helping his readers towards a proper use of their understandings. Gassendi's and Hobbes's logics were in many ways traditional, being divided into four parts, respectively, concerning terms or concepts, propositions, syllogisms, and method. However, they departed from Aristotelian theory and from each other in their conceptions of universals and the intellect. Gassendi, having denigrated logic in his early *Exercitationes,* adopted aspects of Aristotelian logic in the late *Institutio logica.* In particular, he taught that the 'mind' (*mens*) 'abstracts' general ideas by examining singular ideas individually, 'separating out that which all have in common, at the same time disregarding or ignoring mutual differences', thereby forming a 'universal and general idea', which, as in the case of *man,* represents not any particular man but '"man" in general or in common'.[81] In the *Physica* he equated *mens* with the rational soul (and its two faculties, intellect and will), and he argued that intellect must be distinct from imagination and sense because it forms ideas (such as universals, or the 'intelligible magnitude' of the sun as opposed to its imagined size) for which imagination is inadequate.[82] In both places he departed from the usual Aristotelian teaching by contending that the intellect directly cognises singulars, and apprehends universals only through re-flection and comparison. Hobbes, by contrast, rejected any rôle for a faculty of understanding in the use of abstract and universal terms. He reduced universals to concrete 'signs' for a class of objects: 'the name "universal" is not the name of anything existing in nature, nor of an idea or of some phantasm formed in the mind, but is always the name of some vocal sound or name.' This rejection of genuine universals fit hand in glove with his denial of incorporeal agencies and an intellectual faculty. Universal or common names are connected in the imagination and memory with various 'images and phantasms of individual animals or other things'; consequently, 'there is no need to understand the force of a universal with any faculty other than the imaginative one.'[83] The term 'dog' is universal just in so far as various images of particular dogs evoke it. The fact that different dogs can evoke a single word is to be explained by 'their similitude in some quality, or other accident', and this similitude itself consists in the power to produce a certain conception in a perceiver, such as the power to produce the sensation of heat.[84] Finally, Locke, in opposition to both Gassendi and Hobbes, simply dismissed logic by charging that it promotes the abuse of words, and he gave only brief consider-ation to the rôle of the faculties in the acquisition and ordering of knowledge. He focused instead on the use and abuse of words, and he analysed the various forms that knowledge and judgements take in themselves.[85]

## IV. THE FACULTIES AMONG
## THE NEW CORPUSCULARIANS

Among those seeking a 'new' philosophy, corpuscularians (whether atomists or divisibilists) of necessity had to provide a new theory of at least one cognitive faculty, the senses, to replace the Aristotelian theory with its commitment to real qualities and sensible species. Some, like Galileo, while adopting the language of faculties and even envisioning an explanation of sensory qualities through matter in motion, never made the theory of the faculties central to their enterprise.[86] For others, a new theory of the senses, and perhaps of the relation of sense to understanding, was at the core of their new corpuscularian theory of nature. Such was the case with Descartes, Hobbes, and Gassendi.

### 1. Descartes: The senses and the intellect

Descartes adopted various strategies to justify his corpuscularian philosophy and its new theory of the senses. In his early writings he used the new theory of the senses itself as an entry into a new theory of nature; later, he used the deliverances of the intellect to frame a new theory of both nature and the senses.

In *Le monde*, the *Météores*, and the *Dioptrique*, Descartes presented a corpuscularian theory of the senses without the benefit of metaphysical justification (as also in the *Regulae*, XII, published posthumously). Such justification as was given rested on empirical adequacy and conceptual clarity, as Descartes observed in his correspondence.[87] His strategy was to undercut the Aristotelian theory of vision by presenting a corpuscular theory in which the transmission of forms without matter would play no rôle. This corpuscular theory of the senses would then become the Trojan horse by which a general corpuscular theory of nature would enter the mind of the reader. Thus, the *Traité de la lumière* (which forms the first part of *Le monde*) opens with a chapter entitled 'On the Difference between our Sensations and the Things That Produce Them'; in an obvious attack on the Aristotelian theory, it argues that the objects that produce sensations of light need not be 'similar to', or 'resemble', those sensations. The second chapter extends the attack to fire and heat, and, though readers are rhetorically permitted to imagine that heat and light come from the 'form of fire' or the 'quality of heat', the chapter makes clear that such forms or qualities are insufficient to explain the observed phenomena and are superfluous given the existence of an adequate, corpuscularian, account.[88] Subsequent chapters extend this theory of the material basis of qualities, leading ultimately to a corpuscularian description of the earth and the solar system. In the second part of *Le monde* (entitled *Traité de l'homme*), Descartes developed a corpuscular and mechanistic description of human physiology, and especially of the cognitive faculties, including the senses, imagination, and memory; he proposed a mechanistic explanation for association, and a brain-trace explanation for memory (later supplemented by a noncorporeal memory, residing in the soul itself).[89] The *Dioptrique* and *Météores* present allegedly adequate and clear corpuscular accounts of still more phenomena without, as Descartes observed, invoking the 'forms' or 'species' of scholastic philosophy.[90] But they present no direct argument for the corpuscular basis of the account; early on, each work simply introduces certain 'hypotheses', about light and about matter in general, which restrict the proffered explanations to the properties of size, shape, and motion. In the *Discours* Descartes claims that these general hypotheses are justified indirectly, through their explanatory success. He also intimates that a deeper justification is possible, without revealing it there.[91]

In the *Meditationes* and *Principia* Descartes sought to provide a metaphysical justification for his corpuscular physics by appealing to the deliverances of the pure intellect. In opposition both to the Aristotelians and to Hobbes and Gassendi (in their *Objectiones*),[92] Descartes contends that there can be thought without phantasms, and indeed without any activity in the corporeal imagination – a position that was in broad agreement with Platonic and Augustinian theories of cognition. The pure deliverances of the intellect – otherwise known as the clear and distinct perceptions of the understanding – are the source of the basic tenets of metaphysics, including knowledge of the essences of substances (material and mental alike). Having perceived through the intellect that the essence of matter is pure extension, or continuous mathematical quantity,[93] Descartes was in a position to imply in the *Meditationes,* and to develop more extensively in the *Principia,* an account of the senses according to which colour and other sensory qualities in bodies (sounds, odours, tastes, tactile qualities) consist only in certain arrangements of corpuscles possessing the properties of size, shape, motion, and position. That is, he could now rule out, on metaphysical grounds, the Aristotelian doctrine that colour as experienced in sensations is 'wholly similar to' colour as a quality of bodies.[94]

Descartes's mature theory of the faculties and their relations can be gleaned from the *Meditationes* and *Principia,* supplemented by the *Dioptrique* and *Traité de l'homme.* As had the Aristotelians, Descartes opposed positing faculties as entities distinct from the soul; rather, they are powers of the soul (some of which depend on the body, too). But Descartes's theory diverged sharply from that of the Aristotelians. He designated external sense perception, imagination, memory, and pure intellection as modes of a single power of perception (i.e., as operations of the intellect, considered generally). Of these faculties, sense perception, imagination, and memory depend on mind–body interaction, but pure intellect (and will) can operate without any corresponding change in bodily state.[95] Although Descartes casts doubt on the deliverances of the senses early in the *Meditationes* and *Principia,* in the Sixth Meditation and in the later *Principia* he constructs a positive rôle for the senses, in serving to detect ambient benefits and harms, and also in discovering empirical facts of use in the science of nature.[96] In the Sixth Meditation he forges a radical distinction between (pure) intellect and imagination, contending that geometrical figures can be understood independently of the imagination. He argues that both material and immaterial substances can be understood by the intellect in total independence of sensory images or experience.[97] His basic theory of the faculties, including the radical distinction between imagination and pure intellect, was adopted by a host of later Cartesians, including Clauberg, La Forge, Le Grand, and Régis.[98]

The sixth set of *Responsiones* perspicuously summarises Descartes's theory of the processes underlying sense perception.[99] He distinguishes three grades of sense: 'The first extends only to the immediate effects on a bodily organ by external objects; this can consist in nothing but the motion of the particles of the organ, and any change in shape and position resulting from this motion.' As Descartes explained in the *Traité de l'homme* and *Dioptrique*, in the case of vision these effects are caused by the round globules that constitute light pressing on the fibres of the optic nerve, thereby producing a motion in the fibres that causes the pores lining the interior cavity of the brain to open and allow animal spirits to flow rectilinearly from the pineal gland (the seat of mind–body interaction) to the these open pores, so that a perspective image, corresponding to the image received in the eye, is formed on the surface of the gland.[100] This brings us to the second grade, which 'comprises all the immediate effects produced in the mind as a result of its being united with a bodily organ that is so affected'. In the case of vision, this second grade extends only to the perception of light and colour, with the qualification that the colour patch is bounded (which implies it has size and shape); it also includes bodily sensations of pain, pleasure, thirst, and hunger, as well as sensations of sound, taste, smell, heat, cold, and the like, all of which arise from the union of mind and body (see Chapter 25).

The first two grades pertain properly to the sensory faculty. The third grade, which 'includes all of the judgements that we have been accustomed to make from our earliest years about things outside us, on the occasion of motions in a bodily organ', properly belongs to the intellect, but because the judgements take place habitually, without being noticed, people commonly believe that the results of such judgements belong to sense. Presumably, Descartes would include the 'natural' inclination to suppose that colour is a real property of bodies among such judgements. In the sixth *Responsiones* he refers to the *Dioptrique* for his account of size and distance perception, observing that there he shows 'how size, distance and shape can be perceived simply by rationally deriving any one from the others', for instance, by calculating size from visual angle plus distance. This statement makes it seem as if according to Descartes, the perception of size or distance always results from an unnoticed act of judgement. In the *Dioptrique* he indeed does explain how size can be judged from distance plus visual angle ('the size of the images objects imprint in the fund of the eye'); but he also indicates that distance can be known from an act of triangulation, 'an action of thought which, although only a very simple [act of the] imagination, nonetheless comprises reasoning quite similar to that used by surveyors when they measure inaccessible places'. This 'calculation' might simply be an unnoticed judgement, as in the sixth *Responsiones*; but its description as a 'simple imagination' suggests another possibility: that the corporeal processes of the body that underlie imagination are so constructed as to yield the results of this 'calculation' through their mechanical interaction, in such a way that variations in a brain state that are correlated with distance directly cause the mind to perceive distance, just as (he explains) certain brain changes causally linked with the accommodation of eye also cause us to perceive distance.[101] In the *Traité de l'homme,* composed while the *Dioptrique* was in progress, Descartes described a mechanical contrivance by which distance would be represented directly by the variation in a single brain state (the 'tilt' of the pineal gland) yoked to accommodation and convergence; this mechanism permits a psychophysiological explanation of the perception of distance, without unnoticed judgements.[102] Finally, in the continuation of the passage from the sixth *Responsiones,* he distinguishes those unnoticed judgements that typically do accompany the use of the senses from acts of mature reflection by which the trustworthiness of the senses is adjudicated. Presumably, such mature judgements include not only compensation for illusions, as in the example given (of a stick in water), but also the metaphysical judgements that the sensory qualities are not 'similar to' qualities in objects and that the latter qualities arise from the size, shape, and motion of the small corpuscles of which bodies are composed.

### 2. Hobbes: Intellect is imagination

Much as Descartes began philosophising about nature in *Le monde* with a discussion of sensory qualities, it appears that Hobbes began serious thought about natural philosophy by considering the senses. By his own account, on a trip to the continent in the mid-1630s he was amazed to discover that various learned individuals could not agree on an explanation of the basic operation of the senses; upon considering the matter, it 'luckily' occurred to him that the senses operate by motion.[103] In a manuscript of 1646 he wrote, concerning vision, that 'that which I have written of it is grounded especially upon that which about 16 years since I affirmed . . . , that light is a fancy in the mind, caused by motion in the brain, which motion again is caused by the motion of the parts of such bodies as we call *lucid.*'[104] As this doctrine developed in various works composed during the 1630s and 1640s (some published in Hobbes's lifetime, others later),[105] it emerged as the radically materialist thesis that not only are light, heat, and other corporeal qualities nothing but motion, and not only do the nerves and brain operate by motion, but sensation itself is nothing but bodily motion. As he put it, 'Sense, therefore, in the sentient, can be nothing else but the motion of some parts existing inside the sentient; and the parts so moved are parts of the organs by which we sense.'[106] Hobbes could have derived his doctrine of the subjectivity of perceived qualities such as light, colour, and heat from contact with works by Bacon, Galileo, or Descartes; his radical materialism was more singular, and it provoked strong reaction during and after his lifetime.[107] He extended his materialistic account of sense to the other faculties. The resulting account of the faculties formed part of a package of doctrines often discussed in close proximity, including the assertion that the word 'universal' names only other words or names, the reduction of understanding and reason to sense and imagination, the belief that all knowledge arises from the senses, and the denial of incorporeal substances.

An exposition of Hobbes's doctrine of the faculties should begin with light and its reception by the sense of vision and continue on to sensation, imagination, and memory, following Hobbes's own order. By the mid-1630s, Hobbes had adopted the theory that light is an undulation in a medium of fine matter.[108] He explained vision as the consequence of motions set up in the 'organ of sense', which in his earlier writings extended to the optic nerves and brain, and later included the heart.[109] According to his mature analysis, visual 'phantasms' arise when motion induced in the nervous system by light reaches the heart and provokes an outward counter-reaction, namely, a pressure in the animal spirits outward from the heart. In a bit of reasoning that may seem like a pun, Hobbes explained that this outward pressure results in the externalisation of visual phantasms; motions in the internal fabric of the body constitute the apparition of an object present before the eyes. He gave no further analysis of this phenomenon, which he described as the most wondrous of all natural phenomena.[110] Turning to imagination, Hobbes characterised it as decaying sense. He explained the persistence of images in the sensory apparatus using a principle also invoked by Descartes: that bodies tend to remain in their state of motion or rest until acted on by other bodies; once it is set in motion by an impinging object, the internal fabric of the sense organs will continue in motion in the absence of the object, until a subsequent impingement. Consistent with his general dictum that all phantasms or images have their origin in the senses, he held that the images of imagination are copies or compositions from previous sensory phantasms. He considered memory to be a species of imagination, and dreams to be images that arise through inward agitation of bodily parts; in each case, the images must originate in previous sensory phantasms. Finally, he discussed both regulated and unregulated 'traynes of thoughts', or associations of successive images.[111]

Hobbes wrote with apparent contradiction on the status of reason. In *De corpore,* published in 1655 but begun much earlier (ca. 1640), Hobbes wrote that 'philosophy, that is, *natural reason,* is innate in every man; for each and every person reasons continuously to some purpose and in some things.'[112] Yet in the *Leviathan,* published in 1651, he had stated that 'Reason is not as Sense, and Memory, borne with us; nor gotten by Experience onely, as Prudence is; but attayned by Industry; first in apt imposing of Names; and secondly by getting a good and orderly Method.'[113] The seeming contradiction is due to different degrees of terminological nicety. For in *Leviathan,* Hobbes distinguished between the faculty of understanding, which humans share with beasts, and the faculty of reason, which is acquired. Understanding arises in creatures endowed with imagination when the imagination is trained to use 'voluntary' signs, as when a dog learns to come when called by its master; the understanding is the imagination 'raysed' to the use of signs. Although reason also involves the use of signs, such use is marked with the logical strictness characteristic of speech; it is unique to humans, inasmuch as it is unobserved among beasts.[114] In *De corpore,* when Hobbes wrote that reason is innate, he was making a point that he repeated in *Leviathan:* that men left to themselves can achieve a modicum of reasoning, or what he would later call understanding. When in *Leviathan* he restricted reason to the logical reckoning of speech, he likewise was making a point contained in the other work: that right reasoning or true philosophical science comes only with the cultivation of method.[115] Such methodical reasoning is required in philosophy, for philosophic knowledge must be ordered into a deductive system. Nonetheless, as Hobbes protested to Descartes, philosophical reasoning is nothing but trained imagination; it consists only in sense-driven internal vibrations.[116]

Hobbes's investigation of the senses itself of necessity relied on the senses. Hobbes knew that such an investigation required the formation of hypotheses about the microstructures of bodies, sensory media, and the sense organs, nerves, brain, and heart. He couched his hypotheses in the vocabulary of matter in motion. Given his denial that the understanding is a faculty autonomous from the senses, he could not, like his contemporary foe, Descartes, appeal to pure intellect to justify his choice of the corpuscularian hypothesis; he was thus restricted to his own version of Descartes's other justificatory strategy, which appealed to the (as he supposed) conceptual clarity and empirical adequacy of mechanistic explanations. Hobbes at first simply presented his mechanistic approach by way of definition:

philosophy is knowledge of effects from causes or 'generations'; it excludes theology, the study of angels, and indeed the discussion of anything which is not a body or the disposition of the body, all on the grounds that they cannot be explained through the composition and division of their parts (the only 'causal' explanation Hobbes acknowledges).[117] But he realised that such definitions, and the implied choice of explanatory principles, themselves required support. He presented it as self-evident that all change is motion caused by motion through impact,[118] and therefore that all substance is corporeal and that there are no species nor any substantial forms.[119] To support the claim that we have no ideas of incorporeal beings, he observed that all ideas arise from the senses and that the senses can be affected only by bodies in motion.[120] If this pattern of reasoning, from matter in motion to the operation of the senses and back again, be a circle, it is perhaps one of those circles large enough to achieve philosophical stability.

### 3. Gassendi: Between material and immaterial faculties

Although at the outset of his philosophical career Gassendi was not immersed in questions about the operation of the senses – his earliest philosophical writings were directed against the Aristotelians – he spent part of the 1630s investigating the theory of vision.[121] His findings about light and vision agreed with the corpuscularianism of his two contemporaries, Descartes and Hobbes, though Gassendi adopted an Epicurean, 'atomistic' version (he posited indivisible particles moving in a void). Consonant with his commitment to Epicurean philosophy, he interpreted Epicurean *simulacra* in terms of the transmission of particles in rays from each point of an illuminated object so as to permeate the medium with images, which can be received at the retina.[122] His early attempts to follow the atomic philosophy, as far as the fallible natural light of the human mind could trace it, led him to a materialist conception of the minds of human and beast alike, a position that he qualified through the religious teaching that humans possess immaterial souls.[123] In his final work, the *Syntagma*, he advanced arguments for the immateriality of the human mind based on the light of natural reason.[124]

Gassendi's early theory of the faculties is similar in its materialism to that of Hobbes, and indeed his theory of the senses and imagination remained so into the *Syntagma*. Gassendi rejected sensory species, partly on the grounds that as 'forms without matter' they would be incorporeal and hence could not act on corporeal organs of sense.[125] He developed atomistic accounts of the five external senses, and of the nervous processes that properly constitute a 'sensing'.[126] He reduced the variety of internal senses to one, the imagination, conceived as a wholly corporeal power.[127] In the early theory, expressed in the *Disquisitio*, he held, like

Hobbes, that all human cognition can be achieved through the senses and imagination alone, without the activity of an incorporeal agent. In keeping with the background of traditional assumptions surveyed above, he therefore denied that the human mind has ideas of putatively immaterial substances, including the mind itself, God, and angels, and he rejected Descartes's distinction between the intellect and the imagination.[128] His refusal to countenance non-imagistic objects of thought was exemplified in his response to Descartes's distinction between two ideas of the sun – one from the senses, and one known through reasoning, without an image. According to Gassendi, we have only one idea of the sun, that derived from ordinary sense experience, and to the extent that we have an idea of the sun in its proper magnitude, we form this idea by enlarging the first idea so as to take the distance into account.[129]

Gassendi reversed his denial that the imagination/intellect can grasp incorporeal things in the section of his *Syntagma* on the human soul. There he argued that humans have both a lower and a higher soul; the lower one, shared with beasts, is material, and carries out its operations through sense and imagination. The higher one is immaterial.[130] Strikingly, Gassendi argued for the existence of the immaterial soul by countering the very objections he had made to Descartes – as one of Descartes's disciples was quick to notice.[131] He argued that, according to the light of natural reason, it is necessary to posit an immaterial soul to carry out the intellectual operations of grasping universals and other incorporeal things, including God, angels, and the human mind itself; indeed, he now argued that of the two ideas of the sun – sensory and astronomical – the second cannot be grasped by the imagination but requires an immaterial intellect. He did not precisely reverse his position, for he did not describe these intellectual operations as did Descartes: he did not posit an intuitive apprehension of God, the soul, and universal essences. The Gassendist intellect, whether reduced to imagination or not, remained a discursive intellect. According to his later position, the astronomical idea of the sun cannot be known by the senses alone, but it is known discursively. At the same time, Gassendi now argues that because such discursive powers go beyond what the imagination could achieve in itself, they require an immaterial agency.[132]

The change in Gassendi's position exemplifies a generally accepted conception of the relations among the intellect, imagination, and the objects of cognition: those, like Descartes, who distinguish an immaterial intellect from the imagination, also affirm its ability to cognise immaterial substances and the essences of things; those, like Hobbes, who reduce intellect to imagination deny that immaterial substances or universal essences can be directly cognised. Gassendi simply adopted first one, then the other position. Differences over the status of the intellect also led to different justificatory strategies for the corpuscular theory of the senses. Descartes could appeal to the deliverances of pure intellect to justify his physics of matter and motion. Hobbes and the early Gassendi could not and thus were left with the less direct (but philosophically longer lived) strategy of attempting to justify their corpuscularian position on its comparative merits, without the benefit of a previously established, absolute standard of comparison.

## V. THE FACULTIES AMONG RATIONALIST METAPHYSICIANS

The post-Cartesian rationalists of the seventeenth century differed among themselves, and often from Descartes, on the ontology of mind, body, and their relation, but they shared a core position on the cognitive faculties, which underlies their grouping as 'rationalists' as opposed to 'empiricists'. They all affirmed that the intellect can operate independently of the senses, and that in so doing it achieves fundamental knowledge of intelligible objects, including the essences of things. They limited the rôle of the senses to detecting benefits and harms in the ambient environment or to determining empirical facts of use in the science of nature.

### 1. *Spinoza and Leibniz*

In contrast to most major philosophers of the seventeenth century, Spinoza and Leibniz did not give the theory of the faculties philosophical prominence. Together with many others, they were philosophers of substance. But whereas others focused the beam of metaphysical scrutiny on the faculties by which substance allegedly is known, Spinoza and Leibniz began their philosophical arguments directly from statements or assumptions about substance itself. In this regard their approach to metaphysics was like that of the major ancient and mediaeval philosophers.

Spinoza's conception of mind and body as two aspects of a single deterministic order left no room for a unitary soul in possession of various faculties or powers. Given this metaphysics, talk of an array of faculties has to be regarded as a way of talking of the array of ideas, and of the relation of some of them to the array of things. One kind of example is supplied by the absorption of judgement into the idea: 'an idea, insofar as it is an idea, involves an affirmation or negation.'[133] More generally, Spinoza reduced the mind to a collection of ideas, or a single complex idea, identified by the fact that it is the idea of a particular human body.[134] He nonetheless used the language of the faculties in distinguishing sense, imagination, and intellect, and he gave an account of the bodily counterparts for the first two. Sensations have their counterpart in bodily states caused by the impingement of external objects on the sense-organs, and they represent those objects in virtue of the principle that the idea of the cause is implied in the idea of the effect. Within his double-aspect theory of mind–body relation, there is no genuine causation between material sense-organs and independent ideas. Rather, sensory ideas are simply one sort of idea found in the idea that constitutes the human mind – the sort that have as a bodily counterpart some activity in the liquid and soft parts of the body (presumably, animal spirits and the brain), whose current state (in veridical perception) is partly caused by external objects. Spinoza also sketched a material basis for the associative connections formed by the imagination.[135] His strict parallelism further implied that purely intellectual ideas must have their bodily correlates, but he did not characterise these correlates in the *Ethica*.

Spinoza displayed his admiration for the intellect over the senses and imagina- tion in ranking three kinds of knowledge.[136] The first and lowest kind arises in a disordered manner from the senses, or from hearsay, and is mediated by the imagination. The second kind arises from reason and includes the 'adequate' ideas by which the mind apprehends attributes and modes that are common to every- thing, as are the ideas of extension and motion in the case of bodies. These adequate ideas of common properties must be distinguished from the confused ideas that are called universals, such as the ideas of *man, horse,* or even *being* that arise when the images of individual humans, horses, or things (respectively) are confusedly melded together in the imagination. Accordingly, the 'universals' of scholastic Aristotelianism are produced not through intellectual abstraction, but by imaginal confusion.[137] Finally, Spinoza described a third type of knowledge, denominated as 'intuitive', which 'proceeds from an adequate idea of the formal essence of certain attributes of God to the adequate knowledge of the essence of things'.[138] Knowledge of this last kind was the ultimate aim of the *Ethica*. As befit his methodological strategy simply to find and follow adequate ideas, Spinoza had little to say about how intuitive knowledge is possible.

For Leibniz, as for Spinoza, the theory of the faculties did not produce significant argumentation and original thought. In general, Leibniz adopted a simplified Aristotelian division of the faculties and their objects into the external senses, the internal sense (the imagination or common sense), and the intellect.[139] Ontologically, his mature doctrine of individual substance and 'pre-established harmony' precluded a real causal interaction between mind and body, and hence a genuinely interactionist explanation of sense-perception, imagination, or mem- ory.[140] Leibniz focused not on the physiology and ontology of the faculties, but on the epistemic status of their objects. By the external senses we know sensible qualities such as light, colours, and odours; such qualities are cognitively 'clear' (i.e., recognisable) but 'confused' (their content is not further distinguishable). The common sensibles, such as number and shape, are 'found in' the objects of more than one sense, shapes being 'common to colours and tactile qualities'; they are cognised by the imagination or common sense, and are clear and distinct. The common sensibles are the objects of the mathematical sciences, both pure and mixed, though the demonstrations of mathematics require the intellect. Finally, the understanding cognises some objects that are purely intelligible and do not fall under the senses, such as the mind itself, and Leibniz claims to glean from contemplation of the mind the basic notions of metaphysics, including *substance, cause, effect, action,* and *similarity*.[141]

Leibniz strictly distinguished between sense, imagination, and memory on the one hand, and the pure understanding, on the other. Both beasts and humans have imagination and memory and are capable of forming connections between re-peated instances of successive perceptions; upon subsequent occurrences of the first perception, a strong imagination of the other will arise, as when a dog whines in the presence of a stick used previously to punish it. These associative connec-tions (based on habit) guide most human actions, when we act like 'mere empir-ics'.[142] Expectations arising from memory and imagination are distinct from those originating in reason. When we expect daylight after night because of mere past experience, memory and imagination are at work; but when we understand the cause of this succession as does the astronomer, we rely on the intellect or understanding. More generally, Leibniz accorded to the understanding two func-tions that could not be carried out by sense, imagination, and memory. First, the understanding grasps intelligible objects as mentioned. Second, the understanding serves to move from imperfect or finite experiences to necessary and universal truths. Leibniz argued from the actuality of human knowledge of necessary truths in the sciences, to the reality of the intellect as a faculty.

It is generally true that we know [necessary truths] only by this natural light, and not at all by the experiences of the senses. For the senses can indeed make known in some fashion what is, but they cannot make us know what must be or cannot be otherwise. . . . This [further] consideration [from geometry] also shows that there is a *light which is born with us.* For since the senses and induction can never teach us truths that are fully universal, nor what is absolutely necessary, but only what is, and what is found in particular examples, and since we nonetheless know the universal and necessary truths of the sciences – in which we are privileged over the beasts – it follows that we have drawn these truths in part from what is within us.[143]

This natural light is responsible not only for our knowledge of the axioms of mathematics and other necessary truths but also for our ability to draw universal conclusions from a finite number of experiences, as is the case when we judge under what conditions iron will and will not sink in water.

### 2. Malebranche: Sense, judgement, and pure understanding

Among Cartesians, Malebranche developed the theory of the faculties the most extensively and with the greatest originality. He differed from other major Cartesians and from Descartes himself in that his aims were primarily spiritual, rather than theoretical or metaphysical. In his major work, *De la recherche de la verité,* the theory of the faculties provided the organising framework for a diagnosis of the human bent towards error and sin. By making the 'science of man' primary, he hoped to discover how fallen humankind could avoid the errors that divert human thought from its natural object, God.[144]

Malebranche adopted Descartes's division of the faculties into sense, imagination, and pure understanding, his distinction between intellect and will, and his assignment of judgement to the latter. Through the pure understanding we perceive spiritual things, universals, common notions, and God, as well as ourselves upon self-reflection. By the pure understanding the soul 'even perceives material things, extension with its properties; for only pure understanding could perceive a perfect circle, a perfect square, a figure of a thousand sides, and similar things'. Such perceptions are called 'pure intellections', or 'pure perceptions' because 'the mind has no need to form corporeal images in the brain to represent all these things.' Malebranche explained the faculty of imagination by appeal to material images in the brain. The object of imagination is limited to material things: 'since one cannot form images of spiritual things, it follows that the soul cannot imagine them; and this should be noted well.' Finally, the soul has sensations of external objects, either when they make impressions upon the body, or when, 'in their absence, the flow of animal spirits makes a similar impression in the brain'.[145] Of course, the rôle of the brain in imagination and sensation must be understood according to Malebranche's occasionalism, and the soul's ability to exercise pure understanding according to his doctrine that we 'see' intelligible ideas in God (ideas of extension only, for we cognise the soul or God not through ideas, but by their own immediate presence).[146]

Malebranche's elaboration of the relationship between sense and understanding is the most distinctive aspect of his doctrine of the faculties. In the *Recherche,* Descartes's 'three grades of sense' became four, with grade one being partitioned into extra-bodily and bodily stages. Malebranche described his third stage as a passion, or sensation, which occurs in the soul itself on the occasion of brain motions.[147] He altered his description of the fourth stage between the first and second editions of the *Recherche*. At first he described the fourth stage as a rapid, habitual judgement that goes unnoticed and so is regarded as a sensation, even though it actually is a judgement – a description that accords with Descartes's third grade of sense. In subsequent editions, however, Malebranche attributed these 'natural judgements' to God rather than to the human mind; God causes sensations in us corresponding to appropriate optical calculations (e.g., of the size, shape, and distance of objects). Such natural judgements include the belief in real qualities – a naturally arising belief that is, according to Malebranche, followed by a free judgement of the human mind to the same effect, a judgement he hoped to eradicate from his readers.[148] The reassignment of the natural judgements to God makes him an implanter of false conclusions into human minds without their complicity. Malebranche forestalled the theodical question of deceit by observing that these judgements serve only the proper function of the senses, which is to guide the body away from harms and towards benefits.[149] He justified the revised doctrine theoretically by arguing that the finite human mind could not carry out the variety of instantaneous judgements required merely to calculate the size and distance of objects in the field of view. When we open our eyes on a country field, we immediately see a determinate landscape, despite the myriad detail. Thus, God's agency – albeit limited to presenting sensations that accord with such calculations as could be made from the inaccurate perspective projections produced by the imperfect optical apparatus of the human body – is required by the most ordinary of perceptual acts.[150]

Descartes's writings had left unanswered the question of whether sensations are bare signs for their external causes, without intelligible content, or are confused intellectual apprehensions of those causes (i.e., of matter in motion), sometimes seeming to support the former,[151] sometimes the latter.[152] Malebranche denied all intellectual content to sensations. They are not properly deemed confused ideas, for they are not ideas at all; rather, they are modifications of the soul. Unlike ideas, we do not see them in God, but God causes them to occur in the soul in accordance with His general decrees about the relation between bodily states and the arousal of sensations. By contrast, our pure conceptions of bodies – in terms of size, shape, and motion – are ideas that we 'see' in God, by passively receiving them in accordance with His general decision to reveal appropriate ideas to the faculty of understanding on the occasion of the will's desire to judge of them.[153]

Visual perceptions contain both sensations (of light and colour) and ideas (of intelligible qualities, such as size, shape, and motion). The former exist only in our souls, the latter are in God. We 'spread' or 'project' our sensations of colour onto ideas of shape as revealed by God.[154] This projection itself can only be a 'natural judgement'. Malebranche's fourth stage of sense, then, includes not only judgements that objects have a determinate size and distance but also projective judgements that render these shaped objects phenomenally coloured. The content of the perception of shape stems from an idea in God, that of the experience of colour from a sensation produced in us. The natural judgements of stage four thus must serve to explain, as far as can be, how colour sensations in us become phenomenally united with ideas of shape in God.

## VI. THE FACULTIES AND THE CAMBRIDGE PLATONISTS

The Cambridge Platonists valued reason as the image of God in man and as the sure route to knowledge of the divine.[155] Yet they differed from Renaissance Neoplatonists in restricting the immediate object of reason to modes of the human mind (rather than Forms in the divine mind). They gave little systematic attention to the theory of cognition in itself, but discussed the cognitive faculties in the service of other aims, such as refuting the materialism of Hobbes, defending an argument for the existence of God, or diagnosing the contributions of the various faculties to enthusiasm.[156]

More responded to Hobbes's materialistic account of the faculties by trying to show that mere matter could not perform our known mental functions. Of all the matter of the brain, he found the fluid animal spirits to be the most plausible candidate for a materialistic seat of sensation. But he argued that 'no *Matter* whatsoever is capable of such *Sense* and *Perception* as we are conscious to our selves of'. If sensing is performed wholly by the 'common percipient' or 'sensorium' of the brain, then sensory images are found either in one point, or in every point, or in a point-for-point correspondence across the sensorium. If the first be the case, the point receiving the images surely could not subsequently, through material means alone, put the body into motion in reaction to the image received; if the second, the same problem arises on a point-by-point basis; if the third, the unified experience of the whole image goes unexplained.[157] More further argued the unsuitability of fluid, viscous, or hard matter for receiving material images and preserving them, as would be required by imagination and especially memory, or for creating, altering, and experiencing images through imagination and inventive reason.[158] Against Hobbes's claim that 'second notions', including logical and mathematical conceptions, could be seated in matter alone by being equated with mere names or words, he contended that some common and therefore mental basis is required for them, because names differ among languages, but speakers share a common mental content.[159]

In his positive account of the faculties, More devoted great effort to proving that the soul 'is not confined to the Common *Sensorium,* but does essentially reach all the Organs of the Body', and that it has its chief seat in the 'purer Animal Spirits of the fourth Ventricle of the Brain'.[160] His discussion of the operation of the faculties was perfunctory. In opposition to Descartes and his followers, More argued that the qualities and images of things are sensed by the soul as present in the sense organ, and that this sensing is then conveyed, via the animal spirits (the soul's instrument), to the 'Centre of Perception' in the brain, where perception itself occurs.[161] Imagination exercises its function at the seat of the soul in the fourth ventricle of the brain. Memory requires the brain as its instrument, but not for the storage of images which the soul directly consults. Indeed, in remembering we experience only a state of the soul: 'it is plain that the *Memory* is in the *Soul,* and not in the Brain.' More therefore conjectured that the soul itself, through its noncognitive 'plastick power', uses marks in the brain as a kind of 'brachygraphie' or shorthand for things to be remembered. In his positive account of reason or understanding, More simply stated that '*Reason* is so involved together with *Imagination,* that we need say nothing of it apart by it self.'[162] But he elsewhere ascribed to reason the ability to go beyond mere images in grasping geometrical, mathematical, and logical concepts, and in the ideas of immaterial beings including God.[163] In doing so, however, it does not contemplate Forms or essences exterior to itself, but uses its natural capacities and innate notions or ideas.[164]

Cudworth discussed the faculties in defending arguments for the existence of God against the atheistic charge that only material things are humanly cognisable because we know only by way of the senses. But, he countered, 'there is a Higher Faculty in the Soul, of *Reason* and *Understanding*,' beyond sense and imagination. Such a faculty must be acknowledged first on the grounds that without it, we could not form theories of the senses that deny real qualities to external objects and reduce them to 'Magnitude, Figure, Site, Motion, and Rest'. Of the latter, we have not only 'sensible phantasms', but also 'intelligible ideas', though we are likely to confound the two. Of some things, including the meanings of words, our own mind, and God, we have no 'Genuine Phantasm', but only a 'Sence' or 'Intelligible Notion'. The perception of principles, such as that 'Nothing can not act', also depends on understanding rather than sense.[165]

Cudworth used such differences to justify a sharp contrast between the cognitive functions of the senses and intellect. The mind in sensing is partly passive and partly active. It is passive in receiving impressions from the body, active in forming the experienced quality (such as ideas of heat, light, and colours). These sensations are not for knowing truths, or the natures of external things, but for the 'use of the body' (quoting Plotinus).[166] The intellect is for knowing truths and essences, and in doing so it goes beyond the materials of sense. Through the intellect we come to know eternal verities, pertaining to perfect geometrical figures that do not exist in nature and to possibilities that are not actual. To explain such abilities of the human intellect, Cudworth infers the existence of a higher type of mind that contains the archetypes of these thoughts. A mere finite mind, he reasoned, could not generate the possibilities that it knows; these must first be seen by the mind of an 'infinitely fecund' being who really could generate all things. All finite minds, then, 'derive from' and 'participate in' the one infinite mind, 'being as it were Stamped with the Impression or Signature of one and the same Seal'.[167] According to Cudworth, as for More, these eternal verities and other truths have their presence as ectypal ideas that are innate in human minds,[168] and not, as with Ficino and Pico, as Forms in the mind of God apprehended there by lower minds.

## VII. THE COGNITIVE FACULTIES IN LOCKE AND BERKELEY

Locke and Berkeley formulated arguments that draw upon or illustrate common assumptions about the faculties, especially about the rôle of understanding in grasping essences. Discussion of the Molyneux problem raised the question of whether the idea of extension is common to the perceptions of touch and sight.

### 1. Locke: Limits of the understanding

Although Locke's *Essay* was, from its inception, conceived as a book about the human understanding, it was organised around the notion of ideas rather than that of faculties.[169] Its discussion of the faculties arises during Locke's endeavour to produce a general catalogue of simple ideas; having considered various simple ideas received from the external senses, Locke turns to those that arise from 'reflection' – the ideas of the mind's 'powers' to operate on its own ideas. Familiarly enough, Locke divides the 'powers' or 'faculties' of the mind into understanding and will.[170] His list of the 'faculties of the mind' is only partly familiar: without claiming to be exhaustive, it includes perception, retention (divided into contemplation and memory), discerning, comparing, composing, enlarging, and abstracting; elsewhere, he lists reasoning, judging, and knowing as modes of understanding.[171] Like Hobbes and the early Gassendi, Locke did not commit himself to a faculty of pure understanding, capable of cognition independently of the senses and imagination; but unlike them, he did not explicitly reduce understanding to sense and imagination, nor did he promote a materialistic theory of cognition.

In effect, Locke argued that the human mind lacks certain cognitive powers that previous authors had attributed to pure understanding. His contention that all ideas arise from experience, by either sensation or reflection, committed him to denying the claim of the Cartesians – and of the Cambridge Platonists as well – that the understanding has access either to innate ideas or to pure conceptions that are perceived independently of the senses.[172] He was no less at odds with the Aristotelian account of the understanding. Although he shared with the Aristotelians the dictum that there is 'nothing in the intellect that was not first in the senses', he rejected their claim that the human intellect abstracts the real essences of substances from sensory particulars. Locke's discussion of abstraction and general ideas sometimes seems to follow that of 'the schools', as when he says that people make a general idea of *Man* by abstracting so as to 'leave out of the complex *Idea* they had of Peter and James, Mary and Jane, that which is peculiar to each, and retain only what is common to them all', and when he subsequently equates general ideas with 'essences' or 'species'.[173] But whereas the Aristotelian act of abstraction was conceived as a true grasping of an essence or common nature, Locke explains the production of general ideas as merely 'the workmanship of the understanding'.[174] The activity of the understanding in framing abstract ideas of simple properties such as 'white' comes to no more than ignoring what is particular in some specific idea of white, and noting its similarity to other such ideas; in the case of substances, it comes to no more than the grouping of several simple ideas together, as a 'pattern' for sorting subsequent groups of simple ideas. Locke explicitly denies that when he speaks of general ideas as 'essences', he has in mind a 'real essence' in which all individuals in a species 'partake', for he denies that we have knowledge of such essences.[175]

### 2. Berkeley: Against intelligible extension and common sensibles

Berkeley employed the theory of the faculties in promoting and defending his immaterialism. He adopted the now standard division between will and understanding, and divided the origins of occurrent ideas among sense, memory, and imagination.[176] He restricted the scope of pure intellect. Humans know immaterial substances via the intellect – though by way of 'notion'[177] rather than 'idea' – but the intellect does not perceive intelligible extension.[178] This attack on intelligible extension was part of a more general challenge to the existence of matter and the intelligibility of its concept. If successful, it would trim the sails of rationalist metaphysical friends of matter. It would not bother matter's empirical friends, who claimed only that we perceive the sensible extension of matter by both sight and touch. But Berkeley challenged them as well: he denied that visible and tangible extension are instances of a single, common property of being determinately extended, and therefore that the term 'extension' names an ideational content common to the proper objects of touch and vision.

Berkeley's position on sensible extension entailed that all previous theories of vision were in error with respect to spatial perception and the common sensibles. Every author considered thus far held that the ideas of shape, size, and motion received by vision and touch are 'common' – that is, that the idea of a square as known by touch is of an identical type with the idea of a square as received by sight (even if the shape is exhibited with different phenomenal qualities, e.g., colour and texture). The typical and natural explanation of this fact was that one and the same shaped thing causes, or occasions, both ideas, and has its shape represented by both. Berkeley denied that mind-independent material objects exist and that a common ideational content is found in the ideas of sight and touch. The *New Theory of Vision* presents his most extensive arguments for the latter. That work does not endorse immaterialism, and its treatment of the perception of distance and magnitude can be considered independently of immaterialist motivations. But the motivation for treating the problem of 'common sensibles' so extensively – the discussion fills more than one third of the work – becomes intelligible only when its connexion with belief in material objects is made plain. If Berkeley could successfully show that there is no intrinsic connexion between visual and tactual ideas of size, shape, and motion, he would thereby eliminate one of the central arguments for positing a single, material cause of visual and tactual ideas. He would, of course, need to explain why visual and tactual ideas of shape seem similar, but his account of vision was admirably suited to this task: it taught that when a mature perceiver 'sees' distance, size, and shape, this seemingly visual experience is mediated by tactual ideas that have come to be associated (through 'suggestion') with the properly visual ideas that constitute the immediate objects of sight, in such a way that the perceiver no longer notices the visual magnitude and shape but accepts the associated tactual ideas as the object of sight.[179]

### 3. Molyneux's question

In March 1693 William Molyneux wrote to Locke posing his famous question: whether a newly sighted blind person, who could recognise the shapes of objects by touch, would be able at first to do so by sight alone, when presented with a globe and a cube of similar sizes. Molyneux argued that even though the person can distinguish the figures by touch, 'yet he has not yet attained the experience, that what affects his touch so or so, must affect his sight so or so.' Locke agreed, and invited the reader to consider the extensive rôle of 'experience, improvement, and acquired notions' in perception. He held that as a result of judgements made habitual by experience, visual sensations are altered from two-dimensional images to experiences of three-dimensional shapes. A sphere placed before the eyes at first produces only the idea of 'a flat Circle variously shadow'd' (and a cube might produce a variously shadowed hexagon); by 'an habitual custom' of judgement, we subsequently frame the idea of a sphere (or cube).[180] Locke considered these unnoticed judgements to be unique to vision among the senses.[181]

Whether Locke should in fact have agreed with Molyneux's negative reply depends on how one interprets the question posed. If all that is required of the newly sighted is to discriminate one figure from another, then Locke's principles suggest an affirmative reply. Locke held that determinate ideas of such determinables as 'extension, figure, motion, and rest' are 'convey[ed] into our Minds' by both sight and touch. He also attributed to all human minds a native power for discerning sameness or difference of ideas.[182] He should therefore expect a newly sighted person to succeed in discriminating between the visual ideas presented by a sphere and cube, that is, the plane figures of a circle and hexagon.

But Molyneux's task demanded more than mere discrimination of plane figures. He asked whether the newly sighted could 'distinguish and tell, which is the Globe, which the Cube'. Locke's negative answer to this question depends on his belief that the newly sighted would not have acquired the unnoticed judgements that account for perception in three dimensions. He does not say why this lack would preclude success, but he apparently ruled out the possibility that the perceiver could complete the task by noting the similarity between a visually given circle and a tactual sphere (by contrast with a tactual cube). Locke could not, with consistency, argue that the perceiver must learn the connection between identical determinate visual and tactual shapes, because that would have violated his conception that the same determinable, shape, is perceived by both touch and vision.

Leibniz, in his *Nouveaux essais,* agreed with Locke and Molyneux that, if the newly sighted person is not informed that a sphere and a cube lie before him, 'it will not at first occur to him that these types of pictures, which will strike him in the fund of his eyes, and which could have come from a flat painting on the table, represent bodies.' But Leibniz thought that if a newly sighted blind person versed in optics were told which figures to look for, he could discern globe and cube (say, by counting angles on the cube), and that, if given sufficient time, he would, without such prompting, 'by dint of reasoning about the light rays in accordance with optics, be able to understand by the lights and shadows that there is something blocking the rays, and that it must be precisely the same thing that resists his touch'. He explained that the newly sighted can be expected to have this facility because the geometrical figures of touch and sight 'ultimately rest on the same ideas, even though they have no images in common'.[183] Leibniz apparently held that the existence of intelligible ideas of extension (denied by Locke) facilitates the task of comparison. But notwithstanding this disagreement over shared intelligible – as opposed to 'common sensory' – ideas of extension, Locke and Leibniz agree in making the problem turn on the psychological difficulty of the task involved. Neither has a principled reason for denying that the newly sighted could recognise plane or even volumetric visual shapes; they predict failure because of expected difficulty in inferring without practice from two-dimensional images to solids.

By contrast, Berkeley interpreted Molyneux's question so that it applied to plane figures such as squares, and he nonetheless answered it negatively,[184] arguing from his principle that shape is not 'common' to visual and tactual ideas. The immediate visual sensation, or 'proper object of vision', does, on Berkeleyan principles, contain 'visible figures' corresponding to Locke's plane circle and hexagon.[185] But these 'figures' are not, perforce, species of common sensibles. That is, the immediate idea of shape received by vision is not part of the same species of idea, 'ideas of shape', as the immediate ideas of shape received through touch. The phenomenal sameness that we experience arises only in the case of what Berkeley termed the mediate object of vision, which includes the tactual ideas of three-dimensional objects, fused into the visual ideas of light and colour by the associative process of suggestion.[186]

## VIII. PHILOSOPHY AND THE THEORY OF COGNITION

The cognitive faculties were often at the center of philosophical innovation in the seventeenth century. Corpuscularians of necessity framed new theories of sense and imagination; the theory of the intellect was at the crux of metaphysical disputes about the nature of the mind, its ability to know the essences of material things, and to cognise immaterial things. Nonetheless, it would be a distortion to say that the theory of cognition, or the theory of knowledge, dominated and controlled early modern philosophy.

It has been common to mark the seventeenth century as the time when the 'theory of knowledge' attained a central place in philosophy: scepticism and the theory of ideas are alleged to have created the modern epistemological problematic, and epistemology to have become the independent arbiter of metaphysics. Examination of the actual works of those credited (or charged) with the 'epistemological turn'– Descartes, Locke, and Berkeley – suggests otherwise. It is true that Descartes employed sceptical arguments in his *Meditationes,* and that they were presented as a test of the possibility of human knowledge. But these arguments were part of a calculated strategy for purging the senses and uncovering the pure intellect; Descartes's 'Archimedean point', from which he sought metaphysical knowledge, was not founded on the theory of cognition but on the cognitive results of intellection. Malebranche, Locke, and Berkeley were also intensely interested in the power and scope of the intellect. Their projects differ from previous philosophy, and from the direction taken by Spinoza and Leibniz, in that they made the investigation of the knower a fundamental part of the evaluation of metaphysical knowledge. But the theories of cognition, or theories of knowledge, that they developed were not intended to provide independent grounds for adjudicating metaphysics. In Malebranche, the theory of the faculties was itself embedded in a metaphysical theory of the relation between the intellect and the essences of things. Locke, with his project 'to examine our own Abilities, and see, what Objects our Understandings were, or were not fitted to deal with',[187] fits most nearly the picture of epistemology made the autonomous adjudicator of philosophy. But rather than treat the theory of the faculties as an independent ground from which to judge other cognitive claims, Locke examines the senses and intellect by way of internal tests of the faculties against specific metaphysical claims made by others and finds, often grudgingly, that our perception and knowledge fall short of real essences. Berkeley adopts a similar attitude in examining the cognitive basis for knowing material substance, though his discoveries of failure are not presented grudgingly.

It is also a mistake to posit a close relation between seventeenth-century theories of cognition as employed in metaphysical disputes and naturalistic theories of cognition that developed in the eighteenth century and afterwards. It is not that nothing in the writings of Descartes, Hobbes, Malebranche, Locke, or Berkeley could, with hindsight, properly be described as naturalistic psychology; indeed, portions of their theories of the senses and imagination constitute the modern foundation of naturalistic theories of cognition. Furthermore, it may be noted that Descartes's writings of the 1630s, and Hobbes's writings on the faculties in general, employed the strategy of attempting to win support for the corpuscular philosophy by appealing to the 'physics' of sensory stimulation, and that Berkeley attempted to undermine that philosophy through his 'psychology' of sensory perception; to this extent, their works contain an early form of 'naturalised' epistemology. But none of these authors attempted to make the results of an empirically based, natural-scientific theory of cognition the ultimate arbiter of metaphysics or other branches of knowledge. Indeed, in the mature work of Descartes, as in that of Malebranche and Berkeley, the understanding operating in isolation from the senses frames the metaphysical theory of the real. Even Hobbes, within his justification of a mechanical approach to nature, treated as basic the appeal to the 'evidence' of certain claims, as did Locke in his account of knowledge in its various degrees.

At the opening of the seventeenth century, the deepest and most widely shared assumption about the faculties was that an immaterial agency is required for the cognition of immaterial objects. Hobbes made use of this assumption, to the extent that he hoped his argument that all the objects of knowledge are material would remove what had been recognised as the strongest reason for affirming the immateriality of the intellect. The assumption held sway well into the eighteenth century. Indeed, Hume's attack on the view that the mind is able to perceive 'necessary connections', or active powers and agencies, may well have been directed towards a philosophical audience who believed that only an immaterial agency could perceive such connexions or agencies. Kant may have first broken the grip of the assumption. He sought to establish an account of human understanding that precluded its reduction to sense and imagination and that allowed for the cognition of necessary laws, and he endeavoured to do so without appealing to the ontology of the intellect or its objects. It is to Kant that one must look to find the origin of philosophical theories of cognition – or of the conditions on knowledge – that are independent of metaphysics, and so to identify the force behind the 'epistemological turn'. Although earlier philosophers, including Descartes, Locke, and Berkeley, had conceived the project of investigating the knower in order to determine what can be known, it was Kant and not they who molded that investigation, for a time, into the paramount project of theoretical philosophy.

## NOTES

1 Another major faculty, the will, is examined in Chapter 33. It enters the present chapter through its rôle in judgement.
2 R. Rorty 1978, chaps. 1, 3; cf. Ayers 1985.
3 Spinoza, *De int. emen.*; Locke, *Ess.*; Leibniz, *Nouv. ess.*; Berkeley, *Pr. Hum. Kn.* Descartes, *Disc.,* uses 'raison' in its title.
4 Explicitly in Charron *Sag.,* bk. 1; Herbert of Cherbury 1633; Hobbes 1969, p. xiv; and Malebranche, *Rech.*; implicitly in Descartes, *Meds.*

5 Eustachius a Sancto Paulo 1638, pt. 3, 'Physica', III.3, disp. 3 q1 (p. 264); Thomas Aquinas, *Summa th.*, I q78 a4, end; Steneck 1974.

6 Ficino, *Commentarium in Phedrum*, chap. 11 (Ficino 1981, pp. 120–1; see also pp. 122–3). Pico della Mirandola in *Heptaplus*, 4th exp., chap. 2, 5th exp., chap. 6 (Pico della Mirandola 1942, pp. 274, 304), writes that the human intellect partakes of the angelic, which contemplates the intelligible forms (3rd ex., chap. 2, Pico della Mirandola 1942, pp. 252–5; Pico della Mirandola 1965, p. 109).

7 *Heptaplus*, 4th exp., chap. 1, Pico della Mirandola 1942, p. 270 (Pico della Mirandola 1965, p. 119); 5th exp., chap. 6 (Pico della Mirandola 1942, p. 304; 1965, p. 135); Ficino, *Commentarium in Phedrum*, chaps. 7–9 (Ficino 1981, pp. 96–111).

8 Ficino, *Theologia Platonica*, Bk. 18, chap. 4 (Ficino 1964, pp. 193–5; Ficino 1981, pp. 234–5); Marcantonio Genua placed the rational soul in the body not as its informing form, but as a captain in a ship; see Kessler 1988, pp. 524–5.

9 *Collegium Conimbricense* 1600, II.1, q6 a2, concl. 1 (p. 96); II.3, q1 a1 (pp. 133–4); Eustachius a Sancto Paulo 1638, 'Physica', III.1, disp. 1 q6–7 (pp. 182–5); III.4, disp. 1 q2–3 (pp. 279–82); Melanchthon, *Liber de anima* (Melanchthon 1834–60, vol. 13, pp. 9–20); Suárez, *De anima*, I.4.4, I.6.15, I.11.4 (Su. *Op. omn.* 3, pp. 493a, 510a, 553b); Toletus 1594, II.1, q1, concl. 4 (fol. 40rb); II.3, q7, concls. 3–4 (fol. 62vb). See also Thomas Aquinas, *Summa th.*, I q75 a4; q76 a1; q76 a3; q78 a1; Thomas Aquinas 1968b and 1984, q1–2, 11; and on Duns Scotus, Bonansea 1983, pp. 11–36.

10 *Collegium Conimbricense* 1607, 'In Isagogem Porphyrii', pref., q5 a2 (pp. 133–5); Eustachius a Sancto Paulo 1638, 'Physica', III.4, disp. 2 q4–7 (pp. 287–93); Suárez, *De anima*, IV.3–6 (Su. *Op. omn.* 3, pp. 722–38); Toletus 1596, 'In librum Porphyrii', q2 (p. 27b). See also Thomas Aquinas, *Summa th.*, I q76 a5; q84 a7; q85 a1; q85 a3; and on Duns Scotus, Wolter 1990, chaps. 2, 5. These authors differed on whether knowledge pertains only to universals or includes particulars.

11 Thomas Aquinas 1968b; Duns Scotus, *Super libros Aristotelis De anima* (Duns Scotus 1891–95, vol. 3, pp. 472–642); *Collegium Conimbricense* 1600; Melanchthon, *Liber de anima* (Melanchthon 1834–60, vol. 13, pp. 5–178); Rubius 1620; Toletus 1594; Zabarella 1606. Aristotle's *De anima* was itself organised as a treatment of the faculties (primarily, sense and understanding), on which see Kahn 1966.

12 Textbooks: Eustachius a Sancto Paulo 1638, pt. 3, 'Physica', III.3–4 (pp. 228–308); Keckermann, *Systema physicum*, III.15–IV.6 (Keckermann 1614, cols. 1512–1621); Melanchthon, *Initia doctrinae physicae* (Melanchthon 1834–60, vol. 13, p. 197). Toletus 1594, proem, q2, concl. 3 (fol. 4), subsumed the soul in all of its operations under physics; *Collegium Conimbricense* 1600, proem, q1 a2 (pp. 7–9) and Rubius 1620, proem, q1 (pp. 10–12), subsumed the study of the soul considered as separated from the body under metaphysics, while appending treatment of the separable soul to their *De anima* commentaries.

13 In the logical commentaries the most extensive discussion of the intellect and its abstractive powers occurred in the part on Porphyry's *Isagoge*, printed as an introduction to Aristotle's *Categories*: e.g., *Collegium Conimbricense* 1607, q5 a1–2 (pp. 131–5); Rubius 1641, chap. 1, q5 (pp. 37–8); Toletus 1596, q5 (pp. 26b–29a).

14 On the external and internal senses, corporeal phantasms, and the estimative power (which sometimes was considered distinct from imagination, and sometimes not), see *Collegium Conimbricense* 1600, II.5–III.3; Eustachius a Sancto Paulo 1638, 'Physica', tr. III; Keckermann, *Systema physicum*, III.16–29 (Keckermann 1614, cols. 1518–86); Melanchthon, *Liber de anima* (Melanchthon 1834–60, vol. 13, pp. 108–22); Rubius 1620, II.5–III.3; Suárez, *De anima*, Bk. III (Su. *Op. omn.* 3); Toletus 1594, II.5–III.3.

See also Thomas Aquinas, *Summa th.,* I q78 a3–4; Duns Scotus, *De anima,* q1–10 (Duns Scotus 1891–5, vol. 3).

15 Eustachius a Sancto Paulo, 'Physica', III.3, disp. 1 q2 (pp. 230–3); Rubius 1620, II.5–6, q5 (pp. 309, 327). Suárez explains the term 'species intentionales': 'species quidem quia sunt formae repraesentantes: intentionales vero non, quia entia realia non sint, sed quia notioni deserviunt, quae intentio dici solet' (*De anima,* III.1.4, Su. *Op. omn.* 3, p. 614a). He further observes that (sensory) intentional species are 'material' and 'divisible' (III.2.16, p. 619b), even if those of vision are the 'most perfect' because of their subtlety, and those of hearing are 'in a way, spiritual', having the subtlety of air (III.29.1, Su. *Op. omn.* 3, p. 700a).

16 Toletus 1594, II.12, q33 (fol. 109ra–110ra).

17 *Collegium Conimbricense* 1600, II.5–6, q2 a2 (pp. 173–5).

18 *Collegium Conimbricense* 1600, II.5–6, q2 a2–3 (pp. 172–80); Eustachius a Sancto Paulo 1638, 'Physica', III.3, disp. 1 q2; Rubius 1620, II.5–6, q5 (pp. 327–8); Suárez, *De anima,* III.2.9 (Su. *Op. omn.* 3, p. 618a); Toletus 1594, II.12, q34 (fol. 111ra). See also Thomas Aquinas, *Summa th.,* I.78.3; 84.1; Duns Scotus *De anima,* q5 (Duns Scotus 1891–5, vol. 3, pp. 491b–494a). On species as 'forms without matter', see Simmons 1994.

19 *Collegium Conimbricense* 1600, II.1, q1 a6 (pp. 62–3); q6 a2 (pp. 95–8); III.5, q1–6 (pp. 369–408); Eustachius a Sancto Paulo 1638, 'Physica', III.1, disp. 1 q5 (p. 182); III.4, disp. 2 q7–8, 10 (pp. 290–5, 298); Rubius 1620, III.4–5 (pp. 633–735); Suárez *De anima,* IV.2, IV.8.8 (Su. *Op. omn.* 3, pp. 715b–721b, 743a); Toletus 1594, III.4, q10; III.5, q13; III.7, q21. See also Thomas Aquinas, *Summa th.,* I q78 a1; q84 a6–7; 1968b [1984], q4, ad 1; *Quaestiones disputatae de veritate,* q10 a6 ad 7 (Thomas Aquinas 1882– , vol. 22, p. 314a); Duns Scotus, *De anima,* q17 (Duns Scotus 1891–5, vol. 3, pp. 580a–582a); *Ordinatio* I, d3, pt. 3, q3 (Duns Scotus 1950–, vol. 3, pp. 330–8).

20 *Collegium Conimbricense* 1607, pt. 2, 'De interpretatione', chap. 1, q5 a2 (pp. 56–8); chap. 4, q4 a1–2 (pp. 119–27); 'De posteriori resolutione', I.1, q3 a4 (pp. 423–4); but the will can influence the intellect when it is not determined by 'evident cognition', as in matters that depend on faith alone, 'De posteriori resolutione', I.26, q1 a4 (pp. 634–5). Eustachius a Sancto Paulo 1638, pt. 1, 'Dialecticam', I.1, disp. 1 q1 (pp. 110–12); pt. 3, 'Physica', III.4, disp. 1 q11 (pp. 299–300). Toletus 1596, 'Quaestiones in communi', q6 (pp. 18b–19b). The intellectual acts described as the 'simple apprehension' of a universal might be quite complex, involving comparisons with other forms in the possible intellect (e.g., Suárez, *De anima,* IV.3.21–26, Su. *Op. omn.* 3, pp. 728b–730b; Suárez 1964, sec. 6); for a comparison of Aquinas, Scotus, Ockham, and Suárez on this point, see Ross in Suárez 1964, pp. 23–7. Some authors denominated a fourth intellectual operation, ordering or method, which involves structuring an argument or text larger than a syllogism (de Launay 1673, diss. 1, chap. 2, p. 17).

21 *Collegium Conimbricense* 1600, II.5–6, q2 a2, p. 175; III.6–8, q3 a2 (p. 431); Eustachius a Sancto Paulo 1638, 'Physica', III.3, disp. 1 q2 ad 4 (p. 232); Rubius 1620, II.5–6, q3; Suárez, *De anima,* III.1.4–5; 1.8, 2.1–15 (Su. *Op. omn.* 3, pp. 614, 615, 616a–619b); Toletus 1594, II.12, q33 (fol. 109vb). See also Thomas Aquinas, *Summa th.,* I q84 a2; q85 a2.

22 All of the late scholastics canvassed herein say that the species 'represents' or 'is a representation of' an external object, and that it is, in one sense or another, a 'similitude' of the object: *Collegium Conimbricense* 1600, II.6, q2, a2, p. 173: '[Facultem] ab obiecto per sui similitudinem sensui impressam; datur ergo obiecti similitudo, siue species in sensu'; p. 174: 'species candoris, verbi gratia, non est ipse candor materialiter, sed id, quod candorem repraesentat'; Eustachius a Sancto Paulo 1638, 'Physica', III.1,

disp. 1 q2, pp. 230–1: 'cum oculus percipit colorem distantem, aiunt philosophi in oculo esse seu recipi similitudinem quandam ipsius coloris, hoc est, qualitatem quandam quae ab ipso colore per intermedium aerem propagata, & in ipso sensu visus recepta vim habeat ipsum colorem repraesentandi'; Keckermann, *Systema physicum,* III.16 (Keckermann 1614, col. 1522); Rubius 1620, II.6, q3 (p. 324); Suárez, *De anima,* III.2.9 (Su. *Op. omn.* 3, p. 618a); Toletus 1594, II.12, q33 (fol. 109ra). See also Thomas Aquinas *Summa th.,* I q84 a7 ad 2; q85 a1–2; q85 a8 ad 3; *De veritate,* q8 a11 ad 3 (Thomas Aquinas 1882– , vol. 22, pp. 256b–257a); Duns Scotus, *De anima,* q5, resol. (Duns Scotus 1891–95, vol. 3, p.494a).

23 Toletus 1594, II.12, q33, 'sense of the question': 'species est rei simulachrum quod-dam, & imago, obiectum representans' (fol. 109ra); but, q33, concl. 2: 'species non est imagines rerum formales' (fol. 109vb–110ra), and q34, concl. 3: '[species] non est similitudo formalis subiecti' (fol. 111rb). Suárez, *De anima,* III.2.11–15, 20–6 (Su. *Op. omn.* 3, p. 622b) denies that we see species, or that impressed species represent by way of formal similitude, like 'pictures'; characterises species as 'effective' rather than 'formal' representations (vol. 3, p.620b); and admits an 'intentional' similitude between species and object (vol. 3, p.622a). Rubius 1620, II.5–6, q6, pp. 329–32, denies that 'impressed species' in the medium and organs are formal similitudes and images, but allows that when 'expressed' in the act of sensation, they are such. These authors (like many others) repudiated previous denials that species need be posited, especially by Durandus a Sancto Porciano 1571, II, d3, q6 and IV, d49, q2 (fol. 139va, 413rb–vb), but also by William of Ockham, *Quaestiones in librum sententiarum,* III, q2–3 (William of Ockham 1967–86, vol. 6, pp. 43–129): Toletus 1594, II.12, q34 (fol. 111rb); Rubius 1620, II.5–6, q3 (pp. 321–5); Suárez, *De anima,* III.2.9–15 (Su. *Op. omn.* 3, pp. 618a–619b). On the denial of species by Ockham and others, see Tachau 1988.

24 *Collegium Conimbricense* 1600, II.5–6, q2 a2 (p. 176); Eustachius a Sancto Paulo 1638, 'Physica', III.3, disp. 1 q2, 5; Keckermann, *Systema physicum,* III.16, 20; IV.4 ((Kecker-mann 1614, col. 1518–22, 1526–9, 1603); Rubius 1620, II.5–6, q3–7; Suárez, *De anima,* III.1.4, 2.1–26, 28.1–3, 29.1–2 (Su. *Op. omn.* 3, pp. 614a, 616a–622b, 696b–698a, 700); Toletus 1594, II.12, q33–34 (fol. 108r–112r). See also Thomas Aquinas, *Summa th.,* I q78 a3; q84 a2; q85 a2; Duns Scotus, *De anima,* q4–6 (Duns Scotus 1891–5, vol. 3, pp. 488a–498a).

25 Toletus 1594, II.12, q34, concl. 2, fol. 110vb: 'Species habet esse intentionale in medio, & in organo. Pro sensu Conclusionis notandum, quod esse intentionale triplici-ter sumatur. Vno modo, vt distinguitur contra esse reale, & sic logicae proprietates, quae non sunt in rebus, nisi sola Intellectus consideratione, dicuntur habere esse intenti-onale: & sic species non dicitur habere esse intentionale, sed reale: est enim, qualitas quaedam in subiecto existens'; Suárez, *De anima,* III.1.4; 2.1 (Su. *Op. omn.* 3, pp. 614a, 616a); Rubius 1620, II.5–6, q4–5, pp. 326, 328 (he grants them a degree of 'corporeal being'). In his logic Toletus contrasted 'ens reale' with 'ens rationis', not 'intentionale' (1596, 'In librvm Categorivm', 'De praedicamentis in communi', q1, concl. 2, p. 191a); so did *Collegium Conimbricense* (1607, 'In Isagogem Porphyrii', pref., q6, a1–2, pp. 137–44). Ockham, as might be expected, denied that intentional being can be a species of real being: 'illa species non habet esse intentionale vel spirituale, quia hoc dicere includit contradictionem, quia omne ens extra animam est vera et verum esse reale habet suo modo' (William of Ockham, *Quaestiones in librum sententiarum,* III, q2 (William of Ockham 1967–86, vol. 6, p. 60)).

26 Rubius 1620, II.5–6, q5: 'adnotare oportet species istas intentionales sic vocatas, quia cognitionibus (quae intentiones, hoc est, quasi attentiones animae ad cognoscenda

obiecta vocantur) deseruiunt id peculiare habere, quod licet ab obiectis procedant tanquam a principiis efficientibus praecipuisque causis, indifferenter procedunt a qualitatibus actiuis physica activitate, & actione, & etiam ab his, quae nullam actiuitatem physicam, seu naturalem habent, non enim sunt qualitates actiuae physica actiuitate albedo, nigredo, raritas, densitas, & similes, quia nunquam producunt, imo nec producere posse censetur alias sibi similes, nec dissimiles, & nihilominus producunt effectiue species intentionales in sensibus, atque etiam in medio' (pp. 327–8); q.4: 'species sensibiles habere esse corporeum, & non spirituale: sed non corporeum naturale: sed a naturali valde degenerans; & ideo vocatur intentionale, & reuera est esse quoddam diminutum, & respectu esse naturalis obiecti longe inferius; & propterea non est sensibile, quamuis sit medium, vt sentiatur obiectum: itaque esse speciei est proportionatum ad vniendum obiectum potentiae, non tamen vt sentiatur tanquam obiectum' (p. 326). Suárez, III.1.4 (previously quoted), 2.25–6 (Su. *Op. omn.* 3, pp. 614a, 621b– 622b); Toletus 1594, II.12, q34, concl. 2 (fol. 110vb–111rb). See also the use of 'intentional' in *Collegium Conimbricense* 1600, II.5–6, q2, a2–3 (pp. 176, 177); and Eustachius a Sancto Paulo 1638, 'Physica', III.3, disp. 1 q2 (pp. 230–1).

27 AT VI 85.

28 Treatises on optics or *perspectiva* were taught in the Arts faculty at the master's level as part of an advanced course in the mathematical division of speculative philosophy, although a summary treatment sometimes was given as a supplement to the traditional quadrivium (Feingold 1984a, pp. 35, 41–2, 47–8; Freedman 1985, chaps. 3, 6–7). The optical literature was largely inspired by Alhazen 1989 (his *Perspectiva,* translated from the Arabic in the thirteenth century and printed in 1572 under the title *Opticae thesaurus*), which advances a broad conception of 'optics' as a full theory of vision, including what would now be denominated as physical, physiological, psychological, ontological, and epistemological aspects. Alhazen himself drew on an older literature including Ptolemy's *Optica* (Ptolemy 1989), but Alhazen's work was much more widely circulated in the Latin West than was Ptolemy's. Ptolemy, like Plato and Galen, adopted an extramission theory, according to which the visual power extends outward from the eye to 'touch' the seen object. Alhazen championed the intromission view, which had become standard by the late sixteenth century (although extramission theories were still discussed). Works by Pecham (1970) and Witelo (1535) drew heavily on Alhazen and were widely circulated through the sixteenth and into the seventeenth centuries. On the optical tradition and literature, see Lindberg 1967; 1970, pp. 24–32; and 1976, chaps. 5–7. Roger Bacon's synthesis of previous optical work accepted many features of Alhazen's geometrical analysis but combined them with Ptolemy's extramission theory; see R. Bacon 1900, pt. 5. His writings were known to Pecham and Witelo, but his influence on them was not as great as Alhazen's (Lindberg 1976, pp. 116–20).

29 *Collegium Conimbricense* 1600, II.7, q5–7; Suárez, *De anima,* III.18.9–13 (Su. *Op. omn.* 3, pp. 672a–673b); Toletus 1594, II.7, q16, fol. 8[4]va: 'In hac visionis natura Perspectivi suam doctrinam fundant. Nam, quia non videmus nisi recte opposita, dicunt nos per rectas lineas videre; & quia quae videntur, aliqua per lineam directam centro pupillae videntur: aliquae partes vero per lineas lateraliter directas: dicunt, quod videmus per trangulum, seu per pyramidem, quam vocant visualem'; II.12, q34, concl. 4, fol. 112ra: 'Quod de his diximus, etiam intellige de specie producta ab obiecto, vg. colore: cum enim ipsa sit species diffusa, sic ut lumen, quaelibet pars producitur a toto obiecto, ad quod recte, & absque impedimento opponitur. . . . Dicunt etiam, species multiplicari, cum una etiam sit: quia quaelibet pars totum facit cognoscere: totum, inquam a quo dependet, & a quo producta est, & quod oculo opponitur recta: ob id dicitur, multas

species vnius diffundi per medium.' But textbook treatments spoke as if images pass through the air and enter the eye: Abra de Raconis 1646, pt. 1, 'Logica', I.2.2, sec. 2, q4, a2, p. 259: 'species intentionales rerum visibilium sunt ipsae earum imagines, quae in oculo receptae'; Eustachius a Sancto Paulo 1638, 'Physica', III.3, disp. 2 q7, p. 246: 'visio fieret . . . receptis ab obiecto imaginibus seu speciebus intentionalibus'; Keckermann, *Systema physicum*, III.20 (Keckermann 1614, col. 1534 sub).

30 AT VI 128–30; XI 174–6; Hatfield and Epstein 1979.

31 *Collegium Conimbricense* 1600, III.4–8 (pp. 360–459); 'Tractatus de anima separata' (pp. 499–596); Pomponazzi 1516; Rubius 1620, III.4–5 (pp. 633–735); 'Tractatus de anima separata' (pp. 758–94); Thomas Aquinas 1968a; 1968b [1984], q3–5, 11–13; Toletus 1594, III.4–7 (fol. 129r–168v); Zabarella 1606, III (cols. 655–982).

32 Aquinas had specified that the agent intellect creates the intelligible species, while denying that the form in the phantasm is 'transferred' to the intellect: 'Sed virtute intellectus agentis resultat quaedam similitudo in intellectu possibili ex conversione intellectus agentis supra phantasmata, quae quidem est repraesentativa eorum quorum sunt phantasmata, solum quantum ad naturam specei. Et per hunc modum dicitur abstrahi species intelligibilis a phantasmatibus; non quod aliqua eadem numero forma quae prius fuit in phantasmatibus, postmodum fiat in intellectu possibili, ad modum quo corpus accipitur ab uno loco, et transfertur ad alterum' (*Summa th.,* I q85 a1 ad 3; see also q84 a6). The position that the corporeal phantasm, being material, cannot itself be received into or affect the immaterial intellect was accepted by all of the *De anima* commentators here canvassed, but they disagreed on how to characterise the causal rôle of phantasms in the production of intelligible species; Suárez argues for 'material' causation by 'exemplar' (Suárez, *De anima*, IV.2.10–12 (Su. *Op. omn.* 3, pp. 719a–b)); the Coimbran text says the phantasm 'co-operates' to 'excite' the intellect into production (*Collegium Conimbricense* 1600, III.5, q6, pp. 407–9); Rubius 1620 designates the phantasm an 'instrumental' cause ('elevated' by another power) and the agent intellect the 'principal' or 'primary' cause of the production of an immaterial intellectual species in the possible intellect (III.4–5, 'Tractatus de intellectu agente', q3, pp. 646–52); Eustachius describes the phantasm as a 'material' or 'dispositive' as opposed to 'efficient' cause (Eustachius a Sancto Paulo 1638, 'Physica', III.4, disp. 2 q7, pp. 292–3). See also Duns Scotus, *Ordinatio*, I, d3, pars 3, q3 (Duns Scotus 1950–, vol. 3).

33 Thomas Aquinas, *Summa th.,* I q84 a5: 'anima humana omnia cognoscat in rationibus aeternis, per quarum participationem omnia cognoscimus. Ipsum enim lumen intellectuale, quod est in nobis, nihil est aliud quam quaedam participata similitudo luminis increati, in quo continentur rationes aeternae'; he explicitly distinguishes this position from Platonism and other positions in which the eternal types are beheld by the human intellect independently of the senses, or are known innately. See also *Summa th.,* I q79 a3–4; Thomas Aquinas 1968b [1984], q5, resp. and *ad* 6; Thomas Aquinas 1882–, vol. 22, pt. 2, q10, a6 (trans. 1952–4).

34 *Collegium Conimbricense* 1600, III.4–5, q1 a2, 'nuda tabula' (pp. 372, 374); Eustachius a Sancto Paulo 1638, 'Physica', III.4, disp. 2 q7, 'tabula rasa' (p. 291); the agent intellect 'makes' (*fabricare*) intelligible species (pp. 291–2); Rubius 1620, III.4–5, 'Tractatus de intellectu agente', q1–2; Suárez, *De anima*, IV.2.7–18; 7.3; 8.7–8; Su. *Op. omn.* 3, pp. 718a–721b, 739, 742b–743b); Toletus 1594, III.4, q9 concl. 1 (fol. 131v–132r); III.5, q13, concl. 1, 7–8 (fol. 141v, 142vb). See also Thomas Aquinas, *Summa th.,* I q79 a2; q84 a3; Duns Scotus, *Ordinatio*, I, d3, pars 3, q2; and q3, n3, ad 1 (Duns Scotus 1950– , vol. 3, pp. 322–4, 335).

35 Thomas Aquinas, *Summa th.,* I q76 a2; q79 a4–5; Thomas Aquinas 1968b [1984], q3–5;

Duns Scotus, *De anima*, q13 (Duns Scotus 1891–5, vol. 3, p. 546); *Collegium Conimbricense* 1600, III.5, q1, a1–2 (pp. 369–74); Rubius 1620, 'Tractatus de intellectu agente', q4 (pp. 652–3); Suárez, *De anima* IV.8.4–8 (Su. *Op. omn.* 3, p. 741a–743b); Toletus 1594, II.1, q2 (fol. 40vb–48vb); also, Keckermann, *Systema physicum,* IV.4 (Keckermann 1614, col. 1604–5).

36 Theories of cognition specifying the necessity of divine illumination in all knowledge, together with direct knowledge of the soul and, through it, God, were known from the works of Augustine, Roger Bacon, and Bonaventure; Owens 1982, pp. 442, 449–51.

37 The assertion that the agent, or agent and possible, intellects are one was widely cited and discussed in connection with Avicenna and Averroes, e.g., *Collegium Conimbricense* 1600, III.5, q1 a1 (p. 370); Toletus 1594, II.1, q2 (fol. 41); III.4, q10 (fol. 133ra–134ra); III.5, q14 (fol. 143ra–143rb).

38 Zabarella, *Liber de mente agente,* chap. 13 (Zabarella 1606, cols. 935–7). Zabarella's compatriots Telesio and Campanella held that the lower soul actually is material, asserting that the *spiritus* in the brain – considered by many to be the instrument of the sensitive soul – is the sensitive soul itself. On the organic soul in the sixteenth century, see Park 1988; on the concept of 'spirit' in Renaissance physiology in comparison with Descartes's 'animal spirits', Hall 1969, vol. 1, pp. 198–9, 258–9; Hatfield 1992.

39 Pomponazzi 1516, chap. 9 (Pomponazzi 1948, pp. 316–18); in chap. 15 he affirms human immortality by appealing to revelation.

40 *Collegium Conimbricense* 1600, II.1, q6 a2: 'Negari non potest, animam intellectivam esse veram, ac propriam hominis formam, eiusque corpus vt talem informare' (p. 96); but also q1 a6: 'anima intellectiua habet operationes elevatas supra naturam & conditionem corporis ac materiae' (p. 63); Rubius 1620, III.4–5, 'Tractatus de intellectu agente', q4 n63 (p. 652); 'Tractatus de intellectu possibili', q1: 'intellectus possibilis non est potentia organica' (p. 661); Toletus 1594, III, q9 concl. 2 (fol. 132rb); q10 concl. 3: 'Intellectus est vis non organica animae informantis corpus' (fol. 134va). See also Thomas Aquinas, *Summa th.,* I q78 a1; q85 a1.

41 Toletus 1594, III.7, q23 concl. 3: 'Intellectus in corpore non potest habere naturaliter claram & distinctam cognitionem substantiae immaterialis' (fol. 168ra); concl. 4: 'Substantiae immateriales a nobis confusem in hoc statu cognoscuntur' (fol. 168rb); III.7, q21 (fol. 164v, 165r). Eustachius a Sancto Paulo 1638, pt. 3, 'Physica', tr. 4, disp. 2 q4–5, 7, 10 (vol. 3, pp. 287–9, 290–3, 298); Rubius 1620, III.4–5, 'Tractatus de intellectu agente', q2–3 (pp. 637–46); 'Tractatus de intellectu possibili', q5–6 (pp. 680–9); also *Collegium Conimbricense* 1600, III.5, q3, a2, (pp. 383–4); q5, a2 (pp. 402–3); III.8, q7, a2 (p. 449); q8, a2 (pp. 453–5); the Coimbran text states the conclusion clearly only as regards the soul (p. 449). Thomas Aquinas, *Summa th.,* I q87 a3; I q88; Thomas Aquinas 1984, q16. Scotus held that for embodied souls knowledge of God starts from phantasms, but he granted the embodied soul intuitive knowledge – not mediated by phantasms – of its own mental operations: Bonansea 1983, pp. 99–105; and Wolter 1990, pp. 109–22.

42 Ficino, *Theologia Platonica* Bk. 17, chap. 3 (Ficino 1964, p. 159 (Ficino 1981, pp. 230–1)); Pico della Mirandola, *Heptaplus,* 4th exp., chaps. 1–2 (Pico della Mirandola 1942, pp. 270–6).

43 On Albert, see Park 1981. See also the position attributed to Alexander of Aphrodisias, Themistius, and Averroes in Toletus 1594, III.7, q23 (fol. 167).

44 *Sag.,* I.8 (Charron 1635, p. 32); *Sag.,* I.14 (Charron 1635, pp. 50–1).

45 *Sag.,* I.14 (Charron 1635, p. 55).

46 *Sag.,* I.10 (Charron 1635, pp. 37–8).

47 *Sag.,* I.13 (Charron 1635, pp. 43–6).
48 *Sag.,* I.34 (Charron 1635, p. 99).
49 *Sag.,* I.14, 40, 61 (Charron 1635, pp. 55, 144, 197–8).
50 Sanchez 1581, 1618, 1988.
51 Sanchez 1581, p. 55 (as in Sanches 1988).
52 Sanchez 1581, pp. 51, 56–7, 59–67.
53 Sanchez 1581, pp. 68–77.
54 Sanchez 1581, p. 90.
55 *Exercitationes paradoxicae adversus Aristoteleos,* II.6 (Gassendi 1658, vol. 3, p. 201b, sub (Gassendi 1972, p. 94)); *Syntagma,* pt. 1 (Logica), II.v (Gassendi 1658, vol. 1, p. 81a (Gassendi 1972, p. 333)); Glanvill 1661, chap. 22, p. 218; Glanvill 1665, chap. 26, p. 160.
56 *Syntagma,* pt. 1 (Logica), II.v; pt. 2 (Physica), sec. 1, III.viii in Gassendi 1658, vol. 1; Glanvill 1661, chap. 4, pp. 28–31; chap. 21, pp. 211–12; chap. 24, p. 250; 1665, chap. 21, p. 135; 1676, essay 1, p. 21.
57 *Exercitationes,* II.6.6, 8 (Gassendi 1658, vol. 3, pp. 203a–206b, 207b–210b); *Syntagma,* pt. 1 (Logica), II.v (Gassendi 1658, vol. 1, pp. 80b–86a (Gassendi 1972, pp. 329–49)).
58 Mersenne 1625, I.5, pp. 49–56; I.9, pp. 107–13; I.10, pp. 125–6; I.13, pp. 176–8.
59 Mersenne 1625, I.11, pp. 132–3; I.12, pp. 157–8; I.14, p. 186.
60 Mersenne 1625, I.2, p. 18; I.15, pp. 191–5; I.16, pp. 212–13, 221–2.
61 Mersenne 1625, I.2, pp. 14–15; I.5, pp. 50–2; I.10, pp. 126–7; I.11, pp. 150–1; I.16, p. 222.
62 Mersenne 1634, q2, p. 11; also, Letter [p. v]: 'il semble que la capacité des hommes est bornée par l'ècorce, & par la surface des choses corporelles, & qu'ils ne peuvent penetrer plus avant que la quantité, avec une entiere satisfaction.'
63 Mersenne 1625, I.16, p. 224; II.1, pp. 225–34; Gassendi, *Exercitationes,* II.6.8 9 (Gassendi 1658, vol. 3, pp. 208a–209b (Gassendi 1972, pp. 106–7)); *Disquisitio metaphysica,* V.iii.1 (Gassendi 1658, vol. 3, p. 384a (Gassendi 1972, pp. 264–5])); *Syntagma,* pt. 1 (Logica), II.v (Gassendi 1658, vol. 1, pp. 83b–84a (Gassendi 1972, pp. 339–41)); Glanvill 1661, chap. 24, p. 236; Glanvill 1665, chap. 24, p. 153; Apology, p. 174. On Mersenne, see Dear 1988.
64 AT VII 12, 34, 52–3, 130–1, 162, 171–2.
65 Hatfield 1986; 1993; Rozemond, 1993.
66 Of the several notions of method extant in the seventeenth century (see Chapter 7 in this book), the focus here is on method as the means for directing the cognitive faculties in the pursuit of truth.
67 *Collegium Conimbricense* 1607, proem, q6 a2 (pp. 58–60); Rubius 1641, proem, q1 (pp. 2a–3a); Toletus 1596, proem, q1 (pp. 4b–7a); Eustachius a Sancto Paulo 1638, pt. 1, 'Dialecticae', proem, q4 (pp. 10–11).
68 *Nov. org.* I 41, 50.
69 *Nov. org.* I 21.
70 *Nov. org.* I 20, 45–9, 51.
71 *Nov. org.* I.19, 95; II.1–11.
72 *Nov. org.* II.10.
73 AT X 398: 'instrumenta sciendi'.
74 In casting his work as meditations, Descartes adopted a literary mode sometimes aimed at the faculties, and particularly at purging the senses, redirecting the imagination and understanding, and training the will: Ignatius of Loyola, *Exercitia spiritualia,* secs. 1, 3, 10, 20, 45–54, 65–70 (Ignatius of Loyola 1969, trans. in Ignatius of Loyola 1950), and François de Sales, *Introduction à la vie dévote,* II.iv–v (François de Sales 1969, vol. 1, pp.

85–7, trans. in François de Sales 1613); on Descartes's use of the meditative mode, Hatfield 1986, Rorty 1986b.

75 AT VII 155–9; also AT VII 4–5, 9–10, 38–9, 135–6.

76 Spinoza, *De. int. emend.,* Geb. II 13–19 (Spinoza 1985, pp. 16–23).

77 Malebranche, *Rech.* VI.1.1, Mal. *OC* II 246 (Malebranche 1980a, p. 409).

78 Malebranche *Rech.* VI.2.1, Mal. *OC* II 295 (Malebranche 1980a, p. 437).

79 Arnauld and Nicole 1668, 1st disc., pp. 9–13; intro., pp. 39–41 (Arnauld and Nicole 1964, pp. 9–ll; 29–30).

80 Arnauld and Nicole 1668, 1st disc., pp. 14–15 (Arnauld and Nicole 1964, pp. 12–13).

81 Gassendi 1981, I.4 (pp. 86–7).

82 Gassendi, *Syntagma,* 'Physica', sec. 3, memb. 2, IX.2, 4, 5 (Gassendi 1658, vol. 2, pp. 440a–41b, 460a, 461b).

83 Hobbes, *De corp.,* pt. 1, 'Logica', ii.9, Hobbes 1981, pp. 204–7

84 *Lev.* iv (Hobbes 1991, p. 26); *De corp.,* pt. 1, 'Logica', ii.7 (Hobbes 1981, pp. 202–3); on accidents and similitude, see his account of abstract names, 'Logica', iii.3–4 (Hobbes 1981, pp. 226–31).

85 Locke, *Ess.,* III.x.6–7; III and IV, passim.

86 Galilei, *Dialogo sopra i due massimi sistemi del mondo,* 2d Day (Galilei 1890–1909, vol. 7); *Il saggiatore,* sec. 48 (Galilei 1890–1909, vol. 6, pp. 347–51 (Galilei 1960a, pp. 308–13)); Hatfield 1990.

87 AT I 410–11, 420–4, 562–4; II 197–200 (trans. in Descartes 1984–91, vol. 3). For discussion, Clarke 1982, sec. 22; Hatfield 1985, 1989.

88 Descartes 1979, pp. 1–3, 6–9.

89 AT XI 177–9 (*Traité de l'homme*); Descartes 1972, pp. 87–90. AT III 48, 84–5, 143, 425, 598; IV 114; V 220–1.

90 AT VI 112, 239; also ibid., p. 43 (*Discours,* v).

91 AT VI 76–7.

92 Hobbes and Gassendi in AT VII 178, 266–7, 269, 329–32.

93 AT VII 63–90 (Meds. V–VI); *Princ.,* II 3–4.

94 AT VII 81–3 (Med. VI); *Princ.* I 66–71, IV 198–200. Hatfield 1986, p. 68; but cf. Garber 1992a, chap. 4. Descartes clearly intends to exclude colour, and other such qualities, as 'real qualities' through an opposition with genuinely geometrical modes of extension.

95 *Princ.* I 32; AT II 598 (to Mersenne, 16 Oct. 1639); AT VII 56–7, 78–9 (Meds. IV, VI); see also AT X 415–17 (*Regulae,* XII). In making the immaterial mind the seat of sensations Descartes denied the materialist equation of sensation with brain activity, e.g., by Hobbes (AT VII 178) and Gassendi (VII 268–9). As noted previously, he also recognised a wholly noncorporeal form of memory.

96 AT VII 77–83; *Princ.* IV 197–200.

97 AT VII 72–3; also VII 28, 31, 34, 53, 139, 178, 358, 384–5, 387.

98 Clauberg, *Physica,* 'Theoriae corporum viventium', xxxiii–xxxix (Clauberg 1691, vol. 1, pp. 196–203); La Forge 1974, pp. 150, 159, 170, 173, 255, 262–5, 285, 292–4; Le Grand, 'Institution', IX.v.1–13 (Le Grand 1694, pp. 329a–30b); Régis, 'Metaphysique', Bk. 2, I.i.1–iii.1 (Régis 1691b, vol. 1, pp. 296–303).

99 AT VII 436–9.

100 AT XI 151, 170–7 (*De l'homme*), which alone contains the details of pineal flow; VI 81–93, 115–30 (*Dioptrique,* i, v–vi).

101 AT VI 137–8 (*Dioptrique,* vi).

102 AT XI 159–61, 183 (*De l'homme*); Descartes 1972, pp. 61–3, 94.

103 Hobbes, *Lat. Works,* vol. 1, pp. xx–xxi.

104 Hobbes, *Eng. Works,* vol. 7, pp. 468 (*Minute or First Draught of the Optiques*); see also Hobbes in AT III 342. Despite these claims, Hobbes may have given extensive attention to natural philosophy and its foundations only in response to Descartes's *Discours* and *Essais* (especially the *Dioptrique*): Tuck 1988; also Brandt 1928, chap. 4. At the end of the 1646 ms. Hobbes wrote that if his writing 'bee found true doctrine, (though yett it wanteth polishing), I shall deserve the reputation of having beene the first to lay the ground of two sciences; this of *Optiques,* the most curious, and that other of *Natural Justice,* which I have done in my book DE CIVE' (Hobbes, *Eng. Works,* vol. 7, p. 471).

105 On the order of Hobbes's compositions and publications, see Tuck 1988; cf. Brandt 1928, chap. 5–6, and the preface by Tönnies in Hobbes 1969.

106 Hobbes, *De corp.,* IV.xxv.2 (*Lat. Works,* vol 1, p. 31); see also *Lat. Works,* vol. 5, pp. 254, 258 (*Objectiones*); *Elements of Law,* I.ii.8 (Hobbes 1969, pp. 5–6); *Lev.* i (Hobbes 1991, pp. 13–14).

107 On influences, see Brandt 1928, pp. 55–84, and Tuck 1988, pp. 28–37; on the reception of Hobbes's works, see Henry More, *Immortality of the Soul,* I.ix–x, II.i–ii (More 1662d, pp. 38–43, 58–77); Cudworth 1678, p. 761 (sub); Mintz 1962.

108 Hobbes *Excerpta de tractatu optico,* ms., i.4–10 (Hobbes 1969, pp. 212–15); *Tractatus opticus,* published 1644 (*Lat. Works,* vol. 5, p. 217–18); Brandt 1928, p. 48; Tuck 1988, p. 28.

109 Brain: *Elements,* I.ii (Hobbes 1969, pp. 3–7); *Tractatus opticus* (*Lat. Works,* vol. 5, pp. 220–1). Heart and brain: *Excerpta de tractatu optico,* iv.1, 11–16 (Hobbes 1969, pp. 216–17, 218–23); *Lev.* i (Hobbes 1991, pp. 13–14); *De corp.,* IV.xxv.2–4 (*Lat. Works,* vol. 1, p. 318–20).

110 Hobbes, *De corp.,* IV.xxv.1 (*Lat. Works,* vol. 1, p. 316): 'Phaenomenon autem omnium, quae prope nos existunt, id ipsum *to phainesthai* est admirabilissimum, nimirum, in corporibus naturalibus alia omnium fere rerum, alia nullarum in seipsis exemplaria habere'; trans. *Eng. Works,* vol. 1, p. 389.

111 *Elements,* I.iii (Hobbes 1969, pp. 8–12); *De corp.,* IV.xxv.7–9 (*Lat. Works,* vol. 1, p. 322–8); *Lev.* ii–iii (Hobbes 1991, pp. 15–22).

112 *De corp.,* I.i.1 (Hobbes 1981, 172–3): 'philosophia, id est, ratio naturalis, in omni homine innata est.'

113 *Lev.* v (Hobbes 1991, p. 35).

114 *Lev.* ii, iii, v (Hobbes 1991, pp. 19, 23, 31–2, 35–6).

115 *De corp.,* I.i.1-2, ii.1 (Hobbes 1981, pp. 172–7, 192–5).

116 Hobbes, *Lat. Works,* vol. 5, p. 258; also in AT VII 178.

117 *De corp.,* I.i.8 (Hobbes 1981, pp. 188–9).

118 *De corp.,* I.vi.5–6 (Hobbes 1981, pp. 294–7); *De corp.,* II.ix.9, IV.xxv.2 (*Lat. Works,* vol. 1, pp. 111–12, 317–19).

119 *Lev.* i, iv, xxxiv, xlvi (Hobbes 1991, pp. 1–2, 30, 269–70, 463–4).

120 *Elements,* I.xi.5 (Hobbes 1969, pp. 55–6); *Lev.* xxxiv (Hobbes 1991, p. 274).

121 Gassendi 1658, vol. 3, pp. 420–77; Bloch 1971, chap. 1.

122 *Epistolae qvatvor de apparente magnitvdina solis hvmilis et svblimis,* II.iv, viii–xii (Gassendi 1658, vol. 3, pp. 424b–25a, 427a–30a), which postulates an uninverted retinal image; *Syntagma,* pt. 2, 'Physica', sec. 3, VII.v (Gassendi 1658, vol. 2, pp. 377b–82b), which has the image inverted.

123 *Disquisitio metaphysica,* IV.iii.4 (Gassendi 1658, vol. 3, p. 369a (Gassendi 1962, pp. 442–3)).

124 *Syntagma*, pt. 2 (Physica), sec. 3, III.iv, IX.ii–iii (Gassendi 1658, vol. 2, pp. 255–9, 440–54).

125 *Epistolae quatuor*, II.v (Gassendi 1658, vol. 3, p. 425a–b); *Syntagma*, pt. 2, 'Physica', sec. 3, VI.i, VII.v (Gassendi 1658, vol. 2, pp. 337b, 375a).

126 Five senses: *Syntagma*, pt. 2, 'Physica', sec. 3, VII (Gassendi 1658, vol. 2, pp. 353–97, 375a). Material sensory soul: *Syntagma*, pt. 2, 'Physica', sec. 3, VI.iii (Gassendi 1658, vol. 2, p. 345a–b); also *Disquisitio metaphysica*, II.vi (Gassendi 1962, pp. 148–65); Gassendi in AT VII 268–9.

127 *Syntagma*, pt. 2, 'Physica', sec. 3, VIII.ii, iv (Gassendi 1658, vol. 2, pp. 402b–403a, 409–14).

128 *Disquisitio metaphysica*, III.iv; vi.1, 4; VI.i (Gassendi 1962, pp. 236–61, 278–85, 288–93, 518–33).

129 *Disquisitio metaphysica*, III.iii.2 (Gassendi 1962, pp. 224–7, 232–7).

130 *Syntagma*, pt. 2, 'Physica', sec. 3, IX.i (Gassendi 1658, vol. 2, p. 425b).

131 La Forge 1974, p. 263.

132 *Syntagma*, pt. 2, 'Physica', sec. 3, IX.ii, XIV.ii (Gassendi 1658, vol. 2, pp. 440–6, 629a–b).

133 *Eth.* II prop. 49.

134 *Eth.* II props. 13, 15.

135 *Eth.* II props. 13–29.

136 *Eth.* II prop. 40; also *De int. emen.*, Geb. II 10–27.

137 In the *De int. emen.*, Spinoza strictly distinguished imagination from intellect, Geb. II 31–3.

138 *Eth.* II prop. 40.

139 'Lettre touchant ce qui est independant des sens et de la matiere,' (Ger. VI 499–502 (Leibniz 1989, pp. 186–8)).

140 *Disc. mét.* sec. 14; 'System nouveau de la nature et de la communication des substances,' (Ger. IV 483–5); *Mon.* secs. 7–16.

141 'Ce qui est independant' (Ger. VI 501–2); Leibniz to de Volder, 1699, (Ger. VI 194 (Leibniz 1969, p. 522)).

142 *Mon.* sec. 28; *PNG* sec. 5.

143 'Ce qui est independant' (Ger. VI 504–5 (Leibniz 1969, pp. 550–1; Leibniz 1989, pp. 189–91)).

144 *Rech.*, pref., I.i.1 (Mal. *OC* I 20–6, 39–40 (Malebranche 1980a, pp. xxv–xxix, 1–2)).

145 *Rech.*, I.iv.1 (Mal. *OC* I 66–7 (Malebranche 1980a, pp. 16–17)).

146 Malebranche adumbrates his occasionalism early (*Rech.*, I.ii.1, Mal. *OC* I 50, n. (Malebranche 1980a, p. 7, n.)), and explains it together with the doctrine that we see all things in God (*Rech.*, IIIB.vi–vii, Mal. *OC* I 437–55 (Malebranche 1980a, pp. 230–40)). See also *Rech.*, Eclaircissement X (Mal. *OC* III 127–61 (Malebranche 1980a, pp. 612–32)); *Ent. mét.* II.ii–iii, IV.x–xi (Malebranche 1980b, pp. 44–5, 86–91)).

147 *Rech.*, I.x.6–xiii (Mal. *OC* I 129–54 (Malebranche 1980a, pp. 52–66)).

148 *Rech.*, I.vii.4; ix.3; x.6; xiv.2 (Mal. *OC* I 96–7, 119–20, 130, 158–60 (Malebranche 1980a, pp. 34–5, 46–7, 52–3, 68–9)).

149 *Rech.*, I.v; vii.5 (Mal. *OC* I 69–78, 97–100 (Malebranche 1980a, pp. 19–24, 35–6)).

150 *Rech.*, Eclaircissement xvii, secs. 26, 41–3 (Mal. *OC* III 327, 341–8 (Malebranche 1980a, pp. 733–4, 743–8)).

151 Resp. IV, AT VII 233; *Princ.* IV 197.

152 AT VII 41–4 (Med. III), leaves open the possibility that sensations confusedly represent the actual character of their external causes. *Rech.*, IIIA.i.3 attributes the position that

sensation proper contains judgement to Augustine, Descartes, and their followers (Mal. *OC* I 386–7 (Malebranche 1980a, pp. 200–1)); Rodis-Lewis cites La Forge as a follower (Mal. *OC* I 519, n. 308).

153  *Rech.* III.ii.vi, Mal. *OC* I 445 (Malebranche 1980a, p. 234).

154  *Recherche,* Eclaircissement x (Mal. *OC* III 152 (Malebranche 1980a, p. 626)); *Ent. mét.* III.i–vii, V.ii–vi (Malebranche 1980b, pp. 56–61, 106–13).

155  Cudworth, *True Intellectual System,* I.v.1 (Cudworth 1678, p. 733; pp. 638–9); More, *Antidote Against Atheism,* I.xi.12, I.vi–vii (More 1662c, p. 36, 18–21); Benjamin Whichcote and John Smith, in Patrides 1969, pp. 57, 129; 53–6, 143–4.

156  Enthusiasm: More, *Enthusiasmus triumphatus,* secs. 3–10 (More 1662e, pp. 2–7).

157  More, *Immortality of the Soul,* II.ii.3–6, II.vi.4 (More 1662d, pp. 67–8, 85–6).

158  More, *Immortality,* II.ii.7, II.vi.6–7 (More 1662d, pp. 68, 86–7); *Antidote,* I.xi.2–11 (More 1662c, pp. 33–6).

159  More, *Immortality,* I.ii.10 (More 1662d, p. 69): 'it is plain, that there is *a* setled *Notion* distinct from these *Words* and *Names,* as well as those corporeal Phantasmes impressed from the Object.'

160  More, *Immortality,* II.xi.1–3, II.vii–x (More 1662d, pp. 106, [8]8–105).

161  More, *Immortality,* II.x–xi.2 (More 1662d, pp. 101–6).

162  More, *Immortality,* II.xi.3–4 (More 1662d, pp. 106–7).

163  More, *Immortality,* II.ii. 9 (More 1662d, p. 69); *Antidote,* I.iv.2–3, viii.12–14, xi.13 (More 1662c, pp. 14–16, 24–5, 36).

164  More, *Antidote,* I.iii.3, v, vii (More 1662c, pp. 13, 17, 20–1).

165  *True Intellectual System,* I.iv.1 (Cudworth 1678, pp. 634–8).

166  *Eternal and Immutable Morality,* III.ii.1; i.3; generally, III.i–iv (Cudworth 1845, vol. 3, pp. 561, 558, 557–77).

167  *True Intellectual System* I.iv.1 (Cudworth 1678, pp. 732–3, 736–8); also *Immutable Morality,* IV.i–vi (Cudworth 1845, vol. 3, pp. 577–646).

168  *True Intellectual System* I.iv.1 (Cudworth 1678, p. 737); *Immutable Morality,* IV.i.1: 'the intelligible forms by which things are understood or known, are not stamps or impressions passively printed upon the soul from without [by the senses], but ideas vitally protended or actively asserted from within itself' (Cudworth 1845, vol. 3, p. 578); *Immutable Morality,* iv.12: 'all understandings are not only constantly furnished with forms and ideas to conceive all things by, and thereby enabled to understand all the clear conceptions of one another, being printed all over at once with the seeds of universal knowledge, but also have exactly the same ideas of the same things' (Cudworth 1845, vol. 3, p. 628). On Cudworth, see Passmore 1951.

169  On the development of the title, beginning with 'Sic Cogitavit de Intellectu humano', see Locke 1975, p. xiii. The four books of the *Essay* examine the origin of knowledge and ideas (Bk. I), catalogue the variety ideas (Bk. II), investigate the relation between ideas and words (Bk. III), and analyse the relations between ideas constitutive of knowledge and related cognitive states (Bk. IV).

170  *Ess.* II.xxi.5–6.

171  *Ess.* II.vi.2; ix–xi; xxi.20.

172  *Ess.* II.i.2–4. In 'Ce qui est independant'(Ger. VI 501–2; Leibniz 1989, p. 188) Leibniz held that we know immaterial substance through acquaintance with our own minds; Locke held only that we experience the mind's operations, not that we come thereby to perceive the mind to be an immaterial substance (*Ess.* II.i.4; xxxiii.5–6; IV.iii.6).

173  *Ess.* III.iii.7; 12.

174  *Ess.* III.iii.14.

175 *Ess.* III.iii.13–17. Ayers 1991, vol. 2, chaps. 3–7.

176 *Pr. Hum. Kn.,* secs. 1, 27, 30.

177 *Pr. Hum. Kn.,* secs. 27, 140, 142; *Three Dialogues,* III (Berkeley 1948–57, vol. 2, pp. 232–4).

178 *3 Dial.,* I (Berkeley 1948–57, vol. 2, pp. 193–4); see also *Pr. Hum. Kn.,* intro., secs. 7–8.

179 *New Th. Vis.,* secs. 9–11, 25, 50–1.

180 *Ess.* II.ix.8.

181 *Ess.* II.ix.9. Locke does not say why touch, which perceives both its proper objects (such as heat, cold, and solidity, *Ess.* II.iii.1) and the 'Ideas of divers senses' (space, extension, figure, rest, and motion, *Ess.* II.v), does not yield similar judgements; presumably he believed that three-dimensional perception is immediately given with touch and so does not require unnoticed judgements.

182 *Ess.* II.v; II.xi.1.

183 *Nouv. ess.* II.ix.8.

184 *New Th. Vis.,* sec. 133.

185 *New Th. Vis.,* sec. 70, 121; *Theory of Vision Vindicated,* sec. 51; Atherton 1990, pp. 97–8.

186 *New Th. Vis.,* secs. 17, 25, 49, 53, 121-36; *Pr. Hum. Kn.,* secs. 43–4.

187 *Ess.,* epistle, Locke 1975, p. 7.

# 29

# THEORIES OF KNOWLEDGE AND BELIEF

## MICHAEL AYERS

## I. GODS AND GIANTS

### 1. Introduction

Here is a traditional view. The conception of knowledge as an infallible cognitive act was a distinctively seventeenth-century manifestation and consequence of a new obsession with doubt and its resolution. Whereas earlier epistemology, following Plato and Aristotle, had focussed on the move from particular beliefs to general science ('the Problem of Universals'), Cartesian and post-Cartesian epistemology was very differently shaped by a scepticism which extended even to the existence of material objects ('the Problem of Perception').[1] The latter took the form of a new quest for certainty and 'given' foundations which, although dominated by the metaphors of sight[2] and enlightenment, in fact spread a veil – indeed, drove an ontological wedge – between subject and object, a thinking self and an 'external' world. Two schools of philosophy are assigned their origin in this supposedly novel problematic. 'Rationalists' sought a remedy for doubt in quasi-geometrical systems built on supposedly innate axioms evident to the self in independence of the world, while 'Empiricists', with equal egocentricity, looked for the foundations of knowledge in the pure content of sensory experience.

The foregoing, it may be, caricatures a myth which few take seriously any more, but the myth can still do harm.[3] Perhaps the chief thing wrong with it is the postulation of a discontinuity such as to open a way, previously shut off, to philosophical idealism and mind–body dualism. The alleged shift in (or, as some even suggest, invention of)[4] 'theory of knowledge' was in fact the various application and development of existing, largely ancient epistemological theories.[5] In this, the 'new philosophers' were each motivated by some conception of what had been attained and was attainable in physics, but also by considerations drawn from other areas of debate – above all, perhaps, by the politics of religion.[6] There was certainly some novelty, even structural change. Yet there was no sudden transformation of the theory of knowledge by new epistemological concerns or concepts. The 'strong' conception of knowledge later taken to be characteristic of the seventeenth century was drawn directly and consciously from the tradition. First, there were Platonic and Aristotelian accounts of the progress from particular beliefs to systematic knowledge with understanding (*gnosis* or *episteme*, translated *scientia*, 'science'). Second, there were the anti-sceptical arguments developed in the Hellenistic period. These included Epicurean accounts of the criteria of truth and Stoic characterisations of 'clear and evident' cognitive or 'apprehensive' sense-impressions (*phantasiai kataleptikai*). The latter are effectively secure, but beyond them lies the even greater, if less accessible, security of systematic 'science', an overall understanding of experience based on experience.[7]

The distinction between 'rationalists' and 'empiricists' has come increasingly under attack as a construct of Kantian criticism. Yet it is appropriate to bring the distinction to bear on the seventeenth century just because it corresponds to an ancient way of marking an argument about method and scientific knowledge which was among the direct determinants of early modern theories.[8] Both Plato and Aristotle explicitly opposed their own views to doctrines which explained knowledge in terms of perception and memory alone, characteristically maintained that all appearances are equally true, and offered materialist explanations of thought.[9] Plato's own epistemology is triangular, a matter of the inter-relations between the human mind, transcendent universals, and particular sensible things. To achieve 'science', the mind has to apprehend the hierarchical order among immutable and eternal forms, but it needs to be prompted to do so by sensible objects, as a geometer may need diagrams. Reciprocally, universal knowledge is relevant to the sensible world: to have knowledge of the forms is in some way to know why sensible things are as they are. Plato had problems both with the relation between forms and particulars, and with the relation between forms and the mind. As to the latter, he is clear that, in order to apprehend the forms, the mind must be immaterial. That is one point of his famous account of a battle between Gods and Giants, that is, between 'lovers of the forms' (who allow an immaterial mind) and empiricist materialists. Yet his writings are equivocal on the question whether we apprehend the forms in this life or remember apprehending them before birth.[10] The version of the theory authorised by Saint Augustine, however, explains both problematic relations in terms of creation, as well as assigning a mode of existence to universals which avoids setting them up as eternal rivals to God. God creates particular things in accordance with the ideas (essences, eternal truths or archetypes) which constitute divine reason, while human reason is created in the image of divine reason. That explains both why our minds are fitted to apprehend the universal, and why universal knowledge has application to particulars. Just as for Plato, the senses simply prompt the intellect to make such knowledge explicit. It is this theory which was the dominant ancestor of early modern 'rationalism'.

The theory, or its ontology, was incorporated in part into scholastic Aristotelianism. Aristotle had retained universal and intelligible forms in his system, principles of teleological explanation, but bound them into the particulars to which he accorded primary reality. The Augustinian ontology allowed a view of eternal truths about essences which freed them from what is actual. With respect to Platonic epistemology, on the other hand, there can seem to be a certain ambiguity in Aristotle himself. A crucial question concerns the way in which the first principles of science are apprehended (i.e., the premises of the syllogistic 'demonstration' of explicanda which constitutes a developed science). A famous, obscure passage in the *Posterior Analytics* seems to distinguish four stages: (1) sense perception of particulars, (2) memory of particulars perceived, (3) 'experience' (*empeiria*) formed from the memory of many particulars and involving the apprehension of something common to them, and (4) the apprehension of universal explanatory principles, the 'real definitions' (as they came to be known) used as the starting points of scientific demonstration.[11] A traditional interpretation (consonant with the early mediaeval belief that Aristotle's doctrines are in harmony with Plato's) emphasised a qualitative progress from one kind of cognition to another, an intuitive leap of intellect from the multiplicity of experience to the universality of abstract understanding. On the other hand, Aristotle seems to regard the derivation of universal principles from experience as logically a matter of induction. He also presents the steps to science as levels of cognitive capacity: some animals have only perception; some have memory as well, which gives them a small share of experience, and so of prudence (*phronesis*) and a capacity for learning; men have experience to a greater extent, which may, for practical purposes, be as good as, or even better than, 'art' (*techne*); and, finally, art gives us the capacity to explain what experience has taught us, that is, 'science'.[12] This passage suggests that any special faculty of reason or intuition is exercised not so much in universal thought as such, as in understanding things through their essences. It may be significant that Aristotle used a medical example, perhaps attempting to take a middle way between Plato and the empiricism or 'memorism' which seems to have been first developed as medical theory.[13]

Epicurus, however, was firmly empiricist. His 'preconception' (*prolepsis*) is described as 'as it were a perception, or correct opinion, or conception, or universal "stored notion" (i.e., memory) of that which has frequently become evident externally: for example, "Such and such a kind of thing is a man." '[14] Preconceptions such as the preconception of *man* are, it seems, a sort of universalised memories which arise naturally from experience and enable us to bring experience to bear on the particular case, and to make inferences going beyond it. Epicureans distinguished a form of inference employing 'indicative' signs to what is in general unobservable, but more sceptical philosophers (including some medical empiricists) allowed inference only to what is in general observable, based on 'reminiscent' signs arising from experienced constant conjunction. Some Stoics, on the other hand, argued that, although mere resemblance between the present object and what has been experienced in the past may often give rise to psychologically convincing inference, valid scientific inference must be based on a grasp of essences and evident counterfactual conditionals. The possibility of such universal knowledge is not ascribed to forms and the intellect, however, but to human conceptualisation – to abstraction and language.[15] An issue here which became important in the seventeenth century was how far, and how, belief or opinion can be rationally justified while falling short of certain knowledge: in other words, how probability should be dealt with philosophically.

Roughly correspondent to the range of views about the step from observation to science were different estimations of the status and authority of perceptual beliefs. Plato's denigration of the senses for distracting the soul from eternal reality was perhaps more a denigration of inconstant particulars than of the senses' veracity in their own field.[16] It is because of their objects that the senses can at best give rise to true opinion rather than science. For Aristotelians, Epicureans, and Stoics, on the other hand, the deliverances of the senses are foundational. For the Epicureans, that meant that they (and the preconceptions immediately drawn from them) are more dependable than any further product of reasoning. Indeed, for Epicurus all sense impressions are true, a doctrine apparently based on the assumption that the mechanism of sensation will always deliver a material image, composed of atoms, which is appropriate to its causal origin. For example, when a large square tower at a distance appears small and round, the material image, the true object of sense, really is small and cornerless, in virtue of its long journey. As such, the image may naturally give rise to a false belief, yet it is not in fact just the same as an image issuing from a small round tower nearby. So even if the judgement or opinion we form on the basis of any given impression is false, the impression itself is true (i.e., in itself a dependable sign) and should not be rejected, but better interpreted. The need for interpretation does not elevate reason above the senses, since we interpret individual impressions in the light of other impressions and on the basis of experience. Here, 'preconceptions' serve as criteria of truth. Moreover, some impressions are self-evident, so that we may confirm a doubtful judgement about a distant object by approaching the object and seeing it clearly.

The Stoics agreed that sensory beliefs are ultimately corrigible only by the senses themselves, but they developed a more complex view as to how it is done. The ideal *sophos* or 'sage' will have become so by proceeding methodically from the intrinsically trustworthy 'apprehensive' sense-impressions to systematic scientific knowledge. Yet those who assent to apprehensive impressions before achieving science do not so much possess a lower grade of knowledge as suffer from the opposite of knowledge, 'ignorance' (*agnoia*). That is because such assent is 'precipitate', 'changeable and weak', and so not intrinsically immune to sceptical reasoning. The sage will withhold actual assent until possessing the powers of discrimination which come with systematic science. Then assent to apprehensive impressions will itself constitute *episteme,* capable of withstanding the worst the sceptic can do.[17]

Against this background, it is not so surprising that the new philosophers should have fallen at least roughly into two groups, corresponding, indeed, to two possible lines of criticism of Aristotelianism. With few exceptions (Leibniz was one with respect to teleology), they were largely in agreement that forms and teleology should be excluded from physics, that mechanical explanations are paradigms of scientific explanation, and that the only intrinsic attributes of bodies are quantitative, qualities being a matter of the way things appear to perceivers.[18] But were the failings of the Aristotelians due, as Bacon thought, to their being insufficiently attentive to nature as it is open to experience? Were they rationalist spiders spinning their specious teleological and qualitative principles from their own entrails? Or were they, as Descartes seems to suggest in *Meditationes,* blundering empiricists trying vainly to build science from the materials of sense-experience and ignoring the divine gift of mathematics which does not draw on experience at all? On the one hand, the new picture of the physical world was deeply indebted to the ancient theory most like it, the atomism of the empiricist Epicurus. On the other hand, it came in with a programme for mathematising nature at least some of whose proponents saw their most natural justification in a Platonist view of mathematics as a science prior to experience and brought to its interpretation.

If these suggestions are correct, then the revival and development of scepticism does not rate quite the top billing that it often gets in accounts of early modern epistemology. Certainly serious argument for and against scepticism took place, in particular within a debate about religious knowledge across and within the different persuasions. This argument, about the spheres of faith and reason, about natural and revealed theology, about authority and toleration, had some effect on all theories of cognition. Yet we should not summarily conclude that modern epistemology was conceived in a *crise Pyrrhonienne*. Very possibly, every significant epistemologist who was not a sceptic took the trouble to criticise scepticism at least in passing, but that may be poor evidence of underlying motivation. Descartes is only the most remembered (and one of the most dogmatic) of those who found that scepticism could be a helpful foil for constructive argument. Moreover, between dogmatism and scepticism lay a useful space for innovation and the pursuit of natural knowledge. Bacon, much as Descartes did, approved of the sceptics' rejection of established theory while arguing that with the proper aids to the interpretation of experience we can avoid the errors and uncertainty on which scepticism breeds. Yet it is clear that he constructed his method, not to combat scepticism, but in order to replace (above all) Aristotelian natural philosophy with theory more directly answerable to nature itself.

### 2. 'Mitigated scepticism': Mersenne and Gassendi

In the early years of the century, a number of epistemological works were expressly directed against scepticism.[19] In general, they attempted to show that the existence of illusion, error, and disagreement does not undermine the principle that we have faculties which naturally and normally arrive at truth, and that the special circumstances which lead to error can be ascertained and allowed for. In some the argument was couched in the terms of an orthodox interpretation of Aristotelian epistemology, but a striking feature of others was a more Platonic conception of reason and its relation to the senses. Lord Herbert of Cherbury's *De Veritate*[20] is an important, if idiosyncratic, example of the latter. Herbert stresses the existence of innate 'common notions' which are identifiable by their natural evidence and the universal consent of normal, unprejudiced people, and which are employed in the interpretation of experience. An important part of his programme was to install five common notions relating to religion, with the effect of exalting reason over revelation and dogma, and works over faith. Herbert was regarded as a Deist, but other, theologically less suspect English philosophers, in particular the Cambridge Platonists, adopted innatism together with a rational approach to ethics and religion.[21]

Marin Mersenne was another anti-sceptical writer with Platonist leanings whose programme included rather more than the refutation of scepticism, but in his case it was the promotion of a mathematical approach to the physical world. The Aristotelian understanding of mathematics as the science of quantity abstracted from natural change tended to deny it the status of a genuine science, in that it is not knowledge *per causas.* Number is a creature of the mind, while the object of geometry is matter considered simply as the subject of extension. Mathematics says nothing about natural or real essences. For Mersenne, on the other hand, the evidence of maxims (such as 'The whole is greater than the part') and our understanding of mathematics assure us that we have a faculty capable of 'science', the highest degree of knowledge – but that is not all. For although pure mathematics is not directly concerned with natural essences or change, its objects exist as ideas or archetypes in the Creator's mind and, derivatively, in ours. (Indeed, Mersenne seems to have favoured the strongly Platonist argument that, just because its objects change, *physics* cannot be a genuine science.)[22] At the same time, like earlier writers who hoped to improve the standing of mathematics, Mersenne stressed its utility, seeing its applications as reflections of a 'universal harmony' in creation which we can study at the level of appearances. With respect both to this metaphysical conception of a mathematical Creator, and to the epistemological conceptions of enlightenment by God and a resemblance between human and divine reason, Mersenne appealed to the authority of Saint Augustine.

Armed with its luminous truths, reason is in a position to assess the deliverances of sense. Without the judgement of reason, the senses give knowledge only of how things appear. Yet all this rationalism is coupled with what has led to Mersenne's being categorised, not as a rationalist, but with Gassendi as a 'mitigated sceptic'.[23] Essences are unknown to us, and any systematic view of nature can at best be probable. Even the mixed-mathematical sciences of harmonics, astronomy, mechanics, and optics are less than entirely certain in so far as their principles involve assumptions about their natural objects. Their conclusions should therefore be subjected to the test of observation. Nevertheless they represent the best approach to nature that is available to us. In effect, Mersenne employed potentially the most dogmatic of the ancient epistemologies to advance an undogmatic but systematic research programme. Like Bacon's different view, his philosophy is as much as anything concerned with method, the ancient problem of the proper or most productive movement from perception and experience to theory.

The minor paradox of an undogmatic Platonist (minor, since Plato's thought, at least, led into Academic scepticism) is perhaps heightened by comparison with the rather more natural basis of the 'mitigated scepticism' of Mersenne's associate, Pierre Gassendi, in the epistemology of Epicurus. Gassendi drew a distinction between 'science' and 'opinion', but attacked the notion that the objects of science are universal essences or eternal truths outside human minds.[24] He accepted the orthodox use of the term 'science' for the end-product of demonstration from necessary and evident premises, and argued that the term should be extended to knowledge of those premises themselves ('according to the saying that the cause of a quality in something else has that quality itself to a greater degree'). Yet for Gassendi 'necessary' is simply equivalent to 'always true',[25] and the ultimate premises of any chain of demonstration must be known through the evidence of sense. '*Scire per causas*', he claimed, simply means 'to know through certain and evident premises', and no evidence is greater than the evidence of sense on which all other evidence directly or indirectly depends.[26]

As for ancient Epicureans, for Gassendi the 'reason' that corrects mistaken natural sensory judgements is not a separate faculty, but the senses correcting themselves. The correct judgement flows from 'the suffrage of the senses'.[27] Mersenne had claimed that reason brings such maxims as 'The whole is greater than its parts' to bear on the deliverances of sense, and that self-evident truth bestows certainty on the less general proposition that the body is greater than its fingers.[28] Gassendi did not deny a corrective rôle to very general, 'evident' and 'necessary' propositions but insisted that Mersenne's maxim commands belief only because it has been universally observed in particular cases, from infancy, that a whole man is larger than his head, the whole sky is larger than a star, and so on. It is reasoning from less to more general which ought to be called *a priori* ('from what is prior'), he argued, 'since all the evidence and certainty drawn from a general proposition depends on that which has been built up (*collecta est*) from an induction of particulars.'[29] He accepted the principle that maxims need only be understood in order to command assent,[30] but he seems to have interpreted it in the following way: anyone having ordinarily extensive experience of particular wholes and parts who is then presented with, and taught the terms of, the abstract general maxim, will assent to it. The maxim draws together everyone's universal experience.

The opposite of 'evidence' Gassendi called 'obscurity'. Doubtful or uncertain propositions lie equally between the two, while those tending towards evidence are probable. A probable proposition is based on what has usually but not universally been observed, but an otherwise improbable proposition asserted by someone likely to be veracious may also be probable.[31] Our acceptance of the conclusion of a syllogism with only probable premises involves hesitation and is 'opinion' rather than science.[32] Acceptance of another's assertion is 'faith', which is opinion if the authority is human, but equals science in certainty and evidence if the authority is God's, since we have the preconception that God cannot lie. Hence revelation can supply demonstration with premises.

With due apology to such figures as Kepler and Galileo,[33] on the one side, and

Bacon, on the other, it is tempting to see the two friends, Mersenne and Gassendi, as the founders of modern 'rationalism' and modern 'empiricism', respectively.[34] Roughly, Mersenne's (restricted) science and certainty descends from the top down, while Gassendi's is built from the bottom up. On the other hand, their shared anti-dogmatic attitudes and aims were perhaps as important to them as their differences. In particular, neither envisaged an explanatory natural science in the traditional sense, seeing nature as the topic of opinion and probable hypothesis. However that may be, Mersenne's Augustinian rationalism was soon upstaged by that of his protégé Descartes, while Gassendi's main works were published only after Hobbes had constructed an empiricism of a very different kind. That Hobbes was no less dogmatic than Descartes supplies further reason to distinguish the distinction between rationalist and empiricist from the distinction between dogmatist and anti-dogmatist.

### 3. Descartes's 'rationalism'

The formative influence on Descartes was Isaac Beeckman, whose programme for mathematising science antedated Mersenne's.[35] Yet Descartes's epistemology possibly owed its general shape to Mersenne. In effect, at least, he excluded a mitigated scepticism like Mersenne's simply by abolishing the presumption of unknown essences beyond the eternal mathematical truths that are known, thus closing the gap between mathematics and nature. Matter geometrically defined is, as such, a substance capable of separate, concrete existence independent of all but the Creator. By this stroke he broke with Aristotelianism more decisively than Mersenne, according even more significance to mathematics than Augustine or Plato.[36] Yet his move was made within an epistemological framework as broadly Augustinian (apart from his doctrine of the creation of the eternal truths)[37] as Mersenne's. His model for scientific knowledge, its possibility, and its application to the world is constructed round the triangular relation between divine reason, created human reason, and created sensible things. The *cogito* itself has Augustinian connexions,[38] and the Cartesian soul, like the soul in Plato's *Timaeus,* is an essentially rational being, the natural course of whose activity is disturbed and impeded by the sensations and passions consequent on its embodiment.[39] Descartes's version of Christianised Platonism is idiosyncratic and austere, but his project in epistemology was to adapt, modify, and defend an existing structure, and to demolish existing rivals to that structure. He did not sail uncharted seas.

It is significant that Descartes chose to present his theory as a conclusion drawn from a kind of internal re-enactment, in theistic terms, of the Hellenistic debate about the criterion of truth. Accordingly he adopted something like the Stoic conception of assent as a voluntary act, capable of being either wisely suspended or rashly performed in the absence of good reasons.[40] The policy of assenting only to what has the security of science echoes the rule of the Stoic *sophos*. Indeed, the whole train of thought set out in the *Meditationes* mimics (although it significantly diverges from) the scheme advocated by some Stoics. According to the latter, after recognising our natural ignorance in the face of the sceptical critique, we may rise to science on the provisional basis of those impressions which seem clear and evident. We may then, armed with sharper powers to distinguish truth from falsity, descend to our starting points to confirm those which are now indeed evident.

Something like this general framework is sketched out in the *Meditationes,* but with certain crucial differences. First, far from taking their deliverances to be the starting points of science, Descartes characterises the senses as essentially practical capacities which serve their purpose well enough if for the most part they guide us towards what is useful and away from what is physically harmful. The natural, fallible assent to their deliverances (minimally conceived) which is necessary for us to be so guided is accorded some respect as 'what nature teaches', and sensory perceptions are even described as 'clear and distinct enough' for their purpose.[41] Yet the science which supplies post-critical principles of discrimination between true and false natural sensory judgements is founded, not on such judgements, but on innate, purely intellectual principles. That is why Descartes's sceptical rout of the senses is more complete than any Stoic could have accepted, since for him it is only in pure intellect that scepticism meets its match.

According to its avowed aim of showing that room for doubt remains 'so long as we have no foundations for science other than those that we have now', the deliberately inadequate responses offered to the sceptic in Meditatio I presuppose the principle that knowledge is received 'either from the senses or through the senses'.[42] In Meditatio II empiricism is attacked as the source of materialism, or at least of the view that we understand material things best. The distinction between intellect and imagination is drawn both here and, with even more care, in Meditatio VI. Perhaps one target was Aristotelianism.[43] Yet, despite the importance accorded both to material organs and to sensory imagery in Aristotelian psychology, orthodox scholastic Aristotelianism itself emphasised an immaterial intellectual soul, distinct from the imagination, which could reflect on its own nature and operations. Meditatio II does allude directly to the Aristotelian ascription of nutrition, self-movement, and sense perception to the soul, but there is also reference to the Hellenistic view that the soul is a tenuous matter ('like a wind, or fire or ether') permeating the body. Moreover, the argument of Meditatio I passes through well-known Hellenistic topics: the opposition between doubtful beliefs about distant objects and those perceptual beliefs 'about which doubt is quite impossible',[44] madness as an abnormal condition distinguishable from sanity, and dreams as jumbled experience.[45] It is hard to doubt that Descartes, in his attack on empiricist materialism, aimed to preempt such objections as were advanced by two invited critics of the *Meditationes,* Gassendi and Hobbes. At a deeper level, no doubt, he aimed to preempt the charge that his own mechanistic theory of nature was an invitation to atheism. By attacking the Giants, he could emphasise his adherence to the side of the Gods. The authority of Plato and Saint Augustine could shield him from religious reproach.

An interesting case of the pursuit of an Augustinian theme, yet with Hellenistic overtones, is supplied by Descartes's response to the doubt which he allowed to be possible, once one's 'mental vision' is directed elsewhere, even with respect to what is most clearly perceived (e.g., that $2 + 3 = 5$). Such doubt is met with the notorious proof 'that God exists, . . . that everything else depends on him, and that he is no deceiver; and . . . that [therefore] everything which I clearly and distinctly perceive is of necessity true.'[46] The immediate dialectical rôle of this argument is to remove the most cogent of the 'powerful and well thought-out reasons' initially accorded to the sceptic, that is, the possibility of a God who has made me liable to be deceived, or of a deceiving demon 'of the utmost power'. Without that support, the sceptic's position is left merely 'flippant' and 'ill-considered'.[47] Accused of a circular validation of reason by reason, Descartes pointed out that he was not appealing to a particular clear and distinct perception in order to justify all such perceptions including the one appealed to. For, although the doubt in question does indeed extend to the deliverances of the intellect in general, it cannot embrace any *present* clear and distinct perception. We simply cannot doubt what we now perceive to be true. Descartes thus aimed only to set out an argument, capable of being grasped 'by a simple intuition of the mind',[48] for the conclusion that our intellect is a trustworthy faculty, that is, that what the sceptic fears, or threatens us with, is impossible.

Despite this explanation, Descartes's enterprise might well look worthless. For even if it were granted that his argument is both valid and simple enough to be grasped intuitively, as soon as it is no longer so grasped it would seem to fall open to the very same doubt as it refutes. What is the value of such a momentary triumph over scepticism? Yet (not to mention the old point that the sceptic's use of our faculties to undermine our faculties itself lasts, at best, only until we next need to act, or meet a friend) for Descartes the task is simply to show, or clearly to perceive, that reason is self-consistent: that is, that, pressed home, reason validates rather than undermines itself. Having once been thus defeated, scepticism about reason can then be set aside: *Quid enim nunc mihi opponetur?*[49] The argument is, after all, an element in a train of thought demanded of us, just 'once in a lifetime'.[50]

If this explains the structure of Descartes's argument, it does not explain its motive. Why was he not satisfied to establish the pertinent difference between sense and intellect by means of the principle that clear and distinct intellectual perceptions cannot be doubted at the time?[51] The most probable answer is that he responded to the general fideist suggestion that human reason is untrustworthy precisely in order to expound the thesis that knowledge in the full sense involves recognition that its source is God Himself. As he put it, atheists are incapable of science.[52] In other words, Descartes's primary purpose in this argument was to pursue the Augustinian theme that the 'natural light' is itself a form of divine illumination. This, in effect, is the theme of Plato's famous analogy of the sun under its Christian interpretation: God (for Plato, the Good) is, like the sun, both the conserving cause of the objects of knowledge[53] and the source of the light by which they are known. Augustine stated that principles 'are known in God by eternal reasons in the same way as visible things are seen in the sun.'[54] In this context Descartes's argument constitutes an ascent by which we are assured of the relationship between the eternal reasons in God's mind and their appearance in our own. If we cannot gaze directly at the divine sun, we can at least momentarily glimpse it as the source of the light by which we perceive truth. This knowledge validates knowledge in general, including particular judgements of existence arrived at by the rational interpretation of sensation.[55]

Descartes's pursuit of these Platonic-Augustinian-Scholastic concerns also supplies new grounds for a principle of Hellenistic anti-scepticism. Both Epicureans and Stoics asserted vehemently that nature has given us a faculty for recognising truth but left no general argument to certify the point, beyond their claim that scepticism is effectively self-refuting.[56] That is understandable, quite apart from their freedom from any problem about the correspondence between human and divine ideas. Since the Hellenistic natural light is ultimately sensory, the sceptic needs to be defeated at an earlier stage than is necessary for Descartes. There is no independent faculty of reason, and so no possible reasoning, to fall back on.

For Descartes, however, God and intellectual knowledge of God make *scientia* possible for us. His rôle as cause of the objects of knowledge gives Him an equally fundamental place in the content of that science. For physical 'science' requires our recognition of God, not only as the source of knowledge, but as the Creator who maintains both matter and the principles of mechanics in being.[57] Plato's dream in *Phaedo* is fulfilled, according to which the true philosophy will show that

'the ordering mind orders everything and places each thing severally as it is best.'
Yet, despite such dramatic resonances, it was just his austerely geometrical physics
which distinguished Descartes from the mainstream of the Christian Platonism
whose epistemological models he employed. It is not surprising that Henry More
at first saw Descartes as a fairly close ally but later changed his mind.[58] More
postulated immaterial souls in space, and so a less radical divide between souls and
bodies than Descartes.[59] Immaterial 'plastic natures' were called on to explain
what mechanism by itself allegedly could not, the organisation of individuals and
species. When it came to what was fundamental for Descartes, these two Platonists
had rather little in common.

In one respect, however, Descartes's epistemology may be truer to its Platonic
sources and structure than Mersenne's, in that it assigns little worth to belief which
falls short of knowledge, whether natural perceptual belief or probable speculation.
In general, probable opinion appears neither as a stage on the way to knowledge
nor as an acceptable alternative to it, but rather as a distraction to be set aside in
case we confuse it with knowledge.[60] In a well-known (but not prominent)
passage,[61] the consideration that the same phenomena may be susceptible of
different mechanical explanations leads him to concede that any such explanation
may possess only 'moral certainty' sufficient for the purposes of ordinary life. Yet
there is no development of the notion of a sphere in which rationally judged
probability is the best that can be expected. Indeed, he immediately goes on to
claim what seems more than moral certainty for his own hypotheses, since 'the
general features of the universe . . . can hardly be intelligibly explained' in other
ways.

### 4. Rationalism after Descartes

Among Descartes's followers, there were some minor divergences from his epistemology. The authors of the Port-Royal *Logique,* for example, offered an essentially
Cartesian summary of the various forms of cognition.[62] First principles are known
by intellection, when 'the truth needs no mark save the enveloping clarity which
surrounds it and persuades the mind despite any objections.'[63] Other sorts of
conviction are motivated by authority or by reasons. Judgement based on authority, human or divine, is faith. Some reasons may convince; others may be less than
fully convincing. The latter give rise to opinion, which the *Logique,* under the
guidance of Pascal, treated with un-Cartesian seriousness, explaining probability
as something calculable and (given determinately valued ends) with calculable
implications for action.[64] Convincing reasons may be either good or only apparently so. If good, they give rise to science, in which clarity and distinctness is won

by 'long and minute scrutiny' (the *Logique* also includes an account of Cartesian analytic-synthetic method).[65] Motivated by only apparent reasons, judgement is either error or, if true, rash judgement (which Descartes had not distinguished from error). Elsewhere the *Logique* found room for natural sensory judgements which, in virtue of being strictly limited, are free from error.[66] Throughout, an immaterial soul was assumed, empiricism (ascribed to Gassendi and Hobbes) was attacked, and sense and imagination were firmly subordinated to intellect. Apart from the treatment of probability, the only significant divergence from Cartesian doctrine was a reversion to an orthodox view of assent or judgement as a mental act combining predicate-idea with subject-idea – a model which made concepts, rather than truths, the immediate objects of 'perception'.[67] Platonic overtones, however, were muted, with nothing said about the ontological status of the eternal truths.[68]

Three major philosophers developed epistemologies deeply influenced by, but also significantly different from, Cartesian theory. Spinoza, Malebranche, and Leibniz all kept, at least broadly, to Descartes's intellectualist classification of cognitive acts and faculties but found different ways in which to come to terms with the Augustinian thesis of a triangular relation between essences as conceived by God, essences in things themselves, and essences as conceived by us. Much of the detail of their theories will be better examined in Chapter 30, for each theory hinges on a particular metaphysical explanation of objective being and of what an 'idea' is. But something should be said here, in particular with respect to the question, fundamental for all these philosophers, as to just how our minds are related to God's mind and so to the world.

In brief summary, Spinoza went so far as to make the three types or levels of essence one and the same. He identified mind with body, thoughts with their physical basis, and also held that the immediate objects of thoughts are just those bodily processes with which they are identical. As the human mind is thus related to the human body, the divine mind is related to the extended universe as a whole. Indeed, human minds are parts of the divine mind, as human bodies are parts of the extended universe. God knows mathematical truths in and through the extended Nature of which they hold, the immediate object of the divine mind. But such truths hold of the human body no less perfectly than they hold of bodies generally. Thus we can know them, in and through our own body, just as God knows them. In effect, Spinoza drew on a daring, immanentist theology in order to combine the model of divine illumination with a more naturalistic, indeed physicalist account of intellection.

Malebranche, on the other hand, placed his theory of direct apprehension of divine essences within a more conventional view of an immaterial soul and a transcendent God.[69] Like Descartes, he maintained real distinctions between our mind, God's mind, and nature itself; but, like Spinoza, he identified human and divine ideas. In clear and distinct perception we are united to the divine mind. This identification, and the notion of direct access to the divine ideas 'during this life', was fiercely opposed on theological grounds by Arnauld.[70] Finally, Leibniz was as orthodox as Arnauld in his relation to the Augustinian-Cartesian triangle. The innatist version of the model was entirely consonant with his doctrine of pre-established harmony: each monad or soul mirrors the universe by mirroring, in the first instance, its Creator.[71]

With these differences went others, and it may be helpful to draw attention here to some of the issues on which they turn. The Aristotelian intellect had two functions, with different objects: on the one hand, the formation of universal notions and the comprehension of universal truth; on the other hand, the reflexive apprehension of the intellect's own activity.[72] The Augustinian proposal that the universal principles of science are innate elements of human reason brings these two functions closer together. Systematic knowledge, for Descartes, begins with the thinking thing's turning in on itself. Not only the notions of thought and its modes, but also the 'common notions' of substance, identity, duration, and the like, necessary for the intellect's interpretation of the data of sense, are derivable from self-reflection, that is, the reflexivity of thought.[73] The idea of God itself becomes explicit through reflection. The first proof employed in the validation of reason proceeds from the premise that, simply as imperfect thinking things, we possess the idea of a perfect being, 'the mark of the craftsman stamped on his work', a mark which is 'nothing distinct from the work itself'.[74]

Despite (or because of) his more straightforwardly Platonist principles, it is Malebranche who, over Spinoza and Leibniz, offers the greatest contrast to Descartes in these particular respects. Since he held that the human intellect has direct, if limited, access to the divine order of ideas, rather than innately conforming to it, he lacked Descartes's motive for associating universal knowledge with the mind's transparency to itself. Indeed, he sharply distinguished the two functions of intellect, holding that the mind's reflexive awareness (*conscience*) does not constitute an understanding of the self (or of anything else) comparable to the understanding of matter achieved through the perception of its essence in God. We can know that the mind's essence is thought, but we cannot know, except from experience, what modifications of thought are possible.

Although, as it has been seen, Spinoza also attributed our capacity for universal science to our having immediate access to certain divine ideas, he did so in such a way as to suggest that all knowledge is in some sense self-knowledge. Nevertheless, he was no more inclined than Malebranche to start from reflexive awareness in the task of making explicit the foundations of science, or to see in such awareness what for him is the starting point of systematic, ordered knowledge, the idea of substance (or God). For Leibniz, on the other hand, as for Descartes, we draw the idea of substance (as we do other ideas of reason) from our self-awareness, possessing in the unity of consciousness a paradigm of the multiplicity of accidents in a unitary subject.

These differences among rationalist epistemologies are important, but another is even more striking. On the traditional view, *scientia* is abstract knowledge of what is universal and necessary, but particular things possess accidents which, like their existence, are contingent and dependent on God's arbitrary will. Both Spinoza and (perhaps consequentially) Leibniz differed from Cartesians in envisaging a system of necessary knowledge which embraces particulars as such. For both, science is universal and abstract for human beings only because of the limitations of our faculties. For Spinoza, that is because we are unable to comprehend the infinite causal chain of modifications of God or nature which flow from its essence or perfection. For Leibniz, it is because, although the existence of individuals is contingent on God's will, they have individual essences of infinite complexity from which all their attributes flow, and which only God can comprehend. The thought is that someone who possessed a complete concept of an individual would be able to prove analytically every proposition that is true of it: that is, that the predicate is contained in the subject. Consonant with this view was Leibniz's ideal of a formal language in which truth could be calculated with complete evidence.[75] For all their differences, however, the 'rationalists' had something in common: briefly and roughly, a conception of the principles of science as an achievement of the intellect through its access, direct or indirect, partial or complete, to essences as conceived of by God. More important, this resemblance is the mark of the actual, historic bonds between them.

### 5. 'British Empiricism'

Since the next philosophers to be discussed are empiricists and British, it should first be said that the term 'British Empiricism', when taken in its traditional sense to refer to a continuous 'development' from Locke through Berkeley to Hume, is one of the more inept clichés in the historiography of philosophy. No principle, both intelligible and true, can put just these three very differently motivated intellectuals alone on the same island in the sea of early modern philosophy.[76]

Empiricism was flourishing among both English and French new philosophers long before Locke's first thoughts about it, and it continued to do so. The commonplace that empiricism was (or is) a characteristic of British, as opposed to, 'continental' thought[77] should have looked fairly foolish in the era of (say) Cudworth and More, on the one hand, and Bayle and Huet, on the other; or even during the period in which Locke's *Essay* was subjected to considerably rougher criticism in Britain than it was receiving from everyone in France.

If the 'rationalists' are linked by certain themes and principles drawn from the Platonic or Augustinian tradition, particularly as they were enunciated by Descartes, the 'Empiricists' have a similar relation, direct or indirect, to Hellenistic epistemology, although without such an acknowledged modern authority or source. While Bacon or Gassendi might be cited in aid, no empiricist before Locke rivalled Descartes in authority. Bacon's fame rested less on a comprehensive epistemology than on a method of analysing and ordering observations as a stimulus to theory and to the procurement of new observations with foreseeable significance. We should frame determinate questions and force nature to answer them. This emphasis on both directed collection of data and active engagement with the object of study was undoubtedly influential and may even be held to manifest a characteristically 'modern' technological outlook. It helped to shape later conceptions of 'natural history' and experimental method which did not all embody Bacon's optimism as to their outcome in certain and systematic knowledge.[78] Yet, however forward-looking it may now seem to some, Bacon's argument was apparently indebted to Stoic theory[79] and certainly fell within the scope of the ancient concern with the gap between perception and 'science'. Others developed ancient empiricist theory in other ways and with other emphases.

### 6. *The empiricist mechanism of Hobbes*

Hobbes's epistemology, one of the most important of the century, is an attempt to explain reasoning and 'science', by means of a radical nominalism, as achievements of sense and imagination together with the institution of language. His map of cognition is crossed by two intersecting lines, one dividing knowledge from what is less than knowledge, the other dividing what is prelinguistic from what presupposes language. Sensation and imagination give rise to prelinguistic 'knowledge of fact', which is 'sense and memory', 'the knowledge required in a witness'.[80] All thought consists of a sequence of images arising before the mind in a more or less orderly train, the 'discourse of the mind'. The general principle of order or association among images is 'their first *coherence* or consequence at that *time* when they are produced by sense': that is, roughly, their conjunction in experience. The mind may be led along by all sorts of chance associations,[81] but the most important type of association prior to language arises from the experience of cause and effect and involves opinion: 'as for example, because a man hath often seen offences followed by punishment, when he seeth an offence in present, he thinketh punishment to be consequent thereto' in the future.[82] Things so linked in experience are natural signs of each other, each of which will cause in us, as in animals, a 'presumption' about the past or future. Such 'opinion', it seems, is a sort of inclination naturally arising in consciousness. If false, it is 'error'. A chain of alternating opinions constitutes 'doubt', and its final result is 'judgement'. To judge well is to be 'prudent'. All this, no doubt intentionally, more or less corresponds to Aristotle's first three steps to science, which for Aristotle, too, lead as far as human and animal 'prudence'.

The next step involves, not some special faculty of intellect, but language. This introduces a new dimension into the 'consequence or train of imaginations' in so far as names, as experienced, are themselves sensations and images not naturally, but arbitrarily or conventionally associated with other sensations and images. They are thereby capable of serving as 'marks' and 'signs'. As marks they serve to record our experience in virtue of their capacity, when perceived or imagined, to stimulate images like past sensations or images, or to revive such sensations or images. (A record of 'knowledge of fact' is called 'history', natural or civil.)[83] As signs, they make thought public by stimulating images like the speaker's in the listener. Names, together with the copula (whether explicit or embodied in a verb), also make affirmation possible (i.e., predicative assertion and thought), and so truth and falsity in the strict sense. A sentence is true when what is named by the subject is named by the predicate. Finally, names are the means to introducing universality and necessity. A name is universal when it is associated with, and stimulates, the images of many resembling things rather than just one thing. A proposition is necessary when nothing can be imagined which is named by the subject which is not also named by the predicate. A universal, necessary truth such as 'man is an animal' is 'eternal' just because it is equivalent to an open hypothetical relating to language which is true at all times, 'if *man,* then *animal'.*[84]

The language-involving forms of cognition are as follows. Knowledge of first principles is knowledge of the definition of names, while 'science' is 'the knowledge of the consequence of one affirmation to another', a relation which can be set out syllogistically. If there is an incoherent principle as premise, or an error in reasoning or calculating, acceptance of the conclusion is a second sort of mere 'opinion' which is not, strictly speaking, error, but 'absurdity'. Language also makes possible 'faith' or 'belief', which we have when we accept what another says, that is, draw conclusions from their speech.

Sometimes Hobbes wrote as if definitions are merely arbitrary and reasoning is a purely verbal process.[85] He evidently wanted to emphasise that science does not involve a kind of divinely granted access to the nature of things, but depends rather on the methodical use of a tool invented by man. Yet he certainly did not think of science as a purely verbal matter, as appears from his account of definition and, in particular, of 'evidence'. 'Evidence' depends not just on our accepting true sentences, but on our grasping their meaning, on our conceptions.[86]

Truth can become 'evident' only when subject and predicate stimulate appropriate conceptions or images.[87] Syllogistic reasoning involves a chain of such images, corresponding to the definitions of the terms. Thus someone mentally syllogising, 'Man is an animal, an animal is a body, *therefore,* man is a body', is stimulated by the names in the syllogism to form, in order, images of a man speaking or discoursing (i.e., reasoning), of the same man self-moving, and of the same man occupying space. Remembering that 'man', 'animal', and 'body' name the same thing (successively more abstractly considered), the thinker concludes that 'man is a body' is true. Both verbal and non-verbal images are necessary, Hobbes claimed, because it is necessary to think not only of the thing, but of the various names which are applied to it 'propter diversas de re cogitationes', in virtue of different aspects picked out in thought.[88] Of a geometrical example he argued that, although someone without language might recognise the equality of the angles of a particular triangle to two particular right angles, the general rule can be grasped only by a language-user who observes 'that such equality was consequent, not to the length of the sides, nor to any other particular thing in his triangle; but onely to this, that the sides were straight, and the angles three; and that was all, for which he named it a Triangle'.[89] In other words, we perceive the relation in the particular case and we perceive that what matters for the relation is what is named or picked out by certain universal terms, so that our knowing the meaning of the terms enables us to know that whatever satisfies the subject will thereby satisfy the predicate: as Hobbes might have put it, 'if *angles of a triangle,* then *two right angles*'.

Such propositions are analytic: 'every true universal proposition is either a definition, or part of a definition, or demonstrated from definitions.' They are not, however, trivial or *merely* verbal, because names and definitions enable us to analyse the objects of experience and focus on those of their aspects which matter for the purpose of understanding them through their causes. Sensory knowledge takes things in as wholes: by sense we know what the thing is before we turn to its particular attributes or accidents. This is *cognitio quod est. Cognitio causarum,* on the other hand, requires analysis, since 'the cause of the whole is compounded from the causes of the parts.' A 'part' here is not an ingredient but an abstract aspect or 'way of conceiving of a body' (which is Hobbes's definition of an 'accident').[90] Analysis will bring us eventually to the most general or simple concepts (i.e., the basic concepts of geometry and mechanics), a level at which causal principles are 'manifest in themselves' ('Causae . . . universalium . . . manifestae sunt per se'). The definitions which constitute the explications of these simple concepts are the first principles of physics, including moral philosophy (psychology).[91] Civil or political philosophy, however, need not proceed from ultimate principles, since 'the causes of the motions of minds are known not only by reasoning, but also by the experience of each observing its own particular motions.'[92] Elsewhere Hobbes puts geometry and civil philosophy together as fully demonstrable arts, since we ourselves construct their objects (figures and states) knowing how we do so. In physics, on the other hand, we can only demonstrate possible causes, since the natural construction of the objects of physics is known only through its effects.[93] Demonstrated 'science' of any kind, however, is marked out by 'certain and infallible' signs.[94] Knowledge of the causes of sensory appearances enables us to correct those that are deceptive or misleading, and to distinguish what seems from what is, but (as for Gassendi) that is ultimately only to correct sense by sense.[95]

Hobbes was clearly, if perhaps less exclusively than Gassendi, inspired by ancient empiricism.[96] By making universality an attribute of words alone, and discarding the quasi-universal impressions of Epicureans and Stoics, he may seem only to have been tidying up a problematic element in traditional theory.[97] Yet, as with the Stoics, nominalism was also the medium of something like the 'rationalist' conception of *a priori* science as possessing a certainty explicitly in contrast with the fallibility of induction. There is no place in Hobbesian empiricism for the Gassendist principle that all evidence derives from the evidence of sense, since universal propositions may become evident without recourse to sense-experience, solely through our forming images appropriate to their terms. Yet his view *is* 'empiricism'. It is not to be less consistent, but to be more sophisticated for an empiricist to have found a way of recognising that mathematical truths and the like are not, after all, summaries of experience. The modern reader with an ideal, ahistorical conception of 'empiricism' may not disagree just because of Hobbes's suggestion that necessary truths, being analytic, are merely verbal. What may be more disconcerting to that reader, however, is that through his notion of analysis Hobbes extended his explanation of the *a priori* to the principles of physics, embracing a particularly pure, dogmatic, and necessitarian form of mechanism.[98] For Hobbes, some analytic truths capture the essence of things.

### 7. The anti-dogmatism of Locke

Locke evidently read Hobbes, but his wider convictions and purposes were nearer to those of Gassendi, not to speak of other opponents of dogmatism in both religion and natural inquiry active at least since the 1630s.[99] His views sprang from an early sense that arbitrary claims to religious and moral inspiration are a threat to political order, an objection to dogmatism soon confirmed by his active interest in medicine and experimental philosophy. The former led him to a conception of a reasonable ethics and religion, the latter to the view that we cannot know the essences of substantial things.

Locke has traditionally been criticised for failing to carry his empiricist principles to their logical conclusions, later enunciated by Hume. In fact, he himself moved from an empiricism in some ways stronger than Hume's. In the early 1660s,[100] much as Epicurus and Gassendi had done, Locke conflated the acquisition of principles with the acquisition of concepts. Geometry is assimilated to ethics, the 'principles and axioms' of both being given to reason by the senses.[101] In the course of the so-called *Draft A* (1671) of the *Essay concerning Human Understanding,* however, he moved to a conception of universal knowledge as going no further than our ideas, as hypothetical and, in effect, as *a priori*. At first he ascribed our knowledge of geometrical axioms to 'constant observation of our senses espetialy our eys', but soon described them as 'standards', suggesting that at least 'the more general axioms' are 'conteind even in the very signification of the words themselves'.[102] He was coming to see any given 'axiom' as open to alternative interpretations: it can be regarded either as a straightforward empirical summary, liable to empirical refutation, or as a quasi definition which, although founded on experience, is secure just because it is 'barely about the signification of words'. Throughout *Draft A* Locke developed the thought that universal propositions are, if 'instructive', uncertain or, if certain, mere assertions or denials of the identity of ideas, and so 'only verball . . . and not instructive'.[103] Yet, at first left general, this interpretive dilemma was soon restricted (as later in the *Essay* itself) to propositions about substances, with mathematical propositions placed unequivocally in the class of propositions employed as standards, which are certain just because they depend 'on the very nature of those Ideas we have'.[104]

At the same time, Locke was beginning to doubt whether mathematical propositions are merely verbal and to explore the thought that they are instructive just because mathematical ideas (being simple) can be drawn from any and every thing and so have a guaranteed conformity to things.[105] On the other hand, 'any universall proposition . . . only supposes existence . . . which can be knowne noe other way but by our senses.'[106] This issue was unresolved in *Draft A,* but Locke had at least concluded that we know axioms *a priori* or, as he later put it, the angles and figures I contemplate may be 'drawn upon paper, carvd in marble, or only phansied in my understanding'. We know axioms 'not by proofe but by intuition'.[107] Locke's first sustained effort in epistemology thus drew him from an inductivist to an intuitionist theory of *a priori* knowledge. Unlike Hobbes, however, he recognised a distinction between definitional and 'instructive' necessary propositions.

Locke was not a nominalist in the same sense as Hobbes, for he retained the traditional view of knowledge and belief as the quasi-propositional combination of concepts (rather than names) in mental acts of 'affirmation'. Except for mathematics beyond small numbers,[108] there is no sort of thought or cognition for which language is essential.[109] For Hobbes, every idea is particular, and only words are universal. For Locke, 'Words are general . . . when used for Signs of general *Ideas*; and . . . *Ideas* are general, when they are set up, as the Representatives of many particular Things.' For both, universality is a matter of the use a sign is put to.[110] Unlike Hobbes, Locke saw no reason to deny that we can generalise from the particular case to all relevantly resembling cases without being nudged to do so by the universal name. 'Abstract ideas' are simply particular ideas 'partially considered', whether or not named.[111] But he shared with Hobbes the aim of eliminating the eternal truths of the Rationalists.[112]

Armed with this imagist, yet intuitionist, theory of universal knowledge, Locke framed probably the most complex and influential classification of cognition of the century. First, knowledge is the 'perception', and belief[113] the 'presumption', of a relation of 'agreement' or 'disagreement' between ideas. The formal principle of the difference between knowledge and belief, however, is that in knowledge the proposition is evident in itself, whereas a believed proposition is accepted for reasons 'extraneous' to it: for example, someone who follows a geometrical demonstration knows that its conclusion is true, whereas someone who accepts the conclusion on the authority of an expert only believes it.[114] Knowledge and belief do not, as for Plato, have distinct objects: in general, whatever can be believed can be known, and, except for what is immediately evident, whatever can be known can be believed.

Like Mersenne, Locke held that there are degrees, not only of assent, but of knowledge; not only of probability, but of evidence. First comes intuitive knowledge, in which the mind 'perceives the Truth, as the Eye doth light, only by being directed toward it.' Intuition 'leaves no room for Hesitation, Doubt, or Examination.' The second degree is demonstrative knowledge, where the truth is perceived by the aid of one or a chain of 'intermediate ideas'. Doubt is possible at any point in the sequence with respect to connexions not currently in view. Hence, 'Men embrace often Falshoods for Demonstration.'[115] An 'intermediate idea' has affinities with the 'middle term' of a syllogism, but, like Descartes, Locke rejected the view of demonstration as essentially syllogistic.[116] More important, he rejected the pretensions of all proposed analytical methods, like those of Descartes and Hobbes, to uncover principles from which to demonstrate explicanda.[117]

The third degree of knowledge is sensitive knowledge of the existence of external things.[118] It should be stressed, first, that sensitive knowledge is knowledge and not belief: that is, what is known is itself perceived, and not inferred.[119] Second, Locke follows Mersenne in placing the evidence of sense below that of intuition and demonstration and thereby signals his rejection of a general inductivism such as Gassendi's. On the other hand, he did not hold the deliverances of sense to be in need of confirmation by reason or 'science' if they are to withstand scepticism. We can, he said, be 'farther confirmed' in 'the assurance we have from our Senses themselves' by certain general anti-sceptical considerations, such as the involuntariness of our sensations, their evident causal dependence on bodily organs and their interconnectedness. Yet these, even the last, are merely 'concurrent reasons'. The sceptical doubt is unreal, and the senses, as 'the proper and sole judges of this thing', provide 'certainty' and 'an assurance that *deserves the name of Knowledge*'.[120] For Locke, certainty or 'evidence' is bestowed neither by the particular deliverances of sense on the general principles of science, nor *vice versa*, but is possessed, in its appropriate degree, by each perceived proposition in its own right.[121] Finally, it should be noted that we may have 'sensitive knowledge', not only of the existence, but also of the particular 'co-existence' of sensible qualities in the same thing.

Three further epistemological divisions are best explained together: the distinction between 'trifling' (or 'verbal') and 'instructive' (or 'real') propositions (which has been touched on already); the distinction between four propositional relations (or forms of 'agreement') between ideas, which Locke called 'identity', 'relation', 'necessary connexion or co-existence', and 'existence'; and the classification of propositions according to subject-matter, as they are concerned with simple ideas or qualities, with simple or mixed modes and relations, or with substances.

By 'identity' Locke meant not such propositions as 'The author of the *Iliad* was Homer', but tautologies such as 'Gold is gold' and 'Red is not blue', intuitive knowledge of which is achieved by the simple exercise of our faculty of discerning ideas. The category also includes such truths as 'Gold is a metal' or 'Gold is heavy', when these are true by definition.[122] In other words, the category corresponds to that of 'trifling' propositions, and embraces all subject-matters.

The two categories of 'relation' and 'necessary connexion or co-existence' are presented as opposed to identity in being 'instructive'. They together mark Locke's rejection of the view that all necessary propositions are analytic, and of corresponding conceptions of analytic method. His treatment of 'relation' responds to his early difficulty over the informativeness of mathematics.[123] His standard examples of this category are demonstrable geometrical theorems, but they could as well be intuitable axioms (but not, of course, definitions).[124] Metaphysically more exciting examples than the geometrical ones are the propositions that, if anything changes, there must be something with a power to make it change, and that, if anything exists, something must have existed from eternity.[125]

Propositions about natural things, however, fall either under 'existence' or under 'necessary connexion or co-existence'. 'Existence' is self-explanatory, although existential propositions place the greatest strain on the account of knowledge as the perception of a relation between ideas, since they might rather seem concerned with the relation between ideas and reality. The rather complex category 'necessary connexion or co-existence' owes its disjunctive name to its constituents: it includes both particular and universal propositions, the latter of which may be either known or believed (i.e., necessary connexions may be 'perceived', or probable generalisations be inductively based on sensitive knowledge of co-existence). Since it is Locke's contention that a science of substances based on knowledge of their essences is beyond us, he offers few examples of perceived necessary connexions; but possible illustrations are *whatever is solid is impenetrable* and *a body struck by another will move*.[126] Sensitive knowledge that *this* (particular) *is gold* (or *this gold is soluble in aqua regia*)[127] is perception of co-existence, in that the idea of gold has the form *thing ('something', 'substance') which is yellow, heavy, and malleable*.

General beliefs based on experience seem not to fall under 'necessary connexion' (since *ex hypothesi* the connexion in question is not perceived as necessary) but under 'co-existence'. An example of such a general belief would be *gold is soluble in aqua regia,* when that predicate is not part of the thinker's definition of gold. When the predicate *is* part of the definition of the subject, however, the proposition falls under 'identity'. Thus the principle Locke had once applied to all universal propositions, he applied in the *Essay* just to those which are about substances: (virtually without exception) if they are certain, they are trifling, and if they are instructive, they are uncertain. That, of course, is because we do not know the essence of any substance, so that our classification of substances by means of their observable attributes is arbitrary, at best pragmatically justified. With respect to specific material substances such as gold or a horse, we know the 'nominal essence' which we have constructed on the basis of experience, but we do not know the 'real essence' or 'real constitution' (conceived of mechanistically by Locke, in terms of primary qualities of the minute parts) which is responsible for the co-existence of the qualities and powers from which we have selected our definition of the 'sort'. Only if we knew what the observable attributes are 'in the object' would we be in a position to perceive the necessary connexion between them in the present case.[128] In the *a priori* sciences this problem does not arise, since their objects are constructed by us: our ideas of simple or mixed modes themselves, formed without reference to actuality, constitute the subject-matter of the abstract sciences, mathematics, and ethics.[129] In other words, these sciences are possible, as physics is not, just because they deal with mere abstractions.

The impossibility of natural 'science' increases the importance of probability, which Locke explains in terms of degrees of assent: '*Belief, Conjecture, Guess, Doubt, Wavering, Distrust, Disbelief*, etc.'[130] Probability is 'the measure whereby [the] several degrees [of assent] are, or ought to be *regulated*'.[131] As this definition allows, the faculty of assent or 'judgement' does service both as that cognitive faculty or part of human reason by which we arrive at probable beliefs and as our general capacity to form beliefs, however unreasonably. It can issue in false beliefs both because any mere judgement, however reasonable, can turn out to be false, and because judgements can be unreasonable. Only the latter constitute 'error'.

Locke distinguished between two sorts of grounds, and two sorts of objects of assent. The first distinction is between conformity with one's own 'Knowledge, Observation and Experience' and the 'Testimony of others'. The second, between propositions about 'matters of fact' falling within human experience and propositions about what lies 'beyond the discovery of the senses', echoes the ancient distinction between reminiscent and indicative signs. Locke identifies four broad degrees of probability with respect to 'matters of fact': (1) when the general consent of others concurs with the subject's constant experience; (2) when experience and testimony suggest that something is so for the most part; (3) when unsuspected witnesses report what experience allows might as well be so as not; and (4) when 'the reports of History and Witnesses clash with the ordinary course of Nature, or with one another.' In the last case there are, according to Locke, 'no precise rules' for assessing probability.[132] It should be noted that universal *belief* is always treated as second best to a possible *knowledge,* and that their inductive grounding is itself based on the assumption of an underlying necessary connexion:

'For what our own and other Men's constant Observation has found always to be after the same manner, that we with reason conclude to be the Effects of steady and regular Causes, though they come not within the reach of our Knowledge.' Finally, with respect to unobservables, 'a wary reasoning from analogy' with what falls within our experience 'is the only [natural] help we have' and the only ground of probability. This, if somewhat lukewarm, is equivalent to Gassendi's acceptance of 'indicative' signs.[133]

### 8. 'Rationalism' and 'Empiricism' as critical categories

It should be clear from the foregoing that, if the dichotomy between 'Rationalism' and 'Empiricism' is to be a tool in the historiography of philosophy, it needs to be understood in terms of historic doctrines, debts, and allegiances rather than general, abstractly definable approaches in epistemology.[134] If capital letters are reserved for such historical employment of these terms, that is not absolutely to rule out rough characterisations of certain theses, whatever their provenance, as 'rationalist' or 'empiricist' on the basis of their philosophical content. Yet it would be a mistake to assume either (1) that all theses that one might reasonably thus characterise one way or the other together form an ideal, internally consistent system, 'rationalism' or 'empiricism', or (2) that seventeenth-century Empiricists who advanced certain 'rationalist' theses, or Rationalists who advanced 'empiricist' ones, were being in any way inconsistent or untrue to their principles (any more than Conservatives who propose radical, rather than conservative, measures are necessarily being untrue to *their* principles). Questions of philosophical motivation and consistency simply cannot be encapsulated in the lower-case epithets, any more than questions of historical affinity. Unless we recognise that, we may accord too much importance to the question, for example, whether Spinoza and Leibniz, who held that every particular state of affairs flows necessarily from the nature of things, are not thereby essentially more 'rationalist' than Descartes and Malebranche, who attributed even the universal laws of mechanics directly to the will of an omnipotent creator. Hobbes himself might, in this respect, seem closer to pure 'rationalism' than Descartes.[135] Indeed, it might seem an extraordinary paradox, rather than a natural consequence of the Rationalists' Platonism, on the one hand, and the Empiricists' naturalism, on the other, that Descartes and Malebranche are inclined to see laws as contingent in themselves (if flowing necessarily from the immutability or wisdom of the Creator), while Hobbes and Locke favour a strongly necessitarian mechanism.[136] For Locke's *Essay,* too, although an incomparably rich development of available Empiricist theory, notoriously appears to straddle a divide if (like Kant) we hold it up against some ideal of 'consistent' empiricism, rather than read it as a critique of current dogmatism with its own principle of coherence, and with a specific, complex, evolved, largely self-conscious relation to certain ancient and contemporary philosophies. Such central features of its doctrine as intuitionism[137] and the presumption of an intelligible natural order will seem incongruous with the supposed 'empiricist' essence of that doctrine.

Kant himself characterised the dichotomy in a historical way, as between 'the Platonic and the Epicurean schools',[138] yet seemingly without recognising the full implications of that view of it. To accept them is to accept, for example, that Leibniz counts as a 'Rationalist' less because of certain general, abstractly characterisable epistemological assumptions and pretensions, than because he took seriously a very particular, theistic epistemological model, deriving from Plato, Augustine, and Descartes, and allowed it to an extent to shape his philosophy as Malebranche and Spinoza also did, but as Gassendi and Hobbes manifestly did not. Internal evidence for Leibniz's 'Rationalism' is thus (apart from explicit acknowledgement) a matter of the way in which a wide range of his arguments and theses can be seen to be in dialectical relationship with those of other 'Rationalists'. Being a 'Rationalist', like being a fox or an oak-tree, is a largely relational, rather than a purely intrinsic property. That is not to deny Leibniz's susceptibility or loyalty to different, even opposed influences (notably, to Aristotelianism). Nor is it to overlook his readiness to engage in polite debate with, even to make apparent concessions to, a philosopher as different from himself as Locke.

For similar reasons Hobbes and Locke are without doubt 'Empiricists' despite their adherence to mechanism and their development of theories of abstraction in order to account for *a priori* knowledge and 'evidence'. It is true that seventeenth-century Empiricists comprise a somewhat loose-knit group, but that is not surprising since the significant common historical-*cum*-theoretical connexion is with both sceptical and constructive varieties of Hellenistic Empiricism (itself unified by dialectical connexions as much as by shared principles). Yet their theories do have characteristic features in virtue of that relation, as well as sharing a negative, but centrally important common property: God's thoughts are excluded from their epistemology.

This is not, of course, to endorse all the traditional pigeon-holing. There really was a choice facing new philosophers, reasonably described as a choice between Rationalism and Empiricism, but there was also the possibility of deliberate eclecticism or synthesis. Desgabets, for example, was an unorthodox Cartesian who read Descartes's thesis of the creation of the eternal truths as entailing that all propositions are contingent, so that none are knowable *a priori*. Berkeley – classified by Kant as a kind of rationalist[139] but more commonly, since Kant, as an empiricist – was more openly intent on synthesis.

The methodological introduction to Berkeley's *Principles of Human Knowledge* is written around a version of the Empiricists' anti-realist explanation of universal knowledge, while Part I begins with a declaration which at least seems to assign all 'the objects of human knowledge' to sense, reflection, memory, and imagination. It turns out, however, that reflection is an immediate self-awareness so unlike Locke's 'internal sense'[140] as to be assigned to 'pure intellect'.[141] Yet it is not like Cartesian reflection either: its deliverances are carefully characterised as 'experience',[142] and it is not assigned its own innate concepts such that it could function prior to, or independently of, sense perception. The essence of the Berkeleyan soul is to think, but it is quite unlike the Cartesian soul in that thinking necessarily involves sense or imagination.[143] As Berkeley's theory developed, knowledge of reality became the apprehension, whether direct or indirect, of ideas or archetypes in God's mind. Yet that is not, as it is for the Rationalists, a form of cognition different from, and vastly superior to sense perception, but is sense perception itself – the ideas we perceive are precisely ideas of sense, 'exhibited' to us by God.[144] Finally, Berkeley adopted a view of laws as contingent and arbitrary edicts of God, praising Descartes and (as Plato had done) Anaxagoras as predecessors, but employing entirely un-Cartesian reasons. The 'inertness' of bodies is presented as a corollary, not of the geometrical, intelligible essence of matter (which Berkeley rejected), but of their sense-dependence. As experience of volition gives us the notion of action, so experience of sensible things assures us that they are inactive: 'A little attention will discover to us that the very being of an idea implies passiveness and inertness in it.'[145]

Berkeley was clearly on the side of Plato's 'Gods' and could not have been satisfied with Gassendi's or Locke's defensive concession that the soul is probably immaterial – a 'probable Opinion' which Locke does not even attempt to justify and holds to be irrelevant to 'all the great Ends of Morality and Religion'.[146] Berkeley's innovative (if not entirely novel)[147] thesis was that all sensible qualities, including extension, are mind dependent. As his early notebooks confirm, his philosophy developed as an attempt to show, in the light of this thesis, that the fashionable principle of the Empiricist 'Giants' that experience supplies reason with all its concepts leads, not to materialism or scepticism, but to the proof of an immaterial soul; not to atheism, but directly to the existence of God.[148] Kant was by no means the first to attempt a radical synthesis of 'the Platonic and the Epicurean Schools'.

## II. BELIEF BEYOND REASON

### 1. Faith and Reason

The various theories of human knowledge and belief as cognitive achievements, as the natural, properly grounded product of certain faculties with proper objects, constituted the grander, smoother side of seventeenth-century epistemology. Although the preceding account of it has laid some emphasis on the theological motives for some metaphysical theories of knowledge, it has been possible for the most part to present such theories in terms of the ancient, traditional concern with the relation between sense-experience and 'science'. Consequently the seamier side of epistemology has been largely passed over, leaving at least some of the motives for at least some of the arguments and theories unexplained. As historians have made us well aware, the chief motives of seventeenth-century sceptics lay in religion and church politics, and that was often also true of more constructive epistemologists both in their attempts to set out the conditions of knowledge and reasonable belief and, especially, in their accounts of the human proclivity to believe without, against or beyond reason and the operation of our natural faculties. Religious belief and inspiration were problematic in this respect, since there was a division within the armies of controversialists between those who gloried in faith's supposed independence of reason, and those who struggled to identify a reasonable faith. Although there was no such ambiguity about commonplace irrationality and motivated error, there are interesting and important connexions between the theory of error, the topic of the next section, and the theory of faith, the topic of the present one. Together they contributed a good deal to the dialectical shape of seventeenth-century epistemology.

The category of 'divine faith' was commonly included in classifications of cognition within a broader category of 'faith' or assent to testimony. The account given by Aquinas can serve to introduce some main issues. First, since divine faith is a virtue, it cannot be a form of knowledge because there is no virtue in believing what is perceived or known to be so. Unlike knowledge and like opinion, faith arises by an act of will; but, unlike opining, the act is due to 'an interior movement of God's grace' rather than, as the Pelagians held, our own free choice. Faith does not involve rational enquiry into what is believed, but may involve enquiry as to whether we morally ought to believe it, that is, whether it is inspired by God. On the other hand, like knowledge, faith is a firm conviction, whereas opinion is provisional and easily mutable. It is required that our faith extends to certain inessential things, such as that Abraham had two sons, as a means to our believing essential things, the articles of faith, which direct us towards eternal life. Although what is known cannot be an object of faith, something known to some can be a proper object of faith to others, who perhaps cannot conduct the reasoning necessary for knowledge. Some proper objects of faith, however, the mysteries, are so absolutely, being beyond or above human reason.

There is a certain instability in this account. The absolute conviction of faith is supposed to be independent of the content of any proposition on which it is voluntarily bestowed. On the other hand, it is allowed that reasoning is appropriately employed, even if not to justify the proposition, yet to ascertain the obligation to believe it. Yet the two questions hardly come apart. If the proposition concerns what is knowable, a first approach to the question whether it came from God, who cannot lie, might be to consider whether it is true. In any case, if it were known that a proposition comes from God, it would seem to be ruled out as an object of faith as certainly as if we knew its truth directly. If, on the other hand, its divine origin cannot be known, then we cannot know that we ought to believe it. Aquinas himself seems to suggest that the starting point for faith is the probability (or reasonableness of opining) that a proposition is divinely revealed. Faith is our choosing (with the aid of grace) to regard the consequent probability of the proposition itself as certainty. Yet this account again fails to keep the question of whether the proposition comes from God apart from the question of its own direct justification, since the independent probability of what is testified affects the probability that it came from a veracious source. On the other hand, if we choose to believe a proposition as an article of faith, it seems difficult to avoid the vicious circularity of holding it to be an article of faith that all are morally obliged to believe it.[149]

So far Aquinas takes it that faith is the acceptance of what comes to us through others, the recipients of a more direct revelation. It is in his discussion of the latter, 'prophecy', that Aquinas finds room for the metaphor of light 'beyond the natural light of reason'. Unlike faith, prophecy is a form of knowledge. Yet, unlike natural knowledge, it is fitful, a temporary sharing in God's knowledge. Interestingly, Aquinas distinguishes between explicit revelation, in which the divine source of the knowledge is evident to the knower, and mysterious suggestion – a sort of theological 'blindsight'. Only the former is certain knowledge or full prophecy. There is, indeed, a scale of prophecy, ranging from merely being moved to action by the Spirit, through dreams, visions and voices, to the intellectual apprehension of supernatural truth without images. There is also a distinction between prophetic representation (such as a dream) and prophetic light employed in judgement (which might be the interpretation of another's dream).[150]

For Aquinas, reason has two rôles in relation to faith: first, to set the scene by proving God's existence and establishing the credentials of the Christian revelation, and, second, to demonstrate theological conclusions from the articles of faith. On a rather different view, associated with Augustine, with Anselm's *credo ut intelligam* and with Luther, rational theology is never independent of faith – its rôle is to confirm existing faith by explicating what is believed. Any rational 'proof' will be acceptable only to the faithful, through the grace of God.

After Montaigne, the philosophy of faith was closely tied in with attitudes to philosophical scepticism. Montaigne saw the demonstration that we are incapable of knowledge as a condition of true faith, and the source of faith as 'external authority and command'. His conclusion reads like a relativistic advocacy of submission to the locally orthodox religion.[151] Later fideist sceptics, including Montaigne's follower, Pierre Charron, often affirmed the priority of the Catholic church as the most ancient authority.[152] Such writers commonly stressed the many sources of doubt peculiar to religion. First, as had always been obvious, any vehicle of revelation will be capable of a variety of interpretations, so that agreement that the Bible is the word of God leaves it in question just what is to be believed. Second, the evidence commonly offered (as by Aquinas and, indeed, the Bible itself) for the reasonableness of faith consists in certain supposed signs, such as fulfilled prophetic predictions and miracles. Yet the belief in miracles is also (unless for witnesses, when related difficulties arise) a peculiarly problematic instance of assent to testimony. The problems were, perhaps, especially evident at a time when the conception of nature, and so of what is against or above nature, was itself in dispute.[153] There was also the theological issue as to whether the age of miracles is past, in which case all or much of the relevant testimony is itself scriptural. It is therefore not surprising that there were sceptical denials of the possibility of our rationally distinguishing true from false miracles, or of arriving at the correct understanding of scripture. It was, indeed, a question of whether the identity of the Word itself had not been rendered irremediably doubtful to reason by accretions, omissions, and mistranscriptions.[154] Here Catholic apologists deduced the need for an authoritative interpreter.

A Protestant form of fideism, on the other hand, sometimes laid such an emphasis on personal conscience as in effect to make all revelation immediate. In seventeenth-century writers such as Jacob Boehme or the Quaker biblical critic Samuel Fisher, the effect of this emphasis was almost to marginalise scripture. At most they offered a combination of scriptural and prophetic authority, resolving the problem of interpretation by postulating that God directly and infallibly inspires and enlightens the true Christian reader. The interpretive rôle of personal inspiration was emphasised towards mid-century by a group of English writers, including Joseph Mede, John Dury, and William Twisse. Immediate revelation was presented as an independent source of knowledge superior to sense and intellect and the only defence against complete scepticism.[155] Later, such Calvinists as Jean Claude and Pierre Jurieu maintained a similar position, Jurieu presenting divine faith as an unmistakable feeling of certitude without evidence and independent of probabilities.

Thus scepticism was allied, both in Catholic and Protestant apologetics, with a kind of supernaturalist, anti-rational dogmatism. Yet full-blown fideism, while possibly capable of promoting obedience within a church, was ill fitted to bring over those of another persuasion. Debate between faiths led naturally to consideration of probabilities – and with respect to specific claims to revelation no dogmatist could offer more. On the other hand, most agreed that, whatever reason can do to prepare the way, saving faith requires grace. It is therefore not surprising if distinctions become a little blurred. A number of writers in the first half of the century, however, including Grotius, Herbert of Cherbury, and members of the so-called Great Tew circle around Lucius Cary, Lord Falkland, worked on approaches to faith and salvation very clearly opposed to fideism, emphasising the rôle of reason even, in some cases, while admitting that certainty is impossible.[156] William Chillingworth, a friend of Falkland who had converted to Catholicism and then back again, argued that, in matters of religion as in many other things, we must be satisfied with probability, rejecting as absurd the view that faith can have the certainty of knowledge: 'In requiring that I believe something more firmly than it is made to me evidently credible, you require in effect that I believe something which appears to me incredible, and while it does so.'[157] He extended this principle to the identification of uncorrupted revelation, and took the moral content of scripture to supply one of the best arguments for its divine authority. Moreover, no one can possibly know whether he is moved by the spirit of God. He can only say 'these and these Reasons I have to shew, that . . . this or that is the meaning of such a Scripture.'[158] Chillingworth argued for toleration and minimal articles of faith, since God would not require individuals to believe what they lacked the means to make out. What is required is sincere and thorough examination, but no one is infallible and people can sincerely disagree. It was natural for such irenical 'probabilism' to find favour in the English situation, but also for it to have there both Roman Catholic and Calvinist critics.[159]

Those who promoted the new science were interested in another form of religious forbearance. Descartes himself made claims about the relation between faith and reason with a species of toleration in mind. Like Aquinas, he saw faith as a form of assent which is an act of will motivated by divine grace rather than by reasons (although, unlike Aquinas, he held that even in knowledge there is voluntary assent). Like Aquinas, too, he insisted that the basic truths of religion are demonstrable and also agreed that, 'with respect to truths of faith, we should perceive some reason which convinces us that they have been revealed by God.'[160] Even the ignorant, in following authority, need reason to believe that those they follow are less ignorant than themselves. Nevertheless it seems that faith has its own reasons. For the 'formal reason which leads us to assent to matters of faith' consists in an un-Thomistic 'inner light which comes from God'. This light illuminates, not the content of the revelation (which may remain a mystery), but its status as revelation, something which may be not only 'more certain than any natural light', but 'often even, through the light of grace, more evident'.[161] The suggestion that divine grace increases rather than diminishes freedom[162] rests on a similar analogy between grace and reason. Yet that analogy, and Descartes's preference for the model of divine illumination over Aquinas's model of a reasonable (if, thanks to grace, absolute) trust, apparently had a philosophico-political motive. For with it went the possibility of a sharper distinction between the spheres of faith and reason. As faith owes nothing to natural reason, having its own light, so reason owes nothing to faith. The same philosopher who wrote that 'the light of grace is to be preferred to the light of reason' expressed astonishment 'that a theologian should dare to write about the motion of the earth' in the face of Galileo's arguments.[163]

Leading followers of Descartes, while emphatically endorsing the separation of philosophy (including natural theology) from revealed theology, did so without assimilating grace to light and reason. The Port-Royal logicians presented faith as confident trust in authority which, as such, 'supposes some reason', evidently a natural reason. Infinity, however, lies above reason. Thus we should accept the authority of the church, without expecting to understand its doctrine, with respect to those consequences of God's infinite power which constitute the Christian mysteries.[164] Malebranche also returned to the thought that faith is *opposed* to 'evidence': 'to be among the faithful, it is necessary to believe blindly.'[165] While accepting the rôle of reason in natural theology and in establishing the credentials of revelation, these writers effectively denied it a rôle in explicating articles of faith. Malebranche implicitly criticised Descartes for attempting to accommodate the mystery of the Eucharist to his philosophical principles – this was the same mistake that the scholastic Aristotelians had made, and the cause of unnecessary dissension and intolerance among the faithful.[166]

Descartes's claims for reason and natural theology were notably rejected by

Pascal, yet it might seem from the famous (if in outline already fairly trite) 'wager'
that Pascal himself saw faith as justifiable probabilistically. The argument appeals to
the principle that the rationality of any decision depends, not only on the strength
of grounds for expecting the course chosen to turn out successfully (in the case of
belief, grounds for holding it true), but on the value of the ends at stake. It is
therefore rational to do (and believe) whatever may lead to an infinitely valuable
end, eternal life, even if there is only a moderate probability of its doing so
(indeed, of God's existence). Pascal's purpose, however, was to argue not that faith
should or could be guided by such reasons, but that unbelief evidently is not so
guided. The question is ultimately not one for the intellect to determine. Similarly,
miracles are signs which it is sinful to ignore, but which do not convince without
grace. Yet, although this assignment of faith to the heart and to the grace of God
may be characteristic of Port-Royal theology, the wager and the appeal to signs is
included in the Port-Royal *Logique* without Pascal's moral, and others employed
them as if faith were indeed a matter of reasonable, if uncertain, choice.[167] Nicole
states in another work that grace can only serve to strengthen and sustain the best
use we can make of reason,[168] and the *Logique,* presumably, is concerned only
with the latter. Locke later followed Pascal in making it the point of the wager
that the atheist cannot claim that he simply demands a higher or more rigorous
level of proof than the theist. But Locke differed from the Port-Royalists in his
probabilist rejection of the heart as a proper source of certitude beyond what is
supported by reasons for belief.[169]

Despite the philosophical differences between them, the Tew circle's minimalism with respect to doctrine was shared by Hobbes. He, however, undertook
the additional task of proving (consonantly, in a way, with the original constitution
of the Anglican church, but against both Anglican and Presbyterian pretensions to
political authority) that the only ecclesiastical authority with any right to obedience has to be the civil authority.[170] His argument, ostensibly directed against
independent Papal authority, starts from a firm distinction between the spheres of
faith and reason, and an insistence that our senses, experience, and natural reason
'are not to be folded up in the napkin of an implicit faith': 'For though there be
many things in God's word above reason; . . . yet there is nothing contrary to it.'
Faith must itself be founded on reason, but 'when anything therein is written too
hard for our examination, we are bidden to captivate our understanding to the
words; and not to labour in sifting out a philosophical truth by logic, of such
mysteries as are not comprehensible, nor fall under any rule of natural science.'[171]
Since, evidently, 'miracles now cease', alleged personal inspiration can be ignored,
at least by the rest of us. The only thing for reason to establish, therefore, is which

books constitute 'the rules of Christian life'. Rules are laws, so 'the question of the Scripture is the question of what is law throughout all Christendom, both natural and civil.' Since it has been proved that 'sovereigns in their own dominions are the sole legislators', then Scripture is whatever any Christian sovereign establishes as such.[172]

Hobbes's point is that, in so far as an authority is required in matters of faith, only one such authority is possible in a Christian commonwealth. When the ruler is not a Christian, he still remains the authority in all matters of performance, as Christ himself recognised.[173] Apart from a sovereign, the church is just a club which must persuade, and cannot coerce, potential members. Its appeal on matters of interpretation must be (like Saint Paul's) to reason and the hearer's judgement rather than to authority, and its only sanction is exclusion from membership.[174] What is impossible is that a subject should have a divided duty, to a sovereign and to a religious authority separate from the civil sovereign, an idea which for Hobbes is the source of the political evils of his time. It is not possible that subjects should put their salvation at risk by being obedient to the civil law in a Christian commonwealth, since such obedience is consistent both with the evident Laws of Nature and with profession of the one defining principle of Christianity, that Jesus is the Messiah – that is, with the requirements both of works and faith. If these views about the relation between church and state were generally accepted, there would be no reason for sovereigns to be anything but tolerant of different religions.[175] Hobbes confirmed his argument by an elaborately reasoned analysis of scripture itself and its supposed identification of an authoritative church with a civil commonwealth. He set aside the claims of immediate revelation, which must be problematic even to its recipient. For the biblical God speaks only through supernatural visions and dreams which are subjectively no different from the natural 'imaginations' of the false prophets.[176]

Although Hobbes's argument might seem simply to replace the illusory authority of church or inspired conscience with the real authority of the sovereign, in view of his dogmatic system it must be a mistake to class it with those fideistic arguments in favour of an authority which appeal to the supposed general weakness of reason.[177] He emphasised that the sovereign's power and authority extends only to what is to be professed, since belief cannot be commanded. The argument is not epistemological, but political, and authority is required, not to ward off doubt, but to prevent religious or, indeed, any other belief from causing civil strife and sedition. Both those who 'ground their knowledge upon the infallibility of the Church' and those who do so 'on the testimony of the private spirit' wrongly ask how they know, rather than why they believe.[178] The general answer to the right question is easy: belief is due to education. What is important is that what is taught is not pernicious, or interpreted in pernicious ways. Hence it is important to show that Scripture confirms, rather than undermines, 'the power of civil sovereigns, and the duty of their subjects'.[179]

Henry More was a very different English philosopher who also responded to the religious conflicts of the time by arguing for a minimal core of Christian dogma and leaving peripheral questions to the judgement of the individual. Pretences to personal inspiration were brushed aside, while reason, it was thought, can establish Christianity's credentials. Despite his expressed respect for Mede's biblical criticism, More's own efforts at unravelling the biblical code, which included a 'philosophical' interpretation of *Genesis,* relied on their purported reasonableness rather than on any claim to personal inspiration. Yet a more distinctive feature of More's approach was his hard look at the psychology of belief, especially claims to personal illumination. He began by defining inspiration in a way that seems to make the content itself a criterion: 'to be *inspired* is *to be moved in an extraordinary manner by the power or Spirit of God to act, speak, or think what is holy, just and true.'* The only sort of inspiration he envisaged in ordinary seventeenth-century life was a providential 'presage of a mans own heart' in decisions of importance to himself or, 'much more', to the public.[180] But his concern was 'not [with] that which is true, but [with] that which is a mistake', and *Enthusiasmus Triumphatus* is an elaborate natural history of 'enthusiasm' seen as a sort of sickness of the imagination due to physiological causes, sometimes brought on intentionally by such means as 'solemn silence and intense and earnest meditation'. It is mad to put out the light of reason[181] in the fanciful 'expectation of an higher and more glorious Light'. The enthusiast is like someone who advocates breaking lanterns at night-time because their light is inferior to broad daylight. If he takes himself to have a messianic political mission, he is particularly dangerous.

The argument of Spinoza's *Tractatus Theologico-Politicus* is in some respects closely similar to that of *Leviathan,* despite rather different political intentions and very different ethics and epistemology. Unlike Hobbes, Spinoza had a rational, if unorthodox, theology which grounds a conception of God and His relation to the world and human beings. But, like Hobbes, Spinoza approached revealed religion through a reasoned reading of the Bible itself, in which he found nothing not ordinarily intelligible, provided that certain sensible hermeneutic principles are employed capable of uncovering the historic intentions of its various authors.[182] The 'tissue of ridiculous mysteries' is blamed on the twin ideas that there is a light superior to reason, and that 'Reason is a mere handmaid to Theology' –

a view which makes the prophets 'rave with the Greeks'.[183] On the contrary, on the authority of Scripture itself prophecy is a function of the imagination, always requires a sign, and can only give moral certainty. Moreover, biblical signs or miracles 'necessarily happened, like everything else, according to natural laws'. If it could be shown that an event as described in the Bible (making allowance for the beliefs, ignorance of causes and special purposes of the writer) was contrary to nature, it would follow that the passage in question was an interpolation, since what is contrary to nature is contrary to reason, and so absurd.[184] In fact the Bible is a collection of moral teachings, questionably sorted out by later generations,[185] intended to instil piety and obedience to natural and civil law. There can therefore be no duty to believe distinct from the duty 'summed up in love to one's neighbour'. 'Faith' is simply active moral belief which constitutes a kind of knowledge of God: 'Faith consists in thinking such things about God [*de Deo talia sentire*], without which obedience to Him would be impossible, and which the mere fact of obedience to Him implies.'[186] Those who persecute others for their doctrinal beliefs are therefore 'the true enemies of Christ', and virtue is most possible in a tolerant society in which a 'free multitude' is governed by consent with a (preferably democratic) system of checks and balances.[187]

The notion that virtue is impossible without a knowledge of God gives Spinoza a list of seven doctrines essential to salvation. They include, for example, a belief in the forgiveness of sins, without which only despair would be possible. It seems, however, that a person who tries to be just and does not despair thereby implicitly or effectually believes in the forgiveness of sins. Spinoza's view of revealed religion is that, in its benign form, it is a sort of imaginative equivalent to the intellectual moral knowledge which constitutes true virtue and love of God.[188] Like every-thing else, revealed religion flows from God, but, in so far as it is a positive thing comparable with knowledge, there is point in ascribing it to Him more particularly.[189] In effect, faith is justified by 'internal arguments' from the moral content of Scripture, but Spinoza insists that reason and faith have their quite separate spheres, speculative truth and practice.[190]

Locke's view of revelation, as set out in the *Essay, The Reasonableness of Chris-tianity* and other works, had something in common with the views of Hobbes and Spinoza, but his developed epistemology was much more in line with the Anglican probabilist tradition. Like More and Chillingworth, he attempted to combine an acceptance of the Bible as revelation, a critical approach to scriptural interpretation and prophetic claims, a minimalist interpretation of the essential articles of Chris-tian faith, an understanding of Christianity which emphasised its moral teaching and the importance of works as well as faith, and a vindication of reason in the face of fideist-sceptical argument. Some argue that Locke shifted his ground at the end of his life,[191] but the position of the *Essay* is unambiguous enough. Like More, Chillingworth, Hobbes, and Spinoza, he firmly subordinated revelation to reason. When a purported revelation conflicts with what is naturally evident, it must lose its claim to be revelation.[192] Certain revealed truths (such as the Resurrection) lie 'beyond the Discovery of our natural Faculties, and above Reason', but there is little room for mysteries: 'to this crying up of *Faith,* in opposition to *Reason,* we may, I think, in good measure, ascribe those Absurdities that fill almost all the Religions which possess and divide Mankind.' Words without ideas are empty, so that it is impossible even to believe what is not understood.[193]

More fundamentally, although revelation may ground belief that would otherwise be improbable, that is just one natural reason outweighing another: 'It still belongs to *Reason* to judge of the Truth of its being a Revelation, and of the Signification of the Words, wherein it is delivered.'[194] Like Hobbes, Spinoza, and other minimalists, Locke advocated a 'reasonable' approach to Scripture, taking into account the probable circumstances of its authorship. Moreover, the general principle applies as much to 'original' as to 'traditional' revelation: 'If Reason must not examine their Truth by something extrinsical to the Perswasions themselves; Inspirations and Delusions, Truth and Falshood will have the same Measure.'[195] 'Enthusiasm' is ascribed, as by More, to physiology, 'the Conceits of a warmed or over-weening Brain', but More's simile for the advocate of revelation over reason is significantly modified. The enthusiast 'does much what the same, as if he would perswade a Man to put out his Eyes the better to receive the remote Light of an invisible Star by a Telescope'.[196] Divine illumination depends on, and is not separate from, the natural light: indeed,

Light, true Light in the Mind is, or can be nothing else but the Evidence of the Truth of any Proposition; and if it be not a self-evident Proposition, all the Light it has, or can have, is from the clearness and validity of those Proofs, upon which it is received. To talk of any other light in the Understanding is to put ourselves in the dark.[197]

Locke says remarkably little, however, as to what his reasons actually are for accepting the Bible as revelation. He seems to have been in agreement with Chillingworth and Spinoza that the best reasons lie in its moral content. Certainly he held, with both, that '*Reason* must be our last Judge and Guide in every Thing',[198] echoing Chillingworth's basic principle: 'There is one unerring mark of [Love of Truth], *viz.* The not entertaining any Proposition with greater assurance than the Proofs it is built upon will warrant.'[199] The implication of this rule is toleration, 'for where is the Man, that has incontestable Evidence of the

Truth of all that he holds, or of the Falshood of all he condemns; or can say, that he has examined, to the bottom, all his own, or other men's opinions?'[200]

Two of Locke's contemporaries deserve mention for the peculiar forms taken by their advocacy of reasonableness and toleration. One is Pierre Bayle, who is commonly taken for a sceptic but would better be more specifically classified as a critical probabilist and advocate of reasoned examination.[201] Throughout his writings he stressed the limitations of rational argument and the subjectivity or relativity of 'evidence', but without denying, or attempting in general to undermine, their force in determining belief.[202] Still less did he propose setting aside the deliverances of sense or natural feeling. We have to arrive at our religious beliefs, as many other beliefs, through a reasonable assessment of probability, and we have to judge as we find and (as some fideists had insisted) as we feel. But others doing the same may arrive at different conclusions. There is no criterion of truth outside our feelings to decide between us. Bayle did not conclude, sceptically, that both sides should suspend belief, but that neither is in a position to claim the right to persecute the other on the basis of the truth of its own beliefs.

Richard Burthogge argued rather differently for a structurally similar position.[203] Although our senses assure us that things act on us, the conceptions we form of them are necessarily limited, indeed shaped by our faculties themselves, and by language. 'Metaphysical truth', or the conformity of our notions to things as they are in themselves, therefore cannot concern us. The only criterion of truth or 'evidence' we can recognise must be internal to our thought and must lie in the harmony or coherence of our beliefs with one another and with experience. Burthogge did not propose that harmony is a merely subjective criterion, but he took it to be relative, in that any hypothesis, however harmonious, might be supplanted by one that is even more so. Argument and inquiry should therefore be systematic, but undogmatic. Typical of his time, Burthogge drew widely on his philosophical education in constructing a framework for, in the first instance, 'reasonable' theological and exegetical debate, concluding in favour of 'a general toleration'. The resulting epistemology includes perhaps the seventeenth century's clearest statement of a coherence theory of truth, and can seem a startling anticipation of recent anti-foundationalism: 'In science as it is in Arch-work, the Parts uphold one another.'

## 2. Error

The theory of error was central to seventeenth-century epistemology, and no less important for its consequences for later philosophy. It starts, perhaps, from the awkward fact that our cognitive nature, supposedly designed to produce knowledge or at least well-grounded belief, more or less often produces beliefs which are neither one nor the other. Present-day philosophers have come to assume, with Bayle, that our cognitive faculties are essentially fallible, but there is still a problem as to how belief can be motivated by what is seemingly non-cognitive, such as hatred or the expectation of gain. How is such a process related to normal cognition? Yet for philosophers who held that we have at least one faculty which is essentially knowledge-producing and infallible, the problem of error possessed a further dimension.

As this chapter has argued, in the seventeenth century the question of the rôle of the will in cognition was pursued against a dual context. On the one hand, there was the Stoic distinction between perception and judgement, the latter being voluntary even though 'the mind must give way to what is self-evident.'[204] On the other hand, the conception of faith as a moral demand supplied reason for placing at least some belief (even if not knowledge) under the command of the will. Descartes expressed his acceptance of Stoic doctrine in terms of an analogy between error and sin. As sin arises from our freedom to act when we do not clearly apprehend the good, so error is a result of our freedom to judge beyond our clear and distinct ideas. That we cannot but assent to what is self-evident is no limitation on our freedom, since the soul is naturally rational and so most free and self-determined when it is determined by reasons rather than 'external causes'. The special problem of faith is dealt with, as has been seen, by an assimilation of grace and reason. Where neither is present, suspension of belief is the appropriate response. In this way Descartes preserved the conception of an infallible intellectual faculty, gift of an undeceiving God, in the face of the fact of error.

A different classical model was adopted by Hobbes. Epicureans, as it has been noted, took beliefs to arise naturally in the context of sensations and 'preconceptions', while ancient sceptics can similarly seem less to be explaining why it is proper to suspend belief, than to be presenting considerations which will naturally lead to suspense. In the same vein Hobbes explains doubt, not as voluntary suspension of belief, but as a chain of, in effect, alternating inclinations to believe naturally arising as a result of ambiguous experience or, presumably, inconclusive reasoning. 'Judgement' is simply the last, persistent opinion, just as 'will' is 'the last appetite in deliberation'.[205] No distinction is made between considering a proposition and taking up an attitude of belief, disbelief, or something in between. Error is simply the having of false beliefs, to be avoided by that methodical use of language and reasoning which affords 'evidence'. Poor judgement may be motivated in so far as our desires may affect our ability to note significant similarities and make appropriate distinctions.[206]

A similar line was taken by Spinoza against Descartes, although Spinoza followed the Stoics at least verbally in assigning assent to the will. His claim is that the will and the understanding, or rather (since talk of 'faculties' is mere abstraction) volitions and ideas, can no more be prised apart in the human mind than they can in God's: 'In the Mind there is no volition, or affirmation and negation, except that which an idea involves in so far as it is an idea.'[207] To imagine a winged horse is to affirm wings of a horse, but (unless for an imaginative child, a dreamer, or the like, who takes the horse to be present) that will happen in a context such that the subject also perceives what excludes the existence of the horse or perceives that its idea is inadequate. In that case the subject will necessarily either deny or doubt the horse's existence. Just as for Hobbes, for Spinoza suspension of belief is itself a propositional attitude or 'perception'. Error is simply the having of an inadequate idea without perceiving that it is inadequate.

Unlike any of these philosophers, Aquinas had held neither that assent is always voluntary nor that it is never so, and that seems to be the position adopted, somewhat precariously, by Locke. He totally rejected Descartes's doctrine with respect to knowledge or perception. All knowledge is like sense perception, in which we may choose where and how hard to look, but we cannot then choose what we see. Indeed, he endeavours to extend this model to belief generally; 'Assent is no more in our Power than Knowledge. . . . And what upon full Examination I find the most probable, I cannot deny my Assent to.' Nevertheless he wants at least to stress that we have that kind of power over the conduct of enquiry as makes us morally responsible for both belief and ignorance: '*We can hinder both Knowledge and Assent, by stopping our Enquiry,* and not imploying our Faculties in the search of any Truth. If it were not so, Ignorance, Error, or Infidelity could not in any Case be a Fault.'[208] He means, presumably, that we can stop enquiry before 'full examination'. He accordingly suggests that where 'there are sufficient grounds to suspect that there is either Fallacy in words, or certain Proofs, as considerable, to be produced on the contrary side, there Assent, Suspense, or Dissent, are often voluntary Actions.'[209] Unfortunately, it seems, such second-order considerations can lead to a kind of motivated caution which allows us to avoid accepting very many facts we do not like.[210] But the problem for Locke's theorising is that it is difficult to see why second-order grounds do not simply merge with first-order grounds, destroying his apparent, if never clearly articulated, distinction between voluntary suspense and involuntary 'wavering'.[211] In fact, when he comes to identify the causes of error, Locke seems to ignore his official model of two stages, the first voluntary, the second involuntary, in almost the same breath as he endorses it. For example, the same appetites, interests, and passions that motivate voluntary actions are taken to intervene, not only by distorting enquiry, but *between* enquiry and judgement, by distorting our 'measures of probability'.[212] Locke's account has the virtue of not being simplistic, but it is hardly a satisfactory analysis of the perplexing collusion of will and reason which gives rise to motivated belief.

After Locke, the issue of the voluntariness of belief became less prominent (although the sort of view held by Hobbes and Spinoza emerged again in Hume). But the enterprise of explaining error, and the kinds of explanation employed, remained of crucial importance. Some of the ideas which shaped that enterprise throughout the seventeenth century were set out at its beginning by Bacon, in his famous characterisation of four sorts of illusions or 'idols' (*idola*). The first of these, 'illusions of the tribe', are sources of error and prejudice common to all human beings. They include a number of natural inclinations: an attachment to entrenched beliefs despite fresh contrary evidence, an assumption that the whole of reality is like one's partial experience of it, a tendency to match one's beliefs to what is attractive and desirable, and a proneness to abstraction, as if the conceptual dissection of nature explained its operations. But the most damaging of such illusions is the assumption that the senses present reality as it is in itself. The second sort of illusions, 'illusions of the cave' in which each individual lives, are due to mental and bodily peculiarities, cast of mind, education, habits, and other accidents. They include whatever the individual mind 'seizes and dwells upon with its own peculiar satisfaction', as one person loves novelty, another admires antiquity. The third sort, 'illusions of the market-place', are the most harmful of all. These comprise two sorts of linguistic confusion, the assumption that all names stand for things (whereas names like 'fortune' or 'the element of fire' stand only for fictions), and the assumption that all words in use have determinate and constant meanings (whereas words like 'humid' or 'dense' confusedly signify a variety of different attributes). Illusions of the fourth kind, 'of the theatre', are engendered in and by philosophical systems, which Bacon regarded as pretty stories told about the world according to various neat plots or conceptions, as Aristotle 'fashioned the world out of the categories'.[213]

Bacon's list of intellectual vices appears as a polemic aimed at philosophical and religious enemies rather than a general natural history of human unreasonableness and cognitive failure. It stands in sharp contrast to the balanced pros and cons of scholastic disputations and textbooks, in which even presumed error is accorded its due force. Its targets were specific, among them Plato, Aristotle, Gilbert, alchemy, and all those who confuse philosophy and theology. Thus the mind's natural tendency to posit more order than it finds is exemplified by the theory of perfectly circular celestial motions, or the invention of an invisible fourth element to complete a square. Despite the urgency of the purely theoretical question of error for much seventeenth-century epistemology, this general polemical intent and, indeed, a number of Bacon's specific categories remained characteristic of much of the discussion of the causes of error. The prime illusion of the tribe, for example, that the world is as it appears to the senses, figured centrally in corpuscularian rhetoric against both ordinary beliefs and the 'real accidents' of the Aristotelians – most famously, perhaps, as Descartes's 'prejudices of the senses' or 'of childhood'.[214]

Just as striking is the continuity of accusations of linguistic confusion, the negative corollary of the programme of a wide range of philosophers from Wilkins to Leibniz (conducted with more or less optimism as to its consequences if achieved) to establish a universal language of science. Together with the charges of pointless abstraction, and of taking logical distinctions to be natural ones, the mistake of assuming that every name in use has denotation was repeatedly warned against by the new philosophers, often with just Bacon's targets in view.[215] Descartes explains the doctrine [216] that a body can become rarer or more dense in terms of both of Bacon's 'illusions of the market-place', for the mistake is attributed either to philosophers' meaning nothing by talk of a 'substance' underlying geometrical quantity, or to their employing a confused idea of incorporeal substance, while improperly calling it 'corporeal substance'. For Hobbes, too, 'insignificant speech' is the paradigmatic theoretical error, and the phrase 'incorporeal substance' is a prime example of it.[217] Even a work as late as Locke's *Essay* reiterated Bacon's division of the prime sources of language-based error, although it is adapted to suit new concerns. In one kind of case, characteristic of 'the Market and Exchange', speakers 'think it enough, that they use a Word, as they imagine, in the common Acceptation', in order to be assured that it has a clear, unique meaning. In the other kind, they assume that their words stand, not only for ideas, but for 'the reality of Things', 'Things as they really are'. Some of Locke's examples of these faults are just like Bacon's,[218] but many are importantly different. For him the great mistake of the second kind is to suppose that general words such as 'gold' or 'man' achieve a common meaning by naming real species, whereas Bacon regarded the names of substances, in particular of ultimate species, as among the least problematic of all.[219] As for the first kind of linguistic illusion, Locke shared the concern of many writers, including Hobbes and Wilkins, over the regrettable looseness and flexibility of moral language which allowed rhetoricians to teach how to present vice as virtue, good as evil, by shifting the meanings of words. People should be made aware of the 'doubtfulness and uncertainty' of the ordinary use of moral terms, and meanings should be fixed by agreed stipulation. Then, and only then, will rational ethics and political agreement be possible.[220]

Bacon included the force of the imagination and the passions among the sources of error, but he did not particularly stress them. The later, dramatic extension of such explanations is unsurprising, given the Platonist presumption that any wandering from the paths of reason is due to the soul's entanglement with the body. Descartes's debate with the sceptic was intended to demonstrate that error is avoided only when the bodily faculties of sense and imagination are properly subordinated to intellect. Even such an allegedly incoherent or meaningless theory as that of rarefaction is ascribed to the influence of sense.[221] Not that Rationalists denied that sense, imagination and passion are essential to human existence.[222] Descartes's category of pre-critical natural belief, 'what nature teaches', was constructed to cover just this point, while everyone accepted that diagrams can aid, or prompt, abstract thought.[223] And as Spinoza remarked, '[by random experience] I know almost all the things that are useful in life.' But the imagination can impinge improperly on the sphere of intellect. Spinoza gave the example of the Stoics' confusedly imagining immortality in terms of relative impenetrability, so identifying souls with the most subtle bodies.[224] Indeed, he ascribed the whole of popular theology to the mistake of using the imagination to try to conceive of God. Theological disputes have arisen because 'each one has judged things according to the disposition of his brain.'[225]

This human vulnerability to physiology was employed spectacularly, as was seen in the previous section, in More's discussion of 'enthusiasm', an inherently pathological form of the 'superstition' which irritated Bacon and Spinoza. Here a certain sort of error is identified as madness through an analysis of the peculiar workings of the imagination due to habit, physical circumstances, and above all the humours with their attendant passions (melancholy with lust, sanguine with pride). The form of the explanation is readily extended to other kinds of belief, so that sections are included on the 'philosophical enthusiasm' of alchemists and theosophists: 'What can it be but the heaving of the *Hypochondria* that lifts up the Mind to such high comparisons from a supposition so false and foolish?'[226] Happily the condition is curable, if apoplexy does not intervene, by temperance, humility and reason.

Probably the most ambitious of all seventeenth-century treatises on error is Malebranche's *Recherche de la vérité,* which systematically discusses a vast range of natural confusions, pathological delusions and derangements, heresies and philosophical absurdities due in various ways to natural sensory judgements (including value-judgements based on sensory pleasure and pain), to the imagination (often influenced by passions), and to the limitations of the intellect. 'The errors of the senses and the imagination stem from the constitution and nature of the body and are revealed by considering the soul's dependence on it',[227] a task to which Malebranche brings a fairly developed mechanistic physiology. Sense and imagination distract the will from intellectual thought (and so from a virtuous life), but the intellect itself has inherent tendencies to error. It is incapable of grasping the infinite, but is continually drawn to do so, since we have been made to love infinite good. It can only understand even finite subjects part by part, and so falls into confusion without a method. Its continuous apprehension of the general idea of Being through its union with God makes it inherently liable to 'disordered abstraction', the multiplication of abstract entities taken for real ones. Like other, less comprehensive writing in the genre, the whole work is highly polemical and its prime targets are religious and philosophical. Explanation of the errors of Aristotelian physics and metaphysics is particularly unrestrained, some being blamed on sense, others on imagination and yet others on disorderly abstraction. It is, no doubt, with conscious irony that Arnauld diagnoses the principles of Malebranche's own system as 'fancies deriving from childhood prejudices'.[228]

For such empiricists as Hobbes and Locke, for whom intellect is not separable from imagination, the distinction between good and bad functions of the imagination would seem to be even more important than for writers in the Platonist tradition. As it is, the rôle Hobbes assigns to language marks off, in effect, a sphere of reason and so of intellectual error correctable by method, while passions and physiology can be accorded something like their usual blame for leading the mind astray. One engaging idiosyncrasy is his view that a 'good wit' ('by which . . . is meant a *good fancy*'), as well as a bad one, owes something to passion, since it consists in 'celerity of imagining' and 'steady direction to some approved end', neither of which comes without some ambition or 'desire of power'. It is therefore a mistake to ascribe the difference in natural or acquired wit (i.e., in the ability to learn from experience or to employ language effectively) directly to physiology, or 'there would be no less difference of men in their . . . senses, than in their fancies, and discretions.' It is rather those extravagant passions that affect our opinions, such as pride, anger, or melancholy, which are causally related to indisposition of our organs. Like More, Hobbes illustrated his theory by classic tales of madness, and he employed it to attack his bugbears, the 'opinion of being inspired' and the madly 'seditious roaring of a troubled nation' against its protectors.[229]

Definitions of wit and good judgement echoing those of Hobbes appear in Locke's *Essay,* but are unrelated to his main explanations of error.[230] Indeed Locke conceives of the mind's operations on ideas to be independent of any Hobbesian 'train of imaginations'. Judgements based on experience are never treated by Locke as if they were merely an instance of animal habit, the kind of consequence of the customary association of ideas that they are for Hobbes or, for that matter, for their more Platonistically inclined detractors. For Locke, such judgements at least implicitly presume a causal relation: although they may *become* habitual, like the movement from word to idea,[231] they are not *founded* on habit. In general, the topic of the bare 'association of ideas' due to habit and education is a part of the topic of error, the pathology of whatever is 'Extravagant in the Opinions, Reasonings, and Actions of . . . Men' and 'is really *Madness*'.[232] We are back among Bacon's 'illusions of the cave' with a vengeance – and with an appropriate Malebranchian physiology: 'all which seems to be but Trains of Motion in the Animal Spirits, which . . . continue on in the same steps . . . , which by often treading are worn into a smooth path, and the Motion in it becomes easy and as it were Natural.'[233] With a certain restraint (if for greater effect), Locke turns only in the final sections of the chapter to the dire consequences when 'the *idea* of Infallibility be inseparably join'd to [that of] any Person', and of other such 'wrong and unnatural Combinations of *Ideas*' as establish 'the Irreconcilable opposition between different Sects of Philosophy and Religion'. The same polemical moral had been drawn from the same and other Baconian themes in the chapter 'Of wrong Assent, or Error'.[234]

If there seems to have been relatively little variation in the structure and tone of explanations of error during the seventeenth century (although there were new targets, not least when new philosophers turned their weapons on one another), that was soon to change. First, of course, not all philosophical criticism was pathological and could hardly be so in the normal context of debate. Descartes himself had written irenically, while Leibniz, for example, was generally eager to find points of agreement as well as disagreement, truths embedded in the errors of Aristotelians, Kabbalists, Spinoza, Malebranche, Newton, or Locke, not to speak of Descartes. In Berkeley he found 'much . . . that is correct and close to my own view [but] expressed paradoxically.'[235] Although he was second to none in his belief in the efficacy of method,[236] he seems to have recognised even in views he regarded as quite wrong-headed a certain intellectual coherence deserving reasoned response.[237] Berkeley himself found room not only for something like the traditional diagnostic aetiology of error,[238] but for the thought that there is insight as well as illusion in both the assumptions of the vulgar and the modern doctrines which were his philosophical targets. The result constitutes something of a new departure, a dialectic between 'common sense', erroneous philosophy, and true philosophy in which the last is drawn out of the others: 'I do not pretend to be a setter-up of new notions. My endeavours tend only to unite and place in a clearer light that truth which was before shared between the vulgar and the philosophers.'[239]

This faint intimation of a post-traditional, essentially critical philosophy evidently helped to structure the theory which should perhaps count as the first of the 'end of philosophy' philosophies, that of Hume.[240] Hume's scepticism was a sort of apotheosis of seventeenth-century theories of error, following Hobbes in assigning all human thought and inference to the natural working of the imagination, but following the Rationalists in seeing that faculty's products as incoherent and irrational. His own 'system' stands on a different level, taking the form of an associationist pathology of the beliefs, that is, errors, both of the vulgar and of the philosophers.[241] In effect, there is no method for avoiding error, although some errors are better than others in virtue of their usefulness to life.[242]

Hume's theory stimulated Kant's, and another kind of pathology of illusion, whether natural and inevitable or philosophical and pernicious. The concepts of twentieth-century therapeutic and deconstructive philosophy are to that extent in a direct line of descent from More's 'heaving of the hypochondria', not to speak of Bacon's *idola* or Hobbes's 'desire of power'. Yet seventeenth-century reflections on faith and error had as well a rather different, arguably more beneficial product in the outlook which combines a recognition of human fallibility, a sense of the duty of reasoned inquiry and judgement, and an urge towards the political and social toleration of the beliefs of others.

## NOTES

1 The standard opposition between ancient and modern epistemology has been attacked, but with a view less to questioning the received picture of 'post-Cartesian' epistemology than to pointing out that Hellenistic philosophy was centrally concerned with 'the officially modern issue' of the 'grasp of particular facts, of a kind designed to exclude error' (Annas 1990, p. 185). We need to change our view of modern epistemology too.

2 See R. Rorty 1978, especially the introduction and chap. 1, for a recent denunciation of the metaphor of *seeing* (perceiving) necessary truth. Rorty invokes Dewey and Heidegger. Cf. the odd claim of Hacking 1975c, p. 31: 'This dead concept of mental vision is very hard for us to understand.' He adds, 'We still employ the idiom "now I see" when an argument convinces us', as if the metaphor were a quaint survival rather than entirely natural (if not inescapable).

3 The most spectacular example of *philosophical* harm in recent years, perhaps, is Rorty's argument, but cf. the almost blatantly false claim around which much recent epistemology has been shaped, that the 'traditional' or 'standard' definition of knowledge is *justified true belief*. Is that generic view ascribed implicitly to Descartes and Locke just

because they took knowledge in the full sense to involve a peculiar evidence, perspicuity, or mark of truth? Yet 'traditional' epistemology has been *at least* as much concerned with the causal relation between knowledge and its objects, and with knowledge's being the product of our natural faculties.

4 Cf. Rorty's wild claim, 'We owe the notion of a "theory of knowledge" based on an understanding of "mental processes" to the seventeenth century, and especially to Locke' (R. Rorty 1978, p. 3).

5 Richard Popkin, in the opening paragraph of Popkin 1988e, his chapter on 'Theories of Knowledge' in *The Cambridge History of Renaissance Philosophy*, writes, 'The theory of knowledge, as *a* or *the* central branch of philosophy, is a post-Renaissance phenomenon. . . . If epistemology deals with the three basic questions set forth in John Locke's *Essay concerning Human Understanding:* What is the origin, the extent and certainty of human knowledge?, these were not the central issues for most Renaissance thinkers. Most accepted Aristotle's account in *De anima* of how we gain information and form concepts, and Aristotle's account in the *Prior* and *Posterior Analytics* of how the concepts abstracted from sense experience are connected by logical inference to provide knowledge.' Yet, even if orthodox answers were accepted during the Renaissance to questions which later epistemologists answered differently, that does not mean that those answers were not central to the philosophy of the period unless in the trivial sense in which whatever is generally presupposed is thereby not 'central' to current disputes. It certainly does not mean that questioning those answers gave rise to a whole new discipline or pseudo-discipline, epistemology-as-central-to-philosophy. In any case, not a bad description of epistemology is 'the ontology of knowing', and, if epistemology was transformed in the seventeenth century, that was primarily for ontological reasons. The base-line was existing epistemology, including ancient theories hammered out over centuries of controversy by Hellenistic and Roman philosophers apparently obsessed by just the sorts of questions to be asked by Locke, theories on which Locke himself drew heavily and, probably, directly in arriving at the answers he gave. Set beside Popkin's assertion Hussey 1990: 'It is only in the sixth century B.C. that there is hard evidence of general thinking, unburdened by presuppositions, on the nature and limits of human knowledge. But it is better to begin the story earlier." Or, less extremely, Woodruff 1990: 'Much of modern epistemology has tried to answer scepticism, and this tempts us to think of epistemology as second in the order of thought and of history – as the sort of theory given by dogmatic philosophers in answer to what sceptics have already said. But classical scepticism cannot come first in any order of things. . . . In fact, scepticism did not properly emerge until after Aristotle, by which time it could develop against a rich background of dogmatic epistemology.' The present point is that 'modern' is too continuous with 'classical' epistemology for there to be a distinction of kind between them.

6 For some discussion of the epistemology of religion, see Section II of this chapter.

7 According to Cicero, *Academica* II.145, the Stoic Zeno introduced the term *katalepsis* as the third stage in a process compared to that of a hand coming to grasp an object with increasing power, the fourth stage of which is science (Long and Sedley 1987, vol. 1, pp. 253–4).

8 For an account of the origin of the distinction between '*empirikoi*' and '*logikoi*', see Frede 1990.

9 See Plato, *Phaedo* 96b5–8 and *Theaetetus* 151e, and Aristotle, *Met.* IV.5, *de An.* I.2. all cited by Frede.

10 In *Symposium,* cognition of the forms seems to be direct intellectual apprehension; in

*Meno,* it is presented as reminiscence. Arguments in *Parmenides* (e.g., the famous 'third man' argument) may record self-conscious failure to account for the form–particular relation.

11 *Post. an.* B 19 (99b35–100b17). Cf. Barnes's note in Aristotle 1975: 'B 19 is Janus-faced, looking in one direction towards empiricism, and in the other towards rationalism. . . . It is a classic problem in Aristotelian scholarship to explain or reconcile these two apparently opposing aspects of Aristotle's thought.'

12 Cf. Aristotle, *Metaphysics* A 1 and Frede 1990, pp. 238–40.

13 "Memorists", following Galen's 'mnemoneutikoi' (Frede 1990, pp. 226–7). 'Empiricism' was a term in medical theory until modern times.

14 Cited in Long and Sedley 1987, vol. 1, pp. 87–8, from Diogenes Laertius, *Vitae Philosophorum* 10.33.

15 Supposed to be achieved by the method of 'elimination', in such 'evident' judgements as 'If no void, then no movement', or 'If sweat flows through the skin, then there are ducts.' Some Epicureans (whose examples these originally were) argued that essences themselves are known by induction or the method of resemblance too. A cogent Stoic argument against according force to resemblance alone was that it is indeterminate what counts as resemblance. See Long and Sedley 1987, vol. 1, p. 96.

16 And a denigration of the pleasures of the senses, by comparison with the more permanent pleasures of reason and virtue. This aspect of the sense–reason opposition should always be remembered when the motivation of 'Rationalism' is under consideration.

17 Cf. Long and Sedley 1987, vol. 1, pp. 236–59.

18 See Chapter 18 for some of the complexities in Leibniz's relation to the scholastic tradition.

19 Documented in Popkin 1964. Cf. also Dear 1988, chap. 3; Schmitt 1983d; Chapter 32 in this book.

20 Paris, 1624; enlarged ed., London, 1645.

21 For connexions with the advocacy of religious toleration and dogmatic minimalism ('latitudinarianism'), see Part II of this chapter.

22 Dear 1988, p. 54. The present account of Mersenne follows Dear closely. Cf. Chapter 10, sec. III, and Chapter 32, sec. II, for different views of Mersenne.

23 By Popkin 1964, pp. 132–43.

24 Cf. Obj. V to Descartes's *Meds.* (AT VII 319–22).

25 On Gassendi's reductive explanation of the modalities, 'Every man is rich' and 'No man is rich' (since always false) come out as impossible rather than contingent, while 'Some man is rich' and 'Some man is not rich' (since always true) are both necessary. 'Coriscus is playing' is contingent (since sometimes true and sometimes false), but 'The sun is many times greater than the earth' is necessary, although evident only through reasoning based on experience (*Institutio Logica* II.9–13).

26 *Inst. Log.* III.16.

27 Gassendi 1658, vol. 3, p. 7. It is a reasonable assumption that Gassendi agreed with Epicurus (cf. *Inst. Log.* I.11).

28 Mersenne 1625, pp.176–7 (cited in James 1987).

29 *Inst. Log.* III.16.

30 *Inst. Log.* II.15.

31 *Inst. Log.* II.14. Gassendi does not here draw the distinction between reminiscent and indicative signs, perhaps because he is following the Epicurean tendency to treat both in terms of resemblance.

32 *Inst. Log.* III.18. Presumably acceptance of the premises is also opinion.

33 See Chapter 10, Section III, in this book. Neither offered a worked-out epistemology, but wrote from a Platonist-intellectualist viewpoint.

34 Cf. James 1987.

35 On Beeckman's influence, as early as 1618, see, e.g., Schuster 1980, pp. 47–9; Gabbey 1980a, pp. 244–5; and Chapter 18 in this book. According to Schuster, Beeckman was 'virtually the first man in Europe to dream of what was to become the new "mechanical philosophy"' but 'was no builder of systems'.

36 For Plato, mathematical objects do not have the full status of forms, and mathematics is propaedeutic to a higher science from which it receives its first principles (*Republic* V and VI). The last point does have its echoes in Descartes, as we shall shortly see.

37 For a discussion of this doctrine, see Chapters 10 and 12 in this book.

38 Descartes somewhat implausibly claims previous ignorance of Augustine's *si fallor, sum* in *De civitate Dei* xxvi (letters to Colvius and Mersenne, AT III 247 and 261). A similar argument occurs at Augustine, *De Trinitate* X 10.14.

39 A. Rorty 1992 represents this view as 'gross distortion'. Yet, although Descartes, like Plato, saw sensations and passions not only as sources of error and wrong-doing, but also as indispensable in this life, the model of reason impeded by sense and passion is fundamental to the epistemology of both philosophers.

40 Cf. Long and Sedley 1987, vol. 1, pp. 250, 255–7; and Nuchelmans 1983, pp. 47–50.

41 Cf. Med. VI, especially AT VII 82–4. 'What nature teaches' comprises only the belief that *something* external causes the sensation. Roughly (although even this minimal belief can be false in such circumstances as dropsy or pain in a phantom limb), this is assent to materially true, but obscure, ideas.

42 AT VII 18.

43 Cf. Carriero 1987; Garber 1986; and Chapter 32 in this book.

44 Cf. Sextus Empiricus on the Stoic 'cataleptic' impression, cited by Long and Sedley 1987, vol. 1, p. 246: 'The cognitive impression . . . , when it has no impediment . . . , being self-evident and striking, all but seizes us by the hair, they say, and pulls us to assent.'

45 Cf. Long and Sedley 1987, vol. 1, pp. 73–7, 80, 244; Augustine, *De Trinitate* XV 12.21. The proposal that mathematics owes its certainty to its being the abstract science of 'the simplest and most general things' (with no obvious Hellenistic antecedent) may be intended as quasi-Aristotelian, but it is close to Hobbes's view. The emphasis on the certainty of mathematics (explicitly contrasted with the mixed mathematical sciences) suggests Mersennian concerns. Stoics seem to have treated mathematics on a par with empirical science (see Long and Sedley 1987, vol. 1, p. 264). See Chapter 10 in this book, esp. sec. III.

46 Med. III (AT VII 70). There is a large literature on the circle, e.g., Cottingham 1986, pp. 66–73; Curley 1978, chap. 5; Doney 1955; Loeb 1992; Williams 1978, pp. 189–204; Wilson 1978, pp. 131–8. On a possible relation to the thesis that the eternal truths are created, see, e.g., Bréhier 1967; Frankfurt 1970; Kenny 1970.

47 Med. I (AT VII 21f).

48 Resp.II (AT VII 140).

49 Med. V (AT VII 70): 'For what objections can now be raised? That the way I am made makes me prone to frequent error?'

50 Med. I (AT VII 17).

51 Cf. *Meds.* 'Synopsis' (AT VII 12), Resp. III (AT VII 171f).

52 Resp. II (AT VII 141).

53  I.e., as the sun is causally necessary to living things. Cf. Plato, *Res publica* 504–21.

54  *Soliloquies* I.viii, cited by Dear 1988, p. 84. Fonseca, also cited, defended the Augustinian definition of truth as 'the conformity of things with the divine intellect, that is, with the formal reasons of those things which are in the divine mind', commenting that in this life we cannot look at the sun directly, but only see things by its light: we have scientific knowledge only in so far as 'the eternal reasons' are imparted to us 'by the natural light', i.e., the faculty of reason created in us by God (Fonseca 1615, pp. 803–10).

55  In Med.VI the premise that God is no deceiver is used to validate the senses interpreted by reason.

56  Cf., e.g., passages cited by Long and Sedley 1987, vol. 1, pp. 78, 80, 246. The last (from Sextus Empiricus, *Adversus mathematicos*) applies the metaphor of light directly to the senses: 'For nature has given the sensory faculty . . . as our light, as it were, for the recognition of truth.' The sceptic both employs and tries to discard this light.

57  Cf. *Princ.* II 36–7. Indeed, Descartes's doctrine of the creation of the eternal truths makes God the cause, not only of matter and the laws of motion, but of the essence of matter and every first principle of science. The Artificer creates not only His material but His archetypes.

58  Cf. Gabbey 1982; and Chapter 18, Section II, and Chapter 23, Section V, in this book.

59  More 1662d, pp. 19–22.

60  Cf. *Reg.* II (AT X 362): 'In accordance with this Rule, we reject all such merely probable cognition and resolve to believe only what is perfectly known and incapable of being doubted.' That Descartes assigned practical usefulness to probabilities does not weaken this point.

61  *Princ.* IV secs. 204–5.

62  Arnauld and Nicole, *Logique* IV.i.

63  *Logique,* Premier Discours.

64  *Logique* IV.xvi.

65  I.e., IV.ii, which partly employs or paraphrases *Regulae* XIII.

66  *Logique* I.ix.

67  This odd but orthodox doctrine renders propositional content prior to assent problematic but accords with the division of logic into three parts: conception, judgement, and reasoning. But cf. Chapter 4 in this book.

68  But cf. the appeal to Plato and Augustine at *Logique* IV.xiii.

69  Appealing, as might be expected, to Augustine's statement 'mentem rationalem . . . non illuminari nisi ab ipsa substantia Dei (the rational mind is enlightened by nothing but the very substance of God)' (*Rech.* III.2.6).

70  Cf. *Des vrayes et des fausses idées,* chap. 13. For discussion, see Chapter 30 in this book. Beyond the immediate purpose lay objections to Malebranche's conception of grace.

71  *Disc. mét.,* sec. 29.

72  The sole occupation of Aristotle's unmoved mover, as unattached incorporeal intellect, is self-contemplation.

73  Cf. Med. II (AT VII 33): 'Every consideration whatsoever which contributes to my perception of . . . any . . . body, cannot but establish even more effectively the nature of my own mind.'

74  Med. III (AT VII 51). Only later does Descartes rehearse the Ontological Argument, which proceeds, not from our *possession* of an idea with a certain content, but (in this like mathematics) simply from that content.

75  Cf. Ger. IV 295f, Ger. VII 184–9. Degrees of probability would also be calculable (cf. Hacking 1975a, pp. 135–42).

76 For extreme attempts to dissociate the three from one another, see, e.g., Popkin 1959b; Bracken 1974; Loeb 1981 (criticised by Mossner 1959; Ayers 1984). Berkeley did read Locke, and Hume did read Locke and Berkeley, but both read more widely from distinct points of view.

77 That commonplace may be an echo of disputes between followers of Locke and Newton, on the one hand, and Cartesians and Leibnizians, on the other; or may stem from nothing more interesting than a myopic head-count of Great Epistemologists

78 For more on Bacon and his heritage, see Chapter 7.

79 For Stoic scientific method, see Long and Sedley 1987, vol. 1, pp. 259–66.

80 *Lev.* ix.

81 E.g., thinking of Saint Peter when hearing of Saint Andrew, 'because their names are read together'.

82 *Human Nature* IV.1–7.

83 *Lev.* ix.

84 *De corpore* I.iii.7,10.

85 Cf., e.g., Obj. III to Descartes's Med. II (AT VII 178), where he suggested that reasoning is no more than 'the joining of names or appellations in a train by the word *is*' according to conventional definitions.

86 *Human Nature* VI.3.

87 *Human Nature* VI.3.

88 *De corpore* I.iv.8.

89 *Lev.* iv.

90 *De corpore* II.viii.2. Cf I.vi.2: 'I do not mean here parts of the thing itself, but parts of its nature.'

91 *De corpore* I.vi.1–6.

92 *De corpore* I.vi.6–7: i.e., we know what makes people tick from our own case.

93 Cf. *Six Lessons to the Professors of Mathematics in the University of Oxford,* Epistle Dedicatory. *Eng. Works,* vol. 7, p. 183. With respect to the construction of geometrical objects, Hobbes has in mind (e.g.) the definition of a circle in terms relating to its construction by compasses, i.e., as a line each point of which is equidistant from a given point.

94 *Lev.* v.

95 *Human Nature* II.10: 'for as sense telleth me, when I see *directly,* that the colour seemeth to *be* in the object; so also sense telleth me, when I see by *reflection,* that colour is not in the object.'

96 Mediaeval nominalism was another possible influence.

97 Cf. Gassendi, *Institutio Logica* I.4–9.

98 'Pure', in the sense that he took the principles of mechanics to be evident in themselves, in the nature of matter and motion, rather than, as for Descartes, evident as the principles of action of an immutable Creator.

99 E.g., William Chillingworth, Jeremy Taylor, Joseph Glanvill, Robert Boyle. Cf. Van Leeuwen 1963; Woolhouse 1983; and Section II of this chapter.

100 In the MS now known as *Essays* (or *Questions*) *on the Law of Nature* (Locke 1954).

101 Ethics is based on experience in that evidence of design assures us of an intelligent Creator, while experience of human nature reveals His purpose for us.

102 Locke 1990b, p. 22. The knowledge in question is 'that the 3 angles of a triangle are equal to two right ones, or that one side of a triangle being produced the exterior angle is equal to the two interior opposite angles.'

103 Cf. Locke 1990b, p. 55.

104 Locke 1990b, pp. 50–1.
105 Cf. Locke 1990b, p. 57: 'Mathematicall universall propositions are both true and instructive because as those Ideas are in our mindes soe are the things without us.'
106 Locke 1990b, p. 82.
107 Locke 1990b, p. 152–3 (*Draft B,* also 1671). 'Proof' is here used narrowly for empirical grounds: cf. p. 51 (*Draft A*): 'Probable propositions therefor are concernd in and capable of proof but certain knowledge or demonstration makes it self clearly appear and be perceived by the things them selves put togeather and as it were lyeing before us in view in our understandings.'
108 Cf *Ess.* II.xvii.7, which echoes Hobbes, *Lev.* iv on 'numbering'.
109 For Hobbes, truth presupposes names, but for Locke, 'Truth belongs properly to Propositions: whereof there are two sorts, *viz.* Mental and Verbal', corresponding to two sorts of 'signs'. As for Hobbes, names are 'marks' and 'signs' of ideas, but Locke saw ideas themselves as marks and signs. Cf. Chapter 30 in this book.
110 *Ess.* III.iii.11, seems intended as part echo of Hobbes, *De corpore* II.ix. Cf. Ayers 1991, vol. 1, pp. 253–6.
111 Cf. *Ess.* IV.xvii.8: 'The immediate Object of all our Reasoning and Knowledge is nothing but Particulars.' On 'partial consideration', see II.xiii.11 and 13. On the possibility of universal thought without names, cf. IV.v.4. For a fuller discussion of Locke's theory, see Ayers 1991, vol. 1, pp. 49–51 and 242–63.
112 Cf. *Ess.* IV.xii.14: 'Such Propositions are therefore called *Eternal Truths,* not because they are Eternal Propositions actually formed, and antecedent to the Understanding, that at any time makes them; nor because they are imprinted on the Mind from any patterns, that are any where out of the Mind, and existed before: But because being once made, about abstract *Ideas,* so as to be true, they will, whenever they can be supposed to be made again at any time past or to come, by a Mind having those *Ideas,* always actually be true.'
113 Also called 'opinion', 'judgement', and 'assent' (knowledge is a species of mental affirmation, but 'perception' is not a species of 'judgement' or 'assent'). But the terms are not employed interchangeably in all contexts: e.g., 'belief' is sometimes used in a narrow sense, for acceptance of testimony (whereas 'faith' is employed generally, e.g., at *Ess.* IV.xv.3). 'Judgement' is used for the faculty, as well as the act. Cf. Ayers 1991, pp. 312, 316.
114 Cf. *Ess.*IV.xv.3: 'In all the parts of [demonstrative] Knowledge, there is intuition; . . . each step has its visible and certain connexion; in belief not so. That which makes me believe, is something extraneous to the thing I believe.'
115 *Ess.* IV.ii.1–8. Locke evidently did not think that men embrace falsehoods for intuitions.
116 See especially *Ess.* IV.xvii. In geometry, a line drawn for the purpose of a proof would be an intermediate idea. For Descartes's views, see Chapter 6 in this book.
117 See especially *Ess.* IV.vii and xii. At IV.xii.7 he allows algebra as a method for discovery in mathematics, but there is no such concession with respect to physics.
118 The structure of Locke's theory of sensitive knowledge will be explained in Chapter 30 in this book.
119 This is sometimes denied, e.g., by Gibson 1917, pp. 172–6; and Loeb 1981, pp. 55–6, in part because the statement at *Ess.* IV.iv.14 seems grudging, that the perception of '*the particular existence of finite Beings* without us . . . passes under the name of Knowledge.' But even here it is stated that sensitive knowledge goes 'beyond bare probability' (i.e., inferred belief) and provides 'an Evidence, that puts us past doubting'; while

IV.xi.2–3 firmly avers that sensation confers 'an assurance that *deserves the name of Knowledge*'. In fussing over the *name*, Locke both emphasises his rejection of the standardly narrow use of 'knowledge' for apprehension of principles and *scientia* and insists on its difference from 'belief'. Cf. Ayers 1991, vol. 1, pp. 93–5 and 155–65.

120 *Ess.* IV.xi.1–3. We know our own existence by intuition, and God's by demonstration (cf. IV.xi.2).

121 Setting him apart from Gassendi, on the one hand, and Mersenne, on the other. Locke sometimes seems to favour the particular, as at *Ess.* IV.vii.11. Yet this is not Gassendi's inductivism, but the view that 'the immediate object of all our Reasoning and Knowledge is nothing but particulars', whether perceived by the senses or imagined (IV.xvii.8). Occasionally the attack on maxims echoes the Epicurean view of their function as criteria of truth: 'The Mind . . . having drawn its Knowledge into as general Propositions as it can, . . . accustoms it self to have recourse to them, as the Standards of Truth and Falshood' (IV.vii.11).

122 Cf. *Ess.* IV.i.2, IV.viii. The mind cannot have ideas without perceiving 'each what it is, . . . and that one is not another.' The different topic of the identity of individuals is dealt with outside this categorisation of propositions, in II.xxvii.

123 Cf. Kant, *Prolegomena zu einer jeden künftigen Metaphysik,* sec. 3, where the synthetic-analytic distinction is explained with acknowledgements to Locke.

124 *Ess.* IV.xv.1 and IV.v.6. Locke's illustrating intuitive knowledge chiefly by the perception of identity (even using the certainty of tautologies to illustrate the certainty of intuition) might suggest that he did not always keep this point clearly in mind (IV.ii.1). But, of course, unless some propositions falling under 'relation' were intuitable, none would be demonstrable.

125 *Ess.* II.xxi.4, IV.x.3.

126 Cf.*Ess.* II.iv.1 and 5, IV.iii.13. But the tone of IV.iii.13–16, 29, etc. is characteristically pessimistic.

127 Causal powers count as observable qualities for the purposes of Locke's argument (*Ess.* II.xxi.3, II.xxiii.7).

128 *Ess.* II.viii.21 is one passage which identifies secondary qualities with mechanical structure or process. The causal relation between structure and ideas of secondary qualities is represented as peculiarly obscure to us (IV.iii.11).

129 Locke here differs from Hobbes, who was appealing to the alleged fact that we know how actual geometrical figures or political constitutions are brought into existence and can define them accordingly. Note that, although ethics deals in the ideal, according to Locke, its binding force derives from the very real relation between us and our Creator. See notes 92 and 93.

130 *Ess.* IV.xvi.9.

131 *Ess.* IV.xvi.1.

132 Cf. Ayers 1991, vol. 1, pp. 118–20.

133 *Ess.* IV.xvi.12.

134 For a broadly similar view of the 'Rationalist'/'Empiricist' division, see Lennon 1993.

135 Cf. Woolhouse 1988, p. 3.

136 Natural, but not inevitable; witness Spinoza and Leibniz on the one hand, and (perhaps – the issue is not totally clear) Gassendi and Boyle, on the other.

137 The common belief that Locke's intuitionism is 'Cartesian' is criticised in Schankula 1980.

138 Cf. *Kritik der reinen Vernunft* A471 (B499) and A853–4 (B882–3).

139 Kant, *Prolegomena,* Appendix: 'The proposition of all genuine idealists from the ELEA-

TIC SCHOOL to Bishop Berkeley is contained in the formula: "all knowledge through the senses and through experience is nothing but illusion, and only in the ideas of pure understanding and reason is truth." (Kant 1900–   , vol. 4, p. 374). 141 Cf. Berkeley, *Siris* sec. 264: 'sensible and real, to common apprehensions, being the same thing; although it be certain . . . that intellect and reason are alone the sure guides to truth.'

140 Cf. *Ess.* II.i.4.

141 Cf. *3 Dial.* I (Berkeley 1948–57, vol. 2, pp. 193–4); *De Motu,* sec. 53.

142 *Princ.* I 28.

143 Cf. *Philosophical Commentaries,* secs. 318, 539, and 547.

144 *3 Dial.* II (Berkeley 1948–57, vol. 2, p. 214). Cf. Descartes's use of '*menti nostrae exhiberet*' at *Princ.* II 1.

145 *Princ.* I 25.

146 Gassendi 1658, vol. 2, pp. 440a–446b; cf. Locke, *Ess.* II.xxvii.25, IV.iii.6.

147 Cf. Burthogge 1678 and 1694; Collier 1713 (the latter written after 'a ten years pause and deliberation').

148 Cf. Ayers 1996.

149 Thomas Aquinas, *Summa th.* II.II qq1–7.

150 *Summa th.* II.II qq171–4.

151 'Apologie de Raimond Sebond', Montaigne 1922, vol. 2, pp. 324–5 (cited by Popkin 1964, pp. 50–1): 'And since I am not capable of choosing, I accept other people's choice and stay in the position where God put me. Otherwise I could not keep myself from rolling about incessantly. Thus I have, by the grace of God, kept myself intact, without agitation or disturbance of conscience, in the ancient beliefs of our religion, in the midst of so many sects and divisions that our century has produced.'

152 See Popkin 1964, pp. 67–88.

153 For various views of the relation of miracles to nature, see, e.g., Arnauld and Nicole, *Logique* IV.xiv; Spinoza, *Tract. th.-pol.* vi; Leibniz, *Disc. mét.,* sec. 7; and Locke's posthumously published *A Discourse of Miracles* (Locke 1823, vol. 9, pp. 256–65), which expresses a view also taken, if perhaps for different reasons from Locke's, by the Newtonians William Whiston and Samuel Clarke in the first years of the eighteenth century (cf. Harrison 1993).

154 Cf. Chapter 14. For discussion of the radical biblical critics Isaac La Peyrere and Richard Simon, see Popkin 1987b, 1990d *passim.* Locke had two copies of Simon's suppressed *Histoire Critique du Vieux Testament* (Paris 1680 and Rotterdam 1685) among more than a dozen volumes of his works, as well as Jean Le Clerc's defence, *Sentiments de quelques Theologiens de Holland sur l'histoire critique du Vieux Testament* (Amsterdam, 1685) and *Defence des Sentiments . . .* (Amsterdam, 1686).

155 Boehme, Fisher, Mede, Dury, and Twisse (or Twiss) are discussed in Popkin 1990d, pp. 90–119, *et passim.* William Twisse held that 'to know the Scripture to be the Word of God, the Wisdom of God, and the Power of God' is 'peculiar to a regenerate spirit in whom the Spirit of God dwells as the fountain of the life of grace' (*The doubting Conscience Resolved* (London, 1752), p 74, cited by Popkin). Popkin stresses the influence of Mede's *Clavis Apocalyptica* (Cambridge, 1627), and assigns the highest possible importance to the view that inspired interpretation of Scripture gives absolute certainty independent of reason, since he sees it as defining a 'third force' in seventeenth-century epistemology, a response distinct from both rationalism and empiricism to a general sceptical crisis. It is true that both Rationalists and Empiricists argued against it at length.

156 Chillingworth 1687 (first printed 1638) presents extreme scepticism and the Catholic claim to authority as due to the same mistake: 'The ground of your error here, is your not distinguishing, between actual certainty and absolute infallibility. Geometricians are not infallible in their own Science: yet they are very certain of those things, which they see demonstrated' (pp. 326–52). Falkland, John Hales, and Jeremy Taylor expressed similar views to Chillingworth's. Locke was an admirer, and the *Essay* contains many echoes: '*Chillingworth* . . . by his example wil teach both perspicuity, and the way of Right Reasoning better than any Book that I know' ('Mr Locke's Extempore Advice &c', in Locke 1989, pp. 319–27).

157 Chillingworth 1687, p. 334.

158 Chillingworth 1687, pp. 92–5: 'if the Doctrine of the Scripture were not as good, and as fit to come from the Fountain of goodness, as the Miracles, by which it was confirmed, were great, I should want one main pillar of my Faith.'

159 Cf. Sommerville 1992, pp. 109 and 144–6, which cites the early criticism of minimalist views by the Jesuit John Sweet (who himself cites an Anglican treatise of 1596), as well as the Calvinist Francis Cheynell's appeal to 'my heart and conscience' in the interpretation of scripture against a Chillingworth 'runne mad with reason'. However, the unorthodox Calvinist Moise Amyraut, Chillingworth's contemporary, advocated the way of examination.

160 Letter to Clerselier, on Resp. V (AT IX 208).

161 Resp. II (AT VII 147–8). Cf. to Hyperaspistes, August 1641 (AT III 425–6), where he does not rule out that the light of faith should illuminate the mysteries themselves.

162 Med. IV (AT VII 58).

163 To Hyperaspistes (AT III 426); to Mersenne, April 1634 (AT I 288). Descartes's term is 'homme d'Eglise', glossed by Clerselier as 'théologie'. Cf. Letter to Father Dinet (AT VII 598).

164 *Logique* IV.i.

165 Cf *Logique* IV.xii; *Rech.* I.3 (sec. 2); II.2.8 (sec. 3); IV.3 (sec. 3); IV.12; etc. Although the *Logique* asserts that the Christian does *not* obey Christ blindly and unreasonably, there is no real difference from Malebranche since he has the independent justification of the article of faith in mind, while the *Logique* is referring to reasons for trust. Malebranche too states that faith depends on reasoned premises (*Rech.* VI.2.6).

166 *Rech.* III.3.8 (sec. 2): 'We should not, without pressing reasons, undertake intelligible and straightforward explanations of things that the Fathers and Councils have not fully explained. . . . Disputes concerning theological explanations seem to be the most useless and most dangerous of all. . . . Also, obscure and tedious explanations of the faith, which we are not obliged to believe, should not serve as rules and principles in philosophical reasoning.' But perhaps Malebranche thought that Descartes had been given 'pressing reasons' by his critics.

167 Pascal, *Pens.* 418; cf. Arnauld and Nicole, *Logique* IV.xvi. For discussion of Pascal's sources and purpose, see Howells 1984. See Hacking 1975a, pp. 63–73, for a discussion of the (novel) mathematical structure of Pascal's argument.

168 *Les prétendus reformez convaincus de schisme* I.vii.

169 Journal, 29 July 1676 (in Locke 1936).

170 For discussion of Hobbes's relation to the Tew circle, see Sommerville 1992, pp. 135–60.

171 *Lev.* xxxii.

172 *Lev.* xxxiii.

173 *Lev.* xliii.

174  *Lev.* xlii–iii.

175  *Lev.* xliii.

176  *Lev.* xxxvi. Moreover, false prophets, like Pharaoh's magicians, seem to have been as capable of wonders as true ones (cf. Locke 1823, vol. 9, p. 260).

177  As by Popkin 1990d, p. 9–49 and Tuck 1989.

178  A thought extended by Hume to perceptual knowledge (*Treatise* I.iv.2).

179  *Lev.* xliii. Cf. Chillingworth [1635] 1687, p. 119: 'I believed by Fame, strengthened with Celebrity and Consent . . . and lastly by Antiquity.'

180  More 1662e, sec. 31.

181  I.e., 'those *Common notions* that all men in their wits agree upon, or the *Evidence of outward Sense* or else a *clear and distinct Deduction from these*' (More 1662e, sec. 31).

182  *Tract.th.-pol.*, vii–x. For discussion of Spinoza's motives and relation to the clandestine anti-religious *Les Trois Imposteurs*, see Popkin 1990d, pp. 135–48.

183  *Tract. th.-pol.*, Introduction, Geb. III 9.

184  *Tract. th.-pol.* vi.

185  *Tract.th.-pol.* viii–xii. As Spinoza sums up, what we have is 'faulty, mutilated, tampered with, and inconsistent'. Nevertheless 'the expressed opinions of prophets and apostles openly proclaim that God's eternal Word and covenant, no less than the true religion, is Divinely inscribed in human hearts, that is, in the human mind' (Geb. III 158).

186  *Tract. th.-pol.* xiv, Geb. III 175. Cf. Preface: 'the authority of the prophets has weight only in matters of morality, and . . . their speculative doctrines affect us little' (Geb. III 9).

187  Cf. *Tract. the.-pol* xvi: 'The basis and aim of a democracy is to avoid irrational desires, and to bring men as far as possible under the control of reason' (Geb. III 194).

188  The seven doctrines ('*fidei universalis dogmata*') are given in *Tract. th.-pol.* xiv, Geb. III 177–8. It is not entirely clear what status they have for Spinoza. Despite his criticism of philosophical interpretations of scripture, his own closely match his philosophical theory.

189  Cf. *Tract. th.-pol.* i, where it is argued that natural knowledge (in which 'our mind subjectively contains in itself and partakes of the nature of God') is a form of revelation, different from the 'prophetic imaginings' (chap. ii) of Scripture in being intellectual and certain (Geb. III 15–16).

190  *Tract. th.-pol.* xv: 'For as we cannot perceive by the natural light of reason that simple obedience is the path of salvation, . . . it follows that the Bible has brought a very great consolation to mankind. All are able to obey, whereas there are but very few . . . who can acquire the habit of virtue under the unaided guidance of reason.' 'Simple obedience', Spinoza explains, is obedience to moral principles without recognising them as eternal truths (Geb. III 178). Hobbes equally refrains from offering reasons for faith in giving reasoned interpretation – if faith is justified, it is by its consequences: 'I pretend not to advance any position of my own, but only to shew what are the consequences that seem to me deducible from the principles of Christian politics, (which are the holy Scriptures) in confirmation of the power of civil sovereigns, and the duty of their subjects' (*Lev.* xliii).

191  Cf., e.g., Locke 1987, vol. 2, pp. 32–3, 41–3. But grounds for postulating a change of mind are weak – counter-evidence includes the detailed amendment of the *Essay* continued until Locke's death.

192  *Ess.* IV.xviii.5.

193  Cf. *Ess.* IV.xx.18.

194  *Ess.* IV.xviii.8.

195  *Ess.* IV.xix.14; cf.IV.xviii.6.
196  *Ess.* IV.xix.4. The analogy between revelation and aids to sight seems to have been commonplace, also appearing in Boyle and Burthogge. Cf. Lennon 1993, p. 182.
197  *Ess.* IV.xix.13.
198  *Ess.* IV.xix.14.
199  *Ess.* IV.xix.1.
200  *Ess.*IV.xvi.4.
201  On this, see Kilcullen 1988, pp. 54–105.
202  Bayle [1686] 1713 expounds his position, and his general approach is illustrated by discussions in the *Dictionnaire* and *Nouvelles de la République des Lettres* which present both sides of an argument sympathetically and thereby lead to a critical, undogmatic judgement. Cf.'Pomponazzi', on the question of the natural immortality of the soul; or 'Zeno', which sets sceptical argument itself against natural perceptual belief and common sense, preferring the latter while finding the former entirely convincing in its own terms.
203  Burthogge 1678, 1694. For discussion, see Yolton 1956, *passim;* Lennon 1993, pp. 187–90.
204  Cf. Cicero, *Academica* 1.40–1 and 2.37–8; Epictetus, *Discourses* 1.1.7–12 (cited in Long and Sedley 1987, vol. 1, pp. 242, 248, and 391).
205  *Lev.* vi and vii.
206  'Error' is not defined in *Leviathan,* but cf. *De corpore* I.v.
207  *Eth.* II prop. 49. For a development of Spinoza's theory of error and the related aspects of the theory of mind in contrast to that of Descartes, see Curley 1975.
208  *Ess.*IV.xx.16.
209  *Ess.* IV.xx.15.
210  *Ess.* IV.xx.14: 'It is a refuge against *Conviction* so open and so wide, that it is hard to determine when a man is quite out of the verge of it.' We see the phenomenon today in those who regard the theory of evolution, or the connexion of smoking with cancer, as not yet proved.
211  *Ess.* IV.xvi.9.
212  For discussion, see Passmore 1986; Ayers 1991, vol. 1, pp. 104–12.
213  *Nov. Org.* I 38–68.
214  Cf. *Princ.* I.71–3.
215  Cf. Descartes, *Princ.* I.74, II.7; Digby 1645, I pp. 2–4; Arnauld and Nicole, *Logique* I.11–12; Malebranche, *Rech.* III.1.8; Locke, *Ess.* II.xxix, III *passim.*
216  Presumably he had Aristotelian theory in mind (on which, e.g., water expands in becoming air), but Digby is another possible target.
217  Cf. *Lev.* I.v; *De Corpore* I.iii.4, I.v.
218  Cf. *Ess.* III.x.14. Locke concedes that the example (the 'intricate Disputes . . . about *Matter*') is a familiar one.
219  *Ess.* III.ii.3–5; Cf. *Nov. Org.* I.lx: 'Minus vitiosum genus est nominum substantiae alicuius, praesertim specierum infimarum' (A less defective kind of name is that of any [sort of] substance, especially of ultimate species).
220  For an illuminating account of this concern throughout the seventeenth century (and much of the sixteenth), see Skinner 1994. Skinner shows that the real concern behind Hobbes's surprising proposal that the sovereign should be the final authority even for the definitions of moral terms is not a general scepticism, but hostility to *ars rhetorica,* with its employment of allegedly equivocal language to keep argument going on both

sides of any dispute. For Hobbes (as for Epicurus), unless meanings are fixed, *scientia* lacks its starting points. Worse still, disputes never end.

221 Since bodies sensibly appear to expand and contract. Cf. Med. II (AT VII 30).

222 Cf. A. Rorty 1992.

223 Cf. Descartes, Reg. VIII and XII (AT X 395–400, 416–17). Although Med.VI (AT VII 72–3) does not refer to the use of the imagination to stimulate the intellect, there seems no significant change of view. Reg. III (AT X 368) contrasts intellectual intuition with 'the deceptive judgement of the imagination', and *Princ.* I 59 assigns a rôle to the senses in the formation of universal ideas of numbers and figures.

224 Cf. Spinoza, *De int. emen.* 20 and 74.

225 Spinoza, *Eth.* II appendix.

226 *Enthusiasmus Triumphatus* secs. 42–50, in More 1662e.

227 *Rech.* III.1.1 (sec. 1).

228 *Des vrayes et des fausses idées* iv.

229 *Lev.* I.viii.

230 *Ess.* II.xi.2.

231 *Ess.* II.ix.9.

232 *Ess.* II.xxxiii.1.

233 *Ess.* II.xxxiii.6. Cf Malebranche, *Rech.* I.5.4: 'Little by little the animal spirits open and smooth these paths by their continual flow. . . . Now it is in this . . . that *habits* consist.'

234 *Ess.* IV.xx. II.xxxiii first appeared in the fourth edition. Locke's polemical treatment of error and imputations of irrationality and confusion are in tension with his pleas for tolerant and reasoned debate, but he doubtless assumed that those who accepted the latter would avoid irrational error.

235 Written in Leibniz's copy of Berkeley's *Principles of Human Knowledge* (in Kabitz 1932, p. 636, trans. in Leibniz 1989, p. 307).

236 Cf., almost at random, his letter to Elisabeth (G IV 290–5, Leibniz 1989, p. 239): 'I will be asked, what then is this wonderful way that can prevent us from falling? I am almost afraid to say it, it appears too lowly. . . . In brief, it is to construct arguments only in proper form.'

237 For a selection of Leibnizian criticism, see Leibniz 1989, pp. 235–346.

238 Cf. *Pr. Hum. Kn.*, Introduction; I. secs. 4–6, 55–7, 73–4, etc. Berkeley does, however, see the causes of philosophical error as false principles: 'My purpose . . . is, to try if I can discover what those principles are, which have introduced all that doubtfulness and uncertainty, those absurdities and contradictions into the several sects of philosophy' (*Pr. Hum. Kn.*, Introduction, sec. 4). A chief culprit is a false notion of abstraction, the remedy is to strip away words and confront bare ideas.

239 *3 Dial.* III (Berkeley 1948–57, vol. 2, p. 262).

240 Cf. Ayers 1984, 1985.

241 Not to mention physiology, as at *Treatise* I.ii.5. For discussion of Hume's mechanistic physiology of belief and its relation to that of Malebranche and Locke, see Wright 1983, pp. 214–19.

242 Cf. *Treatise* I.iv.4.

# 30

# IDEAS AND OBJECTIVE BEING

## MICHAEL AYERS

### I. INTRODUCTION

It has often been taught, and may in dark corners still be taught, that in the seventeenth century epistemology was transformed by a new notion of 'ideas' as the immediate objects of perception and thought. Henceforward, it was said, philosophy was saddled with 'representative' theories of perception and knowledge that gave rise first to the metaphysical isolation of the mind and then to the thoroughgoing idealism of the following century. In the eighteenth century itself, the realist Thomas Reid saw the Cartesian theory of ideas as the error which, by insinuating a veil or *tertium quid* between the mind and reality, set philosophy on a course leading logically to the scepticism of Hume.[1] Proponents of such an account in the recent past, however, have been less likely to be realists than conceptualists eager to announce that traditional epistemology, in turn, has made way, or ought to make way, for something else, whether for the philosophy of language, for 'naturalism', or for some more refined and elusive form of 'edifying discourse'.

Recent (and some less recent) work on theories of ideas has undermined this influential story.[2] The epistemological debates of the seventeenth century no doubt supplied the seed-bed of later idealism, but there was no sudden, radical departure, least of all by Descartes, from traditional frameworks for dealing with the relation between thought and its objects. As his own explanations emphasise, Descartes's use of the old term 'idea' was only mildly innovative.

For the scholastics in general, following Saint Augustine, 'ideas' were the exemplars or archetypes, both objects and constituents of divine reason, which fulfil the logical rôle of universal essences or 'eternal truths' in accordance with which the particular forms of individual things are created.[3] As such, they are the objects of 'science' (*scientia*). The term 'idea' was also used for the mental archetypes employed by human artificers, but its usage had been extended to a wider range of human thought in the broad sense by both French and English writers in the vernacular before the end of the sixteenth century.[4] On his own account,

Descartes chose the word in order to stress that it is the intellect, rather than the corporeal imagination, which conceives,[5] but it is more specifically appropriate to his Augustinian epistemology.

After Descartes, the term rapidly became common, although far from universal, in the theory of thought. By the early 1650s one of his most persistent critics, Pierre Gassendi, could express a preference for 'idea' over other ancient and scholastic terms – 'species', *notio, praenotio, anticipatio, conceptus, phantasma,* and *imago* – on the grounds that it was by now a familiar and well-used word, less liable to ambiguity than others (in particular 'imago' and 'species').[6] It was used on occasion by Hobbes, by Boyle, and by other writers of very various persuasions. Thus, despite its origin, it soon became neutral in the fundamental dispute as to whether a faculty of pure intellect can operate independently of sense and imagination. Its employment by Gassendi, in accordance with the Epicurean view of sense impressions as signs of their causes, introduced into the debate about thought and knowledge a model significantly different from the scholastic model on which Descartes relied. The tension between these two models is characteristic of the epistemology of Locke, the philosopher who, next to Descartes, did most to popularise the word 'idea'.

Despite fundamental continuities, the new philosophy did stir up the theory of intentionality: first, by dispensing with 'forms' in nature and, second, by postulating a systematic gap of a kind not generally envisaged by Aristotelian philosophy between things as they appear to the senses and things as they are in themselves. Different accounts of what 'ideas' are, and of how they are acquired, reflected different opinions as to whether and, if so, how that gap between sense-experience and 'science' could be bridged. Some held that it could be bridged by methodical refinement of the deliverances of the senses, whereas others called on a higher faculty or function of the mind, with purely intellectual ideas as its object. Yet others were more sceptical. But if there was a general problem as to how ideas represent reality which was more insistent than similar problems had been for Aristotelian scholastics, that was because the ontology of forms or species could no longer be called on as a purported physical explanation of what it is for an object to exist 'objectively' in the understanding, or to be presented or transmitted to the mind. It was not because Descartes's notion of an idea as the immediate object of the understanding set up an unprecedented barrier between thoughts and things. The felt need for a new ontology (or even physiology) of intentionality was a motive the high importance of which in shaping seventeenth-century metaphysics has not, perhaps, been sufficiently recognised.

Unsurprisingly, the two strands, ontological and epistemological, tended to become entwined. Yet it is important to disentangle them, if only to establish that metaphysics remained at the heart of philosophy. The seventeenth century was less obsessed with doubt and certainty than it is often supposed. The New Philosophers were happy enough that sceptical argument should question Aristotelian orthodoxy, but the basis and core of the 'revolution' in philosophy lay with a captivating vision of the natural world rather than with the much maligned, largely traditional 'theory of ideas'.

## II. SCHOLASTIC ANTECEDENTS OF CARTESIAN IDEAS

The scholastic theory of the transmission to the mind of 'forms', 'intentions', or 'species' has been described in Chapter 28. What is relevant here is the intensive theorising about the ontological status of the objects and content of thought, theory stimulated in part by a concern to identify the subject-matter of logic. Aquinas was a dominant influence. On a generic Thomist view, the reception of the form by the intellect, the act of conceiving, gives rise to an internal object of thought, the inner word, *intentio intellecta* or concept, which is distinct from the act of thinking[7] but dependent on it for its existence (its *esse* is *intelligi*). The form thus existing intentionally in the mind can be considered in either of two ways: first, as existing in the knower *qua* accident in a subject, or, second, as the form of the thing known which directs the thought to a particular object. Considered in the first way, it is not itself an object of the act of cognition (although it could be the object of a second-order act).[8] Considered in the second way, it can be regarded as the external object of knowledge itself as it has been received by the mind and is immediately cognised. At the same time, the external thing *as thus conceived of* is not strictly identical with the thing *as it exists in reality* (when it does): rather, there is a likeness in form between the mind and the real object.[9] Aquinas introduced a similarly two-faced mental entity, the product of an act of combining or separating, in order to deal with propositional thought.[10]

This model follows the ordinary ambiguity of terms like 'thought' and 'judgement' as used to mean either a mental operation or its content (cf. the use of 'statement' either for the act of stating or for what is stated). It also allows for our natural talk of 'resemblance' between mental representation and object in so far as the object as conceived of may resemble or fail to resemble the object as it really is. Finally, it allows the same content to be common to different kinds of thought, such as belief and desire. Yet it is understandable that some Aristotelians diverged from Aquinas's ontology. Durandus of Saint-Pourcain, for example, denied that there is a product of the act of conceiving distinguishable from that act as a separate accident of the mind. He achieved a similar economy with respect to propositional thought by running together the acts of conceiving, combining (or dividing), and assenting (or dissenting, or deliberating): all three are included in the last. Their objects have objective existence but can only be said to have real existence in so far as the act in question is veridical or true: that is, contrary to Aquinas's doctrine, what has objective being does not thereby have real being as an accident of the mind distinct from the act of conceiving.

Petrus Aureolus was another to distinguish the act from the *conceptus objectivus* (objective concept). The former is both what makes the object appear and that to which the object appears. The latter is simply that which appears: it is the external object itself as it is conceived of, when there is such an object; otherwise it is an object with a merely intentional or intellectual existence, whose *esse* is *intelligi*. The emphasis is thus placed on the two possible modes of being of objects, rather than on two aspects of an internal mental product of an act of conceiving. This strategy has the advantage of avoiding a multiplication of objects of true thoughts, one internal to the thought, the other external, but does so at the cost of postulating weakly existing objects of such thoughts as lack reference to anything real. A third strategy was proposed by William of Ockham, whose ontology of thought included only real objects and acts of conceiving. The latter are natural signs with built-in direction, and to give their content is to indicate this direction quasi-adverbially. Whether there is something in the direction indicated, that is, whether their objects exist, is another matter.[11]

Another issue had an important influence on Descartes. Early in the seventeenth century, Francisco Suárez, in treating the topic of divine ideas, drew the traditional distinction between the 'conceptus formalis' and the 'conceptus objectivus'.[12] In creatures, the formal concept is always a 'true positive thing inhering as a quality in the mind'. The objective concept, on the other hand, is not always a *vera res positiva* (true positive thing), since we can think of *entia rationis* (beings of reason), such as privations, which can only have objective being. Applying this framework to an understanding of the relation between existence and essence, Suárez argued that, although the essences of creatures are objects of God's intellect before their existence, in order so to 'terminate' his knowledge (which is not to *cause* it),[13] they do not need true or real being but only 'such as is known by science' and is necessary for the truth of 'science'.[14] This he calls 'objective potential being'. God's knowledge that man is a rational animal is knowledge that, if a man is produced, he will be a rational animal, knowledge which abstracts from existence.[15] The essence is nothing at all 'in aliqua ratione veri entis' (in any account of true being),[16] but that does not mean that the eternal truths are dependent on God. If they were, they would be effects of God's will.[17] Suárez's position is that, although, as nothing real, essences neither cause knowledge nor need a creating cause themselves, yet they are in another sense, as possibles, 'real and apt for existence', 'real essences' which are appropriate matter for 'science' and not mere figments of the mind in which they have objective being.[18]

## III. DESCARTES ON IDEAS AND OBJECTIVE BEING

According to Meditatio III,[19] ideas are a sub-class of 'thoughts' (*cogitationes*) in a wide sense. They are such image-like (i.e., representative) thoughts as may enter into other thoughts so as to make them thoughts of this or that in particular. Thus the same content may be willed, feared, affirmed, or denied. Several points can be made about this short passage. First, its makes no reference to any objectless modes of thought in a purportedly exhaustive classification[20] and thereby indicates that Descartes subscribed to the traditional principle (argued, e.g., by Durandus) that all mental acts have objects. Second, it draws no distinction between two types of concept corresponding to the distinction between terms and propositions. The examples are the ideas of a man, a chimera, a goat, and the like, but they are treated as potential objects of judgement in that one might judge that they conform to external things. Third, as explained more fully later in this chapter, although an act of conceiving (i.e., the idea) is separated from the act of judging, the act of conceiving and its content are not treated as they are by Aquinas, as two distinct accidents or modifications of the mind. Rather, they are distinguishable aspects of the same mode of thought.

The conclusion, sometimes doubted,[21] that Descartes ruled out objectless thought receives support from his 'definition' of an idea, in another passage, as 'the form of any given thought (*cuiuslibet cogitationis*), immediate perception of which makes me aware of the thought'.[22] His point is that a thought of any kind is made determinate by its content or object; and that (as Aquinas too had held) in primarily thinking of some object I am only secondarily aware that I am thinking of it. Thus I cannot be aware of my thought without knowing what its object is.[23] This is surely an attempt to explain a universal relation between acts of thought, their objects, and our immediate consciousness of them. The employment here of the form–matter dichotomy[24] shows how a scholastic framework for dealing with intentionality could be retained without the ontology of forms.

What is, in effect, the same form–matter dichotomy is adopted in one characterisation of a systematic ambiguity of the term 'idea', which, Descartes says, can be taken either 'materially, for an operation of the intellect [or] objectively, for the thing represented by that operation'.[25] Descartes's account of this duality in Meditatio III, however, elaborated in his responses to objections, is in different terms. The 'objective reality' of an idea is distinguished from its 'formal reality' with respect to its place on the scale of being. Thus the objective reality of our idea of God is supreme on that scale, but its formal reality is simply that of any mode of thought. A correlative distinction applies to the object itself, which possesses objective existence in so far as it is thought of, or exists in the mind, and formal existence in so far as it exists (if it so exists) in the world, or independently of thought. To be concerned with an idea in so far as it has objective reality, is to be concerned with its object in so far as it has objective being. Hence the two were identified: 'the idea of the sun is the sun itself existing in the intellect – not of course formally existing, as it does in the heavens, but objectively existing, i.e. in the way in which objects normally are in the intellect.'[26]

This last, somewhat blank expansion of the phrase 'objectively existing' echoes Aristotelian explanations of the *sui generis* way in which, say, colour can exist in the medium and in the sense-organ. But for Descartes, only intellect has modifications which are intrinsically representative and support objective existence. Intentionality has been ejected from the material world. Motions in our body may be representative and may be called 'images' or even 'ideas',[27] but only in virtue of their relation to modes of thought. One indivisible intellectual faculty perceives, remembers, imagines, or engages in pure intellection according to how, or whether, it relates to motions in the brain.[28]

Yet if the old notion of objective being was so easy to adapt to dualist metaphysics, it carried the old problems with it. *Which* problems rather depends on whether Descartes's proposal that there is an ambiguity in the term 'idea' meant that there is one thing, the representative mode of thought, which can be considered in two ways, or that there are two distinct things, the representative mode of thought and the object of thought considered as it is represented, both of which can be called 'ideas'. In talking of 'the sun as it exists in the understanding', are we talking simply about the thought, or are we talking about the sun, under its relation to thought? The question could be put as follows. Which is the mere distinction of reason, and which the real distinction:[29] (1) the distinction between the idea as mode of thought and the idea as intentional object of thought or (2) the distinction between the latter (i.e., the thing as it exists in the mind) and the real object (the thing as it exists in reality)? It seems clear that, at least on ordinary realist assumptions, there cannot be one thing, the idea, which is really identical *both* to the mode of thought *and* to the real object.

These are much the same questions as had engaged scholastic philosophers in their attempts to characterise the relations between formal concept, objective concept, and real object. Quite a lot hangs on them from the point of view of epistemology, logic, and ontology. If (2) is taken to be the mere distinction of reason, then the principle that the immediate objects of thought are ideas is consonant with a strong form of direct realism: the immediate objects of thought may be identical with things in the world, even if the way we experience and think of them is not wholly the way they are. Questions then remain as to how it is that incompatible descriptions can apply to the same thing (as it is and as it is thought of), and as to the status of intentional objects of thoughts which have no real objects. If, on the other hand, (1) is taken to be the distinction of reason and (2) the real distinction, those questions may not arise, but there now seems to be a problem as to how thought ever gets outside itself and succeeds in being about things in the world. For it seems a truism that we only conceive of things as they are conceived of.

Descartes himself, in explaining ideas (*qua* intentional objects) as the 'forms' of thoughts, evidently placed the real distinction squarely between the sun as it exists in the mind and the sun as it exists in reality. The same view is present in his insistence to Caterus that, when it is said that the idea of the sun is 'the sun which is thought of', 'no one will take this to be the sun itself with this extrinsic label attached to it', that is, the real sun regarded as extrinsically related to a thought or mind.[30] To talk of the sun which is thought of is simply to talk of the thought itself, giving its specific content, direction, or 'form'. Unfortunately, it seems to follow that I cannot think (immediately) about the real sun (or real God!). Yet any such problem for Descartes's account was not due to his having postulated a third thing, an idea, between act of thought and external object. It is just that, faced with the traditional task of finding an ontological niche for the intentional object, he collapsed it, for plausible reasons, into the act of thought rather than into the real object.

On the other hand, the wider aim of the reply to Caterus was to present objective being as a genuine mode of being, for the reply was a vehicle of Descartes's disagreement with Suárez on the question of whether what has objective being thereby requires a cause. In the *Meditationes* this question arose with respect to the objective reality of the idea of God; but Caterus's criticism hinges on his acceptance of Suárez's doctrine of the eternal truths. Caterus accepted that whatever can be conceived clearly and determinately is an immutable nature or essence and so 'not nothing', a 'real' possibility as opposed to a confused figment of the imagination. Yet what only possesses objective being is also a *mere* possibility, nothing actual or absolute, and so does not require a cause.[31] Descartes limited his response to a narrowly relevant analogy: the objective reality of the idea of God needs a cause just as the idea of a machine needs a cause adequate to its 'objective intricacy', whether that cause be an actual machine or the human intellect. It was only elsewhere that he publicly endorsed the doctrine that the eternal truths are created.[32] His motives for that unpopular thesis are here irrelevant, but it is notably consonant with his view of the origin of our idea of God.

## IV. SOME DISTINCTIONS AMONG CARTESIAN IDEAS

In the course of expounding his epistemology, Descartes applied to 'ideas' several traditional, connected distinctions which were to become subject to a variety of reinterpretations as later philosophers marked out their own positions. It may be helpful to summarise Descartes's use of them.

### 1. Clear and obscure, distinct and confused ideas

Descartes's clear and distinct perceptions or ideas seem chiefly to respond to Stoic clear and evident impressions,[33] which constitute proper and impelling objects of assent and afford a sure criterion of truth. His *prima facie* unhelpful explanation of the terms ('I call a perception "clear" when it is present and accessible to an attentive mind. . . . I call a perception "distinct" which is not just clear, but is so sharply separated and abstracted from all others that it contains absolutely nothing within itself but what is clear')[34] suggests connexions with his proposed method of analysis of the complex into its simple elements, as well as that someone with a clear and distinct idea of $X$ will never confuse $X$ with something else. It is plain that the paradigm of clear and distinct perception is mathematical understanding rather than (as for the Stoics) unimpeded sense-perception. Although clear and distinct perception of one's own existence is both categorical and particular, clear and distinct ideas are characteristically of the essences or eternal truths which Descartes calls 'true and immutable natures'.

### 2. True and false, simple and complex ideas

These two divisions were historically connected through the Aristotelian principle that sentential combination of terms is a necessary condition of truth or falsity. Scholastics disputed whether uncombined 'simple apprehensions' or concepts are capable of truth. Some followed Aristotle in holding that only judgements can be true or false. Others held that to form a concept of something is a cognitive achievement deserving the name of truth. Even on the view that simple apprehensions count as true, however, they cannot be false: for what makes an apprehension an apprehension of *X*, conformity with *X*, also makes it a true apprehension of *X*.[35] Thus (it was argued) it is impossible to have a false idea of God, even though no human idea of Him is adequate.[36]

Descartes, too, held that simple ideas or notions are all in a sense true, and that combination is necessary for falsehood.[37] The combination he had in mind was not, however, essentially sentential or judgemental: indeed, propositional common notions or axioms are included among the 'simple notions'.[38] The simplicity of Descartes's simple notions is better understood in the light of his conception of analytical method. The simple end-product of analysis of what is complex will be clear and distinct perceptions of things, axiomatic 'true and immutable natures' about which we can reason scientifically.

Descartes also held that only judgements can be true or false in the strict sense, but that is not because they are complex, but because they are acts of assent to, or dissent from, a mental content or idea. Ideas are thus true or false in a derivative sense. They possess 'material' as opposed to 'formal' truth or falsity, in that they supply subject-matter or material for assent. Simple ideas are all materially true, but complex ideas are liable to be materially false.

In Meditatio III, our ideas of sensible qualities are characterised as so obscure and confused that we cannot tell whether they are (materially) true or false. Our ideas of heat and cold, for example, present them both as 'real and positive' things, although it may be (as some scholastics argued) that one is a positive quality and the other its privation, or (as Descartes himself wished to argue) that neither is a 'real' quality which could exist as it is represented. In response to Arnauld's traditional objection that an idea cannot be false, Descartes claimed that an obscure and confused idea may be referred 'to something other than that of which it is in fact the idea', by which he presumably meant that what is positive and clear in the idea, the sensation, may be ascribed to a cause supposed like it, whereas its actual cause and object is quite different in character.[39] However that may be, he elsewhere recognised the possibility of referring the sensation indefinitely to whatever in the object causes it, the nature of which is left indeterminate, as unknown.[40] Although this last point is made in terms of actual judgement, it opens the way for there to be a sensory idea of cold, colour, or the like which is materially true (although not clear and distinct), whatever the real nature of its object. What is certain is that no idea can be materially false unless, like sensory ideas, it is complex.[41]

### 3. Adequate and inadequate, complete and incomplete ideas

It was a traditional view that an informative true identical judgement, which distinguishes conceptually between things not really distinct, arises only when the concepts corresponding to each term are inadequate to their object (and, of course, different). Adequate ideas of *A* and *B* would automatically allow us to know whether *A* = *B*. Thus Arnauld objects to Descartes's proof of the real distinction between mind and body on the ground that they may appear distinct only because we have inadequate ideas of them; that is, they may be no more than conceptually distinct.[42] Descartes's response demonstrates his usage: we do have *complete* ideas of them in the required sense (although only God has strictly *adequate* ideas), since we conceive of them as complete beings, that is, capable of existing on their own, as we conceive of them.

## V. TWO FURTHER PROBLEMS FOR DESCARTES AND HIS SUCCESSORS

### 1. *Ideas, sensations, and images in the brain*

Descartes's mind–body dualism led to a significant indeterminacy or ambiguity in his account of ideas of sense and imagination, in particular to the problem of the relation between the idea in the mind and the motion in the brain.

In rejecting the transmission theory of vision, Descartes drew an analogy with motions imparted through a stick which inform a blind man of the physical features of what it touches, although they do not themselves possess those features.[43] With respect to sensible qualities such as light, colours, tastes, and smells, he presents it as a merely providential arrangement that such and such motions in the brain stimulate or produce such and such ideas, and the same model is employed in explanation of the visual perception of position, distance, and size.[44] Yet some part of the transmission theory seems to remain in place. For it is said that the picture on the retina causes a sort of extended picture in the brain which at least to some extent resembles the object of vision, although 'we must not think that it is by means of this resemblance that the picture causes our sensory perception of these objects – as if there were other eyes within our brain with which we could perceive it.'[45] What seems to be proposed is that the brain-picture is constituted by various motions broadly correspondent in their disposition and variety to the disposition and variety of the motions arriving at the retina, but including certain motions due to other elements in the situation than the retinal image, such as the position of the head, disposition of the eyes, the relation between the two retinal images, and so forth. The latter motions, combined with those motions that give rise to sensations of light and colour, give rise to the perception of distance, size, and objective (as opposed to perspectival) shape.[46]

Why did Descartes retain the apparently naive hypothesis of a spatially disposed brain-picture correspondent to the retinal image? As he himself emphasised by an analogy with language, an arbitrarily ordained correlation between brain-motion and sensory idea might take any form, provided only that it is systematic.[47] It is tempting to connect the hypothesis of the brain-image with a different model, according to which the mind arrives at judgements of size and distance by a process of unconscious reasoning from data presented by the senses. For in that case the picture on the pineal gland could be thought to correspond to, or even to be, the sensory datum.

The identification of the visual datum with the corporeal image may seem improbably crude, and hardly consonant with Descartes's own admonitions. Yet he was commonly prepared, in other contexts than optics, not only to explain the mode of representation in sense-perception and imagination as the natural consequence of the intimate union of the soul and the body but also to characterise the relation between intellect and corporeal image in cognitive terms. These passages suggest that sensory ideas actually incorporate an object which is material. The soul 'turns' or 'attends' to the common sense and corporeal imagination, both terms employed in Aristotelian accounts of the active intellect's construction of notions from phantasms by abstraction. In Meditatio VI Descartes draws an argument for the probable existence of body from the nature of imagination: since the imagination, unlike thinking in general, is a faculty I might have been without, it probably involves something other than myself *qua* thinking substance:

So the difference between this mode of thinking and pure understanding may simply be this: when the mind understands, it in some way turns towards itself and inspects one of the ideas which are within it; but when it imagines, it turns towards the body and looks at something in the body which conforms to an idea understood by the mind or perceived by the senses.[48]

Such an explanation accords the intellect a rôle even in sense-perception and at the same time concedes a limited force to the traditional view that sense and imagination require material organs.[49]

The same model seems to be employed for ideas of sensory qualities, which are particularly attributed to the 'intimate union' or 'mixture' of mind and body, and are explained at various places as containing both a sensation and a sort of judgement. The judgement may be either the true judgement that something unknown in external things is the cause of the sensation, or the false judgement that the cause resembles the sensation.[50] Again, in *Passions de l'âme,* the model is used to explain the difference between perceptions of qualities attributed to external objects, on the one hand, and bodily feelings, on the other:

> Thus at the same time and by means of the same nerves we can feel the cold of our hand and the heat of a nearby flame or, on the other hand, the heat of our hand and the cold of the air to which it is exposed. This happens without there being any difference between the actions which make us feel the heat or cold in our hand and those which make us feel the heat or cold outside us, except that since one of these actions succeeds the other, we judge that the first is already in us, and that its successor is not yet there but in the object which causes it.[51]

Yet if the intentional content of sensory perception (what it is 'of') is determined by such a 'judgement', or by the intellect's 'referring' a datum to this or that as its cause,[52] then the datum taken by itself lacks what Descartes assumed, in Meditatio III, to be an essential condition of thought. Seeing the datum as in itself corporeal, a 'cogitatio' only in its being an object of the intellect, would be one way of retaining the principle that all thoughts have intentional objects.[53]

Whatever Descartes's considered view, both the notion of a providential correlation between brain-motions and thoughts and the notion that the immediate object of perception is an image in the brain had important rôles in later philosophy.

### 2. A problem for the theory of innate ideas

In claiming that some ideas are innate, Descartes made it plain that he understood innateness dispositionally: 'We have within ourselves the faculty of summoning up the idea.'[54] A baby does not contemplate metaphysical truths in the womb, but, 'if it were taken out of the prison of the body, it would find them within itself.'[55] In general, what he identified as innate were the simple natures or notions and, through them, all other 'true and immutable natures' of which they are the foundation.[56] In this he was like others in the Platonist tradition. Herbert of Cherbury, for example, based his thesis of innate 'common notions' on an elaborate theory of faculties harmoniously related to their objects. Cambridge Platonists, although speaking graphically of our reading imprinted truths, or of 'heavenly beams' and the like, commonly stressed that sense experience and the employment of reason are necessary to bring what is innate to consciousness.[57] Nevertheless Descartes's theory had certain special features.

First, he employed disparate models to explain innateness. At one extreme, he suggested that the eternal truths, arbitrary creations of God, 'are all *inborn in our minds* just as a king would imprint his laws on the hearts of all his subjects if he had enough power to do so'.[58] Elsewhere, however, he claimed that innate ideas are nothing distinct from our faculty of thinking, which suggests that they constitute, or flow from, what it is to reason. Yet in the latter passage it is also said that even sensory ideas are innate, since the mind is innately disposed to experience pain, colour, and the like on the occurrence of certain corporeal motions.[59] Taken together, these claims seem to imply that reason itself might have operated according to different principles.

Nevertheless, Descartes's identification of innate ideas with the faculty of reason seems generally to have had a very different point. Some innate ideas, at least, are made explicit by a process seeming to have a share in the special security of the *cogito*, in that they are formed through the intellect's reflection on itself and its own operations. Not only may the ideas of substance, duration, and number be directly so formed, but the idea achieved through reflection on our own understanding of things is specifically given as an example of the ideas employed in forming our idea of God.[60] Although my idea of God's infinity is not in just the same way drawn from myself, it is made explicit through consideration of my own finitude *qua* imperfection or negation. Thus the innateness both of the 'common notions' and of ideas relating to incorporeal substance (including God) is more or less closely identified with the power of any thinking thing to reflect on itself.

Descartes's doctrine of innateness invites a cogent objection. If an idea is at any time dispositionally in the soul, it must be so in virtue of what is actual at that time. The principle (not shared by all Platonists) that the essence of the soul is thought implies that all that is actual in the soul at any time is its actual, particular thought at that time. Therefore any alleged innate idea can be in me dispositionally only in virtue of my present thought – yet the idea and the thought may have quite different objects. The proposal that innate ideas are available simply through the mind's capacity to reflect on itself, and so are given with the general reflexivity of thought, would avoid this objection. It is therefore not surprising that Descartes made it, or that his successors further developed it. But such an answer does not plausibly explain the Cartesian innate ideas of extension and motion.[61] Despite the absence of clear and full discussion of this difficulty, it seems to have contributed to the shape of later theories.

## VI. PROBLEMS OF INTENTIONALITY: DIGBY, HOBBES, AND GASSENDI

Some of Descartes's contemporaries among the 'new philosophers' also responded to his two main problems about ideas: (1) the problem of an ontology of thought to replace scholastic forms and (2) the more general problem of the relation between the act of thought, the object 'in the mind' and the real object.

Kenelm Digby, for example, starting from the principle 'that by apprehension, the very thing apprehended is by itself in our soule', asked how a time and place could come to exist materially in another time and place. How could the whole world and more 'be shut up in the little circuite of a man's braine?' How could the same object be corporeally in many brains at once? The only conclusion must be that things in the mind 'are there immaterially,' and 'that what receiveth them, is immateriall'.[62] Incorporeal substances are neither in place nor, more surprisingly, in time.[63] In effect, Digby adopted the same general ontological strategy as Descartes, treating intentionality as *sui generis,* the character of which is evident to us from our own consciousness and which is evidently peculiar to immaterial spirit. Such arguments entered the stock in trade of dualistic mechanism, a partial echo of a narrower Aristotelian argument for the immateriality and immortality of the faculty which apprehends universals.[64]

Despite his premise, Digby also discussed the question whether the 'very thing it selfe is truly in his understanding who rightly apprehendeth it', or whether we should rather 'peremptorily deny the things reall being in our mind, when we make a true and full apprehension of it; accounting it sufficient for our purpose, that some likeness, or image of the thing be there'. He argued that we talk of mere likeness when there 'is but an imperfect unity between a thing, and that which it is said to be like unto'. To make an image of a man *perfectly* like a man would be to make a man. Consequently, 'if the likenesse of a thing, which the objection alloweth to be in our knowledge, doe containe all that is in the thing knowne, then it is in truth, no more a likenesse, but the thing it selfe.'[65] This view of the relationship between resemblance and identity looks more plausible if universal qualities are in question rather than individuals, but it could in any case be asked how an allegedly immaterial image could be perfectly like material man, or an unextended image be like a square.[66] Digby's argument is perhaps more a dismissal of the problem than a theoretical response to it, but, as we shall see, it was a line of thought with some influence.[67]

Materialists, of course, denied any connexion between intentionality and immateriality. Hobbes famously argued that, since the only idea of substance we have through the senses is that of body, the expression 'immaterial substance' is senseless.[68] Yet he also remarked that of all phaenomena touching ourselves, the most wonderful is appearance itself, in that there are patterns (*exemplaria*) of nearly everything in some natural bodies, and none at all in others. These 'appearances' (or 'apparitions'), 'images', 'phantasms', 'conceptions', or 'ideas' are both things in the mind and motions in the innermost organ of, in the first instance, sense. Their intentional content is constituted by the form of motion involved. A motion from an external body causes a reaction which, since the motion is now directed outwards, 'always seems like something situated outside the organ'. What makes this reaction a phantasm or a case of 'seeming' at all, and so different from similarly reactive motions in inanimate things, is that it continues in the organ long after its cause ceases to be present (i.e., there is memory and imagination), so that earlier and later phantasms can be compared, and can constitute a train of thought. Not all ideas are conscious at any one time, because some dominate and blot out others. This heroically mechanist ontology of intentionality is coupled with fairly orthodox assumptions about the distinctions (and ambiguities) involved. Phantasms, as acts of sensation (*sentiendi actus*), are distinguished from 'objects', which are the external bodies themselves. Nevertheless (but as we should expect) colour, heat, smells, empty space, and ghosts are phantasms rather than objects.[69]

A materialist understanding of ideas was also at least implicit in Gassendi's development of Epicurean epistemology, and he objected to Cartesian intellect that it is difficult to see how there could be any representation of space that is not itself extended.[70] But Gassendi's fundamental purpose was anti-dogmatic, so that he was less concerned than Hobbes to propose an ontology of thought.[71] Nevertheless, he advanced a distinctively un-Cartesian account of intentionality through his endorsement of the Epicurean principle that all sensations are true, in being true signs of their causes. On this view, for example, if a visual image diminishes as its object moves further away, although the judgement that the object is getting smaller would be false, the image or idea is itself not false or deceptive, since it appropriately matches the change in the world.[72] Its purpose was anti-sceptical, but for better or worse the argument emphasises the causal element in representation to the extent of suggesting that the true object of any sensation is the total or sufficient mechanical cause of its having the character it has. Since there always is such a cause, all sensations are true.

Before considering later developments of the Epicurean model, however, it is appropriate to examine the bold, spectacularly ingenious responses to our two problems of intentionality, lying within the broadly Cartesian tradition, in the systems of Spinoza, Malebranche, and Leibniz. With these theories may be placed Arnauld's orthodox but impressive critique of Malebranche.

## VII. SPINOZA

Spinoza's astonishing system offered an explanation of two relations, between idea and object and between mind and body, in terms of a single relation between the attribute of thought and the attribute of extension. The fundamental principle of Spinoza's metaphysics is the claim that reality consists of one necessarily existing substance, God or Nature, whose essence is expressed through an infinity of different attributes, each modified in an infinity of ways. Particular or singular things are modes each of which expresses an attribute in a determinate way. Thought and extension are two of the divine attributes. Particular bodies are those modes which express God's essence in a determinate way in so far as He is an extended thing, while particular ideas do the same in so far as He is a thinking thing. God's mind includes ideas of His essence and of everything which follows from it. A human mind is a part of the divine mind, constituted by the idea of a certain mode of God considered in so far as He is extended (together with the idea of that idea, since thought is reflexive). That mode is the human body. The mind–body relation is thus a case of the relation between an idea and its object.

For Spinoza, every particular thing is a link in a chain of causes and effects necessarily determined by the divine essence. He talks as if there is a separate causal chain for each attribute: 'The modes of each attribute have God for their cause only in so far as he is considered under the attribute of which they are modes.'[73] Hence we should not think in terms of causal interaction between mind and body. Yet, despite the separation of the attributes for the purposes of causal explanation, these emanations from God's essence are not really distinct: 'The order and connection of ideas is the same as the order and connection of things.'[74] The same particular thing in God as is an idea under the attribute of thought is also a mode of extension, namely that mode which is the object of the idea: 'A circle existing in nature and the idea of the existing circle, which is also in God, are one and the same thing, which is explained through different attributes.' All this constitutes a neat, if surprising ontological understanding of objective or intentional existence as existence under the attribute of thought, and a strong metaphysical grounding for the traditional definition of an idea as the thing itself in so far as it is thought of. In effect, Spinoza attempts just what was described above as evidently impossible, that is, a coherent theory according to which the real object, the intentional object, and the mode of thought are all three truly identical with one another, distinguished only by distinctions of reason.

Since every human idea has its object within the human body, every idea has a sort of truth. Indeed, all ideas, in so far as they are ideas in God, are true.[75] Falsity exists only in so far as the human mind is constituted by ideas which are incomplete or inadequate. In other words, Spinoza's system presupposes a form of the traditional conception of perfect knowledge as the reflexive knowledge of a perfect being.[76] God understands the necessity with which the modes of His attributes flow from His essence. The human mind, however, as the mere fragment of the divine mind constituted by a certain idea of the human body, perceives effects of other modes on that body, but not the infinite chain of causes and effects perception of which would be requisite for adequate ideas or complete understanding of singular or particular individuals – for understanding them *per causas*. The human idea of the human body is therefore inadequate. Human ideas of other bodies are achieved in sense perception only mediately, in so far as the natures of those bodies are involved in their effects on the perceiver's body, according to the principle that 'knowledge of an effect depends on, and involves, knowledge of its cause.'[77] Since the nature of the affected body is more involved in those effects than the nature of any external affecting body, our ideas of external bodies tell us more about our own body than about the external bodies.[78] Moreover, the effect, the immediate object of our idea, may continue when the affecting body is no longer present, making us believe that it is still present.[79] Such false ideas about external bodies, our own bodies, or our minds are due to ignorance of causes: for instance, if we know why the sun appears only 200 feet away (why it has such an effect on the body), when it is really 600 diameters of the earth away, our idea is not in this respect false, even though the appearance remains.[80]

It is a common-sense objection to Spinoza's system that the object of a thought or experience is conceptually something quite different from its physical basis. Whenever a thought of Socrates occurs, then *ipso facto* a brain-process is caused in just some relevant respect, at whatever remove (involving books, sense, memory, hearsay or whatever), by Socrates. But the immediate object of the thought is Socrates, not, as Spinoza claimed, a physiological process caused by Socrates.

Spinoza's claim becomes more understandable if we suppose him to have had in mind Descartes's conception of the 'intimate union' of soul and body. One part of this conception is the model for sense-perception and imagination, discussed above, according to which the intellect 'inspects' or 'attends to' corporeal images as its immediate objects. Thus Descartes's account of the relation between mind and brain is itself open to the objection under consideration. Spinoza claimed, however, that the soul is the idea of the *body*, not just of the brain or brain-processes, and that suggests the other element in the Cartesian 'intimate union', expressed in the claim that the soul is joined to the whole body, not just to a part of it. Descartes supported this claim by arguing that a complex arrangement of organs is a necessary condition of the union, but there was also the point that the body (or most of it) is the object of a special kind of awareness, in that we experience it as ourselves.[81] Nevertheless, as we have seen, Spinoza's argument requires that an idea have as its immediate object just that affection of the body with which it is identical, that is, its material basis. It is possible that he thought of the whole physical process of perception as it involves organ, nerves, and brain as both physical basis and immediate object of perception.[82] But there does seem to be a crucial indeterminacy in his theory.

Spinoza's position also connects with the Epicurean doctrine that sensations are always true. Epicurus, too, took the material image, rather than the external object, to be the true or immediate object of sense, so that sensory awareness and, indeed, imagination always has an object. Where Spinoza was unique, however, was in his boldly incorporating the intentional relationship into his metaphysics by postulating, not only that the immediate object of an idea or mode of thought is a physiological process, but that the idea, its immediate object and the physiological process are one and the same thing.

Spinoza's inadequate and confused ideas correspond to Descartes's ideas of sense and imagination, but he took some human ideas to be adequate, true, clear and distinct. His metaphysics grounds an extremely neat explanation of how that should be so. Descartes had postulated a special class of innate, purely theoretical ideas which owe nothing to the body. These 'true and immutable natures' correspond to transcendent essences or eternal truths in God's mind and together supply the interpretive structure involved in all other ideas. Spinoza offers a more economical explanation. All human ideas are ideas of affections of the human body, but some are ideas of those affections that are common to all bodies, and so do not constitute the essence of any finite individual. Because such properties are the same in the part as in the whole, in the human body as in bodies in general, they are as complete or adequate in God in so far as He has the idea of the human body as they are in so far as He has the idea of all bodies. In other words, they are adequate in the human mind.[83] All ideas derivable from these adequate ideas, such as the common notions which are the foundation of reasoning, are also adequate. The objects of adequate ideas, the things that are 'fixed and eternal' in God and Nature, appear to us as necessary but are not transcendent universals. In a minor work, Spinoza calls them 'singular': 'although these fixed and eternal things are singular, nevertheless, because of their presence everywhere, . . . they will be to us like universals, or *genera* . . . , and the proximate causes of all things.'[84] His point is that the essences which are the objects of demonstrative 'science' are to be sharply distinguished from man-made universals formed by the imagination, such as the idea of a man or dog. Knowledge of them is knowledge of 'real beings', not merely of abstractions or 'beings of reason'.[85]

There is also, for Spinoza, a kind of intuitive knowledge which involves an adequate idea of a particular 'under the aspect of eternity' (*sub specie aeternitatis*).

This is not a full understanding of it through knowledge of its (infinite) causes, but a general understanding of it as contained in God and flowing necessarily from the divine nature. The aim of life should be to have such an idea of ourselves and our bodies, an intellectual love of God.[86]

Spinoza's distinction between adequate and inadequate ideas follows Descartes in so far as it explains the difference between intellect and imagination in terms of a category of (in effect) innate ideas. Yet it does so in a way that avoids not only the problem of how we know that our innate ideas conform with the essences in God which make them true but also the problem of the relation between those essences and essences in nature. For our adequate ideas are identical with God's adequate ideas and are at the same time identical with their objects. Thus if we form an adequate idea of an eternal thing, we can be sure that its object is not only possible but actual.[87] It will also be seen that the tendency in Descartes to explain certain innate ideas as ideas available to the soul through a kind of reflection on itself has been carried further by Spinoza: even our mathematical and mechanical ideas are possessed through the human mind's perception of itself, that is, of the human body. The same is true of the ideas of metaphysics, among which the idea of God as the truly independent substance is the idea from which demonstrative 'science' must start, mirroring the order according to which the natural world flows from the divine essence.

## VIII. MALEBRANCHE AND ARNAULD

### 1. *Ideas in Malebranche*

Malebranche's theory bears an interesting relation to Spinoza's. Where Spinoza treated not only the distinction between the act of thought and the idea but also the distinction between the idea and the object as mere distinctions of reason, Malebranche treated them both as real distinctions. Where for Spinoza there is really one thing, for Malebranche there are three. First, he argued that an idea, defined as 'the immediate object, or object closest to the mind, when it perceives something', is distinct from the thing of which it is the idea, or which it represents, since ideas may exist of things which do not exist.[88] In any case, since our soul is not in the sky when it sees stars there, and whatever it immediately sees must be joined to it, the stars it immediately sees as in the sky must be distinct from the stars actually in the sky. The errors of the senses typically arise because we take ideas and sensations to be things, that is, what is united or present to the mind to be outside us.[89] Second, Malebranche argued that, although an idea is not a substance, it is certainly something real, and not nothing, since it has properties:

the idea of a square is different from that of a circle. It is also spiritual, since the mind cannot be united to what is extended.

Malebranche then claimed that Aristotelian, innatist, and empiricist explanations of how these ideas come before the mind are unsatisfactory. Yet ideas are not in us essentially. It is indisputable, however, that ideas of His creatures *are* essentially in God, as perfections; 'otherwise He could not have created them.'[90] The only tenable view, therefore, is that it is these that we immediately perceive. We perceive things through God's ideas of them, with which we are united: 'We see all things in God.' Malebranche, in this, at any rate, like Spinoza, returned the word 'idea' to its traditional context in scholastic philosophy, and it is important to see how his doctrine restricts the denotation of the term.

First, there are no 'ideas' (even inadequate ideas) of sensible qualities such as colours, not to speak of pains, for these are sensations, *sentiments,* mere modifications of our own minds which occur together with our perception of extension as an essential element in sense experience.[91] Their essential rôle, according to Malebranche, is to particularise or bound the perception of extension in general, generating the perception of particular bodies.[92] Second, since ideas are essences in God, there cannot be an idea which is not in itself adequate. Inadequacy and obscurity are due to accompanying sensation, which leads us to judge that something exists without exhibiting its essence. Third, since the test for whether we have an idea at all is whether we have the material for a demonstrable 'science' of its object, it is clear, for Malebranche, that we lack an idea of spirit, which we know only by self-consciousness ('*conscience*'). We do not perceive its essence in God, but are simply and directly aware of its modifications in our own case.[93] Thus Malebranche expressly rejected the suggestion, so thoroughly taken up by Spinoza, that ideas of reason become explicit through reflection on ourselves.

### 2. Arnauld's criticisms

Malebranche's theory stimulated one of the most extensive discussions of intentionality of the seventeenth century, Arnauld's polemic *Des vraies et des fausses idées.* Arnauld rejected Malebranche's assumption that it can be asked in general how ideas come before the mind, allowing only that we may inquire into the efficient cause of our having this idea or that. The former question is like asking how minds come to think, whereas it is simply of the nature of the mind to think, and of thought to have an object.[94] He accused Malebranche of using 'idea' in two ways: first, innocuously, for a modification of the soul, the same thing as a perception or thought; and second, perniciously, for a supposed 'representative being' involved in all perception. Malebranche's invention of this chimera, he claimed, was an indirect consequence of the same prejudice of childhood as had been responsible for the scholastic notion of intentional species.

This last charge was elaborated as follows. First, the things children see, normally present before their eyes, are occasionally seen in reflections. These reflections they mistakenly regard as themselves things, like pictures or images, representing objects not themselves seen. Later they recognise that they sometimes perceive things mentally which are not seen literally, and they are led to the assumption that these too are 'seen' by means of representative beings or images of a special sort. That commonplace confusion is compounded with an improved understanding of the soul. For recognition that it is the soul, not the eye, that sees has led to the erroneous view that the object of vision must be present, not just to the eyes, but to the soul. Since no external bodies are ever physically present to the soul, it is concluded that all bodies are seen only by means of representative beings or images (i.e., intentional species). All this involves two false principles: (1) that whatever we perceive is present and united to the soul and (2) that bodies are present to the soul vicariously, by the medium of representative beings like them. Malebranche has uncritically taken over these principles from the Aristotelians. They are the same principles, Arnauld added, that led Gassendi to argue that the soul must be extended in order to receive ideas of extension.

This somewhat insulting diagnosis of Malebranche's error was accompanied by a more rigorous analysis of thought, the chief points of which are as follows. When we perceive, conceive, or think of an object, it can be said to be 'present to the mind' in a certain sense, and to be 'objectively in the mind'. The idea of an object and the perception or thought of an object are the same thing, that is, an essentially representative modification of the mind which, 'although a single being, has two relations: first, with the soul which it modifies, and second, with the thing perceived as it is objectively in the soul'. In the first relation, it is better called a perception, and in the second, an idea. The idea must not be confused with the perceived object, although it can be said to be the perceived object in so far as it is in the mind. It is in an acceptable sense the immediate object of perception, which is a reflexive act: 'For if I think of the sun, the objectively existing sun which is present to my mind is the immediate object of this perception; and the possible or existing sun, which [*scil.,* given that it exists] is outside my mind, is as it were the mediate object of it.'[95] Arnauld presented all this, quite rightly, as an exposition of Cartesian doctrine, appealing to Descartes's definition of an idea as the form of a thought through the immediate perception of which I am conscious of that same thought. By employing this conception of the self-consciousness of thought he managed to maintain the principle that our knowledge of things is mediated by ideas immediately perceived, and that we perceive the real object through the intentional object, while denying that an idea is anything over and above the thought, a distinct object lying between the thought and the thing.

In a famous argument Arnauld claimed that, in confusing the conditions of metaphorical or mental seeing with those of literal seeing, Malebranche had conflated two senses of 'presence', local presence with objective presence. We can think of nothing which is not *ipso facto* 'objectively present' to the mind, but that does not mean that it has to be locally present. Moreover, Arnauld argued, Malebranche is inconsistent in complaining that the sun is too far from the mind to be joined to it, since he holds that even the body cannot be present to the mind in the required sense. However close we supposed the soul were to the sun, it would still, according to Malebranche (and indeed to Arnauld, in another sense), perceive the sun through an idea of it. Moreover, abstract thought is concerned with such objects as a square in general, which are not in space and so neither near to, nor far from the soul. The whole confusion, Arnauld woundingly concluded, arises because the soul is conceived of as if it and all its objects were material.[96] Besides, he argued, why should God take such a strange circuit rather than simply make us have perceptions (i.e., ideas) of bodies?[97]

It is difficult not to sympathise with the main thrust of Arnauld's arguments, both for his common-sensical rejection of Malebranche's exotic ontology of knowing, and for his more general opposition to the reification of ideas. Even his adoption of the problematic principle that we know things only through our ideas of them seems more tenable than Reid found it. If all that it means is that we can think and reason about things only as we conceive of them, it seems no more than an innocuous tautology. Nevertheless there are points to be made on the other side.

First, Arnauld did not come to grips with Malebranche's Platonic motivation, the concern to explain universal knowledge and identify its objects. As Arnauld noted with some enjoyment,[98] Malebranche's thesis was less than clear on the question of the perception of particulars. Yet Malebranche's central claim concerned the objects of *a priori* science, including ethical science: that is, being, number, extension, and order. His denial that we perceive spirit through an idea was thus an inference from, and explanation of, our lack of a demonstrative 'science' of spirit. As for particular bodies, his considered view was that the idea of their essence, extension, is perceived by the intellect, although the qualities which bound and particularise infinite intelligible extension, and which make us judge that particular bodies exist, are mere sensations. Arnauld criticised the view that we see, not the physical man or tree, but an 'intelligible' man or tree, as absurdly circuitous and sceptical. Yet, first, on Malebranche's account an 'intelligible' tree, that is, an idea of a tree, intrinsically represents a tree, so that his theory allows that, in some sense, we perceive real trees. More significantly, the charge of scepticism with respect to the *existence* of bodies was one that Malebranche was explicitly prepared to live with.[99] What he was opposed to was the kind of conceptualism about *essences* advocated by Arnauld. According to Arnauld, in geometrical reasoning we reflect self-consciously on our own perceptions or ideas (i.e., on the form of our thoughts), while abstract numbers, as opposed to numbered things, 'exist only in our soul'.[100] Yet he did not hold that the eternal truths of geometry and arithmetic are *about* our perceptions, since the objects that make them true, on the Augustinian view shared by both philosophers, lie not in human minds, but in God's. It was here in particular that Arnauld's account seemed itself circuitous and sceptical. Malebranche wanted an understanding of the *a priori* sciences which made their eternal objects directly apprehensible by the human mind, not merely available by proxy. Arnauld's claim to allow all objects of thought to be 'present to the mind' (in the relevant sense) could hardly have satisfied Malebranche, in so far as Arnauld himself admitted that, when we think of anything, it is the objectively existing thing, not the real thing, which is immediately 'present to the mind'. His assertion that the objectively existing thing is not itself an entity distinct from our perception of the thing certainly constitutes one way of cutting through the ontological jungle. Yet the implied hard distinction between the thing as it exists in the mind and the thing as it exists in reality seems to pose an epistemological problem.

One of the issues focused on in the dispute was the intentionality of sensations. Malebranche's theory can be seen as an extrapolation from Descartes's tendency to see a sensory idea as composite, a blank datum referred by the mind to an external object and cause. For Malebranche, a sensation, as modification of the mind, has an object, not intrinsically, but in virtue of the circumstances of its occurrence, and in this regard is quite unlike the perception of extension.[101] Arnauld, in response, pursued another Cartesian tendency by insisting on the intrinsic intentionality of all modes of thought, including pleasure and pain. He continued the dispute with Pierre Bayle, who claimed, unconvincingly, that it is possible to have a pain which is not in any part of the body.[102] Yet even if Arnauld was right in this, Malebranche's theory, in its explicit emphasis on the relationship between the intentionality and the spatial content of our perceptual states, helped to clarify what was to become a central theme at a later stage in the history of philosophy.

## IX. LEIBNIZ

Leibniz was another philosopher, like Spinoza and Malebranche, whose theory of knowledge and ideas cannot be disentangled from a radical metaphysics centred on the intentional relation.[103] Like Spinoza, he was dissatisfied with Descartes's form of dualism both because of the problems of interaction between different substances and because of the paradoxical treatment of animals as machines without sensation.[104] He was also committed to a world in which every change occurs in an intelligible way, arising from the nature of the substance involved rather than the intervention of God.[105] Spinoza's immanent and extended God, however, was repugnant to him, as was the account of finite individuals as 'vanishing modifications'. He rejected the latter partly because (like Descartes's own theory) it underrated the substantial unity of living things, but above all because it did not allow for our natural immortality as individual persons, that is, as moral agents with reason and memory.[106]

These motives came together with dissatisfaction with the Cartesian concept of material substance. First, the infinite divisibility of matter makes it impossible to conceive of anything purely material as a genuine unity or, therefore, as a substance.[107] Moreover, Cartesian matter is passive, a feature which, together with the problem of mind–body interaction, encouraged the doctrine of occasionalism. A substance, however, should be active. Leibniz therefore postulated simple substantial individuals which are like 'forms' rather than matter and which do not exist in space. These constitute everything apparently material, and each of them is the principle of unity of an aggregate of other 'monads as' the soul is the principle unifying the body. Reality is thus an infinite hierarchy of dominant and subordinate immaterial substances or souls.[108] Leibniz also argued that interaction between substances is logically impossible, since accidents such as motion, not to speak of sensible species, cannot be transferred from one substance to another. Hence not only spatial but also causal relations are mere appearances – not illusions, but *phenomena bene fundata*. The truth-conditions of propositions concerning such relations lie ultimately in the possession of certain intrinsic properties by simple substances. Indeed, that is where, so he thought, the foundation of all truth must lie.

It is with respect to this feature of his system that Leibniz appealed to intentionality as the unanalysed relation in terms of which other relations are reductively explained. He did so by exploiting certain truisms about perception. If a number of perceivers are all looking at one another, each will differ internally from the others according to its own point of view, that is, according to its spatial relations to the others and the consequent effects of the others on its organs of perception. The perceptual state of each will therefore not only represent the other perceivers more or less well depending on its spatio-causal relations to them, but will also, *ipso facto,* reflect those relations themselves. Leibniz proposed that his form-like and atomic simple substances or 'monads' are quasi perceivers. A pre-established harmony holds between the perceptions of all monads, and a monad exists correspondent to every point in (what appears as) infinitely divisible extension. His reductive claim is that monads and their internal representations are all that is truly real. The representative modifications of monads constitute the sole foundation of true propositions about causal and spatial relations between things rather as (say) A's being off-white and B's being intensely white constitute the sole foundation of the truth that B is whiter than A. The analogy between the intentional relation and a merely 'extrinsic' relation such as *whiter than* holds only in part, however, just because A does not enter into the whiteness of B in the way that the perceived object enters *intentionally* into the perceptual state. Yet the analogy does hold in part, in so far as it would be logically (although not, for Leibniz, metaphysically) possible for any of the mutual perceivers to exist as the sole occupant of a world, but with all the modifications it possesses in the actual world.[109] Each monad internally represents, 'contains', or 'expresses' the universe in the unique way which defines and constitutes both its 'point of view' and its identity or individuality.

Thus Leibniz drew the firmest of real distinctions between the intentional object or *phenomenon* and the real or external object. He himself linked his model to his denial of the transmission of anything like intentional forms from one substance to another. Since there is no interaction in his system, change is explained as the progression within a substance from one perceptual modification to another in accordance with an internal law, force or tendency. Since what determines the state of a substance at any time can only be its own antecedent state, the whole of its future (and, Leibniz held, its past) lies in its present state. This tendency is analogous to desire or appetition in the soul, as 'expression' is analogous to ordinary perception. Nevertheless, there is a great difference between an ordinary monad and a soul in the full sense. The latter is a monad in which perceptions achieve a certain degree of distinctness, coupled with a sort of retained echo, which constitutes sensation and memory. Human souls have not only such perceptions but also apperception, a consciousness or reflective knowledge of their perceptions. Apperception, in ways to be considered, allows us to know the eternal truths, and so to be rational.

Thus animal perception is, for Leibniz, a special case of expression or 'perception' in a wider sense, and the same is true of the asymmetric relation between the soul or form of a living thing and its body (which is also a special case of the relation holding between every monad and the aggregate of its 'subordinate' monads). For, like Spinoza, Leibniz explained the mind–body relation in terms of the intentional relation. Although every substance expresses every other substance, it expresses those substances which make up its own body 'more particularly and perfectly', or 'more distinctly' than it expresses other bodies. The latter it expresses 'according to the relation [they] have to its own body' and especially, in the case of animals, to those parts of its body that constitute organs of sense.[110] The body of a 'dominant' monad undergoes flux; that is, the part of the universe it most distinctly perceives, and through perception of which it perceives the rest of the universe, is constantly changing. Yet every simple substance is itself indestructible and will always dominate some body, however small (something possible just because monads constitute an infinitely divisible, non-spatial continuum or chain). The only indestructibility which is morally significant, however, is the personal immortality available to substances with apperception.[111]

The distinction drawn by Leibniz between bare 'expression', on the one hand, and animal sensation and human consciousness, on the other, makes it difficult to see what is left of the general analogy between expression and perception. Yet it is supposed that expression is always something more than the quasi-causal (but, strictly speaking, pre-established) correspondence or correlation between changes in one monad and changes in other monads.[112] Leibniz clearly did not believe that he could give an account of the kind of correspondence involved, or, for that matter, of the internal order of phenomena within a monad, without presuming that modifications of monads are intrinsically intentional in accordance with the paradigm of conscious perception of things in space. It is evidently from our own case that we are supposed to know what modifications a simple substance can undergo, and the order of which they are capable. Indeed, it is in the conscious unity, in apperception, of our own perceptions, both at one time and over time, that we are provided with an exemplar of the possibility of variety in what is simple, that is, of the metaphysical unity of a substance with all its attributes.[113]

Leibniz was obviously faced with the need to justify the extension of the paradigm to modifications of substances lacking sensation and apperception, and he did so by arguing from the occurrence of unconscious perception in our own case: for example, a sound that we do not consciously hear can nevertheless wake us up. The claim is that everything that affects us is really perceived, unconsciously if not consciously. Yet it can be objected that not every change even in a conscious perceptual state counts as the perception of its cause: the drug that causes visions is not thereby perceived. Subliminal or unconscious perception of a sound in sleep counts as such just because a significant part of the mechanism of conscious hearing is involved, not to speak of the sound's impinging on dreaming consciousness.[114] Another example of *'petites perceptions'* below the level of consciousness, our hearing a multitude of sounds confusedly as one sound, is similarly unhelpful. On what foundation is this notion supposed to be applicable to subjects which never consciously perceive anything at all?

Before pursuing the implications of this last objection, however, it is worth considering a number of distinctions employed by Leibniz with some consistency over a long period in the exposition of his epistemology.[115] First, knowledge (or a notion, or representation) may be either *clear* or *obscure*: it is clear, if it enables us to distinguish the thing represented or known. Clear notions may be either *distinct* or *confused*: distinct, when we can enumerate criteria for distinguishing what is represented, and confused, when we can make the distinction only by some means intrinsically capable of resolution or analysis, but which we have not resolved. Leibniz's prime examples of confused notions are sensory: although we are incapable of further breaking down our sensory representation of red, it is composed of a multiplicity of elements, like the sounds of individual waves in the sound of the sea, corresponding to the multiplicity in what it expresses. Distinctness is a matter of degree: green might be resolved first into a mixture of blue and yellow, and those in turn into the shapes and motions of particles.[116] A distinct notion the elements of which are themselves distinct and incapable of further resolution is *adequate,* as is every simple notion. This account of adequacy enabled Leibniz to hold, rather like Spinoza (but without Spinoza's adequate ideas of individuals *sub specie aeternitatis*), that we only have adequate notions of what is universal, since to have an adequate notion of an individual would require infinite analysis.[117] On the other hand, universal notions are merely abstract and therefore *incomplete,* and it is possible for there to be *complete* notions only of individuals.[118]

Simple or primitive notions or thoughts are *intuitive,* but complex distinct notions are intuitive only if all their parts are held in mind together. When that is beyond us, their analysis employs language as an aid in *symbolic* or 'blind' thought, as in mathematical calculation. Symbolic thinking makes it possible inadvertently to form contradictory notions or *false* ideas. *True* ideas are (as for Suárez, Descartes *et al.*) ideas of real possibilities, and we can know that an idea is true either from the actual existence of its object or by formal demonstration of its possibility, that is, full analysis of the idea by a real, as opposed to nominal definition.[119] Leibniz rejected Spinoza's claim that an adequate idea of an individual would reveal the necessity that it should exist: what makes a true idea of an individual true is God's idea of it as possible, whether or not God has chosen to create it in reality.[120] The relation to God no doubt explains Leibniz's introduction of the term 'idea' at this point in his argument, and indeed he remarked that a false idea is not really an idea. He (of course) firmly rejected the views of Spinoza and Malebranche which identify our ideas (or adequate ideas) with the divine ideas themselves. Against Spinoza, he argued that to identify a soul with an idea in God, and to explain the immortal part of the soul as the eternal truths in God, is to confuse an active reality with abstract potentialities: 'The idea of any animal is a possibility [and the] soul is not an idea, but the source of innumerable ideas.'[121] Against Malebranche, he argued that our ideas are in us as innate capacities which correspond to divine ideas. He nevertheless conceded that, since God is the cause of all our ideas, and 'every effect expresses its cause', He is also their immediate external object: 'the essence of our soul is a certain expression, imitation or image of the divine essence . . . and of all the ideas comprised in it.'[122] The finite universe is thus expressed only mediately.

An important element in Leibniz's notion of an idea is his metaphysical explanation of dispositional innateness. His thesis that a monad at all times expresses its past and future history, unconsciously if not consciously, gave him a way not available to Descartes himself to reconcile the notion of cognitive dispositions with a view of the soul as an essentially perceiving thing. He proposed reserving the term 'idea' for the permanent expression in us 'of some nature, form, or essence' which may become conscious as the occasion demands.[123] Although he recognised the entailment that we always have conceptions of everything we shall ever have thought of, he did not refrain from using the traditional argument for innateness from the possibility of universal or necessary knowledge going beyond experience. He also insisted on the Cartesian thought, rejected by Malebranche, that reflection on ourselves can generate ideas of reason – of 'Being, Unity, Duration, Change, Action, Perception, Pleasure, and hosts of other objects'.[124] Perhaps he would have included extension, motion and the like on the same list, in that they relate to the way we perceive things rather than to anything truly external. At any rate, he claimed that apperception and the ability to reflect goes together with the capacity for a priori reasoning and systematic 'science'.[125]

One great weakness of Leibniz's system is his over-use of the distinctions (or *continua*) between clear and obscure perception and distinct and confused perception, particularly the latter. They are employed, in the ways indicated above, in the explanation of too many other distinctions: between conscious and unconscious perception; between apperception and sensation; between intellect and imagination; between human souls, animal souls, and other simple substances; between current thoughts and cognitive dispositions; between the perceiver's body and other bodies; and even between the organs of perception and other parts of the body.[126] It is difficult to see how all these very different distinctions could be a matter of more and less clear and distinct perception. More decisively, the underlying model is incoherent: every monad maps the whole universe in every detail, yet maps some parts of it more perfectly than others. The analogy with perspectives and points of view may seem to illustrate the second part of the claim but palpably conflicts with the first. The appeal to infinite divisibility (or its monadic correlate) may seem more promising, in that each map brings only a part of the universe above some perceptual threshold and continues to do so however much it is magnified, while the rest of the universe is mapped below that threshold. Thus 'a soul can read in itself only what is distinctly represented there; it cannot unfold all its folds at once, since it goes on to infinity.'[127] Yet, as this quotation demonstrates, such an appeal cannot even look explanatory unless something like self-awareness is built into the model, whereas self-awareness or apperception is just one of the phenomena, peculiar to a few rational souls, that the model is required to explain. Leibniz's alternative to the 'labyrinth' of infinite divisibility constitutes a far more bewildering continuum.

## X. LOCKE

Locke explicitly set aside the question of the physical basis of thought and ideas.[128] Yet his account of representation, broadly Epicurean while retaining the traditional, slippery model of ideas as what exist 'in the mind' as the 'immediate objects' of 'perception' or thought, gave rise to some revealing tensions.

Lockean ideas are either simple or complex. Simple ideas are all acquired in experience and so must necessarily be the product of things operating in a natural way.[129] They are therefore all 'real' and 'adequate' because, 'being nothing but the effects of certain powers in things, fitted and ordained by God, to produce such sensations in us, they cannot but be correspondent, and adequate to those powers.'[130] By the same token they are all 'true' in the chief sense in which ideas can be true:[131] for, 'answering those powers, they are what they should be, *true ideas*.' They are 'marks' which indicate or 'signify distinctions' in things,[132] and are 'signs' in so far as they serve in thought to signify or stand for their normal causes. So the epistemological conception of a sign as a basis for inference is tied in with the logical notion of signification. Ideas are terms in a natural language of thought, and simple ideas are the terms directly grounded on experience. Conventional signs have meaning by association with natural signs, and logic or semiotic is the science of both.[133]

There is no doubt that Locke was developing the Epicurean theme that all sense impressions are true,[134] and his view of illusions is much like Gassendi's. In the case of water which feels hot to one hand and cold to the other, we are invited to take the sensations, not simply as contradictory, but as the different effects (and so signs) of different ratios between motions in the object and motions in each hand. It is as if the corpuscularian hypothesis will allow us to understand how both sensations are veridical.[135] With respect to another possible case, that of the same object's producing different colour sensations in different people 'by the different Structure of our Organs', it is pointed out that each person 'would be able as regularly to distinguish things for his use by those Appearances, and understand, and signify those distinctions . . . as if the Appearances, or *Ideas* in his Mind . . . were exactly the same, with the *Ideas* in other Men's Minds'.[136] In both cases, Locke insists that the rôle of simple sensory ideas as true signs is not impugned.

The radical difference between Lockean and Cartesian ideas lies in more than Locke's jettisoning ideas of pure intellect. For the Lockean simple idea corresponds to Descartes's sensory *datum* or sensation, rather than to his compound sensory idea. Against the Cartesian notion of false ideas, Locke asserts that hypotheses about the unknown cause make no difference to the reference or truth of the idea: 'Nor do they become liable to any Imputation of *Falshood,* if the Mind (as in most Men I believe it does) judges these *Ideas* to be in the Things themselves.'[137] Moreover, Locke generalised the model to all simple ideas, making no distinction at the level of sensitive knowledge between spatial attributes and merely sensory qualities. His distinction between primary and secondary qualities is presented as a hypothesis about essence posterior to sensitive knowledge of existence; in this it is quite unlike the equivalent Cartesian distinction between, in Malebranche's terminology, *sentiments* and *idées*.

Here lies a main point of tension in the theory. For even to express the distinction between primary and secondary qualities requires a notion of representation which is not merely causal. When Locke writes of 'resemblance' between primary qualities and our ideas of them, and says that 'a Circle or Square are the same, whether in *Idea* or Existence', it seems that the comparison is between the intentional object and the real object, the thing as we perceive it and the thing as it is in itself.[138] Take, too, his assumption that the first or primitive use of the names of sensible qualities is for ideas rather than things: in the case of secondary qualities, there 'is nothing like our ideas, existing in the bodies themselves. They are in the bodies, we denominate from them, only a power to produce those sensations in us: and what is sweet, blue, or warm in idea, is but the certain bulk, figure, and motion of the insensible parts in the bodies themselves, which we call so.'[139] Here 'ideas' seem to be attributes of things as we perceive them, not 'like' those attributes as they are in themselves but nevertheless in some sense identical with them. The same entity is blue 'in idea' as is a power or, indeed, a certain aspect of corpuscular structure 'in the bodies', a way of putting it which avoids the hard distinction drawn even by Arnauld between the thing in the mind and the thing in reality. The suggestion that we denominate bodies 'blue' or the like 'from our ideas' reduces to the undeniable point that such words have their primary use for things as they are perceived, rather than for things as they exist independently of perception. All this makes Locke look like a 'direct realist'. Yet his causal model leads him to develop the point quite differently, as if it were as wrong to attribute colours to things as it would be to attribute pains to them: 'Why is whiteness and coldness in snow, and pain not, when it produces the one and the other idea in us?'[140] The analogy with pain, conceived of as a blank 'constitution of the mind',[141] is a crucial indicator of the model employed:

Though fire be call'd painful to the touch, whereby is signified the power of producing in us the idea of pain; yet it is denominated also light and hot; as if light and heat, were really something in the fire, more than a power to excite these ideas in us; and therefore are called qualities in, or of the fire.[142]

The sensation here is a blank effect indicating a power in the object to produce that effect in us, and the name which in its primary employment is the name of the sensation or indicative sign is transferred by a misconception to the power signified. The same misconception makes us call the power a 'quality'. These proposals imply that the name of a primary quality, although similarly employed in the first instance for a sensation having the same status as pain, can nevertheless be employed in just the same sense, if the corpuscularian hypothesis is correct, for an attribute of objects. The natural notion of a resemblance between intentional and real object becomes conflated with the deeply problematic notion of a resemblance between a sensation or 'constitution of the mind' and a physical attribute, between sign and *significatum*.

The same tendency, and the same ambivalence, appears in his famous treatment of the Molyneux problem. What starts as an attempt to explain visual depth in terms of a judgement 'beholding to experience, improvement and acquired no-tions' (rather than to Descartes's 'innate geometry') ends with what could be taken as an assumption that all that sensations of touch and visual sensations have in common is that they are effects of the same cause. The man blind from birth and made to see would not recognise the globe and the cube by sight because 'though he has obtain'd the experience of, how a globe, how a cube affects his touch; yet he has not yet attained the experience, that what affects his touch so or so, must affect his sight so or so.'[143] At the same time, it is difficult to accept that Locke seriously wished to jettison what he called 'ideas of divers senses', a conception which requires that what visual and tactual sensations have in common is that they present the same attributes of things, or share a common content.[144]

The fitful appearances in the *Essay* of what looks like direct realism, appearances strengthened by his having criticised Malebranche at some length,[145] have led to the view that Locke's notion of an idea was essentially the same as Arnauld's.[146] Yet his rejection of Arnauld's position was hardly less explicit than his opposition to Malebranche. Arnauld denounced a principle stated as follows: 'None of the bodies which the mind knows can be present to it in themselves. They must be present to it through images which represent them.' Yet that is just what Locke embraced: 'Since the things the mind contemplates, are none of them, besides itself, present to the understanding, 'tis necessary that something else, as a sign or representation of the thing it considers should be present to it.'[147] The reason for Locke's dissension was not naïveté, but his causal theory of representation.

Simple ideas are all true, but complexity brings the possibility of ideas which are false, inadequate, or 'fantastical'. Ideas of substances are at best framed on the basis of our experience of the concomitant sensible qualities of bodies, together with their powers sensibly to affect and be affected by other bodies. Then they are 'true' and 'real', but they are not 'adequate' or 'complete'[148] since they capture neither the unifying essences from which things' observable properties flow, nor all those indefinitely many properties themselves. Ideas of substances not so based on experience are 'false', 'barely imaginary', and 'fantastical', since (not knowing essences) we can only know from experience what combinations of properties are real possibilities.

In contrast to our ideas of substances, the ideas of modes and relations which constitute the subject-matter of the *a priori* sciences are (provided that they are not self-contradictory) 'true', 'real', and 'adequate' just because they are arbitrary constructions of the mind with no pretensions to correspond to reality. The 'essences' at the basis of such sciences are ideas put together by stipulative definition (the 'nominal essences' of modes are their 'real essences'), while the 'eternal truths' of mathematics and the like are eternal only because they are hypothetical

truths about such abstract ideas – not because they exist or have patterns 'antecedent to the understanding'.[149]

Thus Locke employs a distinction between simple and complex ideas in ways
radically opposed to that of Descartes. Simple ideas are not innate interpretive
principles, true because instilled by God, but phenomenally atomic building
blocks given in experience, dependable links with reality for just that reason.

Something should be said about Locke's famous critique of innate ideas and
knowledge, since it involves an insistence on a strong connexion between intentional content and consciousness. Sometimes Locke seems to assume that innatists
held the impossibly naive belief that children reflect on the maxims of logic 'with
their sucking-bottles, and their rattles,' but such heavy humour was part of an
attack on the dispositionalist theory. He was proposing that innatism only made
sense on an interpretation which made it obviously untenable. He was not
denying that there is a sense in which we can have ideas and knowledge dispositionally.[150] He was claiming that any intelligible conception of dispositional ideas
or principles presupposes their antecedent existence in consciousness and their
retention in the memory: 'If these words (*to be in the understanding*) have any
propriety, they signify to be understood. So that, to be in the understanding, and,
not to be understood; to be in the mind, and, never to be perceived, is all one, as
to say, any thing is, and is not, in the mind or understanding.'[151] The notion of
unperceived impressions is empty. That is because, if it were allowed, every
principle we are capable of perceiving to be true would have to be counted as
innate: 'Since if any one can be said to be in the mind, which it never yet knew,
it must only be because it is capable of knowing it; and so the mind is of all truths
it ever shall know.' The argument is extended to ideas, 'the parts, out of which
propositions are made': 'Whatever idea is in the mind, is either an actual perception, or else having been an actual perception, is so in the mind, that by the
memory it can be made an actual perception again.' Consequently, the only
grounds we could have for holding an idea innate would be if it were actually
perceived from birth or, when first perceived in this life, were perceived with the
'consciousness, that it was known or perceived before' characteristic of memory.
No idea passes either test.[152]

## XI. CONCLUSION: IDEAS AND IDEALISM

Around the end of the century a number of English writers – among them John
Sergeant (a follower of Thomas White, associate of Digby), Henry Lee, and
Edward Stillingfleet – found reason to attack the 'new way of ideas' on grounds

later to become commonplace. Yet, although they suggested that the very notion of an idea, whether Cartesian or Lockean, must mislead its users into a pernicious scepticism, it seems clear that what they really objected to was not so much the term itself as the real or hard distinction between idea and object, that is, between the intentional object and the real object. Yet, as the foregoing discussion has shown, not only does the mere notion of an idea not force such a distinction on its user, but denial of the distinction leads to its own difficulties. Like Digby, Sergeant insisted that 'the same *Ens* or Thing may have diverse *Manners* of existing; one Corporeal, the other Intellectual or Spiritual', arguing that exact likeness is identity in nature, even if not strict numerical identity.[153] Locke made the marginal comment here that the claim 'that a like is the same' is 'nonsense'.[154]

In any case, the same 'scepticism' as drew a hard distinction between idea and thing could be (and to some extent had been) stated just as directly in the terms of the traditional theory of objective being. There were scholastics who asserted firmly enough that logic treats things as they are conceived of, that is, subject to conceptual distinctions.[155] Among the new philosophers, Arnold Geulincx stressed that all knowledge concerns things as they are clothed in the forms of thought and language: for instance, mental affirmation itself projects onto things the forms of subject and predicate.[156] This was a generalisation of a point almost universally brought against Aristotelians by new philosophers, that they mistook the logical forms of our thought for real things. The theme was taken up even more vigorously by Richard Burthogge, whose fundamental epistemological principle is that things are known by us only as they are in our faculties (i.e., sense, imagination, and understanding), and that 'Every Faculty hath a hand, though not the sole hand, in making its immediate Object.'[157] Philosophers recognise that colours and smells are projected onto reality, yet the paradoxes of infinite divisibility show that extension itself is not conceived of as it really is.[158] Moreover, the understanding (i.e., the capacity to employ words in order to bring images to mind, or in place of them) equally 'doth *Pinn* its Notions upon Objects': substance, accidents, powers, similitude, whole, part, cause, effect etc. 'own no other kind of Existence than . . . an Objective one'.[159] To apprehend something through an attribute is to apprehend it imperfectly under a notion or aspect or *modus concipiendi,* and yet we can only apprehend things through their attributes.[160]

Burthogge rejected scepticism, however, since 'cogitable' beings may be evidently grounded in realities. Like Locke, he held that we are unquestionably aware in sensation that external realities are acting on us, summarily preempting sceptical argument from illusions and dreams.[161] Nevertheless, he represented us as separated from 'metaphysical truth' by our inability to get behind our notions. We have to be satisfied with 'logical truth', the defeasible criterion of which is the coherence and harmony of the comprehensive hypothesis we frame, in response to experience, in terms of our notions.[162] He understandably hailed Locke as an ally, but the fact is that he expounded his (as it may be called) 'idealist' view with hardly a mention of so-called ideas, employing much the same terminology as the 'anti-ideists' themselves.

Yet Locke's theory about ideas gave hostages to later idealism in at least one respect not already implicit in the traditional notion of objective being. For the Lockean, quasi-Epicurean view of the simple idea as indicative sign of its external cause did emphasise the separation of what is in the mind from what is in the object. It suited Berkeley, at any rate, to assume for at least some of the time that 'ideas of sense' exist in the mind as blank effects. In this context his claim is simply that their cause is not matter, but God. His attack on the distinction between primary and secondary qualities consequently made great play with Locke's analogy with pain, not to speak of the difficulties in the notion of 'resemblance' between an idea and its cause: 'From our ideas of sense the inference is good to a Power, Cause, Agent. But we may not infer that our ideas are like unto this Power, Cause or Active Being.'[163] Indeed, 'an idea can be like nothing but an idea; a colour or figure can be like nothing but another colour or figure.' Ideas can thus only 'copy and represent' other ideas.[164]

Molyneux's and Locke's conclusion about the man blind from birth was similarly exploited in order to drive a general wedge between ideas of sight and ideas of touch. Tactual extension and visual extension become distinct effects on the same level as colour.[165] In this context Berkeley proposed a radical reinterpretation of the notion of ideas as signs, taking visual ideas in particular to be reminiscent signs of future tactual ideas: 'Visible figures are marks of tangible figures, ... which by nature they are ordained to signify.'[166] This relationship, he argued, constitutes a language in the strict sense, both natural and arbitrary, and an infallible indication of a divine intelligence benevolently conveying the information we need for the purposes of life.[167]

On the other hand, Berkeley made equal play with the notion of objective being or 'existence in the mind'. Ideas are not for him modifications of the soul, but are in effect intentional objects, things-as-perceived.[168] So understanding them, he felt free to identify them on the one hand with sensible things or qualities, and on the other hand with sensations: 'Light and colours, heat and cold, extension and figures, in a word the things we see and feel, what are they but so many sensations, notions, ideas or impressions on the sense.'[169] The common view of colour supplied his paradigm: the mind is not coloured, but 'colours are on all hands taken to exist in it, and nowhere else.'[170] The mode of existence proper to sensible things is objective being: that is, their *esse* is *percipi*.[171] Like Spinoza and Leibniz, Berkeley brought the intentional relationship, unanalysed because presumed to be perspicuous and unanalysable, into the heart of his metaphysics. He did so by according it the generality of the traditional relationship between substance and accident, independent and dependent being. The Aristotelian doctrine that *being* is not a genus, and that 'exists' is predicated in its primary sense of substance and only analogically of accidents, became in Berkeley's system a claim about the relation between minds and bodies:

> *Thing* or *being* is the most general name of all, it comprehends under it two kinds entirely distinct and heterogeneous, and which have nothing in common but the name, to wit, *spirits* and *ideas.* The former are *active, indivisible substances:* the latter are *inert, fleeting, dependent beings,* which subsist not by themselves, but are supported by, or exist in minds or spiritual substances.[172]

It was just because his theory is structured by this complex relationship to traditional ontology that he could present it as a thesis about the senses or meanings of 'exists'.[173]

In denying matter, then, Berkeley was rejecting not simply an allegedly empty speculation as to the unknown cause of ideas, but the notion of the 'real' or 'formal' being of bodies which was traditionally opposed to their objective being: what has objective being, existence in the mind, cannot have any other kind of being. That is the force of his challenge to materialists, if they can, to 'conceive it possible for a sound, or figure, or motion, or colour, to exist without the mind, or unperceived'.[174] It is commonly supposed that he reduced what had previously been regarded as a triadic relation, between the perceiver, the idea, and the sensible object, to a diadic relation, between the perceiver and the idea, chopping off the sensible object.[175] Yet, on the standard view before Berkeley, an idea is not a 'third thing' at all, but something not distinct from the thought itself, or its form. Berkeley dispensed with the 'thing in itself' and formal reality precisely by identifying the idea, not with a thought, but with the sensible object itself, self-consciously 'changing . . . ideas into things'.[176] At the same time, he could claim that he was not so much denying the existence of anything as rejecting the notion of 'a twofold existence of the objects of sense, the one *intelligible,* or in the mind, the other *real* and without the mind'.[177]

In discarding formal existence, however, Berkeley retained a place for a kind of 'distinct' or 'exterior', even 'real' existence, developing in *Three Dialogues between Hylas and Philonous* earlier hints that 'these ideas or things by me perceived, either themselves or their archetypes, exist independently of my mind' in the mind of God. Here Berkeley seems to have been oddly reluctant to decide whether the idea in my mind is identical with the idea in God's mind, or merely resembles it. One motive for this reluctance is perhaps revealed in his discussion of Hylas's claim that 'the same idea which is in my mind, cannot be in yours, or any other mind.' The question is allegedly one of words: 'Some regarding the uniformness of what was perceived, might call it the *same* thing: others especially regarding the diversity of the persons who perceived, might choose the denomination of different things. But who sees not that all the dispute is about a word?' If the second alternative is chosen, then we 'may suppose an external archetype' common to both our ideas 'in that mind which comprehends all things'.[178]

In effect, Hylas's claim raises the question whether the intentional object of your thought can be identical with the intentional object of mine. On the standard notion of objective existence, that would depend on the question whether the intentional object (i.e., the idea) is identified with the real object. But Berkeley interprets the latter question as itself a question as to identity between ideas, ours and God's, and gives an answer reminiscent of the anti-ideists: there is no sharp distinction between likeness and identity. At the same time, he probably saw himself as offering an explanation of the traditional notion of a duality in the notion of an idea: roughly, to attach ideas to persons would be like taking them as *modes* of thought, while to treat them as detachable would be to take them as *objects* of thought.

The same conjunction of distinct models for intentionality – scholastic and Epicurean – as helped to structure Locke's epistemology and Berkeley's metaphysics was again to play a rôle in the arguments of Hume, whose impressions are both things as we perceive them and blank effects of unknown causes. But if it is thus possible to find in seventeenth-century treatments of intentionality some of the material of later idealism,[179] there was no single step or sequential series of steps which led inevitably, or by any kind of dialectical necessity, to the doctrines of Hume or Kant. The earlier arguments were intelligibly motivated, in their context, both by the wider purposes and stances, metaphysical or anti-dogmatic, of their authors, and by the problems (still with us) set by intentionality itself. When Hume, in *his* context, was drawn to launch a sceptical attack on the pretensions of philosophy, and Kant felt the need to come to terms with Hume's challenge, their ingenuity found weapons to hand.

NOTES

1 The theme of *Essays on the Intellectual Powers of Man* II.
2 On ideas in general, see Nuchelmans 1983; Yolton 1984; Ayers 1991, vol. 1, pp. 13–69 (focusing on Locke); Jolley 1990 (on Descartes, Malebranche, Leibniz): Cummins and Zoeller 1992. On Descartes, see Cronin 1966; Lennon 1974b; Costa 1983; Chappell 1986; Normore 1986; Ariew and Grene 1995. On Arnauld, see Laird 1920, pp. 1–14, and 1924; Lovejoy 1923, 1924; Cook 1974; Nadler 1989; Arnauld 1990, pp. 1–41 (S. Gaukroger's introduction). On Malebranche, see Nadler 1992. On Locke, see Ayers 1986; Chappell 1994b.
3 See Chapters 8 and 29 in this book. This theologically gratifying theory of universals combines Platonic, Aristotelian, and conceptualist elements.
4 Descartes was perhaps reacting to passages in Thomas Aquinas, e.g., *Summa th.* I q85 a1, in which Plato's theory of ideas was attributed to a failure to recognise the essential rôle of the body in cognition ('Plato vero, attendens solum ad immaterialium intellectus humani, non autem ad hoc quod est corpori quodammodo unitus, posuit objectum intellectus ideas separatas'). For vernacular usage, Urmson 1967 cites Rabelais and Montaigne; the *Oxford English Dictionary* cites, among others, the lexicographer John Bullokar: '*Idea,* the forme or figure of any thing conceived in the mind' (Bullokar 1616). On the history of the term, see Ariew and Grene 1995.
5 Resp. III (AT VII 181).
6 Gassendi 1658, vol. 1, p. 92 (Gassendi 1981, p. 3).
7 At least, according to some Thomists. See Nuchelmans 1983, p. 13.
8 In other words, it does not figure in cognition like a picture, which presents its object by being seen itself. See Thomas Aquinas, *Summa th.* I q85 a2, where it is argued that if the species or image was itself what is known, rather than a means to knowing something else, then the ancient view would be right that all appearances are true.
9 See Aristotle, *De Anima* 5 and 7 (430a20 and 431a1), for the principle that actual knowledge is identical with its object.
10 See Nuchelmans 1983, p. 15.
11 For discussion of these different scholastic theories, see Nuchelmans 1983, chap. 1; Kretzmann, Kenny, and Pinborg 1982, pp. 435–9.
12 See Suárez *Disp. met.* II.1.1: 'When we conceive of a man, the act which we perform in our minds . . . is called the "formal concept", while the man known and represented by that act is called the "objective concept". [The latter] is doubtless called a "concept" by an extrinsic denomination from the formal concept through which, as it is said, the "object" is conceived – and so it is properly [also] called "objective", because it is not conceived as a form intrinsically terminating the conception, but as an object and subject-matter with which the formal concept is concerned and towards which the mind's gaze is immediately directed.'
13 *Disp. met.* XXXI.2.7: 'Non est enim objectum movens, sed terminans tantum.'
14 *Disp. met.* XXXI.2.7: 'Tale [esse] quale per scientia cognoscitur.'
15 *Disp. met.* XXXI.2.8. Cf. XXXI.12.44–5.
16 *Disp. met.* XXXI.2.4.
17 *Disp. met.* XXXI.12.40: The eternal truths 'are not true because they are known by God, but rather they are thus known because they are true; otherwise no reason could be given why God would necessarily know them to be true. For if their truth came

forth from God himself, that would take place by means of God's will; hence it would not come forth of necessity, but voluntarily.'

18 *Disp. met.* XXXI.12.10; cf. XXXI.12.45.

19 Med. III (AT VII 36f).

20 'Ut prius omnes meas cogitationes in certa genera distribuam . . . inquiram.' 'All' is omitted from Descartes 1984–91.

21 See note 53.

22 Resp. II (AT VII 160).

23 Cf. Med. II (AT VII 33); Resp. III (AT VII 181 and 188).

24 The 'matter' unmentioned but presupposed here is the thought considered without regard to its content. At Resp. II (AT VII 161), he allows the mind to be 'informed' by 'ideas' in the corporeal imagination, but the latter are not, of course, the transmitted 'forms' of objects, but motions (or rather, for Descartes, such forms can only be motions). A complication with the present use of the matter–form distinction is that it can be applied to ideas themselves (rather than to the whole judgement, wish, or whatever), to distinguish acts of conceiving from the content conceived (as in Resp. IV, AT VII 232). For an entirely different interpretation of the Resp. II definition, see Jolly 1990.

25 Med. *Preface* (AT VII). The reading of this use of 'materially' is problematic. It may be drawn from the distinction between the 'material' (i.e., in matter, = real) and the 'intelligible' or 'intentional' existence of forms (in which case, the term is a curious one to use of a modification of the soul – but cf. 'metaphysical matter' at Resp. III, AT VII 175). More probably (as is assumed here), 'materially' is implicitly opposed to 'formally', as in the passages cited in notes 22 and 24. On either interpretation, 'formally' can either be opposed to, or mean effectively the same as, 'objectively', depending on which dichotomy is in use.

26 Resp. I (AT VII 102).

27 See Reg. XII (AT X 414); *Traité de l'Homme* (AT XI 176f). But cf. Resp. III (AT VII 181).

28 Reg. XII.

29 For Descartes's own use of this traditional distinction between distinctions, see *Princ.* I 60–2.

30 Resp. I (AT VII 102). Contrast the view of Petrus Aureolus, cited earlier in the chapter, and Suárez's assertion that the man represented by the formal concept of a man is called the objective *concept* 'by an extrinsic denomination from the formal concept'.

31 Obj. I (AT VII 92–4).

32 In the face of Gassendi's suggestion that to stress the reality of eternal essences is to raise up rivals to God. Obj. V (AT VII 319–21); Resp. V (AT VII 380–2).

33 For relevant Stoic theory, and its probable influence on Descartes, see Chapter 29, Sections I and III. For a seventeenth-century assimilation of Cartesian clear and distinct ideas with Stoic 'cataleptic' (apprehensive) impressions, see Burthogge 1678, s.67: 'Of late the old *Catalepsis* has seen the light again.'

34 *Princ.* I 45.

35 For a seventeenth-century discussion, see Smiglecius 1638, pp. 103–8.

36 Also argued by Arnauld, Obj IV (AT VII 206f).

37 Cf. Reg. XII (AT X 420–3); XIII (AT X 432).

38 Reg. XII (AT X 419); *Princ.* I 48. Cf. Nuchelmans 1983, p. 47.

39 The argument – Med. III (AT VII 43f), Obj. IV (AT VII 206f) and Resp. IV (AT VII 231–5) – is obscure in its details and structure. For various interpretations, see note 41.

40 See Med. VI (AT VII 82); *Princ.* I 70.

41 For discussion of the truth or falsity of sensory ideas, see Wilson 1978, pp. 101–119, and 1990; Beyssade 1992; Schmaltz 1992. Cf. note 53 in this chapter.

42 Obj. IV (AT VII 200–204).

43 *Dioptrique* IV (AT VI 112–14). The analogy was a Stoic one: 'What is seen is reported by means of the stretched air [between object and pupil], as by a walking-stick' (Diogenes Laertius 7.157).

44 Cf. *Dioptrique* VI (AT VI 130), where the correlation is 'ordained by nature'. *Princ.* IV 189–98 ascribes the correlation to the nature of mind and body.

45 *Dioptrique* VI (AT VI 130). Yet an earlier passage (to which this passage refers back) rejects the assumption that 'in order to have sensory perceptions, the soul must contemplate certain images transmitted by objects to the brain' only with a proviso: 'Or at any rate we must conceive the nature of these images in an entirely different manner from that of [Aristotelian philosophers]' (AT VI 112–13).

46 Descartes's account includes an explanation of size-constancy.

47 *Dioptrique* IV (AT VI 112f). But Descartes goes on to express a preference for the analogy with engravings, which, 'consisting simply of a little ink placed here and there on a piece of paper, . . . represent to us forests, towns, people'.

48 Med. VI (AT VII 73). Cf. *Traité de l'Homme* (AT XI 176f).

49 Gassendi assumed this view in arguing against Descartes that the *only* way a geometrical figure can be conceived may be by means of an extended corporeal image (Obj.V, AT VII 331f).

50 Cf. Med. VI (AT VII 81–3), *Princ.* I 70.

51 *Pass. âme* sec. 24.

52 *Pass. âme* sec. 23.

53 In Resp. VI (AT VII 436–9) Descartes distinguishes (1) the motion in the organs; (2) the immediate effects of this in the mind, i.e., perceptions of pain, colours, etc.; and (3) our habitual judgements about external things. For example, on reception of a sensation of colour, 'I judge that a stick located outside me is coloured; and . . . on the basis of the extension of the colour and its boundaries together with its position in relation to the parts of the brain, I make a rational [but now habitual] calculation about the size, shape and distance of the stick.' Here Descartes seems to endorse the conception of a corporeal datum immediately after distinguishing the sensory effect from the motion which causes it.

   With respect to the status of the datum, it has been argued by Margaret Wilson (Wilson 1978) that Descartes gave up the principle that all thoughts or all ideas have intentional objects in *Principia*. She cites *Princ.* I 71 (AT VIIIA 35), 'sensations (*sensus*) of tastes, smells . . . colours and so on . . . which represent nothing located outside thought'. Yet in context the relative clause seems to mean 'which in themselves, apart from the judgement of intellect, represent nothing outside thought'. Descartes was claiming that in a newborn baby the mind does not yet refer such sensations to external objects. (He also claimed, rather awkwardly, that the mind does not yet notice that perceived sizes, shapes, motions, etc. are any different from sensations, *despite* the former's being presented to it as things existing outside thought.) However, Descartes did not say that in our early infancy such sensations did not refer to anything at all, but that they were thoughts through which the mind had sensory awareness of what was happening to the body (*per quas ea sentiebat quae corpus afficiebant*). With respect to her further claim that this passage allows that some *ideas* lack intentionality, Wilson assumes (as elsewhere in her argument) that sensations are themselves straightforwardly ideas for

Descartes, whereas it seems that a sensory idea (except in the rare sense in which ideas are material) is a sensation *as referred to some object* (or at the very least, a thought of sensation). In the process of conscious sensation, a sensory datum enters into an idea (both as an object itself and, characteristically, as referred to an object), but (it seems) there are no objectless ideas. But the interpretive debate is not over: one important issue (see especially Beyssade 1992) concerns the relation between sensations and the perception of spatial properties, an issue in effect pursued by Malebranche (see sec. VIII, and note 101 in this chapter).

54  Resp. III (AT VII 189). Cf. *Notae in programma* (AT VIIIB 358).
55  Letter to Hyperaspistes, August 1641 (AT III 424). Cf. Resp. V (AT VII 375).
56  Cf. letter to Mersenne, 16 June 1641 (AT III 383).
57  For discussion, see Yolton 1956, chap. 2, although Yolton proposes that there are two forms of innatism, 'naive' as well as dispositionalist.
58  To Mersenne, 15 April 1630 (AT I 145). See Chapter 12 in this book for further discussion.
59  *Notae in programma* (AT VIIIB 358f).
60  Med. III (AT VII 44); Resp. III (AT VII 188).
61  Cf. Med. III (AT VII 44–45) where it is said that some elements of my idea of body, 'substance, duration, number and any others of that kind' could have been taken from my idea of myself, whereas extension and its modes 'are not formally contained in me' – if they are in me, it would be *eminenter* (as possible creations).
62  Digby (1645), Bk. I, p. 51.
63  Digby (1645), Bk. I, pp. 89–91.
64  Cf. Arnauld, *Des vrayes et fausses idées* xxxix, who contrasts extrinsic representation by material pictures etc. with intrinsic representation by thoughts, restricting the notion of objective existence to the latter: 'This way of being objectively in the mind is so peculiar to the mind and to thought, in that it constitutes the specific nature of the mind, that one would look in vain for anything like it in what is not mind and thought.'
65  Digby (1645), Bk. II, pp. 3–5. Presumably what lay behind his claim was the thought that we only distinguish the intentional object from the real object (the way we think of the thing from the way it is), if there is reason to say that the one is unlike the other.
66  Just the problem that the doctrine of forms might seem to some to solve.
67  See sec. XI, on Sergeant's anti-ideism and Berkeley's question whether two people can perceive the same idea.
68  *Lev.* xxxiv.
69  For the identification of such intentional objects with phantasms, see *De corp.* IV.xxv.3 and 9, and II.vii.2: 'spatium est phantasma rei existentis, quatenus existentis'. Cf. 'A triangle in the mind arises from a triangle we have seen' (Resp. III, AT VII 193).
70  Cf. Obj. V (AT VII 331f).
71  Although Gassendi's writings (including the late *Institutio Logica*) were mostly explicitly imagist and at least implicitly materialist, in the discussion of the soul in *Syntagma philosophicum,* he conceded the probability of an immaterial intellect. See Gassendi 1658, vol. 2, pp. 440a–446b.
72  Gassendi 1658, vol. 1, pp. 79–86; cf. Lucretius, *De Rerum Natura* IV 499ff.
73  *Eth.* II prop. 6.
74  *Eth.* II prop. 7.
75  *Eth.* II props. 32–5.
76  Cf. *Eth.* I prop. 15, *Eth.* II prop. 3, etc.
77  *Eth.* I ax. 4.

78 *Eth.* II prop. 16 and cors.

79 *Eth.* II prop. 17.

80 *Eth.* II prop. 35 schol.

81 So the famous remark, 'I am not merely present in my body as a sailor is present in a ship' (Med. VI, AT VII 81). Cf. *Pass. âme* secs. 30–44; Chapter 23 in this book.

82 This seems unlikely, given the Cartesians' sharp awareness of a causal process within the body from sense-organ to brain. As Descartes put it, it is the mind, not the eye, that sees.

83 *Eth.* II props 37–9. Cf. *Eth.* II prop. 13 (L2).

84 Cf. *De int. emen.* 101 (Geb. II 36). For Spinoza, all real beings are singular.

85 Cf. *Eth.* II prop. 49 schol.

86 This is the 'third kind of knowledge' of *Eth.* II prop. 40 schol. 2, applied to body and mind at *Eth.* V props. 22–31. Cf. Descartes's ascription of priority to clear and distinct perception in the particular case in the Letter to Clerselier on Gassendi's Objections (AT IXA 206).

87 For another proof of this, see *Eth.* II prop. 34.

88 *Rech.* III.2.1, Mal. *OC* I 413ff.

89 Cf. *Rech.* I.14, Mal. *OC* I 159.

90 *Rech.* III.2.6, Mal. *OC* I 437.

91 *Rech.* III.2.6, Mal. *OC* I 445.

92 *Eclaircissements* X.

93 *Rech.* III.2.7, Mal. *OC* I 451ff.

94 Arnauld (1986) chap. ii.

95 Arnauld (1986) chap. vii.

96 Arnauld (1986) chap. viii.

97 Arnauld (1986) chap. x.

98 Arnauld (1986) chap. xii.

99 *Rech.* I.10; VI.2.6; *Eclaircissements* VI.

100 Arnauld (1986) chaps. vi and xii.

101 Beyssade 1992 brings Descartes's view particularly close to that of Malebranche with the suggestion that, for Descartes, a sensation (such as that of colour) is an idea which possesses reference to an object, not only by being referred to an external cause, but by its integration with the idea of extension – a model which Beyssade sees as avoiding the possibility of sensations being non-intentional modes of thought, or existing otherwise than as ideas. However, there seems to be no clear statement of this proposal by Descartes.

102 For a useful treatment of this point, and of the whole dispute, see Nadler 1992.

103 I here prefer a traditional view of Leibniz's development to the interpretation (attractively argued for in Garber 1985 and accepted by Woolhouse 1993, but criticised by Sleigh 1990a, chap. 5, and Adams 1994, chap. 11) which posits that Leibniz did not arrive at an immaterialist metaphysics (i.e., without quasi-Aristotelian matter) until the 1690s. But cf. Chapter 23 in the present book.

104 See Leibniz's own account of the sources of his philosophy in *Systeme nouveau*, Ger. IV 477–87 (Leibniz 1989, pp. 138–45).

105 See *Nouv. ess.* IV.iii.6.

106 See the remarks on Spinoza in Leibniz 1854, pp. 44–6 (Leibniz 1989, pp. 277).

107 See *Syst. nouv.*, Ger. IV 482, where Leibniz, rejecting the analogy between biological individuals and natural machines, explains Cordemoy's atomism as a confused recognition of the need for unity unsatisfied by Cartesian mechanism.

108 On the question of whether Leibniz held matter to be reducible to immaterial individuals only during the later part of his philosophical career, see note 103.

109 See *Syst. nouv.*, sec. 14 (Ger. IV 484): 'Every substance [represents] the whole universe exactly and in its own way, . . . as if in a world apart, and as if there existed only God and itself.'

110 See *Disc. mét.*, sec. 33; *PNG* sec.4; Ger. II 74 and 90 (to Arnauld, 28 November/8 December 1686, 30 April 1687); Ger. II 172 (to de Volder, 24 March/3 April 1699).

111 *PNG*, sec. 4.

112 Admittedly, Leibniz's principle that every monad expresses the entire universe is the metaphysical equivalent of his physical principle that everything that occurs in any substance has an effect, however minute, on every other substance. At *Disc. mét.* sec. 14, although speaking of the order of 'phenomena' within us (and of 'the world which is in us'), he proposed that the truth-conditions of our perceptions might be regarded as satisfied in virtue of the internal order itself, without bothering about external objects, since it allows reliable prediction on the basis of past experience. His comment ('Nevertheless, it is very true that the perceptions or expressions of all substances mutually correspond in such a way that each one, carefully following certain reasons or laws it has observed, coincides with others doing the same') might suggest that, given law-like order within each monad and correspondence between them, the internal phenomena could be *qualitatively* any sort of modification whatsoever. The note, '*Quid sit Idea*' (Ger.VII 263–4), seems to treat natural (as opposed to conventional) representation as fundamentally a causal relation involving a one-one correspondence between the means of representation and the thing represented. Thus 'every complete effect represents a complete cause, for from knowledge of the effect I can always infer the cause.' Yet his metaphysics relies on there being more to representation than such correspondence.

113 See *Mon.* secs. 8–14. This is the claim denied by Locke and Kant.

114 The case is comparable to the recently identified phenomenon of 'blindsight'.

115 Set out in 1686 at Ger. IV 422–26 ('*Meditationes de cognitione, veritate, et ideis*').

116 See *Nouv. ess.* IV.vi.7.

117 See *Mon.* secs. 36–7; Leibniz 1948, pp. 302–3 (Leibniz 1989, p. 28–9).

118 See Leibniz 1982–91, vol. 8, p. 1999 (Leibniz 1989, p. 32) ('Primae veritates'); Ger. II 277–8 (to de Volder, 1704 or 1705) There is an echo of Descartes, Resp. IV (AT VII 220–3), despite his different conclusions.

119 *Disc. mét.*, sec. 24.

120 *Mon.*, sec. 43.

121 Leibniz 1854, pp. 44–6 (Leibniz 1989, p. 277).

122 *Disc. mét.* secs. 28–9.

123 *Disc. mét.* sec. 26.

124 See *Nouv. ess.*, Preface.

125 Cf. *Mon.*, sec. 30; *PNG*, sec. 5.

126 Even the distinction between action and passion is so explained: in change 'the substance which immediately passes to a . . . more perfect expression [of the universe] exercises its power and *acts*, and the subject which passes to a lesser degree shows its weakness and is *acted upon*' (*Disc. mét.*, sec. 15).

127 *Mon.* sec. 61.

128 *Ess.* I.i.2.

129 *Ess.* IV.iv.4.

130 *Ess.* II.xxxi.2; cf. II.xxx.2, II.xxxii.14.

131 I.e., whenever 'the Mind refers any of its ideas to any thing extraneous to them, they are capable to be called true or false' (*Ess.* II.xxxii.4). The other sense is in relation to other people's (in particular, received) ideas.

132 *Ess.* II.xxxii.14.

133 Cf. *Ess.* IV.xxi.4: 'There are two sorts of signs commonly made use of, *viz.* ideas and words'; *Ess.* IV.v.2: 'Logick; the business whereof is to consider the nature of signs, the mind makes use of for the understanding of things, or conveying its thoughts to others.' Locke's conception of simple ideas as natural signs of their causes is closely connected to his account of sensitive knowledge and answer to the sceptic of the senses. My awareness as I look at a page that something is causing in me the idea (sensation) conventionally associated with the name 'white' constitutes certain knowledge of the existence of the quality which that idea signifies, whatever that quality may be as it is in the object. Thus we have sensitive knowledge of the *existence* of things without knowledge of their *essence*. No inference or reasoned interpretation is involved in 'sensitive knowledge', just because the signification of the simple idea is automatically determined by the natural causal relation.

134 There are particular resonances: e.g., the claim at *Ess.* IV.xi.3 that scepticism of the senses is self-destructive echoes Lucretius, *De rerum natura* IV, 474–99; while IV.xi.2 is close to a claim of the Stoic Chrysippus. Cf. Ayers 1991, vol. 1, pp. 155, 158–9, and 320; and 1994.

135 *Ess.* II.viii.21. The argument implies that heat regarded as 'in the object' is relative to the circumstances of perception. Gassendi (*Syntagma philosophicum* Bk. I, pt. II.v) argued that the same thing's appearing different to different observers is no more a ground for scepticism than the sun's melting some things and hardening others. The different effects correspond to different mechanical relations that the same thing has to organs of sense in different conditions. Contrary sensations are not really contrary, for each is a true sign of a different state of affairs. Again, the argument suggests that the true object of a sensation, whatever beliefs it naturally stimulates, is the interaction between perceiver and object. Since sensation is just such interaction, all sensations are true. Unlike Locke, however, Gassendi concluded here that perceptual knowledge involves reasoned interpretation: with respect to the belief it stimulates, 'the sign may not be reliable, but reason, which is superior to the senses, can correct the perception of the senses, so that it will not accept a sign from the senses unless it has been corrected, and then at last it deliberates, or reaches its judgement of the thing.'

136 *Ess.* II.xxxii.15.

137 *Ess.* II.xxxii.14. At *Le Monde,* chap. I (AT XI 4), Descartes uses the notion of a sign quite differently in explaining sensation: as words can be signs of (and so make us think of) things very different from themselves, so motion in the eye may signify, and stimulate sensory images of, light.

138 *Ess.* II.viii.7, 15, 18 etc.

139 *Ess.* II.viii.15.

140 *Ess.* II.viii.15f.

141 *Ess.* II.xx.2.

142 *Ess.* II.xxxi.2.

143 *Ess.* II.ix.8.

144 *Ess.* II.v. For recent discussion, see Lievers 1992; Ayers 1991, vol. 1, pp. 65–6; Bolton 1994.

145 In *An Examination of P. Malebranche's Opinion of seeing all things in God* (Locke 1823, vol. 9, pp. 211–55).

146 See Yolton 1984.

147 Arnauld 1986, chap. iv; *Ess.* IV.xxi.4. Compare too Arnauld's denial, and Locke's assertion, that the mind is like a camera obscura: Arnauld 1986, chap. v, *Ess.* II.xi.17.

148 For their truth, see *Ess.* II.xxxii.18 and 22–5 (but they are always false if 'looked upon as the Representations of the unknown Essences of Things').

149 *Ess.* IV.xii.14.

150 He discussed both possibilities expressly, the former under the heading of the 'retention' of ideas, the latter under 'habitual knowledge' (*Ess.* II.x.2; IV.i.8f).

151 *Ess.* I.ii.5.

152 *Ess.* I.iv.20.

153 Sergeant 1696, p. 3, and 1697, pp. 20–36; both cited by Yolton 1956, chap. 3. For more on Digby and Sergeant, see Mercer 1993.

154 See Yolton 1951, 1956, for an overview of anti-ideism.

155 Smiglecius 1638 opens with the statement that logic deals with *entia rationis,* things as distinguished by thought.

156 *Logica and Metaphysica ad mentem Peripateticum* (Geulincx 1891–3, vol. 2). For discussion, Nuchelmans 1983, pp. 114–17.

157 Burthogge 1678, pp. 12–15.

158 Burthogge 1678, p. 40.

159 Burthogge 1694, pp. 58ff, and 1678, p. 15.

160 In *Organum,* the example of conceiving of God inadequately through his attributes plays an important rôle, but in *Essay* the point about substance and attribute is cashed out in more Lockean terms (Burthogge 1678, pp. 28–35; Burthogge 1694, pp. 56–7, 67–8).

161 Although both are 'real' in having causes outside the mind, in illusions the causes are unusual, while in dreaming they are 'Causes only, and not Objects as well as Causes' (Burthogge 1694, pp. 78–80).

162 Burthogge 1678, pp. 47–60. For more on Burthogge, see Lennon 1993, pp. 187–9; Yolton 1956 *passim*; Chapter 29, Section II, in this volume.

163 *Th. Vis. Vind.,* sec. 11.

164 *Pr. Hum. Kn.* I, secs. 33, 41.

165 *New Th. Vis.,* secs. 49–138.

166 *New Th.Vis.,* sec. 140. What is rejected is Locke's notion of ideas of sense as 'notes or images referred to *things* or *archetypes* existing without the mind' (*Pr. Hum. Kn.* I, sec. 87).

167 This thesis is most fully worked out in *Alciphron* IV.

168 *Pr. Hum. Kn.* I, sec. 49.

169 *Pr. Hum. Kn.* I, sec. 5.

170 *Pr. Hum. Kn.* I, sec. 49.

171 *Pr. Hum. Kn.* I, sec. 4.

172 *Pr. Hum. Kn.* I, sec. 89.

173 See Ayers 1986.

174 *Pr. Hum. Kn.* I, sec. 22.

175 Cf. Luce 1968, p. 289: 'He maintained a two-term theory of perception, and was up against thinkers . . . who held a three-term theory and put reality outside the mind.'

176 *3 Dial.,* III (Berkeley 1948–57, vol. 2, p. 244).

177 *Pr. Hum. Kn.* I, sec. 86.

178 *3 Dial.,* III (Berkeley 1948–57, vol. 2, pp. 247–8).

179 Of course, there is much more to say about this. An important source for Kant, for example, was Leibniz's conception of space as the form of perception.

# 31

# PROBABILITY AND EVIDENCE

### LORRAINE DASTON

## I. INTRODUCTION

At the outset of the *Nicomachean Ethics,* Aristotle cautioned against confusing the kind of evidence and degree of certainty suitable to various disciplines: 'For it is the mark of an educated man to look for precision in each class of things just so far as the nature of the subject admits: it is evidently equally foolish to accept probable reasoning from a mathematician and to demand from a rhetorician demonstrative proofs.'[1] Seventeenth-century thinkers from the most varied backgrounds and with the most varied objectives made Aristotle's warning their motto but turned it to quite non-Aristotelian ends. Theologians, jurists, historians, and natural philosophers vastly expanded the realm of the probable at the expense of that of the demonstrative and denied the possibility of irrefragable certainty to all disciplines except mathematics and perhaps metaphysics. Whereas Aristotle had hoped for sciences of, *inter alia,* physics and astronomy worthy of the name, grounded in demonstration, the seventeenth-century admirers of the introduction to the *Nicomachean Ethics* doubted that any part of natural philosophy could aspire to such certainty. However, theirs was not a counsel of despair. On the contrary, they regarded contemporary developments in natural philosophy as marked advances over scholastic achievements. They were able simultaneously to demote the new physics to the status of probable knowledge *and* to affirm its superiority to Aristotelian physics because they understood 'probable' in a new way.

In the course of the seventeenth century, the meaning of rational action and belief – and the relationship between the two – changed dramatically. In response to the intellectual crisis created by the revival of the sceptical philosophy and the impasse of Reformation–Counter-Reformation polemics, a continuum of degrees of probability opened up between the philosophical poles of truth and falsehood, episteme and doxa, certainty and ignorance. By defining positions on that continuum, it became possible to be both rational *and* less than certain in matters of contemplation, as well as action. Theologians and natural philosophers, as well as merchants and lawyers, came to couch their arguments in terms of probabilities rather than demonstrations. The very word 'probability' shifted its meaning from an opinion warranted by authority to a degree of belief (or of certainty) proportioned to evidence. Probabilities were held to compel the reasonable man to act — to invest in a risky but lucrative business venture, to undergo a hazardous cure for a worse ailment, and to believe — in God, in the mechanical hypothesis, in the guilt of the accused. These new-style probabilities could be roughly ordered (and later, it was claimed, quantified) and compared; they mirrored both the evidence of testimony and of things; and they in no way implied a rôle for chance in the world. On the contrary, the mathematical probabilists at least were to a man metaphysical determinists of the staunchest sort, insisting that probabilities measured the extent of human ignorance, not the unsteadiness of the causal order.

This essay addresses four major aspects of the new probabilism of the seventeenth century: first, the 'prehistory' of seventeenth-century probabilistic notions; second, how and why the meaning of probability changed and expanded to describe a new kind of provisional rationality; third, the origins and applications of mathematical probabilism; and fourth, the meaning of probability at the turn of the eighteenth century. The first section deals with pre–seventeenth-century notions of chance, credibility, warranted belief, statistical frequencies, and probability so called. The second shows how Hugo Grotius, William Chillingworth, Marin Mersenne, and others responded to the Pyrrhonist challenge and, indirectly, to the stalemated controversy between Catholics and Protestants with a 'mitigated scepticism' that set new standards for rational belief and action. The third describes how the earliest formulations of mathematical probability came to be closely associated with the new reasonableness in the work of Blaise Pascal, Pierre Fermat, and Christiaan Huygens, and how this association influenced the applications of the fledgling mathematical theory. The final section examines the meaning of probability in the culminating work of seventeenth-century probabilism, Jakob Bernoulli's *Ars conjectandi* (1713), and explains the link between probabilism and determinism in this period. With the exception of Bernoulli and Leibniz, whose works were published posthumously, I shall not venture past 1700, except by way of fleeting reference.

## II. THE PREHISTORY OF PROBABILITY

Studies of the prehistory of probability have proliferated in recent years, and scholars have discovered intimations of the concept in pursuits as various as Talmudic law and Renaissance medicine and astrology.[2] Although the setting of odds in a twelfth-century gamble or the rhetorical precepts of Cicero look like

cousins of the post-seventeenth-century notion of probability, the resemblance is
at best partial, and visible only with 20/20 hindsight. The historical fact remains
that none of these promising candidates blossomed into a full-fledged philosophical and mathematical account of probability until circa 1650. The search for the
roots of these developments is plagued by the disjunction between word and thing
in the earlier period: there are both concepts that are similar to what we now
mean by 'probability' and words cognate to 'probability', but they seldom intersect
in the classical, mediaeval, and Renaissance literature.

For example, Aristotle discusses what might be translated as 'chance' (*tyche*) and
'probability' (*endoxa*), but both deviate significantly from our senses of these words.
For Aristotle, chance is primarily the absence of purpose; that is, the absence of
final causes rather than causes in general. This is why chance and (blind) necessity
sometimes figure as synonyms for Aristotle, as in his criticism of Empedocles'
theory of organic forms.[3] Moreover, chance for Aristotle is closely associated with
fortune and with rare events, for it is the nature of good or bad fortune to baffle
'reasonable expectation'.[4] In contrast, reasonable expectation is the essence of the
probable (*eikos*) for Aristotle, and this is why it can serve as the basis for rhetorical
proofs, or enthymemes: 'A probability is a thing that happens for the most part.'[5]
*Eikos* goes hand in hand with *endoxa* – both of which are commonly translated
with the English 'probable' – which latter Aristotle defines as opinions 'accepted
by everyone or by the majority or by the wise – i.e. by all, or by the majority, or
by the most notable and reputable of them'.[6] All of these words and usages capture
some aspect of our 'probability', but in such disparate contexts turned to such
alien ends that only a willful distortion of Aristotle's thought can turn them into a
single, recognisable concept.

The story of seventeenth-century probability consists not only in fusing these
distinct elements, but also in modifying some and eliminating others altogether.
The architects of this new notion of probability were heirs to at least four distinct
intellectual traditions: (1) that of antiquity, best known through the rhetorical
works of Aristotle, Cicero, and various Arabic and Latin commentators; (2)
Thomas Aquinas's influential discussion of the probability of authority (cf. Aristotle's *endoxa*), from which stemmed the theological doctrine of probabilism and its
several variants; (3) the half-folk, half-learned teachings about fortune, crystallised
by Boethius's *De consolatione philosophiae* (A.D. *c.* 520) for centuries' worth of
mediaeval readers; and (4) the hierarchy of proofs evolved by Roman and canon
jurists after the official abolition of the trial by ordeal by the Lateran Council of
1215. In addition to this theoretical background, practical risk-taking in the form
of maritime insurance, gambling, annuities, and other so-called aleatory contracts

presented seventeenth-century thinkers with models for understanding chance. None of these elements was decisive in shaping the seventeenth-century reformulation of probability, but all played their part, and the writings of the new school of probabilists – those of mathematicians such as Blaise Pascal and Jakob Bernoulli, as well as those of philosophers such as John Locke and G. W. Leibniz – are not fully intelligible without them. Therefore, I shall very briefly review them before broaching the seventeenth century proper.

As Aristotle indicated in the passage from the *Nicomachean Ethics* cited earlier, rhetoric was the true home of the probable for classical authors, and it continued to be so for the mediaeval scholars who learned from them. Just as rhetoric was opposed to geometry, the subjects of the trivium to those of the quadrivium, so probable arguments were opposed to demonstrative proofs. Cicero's *De inventione* introduces the notion of the probable (*probabile*) in contradistinction to that of the necessary and distinguishes several related but distinct meanings of the word: that 'which for the most part usually comes to pass' (e.g., mothers love their sons); that 'which is a part of the ordinary beliefs of mankind' (e.g., philosophers are atheists); that which contains an element of analogy to either frequent or commonly believed statements (e.g., just as ships require a harbor for safety, so one friend requires integrity in another for trust).[7] Because the chief aim of rhetoric is persuasion, the difference between the evidentiary weight of things which happen frequently and that of things which are proverbial is of tertiary concern to Cicero and his successors. We are here in the realm of doxa, not episteme. However, Cicero does discern shades of probative force in inferences drawn from various kinds of sensory 'signs', which may imply a conclusion necessarily (as fever implies an illness); probably (as flight from the scene of a murder with an unsheathed bloody sword implies guilt); or even more weakly (as pallor implies pregnancy).[8] Late seventeenth-century works still testify to the longevity of this rhetorical tradition in probability: in the Port-Royal *Logique* (1662), Antoine Arnauld and Pierre Nicole appeal not only to these antique categories, but to the very examples invoked by Aristotle and Cicero.[9]

Thomas Aquinas's elaboration of the sense of probability as opinion formed the basis of the theological doctrine of probabilities that was to culminate in (or deteriorate into) the Jesuit casuistry so bitterly attacked by Pascal in *Les provinciales* (1657). Thomas's problem was a special case of persuasion: the choice among, and reconciliation of, conflicting authorities – a pressing problem by the thirteenth century for Catholic intellectuals faced with a large and growing body of translations from the Greek and Arabic. His solution depends upon the shared etymology of probability, probity, and proof, all stemming from the root '*probatio*'. Probability means an opinion warranted by authority, and such probabilities vary in probative force according to the probity of the authority.[10] This would suggest that it is possible for a 'probable' opinion in Thomas's sense to be in fact false, for even Homer nods, although Thomas does not explicitly admit this. His probable opinions are also wholly divorced from the frequency interpretation of the classical rhetoricians, since what happens rarely could nonetheless be probable in that it does occasionally come to pass.[11]

Although the word 'probabilism' surfaces only in the second half of the seventeenth century, its sense still derives from the Thomistic association of probability with reasonable opinion, for it designates the moral doctrine that accepts the probable opinion of a theological authority as a rule of conduct, even if other, more weighty, authorities contest it. The doctrine is considerably older than the word, having blossomed earlier in the casuist works of Cajetan, François de Vitoria, and others in the sixteenth century. In this confessional literature, 'probable' came to mean 'a plausible opinion, capable of being proved',[12] but by the early seventeenth century the emphasis had shifted from the possibility of proof to the futility of seeking certainty in the moral realm. The Jesuits who taught this brand of probabilism in Catholic institutions throughout Europe in the late sixteenth and early seventeenth centuries echoed Aristotle's sentiments in the *Nicomachean Ethics* concerning the human impossibility of arriving at demonstrations in moral matters, and were pessimistic even about distinguishing more from less probable opinions. It was this laxity that Pascal ridiculed, when he accused certain learned Jesuits of permitting their Indian and Chinese converts to practise idolatry under the guise of 'la doctrine des opinions probables'. But even Pascal's unflattering portrait of Jesuit probabilism in *Les provinciales* never denied the link between a probable opinion and the reasons for holding it: 'An opinion is called "probable" when it is founded upon reasons worthy of consideration . . . for a man particularly dedicated to a studious life does not attach himself to an opinion without being attracted to it by a good and sufficient reason.'[13] The difficulty and, in the case of the Jesuit confessors, opportunity for corruption arose from the relative weighting of several such probable opinions, each supported by plausible reasoning of some learned authority, but none in agreement with the others.

Thus, the Thomist definition of 'probability' as opinion warranted by authority remained the principal sense of the word well into the seventeenth century and lingered even thereafter.[14] There was, however, a technical legal meaning of 'probability' (*probabilitas*) that became increasingly important in the fifteenth and sixteenth centuries, and that indelibly stamped the new probabilism of the seventeenth century. To some extent, the legal doctrine of probabilities undertook the relative weighting of reasons or 'proofs' that was to baffle the Jesuit moralists. When the Fourth Lateran Council abolished the trial by ordeal in 1215, it left jurists with a perplexing problem. Previously, God Himself had presumably vouchsafed the certainty of the verdict that condemned the accused to death. How could fallible mortals presume to judge of life and death with the same certainty?[15] Starting in northern Italy in the thirteenth century, and spreading to France and later to Germany by the fifteenth and sixteenth centuries, the hierarchy of proofs of Roman and canon law solved this problem by requiring a strictly regulated quantity and quality of evidence for conviction of a capital crime. Only 'full' or 'perfect' proofs – the corroborative testimony of two unimpeachable witnesses or a confession – could convict the accused with sufficient certainty. Criminal procedures demanded a proof that was 'full, complete, and clear as noonday'.[16] Because so-called secret crimes such as adultery, heresy, and theft by night lacked witnesses by their very nature, and because even public crimes might lack witnesses unimpeached by age, sex, or relation to the accused, continental courts were driven to regular recourse to confessions extracted by torture in the name of certainty.

However, judges could not order torture with impunity: even here judicial discretion was tightly reined in by rules that specified what kind of circumstantial evidence warranted which degree of suspicion. Taking the rhetorical doctrine of signs as their departure point, late mediaeval jurists constructed a baroque system of categories and weightings of evidence: 'violent' presumptions (e.g., blood-stained clothing), 'close' indices (e.g., testimony of only one witness), 'remote' indices (e.g., a quaver in the voice of the defendant) – all of these 'probabilities' could be summed after a fashion to constrain a judge's opinion or to oblige him to act.[17] Within this 'arithmetic of proof', for example, the testimony of a minor or of a woman might count only a half or one-third that of a fully-qualified male witness. This system survived on the continent well into the eighteenth century, permitting abuses of the sort Voltaire attacked in the Jean Calas case, in which a string of hearsay, rumors, and other remote indices, each valued at one-eighth or one-sixteenth, was summed into the full proof necessary for conviction.[18]

These indices, as they were collectively designated, were imperfect proofs, since they were inferences to causes 'whose effects are uncertain', in contrast to the demonstrations of the sciences in which truths 'necessarily follow, one from another'. Jurists readily admitted that the legal definition of certainty – that is, the corroborative and independent testimony of two unimpeachable witnesses – was a conventional sort of certainty, of a sort different from demonstrative certainty in the sciences.[19] In this regard, legal probabilities were akin to the probabilities of rhetoric and casuistry, in being explicitly opposed to the apodictic certainty of scientific demonstration. But unlike rhetorical and casuist probabilities, legal probabilities were finely subdivided according to the 'proofs' or evidence that engendered them, and proportioned accordingly. That is, legal probabilities came in degrees, and it was even possible to sum various sorts of indices like fractions to constitute a full proof. Of course, the way-stations between doubt and certainty in the mind of the judge hardly exhausted the full mathematical continuum, and the fractional weightings assigned to various kinds of evidence and witnesses were largely arbitrary. Nonetheless, both distinctive aspects of legal probabilities played a rôle in early formulations of mathematical probability.

None of these probabilities was primarily about what we would now call statistical frequencies, although rhetoricians since Aristotle and Cicero had assumed as a matter of course that probable opinion generally follows what happens most of the time, and jurists invoked the 'ordinary' or 'common' to establish presumptions in court. These appeals to belief based on common experience came to be seen as inherently statistical only with Hume's analysis of repeated, identical sensations brightening an idea to the point that belief was irresistible.[20] Empiricism was not a sufficient condition for such a statistical treatment of belief, for even Locke, despite his suggestive account of associations of ideas strengthened by frequently repeated sensations,[21] remained close to the traditional view that it was chiefly the quality rather than the quantity of evidence that mattered. One moral of Locke's King of Siam parable was that not only the constancy and repetition of experience but also its amplitude and variety count in the formation of reasonable beliefs. Although the Dutch ambassador's tales of winter ice-skating on frozen canals conflicted with the unexceptioned experience of generations of Siamese that water is always fluid, the king was nonetheless hasty in dismissing the ambassador as a liar.[22] Similarly, the strong presumption created by testimony that the accused had been seen fleeing the scene of the murder with an unsheathed bloody sword stemmed from reasoning about causes and effects, not about how many times similar testimony had led to convictions. Even the lore of signs, both rhetorical and medical, was as much about the causal connexion between fever and illness as it was about their constant conjunction. After all, constant conjunction alone could hardly have persuaded Aristotle that some signs were 'necessary', in the sense that they could serve as the basis for deduction.[23]

Nor do statistics turn up in an actuarial context before the late seventeenth century, and even then, insurers were notably reluctant to make use of the data and mathematics created for them. Despite the expansion of maritime insurance in the commercial centres of Barcelona, Genoa, Venice, Bruges, Amsterdam, and London from the fifteenth century onward, there is no evidence that insurers ever collected statistics on shipwrecks and other casualties. Indeed, their approach was positively anti-statistical, in that they emphasised the particulars of the captain's integrity, the seaworthiness of the ship, the skill of the crew, the nature of the cargo, the latest news about pirates and warships en route. The absence of any but the roughest correlation between age and annuity prices during this period, and the frequent admonitions to submit each case to a prudent judge, suggest a similarly anti-statistical attitude towards mortality. In an age of notoriously unstable conditions, of plague and piracy, it may not have been unreasonable to fix upon the individual case in all its particularity, rather than to extrapolate from statistics gathered from past experience of dubious relevance. And even if life and seaman-ship had been more settled, the complexity of choosing the correct dependent variable(s) out of a welter of possibilities – mortality correlates with age but also with sex and locale; shipwrecks depend on the season but also on the route – was perhaps also an obstacle to the use of actuarial statistics.[24] However, if insurance and annuity practices did not give rise to statistical probabilities, the legal category to which such agreements belonged, the aleatory contract, did provide an important model for the earliest mathematical formulations of probability.

Before 1660, there was thus very little connexion between the probabilities of belief and statistical frequencies. What statistics existed were demographic, gathered since the mid sixteenth century for either legal or medical purposes – to confirm age or condition, or to monitor the advance of the plague.[25] These statistics were intended as evidence, in both the narrow legal sense of documentary proof and the epidemiological sense of tracking a disease. But they were not probabilistic in the sense that they correlated one variable with the likelihood of another (bills of mortality did not register age at death until 1728, and were therefore of limited utility in constructing life tables), or even in the more primitive sense of being expressed as a proportion (e.g., number of female births to total number of births; number of deaths due to plague to total number of deaths).

Ideas about chance also seldom intersected with those about probability until the seventeenth century. Aside from Aristotle, the chief source of ideas about chance and fortune throughout the Middle Ages was Boethius's *De consolatione philosophiae* (Book II), in which fortune enters in a primarily moral context. What philosophy must console Boethius for is the apparently unjust distribution of 'external' goods such as wealth, health, glory, and beauty to the undeserving by fickle fortune. Philosophy counsels him that just because fortune is so changeable, the wise man would do best to fix his attention upon those goods, such as learning and virtue, which lie within the sphere of his control. Although fortune was not entirely divorced from providence in the mediaeval Christian literature, she was predominantly opposed both to virtue and to rationality, as the long iconographic tradition of the wheel testifies.[26] In contrast to Boethius and to many of the humanists, Machiavelli accepts the inevitability of fortune in a life of action and grants that 'Fortune is the mistrisse of one halfe of our actions', but for him she is still the foe of deliberation and rational calculation: 'I think it is true, that it is better to be heady than wary; because Fortune is a mistresse; and it is necessary, to keep her in obedience to ruffle and force her: and we see, that she suffers her self rather to be mastered by those, than by others that proceed coldly.'[27] Far from being allied with the probabilities of evidence and belief, chance resists reason in both contemplation and action.

## III. THE NEW REASONABLENESS

Out of these disparate notions of warranted opinion, legal proof, demographic data, and mutable chance, seventeenth-century writers fashioned first a philosophical and, eventually, a mathematical theory of probability (or 'doctrine of chances', '*ars conjectandi*', '*géométrie de hasard*', or '*calcul des probabilités*', as it was variously called). The common context which drew these distinct, and sometimes opposed notions together was a polemical one, out of which emerged a new standard of rationality in religion, philosophy, and natural philosophy. This 'reasonableness', as the new brand of rationality was sometimes called, was distinctive in at least three respects: first, it abandoned the ideal of absolute certainty for all human pursuits except mathematics; second, it created an ordered scale (though not a full continuum) of 'certainties' matched to subject matter and evidence; and third, it reversed the justificatory rôles of action and belief, making what we think consistent with what we do, rather than the other way around.

Two controversies intersected to produce the new reasonableness: the Reformation–Counter-Reformation dispute over the foundations of Christian faith, and the revival of academic scepticism in the sixteenth century, with its sharp challenge to all knowledge claims. In the one case, Catholic apologists insisted upon the ambiguity of scripture, while their Protestant opponents attacked the trustworthiness of ecclesiastical tradition as a guide to its meaning. The arguments of both sides turned out to be too powerful, subverting the possibility of any interpretive assumptions whatsoever, one's own as well as those of one's adversaries. In the other case, Michel de Montaigne, Pierre Charron, François de la Mothe le Vayer, and others reformulated the teachings of Sextus Empiricus (A.D. fl. 200) into a devastating attack on the possibility of all knowledge, including that deriving from sense perception and mathematical demonstration. Descartes' *Meditationes* (1641) begins with a sceptical reverie in this extreme vein. The impact of these clashes has been amply documented through the mid seventeenth century, particularly in France and England.[28] I will therefore restrict myself to a brief account of one important response to this theological and epistemological impasse, sometimes described as 'mitigated' or 'constructive' scepticism.

The moderate or constructive sceptics burst upon the philosophical scene *circa* 1625 and can be found on both sides of the confessional divide, numbering Marin Mersenne and Pierre Gassendi among the Catholics, and Hugo Grotius and William Chillingworth among the Protestants. Their strategy was to steer a middle course between religious fideism and philosophical dogmatism, on the one hand, and corrosive scepticism on the other. They accepted the sceptical claim that all or most of our knowledge falls short of complete certainty (Mersenne made a pointed exception for mathematics),[29] but refused to succumb to Pyrrhonism. Rather, they cheerfully turned to the conduct of daily life, in which we often risk all that is dear to us on an uncertain venture. Consistency demands, so they argued, that we follow the same implicit precepts in religion and philosophy, risking belief for a doctrine of comparable likelihood. Many followed Grotius's example in *De veritate religionis christianae* (1627) in citing Aristotle's opening remarks to the *Nicomachean Ethics* with approval,[30] but went further than Aristotle in extending the word 'certainty' to just those domains in which Aristotle had abandoned it. This meant stretching the meaning of the word 'certainty' to include not only the 'absolute' or 'metaphysical' certainty of mathematical demonstration, but also the merely 'moral certainty' of matters of fact and most of human affairs. Some moderate sceptics, such as Robert Boyle and John Wilkins, interpolated another, 'physical', degree of certainty between the moral and mathematical for sensory evidence, and the nomenclature denoting these ordered stages varied slightly from author to author. But their message was the same: by glorifying what the sceptics had rejected as dubious with the title of certainty, albeit a dilute variety of certainty, the moderates emphasised the rationality of believing as well as acting upon a 'proof cogent in its kind, or some concurrence of probabilities'.[31]

This style of reasoning surfaced first in religious apologetics but very quickly spread to natural philosophy, and, at least in England, also to history.[32] William Chillingworth's *Religion of the Protestants* (1638), subtitled 'A Safe Way to Salvation', conceded that the sense of scripture was sometimes opaque to fallible human readers and argued that the Christian faith was also handicapped by a 'great many contingent and uncertain proposals'. But Chillingworth was untroubled by the doubts the sceptics found so damaging: 'But then we say there is no necessity we should be certaine. For if Gods will had been we should have understood him more certainly, hee would have spoken more plainly.' Although these mere 'humane probabilities' may fall short of the certainty of mathematics and metaphysics, Chillingworth contended that they were quite sufficient to 'overcome our will and affections' as Christian discipline demands, for people daily exchange present pleasures for only a 'probable hope' of a future, greater gain.[33] Joseph Glanvill, apologist for the Royal Society and the new experimental philosophy, translated these modest expectations into natural philosophical terms: 'We are to expect no more from our Experiments and Inquiries, than great likelyhood, and such degrees of probability, as might deserve an hopeful assent.'[34] Similar sentiments in the service of Christianity or natural philosophy can be found in the works of Marin Mersenne, Pierre Gassendi, Blaise Pascal, and Robert Boyle, to name only the most influential writers in this vein.

The case of Gassendi is particularly instructive, for he forged the alliance – between probabilism, on the one hand, and empiricism, metaphysical pessimism, and epistemological modesty, on the other – that was eventually to receive its most influential statement from Locke. Although Gassendi's probabilism is sometimes viewed as simply a gradual tempering of his youthful Pyrrhonism, a careful reading of his works reveals that almost all of the essential elements of that probabilism were also present in his earlier writings.[35] These elements included an insistence on sensory givens as the only possible subject matter of reformed natural philosophy; the conviction that our human frailties prevent us from ever attaining certain truth about what is hidden from our senses; and the consolation that we can nonetheless attain a practical sort of certainty, sufficient to establish 'grounds for consent' (*rationi consentaneum*) in both belief and action.[36] Although Boyle, Wilkins, Locke, and others were to integrate these elements with a gradient of certainty and assurance, Gassendi's own use of *probabilitas* (and occasionally, *verisimilitudo*) was too deeply dyed with Platonic and Christian elements to permit any interpretation but one of two incommensurable domains, the probable and the true, the uncertain and the certain. Probable conjectures were the 'shadow' of the truth, and all that post-lapsarian humans were capable of: we cannot aspire to metaphysics, for it is not given to humans to look upon 'the bright shining sun' of truth; we must be content with the 'dawn of probability', that is, a hypothetical science of plausible and revisable explanations of phenomena.[37] The corresponding moral stance was one of extreme modesty and open-mindedness. It is a short step from these sentiments to Locke's rather melancholy view of why we humans are permanently saddled with probabilities, and his defence of tolerance on grounds of fallibility.[38]

This pessimistic brand of probabilism was not always in step with the advancing edge of seventeenth-century natural philosophy, although Gassendi did hope for progress in natural philosophy, and Locke was a confessed admirer of the scientific work of Boyle and Newton. Convinced that the infirmities of the human intellect were incorrigible, Gassendi not only opposed the old dogmatism of the scholastics and what he perceived to be the new dogmatism of Descartes; he also resisted the extension of mixed mathematics to physics as a presumption to unattainable certainty. Here he parted ways with his friend and frequent ally Mersenne.[39] Gassendi practised what he preached, couching his own explanations of natural phenomena in terms of mere probability; interpreting the explanations of others in the same vein, even when they would have sturdily protested;[40] and displaying a disarming readiness to modify or abandon a hypothesis in light of counter-arguments and new evidence.[41]

What might be called the philosophical probabilism of the mid seventeenth century revolved around a new concept of the *kind* of evidence that warrants belief. Thomist probabilities had accrued to opinions because of the probity of those who held them; seventeenth-century probabilities derive primarily from the grounds for holding such opinions. The older 'probability of testimony' did not disappear from the mathematical and philosophical literature of the seventeenth and eighteenth century: not only Locke and Hume but also Condorcet and Laplace attend to the credibility of witnesses. However, it is supplemented with and, increasingly, subordinated to evidence that derived from experience and from argument. Antoine Arnauld and Pierre Nicole distinguish between 'internal' circumstances, which 'belong to the fact itself', and 'external' circumstances, which 'concern those persons whose testimony leads us to believe' the alleged fact.

It is somewhat misleading to call this first variety of evidence that of things, *tout court,* since it also embraced argument. Nor was it solely, or even primarily, the evidence of statistical frequencies. Internal circumstances embrace what ordinarily happens (e.g., 999 notarised documents out of 1,000 are properly dated), but also the reasons for the normal course of affairs (the honour and livelihood of the notaries), *and* any mitigating particulars of the case at hand (*these* two notaries have a shady reputation). This insistence upon irreducibly qualitative features in reasoning about contingent events surfaces in several contexts, and distinguishes philosophical from mathematical probabilism, despite several suggestive similarities. In addition to warning that 'commonplaces which are true in general can be false on particular occasions', the Port-Royal authors despaired of any comparative weighting of conflicting testimony, given the bare possibility of the event reported.[42] Locke's King of Siam parable was meant to show the dangers of relying too heavily on frequencies alone, and he thought it 'impossible to reduce to precise Rules, the various degrees wherein Men give their Assent'.[43] However, mathematicians rushed in where philosophers feared to tread, and the quantitative treatment of evidence became a staple problem in classical probability theory very early on in the works of John Craig, George Hooper, and Jakob Bernoulli.

Although the philosophical probabilists emphasised that rational belief should vary 'as the conformity of our Knowledge, as the certainty of Observations, as the frequency and constancy of Experience', they paid equal attention to the more traditional concern with what Locke described as 'the number and credibility of testimonies'.[44] All of the standard legal guidelines for evaluating legal testimony recur in their works, though without the pretensions to quantification contained in the jurists' arithmetic of proof.[45] Motives, intelligence, integrity, internal consistency, and corroboration must all be sifted before we accept testimony, just as accord with past experience helps decide the internal plausibility of a newly reported fact. These are the reasons for belief, which Leibniz calls 'verisimilitude': he complains that Aristotle and the casuists do not ground probability 'on verisimilitude [*vraisemblance*], as they ought to, authority being only part of the reasons that make for verisimilitude'. It is not testimony per se, but unexamined authority which comes under attack – and more often than not, the authority of the mob rather than that of past sages. Leibniz's plea for a new logic of 'degrees of probability' pitted the probability drawn from the 'nature of things', duly weighed by Copernicus in forming his opinions about cosmology, against those of 'all the rest of mankind';[46] apropos of the interpretation of comets as portents, Pierre Bayle championed the views of 'one clever man', which had withstood all his doubts, to those of 'a hundred thousand vulgar minds, who only follow like sheep'.[47] It is not so much that the evidence of things came to trump that of testimony in the seventeenth century – we are still a long way from Hume, particularly on the subject of miracles[48] – as that testimony was submitted to more severe scrutiny on several counts, following the well-established legal model.

The legal guidelines for evaluating the evidence of both things and witnesses were not novel to the seventeenth century, but sixteenth-century developments in criminal law transformed their import. The intricate system of presumptions, conjectures, and indices had originally been intended to provide certainty, not probability of innocence or guilt. Jurists occasionally admitted that the 'certainty' of the corroborative testimony of two unimpeachable eye-witnesses or of a confession (even if voluntary) was the certainty of convention, rather than of demonstration, but they insisted upon its validity nonetheless. However, in the course of the sixteenth and seventeenth centuries the use of torture to extract confessions in the absence of sufficiently conclusive testimony waned: the new possibility of sentencing suspected criminals to the galleys or to workhouses rather than to execution relieved courts of the burdensome requirement of certainty, and therefore of the necessity of involuntary confessions.[49] Even if the canonical two eye-witnesses were not to be had, jurists could now rest their cases on a tissue of 'probabilities' woven out of the evidence of things and testimony. The evolution of English law during this period followed a parallel course: it is during the seventeenth century that the 'reasonable doubt' criterion for juries emerges.[50] This meant lowering the standard of proof from certainty per se to the 'moral certainty' of the judge so often invoked by the philosophical probabilists.

Although all the philosophical probabilists agreed that certainty eludes human grasp, some were more optimistic than others concerning the alternatives. This is why 'moral certainty' – even though it was uniformly defined as that measure of assurance accruing to beliefs that 'every man whose judgment is free from prejudice will consent unto',[51] and even though it was uniformly applied to the same examples (e.g., matters of fact such as the existence of the city of Rome) – could be both 'mere' moral certainty and all that a reasonable man could desire. Locke understood humans to be condemned to dwell in the 'twilight of probability' as divine chastisement, 'wherein we might not be overconfident and presume; but might by every day's Experience, be made sensible of our short-sightedness, and liableness to error'; Leibniz, confident in his legal training and in the prospects of the new mathematics of chance, replied that such 'degrees of probability' were not just poor substitutes for knowledge, but the genuine article.[52] The authors of the Port-Royal *Logique* resigned themselves to moral certainty, with an audible sigh, as good enough for the 'conduct of life';[53] Descartes, no laxist on standards for scientific certainty, was content to assert a moral certainty equivalent to the existence of the city of Rome for the conclusions of his *Principia philosophiae* (1644).[54] Yet whether or not one chose to see moral certainty as a glass half-full or half-empty, a broad spectrum of philosophical opinion was united in the view that it was the best we mortals could hope for in religion and in natural philosophy, as well as in daily affairs.

This literature of moral certainty brought together almost all of the notions of moral probabilism, legal evidence, risk, and chance that had previously existed apart and assembled them into a powerful argument that hinged on the rationality of trading a certain good for an uncertain one. The term 'moral certainty' and the emphasis upon the necessity to act echoed the casuists; the courtroom supplied Chillingworth, Boyle, Leibniz, and others with their best examples of reasonable decision based upon less than conclusive evidence; gambling and commercial risks were the model against which the hazards of believing in God or the mechanical hypothesis were gauged. Genuine statistical frequencies are absent from this synthesis, but the philosophical probabilists did appeal in a general way to what Locke called 'the frequency and constancy of experience'. The prototypical example of the argument from moral certainty is Pascal's wager, in which libertines are in effect asked to take a gamble on Christianity at odds they could hardly refuse at cards or dice. It is worth examining the form of the wager closely, not because it was original – passages in Chillingworth and in John Tillotson's sermon 'On the Wisdom of Being Religious'(1664) anticipate it in print – but because it is in Pascal that the new philosophical probabilism intersects with the mathematical calculus of probabilities.

## IV. MATHEMATICAL PROBABILISM

In the fragment 'Infini/Rien' of the *Pensées* (posthumous, 1669), Pascal imagines that the chances that God exists or not are equal, like those of getting heads or tails with a single toss of a fair coin. In modern terms, probabilities alone will not incline the reason or will to faith or atheism. But the outcome values are wildly asymmetric, for Christianity teaches us that infinite bliss awaits the faithful, and infinite misery the infidel. (It is one of Pascal's implicit premises that belief in God comes down to embracing Christianity.) Therefore, he argues, he who bets on God stands at best to win the greatest of prizes, and at worst to lose the indulgence of the passions and lusts of this life. Compared with the infinite outcome of salvation, even the most delicious worldly pleasures dwindle to insignificance, but Pascal is not arguing from a comparison of outcome values alone. It is the *product* of the probabilities and the outcome values that forces the choice between bets. For this reason, and because of the infinite outcome values, the arbitrarily chosen probability of God's existence does not weaken the argument: any non-zero value will do.

Here I am concerned with neither the premises nor the rigour of Pascal's argument,[55] but rather with the novel form of rationality it defends, and the risk-fraught situation it assumes. Like the moderate sceptics, Pascal insists that we must act under uncertainty – 'il faut parier'. Neither daily affairs nor religion nor natural philosophy permits us to suspend judgement indefinitely; prudence must prevail where wisdom hesitates. But whereas Chillingworth and others had been content to observe that, as a matter of fact, 'many millions in the world forgoe many times their present ease and pleasure, undergoe great and toylsome labours, encounter great difficulties, adventure upon great dangers, and all this not upon any certaine expectation, but upon a probable hope of some future gaine and commodity',[56] Pascal analysed the structure of the assumptions underlying such conduct and defended its rationality, even in the mundane finite case:

Every gambler wagers with certainty to win with uncertainty, and nonetheless he wagers the finite with certainty to gain the finite with uncertainty, without sinning against reason. There is not an infinite distance between that which one bets and the uncertainty of gain: this is false. There is, it is true, an infinity between the certainty of winning and the certainty of losing, but the uncertainty of winning is proportioned to the certainty of what one wagers according to the proportion of the chances [*hasards*] of gain or loss. And thus it comes to be that if there are as many chances on one side as on the other, the stakes are equal.[57]

Pascal's mathematical description of the relationship between probability and stake is a new element in the probabilism of the seventeenth century, which had been heretofore wholly qualitative. However, the language of what came to be called expectation (i.e., the product of the probability and the outcome value) and the justification of such trades of present certainty for future uncertainty derived from an established category of legal agreements. Sixteenth- and seventeenth-century jurists defined aleatory contracts as those involving some element of chance, in which a good-in-hand was voluntarily exchanged against the possibility of future profit: gambling, insurance policies, annuities, buying the next catch of the fisherman's net, speculating on the wheat harvest two years hence, dowry funds contingent on the daughter's survival to marriageable age – all these counted as examples of such contracts.[58] Aleatory contracts became increasingly important in the fifteenth and sixteenth centuries as a legal loophole for merchants who might otherwise have been suspected of usury: the jurists successfully defended risk as a title to interest. Thus in 1645 Jesuit missionaries were able to extract a special dispensation for Chinese converts charging 30 per cent interest on loans on the condition that 'there is considered the equality and probability of the danger, and provided that there is kept a proportion between the danger and what is received.'[59] The close connexion between the origins of mathematical probability theory and the legal-*cum*-casuist writings on aleatory contracts goes far towards explaining both the distinctive form and domain of applications of the earliest formulations of the theory.[60]

Even a cursory examination of the first documents concerning mathematical probability reveals that they are not about probability *per se,* but rather about expectations – that is, about the 'proportion between the danger and what is received', rather than about what Abraham De Moivre later defined as 'a Fraction whereof the Numerator be the number of Chances whereby an event may happen, and the Denominator the number of all the Chances whereby it may either happen or fail'.[61] Probabilists since De Moivre have *derived* expectation from the product of the probability and the outcome value, but for their forerunners expectation was the prior and fundamental notion. Two examples from the earliest literature on mathematical probability clearly illustrate the centrality of expectation. The first is Pascal's solution to the Problem of Points in his correspondence with Pierre Fermat, July–October 1654 (published 1679). Historians count these letters as the seminal documents in mathematical probability theory, despite suggestive anticipations in Girolamo Cardano's work. Legend has it that it was the mathematical dilettante Chevalier de Méré who posed the problem to Pascal, which became the subject of the famous exchange with Fermat.[62] Two players, Ⓐ and Ⓑ, each stake 32 pistoles on a three-point coin-toss game. When Ⓐ has two points, and Ⓑ one, the game is interrupted. How should the stakes be divided? Although we have only fragments of Fermat's solution, Pascal's fortunately survives in full. Since player Ⓐ is assured of thirty-two pistoles no matter what the outcome of the next round, Pascal argued that only the remaining thirty-two pistoles is at issue. This remainder should be halved, because *le hasard est égal* for both players.[63] Thus Ⓐ should receive 48 pistoles *en justice,* as Pascal later put it. Pascal understood the problem as one in equity, and it is therefore not surprising that he chose to analyse the problem in terms of certain gain, and a remainder to be equitably distributed. Probabilities enter the argument only after Ⓐ's minimum expectation has been established, and then only to endorse halving the residual amount as fair.[64] The Problem of Points was in essence a legal problem, and the first probabilists borrowed their terms of analysis from the legal doctrine of aleatory contracts. This is why expectations were initially more important than probabilities.

The first published treatise on mathematical probability, Christiaan Huygens's *De ratione in ludo aleae* (1657), provides an even more dramatic example of the primacy of expectation. Huygens had heard about, though not read, the Pascal–Fermat correspondence during his 1655 visit to Paris, and his brief treatise posed similar problems on the fair division of stakes and the 'reasonable' price for a player's place in an ongoing game. His 'fundamental hypothesis' was a definition of equal expectations in terms of equity: 'I begin with the hypothesis that in a game the chance one has to win something has a value such that if one possessed this value, one could procure the same chance in an equitable game [*rechtmatigh spel*, in the original Dutch version], that is in a game that works to no one's disadvantage.'[65]

Since later probabilists would define a fair game as one in which players' expectations equalled their stakes, Huygens's inverted definition of expectation in terms of a fair game seems circular. However, Huygens could assume that the notion of a fair game was a self-evident one for his readers, thanks to a well-honed sense of the equitable aleatory contract. Seventeenth-century jurists habitually assessed the trade-offs between various risks and stakes, in the case of annuity prices, wine futures, and other contingent agreements. The fact that Huygens frequently resorted to the legal device of fair exchanges to prove his propositions is further evidence for the intimate link between probabilistic expectation and contract law.

Thomas Bayes, whose seminal and controversial essay was posthumously published in 1763,[66] was the last of the classical probabilists to ground his work on expectations rather than probabilities, but he was old-fashioned even by the standards of the time. By the second decade of the eighteenth century, almost all probabilists had replaced expectation with probability as the prior and fundamental element of their calculus. However, aleatory contracts continued to supply probabilists with the bulk of their applications, and expectation therefore remained at the heart of mathematical probability theory, now rightfully so called. Not only games of chance, but also games of skill, insurance, annuities, future inheritances, and crop futures were grist for the probabilists' mill at the outset, for the focus on expectations made the lack of well-determined probabilities seem less of an obstacle. Moreover, the new rationality of computing and comparing expectations identified the fledgling calculus of expectations (for it was not yet a calculus of probabilities) with the reasonableness of Grotius, Mersenne, Chillingworth, Boyle, and others, although they played no direct rôle in the mathematical developments. Thus did classical probability theory become 'the reasonable calculus', intended by its practitioners as a mathematical codification of sound judgement in uncertain circumstances.[67] This broader sense of expectation as reasonableness bequeathed mathematical probability with yet another set of applications, centring on problems of evidence rather than equity, which united it with the philosophical probabilities of the seventeenth century.

Four works clustered around the turn of the eighteenth century took up the problem of evidence, particularly that of testimony, in the context of the new mathematics of chance: John Craig's *Theologiae christianae principia mathematica* (1699); an anonymous article entitled 'A Calculation of the Credibility of Human

Testimony', published in the *Philosophical Transactions of the Royal Society of London* (1699); Nicholas Bernoulli's *De usu artis conjectandi in jure* (1709); and Jakob Bernoulli's *Ars conjectandi* (posthumous, 1713). The approaches are all so different, and all so speculative in their assumptions, that it would be difficult to understand why mathematical probabilists would have hit upon the topic as a suitable application for their calculus, were it not for the background of legal and philosophical probabilism. As his Newtonian title hints, John Craig's analysis was modelled on mechanics, in that it likened the mind (*Animus*) to a 'moving thing' that moves through a 'space' of degrees of assent, driven by the 'motive forces' of arguments, deriving both from experience and from testimony.[68] Although Craig spoke the physicalist language of 'velocities' of suspicion and belief, his probabilities referred to the decay of conviction as the chain of witnesses grows ever longer and more attenuated: he calculated that the credibility of even the Bible will fade beyond belief after 3,150 years, thus fixing a date for the second coming. In contrast, the author of the *Philosophical Transactions* article (probably the Anglican divine George Hooper),[69] followed the method of Huygenian expectations closely, was exclusively concerned with the evidence of testimony, and calculated that a written tradition 'taken by different Hands, and preserv'd in different Places or Languages' loses its credibility only after 7,000 years, at the earliest.[70] Nicholas Bernoulli, trained both as lawyer and as mathematician, and editor of his Uncle Jakob's posthumous *Ars conjectandi,* took a statistical, if impracticable, tack in his doctoral dissertation on the application of mathematical probability to jurisprudence: the 'degree of credibility' of a witness equals the number of times he has told the truth previously, divided by the total number of times borne witness. But Nicholas then attempted a wholly nonstatistical quantification of the impact of other sorts of evidence, such that the probability of innocence, given $n$ pieces of incriminating evidence, is $(2/3)$.[n71] By far the most subtle and convoluted treatment of the probability of evidence was Jakob Bernoulli's own, in Part IV, Chapter 3, of his *Ars conjectandi,* which distinguished between proofs that might exist – and imply – either necessarily or contingently. Jakob fixed numbers to these proofs by assuming equipossible cases, on analogy with games of chance, but the particulars of his account diverged so sharply from the gambling model that it arguably leads to non-additive probabilities.[72]

As this brief survey of what came to be known as the probability of testimonies shows, the assumptions involved in quantifying the probative force of evidence were neither uniform nor obvious, and a number bordered on the bizarre. Some contemporaries also found the project dubious: Pierre de Montmort reproached

Craig for 'arbitrary' hypotheses and, in the preface to his *Essai d'analyse sur les jeux de hazard* (1713), advised fellow probabilists to give the 'infinity of obscurities' surrounding religion and civil life a wide berth. Yet, in various versions, the probability of testimony remained a staple of the mathematical literature until the early decades of the nineteenth century, cultivated by mathematicians of the calibre of Pierre Simon Laplace and Siméon-Denis Poisson.[73] The problem remained fatally attractive to mathematical probabilists because it was central to the doctrines of the philosophical probabilists of the seventeenth century, who in turn had borrowed it from the jurists. Courtroom judgements founded on compelling but not certain evidence were the paradigm case of the new reasonableness, combining in a weighty matter the elements of unavoidable uncertainty, the necessity to act, and proofs short of demonstration. Thus, credibility derived from evidence, both of things and of witnesses, remained one of the root senses of probability after the onset of the mathematical theory, despite the nearly insuperable obstacles to measuring it. The most plausible approach was statistical – simply totting up the number of times a given kind of evidence had in fact warranted a given conclusion in the past – but even had such voluminous statistics been available (and they were not), it was debatable whether they captured all that was meant by probative force. How was one to put a number to the integrity and intelligence of the witness, or to the intrinsic possibility of the fact in question? It is no accident that eighteenth-century discussions of the probability of testimony concentrated on the problem of miracles, in which intrinsic probabilities could be set at zero, as in Hume's essay 'On Miracles'.

But mathematical probability was not simply philosophical probabilism made numerical, by fair means and foul. Not all of the philosophical senses of probability passed through the filter of quantification, and mathematical probabilism created new senses of the word. It is noteworthy that those senses which did translate from philosophical to mathematical probabilism from early on, such as expectation and the weight of evidence, had already been quantified in some fashion, however arbitrary. In this regard, the common legal context from which both aleatory contracts and fractional proofs sprang is probably less telling for their subsequent mathematical career as expectations and probabilities of evidence than the fact that both were already expressed as numbers. Expectations were (literally) cashed out as money – gambling stakes, insurance premiums, etc. – and evidence had long been evaluated as fractions of a 'full proof'. Even though these 'proto-quantifications' contained a large element of the arbitrary, they appear to have persuaded the mathematicians that they were likely prospects for a fuller treatment.

In contrast, other important senses of philosophical probability, such as degree of analogy or appearance of truth, never found mathematical expression, although they lingered in the eighteenth-century philosophical literature.[74]

The only partial overlap between philosophical and mathematical probabilism at the end of the seventeenth century, as well as the lingering legal associations of both, emerges clearly from Leibniz's one-sided dialogue with Locke over probability and judgement in the former's *Nouveaux essais de l'entendement humain* (composed 1703–5). The relevant passages of Locke's *Essay concerning Human Understanding* (1690) represent philosophical probabilism as it had evolved in the two generations since Grotius and Gassendi.[75] Leibniz's responses are those of a mathematician apprised of the freshest developments in the 'calculus of chances' (he was corresponding with Jakob Bernoulli while writing the *Nouveaux essais*), and at the same time those of a trained jurist steeped in the older legal usage of probability. Between the two of them, the full spectrum of what probability could mean *circa* 1700 unfurls, and the incommensurabilities between philosophical and mathematical probabilism along with it.

Locke's departure point is Gassendi's, namely, the 'State of Mediocrity and Probationership' that condemns humans to probability rather than certainty in most things.[76] Demonstration is to probability as knowledge is to judgement, the one deriving from the 'constant, immutable, and visible connexion' of ideas, the other from the 'appearance of such an Agreement, or Disagreement, by the intervention of Proofs, whose connexion is not constant and immutable'.[77] This psychological emphasis on the mental comparison of ideas prompts Locke to reinterpret the Port-Royal *Logique* distinction between internal and external evidence in subtle ways. Even the purely internal evidence of mathematical demonstration can become external if accepted on authority rather than on the personal experience of intuition, and most of our own views steadily decay in probability because we do not (indeed, cannot) steadily rehearse our grounds for holding them before the mind's eye.[78] It is not only the quality and kind of evidence that makes for probability (though Locke distinguishes among these carefully), but also mental attentiveness and memory for relevant particulars. It is the irremediable deficiencies in these latter faculties that force us to freeze our opinions when we have once sifted the evidence pro and con, and that should, Locke argues, incline us towards modesty and tolerance towards those who refuse to embrace our opinions, for 'tis more than probable, that we are no less obstinate in not embracing theirs.'[79]

However, uncertainty does not imply anarchy in the realm of opinion, and

Locke scrupulously ranks what kind of evidence, both internal and external, warrants what degree of psychological assurance. The highest degree of probability attaches to reports that conform to our own constant observation, and that are attested by all witnesses (e.g., 'the regular proceedings of Causes and Effects in the ordinary course of Nature'), and produces unshakable 'assurance'; the lowest degrees of probability result from singular events reported by untrustworthy and contradictory witnesses, sowing '*Doubt, Wavering, Distrust, Disbelief,* etc.'[80] Although Locke speaks of 'degrees of Assent', there is nothing quantitative in his attempts to rank order either the objective grounds for strength of belief (the probability properly so called, for Locke), nor the subjective belief itself. Nor, as noted earlier, do his appeals to observation and experience readily translate into statistical terms. Far from embracing a mathematical approach to probability, Locke despairs of reducing judgements about conflicting evidence to any 'precise Rules'.[81] There is no refuge from uncertainty, however meticulous our weightings of the probabilities.

Leibniz's reaction is consistently to evade the ineluctable uncertainty in Locke's philosophical probabilism with an appeal to expertise, both legal and mathematical. Yes, we should be wary of accepting opinions on authority (Locke's example concerns confession as an accident of birth), but we should also follow the sage example of judges who trust to expert witnesses.[82] Yes, we should avoid the paralysing scepticism that would result from a continual re-examination of the grounds for our beliefs; but we might also borrow a leaf from the law courts, which keep written records on arguments as an *aide mémoire,* and in any case suspend or revise judgement in light of new arguments, '*in rem judicatum,* as the jurists call it'.[83] Yes, we should be tolerant of opinions different from our own, but only in so far as these are not 'dangerous in relationship to morals or public order', in which case they should be stamped out without hesitation.[84] Yes, we should apportion degrees of assent to evidence at hand, but there do exist precise rules for this, developed 'in considerable detail' by jurists.[85] Indeed, so precise are these rules that they constitute 'a sort of logic' for Leibniz, a logic closely allied to the recent mathematical attempts to quantify the risks of games of chance – attempts which are in turn based on the 'natural mathematics' of taking averages long in use among peasants.[86] At every point, Leibniz tries to exorcise the spectre of genuine uncertainty and unruly judgement raised by Locke with techniques and rules, justifying these latter as the fruit of a venerable tradition of practical reason – be it exercised by jurists, doctors, gamblers, or peasants. These two themes – the apparent routing of uncertainty by recourse to formalism, and the justification of that formalism as practical reason codified – were to stamp the classical interpretation of mathematical probability from Jakob Bernoulli through Laplace.

However, Leibniz's reply to Locke was not simply a mathematical grid ruthlessly imposed upon philosophical probabilism. For Leibniz is still willing to entertain a crowd of meanings for probability, only some of them compatible with seventeenth-century mathematical usage. Probability can still mean the 'appearance of truth' (*vraisemblance*) for Leibniz, an ancient meaning that slipped through the meshes of quantification.[87] Conversely, in his otherwise thorough summary of the mathematical literature to date, Leibniz does not mention the most promising attempts to quantify probabilities, namely, John Graunt's political arithmetic (see the following paragraphs), though he certainly knew of it. Graunt's statistical approach would have suited Leibniz's judicial probabilities as ill as it would have Locke's evidentiary probabilities. Although he ultimately rejects it on metaphysical grounds (nature's variety far outstrips our weak imagination), Leibniz is even willing to consider Locke's position that analogy can be a source of probability. Locke struggles to escape the narrow confines of his empiricism by arguing that our conjectures about things invisible to the senses, be they angels or atoms, can attain probability by their analogy with things we can observe.[88] Moreover, all creation is connected by insensible increments in a great chain of being that warrants such interpolations and extrapolations. Leibniz doubts both the continuity and simplicity that underpin such reasoning, but not its title to be a source of probability.[89] Yet under the pressure from the mathematical probabilism Leibniz so enthusiastically greeted, the probability of analogy soon disappeared, for it proved refractory to even the most determined efforts at quantification. If the mathematicians were selective in their borrowings from the philosophers, they were also creative in stretching the meaning of probability from warranted belief to cover physical possibility and frequency of events. Although it is standard practice among twentieth-century probabilists to distinguish between two senses of probability, subjective and objective,[90] it is possible to refine this distinction further in late seventeenth-century works. By 1700, mathematical probability could mean the strength of an argument (e.g., the weight of evidence in court); the intensity of belief (e.g., the judge's conviction that the accused was guilty); equally possible cases (usually deriving from the physical symmetry and uniform density of a fair coin or die); and the frequency with which certain events occurred (e.g., the annual birth rate). There were obvious difficulties in measuring the first two kinds of probability, despite the sanguinity of many mathematicians; the third applied plausibly only to a very few cases, although some probabilists rather recklessly extended the assumption of equally probable cases to diseases in the human body or the force of evidence; the fourth depended on the existence of an ample body of statistics and stable conditions. The demographic statistics collected since the mid sixteenth century were scanty and intended to serve other ends, but they very soon became the most promising source of mathematical probabilities.

However, the first to draw attention to the potential of these statistics was not a mathematician and was indeed quite ignorant of the nascent calculus of probabilities. John Graunt's *Natural and Political Observations Mentioned in a Following Index and Made upon the Bills of Mortality* (1662) used no more than 'Shop-Arithmetique' and the fragmentary data from the London bills of mortality to make policy recommendations on the advisability of polygamy, quarantine during outbreaks of plague, the overpopulation of London, and various other controversial issues. Ironically, the most influential section of this early tract in political arithmetic, Graunt's mortality table, strayed furthest from the empirical data on which he grounded the authority of his conclusions. Because the bills of mortality of the time did not list age at death, Graunt was driven to shrewd guesswork in order to construct his Baconian-style table of how many died at what age: he noted that approximately one-third of all registered deaths resulted from '*Thrush, Convulsion, Rickets, Teeth,* and *Worms;* and as *Abortives, Chrysomes, Infants, Livergrown,* and *Overlaid* . . . which we guess did all light upon Children under four or five years old', and assumed that the remaining two-thirds died in equal proportions for each decade between the ages of six and seventy-six.[91] Graunt was not exceptional among the early political arithmeticians in distinguishing, in effect, precision from exactitude. William Petty, who also resorted to rough numerical estimates when exact figures were not to be had, ingenuously pleaded that even if his values were false, they were 'not so false as to destroy the Argument they are brought for'. The first political arithmeticians preferred numbers to words not necessarily because they were exact, in the sense that they accurately described housing prices in Paris or the number of potential military conscripts, but rather because they were more precise, serving to sharpen notions better than 'only comparative and superlative Words'.[92]

The mathematicians who seized upon Graunt's table – including Christiaan and Ludwig Huygens, Johann De Witt, Edmund Halley, Leibniz, Jakob and Nicholas Bernoulli – were nevertheless persuaded that the numbers were 'practically near enough the truth',[93] despite the simplifying assumptions. Indeed, the subsequent history of such mortality tables and the probabilistic calculations of life expectancy based upon them is one of quite drastic simplifying assumptions coupled with unshakable confidence in the regularity of human mortality. Johann De Witt proposed an annuity scheme to the Dutch States General that assumed that the chances of dying in any six-month period between the ages of three and fifty-three were equal.[94] De Witt did take the trouble to check his results against the Amsterdam annuity data in a correspondence with mathematician/mayor Johannes Hudde, but judged the discrepancy (18 versus 16 florins) in calculated price to be trivial.[95] Edmund Halley, who published the first empirically derived mortality table in 1693, believed firmly enough that death occurred in regular arithmetic progression to assert that 'Irregularities in the Series of Ages' shown in his table 'would rectify themselves, were the number of years [upon which the data were based] much more considerable, as 20 instead of 5'.[96] Well into the eighteenth century, probabilists calculating the price of annuities, and, later, life insurance premiums, insisted on the simplicity and uniformity of the mortality curve, with only a few dissenting voices.[97]

In the eighteenth century this unflinching belief in the stability of statistical ratios in demography was closely linked to natural theology. There is ample evidence of this connexion in the works of eighteenth-century probabilists and statisticians such as John Arbuthnot, Abraham De Moivre, and Johann Süssmilch: the slight predominance of male over female births, the regularity and uniformity of the mortality curve, the patterns of diseases – all were signs of God's beneficent design.[98] However, vital statistics in the seventeenth century were not given a providential interpretation, and it appears that the arrow of inspiration originally pointed from statistics to natural theology, rather than the reverse. William Derham's Boyle lectures, *Physico-Theology, or A Demonstration of the Being and Attributes of God from His Works of Creation* (1712), exploited the work of the political arithmeticians in his demographic version of the argument from design, but he did not invent the belief in statistical regularities. The rather sudden emergence of this belief is all the more puzzling, in part because it was only selectively applied, and in part because it was diametrically opposed to the fixation upon particulars and changing conditions that characterised the sale of insurance and annuities at the time. The dealers in risk acted as if they lived in a world of mutable particulars, in which regularities were partial at best; the first political arithmeticians and the mathematicians who made use of their work assumed the world was simple, stable, and predictable, at least in the realm of human natality and mortality. In a generation scarred by the last major plague outbreak in London as well as by the Great Fire in the same city, it is striking that Graunt, Halley, and their followers believed that human deaths occurred at regular intervals, but not other familiar disasters like fires and shipwrecks. It is possible that proto-quantification also played a rôle here: since biblical times, death had been linked with the continuous variable of age, and its inevitability made a full enumeration possible. In contrast, the choice of independent variable for fires – type of lodging? trade housed therein? weather? – was neither clear-cut nor easily quantified, and fires did not befall every building.

## V. THE MEANING OF PROBABILITY

Whatever the sources of the belief in selected statistical regularities, they were almost universally professed by the mathematicians, who immediately grasped the relevance of such vital statistics, invented or observed, to measuring probabilities. (The political arithmeticians, however, did not return the favour, and took little notice of mathematical probability theory.) Here the mathematical probabilists diverged sharply from the philosophical probabilists, although not from the jurists. Aleatory contracts remained the chief domain of application, and equity was still the byword among mathematicians. Following the model of mathematical expectation, the Huygens brothers, Leibniz, De Witt, and Jakob and Nicholas Bernoulli set about computing life expectancies and extending their calculus to other kinds of aleatory contracts besides games of chance, although there was some difference of opinion concerning the definition of life expectancy. Halley proudly advertised his Breslau mortality table as the first equitable means of pricing annuities, 'which hitherto has been only done by an imaginary *Valuation*'.[99] After Graunt's work, mathematicians sought statistical probabilities wherever they were to be had and fell back upon the convenient but implausible assumption of equally probable cases only *faute de mieux*.

Despite the ease and eagerness with which the mathematicians made the transition from the probabilities of symmetry to the probabilities of statistics, the relationship between *a priori* probabilities based on equally probable outcomes and *a posteriori* probabilities based on observations remained a vexed one. Bernoulli's and Bayes's theorems were the two most important classical attempts to connect the two, and the difficulties with which they grappled still lie at the heart of debates over valid statistical inference.[100] Only Bernoulli's 'golden theorem', which he intended as his epitaph, falls within the scope of this essay, but it is rich with implications for the subsequent history of the problem. It also plaits the various strands of seventeenth-century probabilism, both philosophical and mathematical, into a single skein.

The theorem was the capstone of the unfinished fourth part of Bernoulli's treatise *Ars conjectandi,* in which he hoped to apply the calculus of probabilities and permutations developed in the first three sections to a wide range of problems in 'civil life', from courtroom evidence to weather prediction. Bernoulli did not doubt that inductive reasoning from effects to causes was both valid and wide-spread: 'even the stupidest man knows by some instinct of nature' that the greater the number of confirming instances, the surer the conjecture. What Bernoulli had spent twenty years pondering was rather the *rate* at which confirming instances increase the probability of the conjecture, and whether this probability 'finally exceeds any given degree of certainty' or instead is bounded by some asymptote.[101] Bernoulli treasured his theorem because it proved that the probability did increase continuously with the number of trials, and more specifically, that a sufficient number of trials could guarantee 'moral certainty' (set by Bernoulli at a probability of .999). Here, as elsewhere in the *Ars conjectandi,* Bernoulli set about quite deliberately quantifying the philosophical probabilism of works like the Port-Royal *Logique:* he tackled the notary problem; put a number to moral certainty; tried to measure the weight of evidence; systematised recourse to past experience as a guide to future expectations. (Bernoulli in fact intended his *Ars conjectandi* to be the pendant to the Port-Royal *Logique,* known as the *Ars cogitandi* in Latin.) His theorem was also a remarkable hybrid of philosophical and mathematical probabilism. In modern notation, Bernoulli showed that as $n \to \infty$, $\lim P(|p - m/n| < \epsilon) = 1$, for $\epsilon$ as small as desired, where:

$$p = a \ priori \text{ probability ('true' ratio)}$$
$$n = \text{the number of trials}$$
$$m/n = a \ posteriori \text{ probability (observed ratio).}$$

Here $p$ is the probability of physical symmetry, likened to drawing balls of different colours from an urn in which they are mixed in unknown proportion; $m/n$ is the probability of statistical frequencies; and $P$ is the probability of warranted belief. Bernoulli's theorem thus represented a grand synthesis of all the then current meanings of probability, both subjective and objective.

However, Bernoulli's own axis of distinction for probabilities was not objective/subjective, but rather *a priori/a posteriori*. Although his Archimedean-style demonstration gave him an impracticable result for the number of trials required to warrant moral certainty,[102] Bernoulli intended his theorem as a practical contribution to empirical natural philosophy. It was a commonplace of seventeenth-century natural philosophy that nature could be investigated in two ways: reasoning from causes to effects, or from effects to causes. Few doubted that the *a priori* method promised greater certainty, but many feared that the *a posteriori* method was the best that mere mortals could hope for. Both the opacity of nature and the obtuseness of the human intellect prevented us from penetrating to the 'hidden springs and principles' of things: 'If Nature were not invelloped in so dense a Cloud of Abstrusity, but should unveil her self, and expose all her beauteous parts naked to our speculation: yet are not the Opticks of our Mind either clear or strong enough to discern them.'[103] There were shades of pessimism – Francis Bacon believed that the strict discipline of method could eventually reveal the 'latent configurations', idols of cave, tribe, marketplace, and theatre notwithstanding; René Descartes abandoned the deductive route only after the general outlines of cosmology had been established; the young Newton asserted that his 'New Theory of Light and Colours' (1672) had been 'deduced' from experiments – but Locke accurately summed up late seventeenth-century philosophical opinion when he abandoned hope of ever discovering the 'real essences' of things we ourselves do not construct.[104] We have indubitable knowledge only about appearances and so are condemned to ply the *a posteriori* method. Defenders of the new experimental philosophy upheld induction not as a perfect but rather as a necessary method and did their best to make a virtue out of that necessity. As the mature Newton admitted, 'Although the arguing from Experiments and Observations by Induction be no Demonstration of general Conclusions; yet it is the best way of arguing which the Nature of Things admits of, and may be looked upon as so much the stronger, by how much the Induction is more general.'[105]

Bernoulli's theorem per se was a part of mathematical probability theory, but its application to *a posteriori* reasoning depended on the urn model of causation he introduced. In the simplest case, an urn is filled with a certain number of black and white balls, from which drawings are made at random and with replacement. Any one ball is equally likely to be drawn as any other. If the ratio of black to white balls is known *a priori,* Bernoulli's theorem tells us the number of drawings necessary to ensure that the observed ratio falls within a certain margin of the true ratio with a given probability. The true ratio corresponds to the 'cause'; the observed ratio, to the 'effect'. Bernoulli believed that this model could be extended to many other cases, from civil life to human mortality. In the case of human diseases, Bernoulli compared the human body to a 'tinder box' filled with diseases, combined in some ratio, like variously coloured balls in an urn. The observed rates of plague, dropsy, gout, and so on were in effect random 'drawings' from their susceptible human urn. The urn model became the hallmark of classical probability theory, eventually applied to phenomena as diverse as birth rates and jury verdicts.

The urn model of causation bore the stamp of these late seventeenth-century musings on the unavoidable and limited character of the *a posteriori* method. Like the hidden causes of nature, the true ratio of coloured balls in the sealed urn could not be ascertained by direct inspection. The curious could only make repeated drawings from the urn, just as natural philosophers blind to the inner workings of nature fell back upon observations of appearances. As the contents of the urn could be guessed from the results of the drawings, so causes could be conjectured from effects. Bernoulli's theorem measured how the conjecture improved as the number of observations increased, that is, the generality of the induction. It thus offered a tentative solution to one central problem of empiricism: how to justify generalising from a restricted set of observations made here and now to all such events everywhere and always. At the same time, it addressed a second major problem: how to choose one conjecture out of a pack of contenders, since empirical confirmation did not guarantee uniqueness. To take a seventeenth-century example, the telescopic observation of the phases of Venus did indeed confirm the Copernican system, but it did not eliminate the Tychonic competition. Bernoulli's theorem measured the probabilities of certain kinds of causal conjectures, making it possible in principle to compare rival hypotheses, and to stack all candidates up against the absolute standard of moral certainty, now quantified. The *Ars conjectandi* thus inspired a mathematics of induction, known as the 'probability of causes', that became one of the principal domains of application for the classical theory of probabilities until the mid nineteenth century.[106]

Although Bernoulli's urn model of causation fitted neatly into the framework of empiricist natural philosophy in some ways, it strained that framework in others. First, Bernoulli's causes were peculiar in being probabilities, rather than, say, Cartesian microscopic mechanisms or Newtonian forces. Second, Bernoulli's effects were peculiar in being repeated, identical, independent, and therefore countable trials, rather than, say, Baconian 'shining instances' which displayed a phenomenon with such clarity that no repetitions were needed. The first peculiarity introduced a chance element into the connexion between cause and effect, in spite of Bernoulli's own staunch determinism. In the urn model, causes 'determined' effects only in a combinatorial fashion. Although the fixed ratio of the coloured balls corresponded to immutable and determinate causes, the relationship between this ratio and any particular drawing was a matter of chance. Necessity obtained only in the longest of long runs, only if 'all events were to be continued throughout eternity'.[107] It is possible that these combinatorial elements may not have been so jarring to ears accustomed to the corpuscularian analogies that likened atoms to letters of the alphabet, in order to show how the permutations of a small number of elements could be made to generate a great variety of effects.[108] However, the second peculiarity, Bernoulli's reinterpretation of effects, implied a severe narrowing of what seventeenth-century writers had meant by empirical evidence. Locke's emphasis on the breadth and variety, as well as sheer bulk, of experience, the force of 'strong' presumptions in a court of law, or imponderables such as the skill of the astronomer wielding telescope or quadrant – all of these considerations were irreproachably empirical, but not easily quantified in the manner demanded by Bernoulli's theorem. And, in fact, empiricist philosophers of the eighteenth century did conceive experience in ever more strictly Bernoullian terms, as a comparison of Locke and Hume on the subject of probability makes clear.[109] Thus the emphasis on *counting* instances introduced by the political arithmeticians had a lasting impact on both philosophical and mathematical probabilism.

These peculiarities of Bernoulli's urn model of causation aside, there was still much that a thoughtful contemporary might have found dubious in Bernoulli's claim that his theorem 'investigated a posteriori cases nearly as accurately as if we had known them a priori'.[110] We are fortunate in having such a witness in Leibniz, with whom Bernoulli corresponded about his discoveries in 1703. In effect, Leibniz attacked the urn model as a crude oversimplification of how we should reason *a posteriori*. In cases as intricate as human morbidity and mortality, what guarantee do we have that diseases do not evolve, emerge, and disappear over time, thus undermining the assumption of a constant underlying probability? Leibniz acknowledged that nature was generally set in 'her own habits', but accepted the possibility of new causes 'because of the very mutabilities of things'. In other words, the composition of the urn might change over time. Leibniz also worried that the number of such causes might be infinite and thereby render Bernoulli's ratios meaningless: the number of balls might be infinite, and their ratios indeterminate. Finally, Leibniz pointed out that the inferred *a posteriori* probability was only one of an infinite number of guesses about the hidden *a priori* probability that fell within the specified margin, just as an infinite number of curves can be traced through any finite set of points.[111]

Bernoulli responded to Leibniz's queries with a mixture of pragmatism, mathematics, and metaphysics. If new causes did emerge, patient observation would eventually reveal them; mathematical methods like Archimedes' approximation made it possible to find determinate ratios even among infinite numbers, and, in any case, God did not create indeterminate entities; and it is reasonable to assume that 'nature follows the simplest paths.'[112] Bernoulli thus skirted knotty mathematical problems concerning the untangling of causes and the convergence of relative frequencies that were to bedevil his successors, from M. J. A. N. Condorcet through Richard von Mises. In order to make the world safe for his theorem, Bernoulli assumed it to be on the whole stable, determinate, and simple, a vision that continued to inspire classical probabilists from De Moivre through Poisson.

The *Ars conjectandi* was the mathematical and philosophical culmination of seventeenth-century probabilism and was the mould in which eighteenth-century probabilism was cast. It presented the mathematical results to date in their most elegant and general form, crowned by Bernoulli's theorem; it defined the domain of applications that occupied probabilists for another century, including the moral sciences; and it solidified, in one context or another, all of the interpretations of probability that were to survive from the rich and varied pre-mathematical usage. What was notably missing from Bernoulli's magisterial work on what came to be known as the 'doctrine of chances' was chance itself. Indeed, classical probabilists from Bernoulli through Laplace were determinists of the strictest persuasion, at least as far as the realm of matter was concerned. Far from signalling a new appreciation of chance in nature, the emergence of mathematical probability went hand in hand with a fortified determinism that denied the very existence of chance. Bernoulli spoke for all when he claimed that: 'Everything that occurs under the sun – past, present, or future – always has the greatest objective certainty in itself' (*in se & objectivè summam semper certitudinem habent*).[113]

This metaphysics was bought at a price by the mathematicians, for it committed them at least officially to a subjective interpretation of probability as a state of mind rather than a state of the world. As we have seen, Bernoulli's theorem appeals to what we would now call objective as well as subjective senses of probability, but his own definition of probability is 'a degree of certainty', related to absolute certainty as fraction to unity. These degrees of certainty vary from person to person, and according to time and place, depending on the state of knowledge. (Bernoulli's subjective probabilities are, however, far closer to the logical probabilities of John Maynard Keynes than to those of latter-day Bayesians of the Bruno De Finetti and Leonard Savage school: a given amount of evidence determines a probability uniquely for all rational subjects.) God has no need of probabilities, and Bernoulli believed that once the science of mechanics had been perfected, probabilities would also be irrelevant to games of chance, for the fall of the die is as necessary as the occurrence of an eclipse. Probabilities, and with them the very category of the contingent, are figments of human ignorance. Mathematical probabilists echoed these sentiments with more or less eloquence for a century thereafter, in the works of De Moivre, Condorcet, and Laplace.

Why did the architects of a mathematics of chance so firmly and unanimously declare their subject matter to be at best an illusion? The answer lies in seventeenth-century standards for applying mathematics to phenomena. These standards not only made determinism compatible with probability theory; they made it seem almost a necessary precondition for that theory. 'Mixed mathematics', in contrast to latter-day applied mathematics, assumed intimate connexions between the form of mathematics and the matter of the phenomena it described. According to the Aristotelian view, which had distinguished proponents well into the eighteenth century, all of mathematics originated from the abstraction of form from matter.[114] For seventeenth-century thinkers, this implied that, within the realm of mixed mathematics, the connexions between cause and effect were as necessary as those between steps in a mathematical demonstration.

In the sixteenth and seventeenth centuries, mixed mathematics expanded to encompass many phenomena previously treated under the qualitative rubric of natural philosophy. Not only was nature (or at least large parts of it) now conceived to be fundamentally mathematical; knowledge of nature was now to be cast in the form of mathematical demonstration: hence the Euclidean format of the Latin sections of Galileo's *Discorsi* (1638) and Newton's *Principia* (1687). Thus, mixed mathematical treatment presupposed necessity. The critical question was whether all phenomena obeyed necessity, and therefore were in principle the subjects of a mathematical science, or whether only some did. Aristotle had narrowly circumscribed the realm of the necessary,[115] and even some enthusiasts of the new mathematical approach to natural philosophy did not entirely part company with him here. Galileo, for example, doubted that there would ever be a true science – that is, a demonstrative, mathematical account – of air currents, because he believed them to be inherently variable.[116] Determinism reigned wherever mathematics applied, but mathematics might not apply everywhere.

As long as such pockets of chance and variability existed, the prospects for a mathematics of chance were dim. Here Girolamo Cardano's promising but flawed attempt to create such a mathematics is extremely instructive. Cardano's *Liber de ludo aleae* (composed *circa* 1520, published posthumously in 1663) is a singular mix of hard-headed advice about gambling (how to unnerve your opponent, lucky streaks, unmasking cheaters) and mathematics. Cardano's personal gambling experience and his mathematical precepts are continually at odds with one another, and eventually vitiate his attempts to calculate chances. He has a clear conception of equiprobable outcomes and can compute the odds for dice games without difficulty. Yet Cardano must confess that the mathematical basis for his calculations is a blatant fiction. He sets the 'circuit' of a fair die – the number of throws necessary to realise all the possibilities – at six throws. Of course, Cardano was fully aware that in practice more than six throws may be required to turn up all six faces: if a given face turns up more or less often than it should within a circuit, 'that is a matter of luck.' For Cardano luck is no illusion: he is a great believer in his own, considers it as fixed a trait in a player as skill, and blames it when events contradict the determinism of his calculations, which, as he himself warns, contribute 'hardly anything to practical play'.[117]

Cardano was no thoroughgoing determinist, and he balked at neither the interventions of chance (small, temporary fluctuations) nor luck (systematic trends or streaks). However, he realised that luck and chance made his calculations all but worthless for the gambler intent on the next throw of the dice. His circuits represent the mixed mathematician's vain attempt to impose necessity on the single contingent event; his admission of failure was also an admission of the reality of chance and luck. Cardano believed that mathematics applied only to the necessary, and that chance events are not necessary. Therefore, the mathematics of chance was a hopeless project, at least at the level of the single event or short run that mattered to his gambling audience. He understood that the discrepancy between calculations and events would disappear in the very long run – that an infinite number of throws would render a calculated outcome 'almost necessary [*proximé necesse*]' – but this was no consolation to the gambler whose fortune was riding on this particular game. In the end, Cardano chose the assistance of Fortuna, not mathematics.

Bernoulli's theorem was a solution to Cardano's problem concerning the discrepancy between calculated probabilities and observed frequencies, but Cardano is unlikely to have accepted it. Bernoulli does not solve the problem of the short run or the individual case; he simply ignores it. He is licensed to do so by an all-embracing determinism that obscured the experience of chance and variability that was so vivid to Cardano. Bernoulli still recognises the terms 'good' and 'bad' fortune, but he redefines them as events less likely to have occurred, not as violations of the causal order. It is the 'hidden causes' of the weather and human mortality that command his attention when he turns to the problem of squaring calculated probabilities with observed frequencies, not the vicissitudes of good and bad fortune. For Bernoulli, the problem is no longer variability in the world, but gaps in our knowledge of the world – knowledge of the hidden causes of next year's weather, the outcome of a game of skill, the 'life and death of future generations'. Bernoulli's theorem did not simply solve Cardano's problem; it changed the problem almost beyond recognition. Eliminating the contingent from his metaphysics permitted Bernoulli to train his sights on the long run, where near-necessity did obtain. This is why determinism, far from stifling mathematical probability, actually promoted it in the late seventeenth century.

## VI. CONCLUSION

Pascal thought his newly invented *géométrie du hasard* oxymoronic.[118] And so it was by contemporary lights: mixed mathematics and chance seemed immiscible. Only the most ambitious, unrelenting determinism could make mathematical probability conceivable under these conditions, and this is why the classical probabilists banished chance. As in all metaphysical sea-changes, the sources of this blanket determinism are various and intertwined, and it goes far beyond the scope of this essay to trace them. Suffice it to point to the suggestive fact that all of the early probabilists, from Pascal through Bernoulli, came from religious backgrounds that embraced a particularly rigorous belief in predestination.

Mathematical probabilism preserved much of philosophical probabilism, particularly its emphasis upon reasonableness, expectation, and evidence. These preoccupations mapped out the domain of mathematical applications for over a century to come, despite the recalcitrance of the subject matter in many cases. But mathematical probabilism also changed the nature of philosophical probabilism through its emphasis on long-term regularities and statistical frequencies. Chance and variability dropped from sight, and induction became a matter of counting instances. The exercise of judgement that Locke and the Port-Royal authors had hesitated to 'reduce to precise rules' became a topic for mathematicians because the evidence to be judged had itself become largely numerical. By transforming the concept of evidence and jettisoning the contingent, the eighteenth-century probabilists parted ways with their seventeenth-century predecessors. Whereas the philosophical probabilists of the early seventeenth century had accepted and enlarged Aristotle's distinction between mathematical certainty and the mere probability of everything else, the mathematical probabilists of the late seventeenth century sought to extend mathematical certainty even to probabilities. The alchemical longing to transform base uncertainty into noble certainty by means of mathematics remained the hallmark of classical probability theory well into the nineteenth century.

## NOTES

1 *Nicomachean Ethics,* 1094b24–26.
2 See Kendall 1956; Rabinovitch 1973; Sheynin 1974; Hacking 1975a; Garber and Zabell 1979; Schneider 1980.
3 *Physics,* 198b10–199a9.
4 *Rhetoric,* 1362a8–11.
5 *Rhetoric,* 1357a.

6 *Topics*, 100b20–21.
7 *De inventione*, I.xxix.44–8.
8 Compare Aristotle, *Rhetoric*, 1357a15–1359a3.
9 See Garber and Zabell 1979 for a further discussion of probability in the classical and mediaeval rhetorical tradition.
10 *Summa th.* I q1 a8 ad2; Byrne 1968, pp. 97–113.
11 Byrne 1968, pp. 155–6 and *passim*.
12 Deman 1936, pp. 455–63.
13 Pascal 1963, pp. 390a–391b.
14 Hacking 1975a, p. 23.
15 Langbein 1976, p. 7.
16 Quoted in Lévy 1939, p. 31; see also Esmein 1882, chap. 3.
17 Allard 1868, chap. 3.
18 Voltaire 1785.
19 Domat 1691–7, vol. 2, pp. 347–8.
20 See Hume, *Treatise*, I.iii.11.
21 *Ess.*, II.xxxiii.5–6.
22 *Ess.*, IV.xv.5.
23 *Rhetoric*, 1357b5–21.
24 Daston 1988, chap. 3.
25 Meuvret 1971.
26 Cioffari 1973; Doren 1922–3.
27 Machiavelli 1640, pp. 349, 352.
28 Popkin 1979; Van Leeuwen 1963.
29 Mersenne 1625, p. 226.
30 Grotius 1627, II.xix, II.xxiii.
31 Boyle 1772, vol. 4, p. 182; Glanvill 1676, p. 47; Wilkins 1699, pp. 5–8.
32 Shapiro 1983, chaps. 3–4.
33 Chillingworth 1638, pp. 73, 79–80, 312.
34 'Of Scepticism and Certainty', in Glanvill 1676, p. 45.
35 Detel 1978, p. 64.
36 Gassendi 1658, vol. 1, p. 78a.
37 Gassendi 1658, vol. 1, p. 286b; vol. 3, p. 259a.
38 *Ess.* IV.xiv.2; IV.xvi.3–4.
39 Mersenne 1625, Preface, pp. 226 and *passim*.
40 Gassendi 1658, vol. 6, pp. 53b–54a.
41 Gassendi 1658, vol. 6, pp. 59b–62b.
42 Arnauld and Nicole 1965, pp. 340–52.
43 *Ess.* IV.xvi.9.
44 *Ess.* IV.xv.6.
45 Compare Locke, *Ess.* IV.xv.6; Arnauld and Nicole 1965, pp. 340–1; Bacon 1857–74, vol. 4, pp. 259–60.
46 *Nouv. ess.* IV.ii.14.
47 Bayle 1911, vol. 1, pp. 134–5.
48 See, e.g., Arnauld and Nicole 1965, pp. 344–6; Locke, *Ess.* IV.xvi.13.
49 Langbein 1976, pp. 46–9.
50 Shapiro 1983, chap. 5; Waldman 1959.
51 Wilkins 1699, p. 8.
52 *Ess.*, IV.xiv.2; *Nouv. ess.*, IV.xiv.2.

53 Arnauld and Nicole 1965, p. 340.
54 *Princ.* IV 205.
55 On this, see, e.g., Hacking 1975a, chap. 8.
56 Chillingworth 1638, p. 312.
57 Pascal, *Pens.* 418.
58 Domat 1691–7, vol. 1 , p. 97.
59 Quoted in Noonan 1957, p. 289.
60 Coumet 1970.
61 De Moivre 1756, pp. 1–2.
62 Hacking 1975a, pp. 49–51.
63 Pascal 1963, pp. 46b–49a.
64 On the rôle of combinatorics, see Raymond 1975.
65 Huygens 1888–1950, vol. 14, p. 60.
66 Bayes 1763.
67 Daston 1988, chap. 2.
68 Craig 1699, defs. 6, 7, 10; Stigler 1986b.
69 The article was reprinted in Hooper 1757, pp. 129–33.
70 Hooper 1699, p. 364.
71 N. Bernoulli 1709, chap. 9.
72 Shafer 1978.
73 Daston 1988, chap. 6.
74 See, e.g., Hartley 1749, vol. 1, pp. 339–40.
75 See *Ess.* IV.xiv–xvi.
76 *Ess.* IV.xiv.2.
77 *Ess.* IV.xv.1.
78 *Ess.* IV.xv.1; IV.xvi.2.
79 *Ess.* IV.xvi.1–4.
80 *Ess.* IV.xvi.6, 9. A pointed exception is made for supernatural events, which are not subject to any of the usual evidentiary strictures, being, Locke contends, the testimony of God and therefore indubitable. See *Ess.* IV.xvi.13–14.
81 *Ess.* IV.xvi.9.
82 *Nouv. ess.* IV.xv.5–6.
83 *Nouv. ess.* IV.xvi.3.
84 *Nouv. ess.* IV.xvi.4.
85 *Nouv. ess.* IV.xvi.9.
86 *Nouv. ess.* IV.xvi.9.
87 *Nouv. ess.* IV.xv.4.
88 *Ess.* IV.xvi.12.
89 *Nouv. ess.* IV.xvi.12.
90 See Nagel 1955.
91 Graunt 1662, pp.14, 57–8.
92 Petty 1690, Preface.
93 Graunt 1662, p. 58.
94 De Witt 1671.
95 Société Général Néerlandaise d'Assurances sur la Vie et de Rentes Viagères 1898, p. 5; Hudde 1679.
96 Halley 1693, p. 599; see also Schmitt-Lermann 1954, p. 55, and K. Pearson 1978, chaps. 1–4.
97 Hacking 1975a, chap. 13.

98  Arbuthnot 1710; De Moivre 1756; Süssmilch 1775; K. Pearson 1978, chap. 9.

99  Halley 1693, p. 600.

100  Hacking 1971c.

101  Bernoulli 1969–89, vol. 3, pp. 249–50.

102  Stigler 1986a, pp. 77–8.

103  Charleton 1654, p. 132 (p. 5 of original).

104  Bacon, *Nov. org.* I 39–67; Descartes, *Disc.* VI; Newton 1672, p. 5004; Locke, *Ess.* III.vi.22.

105  Newton 1952, p. 404.

106  Daston 1988, chap. 5.

107  J. Bernoulli 1969–89, vol. 3, p. 259.

108  See, e.g., Boyle, 'Of the Excellency and Ground of the Corpuscular or Mechanical Philosophy', Boyle 1772, vol. 4, p. 71.

109  See Locke, *Ess.* IV.xv and Hume, *Treatise,* I.iii.11–13.

110  J. Bernoulli 1969–89, vol. 3, p. 249.

111  Ger. Math. III 83–4.

112  Ger. Math. III 87–9.

113  J. Bernoulli 1969–89, vol. 3, p. 239.

114  Aristotle, *Metaphysics* 1078a10–16.

115  *De interpretatione,* 18a27–19a37.

116  Galilei 1890–1909, vol. 8, p. 277.

117  Cardano 1663, vol. 1, pp. 263–4.

118  Pascal 1963, pp. 101A–103B, on p. 103A.

# 32

# SCEPTICISM

## CHARLES LARMORE

In the seventeenth century more than in many other periods of philosophy, scepticism was a fundamentally important philosophical phenomenon. Charron, Pascal, and Bayle are among the greatest sceptical thinkers. And Montaigne as well belongs to this period, for although he died eight years before the century began, he was the central figure in its debate about scepticism. These philosophers argued persistently and imaginatively against the possibility of knowledge in natural science, ethics, and theology, and they developed novel and powerful views of how the sceptical outlook is to be understood. Scepticism was also important because almost every major philosopher who was not a sceptic believed that a decisive feature of his own position was how it differed from scepticism. Some of these philosophers (the 'mitigated sceptics' such as Mersenne and Gassendi) tried to show that a great deal of scepticism could be accepted without abandoning all possibility of knowledge or without leaving reason idle even where knowledge was not possible. Others (such as Bacon and Descartes) tried to work out a new conception of the sources of knowledge which would prove immune to doubt. In general, the issue of scepticism was one around which many of the most important developments in seventeenth-century philosophy crystallised.

The literary sources of seventeenth-century scepticism can be divided into three groups. First, there were the ancient texts – principally Cicero's *Academica* and Saint Augustine's *Contra academicos* – which had been available to the Latin West for centuries and which passed on an account of one of the two principal schools of Greek scepticism, the Academy of Arcesilaus and Carneades. There were, second, those ancient Greek texts which had appeared in Latin translation more recently – Diogenes Laertius's *Lives of the Philosophers* and, more important, the writings of Sextus Empiricus. Sextus's *Outlines of Pyrrhonism* was translated into Latin by Henri Etienne in 1562, and his *Against the Dogmatists* by Gentien Hervet in 1569. These texts were indispensable in providing knowledge of the other Greek school of sceptics – the Pyrrhonists. The third group of sources was the works of sixteenth-century sceptics such as Erasmus (*Moriae encomium*, 1511), Gian Francesco Pico della Mirandola (*Examen vanitatis doctrinae gentium*, 1520),

Agrippa von Nettesheim (*De incertitudine et vanitate scientiarum,* 1526), and Francisco Sanchez (*Quod nihil scitur,* 1581). All of these sceptics made use of Cicero's works, and some had begun to use the ideas in Sextus's writings, but none of them influenced seventeenth-century thought to the extent that Montaigne did.[1]

Seventeenth-century scepticism differed from its ancient models in various respects. One important difference concerned the nature of 'appearances' to which the sceptic is supposed to assent. For the ancient Greek sceptics, appearances were either the observable qualities of things or the way things appear. This was how Montaigne and Charron, Mersenne, and Gassendi generally understood the term as well. But Descartes, and those whom he influenced, came to understand appearances in a third sense, as purely mental 'ideas'. This shift had significant philosophical consequences. Sceptical doubt could now extend, as it had never done for the Greeks, to the very existence of an external world.[2] And the thinking subject could be assumed to be immediately aware only of its own internal states. The 'problem of the external world' and 'subjective self-certainty' are largely post-Cartesian developments. Another important difference between ancient and seventeenth-century scepticism was the relation of the latter to religion. The ancient Pyrrhonists urged conformity to existing customs, religion included. But in the religious controversies which tore apart early modern Europe, scepticism came to play a more partisan rôle.[3] In Montaigne's hands, Pyrrhonian conformism became an argument against Protestant innovation and for allegiance to traditional Catholicism. For Pascal and Bayle, scepticism was a tool for cutting back the pretensions of reason, in order to make room for faith. This was an aim Montaigne voiced as well, but their faith, unlike Montaigne's, tended to leave the sceptical outlook behind, because it was more deeply felt and because it was at odds with established religion.

At the same time, early modern scepticism owed to the ancients the basic forms of its argument and the targets of its attack – the knowability of the real natures of things and of a universally valid morality. The exceptions were limited to scepticism about the very existence of an external world (which appeared with Descartes), the doubt whether what we find evident may not be in fact false (which occurred in Montaigne as well as Descartes), and theological scepticism, such as Bayle's, which could arise only within a Christian framework. Equally important, for many philosophers in the seventeenth century, as for the ancients, scepticism was not just an intellectual exercise but a matter of great practical importance. For Montaigne and his followers, it was itself the proper way of life. For Pascal and Bayle, it was an expression of man's desolation without God. For

Locke and Malebranche, its limited validity pointed to those other areas of life where our greatest concern ought to lie.

## I. MONTAIGNE AND HIS HEIRS

The history of seventeenth-century scepticism must begin near the end of the preceding century, with Montaigne. The most thorough and famous exposition of his scepticism is the twelfth essay of the second book of his *Essais,* the *Apologie de Raimond Sebond.* In the period 1575–76, when he was composing this essay, Montaigne began reading Henri Etienne's translation of Sextus Empiricus's *Outlines of Pyrrhonism.* The last section of the *Apologie,* devoted to the fallibility of the senses, clearly shows Sextus's influence.

Montaigne's scepticism had deeper roots, however, than his discovery of the great manual of ancient Pyrrhonism. It grew out of his increasing dissatisfaction with the neo-Stoicism which he had imbibed from his friend La Boétie, and which he had deployed in his earliest essays. He came to believe, not only that the Stoic ideal of rational self-control and constancy was unattainable but also that what he most wanted to write about was the inconstancy of human action, the diversity and mutability of opinion, and man's general incapacity to order the world and himself as a rational whole. These themes dominate many essays that were written years before the *Apologie.* 'Of the inconsistency of our actions' (*Essais* II.1, 1572–4) sees human life as nothing but a patchwork, a succession of diverse and unstable purposes. And in 'It is folly to measure the true and false by our own capacity' (*Essais* I.27, 1572–4), Montaigne had already begun to draw an epistemological moral from this human condition: we should not try to lay down in advance what is impossible in this world, for that would be to 'assume the advantage of knowing the bounds and limits of God's will and of the power of our mother Nature'.[4] Here is a first expression of the sceptical doubt about how an omnipotent God could have made the world quite different from how we are able to conceive it, a doubt which would return in the *Apologie* (and which would later appear, of course, in Descartes's *Meditationes*). Montaigne's emerging scepticism was directed primarily at the pretensions of Stoicism, although he was also critical of Aristotle, whom he called the 'prince of dogmatists'.[5] The break with neo-Stoicism was gradual, not abrupt. Montaigne discovered the extent and nature of his scepticism as he wrote his essays and as he added to them after the first edition of 1580.[6]

The *Apologie de Raimond Sebond,* especially in the version of the fifth edition of 1588, is a full-fledged sceptical treatise. We have no knowledge, he argues, that goes beyond appearances.[7] What precisely did Montaigne mean by 'appearances'? In the sceptical tradition, ancient and modern, the term has been used to refer to (1) the observable qualities of things, as opposed to their underlying structure, or (2) the way things appear (their apparent qualities), as opposed to how they may be in themselves, or (3) the impressions or ideas of things, as they exist in our minds, and as opposed to anything having extra-mental existence.[8] The sceptic has always been said to assent to the appearances, and to nothing more. But clearly the scope of his assent will differ importantly, depending on which of these three senses is at work. Montaigne's use of the term seems more ambitious than the first interpretation just mentioned, since the doubts about the reliability of the senses, at the end of the *Apologie,* take in not just theories about the ultimate natures of things but also ordinary observations of colours, sizes, and so forth.[9] In general, the second interpretation fits best what Montaigne meant by the 'appearances' that he did not doubt; typically, he questioned whether things are indeed as we perceive them, and not whether there are any external things at all. In one passage near the end of the *Apologie,* however, he equated 'appearances' with 'impressions' (*passions*), which are located in our senses, which are different from objects, and which would have to be compared with objects, if there were to be knowledge of objects.[10] Here the third interpretation, which limits appearances to one's own mental states, is appropriate. At this point, his scepticism extended, as would Descartes's, to the very existence of the external world. However, Montaigne's scepticism was for the most part not as radical as Descartes's. As a rule, 'appearances' meant the way things appear, probably because he considered scepticism as a way of life, which would be difficult to sustain, if judgement were suspended about the existence of everything besides one's own mind. In this he was following in the path of the ancient Pyrrhonists.[11]

Montaigne's sceptical doubts in the *Apologie* are not particularly novel, and few of them are presented in a convincing way. The first sections of the essay refer to the diversity of human opinion and the ease with which men change their opinions. Although these considerations were central to Montaigne's scepticism, and to that of his followers such as Charron and La Mothe Le Vayer,[12] they plainly do not offer a sufficient argument for scepticism by themselves: the fact that one knows something is compatible with there being a wide diversity of opposing views. The last section of the essay shows the influence of his reading of Sextus. Beginning with the supposition that knowledge, if there is any, must come through the senses, he offers a number of reasons for doubting their reliability. We may be lacking certain senses that would give us a different view of the world. The senses may distort, by their mediation, our image of the world. Perceptions while dreaming can be indiscernible from waking experiences. Animals have different sense experiences than we do. We are unable to determine which of our sense experiences merit belief, since any criterion would itself require justification, and that is unavailable, the senses themselves being uncertain and demonstration being open to infinite regress.[13] Although occurring amongst the first four of Sextus's ten tropes, these arguments are not grouped in accord with that classification, but simply follow one another pell-mell. The only doubt without ancient precedent is Montaigne's insistence that because we cannot properly say that omnipotent God cannot do this or that, we should not claim to understand the universe He has created.[14]

The *Apologie de Raimond Sebond* is notable not so much for the sceptical arguments it presents as for its description of the sceptical position itself. Montaigne allied himself with the Pyrrhonists, against the Academic sceptics, such as Carneades, whom he understood to have believed that knowledge beyond the appearances is unattainable and that some opinions can nonetheless be preferred as more probable than others.[15] Following Sextus, he wrote that the thorough sceptic will not conclude even that such knowledge is unattainable but instead keep searching; and against the second belief he made the interesting objection that one proposition cannot be recognised as more probable than another except on the basis of some other proposition known to be true.

But the most important and innovative feature of his scepticism is the motto he proposed for the Pyrrhonist, 'Que sçay-je?'[16] The motto itself occurred first in the edition of 1588, but its rationale had already appeared in the first edition of 1580. Pyrrhonists, he observed, must have difficulty expressing their outlook, since our language 'is wholly formed of affirmative propositions, which to them are utterly repugnant; so that when they say "I doubt", immediately you have them by the throat to make them admit that at least they know and are sure of this fact, that they doubt'.[17] As Montaigne noted, Sextus himself had denied in the *Outlines of Pyrrhonism* (I.206) that the Pyrrhonist asserts the truth of 'I doubt', since such an expression may undermine itself. But Montaigne was far clearer than Sextus about the danger confronting the sceptic here. It is that the assertion 'I doubt' implies knowledge of the fact that one doubts. Montaigne understood the danger better, probably because in the meantime Augustine had exploited this point in order to accuse the sceptic of self-refutation.[18] Most important, he recognised, unlike Sextus, that the sceptic can elude such a counter-argument if he expresses his outlook, not affirmatively ('I doubt'), but rather interrogatively, 'What do I know?' For a question, in contrast to an assertion, implies nothing. It does not imply that one knows that one does not know nor (as Augustine and later Descartes continued the counter-argument) that one knows at least that one exists. This was Montaigne's most significant contribution to scepticism. It was his way of expressing his conviction that scepticism is not really a 'position' at all, like other philosophies, but rather a continual movement of thought. Few thinkers in the seventeenth century were to be as careful in this regard as he.

Montaigne drew two important consequences from his interrogative scepticism. First, he developed a sceptical ethic. The *Essais* rehearse again and again the standard Pyrrhonist view that, unable to extend our knowledge beyond the appearances, we should conform our actions to the existing laws and customs of our society.[19] In the case of religion, if not in other areas, we must thus conform our belief as well. This is the basis of what is often called his 'fideism': he remained a Catholic, not because he could show by argument that this faith is superior to that of the Reformers or to other faiths, but rather because it was the one in which he had been brought up.[20] There is no contradiction, of course, in a sceptic having religious faith, since finding no rational grounds for a belief does not preclude there being other motives for believing it. Indeed, 'Christian Pyrrhonism' was to become a frequent form of thought in the early seventeenth century.[21] Fideistic conservativism, however, is quite compatible with the repression of dissident opinion. Montaigne became an advocate of religious toleration because he broadened the usual Pyrrhonist outlook precisely by insisting upon the sceptic's ongoing search for truth. This is clearest in *Essais* III.8, 'Of the art of discussion'.[22] Our own thinking, he observed, so often contradicts itself that we should welcome discussion with others, however different their opinions may be. Since we are born to search for truth, without ever possessing it, we should not cut anyone out of this conversation, for 'the world is but a school of inquiry'. Every form of tyranny, whether in word or in deed, is therefore abhorrent. This sceptical ethic was Montaigne's second important contribution to scepticism. It replaced, in effect, the ancient sceptical goal of *ataraxia* with the more vigorous ideal of feeling at home in interminable controversy.

Second, Montaigne's interrogative scepticism drew him to self-portraiture, and this turned out to harbour a complexity he did not foresee at the outset. If knowledge of the world eludes us, but if our response to this is to continue searching, then there seems to remain one subject about which we can speak authoritatively, namely, our search itself. Montaigne discovered the availability of this subject only as he wrote his essays and broke with his early neo-Stoicism. By 1580 it was perfectly clear: In the prefatory note to the reader in the first edition of the *Essais* he wrote, 'I am myself the matter of my book', and in the essays he wrote subsequently for Book III, this theme became the centre of attention.[23] He insisted upon complete honesty in his self-portraits, claiming in that prefatory note, 'I want to be seen here in my simple, natural, ordinary fashion, without straining or artifice; for it is myself I portray.'[24] What Montaigne meant by the 'artifice' he aimed to avoid is well explained in the essay 'Of the Inconsistency of our Actions': 'In view of the natural instability of our conduct and opinions, it has often seemed to me that even good authors are wrong to insist on fashioning a consistent and solid fabric out of us. They choose one general characteristic, and go and arrange and interpret all a man's actions to fit their picture.'[25] Artifice consists in giving to the self a coherence it does not actually possess, by choosing just a few of its features as a focus ('the real self') around which all the others are bent into conformity (or else, as Montaigne goes on to say, set down to dissimulation).

In the 1580 account of his project, he proposed to do without artifice, to describe the movement of his thought as it really unfolds. This is because he assumed that the self is like any other object, existing independently of our efforts to describe it. This understanding of self-portraiture remains steadfast through the 1588 edition, from which the passage in II.1 was quoted in the immediately previous paragraph. Of course, if the self is thus an object like any other, Montaigne's general sceptical outlook must extend to it as well. Here, as with other things, we are unable to get beyond appearances. When recounting how Thales stumbled because he was contemplating the heavens, he corrects the Milesian girl who reportedly told Thales to pursue self-knowledge instead: 'Our condition makes the knowledge of what we have in our hands as remote from us and as far above the clouds as that of the stars.'[26]

However, Montaigne's scepticism about self-knowledge moved beyond even this. Two additions to the 1588 edition (which appeared in the 1595 edition, published by his literary executrix, Marie de Gournay) show that he came to doubt whether the appearances of the self are independent of the activity of portraying them. In *Essais* II.18, he wrote:

In modeling this figure upon myself, I have had to fashion and compose myself so often to bring myself out, that the model itself has to some extent grown firm and taken shape. Painting myself for others, I have painted my inward self with colors clearer than my original ones. I have no more made my book than my book has made me – a book consubstantial with its author.[27]

And in *Essais* II.6, he admitted: 'There is no description equal in difficulty, or certainly in usefulness, to the description of oneself. Even so one must spruce up, even so one must present oneself in an orderly arrangement, if one would go out in public. Now, I am constantly adorning myself, for I am constantly describing myself.'[28] These passages assert the inevitability of precisely the 'artifice' it was Montaigne's initial aim to avoid. Self-description always embodies a certain arrangement of the self that is described, since the self to be described always moulds itself with an eye to how it will be described. The point is not that self-knowledge is elusive, as though its object were hidden from us. It is a doubt about whether the notion of self-knowledge makes sense, since the self seems not to be an independent object at all. Self-description is always also self-creation. In describing ourselves, we arrange ourselves into a pattern.[29] There can be this consubstantiality of portrait and model, of course, only because describer and described are one. But Montaigne's ultimate view of the 'unity' of the self (unlike Descartes's) offers no guarantee of the accuracy of self-description; rather, it calls into question the very idea of accuracy. In the seventeenth century, this kind of scepticism fell into oblivion. Most philosophers never imagined that the self could be other than a *res* or substance, even if they would disagree about whether the self is open or resistant to self-knowledge.[30] It would not reappear in any prominent way until the Romantic movement.

Having no male heirs, Montaigne left his friend Pierre Charron the right to bear his coat of arms. But Charron's share in Montaigne's legacy went well beyond this. His massive tome *De la sagesse* (1601, second edition in 1604) was the form in which Montaigne's thought was best known to most philosophers in the seventeenth century. Indeed, so great was the popularity of this book that some, such as Gassendi, preferred it to the *Essais* themselves.[31] In many respects, Charron's book simply made Montaigne's scepticism more accessible, by abstaining from the ancient quotations and digressions which populate the *Essais*. Sometimes it interestingly supplemented Montaigne's themes. At certain points, however, Charron departed from his model. Unfortunately, these differences reflected a neglect of the very elements that make Montaigne's scepticism so subtle.

We have no knowledge, Charron insisted, of what lies behind appearances (by which he meant the way things appear to us): true and false opinions enter by the same door, he wrote, because we have no reliable criterion to distinguish them.[32] But being a good Pyrrhonist, he did not declare that such knowledge is unattainable. Like Montaigne, he urged that the true sceptic continue to search for truth. Also like Montaigne, he argued that the sceptic can live his scepticism only by living a double life. While conforming externally to the given customs and laws of his society, the sceptic will withhold assent to their intrinsic superiority, wherever he finds that doubtful. In an interesting variation on this theme of Pyrrhonist conservativism, Charron observed that doubt by itself is dangerous, since it can easily foster disobedience to the norms whose validity is doubted. What impels the sceptic to conform, he claimed, is the recognition that left to itself thought is unstable and forever fluctuating, incapable of arriving at any fixed point, and thus that life can be lived only within a framework of institutions.[33] This is why Charron could announce that the aim of his book was not to urge a retreat from the world, but rather to prepare men for civil life.[34]

Charron's ideal of the sceptic as one who willingly plays his part in a world of social formalities, while recognising that they are no more than that, had a profound influence on moral thought in seventeenth-century France. During the first half of the century, it inspired a group of thinkers who have since become known as the '*libertins érudits*'. The most important members were François La Mothe Le Vayer and Gabriel Naudé, and Pierre Gassendi for a time. They thought of themselves as '*esprits supérieurs*' or '*esprits forts*', in that their inner freedom set them apart from the unthinking conformism of the multitude and the passionate commitments of dogmatists, both theoretical and political. At times La Mothe Le Vayer wondered whether the ideal of '*l'extérieur au peuple avec réservation du dedans*' is really practicable in the midst of civil life and urged instead a retreat to the private realm. But generally he kept to Charron's position that scepticism is livable only through external compliance with established custom.[35] As the term '*libertin*' indicates, there have long been suspicions that these neo-Pyrrhonian sceptics professed allegiance to the Catholic faith, not out of a genuine fideism, but rather as one more item of outward conformity (the same doubts have arisen about Charron himself). A decisive verdict on their religious sincerity is probably impossible for us to reach (as it may also have been for them).[36] Later in the century, Charron's ideal would turn into that of the *honnête homme* (e.g., Philinte in Molière's *Le misanthrope*), who would show the same willingness to conform without inner conviction but would not have the same devotion to self-examination.

For Montaigne, Charron, and their followers, as for the ancient Pyrrhonists, scepticism was thus an answer to the question how one ought to live. Descartes would later object (despite the similarity between Charron's ideal and his own 'provisional morality' of outward conformity in the absence of moral knowledge) that the notion of a sceptical way of life is a contradiction in terms. Sceptical doubt, he claimed, must be kept apart from the conduct of life, for scepticism itself is unlivable.[37] This difference seems best explained by the fact that the doubt of Montaigne and Charron generally stopped at the way things appear, whereas Descartes believed that sceptical doubt must ultimately encompass the very existence of an external world.[38]

Alongside these continuities with Montaigne, there are also significant differences. One of the most obvious is that the primary theoretical target of Charron's scepticism was no longer Stoicism, but rather Aristotelianism. His sceptical attacks on Aristotle and scholasticism were more frequent and central; his discussion of the unreliability of the senses, unlike Montaigne's, was aimed directly at Aristotle as the one who made the senses the source of all knowledge.[39] One important reason for this shift is that Charron, unlike his mentor, continued to profess loyalty to neo-Stoic ethics. His account of the passions was explicitly based on the writings of the sixteenth-century neo-Stoic Guillaume du Vair, and time and again he insisted, quoting Stoic authorities, that one should live according to nature.[40] Unlike Montaigne, therefore, Charron adopted only a limited moral scepticism: although he claimed that much of morality is no more than a matter of custom and that certain theses of traditional ethics, such as the unity of the virtues, are incoherent (because the possession or exercise of some virtues excludes that of others, and because sometimes one can bring about good only by doing evil),[41] he still believed in reason's ability to discern a core morality of universal validity. Indeed, this allegiance to Stoic natural law formed part of his effort to make ethics independent of religion, by urging that virtue is its own reward.[42] Charron's defence of this core morality is scarcely novel or powerful. And other passages of *De la sagesse* (II.9) expound Montaigne's sceptical ethic, without any appeal to natural law. But there is no mistaking his claims to fundamental moral knowledge.[43]

Morality is not the only area in which Charron cut back on Montaigne's scepticism. As the motto of his scepticism he chose not 'Que sçay-je?' but 'Je ne sçay',[44] showing no apparent awareness of the difficulties that Montaigne had seen in such an affirmative formula. Perhaps Charron was not concerned about the implications of his motto because he believed that knowledge of one's own thoughts and desires is indeed available to the sceptic. He did admit that such self-knowledge is often rendered difficult by the instability of our thoughts, by our interest in deceiving ourselves, and by our tendency to pursue other things in the world precisely in order to avoid reflecting upon ourselves – what Pascal would later call *divertissement*.[45] Yet Charron did not doubt that self-knowledge can eventually be acquired by 'a true, long, and assiduous study of oneself, a serious and attentive examination, not only of one's words and actions, but of one's most secret thoughts'.[46] There is no trace of Montaigne's doubts about the very idea of self-knowledge, no worry whether the self is independent of our efforts to describe it. Another departure from Montaigne is that Charron shared none of his doubts about knowledge of probabilities. He believed that some propositions are discernibly more probable than others, and that the sceptic should 'adhere' to them, though without affirming them.[47]

## II. MITIGATED SCEPTICISM

In important ways, Charron's scepticism was thus less thorough-going than Montaigne's, although he offered no reasons for making it so. Still, *De la sagesse* carried on central elements of Montaigne's thought in a more consumable form, and many philosophers of the seventeenth century did not see any significant difference between them. The scepticism of Montaigne and Charron had many followers, but it also met with considerable resistance. Among its opponents were those who tried to defend Aristotelian and scholastic views about the possibility of knowledge. But the most important anti-sceptics sought instead to work out a third alternative other than scholasticism and scepticism.

There were in general two forms which such a third alternative took. The first was to propose a new conception of the source of knowledge, which would succeed where scholasticism failed, by delivering a 'certain' (that is definitive and indubitable) and ultimate account of nature and of man. This was the path followed by Francis Bacon and René Descartes. In one of his earliest philosophical writings, the *Advancement of Learning* of 1605, Bacon urged that although sceptics, ancient and modern, wrongly condemned the senses altogether as the source of knowledge, their error was understandable, since the only way the 'Logicians' (he plainly meant the Aristotelians) conceived of the senses delivering the principles of demonstrative syllogisms was enumerative induction.[48] Generalisations from what we observe are always liable to be upset by a contrary instance. Bacon's hope was that scepticism could be avoided if the senses could be made to instruct us in a different manner. In later writings, such as the *Novum organon* (1620) and its preface, the *Magna instauratio,* the new method was said to lie in eliminative induction: we can avoid defeat by contrary instances if we seek them out beforehand, believing only those explanations of the phenomena the alternatives to which we have eliminated by crucial experimental tests. Bacon believed that this procedure could yield certainties about the causes of things. (He showed little awareness of the fact that it could do so only if, implausibly, we could list all possible alternative explanations and could have all the relevant data at our disposal.)[49] By assenting only to propositions that had passed such tests, the *Novum organon* claims, we will supposedly avoid the two extremes of hasty assent, typical of the Aristotelians, and the despondent withholding of assent, typical of the Academic sceptics.[50]

Later, I shall discuss Descartes's reaction to scepticism. Before that, I want to examine a second tactic, widespread in the seventeenth century, for cutting a middle way between scholasticism and scepticism. Although agreeing with the sceptics that knowledge about the underlying natures of things is unavailable, proponents of this approach argued that we do have knowledge of appearances (and can acquire a lot more) and that a theory of appearances is the proper task of the sciences. This view, often called 'mitigated' scepticism,[51] was first developed in the writings of Marin Mersenne, particularly in *La vérité des sciences contre les septiques ou pyrrhoniens* (1625), in which he argued against the dangers which the scepticism of Charron and his followers posed both to the sciences and to the Catholic faith.[52] Some of the philosopher-scientists belonging to Mersenne's famous circle of correspondents, most of all Pierre Gassendi, elaborated it further. In these matters, Gassendi's influence upon later thinkers was profound.

However, mitigated scepticism was not all of a piece. It took quite different forms, depending on what was understood to be the domain of 'appearances' and on whether conjectures about what lies behind the appearances were permitted. Generally, Mersenne himself equated the appearances, of which we can have knowledge, with the observable qualities of things, as opposed to their underlying natures, which have been postulated to explain them, but which lie beyond our ken. Occasionally, when considering more radical forms of sceptical doubt, he retreated to talking of the 'appearances' as the way things appear to us, or even as our experiences of things. More constant was his insistence that the sceptical threat would be tamed, if natural philosophy limited itself to finding regularities among the appearances and abstained from speculations about their underlying causes.[53] Physical inquiry, he believed, should follow the path of those mixed sciences, such as optics, which are only a little less certain than mathematics itself and which express observable connexions in mathematical form.[54] One of the most interesting features of Mersenne's anti-Pyrrhonism is his argument why such phenomenal regularities are discernible. Each of Sextus's tropes, he claimed, could be converted into a form of phenomenal knowledge, if we turn the reason for why there is a divergence of perception into a parameter of a regularity: for example, the difference in the perception of the same object among different animal species (the first trope) may be viewed as different sorts of animals regularly perceiving a given object in a specific way.[55] In general, and most vigorously in works subsequent to *La vérité des sciences,* Mersenne opposed any speculation, even conjectural, about the underlying nature of things.[56] This was the central point on which his mitigated scepticism differed from Gassendi's.

An enthusiastic follower of Charron, the young Gassendi disliked Aristotelianism chiefly because of the unsuitability of its ethical thought to the Stoic goal of *ataraxia*.[57] (One important influence of Charron on seventeenth-century Pyrrhonism was the effort to reconcile certain elements of Stoicism with scepticism; it made scepticism less radical in moral matters than it had been in Montaigne and left Aristotelianism to become the paradigm of dogmatism.) Reading Sextus helped Gassendi to broaden his dissatisfaction with Aristotle. His earliest work, the *Exercitationes paradoxicae adversus Aristoteleos,* made use of Sextus's tropes to mount a sustained sceptical attack upon the whole of Aristotle's philosophy, its physics as well as its ethics. Having published the first volume in 1624, he nonetheless withdrew from publication the second volume the following year, despite the fact that it contained his most explicitly Pyrrhonian arguments. This change of mind had probably something to do with his meeting with Mersenne during the winter of 1624–5 (though fear of an Aristotelian backlash was probably also involved). Since Mersenne's *La vérité des sciences* was to appear in 1625, a plausible explanation is that Mersenne convinced him of the weaknesses and dangers in Pyrrhonian scepticism.[58] In any case, Gassendi's subsequent writings charged the Pyrrhonists with a number of mistakes. The *Syntagma philosophicum* (1655), the fundamental epistemological treatise on which he worked continually until his death, proclaimed that a middle way must be found between scepticism and dogmatism.[59] In part he simply followed Mersenne's lead, claiming that we can discern regularities among the 'appearances', by which he usually meant the apparent qualities of things. He also claimed that sometimes – under normal conditions, when the stick has been taken out of the water and we are wide awake – there can be no conceivable doubt that things really are as they appear; so he argued against Descartes in Objectiones V.[60]

Gassendi was not content, however, with an anti-scepticism that dealt simply with phenomenal regularities and, sometimes, with the observable qualities of things. What propelled him beyond Mersenne's programme was his long-standing interest in reconstructing and rehabilitating the thought of Epicurus, an interest which (perhaps largely due to a conversation with Isaac Beeckman in 1629) extended to Epicurean atomism and thus to inferences transcending the domain of appearances.[61] It was an interest favourable to contemporary attempts at mechanical explanation and to Copernican astronomy. Inferences like those of Epicurus, which move from the appearances to their unobservable causes, are permissible, he argued, so long as these postulated causes are analogous to the sorts of things we do observe, so long as they agree with a wide range of phenomena – and, most important, so long as we claim for these explanations no more than probability (*verisimilitudo* or *probabilitas*), never certainty. According to Gassendi,

Sextus and other sceptics had made Epicurus's use of such arguments seem illegitimate, precisely because they overlooked this last qualification.[62] The mature Gassendi's *via media* was thus more ambitious than Mersenne's. Although the true natures of things cannot become the object of *scientia* (that is, certainty, as he believed was demanded by the idea of knowledge, following Aristotle), they do not totally elude us: 'Even if we do not perceive causes that are certain (*certae*) and indubitable (*indubiae*)', he wrote in the *Syntagma*, 'we can still obtain those which have some sort of probability (*speciem aliquam probabilitatis*).'[63] It is important to note that, even if only probable, these conjectures were still meant to be about the ultimate natures of things; Gassendi did not interpret them instrumentally as mere devices for allowing us to predict appearances. In fact, he believed that they might eventually become more than probable, if microscopes could be devised by which we could actually see the atomic structures of things.[64]

Gassendi's overall aim was to replace Aristotelianism with Epicureanism as the official Christian philosophy. For him, Pyrrhonism was chiefly a means to overthrow Aristotle's legacy, first in the area of ethics and then in all domains of thought. His probabilism, although indeed a *via media* between the two, was targeted more against Aristotelian dogmatism than against scepticism. So it is probably wrong to say, as an account of his deepest motivations, that Gassendi was reacting to the 'sceptical crisis' at the beginning of the seventeenth century.[65] Mersenne may have persuaded him to be careful about using Pyrrhonist arguments, but for Gassendi this was a question of means rather than ends. Indeed, the thesis that there was a sceptical crisis in the early seventeenth century seems generally an exaggeration. Sceptics such as Charron lived their scepticism without any sense of crisis at all. There were those like Mersenne who did discern a sceptical crisis, but for Gassendi the principal danger lay elsewhere, with Aristotelianism.

Whatever the exact extent of his influence, Gassendi blazed a path in which many followed. Joseph Glanvill, for example, expressing the views of many of the members of the English Royal Society, urged the same recipe for avoiding the twin dangers of dogmatism and scepticism. Because we can have no infallible knowledge of the underlying natures of things, the Aristotelian ideal of science must forever lie beyond our reach. Yet nothing stands in the way, he argued, of working out hypotheses about this domain and testing them against the phenomena.[66] In fact, Glanvill believed that well-confirmed hypotheses may even be called 'certain', so long as we distinguish 'indubitable certainty', in which no positive reason for doubt has been discovered, from the Aristotelian ideal of 'infallible certainty', in which all possibility of error has been eliminated.[67] The point of this distinction was to indicate that some things can be taken as a settled basis for further inquiry, even though nothing can be held to be immune to revision. It belonged to the spirit of Gassendi's own *via media*. A fallibilist notion of certainty was attractive to a number of other English thinkers as well, such as William Chillingworth and John Wilkins. And it found its most refined development in the methodological thought of Isaac Newton, in his notion of 'experimental certainties'. Newton's distinction between 'experimental certainties' and mere 'hypotheses' is misunderstood if it is taken to assume that experiment can definitively establish any scientific theory. It was aimed at the contemporary conviction (itself more *a priori* than empirical) that every natural phenomenon must be explained by some mechanical (contact-action) hypothesis.[68]

Locke, too, so clearly continued the form of mitigated scepticism advocated by Gassendi and this English tradition that I shall break with strict chronology and discuss Locke, before going on to Descartes.[69] *An Essay concerning Human Understanding* (1690) claimed that a science of the natural world, in the Aristotelian sense of deducing the phenomena from a set of fundamental physical principles known with certainty, lies beyond our reach. Generally our complex ideas of substances – our ideas of the distinctive features of different kinds of things – take in only their observable qualities, which we have seen go together in our experience.[70] We are unable, he wrote, to explain with certainty why these qualities go together, because our knowledge gives out on two fundamental matters.[71] First, we do not know the 'real essences' of things, their underlying structure which is responsible for their observable qualities. And second, even if we did know some real essences, we could not derive the observable qualities from them for the following reason. Our ideas of these qualities tend mostly to be ideas of secondary qualities (colours, sounds, tastes, etc.), which in objects themselves are not as we perceive them to be, but are rather only powers to produce in us such perceptions. So establishing a necessary connexion between real essences and observable qualities would amount to finding one between real essences and ideas. And Locke believed we could never do this, because in general we cannot grasp how bodies can produce anything so different from them ('having no affinity at all') as ideas.[72] Whatever we understand about how bodies affect mind is a matter of inexplicable experiential regularities. His point was not that these are in reality brute regularities, but that their underlying basis lies beyond the limits of our understanding.

Locke was equally sceptical about whether we could know the true nature of mind. Although agreeing that we cannot coherently doubt that we are thinking beings, he insisted against Descartes that this fact leaves open 'what *kind* of being it is' which thinks. Gassendi, in fact, had made the very same criticism of Descartes in Objectiones V.[73] Thus, Locke claimed that it remained undecided whether matter may not have this faculty of thinking – 'it being, in respect of our notions, not much more remote from our comprehension to conceive that GOD can, if he pleases, superadd to matter *a faculty of thinking,* than that he should superadd to it *another substance with a faculty of thinking.*'[74] In other words, the idea that mind and body are distinct substances is no more intelligible to us than the notion of thinking matter (even if in reality the latter is impossible after all).[75] Furthermore, just as Locke also believed that we could not derive the observable qualities of things from their real essences, because we cannot grasp how bodies can act on minds, so he believed that we cannot understand how minds, whatever their underlying nature, can bring about bodily motions.[76] Here, too, we must remain content with the regularities experience teaches us.

Like Gassendi, however, Locke did not recommend that we desist from speculating about the ultimate structure of nature. Indeed, Locke was a partisan of the corpuscularian hypothesis as the best available account of the real essences of bodies, though only so long as it was considered a probability, not a certainty.[77] Locke's conditions for adopting such a conjecture did not differ much from Gassendi's; for example, he, too, claimed that analogy with what we do observe should be our chief guide in proposing underlying structures for the phenomena.[78] But however well confirmed this hypothesis might become, he denied that we could ever come to know, that is – know with infallible certainty, the real essences of things. In this sense Locke was a sceptic about the possibility of a science of nature, indeed a much more dogmatic one than Gassendi, who imagined that one day we might be able to know the underlying structures of things, if sufficiently powerful microscopes were devised.[79]

Beginning with Stillingfleet, Bishop of Worcester and Locke's contemporary, and then Reid, many philosophers have argued that Locke, no doubt contrary to his intentions, had committed himself to an even more radical scepticism because of his 'new way of ideas'.[80] If, as Locke claimed, the immediate object of perception is always an idea, then 'real existence', or the existence of external objects beyond this 'veil of perception', must remain conjectural. Or so his critics have argued. Locke himself did not take the problem of real existence seriously. Conceding that real existence is not as certain as demonstration, he pointed out that demonstrative knowledge itself is not as certain as intuited relations among ideas.[81] Certainty, for Locke, comes in degrees. Real existence must count as certain because there are no conceivable grounds for doubting it: (1) perceiving a real object is experientially different from imagining one, and (2) anyone doubting real existence cannot consistently believe that he is disagreeing with someone claiming knowledge of real existence.[82] The point of this second, very interesting argument is not that the possibility of everything being a dream is experientially equivalent to the supposition of real existence (an anti-sceptical tactic that appears in Leibniz), but rather that it is unintelligible, if advanced controversially. Knowledge of real existence, of course, does not imply knowledge of what real objects are like. Locke believed that we can be certain that our simple ideas of things are true, although real essences of course lie beyond our ken.[83]

Locke's scepticism was thus a limited affair, and yet no less thorough-going for that. Not only did he believe that we cannot understand how mind–body interaction takes place, but he also expressed a similar scepticism about our ability to grasp how one body can causally affect another. The communication of motion in impact, for Descartes the only way in which one body can act on another and the very paradigm of intelligibility, was for Locke just as unintelligible as mind–body interaction, since the only way to conceive it is by way of the obscure idea that motion passes out of one body and into another.[84] Noting our inability to explain mechanical interaction was probably what made Locke open to the possibility that interaction among bodies might be by means other than contact-action. For in his controversy with Stillingfleet he claimed that Newton's work on gravitation had shown that bodies have the power to act on one another at a distance.[85] Such a power, Locke wrote, cannot be derived from our idea of body. Yet he believed it now to be beyond question that such a power is at work in nature. There was therefore some inconsistency in the way Locke tried to accommodate Newton's work in the fourth edition of the *Essay,* saying that 'impulse', or contact, is 'the only way which we can conceive bodies to operate in',[86] as though contact-action were derivable from our idea of body. Instead, the position that Locke had actually come to adopt was that neither contact-action nor action at a distance was derivable from our idea of body, but that both were observably at work in nature.

In sum, Locke's scepticism was directed against the traditional ambitions of natural philosophy. More thoroughly than Gassendi, he argued that we can know neither the real essences of things (both bodies and minds) nor the means by which they interact with one another. He was not denying (as Hume did) that from experience we can detect causal regularities in the world. He was denying that we can do any better, in the project of explaining them, than to 'ascribe them to the arbitrary will and good pleasure of the Wise Architect'.[87]

Locke drew an important lesson from this scepticism. Unlike natural philosophy, morality according to him was capable of demonstration, so that we have good reason to direct our attention more to how we should live than to what is the ultimate structure of nature. 'Morality', he wrote, 'is the proper science and business of mankind in general.'[88] Morality is demonstrable, Locke believed, because (1) the subject of morality, human actions such as murder or gratitude, are things whose ideas ('mixed modes') we fashion ourselves out of simple ideas, and so whose real essence cannot differ from how we conceive them,[89] and (2) human actions are classified as morally right or wrong in terms of their conformity or disagreement with a rule, which may be either civil law, or the law of opinion or reputation, or divine law, the first two being easily knowable, and the third ('the only true touchstone of moral rectitude') as well, so Locke maintained in the *Essay,* since we can prove the existence of a God on whom we depend.[90]

Thus, it is no accident that Locke was not a sceptic about morality. The underlying aim of his mitigated scepticism was precisely to direct our energies to morality as the chief area where certainty is possible.[91] Morality can enjoy this privilege, he believed, because it is to a large extent our own construction. Nature, by contrast, is God's work, done in accord with 'archetypes' lying in His mind. For us, its inner structure must remain an object of conjecture. This is what Locke meant by placing on the title-page of the *Essay* the passage from Ecclesiastes, 'Thou knowest not the works of God, who maketh all things.'

The theme of 'maker's knowledge', the idea that only the maker of a thing can know its inner workings with certainty, because he is in possession of the archetype in accord with which it was made, played an important rôle in the seventeenth-century understanding of scepticism. The claim that we should not presume to know the ultimate structure of nature, since that is God's creation, not ours, figured in the writings of such sixteenth-century sceptics as Montaigne and Sanchez and continued to appear in the works of mitigated sceptics such as Mersenne.[92] Locke's theory of morality can be seen as an attempt to turn this very motif against the moral sceptic.

In this he was not alone. Hobbes had already adopted the same strategy in his own attempt to devise a rational morality. Although agreeing that we cannot know with certainty the causes of natural things, because we did not create them, Hobbes believed that we could achieve this sort of certainty in the area of morality, precisely because there we do create the principles of justice, by means of covenants. His *De homine* of 1658 made this contrast explicitly in Chapter X, Section 5. But the idea of overcoming moral scepticism in this constructivist way shaped his political thought from a very early point and gave it its characteristic form. This was seen by Mersenne himself, who recommended the *De cive* (1642) as the long-awaited refutation of moral scepticism.[93] Hobbes was in fact a member of Mersenne's circle during his long stay in France (1634–7, 1640–51). Yet

Hobbes's argument against moral scepticism drew on a different current of mitigated scepticism, one which was concerned exclusively with morality and whose founder was Hugo Grotius.

Grotius's theory of natural law was a kind of mitigated scepticism in that it, too, aimed to forge a middle way between dogmatism and scepticism, in his case between Aristotelian ethics and the moral scepticism of Montaigne and his followers.[94] Like the epistemology of Mersenne and Gassendi, his strategy was to accept that part of the sceptic's outlook which suffices to refute the dogmatist, but then to show how, contrary to the sceptic, rational inquiry can still be fruitful. He tried to show how a rational morality is possible, even when it is conceded to moral scepticism that what men have called virtue and vice has simply varied from epoch to epoch and from society to society. Near the beginning of the *Prolegomena* to *De jure belli ac pacis* (1625), Grotius summarised Carneades' famous argument against the possibility of natural law, an argument he took to represent the view of moral sceptics in his own time: there can be no natural law, only different laws for different times and places, since men act for their own particular advantage, which varies historically and socially. Grotius agreed that moral diversity is greater than what Aristotelian ethics can handle. But he insisted that in addition to self-interest all men exhibit a minimal sort of 'sociability', impelling them to seek civil peace and to respect each other's property.[95] In the earlier *De jure praedae* (1604–5), he had presented an even more powerful response to the moral sceptic, claiming that self-interest, which Carneades' argument did attribute to all men, suffices as the basis of a morality binding on all.[96] Rational self-interest yields the right of self-preservation and so of acquiring whatever is useful for life. It also points to the need for civil peace, he had continued, if these goals are to be achieved, and this need gives each person the duty to respect the similar rights of others. (He had then supplemented these principles with a *jus gentium,* rules to which there was universal assent.) In either of its versions, Grotius's theory of natural law was quite unlike its Thomist predecessors. It was meant to be a basis for living together to which all could agree, whatever their opinion about Aristotle's more ambitious theory of the virtues, whatever their way of life or religious confession, a basis which would remain valid even if, as he notoriously supposed for the sake of argument, there were no God.[97] Like Montaigne and Charron, Grotius was a horrified witness of nearly a century of religious wars and an advocate of toleration, but on a basis, he believed, much more solid than theirs.[98]

Hobbes's debt to Grotius is manifest. Despite the wide diversity of what people hold to be good, he claimed, everyone is agreed about what is the greatest evil – namely, death.[99] He sought a similarly uncontroversial rule for how people ought to act ('natural law') and claimed to find this in the notion of 'right reason', by which he meant choosing the most efficient means to given ends.[100] This minimalist, basically prudential conception of ends and rational action, along with the recognition that in a moral vacuum (that is, in the absence of a shared morality) people's interests must conflict and violent death will be probable, would move any rational agent to seek peace. And peace could be secured, he believed, only through a common agreement to set up a political authority empowered to create certain mutual obligations. Moral knowledge is attainable, Hobbes was claiming, once we view morality as something we construct on the basis of prudence or rational self-interest: it consists in the articles of civil peace which rational agents, whatever their different desires, would devise. There were some important differences between Hobbes's and Grotius's arguments. Grotius did not believe, for example, that political authority was essential for people to heed this natural law.[101] Nor does he seem to have supposed, as Hobbes did, that self-interest is the only human motive, but rather that (along with natural sociability) it is the only universal one (this is a sign of his greater psychological good sense, but it also makes his argument weaker, since people may have to weigh against one another the demands of self-interest and the claims of other interests, however parochial).[102] Yet despite these differences, Grotius and Hobbes exploited a common anti-sceptical strategy of using scepticism itself as the starting point for the acquisition of knowledge.

Moral anti-scepticism of this sort had a profound influence in the seventeenth century. Spinoza and the early Pufendorf also stood in this tradition.[103] And it underlay Locke's claim that ethics, unlike natural philosophy, can become a science because we ourselves fashion its concepts, although his ethics was not so thoroughly constructivist as Grotius's or Hobbes's, since in its preferred form it appealed to the divine law.[104]

### III. DESCARTES AND SCEPTICISM

Descartes's attitude towards scepticism was fundamentally different from that of the 'mitigated sceptics.' The lesson he drew from scepticism ancient and modern was not that knowledge of the ultimate natures of things lies beyond our capacity, but rather that the Aristotelian view of the sources of knowledge is unsuited to this task. His aim was to devise a new conception of the sources of knowledge, one which would be immune to sceptical doubt, but also powerful enough to yield knowledge of the ultimate structure of reality. The *Meditationes de prima philosophia* (1641) are the authoritative expression of his attitude towards scepticism.[105]

Descartes suggested several times that the sceptical doubts deployed in Meditatio I were not particularly novel.[106] Most of them had indeed figured in the writings of the ancient sceptics and were the stock-in-trade of the neo-Pyrrhonians. But there are two important exceptions. The first is the doubt about the very existence of an external world, which, as I mentioned before, did not belong to the ancient repertoire and was broached only once by Montaigne. The second, for which Descartes did claim some novelty,[107] was indeed unknown to the ancients, but it had many antecedents in Montaigne and mediaeval writers: this was Descartes's supreme doubt concerning an omnipotent God who might have made us err even in what we find to be certain.[108] The real novelty of the scepticism in Meditatio I lay not so much in the doubts themselves, as in the purpose to which Descartes put them. They had the double rôle of discrediting the Aristotelian conception of knowledge while pointing to his own conception as one that is immune to sceptical doubt. This new view of knowledge would enable him, so he claimed in the subtitle of the *Meditationes*, to demonstrate the existence of God and the real distinction between mind and body. His scepticism was thus in the service of a new metaphysics. Since he also believed that these metaphysical truths have important physical implications and that the Aristotelian view of knowledge was what fostered scholastic physics, his scepticism was also meant to secure the foundations of his new physics.[109]

Near the beginning of Meditatio I, Descartes announced that in examining his present beliefs he would treat the slenderest grounds of doubt as sufficient for suspending judgement.[110] This commitment to certainty as indubitability rests on an important, though often misunderstood, assumption about the rational grounds of belief. It does not follow, as some have thought, from Descartes having set aside, at the beginning of the *Meditations*, all merely practical concerns and having turned to the pure pursuit of knowledge.[111] On the contrary, one can be a 'pure enquirer' without adopting the rule of indubitability. The idea of pure enquiry involves the pursuit of (at least) two distinct cognitive goals – the acquisition of truths and the avoidance of falsehoods. But in itself it leaves open how these two goals are to be ranked or balanced against one another.[112] Descartes's unwillingness to run any risk of error shows that for him the second goal always counts for more than the first; that is, it is always better to suspend judgement, if a reason cannot be given against every possibility of a proposition being false, than to accept the proposition on the chance that it may be true. Obviously, there are other ways these two goals can be put together. It is important to see this, if for no other reason than to recognise that giving up Descartes's search for indubitable truths does not require us to abandon the pure pursuit of knowledge.

Descartes proposed that, instead of checking the dubitability of each of his beliefs individually, he would examine the foundations (*fundamenta*) on which they supposedly rest. He summed up these foundations in the following principle: 'Everything which up until now I have taken as most true I have learned either from the senses or through the senses.'[113] For Descartes (as for Charron), this principle expressed a distinctively Aristotelian conception of knowledge. That it was indeed his aim to direct the sceptical attack against the foundations of Aristotelianism is confirmed by what he wrote elsewhere: in the exposition of scepticism in the *Discours* he described this principle as the maxim of the scholastics, and in a letter to Mersenne of 28 January 1641 he claimed that the *Meditationes* aimed at destroying the foundations of Aristotelianism.[114] Of course, Meditatio I was addressed, not just to his scholastic adversaries, but to anyone resolved to think about the basis of his beliefs. The Aristotelian principle was an appropriate starting point even for this larger audience because everyone, according to Descartes, has a natural inclination towards the Aristotelian perspective.[115] (In referring to an examination of 'his' beliefs, Descartes did not mean, of course, his own beliefs, since he had broken with this Aristotelian common-sense outlook long before writing the *Meditationes,* but rather the beliefs of those who still shared that outlook.) Thus, Descartes's decision at the outset of the Meditatio I to focus on the foundations of beliefs does not mean, as some recent critics have charged,[116] that he was unwarrantedly presupposing his own 'foundationalist' idea of knowledge. It reflected instead his conviction that scholasticism was itself foundationalist: the scholastic metaphysics and science he wished to overthrow were nourished by an underlying conception of knowledge as derived from the senses.[117] The progressive effect of this sceptical attack, according to the Synopsis of the *Meditationes,* would be to lead us to detach our mind from our senses (*viam . . . ad mentem a sensibus abducendam*).[118] By this he meant that, once we had recognised the sceptical vulnerability of Aristotelian empiricism, we would be prepared to accept his own non-empiricist foundations of knowledge.

An apparent obstacle to seeing Aristotelian and common-sense empiricism as the target of the scepticism of Meditatio I has to do with how mathematical beliefs are treated here. Being unconcerned about whether their objects exist *in rerum natura*,[119] such beliefs survive the doubt concerning dreaming, but succumb to the subsequent doubt concerning what an omnipotent God might do. Usually it is held that mathematical beliefs are therefore being supposed to have a basis other than the senses, since the reliability of the senses is discredited by the former doubt, and that their status must correspond to Descartes's own view of mathematical knowledge, since the latter doubt returns in Meditatio III to challenge the reliability of clear and distinct perception. But this interpretation is wrong for many reasons.[120] Nowhere in Meditatio I does Descartes represent these mathematical beliefs as being clearly and distinctly perceived or as having any other basis than the senses. On the contrary, the series of doubts proceeds, as we have seen, from the view that *everything* (*Nempe quidquid*) accepted as true rests upon the senses. The Synopsis describes the aim of Meditatio I as leading the mind away from the senses, without mentioning any other purported basis of knowledge as being under scrutiny.[121] Moreover, it is not difficult to understand how an Aristotelian empiricist could maintain the validity of pure mathematics even after the doubt about dreaming has undermined all sense-based beliefs about the natural world: It was Aristotelian doctrine that, once *abstracted* from sense experience, mathematical concepts can be reasoned about independently of their corresponding to anything in nature. It is true that the supreme doubt about an omnipotent God can be made to apply, not just to this abstractionist view of mathematics, but also (as in Meditatio III) to the view that mathematical concepts are innate and mathematical truths clearly and distinctly perceived. But the doubt does not have so broad a scope in Meditatio I, since this alternative view of knowledge has not yet been introduced.

Let us now look more carefully at the series of doubts which Descartes mustered to undermine the reliability of the Aristotelian principle.[122] This section is best understood as a *dialogue* between the Aristotelian (or common-sense person) and the sceptic. The Aristotelian, in response to each doubt voiced by the sceptic, amends his fundamental principle accordingly, but at last is reduced to silence and must admit defeat. Here is an outline of this section as a dialogue:

*Aristotelian:* Knowledge is possible on the basis of the senses.
*Sceptic:* But perception of small and distant objects is fallible.
*Aristotelian:* Nonetheless, perception of close, medium-sized objects is veridical.
*Sceptic:* What of the possibility that you are mad?
*Aristotelian:* I would be mad even to consider that possibility.
*Sceptic:* Nonetheless, you must admit that in the past you have mistaken dreams, which turned out false, for veridical perceptions and indeed that there are no features by which dream perceptions can be distinguished from waking ones. How can you rule out the possibility that any perception of some close, medium-sized object is in fact a dream?[123]
*Aristotelian:* Still, the sensible elements of my perceptions, whether I am awake or dreaming, resemble things in reality.

*Sceptic:* For all you know, these sensible elements could be purely imaginary.

*Aristotelian:* Even so, the simplest elements in these perceptions – mathematical notions of extension, quantity, and magnitude – express truths even if they do not refer to anything in nature: pure mathematics remains certain.

*Sceptic:* Still, there is the possibility of an omnipotent God, who created you and could have given you a nature such that even what you think you know most perfectly is actually false. Or if you think your origin could only have been some natural, more imperfect course of events, you will have all the more reason to wonder whether your nature does not mislead you here.

*Aristotelian:* [silence].

Considering this section a dialogue between the two participants helps us avoid two frequent misinterpretations of Meditatio I. First, it keeps us from wrongly assuming that either the Aristotelian's assertions or the sceptic's doubts express Descartes's own views (although it was certainly Descartes's view that the Aristotelian cannot successfully answer the sceptic's doubts). The Synopsis of the *Meditationes* states that these doubts remain persuasive, only as long as the beliefs questioned are supposed to rest on the foundations currently accepted.[124] Take the doubt concerning dreaming. Unlike the sceptic, Descartes did not believe that dreaming cannot be indubitably distinguished from waking;[125] he believed that the Aristotelian cannot provide a reliable basis for making this distinction. Similarly, this doubt takes for granted that if one does have a waking perception of a close, medium-sized object, then it is veridical (the doubt questions only whether one can know that it is a waking perception). But this is not an assumption Descartes himself believed to be true – far from it, as the *Dioptrique* reveals.[126] Rather, it is the Aristotelian view that perception under normal conditions is not subject to error.

The second, related advantage of this approach is that it allows us to see that the only sceptical doubts taken seriously in Meditatio I are those pointing to possibilities of error the Aristotelian cannot exclude. The possibility of madness is dismissed with the reply that one would have to be mad to take it seriously. This dismissal is best seen, not as Descartes himself refusing to consider this a serious possibility but rather as his recognition that the Aristotelian has no reason to be concerned about it. For Descartes has the sceptic raise another possibility, that of dreaming, that the Aristotelian does not dismiss as ridiculous, because he cannot do so, and the epistemological damage caused by this doubt is *equivalent* to what would have been caused by the possibility of madness. This shows that the possibility of madness is not dismissed, as some critics have objected,[127] because Descartes believed that taking it seriously would thwart his own conception of knowledge. Viewing this section as a dialogue lets us see that it is the Aristotelian (or person of common sense) who dismisses it. Indeed, the *Recherche de la vérité* says just this.[128]

Descartes's technique of having the Aristotelian view of knowledge succumb only to those doubts it cannot rule out expresses a decisive insight in his understanding of scepticism. He appears to have realised that the sceptic's strategy, to remain properly sceptical, must be one of internal demolition. The sceptic must show that the position of those who claim to know undermines itself, that their notion of knowledge is self-contradictory or conflicts with what they claim to know; having to suspend judgement about the true nature of knowledge (as about so much else), he cannot invoke any cognitive standards of his own. Not all sceptics have observed this rule, but it was heeded by many of the ancient sceptics,[129] and Bayle, among the moderns, also had a clear appreciation of it. For Descartes, it was part of his general insistence that the 'order of reasons' be respected.[130]

Indeed, so well did Descartes understand the necessarily internal strategy of the sceptic that in Meditatio II he used it to refute the sceptic himself. The proposition *sum,* he argued, is one that the sceptic cannot coherently doubt. *Sum* is apparently yielded by a premise, *cogito,* but the precise way in which *cogito, ergo sum* represents the collapse of scepticism has always been the subject of great controversy. Any interpretation of *cogito, ergo sum* that views it as an argument in which Descartes advances a premise and draws a conclusion will make it an utterly unpersuasive one.[131] For any reason one supposedly had for not yet knowing the conclusion would surely suffice for one to doubt the premise in this case. This fact has led some to consider *cogito, ergo sum* as not an inference at all, but rather an item of intuitive knowledge.[132] The chief obstacle to this sort of interpretation is, of course, the presence of the word *ergo.* The most promising approach is to regard it as indeed an inference, but not (at least initially) as an argument which Descartes advances on his own.[133] Observe that it is not Descartes himself who advances the premise in Meditatio II. Instead, in the first three formulations of *cogito, ergo sum*[134] the premise is provided, that is, asserted, by the sceptic himself, whatever his intentions, when he expresses his doubt concerning a deceiving God. Descartes thus introduces *cogito, ergo sum,* not as an argument he himself puts forward, but rather as an inference that the sceptic cannot elude. It points to a truth, *sum,* that the sceptic cannot coherently avoid in so far as he doubts.[135] It shows, therefore, that the sceptic's position of suspending judgement about the truth or falsity of all propositions undermines itself because it is self-contradictory. Of course, once he has thus disposed of the sceptic, Descartes is free to assert *cogito, ergo sum* in his own voice. This is what he does in the fourth formulation, which immediately follows the first three.[136]

Descartes's aim was thus to show how the sceptic's position undermines itself from within. In Meditatio II the sceptic is shown to provide the premise of this self-refutation by denying that there is a world or by asserting that there is an evil genius, that is – by claiming that certain things are false. This is because Descartes recommended at the end of Meditatio I that we translate the sceptic's doubts into claims of falsity, in order to learn to give no more credence to doubtful propositions than to false ones.[137] Of course, no true sceptic would ever make such claims (as both Gassendi and later Pierre-Daniel Huet objected); he would instead raise merely possibilities of error.[138] To this extent, radical scepticism might seem to escape incoherence. Nonetheless, inasmuch as the sceptic, in raising these possibilities, says that thus he doubts the propositions in question, he will fall into Descartes's trap. In this regard, the *Principia philosophiae* and even more the posthumous dialogue, *La recherche de la vérité,* offer a sounder version of the self-refutation of the sceptic, since they show that the premise of *cogito, ergo sum* is provided by the sceptic saying that he doubts.[139]

Descartes did not succeed, however, in demolishing Montaigne's scepticism. The sceptic can be said to provide, willy-nilly, the premise of *cogito, ergo sum,* only if his doubt takes the form of an *assertion,* such as 'I doubt' or 'I do not claim to know.' But the apex of Montaigne's scepticism had the form, not of an assertion, but of a question, 'Que sçay-je?' His intention was precisely to elude the clutches of Augustine's proto-Cartesian '*Si fallor, sum.* Although some of Montaigne's followers, such as Charron, missed this manoeuvre, it is odd that Descartes, who knew Montaigne's writings well, showed no awareness of it.[140]

*Sum res cogitans* is thus for Descartes the fundamental certainty that no scepticism can elude. But it serves another function as well. Descartes believed that, by focusing on what it is in the proposition that makes it certain, he could abstract a new standard of knowledge to replace the discredited Aristotelian one. This sort of abstraction has been called his 'intuitionism': we must be able to intuit some propositions as true without appealing to a criterion of truth, for only so can we learn what is the correct criterion.[141] At the beginning of Meditation III, he argued that this abstracted standard is clarity and distinctness of conception.[142] The scepticism by which he overthrew the Aristotelian view of knowledge was the very instrument he used to elicit his own view of knowledge. This new conception rejected the empiricism of Aristotle and the scholastics. This is not because it aimed at generating on *a priori* grounds alone a complete account of the world (Cartesian physics accorded a necessary rôle to experiment).[143] Its non-empiricist character lay rather in providing *a priori* some basic but substantial principles for such an account. For example, Descartes claimed that his ability to know his own existence as a thinking being in the absence of any knowledge of bodies, along with this new standard of clarity and distinctness, yields almost directly the distinction between mind and body as different kinds of substances.[144] This dualism, in turn, rules out the substantial forms of scholastic physics, which, in his view, depend (as in the case of gravity) on the attribution of intentional properties to bodies.[145]

Whatever our standard of knowledge, those things which we seem to know perfectly may still be false, as long as we cannot eliminate the possibility that an omnipotent God has given us a standard of knowledge that leads us astray. That is why the supreme doubt of Meditatio I returns in Meditatio III to confront Descartes's own conception of knowledge, and why it is then formulated (as, of course, it could not be in Meditatio I) as a doubt about the reliability of clear and distinct perception.[146] An idea (a proposition) is clearly and distinctly perceived, if it is recognised as certain; if, that is, we have ruled out all possibility of its being false. So the question is whether the certainty of a belief, the fact that *we* have ruled out every possibility of its being false, guarantees that it is indeed *true*.[147] An omnipotent God may have given us a mind whose best standard of knowledge is unfit for discerning truth.[148]

It is crucial to see how Descartes understood the structure of this doubt. Whenever the meditator of Meditatio III considers the idea of an omnipotent God, he does not see why whatever he clearly and distinctly perceives might not nonetheless be false, and yet whenever he directs his attention instead to what he does clearly and distinctly perceive, he cannot conceive how it could be false. Underlying this predicament is a particular view of assent, which recurs through-out Descartes's writings: when we direct our attention towards a clear and distinct perception and recognise what makes it clear and distinct, he believed, we simply cannot withhold our assent to its truth. We are able to doubt a proposition, only if we do not know that it is certain or if we are no longer attending to what makes it certain.[149] Self-evident propositions, such as *cogito, ergo sum,* cannot be directly doubted at all, because to have them before the mind is necessarily to grasp what makes them certain. Other propositions known to be certain can nonetheless be doubted, to the extent that we remember having shown them to be certain but are no longer attending to these reasons.[150] Thus, the sceptical doubt of Meditatio III involves memory, but not, as some have thought, because it is a doubt about its reliability.[151] The doubt assumes that we correctly remember having shown that a proposition is certain, but, as a doubt about whether what is certain is indeed true, it can arise when we are no longer attending to what makes that proposition certain, because we are thinking instead about what an omnipotent God might do. It is this understanding of assent, of when it is compelled and when it can be withheld, that makes possible Descartes's supreme doubt.

It might seem, then, that self-evident propositions such as *cogito, ergo sum* lie outside the scope of this doubt. In one way this is not so, in another it is. Each of Descartes's formulations of the supreme doubt supposes that everything we clearly and distinctly perceive might be false; no exception is ever made for *cogito ergo sum* or any other self-evident proposition.[152] Yet we cannot even think of such propositions without necessarily assenting to their truth. So in raising this doubt, we cannot have before our mind the fact that by implication the truth of *cogito, ergo sum* is in doubt as well; and, again, no passage in Descartes's writings suggests that we can. The best interpretation is to recognise that Descartes's supreme doubt has the peculiarity of not being logically closed: the fact that this doubt logically implies that self-evident propositions might be false does not mean that thereby these propositions are dubitable.[153] Only this interpretation squares with the two things Descartes says – namely, that the supreme doubt is whether everything clearly and distinctly perceived might be false and that *cogito, ergo sum* cannot be conceived as dubitable.[154]

Descartes claims to dispose of this doubt by proving that a perfect God exists, that God's perfection excludes deception, and thus that He has not given us a standard of truth (clear and distinct perception) that can lead us astray. In short, Meditatio III is chiefly devoted to proving that the certain is also true – *quae clare et distincte percipio, necessario esse vera.*[155] Descartes's understanding of assent plays a vital rôle, not just in the formulation of the supreme doubt, but in this proof as well. A failure to appreciate this is responsible for what has been the most fundamental objection to the proof. This criticism, put very clearly by Arnauld in Obj. IV, is that any proof aiming to resolve this doubt must be either ineffectual or circular: if the premises of such a proof are taken merely as clear and distinct, then the eventual conclusion, 'clear and distinct perception forms an accurate criterion of truth', can also be only clear and distinct, and not necessarily true; the only way for the conclusion to count also as true would apparently be to take its premises as being, not only clear and distinct, but also true, but this would beg the question.[156] Descartes's reply to Arnauld's objection appeals in effect to his view of assent. But the decisive rôle of this view in the proof is even clearer in the reply he later made to Burman's similar objection: the axioms employed in the proof are ones 'he is actually paying attention to. . . . And for as long as he does pay attention to them, he is certain that he is not being deceived, and he is compelled to give his assent to them.'[157] That is, so long as we attend to why the premises are clearly and distinctly perceived and to why they entail the conclusion, we cannot entertain the possibility that the conclusion is certain without being true. This is not because we have begged the question and *assumed* that the premises are true as well as certain. For we could do that only if we could recognise the possibility that the premises are certain without being true, and that means only if we were no longer attending to how the proof works. We find the conclusion true as well as certain, when attending to the proof, because then we simply cannot understand the conclusion any other way. Of course, when we no longer attend to the workings of the proof, assent to the truth of its conclusion is no longer compelled. But this does not mean that there is once again reason to wonder whether after all the conclusion might be false. Even under these circumstances we can recall (and so recognise with certainty) that any such reason has been disposed of.[158] (Descartes was uninterested in arbitrary doubts, which offer no reason for doubt.) The real difficulty facing Descartes's resolution of the supreme doubt is not the dilemma posed by Arnauld. Rather, it is that the premises of his proof, and their entailment of its conclusion, are exceedingly doubtful.

Once the supreme doubt is understood in the way I have outlined, its profound philosophical significance becomes apparent. Since the doubt is about whether the certain is also true, it shows that Descartes declined to *define* the truth of a proposition as its being maximally evident or justifiable under 'ideal conditions'. This is his strongly realist conception of truth.[159] In addition, the rôle of his theory of assent in this doubt suggests that our ability to grasp the distinction between certainty and truth depends on the mobility of our attention and thus on the temporality of our mind (in contrast to God's); indeed, he says just this in Meditatio V.[160] Thus, the lesson that Descartes's supreme doubt may have for us today is that an utterly realist conception of truth can spring, not from a neglect of the human condition, but instead from a recognition of our finitude.

## IV. SCEPTICISM AFTER DESCARTES

Some important thinkers were persuaded that Descartes had indeed worked out a new conception of the sources of knowledge that was at once immune to sceptical doubt and able to produce a science of nature. This seems to have been the view of Antoine Arnauld and Pierre Nicole. *La logique ou l'art de penser,* the so-called Port-Royal Logic which they published in a series of editions from 1660 to 1683, showed little sympathy with scepticism. In one of the introductory discourses, they argued that Montaigne's Pyrrhonism was fuelled simply by a failure of attention: the sceptical argument that nothing can be known because a reliable criterion has not been found is wrong-headed, since we need only attend to some propositions in order to recognise their truth.[161] In this they were following Descartes's 'intuitionist' claim that the standard of truth (clear and distinct perception) is not something with which we begin, but rather something we abstract from cases where we find that we cannot but assent to a proposition.

Arnauld's agreement with Descartes's anti-scepticism included the argument for the real existence of material objects which Descartes had given in Meditatio VI. Here was one of the important points in his long controversy with Malebranche, who, otherwise so close to Descartes, insisted that no argument, not even Descartes's, could *demonstrate* real existence and that indeed this was all for the good. The reason for their disagreement about the force of Descartes's argument was that for Descartes propositions asserting the existence of material objects, unlike mathematical propositions, could not even be certain (much less known to be true), without the knowledge that there is a non-deceiving God. (This is why Meditatio III, which begins with clear and distinct perception in place and asks whether certainty yields truth, makes no mention of clearly and distinctly perceiving material objects). Descartes argued that although we can be certain that our sensible ideas of material objects come from without, our belief that they are caused by bodies, and not by God or some creature more noble than a body, is a matter of natural inclination, not clear and distinct perception. Only because we know there to be a non-deceiving God and because God would be a deceiver if He gave us a natural inclination whose falsity, as in this case, we cannot detect, can we be certain that there are material objects.[162] In the Sixth *Eclaircissement sur la recherche de la vérité,* Malebranche conceded that this argument is the strongest that reason can provide for real existence. But he denied that strictly speaking it is a demonstration. Unlike a real proof, he insisted, it does not rely throughout upon what is recognised to be evident, since it appeals to our natural inclination, and to this extent it does not compel our assent.[163] Actually, Arnauld was right to counter that the argument is perfectly evident (if the truth of the premises is admitted), since it does not appeal to natural inclination, but rather to certainties about the conditions under which we can have a natural inclination.[164] However, the real source of Malebranche's dissatisfaction lay elsewhere, namely in his belief that a demonstration of something's existence must proceed from the ground (*principe*) of that thing, and not, as in this argument, from the impossibility of otherwise explaining something else.[165] We would be able to demonstrate real existence, according to this *Eclaircissement,* only if we could deduce it from God's existence. But that is impossible, since God did not necessarily create the world. Only a necessary being can be proved to exist, so the existence of material objects, he concluded, must remain an article of faith.

Malebranche did not believe that this result was particularly damaging to physical science. In a manoeuvre reminiscent of mitigated scepticism (and anticipating later positivism), he declared that for the purposes of physics we need to make sure only that our reasonings accord with experience, and that to this end statements about bodies can be replaced by statements about sensations.[166] He also believed that the indemonstrability of real existence was a positive blessing. It shows us, he argued in the *Entretiens sur la métaphysique et sur la religion* (1688), that our ultimate concern lies not with bodies, and their relation to our own body, but rather with purely spiritual things.[167] None of this implies, however, that Malebranche was sympathetic to much else in scepticism. A famous chapter in *La recherche de la vérité* (II.3.5) condemns Montaigne for having remained a prisoner of the imagination, unable to discern the truths of reason, such as the essential distinction between mind and matter, which are known by clear and distinct conception. Indeed, Malebranche never exposed to the least sort of doubt the certainties we have about mathematics and essences generally. In this he departed not only from Montaigne, but also from Descartes. He never entertained the possibility that God may have given us a nature whose best standard of truth leads us astray, probably because on his own view our ideas of essences can only be understood as residing in God Himself.[168] In sum, Malebranche's attitude towards scepticism was as complex as the mix of loyalty and defection that characterised his relation to Descartes. In one regard (essences), he believed that Descartes had taken scepticism too seriously, in another (material existence) that he had not taken it seriously enough.

Leibniz, by contrast, believed that in every respect Descartes had taken scepticism too seriously. Like Malebranche, but for different reasons, he refused to entertain the possibility that what we have found to be evident might nonetheless be false. Showing that a proposition is evident, according to Leibniz, amounts to proving that its denial involves a contradiction in terms, and since it is nonsense to suppose that God might have decreed a contradiction, we have no room to wonder whether a proposition for which we have such a proof might nonetheless have been made by God to be false.[169] (Leibniz's argument shows, *a contrario,* how closely Descartes's supreme doubt was connected with his doctrine of the divine creation of the eternal truths, which include the laws of logic). Leibniz differed from Malebranche, however, in believing that doubts about whether there are real objects, and what they are, are just as easy to dismiss. Appearances ('phenomena') count as the way objects really are, he claimed, when they are interconnected with other appearances in a systematic way that permits the successful prediction of other appearances. He admitted that this criterion of reality yields only a 'practical' kind of certainty, sufficient for deciding which appearances should be believed, since 'metaphysically speaking' a dream could be as extensively coherent as a whole life.[170] And he did not think that an appeal to God's veracity, of the sort Descartes had employed at the end of Meditatio VI to buttress an identical criterion for distinguishing dream from reality,[171] could close this metaphysical gap. But if, he argued, our beliefs about real objects go only so far as this 'practical' purpose, then we would not be deceived if there were not actually such objects but only a systematic interconnexion of appearances.[172] Given, then, the nature of our beliefs about real objects, this metaphysical gap according to Leibniz ought to be of no concern to us. 'To seek any other truth or reality than what this [practical certainty] contains is vain, and sceptics ought not to demand any other, nor dogmatists promise it', he wrote in his commentary on Descartes's *Principia*; 'the argument by which Descartes tries to prove that material things exist is weak; it would have been better not to try.'[173] Unlike Malebranche, Leibniz did not believe there was an important lesson to be learned from the dubitability of real existence. Rather, he maintained that such doubts make no sense, once we recognise the nature of our belief in real existence.

Despite their differences, Arnauld, Malebranche, and Leibniz agreed upon a number of points in the question of scepticism. The first was the centrality of Descartes's effort to confute the sceptic: their different views of the merits of scepticism depended directly on their different appraisals of Descartes's anti-sceptical arguments. Second, unlike the mitigated sceptics, they followed Descartes's example in maintaining that a new, non-empiricist conception of knowledge, which Arnauld and Malebranche understood in a far more Cartesian way than Leibniz, had made the scepticism of Montaigne and Charron irrelevant. Indeed, there were many during the second half of the century who viewed the scepticism of the *esprits forts* earlier in the century as not strength but weakness.[174]

It would be wrong, however, to suppose that after 1650 scepticism was a dead issue. Mitigated scepticism flourished in the England of Locke and the Royal Society. It was also well represented in France. Simon Foucher sought to revive 'Academic' scepticism, which he understood in fact as a position rather close to Gassendi's. His chief concern was to show that Cartesianism, far from pointing the way beyond scepticism, succumbs to the usual sceptical charge of internal contradiction: its substantial dualism of mind and matter is incompatible with its understanding of mind–matter interaction in terms of the principles that effects must resemble their causes and that (true) ideas must resemble what they represent. Pierre-Daniel Huet also defended a generally Gassendist position against what he saw as the new dogmatism of the Cartesians.[175] In addition to mitigated scepticism, the second half of the century witnessed two other, truly great contributions to sceptical thought – those of Blaise Pascal and Pierre Bayle.

Pascal did not think of himself as fundamentally a sceptic. But scepticism played a central rôle in his thought. His scepticism does not appear in his early scientific works, but only (and probably not accidentally) after his great conversion of 23 November 1654. It was the subject of the discussion recorded by de Saci (*Entretien avec M. de Saci sur Epictète et Montaigne,* 1655) and formed one of the central themes of the *Pensées.* It focused on the problem of the status of first principles, but Pascal believed that it had fundamental implications for man's self-understanding. Reason, he believed, is exclusively demonstrative, never intuitive.[176] It consists in the capacity to devise proofs, and so (contrary to the dogmatists) it cannot itself show that the first principles underlying such proofs are true. To have recognised this limit to reason, he claimed, was the great and valid insight of the Pyrrhonists.[177] Where they erred, he sometimes objected, was in not acknowledging that, despite this, we have an unshakable certainty that these principles (e.g., that there is an external world; that space, time, and movement exist; and so on) are true.[178] The source of this certainty is not reason, but rather instinct and habit – what Pascal also called more generally the heart.[179]

This objection seems unfair, since Pyrrhonists ancient and modern had granted that, even when reason is mute, there are beliefs about the appearances to which we cannot help but assent. And Pascal, who was a very close reader of Montaigne, knew this full well. As a matter of fact, his quarrel with Montaigne's Pyrrhonism lay instead with what he saw as a failure to appreciate reason's impotence with the proper seriousness, a failure expressed in what he called Montaigne's 'idiotic project' of simply portraying the movement of his thought, without worrying any longer about its truth.[180] Pascal insisted that we ought to worry that our certainty about first principles stems from feeling, not reason. We can overcome this worry and indeed know that these principles are true only once we have come to believe (what for him, however, we can never know) that benevolent God, and not an evil demon nor chance, is the author of our nature.[181] In short, Pascal's allegiance to scepticism was essentially apologetic. He intended his sceptical argument about first principles as an instrument for turning the learned and the *honnêtes hommes* towards religious faith. But he realised that it could fulfill this function only if, unlike Montaigne, they were not content with the sceptical outlook.

Thus, for scepticism to be understood as he wanted it to be, Pascal had to attack this sort of satisfaction with the human condition. That is probably why in his conversation with de Saci he focused his criticism of Montaigne's scepticism upon moral matters, contrasting it, quite appropriately, with the Stoic ethics (Epictetus) against which Montaigne had first worked out his Pyrrhonism. Epictetus, he admitted, had had a just idea of our duties, but he had yielded to pride in presuming that we have it in our power to heed them fully; Montaigne had recognised this incapacity, but, Pascal charged, he had succumbed to laziness and cowardice in no longer striving to obey them.[182] Clearly, this critique of Montaigne's anti-Stoic ethics parallels exactly his objection to what Montaigne had made of epistemological scepticism: he had ceased to care about the theoretical norm that first principles must be known to be true. For Pascal, the proper *via media* between dogmatism and scepticism (in both moral and epistemological matters) was Christian faith and God's grace.

In certain respects, Pascal had a very acute understanding of Montaigne's scepticism. He saw correctly that Montaigne's sceptical ethic, his contentment, followed from more than just his scepticism; it depended also on a general lowering of one's sights, so that ignorance would no longer seem painful. He also discerned, unlike Descartes, the significance of Montaigne's interrogative motto, 'Que sçay-je?' – its resistance to self-refutation.[183] Yet in one important regard Pascal's scepticism had a more restricted scope than any that Montaigne embraced or that Descartes entertained. He seems never to have questioned, in the manner of Descartes's supreme doubt, whether our reason itself might mislead us about the truth.[184] Perhaps this was because for Pascal, reason, being only demonstrative and not also intuitive (as it was for Descartes), could never appear to be a self-sufficient system, about whose relation to truth there could then be raised a fundamental kind of doubt. Instead, Pascal's scepticism turned on the assumption that reason was not self-sufficient, since it could not validate first principles, and that these principles must rather derive from instinct and custom, unless we turn, as Pascal hoped we would, to faith in our creator.[185]

The scepticism of Pierre Bayle embodied the same underlying motivation as that of Pascal: to curb the pretensions of reason, in order to make room for religious faith. But in the range of his scepticism, and in the thoroughness with which he pursued it, Bayle outstripped every other sceptic in the century. Just as important was his understanding of what must be the method of the sceptic, a matter on which only Descartes seems to have been his equal. His early writings of the 1680s, particularly the *Pensées diverses sur la comète* (1682–3), show some of the sceptical themes for which he became famous. There is, for example, his observation that men act more often on the basis of their dominant passions than on their professed principles. This means, as he famously argued in the *Pensées diverses,* that a society of atheists is possible, because the concern for honour would steer them towards right action, even if following through all the consequences of God's non-existence would have drawn them towards remorseless vice.[186] During this period, however, Bayle's scepticism was kept in check by a general allegiance to Cartesianism and, in theological matters, by a particular attachment to Malebranche's version of theodicy. The evident fact that the evil prosper and the good suffer will appear quite compatible with divine providence, he argued, once we recognise with Malebranche that God's wisdom consists in His ruling the world uniformly in accord with simple laws governing the motions of bodies and the psychology of human beings: these laws allow the evil as well as the good to prosper, but it would be contrary to a proper idea of God's perfection to imagine that He ought to intervene to correct the particular effects of these general laws or that He ought to have imposed much more complicated laws, which would have prevented such evils from occurring.[187] At this point in his thought, Bayle still believed that the ways of God could be rationally justified to man.

But in the *Dictionnaire historique et critique* (1696) Bayle surrendered any such confidence in reason. Here he argued relentlessly against reason's capacity to make sense either of the fundamental principles of nature or of the principles on which God has created this world. He also insisted upon the indemonstrability of the real existence of an external world, continuing to appeal to Malebranche on this question, if not on others.[188] Generally the scepticism of the *Dictionnaire* was directed towards fundamental matters, towards the principles of physical science and of theology. As his own careful historical scholarship attests, he did not doubt that straightforwardly empirical questions could be resolved. In this regard, Bayle could thus be seen as standing in the tradition of 'mitigated scepticism'. Indeed, in the article on Pyrrho he described Pyrrhonism simply as the view that we have no knowledge of the underlying nature of things.[189] However, Bayle's doubts ran deeper than either Gassendi's or Locke's. He believed not only that ultimate physical explanations could be at most probable and never certain,[190] and not only that such explanations refer to what we cannot fully understand (for example, he endorsed Locke's view that we know too little about matter to rule out the possibility that God might have 'superadded' to it the power of thought).[191] He also believed that ultimate physical principles turn out, upon reflection, to be self-contradictory. For example, this was the verdict of the discussion of space in his article on Zeno.[192] Space, he argued, cannot consist ultimately of mathematical points (since the addition of extensionless entities to one another cannot produce extension), nor can it consist of extended but indivisible physical points (since anything extended is divisible), nor can it be infinitely divisible (since this would preclude the immediate contiguity of its parts or contrariwise would permit the interpenetration of any two contiguous bodies, and in any case would succumb to the well-known paradoxes of the infinite), nor is any other account conceivable.

Bayle's *Dictionnaire* was even more concerned to show the rational incoherence of theological principles. Generally we understand morality as adherence to a body of simple rules (keeping promises, telling the truth, not injuring others), and to this extent, he conceded, our conception of right and wrong agrees with the Malebranchian view of divine providence. But, he insisted, we also believe that when it is in our power to prevent great harm from befalling another, without our having to do great evil ourselves, we ought to do so even if that requires acting contrary to those simple rules. And yet this is precisely what God, on Malebranche's or any other orthodox account, does not do.[193] Any mother who sent her daughters to a dance, knowing they would fall to temptation, but was satisfied with exhorting them to be virtuous and with threatening to disown them if they did not return as virgins, could not be said to love either her daughters or chastity. Yet, Bayle quipped, this is in effect just how God treated Adam and Eve before the Fall. Nor do we think it a mark of goodness if, instead of preventing someone from falling into a ditch, a person decides to come by an hour later to help him out of it; and yet this fits, according to Bayle, God's apparent 'mercy'. Theodicy is impossible, Bayle concluded, since God's ways are so clearly at odds with our idea of common morality.[194] Manicheanism would be a better explanation than God's omnipotence of what we observe.

The lesson Bayle drew was not, however, the suspension of belief in religious dogma, as many in the eighteenth century would understand him to be recommending.[195] His aim was to show reason's incompetence in speculative matters, most of all theological, in order to give faith its proper function. 'The ways of God are not our ways', he wrote in 'Paulicians', his main article against theodicy. 'Stop at this point, it is a text of Scripture, and do not reason further', for we must accept 'the elevation of faith and the abasement of reason'.[196] Bayle's scepticism can be termed 'fideistic', so long as fideism is understood not as Montaigne's willingness to conform to accepted doctrine, but as Pascal's urgency to have faith resolve what reason leaves unanswered.[197]

For Bayle, reason is more destructive than constructive. It lends itself better, he wrote, to the refutation of opposing positions than to the justification of one's own position.[198] This is because, in its positive employment, reason ultimately undermines itself, collapsing into self-contradiction. (So the fact that reason conflicts with faith, as in the matter of divine providence, ought not to be alarming to faith, he believed.)[199] No doubt this conviction is what let Bayle see with perfect clarity how sceptical argumentation must proceed. It may not appeal to principles not admitted by the position under attack, since such an argument would be irrelevant to partisans of that position and contrary to the sceptic's own professed lack of knowledge of principles. (Merely invoking the variety of opinions about some subject, as Montaigne and his followers were wont to do, is inadequate.) Instead, Bayle claimed, the sceptic must seek to show how the position undermines itself, either because it contains or leads to views which are themselves mutually inconsistent or because it conflicts with views which every reasonable person holds.[200] This view of sceptical procedure is one he shared with Descartes.

Like Pascal, Bayle gave scepticism only instrumental value: it was a means to religious faith, not an end in itself, not an outlook with which one could remain content, as Montaigne believed. Anticipating more recent discussion of 'the paradox of Enlightenment', Bayle predicted that reason, if unchecked, would eliminate not only superstition and barbarism, but eventually every sort of conviction.[201] Against this, he put his trust in the idea that men generally act on the basis of their passions, not their reason, and that God can give men religious faith. Whether he was right that the passions and grace are the only hope depends, of course, upon whether he was right about the fate of reason.

## NOTES

1 For Ciceronian scepticism in the sixteenth century, see Schmitt 1972.
2 On this point, see the important study by Burnyeat 1982. He observes that Augustine (*Contra academicos* III.24) preceded Descartes in this innovation. I shall point out that at one point Montaigne did so as well. Burnyeat also connects this difference between ancient and Cartesian scepticism with another, namely, the fact that the latter, unlike the former, allows appearances to be an object of *knowledge*. There is not much of a connexion here, however, since Mersenne and Gassendi kept the ancient notion of appearances but also made them an object of knowledge.
3 This is one of the central themes of Popkin 1979. There are several points on which I disagree with Popkin (see notes 64 and 65 in this chapter), but no one writing on this subject can fail to acknowledge his debt to this path-breaking book.
4 Montaigne 1962b, p. 178 (Montaigne 1965, p. 132). This thoroughly sceptical essay was written in the period 1572–4, so the common view that Montaigne underwent a 'sceptical crisis' upon reading Sextus is an exaggeration. Rather, Sextus's book confirmed and amplified an outlook he was already elaborating on his own.

5 *Essais* II.12, Montaigne 1962b, pp. 487–8. (Montaigne 1965, p. 376); see also Montaigne 1962b, pp. 521–4 (Montaigne 1965, pp. 403–6) and Montaigne 1962b, p. 554 (Montaigne 1965, p. 429).

6 So gradual was the break that Justus Lipsius, the great neo-Stoic, was led to praise the *Essais* (in their 1580 edition) as the epitome of ancient wisdom. Villey 1908 is famous for having shown how the Stoicism of the earliest essays gives way to scepticism, and how the later essays are marked by a kind of Epicureanism. See also Brush 1966, pp. 35–8. for a critique of some of the oversimplifications in Villey's basically correct scheme, particularly in his view that in Montaigne's 'third period', he ceased being a sceptic.

7 See, e.g., Montaigne 1962b, p. 485 (Montaigne 1965, p. 374).

8 There has been an important controversy between Michael Frede and Myles Burnyeat about whether the first or the second interpretation captures the sense of 'appearances' or *ta phainomena* in ancient Pyrrhonism. See, e.g., Frede 1987; Burnyeat 1984. Both would agree that the third construal of 'appearances' belongs only to modern times.

9 Montaigne 1962b, pp. 571–86 (Montaigne 1965, pp. 443–54); see also Montaigne 1962b, p. 543 (Montaigne 1965, p. 421).

10 Montaigne 1962b, p. 585 (Montaigne 1965, p. 454).

11 On the rôle of this sense of 'appearances' in the ancient Pyrrhonist conception of scepticism as a way of life, and on how Descartes's more radical doubt made scepticism unlivable, see Burnyeat 1982. Burnyeat 1984 (pp. 228, 231) wrongly assigns Montaigne's sense of 'appearances' to the first interpretation; generally it conforms to what Burnyeat himself describes as Pyrrhonist usage.

12 See *Sag.* II.2, Charron 1986, pp. 407–11; La Mothe Le Vayer 1988, pp. 25, 43, 111, 257, 378.

13 Respectively, Montaigne 1962b, pp. 572–3 (Montaigne 1965, pp. 444–5); Montaigne 1962b, pp. 575–6 (Montaigne 1965, p. 446–7); Montaigne 1962b, pp. 580–1 (Montaigne 1965, p. 451); Montaigne 1962b, p. 581 (Montaigne 1965, p. 451); Montaigne 1962b, pp. 585–6 (Montaigne 1965, pp. 454–5).

14 Montaigne 1962b, pp. 493, 507–8 (Montaigne 1965, pp. 380, 392). For some mediaeval antecedents, see Gregory 1974.

15 Montaigne 1962b, pp. 482, 544–5 (Montaigne 1965, pp. 371, 421–2). See also the critique of Carneades at *Essais* III.11, Montaigne 1962b, pp. 1012–13 (Montaigne 1965, pp. 792). In attributing these two doctrines to Carneades, Montaigne was following Sextus Empiricus, *Outlines of Pyrrhonism* I.226–30.

16 Montaigne 1962b, p. 508 (Montaigne 1965, p. 393).

17 Montaigne 1962b, p. 508 (Montaigne 1965, p. 392). It is worth noting that Montaigne pointed out the difficulty of expressing the sceptical position in the context of discussing the inapplicability of our notions of reason and impossibility to God. His idea seems to have been that we can have something in common with God only by becoming proper sceptics, and what we then share will be an inexpressibility in the language of assertion.

18 See Augustine, *De civitate Dei* XI.26.

19 *Essais* II.12, Montaigne 1962b, p. 485 (Montaigne 1965, p. 374) and Montaigne 1962b, p. 562 (Montaigne 1965, p. 436); and *Essais* II.19, Montaigne 1962b, p. 651 (Montaigne 1965, p. 506). The source is Sextus Empiricus, *Outlines of Pyrrhonism* I.17,23.

20 *Essais* I.28, Montaigne 1962b, pp. 180–1 (Montaigne 1965, p. 134); *Essais* II.12, Montaigne 1962b, p. 422 (Montaigne 1965, pp. 324–5).

21 This is a central theme of Popkin 1979.

22 Montaigne 1962b, pp. 899–910 (Montaigne 1965, pp. 703–11).

23 Montaigne 1962b, p. 9 (Montaigne 1965, p. 2); *Essais* III.9, Montaigne 1962b, p. 941 (Montaigne 1965, p. 736); *Essais* III.13, Montaigne 1962b, p. 1050 (Montaigne 1965, p. 821).

24 Montaigne 1962b, p. 9 (Montaigne 1965, p. 2); see also *Essais* III.9, Montaigne 1962b, p. 961 (Montaigne 1965, p. 751).

25 *Essais* II.1, Montaigne 1962b, p. 315 (Montaigne 1965, p. 239).

26 *Essais* II.12, Montaigne 1962b, p. 519 (Montaigne 1965, p. 402).

27 Montaigne 1962b, p. 648 (Montaigne 1965, p. 504).

28 Montaigne 1962b, p. 358 (Montaigne 1965, p. 273).

29 The two passages just quoted tie this mix of self-description and self-creation to portraying oneself 'for others', 'in public'. So Starobinski 1985 is right to say that for Montaigne self-portraiture turns out to be inherently social, mediated by what he thinks others will think of him. But he is not right to conclude (pp. 28–9) that this social mediation ensures his 'honesty' or his 'presence to himself'. Instead, as Montaigne also added to the 1588 edition, 'my style and my mind alike go roaming' (*Essais* III.9, Montaigne 1962b, p. 973 (Montaigne 1965, p. 761)). There is no telling which is prior to the other.

30 In *Rech.* (III.2.7) and also the 11th *Eclaircissement,* Malebranche would argue, against Descartes, that we have no clear idea of the soul's nature and its modifications, but both agreed that the soul is a substance.

31 See Gassendi 1658, vol. 6, pp. 1b–2a. Gabriel Naudé, another of the 'libertins érudits' inspired by Charron, called it the best book since the Bible; see Gregory 1986, p. 72.

32 *Sag.* I.14 and II.2, Charron 1986, pp. 138, 400.

33 *Sag.* I.14, Charron 1986, pp. 140–2.

34 *Sag.,* Preface to the 1601 edition, Charron 1986, p. 35.

35 See La Mothe Le Vayer 1988, p. 49 ('De la philosophie sceptique') for doubts about the ideal of the double life, and pp. 242, 273 for professions of it. The phrase 'l'extérieur au peuple avec réservation du dedans' probably came from Seneca's Epistulae morales V, and this may explain La Mothe's hesitations about it, although he also showed considerable sympathy towards Stoic ethics (see note 43 in this chapter).

36 The term *libertin érudit* was coined by Pintard 1943, who argued that they were not sincere believers. For a similar view (extended to Charron), see Gregory 1986, pp. 86–104. For the opposite interpretation, which sees them as fideists, see Popkin 1979, chap. 5. See La Mothe Le Vayer 1988, pp. 265, 306 for fideistic passages.

37 AT VII 350–1. This claim about the unlivability of scepticism is compatible with his provisional morality (see AT VI 23), since he believed that the search for truth and questions of conduct heed different standards (AT VII 350).

38 Thus, in his *Disquisitio metaphysica* (II.1.ii; Gassendi 1658, vol. 3, pp. 286a–b), Gassendi objected to Descartes that the true sceptic can live his scepticism because, unlike Descartes's sceptic, he assents to the way things appear.

39 On the question in general, see *Sag.,* Preface, Charron 1986, p. 42, and I.43, Charron 1986, p. 291; on the senses, see I.10, Charron 1986, p. 109 and I.13; Charron 1986, p.128.

40 See *Sag.* I.18, Charron 1986, p. 153 and II.3.

41 *Sag.* I.37, Charron 1986, pp. 237–8.

42 *Sag.* III.42, Charron 1986, pp. 799–800.

43 See the discussion of Charron in Berr 1960, pp. 32ff.; and in Horowitz 1974. This reconciliation between scepticism and stoicism appeared among the *libertins érudits* as well. La Mothe Le Vayer 1988 (pp. 14, 128, 302) looked favourably upon Stoic ethics,

urging conformity to nature (pp. 130, 141) and 'la droitte raison' (pp. 61, 129). And for him, too, Aristotle represented the chief dogmatic threat (pp. 62, 245, 310). The situation was similar with Gassendi (see note 57 in this chapter).

44 *Sag.* II.2, Charron 1986, p. 402. He reports having inscribed it on the door of his house in Condom, and it figures on the frontispiece of *De la sagesse.*

45 Respectively, *Sag.* I. Preface, Charron 1986, p. 48; II.1, Charron 1986, p. 376; and I. Preface, Charron 1986, p. 44.

46 *Sag.* I. Preface, Charron 1986, p. 49.

47 *Sag.* II.2, Charron 1986, p. 387.

48 *The Advancement of Learning,* II.13.3–4.

49 For his advocacy of eliminative induction, see *Magna instauratio, 'Distributio operis',* Bacon 1857–74, vol. 1, p. 25; *Nov. org.* I 46. For a sign of worry that the method may be inapplicable, for the reasons given in the text, see *Nov. org.* II 19. And for his hope for certainty, see Van Leeuwen 1963, pp. 1–12. A recent defence of Bacon against these objections is Urbach 1987, pp. 17–58.

50 *Nov. org.* I 67. Bacon made no distinction between Academic and Pyrrhonian scepticism.

51 Mitigated scepticism has also been called 'constructive' scepticism, but the latter term can prove misleading, since one kind of mitigated scepticism, as we shall see, was explicitly 'constructivist'.

52 Mersenne's charge of impiety against Charron and his followers resembles other religiously inspired attacks upon the 'Christian Pyrrhonists' of the same time, particularly the writings of the Jesuit François Garasse. But these forms of anti-scepticism did not share Mersenne's scientific motivations. See Popkin 1979, chap. 6.

53 Mersenne 1625, I.2 (p. 14), I.16 (pp. 212–13), and see the excellent study, Dear 1988, pp. 42–3, 203–6, 224–7.

54 Mersenne 1625, II.1 (pp. 229–31).

55 This is his way of handling most of Sextus's ten tropes, ibid., I.11 (pp. 133–56).

56 See Dear 1988, pp. 41–2.

57 For his high regard for Charron at this time, see his letter of 1621 to Du Four de Pibrac, in Gassendi 1658, vol. 6, pp. 1b–2a: 'Quis Charronio vero sanior judex?' It is in the Preface to Book One of the *Exercitationes* that Gassendi noted the initially ethical basis of his rejection of Aristotelianism (Gassendi 1658, vol. 3, p. 99).

58 See Joy 1987, pp. 32–7.

59 *Syntagma,* Logica, II.5 (Gassendi 1658, vol. 1, p. 79b). On Gassendi's development from the Pyrrhonism of the *Exercitationes* to his later probabilism, see Berr 1960, pp. 105–8, and Popkin 1979, pp. 141–6.

60 Descartes AT VII 332–3. For typical examples of Gassendi's use of the term 'appearance', see earlier in Obj. V, AT VII 277–8, as well as *Disquisitio metaphysica* II.1.ii (Gassendi 1658, vol. 3, pp. 286a–b). And see R. Walker 1983.

61 On Beeckman's influence on Gassendi in this matter, see Rochot 1944, pp. 34–41.

62 For the requirement of analogy, see *Syntagma,* Logica, II.5 (Gassendi 1658, vol. 1, pp. 81b–82b). For his criticism of Sextus's arguments against Epicurus, see *Syntagma, Logica,* II.5 (ibid., pp. 81A–B). The relevant passage from Sextus is *Against the Logicians* II. 337–78, and the sort of passage to which Gassendi referred in claiming that Epicurus's atomism rested on probable arguments is, e.g., Diogenes Laertius, *Life of Epicurus,* X, 34.

63 *Syntagma,* Physica I.iv.1 (Gassendi 1658, vol. 1, p. 286b). For other representative expressions of his probabilism, see *Syntagma,* Logica, II. 4–5 (Gassendi 1658, vol. 1, pp.

78a, 79b, 82b–83a); *Examen philosophiae Roberti Fluddi* (Gassendi 1658, vol. 3, p. 214); *Disquisitio metaphysica* VI.2.i (Gassendi 1658, vol. 3, p. 389a); and his letter to Galileo of November 1632 (Gassendi 1658, vol. 6, p. 53b): 'Quantumcumque enim coniecturae tuae sint verisimillimae, non sunt tibi tamen plusquam coniecturae.' It is not clear from *Post. An.* II.19 or elsewhere that Aristotle himself believed that we could come to know with certainty the true natures of things. But many Aristotelians did maintain this.

64 Gassendi 1658, vol. 2, p. 463b. Popkin 1979, pp. 143, 148 wrongly suggests that Gassendi's hypotheses were not meant to be about the real natures causally responsible for the appearances.

65 It is Popkin's thesis that a 'sceptical crisis' set the basic problem of seventeenth-century philosophy (Popkin 1979, p. 85); this is the context in which he places Gassendi's thought as well (pp. 147–8). See the excellent study by Brundell 1987, pp. 104–6, 137–42, for the argument that it is rather anti-Aristotelianism that lies at the centre of Gassendi's thought.

66 For Glanvill's attack on the Aristotelian ideal of science and his defence of the use of hypotheses, see Glanvill 1665, pp. 141–59. He took Descartes to have been the greatest practitioner of hypothetical science (p. 155), though he also put Gassendi in this camp (pp. 5–6 of the appended reply to Thomas White).

67 Glanvill 1676, p. 47.

68 On this English tradition of mitigated scepticism, see Van Leeuwen 1963. And on Newton's fallibilist notion of certainty, see Larmore 1987b, 1988.

69 For Gassendi's possible influence on Locke, see Cranston 1957, pp. 169–70; Aaron 1971, pp. 31–5.

70 *Ess.* IV.iii.11, IV.xii.9.

71 *Ess.* IV.iii.14.

72 *Ess.* II.viii.10, IV.iii.28; see also IV.iii.6,13.

73 See AT VII 266, 338.

74 *Ess.* IV.iii.6.

75 For the meaning here of Locke's term 'superaddition', see Ayers 1981b; Yolton 1983, pp. 14–28; Jolley 1984, pp. 58–66. It is crucial to see that 'superaddition' is an ontological notion. It refers to a quality or substance that is in principle undeducible from a substance, and not simply to what we are unable to deduce from our idea of that substance. So the idea that superaddition is involved in the present case is no part of Locke's scepticism. His sceptical point is rather that we cannot tell which of the two mentioned kinds of superaddition really obtains.

76 *Ess.* IV.iii.28.

77 *Ess.* IV.iii.16, xii.10.

78 *Ess.* IV.xvi.12.

79 It is significant that Locke brought up the possibility of 'microscopical eyes' discerning the corpuscular nature of bodies, not in order to hope, like Gassendi, that one day this will become feasible, but rather in order to insist that, God not having given us such eyes, our chief business must lie elsewhere than in natural philosophy (*Ess.* II.xxiii.11–12). Here he was expressing his conviction that 'morality is the proper . . . business of mankind', which is discussed later in this chapter.

80 For Stillingfleet, see Locke's 'Second Reply to the Bishop of Worcester' in Locke 1823, vol. 4, p. 360; for Reid, see his *An Inquiry into the Human Mind,* chap. 7, in Reid 1975. For a modern version, see Bennett 1971, pp. 68–70.

81 *Ess.* IV.ii.4,14.

82 *Ess.* IV.ii.14; IV.xi.3: 'He that can doubt so far . . . will never have any controversy with

me; since he can never be sure I say anything contrary to his own opinion'; also *Ess.* IV.xi.8.

83 *Ess.* IV.iv.4.

84 *Ess.* II.xxiii.28. On this passage, see Woolhouse 1983, pp. 171–4.

85 Locke 1823, vol. 4, pp. 467–9.

86 *Ess.* II.viii.11.

87 *Ess.* IV.iii.29.

88 *Ess.* IV.xii.11.

89 *Ess.* II.xxii; III.xi.15–16; IV.xii.8.

90 *Ess.* II.xxviii.4, 7–8; IV.x; IV.iii.18. On Locke's idea of demonstrable morality, see Colman 1983, and also Tully 1980, pp. 8–50. In *The Reasonableness of Christianity* (1695), Locke expressed considerable doubt about whether, without the aid of revelation, a science of morality would ever be elaborated, although he continued to affirm that it was possible in principle.

91 There is reason to believe that Locke began writing the *Essay* as a result of discussions, with Shaftesbury and others, about the principles of morality and revealed religion, discussions to which Locke referred obliquely in 'The Epistle to the Reader' of the *Essay.* See Wolfgang von Leyden's introduction to Locke 1954, pp. 60–1.

92 Montaigne, *Essais* III.11 (Montaigne 1962b, p. 1003; Montaigne 1965, p. 785); Francesco Sanchez, *Quod nihil scitur* (quoted in Gregory 1961, p. 73); Mersenne, *Harmonie universelle* (1636–7) (quoted in Lenoble 1971, p. 384).

93 Popkin 1979, p. 139.

94 On Grotius's work as an answer to moral scepticism, and on Hobbes's position at the intersection of Mersenne's and Grotius's anti-scepticisms, see the path-breaking articles by Tuck 1983, 1987a, and 1987b.

95 *Prolegomena* V–VIII. The source of Carneades' argument is Cicero, *De re publica* III.21 (as transmitted in Lactantius, *Institutiones divinae* V.xvi. 2–4).

96 Grotius 1950, vol. 1, pp. 9–10, 21–2. See also Tuck 1983, pp. 52–5. (Only part of the *De jure praedae* – *Mare liberum,* 1609 – was published in Grotius's lifetime.) In the *Prolegomena* Grotius refused to base the *honestum* on the *utile,* natural law on rational self-interest alone (VI), but he did maintain that the two coincide in their prescriptions (XVI). Tuck 1987a first ignores (p. 105) the *Prolegomena's* rejection of *De jure praedae's* identification of the *honestum* with the *utile,* then downplays (p. 113) it by saying that in both works Grotius makes 'self-preservation' (a blanket term Tuck uses to include both self-interest and sociability) the foundational notion. The continuity in Grotius's thought is better described as, not any particular concept, but a strategy: to point out that core morality which all can reasonably accept, despite the moral controversies that divide them.

97 *Prolegomena* XI. Grotius's abiding aim to find a basis for natural law that no one, not even the moral sceptic, can deny is clear in *Prolegomena* XXXIX.

98 Grotius and his followers, Tuck 1987a (pp. 117–18) writes, 'wished to see the world made safe for the sceptic; the irony was that scepticism itself could not show how the world was to be made safe, for it could not in principle show why the fanatic was *wrong* in holding his moral beliefs and acting upon them, however violently.'

99 *De cive* I.6–7; *De homine* XIII.8–9, XI.6; *Lev.*xv (next-to-last paragraph).

100 That the 'ought' of the natural law for Hobbes is a purely prudential one is clear in *De cive* I.15–II.1 (including footnote added in the 1647 edition) and in *Lev.* iii (paragraphs 4–5), but unfortunately less so in *Lev.* xiv and xv (last paragraph), which has misled some commentators (A. E. Taylor 1965; Howard Warrender 1957) into believing that

Hobbes's natural law consists in moral obligations stemming from God. Hobbes is best seen as claiming that morality can be justified *both* prudentially and as God's command.

101  This was his main criticism of Hobbes's *De cive*. See Tuck 1983, pp. 60–1.

102  For expressions of Hobbes's psychological egoism, see *De cive* I.2, III.21 and *Lev.* xv (paragraphs 16, 31) and xxvii (paragraph 8). In recent times, Hobbes has sometimes been said not to have been a psychological egoist, most notably by Bernard Gert. See his introduction to Hobbes 1972, and also Hampton 1986, pp. 19–24.

103  By the *De iure naturae et gentium* of 1672, Pufendorf had begun to back off from a prudential construction of morality. See Tuck 1979, pp. 156–62, and Tuck 1987a, pp. 105–6. A signal advantage of both Hobbes's moral constructivism and the 'divine imposition' ethics of the mature Pufendorf and Locke was that it overcame moral scepticism at the same time that it cohered with the mechanical philosophy's denial of moral distinctions in nature.

104  Locke's ethics also differed from Hobbes's (if not Grotius's) in that, even in so far as it did not appeal to the divine law, it refused to view morality as a necessarily political construction. Locke held open the other option of appealing to the 'law of opinion', which for him underlay the ancient ethics of the virtues and vices (II.xxviii.10). At *Ess.* I.iii.5 Locke explicitly associated Hobbes with the view that civil law is the sole rule of morality.

105  The *Disc.* and *Recherche de la vérité* give only a rudimentary outline of the stages of doubt. They were meant to be popular writings, as they were written in French instead of Latin, and so do not make the high philosophical demands of the *Meds.* See Descartes, AT VII 247; Gilson 1925, pp. 79, 175, 290.

106  See AT VII 130, 171; VIIIB 367.

107  See Descartes, *Conversation with Burman,* AT V 147 (Descartes 1976, p. 4).

108  See note 14. Burnyeat 1982 (pp. 44–7) gives a more favourable picture of Descartes's understanding of his novelty by running together the two distinct doubts about the external world and about a possibly deceiving God. Descartes gave no sign of seeing the novelty of the first of these.

109  See Garber 1986.

110  AT VII 18.

111  AT VII 17–18, 22 (20–2). A sophisticated example of this view is Williams 1978, pp. 46–7. He claims that the pure inquirer will necessarily try to maximise his 'truth-ratio' (the proportion of his total beliefs that is true). This will indeed lead to a demand for indubitability. But aiming to maximise one's truth-ratio amounts to putting the goal of avoiding falsehoods above that of acquiring truths, and there is no reason why a pure inquirer must do that.

112  These are two distinct goals, for if we pursued only the first, we would believe indiscriminately, trying to get as many truths as possible however many false beliefs we also got in the process; and if we pursued only the second, the best policy would be to believe nothing at all, since we would not care about the truths we missed.

113  AT VII 18 (15–16): 'Nempe quidquid hactenus ut maxime verum admisi, vel a sensibus, vel per sensus accepi.' For the Aristotelian parallel, see *De anima* 432a3–9. In his *Conversation with Burman* (AT V 146 [Descartes 1976, p. 3]), Descartes explained the distinction between *a sensibus* and *per sensus* thus: the former covers what we have seen ourselves, the latter what we have heard from others.

114  AT VI 37; AT III 297–8.

115  See *Resp.* VI (AT VII 441–3); Gilson 1967a, pp. 168–73.

116  See, e.g., Michael Williams 1986.

117 It was, in fact, a commonplace of the modern scepticism preceding Descartes that the
    weakness of the dogmatist stems from his fundamental principles. See Montaigne,
    *Essais* II.12, Montaigne 1962b, p. 522 (Montaigne 1965, p. 404); and Montaigne
    1962b, p. 543 (Montaigne 1965, p. 421); Charron, *Sag.* I.40 and II.2, Charron 1986,
    pp. 278, 402–4.
118 AT VII 12.
119 AT VII 20 (26).
120 The important exception to this sort of interpretation has been Harry Frankfurt 1970,
    pp. 61–7. The arguments in this discussion include some of his.
121 See also Descartes's letter to Vatier of 22 February 1638 (AT I 560 (13–16)), as well as
    Resp. III (AT VII 171–2).
122 AT VII 18–21.
123 The doubt as expressed in the text suggests only that, for all one knows, he may be
    dreaming at any particular time, and not that he may always be dreaming. See
    Frankfurt 1970, p. 51. Wilson 1978, pp. 20–4, urges another construal of this doubt:
    she says that the doubt is not about how to distinguish waking from dreaming, but
    about whether waking experience of physical objects is veridical. There are two
    obstacles to such an interpretation: (1) Descartes always describes this doubt as one of
    distinguishing waking from dreaming (AT VII 19 (20–1), 89 (21)), and (2) his eventual
    resolution of this doubt consists in arguing that if a perception is systematically
    connected with the rest of one's life, this makes it a waking perception (AT VII 90 (5–
    6)). It is assumed throughout this doubt that a waking perception, under the circum-
    stances stipulated (close, medium-sized objects) is veridical – and not because Des-
    cartes believes this, but because he believes the Aristotelian does so. See text at note
    126 in this chapter. Wilson misses here the dialogic structure of Meditatio I.
124 AT VII 12.
125 See, e.g., Med. VI, AT VII 89–90.
126 AT VI 112–13.
127 This is Michel Foucault's criticism in Foucault 1972, pp. 56–8. (Frankfurt offers the
    same interpretation, though not as a criticism, in Frankfurt 1970, p. 38.) In his critique
    of Foucault, Derrida 1967 (pp. 75–85) correctly points out much of the actual dialectic
    of this passage.
128 AT X 511.
129 See Long 1986, p. 90; Annas and Barnes 1985, pp. 41, 45, 53. This was also Hegel's
    interpretation of ancient scepticism. See his *Vorlesungen über die Geschichte der Philoso-
    phie* (Hegel 1969–79, vol. 19), pp. 359, 373, 396.
130 The 'order of reasons' is the theme of the great commentary by Gueroult 1984.
131 A recent version of this interpretation occurs in Kenny 1968, pp. 51–5.
132 Hintikka's famous article 'Cogito, Ergo Sum: Inference or Performance' (Hintikka
    1962) is the best-known modern version of this interpretation. For decisive arguments
    against it, see Frankfurt 1966.
133 This approach has been pioneered by Frankfurt 1970, p. 111, and Curley 1978, pp.
    84–8. However, neither sees Descartes's manoeuvre here as applying to the sceptic his
    very own strategy.
134 AT VII 25 (2–5), (5–8), (8–10).
135 In the Resp. II (AT VII 140–1), Descartes denied that *cogito, ergo sum* is a syllogistic
    inference, with major premise 'Whatever thinks, exists', whereas in *Princ.* I.10 he said
    that this inference assumes the truth of 'in order to think we must be.' Asked by

Burman about the apparent contradiction, Descartes replied (AT V 147) that when this inference is first used to refute the sceptic, the major premise is implicit, not explicit. This may mean that one has innate knowledge of this premise and comes to know that one knows it (to know it 'explicitly') only as a result of knowing directly that *sum* follows from *cogito*. In this way, *cogito, ergo sum* first functions as a direct inference without reference to a major premise.

136 AT VII 25 (11–13).

137 AT VII 22; see also AT VII 461. Kenny 1968, p. 23, quite misunderstands this point. For the correct interpretation, see Gouhier 1954a. However, I do not agree with Gouhier's conclusion that the '*négation méthodique*' is essential to Descartes's rejection of scepticism.

138 See Gassendi, Obj. V (AT VII 257–8) and P.-D. Huet, *Censura philosophiae cartesianae* (1683), cited in Gilson 1925, p. 285. Curley 1978, who comes closest to the interpretation advanced here, sees (p. 86) the sceptic as refuted because the content of the sceptic's doubt contains the assumption *cogito*, but, as Gassendi and Huet would have objected, the sceptic does not assert the doubt as true and so is not in this way asserting *cogito*.

139 *Princ.* I 7; AT X 515.

140 In fact, the manoeuvre is mentioned as late as Silhon's *De l'immortalité de l'âme* (1634). See Popkin 1979, pp. 163–4. And it is still known to Pascal; see note 183 in this chapter.

141 The most important study of Descartes's 'intuitionism', in contrast to Leibniz's 'formalism', is Belaval 1960, especially pp. 23–83. Leibniz's opposition to Descartes's 'intuitionism' is similar to the objection which the sceptic Pierre-Daniel Huet made to it: abstracting the standard of knowledge from an item of knowledge is circular, Huet complained, since that item cannot rightfully be regarded as knowledge except by appeal to the standard. The reply by Pierre-Sylvain Régis, a loyal Cartesian, put the intuitionist case well: a standard of knowledge is a truth, too, and the justification for adopting it can only be a proposition we know independently to be true (see Gilson 1925, pp. 312f.).

142 AT VII 35.

143 See Larmore 1987a.

144 *Princ.* I 7–8.

145 See Gilson 1967a, pp. 143–68.

146 AT VII 35–6.

147 The doubt is not whether we may subsequently have reason to change our mind about whether we have indeed clearly and distinctly perceived some idea. It takes for granted that we know when we have clear and distinct perceptions.

148 Med. I also employs the notion of an evil genius, but not, as some have thought, to express a different kind of doubt. One reason that Descartes used it was his belief that in fact the concept of an omnipotent God excludes this kind of deception (although he proved this only in Med. III). In addition, he viewed the notion of an evil genius as a device we construct to express our liberty to refuse assent to what we recognise as doubtful – which is why he introduces it directly after employing this same liberty (cf. AT VII 12 (10–12)) to treat as false whatever he finds doubtful (AT VII 22), and also why it does not reappear in the version of the doubt in Med. III, which is directed at what is clearly and distinctly perceived or indubitable. Cf. Gouhier 1937, pp. 162–5.

149 See Larmore 1984.

150 Respectively AT VII 145–6; AT VII 146 and IXB 30–1.

151 So little was Descartes concerned here about the reliability of memory that, in reply to Burman's worry that this might be an opening for the sceptic, he said: 'Of the memory I cannot say anything; every man can tell by experience whether he has a good one; if he is in doubt, he should take notes or use similar aids.' (AT V 148). Those who have believed that the reliability of memory is at stake in Med. III range from Leibniz (*Animadversiones in partem generalem Principiorum Cartesianorum* I.5, 13) to Doney 1955. For a decisive refutation of this view see Frankfurt 1962.

152 AT VII 35 (10–13), 36 (29), 53 (17–18), 69 (14–15).

153 For some more detail, see Larmore 1984, pp. 65–6.

154 In *Disquisitio metaphysica* III.1.i (Gassendi 1658, vol. 3, p. 316a), Gassendi noted that Descartes says these two things, but he regarded it as an inconsistency.

155 AT VII 70 (12–13). Frankfurt 1970 (pp. 178–80) and 1978 has argued that this is not the aim of Descartes's proof. For a critique of Frankfurt's position, see Larmore 1984, pp. 63–4, 69–70, and Williams 1978, pp. 35, 198–200.

156 AT VII 214.

157 Descartes, *Conversation with Burman,* AT V 148 (Descartes 1976, p. 6). For Descartes's reply to Arnauld, see AT VII 245–6. Later in the *Conversation* (AT V 178 (Descartes 1976, p. 50)), Descartes says explicitly that without his theory of assent his proof of God would be impossible. (Note that Descartes believed that we can hold in the mind at once, not just a single thought, but also an argument if it is not too long.) On this point, see Larmore 1984, pp. 69–71; also Williams 1983, pp. 337–52.

158 AT VII 70 (13–18).

159 It is what Bernard Williams has called Descartes's 'absolute conception of reality'. See Williams 1978, pp. 64–7.

160 AT VII 69 (16–23).

161 Antoine Arnauld and Pierre Nicole, *La logic; ou, L'art de penser,* Premier Discours, Arnauld and Nicole 1965, pp. 18–20. See also Quatrième Partie, chap. 1 (ibid., p. 292) where they repeat Descartes's claim that, once abstracted from our inability to doubt our own existence, the standard of clear and distinct perception can serve as a rule for testing other propositions. (They do, however, declare that the nature of God's omnipotence and of infinity lies beyond our ken.) The position of Arnauld and Nicole marked an important change in the Jansenist attitude towards scepticism, since Saint Cyran, the founder of the movement, had defended Charron against the attacks of Garasse (see note 52 in this chapter) and Pascal showed considerable sympathy with scepticism. On this change, see Lennon 1977.

162 AT VII 79–80.

163 Mal. *OC* III 60–4 (Malebranche 1980a, pp. 572–4).

164 Arnauld, *Des vraies de des fausses idées,* in Arnauld 1986, pp. 268–9.

165 See particularly his *Ent. mét.* VI.5 in Mal. *OC* XII–XIII 137.

166 *Rech.* VI.2.6 (Mal. *OC* II 377 (Malebranche 1980a, p. 484)).

167 *Ent. mét.* XII.10 (Mal. *OC* XII–XIII 289). There is only a superficial similarity here with Locke's claim that the unavailability of knowledge in natural philosophy shows that our true business lies elsewhere. Because for Locke that is morality, and not pure spirituality, he could not afford to grant that we cannot know that there are material bodies.

168 On the absence in Malebranche of Descartes's supreme doubt about the relation between certainty and truth, see Alquié 1974, pp. 73–82, 143, 226–33. Alquié's book is the best study of Malebranche's complex relation to Descartes generally. He points

out how the disappearance of the supreme doubt is connected with the disappearance of Descartes's cognate doctrine that the eternal truths were created by God.

169 See, e.g., Ger. I 253; and IV 358 (*Animadversiones in partem generalem Principiorum Cartesianorum,* I.13). For English translations, see Leibniz 1969, pp. 181, 185. And see also Leibniz's *Théod.* pt. II secs. 185–6.

170 See, e.g., Ger. I 369–74 (Leibniz 1969, pp. 151–4); Ger. VII 319–22 (Leibniz 1969, pp. 363–5); and *Nouv. ess.,* IV.ii.14, IV.xi.10.

171 AT VII 89–90.

172 Ger. VII 321 (Leibniz 1969, p. 364).

173 Ger. IV 356, 366 (Leibniz 1969, pp. 384, 391) (*Animadversiones* I.4 and II.1).

174 See, e.g., the essay 'Les Esprits forts' in La Bruyère's *Les caractères* (in La Bruyère 1951, pp. 449–81). During this period there was a rapid decline in Montaigne's reputation. See Villey 1972, pp. 164–73.

175 On Foucher, see Watson 1966. On Huet see notes 138 and 141 in this chapter.

176 See Léon Brunschvicg's introduction to the *Pensées* in his edition of Pascal 1967, pp. 294–7. (In the text and notes, references to the *Pensées* are by Lafuma's numbering of the fragments in Pascal 1963.) In the short text, *De l'esprit géométrique* (probably 1656), Pascal oddly exhibited none of this scepticism towards first principles, claiming that they can be perceived by the 'natural light' of 'reason'. See *De l'esprit géométrique* in Pascal 1963, pp. 350, 352. This seems the only place where Pascal extended his notion of reason to cover intuition of first principles.

177 *Pens.* 131.

178 *Pens.* 110.

179 *Pens.* 110, 125, 821, 530. The similarity to Hume is striking, especially since at *Pensées* (821) Pascal traced our confidence in induction to habit (*la coutume*).

180 *Pens.* 780, 680.

181 *Pens.* 131.

182 *Entretien avec M. de Saci sur Epictète et Montaigne,* in Pascal 1963, pp. 295–6. Arnauld and Nicole 1965, pp. 267–9 repeat this indictment of Montaigne.

183 Pascal 1963, p. 293. Pascal understood very well the difference between Montaigne's subtlety and Charron's vulgarisation, of which he had a rather low opinion (*Pensées,* 780).

184 The reference to the possibility of an evil demon in *Pensées* (131) might seem a repetition of Descartes's supreme doubt, but the conviction about first principles which the evil demon is there considered as deceiving is based on feeling (*sentiment naturel*), not reason. Still, there is good reason to think that Pascal was thinking of Descartes here; cf. Marion 1986a, pp. 302ff.

185 *Pens.* 182, 183, 188. On Pascal's view of reason as not a self-sufficient system, see Brunschvicg in Pascal 1967, p. 295–7; and Bénichou 1948, p. 149: 'Toute l'originalité de Pascal consiste justement à n'anéantir ni la raison, ni l'instinct, à se servir de l'un contre l'autre sans bâtir ni sur l'un ni sur l'autre, et finalement à tout remettre, faute de mieux, à l'instinct, en attendant la grâce.'

186 Bayle, *Pensées diverses sur la comète,* CXXXV, CXXXVI, CLXI, CLXXII, CLXXVI, CLXXIX (in Bayle 1984, vol. 2, pp. 9–11, 77, 103–5, 117–9, 125–7). Note the similarity with Locke's view (*Ess.* II.xxviii.10) that, even without appeal to the divine law, a morality of the ancient virtues and vices is possible by reference to 'the law of opinion or reputation'. It should also be noted that here Locke and Bayle were looking back to ancient ideals, and not forward to the quite different idea, popular in the eighteenth century, of 'commercial society'.

187 *Pensées diverses* CCVIII, CCXXXI, CCXXXIV (Bayle 1984, vol. 2, pp. 193–5, 234–5, 239–42). The text by Malebranche on which Bayle was relying was the *Traité de la nature et de la grâce* (1680).

188 'Pyrrho', note B; 'Zeno of Elea' and note H (Bayle 1965, pp. 198, 354, 373–7).

189 'Pyrrho' (Bayle 1965, p. 195).

190 'Pyrrho', note B (Bayle 1965, p. 194).

191 'Dicearchus', note M (Bayle 1965, pp. 72–4).

192 'Zeno of Elea', note G (Bayle 1965, pp. 359–68). This discussion had an important influence on Hume; see *Treatise of Human Nature* (I.ii) and Kemp Smith 1941, pp. 284–90.

193 'Paulicians', notes E, F, and M (Bayle 1965, pp. 175–91). A good discussion of Bayle's defection from Malebranche's theodicy is Riley 1986, pp. 79–99. In this argument and elsewhere, Bayle never doubted that the content of common morality can be discerned independently of any knowledge of God's purposes; on this count, he was a great admirer of Grotius.

194 Leibniz's *Théod.* (1710) was an attempt to rescue theodicy from Bayle's attacks. He argued that God's administration of the world does agree with common morality, once we realise that the evil which occurs is not just a by-product of simple laws (as for Malebranche), but a necessary means for bringing about the most good overall (*Théod.* pt. I secs. 8–10, 24–5; pt. II, sec. 127). However, whether ordinary morality is so single-mindedly consequentialist, so thoroughly given over to *la règle du meilleur*, is debatable. For more on Bayle's critique of theodicy and on the three-way debate on this issue between Malebranche, Bayle, and Leibniz, see Larmore 1993, pp. 121–38.

195 See, e.g., Diderot's article 'Pyrrhonienne ou Sceptique' in the *Encyclopédie*. The most important work to correct this traditional interpretation of Bayle has been Labrousse 1963–4 and also Labrousse 1983.

196 'Paulicians', note E (Bayle 1965, pp. 176–7).

197 Like Pascal the Jansenist, Bayle the Calvinist naturally rejected (*Pensées diverses* CLV (Bayle 1984, vol. 2, p. 64)) Montaigne's view that one should simply conform to the established religion of one's country. For more on this and other differences between Bayle and Montaigne (one more of which I mention later), see Brush 1966, pp. 190, 328–9.

198 'Arriaga', note B; 'Bunel', note E; 'Manicheans', note D; 'Rorarius', note G; 'Simonides', note F; 'Zeno of Elea', note G (Bayle 1965, pp. 27, 42, 151, 231–2, 273, 362).

199 See *Réponse aux questions d'un provincial* (1705), II.CXXXVII.

200 'Spinoza'; 'Second Clarification' (Bayle 1965, pp. 303, 411–12). This is the strategy which in the *Pensées diverses* (Avis au lecteur, Bayle 1984, vol. 1, p. 6) he had called fighting one's adversaries even on their own dungheap (*jusques sur leur propre fumier*).

201 'Takiddin', note A (Bayle 1965, p. 342).

# VII

# WILL, ACTION, AND MORAL PHILOSOPHY

# 33

# DETERMINISM AND HUMAN FREEDOM

## ROBERT SLEIGH, JR., VERE CHAPPELL, AND MICHAEL DELLA ROCCA

### I. INTRODUCTION AND BACKGROUND

Determinism, broadly speaking, is the doctrine that whatever happens in the world is brought about by causes other than itself. In this sense, all the major philosophers of the seventeenth century – with the possible exception of Malebranche – were determinists. But these same philosophers also believed in human freedom. It follows that each of them (again, perhaps excepting Malebranche) was a compatibilist with respect to freedom and determination: each held that being free is logically compatible with being causally determined. Yet their specific teachings on this subject are very different from one another. For they had very different views on the nature and scope of human freedom, and different conceptions of causation.

This chapter concentrates on the teachings of these major figures: Descartes, Hobbes, Spinoza, Malebranche, Locke, and Leibniz. There were, of course, other seventeenth-century thinkers who concerned themselves with freedom and determinism – this was one of the most frequently debated issues of the age. And some of these others, in opposition to the philosophers, were incompatibilists. They held that an action logically cannot both be causally determined and be free, in any proper sense of 'free'. An incompatibilist has two options: adhere to determination and deny that anything or anyone is free (this is hard determinism) or admit free actions and claim that these are undetermined, and thereby reject the doctrine of determinism (this is libertarianism). We know of no seventeenth-century thinker who took the hard determinist position, but quite a few were libertarians. These thinkers belonged chiefly to two groups, both theological in orientation.

---

Vere Chappell is primarily responsible for Sections II, III, and VI; Robert Sleigh is primarily responsible for Sections I, V, VII, and VIII; Michael Della Rocca is responsible for Section IV. A longer version of Section II, by Chappell, was delivered at a British Society of the History of Philosophy conference held at Reading University in October 1991 and was subsequently published, under the title 'Descartes's Compatibilism', in the conference proceedings, Cottingham 1994. Some of the material in Section VII will appear in a different form in a forthcoming article by Sleigh in *Faith and Philosophy*.

There were, on the one hand, the Molinists, who followed the Spanish Jesuit Luis Molina (1535–1600), and, on the other hand, the Arminians, who allied themselves with the Dutch dissident Calvinist Jacob Arminius (1560–1609). The Molinists, as might be expected, were active in the Catholic lands of Europe – France, Spain, and Italy – whereas the Arminians, at first confined to Protestant Holland, came to have influence in Britain as well. We shall not examine the views of these libertarians directly; but since they are criticised by some of the major figures – the Molinists by Descartes, the Arminians by Hobbes and Locke, and both by Leibniz – we shall give some attention to them in our treatments of these philosophers.

The purpose of these introductory remarks is to highlight some of the crucial elements in scholastic thought that influenced seventeenth-century accounts of the nature, extent, and limits of human freedom. No doubt a truly thorough account would commence with the relevant work of *the* philosopher – Aristotle. We begin considerably later, with a brief outline of St. Thomas's mature doctrine of free choice, that is, the doctrine expounded in the second part of the *Summa theologiae* and in *De malo*.

For Thomas, freedom applies to a power of certain individual substances to engage in a certain kind of activity. The actions of created substances may be divided into those that are coerced and those that are not coerced, with the latter divided into those that are natural and those that are voluntary. An activity is coerced when the agent whose activity it is does not contribute to the activity in the manner of a principal efficient cause. If the agent contributes to its own activity in such fashion that the resulting action is not coerced, then the action is said to be spontaneous, and the agent is said to have acted spontaneously. Consider those powers of agents that, when exercised, yield actions that are not coerced. Some of those powers are determined to one outcome and, hence, the actions that result from their exercise are said to occur by a necessity of nature (or by natural necessity); that is, given the circumstances at hand, that power of the agent in question is determined to one specific outcome, if the agent then exercises that power at all. All powers of individual substances lacking cognition fall into this category; the resulting actions are termed natural. Associated with each action is an inclination towards some end, which is the intended goal of the action. If the goal is apprehended by the agent, then the action may be called voluntary in a broad sense that applies to both rational and irrational animals. But in a strict sense, will (*voluntas*) belongs only to agents with rational inclinations (appetites). Hence, in a strict sense, only rational agents have the power to perform voluntary actions, and they do so only when a judgement of the intellect plays a central rôle in causing the volition. Since our topic is human freedom, when we discuss voluntary actions, it will be in this strict sense.[1]

When a rational agent exercises a power of its soul the resulting action is specified by its object, which characterises the particular action it is. Associated with each kind of power possessed by an agent is a general objective which characterises the ultimate goal of all exercises of that power. Thus, truth is the general objective of the cognitive power and the good forms the basis for the general objective of the will. Since an agent can will only what that agent apprehends, the general objective of the will is the good as apprehended, that is, the apparent good. Hence, in Thomas's scheme the thesis that agents never will what does not then and there appear as good to the agent seems to be analytic. It is worth noting that some philosophers in the seventeenth century accepted the thesis but apparently denied its analyticity: Leibniz, for example, characterised the thesis as resulting from a free decree of God.[2]

Given that the universal good − happiness, as it turns out − is the general objective of the will, Thomas concluded that, of necessity, we do not will its contrary. The assumption that what we will of necessity we do not will freely provides the basis for a distinction between voluntary actions and free actions.[3]

As we have noted, Thomas regarded the universal good as the necessary goal of the will. He took the locus of freedom to be the power to choose among various means regarded by the agent as suitable to achieve some desired end. Consider a case in which some human agent performs a free action, say, the agent operates a camera by depressing his right index finger. According to Thomas, the operation of the camera results from an action − the depressing of the right index finger − that is commanded by the agent's will. The willing of that action is itself an action said to be elicited by the will. It is a choice of means to the desired end. In this situation, according to Thomas, freedom applies primarily to the choice of this particular means among numerous others that the agent takes to be available to him, that is, currently within his power. According to Thomas, free actions result from the exercise of a power that is not determined to one outcome. Hence, free actions do not occur by a necessity of nature. Moreover, free actions are those where the agent exhibits some variety of indifference, exhibits self-determination, in virtue of which it is said to be master of its own actions. Most of the expressions used here to formulate these theses are such that translations of them were asserted by most seventeenth-century philosophers, but with a wide variety of meanings attached.[4]

The details of Thomas's mature account of free choice become clearer when one examines a prima facie difficulty that many have noted. Free choice is a power that is not determined to one outcome; still, when a choice occurs, a determination has been made, and, of course, there is a unique outcome. According to Thomas, in order for a choice to be free, the will must be caused to operate by the intellect in virtue of the last practical judgement of the understanding. The objection is this: this theory is a version of an unacceptable thesis, namely, that free choice is compatible with the will's being causally necessitated by circumstances not under the control of the will itself. So Thomas has been accused of advocating intellectual determinism.[5] Thomas's early effort to meet this criticism may be summarised as follows: in order for a choice to be free, the judgement that moves the will to that choice must fall under the power of the one judging. Fortunately, the power to reflect on one's judgements and thereby, in some cases to alter them, belongs to rational beings. Thomas concluded: 'Hence, the entire root of freedom is located in reason.'[6] Even in *De veritate* itself, Thomas emended this theory, attempting to locate some control over the determining judgements in the will. But Thomas's most sophisticated efforts are located in the second part of the *Summa theologiae* and in *De malo*.

In the *Summa,* considering the question whether the will is moved by the intellect, Thomas wrote:

A power of the soul is found to be in potentiality to different things in two ways: in one way with respect to acting or not acting; in another way with respect to doing this or that. For instance, sometimes sight is actually seeing; sometimes not. And sometimes it sees white; and sometimes it sees black. Hence, it requires being moved in two respects, namely, with respect to the exercise or employment of the act, and also with respect to the specification of the act.[7]

This distinction between the exercise and the specification of an act of a power of the rational soul is fundamental to Thomas's mature view; it had a profound impact on ideas about freedom in the seventeenth century. A corresponding distinction was made between two possible kinds of freedom – freedom with respect to exercise (sometimes called freedom of contradiction) and freedom with respect to specification (sometimes called freedom of contrariety). The distinction between exercise and specification pertains to various powers of the soul, intellect and will included. Applied to choice, the distinction is between choosing among a range of apprehended alternatives or not so choosing (exercise), versus choosing one among those apprehended alternatives as opposed to the others (specification). According to Thomas, the specification of an act of a power of the soul – the determination of its species, of its content – is brought about by its object, or, in the case of the will, the object as apprehended by the intellect.[8] But each power of the soul to which the exercise/specification distinction applies is such that the exercise of that power is under the control of the will, including the will itself. Thus, with respect to the question of what moves what in the cases of intellect and will, Thomas drew the following conclusions: the intellect moves itself and the will with respect to specification; the will moves itself and the intellect with respect to exercise.[9]

We may summarise Thomas's mature conclusions concerning the extent of human freedom in schematic form. Since the universal good – complete happiness – is the ultimate goal of the will, we do not have freedom of specification with respect to it, that is, we can not will its contrary. But we do have freedom of exercise even with respect to willing the universal good; the will has the power to avert the intellect from the topic of the universal good.[10] This account of the radical nature of freedom of exercise became a staple in seventeenth-century thought. Thus, for both Locke and Leibniz the presumed ability of the human agent to avert the mind, and thereby suspend the decision-making process, was often presented as the inner bastion of human freedom. Since choice concerns the selection of means, not the selection of the ultimate end, human choice may be free both with respect to its exercise and to its specification. Thomas provided separate accounts to cover each case: the exercise of choice, and the specification of choice. Each account generated criticisms, conjoined with alternatives, from Thomas's scholastic successors. Those criticisms and alternatives reverberated through seventeenth-century thinking on freedom.

Consider freedom of specification with respect to choice. Thomas stood by his thesis that a choice is free with respect to its specification only if the will is moved to that choice by a practical judgement of the understanding. Again, the problem of avoiding an unacceptable intellectual determinism loomed. Thomas's solution seems to be this: a choice that is determined as to specification by a judgement of the intellect is free just in case, at the time of consideration of alternatives and in the circumstances then current, the will had it in its power to bring it about that the intellect consider the course chosen in an alternative fashion such that, had it so considered the course chosen, the intellect would not have determined the will to that choice.[11] The lead idea here is to adhere to intellectual determination, but to insist that the very determining factors remain under the control of the will. Scholastic opponents of this account, Molina and Suárez, for example, found the account wanting and proposed alternatives. The ensuing debate within the scholastic tradition shaped much of seventeenth-century thought on freedom.

Suárez considered the nature of freedom of specification in his *Disputationes metaphysicae,* in a section entitled 'How a Free Cause Is Determined by a Judgement of Reason' (XIX.6). There Suárez argued that a judgement of reason – the last practical judgement of the understanding – is a necessary condition of a free choice of the will, for otherwise the will would, per impossible, select an uncognised object. But he argued that it is not necessary that there be a practical judgement of the understanding that completely determines the will with respect to specification. And, indeed, Suárez went further and argued that it is a necessary condition of the will being free with respect to specification that it not be completely determined with respect to specification by the intellect, operating as an efficient cause. And in paragraph 4 of Section 6 he argues against the kind of counterfactual view of freedom of specification attributed above to Saint Thomas. Against that position and in support of Thomas, Suárez's opponents brought some familiar principles of scholastic philosophy, for example, everything that is moved is moved by another, and the principle of sufficient reason. Suárez, with admirable confidence in his own powers of metaphysical reasoning, concluded that the correct account of free choice yields counterexamples to both principles. Aspects of this debate continued to frame the issues in the seventeenth century.

Consider, next, freedom of exercise with respect to choice. Recall that choice is a function of the will and that, according to Thomas, the will moves itself with respect to exercise. This sounds like as pure a theory of self-determination as one could ask for. But qualifications loom. Thomas noted that since the will is not always willing, it must be caused to exercise its power by something other than itself – something whose causal activity with respect to it in no way compromises its freedom.[12] Not surprisingly, only God can so act on the will, according to Thomas.[13] We need, then, to say something about two distinct modes of divine influence on the created will – God's general concurrence and the special concurrence of grace.

The basic idea of divine general concurrence is this: in the case of an action produced by the active power of a creature, God contributes to the action not only by creating the creature and the power by which the creature operates, and by conserving the creature, its power, and the resulting action, in existence so long as they do exist, but God also causally contributes to the production of the action in such fashion that one and the same action is caused immediately and totally by God in the order of a first cause and immediately and totally by the creature in the order of a second cause.[14] The basic idea of God's special concurrence, that is, grace, is this: no creature is capable of performing an action worthy of supernatural merit without supernatural aid, that is, divine causal input above and beyond the divine causal input that is God's general concurrence.[15]

Since a free choice of a creature is an action of that creature, every free choice of a creature involves God's general concurrence. Since only free actions warrant supernatural merit, every action of a creature worthy of supernatural merit involves God's special concurrence as well as God's general concurrence. But since both general and special concurrence involve input by some agent, that is, God, other than the creature whose choice is under consideration, prima facie both pose threats to the agent's freedom.

At the beginning of the seventeenth century there were two competing theories of general concurrence. One was standardly presented as an elaboration of Thomas's view; the other was presented in opposition to Thomas's view. Here is a typical expression of the alternatives, which forms the question for discussion in Disputation 18 of Diego Alvarez's *De auxiliis divinae gratiae et humani arbitrii viribus, et Libertate, ac legitima eius cum efficacia eorundem auxiliorum concordia* (the *Concordia*): 'Whether the general concurrence of God is an immediate influx into the second cause, or whether it is only an immediate influx with the second cause into its effect'.[16] Alvarez employed standard terminology in describing the first alternative as involving divine premotion and the second as involving only divine simultaneous concurrence. This standard terminology may suggest that on the premotion theory the divine motion said to constitute God's general concurrence temporally precedes the occurrence of that with which God concurs; whereas, on the simultaneous concurrence theory, the relevant divine motion is said to be simultaneous with the occurrence of that with which God concurs. But most of those committed to some doctrine of general concurrence claimed, as Alvarez did in the work cited, that on both theories the divine motion said to constitute God's general concurrence is simultaneous with the occurrence of that with which God concurs.

On the premotion theory, the divine motion has precedence in the causal order, but not the temporal order, to the causal activity of the creature. It is a kind of causing (in the order of the first cause) of the causing of the created agent (in the order of second causes). By contrast, on the simultaneous theory, God's causal activity with respect to general concurrence is directed to causing the effect of an operation of causing by a created agent; it is not directed at causing that operation itself. Neo-Thomists – for example, Báñes – set out the details of the premotion theory, attributing the main ideas to Saint Thomas. The theory of a simultaneous general concurrence, accompanied by a criticism of the premotion theory, was formulated by Molina.[17] Molina objected to the premotion theory on the grounds that no such premotion is required in the case of some secondary causes, for example, fire, and that, when applied to exercises of the will, it is inconsistent with free choice in creatures. If God's general concurrence is understood as

involving divine operation only in the mode of a universal cause – with the
secondary causes operating as particularisers of God's contribution – then Molina's
objection applies only with respect to freedom of exercise. However, there was
widespread agreement among parties to these disputes that God's special concurrence, particularly in the form of efficacious grace, involved divine operation
other than as a universal cause and that God's efficacious grace is directed at the
created agent's causing of an effect (via willing) and not simply at the effect itself.
Hence, prima facie, efficacious grace raises problems relevant to both freedom of
specification and exercise with respect to choices of created agents operating under
its influence.

Just as there were two primary competing theories of general concurrence
extant at the beginning of the seventeenth century, there were also two primary
competing theories of efficacious grace. Our focus is on the relation of efficacious
grace to creaturely freedom. We begin with some brief remarks on the dispute
between Molina and Báñez concerning the nature of creaturely freedom. Consider
Molina's well-known characterisation of a free agent in the *Corcordia:* 'That agent
is said to be free who, all the requisites for acting having been posited, can act or
not act, or so perform one action that he is still able to do the contrary.'[18]

Báñez formulated a number of objections to this account of freedom. In the
first place, Báñez argued that the acceptability of Molina's formulation turns on
how the phrase 'all the requisites for acting having been posited' is construed. He
claimed that Molina's account is acceptable only if the requisites posited are those
that obtain antecedent to the relevant exercise of the will. On Báñez's view, God's
efficacious grace, in the form of a premotion of the exercise of the will, is
simultaneous with that act of the will. He wrote:

If however they [Molina and his allies] understand their definition as concerning the
requisites obtaining at the moment in which the free act is exercised, then it is proven false
that, all these having been posited, it is compossible that the man not choose that good that
God prescribes or advises, because one of the requisites is the actual divine motion by
which the will is moved from not willing to willing.[19]

In the second place, Báñez argued that the extreme form of indifference, which
Molina's characterisation allegedly requires for a free act, is not to be found in any
divine choice, including the decision to create, which all orthodox Christians take
to be free. Hence, Báñez concluded that Molina's characterisation cannot capture
the essence of freedom, since it is admitted that freedom occurs in its most perfect
form in God. This criticism, whatever its merits, had a profound influence on
seventeenth-century thinking about freedom, leading philosophers to consider

two notions of freedom: one, according to which an agent's choice is free to the extent to which it results from rational considerations and is not unduly influenced by passion; another, according to which an agent's choice is free only if it is under the control of the agent.

The essentials of the Molinist response to the second of these criticisms may be found in Suárez's *Disputationes metaphysicae,* where Suárez argues as follows: since there can be no reduction from potency to act with respect to divine actions, there can be no efficient causality with respect to the divine will. Hence, the notions of indifference that characterise, respectively, divine and human free acts are, of necessity, so diverse that different notions of freedom are to be expected.[20]

The Molinist response to Báñez's first criticism may be viewed as a reaction to certain features of Báñez's account of the operation of efficacious grace. As limned in the passage quoted above, that account has this consequence: Where $a$ is some human agent; $w$, some free act of $a$'s will; and $g$, some divine premotion in the form of efficacious grace operating on $a$ with respect to $w$, it is not metaphysically possible that $g$ obtains and $w$ does not occur. Notice that this is a stronger claim than the following: it is not metaphysically possible that grace $g$, which is efficacious relative to $w$ of $a$, act on $a$, and $w$ not occur. The latter claim is trivial, turning on the meaning of the adjective 'efficacious'. And a question naturally arises as to whether grace that is efficacious in its own nature in the way assumed by Báñez is consistent with the claim that an act of will may be the result of divine premotion and yet free. Here the famous fourth canon of the sixth session of the Council of Trent is relevant. It claimed that the following is *de fide* for Catholics: that the will of a created agent, operated on by divine grace, may (however unwisely) resist that grace, if the agent so chooses. So our question was often phrased as a question as to whether the Báñezian theory of efficacious grace is consistent with the teachings of Trent.

The usual response offered by Báñezians featured a distinction between something being possible in the composed sense (*in sensu composito*) and its being possible in the divided sense (*in sensu diviso*). The fact is that a variety of distinctions went under the title 'the composed versus the divided sense'. The basic idea is this. Suppose that a question arises as to whether situation S is possible at time $t$ in circumstances $C_i \ldots C_n$ prevailing at, or just prior to, $t$. We may say that S is possible in the composed sense relative to $C_i$ just in case the state of affairs consisting in the joint obtaining of S and $C_i$ is possible. By contrast, S is possible in the divided sense, but not the composed sense, relative to $C_i$ just in case S's obtaining is possible and $C_i$'s obtaining is possible, but their joint obtaining is not possible. Suppose our question is whether a given agent $a$ was free to elicit volition *w* at *t* in the circumstances prevailing at or prior to *t*, where it is a datum of the question that *a* did not in fact elicit *w* at *t*. Suppose further that it is agreed that if *a* was free to elicit *w* at *t*, then it was possible for *a* to elicit *w* at *t* in the circumstances prevailing at or prior to *t*. Given the distinction between the composed and divided senses of possibility this last supposition requires specification. Traditionally, specification was rendered in terms of what circumstances may be 'divided off' legitimately, that is, what circumstances, among those prevailing, need only be such that *a*'s eliciting *w* at *t* is possible in relation to them in the divided sense. Note that some of the circumstances then prevailing must fall in this category, if triviality is to be avoided. By hypothesis, *a* did not elicit *w* at *t*; if we do not 'divide off' that circumstance, then we reach the result that *a* was not free to elicit *w* at *t* in an utterly trivial way. And, we also trivialise the problem if we allow ourselves to divide off any circumstances we choose. Debates between Báñezians and Molinists centred on what circumstances may be divided off, and what are the grounds for a decision concerning what may be divided off. Our quotation from Báñez suggests one answer that Báñezians employed: divide off all those states of affairs simultaneous with *a*'s eliciting *w*. Note the obvious: this strategy works only if we hold (as Báñez did) that God's special concurrence in the form of efficacious grace – God's premotion of the created will – is simultaneous with that which it premoves. So there were two areas of concern for those who rejected Báñez's approach: first, whether efficacious grace is simultaneous with the act of will of the agent on which it operates; and, second, whether, however efficacious grace is construed, it is legitimate to include it in the items 'divided off'. Molinists argued that on any legitimate construal of God's special concurrence in the form of efficacious grace it is not legitimate to divide it off.[21]

So Molinists insisted that where *a* is some human agent; *w*, some free act elicited by *a*; and, *g*, efficacious grace operating on *a* with respect to *w*, it is metaphysically (and, indeed, physically) possible that *g* obtains and *w* does not occur. Note that the Molinists had a use for the distinction between the composed and divided notions of necessity in solving problems concerning the consistency of divine concurrence and human freedom. According to Suárez, for example, we must distinguish two types of requisites in a case of a created agent's eliciting an act of will: those that are prerequisites of the act, but that are related extrinsically to the act, and those that are intrinsically and essentially included in the act.[22] Let us call them, respectively, extrinsic and intrinsic requisites of the act. In considering whether a given elicited act of the will is free, according to Suárez, we must divide off the intrinsic requisites. In other words, Suárez claimed that Molina's famous characterisation of a free agent should be construed as modified thusly –

'all the *extrinsic* requisites for acting having been posited'. And Suárez held that God's special concurrence in the form of efficacious grace is an extrinsic requisite (where it is a requisite at all), whereas God's general concurrence is an intrinsic requisite of every action of a created agent, and, hence, of every act of will elicited by a created agent.[23]

The differences between Molinists and Báñezians just noted formed the basis for differences between them concerning the proper understanding of God's knowledge. Both sides agreed that God's knowledge of simple intelligence – His knowledge of necessary truths – should be distinguished from God's knowledge derivable from His knowledge of His own will. According to Báñezians, the union of those two varieties of divine knowledge provides a complete survey of God's knowledge. But, according to Molinists, God's knowledge of the free choices of creatures falls into neither category. The relevant propositions are contingent and hence not a component of God's knowledge of simple intelligence. Furthermore, according to the Molinist, were knowledge of a creature's choice derivable from a knowledge of what God wills, then that choice would not be free. Hence, Molinists postulated a third category of divine knowledge – middle knowledge – to complete their account of God's knowledge.

Among the alternative accounts of the operation of efficacious grace on free choice, one that deserves our attention is that of Jansenius in his *Augustinus* (1640). It, too, had a profound impact on seventeenth-century thought about free choice, even though some of its alleged features were deemed heretical.

Jansenius held that efficacious grace is a created entity, functioning in a quasi-causal (and, perhaps, just plain causal) manner as an intermediary between the divine will and the will of the created agent. Moreover, Jansenius agreed with Molina that where $a$ is some human postlapsarian agent; $w$, some free act elicited by $a$; and, $g$, efficacious grace operating on $a$ with respect to $w$ – it is metaphysically possible that $g$ obtains and $w$ is not elicited by $a$. But, according to Jansenius, in the postlapsarian state it never happens that efficacious grace operates on human agent $a$ with respect to will $w$ and yet $a$ fails to elicit $w$. And that it never happens is no accident: Jansenius viewed grace as an affection for God which competes with concupiscence, affection for lower things. Both, according to Jansenius, are *delectationes* that move the will when a choice is made. In this scheme, efficacious grace, *delectatio victrix,* always overcomes lesser motives, always wins the day in virtue of its intrinsic nature. One is tempted to say, that, according to Jansenius, where $a$ is some human postlapsarian agent; $w$, some free act elicited by $a;$ and $g,$ efficacious grace operating on $a$ with respect to $w,$ it is *not* physically possible that $g$ obtains and $w$ is not elicited by $a$. Perhaps, strict adherence to the text of

*Augustinus* suggests that we should resist this temptation.[24] Still, the texts are liable to induce the temptation, and, thus, to suggest a form of compatibilism. Compatibilism would be implied because, on this reading, Jansenius would be construed as asserting that there are human choices that are both physically necessary and yet free. And there are passages in *Augustinus* that suggest that Jansenius's view was that moral responsibility requires freedom from coercion, but not freedom from necessity.[25] Indeed, this very claim constitutes the content of the third of the five propositions that Pope Innocent X claimed to find in *Augustinus*, and which he anathematised.

Although the authors and texts so far cited (aside from Saint Thomas) come from the late sixteenth century and the first half of the seventeenth century, the debates whose features we have noted continued to be the subject of inquiry throughout the century. Note, for example, that Malebranche's last published work, *Réflexions sur la prémotion physique* (1715), is a response – essentially from the Molinist point of view – to Boursier's defence of a version of Báñezianism in his *De l'action de Dieu sur les créatures* (1713). And, although all the authors cited to this point were Catholic, similar issues played out among Protestants. Thus, in *Examen theologicum acromaticum* (1707), the theologian David Hollaz expressed the orthodox Lutheran view in defending an account of general and special concurrence that is basically Molinist; and the same is true of *Theologia didactico-polemica* (1685), an important work of Lutheran theology, written by Johann Andreas Quenstedt. By contrast, a view that is basically Báñezian is expressed in *Corpus theologiae Christianae* (1700), written by the respected and orthodox Reformed theologian, Johann Heinrich Heidegger.

## II. DESCARTES

Descartes is usually taken for a libertarian, and it is true that his writings are full of professions of freedom, human as well as divine. 'That there is freedom in our will', he writes in *Principles* I 39, 'is so evident that it must be counted among the first and most common notions that are innate in us', adding two sections later that 'we have such a close awareness of the freedom . . . which is in us, that there is nothing we can grasp more evidently or more perfectly' (*Princ.* I 41). Notwithstanding his emphasis upon our freedom, however, Descartes clearly held that everything apart from God is caused by factors other than itself. He was therefore a determinist with respect to the created universe, the universe within which human wills are exercised and actions performed. Descartes must, therefore, have been a compatibilist, despite the libertarian flavour of many of his pronouncements. And indeed, there are passages in which he appears explicitly to take the compatibilist's position. Since his accounts both of freedom and causal determination are quite complex, however, his view of the relation between these two is complex as well.

We begin with Descartes's view of freedom. In stating his position, Descartes applies the term 'free' not only to actions but also to the agents who perform actions – the substances of which the actions are modifications. (Sometimes it is the performance that is said to be free, whence the agent is said to act or to do something freely.) An agent may be called free with respect to a particular action, in which case she is free if and only if the action is free. Or she may be called free without qualification, in which case her being free consists in her ability to perform free actions. It is in this latter sense that Descartes speaks, as he sometimes does, of freedom as a power or faculty of agents.[26]

Descartes frequently characterises the actions and the agents which have freedom as 'human' – they are 'human actions' and 'human beings', or 'men'. But this is a loose way of speaking. A man on the Cartesian view is not a single agent or substance but a composite of two distinct substances, a mind and a body. As for the actions ascribed to a man, these fall into three distinct groups. First are those that the mind performs by itself: these are volitions. Second are the purely corporeal operations which belong to the body: these are mere bodily motions, such as the free fall of one's arm, or the beating of one's heart. And third is a class of mixed or composite actions each of which has both a mental and a corporeal part, a volition followed by one or more bodily motions: examples are the voluntary raising of a man's arm and his running in order to catch the bus. It is only the actions in this third category that can properly be said to belong to the whole man, the composite of body and mind.

Sometimes Descartes says that volitions are actions, not of the mind, but of the will, and in this vein he ascribes freedom to the will as well. This is also loose talk on his part. His position is not, as might be supposed, that the will is a substance or agent distinct from the mind. Rather, the will is one of the mind's powers, one of its two principal capacities – the other being the intellect or power of perceiving. Volitions are the will's actualisations, not its properties: they are in fact occasional or episodic properties of the mind, the very mind to which the will itself belongs as a permanent property. So when Descartes says that the will acts, what he means is that the mind exercises its power of willing, thereby performing volitions; it is the mind that is the agent of these performances.

In strict speech, the only actions that are free for Descartes are volitions, and the only free agents are the minds that perform these volitions. Not only is no purely corporeal action ever free; but no composite action is properly said to be free either, even if its mental component, the volition that prompts one to run for the bus for example, is free, strictly speaking.

But volitions are not merely the only free actions for Descartes. It is also his view that every volition is free, and that it is so, furthermore, of necessity. For it is the essence of the will, as he puts it, to act freely: willing is free by nature.[27] Indeed, at several places in his text, Descartes uses the expression 'free decision' (*liberum arbitrium*) as the name of the faculty of will.[28] It is not that men have the power of willing, some of whose exercises are free and some not. Rather, they have just the power of free-willing, or willing freely. Given merely that a man has a will, it follows logically that he has the capacity for free action.

The scope of freedom, however, is not as narrow for Descartes as this restriction of it to volitions might suggest. According to the traditional view, there are only two things that the will does (or, rather, two things that the mind does by willing). It either determines in favour or it determines against some action distinct from its own action of willing – it wills to perform or wills not to perform the action in question. For Descartes, by contrast, willing is a general type of mental activity of which there are a number of different species: 'desire, aversion, assertion, denial and doubt are various modes of willing', he says in one place, noting that judging too, since it just consists in affirming or denying, is an act of the will.[29] Elsewhere he says that all of the soul's 'appetites' are volitions, although other passages make it clear that he wants to distinguish volition not only from bodily appetite but also from that desire which is one of the six primitive 'passions of the soul'.[30] On the traditional view, a man can will to affirm some proposition or to deny it (or will not to do either), and his affirming and his denying are actions – actions, indeed, on the part of the intellect – which are distinct from the action of willing itself: as some scholastic philosophers put it, the affirming is an act 'commanded' by the will, whereas the willing is an act 'elicited' by it. Descartes's position, however, is that affirming and denying and such are among the will's elicited acts; they are its very performances and not merely distinct actions commanded by it. Indeed, for Descartes, there is no generic action of willing, no action that is merely a volition and not also something more specific such as a judgement or appetite.[31] Therefore, the variety of actions that count as free on his view is actually quite wide.

What *is* freedom as Descartes conceives it: wherein does it consist? In several passages, he equates being free with being voluntary.[32] To be voluntary is simply to depend on the will; and depending on the will is usually taken to mean being caused by it – that is, being caused by a volition or action of willing. This cannot be Descartes's understanding of voluntariness, however, since on his view it is volitions themselves that are free. Not only are volitions not caused by volitions, but the only things that are caused by volitions are perceptions and motions of bodies, and none of these is free. Hence when Descartes says (by implication – he never does so directly) that a volition is voluntary, he must mean that it depends on the will, not as one event depends on a second event by which it is caused to occur, but as a modification depends on the substance to which it belongs, or in this case, more specifically, as an action depends on its agent. Volitions are voluntary in the sense that they are the will's, or rather the mind's, own performances.

That this is indeed Descartes's meaning is confirmed by the fact that he also identifies freedom, on occasion, with spontaneity.[33] An action is spontaneous if it is performed by its agent entirely on its own, without being forced or helped or affected by any external factor, or by anything other than its very self. By this definition, to be sure, only the actions of God are spontaneous, properly speaking. So when Descartes attributes spontaneity to the actions of created agents he must be using the word in a qualified or restricted sense, in the way that he uses the word 'substance' when he says that not only God but certain creatures are substances.[34] The actions of creatures, therefore, are spontaneous if they depend on no created entity apart from the agent who performs them. Now the agent by which a human volition is performed is just the human mind; there is neither any need nor any room for any other agent or cause, other than God, to take part in the action of willing. Furthermore, in performing volitions the mind uses only its own power of willing. Whatever, therefore, depends on the will in the way that a volition must do, is bound to depend on the mind to which that will also belongs. In the case of volitions, voluntariness and spontaneity coincide.

Unfortunately, there is a third notion that Descartes appeals to in his efforts to explicate freedom, namely, indifference.[35] An action is indifferent if its agent is able, on the point of performing it, not to perform it, or to perform some other action instead. It is understandable that Descartes should refer to this notion, as well as to spontaneity, in his discussions of freedom. Spontaneity is the essence of freedom according to certain influential thinkers of his time; whereas the Jesuits, following Molina, chose to define freedom in terms of indifference. A proponent of spontaneity whom Descartes knew was Guillaume Gibieuf; Descartes refers to his *De libertate dei et creaturae* (1630) in a letter to Mersenne dated 21 April 1641.[36] A Jesuit with whom Descartes corresponded on the subject of freedom was Denis Mesland.[37] Since Descartes wished to find favour with both parties, he often stressed the similarity of his views to theirs, to the point of using their preferred language when he felt it appropriate to do so. The difficulty is that the notions of spontaneity and indifference appear to yield two different conceptions of freedom.

The situation is complicated by the fact that Descartes uses the word 'indifference' with two distinct meanings. Besides indifference in the sense used by the Jesuits, he introduces his own sense, according to which an action is indifferent only if its agent has no reason to perform it, or if the reasons for and against it are evenly balanced.[38] It is obvious that an action may be indifferent in the one sense without being indifferent in the other; and Descartes says explicitly that a free action need not be indifferent as he uses the word.[39] But there also are passages in which Descartes maintains that actions that are not indifferent in the Jesuits' sense are nonetheless free, owing to their spontaneity. Such actions are those by which a proposition clearly and distinctly perceived is affirmed or assented to; for it is impossible, Descartes contends, for the mind not to assent in such cases, and yet its action is free. In speaking of the cogito, for example, he declares that he 'could not but judge that something so clearly understood was true'.[40] And more generally he says, 'if we see very clearly that a thing is good for us, it is very difficult – and, on our view, impossible, as long as one continues in the same thought – to stop the course of our desire [i.e., volition]'.[41] This is not a point of minor significance in Descartes's philosophy; on the contrary, it is crucial to his epistemological project. For the inability of the mind to be mistaken when it affirms what it clearly and distinctly perceives is the ultimate basis of secure human knowledge.

There are free actions, therefore, which are not indifferent (in the Jesuits' sense): in their case spontaneity is sufficient for freedom. On the other hand, in one of his last pronouncements on the nature of freedom (in a letter dated 9 February 1645, presumably to Mesland – who was, of course, a Jesuit), Descartes explicitly says that the free mind is always indifferent in the sense of being able not to perform any action that it does perform:

I do not deny that the will has this positive faculty [and that] it has it . . . with respect to all . . . actions; so that [even] when a very evident reason moves us in one direction, although morally speaking we can hardly move in the contrary direction, absolutely speaking we can. For it is always open to us to hold back from pursuing a clearly known good, or from admitting a clearly perceived truth, provided we consider it a good thing to demonstrate the freedom of our will by so doing.[42]

There is no consensus among Cartesian scholars as to how this difficulty ought to be dealt with.[43] One obvious strategy is to read the qualification expressed by the phrase 'morally speaking' back into Descartes's earlier statements. The trick is to do this without undermining his entire epistemology. It is not clear if this strategy can be made to succeed, but to pursue that question would take us away from our chief business in this discussion. In any case, the remaining main tenets of the Cartesian view of freedom are clear: that all and only volitions are free actions, that (apart from God) all and only minds are free agents, and that actions and agents are free if and only if they are spontaneous.

Descartes's understanding of freedom is fairly explicit in his works. Not so his conception of causation, however. He does affirm a number of quite general propositions about causal relationships: that 'something cannot arise from nothing'; that 'there must be at least as much [reality] in the efficient and total cause as in the effect of that cause'; that everything depends on God; that corporeal events are governed by laws; that souls and bodies act on one another; and that some of our actions depend on our free will.[44] But though it seems clear that causation is not the same thing in all of these relationships, Descartes says almost nothing about the differences between them. Nor does he do much to explain what causing, or being the cause or a cause of something, or depending on, amounts to in any one of these cases. So an account of Descartes's determinism must of necessity be somewhat speculative.

Since the precise subjects of Cartesian freedom are actions of willing, it is the causal relationships involving these in particular that pertain to the concerns of this chapter – that is, the relationships in which volitions are determined by or depend upon something other than themselves. Volitions, according to Descartes, are subject to three sorts of causes.

First, they are caused by God, in common with everything else in the universe. Descartes distinguishes two aspects of God's causation of things. On the one hand, God is the original creator of substances, and thus of the minds possessing the wills from which volitions are elicited. On the other hand, God concurs in all the operations of substances, including those ascribed to the will. Thus, not only is God the cause of 'all effects', including those that 'depend on human free will', but 'the slightest thought could not enter into a person's mind without God's willing, and having willed from all eternity, that it should so enter.'[45] So God is causally responsible for every mind with its power of willing by having created it; and He is responsible for every volition by concurring in all of the actions of minds.

Second, volitions depend on the minds whose actions they are. This dependence is partly a matter of simply belonging to a substance, in the way that any property does. Since volitions, however, are not merely properties but actions, and therefore events, there is more to their dependence than this. They owe not only their being but their occurrence at particular times to the minds they belong to:

minds produce or perform their volitions as agents, besides possessing them as substances. Furthermore, each volition is produced solely by its own mind (leaving God out of account): this is what makes it a spontaneous and hence a free action. This means not only that no other (created) agent takes part in performing it, but that no (created) factor outside its own mind even affects it. Cartesian minds are thus (God aside) wholly autonomous in performing their volitions. Descartes puts this by saying that the will – that is, the mind – has 'a real and positive power to determine [it]self'.[46]

Finally, volitions are determined by other thoughts that occur in the minds that perform them. The thoughts in question are perceptions, since Descartes does not allow volitions to be caused by other volitions. But not all perceptions are equally effective in causing volitions. Those that are perfectly clear and distinct make it impossible (at least 'morally speaking') for the minds in which they occur not to assent to what they contain, assent being an act of the will. Obscure perceptions, by contrast, may have no effect on the will whatsoever; or if they do affect it they merely incline or dispose the will in one direction or the other, without necessitating its movement (even 'morally speaking') in either. In both of these cases the causal factor, the perception, is an event, whereas the causes of the other two sorts we have noted, God and the mind, are agents. For it is not merely the content of a perception I have, it is also my having it, that either makes me perform a volition or inclines me to do so. But Descartes shows no reluctance in general to count events, as well as agents, as causes. It is true that he never explicitly calls a perception the 'cause' of a free volition. But he regularly uses causal locutions in characterising this relationship. Thus, clear perceptions are said to 'impel' us or the will to perform volitions, as well as to make us incapable of not doing so.[47] And even the passions, which are obscure perceptions and hence merely 'incline' the will without necessitating it, are said to 'incite' and to 'dispose' the soul to this or that action of willing.[48]

It might seem perplexing that perceptions should have causal rôles in willing for Descartes, given his doctrine that volitions are spontaneous actions on the part of the minds they belong to. For a spontaneous action is one that its agent performs all by itself, and a volition is spontaneous just because the mind that produces it is not only not compelled to do so by any external agent, it is not even assisted by anything other than its very self. Such perplexity, however, can be dispelled by recalling that Cartesian perceptions are properties of minds, just as volitions are, and that although no perception is identical with the mind in which it occurs – it is not that very thing – neither is it really distinct from it. In every case in which a perception has any effect on a volition, the perception and the volition are modifications of the same mind, and their interaction takes place entirely within it. Neither, therefore, is an external factor with respect to the other, let alone with respect to the one mind in which both occur.

It is true that minds are not fully responsible, causally, for all their perceptions, in the way that they are for all their volitions. Perceptions are passive states, not actions; and though perceptions need minds to possess and sustain them as properties, they often owe their occurrence to the actions of entities outside the mind, to corporeal agents. But a perception that is caused by an external agent is an obscure perception, and at best it merely inclines the mind in which it occurs to perform a volition. If such a perception were to cause a volition in the sense of (morally) necessitating its occurrence, then Descartes might have to grant that the external cause of the perception was the cause – or at least a partial or contributing cause – of the resulting volition, owing to the transitivity of this kind of causal relation; in that case the volition would not be spontaneous. But no such perception does cause a volition in this sense. And the perceptions that do cause volitions in the sense of (morally) necessitating their occurrence – namely, the ones that are clear and distinct – are none of them caused, even partly, by any external or corporeal factor. They are the productions wholly and solely of the minds they belong to: and that is why the volitions they cause, even though necessitated, are nonetheless spontaneous, and so free.

More needs to be said about how the mind works, on the Cartesian theory, when it performs a volition because of some perception it has, whether clear or obscure. Not much of this, unfortunately, is made explicit by Descartes himself, at least not in any systematic way. But the main lines of what he would or ought to have said on this subject can be worked out from some of his scattered remarks, especially in his last major work, *Les passions de l'âme*.

It is a fundamental principle for Descartes that the human will is naturally oriented towards goodness and truth: the mind has a natural tendency to perform a positive volition when presented with an instance of goodness or truth.[49] This is part of the 'institution of nature' which Descartes appeals to on several occasions.[50] What I call an instance of truth is provided by any proposition which is represented to the mind: the positive volition is one to affirm or assent to the proposition in question. An instance of goodness is provided by any proposition in which an object or situation is represented as being good in some way: the positive volition is one to pursue the object or to realise the situation in question. Mental representations are just perceptions in Descartes's ontology, whether or not they take the form of propositions; and they are formed in the mind by the intellect, which is its perceptive faculty. Perceptions may be generated by corporeal objects outside the mind, including the body with which the mind is united; or they may be produced by the mind itself acting alone, merely in consequence of an act of willing (so that we have one volition causing a perception which in turn causes another volition, even though Descartes does not permit one volition to be caused by another directly).[51] It is another one of Descartes's fundamental principles that the will cannot act except in response to an exercise of the intellect — some perception or representation or idea — so that willing presupposes perceiving: no volition without representation.[52]

When any (propositional) perception is clear and distinct, then the institution of nature is such that the will moves immediately to affirm — that is, to judge to be true — the perception in question. We then say that the perception makes the will act (although strictly speaking, of course, it is the mind that acts). It is, however, only in conjunction with the will's (or the mind's) natural tendency to act, when presented with an instance of truth, that the perception is able to bring about the action of willing. So the institution of nature has to be recognised as a causal factor in such situations as well, a factor deriving ultimately, no doubt, from the creative or concurring action of God.

The situation is more complicated when the perception which 'incites' a volition is obscure, and here the most interesting case to consider is that in which the obscure perception is a 'passion of the soul', in Descartes's special use of that term. For these passions are powerful motivators of human actions, especially those having to do with our bodies: it is their function, Descartes says, 'to dispose the soul to will the things that nature tells us are useful, and to persist in this volition', where 'useful' means 'useful for the purpose of preserving our bodies', usefulness in this sense being one species of goodness.[53] And nature tells us that something is useful by representing it as good in this way, that is, by arranging for us to perceive it as good. Because this perception is obscure, the soul does not respond immediately by willing to pursue the thing perceived as good. What happens rather is that a passion is produced in the soul, the passion of desire in particular: though other passions such as love and joy and hope and courage may be aroused as well, these are effective in moving the will only 'by means of the desire they produce'.[54] It is then this passion that causes the appropriate volition, not by necessitating its occurrence, but by disposing the soul to perform it.

Note that the institution of nature is invoked by Descartes at two points in the process just sketched. For nature first operates by causing a perception of a thing's usefulness to be produced in the soul. And it is by nature's doing again that the passion roused by this perception influences the will. Of course nature is at work also in the intervening process by which the perception gives rise to the passion, for this involves actions on the part of corporeal agents – sense organs, nerves, and brain – all of which are governed by natural laws, the laws of physics in fact. This part of the story is told by Descartes in considerable detail, more detail, certainly, than he provides in the case of the parts dealing specifically with volitions.[55]

We can now address the question of Descartes's compatibilism, the logical consistency of his position that volitions are free with each of his claims regarding their determination by causes. Since he explicitly makes each of these claims – that volitions are caused by God, by the minds in which they occur, and by clear perceptions – while remaining committed to the freedom of every volition, it follows that Descartes is a compatibilist with respect to each of these relationships. But his compatibilism is not merely implicit in his writings, as a logical consequence of his express statements. Descartes also explicitly says, with respect to two of the three ways in question, that there is no conflict between a volition's being free and its being caused. With respect to God, there is, for example, his statement to Elisabeth that 'the free will [or] the independence which we experience and feel in ourselves . . . is not incompatible with a dependence of quite another kind, whereby all things are subject to God'.[56] With respect to clear perception, we have the testimony of the Fourth Meditation that 'neither divine grace nor natural knowledge [both of which are sources of clear perception] ever diminishes freedom; on the contrary, they increase and strengthen it';[57] and Descartes's declaration in the Sixth Replies that 'not only are we free when ignorance of what is right makes us indifferent [in the Cartesian sense of the word], but we are also free – indeed at our freest – when a clear perception impels us to pursue some object'.[58] As for the remaining way in which volitions are caused, namely, by depending on a mind, being so caused is not only not in conflict with, it actually constitutes the freedom of volitions, according to Descartes's equation of freedom with spontaneity: being free entails being caused in this way. In this case, therefore, that freedom is compatible with causal dependence is a consequence *a fortiori*.

Of course, it is one thing for a philosopher to say that there is no incompatibility between two apparently contrary claims in his system, and quite another for his saying this to be justified, or even intelligible. Two problems remain in connection with Descartes's professions of compatibilism in the two cases just noted. How can a volition be free if a clear perception *impels* its performance? And how can a volition be free if, as Descartes says in another letter to Elisabeth, everything that happens comes *entirely* from God, and God is not just the 'universal cause' but 'the total cause of everything'?[59]

The first of these problems is solved if we understand clear perceptions to impel volitions only 'morally speaking' and not absolutely. Alternatively, we could define freedom wholly in terms of spontaneity and give up the requirement of (Jesuitical) indifference. There are difficulties consequent upon both of these alternatives: the one places Descartes's epistemology in jeopardy, the other flies in the face of clear textual evidence. But either or both of these difficulties could, perhaps, be resolved, without doing major damage to the Cartesian system.

The second problem, however, is harder to deal with. For even if we identify freedom with spontaneity, eschewing indifference, we still have to understand how a volition which depends wholly on the mind that performs it can also come entirely from God. Earlier, we set God aside, and defined spontaneity in terms solely of created agents; but now it looks as if that stipulation was illegitimate. For it now looks as if we have two distinct conditions for the performance of any volition, each of which is sufficient as well as necessary: on the one hand, that some created mind produce it; on the other, that it come from God. Furthermore, it must have looked so to Descartes himself on occasion. For in the *Principles* he notes the 'great difficulties' we get ourselves into 'if we attempt to reconcile . . . divine preordination with the freedom of our will' and suggests that the proper response to these difficulties is simply to give up the attempt.[60]

A more satisfactory response, however, would be to consider the action of God to be not sufficient for the performance of any volition, but only necessary therefor. There is some textual basis for thinking that this was in fact Descartes's considered position. For example, in the letter to Elisabeth just cited, he immediately glosses his remarks that everything comes 'entirely from' God and that God is 'the total cause of everything' by saying, in the one case, that 'the slightest thought could not enter into a person's mind without God's willing . . . that it should so enter'; and, in the other, that 'nothing can happen without His will'.[61] In both instances, the original remark connotes sufficiency on the part of God's action, but the gloss implies only its necessity. On the other side, however, these are not the only passages in which Descartes uses the language of sufficiency in speaking of God's causal relation to created things, including free human volitions.[62] It may be that such usages can all be dismissed as rhetorical exaggerations, which Descartes was in general not loath to indulge in. But this would have to be shown in detail before this way of solving the problem could be adopted with confidence.

## III. HOBBES

As we have noted, all the major thinkers whose views we are presenting in this chapter (perhaps excepting Malebranche) were determinists: they held that everything that happens in the world is brought about by antecedent causes. But only Hobbes and Spinoza called much attention to their determinism. Hobbes not only made his commitment to what he called the 'doctrine of necessity' explicit, he flaunted it. One reason he did so may be the connexion he saw between this doctrine and the metaphysical materialism he advocated – Hobbes is, in fact, the only materialist among our six philosophers. But his exaltation of determinism may also have been prompted by his controversy on this subject with an Arminian bishop, John Bramhall of Derry. Bramhall 'hated' (his word) determinism: he thought it morally pernicious as well as intellectually mistaken. And Hobbes was not one to side-step a challenge.

Hobbes's determinism is quite straightforward. As a materialist he takes the only (natural) beings to be bodies, and the only (natural) actions or events to be the motions of bodies. (The qualification 'natural' is called for because Hobbes allows that God exists and acts, but appears – at least in some passages – to exempt Him from the order of nature, even though in other passages he appears to make God a body after all.)[63] Since no motion goes on forever, every action has a beginning in time; and what begins must have a cause distinct from and antecedent to itself. In Hobbes's words, 'Nothing taketh beginning from itself, but from the action of some other immediate agent without itself'.[64] That nothing begins without a cause Hobbes holds to be both necessary and self-evident. He also holds it to be necessary that if some particular *x* causes a particular *y*, then it is necessary that if *x* occurs then *y* ensues. This is what he means when he says that causes necessitate their effects and that every cause is a necessary cause.

But what does Hobbes mean by 'necessary'? Many philosophers – Leibniz, for one – distinguish 'logical' from 'natural' (or 'metaphysical' from 'physical') necessity. The question is, which necessity is it that Hobbes thinks attaches to the causal relation? In one passage he defines 'necessary' as 'that which is impossible to be otherwise, or that which cannot possibly otherwise come to pass',[65] but this merely shifts the question to 'impossible' and 'possible', and these modalities have the same two kinds that necessity does. Although Hobbes does not make this distinction explicitly, it appears to be logical necessity that he takes to characterise the relation of causes to effects. For when he comes in his treatise *De corpore* to define 'cause', he says that when the cause is 'supposed to be present, it cannot be understood but that the effect is produced'.[66] The suggestion is that a cause not followed by its effect is inconceivable, a violation of the laws not merely of nature but of logic. Hobbes's view of the causal nexus is thus the same as that of Spinoza, who holds explicitly that effects follow their causes with logical necessity.

Hobbes holds that every action has a necessary cause. It is important to note that he does not take the necessary cause of a particular action to be another particular action. He acknowledges that we may sometimes call a single particular event a cause: thus 'the last feather' may be said to 'break the horse's back'. But this is really only part of the cause as a whole: the 'last cause' yet not the 'whole cause'. For Hobbes, the 'cause simply' or the 'entire cause' of any action, that which, he says, 'necessitateth and determinateth' it, 'is the sum of all things, which . . . conduce and concur to the [its] production'. Furthermore, since every member of such a 'concourse' of (partial) causes is itself 'determined to be such as it is by a like concourse of former causes', each of which is in its turn determined by another such concourse, and so on; and since all these causes were 'set and ordered by the eternal cause of all things, God Almighty', it follows that the entire cause of every present action is a vast series of collections of partial causes extending back to and including the original action by which God created all things. So God Himself, or more precisely the will of God, though not the whole cause, is nonetheless a partial cause of everything that happens in the world.[67]

Among the things that happen in the world for Hobbes are the actions of human beings. In his view, these, like actions in general, are nothing more nor less than motions of bodies — either of human bodies taken whole or of the various material parts of which such bodies are composed. Hobbes grants that some human actions are voluntary, and that these have special properties which give them moral significance. But these, too, he holds, are merely motions of or in human bodies. It must be noted that Hobbes gives the word 'action' a broad sense, assimilating it to 'event', so that not only the things an agent does but those a patient suffers count as actions: a man engages in an action as much when he accidentally falls from a bridge as when he deliberately jumps. It is true, however, that all of Hobbes's voluntary actions are actions in the narrower sense of performances by an agent. The converse may hold as well, though he is not explicit on this point.

Since in Hobbes's view all actions are caused, and thus determined or necessitated, he is committed to holding that all voluntary actions are determined or necessitated. Indeed, he explicitly says that they are on numerous occasions. What differentiates such actions from those that are involuntary or nonvoluntary is the nature of the cause that determines them. Hobbes defines voluntary actions in what sounds like the standard seventeenth-century way: they are actions which 'have beginning in the will', or which 'proceedeth from the Will'.[68] So a voluntary action is one that has the will for its cause (i.e., for its immediate or last cause: like everything else, the entire cause of a voluntary action is a concatenation of partial causes stretching back to and including the will of God). But Hobbes conceived the will in a manner very different from that of his contemporaries. According to the usual conception, will is 'rational appetite', a power belonging to man's spiritual or intellectual nature and thus distinct from feelings and emotions and from sensual desire or 'animal appetite', all of which are rooted in the body. For Hobbes, however, there is only one kind of appetite in man, and it is of a piece with that found in animals. Indeed, Hobbes recognises only one kind of psychological phenomenon in general. All mental activities, intellectual and sensual, consist of motions, and thus are affections of the human (or animal) body or its parts; and all mental powers are powers to move or be moved.

Hobbes does draw the standard distinction, within the general class of mental phenomena, between 'cognitive' and 'motive' powers. The former yield knowledge or at least conception, whereas the latter have to do with action: Hobbes calls their exercises 'passions', but in their function they are inclinations or motives, that is, factors immediately responsible for the overt actions of men and animals. Hobbes subdivides these passions into positive and negative, according to whether they incline one towards or away from their objects; and he distinguishes several different species of passion under each head: pleasure, love, and desire or appetite on the positive side; pain, hate, and fear or aversion on the negative. One might expect to find willing among Hobbes's specific passions, but that is not how he regards it. Rather, he says, 'will' is what we call the last passion, whatever its specific nature, in a sequence of alternately occurring passions in a process of deliberation. (Thus, there is no special faculty or power of willing in Hobbes's theory, only actions thereof.) It is this last passion which terminates the process, and which immediately precedes the action (or its omission) which was the subject of the deliberation. Will therefore presupposes deliberation, as does voluntary action. Indeed, Hobbes sometimes defines voluntary action as action following deliberation. This makes a problem for him, since he admits that agents sometimes act without deliberation: one may act so suddenly that there is no time to deliberate, or with such assurance that there is no need to. Hobbes solves this problem by pointing out that even in such a case the agent is in some emotional state which causes his action, and that this state is his will, since will is the last appetite before the action, 'and here where is one only appetite, that one is the last.' Besides which, he says, 'no *action* of a man can be said to be without *deliberation,* though never so sudden, because . . . he [will have] had time to *deliberate* all the precedent time of his life, whether to do that kind of action or not'.[69]

Since a voluntary action is caused by a will (i.e., an act of willing), it follows for Hobbes that voluntary actions are necessitated by wills: 'Of *voluntary* actions', he says, 'the *will* is the *necessary* cause'.[70] Of course, to put this accurately we should say that a voluntary action is necessitated by a long chain of partial causes of which willing to do it is only the last link. Furthermore, each of the earlier links in this chain is in turn necessitated by the links that precede it, so that acts of willing are themselves effects of necessary causes. This account of willing was anathema to Bramhall. To begin with, Bramhall, unlike Hobbes, took the will to be a special power of the mind, with its own characteristic nature and way of operating. Second, the will for Bramhall is a 'self-determining power', by which he means not only that acts of willing have no cause other than the will itself, but also that the will is not determined to act by any factors besides itself. Bramhall allows that other factors, such as 'dictates of the understanding' and 'passions and acquired habits', may influence the will to act. But, he says, 'I deny that any of these do necessitate or can necessitate the will of man by determining it physically'.[71] He does admit that the will may be determined 'morally', as 'when some object is proposed to it with persuasive reasons and arguments to induce it to will';[72] and he is even willing to attribute a kind of necessity to the will's response – what he calls 'moral' or 'hypothetical' necessity. But this is not the 'absolute necessity' which is entailed by physical or natural determination, the necessity by which Hobbes, according to Bramhall, holds acts of willing to be produced. For in cases of moral necessitation, Bramhall says, the will still is able to direct its act upon a different object, or suspend it altogether; this it cannot do when the necessitation is natural. Finally, as to the relation between the act of willing and the (overt) voluntary action thereby commanded, Bramhall rejects Hobbes's claim that the former is the 'necessary cause' of the latter. But his actual response to the claim is an *ignoratio elenchi*: he takes Hobbes to mean by 'necessary cause' cause that is itself necessitated (by some further, antecedent cause), rather than cause that necessitates.[73] In another passage, however, Bramhall indicates that he takes this relation too to be one of merely hypothetical necessity. 'The election of our . . . will', he writes, 'produce[s] an hypothetical necessity, that the event be such as . . . the will [hath] elected. But for as much as . . . the will [might] have elected otherwise, this is far from an absolute necessity'.[74]

Hobbes of course had his own criticisms to make of Bramhall's view of willing. The whole idea of moral determination, or of any necessity other than the natural (which, as noted earlier, he evidently took to be not natural in our sense but logical), Hobbes found to be unintelligible. The doctrine of the self-determining will, he charges, violates the maxim that 'nothing taketh beginning from itself', which entails that 'when first a man [has] an appetite or will to something, . . . the cause of his will is not the will itself, but something else not in his own disposing'.[75] Besides which, he suggests, the very idea of a will capable of controlling its own operations – of producing or suspending or directing its acts of willing – is incoherent. For such a will would be a voluntary agent, and its operations voluntary performances; whereas in truth such acts 'proceed not from but are the will: . . . a man can no more say he will will, than he will will will, and so make an infinite repetition of the word will; which is absurd and insignificant'.[76]

Despite his insistence that everything that happens is necessitated, Hobbes does not deny that there is freedom in the world. On the contrary, he explicitly affirms that human beings (as well as animals) are free agents, and that at least some of the actions of these agents are free actions. Obviously, the freedom he allows, whatever its specific nature (a problematic matter which we take up in a moment), must be logically compatible with necessity; and that it is so compatible is indeed a point he frequently stresses: '*Liberty*, and *necessity* are consistent', he says in a famous passage in *Leviathan*.[77] Hobbes was not the only thinker of his time who conceived freedom in this compatibilist way: he cites the Protestant reformers Luther and Calvin and even Saint Augustine as having had the same idea.[78] But the incompatibilist conception promoted by Bramhall and other Arminians had achieved considerable currency in England. For Bramhall and company, the only true freedom was 'freedom from necessity', a freedom to which necessitation by antecedent causes is directly contrary. These thinkers granted the consistency of 'freedom from constraint' with the necessity of action; and this is what they took the compatibilist's freedom to amount to. But they denied that this or any freedom other than freedom from necessity is adequate to ground the practice of morality and the truth of certain doctrines of the Christian religion. For example, they claimed that it would be unjust, for God or man, to punish a sinner whose sins were the product of necessary causes; and to make sinners free in any sense that failed to render their sinning unnecessary would also fail to remove the injustice of punishing them. Although Hobbes thought the chief fault of the incompatibilist's conception of freedom was its intrinsic incoherence, he took pains to rebut this charge of the moral and religious inadequacy of his own conception and sought to show by detailed arguments that the 'inconveniencies' alleged to follow from it in fact did not do so.

One main source of the incoherence Hobbes saw in the incompatibilist's freedom concerns the locus of freedom, the precise subject of which it is or ought to be predicated. Hobbes ascribed freedom both to actions and to agents, and in the case of human beings the proper agent, the true subject of freedom, he insists, is the whole man, not his mind or some particular department thereof. For

Bramhall, by contrast, the primary subjects of freedom are the will, conceived as a special faculty or power of the mind, and the volitions or acts of willing which are the exercises of this faculty. Bramhall did not scruple to ascribe freedom to whole men as well as to their wills, and to overt actions as well as to the acts of willing that produced them. But in each of these cases, he claims, the freedom of the former is derived from and subordinate to that of the latter. For, as he says, 'all the freedom of the agent is from the freedom of the will'. Furthermore, since 'no effect can exceed the virtue of its cause, if the action be free . . . , the power or faculty to will [that action], must of necessity be more free'; and 'if the will be determined, the [action] is likewise determined'.[79] But in Hobbes's view there is no such thing as 'the will', conceived as a special mental faculty. And even if there were, it would simply be an improper use of the English language, he urged, to attribute freedom to it, as if this will were not a power of an agent but itself an agent in its own right – a point also made by Locke some years later. Hobbes also claimed that it is no less 'an absurd speech' to call an act of willing free than it is to call one voluntary.[80]

Apart from making it compatible with necessity, and restricting its application to whole men (or animals) and their overt actions, how does Hobbes conceive of freedom? In several texts he defines freedom (or liberty) as the absence of impediments to motion, or more specifically, as the absence of external impediments, meaning those 'that are not contained in the nature and intrinsical quality of the agent'.[81] As Hobbes notes, even inanimate beings are free by this definition, so that water, for example, 'is said to descend *freely*, or to have *liberty* to descend by the channel of the river, because there is no impediment that way, but not across, because the banks are impediments'.[82] But in his characterisations of the freedom of animate creatures – those which have appetites and can form opinions and thus are voluntary agents – Hobbes includes a reference to their wills, or rather their willings. Thus, 'a FREE MAN is he that in those things, which by his strength and wit he is able to do, is not hindered to do what he has a will to'; and the liberty of such a man 'consisteth in this, that he finds no stop in doing what he has the will . . . to do'. More simply, 'a free agent is he that can do if he will, and forbear if he will'. It follows from this account that every action a voluntary agent actually performs is a free action, or as Hobbes puts it, that 'all voluntary acts are free' (he also takes the converse to be true).[83] For if a man wills to do something, and then actually does it, he must be able to do what he does, by the principle that what is actual is possible. And if he wills to do something, and then is prevented from doing it by some external impediment, he performs, not a voluntary action that is not free, but no action at all, and *a fortiori* no voluntary action.

This all seems quite straightforward; but the situation is complicated by the fact that Hobbes sometimes speaks in a quite different way about freedom, linking it with the deliberation that precedes voluntary action rather than with the impediments that may manifest themselves after deliberation has ended. 'Of a *voluntary agent*', Hobbes says, 'it is all one to say, he is *free,* and to say, he hath not made an end to *deliberating*'; and again, 'we retain the liberty of doing, or omitting, according to the appetite, or aversion [until] deliberation . . . end[s]'.[84] Not only is this way of speaking about freedom different, but what is said about it may actually conflict with what is said in terms of impediments. Bramhall thought it did, and so, too, have some recent scholars. According to Bramhall, it follows from these two statements that 'the same person, at the same time, [may] be free and not free', as when 'a man deliberates whether he shall play tennis: and at the same time the door of the tennis-court is fast locked against him.'[85] Bramhall's point is that the man is free to play tennis because, with the question still under deliberation, the possibility of his doing so is open to him; but that he is not free to play because the locked door impedes his doing so. Hobbes responded to this by denying that the would-be tennis player is not free to play tennis. It is true, he says, that it is impossible for him to play, 'yet it is no impediment to him that the door is shut, till he have a will to play; which he hath not till he hath done deliberating whether he shall play or not'.[86] That is, nothing actually impedes an action for Hobbes until the action has actually been started, or at least attempted or undertaken, and this happens only after deliberation has stopped and a will so to act has occurred. Hobbes's response, however, does not dispose of Bramhall's argument. For one thing, Hobbes cannot consistently restrict what counts as an impediment in this way, in view of other things he holds about freedom. But even if Bramhall's example is deflected by Hobbes's move, there are others which are not. According to A. G. Wernham, if Bramhall's tennis-player 'wills to play tennis and the court is not locked', then 'in so far as he wills to play, he is no longer free to play according as he shall will; but he is still free in so far as he is not hindered to do what he has a will to'. Wernham concludes that Hobbes must recognise two different 'senses' of 'freedom', or, as he also puts it, 'two different kinds of freedom'. The 'still-deliberating' formula, Wernham claims, commits Hobbes to 'a "two-way" freedom (to do or forbear) which excludes will . . . and is abolished by it', whereas the 'absence-of-impediments' formula entails 'a "one-way" freedom which presupposes will'; and an agent may enjoy one of these freedoms and not the other, at the same time and with respect to the same action.[87]

It is unlikely, however, that Hobbes did recognise such different senses of 'freedom' (or kinds of freedom). Not only does he emphasise, in several passages, that 'liberty' means 'the absence of external impediments' 'according to the proper signification of the word', or is 'rightly defined' in this way;[88] but such passages occur in the same works and in close proximity to those in which he links freedom to deliberation. In any case, a careful reading of Hobbes's text provides no basis for the two-freedoms interpretation.

As we have noted, when Hobbes defines 'freedom' merely as 'the absence of external impediments', he is thinking of freedom as a property that may belong to any agent, even an inanimate one. When he wants to focus specifically on the freedom of a voluntary agent, however, he adds a reference to the agent's will. For such an agent, to be free is to be able to do what one wills to do, with 'being able to do' understood as 'not being prevented from doing by any external impediment'. So if $m$ is a voluntary agent, and $d$ is an action, then $m$ is free with respect to $d$ – that is, free to do $d$ – if and only if $m$ both wills to do $d$ and is able to do $d$. Now there are, in Hobbes's view, two different times at which a question as to $m$'s freedom with respect to $d$ (or as to the freedom of $d$ itself) can legitimately be raised. The one (call it $t1$) occurs while $m$ is deliberating whether to do $d$ or not and hence before $m$ has willed either to do or not to do it. The other ($t2$) occurs after $m$ has willed to do $d$ but before he has actually done it (he may only have started doing it, or be trying to do it, or be set to do it, etc.). (No such question arises after $m$ has done $d$, since an action already done is *a fortiori* one that its agent was able to do.) At both times, according to Hobbes's understanding of freedom, $m$ is free to do $d$ if and only if he wills to do $d$ and also is able to do it; so the two cases are in that respect exactly the same. What differentiates them is that in the latter the truth value of the first conjunct of the apodosis of the conditional is already settled, and only the value of the second conjunct remains to be seen; whereas in the former case, while $m$ is still deliberating, the truth of both conjuncts is open. But this is an epistemic or pragmatic difference and not one of semantics: there is no difference in the meaning of 'free' between the two cases.

As for Wernham's example, it fails to establish that Hobbes is committed to two kinds of freedom (or else contradicts himself). For Hobbes admits no sense of 'free' in which an agent is free to play tennis while deliberating whether to play, solely on the basis that the court is not locked against him; and hence there is no Hobbesian sense in which the same agent is not free after he has stopped deliberating and willed to play. What freedom requires, in the one and only way that Hobbes did understand it, is that the player will to play, as well as that there be no impediment to his playing (and the court's being locked, be it noted, is such an impediment, Hobbes's response to Bramhall notwithstanding). This point is confirmed by the fact that Hobbes often expresses his conception of freedom by saying (in effect) that $m$ is free to do $d$ if and only if he is able to do $d$ *if* he wills to do it. And in a passage in *De homine* he makes the requirement of willing explicit: 'When we say someone is free to do this or that, or not to do it, this is always to be understood with this added condition: *if he will*. For to say that someone is free to do this or that whether or not he wills is to speak absurdly'.[89]

There is also this further difference between an agent deliberating whether to do something and one who has already willed to do it – between $m$ at $t1$ and $m$ at $t2$. In the first situation $m$ may well be free, if not in two ways, then at least with respect to two contrary things: doing $d$ and not doing it. For here $m$ is free to do $d$, if he so wills, provided he is able to do it, and free not to do $d$, if he so wills, provided he is able not to do it. And in many cases an agent is able both to do something and not to do it. In the second situation, by contrast, $m$ is free with respect to one thing at most, since having already willed he has ruled out one or the other of doing $d$ and not doing it. And indeed in every instance but one in which Hobbes speaks of the freedom of an agent who 'hath not made an end of deliberating' he characterises it as the freedom 'to do or not to do'.[90] This point no doubt explains why Hobbes says, as he does in one response to Bramhall, that a deliberating agent has more freedom than one who has willed something at the end of a process of deliberation. What he must mean is that such an agent has freedom with respect to more things, namely, the non-performance as well as the performance of some action (assuming the requisite will in each case).

Near the end of his treatise *Of Liberty and Necessity* Hobbes charges: 'That ordinary *definition* of a *free agent*, namely, *that a* free agent *is that, which, when all things are present which are needful to produce the* effect, *can nevertheless not produce it*, implies a contradiction, and is nonsense'. Further on he says that 'the whole controversy' between himself and Bramhall turns on the question whether there is any such thing as a free agent so defined.[91] Bramhall had not himself given this definition in his *Discourse of Liberty and Necessity*, to which Hobbes's treatise was a reply. But in responding to Hobbes's charge he endorsed it and called it 'the very definition which is given by the much greater part of Philosophers and School-men'.[92] Bramhall was not quite correct in this last claim: the definition was in fact first formulated by Molina and hence is not to be found in the works of Thomas Aquinas. Still, it was widely known and repeated in the seventeenth century, having been taken over nearly verbatim by the Dutch Arminians and passed on by them to their English sympathisers, of whom Bramhall was one. The fact remains, however, that Hobbes in his treatment of freedom challenged not only the extreme libertarianism of the Molinist and Arminian sort but the whole scholastic approach to this topic, including the more moderate position of Aquinas himself. Hobbes spends considerable time in his polemic with Bramhall attacking not merely the doctrines but the very terms and distinctions that his contemporaries had learned from Aquinas. What the purveyors of school-learning say, he exclaims, 'especially in the maintenance of free-will, when they talk of *liberty of exercise, specification, contrariety, contradiction, acts elicite and exercite,* and the like [is] but jargon, or that . . . which the Scripture in the first chaos calleth Tohu and Bohu'.[93] Hobbes's own position may be crude, as critics have charged: a little school-learning might have improved it. But there is no doubting its originality.

## IV. SPINOZA

Like so many other features of Spinoza's metaphysics, his determinism is a manifestation of his commitment to the principle of sufficient reason, to the view that every fact must be explicable. Perhaps the clearest expression of this commitment comes in one of his arguments for the existence of God: 'For each thing there must be assigned a cause or reason, as much for its existence as for its non-existence'.[94] Spinoza's determinism follows directly: since each fact must have a cause or reason and since, for Spinoza, the cause or reason of a thing is that which determines it,[95] it follows that each fact is determined to be the case. In particular, the fact that a certain thing exists and that it acts in a certain way is determined.

This does not mean, however, that for Spinoza the existence and action of a thing is due in each case to *external* causes. Spinoza holds that a substance, and only a substance, is capable of determining its own existence and actions. For reasons that we cannot go into here, Spinoza holds that there is only one substance. Spinoza identifies this substance with God.[96]

Besides the self-dependent being or substance, there are, for Spinoza, beings that are dependent on other beings. Each dependent being depends, in particular, on something that is not dependent on other beings, that is, on the one substance, God. Such dependent beings Spinoza calls modes of the substance.[97]

Spinoza divides the modes into infinite and finite. The infinite modes are certain pervasive features found throughout nature. Curley has argued persuasively that these features correspond in Spinoza's system to laws of nature that govern the causal interactions among finite modes.[98] The finite modes are simply things that are not found throughout nature, but whose existence is instead limited in some way. Examples of finite modes include tables, stones, and the minds and bodies of human beings. Spinoza makes clear that not only the existence of finite things but also their actions depend on God.[99]

In addition to depending on God, each finite mode depends on other finite modes and on certain infinite modes. For Spinoza, finite mode $x$ is determined to exist and to act by other finite modes, including, for example, $y$; $y$, in turn, is determined to exist and to act by still other finite modes, and so on ad infinitum.[100] Thus, for Spinoza, there is an infinite causal series of finite modes.[101] Further, finite mode $x$ is dependent on those infinite modes which correspond to the laws of nature governing the causal interaction by which finite mode $x$ comes about.[102] Ultimately, though, God's nature is responsible for the whole series of finite and infinite modes and in this way each finite mode is dependent on God.

Since God's nature is responsible for the whole series of modes and since God's nature could not have been otherwise, this series is the only series that could possibly exist.[103] In this sense, Spinoza holds the view that this is the only possible world. This view can be called Spinoza's necessitarianism.

The claim that Spinoza is a necessitarian is, in our opinion, correct, but, as a matter of interpretation, it is quite controversial.[104] For that reason, we do not rely on this claim. Our examination of Spinoza's notion of freedom takes into account only the completely uncontroversial claim that Spinoza holds that each thing is determined to exist either by itself or by something else and that, in particular, each mode is determined by something beyond itself. We will call this view Spinoza's determinism. We will concentrate on this claim here since, for Spinoza, the fact that a thing is externally determined is sufficient to undermine its freedom. In order to reach this denial of freedom, Spinoza does not appeal to the further claim that the thing exists in the only possible world. (By contrast, as we will see later in this chapter, Leibniz regards necessitarianism as the main threat to freedom. For him, external determination is compatible with freedom, but necessitarianism is not.)

That Spinoza regards external determination as incompatible with freedom is evident from his very definition of 'freedom': 'That thing is called free which exists from the necessity of its nature alone, and is determined to act by itself alone. But a thing is called necessary, or rather compelled, which is determined by another to exist and to produce an effect in a certain and determinate manner.'[105] We can see right away that, for Spinoza, no human being would count as free and that no volition or action of a human being would count as free. Such a volition or action would be a mode and, as such, it would be determined from without. Indeed, for Spinoza it would ultimately be determined by factors extending beyond the human being in question.[106] The action or volition would thus not be free and the human being would not be free with regard to the performance of that action or volition.[107] On Spinoza's definition of freedom, the only thing that can be free is something which is the cause of its own existence and actions. Such a thing is, of course, God, and so only God is free.[108] Although God is free, God cannot be said, according to Spinoza, to act from freedom of the will. This is because the will or, more accurately, particular acts of will are merely modes of God;[109] they are determined, in particular, by God's nature as a thinking thing. Since they are determined by something external, acts of will are not free, even in the case of God.[110]

Spinoza recognises that the belief that we do act freely is widespread and he offers a diagnosis of our failure to appreciate our lack of freedom. For Spinoza, since we are aware of our volitions and actions, but, in many cases at least, unaware of their causes, we reach the mistaken conclusion that we act from freedom of the will. In Letter 58, Spinoza derides 'that famous human freedom which everyone brags of having, and which consists only in this: that men are conscious of their appetite and ignorant of the causes by which they are determined'.[111]

For Spinoza, many passions or affects presuppose such a mistaken belief either in one's own freedom or in the freedom of another person. These include praise and blame, repentance and self-esteem, mockery, disdain, hatred and pity. Since anger is, for Spinoza, borne of hatred, it too must be seen as presupposing a mistaken belief in freedom.[112] For Spinoza, reason demands that these affects, with their false presuppositions, should be abandoned.[113] He also holds that, to the extent that we firmly believe the truth that all human actions are externally determined and hence not performed freely, we will be free of these affects.[114] We will return to this point briefly later.

The claim that blame and anger are to be given up does not, for Spinoza, entail that the practice of punishing those who harm others is likewise to be abandoned. For Spinoza, even though none of us is free, it is still reasonable to act in our own interest. In fact, Spinoza adheres to a version of egoism which claims that the *only* virtuous thing one can do is what will promote one's interests.[115] This provides Spinoza with a reason to endorse punishment of a person who harms others. It is in my interest and the interest of others that such an evil-doer be punished because punishment, Spinoza believes, can prevent that person from harming others in the future. The fact that the evil-doer's actions were externally determined and not free does not undermine the reasonableness of punishment exacted for the sake of the general welfare.[116]

Spinoza's account of human freedom seems rather austere. It is quite surprising, therefore, to find that Spinoza extols the virtues of the free man at the end of Part IV of the *Ethica* and devotes all of Part V to the topic of human freedom. To begin to reconcile such talk with the view just described, it is important to note that, in the *Ethica,* Spinoza's more upbeat claims about human freedom come only after he offers a detailed account of the nature and sources of human action. This fact provides the clue we will use to reconcile the two aspects of Spinoza's thinking on freedom. By tracing out Spinoza's views on the rôles certain psychological states play in action, we will attempt to illuminate the character and limitations of the kind of freedom Spinoza, consistently with the rest of his system, allows human beings to have. We will focus in turn on three such psychological states: desire, belief, and volition.

### 1. Desire

To understand Spinoza's account of desire and its relation to action, it is important to keep in mind his naturalistic program in psychology. Spinoza utterly rejects any view which sees human psychology as governed by no laws or by laws different from those in force throughout the rest of nature.[117] It follows from this naturalism that one can derive a complete account of the workings of human nature by appealing to the kinds of principles that govern the behaviour of objects in general.

For Spinoza, desire, a psychological state of human beings, is simply an instance of the more general phenomenon of striving (*conatus*). *All* things (including rocks, dogs, and human beings) strive to do certain things. This general notion of striving must be understood before one can see how Spinoza applies it to human psychology.

A particular thing, $x$, strives to do $F$, on Spinoza's view, if and only if $x$'s state is such that it will do $F$ unless prevented by causes external to $x$. That Spinoza accepts this account of striving is, perhaps, clearest from the transition from *Ethica* III, proposition 4, to *Ethica* III, proposition 6. In *Ethica* III, proposition 4, demonstration, Spinoza says, 'While we attend only to the thing itself, and not to external causes, we shall not be able to find anything in it which can destroy it'. Here he expresses the view that if external causes do not prevent a thing from continuing to exist, then there is nothing that will bring about the thing's destruction; in other words, if external causes do not destroy a thing, then it will continue to exist.[118] Now in *Ethica* III, proposition 6, partly on the basis of this claim, Spinoza concludes that each thing strives to persist in existence. This indicates that, for Spinoza, what a thing will do if not prevented by external causes is what it strives to do.[119]

But exactly what kinds of things will a thing do unless prevented? The passages cited in the previous paragraph show that, for Spinoza, each thing strives to preserve itself. Spinoza goes on to claim, on this basis, that each thing strives to do whatever will increase what he calls its power of acting (*potentia agendi*).[120]

This latter claim is crucial to understanding the connexion between desire and freedom.

Consider, first, the notion of an increase in power of acting. Spinoza defines acting in the following way:

> I say that we act when something happens, in us or outside us, of which we are the adequate cause, i.e. . . . when something in us or outside us follows from our nature, which can be clearly and distinctly understood through it alone. On the other hand, I say that we are acted on when something happens in us, or something follows from our nature, of which we are only a partial cause.[121]

Since by *Ethica* III, definition 1, an adequate cause is a complete cause, we can say that for Spinoza something is active to the extent to which it is a complete cause of some effect. Similarly, *Ethica* III, dfn. 2, reveals that something is passive to the extent to which it is only a partial cause of some effect.

Activity and passivity, so defined, are clearly matters of degree. Suppose that a stone, at $t_1$, is held in a moving sling. The stone's motion at $t_2$ is a function of its motion at $t_1$ together with the motion of the sling at $t_1$. Let us say that at $t_2$ the sling drops away and so no longer plays a rôle in determining the stone's motion. The motion of the stone at $t_3$ will then solely be a function of the stone's motion at $t_2$ (on the assumption that at $t_2$ no other object interferes with the stone's motion). In this case, we can say that initially (at $t_1$) the stone's motion is determined to a large extent by something apart from the stone (namely, the sling). However, since at $t_2$ the sling is no longer determining the stone's motion, the stone itself becomes more nearly the complete cause or explanation of the stone's motion. To this extent, the stone is more active at $t_2$ than at $t_1$.

Of course, there is a sense in which the stone at $t_2$ is not completely active. Although the stone's state at $t_2$ may suffice for its being in another state of motion at $t_3$, that state at $t_2$ is due in part to external causes that were operative before $t_2$. Thus, the explanation of the stone's motion at $t_3$ will, at some stage, have to appeal to outside causes. However, this undeniable passivity in the stone does not alter the fact that at $t_2$ the stone is less subject to outside forces and relatively more independent than it was previously.

Given this account of degrees of activity, we can define an increase in *power* of acting in the following way: 'An object comes to have a greater power of acting to the extent to which it comes to be able to be active to a greater degree with regard to a certain effect.' In other words, a thing's power of acting increases to the extent to which it becomes less dependent on external things in the production of some effect. A decrease in power of acting can be defined in a corresponding fashion.[122] Thus, when Spinoza says that each thing strives to do whatever will increase its power of acting, his point is that each thing strives to become less dependent on external causes in the above way.

Given Spinoza's naturalism, it follows that a human being, like any other thing, strives to preserve itself (*Ethica III*, proposition 9) and to do whatever will increase its power of acting (*Ethica* III, proposition 12, dem.). This is where desire enters: Spinoza regards desire as the striving of a human being.[123] This means that a human being desires to preserve itself and to do whatever will increase its power of acting.[124]

There are many ways in which a human being's power of acting can increase. Eating nourishing food can make us more independent in the performance of certain physical tasks (such as lifting heavy objects). In this way, such eating can lead to an increase in power of acting. Learning to drive is an action whereby one's power of acting increases: one would no longer be dependent on others – or at least not as dependent on others – say, for getting to work. In general, acquiring new knowledge is a way of increasing one's power of acting. In fact, given that Spinoza holds to a strict thesis of parallelism according to which each mental change is matched by a physical change and vice versa (*Ethica* II, proposition 7), an increase in the body's power of acting is matched by an increase in the mind's power of acting, and vice versa. For this reason, Spinoza often emphasises the importance of cultivating the mind and acquiring more knowledge as a way of increasing one's power of acting.[125]

With this understanding of Spinoza's notion of desire and of increase in power of acting, it is possible to see how Spinoza can coherently make positive claims about human freedom. As *Ethica* I, definition 7, indicates, for one to be free in the performance of one's actions, those actions must not be determined by factors outside oneself. Given Spinoza's determinism, no action of a human being can be completely independent of external causes. Nonetheless, for Spinoza, independence of external causes is a matter of degree: one becomes more independent as one increases one's power of acting. Since Spinoza defines freedom in terms of independence of external causes and since such independence is a matter of degree, it appears that freedom, too, is a matter of degree. Thus, even if human beings cannot be perfectly free with regard to the production of a certain effect, we can, by increasing our power of acting, achieve a greater *degree* of freedom with regard to that effect.[126] (This point applies also to objects in general which are sometimes capable of increasing their power of acting. In this respect, Spinoza is similar to Hobbes who also allows the notion of freedom to apply to objects in general.)

Thus, we have shown that Spinoza can consistently attribute greater or lesser degrees of freedom to human beings, even if he holds that they cannot be absolutely free. In light of this discussion, we can see the sense in which Spinoza is a compatibilist. Although he holds that absolute freedom is incompatible with external determination, he is committed to the view that we can, compatibly with such determination, achieve greater degrees of freedom. This is what Spinoza is committed to, but is it actually what he says in his positive pronouncements on human freedom? The answer is yes.

At the end of Part IV of the *Ethica,* Spinoza introduces the notion of a free man (*homo liber*), one who 'is led by reason' or 'one who lives according to the dictate of reason alone'.[127] As Spinoza makes clear, acting from the guidance of reason alone is doing only those things that are good for oneself.[128] Now for Spinoza that which is good for oneself is that which increases one's power of acting.[129] Thus, Spinoza's free man does only things that increase his power of acting.

Strictly speaking, there can be no such person in Spinoza's system. Each person is inevitably affected by nature in ways that give rise to passions.[130] These passions, Spinoza says, often lead one to do things that harm one or decrease one's power of acting. Spinoza himself seems to recognise that no human being is free to the extent of doing only what leads to an increase in power of acting since, at various points, he qualifies his claims about the free man in an important way. Instead of saying that a free man does only what increases his power of acting, Spinoza says in *Ethica* IV, proposition 73, scholium, that the free man 'strives *as far as he can,* to act well and rejoice'. This passage is a paraphrase of a revealing passage from *Ethica* IV, proposition 50, scholium. There, in speaking of the person he will later call the free man, Spinoza says that this individual 'will strive, *as far as human virtue allows,* to act well . . . and rejoice'. Further, in *Ethica* IV, proposition 73, demonstration, Spinoza characterises the free man as desiring to live more freely. These passages indicate that a free individual achieves independence from external causes as much as possible, but does not achieve perfect independence or, therefore, perfect freedom. For this reason, the freedom of Spinoza's free man must be seen as a matter of degree. In speaking about the free man, Spinoza is not claiming that we can ever be completely free, but is pointing to the fact that we can come to have a greater degree of freedom.[131] This claim does not conflict with Spinoza's uncompromising denials of human freedom which stem from *Ethica* I, definition 7, the definition of freedom. On the contrary, as we have seen, Spinoza's notion of degrees of freedom derives directly from that definition itself. The tension in Spinoza's thought about freedom is merely apparent.

## 2. Belief

By exploring the rôle of desire in human action, we were led to the way in which Spinoza allows that we can have greater or lesser degrees of freedom. By exploring the rôle of *belief* in human action, we can come to see some specific ways in which our ability to increase our freedom is limited. To elicit the rôle of belief, it is necessary to uncover an important modification of the Spinozistic account of desire that we have already presented. On that account,[132] if doing *F* will increase a person *x*'s power of acting, then *x* desires to do *F*. However, it is all too apparent that many of the actions that would in fact aid us are ones we do not desire to perform. This is often because we are unaware of what actions would be beneficial. Spinoza is aware of this difficulty in his account and for this reason he rightly adds a qualification later in the *Ethica*. He says that *if one believes or imagines or judges* that doing *F* will increase one's power of acting, then one desires to do *F*.[133]

Since desire is thus bound up with belief, we can see an important way in which we are prevented from increasing our power of acting and thus our freedom. If we have false beliefs about what will increase our power of acting, then we can fail to avail ourselves of an opportunity to increase our power of acting. In fact, we may, unwittingly, decrease our power of acting. False beliefs can have this result in many ways, but the kinds of cases Spinoza tends to focus on are ones in which our passions blind us to our own interests. Among such cases, Spinoza pays particular attention to ones in which such harmful passions are brought on by a failure to appreciate that human actions are externally determined and hence not performed freely. For example, consider how, for Spinoza, my anger at a person *x* may be generated. Spinoza holds that if I believe that *x* has harmed me or decreased my power of acting and if I do not believe that *x*'s action was externally determined, then I will hate *x*. Hatred, in turn, generates a desire to harm the hated object.[134] Given Spinoza's account of desire as involving belief, we can say that for Spinoza if I hate *x*, I desire to harm *x* at least in part because I believe that harming *x* will benefit me or increase my power of acting.

Spinoza holds that my belief that harming *x* will be beneficial to me is, in fact, false. On his view, each of us has an interest in fostering the welfare of others.[135] Spinoza's arguments for this claim cannot be explored here,[136] but the conclusion he draws from it is important to note. Since, for Spinoza, when we act out of hatred we strive to harm another, we are thereby striving to do what will in fact harm ourselves. This is why Spinoza claims that hate can never be good and that the anger arising from hate is also evil.[137]

Thus, for Spinoza – by virtue of the fact that I fail to realise that *x*'s action, like any other human action, is not freely performed – I come under the influence of hatred and the concomitant false belief that harming $x$ is beneficial to me. In such a case, according to Spinoza, the false belief leads me to act contrary to my own interests, that is, to decrease my power of acting and thus my freedom. Paradoxically then, for Spinoza, by failing to grasp the truth that human beings are not absolutely free or independent of external causes, we lose an opportunity to increase the degree of freedom we do enjoy. To a large extent, our ability to attain the measure of freedom that Spinoza allows that we can have depends on a recognition of the limits of that freedom. For that reason, in outlining techniques for overcoming the harmful effects of the passions, Spinoza emphasises the utility of strengthening one's belief in determinism.[138]

### 3. Volition

In focusing on desire and belief, it may seem that we have omitted the kind of psychological state that is most relevant to action and freedom, namely, willing or volition. As Locke describes volition, it is 'an act of the Mind directing its thought to the production of any Action, and thereby exerting its power to produce it'.[139] On Locke's view, such a volition or willing is not only distinct from any particular belief or desire but is also a necessary condition for an action. If Spinoza does recognise such distinct episodes of willing, then, by focusing on desire and belief, we would indeed have omitted a crucial aspect of his account of action.

Before seeing whether this is so, it is important to separate the question: 'Does Spinoza recognise volitions that are distinct from beliefs and desires?' from the question: 'Does Spinoza recognise a faculty of willing that is distinct from particular willings or volitions?' Such a faculty would be the agency by which an individual wills, but would not itself be a particular willing. Now one can deny that there is any such faculty while claiming that particular volitions are distinct from particular desires, beliefs, and mental states of other kinds. Spinoza does believe that there is no separate faculty of willing (or a separate faculty of intellection).[140] But this leaves open the issue of whether he holds that volitions are distinct from desires and other mental states.

In fact, Spinoza holds that they are not distinct. For Spinoza, volitions are nothing but desires or, rather, those desires in particular that one acts on. Thus, in focusing on desire and belief, we have not neglected a distinct kind of mental state that plays a crucial rôle in action. There is no such distinct state for Spinoza.

To see why this is so, recall that Spinoza defines desire as the striving of a human being and that, for Spinoza, a human being strives to do $F$ if and only if that human being will do $F$ unless prevented by external causes. Given this account, we can see that, for Spinoza, desires (together with the beliefs they presuppose) lead directly to action. If I desire to do *F,* I will do *F,* as long as the world beyond me cooperates. To generate action, there is no need, in Spinoza's account, for a psychological state in addition to the relevant desire and belief.

Note that the line of thought in the preceding paragraph must be modified in an important respect. What we have just said suggests that, for Spinoza, each desire leads to action unless external causes interfere. Spinoza's account of conflicts of desire shows that this is not quite right. I may desire to do *G,* and I may, in addition, desire to do *H.* However, suppose that I know that I cannot do both *G* and *H,* and suppose that, in the end, I decide to act and do act on my desire to do *G.* Spinoza holds that what prevents me from acting on the desire to do *H* is simply the fact that the desire to do *G* has a greater ability to lead to action. As Spinoza puts it, the desire to do *G* restrains the desire to do *H*.[141]

On this account, what prevents me from acting on the desire to do *H* are not so much external causes as a certain *internal* cause, namely, my stronger desire to do *G.* If this is so, then, Spinoza's understanding of conflicts of desires shows that he needs to broaden his account of desire to allow cases in which the fact that one fails to act on a desire is not due to external causes but instead due to internal factors such as competing and stronger desires. How this modification might be carried out is beyond the scope of this discussion.

The important thing to notice here, however, is that even in a case of conflicting desires, the fact that one acts on a certain desire is *not,* for Spinoza, due to a separate volition that favours that desire instead of its competitors. Rather, as just explained, one acts on a certain desire simply because it restrains the competing desire. Thus, even in a case of conflicting desires, Spinoza sees no need for an act of will over and above the particular desires involved.[142]

To the extent that, for Spinoza, a volition is involved in such a case, one must see the volition as simply the more powerful desire that one acts on.[143] This is suggested by *Ethica* III, definitions of the affects 1, in which Spinoza regards volition as a form of desire. In this respect, Spinoza's position seems close to that of Hobbes, who did not regard willing as a distinct kind of mental state, but rather as 'the last appetite in deliberating'.[144]

Spinoza's general position, then, is that my desire to do *F* is one that I act on unless other desires prevent me from doing so. This position is similar to Spinoza's view on the relation between ideas and beliefs. To see this, recall Descartes's view that the fact that the mind entertains the idea that *p* is not, by itself, sufficient for the mind's believing that *p.* For there to be a belief, Descartes holds, there must be an act of will separate from the idea the mind has, an act of will by virtue of which the mind gives its assent to the idea. Thus, for Descartes, belief is a product of the will's being directed positively upon a certain idea and the fact that an idea is not believed is due to the fact that there was no such positive act of will directed at that idea.

Spinoza agrees with Descartes that not all ideas that come before the mind are believed. But he vehemently denies that, in the matter of belief, there is any rôle for acts of will separate from the ideas that are or are not believed. For Spinoza, unlike Descartes, the fact that a given idea is not believed is *not* due to the fact that there was no positive act of will directed at that idea. Instead, the fact that a given idea is not believed is due to the fact that the mind has other ideas which lead one to doubt or deny the idea in question. For Spinoza, if there were no such other ideas which prevent the mind from assenting to the idea in question, then the mind would indeed assent to that idea. Spinoza illustrates this point with his famous example of the idea of a winged horse:

If the mind perceived nothing else except the winged horse, it would regard it as present to itself, and would not have any cause of doubting its existence, or any faculty of dissenting, unless either the imagination of the winged horse were joined to an idea which excluded the existence of the same horse, or the mind perceived that its idea of a winged horse was inadequate. And then either it will necessarily deny the horse's existence, or it will necessarily doubt it.[145]

Thus, for Spinoza, in much the same way that a desire is acted on unless other desires prevent it from being acted on, an idea is believed unless other ideas prevent it from being believed. In both cases, Spinoza does not recognise a separate act of will. His accounts of the mechanism of assent and the mechanism by which we act on a certain desire are elegant and simple in precisely parallel ways.


## V. MALEBRANCHE

Malebranche held a number of bold metaphysical theses, none bolder than the claim that God's will is the only true cause. Obviously this thesis generated a serious – some have said insurmountable – problem for Malebranche concerning creaturely freedom. It is an article of Malebranche's faith, from which he never wavered, that human beings exercise free choices, in virtue of which they are morally responsible for some of their actions. How did Malebranche attempt to reconcile this article of his faith with the metaphysical thesis that God is the only true cause? That is the big question when the topic is Malebranche on freedom.

First, however, it is important to position Malebranche in the ongoing seventeenth-century debate concerning divine determination, natural necessitation, divine foreknowledge, and the bearing of these on creaturely freedom. In order to meaningfully relate Malebranche's views to those of his contemporaries, it is necessary to bracket off Malebranche's leading theses on causality, namely, that God's will is the only true cause, and, hence, that creatures at best are, on occasion, occasional causes. Is that possible without so distorting Malebranche's views as to make the result worthless? We think so. Malebranche was a man of science. When doing physics, when discussing details of the mind–body union, when discussing the phenomena of ordinary life, and when discussing the operation of divine grace, he made causal claims much like those of any well-informed, theologically involved, seventeenth-century scientist. Of course, Malebranche would have parsed these discussions, in strict metaphysical terms, in terms of the operation of occasional causes, rather than in terms of the operation of real causes, unlike most of his seventeenth-century colleagues.

The first point to make is this: Like almost all his Christian colleagues (and perhaps all his Catholic colleagues) Malebranche was not a natural compatibilist. That is, he denied that a choice can occur in virtue of a natural necessity and still be free. In *Réflexions sur le système de la nature et de la grâce,* book I, chapter 14, Arnauld argued that according to Malebranche some free choices are 'a necessary consequence of natural laws'. But, Arnauld continued, the Council of Trent had anathematised compatibilism, so construed. And, in chapter 16, Arnauld identified natural compatibilism as a component in the heresy of Wycliff.[146] Malebranche responded in the second letter of *Lettres du Père Malebranche à un de ses amis.* He accepted Arnauld's claim that Wycliff's position was in error; he did not reject Arnauld's characterisation of that error; but he argued that he did not maintain that some free choices are the necessary consequences of natural laws.[147] This indicates that Malebranche was neither a natural determinist nor a natural compatibilist. Malebranche's denial of natural determinism is reflected in his claim that God's knowledge of determinations of free causes has a different source from God's knowledge of the consequences of natural laws. In a summary of his views on divine providence, Malebranche wrote: 'By his infinite wisdom He [God] knows all the consequences of all possible general laws' and 'By his quality as scrutator of hearts, He foresees all the future determinations of free causes.'[148] In fact, Malebranche was neither a theological determinist nor a theological compatibilist. Denying theological compatibilism has its costs for a Christian philosopher; it requires what some might regard as an excessively attenuated notion of divine providence. We may be reasonably confident that whatever led Malebranche to deny theological compatibilism also led him to deny natural compatibilism. Hence, we focus first on Malebranche's denial of theological determinism and theological compatibilism. For this purpose it will prove useful to outline Malebranche's account of the way in which internal sanctifying grace operates with respect to human choices. We start with a brief description of Malebranche's account of human choice.

Malebranche worked within the familiar framework previously noted, according to which our volition for the highest good, for that which would produce complete happiness, were we to posses it, occurs as a result of a natural necessity and, hence, although voluntary, is not the locus of our freedom. Malebranche's remarks on our natural inclinations introduce a familiar distinction here. In the early pages of the *Recherche* Malebranche wrote:

> Although our natural inclinations are voluntary, nevertheless they are not free with a freedom of indifference . . . , which includes the power of willing, or of not willing, or even of willing the contrary of that towards which our natural inclinations carry us. For although it is voluntarily or freely, i.e., without constraint, that we love the good in general, since we can love only through the will and it is a contradiction that the will can ever be constrained; however, we can not love it freely, in the sense that I have just explained, since it is not in the power of our will to not wish to be happy.[149]

The familiar distinction contained in those remarks can be stated in terms of two notions of freedom – freedom from constraint and freedom of indifference. Clearly, for Malebranche, the heart of the matter is the second notion. Hence, subsequently, when we discuss Malebranche on freedom, it is his notion of freedom of indifference that is the subject. And the locus of freedom of indifference in Malebranche's account is a power that the human mind has with respect to some of its inclinations, the power to consent, or to refuse to consent, to those inclinations. This power to consent or to refuse consent with respect to inclinations is restricted, according to Malebranche, to those inclinations that are not invincible. The connection between non-invincibility and the power whose exercise constitutes freedom of indifference seems to be definitional. Thus, in the *Traité de la nature et de la grâce,* Malebranche wrote: 'This power to love or not to love particular goods . . . this non-invincibility, this is what I call freedom.'[150] The notion of natural necessity and invincibility are closely connected in Malebranche's thinking. It seems that he took the former to imply the latter. And he distinguished both from infallibility, a distinction that looms large in Malebranche's account of divine foreknowledge.[151]

The natural inclination towards the good in general (and also towards self-preservation and the preservation of others) is invincible, persisting while we persist; although voluntary (since a movement of the will), it is not free, since it occurs as a natural necessity.[152] Moreover, our persisting natural inclination towards the good in general brings it about that whenever we perceive a particular object as good, that is, desirable, considered in itself, we experience pleasure at the thought of possessing that good and we have an inclination towards that object, a love of that object.[153] But this love of a particular good is not invincible; we may refuse to consent and thereby dispense with, or diminish, or, at a minimum, not act on, our love for this particular good.

Consider, now, Malebranche's account of the causal structure whereby consentings (or the lack thereof) occur, bearing in mind that the vulgar notion of causality is still the focus of attention here, not the metaphysically purified account that is, in the end, central to Malebranche's metaphysics. First, recollect that, according to Malebranche, what we consent to, when we consent, is the love of (or inclination towards) some particular object that we perceive to be desirable. Furthermore we perceive it to be desirable partly in virtue of the pleasure we experience at the thought of possessing that particular object. The pleasure that engenders love towards a particular object is what Malebranche termed a motive – indeed, physical motive [*motif physique*] with respect to both the love of that object (the inclination towards that object) and the consent with respect to that love (or inclination). The heart of Malebranche's account of freedom is the claim that the very same motive may be efficacious with respect to our love of a particular good, but inefficacious with respect to our consent to that love. In the first Elucidation to the *Recherche* Malebranche wrote: 'Every pleasure or physical motive, although efficacious by itself with respect to the will that it moves, is not efficacious by itself with respect to the consent of the will.'[154]

We are now in a position to formulate some of the basic theses concerning freedom of indifference to which Malebranche appears committed. First, he rejected what he called 'pure indifference', that is, the power to have an inclination towards an object without any motive. And, since what we consent to is an inclination towards an object, we cannot consent without motives for that consent, since, without the motive, there will be no inclination to which to consent. Hence, Malebranche concluded, 'pure indifference' is 'a manifest contradiction'. In the same text Malebranche noted a theological rationale for denying pure indifference: unacceptably, in Malebranche's view, pure indifference would make us independent of those motives that God produces in us 'whereby He knows and can make us will and freely execute all that He wants'.[155]

What about Malebranche's attitude towards what we have called freedom of specification (freedom of contrariety)? The textual evidence seems to indicate that Malebranche denied freedom of specification. In *Méditations chrétiennes et métaphysiques* Malebranche wrote:

When two good objects are presented to your mind at the same time and one appears better than the other, if you choose or determine yourself in that moment, then necessarily you will love the one that appears best to you, supposing that you do not have other alternatives and that you will absolutely to choose. But you can always suspend your consent.[156]

In this passage Malebranche seems to have denied freedom of specification, while affirming freedom of exercise (freedom of contradiction). This passage, and others like it, may suggest that Malebranche's considered view is that in every case every agent has the power not to consent to an inclination it has towards a particular, limited good. But Malebranche recognised that in some cases some agents are so overwhelmed by motives towards some inclination that they do not then have the power not to consent to it.[157] In such a case, according to Malebranche, if the agent then acts on the inclination, the agent acts voluntarily, but not with freedom of indifference, not even freedom of exercise.

Consider, next, a kind of case in which, according to Malebranche, a created agent always has freedom of indifference in the form of freedom of exercise, that is, the case of the operation of internal sanctifying grace. The first of Malebranche's *Quatre lettres du P. Malebranche . . . touchant celles de M. Arnauld* is particularly helpful.[158] Therein Malebranche began by asserting that grace, of the variety that concerns us, comes in two forms: *grâce de lumière* (elsewhere called grace of the Creator) and *grâce de sentiment* (elsewhere called grace of the Redeemer).[159] The latter, *grâce de sentiment,* is the variety of grace that moves the will, and, hence, is the more relevant to freedom.[160] It can also be referred to simply as grace. According to Malebranche, the rôle of grace is to produce in those on whom it is bestowed a love in virtue of which its possessor is disposed 'to prefer true goods to false goods'.[161] Grace, so conceived, functions in competition with other motives in order to bring about a love of true good and consent to that love.

We may come to grips with some of the important features of Malebranche's account of the relation of grace to freedom by considering his explanation of his answer to a fundamental question: are sufficient grace and efficacious grace intrinsically the same? Malebranche wrote: 'It is clear that the actual grace that is called efficacious is not of a different nature from grace that is called sufficient.'[162]

Malebranche held that actual grace, like any other pleasure or physical motive is efficacious by itself with respect to some motion of the will, that is, an inclination or love of something. But, like other motives, actual grace is not invincible, that is, is not efficacious by itself with respect to consent to the inclination efficaciously induced in the will. Whether, on a given occasion, specific actual grace will turn out to be efficacious with respect to a given agent's consent or merely sufficient (and, hence, not efficacious) depends upon free choices of the agent in question in the circumstances then current, according to Malebranche.[163]

Given the constraints orthodoxy imposed on a seventeenth-century Catholic philosopher, the virtues of this scheme are considerable. Note that it permits Malebranche to accept strong Augustinian language concerning the efficacious nature of actual grace. After identifying actual grace, as conceived by Augustine, Malebranche wrote: 'It is efficacious by itself . . . , since it moves the will from the interior and by itself.'[164] Arnauld himself could not ask for stronger language. But, of course, in Malebranche's scheme this remark has substantially less force than Arnauld wanted. Indeed, Malebranche immediately added that, in the respect noted, actual grace is like any other pleasure that creatures experience: 'For every pleasure, precisely in virtue of being pleasure, moves the will towards the object that pleases it.' And then he added: 'But it [actual grace] in no way determines the free movement, that is, consent, of the will.'[165]

This last remark suitably positioned Malebranche's account with respect to the crucial canon four of the sixth session of the Council of Trent, which says, in part: 'If someone were to say that man's free choice, moved and aroused by God . . . can not refuse its consent, if it chooses, . . . let him be anathema.' And, as Malebranche pointed out on occasion, his theory provided the framework for a straightforward account of the compatibility of freedom with the operation of actual grace in sharp contrast with what he viewed as competing Catholic theories, for example, Jansenism and Thomism.[166] Indeed, in terms of the distinctions drawn in our introduction, Malebranche's theory is a version of Molinism, just as Arnauld insisted.[167]

Thus, Malebranche held that God's total causal contribution to creation up to and including the instant at which a free creaturely choice occurs – a consent or non-consent to a volition – is metaphysically and physically consistent with the non-occurrence of that choice. And, as one would expect, he therefore held that God's foreknowledge of creaturely free choices can not consist in God's knowledge of the logical consequences of what He has absolutely decreed. Unlike Molina and Suárez, Malebranche offered no account of the basis of the requisite middle knowledge. In the *Traité de la nature et de la grâce,* he wrote:

God . . . infallibly discerns even the effects that depend upon . . . a free consent of our wills . . . I cannot conceive how God can discern the consequences of actions that do not draw their infallibility from his absolute decrees. I know well that one can make objections against the foreknowledge of future contingents that I admit in God, to which I can not offer clear and evident solutions.[168]

In the fifth letter of *Lettres de Monsieur Arnauld au Révérend Père Malebranche,* Arnauld noted that Malebranche's theory is a version of Molinism.[169] In response, Malebranche made the claim that something like middle knowledge is required in order to provide an account of God's foreknowledge and predestination consistent with creaturely freedom. He immediately went on to disassociate himself from what he termed the semi-Pelagian idea that God utilised His discernment of creaturely merit through His middle knowledge in order to predestine to salvation those who merit it. Malebranche concluded as follows:

Still, I have no doubt whatever that God utilizes His knowledge of the free determinations of our volitions for the establishment of His decrees and the execution of His designs. . . . If that is the view of Molina – something I do not know, since I have not read this author that I am so strongly accused of stealing from – I accept it.[170]

Malebranche's way with divine providence, and, specifically, divine predestination, is what we would expect given his Molinism. On Malebranche's theory, God's causal contribution to creation may include everything relevant to a creaturely choice other than the choice itself (the choice to consent or not to consent to some volition). According to Malebranche, in virtue of what God does contribute relevant to a creaturely choice, that choice thereby occurs infallibly but not necessarily (*Oeuvres complètes* XVI 21–4). Hence, Malebranche concluded, in a typically Molinist way, 'God will always be the master [of the soul] and the first mover.'[171]

To this point our discussion has bracketed off Malebranche's metaphysical thesis about the distribution of efficacious causes among substances. Off with the brackets. In *Réflexions sur la prémotion physique,* Malebranche put his main metaphysical thesis concerning causality thus: 'God alone is the efficacious cause of each real change that happens in the world.'[172] He went on in the same passage to add that nonetheless 'the soul is the unique cause of its own acts, that is, of its free determinations, that is, its consents.'[173] It is perfectly clear that Malebranche held that God is not the true cause of our free choices – our consents or refusals – and that, indeed, we are. After all, some of our consents are sinful and it is crucial to Malebranche's philosophical theology that God is in no way the author of sin –

the efficacious cause of what is sinful. Three pages later, Malebranche committed himself to what is required in order to make these remarks consistent; that is, that creaturely free choice – consent or non-consent to a volition – is not a real change in the soul that is the true cause of that choice, and that the soul, while the true cause of this non-real change, requires for this purpose no efficacity, no power, of the sort Malebranche believed he had established as the sole prerogative of God.

It should be noted that this scheme is as complicated as it appears. It involves three distinct types of causes: an efficacious cause, which is God alone; occasional causes, which do no more than supply occasions on which God exercises efficacious causality; and true causes of non-real changes, which, unlike occasional causes, are not mere occasions for the exercise of divine causality, but which, like occasional causes, possess no efficacious power to exercise. Malebranche made distinct efforts during his philosophical career to make sense of a non-occasional cause that lacks efficacity. The first attempt occurs early in the *Recherche,* where Malebranche claimed that we can, in a sense, be said to be active 'because our soul can determine in various ways the inclination or impression that God gives it. For although it can not arrest this impression, it can in a sense turn it in the direction that pleases it and thus cause . . . all the miseries that are the certain and necessary consequences of sin.'[174] But this account simply will not fit with the rôle Malebranche assigned to God with respect to the causation of our inclinations towards particular goods, according to which God is causally responsible not only for the 'motion' of the inclination, but its particular target as well.[175] And Malebranche seems to have recognised the problem, because in the First Elucidation to the *Recherche* we are offered a different solution – one which presupposes that God is causally responsible for both motion and target in the case of particular volitions.[176]

The account offered in the First Elucidation might be called the 'consent as rest defense'. It is presented in the Elucidation and defended against Arnauld's objections – see especially *Réponse à une dissertation de M. Arnauld.*[177] The basic idea is this. In virtue of causing perception and volition, God causes in us an inclination towards a particular object perceived as good; it is in our power to consent, or refuse consent to that inclination. In the former case we simply give in to that inclination and cease efforts to avoid following it where it leads us – we 'rest' in its object. In the latter case, we pursue other inclinations, thereby refusing to rest in the object of the original inclination. In either case, according to Malebranche, we bring about no new inclination, no new motives, no new perceptions – nothing that requires an exercise of efficacious causality.

Obviously this theory has its problems. There is a difference between consenting to an inclination as opposed to refusing to consent to it. By Malebranche's lights, the ultimate disposition of one's soul may turn on that difference. Yet, according to Malebranche, when the soul passes from a state of indecision to a state of consent (or a state of refusal) no real change has occurred, although, of course, a change has occurred. The crucial problem for Malebranche is the need to establish that the state of consent (or refusal) is of an ontological type, members of which do not require the exercise of efficacious causality in order to come into existence. There are efforts in this direction in Malebranche's writings, but no coherent programme. It is important to realise that some of the considerations Malebranche brought forward in favour of his position in the *Réflexions* are off the mark. For example, Malebranche devoted considerable effort to sustaining the thesis that the state of consent (or refusal) is itself lacking in causal efficacity.[178] But this is irrelevant to the question of whether the human production of states of consent involves efficacious causality on the part of the producer. Were we to infer that no efficacious causality is required in order to produce what is itself lacking in causal efficacity, it would follow on Malebranche's own principles that God lacks causal efficacity.

## VI. LOCKE

Locke's account of human freedom and of the factors that determine our behaviour is more detailed and subtle than those of the philosophers we have considered so far. This account attracted considerable attention at the time of its first publication in the *Essay concerning Human Understanding* (1690); and it was a major force in shaping thinking on the subject, especially in Britain, for a good century afterwards. Locke's treatment of freedom has not, however, received much attention from twentieth-century scholars, despite a lively interest in other areas of his work. The reasons for this neglect are not hard to fathom. Locke originally presented his views on freedom and motivation in *Essay* II.xxi, a chapter that was long, dense, and poorly organised. He then revised this chapter extensively for the *Essay*'s second edition in 1694, and made significant further changes in it for the fourth and fifth editions, published in 1700 and 1706, respectively. In some cases, these changes reflected substantial changes of opinion on Locke's part. But instead of recasting his whole discussion, or even replacing selected portions of it with freshly written material, he kept almost everything he had already published and simply inserted new passages at various points in the existing text. The result is a patchwork, replete with apparent inconsistencies, the ordering principles of which are hidden at best. Only with the 1975 publication of the Clarendon edition of the *Essay*, edited by Peter Nidditch, has it been possible for readers to tell, from a single source, what parts of Locke's discussion were written when, and thus to distinguish the different stages of his thinking, whence the various lines of argument he pursues can be identified and sorted out.[179]

In common with the other leading philosophers of the seventeenth century, Locke was a compatibilist: he not only believed both in freedom and in determinism but explicitly denied that these two preclude each other. In the *Essay*, however, he presents his views on freedom and what he calls 'the determination of the will' more or less independently of one another. He introduces the idea of freedom (or liberty) early in II.xxi, the official subject of which is power. Power in general, Locke says, is an attribute of an individual substance, by which it is able to do or suffer something. The power is active when it enables the substance possessing it to perform an action of some kind; it is passive when it makes the substance liable to be affected in some way. Will is an active power belonging to rational agents; volition or willing is the exercise of this power, that is, the action that having a will enables an agent to perform. Volitions are actions in their own right, but every volition is ordered or directed to some further action of the same agent – what might be called the target of the volition. A volition, more specifically, is either a volition to do or a volition not to do something – to forbear doing it.

When an agent wills to do something, and does it, and does it because she has willed it, she is said to have acted in accord with her will, and her action (that is, the target action) is voluntary. When an agent does not do something she wills to do, or does something else instead of that, then her forbearance or alternative action is involuntary, and she is said to have forborne or acted against her will. Also involuntary are actions performed merely without being willed, though these are not done against the will of the agent. Only the actions of rational agents are voluntary, since only such agents are capable of willing. But involuntary actions are performed by non-rational as well as by rational agents. Indeed, all of the actions of beings without reason or thought are involuntary.

Locke first defines freedom as the property of a rational agent whereby he has the power to act or not to act 'according to the preference or direction of his own mind', that is, in accord with his will.[180] It might appear from this that Locke, like Hobbes, identifies free with voluntary agency – that being free for him just consists in doing or being able to do what one wills. And so a number of commentators have taken him to do. But in fact his position is that voluntariness is merely a necessary condition of freedom. This is the point of his famous example of the man locked in a room with someone he longs to be with. The man 'stays willingly' in the room, that is, his doing so is voluntary. But his staying is not free because, being locked in, 'he is not at liberty not to stay, he has not freedom to be gone'. Hence 'where-ever any performance or forbearance are not equally in a Man's power; where-ever doing or not doing, will not equally follow upon the preference of his mind directing it, there he is not Free, though perhaps the Action may be voluntary'. And again, 'Where-ever . . . compulsion takes away that Indifferency of Ability on either side to act, or to forbear acting, there liberty . . . presently ceases'.[181] Locke's freedom, therefore, includes this liberty of indifference as well as what Descartes and others have called the liberty of spontaneity: freedom means having a choice in addition to choosing. To be free an agent must not only do something because she has willed it, and thus be able to do what she wills; she must also be able, by willing, to do something other than that – her action must be avoidable, she must have an alternative to it.

Things that lack freedom, for Locke, are necessary; the word 'necessary', at least in the chapter on power, just means 'not free'. Necessity, like freedom, is properly a property of agents; but Locke sometimes calls actions with respect to which an agent is 'under necessity' 'necessary actions'. (Although he never makes the parallel move from 'free agent' to 'free action', there is no reason for him – or for us – not to use the latter expression in stating his position.) An action may be necessary because it is done by an inanimate or otherwise non-rational agent; or because its (rational) agent either is compelled by some irresistible internal or external force to do it against his will, or else merely fails to exercise his will with respect to it. Thus, all involuntary actions are necessary for Locke. But likewise necessary are those voluntary actions which an agent cannot avoid doing because of internal or external constraints which prevent him from performing any alternative action, including that of merely forbearing the action he does.

It is important to note that no action is necessary for Locke simply by being the effect of antecedent causes. Locke's use of 'necessary' thus differs from that of Hobbes and other 'classical' compatibilists – Calvin and Hume, for example.[182] For the latter, 'necessary' (when applied to actions) means 'causally determined', and in this sense, they maintain, an action can be necessary *and* free: that is what makes them compatibilists. For Locke, on the contrary, since 'necessary' means 'not free', the same action cannot be both free and necessary. Is Locke then an incompatibilist with respect to freedom and necessity? Is the freedom he advocates the 'freedom from necessity' extolled by Bramhall and his fellow-Arminians? No, for Locke's disagreement with Hobbes and company is only verbal. He believes, as they do and the Arminians do not, that all human actions are causally determined, and hence that all free actions are. So Locke must himself be a compatibilist, and indeed, as we shall see, he so declares himself to be, on several occasions.

Locke claims that it follows from his view of freedom that the 'long agitated' question, '*Whether Man's Will be free, or no*', is 'unintelligible'. It makes no more sense to say that the will is, or is not, free than to say that one's sleep is swift or his virtue square. This is so because '*Liberty,* which is but a power, belongs only to Agents, and cannot be an attribute or modification of the *Will,* which is also but a Power'.[183] This point, that there is a kind of 'category-mistake' involved in attributing freedom to the will instead of to the man or person which is the true subject of human action, was not original with Locke: the same point was made earlier by Hobbes and by the Cambridge Platonist Cudworth.[184] But it is Locke's version of it that has become famous; and it is he who usually is credited with it in standard histories of philosophy.

Having disposed of the will as a subject of freedom, Locke concedes that those who ask 'whether the will be free' may have a different question in mind. What they may mean to ask is not whether the will itself has the property of freedom, but whether an agent possessing a will is free to exercise it: '*Whether a man be free to will*'.[185] For though Locke distinguishes voluntary actions, actions that take place 'consecutive to willing', from the volitions which prompt or give rise to them – the former are overt and physical, the latter covert and purely mental – he nonetheless takes the latter themselves to be actions: they are actions of willing (or acts thereof: Locke draws no principled distinction between actions and acts). And he acknowledges that certain philosophers – he has the Arminians in mind – not only do admit free volitions, but contend that no genuine freedom is possible unless volitions are free. For such philosophers, Locke observes, 'a Man is not free at all, if he be not as free to will, as he is to act, what he wills'.[186] Whether there is any such freedom or not Locke regards as a perfectly intelligible question, and he forthwith proceeds to consider it.

In fact, Locke construes the question here in two ways: what he actually considers are two distinct questions. One is whether a man is free 'in respect of willing any Action in his power once proposed to his Thoughts'. The other is whether 'a Man be at liberty to will either Motion, or Rest; Speaking, or Silence; which he pleases'. It is clear that this distinction of questions is based on the scholastic distinction between the will's freedom of exercise and its freedom of specification, or between the liberty of contradiction and the liberty of contrariety, although Locke does not mention this distinction, by either name. Nor does he dwell upon the difference between the two questions. Since his answer to both turns out to be negative, it suffices for him to conclude simply that a man is not free with respect to his willing, or that no volition is free. But Locke reaches this negative conclusion by different arguments in the two cases, and it is instructive to examine these arguments separately.

Locke takes up the first question, whether agents have the freedom of exercise with respect to their willing, in Section 23 of the chapter. His conclusion is that once a man considers an action, or starts deliberating about it, he 'cannot be free' in respect of willing it. He argues for this conclusion by claiming (1) that such a man is logically bound either to do or not to do the action in question; (2) that he cannot do it without willing to do it; (3) that he cannot not do it without willing not to do it; and hence (4) that it is 'unavoidably necessary' that he will either to do it or not to do it, and so unavoidable that he perform some action of willing, as opposed to not willing at all: there is no logical room for him not to will something.

This is obviously a bad argument – unusual for Locke. The obvious flaw in it was spotted by Leibniz. Leibniz agrees, speaking through Theophile in the *Nouveaux essais,* that 'it is necessary that the action about which one is deliberating must exist or not exist'. But he denies that 'one necessarily has to decide on its existence or non-existence', since 'its non-existence could well come about in the absence of any decision' (Leibniz apparently grants that its existence would not ensue if it were not decided on). In particular, Leibniz has Theophile say, 'one can suspend one's choice, [as] happens quite often, especially when other thoughts interrupt one's deliberation'.[187]

It might seem surprising that Locke should have missed such an obvious point. Even more surprising is the fact that he himself acknowledges the very power of suspension that Leibniz uses against him. He does not do so in his original version of Chapter xxi, in which the argument under discussion first appeared. But Locke's doctrine of suspension (as we shall henceforth refer to it) is a prominent feature of the revised version of this chapter that came out in the *Essay's* second edition – and also of all subsequent versions. And Locke made no change in his argument for this edition, or for the third or fourth editions, either. Finally, in revising his chapter again for the fifth edition, he did add some qualifications to his text, having been brought by his Arminian friend Philippus van Limborch to see a connexion between the doctrine of suspension and his denial of freedom in willing. But Locke evidently failed to see any such connection in the interim period.

We shall have more to say later about Locke's doctrine of suspension and about his correspondence with Limborch on the subject of freedom. First, we need to consider Locke's answer to the second of the questions he raises regarding the freedom of willing. This is the question whether an agent has the freedom of specification with respect to his volitions, the freedom, for example, to will to rise from one's chair as opposed to willing to stay seated. Locke addresses this question in Section 25 of Chapter xxi. 'To ask', he says, 'whether a Man be at Liberty to will either Motion or Rest; Speaking, or Silence; which he pleases, is to ask, whether a Man can will, what he wills; or be pleased with what he is pleased with'. And those who answer this question affirmatively, he continues, 'must suppose one Will to determine the Acts of another, and another to determinate that; and so on in infinitum'; which is, he concludes, an 'absurdity'.[188]

The argument that Locke is relying on here is hardly explicit, but it appears to go something like this: (1) an agent $m$ is free with respect to an action $d$ only if $m$ wills $d$; (2) $m$ wills $d$ only if there is an act of willing $w$, done by $m$, which determines $d$; (3) hence [by (1) and (2)], if $d$ is itself an act of willing, then $m$ is free with respect to $d$ only if $m$ wills (via $w$) an act of willing (namely, $d$); (4) if $d$ and $w$ are acts of willing and $w$ determines $d$, then $w$ and $d$ are distinct, that is, they belong to different 'Wills'; (5) hence (by (1), (2) and (4)), if $m$ is free with respect to $d$ and $d$ is an act of willing, then '[the acts of] one Will . . . determine the Acts of another'; (6) $m$ is free with respect to $d$ only if $m$ is free with respect to $w$; (7) hence (by (1), (2), (4), (6) and parity of reasoning), $m$ is free with respect to $d$ only if there is another act of willing $v$, done by $m$ and distinct from $w$, which determines $w$, and 'so on *in infinitum*'.

If the foregoing is indeed what Locke intended, then he is one of the earliest purveyors of a pattern of reasoning – an *argumentum ad regressum* – that has since been a favourite of anti-libertarians, from Edwards to Ryle. As stated, Locke's argument is valid; its operative premises are (1), (2), (4), and (6). Premises (1) and (2) follow from Locke's definition of free agency and his understanding of voluntary action, respectively. Premise (4) is an instance of the principle that the will is determined by something other than itself (whence 'no will determines itself' – call this the 'heteronomy principle'), which Locke affirmed in almost these words in his initial version of chapter xxi and did not repudiate in any later version.[189] Premise (6) is an instance of the principle that a free action derives or inherits its freedom from the volition which determines it (whence no action is free unless its determining volition is free – call this the 'inheritance principle'). This, however, is not a principle that Locke affirms. Furthermore, it is a principle that is typically held by the very Arminian thinkers – by Hobbes's antagonist Bramhall and by his own correspondent Limborch, for example – that Locke is attacking in this section: indeed, he comes close in a later section to explicitly denying it.[190] This fact pulls the sting from his reasoning here, for it means that he cannot consistently use it against its intended target. Thus, it turns out once again that Locke has no sound basis for concluding that no agent has freedom with respect to his willing, either the freedom of exercise or that of specification.

Basis or no, Locke maintained his position on the freedom of willing through the *Essay*'s first four editions. And even in the fifth edition, where under pressure from Limborch he relented, conceding that 'yet there is a case wherein a Man is at Liberty in respect of willing', he made no change in his argument of Section 25.[191] The problem thus raised for the proper interpretation of Locke's thought again turns on his doctrine of suspension, for the case mentioned in the passage just quoted is that of a man who, while deliberating, 'may suspend the act of his choice from being determined for or against the thing proposed'.[192] Locke introduces this doctrine as he is presenting his 'second thoughts' (in the *Essay*'s second edition) not on freedom but on the factors that determine the will. Before broaching that subject, however, we must lay out his views concerning determination in general.

In general, when Locke says that $x$ determines $y$, he means that $x$ causes $y$. Since he holds that everything that happens in the world is the product of antecedent causes, he holds that everything, including every human action, is determined. In this he is in agreement with Hobbes and Spinoza (and indeed with Descartes, Malebranche, and Leibniz). But unlike these philosophers, Locke offers no defence of this doctrine of universal causation; indeed, he only rarely mentions it in the *Essay*.[193]

Locke also takes for granted, with little notice, a conception of the human will — or rather of volitions, which are the acts or exercises of the will — which was shared by nearly every thinker who considered these matters in mediaeval and early modern times. According to this conception, volitions are crucial links in the causal chains that connect human behaviour, not only with its physical environment, but also with the creative act or acts of God by which (they all believed) the whole universe first came to be. Volitions for these thinkers have two different causal rôles. On the one hand, they are the causes of the voluntary actions that follow them, the actions they determine. On the other, they are the effects of other factors which precede and determine them, both 'motives' within the mind and 'nature' and 'circumstances' outside it. In the former rôle, no volition was supposed to be the sole cause of any voluntary action, or thought to be sufficient therefor. Volitions were taken to be the last links in extended chains of antecedent causes; or better, to be members, in Hobbes's phrase, of 'concourses' of partial causes which themselves belong to series of like concourses all stretching back to God. But volitions are nonetheless, for Locke as for the other thinkers of his day, genuinely causal factors which help both to prompt and to shape or 'specify' voluntary actions, and whose occurrence is necessary for such actions.

Locke does not have much to say about volitions in their rôle as causes of voluntary actions. It is their other rôle, as effects, especially of motives or mental factors, that draws his attention in the *Essay*. Over half of the long chapter on power in the first edition is filled with his discussion of 'what determines the will'; and in the second and following editions, this discussion is significantly expanded. It was on this question that the most important changes in Locke's thinking occurred.

He begins this discussion in the first edition by stating the principle, noted earlier, of heteronomy: 'The Will . . . is determined by something without it self'.[194] He then asks what determines it, and in due course answers that 'Good . . . , the greater Good is that alone which determines the Will'.[195] Since good is identified with happiness and happiness with pleasure (and evil with misery and pain), it follows that what really determines the will is pleasure (and pain, in a negative way). But even this is not the bottom of the matter. For most of the things we do, Locke points out, are motivated not by present pleasure but by the expectation or hope of pleasure to come; and what 'makes us will the doing or omitting any [such] Action . . . is the greater Good appearing to result from that choice in all its Consequences, as far as at present they are represented to our view'.[196] But in order for some good to appear to result from the represented consequences of an agent's future choice, the agent must envisage those consequences and estimate the pleasure they will bring. And this requires the use of his understanding to perform intellectual operations: to make judgements and form beliefs. Thus, Locke's basic position in the first edition of the *Essay* is that it is some cognitive or intellectual factor, some 'judgement of the understanding', that finally determines the will and causes our volitions – at least in the majority of cases.

That this is indeed Locke's meaning was seen by William Molyneux, who in a letter charged his friend with 'seeming to make all Sins to proceed from our Understandings', adding that 'it seems harsh to say, that a Man shall be Damn'd, because he understands no better than he does'.[197] Molyneux is accusing Locke, in effect, of intellectual determinism. Locke later confessed that Molyneux's reaction to his position reinforced doubts he himself had had about it, and encouraged him to seek an alternative. It was the 'second thoughts' resulting from this effort, he says, that caused him to revise his chapter on power for the *Essay*'s second edition.

Locke's new view of motivation is certainly quite different from its predecessor.

What determines the will, he now says, is not 'the greater good in view: But some . . . uneasiness a Man is at present under'.[198] This uneasiness is an occurrent feeling, a kind of pain: it is the feeling that constitutes desire (or at least always accompanies it). In his earlier account, Locke had drawn no clear distinction between desiring and willing. Now he pronounces them 'two distinct Acts of the mind', each with its own kind of object and distinctive phenomenal character.[199] What happens when an agent performs a voluntary action, according to Locke's new view, is that she first desires something and then wills an action designed to attain the object of this desire. Her desiring determines her will, in the sense of causing an act of volition, which in turn produces the action. To desire something, Locke stresses, is not merely to envisage it; it is to feel the pain of not having it. And it is only this feeling of pain, this uneasiness, he says, that actually touches the will, so as to 'set us on work'. Thus ' 'tis uneasiness alone [that] operates on the will'; only uneasiness 'immediately determines' its choice.[200]

In Locke's new account, therefore, what determines the will is some present feeling, and not any cognitive or intellectual state of the agent. So it appears that the intellectualism − if not the determinism − of his earlier position has been repudiated. Such indeed has been the judgement of several commentators. But this appearance is deceptive. For while it is true that a new, non-intellectual factor has been added to the motivational situation in Locke's second view, it is not true that determination by intellectual factors has been removed from it. For agents' judgements of the good and bad attaching to the actions they project continue to play a critical rôle in the motivation of these actions.

In the first place, desire itself contains an intellectual element for Locke. Desire must include a feeling of uneasiness, but it also must have an object, and the desirer must be aware of this object. That is, she must cognise or conceive the thing she desires, and she must conceive it as something good, a source of pleasure − which is to say, she must believe something about it. Second, it is a significant tenet of Locke's new position that desires are capable of being generated by antecedent conceptions and judgements of the goodness of the object desired. Thus, 'due, and repeated Contemplation', he says, is capable of bringing some absent good, which we have recognised as such but have not judged to be essential to our present happiness, 'nearer to the Mind', of giving 'some relish' to it, and raising 'in us some desire; which then beginning to make a part of our present uneasiness, . . . comes in its turn to determine the will'. In this way, Locke continues, 'by a due consideration and examining any good proposed, it is in our power, to raise our desires, . . . whereby [that good] may come to work upon the will, and be pursued'. It follows, he later notes, that it is within 'a Man's power to change the pleasantness, and unpleasantness' of things.[201] This is not the view that Locke had taken in his original version of chapter xxi. Indeed, he explicitly maintained the contrary, saying that it is not 'in [anyone's] choice, whether he will, or will not be better pleased with one thing than another'.[202]

Another feature of Locke's new version of chapter xxi provides even more telling testimony to the importance of intellectual operations in motivation. This is the doctrine of suspension, which made its first appearance there. Locke's new view is that what moves us to will is always some particular uneasiness. But it is a fact of our lives in this world, he observes, that we are beset with a 'multitude of wants, and desires', and thus with 'many uneasinesses', all competing for the will's attention, so to speak, at the same time. Which of these then is the one that wins this competition? 'It is natural', Locke answers, 'that the greatest, and most pressing [uneasiness] should determine the will to the next action'. And so it does, he continues, 'for the most part; but not always. For the mind [has] a power to suspend the execution and satisfaction of any of its desires, and so all, one after the other', and thus keep the will from being determined. That there is such a power Locke claims is 'evident in Experience', a datum that 'every one daily may Experiment in himself'. But the point of suspending one's desires is 'to consider the objects of them; examine them on all sides, and weigh them with others'; and thus 'to examine, view, and judge, of the good or evil of what we are going to do'. In many cases such suspension results in a change in the content or relative strength of the agent's desires, and her will is determined differently from the way it would otherwise have been. But in every case, once, 'upon due Examination, we have judg'd, we have done our duty' as rational beings, 'all that we can, or ought to do, in pursuit of our happiness'.[203]

Thus, Locke's contention is that by suspending her desires an agent is often able to bring her will under the control of her thought and judgement, even if she cannot always do so. This control is not direct: it must be mediated by desire, since only desire is capable of determining the will immediately. But when a volition is produced by a desire that after a process of suspension and examination has been modified or generated by some action of the understanding, then it is ultimately that action that is responsible for the volition. It is the agent's judgement as to what is good or bad for her to do that ultimately determines her will. So again from this perspective it is clear that Locke is still essentially an intellectual determinist in the *Essay*'s second edition, even though he there takes the whole business of motivation to be more complicated than he had initially supposed it to be.

That Locke himself saw no fundamental change in this aspect of his position is shown by the fact that, in his new version of Chapter xxi, he not only retains but reinforces several remarks that he had made in defence of intellectualism in the old one. Not only is it 'not an imperfection in Man, [but] the highest perfection of intellectual Natures', he says in the first edition, to have our wills determined by our judgements of good. It also is no 'restraint or diminution of Freedom, . . . not an Abridgment, [but] the end and use of our Liberty'; and he carries on in this same vein for three more sections.[204] In the second edition, Locke repeats this whole discussion almost verbatim, while interjecting several new comments designed to strengthen or vivify it, especially ones reflecting the new doctrine of suspension. Thus, at the end of the section in which this doctrine is introduced, he maintains that ''tis not a fault, but a perfection of our nature to desire, will, and act according to the last result of a fair Examination'.[205] Again in the following section, in another explicit statement of his compatibilism, he declares that 'were we determined by any thing but the last result of our own Minds, judging of the good or evil of any action, we were not free'. And finally, in a passage added to that same section for the *Essay*'s fifth edition, Locke says that 'every Man is put under a necessity by his constitution, as an intelligent Being, to be determined in willing by his own Thought and Judgement, what is best for him to do: else he would be under the determination of some other than himself, which is want of Liberty'.[206] It is hard to imagine plainer statements of intellectual determinism than these.

As should be evident from the foregoing survey, Locke's doctrine of suspension is entirely in harmony with his account of determination, not only in the *Essay*'s second edition but in the first as well. Its relation, however, to his account of freedom, in both editions (for this account hardly changed from the one to the other), is problematic. We have already noted that this doctrine controverts a premise of one of Locke's arguments for the proposition that agents have no freedom with respect to their volitions. This is the argument to the specific conclusion that there is no freedom of exercise with respect to acts of willing. But is the doctrine of suspension inconsistent with this conclusion itself? And is it inconsistent with the conclusion of Locke's regress argument, that there is no freedom of specification with respect to volitions?

It might be supposed that these questions are moot, in view of Locke's admission to Limborch, also already noted, that the possibility of suspending one's choice in a process of deliberation entails that 'yet there is a case wherein a Man is at Liberty in respect of willing'.[207] But this is not so, for Locke may have been mistaken in making this concession to Limborch. As an Arminian, Limborch was himself convinced, not only that agents could freely determine their volitions, but that no overt voluntary action could be free unless the volition that produced it was free: he believed in and frequently professed the inheritance principle cited earlier. And Limborch thought that the doctrine of suspension committed Locke to this Arminian view.[208] But it is not at all clear that it does. Limborch must have supposed that an agent who suspends her choice in mid-deliberation does so voluntarily, that is, by an act of willing. (And Locke would surely have agreed with this: he would not have thought that a suspension of choice is something that just happens to one during deliberation.) But this volition is a volition to suspend one's choice, or at most one not to will. It is not a volition to will something, and hence not a case of voluntary willing, which both Locke and Limborch maintain a case of free willing would have to be: a free action must at the least be voluntary. Limborch might argue that if stopping one's will can be accomplished voluntarily, then so can starting it up again: an agent who has suspended her choice, examined and judged, can then by willing start deliberating once again, and this time carry the process through to a volition to act. But this new volition would still not be one that the agent had willed. At most she would have willed to reinstate her various desires (perhaps with a new one added or some of the old ones given different strengths), and it would then be one of these desires that brought about her volition to act. Limborch might then claim that willing to start deliberating as to *d,* having judged that *d* is the best thing to do in the situation, is tantamount to willing to will *d*. And perhaps he would be right to do so: he might hold with Aquinas, for example, that 'when you will the means to an end you thereby also [*eodem actu*] will the end'.[209] But that he is right is at the least not obvious; and it is less obvious still that anything in Locke's position commits him to this result.

It is important to note, however, that Locke *could* have accepted the reasoning just attributed to Limborch, consistently with the rest of his position. Some critics have claimed that the doctrine of suspension by itself is incompatible with Locke's determinism, intellectual or otherwise.[210] But this is wrong. An agent who suspends her choice, even one who does so voluntarily, need not be doing anything uncaused: neither her action of suspension nor the volition by which it is produced is ipso facto undetermined. And even if, as Limborch insists and Locke admits in the *Essay*'s fifth edition, an action of suspension requires a volition that is free and not merely voluntary, there is no need for the further volition that is required to produce that free volition to be free itself, or even voluntary. (Limborch would presumably think otherwise, on the basis of the inheritance principle; but there is no reason for Locke to do so.) Locke logically could, therefore, agree with the Arminians that there are free volitions (albeit only in cases of suspension) without becoming an Arminian himself – that is, without adopting even their inheritance principle, much less their indeterminism.

One further complication arising from Locke's advocacy of the doctrine of suspension needs to be mentioned. When, in II.xxi.47 of the *Essay's* second edition, he first calls attention to our power of suspending our desires in mid-deliberation, Locke links this power to freedom (or liberty) in a way that at first sight seems perplexing. In this power, he says, 'lies the liberty Man has'; and again, 'this [power] seems to me the source of all liberty; in this seems to consist that, which is (as I think improperly) call'd Free will'.[211] What these statements suggest is a definition of freedom that is different from the one he has been promoting, or at the least a restriction of the latter to cases involving suspension. (Remember, the only freedom in question at this point is the freedom of overt voluntary actions, those 'consecutive to volition': it is only later that Locke extends freedom to volitions themselves.) But this surely is not Locke's intention. For one thing, he never develops any such suggestion or even repeats it either in the second or in any subsequent edition. He must here be speaking rhetorically, exaggerating the true state of things in order to stress the importance of suspending our desires in our lives as rational and moral agents. What he is literally saying is something like this: that it is by exercising our power of suspension that we can best achieve (as he does say in the very next section) the 'very improvement and benefit of [Freedom]', the 'end and use of our Liberty'.[212]

## VII. LEIBNIZ

No philosopher in the seventeenth century devoted more effort to intellectual problems connected with human freedom than Leibniz. In the preface to the *Théodicée* he wrote: 'There are two famous labyrinths where our reason quite often goes astray: one concerns the great question of the free and the necessary . . . the other consists in the discussion of continuity, and the indivisibles that seem to be its elements. . . . The first perplexes almost all the human race, the other exercises only philosophers.'[213]

Leibniz was well aware that certain original ingredients of his own metaphysical system appear to exacerbate the problems connected with the first of the two labyrinths.[214] We begin with an attempt to locate some ingredients of Leibniz's thinking about freedom by considering his evaluations of views of others on this topic.

Leibniz expressed significant reservations about the views of many philosophers on the topic of freedom. Prominently included in the list of those whose views he criticised are Descartes, Hobbes, Spinoza, the Molinists, Malebranche, and Locke. By contrast, Leibniz frequently aligned himself with Saint Thomas Aquinas on the matter of freedom. Indeed, with the exception of a single corrective theme, we know of no texts in which Leibniz commented on Aquinas on freedom in a negative way. The single corrective theme is expressed in the following passage from Leibniz's observations on King's solution to the problem of evil: 'I do not require that the will always follow the judgement of the understanding, because I distinguish this judgement from those motives that arise from insensible perceptions and inclinations.'[215]

And the corrective point is the emphasis on 'insensible inclinations' as causal factors in the determination of human choices. The corrective point matters; it is not mere detail. Still, it would aid in locating Leibniz's account of human freedom were there sufficient evidence for the thesis that it just amounts to Aquinas's theory, modified to take into account insensible inclinations, and whatever other alterations are required by pertinent differences between their basic metaphysical commitments. But there is not sufficient evidence for this thesis. The problem is that we do not have an adequate grasp of what theory Leibniz took Aquinas to have held. So while comparisons with Aquinas's account are suggestive, in the present state of Leibniz scholarship, they cannot be decisive. Leibniz's fundamental objection to Hobbes and Spinoza is contained in his comments on Hobbes, appended to the *Théodicée,* and in numerous other places. He believed that Hobbes and Spinoza were committed to 'absolute necessity', that is, to the thesis that every state of affairs that obtains does so of necessity, and that every state of affairs that does not obtain, fails to obtain of necessity.[216] And, throughout most of his career, Leibniz took such necessity to be incompatible with freedom, human or divine.

The elements of Descartes's account of human freedom that Leibniz found unacceptable are noted in the following passage from the *Théodicée:*

The Cartesians have been embarrassed on the subject of free choice . . . they considered that all the actions of the soul seem to be determined by what comes from without, following upon impressions of sense, and that ultimately everything in the universe is directed by the providence of God. But from that the objection naturally arose that therefore there is no freedom. To this Descartes replied that we are assured of this providence by reason, but that we are also assured of our freedom by the internal experience we have of it, and that we must believe in both, although we do not see the way to reconcile them.[217]

In Descartes's admonition that we should accept divine providence, accept free choice, and live with any apparent inconsistency between the two, Leibniz saw

unacceptable grist for Bayle's sceptical mill. Since Leibniz accepted divine providence and human freedom he concluded that his duty as a philosopher was to
establish that there is no real inconsistency. Furthermore, Leibniz agreed with
Bayle, that internal experience, in and by itself, cannot establish the reality of
free choice. Leibniz was enamoured of Bayle's weathervane analogy: imagine a
weathervane that at each moment at which it commenced a turn in a certain
direction had a strong desire to turn in exactly that direction. The weathervane
would imagine itself free, whereas, in fact, it was just blowing in the wind.[218]
Leibniz's comments on this analogy are instructive. In *Théodicée,* Section 300,
Leibniz agreed that we cannot prove by internal experience that we are free, since
we cannot know by internal experience that we are not 'determined from without'. But, according to Leibniz, his metaphysical system and, in particular his
principle of spontaneity, 'demonstrates indubitably that in the course of nature
each substance is the sole cause of all its actions, and that each is exempt from all
physical influence of every other substance, except for the ordinary concurrence
of God'. Recall that the immediate problem under discussion is the compatibility
of divine providence with human freedom. Hence, it is a presupposition of
Leibniz's alleged way of establishing consistency that God's ordinary concurrence
in our actions is consistent with those actions being free. We might call the thesis
that in the ordinary course of nature each substance is the sole cause of its own
actions, the principle of spontaneity. It is a central component in Leibniz's account
of freedom. Indeed, it seems quite clear from the discussion in the *Théodicée* from
Section 292 through Section 300 that Leibniz took the principle of spontaneity to
satisfy some necessary condition of human freedom, namely, that the agent is not
causally determined from without. So there is one standard variety of compatibilism that Leibniz rejected. Leibniz's reaction to the account of freedom he associated with Molinism yields one standard variety of libertarianism that he also
rejected. Consider the account of freedom Molina offered in Disputation 2 of the
*Concordia:* 'That agent is said to be free, who, all the requisites for acting having
been posited, can act or not act, or so perform one action that he is still able to
do the contrary.'[219]

   In notes concerning a conversation on the topic of the problem of evil, after a
careful formulation of the principle of sufficient reason, Leibniz set out to criticise
Molina's account of freedom. He wrote: 'This notion of freedom − that is the
power of acting or not acting, all the requisites for acting having been posited, and
all things being equal both in the object and in the agent, is an impossible chimera,
which is contrary to the first principle that I stated.'[220] Then, after claiming that
this account of freedom is not to be found in Aristotle, Augustine, the Master of

Sentences, Thomas, Scotus, and most of the older scholastics, he added: 'It was given currency for the first time by the later Scholastics.'

In an earlier version of this text, Leibniz wrote 'by the Molinists' in place of 'by the later Scholastics'. There is no doubt that we are in the neighbourhood of his major objection to Molina's libertarian account of freedom. And the objection is straightforward: the principle of sufficient reason implies that the conditions required for freedom by Molina cannot be satisfied. Leibniz often formulated this criticism by stating that the Molinist conception of freedom requires an indifference of equipoise, which is inconsistent with the principle of sufficient reason.[221] One might suppose that Leibniz's criticism misses the mark here. A comparison of Molina's conception of freedom, as formulated in the *Concordia,* with the account attributed to him by Leibniz in the passage quoted above, shows that they differ in that Molina's account contains no mention of equipoise, that is, the 'all things being equal' requirement – precisely the point on which Leibniz appears to have focused his criticism. But an examination of some of Leibniz's most carefully crafted criticisms shows that the target is Molina's account of freedom unfettered by a requirement of equipoise.

Consider the following passage from Leibniz's letter of 1711 to the Jesuit, Des Bosses:

I maintain absolutely that the power of determining oneself without a cause, i.e., without a source of the determination implies a contradiction, just as a relation without a foundation implies a contradiction. But, from this, the metaphysical necessity of every effect does not follow for it suffices that the *cause* or reason not be metaphysical necessitating, although it is metaphysically necessary that there be such a cause.[222]

Here there is no mention of a state of equipoise; the idea rejected is that a decision might be made, an action initiated by an agent, without a sufficient reason. Leibniz characterised a sufficient cause or reason for the obtaining of some state of affairs $\alpha$ as a total set of requisites for the obtaining of $\alpha$. The principle of sufficient reason requires that, if $\alpha$ obtains, there is a sufficient reason why it obtains. Put these items together with Molina's characterisation of freedom and it is clear why Leibniz regarded it as an impossible chimera.

Leibniz's criticism of the account of freedom he attributed to the Molinists yields one variety of libertarianism he eschewed, and one kind of indifference he rejected – indifference of equipoise. But it would be rash to draw the conclusion from that alone that therefore Leibniz was a determinist and compatibilist. The principle of sufficient reason requires a reason or cause for each state of affairs that obtains, but there is room within the disjunction – reason or cause – to slip in some version of libertarianism – at any rate, some account of freedom according to which free decisions do not come about in virtue of natural causal necessities, ultimately beyond the control of the agent.

There is much subtle detail in Leibniz's comments in the *Nouveaux essais sur l'entendement humain* on Locke's account of freedom. But the point that needs emphasis is that Leibniz claimed that free choice is the heart of the matter when it comes to freedom. Leibniz saw the inadequacy of the idea that an action is free just in case that action is caused (in part) by a choice of the agent in such fashion that the action would not have occurred had the agent chosen otherwise. Commenting on a characterisation of freedom drawn along these lines Leibniz wrote in a letter to Basnage:

Mr. Jaquelot . . . says that freedom signifies a power to do what one wills, because one wills it in such fashion that if one had not willed it, one would not do it . . . I believe that the most obstinate adversaries of human freedom are obliged to agree that we are free in this sense. I do not know, if even Spinoza would deny it.[223]

In the *Nouveaux essais,* commentating on essentially the same notion of a free action, Leibniz wrote: 'The question is not whether a man can do what he wills to do, but whether his will itself is sufficiently independent.'[224]

Leibniz thought Malebranche's occasionalism and his own theory of the pre-established harmony – including the previously noted principle of spontaneity – both provided accounts whereby the will is 'sufficiently independent' from 'determination from without', provided the 'without' is restricted to the activities of other created substances. And this because both theories deny the possibility of intersubstantial causality among creatures. But Leibniz rejected Malebranche's theory on the ground that it has the unacceptable consequence that God is the author of sin.[225]

The following passage occurs in the *Nouveaux essais* in Leibniz's commentary on Locke's account of freedom:

Freedom of the will is understood in two different senses; one of them is when it is opposed to the imperfection or bondage of the mind, which is an imposition or constraint, but internal like that which comes from the passions; the other sense occurs when freedom is opposed to necessity. Employing the first sense the Stoics said that only the wise person is free . . . It is in this way that God alone is perfectly free, and that created minds are free only to the extent that they are above passion; and this kind of freedom pertains strictly to our understanding. But the freedom of mind that is opposed to necessity concerns the bare will. . . . This is what is called free choice [*le franc arbitre*]; it consists in the view that the strongest reasons or impressions that the understanding presents to the will . . . do not confer upon it an absolute or (so to speak) metaphysical necessity.[226]

Although there are few other texts in which Leibniz explicitly drew a distinction between the two senses of freedom of the will herein adumbrated, nonetheless he utilised the distinction throughout his career. For ease of reference, the first sense noted above may be called freedom of the understanding, and the latter, freedom of the will, even though Leibniz opened the discussion by referring to two senses of freedom of the will. Note that, according to Leibniz, freedom of the understanding is not a purely qualitative concept – it makes sense to say that one being (God) is perfectly free, in this sense, whereas other beings (human beings, for example) are more or less free, in this sense, depending upon the mix of reason and passion in the causation of their choices. And, since a human person will be more or less influenced by passion, depending upon the subject matter of various choices, in this sense, a human person will be freer with respect to some choices than others. In various texts, Leibniz drew up lists in which varieties of persons were compared with respect to freedom in this sense. *Théodicée,* Section 310, is typical. Therein Leibniz noted that 'only God's will ... always follows the judgments of the understanding', whereas all intelligent creatures are subject to passions, even the blessed, although in the case of the blessed the mix of passion and reason moving the will to choice always tends towards the good, not just the apparent good, as it does for us, while we remain pilgrims.

When Leibniz talked about freedom as a perfection, it was freedom of the understanding – the more the better – to which he referred.[227] By contrast, he treated the item in this pair that we are calling freedom of the will as an entry-level variety of freedom, required for freedom of the understanding. And, unlike freedom of the understanding, freedom of the will is a qualitative concept – a given choice is either free or not, in this sense, depending upon whether the conditions that define it are fulfilled. One choice of an agent is not more free than another choice of that agent, nor one agent more free than another, in this sense. Although the two senses of freedom are disparate in significant ways, it will become clear when we focus on the notion of spontaneity, which, according to Leibniz, is a key component of freedom of the will, that the contrast between reason and passion so crucial to freedom of the understanding, has a counterpart that is fundamental to Leibniz's deepest thinking about spontaneity and, hence, freedom of the will.

That freedom of the will is required for freedom of the understanding is central to one of Leibniz's most frequently stated objections to the idea that indifference, in the sense he attributed to Molina, is a component of freedom of the will. The objection is this. God has complete freedom of the understanding. Since freedom of the will is required for freedom of the understanding, God must have freedom of the will. But indifference, in Molina's sense, cannot be attributed to God. Therefore, indifference, in Molina's sense, is not a component of freedom of the will.[228]

A statement of Leibniz's mature analysis of freedom of the will is contained in Section 288 of the *Théodicée*: 'Freedom, as required by the schools of theology, consists in intelligence, which includes a distinct knowledge of the object of deliberation; in spontaneity, in virtue of which we determine ourselves; and in contingency, i.e., in the exclusion of logical or metaphysical necessity.'

This is an accurate, although truncated, statement of Leibniz's mature analysis of the freedom of the will. It is intended to codify a position concerning freedom of the will, which Leibniz held from at least 1700 and perhaps much longer. It is not a position that Leibniz accepted throughout his entire philosophic career. Consider the following passage from a letter to Wedderkopf of 1671: 'Whatever has happened, is happening, or will happen is best, and, accordingly, necessary, but . . . with a necessity that takes nothing away from freedom, because it takes nothing away from the will and from the use of reason.'[229]

A careful reading of the entire letter makes it quite clear that the necessity 'that takes nothing away from freedom', to which Leibniz referred in this context, is metaphysical necessity. At a minimum, the notion of necessity employed in this passage is such that, subsequently, Leibniz wished to disavow his remarks about it; for, subsequently he attached the following comment to his copy of the letter: 'I later corrected this, for it is one thing for sins to happen infallibly, and another for them to happen necessarily.'[230]

The letter to Wedderkopf contains an account of freedom that involves a grade of necessitation that is more severe than the position contained in Section 288 of the *Théodicée*. By contrast, in an important paper entitled 'De necessitate et contingentia', Leibniz seems to offer an account of freedom that is libertarian and thus, apparently, different from the position of Section 288. In this paper, Leibniz claimed that freedom requires not only a lack of metaphysical necessity, which is the claim of Section 288, but an indifference that results from a lack of physical necessity. This is as libertarian a passage as one will find in Leibniz. We believe that it does not represent his mature view. In what follows we will discuss first the requirement of spontaneity and then the third condition cited in Leibniz's analysis of freedom contained in *Théodicée*, Section 288, namely, contingency, and the associated notions of determination and indifference. Discussion of these notions provides an opportunity to explain why we believe that 'De necessitate et contingentia' does not represent Leibniz's mature view on freedom.

The second necessary condition of freedom, contained in Leibniz's classic analysis of *Théodicée,* Section 288, is 'spontaneity, on account of which, we determine ourselves'. In connection with Leibniz's comments on Descartes's views on freedom, we have noted that Leibniz rejected one variety of compatibilism, namely, the thesis that freedom is consistent with determination from outside the agent. We think that it is plausible to suppose that Leibniz thereby meant to claim that causal determination from outside the agent is inconsistent with freedom. Moreover, Leibniz claimed that self-determination is a necessary condition of freedom.[231] Indeed, in his reflections on Bellarmine, Leibniz claimed that 'our freedom consists in the power of determining ourselves to action'. He often touted as one virtue of his principle of spontaneity that it guarantees that when an agent acts spontaneously then that agent is not determined from without and that agent determines himself to action.[232]

Leibniz associated both a negative and a positive thesis with the principle of spontaneity. The negative thesis is the denial of intersubstantial causality among created substances. Here is a carefully crafted version of the positive thesis, formulated by Leibniz in his correspondence with Arnauld: 'Everything happens in each substance in consequence of the first state that God gave it in creating it, and, extraordinary concourse aside, his ordinary concourse consists simply in the conservation of the substance itself, in conformity with its preceding state and with the changes it carries with it.'[233]

Leibniz seems to have held that the changes that the preceding state of a substance 'carries with it [*changemens qu'il porte*]' are, in the case of God's ordinary concourse (i.e., in the nonmiraculous case), outcomes of natural causation, brought about by the exercise of a substance's force.[234] But the texts are curiously vague about the character of the relation between a state of a substance and its predecessor, in virtue of which, according to Leibniz, the former is a consequence of the latter. What kind of consequence, one wants to know. We shall assume that it is a causal consequence, but the texts are less than overwhelming in support of that reading. And, plainly, much is at stake. For how one construes Leibniz's intention on this matter will guide one's understanding of many other central issues in Leibniz's philosophy.

However one construes the relevant notion of consequence, it is quite clear that Leibniz took his principle of spontaneity to have as a straightforward consequence that each individual substance is self-determining and, hence, not determined from without. In letters to Lady Masham and Jaquelot, Leibniz noted that his account 'augments our spontaneity, while not diminishing our choice'.[235] Jaquelot objected that since, on Leibniz's view, the entire sequence of states composing a substance is a consequence of its initial state, that view is inconsistent with freedom. Leibniz responded that on his view preceding states incline, without necessitating, future states, and that, hence, his view is consistent with freedom. He wrote: 'I believe that there is no system in which true freedom, i.e., spontaneity with choice and independence of the soul from everything else except God, appears to greater advantage.'[236]

In most of his writings on this topic, Leibniz confidently asserted that his principle of spontaneity ensures that a creature is never determined from without by other creatures and thereby deprived of freedom. But in a few places Leibniz took seriously the following objection. Granted that Leibniz's principle of spontaneity precludes intersubstantial causal relations among created substances, still his thesis of the pre-established harmony ensures a relation of dependence of the mind on the body, and, more generally, ensures a relation of dependence between a created agent and its external environment, adequate to support the charge that, on Leibniz's theory, a creature is 'determined from without' in a fashion which, although not causal in Leibniz's sense, is, nonetheless, inconsistent with freedom of the will. Leibniz considered the objection that the ground of the will is from items external to the mind. He responded that the internal dispositions of the mind must be included as well, to which he had his opponent reply that present dispositions of the mind arise from past impressions on the body and other past external items. Leibniz responded as follows: 'I concede this concerning some present dispositions of the mind, but not all. For there are certain primitive dispositions in the mind that do not arise from anything external. Therefore we must say that minds in and of themselves, in consequence of their primitive natures, differ among themselves. . . . the root of freedom is in these primitive dispositions.'[237] He made the same points in a letter of 1695 to Thomas Burnett: 'Our primitive determinations do not come from outside . . . ; there is a difference among human souls taken in themselves, whereas most people suppose that their difference arises only from the body.'[238]

It should be clear that Leibniz's efforts to ward off the dreaded 'determination from without' are more complex than is often thought. In order to grasp what he dreaded and what he accepted with equanimity, we need to consider his thinking concerning determination in general, a topic included in our discussion of the third (and last) necessary condition of freedom contained in Leibniz's classic analysis of *Théodicée,* Section 288.

The last condition required for freedom, according to Leibniz's analysis formulated in *Théodicée,* Section 288, is 'contingency, i.e., . . . the exclusion of logical or metaphysical necessity'. It is natural to suppose that had Leibniz meant to exclude physical necessity, as well as metaphysical necessity, he would have said so. Hence, it is natural to suppose that he was a compatibilist in the sense that he thought that a choice might be causally necessitated and yet free. At any rate, it appears that Leibniz was a compatibilist in this sense, at least in his mature period, dating from 1700.[239]

Leibniz distinguished among these varieties of determination: semantical, theological, metaphysical, physical (causal), and conceptual.[240] Let $\alpha$ be some state of affairs that obtains at some time $t$. According to Leibniz, $\alpha$ is semantically determined to obtain whenever the proposition '$\alpha$ obtains at $t$' is true; it is theologically determined to obtain whenever God knows that $\alpha$ obtains at $t$; it is metaphysically determined to obtain at all times after $t$; and it is physically (causally) determined to obtain whenever some state of affairs ($\beta$) obtains such that it is not physically (causally) possible that $\beta$ obtains and $\alpha$ does not obtain at $t$.[241]

Leibniz held that every state of affairs that obtains is both semantically and theologically determined from all eternity. So, for example, Judas's betrayal of Christ was semantically and theologically determined from all eternity, according to Leibniz. And he saw no incompatibility between these varieties of determination and freedom. So, although Judas was semantically and theologically determined from all eternity to betray Christ, his choice, and subsequent action, was free. Furthermore, Leibniz held that metaphysical determination of a choice poses no threat to freedom, provided that it is contingent that the choice in question obtains. And, of course, this explains Leibniz's interest in the third (and last) condition required for freedom: the exclusion of metaphysical necessity.[242]

It is clear that the large question – did Leibniz regard freedom and determinism as compatible – needs to be refined to take into account the various notions of determination he employed. We have covered the cases except for physical determination. Did Leibniz hold that a choice may be physically determined by the obtaining of some state of affairs prior to the obtaining of the choice and yet free? A text that directly addresses this question is '*De necessitate et contingentia*', and the answer expressed therein seems to be – no. Leibniz wrote:

Free or intelligent substances have something greater (than stones) and more marvelous in a kind of imitation of God, so that they are not bound by any certain subordinate laws of the universe, but act as if by a private miracle, on the sole spontaneity of their own power, and, in consideration of some final cause, they interrupt the nexus and course of efficient causes on their will. So it is true that there is no creature that knows the heart who could predict with certainty how some mind will choose in accordance with the laws of nature. . . . From this it can be understood what is that indifference that goes with freedom. Just as contingency is opposed to metaphysical necessity, so indifference excludes not only metaphysical but also physical necessity.[243]

This is a difficult passage to interpret; however it is to be understood, Leibniz's mature position – that expressed consistently in his writings after 1700 – is that freedom and physical determination (and the resulting physical necessity) are compatible.

A central difficulty presented by the quoted passage is the claim that free creatures may 'interrupt the . . . course of efficient causes', and that therefore freedom consists not only in a lack of metaphysical necessity, but, more significantly, in an indifference that results from a lack of physical necessity. Leibniz appears to have denied this claim in his writings on freedom after 1700. Thus, in the preface to the *Théodicée,* touting the virtues of what was to come, Leibniz wrote: 'It will be shown that absolute necessity, which is called also logical and metaphysical, and sometimes geometric, and which alone is to be feared, does not exist in free actions, and, hence, that freedom is exempt not only from constraint, but also from real necessity.'[244]

This is not a stray passage; its point occurs in numerous other texts.[245] Leibniz's point seems to be that only metaphysical necessity, not physical necessity, serves as a threat to freedom; that is, that physical necessity, unlike metaphysical necessity, is compatible with freedom. Consider the following passage from a letter of 1707 to Coste, in which Leibniz set out to establish that the relevant events preceding a choice do not metaphysically determine the choice:

When we propose a choice to ourselves, for example, whether to leave or not, it is a question whether, with all the circumstances, internal or external, motives, perceptions, dispositions, impressions, passions, inclinations taken together, I am still in a state of contingency, or whether I am necessitated to take the choice to leave, for example, i.e., whether in fact this true and determined proposition – in all these circumstances taken together, I will choose to leave is contingent or necessary. I reply that it is contingent, because neither I nor any other more enlightened mind could demonstrate that the opposite of this truth implies a contradiction. And assuming that by freedom of indifference we understand a freedom opposed to necessity (as I have just explained it), I agree with that freedom.[246]

Note that in order for the choice to be free, Leibniz herein required that the relevant conditional lack metaphysical necessity. There is no requirement that it lack physical necessity. And the clear suggestion of the passage (and the entire letter) is that that is all the indifference Leibniz was then prepared to admit.

The compatibilism herein ascribed to Leibniz was an uncommon view in his time. Arnauld strongly criticised Malebranche for holding that an action might be free and yet 'a necessary consequence of the order of nature'.[247] Arnauld associated the thesis that all creaturely actions are a necessary consequence of the order of nature, 'a necessary consequence of natural laws', with the heresy of John Wyclif.[248] Interestingly, Leibniz had a quite different reading of Wyclif; at *Théodicée*, Part I, Section 67, he wrote: 'I am very far from the views of Bradwardine, Wyclif, Hobbes and Spinoza, who advocate, so it seems, this entirely mathematical necessity.'

So Leibniz deplored the necessity he took Wyclif to have advocated in connexion with the actions of creatures, and he would have agreed with Arnauld that necessity as understood by Wyclif is not compatible with freedom, but the notion of necessity deplored is not the one Arnauld had in mind.

A word of caution is in order, however, concerning the interpretation recommended herein. It concerns the ubiquitous notion of the ability to suspend the decision-making process. In the previously quoted passage from *De necessitate et contingentia*, after making his apparently libertarian point, Leibniz wrote: 'So . . . there is no creature that knows the heart who could predict with certainty how some mind will choose in accordance with the laws of nature.'[249]

The point made in this passage does not bear specifically on creaturely inability to predict with certainty when another creature would suspend the decision-making process, but in other writings Leibniz focused on just that situation. In a convoluted piece Leibniz argued that we can safely predict that a creature will choose what appears best to that creature, provided the creature makes a choice as opposed to suspending the decision-making process. Leibniz therein suggested that the real problem of prediction concerns the question of whether the creature will suspend the decision-making process or not.[250]

This concern about predictability of suspension of the decision-making process may strike one as being of epistemological but not metaphysical importance. But in Leibniz's case the epistemological point has metaphysical significance. First, Leibniz took the ability to suspend the decision-making process as a crucial, perhaps even essential, feature of creaturely freedom.[251] Second, Leibniz held that the human mind is so constituted by its creator that it is exactly suited to the discovery of laws of nature. Hence, there is reason to suppose that where Leibniz saw an inability on our part to predict, he saw phenomena not governed by natural law.

The idea that we have this power of suspending our decision-making processes and that it is a crucial feature of our freedom certainly appears in Leibniz's writings after 1700.[252] But the thesis that this power is such that exercises of it are in principle unpredictable by creatures is not to be found. Indeed, a number of the relevant texts suggest that Leibniz then regarded suspension of deliberation as causally ordered in much the same fashion as any other choice is.[253]

According to Leibniz, the basis for a determination that is eternal, for example, semantical or theological, is a conceptual determination. Leibniz put the matter this way in *De necessitate et contingentia*: 'A determination that does not impose necessity on contingent things, but affords certainty and infallibility, in the sense in which it is said that the truth of future contingents is determined – such a determination never begins, but always was, since it is contained from eternity in the very concept of the subject.'[254]

The idea is this. Suppose that the state of affairs $\alpha$ obtains at $t$ just in case individual $a$ has property $f$ at $t$. According to Leibniz, individual $a$ has property $f$ at time $t$ just in case $a$ exists and the complete individual concept of $a$ includes the property of having $f$ at $t$. But if the complete individual concept of $a$ ever includes the property of having $f$ at $t$ then it does so eternally.[255]

Consider the following propositions:

1. Julius Caesar chose to cross the Rubicon in 49 B.C.
2. If Julius Caesar exists at some time, then Julius Caesar chose to cross the Rubicon in 49 B.C.

According to Leibniz, given that (1) is true, the complete individual concept of Julius Caesar includes the property of choosing to cross the Rubicon in 49 B.C. This would seem to have as a consequence that (2) is metaphysically necessary. But, surely, if (2) is metaphysically necessary, then the conditionals whose contingency is required for freedom, according to Leibniz in the 1707 letter to Coste previously noted, turn out to be metaphysically necessary.

Leibniz employed the doctrine of infinite analysis in order to avoid the conclusion that (2) is metaphysically necessary and hence to maintain the consistency of conceptual determination and freedom. Applied to (1), the doctrine of infinite analysis has the consequence that (1) is contingently true because, although the concept of its predicate is contained in the concept of its subject, there is no finite analysis of these concepts that yields an identity, that is, a proposition of the form AB is A, even though there is an analysis of the relevant concepts that converges on such a proposition.[256]

Leibniz developed an alternative account of free choice that should be noted. Its basic idea consists in replacing the third condition required for freedom, that is, contingency, by what we might call possibility in its own nature. The idea is most readily explained in connection with Leibniz's effort to show that God's choice of the best possible world is free. Suppose that the attributes of God relevant to His choice of a world to create are essential to God, that is, it is metaphysically necessary that God has them. That suggests that there is a contradiction in asserting that God chose to create any possible world other than the best possible world. But, then, the choice of the best possible world appears not to be free, because it does not satisfy the contingency condition. One of Leibniz's responses to this argument is that it suffices for freedom, if God's choice is made from among alternatives (i.e., possible worlds) that are internally consistent, that is, 'possible in their own natures', even if only one of them is such that its choice is compatible with God's essential attributes.[257]

In various texts Leibniz extended these ideas to cover nondivine choices – see, for example, *Discours de métaphysique*, Section 13. Thus, according to this account of freedom, even if (2) were metaphysically necessary, Caesar's decision to cross the Rubicon would be free, provided that there were alternatives, each of which was internally consistent, that is, possible in its own nature.

The 'possible in its own nature' strategy was intended to provide some relief with respect to threats to freedom. But Leibniz also noted that considerations similar to those that threaten divine freedom also seem to imply an unacceptable version of necessitarianism. Suppose it is contradictory to hold that God creates any world other than the best possible world. Suppose, further, that whatever possible world is the best, it is so of necessity. Then it seems to follow that it is necessary that if God chooses to create a world then God creates this world, that is, the one that, in fact, is actual. Note that the 'possible in its own nature' strategy will not help with respect to this problem. Leibniz's preferred strategy was to employ the doctrine of infinite analysis as a basis for denying that whatever world is the best, it is so of necessity.[258]

## VIII. POSTSCRIPT

This chapter opened with the following remark: 'Determinism, broadly speaking, is the doctrine that whatever happens in the world is brought about by causes other than itself. In this sense, all the major philosophers of the seventeenth century – with the possible exception of Malebranche – were determinists.' And since these philosophers all ascribed some variety of freedom to human persons, each accepted some version of compatibilism. Yet in the last section of the chapter – the section on Leibniz – we ascribed determinism (and compatibilism) to Leibniz, and noted that determinism and compatibilism were not the common view of the time. That is why Arnauld thought that most of his contemporaries would agree with him that it is heretical to hold (as he took Malebranche to do) that actions of human persons are necessary consequences of the order of nature, that is, necessary consequences of natural laws.

These remarks are not in conflict with one another, if Descartes, Hobbes, Spinoza, Malebranche, Locke, and Leibniz constitute the major philosophers of the seventeenth century. Libertarian positions of various sorts remained alive and well among Catholics philosophising in the scholastic tradition and among many Protestant theologians as well. So Arnauld was undoubtedly right: in terms of numbers, the vote was on his side. What really bothered Arnauld was the metaphysical audacity of these major figures – their willingness, indeed their eagerness, to follow reason based on metaphysical principles wherever it led, unfettered by the absolute requirement of reaching narrowly prescribed 'acceptable' conclusions. And of course, one can understand Arnauld's special contempt for Malebranche, who, Arnauld reasoned, ought to have known better, given his position in the Catholic church.

No doubt our major philosophers were ploughing new ground. Why, then, our initial emphasis on their scholastic background? With the exception of Spinoza and, to a lesser extent, Hobbes, all our major thinkers made an effort to formulate their views in sentences that their audience would find familiar and plausible, at least wherever possible. For the contemporary reader, not to have some grasp of the scholastic tradition is to risk not understanding an essential part of the relevant code. More than that, some of the central scholastic intuitions concerning human freedom had a considerable hold on some of our major philosophers – such as Malebranche, Locke, and Leibniz, whose minds were wrapped up in the primacy of the freedom of exercise (transmuted to the ability to suspend deliberation).

Metaphysical adventuresomeness was not the order of the day for most seventeenth-century philosophers. But it was for these major figures. The intellectual adventures of these thinkers have yet to be fully grasped. One task that needs to be done is to unpack the various concepts of modality that they employed. More daunting is the task of analysing their notions of natural necessity and causality. Until these tasks, and others of comparable difficulty, have been completed, the exact content of the deterministic and compatibilistic theories that arose in the seventeenth century will elude our efforts to determine it.

### NOTES

1 This general account is based primarily on *Summa th.* II.1 q6 aa1–2 and *De malo* q6. For a marvellous discussion of Thomas on human action, see Donagan 1982.
2 Leibniz, *Disc. mét.*, sec. 12.
3 See *Summa th.* II.1 qq7–8 and *De malo* q6.

4 See *Summa th*. II.1 q9 and *De malo* q6.
5 See, e.g., Suárez, *Disp. met*. XIX.6. For a summary of the Thomist response, see Garrigou-LaGrange 1946, vol. 2, chap. iv.
6 *De veritate* q24 a2.
7 *Summa th*. II.1 q9 a1.
8 *Summa th*. II.1 q18 a2
9 *Summa th*. II.1 q9 a3 resp. and *De malo* q6 resp.
10 See, e.g., *Summa th*. II.1 q10 a2 resp. and *De malo* q6 ad 7.
11 See, e.g., *Summa th*. II.1 q13 a6 and q17 a1 ad 3; and *De malo* q6 resp. and ad 15.
12 *Summa th*. II.1 q9 a4.
13 *Summa th*. II.1 q9 a6.
14 Thomas discussed general concurrence in *De potentia* q3 a7; *Summa contra gentiles* Bk. III, chaps. lxvi–lxx; and *Summa th*. I q105.
15 Thomas treated the topic of special concurrence in *Summa th*. II.1 qq109–14 and II.2 qq23–4.
16 Alvarez 1610, p. 113.
17 See, in particular, *Concordia*, disp. 25–8.
18 *Concordia*, disp. 2.
19 Báñez 1942–48, p. 357.
20 *Disp. met*. XIX.4.7.
21 See *Disp. met*. XIX.4.2, 6, and 14.
22 *Disp. met*. XIX.4.10.
23 *Disp. met*. XIX.4.13–14.
24 See Jansenius 1640, vol. 3, Bk. VIII, chap. xx.
25 See, e.g., Jansenius 1640, vol. 3, Bk. VI, chap. iv.
26 AT VII 56; AT VIIIA 19; AT IV 116.
27 AT VII 166; AT XI 359.
28 AT VII 56, 57, 59; AT XI 445; AT V 85.
29 AT VIIIA 17–18; AT VIIIB 363.
30 See AT XI 364, 387.
31 AT VIIIA 17; AT XI 343.
32 AT VII 191; AT VIIIA 18; AT IV 116.
33 AT VII 59; AT IV 175.
34 AT VIIIA 24.
35 AT VIIIA 20; AT IV 173.
36 AT III 360.
37 See AT IV 111, 173.
38 AT VII 58; AT VII 59; AT VII 432–3; AT IV 173.
39 AT VII 58; AT VII 433; AT IV 118.
40 AT VII 58.
41 AT IV 116.
42 AT IV 173.
43 The matter is discussed by, among others, Kenny 1972; Marlin 1985; Moyal 1987; Beyssade 1988; and Petrik 1992.
44 AT VII 40; AT VII 40; AT IV 332; AT VIIIA 61–3; AT XI 354; AT XI 445.
45 AT IV 314.
46 AT IV 116.
47 AT VII 433; AT IV 173.
48 AT IV 295; AT XI 359; AT XI 392.

49  AT I 366; AT VII 166; AT VII 432; AT XI 464.
50  AT VII 87; AT XI 361–2; AT XI 368–70; AT XI 399–400; AT XI 430.
51  AT XI 344.
52  AT VII 60; AT VII 377; AT VIIIB 363.
53  AT XI 372, 430.
54  AT XI 374–8, 436.
55  AT XI 331–42 *et seq.*
56  AT IV 333.
57  AT VII 58.
58  AT VII 433.
59  AT IV 314, emphasis added.
60  AT VIIIA 20.
61  AT IV 314, emphasis added.
62  AT VII 191; AT VIIIA 14; AT VIIIA 20.
63  See *Eng. Works*, vol. 1, p. 10, for the former, and *Lat. Works*, vol. 3, pp. 560–3, for the latter.
64  *Eng. Works*, vol. 4, p. 274.
65  *Eng. Works*, vol. 5, p. 35.
66  *Eng. Works*, vol. 1, p. 122.
67  See, respectively, *Eng. Works*, vol. 4, pp. 247, 268; vol. 1, pp. 121–2; vol. 4, p. 246.
68  *Elements of Law*, p. 62; *Eng. Works*, vol. 3, p. 48.
69  *Eng. Works*, vol. 4, p. 272.
70  *Eng. Works*, vol. 4, p. 274.
71  *Eng. Works*, vol. 5, p. 374.
72  *Eng. Works*, vol. 5, p. 108.
73  *Eng. Works*, vol. 5, pp. 374–6.
74  *Eng. Works*, vol. 5, p. 364.
75  *Eng. Works*, vol. 4, p. 274.
76  *Elements of Law*, p. 63.
77  *Eng. Works*, vol. 3, p. 198.
78  *Eng. Works*, vol. 5, pp. 1–2, 298–9.
79  *Eng. Works*, vol. 5, p. 43.
80  *Eng. Works*, vol. 4, p. 240.
81  *Eng. Works*, vol. 4, p. 273; cf. vol. 2, p. 120 and vol. 3, p. 196.
82  *Eng. Works*, vol. 4, pp. 273–4.
83  Respectively, *Eng. Works*, vol. 3, p. 196; vol. 4, p. 275; vol. 5, p. 365.
84  *Eng. Works*, vol. 4, p. 272; vol. 3, p. 48.
85  *Eng. Works*, vol. 5, p. 346.
86  *Eng. Works*, vol. 5, p. 352.
87  Wernham 1965, p. 119.
88  *Eng. Works*, vol. 3, p. 116; vol. 4, p. 273.
89  *Lat. Works*, vol. 2, p. 95.
90  *Elements of Law*, pp. 61 and 78; *Eng. Works*, vol. 3, p. 48 [twice]; *Lat. Works*, vol. 2, p. 95: the one exception is the passage at *Eng. Works*, vol. 4, p. 273, which prompted Bramhall's charge of inconsistency.
91  *Eng. Works*, vol. 4, pp. 275, 277.
92  *Eng. Works*, vol. 5, p. 385.
93  *Eng. Works*, vol. 5, p. 63.
94  *Eth.* I prop. 11 dem. 2. See also *Eth.* I ax. 3.

95  See, e.g., *Eth.* I prop. 28.

96  *Eth.* I def. 3; prop. 7 dem; def. 6; prop. 14.

97  See *Eth.* I def. 5; prop. 15 dem; prop. 16 and corr.; prop. 25 corr.

98  See *Eth.* I props. 21–3; Curley 1969, chap. 2.

99  See *Eth.* I prop. 25 corr.; prop. 26.

100  *Eth.* I prop. 28; letter 58, Geb. IV 266.

101  We omit here complications arising from the fact that, for Spinoza, the infinitely many extended modes do not causally interact with any of the infinitely many thinking modes; see *Eth.* II prop. 7 schol; *Eth.* III prop. 2.

102  See *Eth.* I prop. 28 schol.

103  *Eth.* I prop. 33.

104  Garrett 1991 discusses the range of competing views while providing a compelling defence of a necessitarian reading of Spinoza.

105  *Eth.* I def. 7.

106  See *Korte ver.* I, chap. 6, §5; *Korte ver.* II, chap. 16.

107  See *Eth.* I prop. 32; *Eth.* II prop. 48.

108  *Eth.* I prop. 17 corr. 2.

109  It is more accurate to speak of particular acts of will than of the will itself since, as we will see, Spinoza denies that there is a faculty of willing.

110  See *Eth.* I prop. 32 and *Eth.* I prop. 32 corr. For some of Spinoza's reservations about how the notion of will is to be applied to God, see *Eth.* I prop. 17 schol.

111  Geb. IV 266. See also *Eth.* I app. (Geb. II 78); *Eth.* II prop. 35 schol.

112  For praise and blame, see *Eth.* I app. (Geb. II 81); *Korte ver.* II, chap. 12, §2. For repentance and self-esteem, see *Eth.* III def. aff. 25–7. For mockery and the like, see *Eth.* IV prop. 50 schol.; *Korte ver.* II, chap. 11, §1. For anger, see *Eth.* III def. aff. 36.

113  *Eth.* IV prop. 50 schol.

114  *Eth.* III prop. 49; *Eth.* V prop. 6.

115  See, e.g., *Eth.* IV prop. 22 corr.

116  See *Eth.* IV prop. 63 corr. and schol.; *Cog. met.* chap. 8 (Geb. I 265); *Korte ver.* II, chap. 18, §5; Letters 58, 78.

117  *Eth.* III pref.

118  We can, for Spinoza, reject the possibility that the thing ceases to exist for no cause at all. For Spinoza, everything has a cause; see, e.g., *Eth.* I ax. 3, and the passage quoted from *Eth.* I prop. 11 dem. 2 at the outset of this section.

119  For a fuller interpretation of *Eth.* III prop. 6 and of Spinoza's notion of striving, see Della Rocca 1996.

120  See *Eth.* III prop. 12 dem. There the claim about striving for increase in power of acting is made for the human mind in particular, but the way in which Spinoza proves this claim indicates that the point would apply to things generally. For the more general claim, see *Korte ver.* I, chap. 5: 'Each thing in itself has a striving to preserve itself in its state, and bring itself to a better one' (Geb. I 40).

121  *Eth.* III def. 2.

122  This and the previous two paragraphs are borrowed from Della Rocca 1996.

123  At one point, Spinoza uses the term 'appetite' for the striving of a human being and seems to restrict the term 'desire' to appetites accompanied by consciousness (*Eth.* III prop. 9 schol.). But, in *Eth.* III def. aff. 1, he indicates that he is also willing to use the term 'desire' more broadly to encompass appetites or human striving in general. I will follow this latter use of the term.

124  We will see later an important way in which Spinoza modifies this general account.

125 See *Eth.* IV prop. 27.
126 Jonathan Bennett 1984, pp. 315–17, and Friedman 1977 also emphasise the importance of degrees of freedom in Spinoza.
127 *Eth.* IV prop. 66 schol.; prop. 67 dem.
128 *Eth.* IV prop. 24 dem.; prop. 63 corr.; prop. 66 schol.
129 See *Eth.* III prop. 39 schol. together with *Eth.* III prop. 11 schol.
130 *Eth.* IV prop. 4 and corr.
131 Cf. *Tractatus politicus,* chap. 2, §§7–11 where Spinoza clearly speaks of human freedom as a matter of degree and contrasts it (in §7) with God's absolute freedom.
132 Which derives from *Eth.* III prop. 12.
133 See *Eth.* III prop. 28; *Eth.* IV prop. 19; *Korte ver.* II, chap. 3, §9. Although such a modification is necessary from the point of view of Spinoza's psychology, it may not fit in well with his naturalistic programme. For it to do so, Spinoza would need to explain how something like the qualification involving belief applies to the strivings of things in general. This he does not do.
134 See *Eth.* III prop. 13 schol.; prop. 39; def. aff. 36; V prop. 5–6.
135 *Eth.* IV prop. 37.
136 See Della Rocca forthcoming.
137 *Eth.* IV prop. 45 corr. 1. See also *Korte ver.* II, chap. 6. In saying that destroying another is never good (in *Eth.* IV prop. 45 dem.), Spinoza seems to be overlooking the possibility (which he himself emphasises in his claims about punishment noted earlier) that although destroying another is an evil, it is, in certain cases, a lesser evil than the alternative. Relatively speaking, such a lesser evil would be a good (see *Eth.* IV prop. 65 and corr.).
138 *Eth.* V prop. 6. For more on Spinoza's techniques for freeing oneself from the passions, see Hampshire 1973; Jonathan Bennett 1984, chap. 14.
139 *Ess.* II.xxi.28.
140 See *Eth.* II prop. 48; letter 2; *Korte ver.* II, chap. 16, §4.
141 *Eth.* IV prop. 7; prop. 15.
142 See *Korte ver.* II, chap. 17, §4.
143 Of course, whether or not one's action successfully realises the desire that one acts on is, in part, up to the external world. In this sense, I can act on a desire without realising that desire.
144 *Lev.* vi. It is interesting to note that in his early work *Cogitata metaphysica,* Spinoza explicitly endorses the view that 'the mind can will nothing contrary to the last dictate of the intellect' (*Cog. met.* II, chap. 12, Geb. I 278).
145 *Eth.* II prop. 49 schol., Geb. II 134. For more on belief and the will in Spinoza, see Curley 1975; Jonathan Bennett 1984, chap. 7; Cottingham 1988.
146 Arnauld 1775–83, vol. 39, pp. 301, 316.
147 Malebranche *OC* VIII 740–1.
148 Malebranche *OC* VIII 716.
149 *OC* I 47 (Malebranche 1980a, p. 5).
150 *OC* V 118–19.
151 See, e.g., *OC* XVI 15.
152 *OC* V 118 (Malebranche 1992b, p. 170).
153 See, e.g., *OC* XVI 17, where Malebranche wrote: 'It is certain that it is necessary that an object pleases before one starts to love it.'
154 *OC* III 32 (Malebranche 1980a, p. 555).
155 Respectively, *OC* III 29 (Malebranche 1980a, p. 553); *OC* XVI 17; *OC* III 29

(Malebranche 1980a, p. 553); *OC* III 29 (Malebranche 1980a, p. 553). See also *OC* XVI 17.

156 *OC* X 66; see also *OC* V 139 (Malebranche 1992b, p. 188); and *OC* VII 353.

157 See, e.g., *OC* V 125 (Malebranche 1992b, pp. 176–7).

158 See *OC* VII 345–75.

159 See *OC* V 131 (Malebranche 1992b, p. 181).

160 See *OC* VII 350.

161 *OC* VII 353.

162 *OC* VII 356.

163 *OC* III 32 (Malebranche 1980a, p. 555); *OC* VII 353–7. See also *OC* XVI 11–24.

164 *OC* XVI 11.

165 *OC* XVI 11.

166 *OC* XVI 11.

167 Arnauld 1775–83, vol. 39, pp. 74–5.

168 *OC* V 145 (Malebranche 1992b, p. 193); see also *OC* XVI 22.

169 Arnauld 1775–83, vol. 39, pp. 74–5.

170 *OC* VII 415–16. This is an instructive passage. Malebranche wrote it in 1687 with his mature views on grace, freedom, predestination, and foreknowledge fully formed. There is ample reason to take him at his word that up to that point he had not read Molina. There is considerable evidence to suggest that Malebranche passed through his entire lifetime without reading Molina. It is entirely salutary that historians of early modern philosophy are paying increasing heed to the late mediaeval and Renaissance background of their subject. But it is important to take into account exactly what the philosopher under investigation knew of that background. It is worth remembering that we are not studying historians of philosophy; for the most part we are studying philosophers, whose familiarity with the texts of those whose names they bandied about may be surprisingly meagre. This is particularly true in matters of philosophical theology where intellectual issues often become politicised, involving disputes among various religious orders within the Catholic church, and between Catholics and Protestants. It is especially true of Molina, who, among non-Jesuit Christian theologians of the seventeenth century, seems to have been frequently mentioned, often vilified, but rarely read.

171 *OC* XVI 43.

172 *OC* XVI 40.

173 *OC* XVI 40.

174 *OC* I 46 (Malebranche 1980a, pp. 4–5).

175 See, e.g., *OC* I 48 (Malebranche 1980a, p. 5); *OC* II 142 (Malebranche 1980a, p. 347).

176 See *OC* III 17–32 (Malebranche 1980a, pp. 547–55).

177 *OC* VII 565–8.

178 See *OC* XVI 40–5.

179 In this chapter, the views attributed to Locke are those maintained in all five of the earliest editions of the *Essay*, unless indicated otherwise: either that the view in question was first introduced in the second, fourth or fifth edition, or that it was abandoned after the first, third, or fourth edition (the second and third editions are virtually identical).

180 *Ess.* II.xxi.8.

181 Respectively, *Ess.* II.xxi.10, 8, 10.

182 For Hobbes's use of 'necessary', see sec. III of this chapter; for Calvin's, see the

*Institutio christianae religionis,* I.xvi.9, II.ii.7, II.iii.5, and II.v.1; for Hume's see *Treatise of Human Nature,* II.iii.1–2, and *Enquiry concerning Human Understanding,* viii.

183 *Ess.* II.xxi.14

184 See *Eng. Works,* vol. 4, p. 265; Cudworth 1838, pp. 24–6.

185 *Ess.* II.xxi.22.

186 *Ess.* II.xxi.22.

187 *Nouv. ess.* II.xxi.23.

188 *Ess.* II.xxi.25–6.

189 See the text in the first edition of *Ess.* II.xxi.29 (Locke 1975, p. 248 n).

190 See the text in the first edition of *Ess.* II.xxi.33 (Locke 1975, pp. 257–8 n) and in the second to fifth editions of *Ess.* II.xxi.50.

191 The quotation is from II.xxi.56, 5th ed. Limborch exerted this pressure on Locke in a series of letters, beginning in 1700, concerning the latter's doctrine of freedom and motivation, as it had been stated in the second edition of the *Essay.* These letters, together with Locke's replies, were first published in Locke 1708; they are included, with English translations and helpful notes, in de Beer's edition of Locke's correspondence; see Locke 1976–92, vol. 7, pp. 167–695 passim.

192 *Ess.* II.xxi.56.

193 See, e.g., *Ess.* IV.x.3. But see Locke 1823, vol. 4, p. 61, and 1990b, pp. 31–2.

194 Text of first edition, *Ess.* II.xxi.29 (Locke 1975, p. 248n). This statement dropped out of subsequent editions, but Locke certainly did not give up the principle.

195 Text of first edition, *Ess.* II.xxi.29 (Locke 1975, p. 251 n).

196 Text of first edition, *Ess.* II.xxi.37 (Locke 1975, pp. 269–70 n).

197 Locke 1976–92, vol. 4, pp. 600–601. Molyneux was evidently a disciple of the libertarian William King, author of the celebrated *De origine mali,* whose criticisms of the *Essay's* account of freedom Molyneux forwarded to Locke: see Locke 1976–92, vol. 4, p. 540.

198 Text of second to fifth editions, *Ess.* II.xxi.31.

199 Text of second to fifth editions, *Ess.* II.xxi.30.

200 Text of second to fifth editions, *Ess.* II.xxi.37, 33, respectively.

201 Text of second to fifth editions, *Ess.* II.xxi.45 (twice), 69, respectively.

202 Text of first edition, *Ess.* II.xxi.28 (Locke 1975, p. 248 n).

203 Text of second to fifth editions, *Ess.* II.xxi.47.

204 Text of first edition, *Ess.* II.xxi.30 (Locke 1975, pp. 250–1 n; note the explicit compatibilism of this last-quoted statement). This continues through the first-edition text of *Ess.* II.xxi.33 (Locke 1975, p. 259 n).

205 Text of second to fifth editions, *Ess.* II.xxi.47.

206 Text of second to fifth editions, *Ess.* II.xxi.48.

207 Text of fifth edition, *Ess.* II.xxi.56; here Locke does not distinguish the freedom of exercise from that of specification.

208 See Locke 1976–92, vol. 7, pp. 368–9 (Locke) and 370 (Limborch).

209 Thomas Aquinas, *Summa th.* II.1 q8 a3 resp.

210 One such is Edmund Law: see King 1781, pp. 214–16 n. 48.

211 Text of second to fifth editions, *Ess.* II.xxi.47.

212 Text of second to fifth editions, *Ess.* II.xxi.48; cf. text of first edition, *Ess.* II.xxi.30 (Locke 1975, pp. 251–2 n).

213 Ger. VI 29 (Leibniz 1951, p. 53).

214 See, e.g., *Disc. mét.,* sec. 13, where Leibniz commenced with the remark: 'But before proceeding further we must try to meet a great difficulty that may arise from the

foundations we have laid.' There Leibniz recognised that his views about the completeness of individual concepts appear to generate problems with respect to freedom.

215 Ger. VI 413 (Leibniz 1951, p. 418).
216 Ger. VI 390 (Leibniz 1951, p. 395).
217 *Théod.*, sec. 292.
218 Bayle, *Réponse aux questions d'un provincial* (1704–6), pt. III, chap. 140, in Bayle 1727, vol. 3.
219 *Concordia* II.14.
220 *Conversatio cum Domino Episcopo Stenonio de libertate* (1677), Leibniz 1982–91, vol. 2, p. 302.
221 Here is a small sample of the texts in which Leibniz made this claim: LAkad. VI.III 132; Ger. I 148 (Leibniz 1969, p. 204); Leibniz 1948, pp. 276–7; LAkad II.I 514–15; Ger. III 402 (Leibniz 1989, p. 194); and Leibniz 1948, pp. 479.
222 Ger. II 420.
223 Ger. III 133.
224 Akad. VI.VI 181.
225 See Robinet 1955, p. 421.
226 *Nouv. ess.* II.xxi.8.
227 See, e.g., *Du franc arbitre* (1678–82), Leibniz 1982–91, vol. 1, pp. 7–10.
228 See, e.g., Leibniz 1948, pp. 125–6.
229 LAkad. II.I 117 (Leibniz 1969, p. 147).
230 LAkad. II.I 118 (Leibniz 1969, p. 147).
231 See, e.g., Leibniz 1948, p. 299; *Nouv. ess.* II.xxi.13; and Ger. II 418.
232 Respectively, Leibniz 1948, p. 299; Ger. VII 108; *Théod.*, sec. 400.
233 Ger. II 91–2.
234 For further statements of the principle of spontaneity, see the *Système nouv.:* Ger. IV 484 (Leibniz 1973, p. 122); 'Metaphysical consequences of the principle of reason', Leibniz 1903, p. 14 (Leibniz 1973, p. 175); *Nouv. ess.* pref., LAkad VI.VI 65; *Mon.*, secs. 11 and 22; and *Théod.*, pt. I, sec. 400.
235 Ger. III 364; Ger. VI 572.
236 Ger. III 471; see also 472.
237 Leibniz 1948, p. 327; italics added.
238 Ger. III 168.
239 Others disagree; see, e.g., Broad 1975, pp. 28–31; Borst 1992; and Paull 1992.
240 The terminology is ours; the ideas are Leibniz's.
241 We discuss conceptual determination later in the chapter.
242 For textual bases for attributing these characterisations and theses to Leibniz, see, e.g., *Théod.*, pt. I, secs. 36, 37, 38, 43; and *Causa dei*, sec. 104.
243 Leibniz 1903, pp. 20–1 (Leibniz 1973, pp. 100–101). As of yet, the editors of the Akademie Edition have declined to fix a particular date after 1677; see Leibniz 1982–91, vol. 3, p. 455.
244 Ger. VI 37 (Leibniz 1951, p. 61).
245 As a small sample, see *Théod.*, secs. 44, 302, 367; Ger. III 401 (Leibniz 1989, p. 194); and Leibniz 1948, pp. 480–1.
246 Ger. III 401 (Leibniz 1989, p. 194).
247 Arnauld 1775–83, vol. 39, p. 301.
248 Arnauld 1775–83, vol. 39, p. 316.
249 Leibniz 1903, p. 20 (Leibniz 1973, p. 100).
250 See Leibniz 1948, pp. 384–6.

251 On the first point, see Leibniz 1948, p. 302. At Leibniz 1948, pp. 125–6, Leibniz noted that the ability to suspend the decision-making process cannot be essential to freedom per se, since suspension is a result of ignorance, which is lacking in God, who is nonetheless free. On the second, see *Disc. mét.*, sec. 16.

252 See, e.g., *Nouv. ess.* II.xxi.47; Ger. VI 413 (Leibniz 1951, p. 418); *Causa dei*, sec. 105, Ger. VI 427 (Leibniz 1951, p. 433).

253 See, e.g., *Nouv. ess.* II.xxi.47 and Ger. VI 413 (Leibniz 1951, p. 418).

254 Leibniz 1903, p. 22 (Leibniz 1973, p. 103).

255 See, e.g., *Disc. mét.*, sec. 8.

256 Leibniz's most forthcoming work on the doctrine of infinite analysis is *Generales inquisitiones de analysi notionum et veritatum* (Leibniz 1903, pp. 356–99 (Leibniz 1973, pp. 47–87)). For an effort to understand the doctrine, see Sleigh 1982. For a critical discussion of Leibniz's use of the doctrine to preserve contingency, see Blumenfeld 1984–5.

257 For a discussion of the possible-in-its-own-nature move, with ample textual references, see Adams 1982. For an effort to characterise the relevant notion, see Sleigh 1990a, pp. 80–3. For a critical discussion of Leibniz's use of the doctrine to preserve freedom, see Blumenfeld 1988–9.

258 See, e.g., Leibniz 1948, p. 336.

# 34

# CONCEPTIONS OF MORAL PHILOSOPHY

## JILL KRAYE

A new conception of moral philosophy began to emerge in the seventeenth century. The discipline was no longer to rest on the foundation of authority, whether classical or Christian; it was to become, instead, a systematic science, grounded on logically rigorous deductions from self-evident principles. This rethinking of the epistemological status of moral philosophy took place against the background of a general reaction against ancient authority on the part of contemporary philosophers such as Descartes and Hobbes. Nevertheless, through-out the century, both in the universities and in the popular mind, the traditional forms of ethics, based on classical philosophy or Christian theology, dominated the scene. Ethical thought within the methodological boundaries set by the past – and the majority of works produced in the seventeenth century fall into this category – was not necessarily intellectually stagnant. While some traditional conceptions remained relatively static, others underwent considerable change, occasionally under the impact of the new ethical ideas put forward by the modernists.

The general pattern followed by traditional moral philosophy in the seven-teenth century had been established during the Renaissance.[1] Classical ethics was represented by the four major schools: Aristotelian, Stoic, Platonic, and Epicurean. Christian ethics, whose primary domain was the field of moral theology, was used as a yardstick against which the classical systems were measured; a few thinkers, however, rejected pagan thought completely and wanted to create an independent Christian moral philosophy. The ethical conceptions embodied in these traditions differed considerably in doctrinal content, at times coming into open conflict. What they had in common was a reliance on some form of authority as the principal means of guaranteeing their validity.

## I. THE ARISTOTELIAN TRADITION

Aristotelian ethics, which had virtually monopolised the teaching of moral philos-ophy in universities since the late Middle Ages, continued to be the central tradition throughout the seventeenth century and beyond.[2] The main, but by no means the only, champions of Aristotelianism in Italy and Spain were the Jesuits, who promoted a blend of Peripatetic and Thomist moral philosophy.[3] In France, the standard philosophy course remained a stronghold of Aristotelianism, and ethics, although regarded as propaedeutic to law rather than to theology, also had a strong Thomist orientation, even when taught by non-Jesuits.[4]

Aristotelian ethics was equally strong in the Protestant universities of northern Europe, from Oxford to Uppsala.[5] Peripatetic philosophy had long been firmly entrenched in Dutch higher education, and in the field of ethics at least remained so even after the Cartesian controversies of the later seventeenth century.[6] Nowhere was the Peripatetic hold on the educational system stronger or longer lasting than in Protestant Germany. Well into the seventeenth century, Germany still had no important representative of modernist views to provide a rallying point for the new philosophy – except for Leibniz, whose position at the court of Hanover placed him at the margins of academic life.[7] In this traditional atmosphere, Aristotelian ethics – one of the least vulnerable parts of the corpus in any case – had little trouble maintaining its privileged place in the syllabus.[8]

Yet not all German Aristotelians were hidebound conservatives. Jakob Thomasius, a prominent professor at Leipzig and one of the teachers who most influenced Leibniz, although a steadfast opponent of modern ideas, was nevertheless committed to reforming contemporary Aristotelianism. He wanted to remove the scholastic accretion of centuries and return directly to the text of Aristotle, understood in its historical context and against the background of other classical philosophical systems.[9] Some insight into the way this programme was conveyed in his teaching of ethics can be gleaned from a 1683 Leipzig dissertation by Johannes Geier, for which Thomasius acted as *praeses*. In the thesis, which explores and defends the Aristotelian doctrine of moral virtue as a mean between two extremes, the fundamental agreement of Aristotle's view with that of many other Greek and Roman philosophers, as well as with the Bible, is set out in learned detail. The arguments put forward against the doctrine by three contemporaries – Hugo Grotius, Thomas Hobbes, and Robert Sharrock – are also discussed and then refuted.[10] Geier displays an unusual willingness to engage in debate with modern philosophers, but his firm endorsement of Aristotle is a mark of the undiminished vigour of Peripatetic ethics in late-seventeenth-century Germany.

Since the time of Thomas Aquinas, philosophers and theologians had sought to resolve the conflicts which inevitably arose between the this-worldly Aristotelian conception of moral philosophy and Christianity.[11] The problem still exercised many seventeenth-century thinkers, particularly Protestants. Some wrote treatises which corrected Aristotelian precepts according to Christian norms, while retaining as much genuine Peripatetic doctrine as possible.[12] Others attempted to play down the differences by finding close parallels between Aristotle and the Bible.[13] The question of whether Peripatetic ethics should be taught in Christian schools was a standard topic in Protestant university disputations and was normally answered in the affirmative.[14] But there were some who argued that Aristotle's notions of the supreme good and of virtue were so contrary to the tenets of faith that they had no place in a Christian education.[15]

On the Catholic side, the compatibility of Aristotelian and Christian ethical notions was usually taken for granted. Theologians such as Bishop Bossuet might maintain that the only true morality was to be found in the Gospels, but they readily conceded that Aristotle's *Ethics* contained a number of valuable doctrines and was well worth studying.[16] The scholastic merger of Thomism and Peripateticism taught at most Catholic universities ensured that Aristotle was always assumed to be in agreement with Christianity, but this could involve considerable hermeneutic gymnastics. For example, the desire to identify Christian good works with the highest good in this life led French professors to explain away Aristotle's commitment to the superiority of contemplation over action by arguing that it applied not to our present condition but to the state of pure nature in which man existed before the Fall.[17]

Traditional commentaries on Aristotle declined in popularity during the seventeenth century, particularly after 1620.[18] Expositions of the *Ethics* shared this general fate, but decreasing numbers were matched by increasing bulk. The massive two-volume commentary written towards the middle of the century by Tarquinio Galluzzi, a Jesuit professor at the Collegio Romano, comprises almost 1,900 folio pages (many of them double-columned) and is probably the largest work ever devoted to the *Nicomachean Ethics*. The vastness of Galluzzi's erudition almost justifies the size of his commentary. He draws on a huge amount of classical, patristic, mediaeval, and Renaissance material, which he fits into a standard scholastic scheme, with summaries, divisions, and explanations of the text (given in both Greek and Latin) followed by a series of *quaestiones*.[19] The *Philosophia moralis* (1698) of Cardinal José Sáenz de Aguirre is not quite on the same monumental scale as Galluzzi's commentary, but it is equally encyclopedic in its sources; and even though written at the very end of the century, it still retained the scholastic format and gave overwhelming preference to Thomas Aquinas as the 'most faithful interpreter' of Aristotle.[20] Samuel Rachelius, the German editor of a 1660 edition of the *Ethics*, presented his commentary in the form of a lengthy – 150 pages – introductory essay, which provided a potted history of philosophy from the Persians and Chaldeans to the Italian Renaissance, as well as an in-depth, and at times critical, analysis of Aristotle's ethical doctrines.[21]

Whereas Latin commentaries on the *Ethics* were sinking under the weight of their own erudition, vernacular treatments managed to stay afloat by striking a lighter tone. In 1627, Francesco Pona delivered a talk to the Academia Filarmonica of Verona on the moral philosophy of 'il maraviglioso Aristotele'. As a man of letters (a few years earlier he had published *La lucerna,* which recounted the bizarrely pornographic adventures of an oil-lamp) rather than a professional philosopher, his aim was not merely to instruct but also to entertain his aristocratic listeners; he therefore promised to present the Peripatetic rose without the scholastic thorns.[22] The market for such simplified, but elegant, versions of the *Ethics* stayed buoyant even after Aristotle's fortunes had waned in the learned world. The writer who best exploited this popular taste was the ex-Jesuit Emanuele Tesauro. Presenting a lively, uncluttered, and mildly Christianised summary of Aristotle's doctrines, Tesauro's *La filosofia morale* (1670) went through twenty-seven editions in the original Italian over the next hundred years and was translated into Spanish, French, Latin, and Russian.[23]

Commentaries on the *Ethics* also appeared in the form of synoptic tables which reduced the text to a series of logically structured and easily memorised diagrams, providing an ideal crib for university students.[24] Some of these tabular commentaries were strange hybrids, retaining typical scholastic features, such as *dubia* and *responsiones,* but transforming them into Ramist dichotomies.[25]

It was, however, a different type of work which took centre stage in university education in the seventeenth century, replacing the commentary as the main vehicle for Aristotelian exposition. Philosophical textbooks, although containing predominantly Peripatetic doctrine and incorporating a good deal of earlier exegesis, differed from commentaries in that they departed from the order in which Aristotle presented a subject, thereby permitting a more methodical arrangement, as well as facilitating the inclusion of non-Aristotelian material. This meant that metaphysics textbooks could offer a systematic treatment of the miscellany of topics bundled together in Aristotle's text, while those in natural philosophy were free to incorporate new scientific discoveries.[26] Ethics textbooks supplemented their Aristotelian core as well, but what they added did not normally derive from contemporary developments in moral philosophy; it came rather from other classical or Christian authorities – the sort of material which had always played a part, although a smaller one, in the commentary tradition. And though the *Ethics* was a more orderly work than the *Metaphysics,*[27] it, too, was subjected to various schemes of reorganisation.

Catholic textbooks usually placed Aristotle's ethical doctrines in a framework loosely modelled on the *Prima* and *Secunda secundae* of Thomas Aquinas's *Summa theologiae*. The paradigm was established as early as 1593, when the Jesuits of Coimbra published their *cursus* on Aristotle's *Ethics*. It was divided into nine *disputationes,* which followed a Thomistic rather than an Aristotelian topical arrangement: the good, the end, happiness, the three principles of human actions (will, intellect, and sensitive appetite), the good and evil of human actions, the passions, the virtues in general, concluding with prudence and the other moral virtues (justice, courage, and temperance). This scheme, adopted in various permutations by most Catholic writers, allowed for significant departures from Aristotle's treatment of ethics. In particular, much space was devoted to scholastic rather than Peripatetic topics such as the will, the passions, and the influence of God, angels, and demons on human actions.[28] Also, the four cardinal virtues, originally a Platonic-Stoic scheme but Christianised by Saint Ambrose and widely adopted throughout the Middle Ages, took precedence over Aristotle's more complex programme of five intellectual and eleven moral virtues. As with later authors, the Coimbra Jesuits' use of a very wide range of sources did not prevent them from consistently endorsing Aristotle's views, usually in the Christianised versions presented by Thomas Aquinas.[29]

One of the most influential French manuals, used in Protestant as well as Catholic countries, was the *Ethica* of the Cistercian Eustachius a Sancto Paulo, first published in 1609 for the philosophy course at the Sorbonne. It covers the same basic Thomistic topics as the Coimbra cursus, but organises them under three main headings: happiness (including the good and the end), the principles of human actions, and human actions themselves (including the passions, virtues, and vices). In subjects not treated by Aristotle (free will or supernatural happiness in the afterlife) the material is taken from Thomas, the Bible, or various patristic and mediaeval writers. Elsewhere, however, Aristotle remains the primary source, even when a non-Aristotelian scheme is endorsed: the definitions of the individual cardinal virtues, for instance, are all taken from the *Nicomachean Ethics.*[30]

The many Catholic textbook writers who followed in Eustachius's footsteps were likewise concerned to draw on Aristotle's authority, even when departing from his arrangement. Chapters might be structured according to a Thomist pattern, but they were supported wherever possible by quotations from Aristotle.[31] Some authors made no bones about the fact that they were pouring Aristotelian wine into Thomist bottles.[32] But others presented their works as if they were commentaries on the *Ethics,* even though their organisation (and some of their material) bore no relation to Aristotle's text.[33] Jacques Channevelle gave perhaps the most accurate description of such textbooks in his title *Ethica seu Philosophia moralis juxta principia Aristotelis,* moral philosophy not according to Aristotle, but according to Aristotelian principles.

Catholic textbooks used a scholastic method of exposition: questions or doubts were raised and then answered; assertions were made and then proved; conclusions were reached and then confirmed. At each of these stages arguments were based on authority or reason. Aristotle was, of course, the primary authority, followed closely by Thomas Aquinas;[34] but the Bible, Church Fathers (especially Saint Augustine), pronouncements of church councils and papal bulls all counted as authoritative.[35] Classical philosophers apart from Aristotle, when not brought in simply to be disagreed with, as they commonly were,[36] tended to play an ancillary rôle in support of the major authorities.[37] Other philosophical schools were, however, given more of a voice in their particular areas of specialisation: Platonists on love, for instance, or Stoics on remedies for the passions.[38]

The second pillar of scholastic argumentation was reason, usually presented in the form of a syllogistic demonstration. Sometimes the syllogisms were based on experience, induction, or logical principles such as Ockham's razor.[39] But frequently the reasons used to prove an argument were taken directly and explicitly from Aristotle, Thomas, or some other authority. In such cases, reason did not have a completely independent validity, but was to some extent validated by its association with authority.[40]

While scholastic disputes dating back to the late Middle Ages were often rehearsed in these textbooks,[41] contemporary philosophical issues were almost never aired. The Jesuit Channevelle joined the anti-Machiavelli campaign (by his time well over a century old) with a rebuttal of the Florentine's 'impious and false' assertion that Christianity had undermined the virtues of courage and magnanimity; but his polemic, which focused on the bravery of Christian martyrs, was essentially religious rather than philosophical.[42] Like other members of his order, Channevelle also used his textbook as a platform to attack Jansenist beliefs on original sin and free will, citing Aristotle – along with Augustine, Thomas, and Pope Innocent X – in support of Jesuit positions.[43]

Protestant textbooks differed from Catholic ones in two important respects: they abandoned, or at least radically simplified, scholastic modes of exposition, favouring a more straightforward presentation of material; and their organisation was not based on the Thomist paradigm, but on systematic schemes designed to serve pedagogical, not theological, purposes. The most common scheme divided ethics into two parts: *eudaimonologia,* dealing with happiness, the goal of ethics; and *aretologia,* dealing with virtue, the means to reach that goal.[44] This arrangement did not deviate as much from Aristotle's as the Catholic textbooks did: *eudaimonologia* usually dealt with *Nicomachean Ethics* I and X.6–8, while *aretologia* was structured around the Aristotelian, rather than the cardinal, virtues.[45]

Bartholomaeus Keckermann's *Systema ethicae* was written for his students at the Danzig Academy, and its aim was to present Aristotelian material in a more methodical fashion than Aristotle himself had done. To this end, he produced for each topic a list of rules, *canones,* which summarised the main points to be studied, remembered, and put into practice.[46] Such lists streamlined Aristotle's teaching, making it easier to assimilate, but in the process the subtlety of his aporetic style of argument was left behind.

The passion for order, characteristic of these systematic manuals, found another outlet in dichotomisation: dividing, subdividing, and subsubdividing every concept or topic in sight. The Calvinist Clemens Timpler, for instance, divided moral virtue into piety, which entailed living according to the rules of Christianity, and probity, which entailed behaving virtuously, either towards oneself (moderate self-love, temperance) or towards others, benefiting them either as individuals (mercifulness, civility) or as members of society (liberality, justice).[47]

Timpler's division of moral virtue into piety and probity was taken over by the Leiden professor Franco Burgersdijck (Burgersdicius). He treated the eleven Aristotelian moral virtues as species of probity but admitted that piety towards God was not a subject which could be learned from Aristotle, the prince of human (but not divine) wisdom. Consequently, his information in this case had to be taken from the Pythagoreans and Platonists. Since, however, he regarded all pagan treatments of piety as deeply inadequate, these were included simply to demonstrate how little we can know of God without supernatural illumination.[48] Burgersdijck composed his ethics handbook because philosophy students were deserting the subject, impatient at the time it took to work through Aristotle's *Ethics.* By producing a well-organised compendium, which covered the same territory but reduced it to a manageable size, he hoped to lure them back.[49] Each of his twenty-four chapters was divided into numbered paragraphs composed of pithy sentences, usually backed up by Aristotelian references. Citations from the Bible, as well as from classical and patristic authors, added a bit of flesh to the Peripatetic bones and filled in the odd gaps such as piety. Unusually for a Protestant, Burgersdijck made considerable (although not uncritical) use of Thomas Aquinas, including – in the manner of Catholic textbooks – a detailed discussion of the passions, which presented a modified version of Thomas's views.[50]

Burgersdijck's student Adriaan Heereboord took over not only his teacher's position at Leiden but also his general approach to ethics. In his natural philosophy textbook, Heereboord concluded each chapter with theses that challenged traditional doctrine; these were partly taken from Descartes and other contemporary philosophers, partly his own.[51] But in his ethical works he showed no sign of modernist sympathies – even his discussion of the passions, where one might have expected some Cartesian influence, was clearly modelled on Burgersdijck's Thomist account.[52] Heereboord seems to have had no interest in new conceptions of moral philosophy; he had chosen Aristotle as his guide in this field and intended to stay within the Peripatetic tradition, making corrections and additions where necessary, but not redrawing the boundaries set by the ancients.[53]

## II. THE STOIC TRADITION

Stoicism, unlike Aristotelianism, was never part of the university philosophy curriculum. Professors of moral philosophy were often knowledgeable about Stoic doctrines,[54] especially after the publication of Justus Lipsius's *Manuductio ad Stoicam philosophiam* (1604), which drew together and explicated the available Greek and Latin sources. But rather than exploring the merits of Stoicism as an alternative ethical system, they focused solely on its weak points – its total rejection of the passions and apparent endorsement of insensibility – which were used to highlight the superiority of the Peripatetic tradition.[55] Yet though the Neostoic revival did not make much headway in the universities, it did succeed in popularising Stoic moral philosophy with large sectors of the literate and cultured public. This audience learned about Stoicism not through textbooks and scholarly Latin treatises but through popular vernacular writings: works of literature and philosophical *haute vulgarisation,* religious tracts, and psychological self-help manuals.[56]

The vogue for Stoicism in France began in the late sixteenth century with Guillaume Du Vair's French version of Epictetus's *Enchiridion*; this frequently reprinted work initiated a spate of translations of Epictetus, Seneca, and, to a lesser extent, Marcus Aurelius, which took Stoic moral philosophy to a large readership.[57] Du Vair also produced elegantly written tracts in which Stoic and Christian themes were skilfully intermingled so as to heighten their similarities and disguise their differences.[58] This sort of Christian Stoicism soon ran into difficulties with those of a more discriminating religious sensibility; but as late as 1688 Nicolas Coquelin still had enough confidence in the essential harmony of the two ethical systems to combine his French translation of Epictetus with a series of moral reflections taken from the New Testament.[59]

The similarity of Stoic and Christian beliefs was an important theme in the abbé d'Aubignac's *Macarise,* a baroque allegorical romance 'containing the moral philosophy of the Stoics under the veil of many pleasant adventures'. In a long preface, d'Aubignac explains the symbolism behind his sprawling narrative: the heroine Macarise stands for Stoicism and her rescuer Prince Cléarte for Zeno; the hero's eventful life (in particular his war against the Moors) represents man's efforts to conquer his passions and attain complete emotional tranquillity. In the telling of the tale, artistic concerns come a poor second to didactic ones: the action is frequently interrupted by long-winded speeches, in which leaden characters present Stoic doctrines (contempt for worldly goods and for death) in terms of Christian dogma (immortality of the soul).[60] The problematic aspects of Stoicism, such as its sacrilegious treatment of the wise man as a god, were no longer a concern, as d'Aubignac explained to the book's dedicatee, Louis XIV, for the sect had now 'voluntarily submitted itself to the Gospels'.[61]

Some French religious thinkers shared this belief that Stoicism, or at any rate some aspects of it, could be converted to the service of Christianity. But in doing so they tended to subordinate its tenets so thoroughly to the demands of faith that the Stoic component became almost unrecognisable. In the writings of the Capuchin Sébastien de Senlis, quotations from Seneca and Epictetus appear side by side with citations from the Bible and patristic writers, the authority of classical antiquity apparently lending support to that of Christian antiquity. In reality, however, the meaning of the Stoic statements is often totally transformed, even deformed, by the religious context in which they occur. Transposing this-worldly pronouncements to a supernatural plane, Senlis changes Stoic virtue from an end in itself to a means of reaching God, Stoic nobility from a disdain for earthly goods to a concern for heavenly ones, and Stoic reason from the master of man to the servant of God. The words remain pagan, but the sense has become completely Christian.[62]

Other religious authors took a more critical, at times hostile, approach towards Stoicism, rejecting as un-Christian its human-centred arrogance and its belief that virtue, not God, was the supreme good.[63] Representative of the attitudes of this group was the treatise *De l'usage des passions* (1641) by the Oratorian Jean-François Senault. The margins of this work are liberally sprinkled with quotations from Seneca; but these are used to incriminate the philosopher and his sect, to demonstrate that the Stoics' futile attempt to repress the passions was a sign of their overbearing pride and their refusal to accept their own humanity. Countering the misguided and morally suspect views of Seneca, Senault used the impeccable authority of Augustine to prove that the passions need only be moderated, with the aid of grace, to be transformed into virtues and thus fulfil God's providential plan for mankind.[64]

In response to such aggressive attacks, the supporters of Stoicism mounted a defensive action. The battle was not between ancients and moderns, but between two opposing ancient conceptions of moral philosophy, with both sides employing the same traditional weaponry. Even Antoine Le Grand, an admirer of Descartes, constructed his passionate defence of passionlessness, as he indicated in the title, 'According to the Views of Seneca'. His opponents were identified as the Peripatetics past and present who had slandered the Stoics, while his allies were 'the greatest minds of antiquity' (Tacitus, Tertullian, Clement of Alexandria), who had all defended the sect. Like Senault, Le Grand was keen to claim Augustine for his side, especially in his dispute with the arch-Augustinians of his day, the Jansenists, over whether original sin had destroyed man's natural capacity to avoid vice, practise virtue, and triumph over the passions.[65]

The Spanish satirist Francisco de Quevedo was unwilling to settle for the authority of a mere Church Father, preferring to call upon the Bible itself. According to Quevedo, the Book of Job was the literal source of Epictetus's philosophy of resignation and of his famous doctrine that only things within our power, such as virtue, were of any value. In an introductory essay to his verse translation of the *Enchiridion* (1635), Quevedo put forward his far-fetched thesis (an oversimplified version of a suggestion in Lipsius's *Manuductio* I.10) that Zeno had learned of the Bible through Phoenician connexions and had transmitted this knowledge to members of his school, who developed the ideas contained there until they reached their culmination in Epictetus. In line with his desire to prove the biblical origin of Stoicism, Quevedo also wanted to minimise any differences between Stoic and Christian morality; he therefore glossed over various areas of conflict, maintaining, for instance, that it was not *feeling* passions but giving in to them which the Stoics had condemned.[66] Quevedo, like Du Vair and many other Christian Stoics, was essentially a religious propagandist, concerned to use Stoicism to promote Christian values; if to do this, improbabilities had to be swallowed and distinctions blurred, it was a price he was more than willing to pay.

Quevedo spent some time at the Spanish court, where he met and became friends with the Italian political writer Virgilio Malvezzi, at the time serving as royal historiographer to Philip IV. Quevedo had already made a Spanish translation of Malvezzi's *Il Romulo,* and the two authors shared an interest in popularising a Christianised form of Stoicism. Malvezzi's belief in disinterested virtue as an end in itself was rooted in Stoic moral philosophy; and one of the key themes in his works was the attempt to overcome the inevitable conflict between Christian morality and the sort of political prudence that was associated, particularly in the works of Lipsius, with Seneca and Tacitus.[67] Malvezzi recognised that even a good prince might occasionally be forced by inexorable circumstances to employ means which were not entirely Christian.[68] But he soundly condemned the Machiavellian strategy of turning religion into a mere instrument of political policy.[69] The Jesuit Sforza Pallavicino, a nephew of Malvezzi, was no devotee of Stoicism: he regarded its ancient followers as the Pelagians or – far worse – the Lutherans and Calvinists of paganism. Yet, partly out of family loyalty and partly out of a typically Jesuit concern to endow pragmatism with religious respectability, he applauded Malvezzi's efforts to reconcile political prudence and Christian piety, claiming that his precepts were more prudent than those of worldly-wise Machiavellians and more pious than those of other-worldly theologians.[70]

In England, too, Stoic moral philosophy was closely connected with Senecan-Tacitean political ideas. In the early years of the seventeenth century, English adherents of Stoicism tended to see the murky moral climate of the court of James I as analogous to that of Rome under Tiberius.[71] Religion, here as elsewhere, also played an important rôle in the reception of Stoicism, with both Catholics and Protestants treating Stoic virtue as a stepping-stone to Christian morality.[72] But, as always, there were problems in reconciling the two sets of values in relation to issues such as the passions. The ex-Jesuit Thomas Wright and the Anglican bishop Edward Reynolds both condemned 'Stoical apathie', not least because Christ himself 'sometimes loved, sometimes rejoyced, sometimes wept, sometimes desired'; moreover, as Wright noted, 'the Scriptures exhort us to these passions. . . . "Be angry, and sinne not."'[73]

The widespread opposition to this Stoic doctrine was equally based on non-religious grounds, above all, the conviction that it was psychologically impossible to repress the passions.[74] As Robert Burton wrote in *The Anatomy of Melancholy*:

> The *Stoicks* are altogether of opinion . . . that a wise man should be *apathes,* without al manner of passions and perturbations whatsoever. . . . *No Mortall man is free from these perturbations:* or if he be so, sure he is either a God, or a blocke. They are born and bred with us, we have them from our parents by inheritance.[75]

For this reason those who believed themselves to have achieved Stoic imperturbability were often portrayed in literature as either fools or hypocrites (or both). The self-deceiving Stoic became a stock figure on the English stage, literally so in the case of Ben Jonson's 'Stoick i' the stocks', the pompous Justice Overdo in *Bartholomew Fair,* whose claim to regard his imprisonment with Stoic detachment – 'I doe not feele it, I doe not thinke of it, it is a thinge without mee' – provokes the scoffing response: 'The Foole is turn'd Philosopher' (IV.vi.95–103). There were, of course, English writers who displayed a more sympathetic attitude towards Stoicism: George Chapman, of Homeric fame, wrote poems based on Epictetus, while John Dryden praised the Stoics as 'the most noble, most generous, most beneficial to human kind, amongst all the sects, who have given us the rules of ethics', although in summarising these rules he was careful to omit those controversial doctrines which had long been criticised by Christian thinkers.[76]

## III. THE PLATONIC TRADITION

Since the time of Augustine, the closeness of Platonism to Christianity had been its strongest selling point. This notion had been given a new lease of life in the late fifteenth century by Marsilio Ficino, whose particular brand of Christian Neoplatonism − emphasising an idealised, mystical notion of love, both of and for God, as the dynamic force in the cosmos − dominated the reading and interpretation of Plato for at least three centuries.[77]

The cleric Julien Davion gave his account of Socratic philosophy, published in 1660, the subtitle, *Le Crayon du Christianisme en la philosophie de Socrate,* and explained that the purpose of the work was to demonstrate that Socrates had been able to perceive, even through the mists of paganism, many Christian truths which present-day *libertins,* despite being illuminated by faith, were too blind to see.[78] Davion shows how Socrates, the most virtuous of pagans, had anticipated Christian dogma, not only on doctrinal issues such as the immortality of the soul and the creation of the world, but also in the sphere of morality: his self-control, modesty, and humility were so near to the spirit of the Gospels that had they been preached in Athens during his lifetime, he would very probably have embraced them. Davion even suggests that Socrates may have been the instrument God used to convey certain Christian truths *avant la lettre* to the gentiles, just as he used Saint Paul, five centuries later, to bring the fully revealed message to the same audience.[79] Ficino's influence comes through most clearly in Davion's belief that the central doctrine of Socrates' teaching was the soul's union with God through love. But Davion balances Ficino's other-worldly mysticism with an emphasis on this-worldly morality, seeing in Socrates' unwillingness, at the end of the *Apology,* to seek revenge on those who had unjustly condemned him to death a prefiguring of Christ's injunction to love one's enemy.[80]

The affinity of Platonism with Christianity was a vital element in the resurgence of interest which occurred around mid-century in England. The poet Thomas Traherne, although trained in Aristotelian moral philosophy at Oxford, turned his back on this tradition when he produced his *Christian Ethicks* (1675), in which he brought together Platonic and Christian treatments of virtue. Traherne made no effort to keep the Platonic strands in his work separate from the Christian ones but instead wove the two into a seamless unity. It was a practical demonstration of his conviction, held by Ficino as well, that 'Faith is by reason confirmed and Reason is by Faith perfected.'[81]

Traherne's fellow Platonic enthusiasts in Cambridge also believed that true philosophy was in fundamental harmony with true religion. Although the light of nature, which had illuminated Plato and his pagan followers, could not reveal the deepest mysteries of theology, it could nevertheless provide insight into the 'first and Radical Principles' of morality.[82] This insight was achieved, according to Ralph Cudworth, not through empirical sense perception, but through knowledge of the ideas of goodness and evil, justice and injustice, which exist innately in the human mind but which derive ultimately from eternal and immutable archetypes in the mind of God. Cudworth based this moral epistemology explicitly on Platonic and Neoplatonic sources, but his motives for constructing the theory were related to contemporary issues. With this one ancient stone he intended to kill two modern birds: voluntaristic theology and ethical relativism.

Near the beginning of *A Treatise concerning Eternal and Immutable Morality*, published posthumously in 1731, Cudworth records the opinion of 'divers Modern Theologers' who contend that 'There is nothing Absolutely, Intrinsically and Naturally Good and Evil, Just and Unjust, antecedently to any positive Command or Prohibition of God; but that the Arbitrary Will and Pleasure of God . . . is the first and only Rule and Measure thereof.' Although Cudworth traces this doctrine back to the 'Scholastick Age', his real opponents are Descartes and the English Puritans, who 'think nothing so essential to the Deity, as Uncontrollable Power and Arbitrary Will'.[83] For Cudworth, however, God's chief attribute is His goodness;[84] he therefore argues that the good is not good because God wills it, but rather that God, who is goodness, wills the good *because* it is good. For Cudworth, goodness and justice are Platonic ideas, that is, real entities, which are what they are 'not by Will but by Nature'. And just as God cannot 'by Meer Will make a Thing White or Black without Whiteness or Blackness', so He cannot make things 'Morally Good and Evil, Just and Unjust, Honest and Dishonest . . . by meer Will, without any Nature of Goodness, Justice, Honesty'.[85]

Even more dangerous to morality was the view that 'Nothing was Good or Evil, Just or Unjust . . . absolutely and Immutably, but Relatively to every Private Person's Humour or Opinion.'[86] According to Cudworth, the first expression of this relativism could be found in the view attributed to Protagoras in the *Theaetetus* (177D): 'Whatsoever any City thinks to be Good and Just, and decrees them such, these things are so in that City.'[87] But what he was actually worried about was the modern version of this theory presented by 'that late Writer of Ethicks and Politicks', who had maintained in his *Leviathan* that in the state of nature 'nothing can be Unjust; the Notions of Right and Wrong, Justice and Injustice have there no Place; where there is no Common Power, there is no Law; where no Law, no Transgression.'[88] Cudworth prescribed the same remedy for ethical subjectivism as he had for theological voluntarism: the epistemology of Plato and Plotinus, which demonstrated the reality, universality, eternity, and immutability of notions such as right and wrong, justice and injustice. In *The True Intellectual System of the Universe* (1678), Cudworth attacked Hobbesian materialism as a pernicious form of atheism; in the *Treatise,* he shows that materialism and atheism are the inevitable concomitants of relativism, for those who believe that notions such as justice and honesty are 'but thin, airy and phantastical Things, that have little or no Entity or Reality in them' do so because they think that 'Matter and Body are the first Original and Source of all Things; that there is no Incorporeal Substance superior to Matter and independent upon it'; and if this is true, 'There cannot possibly be the least Shadow of Argument left to prove a Deity by.'[89] Once again Platonic philosophy provided the antidote to these poisonous doctrines with its ontological principle that 'Mind and Intellect is in it self a more real and substantial Thing, and fuller of Entity than Matter and Body.'[90] Since he regarded Hobbes as a latter-day Protagoras, bent on destroying the foundations of morality and religion, it was natural for Cudworth to use against him what he regarded as the authoritative arguments of Plato, ignoring the fact that his opponent was playing according to an entirely new set of philosophical rules.[91]

Samuel Parker, as a Baconian empiricist and an ardent supporter of experimental science, was deeply suspicious of the Cambridge revival of Platonism, which in his view was 'an ungrounded and Fanatick Fancy'. But while his *Free and Impartial Censure of the Platonick Philosophie* (1666) was highly critical of Platonic epistemology and metaphysics, because they led men away from observation and towards 'Subtle Speculations', it was very sympathetic towards Platonic morality. Indeed, Parker granted Platonism 'Signal Preheminence' over other ethical systems on the grounds that 'the Rules and Directions it prescribes are Sober and Practicable.'[92] This was in striking contrast to the Stoics, the Platonists' 'only Rivals in morality', whose impracticable precepts were based on 'Paradoxes against the convictions of Sense and Experience'.[93] The somewhat unexpected qualities which Parker praises in the Platonists appear to have been chosen primarily to emphasise the deficiencies of Stoicism: he commends the Platonists for their willingness to enjoy life's 'innocent pleasures and sensualities' so that he can condemn the Stoics for their 'scornful & Frierly contempt of every thing'; and he compliments the Platonists for their 'skill in all the Arts of behaviour and conversation' (Plato, he tells us, was 'no Athenian cockney', but rather an accomplished courtier 'admired and envied for the unaffected Gracefulness of his addresses') as a means of criticising the Stoics for their 'insolent and supercilious' conversation and their 'soure and morose behaviour'. When he finally drags in the 'rude and ill-natur'd Pharisees', who 'accounted their own Sect the only School of Sanctity', just as the 'Stoicks esteem'd themselves the only Sons of wisdom, and all other Children, Fools, and Madmen',[94] it becomes clear that the Stoics were standing in for another group much closer to home: the Puritans, those zealous killjoys, convinced of their own election and of the damnation of everyone else. Three years later, Parker, soon to be appointed bishop of Oxford, took his attack on Puritanism out into the open with his Erastian treatise *A Discourse of Ecclesiastical Politie*. What had been presented as a confrontation between the Platonic and Stoic moral philosophy was in reality an attempt to enlist Plato as an ally in Parker's own campaign against contemporary opponents. That he believed such an effort to be worthwhile indicates that ancient authority still carried considerable weight in Restoration England – even among fellows of the Royal Society.

## IV. THE EPICUREAN TRADITION

The process of rescuing Epicurean ethics from its popular image as a philosophical justification for self-indulgent hedonism began in the Renaissance.[95] By the seventeenth century, enough ancient evidence had been uncovered for a few scholars to start calling into question some of the old myths of amoral sensuality. On the other hand, Epicurus's denial of immortality and divine providence and his placing of pleasure above virtue still prevented his entry into the ranks of respectable moral philosophers.[96]

One attempt to remedy this situation came from the pen of the Spanish Neo-Stoic Quevedo, whose *Defensa de Epicuro* (1635) was published together with his treatise on Stoic moral philosophy. The reasons for this odd coupling are revealed in the work itself, which calls on Seneca, a sincere if reluctant admirer of Epicurus, as the star witness for the defence, and tries to rehabilitate Epicureanism by minimising its differences with Stoicism. Where an Epicurean error, such as the denial of providence, had to be admitted, Quevedo palliated the crime by noting that the true doctrine was not available to any pagan philosopher. Another stratagem he employed was to turn the tables on those classical opponents who had slandered Epicurus by directing his own satirical skills against them, with Cicero – not only a bigot but a lawyer to boot – receiving the brunt of the sarcasm.[97]

Similar tactics were used to much greater effect by Pierre Gassendi, the first scholar to succeed in making Epicureanism palatable to a modern audience. As a Catholic priest, he was an unlikely patron of an ancient philosophical system widely regarded as incompatible with Christianity. But his keen interest in the new mechanistic science and attraction to Epicureanism atomism made him want to present the whole philosophy in an acceptable form. Gassendi had begun his philosophical career with a frontal attack on Aristotelianism, the *Exercitationes paradoxicae adversus Aristoteleos* (1624). When this provoked more opposition than support, he changed his strategy and started promoting Epicureanism as an alternative to the entrenched Peripateticism of the schools.[98] Unlike contemporaries, such as Hobbes, who shared his hostility to Aristotle and his sympathy for mechanism, Gassendi did not want to overthrow the authority of the ancients; he merely wanted to replace one ancient authority with another. Because his attitude towards classical philosophy remained traditional (even his scepticism went under the banner of Sextus Empiricus), so did his methods of argumentation and presentation. In his works, Gassendi was every inch the Renaissance humanist, sifting through an enormous amount of ancient evidence and constantly drawing on his skills as a classical philologist to interpret the Greek and Latin texts on which he based his case.[99]

Gassendi had to overcome two major problems before Epicurean physics could replace Aristotelian natural philosophy as the theoretical foundation of seventeenth-century science: he had to rid Epicurus of his damaging reputation as an immoral voluptuary; and he had to purge ancient atomism of its atheistic connotations. The first aim was achieved in his *De vita et moribus Epicuri* (1647). While he by no means denied that Epicurus, like other pagans, held erroneous theological beliefs, Gassendi nevertheless argued that the four main charges which had been levelled against him – impiety, lack of respect for others, devotion to corporeal pleasure as the supreme good, and contempt for learning – were trumped up. Quevedo saw Cicero as the main culprit responsible for libelling Epicurus, but Gassendi pointed the finger of guilt at the Stoics, whose haughty disdain for this rival sect he believed to be motivated by their envy of its popularity.[100] Gassendi removed the other obstacle to the acceptance of Epicureanism in his last and most ambitious work, the *Syntagma philosophicum*, in which he accommodated the corpuscularian hypothesis to the teachings of the church by replacing the infinite, eternal, and self-moving atoms of Epicurus with a finite number of atoms, created and set in motion by God.[101]

Epicurean ethics required similar adjustments before it could be regarded as completely suitable for Christians. So Gassendi, just as he had inserted God into Epicurean atomism, added him to the moral system by postulating that the pleasure principle was part of a grand providential plan. God had ensured the continuing existence of all creatures by making those things which were necessary for their survival pleasurable: 'and the more necessary the action was to be, either for the preservation of the species as a whole or for that of each individual living thing, the more powerful he wanted the pleasure to be.'[102] Gassendi developed his version of Epicurean ethics not only in response to the needs of the church, but also in reaction to the moral implications of Hobbes's materialistic determinism. While Hobbesian psychology used the model of inertial motion to limit human behaviour to a series of necessary reactions to external stimuli, Gassendi safeguarded free will by insisting that although appetite was determined – it naturally followed the good, just as a stone fell downwards – reason remained free. Drawing on the Epicurean calculation of pleasure and pain, he demonstrated that human reason, acting on the basis of an informed understanding of the true nature of happiness (freedom from mental anxiety and bodily pain), had the capacity to overrule the merely reactive movements of the appetite and passions.[103] In this way the Epicurean pleasure principle, safely Christianised by having God as its author, helped Gassendi to avoid the determinism of Hobbes's philosophy.

Gassendi's eloquent defence of Epicurus finally laid to rest the popular misconceptions about the man and his philosophy, establishing unequivocally that he had lived a virtuous life and advocated an entirely virtuous sort of pleasure, one which Christians could indulge in without moral qualms. Backed up by Gassendi's scholarly researches, vernacular writers now promoted Epicurean ethics as a more realistic and agreeable alternative to the rigorous demands of the Stoics, whose moral credentials had been called into doubt by the revelation of their spiteful treatment of Epicurus.[104] Antoine Le Grand, who had previously written in defence of Stoic ethics, switched his allegiance to Epicureanism, although he – like Quevedo – made an effort to reconcile the two schools,[105] presenting Epicurean pleasure as virtually indistinguishable from Stoic virtue.[106] The rehabilitation of Epicurus was so successful that by 1679 the Huguenot Jacques Du Rondel could describe him as a paragon of virtue, temperance, responsible citizenship, and even religious piety: according to Du Rondel, although Epicurus believed that the gods did not concern themselves with the workings of nature, he thought they played a supervisory rôle in moral matters – rather like the elders in a Calvinist community.[107]

Gassendi, drawing on a strong tradition of French Lucretian scholarship, had made extensive use of *De rerum natura* in his expositions of Epicureanism.[108] While the poem's main importance was as a source of natural philosophy, it also contained some Epicurean ethical insights, which became available to a wider audience with the publication of a number of French translations in the second half of the century. Gassendi himself apparently spent his last days revising the French version of Michel de Marolles.[109] Even Molière tried his hand at Lucretius, although the results, unfortunately, do not survive.[110] The French translation of Jacques Parrain begins with a preface in which he tries to neutralise the religious objections that Lucretius's work inevitably aroused. First, he suggests that certain offensive passages on the mortality of the soul (e.g., III.1073–4) should be taken out of context and read in the light of Christian revelation; then, he points out that Lucretius attacked the superstition of ancient polytheism; finally, he falls back on an argument previously used by Quevedo and Gassendi: 'Is there any pagan philosopher the majority of whose opinions are not contrary to our religion?'[111] Parrain went on to write *La Morale d'Epicure* (1695), which consists of his 'réflexions' on ethical maxims taken from Diogenes Laertius's life of Epicurus. Building on Gassendi's condemnation of Zeno and his sect for their deliberate misrepresentation of Epicurean doctrines, Parrain turns his treatise into a sustained invective against the pride, vanity, and hypocrisy of Stoic ethics. Epicurean moral precepts, by contrast, are shown to be reasonable, sincere, and, not infrequently, in conformity with Christianity.[112]

As happened in France, Epicurean moral philosophy entered England on the coat-tails of Epicurean atomism. The English intellectual climate was by no means favourable for either: in the popular mind, the term 'Epicurean' stood for licentious living or atheism. It was Walter Charleton, an enthusiast for the new mechanistic philosophy, who managed to overcome these difficulties and get Epicurus a hearing from the English public. Helped by his royalist connexions and his impeccable religious credentials, Charleton gave English Epicureanism what Gassendi had given the French variety: respectability. He had learned from Gassendi, whose work influenced him greatly, that Epicurean atomism could not be taken up by contemporary science unless certain religious and moral objections to the system were answered. Beginning in 1652, he began to write tracts which publicised the scientific virtues of the atomist hypothesis while condemning and correcting the theological errors associated with it. He presented a sanitised version of the ethical philosophy in *Epicurus's Morals* (1656), prefaced by 'An

Apologie for Epicurus', in which he described the philosopher as a 'Master of Temperance, Sobriety, Continence, Fortitude and all other Virtues', whose reputation had suffered from 'that unjust odium and infamy, which envy and malice . . . have cast upon it'.[113] In Charleton's account of Epicurean ethics, virtue was not the primary means to pleasure, it was the *only* means; and the bulk of the treatise was devoted to showing that each of the cardinal virtues was 'inseparably conjoyned to Pleasure'.[114] This interpretation was given greater currency when repeated a few years later in the third volume of Thomas Stanley's *The History of Philosophy,* which gave a detailed exposition of Epicureanism based on Charleton, Gassendi, and Diogenes Laertius.[115]

The text of Book X of Diogenes Laertius, the most important ancient source for Epicurean ethics, as well as the most sympathetic, was not translated into English until 1688.[116] Lucretius got into English somewhat earlier and was more widely read, but this proved to be a mixed blessing for the Epicurean camp. John Evelyn's pedestrian version of Book I and the anodyne essay which accompanied it made little impact.[117] Thomas Creech's complete version, on the other hand, went through six editions and attracted a good deal of attention. While Creech was a genuine admirer of Lucretius's poetry, he was not a whole-hearted supporter of his philosophy, nor even a half-hearted one: the reason he gave for translating the poem was that exposing the ideas it contained was 'the best method to overthrow the Epicurean Hypothesis (I mean as it stands opposite to Religion)'. Creech complimented the poet on 'his excellent discourses against the fear of Death, his severe dehortations from Covetousness, Ambition, and fond Love', but denounced his denial of providence, which led to 'monstrous Opinions (the Fortuitous concourse of Atoms, the rise of Man out of the ground, like a Pumkin etc.)'. In addition, as a firm believer in the divine right of kings, he condemned the account given by Lucretius in Book V of the rise of societies, for it implied that they are 'founded on Interest alone, and therefore self-preservation is the only thing that obliges Subjects to Duty'. Creech knew that the contemporary resonance of such ideas would not be lost on his readers: 'The admirers of Mr. Hobbes may easily discern that his Politicks are but Lucretius enlarg'd.'[118]

The Hobbesian associations of *De rerum natura* were also noted by Dryden, in the preface to his translation of selected passages from the poem. Commenting on the supreme confidence which Lucretius had in the validity of his own opinions, Dryden wrote: 'I know none so like him, as our Poet and Philosopher of Malmsbury', but while 'our Hobbs' must at least have doubted 'some eternal Truths which he has oppos'd', Lucretius was such a dogmatic atheist that (an unforgivable sin) 'he forgot sometimes to be a Poet.' Dryden was quick to point out the disastrous moral consequences of the Epicurean rejection of immortality ('Who wou'd not commit all the excesses to which he is prompted by his natural inclinations, if he may do them with security while he is alive, and be uncapable of punishment after he is dead!'). He nevertheless found much of practical value in Lucretian ethics, particularly the discussion of love in Book IV, which he described as 'the truest and most Philosophical account both of the Disease and Remedy, which I ever found in any Author'.[119]

In spite of continuing reservations about the theology of Epicureanism,[120] the threat posed by its moral philosophy had been largely defused by the mid-1680s. Sir William Temple's *Garden of Epicurus* (1685) took the now-familiar line, established by Gassendi and promoted by Charleton, that there was an inexorable connexion between pleasure and virtue. He drew attention as well to the large area of common ground between Epicurean and Stoic ethics, although the Stoics received the usual chiding for their slander of Epicurus and their inhuman desire to repress the passions. Instead of Stoic apathy, Temple opted for the Epicurean conception of happiness: mental tranquillity and physical well-being, symbolised by the idyllic life led by Epicurus and his followers in the Athenian Garden. This setting took Temple naturally into the second half of his treatise, an elegant and leisurely disquisition on 'Gardening in the year 1685'. The notorious image evoked by the Garden of Pleasures had now become a wholesome (and very English) vision of the pleasures of gardening.[121]

### V. THE CHRISTIAN TRADITION

Christian ethics, aside from being used as a standard by which the various classical systems were judged, played an independent rôle in the field of moral theology.[122] One of the most popular genres in this area, during the seventeenth century, was casuistry, the application of general moral principles to particular cases, known as *casus conscientiae*, 'cases of conscience'. The genre, which developed during the Middle Ages, went through something of a renaissance in the seventeenth century, with a large number of works being produced by both Catholic and Protestant authors.

Catholics tended to make a strict separation between moral philosophy and moral theology, the latter being left entirely in the hands of theologians.[123] Among theologians, it was the Jesuits who specialised in casuistry, provoking their perennial opponents, the Jansenists, to attack the entire genre as sophistry in the service of moral laxity.[124] Jesuit manuals were aimed at a clerical readership and designed as guides to confessional practice. They took their general ethical principles from the Bible, but the interpretation of these principles relied heavily on a long tradition of scholastic and ecclesiastical exegesis. Consequently, it was *de rigueur* for all points to backed up with a long list of authorities: mediaeval theologians (above all, Thomas Aquinas), church councils (especially Trent), and canon law; biblical citations were relatively scant, references to previous Jesuit commentators abounded.[125] Most of the questions to be resolved were directly related to religious issues – sacraments, heresy, blasphemy – but some occupied the border between theology and ethics: whether physiognomy, chiromancy, and natural astrology were permissible (yes); whether duels were legal (if the cause was just); and even whether a bookseller should sell prohibited or pornographic works (no).[126]

Reformed theologians were initially averse to casuistry, regarding it as a Catholic preserve whose associations with the confessional booth were too close for comfort. By the seventeenth century, however, Protestants had come to see the usefulness of such works and wanted to produce ones which reflected their own theological orientation.[127] Taking as little as possible from their 'papist' predecessors,[128] they fashioned a new type of manual: based almost exclusively on the Bible;[129] shunning the scholastic format adopted by Catholic authors in favour of simple questions and answers or short numbered statements;[130] and aimed, in England at least, at a lay as well as a clerical audience.[131] The distinction between moral theology and moral philosophy, firmly maintained among Catholics, was sometimes blurred by Protestants. The casuistical manual of William Ames, an Englishman who taught in the Low Countries, included detailed discussions of moral virtues such as courage, temperance, and constancy, while Adriaan Heereboord's ethics textbook contained several sections dealing with cases of conscience, in which the views of 'Doctissimus Amesius' were frequently cited.[132]

Ames did not, in fact, believe that moral philosophy was an autonomous discipline. In his view, theology was the sole guide to behaviour, and Scripture the only valid source of ethical precepts. His ethical textbook, entitled *Medulla theologica,* relied entirely on biblical authority and was designed to replace Aristotelian manuals, from which students imbibed such impious doctrines as the conviction that happiness began and ended with man and could be achieved by purely human means. Ames, moreover, rejected the Peripatetic definition of moral virtue as a mean between two extremes, asserting (as Grotius had done) that in virtues such as the love of God, it was maximum intensity rather than moderation which was valued.[133]

Although a few Germans and Scandinavians also attempted to abandon pagan moral philosophy entirely,[134] most Protestants who wrote on Christian ethics took a much less radical position. Daniel Whitby, author of the *Ethices compendium,* was influenced by Ames's *Medulla* and like him insisted that Scripture was a 'perfect and complete rule for our actions'. Notwithstanding, he adopted a number of Peripatetic doctrines and occasionally cited classical as well as biblical texts – his chapter on friendship has far more references to Cicero and Aristotle than to the Bible.[135] Even more compromises with the Aristotelian tradition were made by the Socinian Johann Crell. He wrote two treatises, issued together in 1663: one presented a version of Peripatetic ethics corrected according to the norms of Christianity; the other, entitled *Ethica christiana,* explained all the references to virtues and vices found in the New Testament. Unlike Ames, Crell treated scriptural discussions of moral virtues such as justice and courage as supplements to, rather than as substitutes for, their Peripatetic counterparts, even providing cross-references to the relevant passages in his Aristotelian textbook. Again in contrast to Ames, he not only endorsed the Peripatetic doctrine of the mean, he extended its application to biblical virtues not mentioned by Aristotle, such as spiritual joy and Christian concord. Above all, Crell was careful to point out that Christian virtues did not abolish those discussed in pagan moral philosophy but instead directed them towards their final and true goal.[136]

## VI. FROM TRADITIONAL TO GEOMETRICAL CONCEPTIONS OF MORAL PHILOSOPHY

For the general public and for those in the universities, traditional conceptions of moral philosophy continued to reign supreme. The authority of ancient thought was, however, increasingly challenged by philosophers and scientists operating for the most part outside the academic world. The aim of many of these thinkers was not merely to replace Aristotelian ideas with mechanistic ones but also to establish entirely new criteria of knowledge, which would resolve the dilemmas provoked by the rise of scepticism. One aspect of this epistemological revolution was the attempt to extend the absolute certitude of mathematics to philosophy by adopting the axiomatic method of geometry, with its iron-clad demonstrations and indisputable conclusions. In itself there was nothing particularly new about this idea: since the twelfth century religious apologists addressing Moslems, Jews, or atheists, and therefore unable to rely on arguments based on Christian authority, had sometimes found it useful to write theological works *more geometrico*.[137] Certain seventeenth-century thinkers were attracted to this method for a similar motive: it allowed them to make their case without recourse to classical authority. Moreover, the conclusions they reached – like those of geometry – would not be merely authoritative, they would be irrefutable.

This notion represented a particularly dramatic shift for ethics, traditionally regarded as the least certain of the philosophical disciplines. In *Nicomachean Ethics* I.iii (1094b), Aristotle explains that since the topics dealt with in moral philosophy, such as fine and just actions or the nature of the good, 'exhibit much variety and fluctuation', we have to be content with merely indicating 'the truth roughly and in outline' and with reaching conclusions which are 'only for the most part true' and are not as precise as those of mathematics. Mediaeval Aristotelian commentators, on the basis of this and other passages (e.g., *Metaphysics* VI.i), ranked the different branches of philosophy according to their degree of certitude: mathematics and metaphysics on the top; physics in the middle; and ethics at the bottom.[138] This pecking order was widely accepted by seventeenth-century Aristotelian moral philosophers, who acknowledged that their discipline could not provide the certainty of the speculative sciences.[139]

Nevertheless, the axiomatic method of geometry slowly began to appear in ethical works. One of the first was Niels Hemmingsen's *De lege naturae apodictica methodus* (1562). On the basis of the law of nature, which dictated that those things which preserve nature are required by it, Hemmingsen proposed certain immutable, infallible, and indubitable axioms, such as the principle that virtue was to be sought and vice avoided.[140] Using this and other self-evident axioms, he demonstrated various hypotheses concerning morality. Although some of these demonstrations rested on the foundation of previously proven theorems, as the geometrical method prescribed, others used arguments based on classical or biblical authority.[141] The same sort of mixed method is found in Francesco Pavone's *Summa ethicae* (1620). As in geometrical works, it begins with definitions, which are then used as the basis for a series of propositions. But Pavone's definitions are all taken from classical and mediaeval authorities, while his propositions are organised into typical scholastic *quaestiones*. All that Pavone did, in fact, was to take over a few formal structures from geometry; and his reason for doing so was that he wanted to increase the clarity, not the certainty, of his arguments.[142] As Euclidean axiomatics gained in prestige, geometrical terminology became fairly commonplace in ethics textbooks; but this amounted to little more than the use of fashionable words (*axioma*) for old-fashioned concepts (precept).[143]

It was not the trappings of the Euclidean method which interested Descartes, but the possibility of transferring the certainty and self-evidence of mathematical reasoning to other fields of learning.[144] His stress on starting from clear and evident first principles and reaching indubitable conclusions through rigorous chains of deduction clearly owed much to the geometrical model; he himself even described his physics as 'nothing other than geometry'.[145] It was because the ancients had not followed such strict procedures in their philosophy that they had not been able, according to Descartes, to achieve the solid results which his methodological reform was intended to ensure.

At the beginning of the *Discours de la méthode* (1637) Descartes, while conceding that the ancients' 'writings on morals contain many very useful teachings and exhortations to virtue', compared their works to 'very proud and magnificent palaces built only on sand and mud'.[146] He returned to this metaphor in Part III, describing his 'provisional moral code' as a temporary accommodation to shelter him while rebuilding his philosophical house on more secure foundations. Although he did not go out of his way to admit it, in constructing this new abode he borrowed a few planks from the ancient edifices he had pulled down: his third maxim ('to try always to master myself rather than fortune') has strong Stoic overtones and is based on the Epictetan distinction between things which are within our power and those which are not.[147] Residual admiration for Stoicism later led him to choose Seneca's *De beata vita* as a suitable text for discussion in his correspondence with Princess Elisabeth; but, on rereading the treatise, he discovered that it was 'not sufficiently accurate to deserve to be followed'. Seneca, he complained, had not taught 'us all the principal truths whose knowledge is necessary to facilitate the practice of virtue and to regulate our desires and passions'.[148] Not just the Stoics, but all classical moral philosophers, had failed to deal adequately with the problem of the passions, as he proclaimed in the opening of *Les Passions de l'âme* (1649): 'The defects of the sciences we have from the ancients are nowhere more apparent than in their writings on the passions', which were 'so meagre and for the most part so implausible' that he felt it necessary to depart completely from the paths they had followed.[149]

Descartes's new approach to this problem was based on the conception of moral philosophy he had enunciated in the preface to the French edition of his *Principia Philosophiae* (1644), *Les Principes de la philosophie* (1647): ethics, along with medicine and mechanics, were branches of a philosophical tree, whose trunk was physics and whose roots were metaphysics.[150] Because his treatment of the passions grew out of his physical account of the relation between body and soul, which in turn was grounded on his metaphysical distinction between thinking and extended substance, Descartes believed that he was able to provide those necessary 'principal truths' lacking in Seneca. Unlike the ancients, he was writing not as an orator or a moral philosopher but 'en physicien', as a scientist.[151] Though he was willing to transform the study of the passions into a science, he felt that it was too dangerous to attempt a complete system of morality,[152] nor did he think such an ethical science would ever be able to attain the same level of certainty as mathematics or metaphysics. For all his rejection of Aristotelian philosophy, Descartes maintained the traditional belief that moral knowledge had only a limited certitude, sufficient for all practical purposes, but not as secure as the absolute truths of the speculative sciences.[153]

The task of constructing a Cartesian science of ethics fell to the master's by no means uncritical disciple, Nicolas Malebranche. He, too, believed that there was an epistemological gulf between the speculative truths of geometry and the practical truths of ethics; but in his idiosyncratic brand of Cartesianism, the standard Aristotelian distinction was placed in an Augustinian-Platonic framework: inquiries such as geometry which dealt with relations between pure and unchanging ideas were always self-evident and clear, whereas those such as ethics which concerned relations between embodied and changeable things were necessarily uncertain and 'surrounded by great obscurities'.[154] Nonetheless, at least some moral truths – those which involved only our reason and not our senses – were known to us with the same clarity, distinctness and hence certainty as mathematical concepts, for example, that 'God, having created everything for himself, made our intellect to know him and our heart to love him.'[155]

This 'incontestable principle' became the central axiom from which Malebranche, in his *Traité de la morale* (1684), deduced a science of ethics which would rectify the past mistakes of moral philosophers. Their failure to make any significant progress over six thousand years of human history was due to several factors: a tendency to rely on the authority of other men, whether Aristotle or Descartes, rather than on their own God-given rational faculty; the ease with which they, like all men after the Fall, allowed themselves to be seduced by the senses and imagination rather than make an effort to seek out the less glamorous but far more valuable counsels of reason; finally, their lack of orderly procedures, such as those which guided geometers, who did not attempt to solve complex problems until they had established the simple principles on which they depended.[156] Malebranche's ethical system, by contrast, was logically derived from our reason's clear and distinct knowledge that 'God loves order himself and irresistibly wills that we should love it.' Even though we have only a confused understanding of 'the relations of perfection which are the immutable order which God consults', it is sufficient for us to 'discover that there are some things more perfect, more valuable, and consequently more worthy of love than others' and to regulate our own love and esteem according to this divinely sanctioned hierarchy of values. For

Malebranche, the disinterested and self-sacrificing love of this immutable order was not 'only the chief of all moral virtues but the only virtue . . . the mother virtue, the fundamental, universal virtue', from which all other virtues could be deduced, not with geometrical precision, but by means of a methodical progression from the eternal truths known by the light of reason to their particular manifestations in the temporal order.[157]

Unlike Descartes and Malebranche, Hobbes did not recognise any distinction between speculative and moral certitude. He believed that moral philosophy had the potential to become a completely certain demonstrative science, with a procedure as rigorous and results as infallible as those of mathematics. To achieve this goal ethics would have to be put on a scientific footing, and in Hobbes's view 'the onely Science that it hath pleased God hitherto to bestow on mankind' was geometry.[158] In the first half of his life, his intellectual interests and pursuits were those of a late Renaissance humanist. It was not until his forties that Hobbes began to appreciate the philosophical possibilities of the geometrical method; but with the enthusiasm of a late bloomer, he made up for lost time by developing an ambitious programme for the application of the axiomatised system of Euclid to moral philosophy.[159]

As with other modernists, Hobbes had nothing but contempt for traditional moral philosophy, describing it as a 'counterfeit and babbling form' of ethics, 'exposed and prostitute to every mother-wit'. Its manifest inadequacies had given rise to 'such siding with the several factions of philosophers, that the very same action should be decried by some, and as much elevated by others'. The consequence of centuries of pointless squabbling was 'that what hath hitherto been written by moral philosophers, hath not made any progress in knowledge of the truth', and this in turn had led to 'offences, contentions, nay, even slaughter itself'. 'Geometricians', on the other hand, 'have very admirably performed their part', for all benefits that have accrued to man through astronomy, geography, navigation, 'finally whatsoever things they are in which this present age doth differ from the rude simpleness of antiquity, we must acknowledge to be a debt which we owe merely to geometry. If the moral philosophers had as happily discharged their duty, I know not what could have been added by human industry to the completion of that happiness, which is consistent with human life.' To achieve such results, they would have to employ 'an idoneous principle of tractation', one which, like that of geometry, reached conclusions which no one could deny, since they were based on firmly established principles 'demonstrated by a most evident connexion'.[160] Traditional moral philosophers, the sort who dominated 'the Universities of Christendome', did not ground their doctrines on such scientific procedures, but 'upon certain Texts of Aristotle'. In Hobbes's view, those 'that take their instruction from the authority of books' were 'below the condition of ignorant men', for 'there can be nothing so absurd, but may be found in the books of Philosophers.' The main reason for this was that 'there is not one of them that begins his ratiocinations from the Definitions, or Explications of the names they are to use; which is a method that hath been used onely in Geometry; whose Conclusions have thereby been made indisputable.'[161] Hobbes therefore made exact definitions the cornerstone of his new method. There were to be no 'round quadrangles', no 'incorporeall substances' in his system, only clearly defined, logically sound and consistently used terms. His readers would not have the slightest doubt about the meaning of such crucial words as will, felicity, opinion, liberty, contract, and justice, nor would there be any confusion as to the difference between a right of nature and a law of nature.[162]

While definitions provided the foundation, Hobbes still needed axioms and theorems, the building blocks with which he could construct a truly scientific moral philosophy. Here he turned partly to Galileo, borrowing the concept of inertial motion as the basis for his mechanistic account of human psychology,[163] and partly to a careful scrutiny of himself. It was Hobbes's firm conviction that 'Wisdome is acquired, not by reading of Books, but of Men'; and the best primary source which each man could consult was himself: 'Whosoever looketh into himself, and considereth what he doth, when he does think, opine, reason, hope, feare, &c . . . he shall thereby read and know, what are the thoughts, and Passions of all other men, upon the like occasions.' Hobbes, having read 'in himself, not this, or that particular man; but Man-kind', asked his readers to confirm his results by doing the same, 'for this kind of Doctrine, admitteth no other Demonstration'. So even though he wanted to devise an ethical system which would ensure demonstrative certitude, he could provide no other sanction for the validity of his axioms than the claim that they were founded on 'experience known to all men and denied by none'.[164]

The most important of Hobbes's supposedly self-evident axioms was the 'first and Fundamental Law of Nature; which is, to seek Peace, and follow it', from which he deduced another eighteen laws or 'Theoremes'. The science of these laws, according to Hobbes, was 'the true and onely Moral Philosophy'. What differentiated this conception of moral philosophy from the traditional one was not the content of these laws, which endorsed the standard Christian virtues ('Justice, Gratitude, Modesty, Equity, Mercy'). It was rather that their methodical derivation from the fundamental law of nature demonstrated for the first time the true nature of these virtues, which did not consist, as the previous 'Writers of

Morall Philosophie' (i.e., Aristotle and his followers) had maintained, 'in a mediocrity of passions', but in the fact that they were the 'meanes of peaceable, sociable, and comfortable living'.[165]

Although Hobbes went out of his way to stress that his new ethical science supported rather than undermined conventional morality, even maintaining that its basic premise was tantamount to the Golden Rule,[166] many contemporaries believed that his materialism, determinism, ethical relativism, egoistic psychology, and putative atheism posed a serious threat to Christian values. Some traditional moral philosophers attempted to counter Hobbes's ideas with traditional methods: Cudworth and Gassendi drew on the philosophy of Plato and Epicurus, respectively, to challenge certain assumptions of Hobbesian ethics.[167] Others, however, chose to fight Hobbes on his own ground using his own weapons. Henry More's *Enchiridion ethicum* (1667) is essentially a Christianised version of the *Nicomachean Ethics*. More's treatment of the passions, however, is explicitly Cartesian, while his insistence on the existence of an inclination towards love and benevolence, deriving from what he terms the 'boniform faculty', a divinely inspired moral force within the soul, is an implicit attack on Hobbesian egoism.[168] Like his fellow Cambridge Platonist Cudworth, More frequently drew on the authority of the ancients to support his arguments,[169] although unlike him he cited Aristotle far more than Plato. But More felt it necessary as well to present his case in the same systematic manner as his opponent Hobbes. Therefore, at the beginning of the book he produced twenty-three 'noemata' or axioms, which he claimed were 'immediately true and needed no proof'. These noemata, which played a fairly limited rôle in the work as a whole, were for the most part simply statements of generally accepted moral truths, two of which were identical in content to Hobbes's laws of nature.[170]

A more thorough-going use of the new method of moral philosophy is found in Bishop Richard Cumberland's *De legibus naturae* (1672). He also challenged Hobbes's assumption that men were governed by egoism and self-interest, arguing that human behaviour was instead motivated by benevolence and altruism. After establishing the pursuit of the common good as the fundamental law of nature, Cumberland followed Hobbes's procedure of deducing all rules of morality from this single principle, illustrating his points not with citations from classical philosophers, as More had done, but with examples taken from geometry and algebra.[171] The trend towards mathematical rigour in moral reasoning continued to be a strong force in English ethical thought. Locke's belief that it was theoretically possible for 'the measures of right and wrong' to be derived 'from self-evident

Propositions, by necessary Consequences, as incontestable as those in Mathematicks', was turned into a definite programme by Newton's friend Samuel Clarke, whose Boyle Lectures of 1705 consisted of an exposition, modelled on mathematics, of fifteen propositions concerning morality and religion.[172]

But the most elaborate and consistent attempt to present a geometrical version of moral philosophy was Spinoza's *Ethica ordine geometrico demonstrata* (1677). Methodologically, this work represented the culmination of two seventeenth-century currents: the desire, expressed by Descartes, to integrate ethics into a total philosophical system; and the belief, most forcefully stated by Hobbes, that moral thought could attain the same degree of demonstrative certitude as mathematics. Spinoza carried both these trends to their logical conclusion, treating the ethical sections of the work (III–V) as part of a tightly interlocking structure, grounded on metaphysics (I) and psychology (II) and demonstrated with the full complement of Euclidean paraphernalia: definitions, axioms, postulates, propositions, corollaria, scholia, and lemmata.

The geometrical method suited Spinoza's philosophy in a number of ways. His monistic metaphysics, which stipulated that nothing could be understood except as an aspect of a single substance, readily lent itself to expression in a unified logical structure consisting of necessarily connected and ordered propositions.[173] Furthermore, his conviction that traditional moral philosophers were wrong to treat man's behaviour as 'outside nature' and therefore not subject to 'the common laws of nature' was underscored by his adoption of an approach which demanded that he 'consider human actions and appetites just as if it were a Question of lines, planes, and bodies'. For a philosopher with Spinoza's uncompromising commitment to intellectual honesty, the clarity and precision demanded by the axiomatic form of exposition were obviously attractive, but so too was the fact that by treating 'men's vices and absurdities in the Geometric style' he could 'demonstrate by certain reasoning things which are contrary to reason' and which those who preferred 'to curse or laugh at the affects and actions of men, rather than understand them' proclaimed 'to be empty, absurd, and horrible'.[174] Spinoza was well aware of the resistance his radical new ideas would meet; but he believed that if he could explain and demonstrate his propositions with the same degree of accuracy and certitude as mathematicians achieved, he would be able to convince people to accept notions which they did not find attractive.[175]

Although no one else attempted such a systematic application of the geometrical method to moral philosophy, the modernists eventually succeeded in transforming ethics from an authority-based to a rationally deductive discipline.[176]

They did not, however, achieve the certainty which they sought. Unassailable moral axioms were assailed, irrefutable arguments were refuted and indisputable conclusions were disputed. Far from compelling universal assent, Hobbes's work sparked off heated opposition, while Spinoza did not receive sympathetic attention for over a century. Deductive approaches to moral philosophy were no more effective in producing a consensus on ethical values than the classical traditions they superseded.

## NOTES

1  Kraye 1988.
2  For a survey of the Aristotelian ethical doctrines discussed by early modern moral philosophers (this-worldly contemplation as the supreme good, moral virtue as a mean, the relationship between Aristotelian and Christian ethics), see Kraye 1988, pp. 330–48.
3  For Italy, see R. A. Gauthier 1970, pp. 229–32; and Brizzi 1976, p. 233. For Spain, see Robles 1979, pp. 91–5.
4  Brockliss 1987, pp. 185–7 and 216; R. A. Gauthier 1970, pp. 210–19. The Protestant colleges took a more narrowly Aristotelian approach: see, e.g., Donaldson 1610. It was not, however, until 1644 that ethics became an obligatory part of the Protestant curriculum: Brockliss 1987, p. 186 n. 5.
5  At Oxford, the Laudian statutes of 1636, which remained unchanged for over a century, prescribed the *Nicomachean Ethics* for moral philosophy: Mallet 1968, vol. 2, pp. 319–22. On the strength of Aristotelian ethics at Uppsala in the mid seventeenth century, see R. A. Gauthier 1970, p. 208.
6  Dibon 1954, pp. 15, 59–65; R. A. Gauthier 1970, pp. 220–1. At Leiden, throughout the century, moral philosophy courses were staunchly Peripatetic, as can be gauged from textbooks written by Leiden professors: Burgersdijck 1629; Sinapius 1645; Heereboord 1680. See also Dibon 1954, pp. 59–60, on Petrus Bertius's *Problemata et theoremata ethica*. Student theses at Leiden indicate that even when Aristotelian doctrines were taught in conjunction with those of other classical schools, Peripatetic positions were generally endorsed: see, e.g., Sylvius 1626, sig. A4$^{r\cdot}$ where the Peripatetic account of the supreme good is defended against those of the Epicureans, Stoics, and Platonists; and Vogelsang 1624, sig. A3$^v$; and Le Coq 1626, sigs. A2$^r$–A4$^{r\cdot}$ where the Stoic condemnation of the passions is rejected in favour of Aristotelian moderation.
7  Mercer 1990, pp. 18–29, esp. p. 24.
8  See, e.g., the 1666 statutes of the University of Wittenberg: Friedensburg 1926–7, vol. 2, p. 249; and the ethical theses defended at Wittenberg, with Jacob Martini as *praeses*: Mahnerus 1623. For Helmstedt, see Eichel von Rautenkorn 1654, esp. sig. A3$^{r-v\cdot}$ See also Petersen 1921, pp. 166–79; R. A. Gauthier 1970, pp. 223–9.
9  Mercer 1990, pp. 20–1.
10  Geier 1683. Aristotle's doctrine of virtue as a mean is criticised in Grotius, *De jure belli et pacis,* prolegomena 43–5; Hobbes, *De cive* III.32; and Sharrock, ΥΠΟΘΕΣΙΣ ΗΘΙΚΗ [*Hupothesis ethike*] *de officiis secundum naturae jus,* preface. See also J. Thomasius 1658, a handbook for students which summarises the *Nicomachean Ethics.*
11  Kraye 1988, pp. 342–8.

12 Walaeus 1620; Velsten 1620; Crell 1663; see also R. A. Gauthier 1970, pp. 203–4.

13 Zeisold 1661; see also Petersen 1921, p. 178.

14 See, e.g., Henricides 1627, sig. A3ᵛ: 'An ethica Aristotelis in bene constitutis academiis sit ferenda?'

15 Paulinus 1616; Kelpius and Ericius 1690, p. 74: 'Siluit [Aristoteles] de providentia Dei, de veris actionum humanarum principiis, . . . de vera hujus et futurae vitae beatitate, de ultimo omnium actionum humanarum . . . fine, gloria Dei.'

16 See the *Abrégé de la morale d'Aristote* made for instruction of the dauphin: Bossuet 1964, pp. 317–43.

17 Brockliss 1987, pp. 218–20.

18 Schmitt 1984b, p. 219; Schmitt 1988, p. 804.

19 T. Galluzzi 1632–45; see also R. A. Gauthier 1970, pp. 230–1. Of the few commentaries produced earlier in the century, two were by Scotsmen: Aidius 1614 and Balfour 1620.

20 Sáenz de Aguirre 1698; in his treatise on virtues and vices, closely based on the *Nicomachean Ethics,* he described Thomas as the 'fidelissimus . . . interpres' of Aristotle: Sáenz de Aguirre 1677, p. 139.

21 Aristotle 1660, esp. chap. 8: 'De Aristotele, ejusque in ethicis navata opera, et erroribus quibusdam'; see also Petersen 1921, p. 182.

22 Pona 1627, p. 11.

23 Tesauro 1670; for his handling of Christian themes, see XXI.4: 'Della felicità evangelica'; see also Aricò 1987, pp. 277–85.

24 Stierius 1647, sig. A3ᵛ: 'Praecepta ethicae . . . ex Aristotele . . . collecta, et adjuvandae memoriae causa tabulis synopticis inclusa.'

25 Brerewood 1640.

26 Lohr 1988, pp. 609–38: Schmitt 1988, 1984b; Trentman 1982; Reif 1969.

27 There are only a few structural problems in the *Ethics:* e.g., the discussion of the supreme good is divided between I and X.6–8; and the two books on friendship, VIII and IX, interrupt the account of pleasure, VII.11–15 and X.1–5.

28 Fiering 1981, pp. 80–2.

29 *Collegium Conimbricense* 1957; see, e.g., III.iv.1–2, where an account of 'Diversae philosophorum opiniones' is followed by 'Aristotelis sententia, ejusque comprobatio', ending with a reference to Thomas's *Prima secundae.* The Coimbra ethical *cursus* went through sixteen editions between 1593 and 1631 and was used throughout Europe: Robles 1979, pp. 191–2.

30 Eustachius 1654, III.iii.2; see also Levi 1964, pp. 152–9; Fiering 1981, pp. 79–86. The *Ethica* formed one section of Eustachius's *Summa philosophiae quadripartita,* which went through some thirty editions. For the use of the *Ethica* at Cambridge, see Traherne 1968, pp. xix–xxi.

31 E.g., Bouju 1614, who states in the subtitle: 'Le tout par demonstration et auctorité d'Aristote'; see also R. A. Gauthier 1970, p. 213.

32 Pavone 1633, pp. 2–4, after referring to his work as a compendium of Aristotelian and Thomist moral doctrine, warns the reader, 'Non servamus ordinem quem ille [sc. Aristoteles] in suis moralibus servat'; he does, however, provide an index which keys Aristotle's *Ethics* to the corresponding passages in his work; Melles 1669a, p. 39, after providing a brief summary of the contents of the *Ethics,* states: 'Hoc autem praestabimus cum D. Thoma solitum invententes ordinem.'

33 See Morisanus 1625, p. 670, where the heading 'Disputationes sex, librorum X Ethicorum Aristotelis analysin exhibentes' is followed by Thomist accounts of the passions and the good and evil of human actions.

34 Some authors occasionally (and very cautiously) disagreed with Thomas: Eustachius 1654, pp. 49–50; Dupleix 1610, pp. 31–2.

35 The standard formulae for such arguments were: 'Probatur ex authoritate Aristotelis'; 'Confirmatur ex D. Thoma'; 'Probatur authoritate Scripturae et conciliorum'; 'Probatur ex authoribus sanctis'.

36 Barbay 1680, pp. 104–8, discusses the Stoic and Platonic views of happiness in order to dismiss them in favour of the Peripatetic position; Dupleix 1610, pp. 163–85 and 374–81, does the same with the Stoic and Platonic views of the supreme good and of moral virtues; the Stoic belief that all passions were morally evil was regularly used in this way: Eustachius 1654, p. 82; Channevelle 1666, vol. 2, p. 582; Melles 1669a, p. 99; Barbay 1680, pp. 407–12.

37 Channevelle 1666, vol. 1, p. 10: 'Aristoteli concinit Seneca. . .'; Morisanus 1625, p. 655: 'Probatur ex Aristotele . . . et communi omnium philosophorum opinione'; Melles 1669a, pp. 67–70, cites Boethius, Cicero, Pliny, and Plutarch in support of Thomas.

38 For Plato, see Eustachius 1654, pp. 86–8; and Barbay 1680, p. 420. For Seneca and Epictetus, see Channevelle 1666, vol. 2, pp. 590–5.

39 Pavone 1633, p. 29: 'Probat hanc propositionem experientia'; Channevelle, vol. 1, p. 103: 'Probatur inductione'; Barbay 1680, p. 200: 'Probatur . . . ratione: non sunt multiplicanda entia sine necessitate.'

40 Channevelle 1666, vol. 2, p. 765: 'Ratio . . . est ex Aristotele', and p. 895: 'Probatur non una ratione Philosophi'; Barbay 1680, p. 44: 'Probatur . . . ex natura potentiae vitalis. . . . Hoc argumentum colligitur ex S. Thoma'; Pavone 1633, usually identifies in the margins the sources of his syllogistic arguments.

41 In particular, Scotist-Thomist controversies: over the interconnexion of the moral virtues (Eustachius 1654, p. 111), the superiority of the intellect or the will (Morisanus 1625, p. 663) and the nature of supernatural beatitude (Melles 1669a, pp. 109–14; and Barbay 1680, pp. 115–23).

42 Channevelle 1666, vol 2, pp. 1174–80; see Machiavelli, *Discorsi* II.2.

43 Channevelle 1666, vol. 1, pp. 297–340, esp. p. 340: 'Totus plane noster est Aristoteles, ex cujus principiis libertas indifferentiae probari potest'; see also Brockliss 1987, pp. 222–7.

44 Heereboord 1680, p. 432: 'Receptissima est distributio ethicae in partes duas, in *eudaimonologian* et *aretologian,* id est, in doctrinam de beatitudine . . . et de virtute'; Stierius 1647, p. 1; Heider 1629, p. 48; Bartholinus 1665, p. 6; see also Petersen 1921, p. 171.

45 Burgersdijck 1629, p. 136, rejects the cardinal virtues in favour of Aristotle's grouping; as does Heereboord 1680, p. 746.

46 Keckermann 1607, e.g., pp. 54–72 ('De actionibus virtutem procreantibus, notentur hi canones').

47 Timpler 1607; see also Freedman 1988.

48 Burgersdijck 1629, pp. 134–5; see also Blom 1993.

49 Dibon 1954, pp. 90–116, esp. p. 98.

50 See Burgersdijck 1629, pp. 71–82, esp. pp. 76–7, where he combines the Stoic and Thomist classifications of the passions; see also pp. 108–9, where he rejects Thomas's opinion that justice is located in the will.

51 Heereboord 1663; see also Dibon 1954, pp. 116–19; Thijssen-Schoute 1950, pp. 231–5; and Dibon 1950, pp. 294–8.

52 Heereboord 1680: *Exercitationes ethicae* XVIII–XXI and *Collegium ethicum* XII–XIII. Like Burgersdijck, he was sometimes critical of Thomas: pp. 601, 687.

53 Heereboord 1680, pp. 427, 435 ('ut Aristotelis, quem nobis ducem seligimus, vestigia premamus'), 445, 450, 724 ('ne videamur antiquorum limites refigere') and 746.

54 For a survey of the main ethical doctrines, as discussed in the context of early modern Stoicism (virtue as its own reward, the suppression of the passions, the relationship between Stoic and Christian ethics), see Kraye 1988, pp. 360–74.

55 E.g., Burgersdijck 1629, pp. 60–70; Crell 1663, p. 37; Geier 1683, sigs. C2$^r$–3$^v$; see also nn. 6 and 36 of this chapter.

56 For a bibliography of sixteenth- and seventeenth-century Neostoic works, see Julien Eymard d'Angers 1976, pp. 520–7; on Neostoicism and ethics, see Kraye 1988, pp. 370–4; Morford 1991, pp. 157–80; Lagrée 1994, pp. 96–113.

57 Julien Eymard d'Angers 1976, pp. 3–12, 512–18.

58 Stoic fate, for example, was subtly transformed into Christian providence, and the Stoic exaltation of man's godlike prowess was considerably toned down: Du Vair 1946; see also Abel 1978, chap. 5. Also Colish 1992; Spanneut 1973, pp. 244–51; Lagrée 1994, pp. 119–21.

59 Epictetus 1688.

60 Aubignac 1664, vol. I, pp. 53–65, 115–20; see also Cherpack 1983, pp. 64–7.

61 Aubignac 1664, vol. I, sig. ã3$^v$: 'Elle s'est volontairement soumise à l'Evangile.'

62 See the passages from Senlis 1637, 1638, and 1642 cited by Julien Eymard d'Angers 1976, pp. 276–9.

63 On these writers, most of them Jesuits, Oratorians, and Capuchins, see Julien Eymard d'Angers 1976, pp. 27–8, 233–249, 283–302.

64 Senault 1987, pp. 44, 53–4, 117, 119, 121; see also Julien Eymard d'Angers 1951 and 1976, pp. 373–405. For other anti-Stoic treatments of the passions, see Caussin 1624 and Le Moyne 1640–3; see also Levi 1964, pp. 165–76.

65 Le Grand 1665, sigs. ã5$^v$: 'Les plus grands esprits de l'antiquité ont defendu leur party', and pp. 22–5, for his controversy with the Jansenists; for his Cartesianism, see Le Grand 1672 and 1679a; see also Levi 1964, pp. 155–6, 337. For another Senecan defence of Stoicism, see Testu de Mauroy 1666.

66 Quevedo 1945–60, vol. I, pp. 872–9; in 1641–2, during his imprisonment by the Inquisition, he wrote two further essays portraying Job as the exemplar of Stoic moral philosophy: pp. 1151–1267; see also Ettinghausen 1972; Blüher 1969, pp. 326–70.

67 For his views on virtue, see Malvezzi 1648, p. 18; see also Brändli 1964. For the political dimension of Stoicism, see Lipsius 1589 and Oestreich 1982.

68 Malvezzi 1634, p. 7.

69 Malvezzi 1632, p. 70; see Machiavelli, *Il Principe* XVIII.5.

70 Pallavicino 1644, pp. 145–8; for his critique of Stoicism, see pp. 309, 331 ('La filosofia degli Stoici non solo è falsa, ma pestilente'), 684–5.

71 Salmon 1989.

72 See Thomas Lodge's preface to his translation, Seneca 1614, sig. b4$^v$: 'Would God Christians would endevour to practise his [i.e., Seneca's] good precepts . . . ; and perceiving so great light of learning from a pagans pen, ayme at the true light of devotion and pietie, which becommeth Christians.' John Healey, also a Catholic, translated Epictetus 1610. For Protestant supporters of Stoicism, see Cornwallis 1600 and 1601, Samson Lennard's translation of Charron 1606, and J. Hall 1948.

73 Reynolds 1658, p. 48; T. Wright 1630, pp. 5–16, translating Psalm 4:5. For the rejection of this Stoic doctrine by continental Jesuits, also for religious motives, see Bauer 1987, vol. 2, pp. 453–74.

74 Sams 1944, p. 67; Chew 1988, p. 242.

75 Burton 1989–94, vol. 1, pp. 247–8; see also pp. 107, 165–6; Monsarrat 1984, p. 85.
76 Chapman 1941, pp. 236–41, 243–8, 449–50; Dryden 1900, vol. 2, p. 75. See also Chew 1988, pp. 237–62. On Stoicism and English drama see Monsarrat 1984, pp. 127–252.
77 Kraye 1988, pp. 349–59; Kraye 1994; J. Hankins 1990, vol. 1, pp. 267–359. For the influence of Ficino's Platonic love theory on scholastic treatises on the passions, see Levi 1964, pp. 165–76; also n. 38 of this chapter.
78 Davion 1660, sigs. ē3ʳ, ē7ʳ.
79 Davion 1660, p. 66.
80 Davion 1660, pp. 153, 167–70.
81 Traherne 1968, p. 112; see also Marks 1966.
82 Culverwel 1652, p. 53; cf. Traherne 1968, p. 119.
83 Cudworth 1731, pp. 9–10; AT VII 431–33; see also Muirhead 1931, pp. 58–60.
84 A view also held by Traherne 1968, p. 4.
85 Cudworth 1731, pp. 14–15.
86 Cudworth 1731, p. 39.
87 Cudworth 1731, pp. 42–3.
88 Cudworth 1731, pp. 8–9; *Lev.* xiii, Hobbes 1968, p. 188. See also Zagorin 1992.
89 Cudworth 1731, pp. 288–9, 300.
90 Cudworth 1731, p. 296.
91 See Section VI of this chapter.
92 Parker 1666b, pp. 2, 4.
93 Parker 1666b, pp. 5, 16.
94 Parker 1666b, pp. 14, 16, 27, 29, 34.
95 Kraye 1988, pp. 374–86; Gigante 1988, pp. 367–459.
96 See, e.g., Heider 1629, pp. 95–6; Pallavicino 1644, pp. 51–4; Bartholinus 1665, p. 10.
97 Quevedo 1986, pp. 35–6 (on providence), 38–40 (on Cicero); see also Ettinghausen 1972, pp. 43–56.
98 Gassendi 1959; although the treatise was never completed, the seventh book was to be devoted to a comparison of Epicurean and Aristotelian ethics: see p. 15.
99 Joy 1987, pp. 25–80; Joy 1992; Osler 1993.
100 Gassendi 1658, vol. 5, pp. 167–236.
101 H. Jones 1981, pp. 205–52; H. Jones 1989, pp. 166–85; Brundell 1987, pp. 48–82. For other aspects of Gassendi's Christianisation of Epicureanism, see Osler 1985a; Osler 1991.
102 Gassendi 1658, vol. 2, p. 701: 'Ac tanto esse vehementiorem voluptatem voluerit, quanto ipsa operatio erat magis necessaria futura, sive ad totius generis, sive ad animalis cuiusque singularis conservationem'; see Sarasohn 1982, pp. 242–3.
103 Gassendi 1658, vol. 2, pp. 821–7; see Sarasohn 1985, pp. 369–77.
104 Spink 1960, pp. 133–68; Sarasohn 1991.
105 Le Grand 1669, p. 8: 'Les Stoïques regardent la vertu comme un bien honeste, et les Epicuriens comme delectable'; on his Stoic treatise, see Section II of this chapter.
106 Le Grand 1669 was so keen to overturn the clichés about Epicurean indulgence that he made a point of condemning the 'cuisiniers' of his time as 'ennemies de la santé' and 'sorciers qui enchante l'homme pour le perdre', p. 57.
107 Du Rondel 1679. For a reaction against the post-Gassendian tendency to portray Epicurus as *plus stoïque ques les Stoïques,* see Saint-Evremond 1930, pp. 273–80.
108 He relied heavily on the work of the sixteenth-century editor Denys Lambin; see Brundell 1987, p. 50.

109 Lucretius 1659, sig. ā5$^v$–6$^r$.

110 Spink 1960, p. 148.

111 Lucretius 1682a, vol. 1, sig. ★10$^r$: 'Est-il quelque philosophe payen, dont la pluspart des sentimens n'ayant pas repugné à nôtre religion?'

112 Parrain 1695, pp. 142–3, contrasts 'la dureté stoïcienne', which forbids the wise man to pardon even the smallest faults in others, with the forgiving attitude of Epicurus, which is 'tout à fait raisonnable' and also 'conforme à l'Ecriture sainte', specifically, Ephesians 4:31; see also p. 276, where Epicurus's Principal Maxim XVII (Diogenes Laertius X.144) is compared to the Wisdom of Solomon 1:15.

113 Charleton 1670, sigs. A3$^v$, A4$^v$; the 'Apologie' borrows liberally from Jean-François Sarasin's *Apologie pour Epicure* (1651) and Gassendi's *De vita et moribus Epicuri*; see also Jones 1989, pp. 198–203.

114 Charleton 1670, sig. M6$^v$; see also Fleitmann 1986, pp. 217–19.

115 Stanley 1655–62, vol. 3.

116 Diogenes Laertius 1688; a Greek–Latin edition was published in London in 1664. The text was, of course, widely available in editions printed on the Continent: the Greek *editio princeps* was Basel 1533; the Latin (in Ambrogio Traversari's translation, completed in 1433) was Rome c. 1472; there were also important Greek–Latin editions: Geneva 1570 and 1593 (both printed by H. Stephanus, the latter with notes by Isaac Casaubon); Rome 1594 (edited by Tommaso Aldobrandini); and Book X appeared in Gassendi's *Animadversiones* (1649) and in his 1658 *Opera omnia*: Gassendi 1658, vol. 5, pp. 1–166.

117 Evelyn 1656; see also Jones 1989, pp. 186, 203–4. The first English translation was that of Lucy Hutchinson, made in the 1640s or 1650s, which has remained in manuscript: see Gordon 1985, p. 169.

118 Lucretius 1682b, sigs. b2$^r$–4$^v$, pp. 39–41; see also Mayo 1934, pp. 58–76; Fleischmann 1964; Real 1970; Gordon 1985, pp. 170–80.

119 Dryden 1958, vol. 1, pp. 395–7; see also Fleischmann 1964, pp. 223–7.

120 Its dangers for Christianity were vividly outlined by Richard Bentley in his 1692 Boyle Lectures; see Bentley 1693.

121 Temple 1908; see also Mayo 1934, pp. 90–6.

122 For the influence of Catholic and Protestant moral theology on natural law theory, see Chapter 35 in this volume.

123 See, e.g., Eustachius 1654, p. 150, who declines to discuss the seven deadly sins, a subject which 'ad theologos et praesertim summistas, qui de casibus conscientiae disserunt, pertinet'; see also Brockliss 1987, p. 226.

124 On Jesuit casuistry and Blaise Pascal's Jansenist critique of it in his *Lettres provinciales* (1656–7), see Jonsen and Toulmin 1988, pp. 146–51, 231–49.

125 See, e.g., the frequently reprinted manual of Busenbaum 1688, sigs. ★2$^v$–3$^r$: 'Nihil asserui, nisi vel ex communi doctorum sententia, vel desumptum ex probatissimorum authorum libris.' Among the many fellow Jesuits he cites are Luis de Molina, Francisco Suárez and Gabriel Vázquez.

126 Busenbaum 1688, pp. 97, 196, 442.

127 E.g., on issues such as predestination and good works: see Alsted 1628, pp. 24–7, 143–4; on the power of civil authorities over ecclesiastical matters, see J. Taylor 1660, III.iii.4–5.

128 Ames 1643, sig. B1$^r$, grudgingly admits that 'in a great deale of earth and dirt of Superstition, they [Catholic manuals] have some veins of Silver: out of which, I suppose, I have drawne some things that are not to be despised.'

129 Ames 1643 cites only the Bible; Alsted 1628 uses a few extra-biblical works; J. Taylor 1660 is somewhat more generous in his citation of classical and patristic sources.

130 Alsted 1628 uses a catechistic format; Ames 1643, numbered theses; and J. Taylor 1660, numbered rules.

131 Many English manuals were either written in the vernacular (J. Taylor 1660) or appeared in translation (Ames 1643 is an English version of the 1631 Latin original).

132 Ames 1643, I.viii–xvi; Heereboord 1680, pp. 611–47.

133 Ames 1648, pp. 204, 209–210; Grotius, *De jure belli et pacis,* prolegomena, para. 45; the argument had become commonplace: see, e.g., Dupleix 1610, p. 279. On Ames, see Oldrini 1987, p. 88.

134 Petersen 1921, pp. 167–9; R. A. Gauthier 1970, pp. 205–8.

135 Whitby 1684, pp. 18 (on Scripture), 51 (for the influence of Ames), 207–15 (on friendship).

136 Crell 1663, p. 25; for the doctrine of the mean applied to non-Aristotelian virtues, see pp. 462, 468, 472, and 475.

137 E.g., Nicholas of Amiens's *De arte fidei catholicae* (late twelfth century) (Nicholas of Amiens 1855); Guillaume Postel's *Sacrarum apodixeon, seu Euclidis christiani libri II* (1543); and Jean-Baptiste Morin's *Quod Deus sit* (1635). See Lohr 1986, pp. 53–62; Schüling 1969, pp. 93, 97.

138 Eustratius 1892, pp. 21–2; Odonis 1500, fol. 6$^r$.

139 Berckelius 1623, sig. A2$^v$; Burgersdijck 1629, p. 6; Brerewood 1640, p. 12; Crell 1663, p. 1; Channevelle 1666, vol. 1, p. 27; Sáenz de Aguirre 1677, p. 82; Sáenz de Aguirre 1698, pp. 29–30.

140 Hemmingsen 1562, sigs. B7$^r$, F3$^v$–5$^r$.

141 Hemmingsen 1562, sigs. G4$^r$–5$^r$, where the hypothesis that 'omnium actionum humanarum primum locum obtinere agnitionem Dei' is demonstrated by a syllogism and a quotation from the fourth book of Plato's *Laws* (716D); for his use of Cicero's *De officiis,* see sigs. H2$^v$–3$^r$.

142 Pavone 1633, pp. 4–6. A similar combination of the geometrical and scholastic methods can be seen in works on natural philosophy and metaphysics: e.g., *De motu* (1591) by Galileo's teacher Francesco Buonamici; *Euclides physicus* (1657) and *Euclides metaphysicus* (1658) by Hobbes's friend Thomas White; and the *Physica* (1669–71) of the Jesuit Honoré Fabri. See Helbing 1989, pp. 77–8; De Angelis 1964, pp. 18, 27–9; Boehm 1965.

143 See, e.g., Dupleix 1610, p. 276; Channevelle 1666, vol. 1, p. 3; Melles 1669b, pp. 98, 108, 117–18.

144 *Disc.* II, AT VI 7, 19, 29; *Regulae ad directionem ingenii* II, AT X 366; see also Wolfson 1934, vol. 1, pp. 44–52; Arndt 1971, pp. 49–67.

145 *Les Principes de la philosophie,* preface, AT IX 2–15; Descartes to Mersenne, 27 July 1638, AT II 268: 'Toute ma Physique n'est autre chose que Geometrie'; see also De Angelis 1964, p. 20.

146 AT VI 6–8. For a similar complaint, see Bacon, *Of the Advancement of Learning,* Bacon 1857–74, vol. 3, p. 418.

147 AT VI 22–31; see Epictetus, *Enchiridion,* chap. 1. This distinction continued to be important in Descartes's later work: *Pass. âme,* secs. 144–6, AT XI 436–40; see also Julien Eymard d'Angers, 1976, pp. 469–78; Levi 1964, pp. 281–2; Sorell 1993.

148 Descartes to Elisabeth, 4 August 1645, AT IV 263–8 (K 164–7).

149 *Pass. âme,* sec. 1, AT XI 327–8.
150 AT IX 15.
151 *Pass. âme,* preface, AT XI 326; see also Mesnard 1936, pp. 69–76; Levi 1964, pp. 265–98; Curley 1988, p. 94.
152 Descartes to Chanut, 1 November 1646, AT IV 536 and 20 November 1647, AT V 86–7.
153 *Princ.* IV 205–6, AT IX 323–4; see also Rodis-Lewis 1957, p. 119.
154 *Ent. mét.* VI.I (Mal. *OC* XII–XIII 132 [Malebranche 1980b, p. 129]): 'elles sont environnées de grandes obscuritez'; see also Verga 1964, pp. 35–42, 51–2; Walton 1972, p. 25; Novotny 1977, pp. 452–4.
155 *Rech.* VI.2.6, (Mal. *OC* II 379 [Malebranche 1980a, p. 485]): 'Dieu ayant fait toutes les chose pour lui, il a fait nôtre esprit pour le connoître & nôtre coeur pour l'aimer.'
156 *Rech.* I.3.1, II.2.4, II.3.4, III.1.3, IV.2.3, VI.2.6, (Mal. *OC* I 60–1, 285–6, 345–58, 397–403 and II 18, 380 [Malebranche 1980a, pp. 13–14, 140–41, 178–83, 207–10, 270, 486]).
157 *Traité de la morale* I.i.4 and 6, I.ii.1, I.v.19, (Mal. *OC* XI 18–19, 28, 68 [trans. in Schneewind 1990, pp. 258–9, 261, 267]); see also Walton 1972, p. 60.
158 *Lev.* iv, Hobbes 1968, p. 105.
159 Skinner 1996, esp. pp. 215–57; Kemp 1970, pp. 4–5; Hobbes 1983a, p. 1 (introduction); Kavka 1986, p. 5; Rogers 1988, pp. 195–7; Zagorin 1993, pp. 517–18.
160 Hobbes, *Philosophical Rudiments,* epistle dedicatory and preface, *Eng. Works,* vol. 2, pp. iv–xi; see also *Lev.* v, Hobbes 1968, p. 115: 'Who is so stupid, as both to mistake in Geometry, and also to persist in it, when another detects his error to him?'
161 *Lev.* i, iv–v, Hobbes 1968, pp. 86, 106, 113–14.
162 *Lev.* iv, vi, vii, xiv, xv, Hobbes 1968, pp. 105–10, 126–30, 189, 202.
163 *Lev.* ii, Hobbes 1968, pp. 87–8; see also Kemp 1970, pp. 3–6; Sarasohn 1985, pp. 363–79; Kavka 1986, pp. 7–11; Rogers 1988, pp. 196–7.
164 *Lev.,* introduction, Hobbes 1968, pp. 82–3; *Philosophical Rudiments,* preface, Hobbes, *Eng. Works,* vol. 2, p. XIV; see also Kavka 1986, pp. 6–9.
165 *Lev.* xiv–xv, Hobbes 1968, pp. 189–90, 214–17; see also Sorell 1986, pp. 2–3.
166 *Lev.* xiv, Hobbes 1968, p. 190.
167 See Sections III and IV of this chapter.
168 More 1679b, pp. 32–40 (I.7), 20–4 (I.5); see also Whewell 1862, pp. 61–6; Mintz 1962, pp. 83–90; Fiering 1981, pp. 261–6, 278–9. For Leibniz's notes on and paraphrase of More's *Enchiridion ethicum,* see LAkad. VI.III, pp. 352–63.
169 More 1679b, sig. *5ʳ 'Ne quid . . . authoritatis deesset, non solum verba sed et sententias Veterum . . . frequentissime adhibui.'
170 More 1679b, p. 14 (I.4): 'Principia quaedam immediate vera nulliusque indiga probationis'; cf. noemata XV ('Quod malum tibi fieri nolles, a faciendo illud alteri ipse debes abstinere') and XVI ('Bono bonum compensandum est, non malo') to Hobbes, *Lev.* xiv, xv, Hobbes 1968, pp. 190 ('Quod tibi fieri non vis, alteri ne feceris'), 209 (the fourth law: gratitude). The Golden Rule was often treated as a moral axiom: see, e.g., Culverwel 1652, p. 55; Bartholinus 1665, p. 55; Melles 1669b, p. 111.
171 Cumberland 1672, esp. pp. 4, 22–3, 85–6 (geometry) and 181–2 (algebra); see also Whewell 1862, pp. 75–83; Mintz 1962, pp. 149–50; for Cumberland's place in the history of natural law theory, see Chapter 35 of this book.
172 *Ess.* IV.iii.18; Clarke 1706a.
173 MacIntyre 1984, pp. 141–3.

174 *Eth.* III pref., Geb. II 137–8; Wolfson 1934, vol. 1, pp. 52–60; Kristeller 1984, pp. 2–4; Jonathan Bennett 1984, pp. 16–20; Curley 1988, p. 106; Parkinson 1993, pp. 280–2.

175 *Eth.* I app., Geb. II 83: 'Res enim si intellexisset, illae omnes, teste Mathesi, si non allicerent, ad minimum convinceret.'

176 On the gradual secularisation of moral philosophy, which also began in the seventeenth century, see Attfield 1978, pp. 122–44.

# 35

# DIVINE/NATURAL LAW THEORIES IN ETHICS

## KNUD HAAKONSSEN

The attempt to understand morality in the legalistic terms of a natural law is ancient but is now mostly associated with the formulation given it by Thomas Aquinas in the late thirteenth century. Earlier natural law is commonly seen as leading up to Aquinas's paradigmatic version, whereas later natural law is understood as deriving from it. This approach has resulted in long-standing disputes about the status of Protestant natural law vis-à-vis Thomism, disputes generally centring on the question of the originality of Hugo Grotius, commonly considered 'the father of modern natural law'. It is easy to understand why there should be such disagreements. The sources reveal an extraordinary degree of continuity between scholastic – and not only Thomistic – natural law and the natural law doctrines which dominated Protestant Europe during the seventeenth century and much of the eighteenth. Yet it seemed to moral philosophers of these centuries, and especially to the modern natural lawyers themselves, that something decisively new happened with Grotius. Protestant natural law was seen as a distinct school of moral philosophy until the history of philosophy was redrawn by Kant and by others working in the light of his philosophy.[1]

The resolution of these disputes has in some measure been frustrated by the predominant concentration on the rôle of Grotius. While conveying to Protestant Europe large parts of the natural law material used by the great scholastic thinkers, especially those of sixteenth-century Spain, Grotius's underlying theory contained elements which his successors considered dangerous. In their commentaries on Grotius's text and histories of their discipline, later natural lawyers glossed over or repudiated these elements and ascribed Grotius's novelty to ideas which were in fact not at all new to him but which were important to them. Grotius's true originality must therefore be distinguished from the novelty of subsequent Protestant natural law theory.

## I. SUAREZ

The backdrop to these questions is, of course, scholasticism. Neither as a method nor as a body of doctrine was this a spent force by 1600, and work of various scholastic genres, including commentaries on Aristotle, continued to appear throughout the century. Perhaps the greatest synthesis of scholastic moral-legal theory is a seventeenth-century work, *De legibus, ac Deo legislatore* (1612) by the Jesuit Francisco Suárez. It issued from the Spanish schools which, somewhat removed from the centres of Renaissance humanism and the Reformation, continued not only to teach scholastic doctrine, but to renew it in response to new problems, not least of a colonial and, to use an anachronistic term, international political-legal nature.[2] First of all, it is a carefully argued synthesis of previous doctrines, reflecting some of the most central scholastic disputes, especially that between the Dominicans and the Jesuits over the respective rôles of divine grace and human free will, and that between the nominalist-voluntarist tradition from William of Ockham and the realist-intellectualist tradition from Gregory of Rimini and, most would say, Thomas Aquinas. Of these points, we can only deal with the last.

Like Aquinas, Suárez divides law into four categories: eternal, natural, divine positive, and human positive law.[3] In his analysis of these laws, he does, however, emphasise the rôle of the will of the legislator a good deal more than Aquinas. Law in the strict sense is characterised by being obligatory upon creatures of reason and free will, and this is supposed to require willing on the part of the legislator. Eternal law is only in a tenuous sense a law. On the one hand, it is God's most general will, or providence, for the moral (rational and free-willed) creation, and so it is in a sense a law for the latter. On the other hand, it is only indirectly 'for' God's creatures in as much as they cannot know it in more than the most general sense as part of God's nature.[4] Only when it is promulgated to rational creatures can it be called law proper. This cannot be done directly, knowledge and obligation being temporal effects, and only happens when the eternal law takes the form of one or another of the other three kinds of law.[5] At the same time, Suárez stresses that the eternal law cannot be seen as a law which God imposes upon Himself.[6] Law implies obligation, and obligation implies a superior as legislator, which is a contradiction where God is concerned.

The other forms of law are divided according to the different ways in which they, or those subject to them, participate in the over-arching eternal law.[7] Natural law is simply the way in which the eternal law applies to human moral nature. In the case of positive law, a legislator intervenes. Divine positive law comes about when God acts as a ruler who promulgates his law, in revelation, and binds those subject to it by His will and His power. This is the law of Scripture. It is an addition to nature which can aid man in this life, especially through its institutional forms in the church.[8] In view of God's nature, there can of course be no conflict between this law and eternal or natural law.

Human positive law issues from human rulers[9] and, like other human acts, it has natural law as the moral measure which it may or may not follow in particular cases. (In addition, some human law, of course, is built upon divine law.) Human law is better discussed in conjunction with Suárez's political theory, the basic principle of which is this: Given the nature of the moral creation, humanity has to arrange its affairs in one or other of a number of possible ways; such arrangements are, in other words, enjoined by the law of nature. However, which arrangement is to be adopted is a matter for people to settle among themselves. It is thus a natural necessity arising from the needs of human beings that they live in hierarchies of social groups, minimally the family and *some* sort of wider group. In order to have a coherent social group, there must be an organised concern for the common good, and this requires *some* kind of sovereign authority which in one way or another can legislate and enforce its legislation. In order to make use of the necessary goods of the world, *some* system of property has to be adhered to. This much is according to natural law, but the specific forms property arrangements take have to be agreed upon by people.[10]

Accordingly as far as society, political authority and, by implication, private property are concerned, Suárez can be seen as a kind of contractarian. However, it is important to stress that these social institutions as such are natural and only their specific forms 'artificial', to use the language which was soon to become current in this connexion.

This view of society, political authority and legislation as necessary responses to the needs of human nature is clearly directed against the Reformers' political ideas. Social life and political governance are not to be seen as the necessary means of compensating for fallen man's loss of moral self-government. They are in fact part of the fulfilment of human nature. Original sin just makes it harder to achieve fulfilment in these as in other aspects of the moral life.[11]

The tenuousness of this kind of contractarianism was to persist in much of the debate about the basis for both civil and church government during the following two centuries. It is revealed in Suárez's discussions of the moral position that arises when the contractually instituted forms break down. In situations of extreme hardship the needy have the right to make use of the private property (*dominium*) of others. This right does not derive from any duty on the part of the owners of private property. Rather, private property ceases to exist under such circumstances, and things return to the original common. It is similarly so with sovereign authority (also *dominium*). In cases of extreme need, namely, when government turns tyrannical, the contract transferring sovereignty to it is annulled and sovereignty returns to its original natural source, the community. In both cases the goals set by natural law – broadly speaking, the common good – override what is instituted by contract.

Finally, it should be pointed out that, in his attempts to capture the sense in which the institution of private property is permitted, or licit (*licitum*), under natural law, Suárez helped set in motion the clarification by the modern schools of natural law of the central deontic trichotomy 'obligatory-permitted-forbidden'.[12]

The natural law is the hub of Suárez's system. Apart from the fourfold distinction already mentioned, natural law must be distinguished from *ius gentium*,[13] which again must be kept separate from the *ius civile* or human positive law proper. *Ius gentium* is in effect customary law as found across civil societies. It is thus positive law but not civil law in as much as it does not issue from a sovereign. The category of *ius gentium* provides the framework for Suárez's significant discussions of the laws of war and peace, discussions which, when combined with his in many respects modern concept of sovereignty, must be considered fundamental to what would eventually become international law. Natural law must also be distinguished from law in the metaphorical sense, in which all of nature is 'law-governed' or subject to causal regularity.[14] In this connexion Suárez puts forward the old chestnut, now mainly known from Hume, that the same form of behaviour in an animal and in a person (e.g., promiscuity) has no moral significance in the former case whereas it has in the latter. In other words, natural law proper applies only to moral agents.

Law exists in the mind of the legislator, in the mind of the subject, and in some medium.[15] As far as the last is concerned, Suárez takes the traditional view that the law of nature is promulgated both in human reason and in the Decalogue.[16] In the human mind natural law exists in the form of an act of judgement which precedes and guides the will.[17] In the mind of the legislator, God, law exists as a combination of will and reason, since these are inseparable in Him.[18] It was through this suggestion that Suárez explicitly attempted to reconcile the two sides in one of the greatest scholastic disputes and presented a synthesis which remained at the heart of most natural law thinking for the following two centuries. At one extreme he saw what we now refer to as the intellectualist and realist tradition, where his main reference is Gregory of Rimini. At the other extreme he presented the 'voluntarism' of William of Ockham, Jean Gerson and Peter d'Ailly.[19] Suárez characterises the intellectualist and realist position, as follows:

The natural law is not a preceptive law, properly so-called, since it is not the indication of the will of some superior; but . . . on the contrary, it is a law indicating what should be done, and what should be avoided, what of its own nature is intrinsically good and necessary, and what is intrinsically evil. . . . [T]he natural law is not derived from God as a Lawgiver, since it does not depend upon His will, and . . . in consequence, God does not, by virtue of that law, act as a superior who lays down commands or prohibitions. Indeed . . . Gregory . . . says that even if God did not exist, or if He did not make use of reason, or if He did not judge of things correctly, nevertheless, if the same dictates of right reason dwelt within man, constantly assuring, for example, that lying is evil, those dictates would still have the same legal character which they actually possess, because they would constitute a law pointing out the evil that exists intrinsically in the object.[20]

In contrast to this Suárez formulates the voluntarist thesis in these terms:

That the natural law consists entirely in a divine command or prohibition proceeding from the will of God as the Author and Ruler of nature; that, consequently, this law as it exists in God is none other than the eternal law in its capacity of commanding or prohibiting with respect to a given matter; and that, on the other hand, this same natural law, as it dwells within ourselves, is the judgment of reason, in that it reveals to us God's will as to what must be done or avoided. [Further] that the whole basis of good and evil in matters pertaining to the law of nature is in God's will, and not in a judgment of reason, even on the part of God himself, nor in the very things which are prescribed or forbidden by that law. The foundation for this opinion would seem to be that actions are not good or evil, save as they are ordered or prohibited by God; since God himself does not will to command or forbid a given action to any created being, on the ground that such an action is good or evil, but rather on the ground that it is just or unjust because He has willed that it shall or shall not be done.[21]

Suárez objects to the intellectualist thesis on several grounds. First, there is a difference between a proposition and a law. Furthermore, a judgement about moral values is a judgement of facts, moral facts, and not of itself a guide to action; in order to have any relevance to action, as a law has, something must be added to the judgement.[22] The intellectualist thesis also implies that God Himself is subject to natural law, since it is argumentatively presupposed in His will. Or, to put it differently, if 'good' implies 'is under obligation to', then God is under an obligation to follow the law of nature.[23] However, as mentioned, this is an impossibility, since obligation presupposes a superior, a point underlined by the (question-begging) suggestion that self-command is a meaningless concept.[24] It is thus not only the case that natural law, on this reading of it, could be independent of God; it actually is so.[25] It should be pointed out here that Suárez's formulation of Gregory's view, quoted above, polemically distorts it in a significant way. Gregory did not say, in the passage referred to by Suárez, that without God the dictates of right reason would still have the same 'legal character' (*rationem legis*), nor that they would constitute a *lex ostensiva* etc. He said only that, even without God, there would be sin, or moral evil (*peccatum*).[26] By imputing to Gregory the former view Suárez is in fact suggesting that the earlier thinker had the idea that there could be obligation without God, a point which was obviously taken to be self-evidently absurd.

In view of his own position, Suárez's criticism of the voluntarist thesis is surprisingly muted and poorly formulated. His first point is 'that certain evils are prohibited, because they are evil. For if they are prohibited on that very ground, they cannot derive the primary reason for their evil quality from the fact that they are prohibited, since an effect is not the reason for its cause.'[27] The implication is that either the argument moves in a vicious circle of prohibition and evil quality or it moves in a hierarchy of prohibitions. But, since God is involved, both an infinite regress and an unreasoned fiat are impossible. Consequently, there must ultimately be a reason other than prohibition for the prohibitions of natural law. Suárez finds *a posteriori* confirmation of this point in an attempted *reductio ad absurdum*. If natural law was simply a matter of God's will without the need for reasons, then it was in principle possible that God could allow humanity to hate Him. Hence this 'could be permitted, and it could be righteous' (*posset licere, vel esse honestum*).[28] However, to think that God is rightly the object of hatred is a contradiction in terms. Voluntarism leads to Ockham's notorious paradox.[29] In this argument, much, of course, depends on the notion of the licit. It is surprising that Suárez does not invoke here the clear distinction he makes elsewhere between *permissio facti,* the de facto indifference to an action, and *permissio juris,* the 'active' withholding of disapproval of an action.[30] Only the latter leads to Ockham's paradox, but it is arguable that the imputation to God of this kind of *permissio* is question-begging for a voluntarist in at least one very important situation of God's permission. If we consider the human condition logically prior to, or in abstraction from, God's imposition of the natural law, God's attitude to humanity can hardly be conceived as one of *permissio juris,* since this already contains a moral element. If the human situation prior to the law is amoral, then God's attitude must be understood as a mere *permissio facti*. The question then is whether this *permissio* is consistent with a Christian notion of the God who loves humankind. Clearly Suárez's answer would have been no.

Suárez's own notion of natural law combines elements from both of the extremes he presents and rejects.[31] The heart of the matter is that natural law is both indicative of what is in itself good and evil, and preceptive in the sense that it creates an obligation in people to do the good and avoid the evil. The natural law thus reflects the two inseparable sides of God's nature, namely His rational judgement of good and evil and His will prescribing the appropriate behaviour.[32]

This brings us once more to the question of the necessity of God's willing what is good. We have already seen that there cannot possibly be any obligation upon God, since obligation presupposes a superior. The question then is whether God can be said to derive an ought from his conception of what is good. The answer is that it is uncertain whether Suárez has the conceptual apparatus required to deal with this question. In one sense, God is totally free – free, for example, to create or not to create the known world.[33] If we could conceive of His choice between creating this or another world, or no world at all, as a moral choice, a choice between alternative constellations of goods and evils, then we could see Him as imposing upon Himself certain duties as a consequence of realising one or another set of values. This rather common-sensical view is probably what Suárez intends. The problem is that it amounts to suggesting that human beings can actually understand the eternal law by which God Himself operates and not just its adaptation in the natural law promulgated to humans. If humanity could have this kind of insight, it is not clear why God the legislator should be necessary as the ground of all human morality. On the other hand, having made His choice of creation, He has too little freedom: 'God could not have refrained from willing to forbid that a creature . . . endowed [with reason and knowledge of good and evil] should commit acts intrinsically evil, nor could He have willed not to prescribe the necessary righteous acts.'[34] In other words, the 'ought' is not self-imposed as a result of rationally considering the 'goods', but is the inevitable outcome of the fact that God did choose one set of goods.

In the human world the problem is very different. On the one hand, Suárez is committed to the voluntarist thesis that it is God's will which binds people. In accordance with this he maintains that we are obligated to the natural law under pain of God's punishment. However, such punishment cannot be part of natural law. It depends upon the supernatural, and he explicitly admits that it is a matter of faith. This makes the moral position of unbelievers uncertain – a problem he sidesteps.[35] On the other hand, his adoption also of the intellectualist thesis brings him very close to a clear formulation of the principle that 'good' implies 'ought', that is, that the preceptive force of natural law can be derived from its indicative or demonstrative content, and he calls this natural obligation.[36] Nevertheless, it was impossible for him to pursue this line, for its conclusion would have been that human beings could impose an obligation upon themselves by drawing the said conclusion, and that would in effect have dispensed with God's rôle in Suárez's moral theory.

In his theory of natural law, Suárez generally used the traditional terms *ius naturale*, which to modern ears can mean either natural law or natural right. He had, however, a very clear idea of the distinction between law and right and of their relationship: '*ius* sometimes means the moral power [*moralem facultatem*] to get something [*ad rem aliquam*] or over something [*in re*] . . . which is the proper object of justice. . . . At other times *ius* means law [*legem*] which is the rule of righteous behaviour, and which establishes a certain equity [*aequitatem*] in things and is the rule [*ratio*] of those rights [*iuris*] of the former category [*priori modo sumpti*] . . . which rule [*ratio*] is the very law.'[37] Subjective rights, as they would now be called, are means to the realisation of the goals set by the natural law. They basically encompass our powers, *dominia*, over ourselves (liberty), over the goods of the world (property), and over others, that is, those familial and wider social powers indicated by natural law and generally instituted by contractual or quasi-contractual means. Subjective *iura* are therefore also seen as concessions by the natural law, for 'natural reason not only dictates what is necessary, but also what is permitted [*liceat*].'[38] That is to say, liberty is granted us, but we can give it up or it can be taken from us for an overriding natural-law reason, such as punishment; the world is conceded to us in common, but we can carve it up if private property better serves the common good, and for the same reason lawful authority can take away private property; we have the liberty to marry or not according to our understanding of how best to serve the Lord; and so on.[39] In all cases what is instituted by the use of our *iura* is protected by the natural law – until such time as it may require the dissolution of our institutions.

Suárez distinguishes between negative and affirmative precepts of natural law. The former prohibit that which is in itself evil and the latter prescribe the inherently good. In view of the later uses of similar distinctions, it should be stressed that the two kinds of precepts carry equal obligation.[40]

## II. NATURAL LAW AND PROTESTANTISM

Scholastic natural law theory, as represented by Suárez, was problematic for a number of reasons. Perhaps most fundamental, it was an obvious target for the sort of moral scepticism which had been revived at the Renaissance and which continued to have great influence in the formulations given it by thinkers like Montaigne and Charron. Scholastic natural law seemed to presuppose a degree of knowledge about God, the world, and human nature, which it was only too easy for sceptical criticism to undermine. Not least, it operated with an idea of God and of the relationship between God and man which could hardly be considered 'natural' unless it could be shown to be pervasive outside the Christian world, for example, in the new colonies in the Americas and elsewhere. One of the main points of modern scepticism was that this was not the case. Religious and moral notions were so relative to time and place that no theoretically coherent account could be given of them. Not least, such notions were relative to each person's interest or individual utility. This connexion of an Epicurean theme with Renaissance relativism was made with particular effect when Grotius, in the Prolegomena to his *De iure belli ac pacis* (1625), singled out Carneades as the classical representative of all scepticism.[41] A continuing ambition of modern natural law was therefore to overcome such scepticism. It was still a driving force behind the work of Jean Barbeyrac three-quarters of a century later, his target being Pierre Bayle.

Protestant natural law's answer to scepticism started from its most fundamental objection to scholastic natural law, that it seemed to presuppose a moral continuity and interdependence between God and humanity.[42] For Protestant thinkers, the starting point was the complete discontinuity between God and man, a discontinuity which made it impossible to give a rational account of human morality by reference to God and His eternal law. Only faith could bridge the gulf between humanity and its Creator. This led to a continuing ambiguity in Protestantism towards natural law as a rational account of morals. On the one hand, such an undertaking seemed impossible and pointless, since nothing but faith could sustain morality. On the other hand, precisely the circumstance that no ultimate account seemed attainable put pressure on thinkers to attempt whatever was possible in purely human and temporal terms. Thus, if no amount of calculating human rationality could establish the link between people's behaviour and God's reward or punishment, then they had either to live by faith alone or to find a purely human and temporal foundation for reward and, especially, punishment.

We may see this ambiguity from a different angle. On the one hand, Protestant moral theology, and Luther's in particular, is an ethics of duty par excellence. There is here no room for degrees of perfection and improvement through good works, as in Catholic thinkers like Suárez. Nothing that a person can be or make of himself will justify him before God; only faith justifies, and that only by God's grace.[43] Our duty towards God is thus infinite and we may view our temporal life as a network of unfulfillable duties, which natural law theory may put into systematic form and give such worldly justifications as our limited understanding will permit. On the other hand, if our duty is really infinite and unfulfillable, then it is hard to see it as a possible guide to action; it provides no criterion for what behaviour to choose. We therefore can only live by faith. This strongly antinomian line was adopted by a great many sects at the Reformation and later, and must undoubtedly be regarded as a target no less important than moral scepticism to Protestant natural law theory.

It is in this general perspective that we must view the overwhelming emphasis on duty in modern natural law. Notions of virtue were to be interpreted in terms of duty; rights derived from duty; prima facie supererogatory acts were to be seen simply as special duties.

These general points indicate the logic of the basic ideas. Few thinkers followed this to its full extent, and a large part of the interpreter's task is to account for deviations from it. The first, and in many respects most formidable, stumbling block is Hugo Grotius.

### III. GROTIUS

As just mentioned, Suárez, following tradition, divided *ius naturale* into two basic meanings, a subjective *facultas moralis,* and the 'proper' sense of an objective *lex.* Grotius tried – in vain – to ensure that his breach with tradition would not be lost by introducing at the beginning of the first book of *De iure belli ac pacis* a division of *ius* into three meanings:

[First:] Right signifies meerly that which is just, and that too rather in a negative than a positive Sense. So that the Right of War is properly that which may be done without Injustice with Regard to an Enemy. Now that is unjust which is repugnant to the Nature of a Society of reasonable Creatures. . . .

There is another Signification of the Word Right different from this, but yet arising from it, which relates directly to the Person: In which Sense Right is a moral Quality [*qualitas moralis*] annexed to the Person, enabling him to have, or do, something justly. . . .

There is also a third Sense of the Word Right, according to which it signifies the same Thing as Law [*lex*], when taken in its largest Extent, as being a Rule of Moral Actions, obliging us to that which is good and commendable [*regula actuum moralium obligans ad id quod rectum est*].[44]

*Ius* is first a type of action, namely, any action which is not injurious to others in such a way that social relations break down. In order to determine what is injurious in this way, we have to turn to *ius* as a feature of persons, the second point. This is in itself a complex notion derived from two basic features of human nature,[45] first the *prima naturae* which are the natural drives or instincts for self-preservation, and, second, right reason or sound judgement of what is *honestum,* that is, what makes life with others possible – which is in itself a natural inclination. Considered as a feature of the person, *ius* is the exercise of these two sides of human nature together. When we do so exercise them together, we maintain our own (*suum*) which is

a Right properly, and strictly taken. Under which are contained, 1. A Power either over our selves, which is term'd Liberty; or over others, such as that of a Father over his Children, or a Lord over his Slave. 2. Property. . . . 3. The Faculty of demanding what is due, and to this answers the Obligation of rendering what is owing.[46]

*Ius naturale* is, then, every action which does not injure any other person's *suum,* and that in effect means that it is every *suum* which does not conflict with the *sua* of others.

Grotius's point against scepticism and against religiously inspired antinomianism is that if we claim this much as moral knowledge and act accordingly, we can have society and thereby the basic elements of moral life, while, if we deny it and act on the basis of such denial, we can have neither society nor humanity. This is his 'a priori' argument. In addition we find this reasoning confirmed 'a posteriori' in the history of humankind.[47] It is, therefore, on sound moral grounds that people go to war to protect their rights, which is to say that there are moral reasons independent of religion for the punishment of injustice (injury). This is one of Grotius's main concerns and it makes the title of his main work intelligible.

The *iura* we have sketched are 'perfect rights' and respect for them is 'expletive Justice, Justice properly and strictly taken'.[48] This is the minimal morality which is the foundation for social life. It is, however, not the whole of morals as we normally know it. In addition to the *facultates* by means of which we claim our *sua,* we have vaguer and more dispositional *aptitudines* which may be considered imperfect rights.[49] To these correspond the ability of right reason to judge of *honestum* beyond what is necessary to the very existence of social life, that is, of goods which, in contrast to rights proper, cannot be claimed and, if necessary, defended by force. These imperfect rights are the subject of attributive or distributive justice, and they form the theoretical basis for the rules of charity, or love, which are made into positive law by religions and civil governments.[50]

In the characterisation of *ius,* possessive and attributive features are intertwined. That is to say, *ius* is what a person has or has a claim to, but it is also an ability of the person to judge what he or she has or has a claim to. The latter is not simply the ability to apply a natural law to a specific case, as one might perceive it in scholastic thought, for law does not play any rôle in this part of the argument. The notion of *ius* thus has a certain connotation of a moral power or moral sense.

The conceptual apparatus sketched above forms the basis for most of what Grotius is trying to do in his social and political theory. Individuals with natural rights are the units of which all social organisation is made up. They are people who balance pure self-interest and social inclinations by entering into contractual relations with others about property and about modes of living together, especially about authority. They consider it a right to enforce the obligations arising from such arrangements, that is, to punish their transgression. Over and above this and to varying degrees, they may or may not do good to others by honouring 'imperfect rights'.

The emphasis is on what can be used towards the individual's self-preservation compatibly with the similar striving by others. This is the case with the goods of the world. Originally held in common by humankind, they were gradually divided up into private property because of avarice, population pressure, and other factors. In situations of extreme need, however, the basic rights of the needy defeat the rights of others to private property. Similarly, claims to property right are rendered spurious by non-use – as was the case with Spain's claims to vast tracts of lands and goods in foreign parts, which Dutch trading companies could well find use for, not to speak of claims to ownership of the high seas, the use of which was clearly not improved by being held exclusively by any one power.[51] Furthermore, people could make use of their rights in extreme ways to secure their self-preservation, for instance, by selling themselves into slavery or submitting to tyrannical government. These and similar political concerns were among the primary motivations of Grotius's enterprise.

The honouring of rights, perfect and imperfect, is in itself good, and as a consequence we can consider such behaviour as being prescribed by the Author of our nature. Such prescription is *lex,* the third sense of *ius naturale.* Grotius hastens to add that the behaviour prescribed by God is obligatory in itself – that is, without God – and that this distinguishes it from divine positive law as well as from human law.[52]

In this light we can make proper sense of a famous and controversial passage in the Prolegomena to Grotius's major work. Having given a brief sketch of *ius naturae* as encompassing both negative or perfect rights and positive or imperfect rights, he declares that all this 'would apply though we should even grant, what without the greatest Wickedness cannot be granted, that there is no God, or that he has no Care of human Affairs.' However, since Christians, at least, believe in God and His care for human affairs, 'this now becomes another Original of Right [*juris*], besides that of Nature, being that which proceeds from the free Will of God.'[53]

The controversial point is whether Grotius is maintaining anything other than the old notion going back to Gregory of Rimini, if not further, which we considered above. He obviously is. The scholastic point was that human beings have the ability to understand what is good and bad even without invoking God but have no obligation proper to act accordingly without God's command. Grotius is suggesting that people unaided by religion can use their perfect – and even imperfect – rights to establish the contractual and quasi-contractual obligations upon which social life rests. God is simply an additional source perceived by Christians – though it should of course be remembered that he held the basics of Christianity to be open to rational understanding.[54] Grotius's separation of natural law from the Christian religion is underlined in several ways. For instance, he firmly denies that natural law can be identified with either the Old or the New Testament,[55] in sharp contrast to Suárez, who saw the Decalogue as containing the natural law.

Much of Grotius's natural rights theory originated in his attempt to justify the claims of Dutch traders to operate in the colonies of Spain. In fact, the nucleus of his theory is already formulated in the first four laws of nature in his unpublished work *De Indis* (begun in 1604),[56] except that he there gave natural law an unusual voluntarist foundation which was rejected in his later work.[57] Much of the energy of his argument was generated by the analogy between sovereign states and individuals, which leads to a view of the natural state of man as morally similar to the situation of states amongst each other. The subsequent development of the argument in the great treatise *De iure belli ac pacis* had several additional concerns: the proof of an undeniable core of morality against sceptics and antinomian radicals; proof that a legal, including an international, order was possible independently of religion, *pace* Europe's warring confessions; proof that absolutist government could be legitimate; proof of the circumstances under which war was justified, namely in defence of rights and of the means to their maintenance; and much else.

Grotius's legacy was rich and varied, and both he himself and his ideas became European phenomena in several areas, especially church politics and philosophy. Grotius thought that the state *needed* and was justified in enforcing only two beliefs: that there is a God and that He cares for his creation. This conviction inspired Grotius's life-long schemes for reunification of the Christian churches and his rapprochement with Catholicism, while remaining an Arminian; these eirenic and liberal doctrines inform his theological works, notably the influential *De veritate religionis christianae.*[58] His early impact in England was particularly important. His ideas played a central rôle in the Great Tew circle and were taken up by John Selden and Thomas Hobbes.[59] Selden took the idea of man's natural freedom from moral laws a great deal further than Grotius, so far, in fact, that the only way in which moral community could be understood was as an effect of God's positive imposition and enforcement of the moral law as promulgated in the precepts given to the sons of Noah.[60]

## IV. HOBBES

The relationship between Grotius and Hobbes is a complex matter. However, as far as concerns the rôle of natural jurisprudential concepts in their ethics, it has proved a particularly fruitful suggestion to see the *Elements of Law, De cive* and *Leviathan* as descendants of *Mare liberum, De iure belli ac pacis* and *De veritate religionis christianae.*[61] Like Grotius, Hobbes labours under a prima facie ambiguity. On the one hand, they both write from a basic theistic standpoint according to which life and morals are part of the divine dispensation. On the other hand, they intend to account for the moral aspect of this dispensation in such a way that it explains how people without theistic beliefs can have a moral life. According to Grotius, the dispensation consists partly of the world provided for our use and partly of human nature with an urge and an ability to limit such use to the socially sustainable. According to Hobbes, humanity is also given the world for use, but the extent and form of this use is not limited by either a tendency towards sociability or an ability to judge from the other person's point of view. From the hand of nature, we all have an unlimited 'Right to every thing; even to one anothers body'. This '*Jus Naturale,* is the Liberty each man hath, to use his own power, as he will himselfe, for the preservation of his own Nature; that is to say, of his own Life; and consequently, of doing any thing, which in his own Judgement, and Reason, hee shall conceive to be the aptest means thereunto.'[62] This right is being exercised by persons who, according to Hobbes's elaborate anthropology, inevitably are concerned with self-preservation above all else. Human life consists in the satisfaction of a wide variety of desires, and the precondition for the satisfaction of any desire is to be alive. In view of the basic physical and intellectual equality among individuals in pursuit of self-preservation, the exercise of one's right to everything would be self-defeating, creating a war of everyone against everyone.[63] In the interests of self-preservation, people therefore tend to heed certain precepts which limit their natural liberty or rights. These precepts are the laws of nature:

A Law of Nature, (*Lex Naturalis*,) is a Precept, or generall Rule, found out by Reason, by which a man is forbidden to do, that, which is destructive of his life, or taketh away the means of preserving the same; and to omit, that, by which he thinketh it may be best preserved.[64]

The content of the basic laws of nature is that everyone should seek peace, or live sociably, in as far as at all possible, by laying 'down this right to all things; and [being] contented with so much liberty against other men, as he would allow other men against himselfe.'[65]

The rights of nature are not dependent upon any basic moral principle or law. By recognising the laws of nature as heuristically obligatory, people do, however, create a kind of opposition between right and law in the sense that the latter limits the former, that is, commits the person to definite forms of action by ruling out endless others. The obligation is only heuristic and, if the law-regulated behaviour does not serve self-preservation, the basic right to self-defense in the interest of preservation remains to be asserted by the individual.[66]

There are, in other words, nowhere any obligations corresponding to the rights of nature; they are the primary moral feature of persons. But by recognising an obligation to the laws of nature, people will strive to establish a realm of matching rights and obligations, namely those of contractual relations which are the basis for civil society. The rest of the laws of nature specify the virtues which are required for the maintenance of such a system. The most important is '*That men performe their Covenants made*', which is 'the Fountain and originall of Justice'.[67] The others specify a number of essentials of sociability.[68]

With this line of argument, Hobbes took the Grotian idea of subjective rights as the primary moral feature of human personality to the limit. To his contemporaries, it seemed a scandalous attempt to make out morals to be nothing but a human invention for self-serving purposes. To modern scholars, it has rather seemed odd that he chose to couch such a program in the antiquated language of natural law – to some, so odd that they deny that this in fact was his programme and instead interpret him as a 'genuine' natural lawyer; while to others, the traditional language is little more than a radical thinker's bow to conventional wisdom, probably with an eye to his own safety and quiet.[69] Behind much of this debate may lie an anachronistic assumption that Hobbes had to find his way among the same concepts of obligation as we do, that is, roughly that it is either an implication of some kind of undeniable good, or that it is a special self-imposed necessity. There is no doubt that Hobbes took a decisive step in the direction of the latter with his theory of the contractual foundations for the common moral virtues and institutions. At the same time, it is undeniable that this theory is situated within a doctrine of natural law and natural rights – and this is neither traditional nor modern.

As already mentioned, Hobbes saw the world in a general theistic perspective, and there seems to be no good reason to doubt his profession of a Christian interpretation of this nor that he meant his deterministic metaphysics to be a philosophical elaboration of Calvinist necessitarianism. If anything, this only increases the difficulty of understanding his willingness to describe the rational precepts, or laws of nature, as divine commands for the direction of human behaviour. However, when the issue is at the focus of discussion his words are carefully chosen:

> These dictates of Reason, men use to call by the name of Lawes; but improperly: for they are but Conclusions, or Theoremes concerning what conduceth to the conservation and defence of themselves; wheras Law, properly is the word of him, that by right hath command over others. But yet if we consider the same Theoremes, as delivered in the word of God, that by right commandeth all things; then are they properly called Lawes.[70]

So the legal quality of the precepts depends upon our consideration, and in such consideration the crucial concept is the 'right' by which God commandeth. Generally, such authority arises from one or another form of contractual authorisation, but since humanity, apart from a few and exceptionally inspired individuals, can have no communication with God, this cannot be the basis for divine moral authority.[71] Rather, it arises from God's irresistible power. God is in the same situation as all other moral agents in having a right to everything; but in contrast to other agents, He has the irresistible power to maintain this right successfully:

> Seeing all men by Nature had the Right to All things, they had Right every one to reigne over all the rest. But because this Right could not be obtained by force, it concerned the safety of every one, laying by that Right, to set up men (with Soveraign Authority) by common consent, to rule and defend them: whereas if there had been any man of Power Irresistible; there had been no reason, why he should not by that Power have ruled, and defended both himselfe, and them, according to his discretion. To those therefore whose Power is irresistible, the dominion of all men adhæreth naturally by their excellence of Power; and consequently it is from that Power, that the Kingdome over men, and the Right of inflicting men at his pleasure, belongeth Naturally to God Almighty; not as Creator, and Gracious; but as Omnipotent.[72]

Those who understand this situation will see everything they do towards their self-preservation, and especially their adherence to the precepts of reason, as done with the connivance of the irresistible power that could have ordered entirely otherwise. Those who do not, or will not, see it this way are enemies of this natural kingdom of God – but they still have the precepts of natural reason.

For Grotius, there were two reasons why men in the state of nature could agree not only *that* others have the right to self-preservation and the rights that follow therefrom, but also to a significant extent *what* those rights are in particular circumstances. First, transgressions against such rights are inherently wrong – so inherently wrong that not even God could make them acceptable. Grotius is, in anachronistic terms, a realist. Second, men have the moral power to recognise such objective values, as already pointed out. This means that they have the ability to see what is good for others, as well as for themselves, and it is common knowledge among them that this is so. By contrast, Hobbes gave a completely subjectivist account of what is good and bad and of moral judgement. Of course, he introduced into this scheme his notion of natural law as right reason bidding individuals to close off some of their endless possibilities or rights by seeking peace with others. In itself, however, this does not help as long as we have no objective standard for recognising when others are or are not doing this, and a consequent common or intersubjective knowledge that this is happening. Only when the natural law has become institutionalised, that is, has become the sovereign's law, do we have such a standard and such common knowledge. Hobbes had to seek a political solution, the creation of an absolute sovereign, to the impasse in his moral theory. For Grotius, the political establishment secures and extends the particular social arrangements which are direct expressions of the minimal morality of the natural state.[73]

This has led to extensive discussions, using modern notions from the theory of games like the prisoner's dilemma, as to whether Hobbesian individuals could rationally engage in contractual relations at all.[74] Hobbes himself seems to have taken the line that individuals in nearly all circumstances had to work together in order to preserve themselves. Any breach of trust would so tarnish a person's trustworthiness that his chances of future cooperation would be greatly diminished, and this was a sufficiently dangerous prospect to keep people cooperative in all but the most extreme personal danger.[75] The appropriate question is whether the state of nature could exist.

In contrast to Grotius, Hobbes had an elaborate metaphysics and moral psychology, and these theories forced him to try to do without even the minimal moral equipment of the Dutchman. Whatever the philosophical merit of his attempt, historically the price he paid was high. To contemporaries and most successors, he seemed to have arrived at a scepticism (relativism) even worse than the Renaissance variety which Grotius had seen as his target; natural law seemed to have been largely emptied of meaning and it had become exceedingly difficult to see how human nature, on Hobbes's account of it, would even allow the formation of social relations. At the same time, Grotius's 'realism', though not his 'cognitivism', was seen as a relic of scholasticism. These were among the problems which Samuel Pufendorf faced.

## V. THE GERMAN DEBATE

Samuel Pufendorf must be seen partly in the wider European context, partly as a major participant in a more local debate. In both arenas, the situation was extraordinarily complex and beyond easy summary. In Germany, Pufendorf was part of the Lutheran reaction to Grotius, which had begun somewhat later than the reactions in England and Holland and only gained momentum after the mid-century.[76] The German debate principally concerned the relationship between natural law and moral theology, with most orthodox Lutherans insisting that the former was based on or part of the latter. The source for this view was a Protestant Aristotelianism considerably resembling scholastic Aristotelianism.[77] The original reformers, not least Luther, had revolted against the scholastic *imago Dei* doctrine. That is to say, they had rejected the possibility that men could have any rational knowledge of God's nature on the basis of which they could draw moral lessons for themselves – technically expressed, for example, as a denial that we can know that the natural law 'participates' in God's eternal law. Only faith and grace could guide and save humankind. Apart from being less than helpful as a social philoso-phy for troubled times,[78] this tendency in Lutheran thinking flew in the face of a metaphysics and anthropology which, being of a basically Aristotelian bent, had great difficulty in giving up a teleological view of human nature. This kept alive the *imago Dei* notion, which was in fact central to much Lutheran orthodoxy in the seventeenth century. With it went the idea that the natural law could only be derived from that original state of innocence in which man was closest to being in the Maker's image. While the Lutherans, more than their scholastic predecessors, emphasised the debilitating effect of the Fall upon man's moral faculties, they held that with the help of God's revealed word man could gain sufficient insight into the law to secure social living in the here and now – the hereafter being an entirely different question. Allowing for a great many variations, it is this basic theme of the dependence of natural law upon revealed religion which is one of Pufendorf's main targets.[79]

These disputes were by no means divorced from the wider philosophical themes discussed above. The orthodox well understood that their main enemy was a theological voluntarism. Disregarding, or perhaps misunderstanding, Grotius's potentially radical rights-based theory, they therefore often invoked his notable realism in their support. This must always be borne in mind when we find Pufendorf and his followers claiming to be Grotius's true successors. This was a polemical ploy and a misleading half-truth.

## VI. PUFENDORF

Pufendorf took his stand against the Lutherans of his day by insisting on Luther's own assertion of the rational and moral gulf between God and man. However, while the reformer was led from this to a suspicion and neglect of natural law, the natural lawyer saw the possibility of developing it as a complete science of morals, sharply separate from moral theology and analogous to the new deductive science. This insistence on the scientific character of natural law, inspired by Cartesianism and by Hobbes, is a renewal of Grotius's ambition to use mathematics as the guiding ideal for natural law, an ideal mostly submerged by his humanist learning.[80]

Pufendorf's scientific ambition is patent in his early work, the *Elementa* (1660), which is intended to lay the foundations for natural jurisprudence as a hypothetico-deductive system and is cast in the form of one book of twenty-one definitions and another of two axioms and five observations. By the time of his major work, *De iure,* such formalities have been laid aside, but the substantial point is largely retained.

Just as God chose to create the physical world in such a way that it follows certain laws discoverable by the physical sciences, so He created a moral world which has certain permanent features, namely, those of basic human nature. Beyond presupposing human nature as empirically given, however, moral science is not empirical. What makes it properly scientific is that it is an *a priori,* demonstrative or deductive discipline which in principle can give us certain knowledge analogous to that of mathematics.[81] This is because human nature in fact *creates* morals.

The basic features of human nature are a constant concern for self-preservation, recognition of one's insufficient ability to provide such security alone, a certain sociability, and a mutual recognition of these features in each other.[82] Given such a nature, groups of people will invent a language in which to articulate the recognition of their situation and to deduce basic rules enabling them to live together and, from these, more particular rules and institutions. While the root of morals is God's will in choosing human nature as He did, the rest of morals is thus a human creation of which we have 'maker's knowledge', that is, demonstrative knowledge. In this respect, as in many others, Pufendorf's theory is clearly a precursor of Locke's in the *Essay concerning Human Understanding.*

The moral and the physical world are two self-contained spheres, which is to say that there is no moral quality or purpose inherent in the physical world. Values are not amongst the natural qualities. The *entia moralia* are simply 'modes' which are introduced into the natural world at one spot, human nature. In order for things or events in nature to acquire value, they have to be related to a norm, and this can only be done by beings who can understand norms as prescriptions for actions, and who can act upon this understanding, that is, beings of intellect and free will who may or may not follow the prescription and thereby do either right or wrong. Value is thus imposed upon that which in itself is morally neutral, when a rule is prescribed to guide a will. The human will can give such guidance to itself when it enters into pacts and promises and thus undertakes obligations; and one human will can guide another by legislating for it. These human impositions are, however, no more than deductions from the basic law of nature which is inherent in human nature and as such a manifestation of God's will. Without the guidance of natural law, human volition and human action would be natural, non-moral phenomena like those we find in the rest of the animal creation.[83]

It should be stressed that Pufendorf's voluntarism in the first instance is onto-logical. It was in His choice of creation that God exercised His free will. However, once He had included a human nature of the sort He did, a certain set of moral entities was naturally fit to provide guidance for this nature.[84] The standard charge against voluntarism, that it makes God's prescription of natural law appear an arbitrary imposition, was thus in some measure misconceived; and a parallel complaint about the arbitrary choice of human nature would be impossible since we have no means of knowing God's motives for creation. This train of reasoning we have already met with in Suárez (and it is to be found again in Locke), but in Pufendorf it was further strengthened by his particular understanding of Lutheran-ism – which contrasted so sharply with that of his contemporaries – as well as by his concern to make natural law independent of theology.

From the preceding, it should be clear that Pufendorf was also a moral volunta-rist for whom the basis for morality was the will or law of a superior. This does not, however, follow from his ontological voluntarism and has to be argued separately. After all, God might, for instance, have chosen human nature in such a way that men would primarily recognise a more or less extensive complement of subjective rights in each other, while any moral guidance beyond that would be derivative from such rights.[85] This would have brought Pufendorf very close to the standpoint of Grotius. Pufendorf's texts do, however, make it clear that he subscribes to a voluntarism according to which law is logically and causally primary, while obligation, duty, and right are derivative.

First of all, Pufendorf suggests that 'good' and 'evil', 'justice' and 'injustice' are conceptually derived from 'law'.[86] Second, he maintains that without law there is no possibility of moral judgement. There is no separate moral faculty or conscience, and moral judgement consists in nothing more than the correlation of action, legal prescription, and reaction of law-giver (reward/punishment).[87] Concerning the relationship between law and rights, Pufendorf's basic definition of *ius* must be remembered: it is a 'Power of acting granted or left free by the Laws'.[88]

Pufendorf uses *ius* in the sense of subjective rights to refer to four different categories of deontic powers: power over one's own actions (or *libertas*); power over another person's actions (or *imperium*); power over one's own things, property (or *dominium*); power over another person's property (or *servitus*).[89] The three last are adventitious; that is, they are instituted by men through contractual and quasi-contractual arrangements, and they thus presuppose the first power. *Libertas* encompasses the absence of subjection in a human being's command of his physical and moral personality – his life, actions, body, honour, and reputation. This right, or cluster of rights, does not depend on the agreement of others; it exists in a person by nature or innately. In fact, it exists ante-natally, in as much as a foetus has rights as soon as it is a recognisably human organism. The natural or innate character of *libertas* does not, however, mean that it is *sui generis* and independent of natural law. A clue is given in a passage concerning the rights of the foetus. There Pufendorf makes it quite clear that such rights exist due to the fact that other people have duties, imposed by natural law, to respect such rights. In order to appreciate Pufendorf's way of thinking, we must distinguish between the obligator, that is, the person to whom one is bound in obligation, and the beneficiary of an obligation. The two can be one person, as when *A* promises *B* to do something for him or her. However, in the case of *libertas* the obligator is God to whom we are obligated to obey the law of nature by, *inter alia,* respecting the *libertas* of our neighbour, but it is the neighbour who is the beneficiary of this obligation, his benefit being his *libertas.* This also explains why it is that in the state of nature there is no right of punishment in man. Such a right is an authority over others, but prior to agreements no man has any authority over another, and the only authority in the state of nature is God. Man does have a right of self-defence as part of the basic right to self-preservation, but Pufendorf is careful to distinguish this from the right to punish – in opposition to Hobbes.[90]

In this account, a right is that which there is a duty to yield, whether to oneself or to others. Rights are, however, also related to duties and law in a different way. That which we have a duty to do, we must have a right to do, and in this sense a right is a moral power to act, granted by the basic law of nature in order to fulfil the duties imposed by this law. Rights thus have a positive as well as a negative side, both of which are derived from duties conceived as impositions of natural law.

The reason for Pufendorf's obvious fear of considering rights as primary over law was that he saw such a position as a version of scholastic essentialism – the view that moral values were inherent in nature prior to God's moral legislation. This was exactly the view he vehemently criticised in Grotius.[91]

Of course, one can rescue the thesis of the primacy of rights by resorting to the circumstance that the natural law is dependent on God's right to legislate, that is, to obligate those subject to the law. That, however, trivialises the thesis as far as human morals are concerned, and to assimilate God's and man's 'right' is furthermore most un-Pufendorfian.

The vexed question whether Pufendorf subscribed to the thesis of the correlativity of rights and obligations must then be answered in the affirmative, though with two important cautions which make the thesis different from that normally held. First, the thesis is, in the present context, only philosophically interesting concerning natural rights, since adventitious institutions may be made to include rights unsecured by obligations. Second, and more important, in the case of *libertas* there are indeed correlated obligations, but they are not directly to the rights-holder, they are to God.

The character of Pufendorf's theory is in fact evident from the very structure employed in *De iure* and *De officio*. The basic natural law is that, given human nature, we should live sociably. This means that we must fulfil certain offices, *officia*. In order to do so, people need certain powers. Disregarding the obvious physical powers, for example, of speech or procreation, the basic moral powers are the four groups of rights mentioned above, *libertas* being the fundamental one. In order for these rights to be effective, there must be specific duties (also mostly called *officia*) to respect them. As far as *libertas* is concerned, these duties are imposed by the basic law of nature; as far as the other rights are concerned, the duties are directly or derivatively self-imposed by contractual or quasi-contractual means or imposed by authorities established in this way. *Officia* in the broader sense are thus not simply 'duties', as the term is normally rendered in English. They are the offices of life which encompass clusters of specific duties and rights, and we are bound to them by an *obligatio*, or moral necessity.

The basic offices of life fall into three categories, that of being a human being *tout court*, that of being a member of a family (as spouse, parent, child, sibling, master, servant), and that of being a member of a political society (as citizen, sovereign, all manner of magistrates, soldier, etc.). These three groups of offices provide the basis for Pufendorf's tripartite division of his material into analyses of the specific natural jurisprudential relations of persons as persons, of 'oeconomical' (household) relations in the traditional sense, and of civic relations. Self-consciously inspired by Stoicism, this theory fitted directly into the Christian Stoicism of the Enlightenment and lived on in the popular practical ethics of the eighteenth century as Pufendorf's most pervasive legacy – though often on very different philosophical foundations.[92]

It remains to consider the *obligatio* or moral necessity of the law of nature. Pufendorf provides a dual foundation for natural law, namely, a Hobbesian idea of man's need for self-preservation and a Grotian idea of man's social nature. It is debatable whether and to what extent the latter is an independent principle, or whether it really reduces to the former.[93] On the latter view, man's sociability is not an independent principle but a means towards self-preservation; he is de facto social, rather than *sociabilis,* inherently sociable. It is argued that this is often obscured by Pufendorf's attempts to distance himself from Hobbes, and it is at any rate certain that the polemics of the time soon forced him to seek such distance. However, Pufendorf did see very clearly that obligation for self-interested persons easily becomes conceptually confused with the threat of the use of superior power. Such threat is indeed of the essence of obligation, but the distinguishing characteristic of the latter is that there are morally good reasons for the threat of sanctions. The moral necessity in obligation consists in the obligee's rational insight into the justifiability of the obligator's imbuing him with fear through threat of sanctions if the obligation is breached.[94] This side of Pufendorf's argument points to an independent status for the principle of sociability.

There is thus a fundamental ambiguity in Pufendorf's theory of the obligation to natural law. If the emphasis is on self-preservation, then obligation reduces to self-interest in the mode of Hobbes, which Pufendorf evidently wanted to avoid. If the emphasis is on inherent sociability, then an interesting dilemma arises. Sociability can be understood as a given, ultimate feature of human nature. This would dispense with any rôle for the deity, except as creator. Morals would thus be entirely self-contained as a human enterprise, and the discipline dealing with it, natural jurisprudence, would be completely segregated from all theology. The latter was one of Pufendorf's main concerns, and there is therefore a strong case for reading him in this way. However, in that case it would make no sense to talk of sociableness as a *law,* and there would be no meaning in talking of obligation to it, let alone in invoking God. Pufendorf does all of this. If, on the other hand, sociability is God's will for humanity, then the question of our obligation to God arises in all its sharpness after all.

## VII. REACTIONS TO PUFENDORF

These ambiguities gave rise to a debate which lasted for a generation or more and which was as fierce as any in the history of philosophy. It also helped to secure for Pufendorf an influence which was European in scope and lasted well into the eighteenth century.[95] The central problems concerned the rôle of God in the moral world and, consequently, the relationship between moral theology and natural law (or, in modern parlance, ethics). On the one hand, Pufendorf was accused of excluding God from human morals by making the content of the latter entirely dependent upon human nature and its exertions. In this regard the accusations ranged from Hobbist (and Spinozistic) self-interest to mistaken reliance on the principle of sociability. On the other hand, Pufendorf was charged with ascribing to God, if not too large a rôle, at least a mistaken one by making all obligation dependent upon God's will.

The critics were many, but one of the most important was Leibniz, who concentrated the central points in a long letter, subsequently appended to Jean Barbeyrac's influential French edition of Pufendorf's *De officio* together with Barbeyrac's answer to it.[96] Leibniz's first point is that Pufendorf confines natural law (or morals) as we know it to this life. Yet, the very fact of moral striving in earthly life points to a completion in a future life. Pufendorf allows some rôle for God, but the notion itself of divinity implies transcendent vengeance and reward.[97] The second criticism is that Pufendorf limits the scope of natural law to overt action, while 'that which remains hidden in the soul' is a matter for moral theology, 'whose principle . . . is revelation.' However, the moral agent is one and the moral status of external actions cannot be separated from 'the internal movements of the soul'.[98] In that case, natural law would be concerned with nothing but human justice in isolation from that which, as we shall see in the following section, gives the notion of justice its moral content, namely, the divine justice which encompasses goodness and which is the true object of the soul's moral striving.

Third, Leibniz, like many Lutheran scholastics, is severely critical of Pufendorf's voluntaristic account of the obligation to natural law. First, if justice is simply a matter of God's will, then there is no rational account of why we should praise God as just. It is because 'justice follows certain rules of equality and of proportion [which are] no less founded in the immutable nature of things, and in the divine ideas, than are the principles of arithmetic and of geometry' that universal or divine justice encompasses the idea of truth in terms of which we can praise God as truly just. Otherwise, Pufendorf would have to follow the 'unheard-of paradox by which Descartes showed how great can be the errors of great men', namely, that truth itself is a matter of divine will.[99] Pufendorf had, of course, appealed to the justice of God's reasons for imposing the natural law, thus invoking a norm which is prior to God's will. But, Leibniz says, 'if the source of law is the will of a superior and, inversely, a justifying cause of law is necessary in order to have a superior, a circle is created, than which none was ever more manifest.'[100] Pufendorf tried to forestall criticism of this apparent breach of his own principle and prima facie blurring of his sharp division between natural law and revealed religion in the following manner. When he talks of sanctions being imposed justly, he means that they must come from someone with authority over the obligee. One agent's authority over another stems either from agreement by the latter or from some extraordinary benefit rendered by the former. Agreement with God being out of the question, Pufendorf rests his case on God's extraordinary good to humankind, in the free gift of creation as moral and social beings with the capacity to enjoy creation as we find it in ourselves, in others and in the rest of the world. The natural reaction to this is gratitude for the gift, which is shown by looking after it as specified in the law of nature. Without presuming knowledge of God's motives, we are thus under a rational obligation to Him.[101]

This argument does not quite get to the bottom of Leibniz's objection, for it is presupposed that man has the ability to recognise the goodness of God's gift independent of the law of nature, since this is the foundation of the obligation to the law. However, 'good' and 'evil' are only given meaning by the law of nature, and it is only through the latter that we have a capacity for moral knowledge. On this basis, Leibniz rejects Pufendorf's idea that the force of divine sanctions and the reasons of God's justice, while severally necessary, are conjointly sufficient for obligation to natural law.[102]

If Pufendorf had kept to the idea that human sanctions against ingratitude for 'God's gift' would do as the foundation for natural law, he would indeed have minimalised the rôle of God and he would have provided the possibility of a purely human or social account of how we come to learn about 'good' and 'evil' or develop our moral powers (whether innate or purely acquired). Locke toyed with such thoughts, as we will see, and they were at the centre of the moral philosophy of the Enlightenment. The way was cleared for it in a somewhat circuitous manner through a return by several late-seventeenth-century natural lawyers to some scholastic points, especially the distinction between the goodness and the obligation of natural law, which we have already met with in Suárez.

In his native Germany, Pufendorf remained for long the focus of the debate about the relationship between natural law and revealed religion, the main support for his sharp separation of the two being provided by his most outstanding disciple, Christian Thomasius.[103] In a host of works, but most importantly in the *Institutiones jurisprudentiae divinae* (1688), Thomasius maintained the independence of natural law by delimiting the voluntaristic element to the bare minimum outlined above, arguing in effect that we cannot rationally know more about God's authorship of the law than the mere fact, and that we can learn the rest from human rationality considered as a social practice. After a prolonged pietistic crisis of doubt about the adequacy of his own or any other rational reply to the criticisms of voluntarism, Thomasius radically restated his position in *Fundamenta juris naturae et gentium* (1705). He here reduces the status of *ius naturae* from one of law proper to that of divine advice or a matter of conscience and stresses the rôle of positive law and social morality. This is the basis for his well-known distinction between *honestum, justum,* and *decorum,* respectively.

In the French- and English-speaking worlds Pufendorf's impact was mediated by the Huguenot refugee Jean Barbeyrac, who provided grand editions and French translations not only of Pufendorf, but also of Grotius and Cumberland.[104] The French editions of Grotius and Pufendorf subsequently became the basis for English ones, which had significant influence in the English-speaking world, especially in Scotland.[105] It was Barbeyrac more than anyone who streamlined the natural jurisprudential debate from Grotius onwards and delivered it to the eighteenth century as a coherently developing tradition, which was the most important modern school of moral thought and whose primary objective was to combat modern scepticism, especially that of Pierre Bayle.[106]

## VIII. LEIBNIZ

Throughout the seventeenth century, there were strong currents of moral realism, of partly Platonic, partly scholastic-Aristotelian provenance. While opposing voluntarism of the Cartesian, Hobbesian, and other varieties, these nevertheless had to find room somewhere for the voluntarist element required of any acceptable form of Christianity or of any natural religion compatible with Christian thought. In Germany, the greatest representative of this tendency was Gottfried Wilhelm Leibniz. Of his copious writings on natural law, only a few were published in his lifetime, and of these the best-known piece was mainly critical in character.[107]

The criticisms of Pufendorf's voluntarism, considered above, were based on the idea of a universal jurisprudence. The object of this was a justice that was universal for all rational beings and thus common between God and human beings. Since God cannot be indebted to humans, let alone be thought to harm them, this justice cannot be conceived in terms of the two traditional stricter forms of justice, giving each one his due and refraining from harm to others. Universal justice is a form of love or benevolence, though understood not as an emotive state but as an active principle guided by rational judgement. This is what Leibniz calls *caritas sapientis,* the charity of the wise person. He thus transposes the issue of voluntarism to the spheres of rational theology and moral psychology: In God, and in pale imitation in humanity, wisdom and will come together as 'the measure of justice', while 'power', Hobbes's master principle as Leibniz read him, is nothing but the temporal efficient cause:

> Justice is nothing else than that which conforms to wisdom and goodness joined together: the end of goodness is the greatest good, but to recognize it wisdom is needed, which is nothing else than knowledge of the good. Goodness is simply the inclination to do good to everyone, and to arrest evil. . . . Thus wisdom is in the understanding and goodness in the will. And justice, as a consequence, is in both. Power is a different matter, but if it is used it makes right become fact, and makes what ought to be also really exist, in so far as the nature of things permits. And this is what God does in the world.[108]

## IX. CULVERWEL

The concept of natural law had an even more tenuous position in the Platonic-Aristotelian ethics of the so-called Cambridge Platonists.[109] In one of their eclectic students, Nathaniel Culverwel, there is, however, a more concerted attempt at compromise.[110] On the one hand, Culverwel was a Calvinist who had to reject the Platonists' theory of innate ideas as a trace of God's hand in the human mind and the associated notions of the soul as living or participating in the divine mind and therefore having an inherent goodness. On the other hand, he had to agree with the Platonists that goodness and justice could not simply be understood as effects of God's will; there was such a thing as inherently good and just behaviour. For this to make sense, there must be an over-arching eternal law, to be understood as a purely conceptual link between God and the natural law prescribed for humanity. Against this uneasy background, Culverwel drew well-known distinctions with origins in Suárez – between mere precepts discovered by reason in the nature of things and laws of nature prescribed for humans, between the matter and the form of the law of nature; between natural and moral good, and between the natural obligation of rational precepts and the moral obligation of law proper.[111] Sadly, he is even further than his intellectual master, Suárez, from clarifying 'natural obligation', which seems to signify no more than recognition of natural goodness.

## X. CUMBERLAND

The search for a way between realism and voluntarism is pursued also by Richard Cumberland in his attempt to refute Hobbes.[112] He argues that only by serving the common good of the universal moral community of God and humanity, past, present and future, will we serve our own good. We have a natural inclination, benevolence, to do this, and we develop rational precepts to guide this inclination. We will eventually appreciate that benevolent behaviour is also God's will and thus see that the rational precepts are proper laws of nature, that the inclinations are virtues, and that the common good is not only a natural, but a moral good. The obligation to the basic law of nature concerning the promotion of the common good arises from the individual unifying his particular will with the general will of God. When Cumberland uses the traditional formulation that man's obligation stems from God's will, he means that obligation arises from our seeing that our will is part of God's general will. However, since moral goodness is defined in terms of law, and since God cannot be subject to law, Cumberland is caught in the traditional dilemma. He takes the line that God's supreme reasoning and willing takes place *as if* He were following a law, and in His complete goodness and wisdom He binds himself to will the common good of the moral universe He has created. God is thus a sort of moral intuitionist who can undertake self-obligation to moral goodness, and this is the ultimate ground of all moral obligation. While this is at best a marginal advance on attempts like those of Suárez and Culverwel, the formulation is so thoroughly anthropomorphic that this notion of *God's* ability to derive 'ought' from 'good' begs to be transferred to humanity. If human moral ability is made as closely in God's image as he thinks, cannot humans make the same sort of inference, albeit imperfectly? Several thinkers such as Shaftesbury, Clarke, and Hutcheson set about exploring this possibility, some of them obviously inspired in part by Cumberland.

Cumberland's theory of natural law and its obligation as based upon love, benevolence, and human beings sharing in the will of God presupposes a moral community of humanity with God. Traditionally, this was associated with innatism and often with Catholicism. The 'empiricist' critique of innatism is thus often used as part of anti-popish polemics, for example, in Locke. Cumberland is of some significance in this connexion. His combination of a strong critique of innate ideas and assertion of the moral community with God was a contributing factor in the formation of the kind of empirically based natural providentialism, or natural religious teleology, which soon became the framework for natural law thinking and, indeed, for the mainstream of Enlightenment moral thought, not least in Scotland. In England, this line of thought was associated with strong elements of latitudinarian theology and became entangled in the deistic debates, where one finds widespread use of Cumberland.

## XI. LOCKE

For Cumberland, the loss of innate ideas of morals was amply compensated for by the knowledge acquired by reason and experience of the moral community in this world and the next. Despite his reputation as the great 'empiricist' philosopher, there was no such easy replacement of innate with empirical knowledge in John Locke's theory of morals.[113] Locke originally thought of natural law in traditional voluntarist-cum-realist terms, as we see from his unpublished *Essays on the Law of Nature* (1663),[114] although even then he rejected innatism. During the subsequent quarter of a century, as his epistemology and theology developed, the status of morals had to be rethought. However, Locke never published a comprehensive statement of his moral theory, and the partial presentations in *An Essay concerning Human Understanding* (1689), the *Two Treatises of Government* (1690), and the works on education and religion left his contemporaries dissatisfied and confused, a condition matched by the disagreements among modern scholars even when they have been able to make use of Locke's correspondence and unpublished manuscript materials.[115] The disputes centrally concern the relationship between reason and revelation, as we shall see.

In much of his philosophy relating to morals Locke is working out a programme similar to Pufendorf's and, in view of Locke's stated admiration for the German thinker, he is likely to have been doing so with some degree of self-consciousness.[116] Like Pufendorf, Locke argues, as part of his criticism of innate ideas, that moral phenomena are created by moral agents and imposed upon nature which, in abstraction from such activity, is value-neutral. Moral ideas are mixed modes, that is complex ideas deliberately put together from simple ideas so as to order our understanding of particular events and thus facilitate our behaviour in the world. Like Pufendorf, he stresses the social aspect of this activity. Unless we arrange the particular events of life into groups and categories, we shall have difficulty in communicating with and thus relating to others. The clear definition and labelling of moral ideas is thus important in order to achieve some communal or social stability in such ideas. In short, morals is a mental construct used in social communication through the medium of language. Different individuals and, especially, groups of individuals can make different constructions and thus have different moral languages. Since morals is human-made, it can, as in Pufendorf, be a demonstrative science, for deductive proof consists in bringing ideas, over which we have command, into relationship to each other in the same way as we do in mathematics. The science of morals is thus a hypothetico-deductive system concerned with formal coherence. Whether anything corresponds to it in the empirical world of the senses is an entirely different question which does not strictly pertain to the science as such:

The Truth and Certainty of *moral* Discourses abstracts from the Lives of Men, and the Existence of those Vertues in the World, whereof they treat: Nor are Tully's Offices less true, because there is no Body in the World that exactly practices his Rules, and lives up to that pattern of a vertuous Man, which he has given us, and which existed no where, when he writ, but in *Idea*.[117]

Proof in morals consists more particularly in relating moral ideas and types of ideas to laws. In order for a rule to be a law, it has to issue from a lawmaker, that is, an authority who can back up the rule with reward and punishment. Laws are divided according to their type of enforcement into three kinds, the divine or natural law stemming from God; the civil law imposed by governments; and the law of opinion or reputation arising in a given social group.[118]

All these forms of law are complex moral ideas which the mind constructs. The thing which, so to speak, anchors moral ideas in the world of action and thus makes the laws into practical principles is human beings' native desire for happiness and aversion to pain. The core of personality or agency is self-consciousness, which implies a concern for maintenance of the self, and this expresses itself in such desire and aversion.[119] However, what counts as happiness and pain depends upon people's understanding of life, that is, upon their moral ideas. 'Hence naturally flows the great variety of Opinions, concerning Moral Rules, which are to be found amongst Men, according to the different sorts of Happiness, they have a Prospect of, or propose to themselves.'[120] It is the happiness or pain which we understand a lawmaker to attach to his rules as reward or punishment which make these rules into laws guiding our conduct and defining or demonstrating what is morally good or evil:

*Morally good and Evil,* then, is only the Conformity or Disagreement of our voluntary Actions to some Law, whereby Good or Evil is drawn on us, from the Will and Power of the Law-maker; which Good and Evil, Pleasure or Pain, attending our observance, or breach of the Law, by the Decree of the Law-maker, is that we call *Reward* and *Punishment.*[121]

All this amounts to a straightforward relativistic theory of morals, and Locke is in fact proud that he can account so economically for the moral diversity which history and geography exhibit. The question is, however, whether he can anchor the divine or natural law in something sufficiently permanent and universal to give him an absolute moral standard or a natural/divine law proper. This is where the main controversies arise. The central question is whether Locke did, or could, deliver something which, by his own standards, would be considered a rational argument for the proposition that God is a lawmaker for humanity in the sense outlined above, or whether he relied, or had to rely, on revelation at this point. The problem is compounded by evidence that Locke himself was uncertain and that his views changed over time. The most coherent line of argument in his main philosophical works is as follows.

Of all our ideas, two particular ones have a special veridical status, our knowledge of the self and our knowledge of God. The self considered not as some kind of substance but as self-consciousness is undeniable, and any attempt at denial is self-refuting. From this idea of the self and its properties of perception and reason, Locke argues causally or demonstratively to the existence of '*an eternal, most powerful, and most knowing Being*'.[122] Whatever we, from a post-Humean and post-Kantian perspective, may think of such an argument, it was of course entirely traditional, and there is little to suggest that Locke saw his own epistemology as undermining it.

Having established that the relationship between God and man is one of dependence, the question is whether this can be shown to mean that God is lawmaker. Commonly this is taken to mean that Locke would have to show that there is an afterlife for the self, and that God holds the promise of reward and threat of punishment in eternity. It seems clear that Locke did not think these things could be shown by reason, and it is commonly pointed out that he in fact undermines the usual arguments for the immortality of the soul.[123] But are such arguments in fact necessary in his scheme of things? First, immortality.

The basic point in Locke's account of the self in terms of self-consciousness is to get rid of ideas of substance, whether material or immaterial, so that agency can be understood as continuous across changes of substance. And he explicitly links this to the idea of reckoning at the Great Day, when every one shall *receive according to his doings, the secrets of all Hearts shall be laid open.* [note: 'cf. 1 Cor. 14: 25 *and* 2 Cor. 5: 10'] The Sentence shall be justified by the consciousness all Persons shall have, that they *themselves* in what Bodies soever they appear, or what Substances soever that consciousness adheres to, are the *same,* that committed those Actions, and deserve that Punishment for them.[124]

In other words, while we cannot know anything of the immortality of the self as a substance, we can know that there is no reason why the self considered as self-consciousness should not continue to live.

Further, since, in an un-Lockean metaphor, it is of the essence of the self, understood as self-consciousness, to be concerned with self-preservation, or the security of pleasure and the avoidance of pain, it is rational to assume that an infinitely more powerful being, upon whom we demonstrably depend for our very existence, has rewards and punishments in store for us, if he has any views on how we should behave. In other words, if it is rationally ascertainable that the creator has intentions for his rational creatures, then it is a rational conclusion on the part of these creatures that they should 'play safe' by assuming that sanctions are attached to these intentions.[125] It does not, of course, follow that humanity as a matter of fact generally is rational and plays safe.[126]

Can God's intentions towards humanity, or the content of the law of nature, be discovered by human reason? In the *Essay* Locke makes only a few general remarks to the effect that the law of nature is to secure the public happiness, the preservation of society, the benefit of all, that it is a 'Rule whereby Men should govern themselves', and the like.[127] However, in *The Second Treatise of Government* he makes it clear that the fundamental law of nature is to preserve humanity in others as well as in oneself.[128] It is for this purpose that we must understand the rest of our moral powers, namely our rights in ourselves and in the world around us as well as the further rights which we create by contractual means. For Locke, as for Pufendorf, natural rights are powers to fulfil the basic duty of natural law.[129]

There is, however, an immensely important difference between the two thinkers here. In contrast to Pufendorf, Locke consistently maintains that among the rights entailed by the law of nature is the right or '*Power to Execute* that Law'.[130] He is clearly aware that this may be controversial, admitting that it 'will seem a very strange Doctrine'.[131] The point is that he has achieved too much rather than too little by means of reason, both for his own taste and for that of his contemporary readers. He has come dangerously close to making natural law independent of the divinity considered as a lawmaker as opposed to a mere creator. If we, unaided by revelation, can understand that the divinity has a *ius creatoris* over us consisting in our duty to obey the law of nature and if this rationally understood law entails a right on those who are subject to it to sanction it, then the divinity's additional sanction, which is simply rationally *possible,* would appear to be deprived of much of its immediate relevance to the conduct of ordinary human affairs. And Locke does of course try to show that we, through our institutional arrangements, have a tolerable ability to sanction the law ourselves.

The need for sanctions of natural law arises because we, despite our rational abilities, all too frequently follow our immediate desires rather than the rational necessity of the good pointed out by natural law. In view of the prima facie hedonism we earlier found in Locke, this divergence between what is desired and what is good is in need of explanation. The background to this is that Locke does not identify desire and will in the manner of Hobbes (II.xxi.30) and while he defines 'good' in terms of 'pleasure', as we have seen, he does not, like Hobbes, define 'good' in terms of 'being desired.' He thus leaves an opening for objects of will that are not presently desired and thus for goods that, while pleasant, are not currently pleasing. In this view, we have a liberty to will some good other than what we desire at the moment (II.xxi.38). The law of nature points out what the highest good is, namely, the pleasures of a possibly eternal life, but the law does not constrain the will to do the good and thus terminate the individual's liberty.[132] Liberty consists in having compliance with the law as a rational option. This leaves scope for error and thus raises the need not only for sanctions but also for education. The most common error is that we remain satisfied with the goods of this life (II.xxi.40), which, it might appear, we can secure through our own execution of the law of nature. Only the prospect of the incomparably greater pleasures of eternity can tear us from such erroneous inferences.

Much has been made of Locke's failure to fulfil his promise of a fully worked out theory of natural law. It has been suggested that he was so dissatisfied with his arguments concerning immortality and divine sanctions that he despaired of providing a rational foundation for natural law. In keeping with his increasingly Socinian leanings in theology, he ended by relying entirely on revelation.[133] In contrast, I want to suggest that Locke's natural law doctrine, as interpreted here, fitted some aspects of Socinianism exceedingly well. Any further elaboration of the theory would inevitably have strengthened the already fierce criticism of him for Socinianism and, since the latter was a serious crime, he was well advised not to pursue the matter further than he did in his anonymous works, leaving the final indications of his standpoint to the posthumous *Paraphrase and Notes on the Epistles of St. Paul.*[134]

The net result of the deliberations in the *Essay* was that immortality was rationally possible and that, given our demonstrable dependence upon an almighty creator and given the character of humanity, it was reasonable to fear that divine sanctions were attached to the law of nature.[135] But although it was often asserted that God in fact holds such sanctions in store for us, it was never suggested that this could be proved. In the theological works and especially in the *Paraphrase,* Locke repeatedly and emphatically reaffirms that the law of nature can be understood by natural reason and that it therefore is given for all humankind irrespective of religion.[136] However, the divine sanction of the natural law in an afterlife, which reason could only show to be a sensible expectation and a rational possibility, was affirmed to be a reality by revelation. More particularly, it was Christ's special mission to teach this to humanity. Christ in fact re-promulgated the law of nature, which had previously only been known partially by natural reason or through God's word to Moses, and taught it and its attendant sanctions more perspicuously than these other sources could. In this connexion, Locke strongly emphasises that reason, represented by philosophy, had in fact not developed a full system of morals, but he does not deny the possibility of such a philosophical enterprise. It could, of course, never be very effective with the bulk of humankind who are incapable of rational demonstration and rather need direct commands backed by sanctions. The mission of Christ was therefore at once to make clear to humanity what it had been fumbling for and, especially, to make it an effective force in people's lives by declaring the sanctions attaching to the moral law. However, Locke equally emphasises that the revelation of the law itself, like all revelation, is subject to control by reason.[137] In other words, Locke's philosophical arguments in the *Essay* neatly left theoretical room for exactly the practical rôle of Christ in the world which Socinian theology had allotted him – to be the teacher of, more than the lawmaker for, humanity. It was clearly implied that his lessons would provide valuable guidance in the exercise of our natural duty-cum-right to impose our own preliminary sanctions, asserted in the second *Treatise.*

On the interpretation suggested here, it is possible that Locke worried about his arguments in the *Essay* and, not least, the 'very strange Doctrine' in the (anonymous) second *Treatise,* not because they were weak, but because they were so strong that they drastically reduced the rôle of a divine legislator, let alone of revelation.

## XII. CONCLUDING OUTLOOK

The division between the present chapter and its equivalent in the companion volume on eighteenth-century philosophy is rather artificial.[138] The history of natural law theory is to a significant degree a story of the continuities in moral thought. By the same token, it accounts for the framework within which innovation took place. By the early years of the eighteenth century natural law was established as the most important form of academic moral philosophy in most of Protestant Europe – Germany, the Netherlands, Switzerland, Scandinavia; and it was fast gaining ground in Scotland, in the academies of the rational dissenters in England and, eventually, in the North American colleges.[139] As the 'core curriculum' in practical philosophy, natural law became the seed-bed for new academic disciplines, notably political economy, and for political reforms, especially law reform in Germany. Seventeenth-century natural law had received much of its inspiration from the need to settle confessional and colonial conflicts, and its eighteenth-century successors produced recognisably modern systems of the law of nations in response to great European wars. Seen in this perspective, it is hardly surprising that the theoretical aspects of natural law should continue to be a prominent part of philosophical endeavour.

The great questions which late seventeenth-century natural law theory, especially that of Pufendorf and Locke, had stated so forcefully were, in effect, in what sense and to what extent morals could be accounted for as a human construct without lapsing into 'scepticism', that is, relativism. This sent moral philosophers in two directions, often at once. On the one hand, they sought out moral powers in individual human nature which, whether in the shape of moral sense, conscience or reason, were both veridical and motivating. On the other hand, they traced the evidence for the collective effects of such moral powers in the moral institutions of humankind, ranging from money or the family to civil society or the international community. When interpreted in terms of providence, the collective evidence certified the veridicity of the moral powers. This teleological or providential naturalism formed the mainstream of Enlightenment moral philosophy. But when the sense of purpose was lost to the criticism of a Hume and a Smith, providential naturalism turned into the natural history of civil society, and the veridicity of the moral faculty was reduced to a question of what was minimally required for the existence of social life. This was answered by a theory of negative justice harking back to Grotius's idea of perfect rights. Such ideas were, however, exceptions in a sea of Christian-Stoic or neo-Aristotelian teleology, in which rights remained derivative powers in the service of the duties imposed by natural law. Within this framework, it was next to impossible to reach a philosophically coherent idea of the rights of man – let alone woman – as the primary feature of moral agency. In so far as it was reached, it was via a notion of autonomy or self-legislation which was the philosophical, if not the historical, death of natural law thinking proper.[140]

## NOTES

1 See Tuck 1987a.
2 See Green and Dickason 1989; Holzgrefe 1989; Pagden 1981, 1987; Scott 1934. For the context, see also Hamilton 1963.
3 *De legibus* I.3.v–vi. The complete Latin text can be found in Suárez 1971–81; a partial Latin text with English translation can be found in Suárez 1944, vol. 2.
4 *De legibus* II.1.xi.
5 *De legibus* II.4.ix–x.
6 *De legibus* II.2.viii.
7 *De legibus* I.3.vii–viii.
8 *De legibus* I.3.xiv–xvi.
9 *De legibus* Book III.
10 For the further development of the theory of property in modern natural law, see Buckle 1991; Horne 1990, chap. 1.
11 For Suárez's general programme of criticism of the 'heretics', see *De legibus* I.18.ix–x.
12 See Hruschka 1986.
13 *De legibus* II.17–20.
14 Cf. Chapter 21 in this volume.
15 *De legibus* I.4.iv.
16 *De legibus* II.Introd.
17 *De legibus* I.4.v.
18 *De legibus* I.4.vi; II.1.viii.
19 *De legibus* II.6.iii–iv; etc.
20 *De legibus* II.6.iii.
21 *De legibus* II.6.iv.
22 *De legibus* II.6.vi. The reader may want to consider the transposition of this point to Hume's *Treatise* III.1.i.
23 *De legibus* II.5.vii.
24 *De legibus* II.6.i.
25 *De legibus* II.5.viii.
26 *Lectura super primum et secundum sententiarum*, d. 34, q. 1. art. 2, in Gregory of Rimini 1978–87, vol. 6.
27 *De legibus* II.6.xi.
28 *De legibus* II.6.xi. Cf. the further discussion at II.6.xiv–xix. Although unacknowledged in Suárez, the example is well known from Ockham's extreme formulation of his voluntarism.
29 'If God could command this [that He be not loved for a certain time] – and it seems that He can do it without contradiction – then I maintain that the will in this situation cannot perform such an act, because merely by performing such an act the will would love God above all and consequently would fulfil the divine precept. For to love God above all means to love whatever God wills to be loved. But by the mere fact of loving God in this way one would not (according to our assumption) fulfil the divine command. Consequently by loving God in this manner one would love God and not love God; one would fulfil the precept of God and not fulfil it.' *Quodlibeta*, III, Q. xiii, Ockham 1967, p. 147. Whether Ockham in fact subscribed to the extreme form of voluntarism suggested by Suárez is at least doubtful; see Kilcullen 1994. The voluntarist

interpretation of Ockham may be part of a polemical tradition ratified and effectively conveyed by Suárez.

30 *De legibus* I.15.vii and II.14.xiii–xix.

31 *De legibus* II.6.v and xi.

32 *De legibus* II.6.xiii.

33 *De legibus* II.6.xxiii.

34 *De legibus* II.6.xxiii.

35 *De legibus* II.9.ii–iii.

36 *De legibus* II.9.iv–vii. II.15.xviii.

37 *De legibus* II.17.ii; p. 326; cf. I.2.

38 *De legibus* II.18.ii; p. 335.

39 *De legibus* II.14, esp. xiii–xix. II.18.ii–iii.

40 *De legibus* II.9.ix. II.10.i. II.13.iv.

41 'This Man (Carneades) having undertaken to dispute against Justice, that kind of it, especially, which is the Subject of this Treatise, found no Argument stronger than this. Laws (says he) were instituted by Men for the sake of Interest; and hence it is that they are different, not only in different Countries according to the Diversity of their Manners, but often in the same Country, according to the Times. As to that which is called NATURAL RIGHT, it is a mere Chimera. Nature prompts all Men, and in general all Animals, to seek their own particular Advantage: So that either there is no Justice at all, or, if there is any, it is extreme Folly, because it engages us to procure the Good of others, to our own Prejudice.' Grotius 1735, and 1738, Prol. 5. Presumably such use of Epicureanism by a sceptic strawman helped dissolve the Christianised Epicureanism of the Renaissance and thus prepare the way for Gassendi and Hobbes; cf. Kraye 1988, pp. 382–6.

42 For a comprehensive survey of Reformation principles, their context and social and political implications, see Skinner 1978, vol. 2, chaps. 1, 3, and 7. For the major figures, see McGrath 1985; Höpfl 1985; Stephens 1986.

43 Cf. McGrath 1986, vol. 2.

44 Grotius 1735, and 1738, I.1.iii–iv and ix. For the earlier history of *ius,* see esp. Tierney 1987, 1988, 1989, and 1991; Villey 1975.

45 Grotius 1735, and 1738, I.2.i.

46 Grotius 1735, and 1738, I.1.v.

47 Grotius 1735, and 1738, I.1.xii; Prol. XL–XLI.

48 Grotius 1735, and 1738, I.1.viii.

49 Grotius 1735, and 1738, I.1.iv.

50 Grotius 1735, and 1738, II.17.ix; II.25.iii (3); III.1.iv (2); III.13.iv; cf. I.2.viii (3); II.1.xiii; II.12.ix (2). For the rules of charity, see Schneewind 1987, pp. 140–1; for the great historical significance of the distinction between perfect and imperfect rights, see Haakonssen 1985b.

51 Grotius, 1950; Tuck 1993, pp. 169–79.

52 Grotius 1735 and 1738, I.1.ix–x.

53 Grotius 1735 and 1738, Prol. XI–XII.

54 Grotius 1679 and 1805.

55 Grotius 1735 and 1738, Prol. XLIX, LI.

56 Chapter 12 of this work was published in 1609 as *Mare liberum*. The full work was only rediscovered in the nineteenth century and published as *De iure praedae* (1868). See Knight 1925, chap. 5. For the development of Grotius's ideas, see above all Tuck 1993, chap. 5.

57 See Grotius 1950, vol. 1, pp. 8–9; and Tuck, 1993, pp. 172–3.

58 See Grotius 1679 and 1805. As Swedish ambassador in Paris from 1635 to 1645, Grotius was at the centre of European diplomacy, politics, and intellectual life; Knight 1925, chap. 11. For a possible attempt by Sweden's rival, Denmark, to attract him, see Carlsen 1938.

59 For the connexions with Tew and Selden, see Trevor-Roper 1987a, chap. 4; Tuck 1979, chaps. 4–5; and Tuck 1993, pp. 205–21 and 272–8.

60 Selden 1640. Cf. Selden 1663; Crowe 1977a; Sommerville 1984; Tuck 1979, chap. 4; Tuck 1982; Tuck 1993, pp. 205–21.

61 See Tuck 1983, 1988, and 1989. Tuck even suggests that Hobbes, like Grotius, primarily sought an answer to scepticism; see especially Tuck 1987b. This has been subjected to criticism by Perez Zagorin 1993.

62 *Lev.* xiv, Hobbes 1968, pp. 190 and 189; cf. *De cive*, I.10 and *The Elements of Law*, XIV.10.

63 Hobbes, *The Elements of Law*, XIV.10–12; *De cive*, I.11–13; *Lev.* xiii.

64 *Lev.* xiv, Hobbes 1968, p. 189; cf. *The Elements of Law*, XV.1 and *De cive*, II.1.

65 *Lev.* xiv, Hobbes 1968, p. 190; cf. *The Elements of Law*, XV.1–2 and *De cive*, II.2–3.

66 *Lev.* xiv, Hobbes 1968, p. 190.

67 *Lev.* xv, Hobbes 1968, pp. 201–2; cf. *The Elements of Law*, XVI.1 and *De cive*, III.1.

68 Hobbes, *The Elements of Law*, XVI–XVII; 1983, III; *Lev.* xv.

69 The most important proponents of the former view are Warrender 1957 and Martinich 1992, but see also Taylor 1965 and Hood 1964, as well as the discussions in K. C. Brown 1965. Particularly important discussions of Hobbes on obligation are Oakeshott 1975, chap. 1, and T. Nagel 1959. The latter view has taken many forms, but see esp. Peters 1956; Watkins 1965; Goldsmith 1966; McNeilly 1968; Gauthier 1969; Hampton 1986. For particularly useful general assessments, see Raphael 1977; Sorell 1986; Tuck 1989; Baumgold 1988.

70 *Lev.* xv, Hobbes 1968, pp. 216–17. Cf. Hobbes's explanation to Bishop Bramhall: 'After I had ended the discourse he mentions the laws of nature, I thought it fittest in the last place, once for all, to say they were the laws of God, then when they were delivered in the word of God; but before, being not known by men for any thing but their own natural reason, they were but theorems, tending to peace.' *Eng. Works*, vol. 4, pp. 284–5. See also *The Elements of Law*, XVIII.1 and *De cive*, IV.1.

71 Hobbes, *The Elements of Law*, XV.11; *De cive*, II.12; *Lev.* xiv, Hobbes 1968, p. 197.

72 *Lev.* xxxi, Hobbes 1968, p. 397; cf. *De cive*, XV.5.

73 Tuck 1989, pp. 63–4.

74 Most of this debate originates from Gauthier 1969.

75 *Lev.* xv, Hobbes 1968, pp. 204–5.

76 Reibstein 1953–4. For Pufendorf's background, see especially Döring 1988 and 1992.

77 Petersen 1921.

78 Cf. Suárez's polemic against the Lutherans as simple and dangerous antinomians, *De legibus* I.18.ii. For a different view of the place of natural law in the reformers, see McNeill 1946.

79 The orthodox position was significantly clarified in the intense polemic which followed Pufendorf's two main natural law works from 1672 and 1673 and his defence of them, esp. in *Eris Scandica* in 1686 (Pufendorf 1672, 1927, and 1706b). The most extreme and clear position was that of Valentin Alberti 1678 and 1687. Cf. Osterhorn 1962.

80 Concerning the connexions between natural law and the methodological discussions, see Röd 1970. For Pufendorf, also Denzer 1972, pp. 279–96, and, for his teacher, Erhard Weigel, Röd 1969. For general studies of Pufendorf, see, in addition to Denzer

1972, Krieger 1965; Laurent 1982; Palladini 1990; Goyard-Fabre 1994; Welzel 1958. For his biography and background, Döring 1992. More specialised, valuable studies include Diesselhorst 1976; Hruschka 1984; Lezius 1900; Rabe 1958; Zurbuchen 1991.

81 Pufendorf 1967; 1749, I.2.

82 Pufendorf 1967; 1749, II.3, esp. x–xi and xv–xvi.

83 Pufendorf illustrates his point in the manner we have already encountered in Suárez by suggesting that actions which are physically identical in man and in beast have completely different moral import. 1967 and 1749, I.2.vi.

84 *Elementorum jurisprudentiae universalis libri duo* I.xiii.14, in Pufendorf 1931.

85 A succession of Swedish commentators seem to subscribe to something like this view; Hägerström 1965; Olivecrona 1971 and 1977; Mautner 1989.

86 *De officio hominis et civis juxta legem naturalem libri duo* I.2.xi and xiii, in Pufendorf 1927 and 1991.

87 Pufendorf 1967 and 1749, I.3.iv.

88 Pufendorf 1967 and 1749, I.6.iii.

89 Cf. Olivecrona 1977; Mautner 1989.

90 Pufendorf 1967 and 1749, VIII.3.i–ii. Cf. p. 1348.

91 Pufendorf 1967 and 1749, I.2.vi. I.6.iv.

92 Haakonssen 1996, chaps. 2 and 10.

93 For the latter view, see Palladini 1990.

94 Pufendorf 1967 and 1749, I.6.v.

95 For some overviews, see Derathé 1988, esp. pp. 78–84; A. Dufour 1986; Haakonssen 1996 and forthcoming b; Hammerstein 1986; Hont 1987; Luig 1972; Mautner 1986; J. Moore 1988; Thieme 1979. For important aspects of the more immediate impact of Pufendorf, see Bazzoli 1979; Foss 1934; Krieger 1965; Lindberg 1976; Meylan 1937; Moore and Silverthorne 1983 and 1984; Osterhorn 1962; Palladini 1978, 1984, and 1990; Rüping 1970; Sève 1989; Tamm 1986.

96 Leibniz 1718. Barbeyrac says (p. 429) that he 'has learned' that Leibniz's letter was previously published, with the author's name, in A. A. Pagenstecher's edition of the Latin *De officio*, Groeningen, 1712. The Latin text is found in Leibniz 1768, vol. 4, part 3, pp. 275–83, and is translated in Leibniz 1972, pp. 64–75. For discussion of Leibniz's criticism of Pufendorf, see esp. Sève 1989, pp. 49–63. Concerning Barbeyrac's partial defence of Pufendorf, see Meylan 1937, esp. pp. 190–8. Leibniz's attack on Pufendorf was parallelled by one on the strongly theocratic voluntarism of Heinrich von Cocceji and his son Samuel. For the discussion, which rehearsed several of the arguments set out here, see Samuel von Cocceji's dissertation (Cocceji 1699); Leibniz's anonymous journal-article (reprinted as 'Observationes de principio juris' in Leibniz 1768, vol. 4, pp. 270–5); and Cocceji's rejoinder (Cocceji 1702, Part II, pp. 5–51). Cf. Haakonssen 1996; Schneider 1979. For a splendid analysis of the younger Cocceji's later work, see Reynolds 1993; and for his significance for later thought, esp. Adam Smith, Haakonssen 1996, chap. 4.

97 Leibniz 1718, p. 441; Leibniz 1768, vol. 4, part 3, pp. 276–7 (Leibniz 1972, p. 67).

98 Leibniz 1718, p. 447–8; Leibniz 1768, vol. 4, part 3, p. 277 (Leibniz 1972, p. 68).

99 Leibniz 1718, p. 466; Leibniz 1768, vol. 4, part 3, p. 280 (Leibniz 1972, p. 71).

100 Leibniz 1718, p. 485; Leibniz 1768, vol. 4, part 3, p. 281 (Leibniz 1972, pp. 73–4).

101 See Schneewind 1987, p. 145.

102 Leibniz 1718, pp. 487–8; Leibniz 1768, vol. 4, part 3, p. 282 (Leibniz 1972, pp. 74–5).

103 Concerning Pufendorf and Thomasius, see Pufendorf 1897; Haakonssen forthcoming b; Schneiders 1971. See also Barnard 1966 and 1971; Rüping 1968.

104 Pufendorf 1706a and 1707; Grotius 1724; Cumberland 1744. Cf. Othmer 1970; Meylan 1937; Moore 1988.

105 Forbes 1975, chap. 1, and Forbes 1982; Haakonssen 1985a; Medick 1973; Moore and Silverthorne 1983 and 1984. There had been earlier English editions of Grotius and the shorter Pufendorf. For France and the French-speaking world, see Derathé 1988; Dufour 1976; Meylan 1937.

106 Barbeyrac 1749; Moore 1988. For Barbeyrac's own contribution to moral and political theory, see Hochstrasser 1993.

107 See, especially, the letter cited in note 96. In addition to Sève 1989, see also Schneider 1967; Schneiders 1966.

108 'Meditation sur la notion commune de la justice', in Leibniz 1885, pp. 41–70, esp. p. 47 (Leibniz 1972, p. 50).

109 See, e.g., Henry More 1690, Book III. Richard Hooker was a crucial link between scholasticism and English ideas of natural law; see Munz 1952. Cf. Passmore 1951.

110 Culverwel 1971; Greene and MacCallum 1971; Haakonssen 1988.

111 Culverwel 1971, pp. 49–53.

112 Cumberland 1727; Haakonssen forthcoming a; Kirk 1987.

113 For a rather naïve attempt to combine Locke and Cumberland, see James Tyrrell 1701.

114 Locke 1954, pp. 111–13 and Essay 6. For a recent, somewhat different translation of this work, see Locke 1990a.

115 The most comprehensive modern discussion of Locke's moral theory is Colman 1983. Valuable brief introductions are Dunn 1984 and Thiel 1990. In the Locke manuscripts there is an important overview of the main points in his moral theory, 'Of ethics in general', in King 1830, vol. 2, pp. 122–39.

116 See Locke 1989, para. 186 (p. 239); 'Mr. Locke's extemporè advice &c', in ibid., p. 322; and letter to the Countess of Peterbough, letter no. 2320, in Locke 1976–92, vol. 6, pp. 212–16, here at p. 215.

117 *Ess.* IV.iv.8.

118 *Ess.* I.iii.12; II.xxviii.5–10.

119 *Ess.* II.xxvii.17–18.

120 *Ess.* I.iii.3–6, quotation from the last paragraph.

121 *Ess.* II.xxviii.5.

122 *Ess.* IV.ix and IV.x.1–6, quotation from the last paragraph.

123 E.g., Wootton 1990, p. 49.

124 *Ess.* II.xxvii.26.

125 *Ess.* II.xxi, esp. 38.

126 *Ess.* II.xxvii.26; IV.iii.28; IV.xii.13, see also Bodleian MS. Locke f.3, fos. 201–2, 'Lex naturae' (Journal entry 15 July 1678), printed in Leyden 1956, p. 35.

127 *Ess.* I.iii.6; II.xxviii.8.

128 Locke 1967a, *Second Treatise,* chap. 2, paras. 6–7.

129 Cf. Tully 1980.

130 Locke 1967a, II.2.vii.

131 Locke 1967a, II.2.ix; again II.2.xiii and II.16.clxxx.

132 Concerning this conception of liberty, see the fine analysis in Tully 1993, pp. 294–8.

133 Wootton 1990; cf. Tully 1993, chap. 6.

134 Concerning the danger of being accused of Socinianism, see Moore 1991 and the literature cited there. Cf. also Spellman 1988.

135 See the tellingly hypothetical formulations in 'Morality', a manuscript printed in

Sargentich 1974, here p. 27; and the refrain of reasonable expectations in the pungent, brief journal-entry, '*Lex naturae*', printed in Leyden 1956, p. 35.

136 This is denied in Wootton 1990, pp. 42–3, but see Locke 1824, pp. 11–15 and Locke 1987, e.g., vol. 2, pp. 496–7, 501, 687–8, 767. Cf. also the Introduction by Wainwright, Locke 1987, vol. 1, pp. 46–7.

137 Locke 1824, pp. 138–47.

138 See Darwall, forthcoming.

139 It was, at least in periods, practised with some distinction at Cambridge, and it had a significant impact in parts of Catholic Europe.

140 Haakonssen 1996, chap. 10.

# 36

# REASON, THE PASSIONS, AND
# THE GOOD LIFE

SUSAN JAMES

## I. INTRODUCTION

That the passions are both wayward and destructive is one of the commonplaces of seventeenth-century thought. Plays, religious tracts, meditational manuals, educational handbooks, maxims, and philosophical treatises all emphasise this conviction, remorselessly probing the hazards posed by our emotions and desires. To be passionate is to be blinkered and impressionable, vulnerable and a threat to others. At the same time, it is part of our natural condition, an endowment with which we are born and which we rarely escape.

This fundamental fact about human nature is held to be compatible with a vast diversity of temperaments. Among the many factors that may have a hand in shaping our individual emotional dispositions are the circumstances of a child's conception, the social position of its family, its experiences in the womb, the climate in which it grows up, its education, the chance associations and repetitions of events it encounters, and the presence or absence of divine grace.[1] But the processes by which our passions are channelled or modified do not usually create well-rounded and balanced personalities. On the contrary, adults are often left with powerful contradictory affections and thus remain vulnerable to destructive conflicts of emotion. Sometimes, as seventeenth-century drama vividly reminds us, this flaw in human nature can be the cause of tragedy; and at a less apocalyptic level its effect is to make people inconstant and restless, driven from one emotion to the next as waves on the sea are driven by the wind.[2]

The view that our passionate responses are liable to be destructive was, of course, far from novel in the seventeenth century, and writers who maintained it allied themselves more or less self-consciously with a range of traditions stemming from antiquity. The same is true of those who adhered to the widespread belief that the passions are opposed to reason and virtue. Implicit in the contest between passion and reason is a comparison between people as they are and people as they might be; between those who are tugged about by changeable emotions and others who are able to submit their feelings and desires to the controlling power of reason. The struggle between these ways of life, and the moral qualities of each, are expressed in a series of ubiquitous sensory metaphors. The light of reason is obscured by passions which cloud our vision and darken our sight.[3] Alternatively, while the passions are like the sound of an untuned lute, reason overcomes discord and replaces it with harmony.[4] The pervasive tension that these metaphors convey is also intertwined with a further conflict between passion and virtue, an opposition which derives some of its plausibility from the classical identification of virtue with reason, to which many seventeenth-century writers adhered. (If rationality is a part of virtue, and reason is opposed to passion, irrational or passionate behaviour emerges as vicious.) But this second contrast also gains force from the way that particular passions are characterised. A glance at the standard classifications reveals a number of central examples, such as anger, hatred, envy, fear, and ambition, which are readily construed as impediments to virtue. In addition, some less obviously anti-social emotions such as love, pity, hope, fidelity, and generosity were widely interpreted as two-edged swords, unstable powers for either good or evil. The equation of passion with immorality is therefore to some extent intuitively accessible.

Since the incompatibility of virtue and untrammelled passion tended to be taken for granted, one issue that exercised all writers concerned with the proper place of emotion and desire in a moral life was how the passions could be controlled. This problem will be discussed in sections II and III, but it may be helpful to begin by sketching the repertoire of solutions over which debate ranged. Central to all of these was the belief that the subjugation of the passions was an achievement, the outcome of a delicate and complex process of transformation which was rarely, if ever, completed. Self-discipline, aided by other people's judicious interventions, could moderate and sometimes extinguish our ordinary passions. But the danger of their breaking out again remained, a threat to both individual integrity and social order. The project of containing them within acceptable limits was therefore conceived as an endless task, requiring perpetual ingenuity and vigilance.

Among the available methods for controlling the passions, the most widely favoured approach appealed to the power of rationality.[5] The supposition that reason could, and should, gain the upper hand over the passions was so taken for granted in the seventeenth century that Hume's inversion of this commonplace – his celebrated claim that reason is and ought only to be the slave of the passions – was to come as a startling challenge to established pieties.[6] In the meantime, however, moral philosophers were preoccupied by the question of what was needed to make a person act on their rational judgements rather than their passions. To be rational, it was agreed, it was important to be educated by somebody who understood what reasoning consisted in; but while education could set one on the right path, it could not actually inculcate the goal of rationality.[7] To follow reason and thereby master one's passions required perfect self-discipline; and while a teacher could instill habits conducive to such control, the control itself had to come from within. The task of learning to be rational was therefore ultimately a task of self-education, one aided according to some authors by divine grace.[8] It was also a task which, because it involved the subjugation of powerful natural dispositions, was at best extremely arduous.

Partly because the demands of rationality were so great, there was also said to be a range of more pragmatic means of controlling the passions.[9] A significant feature of many of these techniques was that, while one could employ them on oneself, they could also be used to manipulate the passions of others. By exciting fear, a ruler could dampen the ambition of citizens and ensure their good behaviour, while a priest could improve the moral fibre of his flock. Equally, by cultivating laudable desires and stamping out less worthy yearnings, a teacher could direct the hopes and aspirations of his pupils. Because the same methods could be perfected and applied in a variety of institutional contexts, they held out to societies recently torn by civil and religious war the hope of social order.

The view that it was possible to control the passions had given rise in antiquity to a further debate about their place in a virtuous life. Was the virtuous man altogether devoid of passion, as the Stoics claimed? Did he experience only moderate and appropriate passions, as the Aristotelians held? Or did he feel some passions intensely (such as a kind of unifying love) and others not at all, as the Platonists suggested? Seventeenth-century writers inherited and pursued these questions,[10] but they naturally tended to address the versions of them that cohered best with their other beliefs. A few philosophers aligned themselves directly with their classical forebears, but most early modern discussions of these alternative conceptions of the good life were refracted through Christian doctrines which subtly altered their shape. To take an obvious example, the sublime love of Platonic virtue and piety was usually interpreted as love of the Christian God.

Nevertheless, the moral philosophy of this period still bears many traces of its classical heritage, among them the sheer variety of conceptions of virtue that continue to be defended. Arguments for variants of the three images of the good life outlined above were interwoven with opinions about the extent to which the passions can be controlled, to produce articulations of virtue ranging from the yearningly utopian to the politically pragmatic, and from the implicitly secular to the profoundly religious. In all of these the passions are an important consideration, a feature of the ethical landscape which must be accommodated or reshaped.

The wish to place an ethical account of the passions on firm foundations, thereby going beyond the rather *ad hoc* and moralising handbooks which remained popular throughout the period,[11] gave rise in the seventeenth century to some outstanding and innovative systematic philosophy. It was balanced, however, by the rather more quizzical approach adopted by writers who doubted whether it was possible to give a general account of the subject and, even if this could be done, whether such an account would prove persuasive. These hesitations are expressed in the use of particular literary forms. The *Maximes* of Rochefoucauld[12] and the *Caractères* of La Bruyère[13] display a fragmentation and lack of system deliberately foreign to the philosophical treatise or discourse. Moreover, these forms are used to voice a pervasive scepticism about the ideal of rationality favoured by more scientifically inclined thinkers, and to draw attention to the complexity, unpredictability, and variety of our passionate impulses. The *moralistes'* observant and unblinking insights into the foibles of humanity exhibit an acuity and precision that go far beyond the tables of passions constructed by so many philosophers of the same period. But from the perspective of the latter, the *moralistes* represent a retreat from generality to particularity, from explanation to mere reportage. The co-existence of these two approaches is symptomatic of an ancient but unresolved disagreement about the power of reason to quell the passions, and thus about the relevance of reasoning to moral philosophy.

## II. VIRTUE AS REASON

The conviction that the passions could be quelled by reason was frequently complemented in the seventeenth century by a belief in the possibility of a science of ethics. Many philosophers held that rational enquiry could yield knowledge of the principles in accordance with which a good life should be lived and that these principles could be used to regulate behaviour. The haphazard stabs at virtue to which our passions sometimes incline us would give way to a rational and consistent comprehension of the good. Embodied in this view are two central claims, each of great importance and complexity. First, it is assumed that there are two distinct kinds of judgement: rational, scientific judgements that constitute ethics and irrational judgements inspired by our passions. Second, it is held that a knowledge of ethical truths enables us – or at least helps us – to control our passions. The elucidation and questioning of these claims is a recurrent theme of ethics in the early modern period.

As we have seen, the habit of opposing passion and reason made it seem natural to describe the passions, along with the actions to which they gave rise, as irrational. This label carries connotations of impetuousness and lack of reflection. Although some of what was regarded as passionate behaviour does indeed answer to such a description, it would be a mistake to take this as definitive. Far more important to seventeenth-century philosophers is the fact that our passions, and the actions to which they give rise, are grounded on informal inductive inferences. The feelings and desires which prompt us to seek some things and avoid others are the fruit of our experience. (To take Descartes's example, we only feel afraid of a wild animal and act to avoid it if our experience leads us to believe that it is dangerous.)[14] This method of forming judgements has various practical advantages; it enables us to work out how things are useful or damaging to us. Nevertheless, many seventeenth-century theorists of the passions regard it as a perilously unstable and irrational procedure[15] which should, as far as possible, be modified.

This stance is grounded on the assumption that everyone has, as part of their character, a set of emotional dispositions or passions: a person may, for example, be ambitious, generous, prone to hatred, or easily infatuated. The presence of these passions explains an agent's patterns of action, so that an ambitious man, for example, will act with a certain determination and even ruthlessness to achieve success.[16] To describe him as ambitious is to acknowledge that he is attracted to a particular type of goal which we can describe simply as success, and a component of this attraction is his belief that the realisation of success will yield some sort of satisfaction or happiness. Passions thus have beliefs built in to them. But because they are incorporated into passions, these beliefs are not held in an open-minded fashion. The strength of our passions ensures that we hold some beliefs strongly and unreflectively; and it ensures at the same time that we are resistant to the suggestion that our beliefs about how to achieve happiness are mistaken. An ambitious man is not someone who is wondering what sort of ends are likely to prove most rewarding in life; by virtue of being ambitious, he is already committed to the pursuit of success and already desires to achieve it. His belief that it will bring him satisfaction may be wrong; but, while the passion lasts, he will not consider this possibility in a cool and objective manner. When we reason inductively, therefore, we do not make inferences on the basis of beliefs derived from experience by some neutral means, which we continue to hold open to revision in the light of the evidence. Instead, we reason from beliefs which already reflect our loves, hates, hopes, and fears, and to which we are emotionally committed.

If this is why our everyday inferences are suspect, it may seem that our best hope is to improve our capacity for inductive reasoning by learning to take a more open-minded view of the available evidence. On the basis of experience we may then revise our conceptions of the goals most likely to yield satisfaction, and alter our passions accordingly. Seventeenth-century theorists tend to agree that this is a generally beneficial strategy. They allow that people possessed of some experience and a degree of inductive discipline are more likely to realise their goals and find satisfaction in them than those who give their passions full sway. And they allow that comparatively cautious and prudent people are better equipped to act morally than the impetuous and volatile.[17]

A number of philosophers deny, however, that even the most careful inductive reasoning is sufficient for the good life. Two connected reasons are given for this conclusion, the first of which concerns our knowledge of the ends that are consonant with virtue. When we reason inductively, we pursue ends that we believe will bring us satisfaction and call these ends good. But mere experience cannot assure us that the ends we describe as good coincide with the true good, the end of a fully ethical life.[18] Second, it is held to be extremely improbable that, on the basis of inductive reasoning, it will be possible to avoid the moral failings to which our passions make us prone. The overwhelming likelihood remains that one will at some stage act on a passionate impulse at odds with the demands of morality.

How are these pitfalls to be avoided? The only remedy, it was generally agreed, lay in the construction of a science of ethics. As Hobbes explains, echoing the general consensus of opinion, our everyday decisions and actions are the result of reasoning about 'particular things' – reasoning based on inductively grounded premises.[19] Since the truth of the ensuing conclusions is conditional on that of the premises, and the premises are not known for certain, the conclusions themselves are not known for certain and are examples of 'opinion' as opposed to 'knowledge'.[20] Reasoning of this kind, Hobbes says, is what people often have in mind when they talk about understanding. But it is to be contrasted with another mode of inference which constitutes reasoning in the true sense.

Reasoning of this latter kind proceeds not from inductive generalisations but from evident and universal premises. For example, in geometry, 'the only science that it hath pleased God hitherto to bestow on mankind', proofs move by a series of deductive steps from axioms and definitions to conclusions.[21] Most seventeenth-century philosophers shared Hobbes's view that this mode of reasoning is best exemplified by arithmetic and geometry. But many also agreed that there is in principle nothing to stop us from reasoning in the same way about what is and is not truly good, and thus arriving at a science of ethics.[22]

The premises of such a science would need, first of all, to be self-evident. But more specifically, they would have to include propositions about the proper ends of action and the proper means to those ends. Imagine, for example, a man moved by ambition to seek high office, who pauses to wonder whether it would be right to allow his name to go forward. It would be irrational for him to arrive at his decision inductively by considering, for instance, whether the pursuit of such goals has, in his experience, brought satisfaction, or how he has responded to failure in the past. Equally, it would be irrational for him to act on his current desires. Rather than treating his passions as data to be taken into account, he must stand back from them and try to deduce a conclusion about what to do from some self-evident principles. He must assess his ambition to hold office in the light of a general account of the ends it is good to pursue and the means by which it is good to pursue them.

In their search for truly human ends, seventeenth-century writers usually appealed to the dictates of human nature. They tended to take it as axiomatic that people strive for some specific goal such as pleasure (Locke), power to persevere in their being (Spinoza), or self-preservation (Hobbes), and further assumed that reason requires us to pursue these ends.[23] For example, if we are naturally disposed to preserve ourselves, it would be self-defeating and thus irrational to attempt to fly in the face of this aspect of our nature. However, as the very diversity of these theories suggests, it is not at all obvious that the human ends they identified were self-evident or beyond doubt. Moreover, they were too coarse-grained to provide more than a minimal guide to action. The injunction to preserve ourselves would, for instance, only prevent a man from running for office if such a course would be suicidal or reckless. Beyond that, it gives him no guidance as to what to do.

To defend themselves against this straightforward objection, many seventeenth-century theorists appealed to more elaborate accounts of our truly human ends. The end of self-preservation, for example, involved more than just staying alive; to preserve oneself was also to make one's life, and one's way of life, secure.[24] By this means, it was of course possible to formulate comparatively substantial premises from which a greater range of conclusions could be deduced. But all such attempts to enrich the foundations of a science of ethics remained constrained by the requirement that its premises should be self-evidently true, and this meant that interpretations of the ends prescribed by reason were beset by two dangers. On the one hand, they might be suitably obvious and uncontentious but prescribe too few courses of action. On the other hand, they might discriminate between more courses of action at the expense of their own indubitability.

In fending off this line of objection, philosophers often appealed to the view that, as well as yielding an account of our truly human ends, reason prescribes the proper means by which these ends should be achieved. Rational deliberation alters one's beliefs about the means it is appropriate to employ. For example, because reason is impervious to the perspective of the present and makes no distinction between short- and long-term ends, a man who reasons will give as much weight to his future states as to his immediate goals. He will therefore regard certain instrumental courses of action, such as those which will satisfy his immediate desires at the expense of his long-term interests, as irrational.[25]

By specifying both rational ends and rational means, a science of ethics could, it was thought, offer a comprehensive guide to action. Many seventeenth-century philosophers did not doubt that this project could be carried through. But their works nevertheless testify to the difficulty of pinning down any agreed principles from which useful, prescriptive conclusions could be derived.[26] The non-existence of an available and accepted ethical science sustained the suspicion that the enterprise of constructing one lay at the edge of human capabilities. More specifically, it implied that the art of reasoning from the existing fragments of such a science was complex and intricate, demanding deductive talents of a high order. To act rationally, it was constantly stressed, one needed to be skilled in the art of reasoning.

What was not so much emphasised in this drive towards scientificity was that the need to interpret specific events and relate them to ethical principles requires a shrewd inductive sense. Consider, for example, Hobbes's view that the rational man ought to seek peace as long as he has hope of obtaining it.[27] The argument for this precept purports to be deductive. But in order to apply it – in order to know in a particular situation whether to seek peace or resort to the advantages of war – one needs a reliable assessment of the likelihood of obtaining peace. Hobbes believed that peace could only be obtained if other people were willing to keep their promises.[28] But how can one judge whether they are going to do so? This kind of information cannot be reached by deductive arguments from universal premises. Rather, we acquire it inductively, by appeal to local knowledge and experience.

It is therefore an oversimplification to claim that the difference between reason and unreason in ethics is the difference between deductive and inductive reasoning. The point is rather that, whereas irrational people act solely on inductive generalisations drawn from experience, those who are rational rely on a mixture of both types of argument. For a rational man, deductive inference plays the major rôle, furnishing general precepts to guide him. Induction then enters at a later stage and enables him to apply these precepts in his daily life.

### III. THE POWER OF REASON

Seventeenth-century philosophers were encouraged to persevere in their attempts to articulate a science of ethics by their belief that reason can conquer the passions. A science of ethics would be worth having if it offered a way to keep the passions in check. There remained a problem, however, about the relation between ethical knowledge and passionate inclinations. What is it about deductively grounded conclusions that makes them able to resist passionate judgements? Why will a man who has ethical knowledge be better at controlling his passions than one who is good at inductive reasoning? In short, why is reason the most effective way to control the passions?

One prevalent answer to this question draws on the deeply held belief that rational judgements have an exceptionally strong cognitive hold over us. Once we understand something with the clarity that attaches to ideas that are distinct or adequate, whether they are intuitively grasped premises or the outcome of deductive inference, we can neither deny nor ignore it. The quality of these ideas makes them compelling so that, having reasoned our way to a conclusion, we find it difficult to discount it or to muster convincing reasons against it. Whereas passionate judgements are easily altered, rational ones are strong and unshakeable.

This view is sometimes supported by an appeal to intuition: for example, once you know how to add, it just seems obvious that 2 + 5 cannot be anything but 7.[29] The belief that rational judgements have a kind of force or power which enables them to oppose the passions is also defended by an appeal to the conception of reason as active and the passions as passive. This line of argument is widely used;[30] but it is particularly clear in the work of Spinoza, who argues explicitly that when we reason we act, and that when we are subject to passion we are acted on.[31] In Spinoza's view, our passions are principally responses to external things of which our knowledge is partial. For instance, when we fall in love, the object of our passion is another person of whom we have only limited experience. On the basis of this partial experience we form what Spinoza calls inadequate ideas, which play a causal rôle in the processes by which we arrive at judgements, and consequently affect what we do. When this happens, we are acted on and our judgements are passionate. By contrast, when we reason from one adequate idea to another, the mind exercises a capacity to generate ideas out of itself which does not causally depend on our continuing experience of objects in the world. The mind is able to think independently, or, as Spinoza says, it acts.[32]

This way of interpreting the difference between the thinking that rational people engage in and the thinking that is the preserve of the passionate illuminates a sense in which rational people are able to control and advance the processes of their own thought, whereas passionate people are responsive to, and constrained by, the partial ideas they derive from experience. In this sense, rational people are agents, while passionate people are not.

If reasoning is intrinsically forceful, a rationally grounded judgement such as that I ought not to steal will be hard to ignore. How, though, does this judgement bear on my actions? For example, if I find a purse and at least entertain the idea of picking it up and keeping it, how will my reason prevent me from doing so? Some philosophers regard this as a misleading question in so far as it implies a separation between judgement on the one hand and action on the other. For Spinoza there is no such gap.[33] If rational deliberation leads us to conclude that it is wrong to steal we will not steal; we may imagine ourselves stealing but we will not do so. This view of the matter relies heavily on the idea that rational judgements have cognitive power. But it also traces that power to the structure of a science of ethics. As a scientifically derived conclusion, the rational judgement that it is wrong to steal does not stand unsupported; it is inferred from incontrovertible premises and gives rise to further conclusions, both of which serve as reasons for it. They impart to it a strength which outweighs both the desire to steal and any reasons that can be given in support of such a course of action.

For some writers, this is all there is to be said about the connexion between rational judgement and moral action. Others (more sensitive to the objection that no amount of cognitive grasp will reliably counter the strength of feeling that attaches to our passions) acknowledge the need to provide a fuller account of the motivating power of reason. The problem, as they see it, is that just as a prudent inductive reasoner remains vulnerable to his affections – he may suddenly fall in love and fling caution to the winds – so the deductive reasoner may be swept off course by a particularly strong gust of desire or anger. When this happens, it is not obvious that a rational understanding of what he ought to do will be enough to prevent him from acting on his passion.

One response to this difficulty simply allows that humans cannot become invincibly rational. Despite our best efforts, it is always possible that our passions may get the better of us.[34] A second and less quietist answer bolsters the forces on the side of reason. In terms deeply indebted to Stoicism, some philosophers claim that the process of reasoning brings with it a superlative happiness, compared with which the satisfactions derived from the passions pale into insignificance.[35] The exercise of our reason, our most fully human capacity, gives rise to an unequalled joy which is sustained when we act rationally but undermined when we are irrational. According to this picture, we may not start out with any inclination to pursue reason; but once we begin to do so we are rewarded with intellectual pleasures, and the prospect of more of these moves us to become still more rational. So we have both cognitive and emotional reasons for acting as reason dictates, which together defeat our passions.

Although this last analysis of the strength of reason is designed to explain how reason can conquer passion, it tends to subvert the very opposition between them. Like their classical forebears, seventeenth-century advocates of this view hold that the pleasures of reasoning are not passions.[36] But in allowing that reasoning is not devoid of emotion, they reinforce the similarities between passionate and rational thinking. We have seen that the cognitive content of our everyday judgements is indelibly coloured by passion. Likewise, our rational inferences are suffused with joy.

The problem of what gives reason its strength, and the related problem of how strong it can become, are therefore vexed questions in seventeenth-century moral philosophy, so that an air of inconclusiveness hangs over discussions about the extent to which reason can control the passions. A comparable irresolution afflicts a parallel set of arguments, centring on the claim that the will, rather than the reason, is what moves us to act. According to this view, championed in the seventeenth century by the followers of Descartes, reason itself is powerless to move us, but our rational judgements give rise to volitions, on which we act.[37] This analysis draws on the idea that rational judgements are stronger and more forceful than their passionate counterparts, and adds the claim that the force of a judgement is transferred to the corresponding volition. If I have a clear conviction that it is wrong to steal and a weak desire to keep the purse I have found, I will have a strong volition not to steal and a weak volition to steal, of which the former will win out. To control my passions I therefore need to be able to control my volitions. But these in turn are responsive to the judgements of my understanding. Like the previous argument we considered, this rules out the possibility that I may understand that I ought not to steal but do so nonetheless. And as before, the problem of weakness of will remains to haunt us.

## IV. THE MORAL POWER OF REASON

Despite significant differences between them, the view that the passions can be controlled directly by reason, and the view that they can be controlled by the combination of reason and will, alike give rise to conceptions of virtue in which reasoning plays an absolutely central part. Both hold that, to lead a moral life, one must have one's passions under control so that one can pursue the truly moral ends that the science of ethics reveals to us. Beyond this the two arguments diverge, but not as much as may at first appear.

According to the first view, exemplified by Spinoza, we are virtuous in so far as we are rational. At first glance, this doctrine may appear to abandon any substantive conception of the good life in favour of a purely procedural conception of virtue. But this is not the case. When we pursue the only true good – that is, when we reason – we arrive at truths about how to live. We learn, for example, that many of our everyday emotions, and hence some kinds of relationship with other people, are inappropriate, in that they are the outcome of a mistaken conception of the world and our place in it.[38] Equally, as we gain a more accurate understanding of the world, we come to see what kinds of feelings and relations are constitutive of the good life.[39] Understanding, the end at which we aim if we are rational, contains within it a substantive and familiar picture of virtue: the virtuous man, as Spinoza portrays him, is generous, steadfast, and honourable.[40] When we are rational, we understand what a good life involves. And when we understand what it involves, we act virtuously.

According to the second view, exemplified by Descartes, virtue requires that we should be able to control our passions by the use of the will. *Générosité*, which is 'as it were the key to all the other virtues',[41] consists in a person's 'firm and constant resolution to use his freedom well – that is, never to lack the will to undertake and carry out what he judges to be best'.[42] Once again, this view seems to give up a substantive conception of virtue. As before, however, a man who possesses *generosité* understands certain things about himself which shape his picture of what he can and cannot do, and contribute to his understanding of the good life. Most important, he knows that 'nothing belongs to him but this freedom to dispose his volitions, and that he ought to be praised or blamed for no other reason than his using this freedom well or badly'.[43] Administering a well-known Stoic medicine, Descartes assures us that, once we realise that most things depend on objects and states of affairs over which we do not have sole control, we will cease to value them and concentrate our attention on our volitions, which are within our power. The values of a man who possesses *générosité* will thus be strictly circumscribed; he will not pine for things he cannot have or set himself unattainable goals, and he will no longer feel such passions as envy, hatred, jealousy, fear, or anger, which are themselves failures of *générosité*. In addition, the understanding that people are all the same in possessing only the freedom to control their volitions breeds, so Descartes claims, various aspects of good character. The wise man esteems others, towards whom he is courteous, gracious, and obliging.[44]

For these writers, rationality gives rise to a kind of self-control which is itself equated with virtue. A rational man is not simply one who is able to restrain his passions sufficiently to act in a cool and calculating manner. He also understands specific truths about himself and his relations with the rest of the world which reveal to him, and move him to conform to, the particular patterns of feeling and behaviour that constitute virtue. The persuasiveness of this view depends in part on the fact that its exponents draw on conventional interpretations of what it is to be virtuous. For example, if rational argument leads us to the conclusion that we should be courteous, and we are already persuaded that courtesy is a characteristic of a virtuous life, we may find ourselves agreeing that rationally grounded conclusions have some moral force and that we ought to do what reason dictates. But if reason were to recommend a course of action at odds with our interpretation of the good life, this might not be nearly so clear. Carefully chosen cases can be used to paper over the gap between rationality and virtue. But the question of whether they were enough to close it remained highly contentious in seventeenth-century moral philosophy.

The limitations of arguments for the straightforward identity of virtue and reason were keenly appreciated by a number of philosophers concerned with the status of the Law of Nature. We saw earlier that advocates of ethical science frequently posited a goal of human existence, such as self-preservation, which they took to be part of human nature – a constant and inescapable disposition of all human beings. These premises, and others like them, were widely interpreted as part of the Law of Nature that reason reveals to us, so that the science of ethics was seen as a branch of Natural Law. Writers in this tradition took it for granted that we can grasp the content of Natural Law by reasoning, and that to act in accordance with it is to act rationally. They also accepted that to act in accordance with the Law of Nature is to act morally.[45] But they felt a pressing need to explain what gives this law its moral status, and thus why it is that we are morally obliged to act as reason dictates. The question at stake here is no longer what makes rational judgements prevail over passionate ones. Rather, it is the question of how rational judgements can have a distinctively moral force capable of grounding obligations. As far as the opposition between reason and the passions is concerned, this issue is of crucial importance. Unless rational judgements possess moral authority, it is not clear that we are under any obligation to act on them. And if we are not morally obliged to act rationally, the case for saying that we are subject to an ethical requirement to use reason to control our passions collapses.

This problem was usually addressed in a theological context. Almost without exception, it was allowed that reason reveals to us the characteristics of a Judeo-

Christian God, the perfect and beneficent creator of the universe, and that the pronouncements of reason coincide with the principles of a Christian life.[46] Against this background, however, several distinct accounts of the relation between reason and morality continued to be elaborated and discussed. According to an influential voluntarist strand of argument, our moral obligation to obey the Law of Nature derives from the fact that the law is willed by God. We ought to obey the prescriptions of Natural Law because they specify what is good. And they specify what is good simply because they are what God wills.

While several versions of this view were proposed, some less bald than others, it was Descartes, above all, who was identified by his contemporaries as an exponent of pure voluntarism and singled out by critics of this position who objected to its apparent arbitrariness.[47] Voluntarism seemed to them to have implications that were patently ridiculous. For instance, if God is omnipotent and can will anything he likes, any state of affairs at all must be good if God happens to command it. The absurdity of this conclusion was taken as evidence that voluntarism had failed to provide an adequate explanation of the moral force of Natural Law.[48]

Applied to the most strident formulations of the doctrine, this criticism may indeed be justified. But it does not so obviously damage a more subtle version, according to which our obligation to do what God commands because He demands it stems from other characteristics of God, logically independent of His omnipotence. Locke, for example, reminds us that God is a legislator, the author of the Law of Nature, and our creator. Since we depend on Him for our existence, He is a superior to whom we are rightly subject; and what we are rightly subject to is nothing other than the law He has made. God's right to command us, and our correlative obligation to obey Him, are here traced to the fact that we are His creatures,[49] and in so far as this claim is persuasive, the arbitrariness of our obligation is purportedly dispelled.

Arguments of this kind go some way towards meeting the objection that voluntarism makes morality a matter of divine caprice. But there remained critics who believed that this approach was irreparably flawed. In their view, moral properties are not dependent on the will of God but are fixed in the immutable nature of things. Reason tells us that, just as objects have natural properties, so they have moral ones which, taken together, form a moral order. This order not only obliges human agents; it also constrains God Himself, who is bound to abide by what Cudworth called 'eternal and immutable morality'.[50] What, though, is the source of God's obligation? In the first place, God conforms His will to the moral order because He understands it, and thus has a perfect grasp of what is by its nature good and right. For Him, the truth is its own motivation, and no further obligation is conceivable. Similarly, a completely rational human agent would be moved by the force of reason itself to act in accordance with the moral order, and in so far as we are rational we are under this obligation.[51]

From God's perspective, therefore, the intrinsic moral qualities of things determine the content of the Law of Nature. If humans were able to climb to God's vantage point, they, too, would perceive that Natural Law is to be obeyed because it accurately reflects the independent moral order. As things are, however, they have a further and vitally important reason for obeying Natural Law, namely, that in doing so they are following the commands of God. Their obedience is thus doubly determined by their limited capacity to understand the moral order and their greater capacity to understand the obligations engendered by their relation to the divine.

Despite the fact that this account of our obligation to obey Natural Law appeals to a moral standard independent of both God and humanity, its champions did not regard it as in the least threatening to established religion. On the contrary, they were anxious to show that it complemented and reinforced the tenets of Christianity. Nevertheless, their view left a conceptual space for an altogether non-theistic account of the relation between reason and morality: one which simply dropped any mention of God as a source of obligation, and appealed entirely to our rational understanding of the moral order. This spectre was raised by Hobbes and continued to haunt philosophers and moralists throughout the century.

Much of Hobbes's account of the Law of Nature is perfectly conventional.[52] But when he comes to discuss our duty to obey it, he studiously avoids the claim that we are obliged to do so because it is the law of God. Instead, he offers a completely secular justification for this course of action: to follow the law is to follow the most effective policy of self-preservation; and it is obvious that no value can ever override that of survival. Our obligation to obey Natural Law is thus rooted in prudential considerations of self-interest, and, in cases of conflict, is deaf to the demands of the common good. Many of Hobbes's contemporaries found the implications of this theory deeply disturbing. Beneath the mild manner of Locke's remark that a 'Hobbist, with his principle of self-preservation, whereof he himself is to be judge, will not easily admit a great many plain duties of morality'[53] lay a profound feeling of unease. Some attempted to dismiss it with the objection that Hobbes had neglected to distinguish a prudential question – What *reason* have we got to follow the law of nature? – from a moral one – What *obliges* us to follow the law of nature? (Cudworth, for example, complains that, 'according to this civil (or rather uncivil) philosopher' no law can be unjust.)[54] But the problem posed by his work was not easily dealt with and continued to exercise philosophers and moralists throughout the century.

Despite their many differences, seventeenth-century philosophers largely agreed that we must restrain our passions if we are to lead good lives, and that the most reliable way to do this is by reasoning. They were, however, less clear about the justification for their position. As we have seen, they held several divergent views about why we are morally obliged to do what reason dictates. Moreover, this debate bore directly on the question of why we should control our passions. According to one strand of thought, we are required to do so by the immutable moral order and by God. But according to another, our moral obligation is prudential. Embodied in these interpretations are different understandings of the normative character of the passions. For example, advocates of the first view will tend to regard at least some passions as immoral, opposed to virtue and the good life. By contrast, advocates of the second view may be inclined to argue that our passions are more misguided than immoral – imprudent impulses which may threaten our preservation, and which it is therefore in our interest to control. Although both these pessimistic assessments of the passions continued to be discussed, they began to be juxtaposed, towards the end of the seventeenth century, with a more confident reading of human nature according to which our emotional dispositions are essentially benign. As Shaftesbury insists in his *Characteristics,* there is no need to portray man's nature outside the bounds of law 'under monstrous visages of dragons, Leviathans and I know not what devouring entities'.[55] Once this view was taken up, the ethical questions surrounding the passions underwent a notable shift. The problem of how the passions were to be controlled gave way to a consideration of the contribution they make to the virtuous life.

## V. THE PLACE OF PASSION IN A VIRTUOUS LIFE

The problems so far discussed are complicated by their connexions with a further debate concerning the rôle of the passions in a virtuous life. Do virtuous people experience moderate passions? Or does reason control the passions to the extent of getting rid of them altogether? Seventeenth-century writers were heirs to a long-standing dispute over this issue between the advocates of two traditions, one Stoic, the other Aristotelian. According to the Stoics, it is possible to overcome the passions altogether; the struggle between the rational and emotional aspects of human nature can be so thoroughly won by reason that we no longer experience any passions at all.[56] By contrast, Aristotle held that, even if it were possible, it would be undesirable to quell the passions completely.[57] Instead, reason should control them in such a way that our emotions are appropriate to their objects. Because the first of these claims was never espoused without qualification during the seventeenth century (even its most ardent advocates allowed that the ideal of a completely rational and hence passion-free life is unattainable), the two positions are sometimes hard to distinguish. Nevertheless, the difference between them is clear enough. While the Stoics believed that the passions are incompatible with reason and virtue, defenders of an Aristotelian tradition held that the passions can, and must, play a part in any good life.

The most rigorous and sustained exposition of the neo-Stoic position in this period is perhaps given by Spinoza, who portrays virtue as a tranquil and passion-free condition, devoted to what he calls the intellectual love of God.[58] In everyday life, Spinoza argues, our partial and inadequate understanding of the world and of ourselves leads us to respond passionately to the things around us. We experience desire (*cupiditas*) for certain objects and states of affairs and pursue them with the aim of securing joy (*laetitia*) and avoiding sadness (*tristitia*).[59] However, as we begin to reason we grasp certain adequate truths which change our attitudes. For example, our feelings for others are normally based on the assumption that their actions are within their control, so that it is appropriate to praise or blame, love, or hate them for what they do. We take it that they are in general able to choose whether or not to act, and identify something about them – some constellation of passions for instance – as the cause of their action. But rational enquiry will show us that these assumptions are mistaken. This is partly because actions, like all other events, are causally determined.[60] But it is also because the antecedent constellation of passions is only one factor in a nexus of causes, so that to fix on it as *the* cause is to take a partial and shortsighted view. Once we understand that human action is part of a closed, deterministic system, we will realise that things could not have been otherwise and will also see that our passionate responses to the events of everyday life are inappropriate.

This realisation is, in Spinoza's view, one of the main insights enabling us to overcome our passions. It defuses our emotional responses to particular events so that we no longer feel grief, envy, anger or despair, and frees us from affects which presuppose contingency, such as expectation, disappointment, hope, and fear.[61] Moreover, as our rational understanding of the world grows, we become progressively more detached from the details of our own and other people's lives, and increasingly concerned with the workings of the whole system of which we are part. This shift of attention is at the same time an emotional withdrawal. As people become more rational, they come to see particular individuals and events as comparatively insignificant and therefore cease to have strong feelings about them. In this way, Spinoza believes, the wise approach (but never attain) a condition of pure virtue in which they are entirely dispassionate.[62]

By delineating the content of understanding, Spinoza aims to show how rational people are able to overcome passion. But he is nevertheless emphatic that a rational life is not altogether devoid of emotion. There are, in his view, two types of emotion, one passionate and the other not. When rational people strive to understand, they experience a rational emotion which is comparable to *cupiditas* in that it is a *desire* to understand but is nevertheless not a passion. Equally, as their understanding increases, they experience a kind of joy which, like *laetitia,* is an emotion, but is not a passion. This delight in the exercise of their own power of reasoning resembles the passions, in so far as it is a feeling (though it far exceeds any pleasure known to ordinary people), but is free from the destructive traits by which the passions are sullied.[63]

Whilst the Stoic ideal attracted advocates such as Antoine Le Grand,[64] as well as prominent sympathisers such as Descartes,[65] the idea of a life free from passion was frequently dismissed as incoherent. Much criticism stemmed from the fact that it was widely interpreted as a life altogether free from emotion, and such a goal was regarded as inconceivable. In the first place, it was argued, it could not possibly be equated with virtue, for a person who neither felt nor expressed any emotion would be more monstrous than virtuous. What could be more reasonable, as Coëffeteau asks in his *Tableau des Passions Humaines,* 'than to see a man touched with pity and compassion at the misery of his fellow creature? Of his friend? Of his parent? Would not a mother be inhuman if she were to see her child in the grip of wild beasts, shipwrecked, tied to a wheel, torn by some other torture, or only seized by a violent illness, without feeling her heart filled with sadness?'[66]

To some extent, this objection was the result of a misunderstanding. Defenders of Stoicism were not committed to the view that, in overcoming passion, we overcome emotion altogether; instead we make way for rational emotions, including rational desires which can motivate us to act. However, this reply failed to satisfy most critics, who did not accept the distinction between passions and rational emotions on which it rests.[67] All that had happened, in their view, was that passions had been reintroduced under another name, thereby implicitly conceding their objections. Many of these opponents, including Senault and Coëffeteau, regarded this capitulation as particularly evident in the Stoic claim that a virtuous man, while he experienced no passions, nevertheless experienced the physical symptoms of passions – he might blush, tremble, laugh, or weep. For why, they wanted to know, should he display the outward signs of an emotion he did not feel?[68]

According to their critics, the Stoics had fallen prey to pride and failed to appreciate that the passions are useful and indeed vital to our survival and well-being. As Senault sternly writes, 'There is no passion which is not serviceable to virtue, when they are governed by reason, and those that have cryed them down, make us see they never knew their use or worth.'[69] Instead of embarking on a futile struggle to extinguish them, we should employ our powers of reasoning to moderate and guide them. While we must curb their natural tendency to excess and fluctuation, the passions remain, as Henry More wrote, 'lamps and beacons to conduct and excite us to our journey's end'.[70]

Since the proponents of the Aristotelian position agreed that both 'good' emotions such as compassion, and 'bad' ones such as hatred can be beneficial in some circumstances and destructive in others, they held that all passions have their uses, provided they are kept within the bounds of reason. To quote Senault again, 'Love and hatred, desire and eschewing, are rather virtues than passions when governed by reason. Provided they love nothing but what is lovely, and hate nothing but what is hateful, they deserve praise rather than reproach.'[71] The justification for this latter view was held to be obvious: the characteristic of reason which made it uniquely able to control the passions was quite simply its ability to guide us to true conclusions. By reasoning we can gain a correct understanding of the properties of objects and states of affairs. And this correct understanding will in turn enable us to know what emotions are appropriate. While theorists tended to depart from Aristotle's view that rational emotions were always a mean between two irrational extremes,[72] they agreed that the appropriate response to a situation will always be determined by its characteristics and their implications.

This thesis clearly possesses an intuitive attractiveness. As the seventeenth-century critics of Stoicism were fond of pointing out, it is hard to envisage a morally virtuous life in which the usual range of emotions have been displaced by a consuming preoccupation with understanding. But it also drew support from a range of Christian doctrines. The belief that God's creation partakes of His perfection gave rise to a widespread view that everything God has created has a use and plays a part in the proper functioning of the universe. The passions are thus 'not maladies but instruments of virtue', they are 'budding virtues' with which God has endowed us, waiting to be cultivated by reason.[73] The Bible, moreover, furnished further evidence for the view that passion is an essential ingredient of virtue. Adam was held to have experienced rationally governed emotions before the Fall.[74] Still more persuasive, Christ, the incarnation of virtue, clearly felt joy, grief, and anguish during his sojourn on earth.[75] Aspects of Christian teaching therefore helped to sustain the view that the passions are at least potentially benign. At the same time, sectarian divisions within Christianity kept alive a further series of debates about which of the passions are intrinsic to a godly life. Rather than allowing that all passions have their place, some theorists singled out particular emotions as definitive of Christian virtue, arguing that the cultivation of virtue is a process of selection as well as control. One must prune or weed out some emotions while allowing others to grow.

Perhaps the most striking example of this kind of interpretation is the Augustinian emphasis on the centrality of love, which remained extremely influential. Some aspects of this widely held view will be discussed in sections VII and VIII of this essay, but it is worth noting that a number of quite diverse seventeenth-century theorists identified love with virtue.[76] A somewhat different picture of the virtuous life derives from Calvin's interpretation of the wretchedness of humanity. According to Calvin, the conviction that God is merciful gives a virtuous person grounds for hope. But this passion will be intermittently eclipsed by fear of divine wrath, shame at human corruption and longing for salvation.[77] These powerful emotions, which find their proper expression in groans, tears, and cries to God, are all a necessary part of repentance, so that a person who does not experience them cannot count as virtuous.[78] But they contribute to a conception of virtue as an emotionally unstable state, and to a portrait of a godly life as an unending struggle. The contrast with the Stoic or Aristotelian models could hardly be more marked. In place of serene tranquillity, or moderate emotion, the Calvinist tradition holds out a conception of virtue marked by extreme passions which at times come close to desperation. For writers influenced by this tradition,[79] strong and uncontrollable passions were not always a falling away from reason; in some cases they were a rational response to the human condition.

## VI. OTHER WAYS OF CONTROLLING THE PASSIONS

To keep one's passions forever on the leash, under the controlling hand of reason, is acknowledged to be extremely difficult. Reason is weak and our capacity for understanding limited. There is a further flaw in our nature, moreover, which prevents us from making moral progress: the fact that, in spite of their certainty, rational arguments do not always persuade us. We have already seen that seventeenth-century proponents of a science of ethics hold for the most part to the official position that deductively grounded truths are persuasive. To continue to ask why we should accept them would be to miss the point. Yet this philosophical stance was cross-pressured by the recognition that ethical science had not had an overwhelming impact on the community at large. Many people were unable to understand it, others understood it but remained unmoved, and even its most fluent practitioners sometimes failed to act on the conclusions of their own proofs. The tension between these views reveals a deep ambivalence in seventeenth-century conceptions of the place of reason in human nature. On the one hand, reason distinguishes us from the beasts, and in this sense all persons are rational. On the other hand, rationality is the fruit of education and character, an exceptional attainment as rare as the phoenix.[80]

Since our ability to think and behave rationally is so limited, it would be utopian to rely entirely on reason to control the passions. Seventeenth-century philosophers and moralists therefore supplemented their appeal to the powers of the intellect with a catalogue of techniques for directing and restraining our emotional dispositions. If, as Descartes puts it, what we call virtues are 'habits in the soul which dispose it to have certain thoughts',[81] such habits need to be cultivated and perfected. For this there existed various exercises, some of which discerning people could apply to themselves,[82] and many of which could be used to mould the passions of other people.

These latter methods presupposed the existence of a rational, educated élite, in a position to manipulate the emotions and desires of the morally less well-endowed. They thus assumed a vital distinction between the knowledgeable and powerful, and the comparatively ignorant and powerless.[83] In politics, this divide was held to lie between statesmen and ordinary citizens; it was acknowledged that the security and stability of the polity depended both on the existence of temperate rulers and on their ability to channel and defuse the passions of the populace.[84] But there was also in this respect a significant division between men and women. Although women, by virtue of their humanity, were held to be rational, their capacity to use reason to control their passions was regarded as inferior to that of men,[85] an attitude not undermined by the existence of 'femmes fortes' or 'exceptional women' whose moral or intellectual attainments could be ranked alongside those of male heroes. Just as there could be exceptional children, wise beyond their years, so some women might overcome the limitations of their sex. But women as a group were generally, though not universally, held to be inconstant and dangerous, and thus rightfully kept under the control of their fathers or husbands.[86]

Of the various techniques recommended for restraining the passions, some are closely associated with reasoning while others are presented as alternatives to it. At one end of the spectrum, we are invited to become more self-aware about our intellectual limitations and to learn to suspend judgement whenever we are in doubt. To some extent, the suspension of judgement is an aspect of rationality – it is the ability to recognise the limits of demonstrability,[87] to see when a conclusion is less than certain and to remain sufficiently open-minded not to arrive at a judgement in advance of adequate evidence. At the same time, however, it is a practical knack of countering our natural disposition not only to form over-hasty judgements, but to act on them. It is the ability to treat our own judgements circumspectly rather than regarding them as final.[88]

Teachers and philosophers could, and did, discourse about the art of suspending judgement, but it was understood that, since the only judgement we can suspend is our own, individuals must cultivate this kind of self-control in themselves. By contrast, the procedure known as the separation of ideas could also be used to reverse the natural dispositions of other people. According to a number of seventeenth-century philosophers, many of our emotional responses are the fruit of chance associations of ideas.[89] But we can set ourselves to undo particular connexions and replace them with others. Descartes, who holds that both mental representations and passions are correlated with particular movements of the pineal gland, advocates a version of this technique – the separation of the motion that produces a representation (for instance of a particular dish) from the motion that produces an accompanying passion (such as revulsion). Significantly, he compares the process by which this is achieved to the training of gun-dogs. 'Since we are able, with a little effort, to change the movements of the brain in animals devoid of reason, it is evident that we can do so still more effectively in the case of men. Even those who have the weakest souls could acquire absolute mastery over their passions if we employed sufficient ingenuity in training and guiding them.'[90] This exercise, too, can be seen as an aspect of rational behaviour. But it is understood to involve a specific practical skill at which rational people may be more or less adept and in which they can be trained.

For those who are unequal to the strenuous demands of reasoning, there is a further para-rational method for controlling the passions. As Spinoza puts it, 'The best thing, then, that we can do, as long as we do not have perfect knowledge of our affects, is to conceive a correct principle of living, or sure maxims of life, to commit them to memory, and to apply them constantly to the particular cases encountered in life. In this way our imagination will be extensively affected by them, and we shall always have them ready.'[91] Maxims themselves varied greatly. They could be substantive, in the manner of the Ten Commandments, or procedural, as when Spinoza recommends us to remember that the 'highest satisfaction of mind stems from the right principle of living'.[92] They could be general, as when Hutcheson urges us to attend to the disasters to which our passions lead us, or comparatively specific, as when he instructs us to remember that entertainments are not an important part of the services we perform for our friends.[93] In all these cases, the advantage of maxims is supposed to be that, because they can be comparatively easily learned and applied, they can function both as a digest of a more complicated set of moral principles, and as a guide for people who might otherwise yield to their passions. Many authors seem to take it for granted that such rules are compiled by experts in reasoning for the use of the less skilled, a view which perpetuates the conception of a divide between a rational élite and the hoi polloi. Thus, when philosophers confidently lay down rules for the inculcation of correct conduct, they align themselves with the wise, the people who can interpret the demands of reason to everyone else.[94]

Many moral theorists of the seventeenth century recognised that the techniques for combatting the passions so far outlined were of only limited use, and that it was sometimes necessary to abandon any appeal to reason and to counter passion with passion. One could appeal to one dominant passion, as Hobbes recommends when he reminds us that 'the passion to be reckoned with is fear.'[95] Alternatively, one could pit particular affections against each other: fear against ambition; love against anger; hope against despair, and so on.[96] While the trick of arousing one passion to quell another was a recognised aspect of the art of political rule, it could also play a part in the quest for individual virtue. Hutcheson, for example, offers a striking reminder of this fact when he suggests that, if our children are worthless, we should restrain our natural affection for them by contemplating their vices.[97] Here, one passion is used to overcome another in the name of an impartiality which is itself seen as a feature of the good life.

A variant of this method of directing our emotions, which gained currency in the latter half of the seventeenth century, was the attempt to control passions by appealing to interests. The early French writers on the interests of princes who first made this idea central to political theory often assume, as in the case of Rohan, that it is definitive of wise princes that they are governed not by passion but by a sense of their best interests, a sense to which reason is said to guide them.[98] Interests thus come to be interposed between reason and passion in a model that lays emphasis on the prudential aspects of action.

In some quarters, these latter techniques for limiting passion were seen as dangerous capitulations to rhetoric (itself the art of arousing the passions) which permitted persuasive orators to play upon the emotions of their audiences for their own ends, and 'as the devil undid man by means of woman, gain reason by means of passion'.[99] For the most part, however, it was agreed that the manipulation of the passions was a necessary part of social life, essential to the inculcation of order. It formed part of the education of children, whose passions had to be directed if they were to learn to internalise the requirements of reason. In addition, it could be used in religious and secular contexts to control the emotions of adults who could not be relied upon to do so for themselves. The many techniques recommended for controlling the passions were consequently not neatly allocated to specific contexts or audiences, and they came together in conventions such as Christian meditation, which made use of all available means to work on the emotions and direct them into suitably pious channels. Meditational manuals such as Ignatius Loyola's *Exercitia spiritualia* continued to exert an enormous influence on Roman Catholic communities,[100] matched, for Protestants, by the works of such authors as Thomas Wright, Richard Baxter, or Thomas Traherne.[101] Codified practices for shaping the emotions were thus a part of everyday life. Equally, if less didactically, some authors drew attention in a more informal style to the follies into which our passions lead us. La Bruyère, for example, points out that there are people who like to be forced (*forcés*) by a demonstration to a particular conclusion,[102] and others who are more susceptible to the approach exemplified by his *Caractères*, in which he teases his readers into an awareness of the comically petty feelings and habits that go to make up society, implicitly offering them the means to greater self-knowledge.

## VII. BEYOND THE BOUNDS OF REASON

### 1. *Grace and virtuous action*

As we have seen, techniques for directing the emotions and desires were widely regarded as surrogates for active reasoning. They enabled people who would otherwise remain victims of their passions to approximate more closely to a standard of rational behaviour. Many advocates of such exercises did not doubt that this standard was simultaneously one of virtue, and that in order to lead a moral life it was sufficient to follow reason. But there were also theorists of the passions who believed that this was not enough: one might cultivate one's ability to control one's passions, and enlarge one's knowledge of ethical science to the utmost – and still fall short of virtue. The importance of these writers lies in the fact that they identified various feelings and emotions akin to passions as intrinsic features of a morally commendable life, thereby blurring the opposition between passion and virtue around which so much discussion in this area was organised.

Philosophers of this type can be roughly divided into two groups. First, there

are those who believe that the problem is one of motivation: we cannot attain the
ideal of a virtuous life by reasoning alone because, sullied as we are by Adam's fall,
we lack the ability to follow its dictates consistently. Second, there are advocates
of the epistemological view that certain important moral truths lie beyond the
reach of human reason. Even if we were able to follow reason effortlessly, we
could still fall short of virtue by failing to understand and act on these truths,
which can only be derived from some extra-rational source of knowledge.

To appreciate the significance of these lines of argument, it is important to
realise that they were entwined in a volatile theological debate about whether the
pursuit of reason is a reliable route to eternal salvation. A century earlier, Luther
had argued that, because we are fallen creatures, our reason cannot enlighten us as
to how God wishes us to act. Equally, our attempts at right action are distorted by
wickedness, and nothing we do can justify us in God's sight. We cannot, therefore,
be saved by our works, and our burden of sin can never be shed; but this may cease
to count against those who realise a completely passive faith in the righteousness of
God and the possibility of being redeemed through grace. By the mediation of
Christ, God can give to those who struggle for faith a further and unmerited kind
of sudden righteousness which 'swallows up all sins in a moment'.[103]

According to this Lutheran view, the ideal of virtue is replaced by that of
righteousness, the quality possessed by those awarded the grace to lead a godly
and hence a moral life. But while virtue had traditionally been regarded as an
achievement, the fruit of an active process of learning and self-discipline, the
concept of righteousness embodies a deliberate negation of these characteristics.
The righteous Christian is seen as inhabiting both the realm of Christ and the
realm of worldly things. In the latter, he or she must reason as best they can about
mundane matters and act as rationally as possible. But they must not entertain the
illusion that activity of this kind has any bearing on true morality – the law laid
down for us by God – or consequently on the afterlife. Anyone who aspires to
lead a moral life must try instead to cultivate a passive and unreasoning faith, in
the hope that God will give them the 'alien righteousness, instilled in us without
our works by grace alone' which is the only means to salvation.[104] Righteousness
therefore has nothing to do with reason and the associated conception of the
active self. In Augustinian vein, Luther adds to the dichotomy of active reason
versus passive emotion a third term – a morally commendable form of passivity.[105]

Luther's unyielding denigration of reason was in general opposed by Roman
Catholics. But it also had antagonists within the ranks of Protestantism. Calvin,
although he shared the belief that nothing we do can have any effect on our
salvation, resisted the view that our reason is so corrupted as to be morally

worthless. Corrupted it certainly is, but we nevertheless retain *scintillae* or sparks of reason which we must fan to the best of our ability in order to work out what we ought to do. Reason thus plays a significant rôle in our attempts to lead good lives, although it is powerless to affect what happens to us after death.[106]

There was, therefore, a dispute among Protestants as to how much insight reason provides into the moral rules by which God intends people to live. But this debate was by no means confined to Protestantism, and the same question was also raised within the Catholic church. Indeed, some of the richest philosophical discussions of the problem arose out of a strong Augustinian tradition within French Catholicism, a tradition that came to be associated during the 1640s with the name of Cornelius Jansenius. Like Luther, Jansenius was deeply influenced by Augustine (he entitled his *magnum opus* the *Augustinus*) and consequently advocated a form of Christianity alive to the wretched condition of fallen man.[107] In common with many Protestants, his followers believed that the established church displayed a misplaced confidence in a Pelagian conception of humans as free and rational, equipped with the means to ensure their own salvation. In taking this view, they argued, the church was not only guilty of encouraging the sins of pride and vanity. It was also failing to acknowledge the message of the New Testament, that humans are powerless without the help of Christ, who intercedes for them and redeems them.[108]

Jansenists thus shared with Protestants the belief that Christians had strayed from the ideal of a morally commendable life as a life of piety and humility, informed by the Christian virtues of faith, hope, and charity. But their efforts to rejuvenate this model reawakened a long-standing tension between the demands of reason on the one hand and those of faith and grace on the other. If faith in the Bible was all that a moral life required, reason seemed on the face of things to be largely redundant. If reason alone was sufficient, faith seemed overridden. For those who were not prepared to give up reason completely, a reconciliation of these ideas was urgently needed.

A first conciliatory argument focused on the claim that we are unable to realise the ideal of virtue because we lack the power to act as reason commands. This rather commonplace observation is often left to speak for itself but in the philosophy of Malebranche it is developed into a more refined analysis of the precise point at which reasoning lets us down. Malebranche's discussion revolves around an account of the relationship between the understanding and the will. By endowing us with understanding, God has given us the capacity to acquire ideas; but these are passive in that, by themselves, they do not move us to do anything.[109] In order that we may act, God has equipped us with a natural impulse towards the good[110] which gives rise to pleasure when it is satisfied.[111] Because we are fallen, yet retain some remnant of our uncorrupted nature, we are able to experience pleasure in two kinds of object. First, by virtue of what Malebranche calls concupiscence, we take pleasure in the familiar objects of our passions.[112] Second, we have the ability to experience a higher pleasure of which the object is God. Our natural weakness ensures that we are usually drawn away from this latter pleasure by our passions, and that our attempts to keep these in check are sporadic.[113] But we can be aided in this struggle by what Malebranche calls grace of feeling, or the grace of Jesus Christ.[114] This grace is 'given to balance the pleasures of concupiscence', and Malebranche describes it as a weight in a scale which may or may not be heavier than our countervailing passionate desires, and thus may or may not move an agent to right action. For 'although this grace be always efficacious by itself, it depends, or rather the effect depends, on the actual dispositions of him to whom it is given. The weight of concupiscence resists it: and sensible pleasures, which draw us to the creatures that seem to produce it in us, hinder the pleasure of grace from uniting us strictly to him who alone is capable of acting in us and of making us happy.'[115]

In this account, Malebranche self-consciously opposes the view that reason is its own motivation – that the very force of its conclusions moves us to action. Equally, he opposes the widespread belief that the process of reasoning gives rise to a pleasure of sufficient intensity to outweigh the passions. Understanding, as he sees it, is a form of intellectual activity which is, so to speak, confined to the mind, and is therefore powerless to move the body to act. Playing on the metaphors of passivity and activity, he presents understanding as active in so far as it is a kind of thinking, yet inert in the material world where it has to be complemented by the will. Again, by presenting virtuous action as the outcome of a partnership between a human agent, whose task is to learn to reason correctly, and Jesus Christ, who gives grace of feeling, Malebranche emphasises the passivity of human desires and contrasts them with the active, intervening rôle of the Redeemer.

## 2. Passionate knowledge

In one sense, Malebranche's view that without grace people lack the desire to follow the dictates of understanding is a cautious one. Although understanding is held to be powerless in moving us to action, its speculative reach is undiminished, and an appreciation of morality lies within its grasp. This assumption is challenged by the advocates of a second line of argument, who attack reason in its citadel, so to speak, by casting doubt on the belief that it can give us the kind of understanding of God which is vital to both morality and salvation.

A number of versions of this doctrine were developed during the seventeenth century. Although they defy easy classification, two main variants attracted widespread attention and played a central part in influential philosophical debates. On the one hand, the belief that reason cannot provide us with moral knowledge is characteristic of the strictest forms of predestinarian Protestant thought. On the other hand, there is a cluster of interpretations of the doctrine which are basically Platonist in allegiance, drawing from chronologically scattered sources the common conviction that because reason yields only one, relatively poor, kind of knowledge, the mind must move out beyond it to a knowledge more akin to feeling. Only Love or knowledge of the heart can yield true insight into the nature and commands of God, and thus into the Good.

Among the defenders of this Platonist tradition were some writers who wore their colours on their sleeves. John Smith, for example, who belonged to the group of philosophers known as the Cambridge Platonists, followed their practice of reworking a series of doctrines attributed to Plato and Plotinus in the name of true (Protestant) Christianity. His argument for the limitations of reason[116] displays what is by now a familiar concern with the rôle of piety in the lives of true Christians. To possess moral knowledge, he implies, is to be able to act rightly; and to act rightly is to lead the kind of godly life described in the New Testament. But this kind of knowledge is not supplied by a science of ethics. 'It is but a thin, aery knowledge that is got by mere speculation, which is ushered in by syllogisms and demonstrations; but that which springs forth from true goodness . . . brings such a divine light into the soul, as is more clear and convincing than any demonstration.'[117]

At the root of this contrast lies the view that reason is speculative and hence divorced from action; it yields only passive understanding rather than the active engagement with the world that characterises a life of moral virtue. To some extent, Smith agrees with Malebranche that what we lack is the motivation to do what reason recommends. But he goes further than this and suggests that we must transcend speculative rationality completely to achieve knowledge of an altogether different kind. Smith starts from the fact that 'there are some radical principles of knowledge that are so deeply sunk into the souls of men, as that the impression cannot easily be obliterated'. And of these, 'The common notions of God and virtue . . . are more perspicuous than any else.'[118] These impressions, however, grow faint and inefficacious if we do not put them into practice by leading virtuous lives; and they are especially prone to be weakened by our bodily passions. To retain our natural grasp of virtue, we must withdraw from sensuous encounters, for only then can we begin to acquire the knowledge of the divine world which will subsequently protect us from our passions.[119]

Anyone who is able to take this advice has already embarked upon an ascent through four types of knowledge and has passed beyond the lowest level, where reason is subject to passion, to the second phase. Here, reason has won enough ground for a person to have clear and steady impressions of virtue and goodness. From this point they may rise to a third level at which 'their inward sense of virtue and moral goodness [are] far transcendent to all mere speculative opinions of it', but not yet so secure as to be proof against pride, conceit, and other varieties of self-love. And, finally, a person 'running and shooting up above his own logical or self-rational life' may achieve union with God.[120]

For Platonists, the transformation embodied in these four stages has a mystical quality; those who have not yet gained divine knowledge must have faith in the possibility of doing so, while lacking a more than schematic sense of what they are striving to achieve. And among the claims they must take on trust is the view that it is possible to acquire a non-propositional kind of knowledge. In their efforts to explain this idea, writers such as Smith and More play upon a variety of conventional contrasts. They are emphatic that moral knowledge is not mere knowledge *that* certain things are the case, but knowledge of *how* to live a virtuous life. But at the same time they undermine the sceptical contrast between sensing and knowing by using metaphors of sight and taste to convey the quality of divine truth.[121] Finally, Smith takes up a common play on the opposition between knowledge and feeling and reverses their traditional associations with the head and the heart. 'That is not the best and truest knowledge of God', he tells us, 'which is wrought out by the labour and sweat of the brain, but that which is kindled within us by an heavenly warmth in our hearts.'[122] The best knowledge – knowledge of God and morality – originates in the heart, the seat of the emotions.

This assimilation of reason to emotion, of knowledge to love, offers writers in the neo-Platonist tradition a way out of the impasse created by the view that reason is powerless to motivate us to act. They allow that this is indeed a problem for mere speculation. But they argue that, once we transcend the passive reasoning of syllogisms and demonstrations, we can approach a kind of knowledge of God and his order (also confusingly sometimes called a kind of reason) which incorporates a love strong enough to bring our wills into conformity with that of God.

Writers who identified themselves as Platonists were by no means alone in arguing that knowledge lies beyond the reach of reason. Indeed, any distinction between Platonists and non-Platonists in this matter is a somewhat artificial one, given that Plato's doctrines had been widely adapted by Christian thinkers whose works were then invoked both by self-confessed Platonists and by Christian authors in general. Augustine, in particular, had made some aspects of Platonism his own, and had justified his borrowings by the judgement that Plato was the most nearly Christian of the pagan philosophers.[123] In the seventeenth century, the similarity between philosophers in the Augustinian tradition and authors who identified themselves as Platonists emerges particularly clearly in the works of French writers sympathetic to Jansenism. Unsurprisingly, the latter group tend to reflect the Augustinian emphasis on man's fallen nature. And, partly because they regard human corruption as central to our own self-understanding, they share with the Platonists the view that there are moral truths that reason is incapable of discerning. By far the most sustained and original treatment of this theme is that of Pascal, who brings to it a rhetorical clarity foreign to the sermons and discourses of English Platonism in this period. Like other Augustinian writers before him, Pascal places reason in a hierarchy of types of knowledge and value. But he goes on to delineate its limits in its own terms. Confronting the advocates of the belief that we can grasp the requirements of a moral life by reasoning, he appeals to reason itself to explain just how their view is deficient.

In his *Pensées* Pascal distinguishes three orders of *grandeur,* or greatness – the order of the flesh, the order of the mind, and the order of charity – each of which constitutes a system of values and ends.[124] The carnal order allots value to worldly things and recognises the *grandeur* of those who wield temporal power. The order of the mind esteems intellectual achievements such as argument and discovery, and its *grandeur* is exemplified, in Pascal's view, by Archimedes. Finally, the order of charity or the will values only divine things. Its *grandeur* – wisdom – resembles the wisdom of God and its exemplars are Christ and the saints.[125] Each order also incorporates a method of investigation and justification. Unsurprisingly, perhaps, the values of the carnal order are recognised by the eyes, and more generally by the senses. Reason, the 'eyes of the mind', enables us to appreciate and justify intellectual achievement. And, lastly, faith, 'the eyes of the heart', reveals to us the religious values of the order of charity.[126]

These three moral schemes are on the one hand incommensurable, in the sense that the values embedded in one order cannot be appreciated from the perspective of a lower order, and yet on the other hand they can be compared. When the comparison is made, wisdom far outstrips either carnal or intellectual greatness, and Pascal assumes that this supreme value is the only end of a truly moral life, the only source of real happiness. We should, therefore, make it our goal. But this conclusion obviously poses a problem. If we are burdened with the unenlightened values of the body or the intellect, we shall be unable to appreciate the significance or rewards of wisdom, and will therefore have no reason to pursue it.

The resolution of this dilemma is a prominent theme of the *Pensées*. Implicitly taking the view that one can only ascend the hierarchy of orders one stage at a time, Pascal concentrates on the plight of those who inhabit the order of the intellect and confidently put their trust in reason. The only way to convince them of the poverty of their ends is to borrow their own tools and persuade them by reasoned argument that they have rational grounds for distrusting reason.[127] Pascal accordingly offers several kinds of grounds for doubting its sufficiency. The least ambitious – a familiar repertoire of Pyrrhonist tropes – are designed to persuade us that reason is extremely unreliable.[128] They are complemented by a more telling discussion of the psychological difficulty we encounter in trying to excise all non-rational elements from our judgements. The capacity of humans to conform to reason is jeopardised by the fecundity of the imagination, which all but swamps it with vivid yet extraneous items of evidence. The philosopher standing on a wide plank over a ravine, for example, is, despite himself, prey to an irrational fear of falling. While his reason assures him that the danger of losing his balance is negligible, his imagination portrays this terrifying possibility in lurid colours.[129]

Humans are thus burdened by emotional and cognitive dispositions which make it extremely difficult for them to reason, so much so that it would be fruitless to try to explain their behaviour as the outcome of rational judgement. Equally, it would be a sign of vanity to suppose that they are capable of becoming rational, since dispassionate inspection reveals that they are powerless to reform their natures. This pessimistic view, so commonly enunciated by Christian moralists, is elaborated in the *Pensées* when Pascal embarks upon a further argument to the effect that, even if we were capable of using our reason properly, it would not meet the standard of certainty usually claimed for it. Here the criticism of reason shifts from a psychological to an epistemological plane, and once again Pascal follows in the footsteps of Pyrrhonism.

The chief obstacle standing in the way of certainty is, Pascal claims, the first principles from which reasoning proceeds. For the conclusion of a syllogism to be secure, its premises must be certain; but the first principles on which all our reasoning is ultimately founded are not themselves known by reason. Thus, if the art of demonstration is not to be undercut, their truth must be guaranteed by some other means. What could this be? One possibility would be to claim, as Descartes did, that first principles are known by intuition. But Pascal argues that this is tantamount to dogmatism, since the intuition that the principles are true does not amount to proof, and reason tells us that we should not be prepared to accept unproven propositions. Another way out would be to draw the sceptical conclusion that there is no justification for first principles. But Pascal argues that this, too, is unsatisfactory because we are by nature incapable of suspending belief about such fundamental matters.[130]

The proper response to this difficulty is to allow that, while we do indeed know the first principles on which we base demonstrations, we do not know them by means of reason. Instead, our knowledge of them flows from another cognitive principle associated with instinct, feeling and the heart. 'We know the truth not only through our reason, but also through our heart. It is through the latter that we know first principles, and reason, which knows nothing about them, tries in vain to refute them. . . . Principles are felt, propositions proved, and both with certainty though by different means.'[131] While it is not at all clear that Pascal has here escaped the dependence on intuition which he earlier condemned as dogmatism, it is clear that he wishes to defend the cognitive status of a certain kind of feeling. He seeks to persuade us that, since we already depend on diverse cognitive principles, we should not shrink from admitting that reason is only one source of knowledge.

At the same time, sober and unflinching reflection on our state should, in Pascal's view, convince us that we are incapable of gaining more than a very modest knowledge of nature.[132] But once we realise that anything more is beyond our grasp, we will be prone to suffer a kind of frustration in the face of our own impotence. Our limited powers of reasoning are sufficiently strong to enable us to understand the difference between knowledge and opinion. And this understanding in turn enables us to conceive the possibility of a complete and securely founded knowledge, guaranteed by reason through and through. Such cast-iron certainty is the object of intense desire. But the very powers of reasoning which enable us to conceive it also show us that it can never be attained.[133]

Reason thus has the special characteristic of revealing its own limits, and although Pascal occasionally discusses this in a matter-of-fact tone of voice as something we must just settle down and accept, he more often speaks of the juxtaposition of power and powerlessness as a source of anguish. 'We desire truth, but find in ourselves nothing but uncertainty. We seek happiness, but find only wretchedness and death. We are incapable of not desiring truth and happiness and incapable of either certainty or happiness. We have been left with this desire as much as a punishment as to make us feel how far we have fallen.'[134]

Yet out of anguish comes a new kind of understanding. For once we ask ourselves why we have both an ability to reason and an inability to carry our reason to its natural conclusion, we shall see, according to Pascal, that this paradoxical state of affairs must be explained by the Fall. 'Is it not as clear as day that man's condition is dual? The point is that if man had never been corrupted, he would, in his inno-cence, confidently enjoy both truth and felicity, and, if man had never been any-thing but corrupt, he would have no idea either of truth or bliss. But unhappy as we are . . . we have an idea of happiness but we cannot attain it. We perceive an image of the truth and possess nothing but falsehood, being equally incapable of absolute ignorance and certain knowledge; so obvious is it that we once enjoyed a degree of perfection from which we have unhappily fallen.'[135]

In order to understand ourselves, we must acknowledge the duality within our nature. But Pascal goes on to insist that this correct self-description is not suscepti-ble to rational justification. It will, first of all, only be acceptable to those who believe the story of the creation told in the Bible, and since the truth of this story cannot be demonstrated, such a belief must rest on faith. Moreover, when we accept the story of the Fall, we accept the doctrine of the transmission of sin. And, as Pascal comments, 'nothing is more shocking to our reason than to say that the sin of the first man has implicated in its guilt men so far from the original sin that they seem incapable of sharing it. This flow of guilt does not seem merely impossible to us but indeed most unjust.'[136] Nothing in reason can convince us of the veracity or the justice of God's decree that Adam's sin should be transmitted. But unless we accept its veracity we are left with no way of explaining our dual nature. And to accept its veracity without accepting its justice would be to settle for an unjust God – a possibility not contemplated by Pascal. In his view, therefore, we are committed to accepting both that Adam and Eve fell from grace and that their sin descends to us. But in doing so we abandon reason, which is powerless in this arena, for faith.

It is therefore by turning inward upon ourselves that we are able to understand the contradictions that are part of our nature and see how to resolve them. Pascal's stress on self-knowledge here owes much to Montaigne, and although he fiercely repudiates the secular tone and argument of the *Essais*,[137] he shares the view that self-knowledge gives rise to both practical and philosophical benefits, and may even lead one to the truth. To achieve self-understanding in this latter sense, however, one must recognise the limits of reason and submit to faith. God will help any who sincerely attempt to conquer the polar vices of pride and despair[138] and set themselves to believe the central truths of Christian religion. For He will give them grace – the overwhelming desire to love God and lead a pious life – which will enable them to conform to the laws of Christian morality.

This conclusion muddies the opposition between reason and passion. To be sure, the passions remain destructive of both rationality and piety. But reason, the surviving fragment of our prelapsarian condition, appears in a more equivocal light. While it is still acknowledged to be active, its controlling quality is no longer seen as the benevolent means to virtue. Instead, our ability to use reason to quash the passions is now presented as one aspect of an undue confidence, arrogance, and pride, itself a consequence of our fallen nature. Our busy attempts to impose rational order on the world are therefore self-defeating in that they conceal from us the centrality of faith and thus ensure that our attempts to gain knowledge of the moral law laid down by God are perpetually frustrated. Virtue will not, then, be achieved by means of the active processes of reasoning. Rather, it issues from a constructive form of passivity which Pascal describes as submission.[139] To be passive therefore need not be a bad thing. On the contrary, it is only through submission that we can transcend the order of the mind and recognise the supreme values embodied in the order of charity.

Throughout the seventeenth century, philosophers continued to address a collection of problems which they had inherited from their predecessors about the relation between the passions and the good life: How do the passions threaten virtue? How can they be kept under control? What passions, if any, do virtuous people display? Much of this discussion was carried on within an established framework which opposed reason and virtue to passion and vice; a context in which the passions tended to be regarded as dangerous, amoral forces. But during the same period this deeply entrenched view was subjected to a variety of conflicting pressures which eventually contributed to its displacement. First, as we have seen, a number of arguments served to muddy the distinction between reason and passion, and that between the associated notions of activity and passivity. An emphasis on the suggestion that what had generally been classified as reasoning might itself be imbued with emotion served to reshape the philosophical landscape and strengthened the view that passion plays an essential part in our understanding of the good. At the same time, philosophers began to reassess the conventional wisdom that our emotions are predominantly destructive and treacherous. Building on the view that they are 'buds of virtue' created in us by God, they came to see at least some of the passions in a more optimistic light. This shift is reflected in the emergence and increased use of distinctions such as those between passions and interests, and between calm and uncalm passions, which could in turn be employed to provide more refined accounts of the connexion between virtue and the emotions. In the seventeenth century itself, these changes remained tentative. But we can see in retrospect that they paved the way for the transformations in moral and psychological thinking known as the Enlightenment.

## NOTES

1 For discussions of factors that can affect our passions see, e.g., Charron, *Sag.*, Bk. I, chap. 42, Charron 1986, pp. 285–90; Descartes, *Pass. âme* sec. 161; Wright 1630, p. 327; Malebranche, *Rech.* II.I.7.1 and 6, *OC* I 232–4 and 249–55.

2 This simile is widely appealed to. See Spinoza *Eth.* III prop. 59; Glanvill 1670, p. 18.

3 The centrality of this metaphor has been much discussed. See, e.g., Judowitz 1993, pp. 63–86. The 'light of nature' is widely treated as a synonym for reason as, e.g., in the title of Culverwel's work 'An Elegant and Learned Discourse of the Light of Nature'.

4 See, e.g., Pierre Charron, *Sag.*, Bk. II, chap. 1, Charron 1986, p. 380; and More 1690, Epistle to the Reader. For the relation between music and the passions see Duncan 1993, pp. 100–1.

5 See sections II and III of this chapter.

6 Hume, *A Treatise of Human Nature*, Hume 1978, p. 415.

7 See Locke 1968, secs. 42, 72, 73.

8 See sec. VIII.

9 See sec. VI.

10 See secs. V and VII.

11 Eclectic, sixteenth-century discussions of the passions continued to be popular. See, e.g., Vives 1990; Charron, *De la Sagesse*. Among seventeenth-century works which answer to this description see, e.g., Caussin 1630; Cureau de la Chambre 1658; Wright 1630; Charleton 1674; More 1690.

12 La Rochefoucauld 1967.

13 La Bruyère 1990.

14 Descartes, *Pass. âme* sec. 47.

15 Charron, *Sag.*, Bk. I, chap. 14, Charron 1986, pp. 143, 127; Pascal, *Pens.* 44.

16 Spinoza, *Eth.* III prop. 39.

17 Otherwise there would be no point in the methods described in section VI of this chapter.

18 Hobbes 1968, p. 120; Descartes, *Pass. âme* sec. 56; Spinoza, *Eth.* IV pref.

19 Hobbes 1968, p. 112. See also More 1690, pp. 79–80.

20 Hobbes 1968, p. 132; cf. Descartes, *Regulae*, rule 2, AT XI 362–3.

21 Hobbes 1968, p. 105.

22 E.g., Spinoza's *Ethica* purports to be such a science. Descartes describes the science of morals as the highest and most perfect moral system: *Princ.*, Preface to the French edition. Locke supposes that morality, as well as mathematics, is capable of demonstration, *Ess.* IV.xii.18, as does More 1690, pp. 20–1.

23 Hobbes 1968, pp. 160–1; Spinoza, *Eth.* III prop. 7; Locke, *Ess.* II.xx.3.

24 Hobbes 1968, p. 161.

25 Spinoza, *Eth.* IV prop. 62; Locke, *Ess.* II.xxi.60.

26 This lack of a set of agreed moral principles is acknowledged by Locke, *Ess.* IV.xii.8. Descartes concedes that these can only be known by God; see his letter to Elisabeth, 15 September 1645, AT IV 290–1. See Levi 1964, pp. 287–8.

27 Hobbes 1968, p. 190.

28 Hobbes 1968, pp. 190–3.

29 See, e.g., Descartes, *Princ.* IV 206 and *Regulae*, rule 3 (AT XI 366–7); Locke, *Ess.* IV.ii.1.; Hobbes 1968, p. 410.

30 Descartes, letter to Regius, May 1641, AT III 371–2; Woolhouse 1993, chaps. 8 and 9. Cudworth 1845, vol. 3, pp. 586–7 (Bk. III, chap. 2); More 1690, pp. 12–13.

31 Spinoza, *Eth.* III prop. 3.

32 Spinoza, *Eth.* II prop. 29 cor.

33 Spinoza, *Eth.* II props. 48, 49; cf. Hobbes 1968, p. 127.

34 See, e.g., La Rochefoucauld 1967, Maxim 5: 'La passion fait souvent un fou du plus habile homme, et rend souvent les plus sots habiles.'

35 Spinoza, *Eth.* V prop. 32; Descartes makes a closely related point, *Pass. âme* sec. 148; La Forge 1666, pp. 356–8 (chap. 21); More 1690, pp. 4–7.

36 Spinoza, *Eth.* III prop. 58; La Forge 1666, pp. 356–7 (chap. 21).

37 See Chapter 27 in this book.

38 The relevant mistakes here are the ones to which Spinoza draws attention in the *Ethica*.

39 See, e.g., *Eth.* III prop. 49, V prop. 6.

40 Spinoza, *Eth.* IV prop. 18, prop. 37 schol. 1.

41 Descartes, *Pass. âme* sec. 161.

42 Descartes, *Pass. âme* sec. 153.

43 Descartes, *Pass. âme* sec. 153.

44 Descartes, *Pass. âme* sec. 156.

45 For discussion of this theme, see Chapter 35 in this book.

46 For a significant exception, see Grotius 1925, vol. 1, p. 9 (*Prolegomena*); Crowe 1977b, pp. 223–8.

47 See Cudworth, *Treatise concerning Eternal and Immutable Morality*, Bk. I, chap. 3, Cudworth 1845, vol. 3, p. 536; Muirhead 1931, pp. 59–60.

48 See, e.g., Shaftesbury 1900, vol. 1, pp. 60–1.

49 Locke 1954, pp. 133, 187.

50 This is the title of Cudworth's work on the subject. Among other advocates of the same view, see Stillingfleet 1659, chap. 1, in Stillingfleet 1710, vol. 4, p. 15: 'The Law of Nature binds indispensably, as it depends not upon any arbitrary constitutions, but is founded on the intrinsical nature of good or evil in things themselves.' See also Shaftesbury 1900, vol. 1, p. 264.

51 See Clarke 1738, vol. 2, pp. 608–9; Cudworth, *Treatise concerning Eternal and Immutable Morality*, Bk. I, chap. 2, Cudworth 1845, vol. 3, pp. 530–6; Colman 1983, chap. 2.

52 Central to Hobbes's argument is the conventional view that it is rational to adhere to the laws of nature, which specify the best means to our most fundamental goals. (Thus, 'Endeavour peace as far as you have hope of obtaining it' tells us how to preserve ourselves.) On the one hand, 'though improperly called laws', the laws of nature are but theorems. That is to say, they are precepts which, because they are rationally grounded, are universally applicable. On the other hand, they are also the laws of God; by endowing us with reason, God has given us the means to work out the precepts by which He intends us to be ruled. Hobbes 1968, pp. 190–1, 409–10.

53 King 1830, p. 191. For a less temperate attack on Hobbes's position see More 1690, pp. 31–2.

54 Cudworth, *Treatise concerning Eternal and Immutable Morality*, Bk. I, chap. 1, Cudworth 1845, vol. 3, p. 528.

55 Shaftesbury 1900, vol. 2, p. 83.

56 For texts and commentary see Long and Sedley 1987, secs. 63, 64, 65.

57 Aristotle, *Nicomachean Ethics*, Bk. II.

58 Spinoza, *Eth.* V props. 15ff.

59 Spinoza, *Eth.* III props. 9, 11.
60 Spinoza, *Eth.* I prop. 29; II prop. 44.
61 Spinoza, *Eth.* IV prop. 47.
62 For the limits of this view see *Eth.* IV props. 4, 6.
63 Spinoza, *Eth.* IV prop. 59; see also Descartes, *Pass. âme* secs. 147 and 148 and *Princ.* IV 190. See also La Forge 1666, pp. 259–60 (chap. 21); Levi 1964, pp. 284ff.
64 Le Grand 1662.
65 Descartes's debts to Stoicism are evident in his analysis of *générosité*; see *Pass. âme* secs. 153–6. See Rodis-Lewis 1987b, pp. 43–54.
66 Coëffeteau 1630, p. 33. See also Descartes, *Pass. âme* secs. 168, 182.
67 See, e.g., Senault 1649, p. 125.
68 Coëffeteau 1630, p. 42; Senault 1649, p. 125.
69 Senault 1649, p. 8. See also More 1690, p. 34.
70 More 1690, p. 83.
71 Senault 1649, p. 144.
72 More 1690, pp. 146–7; Perkins 1966, p. 164.
73 Senault 1649, p. 126; Wright 1630, Bk. I, p. 15.
74 This view is widespread. See, e.g., Senault 1649, pp. 39–40 (5th Discourse).
75 Senault 1649, pp. 46–7 (6th Discourse).
76 See Coleman 1994; Kraye 1994. In England, this tradition was associated with the Cambridge Platonists. See, e.g., More 1690, pp. 40, 41; Norris 1694, a work dedicated to Cudworth's daughter, Lady Damaris Masham. See Muirhead 1931; Strier 1983, chap. 8. For Augustinianism in France, see Levi 1964, chap. 8; Rodis-Lewis 1990, pp. 101–26; Sellier 1970.
77 Calvin 1961, vol. 1, pp. 562–9.
78 Calvin 1961, vol. 1, pp. 607–9.
79 Ames 1639, Bk. I, pp. 44–7; Bk. II, pp. 20–1. Perkins 1966, p. 73.
80 This is especially an inheritance from the classical rhetorical tradition according to which *ratio* in the absence of *eloquentia* lacks any power to motivate action or even to induce belief. See especially the opening of Cicero, *De inventione.* Among seventeenth-century philosophers, Locke is a good example of someone who appreciates that most people manage most of the time without any grasp of formal deductive reasoning. See *Ess.* I.ii.12. See Atherton 1993.
81 Descartes, *Pass. âme* sec. 161.
82 Descartes, *Pass. âme* sec. 161. See also Malebranche, *TNG*, Discours III, xv, *OC* V 250.
83 See Charron, *Sag.,* Bk. I, chap. 52, Charron 1986, pp. 335–8; Bk. II, Preface, Charron 1986, pp. 369–70; Malebranche, *TNG*, Discours III, xiv, *OC* V 250.
84 This is assumed by the authors of didactic advice books to princes, which continued to be written in the seventeenth century. See, e.g., La Mothe le Vayer 1662, vol. 1, pp. 847–72. See also Senault 1649, pp. 135–6; Charron, *Sag.,* Bk. I, chap. 49, Charron 1986, pp. 321–8.
85 Maclean 1977, chap. 2.
86 Le Moyne 1668; Maclean 1977, chap. 3.
87 See, e.g., Descartes, Med IV, AT VII 59–60.
88 E.g., Descartes, letter to Mesland, 2 May 1644, AT IV 115–16; Malebranche, *TNG*, Discours III, xvi, *OC* V 251–2.
89 See, e.g., Malebranche, *Recherche*, II.I.5, *OC* I 222–3; Locke, *Ess.* II.xxxiii.7; Spinoza, *Eth.* III prop. 16.

90  Descartes, *Pass. âme* sec. 50. See also Spinoza, *Eth.* V prop. 10; Locke, *Some Thoughts concerning Education,* Locke 1968, p. 115.

91  Spinoza, *Eth.* V prop. 10.

92  Spinoza, *Eth.* V prop. 10.

93  Hutcheson 1728, p. 168.

94  Among many examples see Bacon, *The Advancement of Learning,* Bacon 1857–74, vol. 3, p. 439; Malebranche, *Traité de Morale,* I.xiii.12.

95  Hobbes 1968, p. 200.

96  See, e.g., Senault 1649, p. 117; Bacon, *The Advancement of Learning,* Bacon 1857–74, vol. 3, p. 438; Charron, *Sag.,* Bk. 2, chap. 1, Charron 1986, p. 381.

97  Hutcheson 1728, p. 107.

98  Rohan 1638. See Hirschman 1977, pp. 311–54; Keohane 1980, pp. 155–63.

99  Senault 1649, pp. 172–3. For the dangers of rhetoric, see Descartes, *Pass. âme* sec. 48.

100  Ignatius of Loyola 1989; François de Sales 1971.

101  Baxter 1673; Traherne 1675; Wright 1630. See Kaufmann 1966.

102  La Bruyère 1990.

103  Luther 1955–86, vol. 31, p. 298; see Cranz 1959, p. 126; Skinner 1978, vol. 2, pp. 1–12.

104  Luther 1955–86, vol. 31, p. 299. See Gerrish 1962.

105  For some antecedents of this view, see Skinner 1978, vol. 2, pp. 22–3.

106  Calvin 1961, pp. 270, 273–4.

107  Jansenius 1640.

108  See Sedgwick 1977; Hildesheimer 1991.

109  Malebranche, *Rech.,* Preface, *OC* I 43.

110  Malebranche, *Rech.,* *OC* I 45; *TNG,* Discours III.xviii, *OC* V 253.

111  Malebranche, *TNG,* Discours III.iv, *OC* V 243.

112  Malebranche, *TNG,* Discours II.xxxi, *OC* V 222.

113  Malebranche, *TNG,* Discours III.xiii, *OC* V 249.

114  Malebranche, *TNG,* Discours III.xv, *OC* V 250.

115  Malebranche, *TNG,* Discours III.xx, *OC* V 254.

116  Smith 1969, pp. 128–44.

117  Smith 1969, p. 130.

118  Smith 1969, p. 138.

119  Smith 1969, p. 139.

120  Smith 1969, p. 142.

121  Smith 1969, p. 128.

122  Smith 1969, p. 129.

123  *De civitate Dei* VIII.ii, Augustine 1972, p. 313.

124  Pascal, *Pens.,* 308, 933.

125  For the antecedents of this idea, see Topliss 1966, pp. 129–36.

126  Pascal, *Pens.,* 308.

127  Pascal, *Pens.,* 188. Pascal attributes this view to Augustine. See Sellier 1970.

128  Pascal, *Pens.,* 21.

129  Pascal, *Pens.,* 44.

130  Pascal, *Pens.,* 110, 131.

131  Pascal, *Pens.,* 110. See also 513.

132  Pascal, *Pens.,* 199.

133  Pascal, *Pens.,* 131.

134 Pascal, *Pens.,* 401.
135 Pascal, *Pens.,* 131.
136 Pascal, *Pens.,* 131.
137 Pascal, *Entretien avec M. de Saci,* in Pascal 1963, p. 293.
138 Pascal, *Pens.,* 354.
139 Pascal, *Pens.,* 167, 170, 188.

# BIOBIBLIOGRAPHICAL APPENDIX

## ROGER ARIEW AND DANIEL GARBER

This section contains entries for some of the most important philosophers, understood broadly, in the period covered by this volume. We sought to include all of the main figures discussed in this history, along with some others who may be of interest to readers. This is particularly true of many of the women included. The first part of each entry contains a brief biographical sketch, including a list of the main works of philosophical significance in their main editions and, when available, an indication of the most important modern editions. The second part contains a brief selection of secondary literature. We have given complete bibliographical citations so that the reader does not have to refer forward to the bibliography to find that information. These biographical and bibliographical entries are not intended to be comprehensive and complete. Rather, they give background information and serve as a starting place for further investigation.

ALSTED, JOHANN HEINRICH b. Ballersbach (Herborn), 1588; d. Weissenburg (Transylvania), 1638. Calvinist philosopher, theologian, and pansophist whose textbooks on methodology and education were widely read. Taught at the University of Herborn from 1608 to 1629, where he became professor of philosophy in 1615 and of theology in 1619. Attended the Synod of Dordrecht in 1618. Attracted students from all over Europe, the most famous of whom was Amos Comenius. Interested in the kabbalah and in Lull's interpretation of it, which he summarised in his *Clavis artis Lullianae* (Strasbourg, 1609) and which influenced his early encyclopaedic projects. In his *Systema nemonicumm duplex* (Frankfurt, 1610), presented his art of memory and an outline of all metaphysical knowledge. His life-long goal was to organise in a systematic fashion all knowledge so that it might be more easily learned and taught. To this end, he wrote the *Panacea philosophica; id est, facilis, nova et accurata methodus docendi et discendi universam encyclopaediam* (Herborn, 1610); *Theatrum scholasticum, in quo consiliarius philosophicus proponit et exponit* (Herborn, 1610); the *Trigae canonicae* (Frankfurt, 1612) and the *Philosophia digne restituta* (Herborn, 1612) in which he most clearly presents the theory behind his encyclopaedic projects; the *Compendium logicae harmonicae* (Herborn, 1613); the *Cursus Philosophici Encyclopaedia libris XXVII* (Herborn, 1620), his first massive encyclopaedia; and the *Compendium lexici philosophici* (Herborn, 1626); *Summa casuum conscientiae, nova methodo elaborata* (Frankfurt, 1628). When his work was disrupted by the Thirty Years' War, accepted an invitation in 1629 from Gabriel Bethlen, the prince of Transylvania, to join a new academy in Weissenburg. His most influential work is probably the huge *Encyclopaedia* (Herborn, 1630, repr. Stuttgart-Bad Cannstatt: Frommann, 1989), which sets forth in seven volumes an account of all knowledge, organised by topic, ranging from metaphysics and physics to jurisprudence and zoology, and which draws upon an impressive range of ancient, Neoplatonic Renaissance, and early modern sources and has an extensive index. There is no standard edition.

Secondary Sources: Kvačala, J. (1889), 'Johann Heinrich Alsted', *Ungarische Revue* 9:628–42.Wundt, M. (1939), *Die Deutsche Schulmetaphysik des 17: Jahrhunderts,* Tübingen: J. C. B. Mohr, pp. 81–2. Rossi, P. (1960), *Clavis Universalis: Arti mnemoniche e logica combinatoria da Lullo a Leibniz,* Milan: Riccardo Ricciardi. Loemker, L. E. (1961), 'Leibniz and the Herborn Encyclopedists', *Journal of the History of Ideas* 22:323–38. Clouse, R. G. (1969), 'Johann Heinrich Alsted and English Millenarianism', *Harvard Theol. Review* 62. Staedke, J. (1978), 'Alsted', *Theol. Realenzyklopädie,* Berlin and New York: de Gruyter, vol. 2, pp. 299–303. Webster, C. (1970–80) 'Johann Heinrich Alsted', in *DSB*. Schmidt-Biggemann, W. (1983), *Topica universalis: Eine Modellgeschichte humanistischer und barocker Wissenschaft.* Hamburg: Meiner. Schmidt-Biggemann, W. (1989), Vorwort to *Encyclopaedia universa,* repr. Stuttgart: Frommann, pp. i–xviii. [Christia Mercer]

ARNAULD, ANTOINE (Le grand Arnauld) b. Paris, 1612; d. Liège, 1694. Theologian, philosopher. The leading spokesperson for the Catholic Jansenist movement in France, and one of the more outspoken and orthodox defenders of Cartesian philosophy in the seventeenth century. Received his doctorate in theology in 1641; admitted to the Sorbonne in 1643. Author of sympathetic but critical *Quartae Objectiones* to Descartes's *Meditationes de prima philosophia* (Paris, 1641). Influenced by St. Cyran (Jean Duvergier du Hauranne), spiritual counsellor to Port-Royal. Wrote *De la fréquente communion* (Paris, 1643), an indictment of Jesuit doctrine, and *Apologie de Monsieur Jansenius* (Paris, 1644). Persecuted by Jesuits, Vatican, French church, Parlement, Université de Paris, and the King for theological views. Expelled from Sorbonne, 1656. Composed *Gramaire générale et raisonnée* (published Paris, 1660) with Claude Lancelot; and *La Logique, ou l'art de penser* (Port-Royal Logic, published Paris, 1662) with Pierre Nicole. Went into exile in the Netherlands in 1679. Defended Descartes's philosophy in the *Examen d'un écrit qui a pour titre: Traité de l'essence du corps et de l'union de l'Ame avec le corps, contre la philosophie de M. Descartes,* written in 1680, but published posthumously. Engaged in public debate over Malebranche's theory of ideas and doctrine of grace and divine providence with *Des vraies et des fausses idées* (Cologne, 1683), *Défense de M. Arnauld contre la réponse au livre des vraies et des fausses idées* (Cologne, 1684), *Réflexions philosophiques et théologiques sur le nouveau système de la nature et de la grâce* (Cologne, 1685), and numerous letters. Corresponded with Leibniz regarding his *Discours de métaphysique* from 1686 to 1690. Published *Dissertation sur le prétendu bonheur des plaisirs des sens* in Cologne, 1687. The standard edition of his works is Arnauld (1775–83), *Oeuvres de Messire Antoine Arnauld, docteur de la maison et société de Sorbonne* (43 vols.), Paris.

Secondary Sources: *BHPC.* Zimmermann, C. (1911), 'Arnauld's Kritik der Ideenlehre Malebranches', *Philosophisches Jahrbuch* 24:3–47. Lovejoy, A. O. (1923), 'Representative Ideas in Malebranche and Arnauld', *Mind* 32:449–61. Laird, J. (1924), 'The Legend of Arnauld's Realism', *Mind* 33:176–9. Sainte-Beuve, C. A. (1928), *Port-Royal* (7 vols.), Paris: La Connaissance. Church, R. W. (1931), *A Study in the Philosophy of Malebranche,* London: George Allen and Unwin. Rodis-Lewis, G. (1950), 'Augustinisme et Cartésianisme à Port-Royal', in E. J. Dijksterhuis et al. (eds.), *Descartes et le Cartésianisme hollandais,* Paris: Presses Universitaires de France. Laporte, J. (1951–2), *La Morale de Port-Royal* (2 vols.), Paris. McRae, R. (1965), '"Idea" as a Philosophical Term in the Seventeenth Century', *Journal of the History of Ideas* 26:175–90. Verga, L. (1972), *Il pensiero filosofico e scientifico di Antoine Arnauld,* Milan: Vita e Pensiero. Cook, M. (1974), 'Arnauld's Alleged Representationalism', *Journal of the History of Philosophy* 12:53–64. Radner, D. (1976), 'Representationalism in Arnauld's Act Theory of Perception', *Journal of the History of Philosophy* 14:96–8. Sedgwick, A. (1977), *Jansenism in Seventeenth-Century France,* Charlottesville: University of Virginia Press. Gouhier, H. (1978), *Cartésianisme et Augustinisme au XVIIe siècle,* Paris: J. Vrin. Yolton, J. (1984), *Perceptual Acquaintance from Descartes to Reid,* Minneapolis: University of Minnesota Press. Nadler, S. (1988), 'Arnauld, Descartes, and Transubstantiation: Reconciling Cartesian Metaphysics and Real Presence', *Journal of the History of Ideas* 59:229–46. Nadler, S. (1989), *Arnauld and the Cartesian Philosophy of Ideas,* Princeton: Princeton University Press. Ndiaye,

A. R. (1990), *La Philosophie d'Antoine Arnauld*, Paris: Vrin. Kremer, E. (ed.) (1994), *The Great Arnauld and Some of his Philosophical Correspondents*, Toronto: University of Toronto Press. Nadler, S. (1994), 'Dualism and Occasionalism: Arnauld and the Development of Cartesian Metaphysics', *Revue Internationale de Philosophie* 48:421–40. [Steven Nadler]

ASTELL, MARY b. Newcastle-upon-Tyne 1666(68); d. Chelsea 1731. Social and political philosopher, feminist philosopher, metaphysician, rational theologian. Educated by her uncle, a clergyman, but could read neither French nor Latin. Her circle of friends included Elisabeth Elstob and Lady Mary Wortley Montagu. *A Serious Proposal to the Ladies for the Advancement of Their True and Greatest Interest* (London, 1694) was published anonymously, yet soon gained Astell notoriety. It suggested the founding of a women's college and argued for women's intellectual abilities. The Cambridge Platonist, John Norris, introduced her to the ideas of Malebranche. Their correspondence, including Astell's objections to Occasionalism, is the substance of *Letters concerning the Love of God between the Author of the Proposal to the Ladies and Mr. John Norris* (London, 1695). Her treatment of divine love in *Letters* was praised by Leibniz. *A Serious Proposal to the Ladies Part II Wherein a Method Is Offer'd for the Improvement of Their Minds* (London, 1697) drew on Cartesian method and *La logique ou l'art de penser* of Port Royal to show women how to improve their minds on their own. *Some Reflections upon Marriage* (London, 1700) treated women's subordinate position within marriage. *The Christian Religion as Profess'd by a Daughter of the Church of England* (London, 1705) was a response to Locke's *Reasonableness of Christianity*, and his essays on Norris and Malebranche, and to Damaris Masham's attack on Norris's Platonism in her *Discourse concerning the Love of God*. Other works include *Moderation Truly Stated* (London, 1704); *A Fair Way with the Dissenters and Their Patrons* (London, 1704); *An Impartial Enquiry into the Causes of Rebellion and Civil War in This Kingdom* (London, 1704); *Bar'lemy Fair or an Enquiry after Wit* (n.p., 1709); Preface to *The Letters of the Right Hon. Lady M--y W--y M----e* [Lady Mary Wortley Montagu] . . . (n.p., 1763).

Secondary Sources: Ballard, G. (1752), *Memoirs of several Ladies of Great Britain . . .* , Oxford: W. Jackson; repr. ed. R. Perry, Detroit: Wayne State University Press, 1985. Hays, M. (1803), *Female Biography; or Memoirs of illustrious and celebrated women, of all Ages and Countries* (6 vols.), London: R. Phillips. Smith, F. (1916), *Mary Astell*, New York: Columbia University Press. Stenton, D. (1957), *The English Woman in History*, New York: Macmillan. Smith, H. (1982), *Reason's Disciples: Seventeenth-Century English Feminists*, Urbana: University of Illinois Press. Ferguson, M. (ed.) (1985), *First Feminists: British Women Writers 1578–1799*, Bloomington: Indiana University Press. Perry, R. (1987), *The Celebrated Mary Astell: An Early English Feminist*, Chicago: University of Chicago Press. Squadrito, K. (1991), 'Mary Astell', in M. W. Waithe (ed.), *Modern Women Philosophers, 1600–1900*, Dordrecht: Kluwer. Atherton, M. (1992), 'Cartesian Reason and Gendered Reason', in L. Antony and C. Witt (eds.), *A Mind of One's Own: Feminist Essays on Reason and Objectivity*, Westview Press. [Eileen O'Neill]

BACON, FRANCIS (Verulam, Verulamus) b. London, 1561; d. London 1626. English lawyer, parliamentarian, essayist. Educated at Trinity College, Cambridge 1573–5, enrolled at Gray's Inn and spent a few years in Paris. Became a barrister, 1582. Entered parliament in 1584 and held various political and judicial offices in government: solicitor general, 1607; attorney general, 1612; lord keeper, 1617; and lord chancellor, 1618. He was knighted 1603, made Lord Verulam 1618, and Viscount St. Albans 1621. His political career ended in 1621, when he confessed to bribery. From his earliest days at Cambridge he was preoccupied with a philosophy and method of investigation that would entail a decisive break with the past. He first turned to Platonic philosophy to counter Peripatetic doctrines and practices, then thought to supplant all past and present theories by a thoroughly naturalistic and materialistic philosophy. The axioms of his new philosophy would be statements of natural causes and laws derived from scientific observation and experiment. His views were enormously influential on later seventeenth-century thought, particularly in English natural philosophy and its organisation in institutions like the Royal Society. Wrote *Essays* (London, 1597–1625); *The Advancement of Learning* (London, 1605; expanded Latin version, *De dignitate et augmentis scientarum*, London, 1623); *De sapientia veterum* (London, 1609); *Instauratio magna* and *Novum organum* (London, 1620); *History of Henry the Seventh* (London, 1622); *New Atlantis* (1624, but published London, 1627); and *Sylva sylvarum* (London, 1626). The standard edition of his writings (1857–74), *The Works*, ed. J. Spedding, R. L. Ellis, D. D. Heath (14 vols.). London: Longmans, repr. Stuttgart: Frommann, 1989; vols. 8–14 have the title page: *The Letters and the Life of Francis Bacon.*

Secondary Sources: Anderson, F. H. (1948), *The Philosophy of Francis Bacon,* Chicago: University of Chicago Press. Gibson, R. W. (1950), *Francis Bacon: A Bibliography of His Works and of Baconiana,* Oxford: Scrivener's Press. Farrington, B. (1964), *The Philosophy of Francis Bacon,* Liverpool: Liverpool University Press. Rossi, P. (1968), *Francis Bacon: From Magic to Science,* London: Routledge. Vickers, B. (1968), *Francis Bacon and Renaissance Prose,* Cambridge: Cambridge University Press. Jardine, L. (1974), *Francis Bacon: Discovery and the Art of Discourse,* Cambridge: Cambridge University Press. Stephens, J. (1975), *Francis Bacon and the Style of Science,* Chicago: University of Chicago Press. Vickers, B. (1978), *Francis Bacon,* Harlow, Essex: Longman Group. Bacon, Francis (1985), *Sir Francis Bacon: The Essays or Counsels, Civill and Morall,* ed. M. Kirnan, Oxford: Oxford University Press. Urbach, P. (1987), *Francis Bacon's Philosophy of Science,* La Salle, Ill.: Open Court. Perez-Ramos, A. (1988), *Francis Bacon's Idea of Science and the Maker's Knowledge Tradition,* Oxford: Oxford University Press. Martin, J. (1992), *Francis Bacon, the State, and the Reform of Natural Philosophy,* Cambridge: Cambridge University Press. [Roger Ariew]

BARROW, ISAAC b. London, 1630; d. London, 1677. Mathematician and divine. Most of Barrow's adult life was spent at Cambridge. A student of Trinity College, he graduated B.A. in 1648, was elected fellow the following year, and graduated M.A. in 1652. Renowned for his royalist sympathies, Barrow was denied the appointment of Regius Professor of Greek and, as a result, in 1655 embarked on a long tour of the Continent. Prior to his departure, Barrow sent to press his compact edition of Euclid's *Elements* (in Latin, Cambridge, 1657; English version, London, 1660), which became a popular textbook. Following the Restoration, Barrow finally received the Greek professorship, to which he added in 1662 the Gresham Professorship of Geometry. He resigned both positions a year later, following his election as first Lucasian Professor of Mathematics at Cambridge. His three major scientific publications correspond to his public lectures, as Barrow declined revising them. *Lectiones mathematicae XXIII* were delivered between 1664–6 and first published in London, 1683 (English trans. London, 1734); *Lectiones geometricae* were delivered during 1667–8 and published in London, 1670 (English trans. London, 1735; another version by J. M. Child, Chicago: Open Court, 1916); *Lectiones opticae* were delivered during 1668–9 and published later in London, 1669 (English trans: *Isaac Barrow's Optical Lectures,* trans. H. C. Fay, ed. A. G. Bennett and D. F. Edgar, London: Worshipful Company of Spectacle Makers, 1987). His epitome of Archimedes, Theodosius, and Apollonius, written in 1653, appeared as *Archimedis Opera; Apollonii Pergaei Conicorum libri IIII; Theodosii Sphaerica,* London, 1675. Barrow resigned his professorship in 1669 – arranging for Isaac Newton to succeed him – in order to devote himself to his preferred vocation, theology. He was appointed Royal Chaplain and, in 1673, Master of Trinity College. Barrow became a renowned preacher and apologist for the Church of England. His sermons were collected after his death (they appeared in 1683–7), and his influential *Treatise on the Pope's Supremacy* also appeared posthumously. The standard edition is Barrow (1859), *The Theological Works of Isaac Barrow,* ed. A. Napier, 9 vols. Cambridge: Cambridge University Press. His scientific works collected in *The Mathematical Works of Isaac Barrow,* ed. William Whewell, Cambridge: Cambridge University Press, 1860.

Secondary Sources: Whewell, William (1859), 'Barrow and His Academical Times', in Napier's edition. Osmond, Percy H. (1944), *Isaac Barrow, His Life and Times,* London: Society for the Promotion of Christian Knowledge. Simo, Irène (1964), 'Tillotson's Barrow,' *English Studies* 45:193–211. Simo, Irène (1967–76), *Three Restoration Divines,* Paris: Les Belles Lettres. Strong, E. W. (1970), 'Barrow and Newton,' *Journal for the History of Philosophy* 9:155–72. Spada, Marina Frasca (1984), 'Barrow e Hume sulla geometria: una teoria "classica" e una intuizione relativistica,' *Rivista di filosofia* 75:353–68. Feingold, Mordechai (ed.) (1990), *Before Newton: The Life and Times of Isaac Barrow,* Cambridge: Cambridge University Press. Feingold, Mordechai (1993), 'Newton, Leibniz, and Barrow Too: An Attempt at a Reinterpretation,' *Isis* 84:310–38. [Mordechai Feingold]

B A S S O , S E B A S T I E N (Basson, Bassonus) b. Lorraine; fl. ca. 1560–1621. French physician and natural philosopher. Educated at Pont-à-Mousson (founded 1572). Later visited Rome. Served as tutor to Carolus Tonardus, dominus d'Ison, a French Protestant gentleman. Little is known of Basso's life beyond the details offered in his single known publication: *Philosophiae naturalis adversus Aristotelem, Libri XII* (Geneva, 1621; Amsterdam, 1649). Basso combines Epicurean and Stoic ideas in his critique of Aristotle. The smallest particles of the elements are atoms, but the space between them is filled by a universal fluid, excluding vacua. Although a geocentrist, Basso offers a mechanical account of planetary motion. Frequently cited by later writers, including Descartes.

Secondary Sources: Lasswitz, Kurd (1890), *Geschichte der Atomistik vom Mittelalter bis Newton* (2 vols.). Hamburg and Leipzig: L. Voss, vol. 1, pp. 467–81. Gregory, Tullio (1964), 'Studi sull'atomismo del seicento. I. Sebastiano Basson', *Giornale critico della Filosofia Italiana* 18:38–65. Kubbinga, H. H. (1984), 'Les premières théories moléculaires: Isaac Beeckman (1620) et Sébastien Basson (1621)', *Revue d'Histoire des Sciences* 37:215–33. Nielsen, L. F. (1988), 'A Seventeenth-Century Physician on God and Atoms: Sebastian Basso', in N. Kretzmann (ed.), *Meaning and Inference in Medieval Philosophy,* Dordrecht: Kluwer, pp. 297–369. [Peter Barker]

B A Y L E , P I E R R E b. Le Carla (southern France), 1647; d. Rotterdam, 1706. Philosophical sceptic and religious writer. Born in Calvinist family. Educated at home, in Protestant academies, and at Jesuit college in Toulouse. Temporary conversion to Catholicism, 1669–70, followed by return to Calvinist faith and flight to Geneva. Professor of Philosophy at Protestant Académie de Sedan, 1675–81; on its abolition, moved to Rotterdam and became Professor of Philosophy at the Ecole Illustre. Published *Lettre sur la comète* (Rotterdam, 1682), expanded as *Pensées diverses sur la comète* (Rotterdam, 1683). In aftermath of Revocation of the Edict of Nantes (1685), published *Commentaire philosophique sur ces paroles de Jésus-Christ 'Contrains-les d'entrer'* (Amsterdam, 1686), a defence of religious toleration. He is best known for his *Dictionnaire* project. The project was preceded by the *Projet et fragmens d'un Dictionnaire critique* (Rotterdam, 1692). The *Dictionnaire historique et critique* itself was first published in Rotterdam, dated 1697 (it actually appeared in December 1696); it contains a full presentation of his scepticism. It appeared in many later editions, most importantly the second (Rotterdam, 1702) and the fourth (Rotterdam, 1720). The authoritative edition of the *Dictionnaire* is the fifth edition of Amsterdam, Leiden, The Hague, and Utrecht, 1740; English translation, London, 1734–8. (Though the editors represent this as the fifth edition, it is actually the eighth.) His other works were collected in *Bayle* (1727), *Oeuvres diverses,* The Hague [repr. Hildesheim: Olms, 1964–8]. There is a critical edition of the *Pensées diverses,* Bayle (1984), *Pensées diverses sur la comète,* ed. A. Prat and P. Rétat (2 vols.), Paris: Nizet.

Secondary Sources: Devolvé, Jean (1906), *Essai sur Pierre Bayle,* Paris: Alcan. Dibon, Paul (ed.) (1959), *Pierre Bayle, le Philosophe de Rotterdam,* Amsterdam: Elsevier. Labrousse, Elisabeth (1963–4), *Pierre Bayle* (2 vols.), The Hague: Nijhoff. Brush, Craig (1966), *Montaigne and Bayle. Variations on the Theme of Scepticism,* The Hague: Nijhoff. Popkin, Richard (1980), *The High Road to Scepticism,* San Diego: Austin Hill Press. Labrousse, Elisabeth (1983), *Bayle,* Oxford: Oxford University Press. Labrousse, Elisabeth (1987), *Notes sur Bayle,* Paris: Vrin. [Charles Larmore]

BEECKMAN, ISAAC b. Middelburg, 1588; d. Dordrecht, 1637. Natural philosopher, mechanicist, teacher. Apprenticed in his father's trades, making candles and hydraulic devices, he also studied theology at Leiden (1607–10) and Saumur (1612). Obtained M.D. at Caen ('*Theses de febre tertiana intermittente . . .*', 1618). Assistant headmaster under his brother at a series of schools in the Netherlands (1618–27); rector of the Latin school in Dordrecht (1627–37). Strongly influenced by the Reformed Church and by Ramism, via his teacher Rudolph Snel. Committed to a 'picturable' explanation of nature (see van Berkel 1983). Sought to educate craftsmen in science. A moderate Copernican and a corpuscularian, he proposed a principle of inertia and investigated such topics as the aether, falling bodies, and music. Although he never published anything beyond his M.D. thesis, his work was known to Gassendi and Mersenne, to his students Jan de Witt and George Ent, and most especially to Descartes, who collaborated with him. His brother published excerpts of his scientific diaries in *D. Isaaci Beeckmanni medici et rectoris apud Dordracenos mathematico-physicarum meditationum, quaestionum, solutionum centuria* (Utrecht, 1644); the standard, complete edition is Beeckman (1939–53), *Journal tenu par Isaac Beeckman de 1604 à 1634*, The Hague: Nijhoff.

Secondary Sources: Dijksterhuis, E. J. (1924), *Val en Worp*, Groningen: Noordhoff. Hoeven, J. van der (1933), 'Een brief van Justinus van Assche aan Isaac Beeckman', *Bijdragen tot de Geschiedenis der Geneeskunde* 13:17–23. Hooykaas, R. (1951), 'Science and Religion in the 17th Century: Isaac Beeckman (1588–1637)', *Free University Quarterly* 1:169–83. Lieburg, M. J. van (1982), 'Isaac Beeckman and his diary-notes on William Harvey's theory on blood circulation (1633–4)', *Janus* 69:161–83. Berkel, K. van (1983), *Isaac Beeckman (1588–1637) en de Mechanisering van het Wereldbeeld*, Amsterdam: Rodopi. Cohen, H. F. (1984), *Quantifying Music: The Science of Music at the First Stage of the Scientific Revolution, 1580–1650*, Dordrecht: Reidel. Buzon, F. de (1985), 'Science de la nature et théorie musicale chez Isaac Beeckman (1588–1637)', *Revue d'Histoire des Sciences* 38:97–120. Kubbinga, H. H. (1988), 'The First "Molecular" Theory (1620): Isaac Beeckman (1588–1637)', *Journal of Molecular Structure* 181(3/4):205–18. Kubbinga, H. H. (1989), 'Nouveau: Le *Catalogus . . . librorum* d'Isaac Beeckman', *Revue d'Histoire des Sciences* 42:173–5. [Joella Yoder]

BENTLEY, RICHARD b. Oulton, Yorkshire, 1662; d. Cambridge, 1742. Classical scholar and divine. After graduating B.A. from St. John's College, Cambridge, in 1680, Bentley was briefly a schoolmaster before accepting in 1683 the invitation of Edward Stillingfleet, dean of St. Paul's, to serve as tutor to his son. He remained in Stillingfleet's household for six years, considerably improving his classical and theological learning, and then accompanied his pupil to Oxford where he benefitted from study in the Bodleian library. In 1691 a request to comment on John of Malala's *Chronicon,* then at the Oxford press, produced his *Epistola ad Joannem Millium* (Oxford, 1691), a brilliant tour de force of classical learning, which immediately established his European-wide reputation. In the following year he was appointed first Boyle lecturer, and the ensuing publication of the eight sermons under the collective title, *The Folly and Unreasonableness of Atheism* (London, 1692) benefitted from the advice of Isaac Newton. Bentley was made Prebendary of Worcester in 1692 and two years later was appointed Royal librarian. In 1697, he contributed a short treatise to William Wotton's second edition of *Reflections of Ancient and modern Learning* (London, 1697), in which he exposed as forgery the *Letters of Phalaris.* Following a rebuttal by the recent editor of the work, Charles Boyle, and his Christ Church cronies, Bentley published his brilliant *Dissertation on the Letters of Phalaris* (London, 1699). In 1700 he was elected master of Trinity College, Cambridge, which he ruled for over four decades, often facing bitter opposition from the fellows. During that time, however, Bentley published his Horace (Cambridge, 1711), Terence (London, 1726), and Manilius (London, 1739); saw through the press the second edition of Newton's *Principia* (Cambridge, 1713); and published a 'corrected' version of Milton's *Paradise Lost* (London, 1732). The standard edition is *The Works of Richard Bentley,* ed. Alexander Dyce, 3 vols. (London, 1836); *The Correspondence of Richard Bentley,* ed. Christopher Wordsworth, 2 vols. (London, 1842).

Secondary Sources: Monk, James H. (1833), *The Life of Richard Bentley*, 2d ed., 2 vols., London: Rivington. Jebb, R. C. (1882), *Bentley*, London: Macmillan. Bartholomew, Augustus T. (1908), *Richard Bentley, D. D.: A Bibliography of his Works*, Cambridge: Bowes and Bowes. Fox, Adam (1954), *John Mill and Richard Bentley*, Oxford: Blackwell. White, R. J. (1965), *Dr. Bentley: A Study in Academic Scarlet*, London: Eyre and Spottiswoode. Brink, C. O. (1986), *English Classical Scholarship*, New York: Oxford University Press. Levine, Joseph M. (1991), *The Battle of the Books*, Ithaca: Cornell University Press, pp. 47–84. [Mordechai Feingold]

BERKELEY, GEORGE b. Kilkenny, Ireland, 1685; d. Oxford, 1753. Philosopher and divine. Pupil at Kilkenny College (1696–1700). Entered Trinity College, Dublin, 1700 (B.A., 1704; M.A., 1707). In 1707, published *Arithmetica* (Dublin) and *Miscellanea Mathematica* (Dublin); was elected Fellow of Trinity College. Worked out his immaterialist system in his notebooks (the *Commonplace Book* or *Philosophical Commentaries*, written circa 1707–9, not published until 1871). Published *An Essay towards a New Theory of Vision*, in Dublin, 1709; was ordained deacon. Published *A Treatise concerning the Principles of Human Knowledge* in Dublin, 1710 (rev. ed., London, 1734); was ordained an Anglican priest. Appointed Junior Lecturer in Greek, 1712; published *Passive Obedience*. Went to London in 1713; presented at court by Swift; became acquainted with Pope, Gay, Addison, and Steele; wrote articles for Steele's *Guardian*. Published *Three Dialogues between Hylas and Philonous* (London, 1713; revised ed., London, 1734). Travelled in France and Italy as chaplain to the Earl of Peterborough (1713–14). Made second tour of France and Italy (1716–20) as companion and tutor to the son of the Bishop of Clogher. While in France, wrote *De Motu* (London, 1721). Returned to Ireland, 1721, was made Doctor of Divinity and appointed Divinity Lecturer at Trinity College. Executor and legatee of the will of Esther van Homrigh (Swift's 'Vanessa'), 1723. Made Dean of Derry in 1724. Soon thereafter went to London to promote the project of founding a college in Bermuda to train the sons of the colonists and the Indians from the mainland in religion and the useful arts. Received, in 1726, a royal charter for the college and a pledge of £20,000 from Parliament. Married Anne Forster, in 1728, and sailed for America. Spent 1729–31 in Newport, Rhode Island, awaiting the promised funds. While in Newport, wrote *Alciphron: or the Minute Philosopher* (London, 1732), and exerted considerable influence on the philosophical views of Samuel Johnson of Connecticut (later first president of King's College, New York – now Columbia University). Gave up the Bermuda project when it became clear that the monies pledged were not to be paid; returned to England in 1731, remaining there for three years. Published *The Theory of Vision, or Visual Language Vindicated and Explained* (London, 1733) and *The Analyst* (London, 1734). Was made Bishop of Cloyne, in southern Ireland, in 1734. Earnestly sought ways to relieve the poverty and disease he found in his diocese (set out his economic proposals in sets of queries, published as *The Querist*, 1735–7); experimented with tar-water and became persuaded of its medicinal value. Declined nomination for vice-chancellorship of Dublin University (1741). Published the *Siris* (Dublin and London, 1744). Retired in 1752, removing with his family to Oxford, where he is interred in the chapel of Christ Church. The standard edition of his works is Berkeley (1948–57), *The Works of George Berkeley*, Edinburgh, London: T. Nelson.

Secondary Sources: Luce, A. A. (1949), *The Life of George Berkeley, Bishop of Cloyne*, Edinburgh: Nelson. Johnston, G. A. (1923), *The Development of Berkeley's Philosophy*, London: Macmillan. Luce, A. A. (1945), *Berkeley's Immaterialism*, Edinburgh: Nelson. Warnock, G. J. (1953), *Berkeley*, London: Penguin. Gueroult, M. (1956), *Berkeley: quatre études sur la perception et sur Dieu*, Paris: Aubier. Luce, A. A. (1967), *Berkeley and Malebranche*, 2d ed., Oxford: Oxford University Press. Jessop, T. E. (1973), *A Bibliography of George Berkeley*, 2d rev. ed., The Hague: Nijhoff. Tipton, I. C. (1974), *Berkeley: The Philosophy of Immaterialism*, London: Methuen. Pitcher, G. (1977), *Berkeley*, London: Routledge and Kegan Paul. Grayling, A. D. (1986), *Berkeley: The Central Arguments*, La Salle, Ill.: Open Court. Winkler, K. (1989), *Berkeley: An Interpretation*, Oxford: Oxford University Press. Atherton, Margaret (1990), *Berkeley's Revolution in Vision*, Ithaca: Cornell University Press. [Charles McCracken]

BERNIER, FRANÇOIS b. Joué, Anjou, 1620; d. Paris, 1688. Traveller, philosopher, physician. Philosophically most important as a proponent of the views of Gassendi. In 1642 shared Gassendi's philosophy lessons for Chapelle, perhaps with Cyrano de Bergerac and Molière. Took a medical degree at Montpellier in 1652. Defended Gassendi against the astrologist J.-B. Morin, especially in *Anatomia ridiculi muris* (Paris, 1651) and *Favilla ridiculi muris* (Paris, 1653). Left the year after Gassendi's death (1655) for trip to Middle East and ten-year stay on the Indian subcontinent, which led to his *Mémoires du sieur Bernier sur l'empire du grand Mogul* (Paris, 1670–1), his most popular work, with many editions and translations. Hilarious defence of the new philosophy against Aristotelianism in his *Requeste . . . presentée à la Cour souveraine du Parnasse . . .*, published by G. Gueret in *La Guerre des auteurs anciens et modernes* (The Hague, 1671). Most important work was the *Abregé de la philosophie de Gassendi,* consisting of translation, resumé, and interpretation of *Gassendi's Syntagma* (first complete edition, Lyon, 1678, with one-volume proto-editions in 1674 and 1675; second edition, in seven volumes, Lyon, 1684). Departed from Gassendi's views on several important points set out in his *Doutes de M. Bernier sur quelques uns des principaux chapitres de son Abrégé de Gassendi* (Paris, 1682), a version of which he published with the later *Abrégé.* Criticism of Cartesianism in his *Eclaircissement sur le livre de M. de la Ville,* published by Bayle in his *Recueil de quelques pieces curieuses concernant la philosophie de M. Descartes* (Amsterdam, 1684). Contact with Locke and Bayle, among others.

Secondary Sources: Lens, L. de (1872), 'Notice Sommaire sur François Bernier', in M. C. Port, *Dictionnaire historique, géographique, et biographique de l'Anjou,* 21e livraison, Novembre, 1872. Lens, L. de (1873), *Documents inédits ou peu connus sur François Bernier,* Angers. Lennon, T. M. (1993), 'François Bernier', in *Ueberwegs Grundriss der Geschichte der Philosophie,* Basel: Schwabe and Co., vol. 2, pp. 242–52. Murr, S. (ed.) (1992), *Corpus* 20/21:1–295. Lennon, T. M. (1993), *The Battle of the Gods and Giants: The Legacies of Descartes and Gassendi, 1655–1715,* Princeton: Princeton University Press. [Thomas Lennon]

BERNOULLI, JAKOB b. Basel, 1654; d. Basel, 1705; and JOHANN b. Basel, 1667; d. Basel, 1748. Natural philosophers, mathematicians. Jakob studied philosophy and theology at Basel, spent his early years travelling in France and the Netherlands, then settled at the University of Basel, becoming professor of mathematics in 1687. Johann completed a doctoral dissertation in medicine at Basel (*De motu musculorum,* 1694), received his mathematics education privately from his brother, and was professor of mathematics at the University of Groningen (1695–1705) until he succeeded Jakob at Basel. The first students of the Leibnizian calculus, they greatly expanded its power, especially in the realm of differential equations. Founded the field of rational mechanics through their study of curves defined by physical properties, such as the brachistochrone and the sail curve. Intense sibling rivalry pushed them to outdo each other on the same topic, as in the case of the isoperimetric problem which underlies the calculus of variations. Jakob also codified and extended contemporary thought on probability in his *Ars conjectandi* (Basel, 1713). In the early 1690s, Johann taught the new calculus to the Fatio de Duillier brothers in Geneva and to Pierre de Varignon and the Marquis de l'Hospital in France. In addition, their research was continued by succeeding generations of Bernoullis, especially Johann's son Daniel (1700–82). G. Cramer's editions of their works were the standards until recently: Bernoulli, Jakob (1744), *Opera* (2 vols.), Geneva; Bernoulli, Johann (1742), *Opera* (4 vols.), Geneva. The standard edition of their writings will be, when completed, *Die gesammelten Werke der Mathematiker und Physiker der Familie Bernoulli* (1955–    ), edited under the auspices of Der Naturforschenden Gesellschaft in Basel, Basel: Birkhäuser. Currently three volumes of Jakob Bernoulli's writings have appeared in that series, Bernoulli 1969–89.

Secondary Sources: Fleckenstein, J. O. (1949), *Johann und Jakob Bernoulli,* Basel: Birkhäuser. Hofmann, J. E. (1956), *Über Jakob Bernoullis Beiträge zur Infinitesimal mathematik,* Geneva: Institut de Mathématiques de l'Université. Dietz, P. (1959), 'Die Ursprünge der Variationsrechung bei Jakob Bernoulli',

*Verhandlungen der Naturforschenden Gesellschaft in Basel* 70:81–146. Hacking, I. (1975), *The Emergence of Probability*, Cambridge: Cambridge University Press. Heimann, P. M. (1977), 'Geometry and Nature: Leibniz and Johann Bernoulli's Theory of Motion', *Centaurus* 21:1–26. Shea, W. R. (1988), 'The Unfinished Revolution: Johann Bernoulli (1667–1748) and the Debate between the Cartesians and the Newtonians', pp. 70–92 in W. R. Shea (ed.) (1988), *Revolutions in Science: Their Meaning and Relevance*, Canton, Mass.: Science History. Hess, H.-J., and Nagel, F. (eds.) (1989), *Der Ausbau des Calculus durch Leibniz und die Brüder Bernoulli*, Symposion der Leibniz-Gesellschaft und der Bernoulli-Edition der naturforschenden Gesellschaft in Basel, 15. bis 17. Juni 1987 (Studia Leibnitiana, Sonderheft 17), Stuttgart: Franz Steiner. Sylla, E. (1990), 'Political, Moral, and Economic Decisions and the Origins of the Mathematical Theory of Probability: The Case of Jacob Bernoulli's *The Art of Conjecturing*', pp. 19–44 in G. M. Furstenburg (ed.) (1990), *Acting under Uncertainty: Multidisciplinary Conceptions*, Dordrecht: Kluwer. [Joella Yoder]

BOURDIN, PIERRE b. 1595; d. 1653. Jesuit French mathematician. Became professor of Letters at the college of La Flèche right after Descartes left (1618–23), returned to La Flèche in 1633 as a professor of Rhetoric, and taught mathematics there in 1634. Sent to Paris in 1635, to the Collège de Clermont, where he remained until his death. Published several mathematics texts: *Prima geometriae elementa* (Paris, 1639); *Geometria, nova methodo* (Paris, 1640); *L'introduction à la mathématique* (Paris, 1643); *Le cours de mathématique* (3d ed., Paris, 1661; the two other editions were anonymous editions from circa 1631–45); and posthumously, *L'architecture militaire ou l'art de fortifier les places regulières et irregulières* (Paris, 1655) and *Le dessein ou la perspective militaire* (Paris, 1655). Bourdin's mathematics, like most seventeenth-century Jesuit mathematics, can be characterised by its practical disposition. Bourdin's *Cours de mathématique* contains discussions of fortification, terrain, military architecture, and sections on cosmography and the use of the terrestrial globe. In his cosmology, represented by *Sol flamma sive tractatus de sole, ut flamma est, eiusque pabulo sol exurens montes* (Paris, 1646) and *Aphorismi analogici parvi mundi ad magnum, magni ad parvuum* (Paris, 1646), Bourdin follows the then-fashionable system of Tycho Brahe. He is a severe critic of the philosophy, and especially of the sceptical method of Descartes, in his *Objectiones Septimae*, published first in the second edition of Descartes's *Meditationes* (Amsterdam, 1642). [Roger Ariew]

BOYLE, ROBERT, b. Lismore, County of Munster, Ireland, 25 January 1627; d. London, 30 December 1691. Natural philosopher. One of the foremost experimental and mechanical philosophers of his day. Educated at Eton and then privately at Geneva and on the 'Grand Tour'. Conversion experience about 1641 during a thunderstorm. Returned to England in 1644 when Irish rebellion and Civil Wars affected the family fortunes. Under the pragmatic reformist influence of Samuel Hartlib, cultivated an interest in alchemy with a view to medical and agricultural improvements, referred to himself as member of an 'Invisible' College of improvers. Wrote but did not publish various devotional and ethical works: *Seraphick Love*, ca. 1648 published London, 1659; *Aretology*, 1645, published in Boyle (1991); *The Early Essays and Ethics of Robert Boyle*, ed. J. T. Harwood, Carbondale and Edwardsville: Southern Illinois University Press. Visited Irish estates, 1652–3, and taught himself anatomy. About 1656 settled in Oxford and became a leading member of the circle of experimental natural philosophers who were to form the core of the Royal Society of London (from 1660). Published results of experiments with an air-pump, *New Experiments Physico-Mechanicall, Touching the Spring of the Air* (Oxford, 1660; 2d ed., Oxford, 1662) provided evidence for Boyle's Law. Controversies with Hobbes and Francis Linus, 1661–2, over the existence of vacuum and the nature of the 'spring' of the air, and with Spinoza over interpretation of experiments. From 1661 to 1689 a governor of the Society for the Spread of the Gospel in New England. Announced his mechanical and corpuscularian philosophy in *Certain Physiological Essays* (London, 1661). Rejected Aristotelian and Paracelsian concepts of elements in *The Sceptical Chymist* (London, 1661). Other major statements of his philosophy are the *Origine of*

*Formes and Qualities* (Oxford, 1666), and *Experiments, Notes &c. about the Mechanical Origine or Production of Divers Particular Qualities* (London, 1675). A subscriber to the philosophical reforms of Francis Bacon; many of his works are accounts of experimental results intended to provide data for a future 'Great Instauration'. Otherwise the major part of his output is concerned with natural theology, for example: *Some Considerations about the Reconcileableness of Reason and Religion* (London, 1675), *Disquisitions concerning the Final Causes of Natural Things* (London, 1688), *The Christian Virtuoso* (London, 1690). Controversy with Henry More in 1672 over interpretation of experimental results and nature of God's providence. Turned down presidency of the Royal Society in 1680 because of religious scruples against oath-taking. Founded 'Boyle Lectures' on natural theology by the terms of his will. The standard edition of his writings is Boyle (1772), *The Works of the Honourable Robert Boyle*, ed. T. Birch (6 vols.), London. There is a new edition in progress, edited by E. B. Davis and M. Hunter.

Secondary Sources: More, L. T. (1944), *The Life and Works of the Honourable Robert Boyle*, London: Oxford University Press. Fulton, J. (1969), *A Bibliography of the Honourable Robert Boyle*, 2d ed., Oxford: Oxford University Press. Van Leeuwen, H. G. (1963), *The Problem of Certainty in English Thought, 1630–90*, The Hague: Nijhoff, pp. 91–106. Hall, A. R., and M. B. Hall (1964), 'Philosophy and and Natural Philosophy: Boyle and Spinoza', in *Mélanges Alexandre Koyré*, vol. 2, pp. 241–56. McGuire, J. E. (1972), 'Boyle's Conception of Nature', *Journal of the History of Ideas*, 33:523–42. Webster, C. (1975), *The Great Instauration: Science, Medicine and Reform, 1626–60*, London: Duckworth. Oakley, F. (1984), *Omnipotence, Covenant and Order: An Excursion in the History of Ideas from Abelard to Leibniz*, Ithaca: Cornell University Press, pp. 72–92. Alexander, P. (1985), *Ideas, Qualities and Corpuscles: Locke and Boyle on the External World*, Cambridge: Cambridge University Press. Shapin, S., and S. Schaffer (1985), *Leviathan and the Air Pump: Hobbes, Boyle and the Experimental Life*, Princeton: Princeton University Press. Shanahan, T. (1988), 'God and Nature in the Thought of Robert Boyle', *Journal of the History of Philosophy* 26: 547–69. Boyle (1991), *The Early Essays and Ethics of Robert Boyle*, ed. J. T. Harwood, Carbondale and Edwardsville: Southern Illinois University Press. Osler, M. J. (1991), 'The Intellectual Origins of Robert Boyle's Philosophy of Nature: Gassendi's Voluntarism and Boyle's Physico-Theological Project', in R. Ashcraft, R. Kroll, and P. Zagorin (eds.), *Philosophy, Science, and Religion, 1640–1700*, Cambridge: Cambridge University Press. Hunter, Michael (ed.) (1994), *Robert Boyle Reconsidered*, Cambridge: Cambridge University Press. Hunter, Michael (ed.) (1994), *Robert Boyle by Himself and His Friends*, London: Pickering and Chatto. Sargent, Rose-Mary (1995), *The Diffident Naturalist: Robert Boyle and the Philosophy of Experiment*, Chicago: University of Chicago Press. [John Henry]

BRUNO, GIORDANO (Filippo) b. Nola, near Naples, 1548; d. Rome, 1600. Italian Humanist and philosopher. Entered Dominican monastery at Naples, studying theology, 1565; ordained 1572; Doctor of Theology 1575. Suspected of heresy, 1576; fled to Rome and to other Italian cities. Quarreled with Calvinists at Geneva, 1578–9. Visited Toulouse, 1579–81, where he lectured on Aristotle, and Paris, 1581–3; published *Ars memoriae* (Paris, 1582), *De umbris idearum* (Paris, 1582), and *Candelaio* (Paris, 1582). Went to England, 1583–5; published *La cena de le ceneri* (London, 1584), *De la causa, principio e uno* (London, 1584), *De l'infinito universo e mondi* (London, 1584), and *Lo spaccio de la bestia trionfante* (London, 1584), and *De gli eroici furori* (London, 1585). After returning to Paris, 1585, he visited Prague and various German cities and lectured on Aristotle's logic. Published his Latin cosmological poems in 1591. Went to Venice in 1591 and was delivered to the Inquisition. Conveyed to Rome in 1593 and put on trial over many years, ultimately refusing to recant. He was executed in 1600. The standard editions are Bruno (1879–91), *Opere latine*, ed. F. Fiorentino, et al., Naples and Florence: Morano and Bruno (1957), *Dialoghi italiani*, ed. Giovanni Gentile and Giovanni Aquilecchia, Florence: Sansoni.

Secondary Sources: Badaloni, N. (1988), *Giordano Bruno: tra cosmologia ed etica*, Bari: De Donato. Nelson, J. C. (1958), *Renaissance Theory of Love: The Context of Giordano Bruno's 'Eroici furori'*, New York: Columbia University Press. Michel, P.-H. (1973), *The Cosmology of Giordano Bruno*, Ithaca:

Cornell University Press. Yates, F. A. (1964), *Giordano Bruno and the Hermetic Tradition*, Chicago: University of Chicago Press. Yates, F. A. (1966), *The Art of Memory*, Chicago: University of Chicago Press. Védrine, H. (1967), *La conception de la nature chez Giordano Bruno*, Paris: Vrin. Papi, F. (1968), *Antropologia e civiltà nel pensiero di Giordano Bruno*, Florence: La Nuova Italia. Aquilecchia, G. (1971), *Giordano Bruno*, Rome: Istituto della Enciclopedia Italiana. Ingegno, A. (1978), *Cosmologia e filosofia nel pensiero di Giordano Bruno*, Florence: La Nuova Italia. Ciliberto, M. (1979), *Lessico di Giordano Bruno*, 2 vols., Rome: Edizioni dell'Ateneo and Bizzarri. Blum, P. R. (1980), *Aristoteles bei Giordano Bruno*, Munich: Fink. Ingegno, A. (1985), *La sommersa nave della religione: Studio sulla polemica anticristiana del Bruno*, Naples: Bibliopolis. Bernart, L. de (1986), *Immaginatione e scienza in Giordano Bruno*, Pisa: E. T. S. Editrice. Ordine, N. (1987), *La cabala dell'asino: asinità e cognocenza in Giordano Bruno*, Naples: Liguori. Spruit, L. (1988), *Il problema della conoscenza in Giordano Bruno*, Naples: Bibliopolis. Gatti, H. (1989), *The Renaissance Drama of Knowledge: Giordano Bruno in England*, London: Routledge. [Roger Ariew]

BURGERSDIJCK, FRANCO b. Lier, near Delft, 1590; d. Leiden, 1635. Dutch theologian and philosopher. Studied classics, rhetoric, and dialectic at Amersfort and philosophy at Delft, 1604–10. Matriculated at Leiden and studied theology, 1610–14; travelled in France and Germany, 1614. Studied theology and taught philosophy at Saumur, 1616–19. Matriculated again at Leiden, 1619; became professor of philosophy, 1620–35; taught logic and ethics from 1620, and physics from 1628; rector of the university, 1629, 1630, 1634. His textbooks on the parts of philosophy were widely used and reprinted many times: *Idea philosophiae naturalis* (Leiden, 1622); *Idea philosophiae moralis* (Leiden, 1623); *Institutionum logicarum, libri duo* (Leiden, 1626); *Institutionum logicarum synopsis sive rudimenta logica* (Leiden, 1632); *Institutionum metaphysicarum, libri duo* (Leiden, 1640); *Idea oeconomicae et politicae doctrinae* (Leiden, 1644).

Secondary Sources: Dibon, Paul (1954), *La philosophie néerlandaise au siècle d'or*, Paris: Elsevier, vol. 1. Bos, E. P., and H. A. Krop (eds.) (1993), *Franco Burgersdijk (1590–1635): Neo-Aristotelianism in Leiden*, Amsterdam: Rodopi. [Roger Ariew]

BURNET, THOMAS b. 1635 in Crofts, Yorkshire; d. 1715. Natural philosopher and divine. Educated at Cambridge (M.A. 1658), Burnet was fellow of Christ's College from 1657 to 1678, and served as proctor in 1667. Travelled on the Continent as guardian to young aristocrats. In 1681 he published the most thorough attempt to date to reconcile the Bible with the new science under the title *Telluris Theoria Sacra* (London, 1681), which benefitted from Newton's comments. A revised English edition appeared three years later (London, 1684). The second part was published in London, 1689, and the whole was translated that year as *The Theory of the Earth* (London, 1689). The book elicited a wave of criticism and Burnet sought to respond to these with his *Archaeologiae Philosophicae* (London, 1692), a further attempt to reconcile his cosmogony with the book of Genesis. It was widely believed that these works cost Burnet the archbishopric of Canterbury for he never rose higher than the mastership of the Charterhose, to which he was appointed in 1685. Burnet's critique of Locke, the *Remarks upon an Essay concerning Human Understanding*, appeared in London, 1697, and it was followed by two additional installments (London, 1697 and 1699). Two other works, *De fide et officiis Christianorum* and *De statu mortuorum at resurgentium*, were published posthumously. There is no standard edition of his writings.

Secondary Sources: Nicolson, Marjorie H. (1959), *Mountain Gloom and Mountain Glory*, Ithaca: Cornell University Press, pp. 184–270. Jacob, Margret C., and W. A. Lockwood (1972), 'Political Millenarianism and Burnet's *Sacred Theory*', *Science Studies* 2:265–79. Grave, S. A. (1981), *Locke and Burnet*, Perth: Philosophical Society of Western Australia. Mirella Pasini (1981), *Thomas Burnet: una storia del mondo tra ragione, mito e rivelazione*, Florence: La Nuova Italia. Gould, Stephen J. (1987), *Time's Arrow Time's Cycle*, Cambridge, Mass.: Harvard University Press. [Mordechai Feingold]

BURTHOGGE, RICHARD b. Plymouth ca. 1638; d. ca. 1703. Physician, metaphysician. Attended university at Oxford from 1654 and graduated in 1658 (B.A.); studied medicine at Leiden from 1661–2, where he took his M.D. in 1662; in Leiden he was probably influenced by Geulincx. Returned to England to practice as physician in Devonshire. Champion of religious toleration. His philosophy is sometimes said to contain views anticipating those of Kant. Corresponded with Locke from 1694. Published *TAΓAΘON, or Divine Goodness Explicated and Vindicated from the Exceptions of the Atheist* (London, 1670? or 1672?); *Causa Dei, or an Apology for God* (London, 1675); *Organum Vetus et Novum; or a Discourse of Reason and Truth* (London, 1678); *Prudential Reasons for Repealing the Penal Laws against All Recusants, and for a General Toleration* (London, 1687); *The Nature of Church-Government, Freely Discussed and Set Out* (London? 1690); *An Essay upon Reason, and the Nature of Spirits* (London, 1694; repr. New York: Garland, 1976), the last dedicated to Locke. *Of the Soul of the World, and of Particular Souls. In a Letter to Mr. Lock* (London, 1699); *Christianity a Revealed Mystery* (London, 1702). Modern edition of his philosophical works: Burthogge 1921; contains reprints of *Organum Vetus et Novum, Of the Soul of the World,* and selections from *An Essay upon Reason.* Letters to Locke published in Locke 1976– , vol. 5, pp. 51, 78; vol. 6, pp. 684–6; vol. 7, pp. 709–11; 777–80.

Secondary Sources: Lyon, G. (1888), *L'Idéalisme en Angleterre au XVIIe siècle,* Paris: Alcan, pp. 72–96. Cassirer, E. (1906), *Das Erkenntnisproblem in der Philosophie und Wissenschaft der neueren Zeit,* Berlin: B. Cassirer, vol. 1, pp. 543–53. Lovejoy, A. O. (1908), 'Kant and the English Platonists', in *Essays Philosophical and Psychological in Honor of William James,* New York: Longmans, Green, pp. 265–302. Landes, M. W. (1921), 'Introduction' to Burthogge 1921. Grünbaum, J. (1939), 'Die Philosophie Richard Burthogges', Bern, Ph.D. diss. Yolton, J. W. (1959), *John Locke and the Way of Ideas,* Oxford: Oxford University Press, pp. 20–2; 46–8. Thiel, U. (1983), *Lockes Theorie der personalen Identitaet,* Bonn: Bouvier, pp. 76–9, 110, and 173; Lennon, T. (1993), *The Battle of the Gods and Giants,* Princeton: Princeton University Press, pp. 187–90. [Udo Thiel]

CAMPANELLA, TOMMASO, O. P. b. Calabria, 1568; d. Paris, 1639. Italian theologian, philosopher, and poet. Entered the Dominican order, 1582. Published *Philosophia sensibus demonstrata* (Naples, 1591). Censured for holding the views of Bernardino Telesio. In 1594, after visiting Rome and Florence, he met Galileo at Padua. Tortured by the Inquisition. Imprisoned at Rome and forced to retract. Arrested in 1599 by the Spanish authorities in southern Italy. Wrote *Città del Sole* (circa 1602). Imprisoned at Naples and condemned to life imprisonment in 1603. He wrote a number of works in prison, including: *De sensu rerum et magia* (Frankfurt, 1620) and *Apologia pro Galileo* (Frankfurt, 1622). Freed in 1626, but re-imprisoned; eventually released by Urban VIII. Fled to Paris 1634, obtaining the patronage of Cardinal Richelieu, and publishing many of his earlier works, including: *Medicinalium juxta propria principia libri septem* (Lyon, 1635), *Disputationum in Quatuor Partes Suae Philosophiae Reales Libri Quatuor* (Paris, 1637), *Universalis Philosphiae, seu Metaphysicarum Rerum Iuxta Propria Dogmata* (Paris, 1638), *Philosophia Rationalis Partes Quinque* (Paris, 1638), and *Atheismus triumphatus* (Paris, 1647). The latest editions of his works are Campanella (1951), *Opusculi inediti,* Florence: Olschki; Campanella (1954), *Opera,* Milan: Mondadori; and Campanella (1975), *Opera Latini, Francofurti impressa annis 1617–30,* Turin: Bottega d'Erasmo.

Secondary Sources: Firpo, L. (1940), *Bibliographia degli scritti di Tommaso Campanella,* Turin: Unione Tipografico-Editrice Torinese. Firpo, L. (1947), *Ricerche campanelliane,* Florence: Sansoni. Di Napoli, G. (1947), *Tommaso Campanella, filosofo della restaurazione cattolica,* Padua: CEDAM. Walker, D. P. (1958), *Spiritual and Demonic Magic from Ficino to Campanella,* London: Warburg Institute. Corsano, A. (1961), *Tommaso Campanella,* Bari: Laterza. Badaloni, N. (1965), *Tommaso Campanella,* Milan: Feltrinelli. Femiano, S. (1968), *La metafisica di Tommaso Campanella,* Milan: Marzorati. Bonansea, B. (1969), *Tommaso Campanella: Renaissance Pioneer of Modern Thought,* Washington, D.C.: Catholic University of America Press. Amerio, R. (1972), *Il sistema teologico di Tommaso Campanella,* Milan and Naples:

Ricciardi. Bock, G. (1974), *Tommaso Campanella,* Tübingen: Niemeyer. Cassaro, A. (1983), *L'Atheismus triumphatus di Tommaso Campanella,* Naples: D'Auria. Negri, L. (1990), *Fede e ragione in Tommaso Campanella,* Milan: Massimo. Ernst, G. (1991), *Religione, ragione e natura: ricerche su Tommaso Campanella e il tardo Rinacimento,* Milan: Angelli. [Roger Ariew]

CASAUBON, MERIC b. 1599, Geneva; d. 1671, Canterbury. Scholar and divine. The son of the great humanist scholar Isaac Casaubon, Meric was educated at Christ Church, Oxford, and received his M.A. in 1621. His first two publications consisted of a defence of his father against his Catholic critics, and these curried favour with both James I and his bishops. In 1628, Meric was given a prebend at Canterbury, and he received several other livings during the 1630s. His publications during this period included an edition of Optatus (London, 1631) and a translation the *Meditations* of Marcus Aurelius (London, 1634). Following the Puritans' coming to power Casaubon forfeited all his positions, and in 1647 he settled in Sussex, where he remained until the Restoration, dedicating himself to literary work. His *Quatuor linguis commentationis pars prior* appeared in London, 1650, followed by editions of Hierocles (London, 1655) and Epictetus (London, 1659). He covered different ground with the publication in *A Treatise concerning Enthusiasme* (London, 1655, 2d ed., London, 1656), a sober analysis of the varieties of religious and philosophical zeal. Four years later, he also published John Dee's conversations with angels, *A True & Faithful Relation of What passed for many Yeers between Dr. John Dee . . . and Some Spirits* (London, 1659). With the Restoration of Charles II, Casaubon recovered his several livings and returned to Canterbury. It was during the 1660s that his defence of humanist learning and religion against the new philosophies appeared: *Of Credulity and Incredulity* was published in two parts between 1668 and 1670, *Of Credulity and Incredulity in Things Natural, Civil, and Divine* (London, 1668), and *Of Credulity and Incredulity in Things Divine & Spiritual* (London, 1670); the *Letter . . . to Peter du Moulin concerning Natural Experimental Philosophie* appeared in Cambridge, 1669, while his treatise 'On Learning' (written in 1667) remained in manuscript until it was published in part in 1980 in Spiller 1980.

Secondary Sources: Spiller, Michael R. G. (1980), *'Concerning Natural Experimental Philsophie': Meric Casaubon and the Royal Society,* The Hague: Nijhoff. Michael Hunter (1982), 'Ancients, Moderns, Philologists and Scientists,' *Annals of Science* 39:187–92. [Mordechai Feingold]

CATERUS, JOHANNES (de Kater, Johan) b. Haarlem (?); d. Alkmaar, 1656. Theologian. Catholic priest in the Netherlands. Named canon in Haarlem and Archpriest of Alkmaar, 1632. Received manuscript of *Meditationes de prima philosophia* from Descartes's Dutch friends, the priests Bannius and Bloemaert; composed *Primae Objectiones* (1640), in which he offers Thomistic critique of Descartes's work. By 1650, ceased to perform ecclesiastical functions, but retained posts.

Secondary Sources: Monchamp, G. (1886), *Histoire du Cartésianisme en Belgique,* Brussels: Hayez. Descartes (1936–63), *Descartes: Correspondance,* ed. Adam, C., and G. Milhaud (8 vols.), Paris: Alcan and Presses Universitaires de France (see vol. 4). Mazzarella, P. (1952), 'Considerazioni intorno alla polemica Caterus-Cartesio', *Sophia* 20:310–21. Gilson, E. (1967), *Etudes sur le rôle de la pensée médiévale dans la formation du système cartésien,* Paris: Vrin. [Steven Nadler]

CAVALIERI, BONAVENTURA b. Milan, c. 1598; d. Bologna, 1647. Mathematician, theologian. Educated by the Jesuati order, which he entered in 1615 and for which he briefly taught theology. His mathematics teacher, Benetto Castelli, introduced him to Galileo, to whom he then addressed over 100 letters concerning his mathematical ideas. From 1629 until his death, he was both professor of mathematics at the University of Bologna and prior of the local Jesuati monastery. Introduced and continually refined a method for solving geometrical problems using indivisibles (*Geometria indivisibilibus continuorum nova quadam ratione promota,* Bologna, 1635; *Exercitationes geometricae sex,* Bologna, 1647).

Because of the obscurities and internal inconsistencies in his books, his ideas have been conflated with still another variant of the method made by his follower, Evangelista Torricelli (see Andersen 1985). Also studied logarithms, burning glasses, and many aspects of the theory of conics. Wrote on astrology under the pseudonym Silvio Filomantio (*Trattato della ruota planetaria perpetua e dell'uso di quella*, Bologna, 1646). Modern editions of his writings are Cavalieri, B. (1985), '*Opere inedite*. A cura di Sandra Giuntini, Enrico Giusti, Elisabetta Ulivi', *Bollettino di Storia delle Scienze Matematiche* 5(1/2):1–352; and Cavalieri, B. (1987), *Carteggio*, ed. Giovanna Baroncelli (Archivio della corrispondenza degli scienziati italiani, 3), Florence: Olschki.

Secondary Sources: Piola, G. (1844), *Elogio di Bonaventura Cavalieri*, Milan. Masotti, A. (1948), 'Commemorazione di Bonaventura Cavalieri', *Rendiconti dell'Istituto Lombardo di scienze e lettere, parte generale e atti ufficial* 81:43–6. Cellini, G. (1966), 'Gli indivisibli nel pensiero matematico e filosofico di Bonaventura Cavalieri', *Periodico di matematiche,* ser. 4, 44:1–21. Cellini, G. (1966), 'Le dimostrazioni di Cavalieri del suo principio', *Periodico di matematiche,* ser. 4, 44: 85–105. Arrighi, G. (1973), 'La *Geometria indivisibilibus continuorum* di Bonaventura Cavalieri nella ritrovata stesura del 1627', *Physis* 15:133–47. Ariotti, P. E. (1975), 'Bonaventura Cavalieri, Marin Mersenne, and the relecting telescope', *Isis* 66:303–21. Giusti, E. (1980), *Bonaventura Cavalieri and the Theory of Indivisibles,* Bologna: Cremonese. Andersen, K. (1985), 'Cavalieri's Method of Indivisibles', *Archive for History of Exact Sciences* 31:291–367. Cioffarelli, G. (1987), 'Il *Trattato della sfera* di Bonaventura Cavalieri nel edizioni di Urbano Daviso', *Boll. Stor. Sci. Mat.* 7:3–59. Ulivi, E. (1987), 'Le fonti di Bonaventura Cavalieri: La costruzione delle coniche fino allo *Specchio ustorio* (1632)', *Boll. Stor. Sci. Mat.* 7:117–79. Festa, E. (1990), 'La querelle de l'atomisme: Galilée, Cavalieri et les jésuites', *Recherche* 21:1038–47. De Gandt, F. (1991), 'Cavalieri's Indivisible and Euclid's Canons', in *Revolution and Continuity: Essays in the History and Philosophy of Early Modern Science,* ed. P. Barker and R. Ariew, Washington, D.C.: Catholic University Press of America, pp. 157–82. [Joella Yoder]

CAVENDISH, MARGARET LUCAS, Duchess of Newcastle b. St. John's, Essex, 1623–4; d. London, 1673–4. Metaphysician, natural philosopher, gender theorist, literary figure. Tutored at home in music, reading, and writing. From 1643 to 1645, maid of honour to Queen Henrietta-Maria. Through her marriage to William Cavendish, became a member of the 'Newcastle Circle' of philosophers influenced by materialism, which included Hobbes, Digby, Mersenne, Gassendi. While in exile in Paris, Rotterdam, and Antwerp, during the 1640s and 1650s, met such figures as Descartes and Roberval. Became the first woman to attend a session of the Royal Society of London. Corresponded with Glanvill about witchcraft and with Christiaan Huygens about 'Rupert's exploding drops'. Her early writings on metaphysics and natural philosophy include *Philosophical and Physical Opinions* (London, 1655) and *Natures Pictures Drawn by Fancies Pencil to the Life* (London, 1656). Responded to Descartes, Hobbes, Van Helmont, and More in *Philosophical Letters: Or, Modest Reflections upon some Opinions in Natural Philosophy* (London, 1664). Criticised experimental and empiricist philosophy in *Observations upon Experimental Philosophy* (London, 1666), to which she appended possibly the first piece of science fiction in English, *The Description of a new World, called The Blazing World*. Her most mature views appear in *Grounds of Natural Philosophy* (London, 1668). *Orations of Divers Sorts* (London, 1662) contains some of her views on woman's nature and gendered virtues. Her autobiography is contained in her *The Life of the Thrice Noble, High and Puissant Prince William Cavendishe, Duke, Marquess and Earl of Newcastle* (London, 1667). There is no standard edition of her works.

Secondary Sources: Ballard, G. (1752), *Memoirs of Several Ladies of Great Britain . . . ,* Oxford: W. Jackson. Meyer, G. D. (1955), *The Scientific Lady in England 1650–1760,* Berkeley: University of California Press. Grant, D. (1957), *Margaret the First: A Biography of Margaret Cavendish, Duchess of Newcastle, 1623–73,* London: Rupert Hart-Davis. Kargon, R. H. (1966), *Atomism in England from Hariot to Newton*, Oxford: Clarendon Press. Merchant, C. (1980), *The Death of Nature*, San Francisco: Harper and Row. Smith, H. (1982), *Reason's Disciples: Seventeenth-Century English Feminists*, Urbana: University of Illinois Press. Sarasohn, L. T. (1984), 'A Science Turned Upside Down: Feminism and the Natural Philosophy of Margaret Cavendish', *Huntington Library Quarterly*, 47:4. Ferguson, M. (ed.) (1985), *First Feminists: British Women Writers 1578–1799*, Bloomington: Indiana University Press. Alic, M. (1986), *Hypatia's Heritage: A History of Women in Science from Antiquity through the Nineteenth Century*, Boston: Beacon Press. Schiebinger, L. (1989), *The Mind Has No Sex? Women in the Origins of Modern Science*, Cambridge, Mass.: Harvard University Press. Schiebinger, L. (1991), 'Margaret Cavendish, Duchess of Newcastle', in M. E. Waithe (ed.), *Modern Women Philosophers, 1600–1900*, Dordrecht: Kluwer. [Eileen O'Neill]

CHARLETON, WALTER b. Shepton Mallet, Somerset, 13 February 1620; d. London, 6 May 1707. Natural philosopher and physician. Entered Magdalen Hall, Oxford in 1635, graduated M.D. in January 1643 and became physician-in-ordinary to Charles I. In 1650 he published *Spiritus gorgonicus*, a medical treatise about 'the stone', and *A Ternary of Paradoxes*, a translation of three short medical tracts by J. B. Van Helmont. In self-imposed exile in France during the Civil War period, he became a friend of Thomas Hobbes, and rapidly absorbed the details of Cartesian and Gassendist natural philosophy. Published one of the earliest exercises in the English tradition of natural theology in London, 1652: *The Darknes of Atheism Dispelled by the Light of Nature*. His *Physiologia-Epicuro-Gassendo-Charltoniana* (London, 1654), a major means of disseminating Gassendi's philosophy in England, was a translation and paraphrase of the physical part of Gassendi's (Lyon, 1649) *Animadversiones*, with additions drawn from the then unpublished *Syntagma philosophicum* (Lyon, 1658). Published *Epicurus's Morals, a defence*, in London, 1656, and *The Immortality of the Soul* in London, 1657. Many of his other works concentrate on medical matters, including *Natural History of Nutrition, Life and Voluntary Motion* (London, 1659), *Exercitationes pathologicae* (London, 1661), *A Natural History of the Passions* (London, 1674), *Enquiries into Human Nature* (London, 1680). Other non-medical works include the misogynistic fable of carnal love, *The Ephesian Matron* (London, 1659), the eulogistic *Imperfect Pourtraicture of His Sacred Majesty Charles the II* (London, 1661), and his study of Stonehenge, *Chorea gigantum* (London, 1663). An active original member of the Royal Society of London, he later absented himself and became more prominent in the Royal College of Physicians, of which he was president, 1689–91. After this, his career unaccountably went into major decline; there are reports of his final years being spent in financial and emotional distress.

Secondary Sources: Kargon, R. H. (1964), 'Walter Charleton, Robert Boyle, and the acceptance of Epicurean Atomism in England', *Isis* 55:184–92. Kargon, R. H. (1966), *Atomism in England from Harriot to Newton*, Oxford: Oxford University Press, pp. 77–92. Gelbart, N. R. (1971), 'The Intellectual Development of Walter Charleton', *Ambix* 18:149–68. Sharp, L. (1973), 'Walter Charleton's Early Life, 1620–59, and Relationship to Natural Philosophy in Mid-Seventeenth-Century England', *Annals of Science*, 30:311–43. Osler, M. J. (1979), 'Charleton and Descartes on Nature and God', *Journal of the History of Ideas*, 44:549–60. Fleitmann, S. (1986), *Walter Charleton (1620–1707), Virtuoso: Leben und Werk*, Frankfurt am Main, Bern, New York: Lang. [John Henry]

CHARRON, PIERRE b. Paris, 1541; d. Paris, 1603. Pyrrhonist philosopher. Studied classics at the Sorbonne and jurisprudence at Orléans/Bourges; doctor of law, 1571. Studied theology and ordained, 1576. In 1589, began close association with Montaigne, who made him his adopted son. Wrote *Les Trois Véritez contre les athées, idolâtres, juifs, mahométans, hérétiques et schismatiques* (Paris, 1593), and his most important work, *De la sagesse* (Bordeaux, 1601, 2d edition, 1604). *Petit traicté de sagesse* was published posthumously and included replies to critics. There is a recent edition of *De la sagesse* (Paris: Fayard, 1986).

Secondary Sources: Sabrié, Jean-Baptiste (1913; reprint 1970), *De l'Humanisme au rationalisme: Pierre Charron, l'homme, l'oeuvre, l'influence,* Geneva: Slatkine Reprints. Rice, Eugene (1958), *The Renaissance Idea of Wisdom,* Cambridge: Harvard University Press, pp. 178–207. Soman, Alfred (1970), 'Pierre Charron: A Revaluation', *Bibliothèque d'humanisme et Renaissance* 32: 57–79. Popkin, Richard H. (1979), *The History of Scepticism from Erasmus to Spinoza,* Berkeley: University of California Press, pp. 55–62. Gregory, Tullio (1986), *Etica e religione nella critica libertina,* Naples: Guida. [Charles Larmore]

CHILLINGWORTH, WILLIAM b. Oxford, 1602; d. Chichester, 1644. Theologian and religious controversialist. Educated at Trinity College Oxford: B.A. 1620, M.A. 1623; Fellow of Trinity 1628. In 1628 renounced his allegiance to the Church of England, resigned his fellowship, and became a Roman Catholic. Entered a Catholic seminary, probably in Douai, possibly in St. Omer, but found the life uncongenial and returned to England. No clear religious allegiance in early 1630s but returned to Church of England by 1635. From 1634 lived in Viscount Falkland's house at Great Tew in Oxfordshire. In Oxford and London, 1638, published chief work, *The Religion of Protestants a Safe Way to Salvation,* directed against the Jesuit Edward Knott; in the same year appointed chancellor of Salisbury Cathedral. Sided with royalist party during the Civil War. There is no modern edition of his works: a widely cited older edition is Chillingworth (1727), *The Works of William Chillingworth,* London. Orr 1967 (see below) contains a list of unpublished writings.

Secondary Sources: Des Maizeaux, P. (1725), *An Historical and Critical Account of the Life of William Chillingworth,* London. Orr, R. R. (1967), *Reason and Authority: the Thought of William Chillingworth,* Oxford: Oxford University Press. [John Milton]

CHRISTINA, Queen of Sweden b. Sweden, 1626; d. Rome, 1689. Maxim writing moralist influenced by Scepticism, Stoicism, Hermeticism, and Quietism. Upon the death of her father, Gustavus Adolphus, inherited the throne of Sweden and held an absolutist theory of monarchy. Began her education at the age of seven in accordance with the system of Comenius. Knew seven languages including Latin and Greek, read medical treatises, studied astronomy with Lubenitz, and conducted alchemical experiments. Studied the ancients and such modern philosophers as Lipsius, Descartes, Gassendi, and La Rochefoucauld. Filled her court with scholars like Isaac Vossius, Nicholas Heinsius, Hermann Conring, Pierre Daniel Huet, and Johannes Freinshemius; attracted such visitors as Grotius and Descartes. Corresponded and met with Arnauld, Gassendi, Pascal, Miguel Molinos, Claude Saumaise, Isaac La Peyrère, Anna Maria van Schurman, Anne Dacier, and Madeleine de Scudéry. In 1654 decided to abdicate the throne, and at Innsbruck, in 1655, publicly converted to Catholicism. In France, in 1656, held an academy which discussed the nature of love; her Italian academies focused on scepticism, cosmology, and natural philosophy. In 1657, caused debates regarding international law by using her 'sovereign right' to order the death of her servant, Monaldescho, while in a foreign country. Made several unsuccessful attempts to gain political power in Sweden (1660; 1668), Poland (1667–8), and Turkey (1670–2) in the hopes of effecting international peace and religious tolerance. In the 1670s and 1680s, composed the numerous versions of her maxims. In her final years, was a patroness of artists and musicians, e.g., Corelli and Scarlatti, and held academies in natural philosophy in Rome. There is no standard edition of her writings. Two collections of maxims, the earlier *Ouvrage de loisir* (c. 1670–80) and the later *Les Sentiments héroïques* (c. 1670–80), exist in a number of versions in manuscript. Both appear, together with *Réfléxions diverses sur la Vie et sur les Actions du Grand Alexandre, Les Vertues et vices de Caesar,* a sampling of her correspondence, and her unfinished autobiography in J. Arckenholtz (1751–60), *Mémoires concernant Christine, reine de Suède pour servir d'éclaircissement à l'histoire de son regne et principalment de sa vie privée, et aux evenements de son tems civile et literaire* (4 vols.), Leipzig and Amsterdam. A manuscript secretarial draft of the maxims at the Royal Library, Stockholm, is published in Christina (1959), *Drottning Kristina Maximer – Les Sentiments Heroiques,* ed. Sven Stolpe (Acta Academiae Catholicae Suecanae), Stockholm: Bonniers; this is generally considered the most authoritative version, though Susanna Akerman has recently discovered a later edition (c. 1683) in the Herzog August Bibliotek, Wolfenbüttel, that may supersede all others. Her notes on the maxims of La Rochefoucauld have recently been published in La Rochefoucauld (1967), *La Rochefoucauld – Maximes . . .* , ed. J. Truchet, Paris: Garnier. Her letter to Terlon of 2 February 1686, on tolerance of French Huguenots was published in *Nouvelles de la Republique des Lettres.*

Secondary Sources: Gualdo Priorato, G. (1658), *The History of the Sacred and Royal Majesty of Christina Alessandra Queen of Swedland . . .* , London. Cassirer, E. (1939), *Descartes: Lehre – Persönlichkeit – Wirkung,* Stockholm: Behmann-Fischer. Stolpe, S. (1960–1), *Drottning Kristina,* Stockholm: Askild och Kärnekull; trans. R. M. Bethel (1966), *Queen Christina,* London: Burns and Oates. Platen, Magnus von, ed. (1966), *Queen Christina of Sweden: Documents and Studies, Analecta Reginensia* I, Stockholm. Oestreich, G. (1982), *Neostoicism and the Early Modern State,* Cambridge: Cambridge University Press. Setterwell, M. (1985), 'Role-playing in Maxim Form – A Comment on Queen Christina's Maxims', *Scandinavian Studies* 2. Atkinson, J. L. (1989), 'Sovereign between Throne and Altar', in K. Wilson and F. Warnke (eds.), *Women Writers of the Seventeenth Century,* Athens, Ga.: University of Georgia Press. Akerman, S. (1991), 'Kristina Wasa, Queen of Sweden', in M. E. Waithe (ed.), *Modern Women Philosophers, 1600–1900,* Dordrecht: Kluwer. Akerman, S. (1991), *Queen Christina of Sweden and Her Circle,* Leiden: Brill. [Eileen O'Neill]

CLARKE, SAMUEL b. Norwich, 1675; d. London, 1729. Philosopher and divine. Educated at Gonville and Caius College, Cambridge (B.A. 1695). Clarke was one of the first to master Newton's *Principia.* In 1697, he translated Jacques Rohault's *Traité de physique* into Latin, under the title *Jacobi Rohaulti Physica* (London, 1697; trans. John Clarke, London, 1723), adding to it extensive annotations that 'corrected' Descartes, often through incorporation of Newtonian principles. Clarke was chaplain of Bishop John Moore of Norwich between 1698 and 1710 and published several theological works before his appointment as Boyle lecturer in 1704, and again in 1705. The two sets of sermons were published separately as *A Demonstration of the Being and Attributes of God* (London, 1705) and *A Discourse concerning the Unchangeable Obligations of Natural Religion* (London, 1706) and soon collected under the title *A Discourse concerning the Being and Attributes of God, the Obligations of Natural Religion, and the Truth and Certainty of the Christian Religion* (London, 1706), wherein, in addition to proffering a cosmological argument for the existence of God, Clarke expounded his 'intellectualist' ethical theory. Clarke's Latin translation of Newton's *Opticks* appeared in London, 1706, the year in which he also moved into a living in London. For the next quarter of a century he was embroiled in various theological disputes, including one with Henry Dodwell over the immortality of the soul and the notorious and protracted Trinitarian controversies of 1712–29. With the ascension of George I to the English throne, Clarke became intimate with Princess Caroline, who served as the conduit for the Leibniz–Clarke exchange, which appeared shortly after Leibniz's death under the title *A Collection of Papers, Which Passed between the Late Learned Mr. Leibnitz and Dr. Clarke in the years 1715 and 1716* (London, 1717). His theological and philosophical writings were collected in *The Works of Samuel Clarke,* 4 vols. (London, 1738).

Secondary Sources: Hoskin, Michael A. (1961), '"Mining All Within": Clarke's Notes to Rohault's *Traité de Physique*', *The Thomist,* 24:353–63. J. P. Fergusson (1976), *Dr. Samuel Clarke an Eighteenth-Century Heretic,* Kineton: Roundwood. Attfield, Robin (1977), 'Clarke, Collins, and Compounds', *Journal of the History of Philosophy* 15:45–54. Barber, W. H. (1979), 'Voltaire and Samuel Clarke', *Studies on Voltaire and the Eighteenth Century* 179:47–61. Shapin, Steven (1981), 'Of Gods and Kings: Natural Philosophy and Politics in the Leibniz-Clarke Disputes', *Isis* 72:187–215. Stewart, Larry (1981), 'Samuel Clarke, Newtonianism, and the Factions of Post-Revolutionary England', *Journal of the History of Ideas* 42:53–72. Moorcavallo, Bruno (1985–6), 'Samuel Clarke e la cultura inglese tra il XVII e il XVIII secolo', *Studi Settecenteschi* 7–8:27–53. Vailati, Ezio (1993), 'Clarke's Extended Soul', *Journal of the History of Philosophy* 31:387–403. Attfield, Robin (1993), 'Clarke, Independence and Necessity', *British Journal of the History of Philosophy* 1:67–82. [Mordechai Feingold]

CLAUBERG, JOHANN (Claubergius) b. Solingen, Westphalia, 1622; d. Duisburg, 1665. Widely known philosopher and Calvinist theologian whose writings on the Cartesian philosophy propagated that philosophy, especially in Germany. Studied in Bremen, where he taught upon completion of his university studies. At the University of Groningen, the Netherlands, worked with the anti-Cartesian Martinus Schoock and with Descartes's friend, Tobias Andreae. After a trip to France in 1646 and then to England, published *Elementa philosophiae sive ontosophia* (Gronigen, 1647), which combines the philosophy of Aristotle with more modern doctrines. Upon hearing the lectures of Johannes de Raey in Leiden, partly converted to the Cartesian philosophy and developed a version of occasionalism. He presented that philosophy in scholastic terms, de-emphasised its more controversial doctrines, and thereby made it more palatable to traditionalists. In 1649, despite controversy about his Cartesianism, acquired a position as professor of philosophy and assistant professor of theology at the Calvinist University of Herborn. He became professor of philosophy (1651) and of theology (1655) in Duisburg where the Calvinist Gymnasium was being converted to a university. Published *Logica vetus et nova* (Amsterdam, 1654, 1658) and *De cognitione Dei et nostri* (Duisburg, 1656). From his home in Duisburg, remained in contact with the philosophers and theologians of the Cartesian school in France and in the Netherlands. The changes made to the second edition of his *Ontosophia*, entitled *Metaphysica de ente quae rectius Ontosophia* (Duisburg, 1664), reveal his greater acceptance of the Cartesian philosophy. Published *Physica* (Amsterdam, 1664). His writings on the philosophy of Descartes, especially *Defensio Cartesiana* (Amsterdam, 1652), *Initiatio philosophi, seu dubitatio Cartesiana* (Duisburg, 1655), and *Paraphrasis in R. Des Cartes Meditationes de prima philosophia* (Duisburg, 1658), helped spread Cartesianism throughout Germany and secured his own reputation as a literary figure. The standard edition of his writings remains Clauberg (1691), *Opera omnia philosophica*, Amsterdam.

Secondary Sources: *BHPC* I. Mueller, H. (1891), *Johannes Clauberg und seine Stellung im Cartesianismus,* Jena: Frommannsche Buchdruckerei H. Bohle. Bohatec, J. (1912) *Die Cartesianische Scholastik in der Philosophie und Theologie der reformierten Dogmatik des 17. Jahrhunderts,* Leipzig: Deichert. Molhuysen, P. C. (1913–24) *Bronnen tot de geschiedenis der Leidsche Universiteit,* 7 vols., The Hague: Nijhoff, vol. 2. Brosch, P. (1926), *Die Ontologie des J. Clauberg,* Greifswald: Hartmann. Wundt, M. (1939), *Die deutsche Schulmetaphysik des 17. Jahrhunderts,* Tübingen: J. C. B. Mohr. Balz, A. G. A. (1951), 'Clauberg and the Development of Occasionalism', in his *Cartesian Studies,* New York: Columbia University Press. Thijssen-Schoute, C. L. (1954), *Nederlands Cartesianisme,* Amsterdam: North-Holland. Weier, W. (1970), 'Cartesianischer Aristotelismus im siebzehnten Jahrhundert', *Salzburger Jahrbuch für Philosophie* 14:35–65; Viola, E. (1975), 'Scholastica e cartesianesimo nel pensiero di J. Clauberg', *Rivista di Filosofia Neoscolastica* 67:247–66; Weier, W. (1982), 'Der Okkasionalismus des J. Clauberg und sein Verhältnis zu Descartes, Geulincx, Malebranche', *Studia Cartesiana* 2:43–62. Verbeek, T., (1992) *Descartes and the Dutch: Early Reactions to Cartesian Philosophy, 1637–50,* Carbondale: Southern Illinois University Press. [Christia Mercer]

CLERSELIER, CLAUDE b. Paris (?), 1614; d. Paris, 1684. A lawyer and member of the Parlement of Paris, Clerselier was the brother-in-law of Pierre Chanut, a close friend of Descartes, and he was the father-in-law of Jacques Rohault, later to become an advocate for Cartesian physics. Clerselier is best known for the help he rendered Descartes in making his philosophy public, both during Descartes's life and after. By 1644 Clerselier was known as a close and devoted friend of Descartes, Baillet reports. He translated the *Objectiones et Responsiones* to the *Meditationes* into French (Paris, 1647), and reviewed and corrected Picot's French translation of Descartes's *Princ. Phil.* (Paris, 1647). After Descartes died, Chanut, to whom the papers were entrusted, passed the responsibility for editing them to Clerselier.

Clerselier collected Descartes's correspondence and published it in three volumes under the title *Lettres de Mr Descartes*, vol. 1 (Paris, 1657), vol. 2 (Paris, 1659), and vol. 3 (Paris, 1667). In addition to his prefaces, these volumes included a number of Clerselier's own letters, written after Descartes's death to other Cartesians. These letters are important sources of information about discussions among the early French Cartesians, including early discussions of occasionalism. Together with Louis de La Forge, Clerselier also published an edition of Descartes's *Traité de l'homme*, under the title *L'Homme de RENE DESCARTES* (Paris, 1664); when a second edition was published in Paris in 1677, Clerselier added the *Traité de la Lumiere 'du mesme Autheur'*. When he died, he had not yet published everything of Descartes's he had intended to, leaving that task, never to be finished, to Jean-Baptiste Legrand. Clerselier is also responsible for editing a posthumous edition of the writings of his son-in-law, Jacques Rohault, *Oeuvres posthumes de Mr. Rohault*, (Paris, 1682). His editions of Descartes's letters and *Le Monde* (*Traité de l'homme* and *Traité de la Lumiere*) form the basis of the modern AT edition of those texts. His prefaces to the three volumes of the letters are reprinted in AT V 743–81.

Secondary Sources: Baillet, A. (1691), *La Vie de M. Descartes* (2 vols.), Paris, vol. 2, pp. 241–2. *BHPC* I 504–6. Balz, Albert G. A. (1951), *Cartesian Studies*, New York: Columbia University Press, pp. 28–41. Clair, Pierre (1984), 'Clerselier, Claude', in D. Huisman (ed.), *Dictionnaire des philosophes*, Paris: Presses Universitaires de France, p. 558. [Daniel Garber]

COCKBURN, CATHARINE TROTTER b. London, 1679; d. Long Horsley, 1749. A dramatist and writer of metaphysical, epistemological, and moral essays. She studied French, Latin, Greek, and logic and was something of a child prodigy. Forced to support herself by the time of her adolescence, she became a successful playwright. She published anonymously *A Defence of the Essay of Human Understanding, written by M*r *Locke* (London, 1702) against three published, critical responses to the *Essay* by Thomas Burnet. Her defence was praised by Toland, Tyrell, Leibniz, Norris, and Locke himself. In 1726 and 1727, she again defended Locke, this time responding to Dr. Holdsworth. In 1737, she offered a defence of her views (which she shared with Samuel Clarke) on the grounding of moral virtue and obligation. This work, *Remarks upon Some Writers in the Controversy concerning the Foundation of Moral Virtue and Moral Obligation*, was printed in *The History of the Works of the Learned* (London, 1743). Her final philosophical work was a defence of Clarke's views entitled *Remarks Upon the Principles and Reasonings of Dr. Rutherford's Essay* (London, 1747). The standard edition of her works is Cockburn (1751), *The Works of Mrs. Catharine Cockburn, Theological, Moral, Dramatic and Poetical*, London.

Secondary Sources: Allibone, S. (1710), *A Critical Dictionary of English Literature and British and American Authors* [repr. Detroit: Gale Publishing Co., 1965]. Stenton, D. M. (1957), *The English Woman in History*, London: Allen and Unwin. Waithe, M. E. (1991), 'Catharine Trotter Cockburn', in M. E. Waithe (ed.), *Modern Women Philosophers, 1600–1900*, Dordrecht: Kluwer. Bolton, M. (1993), 'Some Aspects of the Philosophy of Catharine Trotter', *Journal of the History of Philosophy* 31:565–88. [Eileen O'Neill]

COLLIER, ARTHUR b. Langford Magna, Wiltshire, 1680; d. Langford Magna, 1732. Metaphysician, theologian. Educated at Salisbury and Oxford; ordained Anglican priest (1704). Was rector of Langford Magna (from 1704 to 1732), as his father, grandfather, and great-grandfather had been before him. Deeply influenced by Descartes and Malebranche, and above all by John Norris, rector of the nearby church at Bemerton, whom he almost certainly knew personally. Published *Clavis Universalis; or, A New Inquiry after Truth. Being a Demonstration of the Non-Existence or Impossibility of an External World* (London, 1713), which gave nine arguments against the existence of matter (he was not at the time acquainted, it seems, with Berkeley's views); *A Specimen of True Philosophy; In a Discourse on Genesis* (Sarum, 1730), which argued that the visible world exists in the mind, the mind in the Logos, and the Logos in God; and *Logology, or a Treatise on the Logos, in Seven Sermons on John 1:1, 2, 3, 14* (London,

1732), which denied the consubstantiality of the first two members of the Trinity and defended the Apollinarian doctrine that in the Incarnation Christ did not unite himself to a human soul. Impoverished by his own impracticality, it was said, and his wife's extravagance, he sold the advowson of the Langford Magna church, which his family had held for a century, to Corpus Christi College, Oxford, for sixteen hundred guineas. His philosophical works were ignored by his countrymen, but an abstract of *Clavis Universalis* in the *Acta Eruditorum* (1717), and a translation of it (Rostock, 1756) by J. C. Eschenbach (published with his translation of Berkeley's *Three Dialogues*), brought his views to the attention of some German philosophers, among them Wolff, Bülffinger, and possibly Kant. *Clavis Universalis, A Specimen of True Philosophy*, and extracts from *Logology* are reprinted in Parr, S. (1837), *Metaphysical Tracts by English Philosophers of the Eighteenth Century*, London.

Secondary Sources: Benson, R. (1837), *Memoirs of the Life and Writings of the Rev. Arthur Collier, M.A.*, London. Lyon, G. (1888), *L'Idéalisme en Angleterre au XVIIIe siècle*, Paris: Alcan. Lovejoy, A. O. (1908), 'Kant and the English Platonists', in *Essays Philosophical and Psychological in Honor of William James . . . by His Colleagues at Columbia University*, New York: Longmans. Johnston, G. A. (1923), *The Development of Berkeley's Philosophy*, London: Macmillan, Appendix I. Muirhead, J. H. (1931), *The Platonic Tradition in Anglo-Saxon Philosophy*, London: Allen and Unwin. Vleeschauwer, H. J. de (1938), 'Les Antinomies kantiennes et la *Clavis Universalis* d'Arthur Collier', *Mind* 47:303–20. Jordak, F. E. (1978), 'Arthur Collier's Theory of Possibility', *Idealistic Studies* 8:253–60. McCracken, C. J. (1983), *Malebranche and British Philosophy*, Oxford: Oxford University Press. McCracken, C. J. (1986), 'Stages on a Cartesian Road to Immaterialism', *Journal of the History of Philosophy* 24:19–40. [Charles McCracken]

CONWAY, ANNE (née Finch), Viscountess Conway b. Kensington House (now Kensington Palace), London, 1631; d. Ragley Hall, Warwickshire, 1679. Metaphysician, theologian. Precluded by her sex from following her half-brothers John and Heneage Finch to Oxford, she learned Latin and Greek at home, and avidly read books of philosophy and theology. Met Henry More, tutor to her half-brother John, in about 1649. Was for three decades More's intimate friend – a friendship Platonic twice over, both chaste and rooted in a shared enthusiasm for Platonism. Married, 1651, to Edward Conway, later third Viscount Conway and Killultagh, first Earl of Conway. More spent much time at Ragley Hall, the Conway seat, also frequented by other Platonists, Cudworth, Whichcote, and Glanvill, among them. Franciscus Mercurius Van Helmont, the Flemish Platonist, settled at Ragley in 1671 where he tried, by 'occult medicine', to cure Conway of chronic, debilitating headaches that had begun in girlhood and increased in severity for the rest of her life. Van Helmont stayed at Ragley until Conway's death; he failed to relieve her suffering but exerted strong influence over her philosophical and theological views. In 1676, to the consternation of her family and More, she became a Quaker (Van Helmont had declared himself a Quaker in 1676, though his relationship to the society proved stormy). At death, she left a notebook setting out a metaphysical system according to which reality is a hierarchically ordered chain of beings, each of which has some measure of life and sentience or thought. More and Van Helmont had the work translated into Latin; it appeared as *Principia Philosophiae Antiquissimae et Recentissimae: De Deo, Christo et Creatura; id est, de Spiritu et Materia in genere* (Amsterdam, 1690); an English retranslation from the Latin was published (London, 1692) as *The Principles of the Most Ancient and Modern Philosophy, concerning God, Christ, and the Creatures, viz. of Spirit and Matter in General; whereby may be resolved all those Problems or Difficulties, which neither by the School nor Common Modern Philosophy, nor by the Cartesian, Hobbesian, or Spinosian, could be discussed*. Introduced to her ideas by Van Helmont, Leibniz showed keen interest in Conway's views, praising her, in his *Nouveaux essais*, as one of the most acute of those 'who have held that all things have life and perception'. The only modern edition is Conway (1982), *Principles of the Most Ancient and Modern Philosophy*, The Hague: Nijhoff, which contains the text of both the 1690 Latin and the 1692 English versions. Most of Conway's extant letters are in Nicolson 1930, with an excellent biographical account of Conway; her correspondence with More about Cartesianism is in Gabbey, Alan (1977), 'Anne Conway et Henry More, Lettres sur Descartes', *Archives de philosophie*, 40:379–404.

Secondary Sources: Powicke, F. J. (1926), *The Cambridge Platonists*, London: Dent. Owen, G. R. (1937), 'The Famous Case of Lady Anne Conway', *Annals of Medical History* 9:567–71. Politella, J. (1938), *Platonism, Aristotelianism, and Cabalism in the Philosophy of Leibniz*, Philadelphia: University of Pennsylvania Press. Walker, D. P. (1964), *The Decline of Hell*, Chicago: University of Chicago Press. Hutin, S. (1966), *Henry More*, Hildesheim: Georg Olms. Coudert, A. (1975), 'A Cambridge Platonist's Kabbalist Nightmare', *Journal of the History of Ideas* 36:634–52. Coudert, A. (1976), 'A Quaker-Kabbalist Controversy', *Journal of the Warburg and Courtauld Institutes* 39:171–89. Merchant, C. (1979), 'The Vitalism of Anne Conway: Its Impact on Leibniz's Concept of the Monad', *Journal of the History of Philosophy* 17:255–70. Merchant, C. (1980), *The Death of Nature*, San Francisco: Harper and Row. Fraser, A. (1985), *The Weaker Vessel*, New York: Vantage. Duran, J. (1989), 'Anne Viscountess Conway: A Seventeenth-Century Rationalist', *Hypatia* 4:64–79. [Charles McCracken]

CORDEMOY, GÉRAULD DE b. Paris, 1626; d. Paris, 1684. Originally trained as a lawyer, a profession which he followed in later life, Cordemoy became one of the most important French followers of Descartes. From 1657, Cordemoy was known as a participant in various Cartesian academies, including those of Maignan, Bourdelot, Rohault, Lamoignon, and Montmort, as well as the Cartesian salon of Mme de Bonnevaux. Cordemoy is reputed to have been among the inner circle present at the reburial of Descartes's remains in Paris on 24 June 1667. In 1673, Cordemoy was named lecteur ordinaire du dauphin, and probably at that time began working on a history of France that was left incomplete at his death. In 1675, Cordemoy was elected to the Académie Française. His first publication was the anonymous *Discours de l'Action des corps*, published as an appendix to the 1664 Paris edition of Descartes's *Le monde*; it had been first presented as a *conférence* at the Montmort academy. This short essay then appeared as the second discourse in a book that Cordemoy published under his own name, *Le Discernement du Corps et de l'Ame en six discours . . .* (Paris, 1666). This came out in a second Paris edition in 1670 and was reprinted in 1671, 1679, 1680, 1683, and later, sometimes under somewhat different titles; a Latin edition was published in Geneva in 1679. In this work, Cordemoy advocated a Cartesian physics, explaining everything in the physical world in terms of size, shape, and motion, and like many contemporary Cartesians, advocating an occasionalist account of causality. But unlike other Cartesians, Cordemoy advocated atoms and the void, an innovation that was not well received by other Cartesians. Other important works include the *Discours physique de la Parole* (Paris, 1668), published in a second edition in 1671 and 1677, with later editions, including translations into Latin and English. In this work Cordemoy presents a Cartesian theory of language and communication. Also important are *Lettre Ecrite à un sçavant Religieux* ('*Lettre . . . au R. P. Cossart . . .* ') (Paris, 1668), in which he defends Cartesian orthodoxy against certain religious attacks concerning Descartes's account of animals, and the consistency between his system and the book of Genesis, and two metaphysical treatises, published posthumously in *Divers Traitez de Metaphysique, d'Histoire, et de Politique* (Paris, 1691), which also includes other posthumously published writings on history and politics. His inaugural lecture at the Académie Française was published under the title *Discours Prononcez à l'Academie Françoise Le XII. de Decembre M.DC.LXXV . . .* (Paris, 1676). His *Histoire de France* was published posthumously by his son Louis Gérauld Cordemoy, vol. 1 (Paris, 1685), and vol. 2 (Paris, 1689). A collected edition of his writings came out as *Les Oeuvres de Feu Monsieur de Cordemoy* (Paris, 1704). There is a modern edition of some of the texts of particular philosophical interest, Cordemoy (1968), *Oeuvres philosophiques*, Paris: Presses Universitaires de France, including the *Discernement*, the *Discours physique*, the *Lettre . . . au R. P. Cossart . . .*, the two *Traités de métaphysique*, and an essay on politics, *De la Réformation d'un Etat*.

Secondary Sources: A eulogy by Jean Racine can be found in *Discours prononcez a l'Academie françoise le 2. ianvier 1685* (Paris, 1685). A fuller biographical study is found in the editors' introduction to

Cordemoy, Gérauld de (1968), *Oeuvres philosophiques,* ed. P. Clair and F. Girbal, Paris: Presses Universitaires de France. See also Prost, J. (1907), *Essai sur l'atomisme et l'occasionalisme dans la philosophie cartésienne,* Paris: Paulin. Mouy, Paul (1934), *Le développement de la physique cartésienne 1646–1712,* Paris: Vrin, pp. 101–6. Balz, Albert G. A. (1951), *Cartesian Studies,* New York: Columbia University Press, pp. 3–27. Battail, Jean-François (1973), *L'avocat philosophe Géraud de Cordemoy,* The Hague: Nijhoff. [Daniel Garber]

CUDWORTH, RALPH b. Allen in Somersetshire, 1617; d. Cambridge, 1688. Theologian, metaphysician, moral philosopher, scholar of ancient Greek and Hebrew. A leading Cambridge Platonist. Entered Emmanuel College, Cambridge, 1632; B.A. 1635, M.A. 1639. Elected Fellow, 1639, popular tutor. *Discourse concerning the True Notion of the Lord's Supper,* 1642. Bachelor of Divinity, 1644, defending theses on the eternity of good and evil and on the existence of incorporeal substances that are immortal by nature. Master of Clare Hall and Regius Professor of Hebrew, 1645. Preached a sermon before the House of Commons, 1647, arguing against divisions among Christians stemming from dogmatism over ritual and Church government. Doctor of Divinity, 1651, with a disputation on the rational and immutable nature of good and evil. Left the University, 1651–4, returned as master of Clare Hall, 1654–88. His daughter, Damaris Cudworth, later Lady Masham, b. 1658. Received vicarage of Ashwell in Hertfordshire, 1662. Was composing a work on moral good and evil mid-1660s; abandoned upon hearing of Henry More's *Enchiridion ethicum.* More a fellow in Clare Hall. In 1671 Cudworth completed *The True Intellectual System of the Universe, wherein All the Reason and Philosophy of Atheism Is Confuted* (London, 1678; Latin translation Leiden, 1733). Criticised for presenting atheistic arguments too forcefully. Polemical against Hobbes. Sympathetic towards Descartes. Deeply influenced by Neoplatonic writings, ancient, Christian, and Florentine. Coleridge dubbed him a 'Plotinist' rather than a 'Platonist'. Prebend at Gloucester, 1678. Posthumous works, *A Treatise concerning Eternal and Immutable Morality* (London, 1731); *A Treatise of Free Will* (London, 1838). Facsimile editions of the collected works, under preparation by B. Fabian, Hildesheim: Olms, 1977–

Secondary Sources: Wise, T. (1706), *A Confutation of the Reason and Philosophy of Atheism; Being in a Great Measure either an Abridgment or an Improvement of What Dr. Cudworth Offer'd to that Purpose in His True Intellectual System of the Universe* (2 vols.), London. Janet, P. A. R. (1860), *Essai sur le médiateur plastique de Cudworth,* Paris: Ladrange. Tulloch, J. (1874), *Rational Theology and Christian Philosophy in England in the Seventeenth Century,* 2d ed. (2 vols.), Edinburgh and London: Blackwood, vol. 2, pp. 193–302. Lowrey, C. E. (1884), *The Philosophy of Ralph Cudworth: A Study of the True Intellectual System of the Universe,* New York: Phillips and Hunt. Powicke, F. J. (1926), *The Cambridge Platonists,* London, Dent, chap. 4. Muirhead, J. H. (1931), *The Platonic Tradition in Anglo-Saxon Philosophy,* New York: Macmillan, pt. 1, chaps. 2–3. Cassirer, E. (1932), *Die Platonische Renaissance in England und die Schule von Cambridge,* Leipzig and Berlin: Teubner; trans. J. P. Pettegrove (1953), *The Platonic Renaissance in England,* Austin: University of Texas Press. Aspelin, G. (1943), *Ralph Cudworth's Interpretation of Greek Philosophy,* Acta Universitatis Gotoburgensis, vol. 49. Passmore, J. A. (1951), *Ralph Cudworth: An Interpretation,* Cambridge: Cambridge University Press. Gysi, L. (1962), *Platonism and Cartesianism in the Philosophy of Ralph Cudworth,* Bern: H. Lang. [Gary Hatfield]

CULVERWEL, NATHANAEL. b. Middlesex (?); d. Cambridge (?), 1651? Very little is known of Culverwel's life. He is known to have entered Emmanuel College, Cambridge, in 1633, receiving the B.A. in 1636, the M.A. in 1640, and was elected fellow in 1642. At Cambridge he was a contemporary of others who came later to be known as the Cambridge Platonists, including Benjamin Whichcote and Ralph Cudworth. After the successful publication of his posthumous treatise, *Spiritual Opticks: Or a Glasse Discovering the Weakness and Imperfection of a Christians Knowledge in This Life* (Cambridge, 1651), William Dillingworth was encouraged to publish a collection of college exercises and sermons, including the *Spiritual Optics* among other things, entitled *An Elegant and Learned Discourse of the Light of Nature with several other Treatises* (London, 1652), reprinted a number of times in the years following. This was one of the earliest publications by a member of the Cambridge Platonists. Culverwel rejected innate ideas, though he emphasised the certainty and self-evidence of first principles, and argued that sensation, though uncertain, is essential for knowledge. In moral philosophy, he argued that morality is grounded in divine commandment.

Secondary Sources: De Pauley, William C. (1937), *The Candle of the Lord; Studies in the Cambridge Platonists* (New York: Macmillan). O'Brien, Margaret Townsend (1951), 'Nathaniel Culverwel: An Aristotelian among Platonists' (Ph.D. diss., Radcliffe College, Cambridge, Mass., Passmore, John (1967), 'Culverwel, Nathaniel', in *EP.* Further bibliography can be found in George R. Guffey (1969), *Traherne and the Seventeenth-Century English Platonists, 1900–1966* (London: Nether Press). [Daniel Garber]

CUMBERLAND, RICHARD b. London, 1632; d. Peterborough, 1718. Moral philosopher, antiquarian, divine, friend of Pepys. Educated Magdalene College, Cambridge, from 1649: B.A. 1653, Mass. 1656, B.D. 1663, D.D. 1680. Fellow of Magdalene 1653–8. A 'survivor' of both Restoration and Revolution, rose in the Church of England to become bishop of Peterborough in 1691 as part of the Revolution-settlement of the church. His only work in philosophy, *De legibus naturae. Disquisitio philosophica, in qua earum forma, summa capita, ordo, promulgatio & obligatio e rerum natura investigantur; quinetiam elementa philosophiae Hobbianae, cum moralis tum civilis, considerantur & refutantur* (London, 1672), seeks to refute Hobbes's moral philosophy. English translations in London, 1727, and London and Dublin, 1750, secured continuing impact on British moral thought. Most important modern language version is Barbeyrac's annotated French translation, Cumberland, *Traité philosophique des loix naturelles,* trans. J. Barbeyrac (Amsterdam, 1744), reinforcing his European reputation as one of the three founders of modern natural law, the others being Grotius and Pufendorf. James Tyrrell, *A Brief Disquisition of the Law of Nature* (London, 1701), which presents itself as an exposition of Cumberland's views, contains too much of Tyrrell himself, and of Locke, to give an adequate picture of Cumberland.

Secondary Sources: Ringmacher, D. (1693), *Cumberlandus illustratus sive Disquisitio philosophica de lege naturae fundamentali ad mentem Rich. Cumberlandi, Angli, instituta, et quatuor disputationibus,* Ulm. Squire Payne (1720), 'A Brief Account of the Life, Character and Writings of the Author', in R. Cumberland, *Sanchoniatho's Phoenician History, translated from the first book of Eusebius De praeparatione Evangelica,* London (French trans. in Cumberland (1744), *Traité Philosophique des loix naturelles,* Amsterdam). Barbeyrac, J. (1744), Preface, in R. Cumberland, *Sanchoniatho's Phoenician History.* Maxwell, J. (1727), 'Two Introductory Essays' and 'Appendix' in Cumberland (1727), *A Treatise of the Laws of Nature,* London. Spaulding, F. G. (1894), *Richard Cumberland als Begründer der Englischen Ethik,* Leipzig. Albee, E. (1901), *A History of English Utilitarianism,* London: George Allen and Unwin, New York: Macmillan (2d ed., 1957). Sharp, F. C. (1912), 'The Ethical System of Richard Cumberland and Its Place in the History of British Ethics', *Mind* 21:371–98. Forsyth, M. (1982), 'The Place of Richard Cumberland in the History of Natural Law Doctrine', *Journal of the History of Philosophy* 20:23–42. Kirk, L. (1987), *Richard Cumberland and Natural Law. Secularisation of Thought in Seventeenth-Century England,* Cambridge: J. Clarke and Co. Haakonssen, K. (1988), 'Moral Philosophy and Natural Law: From the Cambridge Platonists to the Scottish Enlightenment', *Political Science* 40:97–110. Haakonssen, K. (1995), 'The Character and Obligation of Natural Law according to Richard Cumberland', in M. A. Stewart (ed.), *Studies in Seventeenth-Century Philosophy,* Oxford: Oxford University Press. [Knud Haakonssen]

CUREAU DE LA CHAMBRE, MARIN b. Saint Jean d'Assé (near Mans), 1594 or 1596; d. Paris, 1669. Cureau was trained as a physician at Montpellier, and practised at first in Mans. In 1634, he was made the personal physician to Pierre Séguier, then Garde des Sceaux, later Chancelier de France. At that time, he moved to Paris, where he resided in Séguier's household for the rest of his life. In subsequent years he became the 'démonstrateur-opérateur pharmaceutique' at the Jardins du Roi (1635), a member of the Académie Française (1635), a physician to the 'Grande Chancellerie' (1635), counsellor and physician to Louis XIII (1640), ordinary physician to Louis XIV (1650, passed in 1664 to his son François), and a member of the Académie des Sciences (1666). His writings include a number of medical tracts, some number of occasional pieces, and several pieces on light and colour, including *Nouvelles pensées sur les causes de la lumière, du débordement du Nil et de l'amour d'inclination* (Paris, 1634), *Nouvelles observations et conjectures sur l'iris* (Paris, 1650), and *La lumière* (Paris, 1657). He was best known, though, for his voluminous psychological writings, including: *Les caractères des passions, volume I: amour, joie, rire, désir, espérance* (Paris, 1640); *Les caractères des passions, volume II: des passions courageuses . . .* (Paris, 1645); *Les caractères des passions, volumes III et IV: haine, douleur . . .* (Paris, 1659); *Les caractères des passions, volume V: larmes, crainte, désespoir* (Paris, 1662); *Traité de la connoissance des animaux . . .* (Paris, 1647); *L'art de connoistre les hommes. Première partie où sont contenus les discours préliminaires . . .* (Paris, 1659); *Le système de l'âme* (second part of *L'art de connoistre les hommes*) (Paris, 1664). *L'art de connoistre les hommes. Partie troisième qui contient la défense de l'extension des parties libres de l'âme* (Paris, 1666); *Discours de l'amitié et de la haine qui se trouvent envers les animaux* (Paris, 1667). A number of these also appeared in English editions shortly after they were published. The *Traité de la connoissance des animaux* has been published in a modern edition, ed. O. Le Guern (Paris: Fayard, 1989). There is no standard modern edition of his writings.

Secondary Sources: Kerviler, René (1877), *Marin et Pierre Cureau de la Chambre (1596–1693): étude sur leur vie et leurs ecrits,* Le Mans: Pellechat. Foerster, Ilse (1936), *Marin Cureau de La Chambre (1594–1675). Ein Beitrag zur Geschichte der psychomoralischen Literatur in Frankreich,* Breslau: Priebatsch. Balz, Albert G. A. (1951), *Cartesian Studies,* New York: Columbia University Press, pp. 42–64. Connell, D. (1978), 'Cureau de La Chambre, source de Malebranche', *Recherches sur le XVIIème siècle* 1978 no. 2: 158–72. Darmon, Albert (1985), *Les corps immatériels: Esprits et images dans l'oeuvre de Marin Cureau de la Chambre (1594–1669),* Paris: Vrin. Wright, John P. (1991), 'The Embodied Soul in 17th-century French Medicine', *Canadian Bulletin of Medical History* 8:21–42. [Daniel Garber]

DANIEL, GABRIEL b. Rouen, 1649; d. Paris, 1728. A Jesuit, Daniel taught rhetoric, philosophy, and theology at Rennes, and eventually became the librarian of the Jesuits in Paris. Louis XIV also honoured him with the title of 'historiographe de France'. Among the many books he wrote, the more important philosophically were his attacks on Descartes and Cartesianism, the satiric *Voiage du Monde de Descartes* (Paris, 1690), followed by the *Nouvelles difficultés proposées par un péripatéticien à l'auteur du Voyage du monde de Descartes* (Paris, 1693), a sequel to the *Voiage*. In these enormously popular books, which appeared in many editions in many languages, the author imagines travelling as a disembodied Cartesian soul through the Cartesian heavens, guided by the good Father Mersenne, encountering a variety of philosophers, including, eventually, Descartes himself, and discussing a variety of issues from the Cartesian philosophy. In general, Daniel was critical of Descartes's thought. Daniel also wrote a response to Pascal's *Lettres provinciales* entitled *Entretiens de Cléandre et d'Eudoxe sur les Lettres provinciales de Pascal* (Cologne and Rouen, 1694), and his important *Histoire de France* (vol. 1, Paris, 1696; 3 vols., Paris, 1713). Daniel left many more publications, largely in theology. There is no modern edition of his writings.

Secondary Sources: *BHPC* I 576–7. Sortais, Gaston (1929), *Le cartesianisme chez les Jésuites français au 17ᵉ et 18ᵉ siècles (Archives de philosophie,* vol. 6, no. 3), Paris: Beauchesne. Bourke, Vernon (1937), 'An Illustration of the Attitude of the Early French Jesuits Towards Cartesianism', in *Cartesio nel terzo centenario nel 'Discorso del Metodo,* in *Rivista di filosofia neo-scolastica* 20(supp):129–37. Rosenfield, Leonora Cohen (1957), 'Peripatetic Adversaries of Cartesianism in 17th-Century France', *Review of Religion*

22:14–40. Rosenfield, Leonora Cohen (1968), *From Beast-Machine to Man-Machine,* 2d ed., New York: Octagon Books, pp. 86–90. [Daniel Garber]

DESCARTES, RENÉ (Cartesius, Renatus Pictus, René du Perron) b. La Haye, 1596; d. Stockholm, 1650. Metaphysician, natural philosopher, mathematician. One of the central figures of the century and founder of a school of thought. Educated at the Jesuit College of La Flèche ca. 1606 to ca. 1614; degree in law from Poitier 1616. Made the acquaintance of Beeckmann at Breda in 1618. Had a series of dreams (on 10 November 1619) about the unity of science. Composed but did not finish *Regulae ad directionem Ingenii* ca. 1618–28 (published posthumously in Dutch translation 1684 and in Latin, in the *Opuscula Posthuma,* Amsterdam, 1701). Matriculated at Leiden University 1630. Learned of Galileo's condemnation and suppressed the publication of *Le Monde ou traité de la lumière* (published posthumously, Paris, 1664). Published *Discours de la Methode* with *Dioptrique, Meteores,* and *Geometrie* as samples of the method (Leiden, 1637, Latin translation Amsterdam, 1644); disputed with scholastics and Jesuits (Fromondus, Plempius, Morin, Bourdin). Published *Meditationes de Prima Philosophia,* appending to it sets of objections and replies (Paris, 1641, Amsterdam, 1642, with French translation Paris, 1647). Quarrelled with Voëtius, Rector of Utrecht University, 1641–3. Judgement pronounced against him by the Utrecht magistrates 1643. Published *Principia Philosophiae* (Amsterdam, 1644, French translation Paris, 1647); reconciled with Jesuits. Had troubles with Leiden University similar to those in Utrecht. Published *Passions de l'âme* (Paris, 1649). Went to Sweden at the invitation of Queen Christina, 1649. His significant correspondence (with Beeckman, Mersenne, Huygens, Regius, Elisabeth, Arnauld, More, and others) was published posthumously in three volumes by Clerselier 1657, 1659, and 1667. The standard edition of his writings is AT.

Secondary Sources: Baillet, A. (1691), *La Vie de Monsieur Descartes* (2 vols.), Paris. BHPC. Gilson, E. (1913), *Index scolastico-cartésien,* Paris: Félix Alcan. Gilson, E. (1967), *Etudes sur le rôle de la pensée médiévale dans la formation du système cartésien,* Paris: Vrin. Sebba, G. (1964), *Bibliographia Cartesiana, a Critical Guide to the Descartes Literature 1800–1960,* The Hague: Nijhoff. Alquié, F. (1950), *La découverte métaphysique de l'homme chez Descartes,* Paris: Presses Universitaires de France. Gueroult, M. (1968), *Descartes selon l'ordre des raisons* (2 vols.), 2d ed., Paris: Aubier; trans. R. Ariew (1984–5), *Descartes' Philosophy Interpreted according to the Order of Reasons* (2 vols.), Minneapolis: University of Minnesota Press. Frankfurt, H. (1970), *Demons, Dreamers, and Madmen,* Indianapolis: Bobbs-Merrill. Vrooman, J. R. (1970), *René Descartes, A Biography,* New York: Putnam. Rodis-Lewis, G. (1971), *L'oeuvre de Descartes* (2 vols.), Paris: Vrin. Gouhier, H. (1972), *La pensée religieuse de Descartes,* 2d ed., Paris: Vrin. Curley, E. M. (1978), *Descartes against the Skeptics,* Cambridge: Harvard University Press. Gouhier, H. (1978), *La pensée métaphysique de Descartes,* 3d. ed., Paris: Vrin. Wilson, M. (1978), *Descartes,* London: Routledge and Kegan Paul. Beyssade, J.-M. (1979), *La philosophie première de Descartes,* Paris: Flammarion. Marion, J.-L. (1981), *Sur l'ontologie grise de Descartes,* 2d ed., Paris: Vrin. Marion, J.-L. (1981), *Sur la théologie blanche de Descartes,* Paris: Presses Universitaires de France. Garber, D. (1992), *Descartes' Metaphysical Physics,* Chicago: University of Chicago Press. [Roger Ariew]

DESGABETS, ROBERT b. Ancemont (Verdun), 1610; d. Breuil, 1678. Philosopher, theologian, physiologist. Important primarily as an advocate of what he saw as a purified version of Cartesianism in that 'Descartes sometimes ceased to be a good Cartesian'. Entered the Benedictine order in 1636 and served in various ecclesiastical posts thereafter. Involved in the theorising and experimentation concerning transfusion of blood, particularly in the Montmort académie in 1658. Defended the orthodox Cartesian against the Cartesian atomism advanced by Cordemoy in 1666; the document is still unpublished but discussed extensively in Prost 1907. Participated in discussion of Cartesianism with Cardinal de Retz in Commercy during 1677 – first published in Cousin 1845 (v. 'Procès-verbal . . .', 'Le cardinal de Retz . . .'). Defended, to the dismay of the author, Malebranche's *Recherche* against

Foucher's *Critique de la recherche de la vérité* in his *Critique de la critique* . . . (Paris, 1675). Otherwise, his major works are all posthumously published in Desgabets (1983), *Oeuvres Philosophiques inédites,* ed. J. Beaude, Amsterdam: Quadratures, with an important introduction by G. Rodis-Lewis.

Secondary Sources: Lemaire, P. (1901), *Le cartésianisme chez les bénédictins. Dom Robert Desgabets, son système, son influence et son école.* Paris: Alcan. Prost, J. (1907), *Essai sur l'atomisme et l'occasionalisme dans la philosophie cartésienne.* Paris: H. Paulin. Beaude, J. (1974), 'Desgabets et son oeuvre. Esquisse d'un portrait de Desgabets par lui-même', *Revue de Synthèse* (January–June 1974): 7–17. Armogathe, J.-R. (1977), *Theologia Cartesiana: L'explication physique de l'Eucharistie chez Descartes et dom Desgabets.* The Hague: Nijhoff. Beaude, J. (1979), 'Cartésianisme et anticartésianisme de Desgabets', *Studia Cartesiana* 1:1–24. Watson, R. A. (1987), *The Breakdown of Cartesian Metaphysics,* Atlantic Highlands, N.J.: Humanities Press. [Thomas Lennon]

DIGBY, KENELM b. Gayhurst, Buckinghamshire, 1603; d. London, 1665. Digby led an active and colourful life, for which he was admired as much, perhaps, as for his intellectual accomplishments. Born a Catholic, Digby was at Oxford from 1618 to 1620, after which he travelled to France, Italy, and Spain, returning to England in 1623. In 1625 Digby married the love of his life, Venetia Stanley, whose death in 1633 led him to withdraw from society and turn to study. By the mid-1630s, the troubles in England had led him to move to France, where he lived in exile for many years. Although a Catholic, and a royalist (he briefly converted to Protestantism in 1630, though he reconverted to Catholicism by 1635), he was able to travel freely in England and did so; in 1648 and 1655–6 he negotiated with Cromwell for the toleration of Catholicism in England. While living in France, he was part of the Mersenne circle, met and corresponded with Descartes in Holland, and was close to other English exiles, among them Thomas Hobbes, to whom he introduced Descartes's works. After the Restoration in 1660, Digby returned to England and became a member of the new Royal Society. His most important philosophical work is the *Two Treatises. In the one of which the Nature of Bodies; in the other, the Nature of Mans Soule; is looked into: in the way of discovery, of the Immortality of Reasonable Soules* (Paris, 1644). The first treatise presents an account of the physical world that is generally mechanist, though it contains recognisably Aristotelian features. The second treatise puts forth an argument for the existence of an immaterial and immortal soul; Digby identifies a number of features of the soul that it could not have if it were merely material. Also important is his *Observations upon Religio Medici* (London, 1643), a response to Sir Thomas Browne's *Religio Medici* (London, 1642). His most popular work was probably an account of the weapon salve, which cures wounds when spread on the weapon that caused them, *Discours fait en une célèbre assemblée, par le Chevalier Digby . . . touchant la guérison des playes par la poudre de sympathie* (Paris, 1658), reprinted often, and translated into a number of languages. Also popular were a number of collections of alchemical recipes purporting to have been taken from his manuscripts and published after his death. There is no modern edition of his writings.

Secondary Sources: Dobbs, Betty Jo Teeter (1971–4), 'Studies in the Natural Philosophy of Sir Kenelm Digby', *Ambix* 18:1–25, 20:143–63, 21:1–28. Henry, John (1982), 'Atomism and Eschatology: Catholicism and Natural Philosophy in the Interregnum', *British Journal for the History of Science* 15:211–39. Krook, Dorothea (1993), *John Sergeant and His Circle,* Leiden: Brill, chap. 3. Hall, M. B., 'Digby, Kenelm', in *DSB.* [Daniel Garber]

DU HAMEL, JEAN b. (?); d. Paris, 1705. Du Hamel was a professor of philosophy at the Collège du Sorbonne-Plessis from 1668 to about 1690. Outside of this, nothing is known of his life. He is important largely as a scholastic adversary of Descartes. His *Réflexions critiques sur le système cartésien de la philosophy de Mr. Regis* (Paris, 1692) gathers together a variety of standard arguments against Descartes in the air in the late seventeenth-century university. This was followed a few years later by the *Lettre de M. Du Hamel, . . . pour servir de réplique à M. Régis* (Paris, 1699). Most important, though, is his

*Philosophia universalis, sive commentarius in universam Aristotelis philosophiam ad usum scholarum comparatam quaedam recentiorum philosophorum ac praesertim Cartesii propositiones damnatae ac prohibitae* (Paris, 1705). This work is one of the very last Aristotelian philosophy courses to be published in France, and is particularly important for its systematic attack against the Cartesian philosophy from a scholastic point of view. It includes an appendix of some of the principal condemnations relating to issues in Descartes's philosophy, going as far back as the Condemnation of 1277. In addition to these works, a number of theses at which he presided survive. There is no modern edition of his writings.

Secondary Sources: Jourdain, Charles (1887), *Histoire de l'Université de Paris au XVIIe et au XVIIIe siècle,* Paris, pièces justificatives, pp. 133–4. Rosenfield, Leonora Cohen (1957), 'Peripatetic Adversaries of Cartesianism in 17th Century France', *Review of Religion* 22:14–40. Gilson, Etienne (1967), *Etudes sur le rôle de la pensée médiévale dans la formation du système cartésien,* 3d ed., Paris: Vrin, pp. 316–17. [Daniel Garber]

DU HAMEL, JEAN-BAPTISTE b. Vire, 1624; d. Paris, 1706. Duhamel entered the Oratorians in 1643, leaving ten years later in 1653 to become the curé of Neuilly-sur-Marne, then later the almonier to Louis XIV and the chancelier of the church of Bayeaux. In 1666 Colbert named him the secretary of the Académie des Sciences. He is best known in philosophy for his textbooks which attempt to reconcile various old and new schools of philosophy. These works include his *De consensu veteris et novae philosophiae* (Paris, 1663) and his *Philosophia vetus et nova ad usum scholae accomodata* (4 vols.) (Paris, 1678). Other philosophical works include the *De mente humana* (Paris, 1672). In addition, Du Hamel wrote a number of works on physics, mathematics, and theology. He spent his last years working on a history of the Académie des Sciences and the Bible. There is no standard edition of his writings.

Secondary Sources: *BHPC* I 556–7. Vialard, Augustin (1884), *J.-B. Du Hamel,* Paris: G. Téqui.Rosenfield, Leonora Cohen (1957), 'Peripatetic Adversaries of Cartesianism', *Review of Religion* 22:14–40. [Daniel Garber]

DUPLEIX, SCIPION b. Condom, 1569; d. (?), 1661. Scholastic philosopher and French historian. Studied at the Collège de Guyenne at Bordeaux, became maître des requêtes of Marguerite de Valois and followed her to Paris in 1605. He then became king's historian, in the service of Cardinal Richelieu. His historical writings have been strongly criticised; this was so even in his own time. From 1603 to 1610, he wrote an extremely well-received French-language philosophy textbook: *Corps de philosophie* (Geneva, 1623 with more than ten other editions up to Rouen, 1645), containing *La Logique* (Paris, 1603), *La Physique* (Paris, 1603), *La suite de la physique* (Paris, 1604), *La Metaphysique* (Paris, 1610), *L'Ethique* (Paris, 1610), *Les causes de la veille et du sommeil, des songes et de la vie et de la mort* (Paris, 1606), and *La curiosité naturelle redigée en questions, selon l'ordre alphabetique* (Paris, 1606), English transl., *The Resolver or Curiosities of Nature* (London, 1635). These treatises were also published separately several times; the first five were republished recently, Paris: Fayard, 1984–94. During a period when most scholastics leaned towards Thomism, he was rather eclectic, defending other doctrines, those of John Duns Scotus and Julius Scaliger, for example. In his textbook, he often responded with disdain to the doctrines of 'Saint Thomas Aquinas and his followers'. His historical work, most of which was also published several times, included *Les lois militaires touchant le duel* (Paris, 1602); *Mémoires des Gaules* (Paris, 1619); *Histoire générale de la France,* 3 vols. (Paris, 1621–8); *Histoire de Henri III* (Paris, 1630); *Histoire de Henri le Grand* (Paris, 1632); *Histoire de Louis le Juste* (Paris, 1633); *Continuation de l'histoire du règne de Louis le Juste* (Paris, 1648); *Histoire Romaine depuis la fondation de Rome* (Paris, 1644); *Liberté de la langue françoise dans sa pureté* (Paris, 1651). [Roger Ariew]

ELISABETH OF BOHEMIA, Princess Palatine b. Heidelberg, 1618; d. Herford, 1680. Philosophical correspondent of Leibniz, Malebranche, and other notable philosophers. Eldest daughter of Elector

Palatine and King of Bohemia, Frederick V, and Elizabeth Stuart, daughter of King James I of England, who in 1620 lost the throne of Bohemia and the Palatine possessions to Catholic forces. Lived with relatives in Silesia and at nine rejoined her family, who eventually found refuge in Holland. Tutored at the Prinsenhof in Leiden in Scripture, Latin, Greek, French, German, English, mathematics, the sciences, history, and law. In 1642, read Descartes's *Meditationes*. Descartes expressed a desire to meet her, which probably first took place at the court of her mother in The Hague. On 6 May 1643, she began an extensive philosophical correspondence with Descartes that lasted until the latter's death in 1650. They discussed mind–body interaction, free will, and divine providence, the sovereign good, impartiality in ethics, the immortality of the soul, and the doctrine of the passions. In 1644, Descartes dedicated his *Principia Philosophiae* to her; his *Passions de l'âme* (Paris, 1649) was first composed for her. In 1646, after a scandal that resulted in the murder of Monsieur L' Espinay at the hands of her brother Philip, she was sent by her mother to relatives in Grossen, then to Heidelberg, and finally to Cassel, where she attempted to interest German professors in Descartes's work. In 1667, she entered a Protestant convent at Herford and eventually became the abbess. In 1670, invited her former learned correspondent, Anna Maria van Schurman, and the religious reformer Jean de Labadie to settle in Hereford. Later invited Quaker leaders William Penn and Robert Barclay to her convent and exchanged letters with both. In the last years of her life, corresponded with Malebranche and with Leibniz; was impressed with the mystical philosophy of Jacob Böhme. Her letters are published in the following editions: Descartes 1964–74; Malebranche 1958–84; Penn, W. (1981), *Papers of William Penn*, ed. M. Dunn and R. Dunn, Philadelphia: University of Pennsylvania Press; *Reliquiae Barclaianae: Correspondence of Colonel Barclay and Robert Barclay of Urie and His Son Robert, including Letters from Princess Elizabeth of the Rhine, the Earl of Perth, the Countess of Sutherland, William Penn, George Fox and Others . . .* (London, 1870).

Secondary Sources: Foucher de Careil, L. (1862), *Descartes et la Princesse Palatine, ou de l'influence du cartésianisme sur les femmes au XVIIe siècle*, Paris: Auguste Durand. Foucher de Careil, L. (1909), *Descartes, la princesse Elisabeth et la reine Christine*, Paris: Felix Alcan. Godfrey, E.[ Jessie Bedford, pseud.] (1909), *A Sister of Prince Rupert: Elizabeth Princess Palatine and Abbess of Herford*, New York: John Lane Co. Adam, C. (1917), *Descartes, ses amitiés féminines*, Paris: Boivin. Néel, M. (1946), *Descartes et la princesse Elisabeth*, Paris: Elzévir. Petit, L. (1969), *Descartes et la princesse Elisabeth*, Paris: A. G. Nizet. Zedler, B. (1989), 'The Three Princesses', *Hypatia* 4: 1. Schiebinger, L. (1989), *The Mind Has No Sex? Women in the Origins of Modern Science*, Cambridge, Mass.: Harvard University Press. Harth, E. (1992), *Cartesian Women: Versions and Subversions of Rational Discourse in the Old Regime*, Ithaca: Cornell University Press. [Eileen O'Neill]

EUSTACHIUS A SANCTO PAULO (Eustache de Saint-Paul, Asseline) b. Paris, 1573; d. Paris, 1640. French scholastic philosopher and theologian. Studied at the Sorbonne and received his doctorate in 1604. Entered the Cistercian congregation of the Feuillants (1605), where he held various prominent functions. Very influential in the French Catholic revival. Wrote two classical textbooks, *Summa philosophiae quadripartita de rebus dialecticis, moralibus, physicis, et metaphysicis* (Paris, 1609 and more than a dozen editions until 1649, with the *Ethica* being published separately until 1693), a work that Descartes held to be the typical 'scholastic' textbook in philosophy, and *Summa theologiae tripartita* (Paris, 1613–16). He also wrote *Addresse spirituelle contenant une facile pratique de se perfectionner en la voye au salut* (Paris, 1624) and *Exercices spirituels contenant plusieurs méditations très efficaces pour retirer les âmes du péché et les avancer aux vertus chrestiennes et religieuses et à la parfaite union d'amour avec Dieu* (Paris, 1630).

Secondary Sources: Lejeune, Antoine de Saint-Pierre (1646), *Vie du R. P. Eustache de Saint-Paul Asseline*. Paris; Standaert, M (1961), 'Eustache de Saint-Paul Asseline', in Marcel Viller et al. (eds.) (1932–95), *Dictionnaire de spiritualité ascetique et mystique* (17 tomes in 21 vols.), Paris: Beauchesne, t. 4, col. 1701–5; Gilson, E. (1982), *Index scolastico-cartésien*, 2d ed., Paris: Alcan. [Jean-Robert Armogathe]

FABRI, HONORÉ (Fabry, Fabrius) b. Virieu-le-Grand, Ain, 1608; d. Rome, 1688. Natural philosopher, mathematician, theologian. Entered Jesuit order 1626; studied at Collège de la Trinité, Lyon 1628–36; studied at Collegio Romano 1632–3. Ordained 1635; taught at Jesuit colleges at Arles 1636–8, Aix-en-Provence 1638–9; professor of philosophy and mathematics at Lyon 1640–6. Published *Philosophiae tomus primus* based on his lectures (Lyon, 1646), also *Tractatus physicus de motu locali* (Lyon, 1646); criticises Descartes's concept of subtle matter. After year at Jesuit residence in Fréjus, Var, moved to Rome 1647, which remained his chief residence, and entered Jesuit Minor Vatican Penitentiary. Defended Jesuits against Pascal's criticisms 1659; criticised Christiaan Huygens's ring interpretation of the appearance of Saturn 1660, backed down 1665. Rumoured to have been involved in placing of Descartes's works on Index 'donec corrigantur' 1663. Discussed motion of earth (rejected for lack of conclusiveness) and Grimaldi's work on light in *Dialogi physici* (Lyon, 1669); published major work on natural philosophy, *Physica,* in same year (Lyon, 1669). Wrote major defence of probabilism 1670, for which suffered short term of imprisonment in 1672. Rehabilitated thereafter, although the book remained on the Index.

Secondary Sources: Sommervogel, C., et al. (1890–1932), *Bibliothèque de la Compagnie de Jésus* (11 vols.), Brussels: Schepens, entry in 3:512–22. Fellmann, E. A. (1959), 'Die Mathematischen Werke von Honoratus Fabry', *Physis* 1:6–25, 73–102. Boehm, A. (1965), 'L'Aristotélisme d'Honoré Fabri', *Revue des sciences religieuses* 39:305–60. Fellmann, E. A. (1971), 'Fabri, Honoré', in *DSB.* Lukens, D. C. (1979), 'An Aristotelian Response to Galileo: Honoré Fabri, S.J. (1608–88) on the Causal Analysis of Motion', Ph.D. diss., University of Toronto. Caruso, E. (1987), 'Honoré Fabri gesuita e scienziato', in *Miscellanea scentesca: Saggi su Descartes, Fabri, White* (Universita' degli Studi di Milano Facolta' di Lettere e Filosofia, Quaderni di Acme 8), Milan: Cisalpino-Goliardica, pp. 85–126. [Peter Dear]

FÉNELON, FRANÇOIS DE SALIGNAC DE LA MOTHE b. Sarlat (Périgord), 1651; d. Cambrai, 1715. Born into nobility, Fénelon was educated at home before attending the Jesuit college at Cahors (1663–5?), then the Collège du Plessis in Paris (1666?), entering the Séminaire de Saint-Sulpice in 1672 or 1673. He was ordained in 1674 or 1675 and received a doctorate in theology from the Université de Cahors in 1677. He served in the parish of Saint-Sulpice from 1675 to 1678, then became the Superior in the Congrégation des Nouvelles Catholiques from 1678 to 1689, where he dealt with the instruction of Protestent women who had converted to Catholicism and was involved in other efforts to convert the Protestants that followed the revocation of the Edict of Nantes in 1685. By the late 1680s, Fénelon was a protégé of the powerful Bishop Jacques-Bénigne Bossuet, and from 1689 to 1699 he served as the tutor to the grandson of Louis XIV, the duc de Bourgogne. In 1693, he was elected to the Académie Française, and in 1695 he was made archbishop of Cambrai. During these years he was associated with Mme Guyon, under attack for quietism. This led to a break with Bossuet and his banishment by the king to Cambrai in 1697, where he was to remain until his death. The king also dismissed him as tutor in 1699; that same year the Pope condemned a number of propositions found in Fénelon's work. Fénelon was a prolific author, writing in a number of different genres. His first important work was connected with his work at the Congrégation des Nouvelles Catholiques, the *Traité de l'Education des filles* (Paris 1687); there were other pedagogical writings connected with his role as tutor. Also important are his political writings, some of which are connected with his role as royal tutor; these include *Lettre à Louis XIV* (1693–4?) and *Examen de conscience sur les devoirs de la royauté* (1697?), both published after his death. Of the numerous religious writings, the most important was a defence of a variety of mysticism (*L'Explication des Maximes des Saints sur la vie intérieure* (Paris, 1697)), written in defence of his views during the unfortunate 1690s. He is also the author of an important didactic novel, . . . *Les Avantures de Télémanque, fils d'Ulysse* (Paris, 1699), written for his royal student. Fénelon also left a voluminous correspondence, much of which has been published. In 1687, at the request of Bossuet, Fénelon composed a response to Malebranche, *Réfutation du système de la nature et de la grâce,* which remained unpublished until after his death. His most important philosophical work was the *Démonstration de l'existence de Dieu, Tirée de la connoissance de la Nature et proportionée à la faible intelligence des plus simples.* Part I, written during his years at Cambrai, was published in Paris, 1712; an expanded edition, including what was represented as a part II, actually a previously unpublished independent work, written probably in the late 1680s and showing the clear influence of Cartesian ideas, appeared in Paris, 1718, after the author's death, with a new edition containing yet more early material published in Paris, 1731. There were a number of collected editions of his writings after his death. Most important are Fénelon (1820–30), *Oeuvres,* ed. J. E. M. Gosselin and A. Caron (35 vols.), Versailles; Fénelon (1848–52), *Oeuvres complètes de Fénelon . . .* (10 vols.), Paris; Fénelon (1870–8), *Oeuvres de Fénelon . . . ,* ed. Aimé Martin (3 vols.), Paris. The complete correspondence is in the process of being published in Fénelon (1972–    ), *Correspondance de Fénelon,* ed. J. Orcibal, Paris: Klincksieck. There is no complete modern edition of his writings, though the first volume of an edition has appeared in the *Pleiade* series, Fénelon (1983–    ), *Oeuvres,* ed. J. Le Brun, Paris: Gallimard. There is a new critical edition of his most important philosophical work, Fénelon (1990), *Traité de l'existence de Dieu,* ed. J.-L. Dumas, Paris: Editions Universitaires. There are also modern editions of his literary and spiritual works.

Secondary Sources: *BHPC* II 264–304. Carcassonne, Ely (1946), *Fénelon, l'homme et l'oeuvre,* Paris: Boivin. Goré, Jeanne-Lydie (1957), *L'itinéraire de Fénelon: Humanisme et Spiritualité,* Paris: Presses Universitaires de France. Gouhier, Henri (1977), *Fénelon Philosophe,* Paris: Vrin. Davis, James Herbert, Jr. (1979), *Fénelon,* Boston: Twayne. Cognet, Louis (1991), *Crépuscule des Mystiques,* Paris: Desclée. [Daniel Garber]

FLUDD, ROBERT b. Bearsted, Kent, England, 1574; d. London, 1637. Born to a prosperous family, Fludd received a traditional education at St. John's College, Oxford, and received an M.D. degree in 1605 from Christ's Church, Oxford. A successful practitioner of medicine, Fludd nevertheless found time to engage in philosophical debates and to conduct and direct experiments in his own chemical laboratory. A loyal member of the Church of England, Fludd also defended the elusive Rosicrucians who called for a new learning to be based upon Christian doctrine and a new reading of Scripture. Thus despite his ties to the most conservative and most traditional institutions of seventeenth-century England – the university, the profession of medicine, and the Church of England – Fludd was remarkably innovative in his calls to reform human knowledge. Fludd is chiefly remembered for his defence of the occult sciences and his call to include astrology, alchemy, and natural magic within the embrace of university learning. In doing so, Fludd encountered the bitter criticisms of his contemporaries, including Pierre Gassendi, Johannes Kepler, and Marin Mersenne. As a critic of Aristotelian and Galenic orthodoxies in the universities, Fludd turned to Scripture and Hermetic and Platonic texts for inspiration and authority. Fludd's philosophy leaned heavily on the analogy of the macrocosm and microcosm, a heavily used concept of Hermeticists and alchemists. Indeed, his most prominent published work was a two-part explication of this analogy, the *Utriusque cosmi majoris scilicet et minoris, metaphysica, physica atque technica historia* (Oppenheim and Frankfurt, 1617–21), which appeared in a number of parts. Also important is an early work defending the Rosicrucians, *Apologia compendiaria Fraternitatem de Rosea Cruce suspicionis maculis aspersam varitatis quasi Fluctibus abluens et abstergens* (Leiden, 1616); there was a second, expanded edition published under the title *Tractatus apologeticus integritatem Societatis de Rosea Cruce defendens* (Leiden, 1617). Also interesting are his responses to Kepler, *Veritatis proscenium . . .* (Frankfurt, 1621), to Mersenne, *Sophiae cum moria certamen* (Frankfurt, 1629), and Gassendi, *Clavis philosophiae et alchemiae* (Frankfurt, 1633). There are also a number of medically related texts, the *Anatomiae Amphitheatrum . . .* (Frankfurt, 1623) and *Medicina catholica, seu Mysticum artis medendi sacrarium* (Frankfurt, 1629–31). His final major work, *Philosophia Moysaica,* appeared posthumously in Gouda, 1638. A modern edition and English translation of the *Utriusque cosmi majoris* (ed.

Patricia Tahil and Adam McLean, Grand Rapids: Phanes Press, 1992) is available. Readers should also consult the recent edition of a Fludd manuscript by Allen Debus (1979), *Robert Fludd and His Philosophicall Key*, New York: Science History Publications.

Secondary Sources: Recent biographies include: Huffman, William (1988), *Robert Fludd and the End of the Renaissance*, London: Routledge. Hutin, Serge (1971), *Robert Fludd (1574–1637), alchimiste et philosophe rosicrucien*, Paris: Editions de l'Omnium litteraire. See also: Pagel, Walter (1935), 'Religious Motives in the Medical Biology of the Seventeenth Century', *Bulletin of the Institute of the History of Medicine*, 3:97–132. Yates, Frances (1964), *Giordano Bruno and the Hermetic Tradition*, Chicago: University of Chicago Press. Debus, Allen (1965), *The English Paracelsians*, New York: Franklin Watts. Yates, Frances (1972), *The Rosicrucian Enlightenment*, London: Routledge and Kegan Paul. Debus, Allen (1977), *The Chemical Philosophy: Paracelsian Science and Medicine in the Sixteenth and Seventeenth Centuries*, New York: Science History Publications. [Martha Baldwin]

FONTENELLE, BERNARD LE BOVIER DE b. Rouen, 1657; d. Paris, 1757. Man of Letters, historian, scientist, philosopher of science. A seminal figure of the early Enlightenment and the first modern populariser of science. Educated at the Jesuit collège in Rouen; studied law; pursued an unsuccessful career as a lawyer. Produced libretti for two tragic operas (*Psyché*, Paris, 1678; *Bellérophon*, Paris, 1679). Composed the *De l'origine des fables* 1680 (published Paris 1724; critical edition ed. J. R. Carré, Paris: Alcan, 1932). Wrote the modestly successful *Lettres galantes* (Paris, 1683; revised Paris, 1685). Created his literary reputation with the two-part *Nouveaux dialogues des morts* (part I: Paris, 1683; part II: Paris, 1684). Published *Histoire des oracles* anonymously in Paris, 1686 (critical edition, ed. L. Maigron, Paris: E. Cornély, 1908). Published the satirical *Relation de l'ile de Bornéo* in *Nouvelles de la République des Lettres* (1686). Turned to the popularisation of science with *Entretiens sur la pluralité des mondes* (Paris and Lyon, 1686) (critical edition, ed. R. Shackleton 1955, Oxford: Oxford University Press), which popularised a Copernican (heliocentric) astronomy based on Cartesian vortices. Published *Poésies pastorales* containing the controversial 'Digression sur les Anciens et les Modernes' (Paris, 1688). Elected to the Académie Française 1691. Became perpetual secretary of the Académie Royale des Sciences 1697, and began writing his remarkable *éloges*. Elected to the Académie des Inscriptions 1701. Between 1699 and 1740, he worked almost exclusively on the *Histoire de l'Académie royale des sciences*. The first volume, for the year 1699, appeared in Paris, 1702. In all, forty-two volumes appeared. Of particular interest is the *Histoire de l'Académie royale des sciences . . . depuis son établissement en 1666, jusqu'à 1699* (Paris, 1733), covering the early years of the Académie. The first collection of his celebrated *éloges* appeared as *Histoire du renouvellement de l'Académie* (Paris, 1708), followed by expanded collections in 1717, 1722, and 1733. Published *Eléments de la géométrie de l'infini* (Paris, 1727), and his Cartesian physics, *Théorie des tourbillons cartésiens* (Paris, 1752), a strong presentation of the mechanical philosophy in physics. The *Traité de la liberté*, on religion and metaphysics, is ascribed to Fontenelle, as are four other pamphlets that appeared together with it as a sceptical tract under the title *Nouvelles libertés de penser* (Amsterdam and Paris, 1743). The standard edition of his works is Fontenelle (1825), *Oeuvres de Fontenelle*, ed. G. Depping (5 vols.), Paris, which does not include the *Histoire de l'Académie royale des sciences*.

Secondary Sources: Maigron, L. (1906), *Fontenelle, l'homme, l'oeuvre, l'influence*, Paris: Plon-Nourrit. Carré, J.-R. (1932), *La Philosophie de Fontenelle ou le sourire de la raison*, Paris: Alcan. Consentini, J. W. (1953), *Fontenelle's Art of Dialogue*, New York: King's Crown. Marsak, L. M. (1959), 'Bernard de Fontenelle, The Idea of Science in the French Enlightenment', *Transactions of the American Philosophical Society*, vol. 49, pt. 7. [David Lux]

FOUCHER, SIMON b. Dijon, 1644; d. Paris, 1696. Theologian, philosopher. A critic of Cartesian philosophy and proponent of academic scepticism. Honorary canon at Sainte Chapelle in Dijon.

Moved to Paris, obtained bachelor's degree in theology at Sorbonne; became chaplain on Rue Saint-Denis. In Paris, came into contact with Rohault and other Cartesians. According to Baillet, he was asked to give funeral oration upon return of Descartes's remains to Paris in 1667. Acquaintance with Leibniz on latter's stay in Paris in 1672–6, followed by philosophical correspondence from 1676 to 1695 (letters published in *Journal des Sçavans*, 1692–6). Published *Dissertations sur la recherche de la vérité, ou sur la logique des academiciens* in Dijon, 1673. Engaged in polemic with Malebranche over theory of ideas and Cartesian metaphysics in *Critique de la recherche de la vérité* (Paris, 1675) and *Réponse pour la critique à la préface du second volume de la recherche de la vérité* (Paris, 1676). Composed expositions and defences of Academic philosophy, *Dissertations sur la recherche de la vérité ou La logique des academiciens* (Paris, 1673), *L'apologie des academiciens* (Paris, 1687), and *L'histoire des academiciens* (Paris, 1693). Responded to Desgabets's response to his critique of Malebranche in *Nouvelle dissertations sur la recherche de la vérité, contenant la réponse à la critique de la critique de la recherche de la vérité* (Paris, 1679).

Secondary Sources: Baillet, A. (1691), *La vie de Monsieur Descartes*, Paris. BHPC. Rabbe, F. (1867), *Etude philosophique sur l'abbé Simon Foucher*, Paris: Didier. Gouhier, H. (1927), 'La première polemique de Malebranche', *Revue d'histoire de la philosophie*, 1:168–91. Popkin, R. H. (1957), 'L'abbé Foucher et le problème des qualités premières', *Bulletin de la societé d'étude du XVIIe siècle* 33:633–47. Popkin, R. H. (1965), 'The High Road to Skepticism', *American Philosophical Quarterly*, 2:18–32. Watson, R. A. (1966), *The Downfall of Cartesianism*, The Hague: Nijhoff; reissued in Watson (1987), *The Breakdown of Cartesian Metaphysics*, Atlantic Highlands, N.J.: Humanities Press. Watson, R. A. (1969), 'Introduction', in Simon Foucher, *Critique de la recherche de la vérité*, New York: Johnson. Radner, D. (1978), *Malebranche*, Amsterdam: Van Gorcum. Lennon, T. M. (1980), 'Philosophical Commentary', in Nicolas Malebranche, *The Search after Truth*, trans. T. M. Lennon and P. Olscamp, Columbus: Ohio State University Press. [Steven Nadler]

FROMONDUS, LIBERTUS (Libert Froidmont) b. Haccourt, 1587; d. Louvain, 1653. Professor at the University of Louvain, first rhetoric (1609–14), then philosophy (1614–28), then after receiving his doctorate in 1628, theology (1628–53). Succeeded his friend Jansenius in chair in Sacred Scripture; shortly after helped in the publication of the main text of the Jansenist movement, Jansenius's *Augustinus* (Louvain, 1640). Published *Meteorologicorum libri VI* (Antwerp, 1627). Published *Labyrinthus sive de compositione continui* (Antwerp, 1631), an attack on contemporary Epicurean atomism, particularly at Louvain, which he continued in a pamphlet, *Causae desperatae Gisb. Voetii . . . adversus spongiam . . . D Corn. Hansenii . . . crisis* (Antwerp, 1636). Attacked Copernicanism in *Ant-Aristarchus* (Antwerp, 1631) and *Vesta, sive Ant-Aristarchi vindex . . .* (Antwerp, 1634). He was one of the small circle of savants who corresponded with Descartes on the publication of the *Discours*. Other scientific and philosophical works include *Brevis anatomia hominis* (Louvain, 1641); *Chrysippus, sive de libero arbitrio* (Louvain?, 1644); *Philosophiae christianae de anima libri quatuor* (Louvain, 1649). He also left a number of theological writings and biblical commentaries.

Secondary Sources: Monchamp, Georges (1892), *Galilée et la Belgique*, Saint-Troud: Moreau-Schouberechts. Ceyssens, Lucien (1957), *Sources relatives aux débuts du jansénisme et de l'antijansénisme (1640–3)* (Bibliothèque de la Revue d'histoire ecclésiastique, 31), Louvain: Bibliothèque de l'Université. Ceyssens, Lucien (1964), 'Le janséniste Libert Froidmont', in Ceyssens, *Jansenistica Minora*, Malines: Editions Saint-François, vol. 8. [Jean-Robert Armogathe and Daniel Garber]

GALILEI, GALILEO b. Pisa, 1564; d. Arcetri (near Florence), 1642. Italian natural philosopher. Studied at Pisa, becoming lecturer in mathematics, 1592; wrote *De motu*, 1590–2. Became lecturer in mathematics at Padua, 1592–1610. Constructed a telescope and made observations of the moon and the moons of Jupiter, which he described in *Siderius nuncius* (Venice, 1610). Moved to Florence as 'Chief Philosopher and Mathematician' to the court of the Grand Duke of Tuscany (1610–42).

Published *Discorso intorno alle cose che stanno in su l'acqua* (Florence, 1612) and *Letters to Mark Welser* on sunspots (Rome, 1613); wrote *Letter to Castelli* on the relation between science and faith (Rome, 1613) and *Letter to the Grand Duchess Christina* on the use of biblical quotations in matters of science (1615; published with Latin trans., Strassburg, 1636). Denounced to Inquisition for support of Copernican theory, 1615; went to Rome to defend theory, 1615–16. Church condemned Copernicanism, 1616. Published *Il Saggiatore* (Rome, 1623) and *Dialogo sopra i due massimi sistemi del mondo* (Florence, 1632). In 1633, he was summoned to Rome, forced to retract his views, and confined for life, first at Rome, then at Arcetri. Published *Discorsi e dimostrazioni matematiche intorno a due nuove scienze* (Leiden, 1638). The standard edition of his writings is Galilei (1890–1909), *Opere*, ed. A. Favaro (20 vols.), Florence: Barbera.

Secondary Sources: Caverni, R. (1891–1900), *Storia del metodo sperimentale in Italia* (6 vols.), Florence: Cirelli (repr. Bologna, 1970). Santillana, G. de (1955), *The Crime of Galileo*, Chicago: University of Chicago Press. Drake, S. (1970), *Galileo Studies*, Ann Arbor: University of Michigan Press. Clavelin, M. (1974), *The Natural Philosophy of Galileo*, Cambridge Mass.: MIT Press. Koyré, A. (1978), *Galileo Studies*, Atlantic Highlands, N.J.: Humanities Press. Drake, S. (1978), *Galileo at Work*, Chicago: University of Chicago Press. Galluzzi, P. (1979), *Momento: studi galileiani*, Rome: Edizioni dell'Ateneo and Bizzarri. Carugo, A. and Crombie, A. C. (1983), 'The Jesuits and Galileo's Ideas of Science and of Nature', *Annali dell'istituto e Museo di storia della scienza di Firenze*, 8: 3–68. Wallace, W. A. (1984), *Galileo and His Sources*, Princeton: Princeton University Press. Redondi, P. (1987), *Galileo Heretic*, Princeton: Princeton University Press. Blackwell, R. J. (1991), *Galileo, Bellarmine, and the Bible*, Notre Dame: University of Notre Dame Press. Wallace, W. A. (1992), *Galileo's Logic of Discovery and Proof*, Dordrecht: Kluwer. [Roger Ariew]

GASSENDI, PIERRE (Gassend, Gassendus) b. Champtercier, Provence, 1592; d. Paris, 1655. Philosopher, theologian, humanist scholar, experimental physicist, and astronomer. The century's most prominent advocate of Epicureanism, especially of its atomist ontology and empiricist epistemology. Received a doctorate in theology in 1614 and was ordained a priest two years later. Conducted astronomical observations from 1618 until his death. Argued against Aristotelianism in his first extant work, the *Exercitationes paradoxicae adversus Aristoteleos* (part I, Grenoble, 1624; part II published posthumously). Began his life's main project of the Christian rehabilitation of Epicurus ca. 1626. Travelled to the Low Countries in 1628–9, meeting Beeckman and Van Helmont, among others. Spent five extended periods in Paris, totalling some fifteen years. Early on, he became acquainted with Mersenne there and later knew Hobbes and Pascal, among others; was identified with the libertinage érudit of the Tétrade; finally was appointed to the chair of mathematics (astronomy) at the Collège Royal. Corresponded with Galileo 1625–37; first published principle of inertia, in defence of Copernicanism, *De motu impresso a motore translato epistolae duae* (Paris, 1642). Wrote *Objectiones Quintae* to Descartes's *Meditationes* (Paris, 1641), which were also published with Descartes's replies and his long rebuttals of those replies in *Disquisitio metaphysica* (Amsterdam, 1644). The first part of two decades of work on Epicurus appeared as *De vita et moribus Epicuri* (Lyon, 1647), and *Animadversiones in decimum librum Diogenis Laertii* (Lyon, 1649). His principal work is the *Syntagma philosophicum*, published posthumously in his *Opera omnia* (Lyon, 1658), which is still the standard edition of his works.

Secondary Sources: Bougerel, J. (1737), *Vie de Pierre Gassendi*, Paris. Rochot, B. (1944), *Les Travaux de Gassendi sur Epicure et l'atomisme: 1619–58*, Paris: Vrin. Gregory, T. (1961), *Scetticismo ed empirismo: Studio su Gassendi*, Bari: Laterza. Bloch, O. R. (1971), *La Philosophie de Gassendi: Nominalisme, matérialisme, et métaphysique*, The Hague: Nijhoff. Jones, H. (1981), *Pierre Gassendi, 1592–1655: An Intellectual Biography*, Nieuwkoop: De Graaf. Joy, L. S. (1987), *Gassendi the Atomist*, Cambridge: Cambridge University Press. Brundell, B. (1987), *Pierre Gassendi: From Aristotelianism to a New Natural Philosophy*, Dordrecht: D. Reidel. Osler, Margaret J. (1994), *Divine Will and the Mechanical Philosophy:*

*Gassendi and Descartes on Contingency and Necessity in the Created World,* Cambridge: Cambridge University Press. [Thomas Lennon]

GEULINCX, ARNOLD (Arnout) b. Antwerp, 1624; d. Leiden, 1669. Metaphysician, moralist, logician. Studied at Louvain, where he also taught philosophy from 1646 until 1658. In that year he was dismissed, probably for religious reasons, and went to Leiden, where he acquired a doctorate in medicine and taught logic, first as lecturer and later as professor extraordinary. Apart from *Quaestiones quodlibeticae in utramque partem disputatae* (Antwerp, 1653; Leiden, 1665) and the *Disputatio medica inauguralis de febribus* (Leiden, 1658), Geulincx himself published two works on logic – *Logica fundamentis suis, a quibus hactenus collapsa fuerat, restituta* (Leiden, 1662), and *Methodus inveniendi argumenta quae solertia quibusdam dicitur* (Leiden, 1663) – and the *De virtute et primis ejus proprietatibus tractatus ethicus primus* (Leiden, 1665), the first part of his *Ethica,* which he also translated into Dutch (Leiden, 1667). Other treatises were published posthumously: the complete *Ethica* (Leiden, 1675), *Physica vera* (Leiden, 1688), *Compendium physicae* (Franeker, 1688), *Annotata praecurrentia ad Renati Cartesii Principia* (Dordrecht, 1690), *Annotata maiora in Principia philosophiae Renati des Cartes* (Dordrecht, 1691), *Metaphysica vera et ad mentem Peripateticam* (Amsterdam, 1691). The standard edition is Geulincx (1891–3), *Opera philosophica,* ed. J. P. N. Land. (3 vols.), The Hague: Nijhoff.

Secondary Sources: Van der Haeghen, V. (1886), *Geulincx: Etudes sur sa vie, sa philosophie et ses ouvrages,* Ghent: Hoste (this contains a bibliography of Geulincx's works). Land, J. P. N. (1895), *Arnold Geulincx und seine Philosophie,* The Hague: Nijhoff. Terraillon, C. (1912), *La morale de Geulincx dans ses rapports avec la philosophie de Descartes,* Paris: Alcan. De Vleeschauwer, H. J. (1953–4), 'Les antécédents du transcendentalisme: Geulincx et Kant', *Kant-Studien* 45:245–73. De Vleeschauwer, H. J. (1957), *Three Centuries of Geulincx Research* (Communications of the University of South-Africa, 1), Pretoria: University of South Africa. Mancini, I. (1957), 'Una battaglia contro la metafisica classica nel seicento: Arnoldo Geulincx', *Rivista di filosofia neoscolastica.* 49:476–500. De Vleeschauwer, H. J. (1958), 'L'opera di Arnold Geulincx: Bibliografia e evoluzione', *Filosofia* 9:197–220, 592–615. De Lattre, A. (1967), *L'occasionalisme d'Arnold Geulincx: Etude sur la constitution de la doctrine,* Paris: Minuit. Cooney, B. (1978), 'Arnold Geulincx. A Cartesian Idealist', *Journal of the History of Philosophy,* 16:167–80. Nuchelmans, G. (1988), *Geulincx' Containment Theory of Logic* (Mededelingen van de Koninklijke Nederlandse Akademie van Wetenschappen, Afdeling Letterkunde, Nieuwe reeks, deel 51, no. 8), Amsterdam-Oxford-New York: North-Holland. [Gabriel Nuchelmans]

GILBERT, WILLIAM b. Colchester, Essex, England, 1544; d. London, 1603. Natural philosopher and physician. Educated at St. John's College, Cambridge (M.A. 1564). Elected fellow of the college and served as its mathematical examiner and senior bursar. Moved to London to practice medicine two or three years after he had obtained M.D. at Cambridge, in 1569. Elected fellow of the Royal College of Physicians in 1577; later served several times as censor and treasurer of the College before being elected its president in 1600. In that year he also published his ground-breaking treatise, *De Magnete* (London, 1650). His *De mundo nostro sublunari philosophia nova* was published posthumously in Amsterdam, 1651 [repr. Amsterdam: Menno Hertzberger, 1965].

Secondary Sources: Roller, Duane H. D. (1959), *The De Magnete of William Gilbert,* Amsterdam: Hertzberger. Kelly, M. S. (1965), *The De Mundo of Wiliam Gilbert,* Amsterdam: Menno Hertzberger. Abromitis, Lois I. (1977), 'William Gilbert as Scientist', Ph.D. diss., Brown University. Kay, Charles D. (1982), 'William Gilbert's Renaissance Philosophy of the Magnet', Ph.D. diss., Pittsburgh. Carter, Richard B. (1982), 'Gilbert and Descartes: The Science of Conserving the Compound Body', *Zeitschrift fur Allgemeine Wissenschaftstheorie,* 13:224–33. Gad Freudenthal (1983), 'Theory of Matter and Cosmology in William Gilbert's *De Magnete'*, *Isis* 74:22–37. Pumfrey, S. P. (1987), 'William Gilbert's Magnetical Philosophy, 1580–1674', Ph.D. diss., University of London. [Mordechai Feingold]

GLANVILL, JOSEPH b. Plymouth, 1636; d. Bath, 1680. Divine and polemicist. Studied at Oxford 1652–60 (M.A. 1658). While still at Oxford, he became an admirer of Henry More, whose *The Immortality of the Soul* pre-empted Glanvill's own book on the subject. Failing to find advancement at Oxford, in 1660 Glanvill accepted a living in Essex. In London, in 1661, he published his first book, *The Vanity of Dogmatizing,* in which he assaulted scholaticism as well as his alma mater. A year later, he published *Lux Orientalis* (London, 1662) and received a vicarage in Somersetshire. He was to remain in that county for the rest of his life, primarily at the Abbey Church in Bath. In response to Thomas White's censure of *Vanity,* Glanvill recast the book and published it under the title *Scepsis Scientifica* (London, 1665). In a shrewd dedication to the Royal Society, he joined a personal vindication with a defence of the nascent Society, and the grateful assemply promptly conferred a fellowship on Glanvill. In London, in 1668, he published *Plus Ultra,* another defence of the new science as well as of the author's reputation from charges of religious heterodoxy. This book, however, embroiled him in a bitter and protracted dispute with Henry Stubbe. When the dust settled, half a dozen books later, Glanvill's career as an apologist for the new science was largely over. Among his later works, mention should be made of *Some Philosophical Considerations Touching Witches and Witchcraft* (London, 1666); later editions are published under the title *A Blow at Modern Sadducism.* Henry More published an expanded version, including some of his own writings on the same subject under the title *Saducismus triumphatus; or, Full and plain evidence concerning witches and apparitions* (London, 1681; 2d ed., London, 1682; 3d ed., London, 1689). Also of interest are *Essays on Several Important Subjects* (London, 1676); *An Essay concerning Preaching* (London, 1678). There is no collected edition of his writings. There are numerous modern reprints of his works, but no modern edition.

Secondary Sources: Cope, Jackson I. (1956), *Joseph Glanvill Anglican Apologist,* St. Louis: Washington University. Jobe, Thomas H. (1981), 'The Devil in Restoration Science: The Glanvill-Webster Debate', *Isis* 72:342–56. Talmor, Sascha (1981), *Glanvill: The Uses and Abuses of Scepticism,* Oxford: Pergamon. Steneck, Nicholas H. (1981), '"The Ballad of Robert Crosse and Joseph Glanvill" and the Background to *Plus Ultra*', *British Journal for the History of Science,* 14:59–74. Lupoli, A. (1984), '"Scetticismo moderato" e aristotelismo antiscolastico: La polemica tra Joseph Glanvill e Thomas White', in *La storia della filosofia come sapere critico: studi offerti a Mario Dal Pra,* Milan: Angeli. Sutliff, Kristene G. (1985), 'The Influence of the Royal Society on the Prose Style of Joseph Glanvill', Ph.D. diss., Oklahoma State University. Pauschert, Uwe (1994), *Joseph Glanvill und die Neue Wissenschaft des 17. Jahrhunderts,* Frankfurt: Lang. [Mordechai Feingold]

GOCLENIUS, RUDOLPHUS (Rudolf Göckel) b. Corbach, 1547; d. Marburg, 1628. German philosopher. First studied at Corbach, then at the University of Marburg, 1564, and the University of Wittenberg, 1568. Became magister at Marburg in 1571. Rector of Stadschule, Corbach, 1573–5; rector of Stadschule, Kassel, 1575–81. Professor of natural philosophy at Marburg, 1581; from 1589, professor of logic; taught mathematics, 1598–1609; and from 1603 also held the chair of ethics. Many times dean; rector in 1611. Published his most famous work, the *Lexicon philosophicum* (Frankfurt, 1613). Also published numerous works, probably intended for scholastic use, including *Organon cum sylloge annotationum* (Marburg, 1590), *De sensu et sensibilibus* (Frankfurt, 1596), *Organon per theoremata* (Frankfurt, 1597), *Problemata logica* (Frankfurt, 1597), *Isagoge in Organon Aristotelis* (Frankfurt, 1598), *Isagoge in peripateticorum et scholasticorum primam philosophiam* (Frankfurt, 1598). [Roger Ariew]

GOURNAY, MARIE LE JARS DE b. Paris, 1565; d. Paris, 1645. Editor of Montaigne's *Essais;* writer of feminist, moral, and theological tracts; translator, literary and philological theorist, poet, and novelist. An autodidact, she mastered Latin and translated Diogenes Laertius's *Life of Socrates* in her youth. At eighteen or nineteen became an admirer of the early essays of Montaigne, secured a meeting with him in 1588, and became such an intimate friend that he referred to her as his 'adopted daughter.' This inspired her novel *Le Proumenoir de Monsieur de Montaigne* . . . (Paris, 1594, 1595, 1599; Chambéry, 1598; repr. Delmar, N.Y.: Scholars' Facsimiles and Reprints, 1985). In 1594, Montaigne's widow sent her the final manuscript of his *Essais*; Gournay published an edition of it, together with a long 'Préface' defending the work against all contemporary criticisms, in Paris, 1595. There are six versions of the preface: shortened ones in the editions of 1598, 1600, 1604, 1611; versions of the original longer one in the editions of 1617, 1625, 1635. Defended the Jesuits against the charge that they were responsible for the assassination of King Henry IV in *Adieu de l'âme du roy de France . . . avec La Défence des Pères Jésuites* (Paris and Lyon, 1610); was herself attacked in the *Anti-Gournay* (n.d.) and in *Remercîment des beurrières* (Niort, 1610). Published classical translations in *Versions de quelques pièces de Virgile, Tacite et Saluste* . . . (Paris, 1619) and a feminist tract, *Egalité des hommes et des femmes* (n.p., 1622), reprinted in all collected works. Her first collection of essays, *L'Ombre de la Damoiselle de Gournay* (Paris, 1626), included literary and philological essays, essays on education, morals, feminist issues, as well as poetry and translations from the *Aeneid* and the works of Tacitus, Sallust, Ovid, and Cicero. Expanded editions later appeared under the title *Les Advis ou Les Presens de la Demoiselle de Gournay* (Paris, 1634, 1641). Became well known for her defence of old terms in the French language and the poetry of the Pléiade against Malherbe and other Moderns. During her last years, participated in the salons of the Duchess de Longueville and the Comtesse de Soissons; her own salon included La Mothe le Vayer, Abbé de Marolles, and Guillaume Colletet and was, arguably, the seed from which the French Academy grew. Corresponded with Anna Maria van Schurman, Justus Lipsius, Saint Francis de Sales, La Mothe le Vayer, Abbé de Marolles, Madame de Loges, Guez de Balzac, and Cardinal Richelieu. Her correspondence with Lipsius appears in Payen, J.-F. (1862), 'Recherches sur Montaigne: Correspondance relative à sa mort,' *Bulletin du Bibliophile*. Some of her writings have been reprinted in Gournay (1987), *Fragments d'un discours féminin,* ed. E. Dezon-Jones, Paris: Corti.

Secondary Sources: Somaize, A. de (1660), *Le Grand Dictionnaire des Précieuses,* Paris. La Forge, J. de (1663), *Le Cercle des femmes sçavantes,* Paris. Baillet, A. (1694), *Jugemens des Savans sur les principaux ouvrages des auteurs,* 8 vols., Paris. Bayle, P. (1697) *Dictionnaire Historique et Critique,* Paris. *Menagiana* (1754), 4 vols., Paris. Sainte-Beuve, C.-A. (1828), *Tableau historique et critique de la Poésie Française et du Théâtre Français au XVIe siècle,* Paris. Feugère, L. J. (1860), *Les Femmes poètes du XVIe siècle,* Paris. Bonnefon, P. (1898), *Montaigne et ses amis,* Paris: Colin. Schiff, M. (1910), *La Fille d'Alliance de Montaigne, Marie de Gournay,* Paris: Champion. Richards, S. A. (1914), *Feminist Writers of the Seventeenth Century* , London: University of London, M.A. thesis. McDowell Richardson, L. (1929), *The Forerunners of Feminism in French Literature from Christine of Pisa to Marie de Gournay,* Baltimore: Johns Hopkins University Press. Ilsley, M. H. (1963), *A Daughter of the Renaissance: Marie Le Jars de Gournay, Her Life and Works,* The Hague: Mouton. Albistur, M. and D. Armogathe (1977), *Histoire du féminisme français,* tome 1, Paris: Des femmes. Bijvoet, M. (1989), 'Editor of Montaigne: Marie de Gournay,' *Women Writers of the Seventeenth Century,* ed. K. Wilson and F. Warnke, Athens, Ga.: University of Georgia Press. Zedler, B. (1989), 'Marie Le Jars de Gournay,' *A History of Women Philosophers,* vol. 2, ed. M. E. Waithe, Dordrecht: Kluwer. [Eileen O'Neill]

GROTIUS, HUGO (Huig de Groot) b. Delft, 1583; d. Rostock, 1645. 'The father of modern international law', humanist scholar and man of action: historian, theologian, legal philosopher, editor of classical texts, Latin poet, lawyer, politician, diplomat. Educated University of Leiden from 1694; doctor of law, University of Orleans 1598. Member of diplomatic missions to France 1598 and 1599. Barrister in the Hague 1599. Defence of his country's right to free trade overseas in *De Indis* (1604–5). This work was only rediscovered and published in 1868 as *De iure praedae,* though Chapter 12 appeared as the controversial *Mare liberum* (Leiden, 1609); see esp. John Selden's reply, *Mare clausum* (London, 1635). Historiographer of Holland 1606. Leading role in negotiations with England 1613 and 1615 about East India trade. Rapid republican career (Pensionary of Rotterdam 1613) under Jan van

Oldenbarnevelt ended abruptly 1619 with the latter's execution for treason and Grotius's sentence to life imprisonment and famous escape to Paris (1621). *De iure belli ac pacis* published Paris, 1625. Lifelong schemes for reunification of the Christian churches; rapprochement with Catholicism; hugely influential *De veritate religionis christianae* appeared in Leiden, 1627. Attempted return to Amsterdam 1631; outlawed, fled to Germany 1632–4. Councillor to Queen Christina of Sweden, her ambassador to France 1634. In Paris from 1635, recalled 1645, left Stockholm without prospects or clear destination, died following shipwreck. Huge *oeuvre* in nearly all humanistic disciplines. There is no standard edition of works. For the correspondence, see Grotius (1928–      ), *Briefwisseling*, The Hague: Nijhoff (vols. 1–11); Assen/Maastricht: van Gorcum (vol. 12); The Hague: Instituut voor Nederlandse Geschiedenis (vol. 13).

Secondary Sources: Brandt, K. and A. van Cattenburgh (1727), *Historie van het Leven des Heeren Huig de Groot* (2 vols.), Dordrecht and Amsterdam. Burigny, J. L. de (1752; Engl. trans. 1754), *Vie de Grotius,* Paris. Knight, W. S. M. (1925), *The Life and Works of Hugo Grotius* (Grotius Society Publications no. 4), London: Sweet and Maxwell. Vollenhoven, C. van (1931), *The Framework of Grotius' Book De Jure Belli ac Pacis (1625),* Amsterdam: North-Holland. Chroust, A.-H. (1943). 'Hugo Grotius and the Scholastic Natural Law Tradition', *The New Scholasticism* 17:101–33. Ter Meulen, J., and P. J. J. Diermanse (1950), *Bibliographie des écrits imprimés de Hugo Grotius,* The Hague: Nijhoff. *Grotiana* (edited by Vereeniging voor de uitgave van Grotius), vols. 1–10, The Hague, 1928–42. Diesselhorst, M. (1959), *Die Lehre des Hugo Grotius vom Versprechen,* Cologne and Graz: Böhlau. Remec, P. P. (1960), *The Position of the Individual in International Law according to Grotius and Vattel,* The Hague: Nijhoff. Hägerström, A. (1965), *Recht, Pflicht und bindende Kraft des Vertrages nach römischer und naturrechtlicher Anschauung,* ed. K. Olivecrona, Stockholm: Almqvist and Wiksell, and Wiesbaden: Harrassowitz. Dumbauld, E. (1969), *The Life and Legal Writings of Hugo Grotius,* Norman: University of Oklahoma Press. Tuck, R. (1979), *Natural Rights Theories.* Cambridge: Cambridge University Press, chap. 3. Edwards, C. S. (1981), *Hugo Grotius. The Miracle of Holland.* Chicago: Nelson-Hall. Haggenmacher, P. (1983), *Grotius et la doctrine de la guerre juste,* Paris: Presses Universitaires de France. Tuck, R. (1983), 'Grotius, Carneades and Hobbes', *Grotiana,* n.s. 4:43–62 (1984), *The World of Hugo Grotius (1583–1645),* Amsterdam and Maarssen: APA-Holland University Press. Haakonssen, K. (1985), 'Hugo Grotius and the History of Political Thought', *Political Theory* 13:239–65. Paech, N. (1985), *Hugo Grotius,* Berlin: Argument-Verlag. Buckle, S. (1991), *Natural Law and the Theory of Property. Grotius to Hume,* Oxford: Oxford University Press, chap. 1. Tuck, Richard (1993), *Philosophy and Government 1572–1651,* Cambridge: Cambridge University Press. *Grotiana,* N. S., vol. 1 (1980–      ), Assen: van Gorcum. [Knud Haakonssen]

HEEREBOORD, ADRIAAN (Adrianus) b. Leiden 1614; d. Leiden 1661. Logician and early Cartesian philosopher. Professor of logic and ethics at the University of Leiden. Converted to Cartesianism in 1644, engaged in controversy with the anti-Cartesians Jacobus Revius and Adam Stuart, and helped to gain Cartesianism a foothold in the Netherlands. Probably the author of the preface to Descartes's *Notae.* Like his contemporary Cartesians in Leiden, Johannes Clauberg and Johannes de Raey, he was prepared to reconcile elements of the Cartesian system with those of Aristotle. Works include *Disputatio ethica, Disputatio physica de mundo, Disputatio logica* (Leiden, 1642); *Parallelismus Aristotelicae et Cartesianae philosophiae naturalis* (Leiden, 1643); *Sermo extemporaneus de recta philosophice disputandi ratione* (Leiden, 1648); *Meletemata philosophica in quibus pleraeque res metaphysicae ventilantur* (Leiden, 1654); *Philosophia rationalis, moralis et naturalis* (Leiden, 1654); *Praxis logica,* and *Philosophia pneumatica* (Leiden, 1659); and *Philosophia naturalis cum commentariis peripateticis antehac edita . . .* (Leiden, 1663), which includes a discussion of Descartes. There is no standard edition.

Secondary Sources: *BHPC* I. Bohatec, J. (1912), *Die Cartesianische Scholastik in der Philosophie und Theologie der reformierten Dogmatik des 17. Jahrhunderts,* Leipzig: Deichert. Molhuysen, P. C. (1913–24), *Bronnen tot de geschiedenis der Leidsche Universiteit,* 7 vols., The Hague: Nijhoff, vol. 2. Sassen, F. L. R.

(1942–3), 'Adriaan Heereboord: de opkomst van het cartesianisme in Leiden', *Algemeen Nederlands Tijdschrift voor Wijsbegeerte* 36:12–22. Thijssen-Schoute, C. L. (1954), *Nederlands Cartesianisme,* Amsterdam: North-Holland. De Dijn, H. (1973), 'Spinoza's Geometrische Methode van Denken', *Tijdschr Filosof* 35:707–65. De Dijn, H. (1983), 'Adriaan Heereboord en het Nederlandse Cartesianisme', *Algemeen Nederlands Tijdschr voor Wijsbegeerte* 75:56–69. Verbeek, T. (1992), *Descartes and the Dutch: Early Reactions to Cartesian Philosophy, 1637–50,* Carbondale: Southern Illinois University Press. [Christia Mercer]

HERBERT OF CHERBURY (Edward Herbert, first Baron Herbert of Cherbury) b. Eyton-on-Severn, 1583; d. London, 1648. Herbert led a colourful life and was an active participant in the politics of his day. Born into a prominent family, Herbert studied at University College, Oxford, from 1596 to 1600. The next years were spent in court politics and public service, first under Elizabeth, then, in 1603, under James I, and in travelling on the Continent, where, among other events, he was entertained by Henri IV of France, and became a volunteer in the army of the Prince of Orange. In 1619, he became the English ambassador in Paris, a position that he held until 1624, when he was abruptly recalled by James because of a disagreement over policy. Back in England, he maintained his active interest in politics for a number of years, until the growing political troubles made it impossible. Though he had been associated with the monarchy in his earlier years, he did his best to remain neutral in the growing battles between Parliament and the Royalists, trying to keep his library and possessions from falling into the hands of either party. In late 1644, Herbert retired to his London house, where he remained, immersed in his studies, until his death four years later. The first of Herbert's philosophical writings is his *De veritate, prout distinguitur a revelatione, a verisimili, a possibili, et a falso* (Paris, 1624), written while he was ambassador in France. In this work, Herbert presents an account of knowledge grounded not in the senses or in tradition, but in innate common notions. He expanded this work in his last years, adding in the third London edition (1645) chapters dealing with error (*de causis errorum*) and religion (*de religione laici*). In the latter, he extends his general account of truth to religion, rejecting revelation and tradition, and grounding religion in a small number of innate religious truths, common to all. These themes are further developed in the posthumously published *De religione gentilium* (Amsterdam, 1663) and *A Dialogue between a Tutor and His Pupil* (London, 1768). In the former, he presents a kind of natural history of religion, arguing that all religions are grounded in his innate religious truths. In the latter, he presents a defence of his rejection of revelation and argues that reason leads us to truth in religion. While widely discussed, his philosophy had few real followers. In addition to these writings, Herbert wrote histories and an autobiography presenting a romantic and extravagant view of his life up until the time he left Paris in 1624. He also wrote poetry and is counted among the followers of John Donne, a family friend, though as a poet, his reputation was eclipsed by that of his rather more reclusive brother, George Herbert. There are facsimile editions of *De veritate,* 3d ed. (Stuttgart: Friedrich Frommann, 1966), of *De religione gentilium* (Stuttgart: Friedrich Frommann, 1967), and of *A Dialogue . . .* (Stuttgart: Friedrich Frommann, 1971). There are no modern editions of his philosophical works, but there are modern translations of *De veritate,* trans. Meyrick H. Carré, Bristol: Arrowsmith, and *De religione laici,* trans. H. R. Hutchenson, New Haven, Conn.: Yale University Press.

Secondary Sources: Rossi, Mario (1947), *La vita, le opere, i tempi di Edoardo Herbert di Chirbury* [*sic*], Florence: Sansoni. Mosner, E. C. (1967), 'Herbert of Cherbury', in *EP.* Bedford, R. D. (1979), *The Defence of Truth: Herbert of Cherbury and the Seventeenth Century,* Manchester: Manchester University Press. Hill, Eugene D. (1987), *Edward, Lord Herbert of Cherbury,* Boston: Twayne Publishers. Lagree, Jacqueline (1989), *Le salut du laic : Edward Herbert de Cherbury: Etude et traduction du De religione laici,* Paris: Vrin. Popkin, Richard H. (1989), *The History of Scepticism from Erasmus to Spinoza,* Berkeley: University of California Press, chap. 8. Butler, John (1990), *Lord Herbert of Chirbury* [*sic*] *(1582–1648): An Intellectual Biography,* Lewiston, N.Y.: Mellen. [Daniel Garber]

HILL, NICHOLAS b. London, c. 1570; d. Rotterdam, c. 1610. Philosopher. Very little is known about Hill's life. He studied at St. John's College, Oxford, and was elected fellow of the college in 1590. However, he was ejected a couple of years later, presumably on account of his conversion to Catholicism, and he probably moved to London. He appears to have been patronised by the earl of Northumberland and Sir Walter Raleigh. Hill may have also been involved in the strange conspiracy of Robert Basset, who laid claim to the English throne, and subsequently found it prudent to flee England c. 1600. He may have practised medicine in Holland, where he is reputed to have died. His only publication was *Philosophia Epicurea, Democritiana, Theophrastica proposita simpliciter, non edocta* (Paris, 1601; another edition, Geneva, 1619), an early contribution to the revival of atomism and a work influenced by the cosmology of Giordano Bruno.

Secondary Sources: McColley, Grant (1939), 'Nicholas Hill and the *Philosophia Epicurea,*' *Annals of Science* 4:390–405. Jean Jacquot (1974), 'Harriot, Hill, Warner and the New Philosophy,' in John W. Shirley (ed.), *Thomas Harriot, Renaissance Scientist,* Oxford: Oxford University Press, pp. 107–28. Hugh Trevor-Roper (1988), 'Nicholas Hill, the English Atomist,' in his *Catholics, Anglicans and Puritans: Seventeenth-Century Essays,* Chicago: University of Chicago Press. [Mordechai Feingold]

HOBBES, THOMAS b. Malmesbury, Wiltshire, 1588; d. Hardwicke Hall, Derbyshire, 1679. Author of comprehensive philosophical system, humanist scholar, polemicist in politics, science, and theology. Educated at Westport Church, at a private grammar school in Malmesbury and at Magdalen Hall, Oxford, 1602–8. B.A. 1608. Spent most of his life as tutor, secretary, financial manager in the service of the earls of Devonshire and their kinsmen, the earls of Newcastle. Met the elderly Bacon in the 1620s. Extensive tutorial travels in Europe brought direct contact with intellectual and political movements and many leading thinkers of the time. First publication a translation of Thucydides, the *Eight bookes of the Peloponnesian warre* (London, 1629). From 1628, focus on the great philosopher-scientists, including Galileo, whom he visited in 1636; Gassendi; and Mersenne, to whose circle he belonged while in Paris in 1635 and who acted as go-between in discussions with Descartes. First formulation of philosophical ideas commonly supposed to be the anonymous *Short Tract on First Principles* (ca. 1630–36?), but there is no clear evidence of authorship. After 1637, political upheavals in England turned Hobbes's attention to political theory. *The Elements of Law, Natural and Politic* (written in 1640; unauthorised publication in two parts in London, 1650, as *Human Nature: or the Fundamental Elements of Policy* and *De Corpore Politico: or the Elements of Law, Moral and Politic;* first complete edition London, 1889) gave theoretical support to royalist argument in the dispute between king and Parliament; this led Hobbes to seek exile in Paris from 1640 to 1651, rejoining the Mersenne circle, where hostile relations with Descartes eventually softened. Contributed the 'Objectiones tertiae' published with Descartes's *Meditationes* (Paris, 1641), began to publish his own system with *Elementorum philosophiae sectio tertia De Cive* (Paris, 1642; English trans. *Philosophical Rudiments concerning Government and Society,* London, 1651, not by Hobbes, as often supposed); section one, *Elementorum philosophiae sectio prima De Corpore* was not published until 1655 in London (English trans. *Elements of Philosophy, The First Section, concerning Body,* London, 1656), and section two, *Elementorum philosophiae sectio secunda De Homine,* not until 1658 in London (partial trans. in Hobbes 1972; corresponds to *Human Nature*). Wrote criticism of Thomas White (1642–3, only published this century, Paris, 1973), contributed *Tractatus opticus* to Mersenne's *Universae geometriae mixtaeque mathematicae synopsis* (Paris, 1644; English trans. 'Thomas Hobbes: *Tractatus opticus*', ed. F. Alessio, in *Rivista critica di storia della filosofia* 18(1963):147–288). In 1646, he became mathematics tutor to the prince of Wales, later Charles II. Seriously ill and near death in 1647. His views antagonised royalist exiles and French government, culminating in publication of *Leviathan, or the Matter, Forme, and Power of a Commonwealth Ecclesiasticall and Civill* (London, 1651; Latin trans. with significant changes London, 1668) which rejected episcopacy (Anglicanism). In 1652, reconciled to the Commonwealth, he returned to England; close to moderate Cromwellian line in church politics; friendly with John Selden in last years. Dislike of both Presbyterianism and Anglicanism led to ongoing theologico-political feuds. A private interchange on free will and determinism with Bishop John Bramhall from 1645 became a public confrontation with Anglicanism upon the unauthorised publication of Hobbes's papers in 1654. A long-running disagreement over geometry incorporated a fierce dispute with Oxford Presbyterianism. Meanwhile, he also wrote extensively on politics, especially on relationship of church and state. The Restoration (1660) saw an *ad hoc* alliance of Anglicanism and Presbyterianism, which, accusing Hobbes of heresy, caused him to fear for his safety. Hobbes was protected by the earl of Arlington, a ministerial colleague of Anthony Ashley Cooper (later earl of Shaftesbury), who had John Locke as an adviser. The two philosophers may have met. Hobbes wrote a series of works, all published posthumously, including *A Dialogue between a Philosopher and a Student of the Common Laws of England* (written 1666?; published London, 1681 with an abridgement of Aristotle's *Rhetoric,* 'The Art of Rhetoric', from 1637) and *Behemoth, or the Long Parliament* (written before 1671; published London, 1679). He wrote two autobiographical accounts, published in 1679 and 1681. Collected works: *Thomae Hobbes Malmesburiensis opera philosophica, quae Latine scripsit, omnia* (Amsterdam, 1668). The standard editions are Hobbes (1839–45), *Opera philosophica quae Latine scripsit omnia,* ed. Sir William Molesworth (5 vols.), London, for the Latin writings, and Hobbes (1839–45), *The English Works of Thomas Hobbes of Malmesbury,* ed. Sir William Molesworth (11 vols.), London, for the English writings. A new collected edition is in progress from Oxford University Press.

Secondary Sources: Blackbourne, R. (1681), *Vitae Hobbianae Auctarium,* London. Aubrey, J. (1898), 'The Life of Thomas Hobbes', in *Brief Lives,* Oxford: Oxford University Press, vol. 1, pp. 321–403. Brandt, F. (1928), *Thomas Hobbes's Mechanical Conception of Nature,* Copenhagen: Levin and Munksgaard. Strauss, L. (1936), *The Political Philosophy of Hobbes,* Oxford: Oxford University Press. MacDonald, H. and M. Hargreaves (1952), *Thomas Hobbes: A Bibliography,* London: Bibliographical Society. Warrender, H. (1957), *The Political Philosophy of Hobbes,* Oxford: Oxford University Press. Macpherson, C. B. (1962), *The Political Theory of Possessive Individualism. Hobbes to Locke,* Oxford: Oxford University Press. Mintz, S. I. (1962), *The Hunting of Leviathan,* Cambridge: Cambridge University Press. Brown, K. (ed.) (1965), *Hobbes Studies,* Oxford: Blackwell. Watkins, J. W. N. (1965), *Hobbes's System of Ideas,* London: Hutchinson. Goldsmith, M. M. (1966), *Hobbes's Science of Politics,* New York: Columbia University Press. McNeilly, F. S. (1968), *The Anatomy of 'Leviathan',* London: Macmillan. Gauthier, D. F. (1969), *The Logic of Leviathan,* Oxford: Oxford University Press. Pocock, J. G. A. (1972), 'Time, History, and Eschatology in the Thought of Thomas Hobbes', in Pocock, *Politics, Language and Time,* London: Methuen, pp. 148–201. Oakeshott, M. (1975), *Hobbes on Civil Association,* Oxford: Blackwell. Sacksteder, W. (1982), *Hobbes Studies (1879–1979): A Bibliography,* Bowling Green, Ohio: Philosophy Documentation Center. Shapin, S., and S. Schaffer (1985), *Leviathan and the Air-Pump,* Princeton, N.J.: Princeton University Press. Hampton, J. (1986), *Hobbes and the Social Contract Tradition,* Cambridge: Cambridge University Press. Johnston, D. (1986), *The Rhetoric of 'Leviathan',* Princeton: Princeton University Press. Kavka, G. S. (1986), *Hobbesian Moral and Political Theory,* Princeton: Princeton University Press. Baumgold, D. (1988), *Hobbes's Political Theory,* Cambridge: Cambridge University Press. Tuck, R. (1989), *Hobbes,* Oxford: Oxford University Press. Lloyd, S. A. (1992), *Ideals and Interests in Hobbes's* Leviathan, Cambridge: Cambridge University Press. Martinich, A. P. (1992), *The Two Gods of* Leviathan, Cambridge: Cambridge University Press. [Knud Haakonssen]

HOOKE, ROBERT b. Freshwater, Isle of Wight, 1635; d. London, 1703. Natural philosopher and early member of Royal Society, noted for his experimental abilities and for suggesting many important physical principles, although he failed to develop any of them systematically. Educated at Westminster School 1649–53; attended Christ Church College, Oxford, 1653, receiving M.A. in 1663. While at Oxford, became active in the intellectual circles which eventually became the Royal Society. Propounded law of elasticity in 1660 and later assisted Boyle with his construction of an air pump. Made curator of experiments by the Royal Society in 1662, elected a fellow of the Royal Society in 1663. Conducted numerous experiments and published many pamphlets and treatises in all areas of natural philosophy, including pneumatics, statics, optics, microscopy, geology, and meterology. Became lecturer in mechanics at Gresham College in 1664 in a position endowed by Sir John Cutler, named professor of geometry at Gresham College in 1665. Published *Micrographia, or Some Physiological Descriptions of Minute Bodies* (London, 1665), recording numerous microscopic observations and physical speculations. Proposed plan for rebuilding city after London fire in 1666 and was made surveyor in 1667, with responsibility for assisting in the supervision of the reconstruction. Reported attempt at a telescopic determination of parallax of fixed star in his *Attempt to Prove the Motion of the Earth by Observations* (London, 1674). Became secretary of the Royal Society upon Oldenburg's death in 1677, an office he held until 1682. Corresponded with Newton in 1678–9 and suggested the inverse square law for attractive forces as well as, arguably, the law of universal gravitation. Published *Lectiones Cutlerianae* on various topics in physics, London, 1679. Engaged in numerous disputes throughout his career, including a quarrel with Newton over optical matters (1672–6), a series of bitter exchanges with Hevelius on astronomy (1668–72), a fight with Huygens and Oldenburg on priority for invention of the spiral watch spring (1675–7), and again with Newton over priority for laws of mechanics (1686–8). The last fifteen years of his life were marked by ill health, and he died in his rooms at Gresham College in 1703. There is no complete edition of his works, but collections are available in Hooke (1705), *Posthumous Works of Robert Hooke,* ed. R. Waller, London; Hooke (1726), *Philosophical Experiments and Observations of the Late Eminent Dr. Robert Hooke,* ed. W. Derham, London; and Gunther, R. W. T. (1923–67), *Early Science in Oxford* (15 vols.), Oxford: for the subcribers, vols. 6–7, 8, 10, and 13. His diary for 1672–80 is published as Hooke (1938), *The Diary of Robert Hooke,* ed. H. W. Robinson and W. Adams, London: Wykeham; for the years 1688–90 it is found in vol. 10 of Gunther 1923–67.

Secondary Sources: Andrade, E. N. da C. (1950), 'Robert Hooke', *Proceedings of the Royal Society* 201A:439–73. Espinasse, M. (1956), *Robert Hooke,* Berkeley: University of California Press. Keynes, G. (1960), *A Bibliography of Dr. Robert Hooke,* Oxford: Oxford University Press. Hesse, M. B. (1966), 'Hooke's Philosophical Algebra', *Isis* 57:67–83. Westfall, R. (1967), 'Hooke and the Law of Universal Gravitation', *British Journal for the History of Science* 3:245–61. Centore, F. F. (1970), *Robert Hooke's Contributions to Mechanics: A Study in Seventeenth-Century Natural Philosophy,* The Hague: Nijhoff. Oldroyd, D. R. (1972), 'Robert Hooke's Methodology of Science as Exemplified in his Discourse of Earthquakes', *British Journal for the History of Science* 6:109–30. Oldroyd, D. R. (1980), 'Some "Philosophical Scribbles" Attributed to Robert Hooke', *Notes and Records of the Royal Society* 41:145–67. Hunter, M. (1989), *Establishing the New Science: The Experience of the Early Royal Society,* Woodbridge, Suffolk: Boydell, pp. 185–244, 279–338. Hunter, M., and S. Schaffer (eds.) (1989), *Robert Hooke: New Studies,* Woodbridge, Suffolk: Boydell. [John Henry and Douglas Jesseph]

HUET, PIERRE-DANIEL b. Caen, 1630; d. Paris, 1721. Literary scholar, linguist, exegete, scientist, bishop. An important Christian sceptic and Cartesian critic. Gained an early reputation as a philologist, literary figure, and scientist. Educated first at the Jesuit Collège du Mont in Caen 1638–46. Left the law faculty of the university in Caen without a degree 1650. Travelled with Samuel Bochart to the court of Christina of Sweden, where he began work on an edition of Origen's commentaries 1652. Elected to membership in the Académie du Grand Cheval in Caen 1653. Published *De Interpretatione Libri duo: quorum prior est de optimo genere interpretandi: alter de claris Interpretibus* (Paris, 1661), a work on exegetic methods. Founded an academy of sciences in Caen 1662. Published the *Origenis commentaria in Sacram Scripturam* (Rouen, 1668). Published an essay on literary history, *Traité de l'origine des romans* (Paris, 1670). Named sous-précepteur au Dauphin 1670. Elected to the Académie Française 1674. Ordained priest 1676. Published *Animadversiones in Manilium et Scaligeri notas* (Paris, 1679). Published

*Demonstratio Evangelica* (Paris, 1679), a flawed attempt at an axiomatic development of faith. Became Abbé d'Aunay 1680. Attacked Cartesians in the *Censura philosophiae cartesianae* (Paris, 1689). Named bishop of Soissons 1685, bulls withheld, named bishop of Avranches 1689, invested 1692. Published the *Alnetanae questiones de concordia rationis et fidei* (Caen, 1690). Treated the geography of the terrestrial paradise in *Traité de la situation du paradis terrestre* (Paris, 1691). Composed the sceptical *Traité philosophique de la foiblesse de l'esprit humain* (written 1692; published Amsterdam, 1723). Published the polemical *Nouveaux mémoires pour servir à l'histoire du cartésianisme* (n.p., 1692). Remitted bishopric of Avranches 1699. Named Abbé de Fontenay 1699; soon retired to the Jésuites de la Maison Professe in Paris, whose library he endowed with 9,000 volumes (now at the Bibliothèque Nationale). Published *Les origines de la ville de Caen et des lieux circonvoisins* (Rouen, 1702; rev. ed., Rouen, 1706); *Dissertations sur diverses matières de religion et de philosophie* (Paris, 1712); *Histoire du Commerce et de la Navigation des Anciens* (Paris, 1716). Published his autobiography, *Commentarius de Rebus ad eum pertinentibus* (Amsterdam, 1718; English trans., John Aiken, London 1810; French, Charles Nisard, Paris 1853). Many selections from his writings have been edited, two are by P. J. d'Olivet, *Huetiana* (Paris, 1722), and D. Aubery, *Daniel Huet, évêque d'Avrances* (Paris: Bonne Press, 1943).

Secondary Sources: Barthomèss, C. (1850), *Huet évêque d'Avranches ou le scepticisme théologique*, Paris. Tolmer, L. (n.d. [1949]), *Pierre-Daniel Huet (1630–1721), Humaniste-physicien*, Bayeux: Colas. Brennan, Katherine Stern (1981), 'Culture and Dependencies: The Society of the Men of Letters of Caen from 1652 to 1705', Ph.D. diss., Johns Hopkins University. Lux, D. S. (1989), *Patronage and Royal Science: The Académie de Physique in Caen*, Ithaca, N.Y.: Cornell University Press. [David Lux]

HUYGENS, CHRISTIAAN b. The Hague, 1629; d. The Hague, 1695. Natural philosopher, mathematician, astronomer. Primarily privately taught; attended van Schooten's mathematics lectures at Leiden; law degree from a college in Breda. His father, Constantijn, was a friend and correspondent of Descartes and launched Christiaan's international career by sending Mersenne the teenager's proof that projectiles follow a parabolic path. Created a new geometrical technique for approximating pi (*De Circuli Magnitudine Inventa*, Leiden, 1654). Invented the pendulum clock (*Horologium*, The Hague, 1658) and used his discovery of the isochronism of the cycloid and his theory of evolutes to build a mathematically improved version (*Horologium Oscillatorium*, Paris, 1673). Wrote the first published treatise on probability, in which he introduced the concept of expectation (*Tractatus de ratiociniis in aleae ludo*, Leiden, 1657). Argued that Saturn, whose largest moon he had discovered, was surrounded by a ring (*Systema Saturnium*, The Hague, 1659). Analysed the impact of bodies, refuting Descartes's laws and advocating the relativity of motion (*De motu corporum ex percussione*, pub. posthumously but presented in outline in 1669). Maintained a wave theory of light and a modified vortex explanation of gravity (*Traité de la lumière . . . avec un discours de la cause de la pesanteur*, Paris, 1690). Leading member of the Académie Royale des Sciences; first foreign member of the Royal Society of London. Analysed centrifugal force; investigated the optical properties of lenses, especially aberration; invented the spiral spring watch (this was contested by Hooke); participated in the development of the air pump and microscope; corresponded with Leibniz and l'Hospital over the calculus and questions in physics. The standard edition of his writings is Huygens (1888–1950), *Oeuvres complètes*, The Hague: Société Hollandaise des Sciences and Nijhoff.

Secondary Sources: Harting, P. (1868), *Christiaan Huygens in zijn Leven en Werken geschetst*, Groningen: Gebroeders Hoitsema. Geer, P. van (1907–12), 'Hugeniana Geometrica', *Nieuw Archief voor Wiskunde*, ser. 2, 7:215–26, 438–54; 8:34–63, 145–68, 289–314, 444–64; 9:6–38, 202–30, 338–58; 10:39–60, 178–98, 370–95. Brugmans, H. L. (1935), *Le séjour de Christian Huygens à Paris et ses relations avec les milieux scientiques français suivi de son journal de voyage à Paris et à Londres*, Paris: Droz. Bell, A. E. (1947), *Christian Huygens and the Development of Science in the Seventeenth Century*, London: Arnold. Dijksterhuis, E. J. (1961), *The Mechanization of the World Picture*, Oxford: Oxford University Press. Elzinga, A. (1972),

*On a Research Program in Early Modern Physics,* Göteborg: Akademiförlaget. Frankfourt, U. I., and A. M. Frenk (1976), *Christiaan Huygens,* trans. [French] I. Sokolov, Moscow: Editions Mir. Bos, H. J. M., et al. (1980), *Studies on Christiaan Huygens: Invited Papers from the Symposium on the Life and Work of Christiaan Huygens, Amsterdam, 22–5 August 1979,* Lisse: Swets and Zeitlinger. Burch, C. B. (1981), 'Christiaan Huygens: The Development of a Scientific Research Program in the Foundations of Mechanics', Ph.D. diss., University of Pittsburgh. *Huygens et la France: Table ronde du Centre National de la Recherche Scientifique, Paris, 27–9 mars 1979* (1982), intro. René Taton, Paris: Vrin. D'Elia, A. (1985), *Christiaan Huygens: Una biografia intellettuale,* Milan: Angeli. Yoder, J. G. (1988), *Unrolling Time: Christiaan Huygens and the Mathematization of Nature,* Cambridge: Cambridge University Press. Shapiro, A. E. (1989), 'Huygens' *Traité de la lumière* and Newton's *Opticks:* Pursuing and Eschewing Hypotheses', *Notes and Records of the Royal Society of London* 43:223–47. [Joella Yoder]

JUNGIUS, JOACHIM b. Lübeck, 1587; d. Hamburg, 1657. Logician, mathematician, natural philosopher. Studied at Rostock, Giessen, and Padua, where he took a degree in medicine in 1618. In 1628, he became rector of the Gymnasium at Hamburg. For his pupils he wrote the *Logica Hamburgensis,* published in Hamburg, 1635 (the first three books) and Hamburg, 1638, and, in a modern edition, with German translation, ed. R. W. Meyer, Hamburg: J. J. Augustin. This handbook of logic, a number of theses, and the *Geometria empirica* (Hamburg, 1627) are the only works published during Jungius's lifetime. Of the many manuscripts he left some were published posthumously: *Doxoscopiae physicae minores* (Hamburg, 1662), *Isagoge phytoscopica* (Hamburg, 1678), *Harmonica* (Hamburg, 1678), *Mineralia* (Hamburg, 1689), *Phoranomica* (Hamburg, 1689), *Historia vermium* (Hamburg, 1691), *Opuscula physica botanica* (Hamburg, 1747). In 1691 a fire in the house of Johannes Vagetius, one of Jungius's pupils, destroyed most of the remaining manuscripts; further damage was caused by the Second World War. Modern editions of source material are available in Jungius (1977), *Joachimi Jungii Logicae Hamburgensis additamenta,* ed. W. Risse, Göttingen: Vandenhoeck and Ruprecht, and Jungius (1982), *Joachim Jungius: Praelectiones physicae, Historisch-kritische Edition,* ed. C. Meinel, Göttingen: Vandenhoeck and Ruprecht.

Secondary Sources: Guhrauer, G. E. (1850), *Joachim Jungius und sein Zeitalter,* Stuttgart-Tübingen. Vogel (or Fogel), M. (1658), *Historia vitae et mortis Joachimi Jungii,* Argentorati. Meyer, A. (ed.) (1929), *Beiträge zur Jungius-Forschung,* Hamburg (with bibliography). Joachim Jungius-Gesellschaft der Wissenschaften (1958), *Die Entfaltung der Wissenschaft, zum Gedenken an Joachim Jungius,* Hamburg: Augustin. Kangro, H. (1969), 'Joachim Jungius und Gottfried Wilhelm Leibniz: ein Beitrag zum geistigen Verhältnis beider Gelehrten', *Studia Leibnitiana* 1:175–207. Trevisani, F. (1978), 'Geometria e logica nel metodo di Joachim Jungius (1587–1657)', *Rivista critica di storia della filosofia* 33:171–208. Schupp, F. (1980), 'Theoria-Praxis-Poiesis'. Zur systematischen Ortsbestimmung der Logik bei Jungius und Leibniz', *Studia Leibnitiana,* Supplementa 21:1–13. Meinel, Chr. (1984), *In physicis futurum saeculum respicio: Joachim Jungius und die naturwissenschaftliche Revolution des 17. Jahrhunderts* (Veröffentlichungen der Joachim Jungius-Gesellschaft der Wissenschaften, Hamburg, 52), Göttingen: Vandenhoeck und Ruprecht. [Gabriel Nuchelmans]

KECKERMANN, BARTHOLOMAEUS b. Danzig, 1571/73; d. Danzig, 1608/9. Protestant theologian, metaphysician. Attended university at Wittenberg (from ca. 1590), Leipzig, and Heidelberg where he took his M.A. (1594). At Heidelberg he taught at the Collegium Sapientiae (from 1597) and, in 1600, he became professor of Hebrew. Returned to Danzig in 1602 where he took up the position of professor of philosophy and rector at the reformist gymnasium. Regarded as the father of modern 'systematic theology'. In philosophy he defended Aristotle against the Ramist School. Wrote textbooks in logic, metaphysics, and ethics, some of which had a considerable influence in susbsequent university teaching during the first half of the seventeenth century, in both Germany and England. Keckermann

1440

*Biobibliographical appendix*

published *Systema logicae* (Hanau, 1600); *Gymnasium logicum* (London, 1606); *Praecognitorum logicorum tractatus III* (Hanau, 1606); *Systema ethicae* (Heidelberg, 1607; London, 1607); posthumously: *Scientiae metaphysicae compendiosum systema* (Hanau, 1609); *Systema physicum* (Hanau, 1612). His metaphysical textbooks were published together posthumously in two volumes: *Systema systematum* (Hanau, 1613). The standard edition of his works is Keckermann 1614, *Operum omnium quae extant tomus primus et secundus* (2 vols), Geneva. Nine letters by Keckermann were published by Th. Schieder (1941), 'Briefliche Quellen zur politischen Geistesgeschichte Westpreussens vom 16.–18. Jahrhundert', in *Altpreussische Forschungen* 18:262–76.

Secondary Sources: Althaus, P. (1914), *Die Prinzipien der ref. Dogmatik im Zeitalter der aristotelischen Scholastik*, Leipzig: Deichert, pp. 18ff., 76ff. Tellkamp, A. (1927), *Über das Verhältnis John Lockes zur Scholastik*, Münster i. W.: Aschendorff. Van Zuylen, W. H. (1934), *Bartholomaeus Keckermann. Sein Leben und Wirken*, diss., Tübingen. Wundt, M. (1939), *Die Deutsche Schulmetaphysik des 17. Jahrhunderts*, Tübingen: Mohr, pp. 70–2, 144–5, and see index. Risse, W. (1964–70), *Logik der Neuzeit*, Stuttgart: Frommann, vol. 1, pp. 440–50. Büttner, M. (1973), *Die Geographia Generalis vor Varenius*, Wiesbaden: Steiner, pp. 172–205. Vasoli, C. (1983), 'Logica ed "enciclopedia" nella cultura tedesca del tardo cinquecento e del primo seicento: Bartholomaeus Keckermann', in *Atti del Convegno internazionale di storia della logica*, ed. V. M. Abrusci et al., Bologna: CLUEB, pp. 97–110. Vasoli, C. (1984), 'Bartholomaeus Keckermann e la storia della logica', in *La Storia della Filosofia come sapere critico: Studi offerti a Mario Dal Pra*, ed. N. Badaloni, Milan: Angeli, pp. 240–59. Muller, R. A. (1984), 'Vera philosophia cum sacra theologia nusquam pugnat: Keckermann on philosophy, theology and the problem of the double truth', in *Sixteenth Century Journal* 15:341–65. Schmitt, C., Q. Skinner, and E. Kessler (eds.) (1988), *The Cambridge History of Renaissance Philosophy*, Cambridge: Cambridge University Press, esp. pp. 632–7. [Udo Thiel]

KEPLER, JOHANNES b. Weil der Stadt, in the Duchy of Württemberg, 1571; d. Regensburg, 1630. Scientific reformer, astronomer and mathematician, remembered today as the discoverer of three laws of planetary motion. Eyesight damaged by smallpox at age four. Raised by grandparents, attended Lutheran seminaries at Adelberg 1584, Maulbronn 1586, University of Tübingen, 1589. Began a lifelong friendship with Michael Maestlin who converted him to Copernicanism. A sincere Christian, his reservations about the Augsburg confession precluded the church career for which he originally trained. In later life, he was excluded from communion by the pastor of the Lutheran congregation at Linz. In Graz, 1594–1600, he served as mathematics teacher at the Protestant seminary, and as district mathematician, achieving notable success in predicting the weather and Turkish invasions. While his prognostications secured him increasingly powerful patrons, his intellectual reputation was founded upon the *Prodromus Dissertationum Cosmographicarum seu Mysterium Cosmographicum* (Tübingen, 1596; 2d ed. with new notes, Frankfurt, 1621) in which he accounts for the numbers, sizes, and distances of the planetary orbits by inscribing and circumscribing the corresponding spheres in the Platonic regular solids. Following this work he conceived a general plan for the reform of the middle sciences based on a quasi-theological vision of divine harmony and geometrical order. Although able to remain in Graz for two years after the expulsion of other Protestant intellectuals, he was finally compelled to leave in 1600. Moving to Prague, he became an assistant to Tycho Brahe and wrote the *Apologia pro Tychone contra Ursum*, unpublished during Kepler's lifetime, but offering valuable evidence of his acquaintance with ancient authorities and his views on methodology. On Tycho's death in the following year, Kepler succeeded him as Imperial Mathematician to Rudolf II, and began an ambitious programme of publication. In *De Fundamentis Astrologia Certioribus* (Prague, 1602), Kepler reformed the ancient astrological doctrine of aspects. In his *Ad Vitellionem Paralipomena, quibus Astronomiae pars Optica traditur* (Frankfurt, 1604), he offered a law of refraction and discussed many optical effects important to astronomy. He wrote astrological works on the great conjunction of 1603 and the nova of 1604 while preparing his major work on astronomy. Published in Prague in 1609, and dedicated to the Emperor, the *Astronomia Nova ΑΙΤΙΟΛΟΓΗΤΟΣ seu Physica coelestis tradita commentariis de motibus stellae Martis* substituted physical reasoning for the geometrical models of all previous astronomical theories and argued the superiority of elliptical orbits with the sun at one focus over the epicyclic geocentrism of Ptolemy, Brahe's geo-heliocentrism, and indeed the partly realised heliocentrism of Copernicus. The first two of Kepler's laws of planetary motion are conventionally located in this work, although the modern reader may be hard pressed to locate succinct statements of either. Responded favourably to Galileo's telescopic discoveries in the *Dissertatio cum Nuncio Siderio* (Prague, 1610) and returned to refraction and the telescope in the *Dioptrice* (Augsburg, 1611). After the forced abdication and subsequent death of Rudolf, Kepler became mathematician to the states of Upper Austria at Linz, while nominally retaining his imperial position. Failed in an attempt to introduce the Gregorian calendar to the German states (1613). Contributed to the origins of the calculus in *Nova Stereometria Doliorum* (Linz, 1615). Presented the culmination of his harmonic approach to cosmology in *De Harmonice Mundi* (Augsburg, 1619), including the third law of planetary motion. The book was dedicated to James I of England, but Kepler declined a subsequent invitation to his court. *Epitome Astronomiae Copernicanae* (Linz and Frankfurt, 1618–21) further presented his ideas on physical astronomy and showed that the Galilean satellites of Jupiter obeyed his laws of planetary motion. Pioneered the use of logarithms in Germany. Secured the release of his mother from protracted charges of witchcraft, 1621. His last major project, the *Tabulae Rudolphinae* (Ulm, 1627), quickly replaced the Alfonsine Tables as the standard work, also included tables of logarithms, atmospheric refraction, and Kepler's enlargement of Tycho's star catalogue, with 1005 entries. Entering the service of Wallenstein in 1628, Kepler moved to Sagan in Silesia, and died of a fever while travelling, at Regensburg in 1630. A satirical fantasy, *Johannes Keppleri Somnium,* appeared posthumously in 1634. C. Frisch edited *Johannis Kepleri Astronomi Opera Omnia,* 8 vols. (Frankfurt, 1858–71). A new and more comprehensive edition, *Johannes Kepler Gesammelte Werke,* began to appear at Munich in 1937, originally under the direction of W. von Dyck and M. Caspar, and has now reached 20 vols. There is also a recent English translation of the *Astronomia Nova,* Kepler (1992), *New Astronomy,* trans. W. H. Donahue, Cambridge: Cambridge University Press.

Secondary Sources: Horrox, J. (1673), *Astronomia Kepleriana, defensa et promota,* Oxford. Small, R. (1804), *An Account of the Astronomical Discoveries of Kepler,* London [repr. Madison: University of Wisconsin Press, 1963]. Bethune, J. D. (1830), *The Life of Kepler,* London. Baumgardt, C. (1951), *Life and Letters of Kepler,* New York: Philosophical Library. Caspar, M. (1959), *Kepler,* trans. C. D. Hellman, London and New York: Abelard-Schuman. Koyré, A. (1961), *La révolution astronomique,* Paris: Hermann. Caspar, M., Rothenfelder, L., and List, M. (1968), *Bibliographia Kepleriana,* 2d ed., Munich: Beck. Hübner, J. (1975), *Die Theologie Keplers zwischen Orthodoxie und Naturwissenschaft,* Tübingen: Mohr. Simon, G., *Kepler: Astronome-Astrologue,* Paris: Gallimard. Chevalley, C. (1980), *Kepler: Les fondements de l'optique moderne,* Paris: Vrin. Field, J. (1984), 'A Lutheran Astrologer: Johannes Kepler', *Archive for History of Exact Sciences* 31:189–272 (includes a translation of *De Fundamentis Astrologiae Certioribus*). Seconds, A. (1984), *Jean Kepler: Le secret du monde,* Paris: Belles Lettres. Jardine, N. (1984), *The Birth of History and Philosophy of Science: Kepler's Defense of Tycho against Ursus with Essays on Its Provenance and Significance,* Cambridge: Cambridge University Press. Field, J. (1987), *Kepler's Geometrical Cosmology,* Chicago: University of Chicago Press. Stephenson, B. (1987), *Kepler's Physical Astronomy,* New York: Springer. [Peter Barker and Douglas Jesseph]

KIRCHER, ATHANASIUS b. Geisa, Abbacy of Fulda (Thuringia), 1602; d. Rome, 1680. A scholar of encyclopaedic learning and interests, his published writings were verbose and wide-ranging. His interests span the subjects of archaeology, musicology, hieroglyphics, medicine, geology, acoustics, mathematical machines, comparative religion, magnetism, and Oriental linguistics. Although raised in Germany and trained in its Jesuit schools, Kircher spent most of his adult life in Rome, where he taught at the Jesuit-run Collegio Romano. Despite the strong commitment of the Society of Jesus to Aristotelian learning and natural philosophy, Kircher's writings evince the heavy influence of Hermetic and Neoplatonic ideas. Religious irenicism also significantly affected this Jesuit, who sought common origins for mankind and believed that all humans worshipped essentially the same god. Like many of his contemporaries, he believed that all human languages descended from an original universal language lost to mankind in his early history. Although he enjoyed a fair, if not unblemished, reputation for erudition among his contemporaries, Kircher and his works were sharply eclipsed after his death. A full modern biography of this complex man has not yet been written. Kircher's published books number more than thirty titles. Most important among these are *Magnes, sive de Arte Magnetica* (Rome, 1641), *Ars magna lucis et umbrae* (Rome, 1646), *Musurgia universalis* (Rome, 1650), *Oedipus Aegyptiacus* (3 vols., Rome, 1652–4), *Mundus subterraneus* (Amsterdam, 1665), *Polygraphia Nova* (Rome, 1663), *Arca noe* (Amsterdam, 1675). Modern editions include a facsimile reprint of the *Phonurgia nova* (New York, 1966) and a recent translation (1987) of his *China Illustrata,* trans. Charles van Tuyl, Muskogee, Okla.: Indian University Press, Balcone College.

Secondary Sources: Godwin, Joscelyn (1979), *Athanasius Kircher, A Renaissance Man and the Quest for Lost Knowledge,* London: Thames and Hudson. Brauen, Fred (1982), 'Athanasius Kircher (1602–80)', *Journal for the History of Ideas* 43:129–34. *Enciclopedismo in Roma Barocca: Athanasius Kircher e il Museo del Collegio Romano tra Wunderkammer e Museo Scientifico* (1986), Venice: Marsilio. Rivosechhi, Valerio, *Esotismo in Roma Barocca: Studi sul Padre Kircher,* Roma: Bulzoni. Iversen, Erik (1993), *The Myth of Egypt and Its Hieroglyphics in the European Tradition,* Princeton: Princeton University Press. [Martha Baldwin]

LA FORGE, LOUIS DE b. La Flèche, 1632; d. 1666(?). The son of a physician, he probably studied at La Flèche, though possibly at the Université d'Angers. Married in 1653, at which time he was identified as a 'docteur en medecine'. Shortly after his wedding, moved to Saumur, a city with an active Oratorian community sympathetic to Cartesian ideas. La Forge became an ardent Cartesian. Together with Gérard van Gutschoven, he provided the illustrations for the 1664 edition of Descartes's *Traité de l'homme,* which appeared with La Forge's extensive annotations. His main work is *Traitté de l'esprit de l'homme* (Paris, 1666), which is intended to carry Descartes's programme in *L'homme* further by discussing in detail the mind and its union with the body. This work is an important statement of the doctrine of occasionalism, which came to dominate the Cartesian school. La Forge (1974), *Oeuvres Philosophiques,* ed. P. Clair, Paris: Presses Universitaires de France, contains a modern edition of his *Traitté de l'esprit de l'homme,* together with a bibliography and biographical sketch.

Secondary Sources: Prost, J. (1907), *Essai sur l'atomisme et l'occasionalisme dans la philosophie cartésienne,* Paris: Paulin. Balz, Albert G. A. (1951), *Cartesian Studies,* New York: Columbia University Press, pp. 80–105. *BHPC* I, chap. 24. Watson, Richard A. (1966), *The Downfall of Cartesianism 1673–1712,* The Hague: Nijhoff, pp. 70–3. Isolle, J. (1971), 'Un disciple de Descartes: Louis de la Forge', *Dix-sept. siècle* 92:99–131. P. Claire (1979), 'Le matérialisme hobbien vu par Louis de la Forge', *Revue international de philosophie* 33:529–30. [Daniel Garber]

LA MOTHE LE VAYER, FRANÇOIS b. Paris, 1588; d. Paris, 1672. Born into a legal family, man of letters, occasional diplomat, and substitute to the procureur-général of the Parlement de Paris 1626. Married to the daughter of the Scottish erudite Adam Blackwood, widow of the Scot George Criton, professor of Greek at the Collège Royal. Member of the Académie Française (1638) and supported by Richelieu. Named preceptor of duke of Orléans (1647) and of King Louis XIV (1652). Widowed; remarried 1664. Continued writing until age eighty-two. His first published work was *Dialogues faits à l'imitation des anciens,* published in two parts, probably in Paris, 1630–3 (?), with false title-pages indicating Frankfurt, 1604 and 1506, respectively. It offers, even more decisively than Charron, a classic exposition of seventeenth-century fideism underpinned by Pyrrhonian scepticism and Middle Stoicism. Later works stress this (*Discours de la contrariété d'humeurs qui se trouve entre certaines nations* (Paris, 1636)) and reiterate his admiration for pagan self-control and submission to the realities of this life (*De la vertu des payens* (Paris, 1642); *De la liberté et de la servitude* (Paris, 1643)). Works published during his tenure as royal tutor include the *Geographie, Morale, Rhétorique, œconomique, Politique, Physique,* and *Logique du Prince* (Paris, 1651–8). His writings are collected in La Mothe le Vayer (1756–9), *Oeuvres* (14 vols.), Dresden; there is also a modern edition of the *Dialogues* (Paris: Fayard, 1988).

Secondary Sources: Etienne, M. (1849), *Essai sur La Mothe le Vayer*, Rennes. Kerviler, René (1879), *François de La Mothe le Vayer, précepteur du duc d'Anjou et de Louis XIV,* Paris. Pintard, René (1943), *Le Libertinage érudit dans la première moitié du XVIIe siècle,* Paris: Boivin. Pintard, René (1943), *La Mothe le Vayer, Gassendi, Guy Patin. Etudes de bibliographie et de critique, suivies de textes inédites de Guy Patin,* Paris: Boivin. Julien Eymard d'Angers, Father (1954), 'Stoicisme et libertinage dans l'oeuvre de François La Mothe le Vayer', *Revue des sciences humaines,* n.s. fasc. 75:259–84. Comparato, Vittor Ivo (1981), 'La Mothe le Vayer dalla critica storica al pirronismo', in Tullio Gregory et al. (eds.), *Ricerche su letteratura libertina e letteratura clandestina nel Seicento,* Florence: La Nuova Italia. Taranto, D. (1987), 'Sullo scetticismo politico di La Mothe le Vayer', *Il pensiero politico* 20:179–99. [Peter Miller]

LAMY, BERNARD b. Mans, 1640; d. Rouen, 1715. Lamy was particularly important as an advocate for Cartesian philosophy within the French university. Lamy was educated first in the Oratorian college in Mans (1657–8), then entered the Oratorian house in Paris (1658–9), before attending the Oratorian collège at Saumur (1659–61). After collège, he taught belles lettres at Vendôme (1661–3) and Juilly (1663–8), where he was probably exposed to Cartesianism, perhaps by Nicolas-Joseph Poisson. Now a priest, Lamy returned to Saumur in 1669, first as a student of theology, then as a teacher of philosophy (1671–3). In 1673, he moved from Saumur to Angers. At Angers he got into considerable trouble for his Cartesianism and for following the teaching of Michel de Bay (Baïus). Expelled from Angers in 1675 for continuing to teach Cartesianism after the ban by Louis XIV, he was exiled to St. Martin-de-Miséré until 1676, when he was sent to Grenoble. In 1677 he was given a chair in theology at the seminary of Grenoble by the bishop Etienne Le Camus. Lamy was in Paris from 1686 to 1689. After an altercation with the archbishop of Paris over his *Harmonia sive concordia quatuor evangelistarum . . .* (Paris, 1689), he was sent to Rouen in 1689, where he stayed for the rest of his life. Lamy was a prolific author whose popular books went through many editions and translations during his life and afterwards. There are a number of scientific and mathematical works, including *Traités de mécanique, de l'équilibre des solides et des liqueurs* (Paris, 1679; nouv. éd. 1687); *Traité de la grandeur en général . . .* (Paris, 1680); *Les élémens de géométrie* (Paris, 1685); *Traité de perspective où sont contenus les fondements de la peinture* (Paris, 1701). During his later years, he was particularly interested in theological issues and published a number of books on those subjects: *Apparatus ad Biblia Sacra* (Grenoble, 1687); *Démonstration de la vérité et de la sainteté de la morale crétienne* (Paris, 1688); *Harmonia sive concordia quatuor evangelistarum . . .* (Paris, 1689); *Traité historique de l'ancienne Pâque des juifs . . .* (Paris, 1693). But he is best known for two pedagogical books, *L'art de parler* (Paris, 1675; 2d ed., Paris, 1676; 3d ed., Paris, 1688; 4th ed., Amsterdam, 1699 and Paris, 1701) and *Entretiens sur les sciences* (Grenoble and Paris, 1683; 2d ed., Lyon, 1694; 3d ed., Lyon, 1706). (He is also the author of a book on poetics, *Nouvelles réflexions sur l'art poétique . . .* (Paris, 1678).) *L'art de parler* was a manual of rhetoric and was widely read and often reprinted. The *Entretiens sur les sciences* is a pedagogical manual, which discusses the proper way to teach a variety of subjects to young students. It shows the clear influences of the Augustinianism of his order, and more recent Cartesian and Malebranchist ideas. There is a modern edition of his *Entretiens sur les sciences,* Lamy 1966. There is no collected edition of his works, or standard modern edition.

Secondary Sources: *BHPC* I 473–7; II 339–44. Girbal, François (1964), *Bernard Lamy (1640–1715). Etude biographique et bibliographique avec les textes inédites,* Paris: Presses Universitaires de France. [Daniel Garber]

LAMY [OR LAMI], DOM FRANÇOIS b. Beauce (Diocese of Chartres), 1636; d. Saint-Denis, 1711. Born of noble ancestry, he bore arms before deciding to join the Benedictines. He was ordained in 1659. Of a quarrelsome nature, Lamy was known for the disputes he got into with philosophers and theologians, including Arnauld, Nicole, and Leibniz; though in many ways a Malebranchist, he fought with even Malebranche himself. His most important philosophical work is *De la connoissance de soi-mesme* (Paris, 1694–8), which shows the deep influence of Malebranche's *De la recherche de la vérité* in its emphasis on the passions, the illusions of the senses, and the imagination. Lamy's metaphysics is more prominent in *Lettres philosophiques sur divers sujets importans* (Paris, 1703) and *Les premiers élémens des sciences, ou Entrée aux connoissances solides . . .* (Paris, 1706), again deeply influenced by Malebranche, and arguing for a Malebranchist view of the relation of mind to body and to God, and defending Malebranche's occasionalism, among other views. Also important is Lamy's refutation of Spinoza, *Le Nouvel athéisme renversé, ou Réfutation du sistème de Spinosa, tirée pour la plupart de la conoissance de la nature de l'homme* (Paris, 1696). There is no collected edition of his writings, nor is there a modern edition of his works.

Secondary Source: *BHPC* II 363–73. [Daniel Garber]

LAMY, GUILLAUME b. Coutances, 1644(?); d. Paris, 1682(?). Natural philosopher, physician, professor of anatomy. Critic of Aristotelian and Cartesian metaphysics; sympathetic to Epicurean atomism. Received M.A. prior to 1668; doctor of medicine, Paris 1672; doctor regent of anatomy, University of Paris. *Lettre à M. Moreau contre les prétenduës utilités de la transfusion du sang* (Paris, 1667). *De principiis rerum* (Paris, 1669 and 1680) discusses Aristotle, Descartes, and Epicurus (via Lucretius). *Discours anatomiques* (Rouen, 1675, 2d ed., Brussels 1679, 1685) is anti-Galenist and anti-teleological, and opposes human-centred interpretation of nature. Honoured by the Medical Faculty of Paris 1676. *Explication mécanique et physique des fonctions de l'âme sensitive* (Paris, 1677, Paris, 1678; 2d ed., Paris, 1681, Paris, 1687) emphasises speculative nature of such explications. Popular with public, frequently engaged in medical polemic. Often obliged to defend anti-teleological anatomy from charges of impiety.

Secondary Sources: Revéillé-Parise, J. H. (1851), 'Etude biographique: Guillaume Lamy', *Gazzette médicale de Paris* 6:497–502. Busson, H. (1948), *La religion des classiques,* Paris: Presses Universitaires de France, pp. 147–64. Roger, J. (1963), *Les sciences de la vie dans la pensée francaise du xviii*ᵉ *siècle,* Paris: Colin, pp. 271–3 and passim. Landucci, S. (1978), 'Epicureismo e anti-finalismo in Guillaume Lamy', *Rivista Critica di Storia della Filosofia* 33:153–67. Kors, A. (forthcoming), *Atheism in France 1650–1729,* vol. 2, *Naturalism and Disbelief,* Princeton: Princeton University Press. Plantefol, L., 'Guillaume Lamy', in *DSB.* [Gary Hatfield]

LA SABLIÈRE, MARGUERITE HESSEUB DE b. Paris, 1630(?) 1640(?); d. Paris, 1693. Salonnière, student of natural philosophy and moral maxim writer. Educated in her youth in literature and the arts, including Latin and Greek, she was later taught mathematics, physics, and astronomy by two members of the French Academy: Joseph Sauveur and Giles Persone de Roberval. François Bernier taught her natural history, anatomy, and the doctrines of Descartes and Gassendi; they studied astronomy together. For her, he wrote the *Abrégé de la philosophie de Gassendi* (1674, 1675, 1678). From 1669 to 1680, her salon on the rue Neuve-des-Petits-Champs attracted such notables as La Fontaine, Molière, Racine, Huet, Perrault, Fontenelle, Bernier, Roberval, Mme de Maintenon, Marquise de Lambert, Ninon l'Enclos, Marquise de Sévigné, Mme de Lafayette, and Queen Christina of Sweden.

Bayle described her renown as an intellect in the *Nouvelles de la République des Lettres,* Sept. 1685. La Fontaine addressed to her his 'Discours à Madame de La Sablière' in Book IX of his *Fables,* wherein he argued against Descartes's doctrine of the beast-machine. Boileau attacked what he took to be the intellectual pretensions of the women of her salon in his *Satire sur les femmes* (1694); he portrayed her as ruining her sight and complexion by observing Jupiter at night, astrolabe in hand. Perrault defended her intellectual and moral virtues in his *Apologie des femmes* 1694. In the 1680s, converted to Catholicism and spent the last years of her life in seclusion at Les Incurables tending the sick. Of her published writing, we have only the maxims attributed to her which appeared in La Rochefoucauld 1705; her *Pensées chrétiennes* and some letters appear in Menjot-d'Elbenne, S., Vicomte (1923), *Mme de la Sablière, ses pensées chrétiennes et ses lettres à l'abbé de Rancé,* Paris: Plon-Nourrit.

Secondary Sources: Pellisson et d' Olivet (1743), *Histoire de l'Academie française,* Paris. Walckenaer, C.-A. (1820), *Histoire de la vie et des ouvrages de J. de la Fontaine,* Paris: A. Nepveu. Monmerqué (1862), *Lettres de Madame de Sévigné,* éd. des grands écrivains, Paris: Hachette. Menjot-d'Elbenne, S., Vicomte (1923), *Mme de la Sablière, ses pensées chrétiennes et ses lettres à l'abbé de Rancé,* Paris: Plon-Nourrit. Ogilvie, M. B. (1986), *Women in Science: Antiquity through the Nineteenth Century,* Cambridge, Mass.: MIT Press. [Eileen O'Neill]

LE CLERC, JEAN b. Geneva, 1657; d. Amsterdam, 1736. After theological studies in Geneva, he travelled extensively in Europe, read Spinoza's *Tractatus theologico-politicus,* and started a correspondence with the Remonstrant theologian Philippus van Limborch (1633–1712). In 1683 he settled permanently in Amsterdam, where he became a minister of the Remonstrant Brotherhood and was given a chair in philosophy at their seminary. In his own philosophical views, he was basically Cartesian, but not dogmatically so, modifying and correcting Descartes's thoughts in the light of Locke, Boyle, and Newton, as well as the Platonism of Cudworth. He also believed that a consistent application of Descartes's principles was of very great use in establishing the truth of the Christian religion. His main philosophical works include *Logica sive ars ratiocinandi* (Amsterdam, 1692; reprinted many times, also in London and Cambridge); *Physica sive de rebus corporeis* (Amsterdam, 1695; repr. many times in Leiden, Amsterdam, London, and Leipzig); *De l'incrédulité où l'on examine les motifs et les raisons générales qui portent les incrédules à rejeter la religion chrétienne* (Amsterdam, 1696; repr. several times until 1733; English translation: *A treatise on the causes of incredulity,* London 1697, 1720), as well as editions of Erasmus (*Opera omnia,* 10 vols., Leiden 1703–6) and Hugo Grotius (*De veritate religionis christianae,* Amsterdam 1709). Even more important was Le Clerc's work as a journal editor. In 1686 he started the *Bibliothèque universelle* (25 vols. until 1693), which in 1703 was followed by the *Bibliothèque choisie* (26 vols. until 1713) and in 1714 by the *Bibliothèque ancienne et moderne* (29 vols. until 1730). These journals were instrumental in spawning debates in which Leibniz and Bayle, among others, participated. They also were a channel for the spread of English ideas to the continent, where people learned about Locke, the Cambridge Platonists, Berkeley, and others by reading Le Clerc's abstracts. His extensive correspondence is a testimony of his friendship with many famous contemporaries. The main edition of his works remains Le Clerc (1698), *Opera philosophica* (4 vols.), Amsterdam (repr. 1704, 1710, 1722, and 1726). Some of his correspondence appears in Le Clerc (1959), *Lettres inédites de Le Clerc à Locke,* ed. G. Bonno, Berkeley: University of California Press; Le Clerc and Limbroch (1984), *Arminianesimo e tolleranza nel Seicento olandese: Il carteggio Ph. van Limbroch / Jean Le Clerc,* ed. Luisa Simonutti, Florence: Olschki, 1984; Le Clerc (1987– ), *Epistolario,* ed. M. Sina (2 vols. to date), Florence: Olschki.

Secondary Sources: Haag, E. and E. (1846–58), *La France protestante* (10 vols.), Paris, vol. 6, pp. 464–70. Reesink, H. J. (1931), *L'Angleterre et la littérature anglaise dans les trois plus anciens périodiques de Hollande de 1684 à 1709,* Paris (diss. Amsterdam). Barnes, Annie (1938), *Jean Le Clerc et la République des Lettres,* Paris. Vernière, P. (1954), *Spinoza et la pensée française avant la Révolution* (2 vols.), Paris: Presses Universitaires de France, vol. 1, pp. 73–81. Colie, R. L. (1957), *Light and Enlightenment: A Study of the*

*Cambridge Platonists and the Dutch Arminians,* Cambridge: Cambridge University Press. Bots, H. (1977), 'L'esprit de la République des Lettres et la tolérance dans les trois premiers périodiques savants hollandais', *XVIIe siècle* 116:43–57. Pitassi, M. C. (1987), *Entre croire et savoir: Le problème de la méthode critique chez Jean Le Clerc,* Leiden: Brill. [Theo Verbeek]

LEIBNIZ, GOTTFRIED WILHELM b. Leipzig, 1646; d. Hanover, 1716. Metaphysician, natural philosopher, theologian, mathematician. Attended university at Leipzig (1661–6) and Altdorf (1666–7), graduating with degrees in law and in philosophy. Invited to join the faculty at Altdorf; chose instead to go into public service. Entered the service of the elector of Mainz and occupied a number of positions in Mainz and Nuremberg. Sent on diplomatic business to Paris (1672–6), where he met Huygens and others and did the basic work on his differential and integral calculus. Returned to Germany in 1676, and along the way, stopped in England and Holland, where he met Spinoza. Returned to the court of Hanover as counsellor; served as mining engineer (unsuccessfully supervising the draining of the silver mines in the Harz mountains), as the head librarian, as adviser and diplomat, and as court historian. Wrote, but did not publish, 'Discours de métaphysique', in 1686, and *Dynamica,* 1689–91; published 'Système nouveau de la nature' (*Journal des Scavants,* 1695), and 'Specimen Dynamicum' (*Acta Eruditorum,*1695); wrote, but did not publish, 'De rerum origine radicali' (1697); published 'De ipsa natura' (*Acta Eruditorum,* 1698). Finished *Nouveaux essais sur l'entendement* in 1704 but did not publish it. Published *Théodicée* (Amsterdam, 1710); wrote, but did not publish, 'Principes de la nature et de la grâce' and 'Monadologie', both 1714. Maintained an extensive circle of correspondents, including Foucher, Arnauld, Malebranche, Huygens, De Volder, Des Bosses, Burnett, Lady Masham, and Clarke. The current standard edition of his philosophical writings is Leibniz (1875–90), *Die philosophischen Schriften* (7 vols.), ed. C. I. Gerhardt, Berlin: Weidmannsche Buchhandlung; it will eventually be replaced by Leibniz (1923–    ), *Sämtliche Schriften und Briefe,* ed. Deutsche [before 1945, Preussische] Akademie der Wissenschaften, Berlin: Akademie Verlag. Other important collections of his writings include Leibniz (1768), *Leibnitii opera omnia,* ed. L. Dutens (6 vols.), Geneva; Leibniz (1849–63), *Mathematische Schriften,* ed. C. I. Gerhardt (7 vols.), Berlin and Halle: A. Asher et comp. and H. W. Schmidt; Leibniz (1903), *Opuscules et fragments inédits,* ed. L. Couturat, Paris: Alcan; and Leibniz (1948), *Textes inédits d'après les manuscrits de la bibliothèque provinciale de Hanovre,* ed. G. Grua (2 vols.), Paris: Presses Universitaires de France. Numerous translations are available in many languages.

Secondary Sources: Guhrauer, G. E. (1842), *Gottfried Wilhelm Freiherr von Leibniz: Eine Biographie* (2 vols.), Breslau. Bodemann, E. (1889), *Der Briefwechsel des Gottfried Wilhelm Leibniz in der Königlichen Öffentlichen Bibliothek zu Hannover,* Hanover. Bodemann, E. (1895), *Die Leibniz-Handschriften der Königlichen Öffentlichen Bibliothek zu Hannover,* Hanover. Couturat, L. (1901), *La logique de Leibniz,* Paris: Alcan. Fischer, K. (1920), *G. W. Leibniz: Leben, Werke, und Lehre,* 5th ed., Heidelberg: Winter. Russell, B. (1937), *A Critical Exposition of the Philosophy of Leibniz,* 2d ed., London: Allen and Unwin [1st. ed. 1900]. Ravier, E. (1966), *Bibliographie des Oeuvres de Leibniz,* reprinted Hildesheim: Olms. Gueroult, M. (1967), *Leibniz: Dynamique et métaphysique,* Paris: Aubier. Müller, K. (1967), *Leibniz-Bibliographie: Verzeichnis der Literatur über Leibniz,* Hanover: Klostermann. Müller, K., and G. Krönert (1969), *Leben und Werk von G. W. Leibniz: Eine Chronik,* Frankfurt: Klostermann. Ishiguro, H. (1972), *Leibniz's Philosophy of Logic and Language,* Ithaca: Cornell University Press. Broad, C. D. (1975), *Leibniz: An Introduction,* Cambridge: Cambridge University Press. Aiton, E. J. (1985), *Leibniz: A Biography,* Bristol: A. Hilger. Robinet, A. (1986), *Architectonique disjonctive automates systématiques et idealité transcendentale dans l'oeuvre de G. W. Leibniz,* Paris: Vrin. Mates, B. (1986), *The Philosophy of Leibniz: Metaphysics and Language,* Oxford: Oxford University Press. Wilson, C. (1989), *Leibniz's Metaphysics: A Historical and Comparative Study,* Princeton: Princeton University Press. Sleigh, R. (1990), *Leibniz and Arnauld,* New Haven, Conn.: Yale University Press. Adams, Robert (1994), *Leibniz: Determinist, Theist, Idealist,* Oxford: Oxford University Press. Rutherford, Donald (1995), *Leibniz and the Rational Order of Nature,*

Cambridge: Cambridge University Press. Jolley, Nichloas (ed.) (1995), *The Cambridge Companion to Leibniz,* Cambridge: Cambridge University Press.[Roger Ariew]

LOCKE, JOHN b. Wrington, Somerset, 1632; d. Oates, Essex, 1704. Metaphysician, moral and political philosopher, philosopher of education, economic theorist, theological polemicist, medical doctor, intellectual in politics, and public servant. Educated Westminster School 1647–52, Christ Church, Oxford 1652–8, magister 1658. Remained at Christ Church as student (life-fellow; position withdrawn 1684 by King), studying medicine for years, worked closely with Thomas Sydenham, friend of Boyle, deeply influenced by Descartes, and especially Gassendi, in later 1660s; elected fellow of the Royal Society, 1668. Early conservatism shown in two works only published this century, *Two Tracts on Government* (1660 and 1661; published as Locke 1967b) and lectures on the law of nature delivered as censor of moral philosophy at Christ Church in 1664 (Locke 1954, Locke 1990). In 1667, he joined household of Anthony Ashley Cooper (from 1672 1st Earl of Shaftesbury) as physician and political adviser, remained closely associated with him until his death in 1683. Locke was member of Council of Trade in 1672 when Shaftesbury was lord chancellor. This association saw a drastic change in his political views, and already in 1667 he wrote an essay defending toleration (published in Locke 1961). Worked intermittently on philosophy but chiefly concerned in 1670s and early 1680s with assisting Shaftesbury and his circle in attempts to enforce constitutional limits on the crown's authority and in efforts, from 1679, to exclude the Catholic James, Duke of York, from succession. Like Algernon Sidney and James Tyrrell, Locke wrote against royal absolutism as presented by Sir Robert Filmer. Exact date of *Two Treatises of Government* still disputed, but manuscript kept until safer times. After Shaftesbury's death in exile in Holland in 1683, Locke followed him there later that year. Established wide contacts among the Dutch Arminians and other liberal Protestants, especially after revocation of Edict of Nantes (1685). Being excluded from active politics, he wrote *Essay concerning Human Understanding* and *Epistola de tolerantia.* After Revolution he could return to England in 1689, immediately publishing *Epistola* (Gouda, 1689, with an English trans., London, 1690) and the *Two Treatises of Government* (London, 1690), both anonymously. The *Essay* (London, 1690) was published under his name at the end of the year. Though not uncontroversial (especially important was a dispute with Edward Stillingfleet that began in 1697 and extended through a number of exchanges), it was an immediate success, appearing in four London editions during Locke's lifetime (1690, 1694, 1695, 1700), sometimes with significant revisions, in Latin, French, and in an abridged edition; a fifth edition, in preparation at the time of Locke's death, appeared posthumously in 1706. It was to prove one of the seminal texts of the Enlightenment. Locke was deeply involved in economic and monetary policies of the new government, served on the Board of Trade, and left a significant number of writings on economic questions. His defence of religious toleration extended in polemics: *A Second Letter concerning Toleration* (London, 1690) and *A Third Letter for Toleration* (London, 1692). In London, 1693, appeared *Some Thoughts concerning Education* and in London, 1695, *The Reasonableness of Christianity.* Accused of Socinianism, he defended himself in *A Vindication of the Reasonableness of Christianity* (London, 1695) and *A Second Vindication of the Reasonableness of Christianity* (London, 1697). All his works, except the *Essay,* remained anonymous during his life. By 1700 ill health curtailed his public appointments. He spent the last years of his life living in the household of Lady Damaris Masham at Oates. The old standard edition: *The Works of John Locke* (10 vols.), London, 1823. A new edition was started in 1975 and is still in progress: *The Clarendon Edition of the Works of John Locke,* gen. ed. M. A. Stewart, Oxford: Oxford University Press, which includes nine volumes of correspondence, ed. E. S. de Beer.

Secondary Sources: Le Clerc, J. (1705), *Eloge historique de feu Mr. Locke par Mr. Jean Le Clerc,* in *Bibliotheque Choisie,* VI, and in *Oeuvres diverses . . . ,* 1710; English trans. *The Life and Character of Mr. J. Locke . . . ,* London, 1906. King, Peter (1830), *The Life of John Locke* (2 vols.), London. Yolton, J. W. (1956), *John Locke and the Way of Ideas,* Oxford: Oxford University Press. Cranston, M. (1957), *John*

Locke: A Biography, London: Longmans, Green. Long, P., *A Summary Catalogue of the Lovelace Collection of the Papers of John Locke in the Bodleian Library*, Oxford: Oxford University Press. Macpherson, C. B. (1962), *The Political Theory of Possessive Individualism. Hobbes to Locke*, Oxford: Oxford University Press. Harrison, J. R., and P. Laslett (1965), *The Library of John Locke*, Oxford: Oxford University Press. Dunn, J. (1969), *The Political Thought of John Locke*, Cambridge: Cambridge University Press. Yolton, J. W. (ed.) (1969), *John Locke: Problems and Perspectives*, Cambridge: Cambridge University Press. Yolton, John W. (1971), *John Locke and Education*, New York: Random House. Mackie, J. L. (1976), *Problems from Locke*, Oxford: Oxford University Press. Tully, J. (1980), *A Discourse on Property: John Locke and His Adversaries*, Cambridge: Cambridge University Press. Vaughn, K. I. (1980), *John Locke, Economist and Social Scientist*, Chicago: University of Chicago Press. Hall, R., and R. Woolhouse (1983), *Eighty Years of Locke Scholarship: A Bibliographical Guide*, Edinburgh: Edinburgh University Press. Colman, John (1983), *John Locke's Moral Philosophy*, Edinburgh: Edinburgh University Press. Ashcraft, R. (1986), *Revolutionary Politics and Locke's Two Treatises of Government*, Princeton, N.J.: Princeton University Press. Thompson, M. P. (1987), *Ideas of Contract in English Political Thought in the Age of John Locke*, New York: Garland. Spellman, W. M. (1988), *John Locke and the Problem of Depravity*, Oxford: Oxford University Press. Ayers, M. (1991), *Locke* (2 vols.), London: Routledge. Yolton, J. W. (1991), *Locke and French Materialism*, Oxford: Oxford University Press. Harris, Ian (1993), *The Mind of John Locke: A Study in Political Theory in Its Intellectual Setting*, Cambridge: Cambridge University Press. Tully, James (1993), *An Approach to Political Philosophy: Locke in Contexts*, Cambridge: Cambridge University Press. Chappell, Vere (ed.) (1994), *The Cambridge Companion to Locke*, Cambridge: Cambridge University Press. Marshall, John (1994), *John Locke: Resistance, Religion, and Responsibility*, Cambridge: Cambridge University Press. [Knud Haakonssen]

MALEBRANCHE, NICOLAS b. Paris, 1638; d. Paris, 1715. Philosopher, priest. Educated in scholasticism, including three years at the Sorbonne. Permanently entered the Oratory in 1660 (ordained in 1664); there absorbed one of his two major influences: Augustine. A chance discovery in 1664 of the treatise *L'homme* led to the other: Descartes. His first, longest, and most important work appeared in two volumes in Paris, 1674–5: *De la recherche de la vérité, ou l'on traite de la nature de l'esprit et de l'usage qu'il en doit faire pour éviter l'erreur dans les sciences*. This work appeared in a number of later editions with significant changes, particularly an increasingly long series of *Éclaircissements* that occupied fully a third of the text by the 6th and last ed. Paris, 1712. In this work, Malebranche presents and defends the two doctrines for which he is best known, the extreme occasionalism that denies all causal efficacy to finite things, including minds' internal activities; and his claim that we see all things in God. The *Recherche* elicited two spirited attacks, Simon Foucher's *Critique de la recherche de la vérité* (Paris, 1675) and Antoine Arnauld's *Des vraies et des fausses idées* (Cologne, 1683). Though he disclaimed a taste for polemic, Malebranche engaged in lengthy and sometimes bitter debate with these two antagonists, as well as others, including La Ville [Le Valois] (transubstantiation, 1680), Leibniz (laws of collision, 1686), Régis (horizontal moon, pleasure, 1690), François Lamy (Quietism, 1697). Other important works that develop his metaphysical, epistemological, and theological ideas include *Traité de la nature et de la grâce* (Amsterdam, 1680); *Traité de morale* (Cologne, 1683); *Entretiens sur la métaphysique* (Rotterdam, 1688), expanded with the addition of the *Entretiens sur la mort* (Paris 1696); and *Entretien d'un philosophe crétien et d'un philosophe chinois sur l'existence et la nature de Dieu* (Paris, 1708). Like the *Recherche*, these works went through numerous editions with significant changes. Malebranche also worked in microscopy, influentially discussed the infinitesimal calculus and was elected to the Académie des sciences in 1699. The now standard modern edition of his writings is Malebranche (1958–84), *Oeuvres complètes*, ed. André Robinet (20 vols.), Paris: Vrin.

Secondary Sources: André, Y. M. (1886), *La vie du Père Malebranche, prêtre de l'Oratoire, avec l'histoire de ses ouvrages*, Paris: Poussielgue. Easton, P., Lennon, T. M., and Sebba, G. (1992), *Bibliographia Malebran-*

*chiana: A Critical Guide to the Malebranche Literature Since 1989*, Carbondale: Southern Illinois University Press. Gouhier, H. (1926), *La vocation de Malebranche*, Paris: Vrin. Church, R. W. (1931), *A Study in the Philosophy of Malebranche*, London: George Allen and Unwin [repr. Geneva: Slatkine Reprints, 1970]. Gouhier, H. (1948), *La philosophie de Malebranche et son expérience religieuse*, 2d ed., Paris: Vrin. Gueroult, M. (1955–9), *Malebranche* (3 vols.), Paris: Aubier. Dreyfus, G. (1958), *La volonté selon Malebranche*, Paris: J. Vrin. Rodis-Lewis, G. (1963), *Nicolas Malebranche*, Paris: Presses Universitaires de France. Rome, B. K. (1963), *The Philosophy of Malebranche*, Chicago: Henry Regnery. Robinet, A. (1965), *Système et existence dans l'oeuvre de Malebranche*, Paris: Vrin. Connell, D. (1967), *The Vision in God: Malebranche's Scholastic Sources*, Louvain-Paris: Nauwelaerts. Walton, C. (1972), *De la recherche du bien: A Study of Malebranche's Science of Ethics*, The Hague: Nijhoff. Alquié, F. (1974), *Le cartésianisme de Malebranche*, Paris: Vrin. Radner, D. (1978), *Malebranche: A Study of a Cartesian System*, Assen: Van Gorcum. McCracken, C. J. (1983), *Malebranche and British Philosophy*, Oxford: Oxford University Press. Jolley, Nicholas (1990), *The Light of the Soul: Theories of Ideas in Leibniz, Malebranche, and Descartes*, Oxford: Oxford University Press. Nadler, Steven (1992), *Malebranche and Ideas*, Oxford: Oxford University Press. [Thomas Lennon]

MASHAM, LADY DAMARIS CUDWORTH b. Cambridge, 1658; d. Oates, Essex, 1708. Author of two published books on philosophical theology, the grounds of moral virtue, knowledge and education. Daughter of the Cambridge Platonist Ralph Cudworth, she became acquainted with Locke around 1682 and studied divinity and philosophy with him. After a romantic involvement with Locke, she became the second wife of Sir Francis Masham, Baronet, of Oates in 1685. (In 1691, the ailing Locke came to live in their household until his death in 1704.) The Platonist and defender of Malebranche, John Norris of Bemerton, began to correspond with her in 1684 and dedicated *The Theory and Regulation of Love* (1688) and *Reflections upon the Conduct of Human Life* (London, 1690) to her. In opposition to Norris's *Discourse concerning the Measures of Divine Love* in his *Practical Discourses* . . . vol. III (London, 1693) and *Letters concerning the Love of God* (London, 1695), which argue that since God is the sole cause of our pleasures, he should be the sole object of our love, Masham anonymously published *Discourse concerning the Love of God* (London, 1696). It was translated into French by Coste in 1705. Mary Astell responded to this work, as well as to Locke, in *The Christian Religion as Profess'd by a Daughter of the Church of England* (London, 1705). Masham's views on the education of women, the relative merits of reason and revelation, and the basis of moral virtue were published in *Occasional Thoughts in Reference to a Vertuous or Christian Life* (London, 1705). Masham's correspondence with Locke appears in Locke 1976. Her letters to Leibniz on metaphysical issues, including a defence of her father against Bayle's charge that Cudworth's system led to atheism, are found in Leibniz's published correspondence (Ger. III 336–75). She also sent a defence of her father to Jean Le Clerc for possible publication. She wrote an essay on Locke for the *Great Historical Dictionary*. The manuscript of her biography of Locke is extant, Universitiets-Bibliotheek Amsterdam, Remonstrants's MSS. J. 57a.

Secondary Sources: Ballard, G. (1752), *Memoirs of Several Ladies of Great Britain . . .*, Oxford. Lois Frankel (1991), 'Damaris Cudworth Masham', in M. E. Waithe (ed.), *Modern Women Philosophers, 1600–1900*, Dordrecht: Kluwer. Atherton, M. (1992), 'Cartesian Reason and Gendered Reason', in Antony, L., and Witt, C., (eds.), *A Mind of One's Own: Feminist Essays on Reason and Objectivity*, Westview Press. Hutton, S. (1993), 'Damaris Cudworth, Lady Masham: Between Platonism and Enlightenment,' *British Journal for the History of Philosophy* 1:29–54. [Eileen O'Neill]

MERSENNE, MARIN b. Oizé, Maine, 1588; d. Paris, 1648. Mathematician, musician, natural philosopher. The chief philosophical intelligencer of his time and promoter of mathematical sciences of nature. After elementary grammar training, entered the Jesuit college of La Flèche soon after its founding in 1604; left ca. 1609 to study at the Sorbonne and Collège Royal until 1611, when he entered the order of Minims. Entered Minim convent in Paris in 1619, where he lived for the remainder of his life. Published several apologetic works, most with significant natural philosophical content, between 1623 and 1625, including *Quaestiones in Genesim* (Paris, 1623), *L'impieté des deistes* (Paris, 1624), and *La verité des sciences* (Paris, 1625). Published *Synopsis mathematica* (Paris, 1626), a *vade mecum* of classical geometry, optics, and mechanics, issued in a second edition as *Universae geometriae mixtaeque mathematicae synopsis* (Paris, 1644), with an optical treatise by Thomas Hobbes. Among his works devoted to music were *Traité de l'harmonie universelle* (Paris, 1627) and *Harmonie universelle* (Paris, 1636–7). Acted as the centre of a correspondence network among many philosophers throughout Europe. Championed the works of Galileo, publishing *Les mechaniques de Galilée*, a French paraphrase of an early Galilean work on statics, in Paris, 1634, and *Les nouvelles pensées de Galilée*, paraphrasing material from Galileo's *Discorsi*, in Paris, 1638/9. Served as Descartes's link to the learned world in 1630s and early 1640s, assisting in publication of the *Discours* (Leiden, 1637) and soliciting the 'Objectiones' to the *Meditationes* (Paris, 1641). In 1645 brought news of the Torricellian experiment back to France from a trip to Italy, also reported in *Novarum observationum . . . tomus III* (Paris, 1647). Other compendia of mathematical sciences were the *Cogitata physico-mathematica* (Paris, 1644), and *L'optique et la catoptrique* (Paris, 1651). The publication of Mersenne's extensive surviving correspondence has recently been completed, Mersenne (1932–88), *Correspondance du P. Marin Mersenne, religieux minime,* ed. C. de Waard et al. (17 vols.), Paris: Beauchesne (vol. 1), Presses Universitaires de France (vols. 2–4), *CNRS* (vols. 5–17). There is no standard edition of his other writings.

Secondary Sources: De Coste, H. (1649), *La vie du R. P. Marin Mersenne, théologien, philosophe et mathématicien, de l'ordre des Pères Minimes,* Paris [repr. in Philippe Tamizey de Larroque, *Les correspondants de Peiresc,* Geneva: Slatkine, 1972, vol. 2, pp. 436–97]. Thuillier, R. (1709), *Diarium patrum, fratrum et sororum Ordinis Minimorum Provinciae Franciae,* Paris [repr. Geneva: Slatkine, 1972, entry in vol. 2, pp. 90–113]. Lenoble, R. (1971), *Mersenne ou la naissance du mécanisme,* Paris: Vrin. Crombie, A. C. (1974), 'Mersenne, Marin', in *DSB.* Duncan, D. A. (1981), 'The Tyranny of Opinions Undermined: Science, Pseudo-Science and Scepticism in the Musical Thought of Marin Mersenne', Ph.D. diss., Vanderbilt University. Dear, P. (1988), *Mersenne and the Learning of the Schools,* Ithaca: Cornell University Press. [Peter Dear]

MOLINA, LUIS b. Cuenca, 1536; d. Madrid, 1600. Jesuit theologian and philosopher. Studied law at Salamanca 1551–2 and philosophy at Alcalá 1552–3. Entered the Company of Jesus in 1553. Studied philosophy (1554–8) and theology (1558–62) at Coimbra. Taught philosophy at Coimbra (1563–7, while Fonseca was teaching logics and Aristotle's metaphysics). Professor of theology at Evora, for twenty years, then in the College of Cuenca (1591–1600; published his lectures). Called to Madrid (1600) to teach moral theology. His main work is *Concordia liberi arbitrii cum gratiae donis, diuina praescientia, prouidentia, praedestinatione et reprobatione ad nonnullos primae partis diui Thomae articulos* (Lisbon, 1588, numerous additions and revisions in the various re-editions, the main one being Antwerp, 1595; critical edition by J. Rabeneck (Madrid: La Sapientia, 1953)). The *Concordia* is a highly original attempt to solve the grace/liberty problem in Catholic theology. Other works by Molina include his *Commentaria in primam d. Thomae partem* (Cuenca 1592) and his *De iustitia et iure,* 6 vols. (Cuenca, 1593–1609); early writings published by F. Stegmüller in *Beiträge zur Geschichte der Philosophie und Theologie der Mittelalters* vol. 32, 1935.

Secondary Sources: Vansteenberge, E. (1903–50), 'Molinisme', in E. Mangenot, A. Vacant, and E. Amann (eds.), *Dictionnaire de théologie catholique,* Paris: LeTouzey et Ané. Stegmüller, F. (1935), *Geschichte des Molinismus,* Münster: Aschendorff. Pegis, Anton C. (1939), 'Molina and Human Liberty', in Gerard Smith, S.J. (ed.), *Jesuit Thinkers of the Renaissance,* Milwaukee: Marquette University Press. Rabenek, J. (1950), 'De vita et scriptis Ludovici Molina', *Archivum Historicum Societatis Iesu* 19:75–145.

Smith, Gerard, S.J. (1966), *Freedom in Molina,* Chicago: Loyola University Press. Queralt, A. (1975–6), 'Libertad humana en Luis de Molina', *Archivo teologico granadino* 38:5–156 and 39:5–100. Freddoso, Alfred (1988), 'Introduction', in Molina (1988), *On Divine Foreknowledge,* Ithaca: Cornell University Press. Craig, William L. (1988), *The Problem of Divine Foreknowledge and Future Contingents from Aristotle to Suárez,* Leiden: Brill, chap. 7. [Jean-Robert Armogathe]

MONTAIGNE, MICHEL DE b. Montaigne (near Bordeaux), 1533; d. Montaigne, 1592. Philosopher and essayist. Educated by private tutor and at Collège de Guyenne. Studied law at Bordeaux, becoming counselor to Parlement of Bordeaux. Close friendship with La Boétie, 1558–63, ending with his death. After following royal court, retired to his estates, 1571. Beginning of interest in scepticism, upon reading Sextus Empiricus, 1576. Published first two books of *Essais,* Bordeaux, 1580. Mayor of Bordeaux, 1581–5, followed by permanent retirement. Published in Paris, 1588, third book of *Essais,* along with additions to first two books. Posthumous publication, Paris, 1595, by Marie de Gournay (his literary executrix) of the 'Bordeaux copy' of the *Essais,* containing his final additions to the 1588 edition. The best French edition is Montaigne (1962), *Oeuvres complètes,* ed. Albert Thibaudet and Maurice Rat, Paris: Gallimard, which identifies the different strata belonging to the 1580, 1588, and 1595 editions. There is an excellent translation into English by Donald Frame, Montaigne (1965), *Complete Essays of Montaigne,* Stanford: Stanford University Press.

Secondary Sources: Villey, P. (1933), *Les sources et l'évolution des Essais de Montaigne* (2d ed.), Paris: Hachette. Freidrich, H. (1949), *Montaigne,* Bern: Francke. Frame, D. (1965), *Montaigne. A Biography,* London and New York: Harcourt Brace and World. Brush, C. (1966), *Montaigne and Bayle. Variations on the Theme of Scepticism,* The Hague: Nijhoff. Starobinski, J. (1982), *Montaigne en mouvement,* Paris: Gallimard. Screech, M. A. (1983), *Montaigne and Melancholy,* London: Duckworth. Boutaudou, C. (1984), *Montaigne. Textes et débats,* Paris: Union générale d'édition. [Charles Larmore]

MORE, HENRY b. Grantham, Lincolnshire, October 1614; d. Cambridge, 1 September 1687. Metaphysician, natural philosopher and theologian. Educated at Eton and, from 1631, Christ's College, Cambridge, More rejected the Calvinism of his family upbringing in favour of a more liberal Anglicanism. Graduated B.A. in 1636, M.A. in 1639. Ordained and took up fellowship at Christ's in 1641. *Psychodia Platonica; or, a Platonicall Song of the Soul* (Cambridge, 1642) shows the influence of Neoplatonism on his theology. *Democritus Platonissans; or, an Essay upon the Infinity of Worlds out of Platonick Principles* (Cambridge, 1646) attempted to marry Neoplatonism with the new philosophy of Copernicus, Galileo and Descartes. Correspondence with Descartes, 1648–9, reveals clear differences in their thought, despite More's admiration for Descartes. Controversy with Thomas Vaughan, 1650–1, about the correct interpretation and representation of Platonism. *An Antidote Against Atheisme* (London, 1653) was his first attempt to develop a systematic natural theology drawing upon Cartesian philosophy. Supplemented in the same year by *Conjectura Cabbalistica* (London, 1653), and later by *The Immortality of the Soul* (London and Cambridge, 1659), which fully developed his concept of the 'Spirit of Nature', an architectonic principle responsible for all physical change. Revised versions of these three works together with *Enthusiasmus triumphatus* (London and Cambridge, 1656) and the Descartes corespondence, appeared in *A Collection of Several Philosophical Writings* (London and Cambridge, 1662). After concentrating on apologetic religious writing for nearly a decade, published *Divine Dialogues* (London, 1668), a redaction of his theology and philosophy presented in the context of a discussion on the nature of divine providence. The *Enchiridion metaphysicum* (London and Cambridge, 1671) was a more forceful restatement of his philosophy which drew an attack from Robert Boyle in his *Hydrostatical Discourse* (London, 1672). *Opera omnia* (London, 1675–9) consisted of Latin translations of his earlier works together with new material, including two attacks upon the philosophy of Spinoza. Subsequent publications all directly concerned with theology except for his edition of Joseph Glanvill's *Saducismus*

*Triumphatus; or, Full and Plain Evidence concerning Witches and Apparitions* (London, 1681), with numerous additions by More, which extends earlier attempts to prove the existence of the spiritual realm. More inspired a number of disciples but his most able follower, Lady Anne Conway, eventually rejected his strict dualism in favour of a monistic spiritualism.

Secondary Sources: Ward, R. (1710), *The Life of the Learned and Pious Dr. Henry More*, London. Cassirer, E. (1953), *The Platonic Renaissance in England*, Austin: University of Texas Press. Colie, R. L. (1957), *Light and Enlightenment: A Study of the Cambridge Platonists and Dutch Arminians*, Cambridge: Cambridge University Press. Lichtenstein, A. (1962), *Henry More: The Rational Theology of a Cambridge Platonist*, Cambridge, Mass.: Harvard University Press. Pacchi, A. (1973), *Cartesio in Inghilterra: Da More a Boyle*, Bari: Laterza. Cristofolino, P. (1974), *Cartesiani e sociniani: Studio su Henry More*, Urbino: Argalia. Gabbey, A. (1977), 'Anne Conway et Henry More, Lettres sur Descartes', *Archives de Philosophie*, 40:379–404. Gabbey, A. (1982), 'Philosophia Cartesiana Triumphata: Henry More, 1646–71', in T. M. Lennon, J. M. Nicholas, J. W. Davis (eds.), *Problems in Cartesianism*, Kingston and Montreal: McGill-Queen's University Press, pp. 171–249. Hutton, S. (ed.) (1990), *Henry More (1614–87): Tercentenary Studies*, Dordrecht: Kluwer. Hall, A. R. (1990), *Henry More: Magic, Religion and Experiment*, Oxford: Blackwell. Nicolson, M. H., and Hutton, S. (1992), *The Conway Letters: the Correspondence of Anne, Viscountess Conway, Henry More, and their Friends, 1642–84*, rev. ed., Oxford: Oxford University Press. [John Henry]

NEWTON, SIR ISAAC b. Woolsthorpe, Lincolnshire, 1642; d. London, 1727. Natural philosopher, mathematician, alchemist. The foremost mathematician and natural philosopher of the late seventeenth century. Attended Trinity College, Cambridge 1661–4, B.A. 1665. Granted scholarship to Trinity in 1665; composed a notebook *Quaestiones quaedam philosophicae* (1664) dealing with the 'new philosophy'. Spent most of 1665–6 in Lincolnshire due to plague at Cambridge. Undertook intensive mathematical research 1665–6, culminating in unpublished 'October 1666 Tract' on the calculus. Elected Fellow of Trinity College, 1667; 1667–8 researches in optics resulted in first reflecting telescope. Assisted Isaac Barrow with editing of *Lectiones opticae* in 1669 and later composed several mathematical treatises, including *De analysi per aequationes numeri terminorum infinitas* (published London, 1711) and *De methodis serierum et fluxionum* (published in English translation, London, 1736). Succeeded Barrow as Lucasian Professor of Mathematics at Cambridge (1669), composed and delivered lectures on optics (1670–2). Sent reflecting telescope to Royal Society in 1671, elected to Royal Society in 1672. Communicated letter on 'New Theory of Light and Colours' to Royal Society in 1672, sent second paper on optics to Royal Society in 1675. Engaged in dispute with Hooke, Pardies, Linus, Lucas, and Huygens on optical issues (1672–8). Engaged in alchemical research from mid-1670s through 1690s. Composed, but did not publish, treatise 'De Motu' (1684); later revised and expanded this into *Principia mathematica philosophiae naturalis* published in London, 1687. In 1686–8 engaged in bitter dispute with Hooke over priority for the inverse square law. Suffered severe mental breakdown in 1693. Became Warden of the Mint in 1696 and moved to London, named Master of the Mint in 1700. Elected President of the Royal Society in 1703, knighted in 1705. Published *Opticks*, London, 1704 (with mathematical appendices on quadrature and classification of curves). Engaged in priority dispute with Leibniz over the calculus, 1703–15. Published *Arithmetica Universalis* (Cambridge, 1707; English translation, London, 1720). Published second edition of *Principia* in London, 1713, third edition in London, 1726 (English translation, London, 1729). Years of theological research resulted in the posthumous publication of *The Chronology of Ancient Kingdoms Amended* (London, 1728) and *Observations Upon the Prophecies of Daniel and the Apocalypse of St. John* (London, 1733). There is no standard edition of his works, but the following may be consulted. The authoritative edition of the *Principia* is Newton (1972), *Isaac Newton's Philosophia Naturalis Principia Mathematica: The Third Edition with Variant Readings*, ed. Alexandre Koyré and I. Bernard Cohen (2 vols.), Cambridge, Mass.: Harvard University Press. His mathematical papers are available in Newton (1967–81), *The Mathematical Papers of Isaac Newton*, ed. D. T. Whiteside (8 vols.), Cambridge: Cambridge University Press. His optical works are being published in Newton (1984– ), *Optical Papers of Isaac Newton*, ed. A. E. Shapiro. Cambridge: Cambridge University Press. Convenient collections of his papers, published and unpublished, are available in Newton (1962), *Unpublished Scientific Papers of Isaac Newton*, ed. A. R. Hall and M. B. Hall. Cambridge: Cambridge University Press, and Newton (1978), *Papers and Letters on Natural Philosophy*, ed. I. Bernard Cohen. Cambridge, Mass.: Harvard University Press. His early notebook (1664) is transcribed in Newton (1983), *Certain philosophical questions: Newton's Trinity Notebook*, ed. J. E. McGuire and Martin Tamny, Cambridge: Cambridge University Press. Correspondence is available in Newton (1959–77), *The Correspondence of Isaac Newton*, ed. H. W. Turnbull, J. F. Scott, A. R. Hall, Laura Tilling (7 vols.), Cambridge: Cambridge University Press.

Secondary Sources: Maclaurin, C. (1748), *An Account of Sir Isaac Newton's Philosophical Discoveries*, London. Cohen, I. B. (1956), *Franklin and Newton*, Philadelphia: American Philosophical Society. Manuel, F. E. (1963), *Isaac Newton, Historian*, Cambridge, Mass.: Harvard University Press. Herivel, J. W. (1965), *The Background to Newton's 'Principia'*, Oxford: Oxford University Press. Koyré, A. (1968), *Newtonian Studies*, Chicago: University of Chicago Press. Manuel, F. E. (1968), *A Portrait of Isaac Newton*, Cambridge, Mass.: Harvard University Press. Westfall, R. W. (1971), *Force in Newton's Physics*, New York: American Elsevier. Cohen, I. B. (1971), *An Introduction to Newton's 'Principia'*, Cambridge, Mass.: Harvard University Press. Manuel, F. E. (1974), *The Religion of Isaac Newton*, Oxford: Oxford University Press. Dobbs, B. J. T. (1975), *The Foundations of Newton's Alchemy*, Cambridge: Cambridge University Press. Wallis, P., and Wallis, R. (1977), *Newton and Newtoniana: 1672–1975*, London: Dawson. McMullin, E. (1978), *Newton on Matter and Activity*, Notre Dame: Notre Dame University Press. Harrison, J. (1978), *The Library of Isaac Newton*, Cambridge: Cambridge University Press. Cohen, I. B. (1980), *The Newtonian Revolution*, Cambridge: Cambridge University Press. Hall, A. R. (1980), *Philosophers at War*, Cambridge: Cambridge University Press. Westfall, R. W. (1980), *Never at Rest*, Cambridge: Cambridge University Press. King-Hele, D. G., and Hall, A. R. (eds.) (1988), *Newton's 'Principia' and its Legacy*, London: Royal Society. Dobbs, B. J. T. (1991), *The Janus Faces of Genius: The Role of Alchemy in Newton's Thought*, Cambridge: Cambridge University Press. [John Henry and Douglas Jesseph]

NICOLE, PIERRE b. Chartres, 1612; d. Paris, 1695. Theologian, moralist, political philosopher. One of the most prominent writers affiliated with the Jansenists at Port-Royal. Studied theology at Sorbonne; withdrew to become a *solitaire* at Port-Royal des Champs. After 1654, served as secretary to Arnauld. Collaborated with Arnauld on *La Logique, ou l'art de penser* (Paris, 1662). Taught at 'little schools' associated with Port-Royal. Wrote *De la foi humaine* (Paris, 1664), *La perpetuité de la foi de l'eglise catholique touchant l'eucharistie* (Paris, 1669, with Arnauld), and *Essais de morale* (composed in the 1670s). Went into exile with Arnauld in 1679, but soon returned after making peace with the Archbishop of Paris, Harlay de Champvallon. The standard editions of Nicole's important works are Nicole (1730), *Essais de morale* (13 vols.), Paris, and Nicole (1755), *Oeuvres de controverse de M. Nicole* (6 vols.), Paris.

Secondary Sources: Sainte-Beuve, C. A. (1928), *Port-Royal* (7 vols.), Paris: La Connaissance. Seillière, E. (1929), 'Pierre Nicole et la doctrine de la grâce', *Séances et Travaux de l'Académie des Sciences Morales et Politiques*, 2:275–87. Rodis-Lewis, G. (1950), 'Augustinisme et Cartésianisme à Port-Royal', in E. J. Dijksterhuis et al. (eds.), *Descartes et le Cartésianisme hollandais*, Paris: Presses Universitaires de France. Rodis-Lewis, G. (1950), 'L'intervention de Nicole dans la polémique entre Arnauld et Malebranche', *Revue Philosophique de la France et de l'Etranger*, 140:483–507. Laporte, J. (1951–2), *La doctrine de Port-Royal* (2 vols.), Paris: Presses Universitaires de France. James, E. D. (1972), *Pierre Nicole Jansenist and Humanist. A Study of His Thought*, The Hague: Nijhoff. Sedgwick, A. (1977), *Jansenism in Seventeenth*

*Century France,* Charlottesville: University of Virginia Press. Dominicy, M. (1985), *La naissance de la grammaire moderne: Langage, logique et philosophie à Port-Royal,* Brussels: Mardaga. Nadler, S. (1988), 'Cartesianism and Port-Royal', *Monist,* 71:573–84. [Steven Nadler]

NORRIS, JOHN b. Collingbourne-Kingston, Wiltshire, 1657; d. Bemerton, Wiltshire, 1711. Metaphysician, theologian, poet. Educated at Winchester (1670–6) and Exeter College, Oxford (B.A., 1680; M.A., 1684); fellow of All Souls College, Oxford (1680–9). Drawn early to Platonism; corresponded (from 1684) with Henry More and Lady Damaris Masham. Took holy orders (1684). Rector of Newton St. Loe, Somerset (1689–91). Rector of Bemerton (1691–1711), a benefice Locke obtained for him, at the instigation of Lady Masham, from the earl of Pembroke; a subsequent misunderstanding over a letter that Locke had entrusted to him for delivery to Lady Masham led to a permanent rupture in his relations with Locke. Published, in addition to philosophical and theological works, volumes of sermons, poems, controversial writings and correspondence. Some had many printings, leading the bookseller John Dunton to say of him, 'He can turn Metaphysicks into Money'. *Poems and Discourses* (London, 1684), his first important work, showed him close to the Cambridge Platonists. *The Theory and Regulation of Love* (Oxford, 1688), *Reason and Religion* (London, 1689), and *Reflections upon the Conduct of Human Life* (London, 1690) revealed the growing influence of Malebranche on him. Amiable in person, but zealous in controversy, he criticised Locke's 'new way of ideas' from a Malebranchean perspective in *Cursory Reflections upon a Book Call'd an Essay concerning Human Understanding,* appended to *Christian Blessedness* (London, 1690); assailed the Quakers' 'gross notion' of inner light in *Two Treatises concerning the Divine Light* (London, 1692); combatted John Toland's deistic views in *An Account of Reason and Faith in relation to the Mysteries of Christianity* (London, 1697); and replied to Henry Dodwell's denial of the natural immortality of the soul in *A Philosophical Discourse concerning the Natural Immortality of the Soul* (London, 1708). A Tory and High Churchman, he opposed the Toleration Act of 1689 in *The Charge of Schism Continued* (London, 1691) and probably authored an anonymous High Church defence, *The Distinction of High Church and Low Church* (London, 1705). He corresponded with a number of learned women – Mary Astell, Lady Mary Chudleigh, Elizabeth Thomas, as well as Damaris Masham – about philosophy, urging them to study the works of Malebranche and to learn French, if need be, to do so. His chief philosophical work was *An Essay towards the Theory of the Ideal or Intelligible World* (London, vol. 1, 1701; vol. 2, 1704), a closely reasoned book that showed him well deserving of the sobriquet 'the English Malebranche'. The series 'British Philosophers and Theologians of the 17th and 18th Centuries' (1976–9, ed. R. Wellek, New York: Garland), reprints the following works by Norris: *A Collection of Miscellanies* (includes *Poems and Discourses* and *An Idea of Happiness*), *Christian Blessedness* (includes *Cursory Reflections upon a Book call'd an Essay concerning Human Understanding*), *Treatises on Several Subjects* (includes *Reason and Religion, Reflections upon the Conduct of Human Life, The Charge of Schism Continued,* and *Two Treatises concerning Divine Light*), and *An Essay towards the Theory of the Ideal or Intelligible World.*

Secondary Sources: Lyon, G. (1888), *L'Idéalisme en Angleterre au XVIIIe siècle,* Paris: Alcan. Powicke, F. J. (1893), *A Dissertation on John Norris,* London: G. Philip. MacKinnon, F. I. (1910), *The Philosophy of John Norris of Bemerton* (Philosophical Monographs, 2), Baltimore: Psychological Review Publishing Co. Muirhead, J. H. (1931), *The Platonic Tradition in Anglo-Saxon Philosophy,* London: Allen and Unwin. Ryan, J. (1940), 'John Norris, a Seventeenth Century Thomist', *New Scholasticism,* 14:109–45. Walton, G. (1955), *Metaphysical to Augustan: Studies in Tone and Sensibility in the 17th Century,* London: Bowes and Bowes. Johnston, C. (1958), 'Locke's Examination of Malebranche and John Norris', *Journal of the History of Ideas,* 19:551–8. Hoyles, J. (1971), *The Waning of the Renaissance 1640–1740: Studies in the Thought and Poetry of Henry More, John Norris and Isaac Watts,* The Hague: Nijhoff. Acworth, R. (1979), *The Philosophy of John Norris of Bemerton,* Hildesheim: Georg Olms. McCracken, C. J. (1983), *Malebranche and British Philosophy,* Oxford: Oxford University Press. [Charles McCracken]

OLDENBURG, HENRY (Grubendol) b. Bremen, ca. 1615; d. Charlton, Kent, 1677. Natural philosopher, man of letters. Secretary of the Royal Society in its early years, correspondent with nearly every scientific and philosophical luminary of his era. Educated at the Gymnasium Illustre in Bremen 1633– 9, receiving Master of Theology in 1639. Attended the University of Utrecht in 1641, but took no degree. From 1642–53 his whereabouts and activities are uncertain, but he seems to have travelled widely and was probably a private tutor. Appointed emissary to Cromwell by Bremen government in 1653 and went to England, where he made the acquaintance of Milton and his circle. Became a tutor to Boyle's nephew Richard Jones and accompanied him to Oxford in 1656, where he met John Wilkins, John Wallis, and others who introduced him to the 'new experimental learning'. Made the continental tour with Richard Jones in 1657 and seems to have visited learned societies. Joined the precursor to the Royal Society in 1661 and (along with Wilkins) was made secretary to the Royal Society in 1663. As secretary he carried on a voluminous correspondence with men of learning throughout Europe, kept minutes of the Royal Society meetings, and published the *Philosophical Transactions of the Royal Society*. His frequent contact with learned men on the continent aroused suspicion and he was imprisoned in the Tower of London for three months on charges of espionage and treason in the summer of 1667. Undertook numerous translations of works after 1670, including Latin versions of Boyle's works and an English translation of Nicolaus Steno's *Prodromus*. Engaged in acrimonious dispute with Hooke in 1675–6, who complained that Oldenburg had not properly credited him with invention of the spiral watch spring but had instead given the idea to Christiaan Huyghens. Remained active in the Royal Society until his death in 1677. His correspondence is available in Oldenburg (1965–86), *The Correspondence of Henry Oldenburg*, ed. A. Rupert Hall, Marie Boas Hall (13 vols.), vols. 1–9 Madison: University of Wisconsin Press; vols. 10–11 London: Mansell; vols. 12–13 London: Taylor and Francis.

Secondary Sources: Mackie, D. (1948), 'The Arrest and Imprisonment of Henry Oldenburg', *Notes and Records of the Royal Society*, 6:28–47. Hall, A. R., and Hall, M. B. (1962), 'Why Blame Oldenburg?' *Isis* 53:482–91. Hall, A. R., and Hall, M. B. (1963), 'Some Hitherto Unknown Facts about the Private Career of Henry Oldenburg', *Notes and Records of the Royal Society* 18:94–103. Hall, M. B. (1965), 'Henry Oldenburg and the Art of Scientific Communication', *British Journal for the History of Science* 2:227–90. Hall, A. R., and Hall, M. B. (1968), 'Further Notes on Henry Oldenburg', *Notes and Records of the Royal Society* 23:33–42. Hall, A. R. (1970), 'Henry Oldenburg et les relations scientifiques au XVIIe siècle', *Revue d'histoire des sciences* 23:285–304. Henry, J. (1988), 'The Origins of Modern Science: Henry Oldenburg's Contribution', *British Journal for the History of Science* 21:103–9. Shapin, S. (1988), 'O Henry,' *Isis* 78:417–24. [Douglas Jesseph]

PARDIES, IGNACE-GASTON b. Pau, 1636; d. Paris, 1673. Physicist and mathematician. Known primarily as a helpful critic of Newton's colour theory; also recognised for skill with instruments, his imaginative syntheses in physics, and his rôle in the animal soul debate. Entered the Jesuit novitiate at Fontanieux after completing the first stage of his education at the Jesuit Collège of Saint Louis in Pau 1652; studied and taught at Toulouse, developing considerable mathematical skill 1654–6; taught humanities at the Collège de la Madeleine in Bordeaux 1656–65; student in the faculty of theology in Bordeaux 1660–4; taught philosophy at La Rochelle 1666–8, Bordeaux 1668–70, and the Collège Clermont in Paris 1670–3. Though he presented himself as a follower of the schools, Pardies was suspected of Cartesian sympathies by his contemporaries, particularly with respect to his theory of motion and his account of animal souls. Combining his own scientific research with teaching and his own studies in theology, produced his first scientific work, *Horologium thaumanticum duplex* (Bordeaux, 1662); published *Dissertatio de motu et natura comentarum* (Bordeaux, 1665), *Theses mathematicae ex mechanica* (Paris, 1669), *Discours du mouvement local* (Paris, 1670), *Elémens de géométrie* (Paris, 1671), *Discours de la connaissance des bestes* (Paris, 1672), *Lettre d'un philosophe à un cartésien de ses amis* (Paris,

1672) (this work is of disputed authorship), *Deux machines propres à faire les quadrans avec une très grande facilité* (Paris, 1673), *La statique ou la science des forces mouvantes* (Paris, 1673), and, posthumously, *Atlas céleste* (Paris, 1674). His mathematical works were published in a single edition, *Oeuvres de mathématiques* (Paris, 1691). Many of his most important ideas were communicated in his correspondence, much of which remains unpublished. Published letters can be found in collections of the correspondence of Newton, Huygens, and Oldenburg.

Secondary Sources: Ango, P. (1682), *L'optique,* Paris. Sortais, Gaston (1929) *Le cartesianisme chez les Jésuites français au 17ᵉ et 18ᵉ siècles* (*Archives de philosophie,* vol. 6, no. 3), Paris: Beauchesne, pp. 52–3. Rosenfield, Leonora Cohen (1968), *From Beast-Machine to Man-Machine,* 2d ed., New York: Octagon Books, pp. 80–6, 219–21, 331–2. Ziggelaar, A. (1971), *Le physicien Ignace Gaston Pardies S.J.* (1636–73), vol. 26 of Bibliotheca Universitatis Havniensis, Odense. [David Lux]

PASCAL, BLAISE b. Clermont-Ferrand, 1623; d. Paris, 1662. Mathematician, physicist, religious writer. Educated at home by his father. Published an *Essai pour les coniques* in 1640 and invented a calculating machine in 1642. Met Descartes in Paris in 1647. Also in 1647, devised experiment of Puy-de-Dôme (performed the following year by his brother-in-law Florin Périer), intended to show the real existence of a vacuum in nature. Wrote in 1651 *Traité du vide,* of which the methodological preface survives. Corresponded with Fermat in 1654 about the mathematics of games of chance. Had a mystical experience on 23 November 1654 (described in his *Mémorial*), after which he devoted himself to God and the Jansenist cause. Retreated to Port-Royal in 1655, where he conducted the *Entretien avec M. de Saci sur Epictète et Montaigne* (published in 1728). Wrote *Lettres provinciales* in 1656–7, and in 1658 began the composition of an *Apologie de la religion chrétienne* unfinished at his death, and published first in 1670 as *Pensées.* The edition of the *Pensées* most faithful to Pascal's intentions, which contains the now standard numbering of the fragments, is found in Pascal (1963), *Oeuvres complètes,* ed. Louis Lafuma, Paris: Editions du Seuil. There is a new complete edition currently in progress, Pascal (1964–     ), *Oeuvres complètes,* ed. Jean Mesnard (4 vols. to date), Paris: Desclée De Brouwer, but it has not yet published its edition of the *Pensées.*

Secondary Sources: Périer, Gilberte [Pascal's sister] (1686), *La Vie de Monsieur Pascal.* Brunschvicg, L. (1945), *Descartes et Pascal lecteurs de Montaigne,* Neuchâtel: La Baconnière. Bénichou, P. (1948), *Morales du grand siècle,* Paris: Gallimard, pp. 121–213. Mesnard, J. (1951), *Pascal, l'homme et l'oeuvre,* Paris: Boivin. Brunschvicg, L. (1967), introductory material in Pascal, *Pensées et opuscules,* Paris: Hachette. Krailsheimer, A. J. (1980), *Pascal,* Oxford: Oxford University Press. [Charles Larmore]

POIRET, PIERRE b. Metz, 1646; d. Rijnsburg, 1719. Lived on the eastern and northern periphery of French intellectual activity, educated in Basle, ending up, significantly, in Amsterdam for thirty years, before moving to Rijnsburg, near Leiden, where he died. Early on, he studied the philosophy of Descartes and also theology, becoming a minister in Heidelberg in 1668. His own theology was of a mystical sort – short of Boehme, most of whose work he found unintelligible, but extensive enough to incur the disapproval of his pastoral colleagues in Hamburg around 1688. He was well enough known in the period; his work, mostly in Latin, was translated into English and German. Began with the Cartesian-inspired *Cogitationum rationalium de Deo, anima et malo* (Amsterdam, 1677), but under the influence of Antoinette Bourginon and other mystics, he came to reject Descartes in the rest of his work. Bayle said of him that he was 'so devoted a Cartesian as to suspend all terrestrial business in order to attend better to the celestial.'

Secondary Sources: *BHPC* II 305–14. Jungst, Walter (1912), *Das Verhaltnis von Philosophie und Theologie bei den Cartesianern Malebranche, Poiret und Spinoza. Eine philosophiegeschichtliche Untersuchung,* Leipzig: Quelle and Meyer. Hirsch, Emanuel (1949), *Geschichte der neueren evangelischen Theologie im Zusammen-*

*hang mit den allgemeinen Bewegungen des europaischen Denkens,* Gutersloh: C. Bertelsmann, chaps. 8 and 9. Rodis-Lewis, G. (1981), 'Polémiques sur la création des possibles et sur l'impossible dans l'école cartésienne', *Studia Cartesiana* 2:105–23. [Thomas Lennon]

POISSON, NICOLAS-JOSEPH b. Paris, 1637; d. Lyon, 1710. Poisson, an Oratorian from 1660, was an enthusiastic follower of Descartes in his early years and planned to write a commentary on the whole of Descartes's corpus. Clerselier, who made available to him the manuscripts of Descartes which he held, also urged him to write a biography of Descartes. Poisson's first publication was an edition and translation into French of Descartes's early *Compendium musicae* and the long letter to Huygens which was known as the *Traité des mechaniques,* with an introduction and commentary; this appeared under the title: *Traité de la Mechanique composé par Monsieur Descartes. De plus L'Abregé de Musique du mesme Autheur mis en François. Avec les Eclaircissements necessaires Par N.P.P.D.L.* [i.e., Nicolas-Joseph Poisson, Prestre de l'Oratoire] (Paris, 1668). Two years later, he published his *Commentaire ou Remarques sur La Methode de René Descartes où on établit plusieurs Principes generaux, necessaires pour entendre toutes ses Oeuvres* (Vendôme, 1670). But the growing controversy over Descartes's thought induced Poisson to give up these Cartesian projects and turn back to theological and ecclesiastical matters, which, for the most part, occupied him for the rest of his life. There is a modern edition of his commentary on Descartes's music theory, Descartes (1990), *Abregé de musique . . . Suivi des Eclaircissements physiques sur la musique de Descartes du R. P. Nicolas Poisson,* trans. and ed. P. Dumont (Paris: Meridiens Klincksieck), and a reprint edition of the commentary on Descartes's *Discours de la méthode* (New York: Garland, 1987).

Secondary Sources: Cléments (abbé) (1898–9), 'Le cartésianisme á Vendôme. Le P. Nicolas-Joseph Poisson, supérieur du collège de l'Oratoire', *Bulletin de la société du Vendômois.* [Daniel Garber]

PUFENDORF, SAMUEL (Freiherr von) b. Dorf-Chemnitz (Saxony), 1632; d. Berlin, 1694. Legal philosopher, historian. Attended the Prince's School at Grimma from 1645 to 1650. Attended university at Leipzig (from 1650) where he briefly studied theology, but then turned to law and natural philosophy. He moved to the University of Jena, where he studied ethics and politics, and especially natural law. Under the supervision of Erhard Weigel, who also taught Leibniz, he studied Descartes, Galileo, Grotius, and Hobbes. In 1658, Pufendorf left Jena as magister artium and became tutor in the house of the Swedish ambassador in Copenhagen, Coyet. Soon after his arrival, war broke out between Sweden and Denmark, and Pufendorf was imprisoned for eight months. During this time, he wrote his first work on natural law, *Elementorum Jurisprudentiae Universalis Libri Duo* (The Hague, 1660). After his release in 1659, he went to Holland and studied at the University of Leiden. In 1661, he took up the chair of natural and international law at the University of Heidelberg – the first chair of this kind in Germany. Here, he developed his own natural law theory. He also worked on constitutional and political problems, and in 1663 published two dissertations, *De Obligatione erga patriam* and *De Rebus Gestis Philippi Amyntae.* In 1667 he published (anonymously) a work on the condition of the Holy Roman Empire, *De Statu Imperiui Germanici* (Geneva); a posthumous edition of this work, with alterations prepared by Pufendorf, was published in Berlin in 1706. In the winter of 1668/9 he took up a professorship of international and natural law at the University of Lund in Sweden. Here he wrote and published his main works on natural law, *De jure naturae et gentium* (Lund, 1672) and an abstract of this huge work, *De officio hominis et civis juxta legam naturalem* (Lund, 1673). Both works had an immense impact in eighteenth-century thought. To defend himself against the charge of heresy, Pufendorf published *Eris Scandia, quae adversus libros de jurae naturae et gentium objecta diluuntur* (Frankfurt, 1686). Since 1677 Pufendorf had been court historian in Stockholm and wrote extensively on history; he published his *Einleitung zu der Historie der vornehmsten Reiche und Staaten so itziger Zeit in Europa sich befinden* (2 vols.) (Frankfurt 1682–5), and a large history of Sweden from the time of Gustav Adolf onwards: *Commentariorum de rebus Sueciis libri 26* (Utrecht, 1686). In 1688, Purfendorf took up the position of court historian for the elector of Brandenburg in Berlin, where he lived until his death. He wrote, but did not publish, a history of the time under the elector, *De Rebus Friderici Wilhelmi Magni Electoris Brandenburgici commentariorum libri 19* (completed 1692; published posthumously in Berlin, 1695). He also wrote, but did not publish, two works on church politics, *De habitus christianae religionis ad vitam civilem* (published posthumously in Bremen, 1697) and a plea for the unity of Protestants, *Jus feciale Divinum sive de consensu protestantium* (published posthumously in Lübeck, 1695). Pufendorf's letters are published in Pufendorf 1893, 1894, 1897. There are a variety of modern editions of his work.

Secondary Sources: Lezius, F. (1900), *Der Toleranzbegriff Lockes und Pufendorfs*, Leipzig: Dieterich. Rabe, H. (1958), *Naturrecht und Kirche bei Samuel Pufendorf*, Tübingen: Fabianverlag. Welzel, H. (1958), *Die Naturrechtslehre Samuel Pufendorfs*, Berlin: de Gruyter. Wolf, E. (1963), *Grosse Rechtsdenker der deutschen Geistesgeschichte*, Tübingen: Mohr, pp. 311–70. Krieger, L. (1965), *The Politics of Discretion: Pufendorf and the Acceptance of Natural Law*, Chicago: University of Chicago Press. Denzer, H. (1972), *Moralphilosophie und Naturrecht bei Samuel Pufendorf*, Munich: Beck. Medick, H. (1973), *Naturzustand und Naturgeschichte der buergerlichen Gesellschaft. Die Urspruenge der buergerlichen Sozialtheorie als Geschichtsphilosophie und Sozialwissenschaft bei Samuel Pufendorf, John Locke und Adam Smith*, Göttingen: Vandenhoeck und Ruprecht. Tuck, R. (1979), *Natural Rights Theories. Their Origin and Development*, Cambridge: Cambridge University Press, pp. 156–62. Laurent, Pierre (1982), *Pufendorf et la loi naturelle*, Paris: Vrin. Nutkiewicz, M. (1983), 'Samuel Pufendorf: Obligation as the Basis of the State', *Journal of the History of Philosophy* 21:15–29. Denzer, H. (1983), 'Leben, Werk und Wirkung Samuel Pufendorfs', *Zeitschrift für Politik* 30:160ff. Schneewind, J. B. (1987), 'Pufendorf's Place in the History of Ethics', in *Synthese* 72:123–55. Döring, D. (1988), 'Samuel Pufendorf (1632–94) und die Leipziger Gelehrtengesellschaften in der Mitte des 17. Jahrhunderts', *Lias* 15:13–48. Buckle, S. (1991), *Natural Law and the Theory of Property: Grotius to Hume*, Oxford: Oxford University Press, pp. 53–124. Döring, D. (1992), *Pufendorf-Studien*, Berlin: Duncker und Humboldt. [Udo Thiel]

R A E Y , J O H A N N E S D E (Raei) b. Wageningen, 1622; d. Leiden, 1702. Natural philosopher and early proponent of Cartesianism who converted many thinkers to that philosophy. Despite his embrace of the new philosophy, he never abandoned Aristotelian thought. Studied in Utrecht with Henricus Regius and in Leiden, where he graduated in 1647 both in philosophy and in medicine. Publicly proclaimed the Cartesian philosophy and engaged in many heated debates (e.g., with Adam Stuart). Acquired a chair in philosophy at Leiden in 1659 and a professorship in Amsterdam in 1668. Soon returned to Leiden where he was a respected and influential lecturer on Cartesianism. His most important book, *Clavis philosophiae naturalis, seu introductio ad contemplationem naturae Aristotelico-Cartesiana* (Leiden, 1654), argues for the reconciliation of the philosophy of Aristotle with that of Descartes. The text was widely read and, for example, influenced the young Leibniz. It was significantly revised and retitled for its second edition, *Clavis philosophiae naturalis aristotelico-cartesiana* (Amsterdam, 1677). In this later period, criticises what he considers the extreme Cartesianism of people like Henricus Regius and Spinoza. Other works include *Disputationes physicae ad problemata Aristotelis* (Leiden, 1651–2); *De sapientia veterum* (Amsterdam, 1669); and *Dictionarium geographicum* (Amsterdam, 1680). There is no standard edition.

Secondary Sources: BHPC I. Bohatec, J. (1912), *Die Cartesianische Scholastik in der Philosophie und reformierten Dogmatik des 17. Jahrhunderts*, Leipzig: Deichert., repr. Hildesheim: George Olms, 1966. Molhuysen, P. C. (1913–24), *Bronnen tot de geschiedenis der Leidsche Universiteit* (7 vols.), The Hague: Nijhoff, vol. 2. Mercer, C., 'The Seventeenth-Century Debate between the Moderns and the Aristotelians', *Studia Leibnitiana*, Supplement 27. Mercer, C. (forthcoming), *Leibniz's Metaphysics: Its Origins and Development.* Verbeek, T. (1992), *Descartes and the Dutch: Early Reactions to Cartesian Philosophy, 1637–50,* Carbondale: Southern Illinois University Press. [Christia Mercer]

RÉGIS, PIERRE-SYLVAIN b. Salvetat, Agenais, 1632; d. Paris 1707. Metaphysician, theologian, natural philosopher. An important figure in developing and defending Cartesianism, as a student and follower of the physicist Jacques Rohault, he gained an early public reputation as Cartesian expositor through public lectures and short articles in the *Journal des Savants.* Discouraged from teaching publicly by Louis XIV's disapproval in 1680, he refrained from public lecturing until 1699, when he was admitted to the reformed Académie Royale des Sciences. In his *Système de philosophie, contenant la logic, la metaphysique, la physique, et la morale* (Paris, 1690), offered a strongly empirical approach to Cartesianism (leading to a dispute with Malebranche), a distinctive metaphysics (part 2) in which the soul in this life depends on the body for both action and knowledge, and an extensive treatment of ethics (part 4) that owes a great deal to Hobbes and Spinoza. This work presents his logic (part 1), metaphysics (part 2), and his ethics (part 4) as complete and certain while his physics (part 3) is presented as self-evident but probable. Made notable polemical attacks against Pierre-Daniel Huet, Malebranche, Jean-Baptiste Du Hamel, and Spinoza. His *Réponse au livre qui a pour titre P. Danielis Huetii, . . . Censura Philosophiae Cartesianae . . .* (Paris, 1691) points out Huet's failure to distinguish categories of doubt. His *Réponse aux réflexions critiques de M. Du Hamel . . .* (Paris, 1692) argues (against Du Hamel) that knowledge of real objects does not require resembling ideas. In his last work, *L'usage de la raison et de la foy, ou l'accord de la foy et de la raison* (Paris, 1704), he argued that reason and faith do not conflict, with reason infallible in the world of nature and faith infallible in matters of grace.

Secondary Sources: Damiron, J. P. (1846), *Essai sur l'histoire de la philosophie en France au XVIIe siècle,* Paris. BHPC. Mouy, P. (1934), *Le développement de la physique cartésienne 1646–1712,* Paris: Vrin. Watson, R. A. (1987), *The Breakdown of Cartesian Metaphysics,* Atlantic Highlands, N.J.: Humanities Press. [David Lux]

REGIUS, HENRICUS (Hendrick de Roy) b. 1589; d. 1679. Studied in Franeker, Groningen, Leiden, and abroad (Paris, Montpellier, Valence, Padua); professor extraordinary of theoretical medicine and botany in Utrecht in 1638 and ordinary professor in 1639; obtained the right to lecture on physical problems in 1641, which he lost one year later as a consequence of the crisis at Utrecht over the teaching of Descartes's philosophy, of which he had been the centre. Regius was the first professor to support Descartes publicly. Later Descartes broke with him because he could not agree with certain of the ideas expressed in Regius's *Fundamenta physices* (Amsterdam, 1646; later editions under the title *Philosophia naturalis*). Regius followed the *Fundamenta* with a short placard, *Explicatio mentis humana* (Utrecht, 1647), which Descartes, in turn, answered in his *Notae in programma quoddam* (Amsterdam, 1648). His other important works include the *Physiologia sive cognitio sanitatis* (Utrecht, 1641), the *Fundamenta medicinae* (Utrecht, 1647), the *Brevis explicatio mentis humana sive animae rationalis* (Utrecht, 1648), and *De affectibus animi dissertatio* (Utrecht, 1650). There is no modern edition of his writings. The *Explicatio* can be found with Descartes's response in AT VIIIB.

Secondary Sources: Vrijer, M. J. A. de (1917), *Henricus Regius: een 'Cartesiaansch' hoogleeraar aan de Utrechtsche Hoogeschool,* The Hague: Nijhoff. Thijssen-Schoute, C. Louise (1954), *Nederlands Cartesianisme,* Amsterdam: North-Holland, pp. 2–19, 120–2, 125, 187, 239–41, 263–8. Dechange, Klaus (1966), *Die frühe Naturphilosophie des Henricus Regius (Utrecht 1641),* Münster: Inaug. Diss. Rothschuh, K. (1968), 'Henricus Regius und Descartes: neue Einblicke in die Physiologie des Henricus Regius (1640–1)', *Archives Internationales d'Histoire des Sciences* 21: 39–66. Farina, Paolo (1975), 'Sulla Formazione scientifica di Henricus Regius: Santori ɔ e il Statica Medicina', *Rivista Critica di Storia della Filosofia* 30:363–99. Farina, Paolo (1977), 'Il corpuscolarismo di Henricus Regius: materialismo e medicina in un Cartesiano olandese del Seicento', in Ugo Baldini *et al.* (eds.), *Ricerche sull'Atomismo di Seicento: Atti del Convegno di Studio di Santa Margharita Ligure (14–16 ottobre 1976),* Florence: La Nuova Italia, pp. 119–78. Verbeek, Theo (1988), *La querelle d'Utrecht,* Paris: Les impressions nouvelles. Paul Dibon (1990), 'Sur deux lettres de Descartes à Regius', in Dibon, *Regards sur la Hollande du siècle d'or,* Naples: Vivarium. Hohn, H. B. (1990), *'De Affectibus Animi' 1650: Die Affektlehre des Arztes Henricus Regius (1589–1679) und sein Verhältnis zu zeitgenössischen Philosophen* (Arbeiten der Forschungsstelle des Instituts für Geschichte der Medizin der Universität zu Köln, Band 54), Köln: Kölner medizinhistorische Beiträge. Verbeek, Theo (1992), *Descartes and the Dutch,* Carbondale: Southern Illinois University Press. Verbeek, Theo (1992), ' "Ens per Accidens": Le origini della Querelle di Utrecht', *Giornale Critico della Filosofia Italiana* 71:276–88. Verbeek, Theo (ed.) (1993), *Descartes et Regius. Autour de l'explication de l'esprit,* Amsterdam: Rodopi. Verbeek, Theo (1994), 'Regius's *Fundamenta Physices*', *Journal of the History of Ideas* 55:533–51. [Erik-Jan Bos]

ROHAULT, JACQUES b. Amiens, 1618; d. Paris, 1672. French Cartesian philosopher, physicist, mathematician. Educated in conventional scholastic philosophy at Paris, later adopted and defended the Cartesian philosophy as the foundation of mechanics. Friend to Clerselier whose daughter, Geneviève, he married. He became an important defender of the Cartesian system; his public lectures and experiments attracted many to his Cartesian conferences in Paris, including Pierre-Sylvain Régis. His celebrated *Traité de physique* (Paris, 1671) underwent numerous editions, and was published in France, London, Amsterdam, Geneva, Cologne, and Leiden (English translation, J. Clarke, London, 1723, *A System of Natural Philosophy;* reprinted with introduction by L. Laudan, New York: Johnson Reprint Corporation, 1969). This work became a standard physics textbook not only on the Continent but also in England at both Cambridge and Oxford (Latin translations, T. Bonet, Geneva, 1674; S. Clarke, London, 1697). Samuel Clarke's Latin edition incorporated the Newtonian conception of physics in footnotes, which set the Cartesian mechanics against that of Newton. In *Entretiens sur la philosophie* (Paris, 1671) he defends Cartesian doctrine against various theological objections, such as Descartes's account of transsubstantiation – critical edition by P. Clair in Rohault (1978), *Jacques Rohault: 1618–72: bio-bibliographie, avec l'edition critique des Entretiens sur la philosophie,* Paris: CNRS. Despite his many scientific accomplishments, and despite his distinguished reputation among his comtemporaries, such as Clerselier, Oldenburg, and Huygens, he was never accepted into the Académie des Sciences. There is no standard edition of his works, though Claude Clerselier did publish a collected edition of his writings, Rohault (1682), *Oeuvres posthumes de Mr. Rohault,* Paris.

Secondary Sources: Mouy, P. (1934), *Le Développement de la physique cartésienne, 1646–1712,* Paris: Vrin. Balz, Albert (1951), 'Clerselier, 1614–84, and Rohault, 1620–75', in *Cartesian Studies,* New York: Columbia University Press, pp. 28–41. Hoskin, M. (1961), ' "Mining All Within": Clarke's Notes to Rohault, *Traité de physique*', *The Thomist* 34:353–63. Armogathe, J.-R. (1977), *Theologia Cartesiana,* The Hague: Nijhoff. Rohault, Jacques (1978), *Jacques Rohault: 1618–72: bio-bibliographie, avec l'edition critique des Entretiens sur la philosophie,* ed. Pierre Clair, Paris: CNRS. Gouhier, H. (1978), *Cartésianisme et Augustinisme au XVIIe siècle,* Paris: Vrin. Tournadre, G. (1982), *L'orientation de la science cartésienne,* Paris: Vrin. [Patricia Easton]

SABLÉ, MARQUISE MADELEINE DE SOUVRÉ DE b. Tourraine, 1598/1599; d. Paris, 1678. Jansenist maxim writer and 'Cartesian' salonist. A *précieuse,* but also a *femme savante,* whose interest in scholastic and modern philosophy and grammar led Arnauld to send her the preliminary discourse of *La Logique.* Assisted in the preparation of the first edition of Pascal's *Pensées* and apparently was consulted by La Rochefoucauld when he was composing his *Maximes.* Her salon, most noted for its focus on moral maxims, included La Rochefoucauld, Madame de Lafayette, Voiture, the duchess of Longueville, Arnauld d'Andilly, the princess de Guéméné, Mademoiselle de Choisy and the Comtesse de Maure. Documents from the salon, including her 'Pour les enfants qu'on ne veut pas faire étudier à fond', appear in Sablé (1865), *Les Amis de la Marquise de Sablé: Recueil de Lettres des principaux habitués de son salon*, ed. E. de Barthélemy, Paris: Dentu. Her maxims were published in her *Maximes et Pensées Diverses* (Paris, 1678) and as *Maximes de madame la marquise de Sablé* were published along with the *Pensées diverses de L. M. L. D.* [l'abbé d'Ailly, chanoine de Lisieux] (Paris, 1678). The latter two works were reprinted with the *Maximes du duc de la Rochefoucauld* in La Rochefoucauld, *Réflexions ou Sentences et Maximes morales de Monsieur de la Rochefoucauld, Maximes de Madame la marquise de Sablé. Pensées diverses de M. L. D. et les Maximes chrétiennes de M\*\*\*\** [Madame La Sablière] (Amsterdam, 1712). Cartesian doctrines were discussed in her salon; she was particularly concerned about the consistency of the doctrine of the Eucharist with Cartesianism. She and the Princess de Guéméné apparently triggered the theological debate which led to the *fréquente communion* affair documented in the preface to Antoine Arnauld, *De la fréquente communion* (Paris, 1643). She had first become influenced by Jansenism through the efforts of Mère Angelique Arnauld and Mère Agnès Arnauld of Port-Royal in 1640; she did not settle into its monastery in Paris until 1655, or, on some accounts, until after the death of the Comtesse de Maure in 1663.

Secondary Sources: Cousin, V. (1854), *Madame de Sablé: Nouvelles Etudes sur la société et les femmes illustres du dix-septième siècle*, Paris: Didier. Ivanoff, N. (1927), *La Marquise de Sablé et son Salon*, Paris: Presses Modernes. Picard, R. (1943), *Les Salons littéraires et la société française 1610–1789*, New York: Brentano's. Gibson, W. (1989), *Women in Seventeenth-Century France*, New York: St. Martin's Press. [Eileen O'Neill]

SCHURMAN, ANNA MARIA VAN b. Cologne, 1607; d. Wieuwerd (Friesland), 1678. One of the most famous female scholars of the seventeenth century, known as 'Sappho' and the 'Tenth Muse'. Born into a highly religious Reformed family that settled in Utrecht, she was educated by her father in Greek, Latin, arithmetic, geography, astronomy, and music. Gained attention in her youth for her artistic, poetic, and musical talents; in her late twenties, under the mentorship of Gisbertus Voetius, professor of oriental languages and theology, became the first female student at a Dutch university. Under his guidance, studied Hebrew, Arabic, Chaldee, Syriac, and Ethiopian and wrote the first Ethiopian grammar. Her correspondence with the Calvinist theologian André Rivet on the appropriateness of scholarship for women and her syllogistic arguments in defence of women's education were published in *Amica dissertatio inter Annam Mariam Schurmanniam et Andr. Rivetum de capacitate ingenii muliebris ad scientias* (Paris, 1638); reprinted as *Dissertatio logica de ingenii muliebris ad doctrinam et meliores litteras aptitudine, cui accedunt epistolae aliquot (Schurmanniae ipsius et Riveti) ejusdem argumenti* (Leiden, 1641 and 1673); French translation, *Question célèbre . . .* (Paris, 1646); English translation, *The Learned Maid, or, Whether a Maid May Be a Scholar? A Logick Exercise . . .* (London, 1659). Corresponded with the physician and Deputy to the States-General, Johan van Beverwijck, on the respective rôles played by God and medicine in controlling life and death. These letters were published posthumously in *Lettres de la très fameuse demoiselle Anne-Marie Schurmans, academicienne de la fameuse Université d'Utrecht, traduites du holandois par Madame De Zoutelandt . . .* (Paris, 1730), and her treatise on this topic was published separately as *De vitae termino* (Leiden, 1639; Rotterdam, 1644; Leiden, 1651); Dutch version, *Paelsteen van den tijt onzes levens* (Dordrecht, 1639). This treatise, her dissertation and correspondence with such figures as Richelieu, Gassendi, Mersenne, Spanheim, Heinsius, Saumaise, Constantijn Huygens, Elisabeth of Bohemia, Bathsua Makin, and Marie de Gournay appear in *Nobliss. Virginis Annae Mariae à Schurman, Opuscula. hebraea, graeca, latina, gallica, prosaica et metrica* (Leiden, 1648); reprinted 1650, 1652, 1794. Had contact with Descartes and Queen Christina of Sweden, but came to spurn both for religious reasons. By the 1650s, she had given up her studies. Became interested in the French Pietist mystic Jean de Labadie, whose community in Amsterdam she joined in 1669. The community was persecuted and forced to move to Herford (at the invitation of the Abbess Elisabeth of

Bohemia), then to Altona, and finally back to the Netherlands in Wieuwerd. Her autobiography and defence of the theological views of Labadism were published as *Eucleria: seu Melioris partis electio* . . . (Altona, 1673). Along these lines she also published *Korte Onderrichtinge Rakende de Staat* . . . (Amsterdam, 1675). Johann Gabriel Drechssler of Halle charged that her demand for inner illumination demeaned the authority of the Bible and implied the uselessness of human arts and sciences. She defended herself in her Dutch work *Euchleria II* (Amsterdam, 1684); Latin (Amsterdam, 1685); German, with Part I (Dessau, 1783). Other works include *Mysterium magnum oder Grosses Geheimnis* (Wesel, 1699) and *Uitbreiding over de drie eerste Capittels van Genesis* (Groningen, 1732).

Secondary Sources: Beverwyck, J. van (1639), *Van de Wtnementheyt des vrouwelicken Geslachts,* Dordrecht. Fischer, K. (1887), *History of Modern Philosophy: Descartes and His School,* New York: Scribner's. Birch (Pope-Hennessy), U. (1909), *Anna van Schurman: Artist, Scholar, Saint,* London: Longmans, Green and Co. Albistur, M. and D. Armogathe (1977), *Histoire du féminisme français,* Paris: Des femmes, tome 1. Irwin, J. L. (1980), 'Anna Maria van Schurman: The Star of Utrecht', in J. R. Brink (ed.), *Female Scholars: A Tradition of Learned Women Before 1800,* Montréal: Eden Press. Irwin, J. L. (1989) 'Anna Maria van Schurman: Learned Woman of Utrecht', in K. Wilson and F. Warnke (eds.), *Women Writers of the Seventeenth Century,* Athens, Ga.: University of Georgia Press. [Eileen O'Neill]

SCUDÉRY, MADELEINE DE [known as 'Sapho'] b. Havre, 1607; d. Paris, 1701. Précieuse, salonnière, novelist, and writer of moral essays and dialogues. Moved to Paris in 1637, where she took part in the salon of Madame de Rambouillet. In 1641, began writing her multi-volume novels under the name of her brother, Georges de Scudèry. Contributed to the *querelle des femmes* with her publication of *Les Femmes illustres ou les harangues héroïques* (Paris, 1642), under her brother's name. Began her own salon, the *Samedi,* in 1653, which until its demise around 1659 was frequented by members of the *Académie française* such as Gilles Ménage and Paul Pellisson, as well as by Mme de Sévigné, Mme de Sablé, Mme de Lafayette, and Mme de Maintenon. Awarded first prize by the *Académie française* for her essay *Discours de la gloire* (Paris, 1671), which was translated by Elizabeth Elstob as *An Essay upon Glory* (London, 1708). Anonymously published *Conversations sur divers sujets* (2 vols.) (Paris, 1680), which is translated as *Conversations upon Several Subjects* (2 vols.) (London, 1683). These anonymous publications follow: *Conversations nouvelles sur divers sujets* (2 vols.) (Paris, 1684); *Conversations morales ou la morale du monde* (2 vols.) (Amsterdam, 1686); *Nouvelles conversations de morale* (2 vols.) (The Hague, 1688); *Entretiens de morale* (2 vols.) (Paris, 1692). In 1684, she was elected to the Academy dei Ricovrati of Padua. Her correspondence can be found in Scudéry (1806), *Lettres de Mesdames de Scudéry, de Salvan de Saliez, et de Mademoiselle Descartes,* Paris: Collin, and in Rathery and Boutron (1873), *Mademoiselle de Scudéry: sa vie et sa correspondance avec un choix de ses poésies,* Paris: Techener.

Secondary Sources: Somaize, A. de (1660), *Le grand dictionnaire des précieuses,* Paris. Bosquillon (1701), 'Eloge de Mlle de Scudéry', *Journal des Savants,* July 11. Cousin, V. (1858), *La Société Française au XVIIe Siècle d'après le grand Cyrus de Mlle de Scudéry* (2 vols.), Paris: Didier et Cie. Magne, E. (1927), *Le Salon de Mlle de Scudéry ou Le Royaume de Tendre,* Monaco: Société des Conférences. McDougall, D. (1938), *Madeleine de Scudéry, Her Romantic Life and Death,* London: Methuen. Mongrédien, G. (1946), *Madeleine de Scudéry et son salon,* Paris: Tallandier. Adam, A. (1958), *Histoire de la littérature français au XVIIème siècle* (5 vols), Paris: Del Duca. Adam, A. (1959), 'La Préciosité', *Cahiers de l'Association des Etudes françaises,* 1. Lougee, C. (1976), *Le Paradis des Femmes: Women, Salons, and Social Stratification in Seventeenth-Century France,* Princeton: Princeton University Press. Niderst, A. (1976), *Madeleine de Scudéry, Paul Pellisson et leur monde,* Paris: Presses Universitaires de France. Aronson, N. (1978), *Mademoiselle de Scudéry,* Boston: Twayne. Aronson, N. (1984), 'Les femmes dans "Les conversations morales" de Mlle de Scudéry', in W. Leiner (ed.), *Onze nouvelles études sur l'image de la femme dans la littérature française du dix-septième siècle,* Tubingen/Paris: Editions Jean-Michel Place. Venesoen, C.

(1986), 'Madeleine de Scudéry et la "Defence du sexe" ', *Papers on French Seventeenth-Century Literature* 13 (25). Goldsmith, E. (1988), *Exclusive Conversations: The Art of Interaction in Seventeeth-Century France,* Philadelphia: University of Pennsylvania Press. [Eileen O'Neill]

SENNERT, DANIEL b. Breslau, 1572; d. Wittenberg, 1637. Physician, medical teacher, chemist, natural scientist. Attempted to reconcile Aristotle, Galen, Paracelsus, and atomism. Schooled in Breslau, enrolled at Wittenberg 1593; M.A. 1598. Studied medicine for three years at Leipzig, Jena, and Frankfurt an der Oder. Practised briefly in Berlin under Johann Georg Magnus. Doctor of Medicine, Wittenberg 1601; professor of medicine, Wittenberg 1602–37. Sennert was a prolific writer, whose numerous books and pamphlets were often reprinted. Selected works include *Institutionum medicinae libri V* (Wittenberg, 1611; 2d ed., Wittenberg, 1620; 3d ed., Wittenberg, 1628). *Epitome naturalis scientiae* (Wittenberg, 1618; 2d ed., Wittenberg, 1624; 3d ed., Oxford, 1632; others, 1683, 1641, 1650, 1651, 1653, 1664; English translation London, 1659). *De chymicorum cum Aristotelicis et Galenicis consensu ac dissensu liber: cui accessit appendix de constitutione chymiae* (Wittenberg, 1619; Wittenberg, 1629). *Practicae medicinae* (Wittenberg, 1628; Lyon, 1632; Wittenberg, 1636). Many other medical works and disputations. His works are collected in *Opera omnia* (3 vols.) (Venice, 1641), which was often reprinted.

Secondary Sources: Lasswitz, K. (1879), 'Die Erneuerung der Atomistik in Deutschland durch Daniel Sennert und sein Zusammenhang mit Asklepiades von Bithynien', *Viertelijahrsschrift für wissenshaftliche Philosophie* 3:408–34. Lasswitz, K. (1890), *Geschichte der Atomistik vom Mittelalter bis Newton* (2 vols.), Hamburg and Leipzig: Voss, vol. 1, pp. 436–54. Ramsauer, R. (1935), *Die Atomistik des Daniel Sennert,* Kiel: Ramsauer. Gregory, Tullio (1966), 'Studi sull'atomismo del seicento. II, David van Goorle e Daniel Sennert', *Giornale critico della Filosofia Italiana,* 20:44–63. Brentini, P. (1971), *Die Institutiones medicinae des Daniel Sennert (1572–1637),* Zurich: Juris. Neibyl, P. H. (1971), 'Sennert, van Helmont, and Medical Ontology', *Bulletin of the History of Medicine* 45:115–35. Eckart, W. (1983), " 'Auctoritas" versus "Veritas" or: Classical Authority and Its Role for the Perception of Truth in the Work of Daniel Sennert (1572–1637)', *Clio Medica* 18:131–40. Kangro, H., 'Daniel Sennert', *DSB.* [Gary Hatfield]

SERGEANT, JOHN b. Barrow-upon-Humber (Lincolnshire) 1622; d. 1707. Metaphysician, Roman-Catholic controversialist. Attended university at Cambridge (from 1639) where he took his B.A. in 1642/3. Conversion to the Roman Catholic Church in the mid-1640s. Went to the English College in Lisbon and was ordained a priest. In 1652, he was sent on a mission to England. During the Glorious Revolution he practised as physician under assumed names. In philosophy, Sergeant saw himself as working in the Aristotelian-Thomistic tradition. Best known as a critic of Descartes and Locke. Published *Sure-Footing in Christianity, or Rational Discourses on the Rule of Faith* (London 1665); *Catholick Letters* (London 1688); *The Method to Science* (London 1696); *Solid Philosophy Asserted* (London 1697); *Non Ultra: Or, A Letter to a learned Cartesian* (London 1698); *Transnatural Philosophy; or, Metaphysicks* (London 1700); *The Literary Life of John Sergeant. Written by Himself in Paris, 1700, at the Request of the Duke of Perth,* ed. John Kirk (London 1816). A letter by Sergeant to John Locke is published in Locke 1976– , vol. 5, pp. 635–7.

Secondary Sources: Bradish, N. C. (1929), 'John Sergeant, a Forgotten Critic of Descartes and Locke', *Monist* 39:571–92. Yolton, J. W. (1951), 'Locke's Unpublished Marginal Replies to John Sergeant', *Journal of the History of Ideas* 12:528–59. Yolton, J. W. (1956), *John Locke and the Way of Ideas,* Oxford: Oxford University Press, pp. 76–87, 103–13. Cooney, B. (1972–3), 'John Sergeant's Criticism of Locke's Theory of Ideas', *Modern Schoolman* 50:143–58. Thiel, U. (1983), *Lockes Theorie der personalen Identitaet,* Bonn: Bouvier, pp. 24–7, 34, 48–9, 120–5. Glauser, R. (1988), 'John Sergeant's Argument against Descartes and the Way of Ideas', *Monist* 71:585–95. Krook, Dorothea (1993), *John Sergeant and His Circle,* Leiden: Brill. [Udo Thiel]

SOPHIE, ELECTRESS OF HANOVER b. The Hague, 1630; d. Herrenhausen, 1714. Philosophical correspondent of Leibniz, and mother of Sophie Charlotte, Queen of Prussia (who was herself a philosophical interlocutor of Leibniz, Toland, and Bayle). Youngest daughter of Elector Palatine, Frederick V, and Elizabeth Stuart; sister of Elisabeth of Bohemia. Tutored at Leiden, spent her youth at The Hague and Heidelberg until her marriage to Ernst August in 1658. Corresponded with Leibniz from 1684 to 1714; more than three hundred letters are extant. She pressed Leibniz on his belief in the multiplicity of individual substances and in the immateriality of rational thought, and discussed with him the philosophical views of Matheus Molanus, John Toland, Damaris Masham, John Locke, Catherine Trotter Cockburn, Pierre Bayle, Franciscus Mercurius Van Helmont, Jacques Bossuet, Anthony Collins. Her correspondence with Leibniz appears in Leibniz (1874), *Correspondance de Leibniz avec l'électrice Sophie de Brunswick-Lunebourg,* ed. O. Klopp (3 vols.), Hanover: Kindworth; other letters appear in Sophie (1927), *Briefwechsel der Kurfürstin Sophie von Hanover,* Berlin and Leipzig: K. J. Koehler.

Secondary Sources: Sophie (1879), *Memoiren der Herzogin Sophie, nachmals Kurfürstin von Hanover,* ed. A. Kocker, Leipzig: S. Hirzel; English trans. (1888), *Memoirs of Sophia, Electress of Hanover 1630–80,* London: Bentley. Foucher de Careil, L. A. (1876), *Leibniz et les deux Sophies,* Paris: Germer-Bailliére. Baily, F. E. (1936), *Sophia of Hanover and Her Times,* London: Hutchinson and Co. Kroll, M. (1973), *Sophie: Electress of Hanover: A Personal Portrait,* London: Gollancz. Zedler, B. (1989), 'The Three Princesses', *Hypatia* 4:1. [Eileen O'Neill]

SORBIERE, SAMUEL b. St. Ambroix, 1615; d. Paris, 1670. Physician, Gassendist, translator, biographer. Studied medicine at Paris and practised in Holland until 1650. In 1653 he converted from Protestantism to Catholicism. He returned to Paris in 1656 and became an early member of the Montmor Academy, which met regularly to discuss scientific questions. He travelled to England where he met Hobbes and Oldenburg and attended meetings of the Royal Society (recounted in his *Relation d'un voyage en Angleterre,* Paris, 1664). His medical works gained little esteem from his contemporaries and include *Discours sceptique sur le passage du chyle et sur le mouvement du coeur* (Leiden, 1648); and *Discours de M. de Sorbière, touchant diverses expériences de la transfusion du sang* (Paris, 1668). A strong anti-Cartesian, he was a great admirer of Gassendi and Hobbes. He published little of philosophical significance himself, but edited and translated works which supported the Gassendist cause. He edited Gassendi's *Disquisitio metaphysica adversus Cartesium* (Amsterdam, 1644); he wrote the biographical prefaces to Gassendi's *Opera omnia* (Lyon, 1658) and Gassendi's *Syntagma Philosophiae Epicuri* (The Hague, 1659). He also translated works by Thomas More (*L'Utopie,* Amsterdam, 1643); and by Thomas Hobbes (*Le corps politique,* Leiden, 1652); *Elemens philosophiques du citoyen,* Amsterdam, 1649). He began but never completed a translation of Sextus Empiricus.

Secondary Sources: Brown, H. (1934), *Scientific Organizations in Seventeenth-Century France (1620–80),* Baltimore: Williams and Wilkins. Graverol, F. de (1709), *Memories of the Life of S. Sorbière,* London. Balz, Albert (1951), 'Samuel Sorbière, 1615–1670', in *Cartesian Studies,* New York: Columbia University Press, pp. 65–79. Popkin, R. (1953), 'Samuel Sorbière's Translation of Sextus Empiricus', *Journal of the History of Ideas* 14: 617–21. Lennon, T. M. (1993), *The Battle of the Gods and Giants,* Princeton: Princeton University Press. [Patricia Easton]

SPINOZA, BENEDICTUS DE b. Amsterdam, 1632; d. The Hague, 1677. Dutch Jewish philosopher. Went to rabbinical school, where he learned Hebrew and read the works of Jewish thinkers, such as Maimonides. Learned Latin and sought instruction in natural philosophy and in the philosophy of Descartes. Excommunicated in 1656. Moved to Ouwerkerk, a village south of Amsterdam, where he supported himself by making lenses, then to Rijnsburg in 1660. He moved to Voorburg, near The Hague, in 1663, and ultimately resided in The Hague itself. Published *Cogitata Metaphysica* and *Renati*

*Des Cartes Principiorum Philosophiae Pars I et II, More Geometrico demonstratae* (Amsterdam, 1663). Corresponded with Henry Oldenburg, secretary of the Royal Society. Published *Tractatus Theologico-Politicus* in 1670; actually published in Amsterdam, it appeared under the name of a fictitious publisher in Hamburg. Refused the professorship of philosophy at the University of Heidelberg, 1673. His *Opera Posthuma* (Amsterdam, 1677, also published in Dutch translation under the title *De Nagelate Schriften*, Amsterdam, 1677), included *Ethica, ordine geometrico demonstrata, Tractatus politicus,* and *Tractatus de Intellectus Emendatione.* The standard edition of his writings is Spinoza 1925.

Secondary Sources: Joachim, M. M. (1901), *A Study of the Ethics of Spinoza,* Oxford: Oxford University Press. Wolfson, H. A. (1934), *The Philosophy of Spinoza* (2 vols.), Cambridge, Mass.: Harvard University Press. Hampshire, S. (1962), *Spinoza,* New York: Penguin. Deleuze, G. (1968), *Spinoza et le problème de l'expression,* Paris: Minuit. Gueroult, M. (1968–74), *Spinoza* (2 vols.), Paris: Aubier. Curley, E. (1969), *Spinoza's Metaphysics,* Cambridge, Mass.: Harvard University Press. Matheron, A. (1969), *Individu et communauté chez Spinoza,* Paris: Minuit. Matheron, A. (1971), *Le Christ et le salut des ignorants chez Spinoza,* Paris: Aubier. Macherey, P. (1979), *Hegel ou Spinoza,* Paris: Maspera. Alquié, F. (1981), *Le rationalisme de Spinoza,* Paris: Presses Universitaires de France. Bennett, J. (1984), *A Study of Spinoza's Ethics,* Cambridge: Cambridge University Press. Curley, E. (1988), *Behind the Geometrical Method,* Princeton: Princeton University Press. Donagan, A. (1989), *Spinoza,* Chicago: University of Chicago Press. Yovel, Y. (1989), *Spinoza and Other Heretics,* 2 vols., Princeton: Princeton University Press. Negri, A. (1991), *The Savage Anomaly: The Power of Spinoza's Metaphysics and Politics,* Minneapolis: University of Minnesota Press. [Roger Ariew]

STILLINGFLEET, EDWARD b. Cranborne, Dorset, 1635; d. London, 1699. Scholar and divine. A year after graduating M.A. at Cambridge (1656), Stillingfleet received the rectory of Sutton. His first book was *Irenicum: A Weapon-Salve for the Churches Wounds . . . : Whereby a Foundation Is Laid for the Churches Peace, and the Accomodation of Our Present Differences . . .* (London, 1659), a book intended to promote peace between warring Protestant sects, particularly the Presbyterians and the Episcopalians. Stillingfleet followed this with a greatly admired defence of the authority of Scripture, *Origines sacrae* (London, 1662), and, two years later, *A Rational Account of the Grounds of the Protestant Church* (London, 1664). Church dignities soon followed, and from 1667 Stillingfleet was living in London, where he became a popular preacher. He was made dean of St. Paul's in 1678 and elected bishop of Worcester in 1689. Were it not for his bad health, he would have probably followed Tillotson in 1694 as archbishop of Canterbury. An indefatigable apologist of the Church of England, Stillingfleet nevertheless found time to compose more scholarly works such as *Origenes Britannicae* (London, 1685). During 1696–7 Stillingfleet was engaged in a dispute with John Locke over the latter's alleged impugning of the doctrine of trinity in his *Essay concerning Human Understanding.* The dispute begins with Stillingfleet's *A Discourse in Vindication of the Doctrine of the Trinity: With an Answer to the Late Socinian Objections against It from Scripture, Antiquity and Reason* (London, 1697), part of an answer to John Toland's celebrated pamphlet, *Christianity Not Mysterious* (London, 1696). In the course of his argument, Stillingfleet associated Locke's view of substance with Toland's sceptical view of religion, which elicited a reply from Locke. This began an exchange of pamphlets between the two of them that constitutes one of the most important documents for understanding Locke's *Essay.* Locke contributed three letters to this exchange: *A Letter to the Right Rev. Edward Ld. Bishop of Worcester . . .* (London, 1697), *Mr. Locke's Reply to the Right Rev. the Lord Bishop of Worcester's Answer to his Letter* (London, 1697), and *Mr. Locke's Reply to the Right Rev. the Lord Bishop of Worcester's Answer to his Second Letter* (London, 1699). Stillingfleet contributed two letters: *An Answer to Mr. Locke's Letter, concerning Some Passages Relating to His Essay of Humane Understanding* (London, 1697), and *An Answer to Mr. Locke's Second Letter; Wherein His Notion of IDEAS is prov'd to be Inconsistent with it self, and with the ARTICLES of the CHRISTIAN FAITH* (London, 1698). Locke's letters are reprinted most recently in Locke 1823. Stillingfleet's appear, together with the rest of his work, in *The Works of That Eminent and Most Learned Prelate, Dr. Edw. Stillingfleet, Late Lord Bishop of Worcester* (6 vols.) (London, 1710). His *Miscellaneous Discourses on Several Occasions* (London, 1735) was published posthumously by his son, the Reverend James Stillingfleet. There is no modern edition of Stillingfleet's writings.

Secondary Sources: Goodwin, Timothy (1708), *The Life and Character of . . . Edward Stillingfleet*, London. Popkin, Richard H. (1971), 'The Philosophy of Bishop Stillingfleet', *Journal of the History of Philosophy* 9:303–19. Carroll, Robert T. (1975), *The Common-Sense Philosophy of Religion of Bishop Edward Stillingfleet, 1635–99*, The Hague: Nijhoff. Fishman, Joel H. (1978), 'Edward Stillingfleet, Bishop Of Worcester', Ph.D. diss., University of Wisconsin. Reedy, Gerard (1984), 'Barrow, Stillingfleet, and Tillotson on the truth of Scripture', in *Greene Centennial Studies*, ed. Paul J. Korshin and Robert R. Allen, Charlottesville: University Press of Virginia. Reedy, Gerard (1985), *The Bible and Reason*, Philadelphia: University of Pennsylvania Press. Hutton, Sarah (1992), 'Edward Stillingfleet, Henry More, and the Decline of "Moses Atticus" ', in *Philosophy, Science, and Religion in England 1640–1700*, ed. Richard Kroll et al., Cambridge: Cambridge University Press. [Mordechai Feingold]

STURM, JOHANN CHRISTOPH (Sturmius) b. Hilpoltstein, 1635; d. Altdorf, 1703. Mathematician, natural philosopher, Cartesian, occasionalist, whose eclectic tendencies and good knowledge of ancient philosophy led him to criticise some Cartesian teachings and to combine others with ancient philosophy, especially the philosophy of Aristotle. Educated in Weissenburg (Franken); Nuremberg; Jena, where he received an M.A. (in 1658) and where he taught philosophy and mathematics; and in Leiden (1660). Returned to Jena, resumed lecturing in mathematics and philosophy, and added theology to the course of his studies. Worked as a private schoolmaster in Nuremberg, served for five years as Pastor in Deiningen (1664–9). Trip to Holland led to an interest in the Cartesian philosophy and to attempts to combine parts of the Cartesian system with the philosophy of Aristotle. Upon the death of Abdias Trew, received a position as professor of mathematics and physics in Altdorf. Despite numerous offers from abroad, remained in Altdorf for the rest of his life. Corresponded with many prominent intellectuals, including Leibniz. Wrote and published essays, letters, and books on a number of topics including *Scientia cosmica* (Altdorf, 1670), *De authoritate interpretum naturae ac speciatim Aristotelis dissertatio . . .* (Altdorf, 1672); *De Cartesianis et Cartesianismo* (Altdorf, 1677), *Ad virum celeberrimum Henricum Morum epistola qua de ipsius principio hylarchico seu spiritu naturae . . .* (Nuremberg, 1676); *Philosophia eclectica* (Altdorf, 1686); *Mathesis enucleata* (Nuremberg, 1689), which went through several editions and was translated into English in 1700; *Mathesis compendiaris* (Nuremberg, 1693). There is no standard edition.

Secondary Sources: Apin, S. J. (1728), *Vitae professorum philosophiae qui a condita Academia Altorfina . . . clarverunt*, Altdorf. Baku, G. (1891), 'Der Streit ueber den Naturbegriff am Ende des 17. Jahrhunderts', *Zeitschrift fuer Philosophie und philosophische Kritik* 98:162–90. Bohatec, J. (1912), *Die Cartesianische Scholastik und reformierten Dogmatik des 17. Jahrhunderts*, Leipzig: Deichert. Mercer, C. and Sleigh, R. C. (1995), 'Metaphysics: The Early Period to the *Discourse on Metaphysics*', in N. Jolley (ed.), *Cambridge Companion to Leibniz*, Cambridge: Cambridge University Press. [Christia Mercer]

SUÁREZ, FRANCISCO, S.J. b. Granada, 1548; d. Lisbon, 1617. Spanish Jesuit philosopher, theologian, jurist. Entered Society of Jesus, 1564. Studied law, philosophy, and theology at Salamanca. Taught philosophy at Segovia, 1571–4. Taught theology at Valladolid, 1574–5; at Segovia and Avila, 1575–6; at Valladolid, 1576–80; at Collegio Romano, 1580–5; at Alcalá, 1585–93; at Salamanca, 1593–7; at Coimbra, 1597–1616. Visited Rome, 1604–6. Prominent in the Counter-Reformation revival of scholasticism. Wrote *De legibus* (Coimbra, 1612) and the monumental *Disputationes metaphysicae* (Salamanca, 1597), perhaps the most important work in late scholastic thought, as well as commentaries and treatises on many works of Aristotle. The standard edition of his works is Suárez (1856–78), *Opera Omnia*, ed. D. M. André (28 vols.) (Paris).

Secondary Sources: Werner, K. (1889), *Franz Suarez und die Scholastik der letzen Jarhhunderte* (2 vols.), Regensburg: G. Manz. Masi, R. (1947), *Il movimento assoluto e la positione secondo Suarez*, Rome: Facoltà di Filosofia del Pont. Ateneo Lateranense. Alcorta, J. I. (1949), *La theoria de los modos in Suárez*, Madrid: Consejo Superior de Investigaciones Científicas, Instituto 'Luis Vives' de Filosofia. Iturrioz, J. (1949), *Estudios sobre la metapfisica de Francisco Suárez*, Madrid: Ediciones Fax. Hamilton, B. (1963), *Political Thought in Sixteenth-Century Spain: A Study of the Political Ideas of Victoria, De Soto, Suárez, and Molina*, Oxford: Oxford University Press. Wilenius, R. (1963), *The Social and Political Theory of Francisco Suárez*, Helsinki: Societas Philosophicae Fennica. Ernst, W. (1964), *Die Tugendlehre des Franz Suarez*, Leipzig: St. Benno-Verlag. Cronin, T. J. (1966), *Objective Being in Descartes and Suarez*, Rome: Analecta Gregoriana. Lewalter, E. (1967), *Spanisch-jesuitische und deutsch-lutherische Metaphysik des 17. Jahrhunderts*, 2d ed., Darmstadt: Wissenschaftliche Buchgesellschaft. Seigfried, H. (1967), *Warheit und Metaphysik bei Suarez*, Bonn: Bouvier. Lohr, C. (1976), 'Jesuit Aristotelianism and Sixteenth-Century Metaphysics', in G. Fletcher and M. B. Schuete (eds.), *Pardosis: Studies in Memory of Edwin A. Quain*, New York: Fordham University Press, pp. 203–20. Andrés, M. (1976–7), *La teologia española en el siglo XVI* (2 vols.), Madrid: La Editorial Católica. *Simposio Francisco Suárez* (1980), *Cuardenos salamantinos de filosofia* 7:3–394. Castellote, S. (1982), *Die Antropologie des Suarez*, 2d ed., Freiburg i. Br.: Alber. Courtine, J.–F. (1990), *Suarez et le système de la métaphysique*, Paris: Presses Universitaires de France. [Knud Haakonssen]

SUCHON, GABRIELLE b. Semur, 1631; d. Dijon, 1703. Feminist social and political philosopher, metaphysician, and theologian. For some years a Dominican nun, then renounced her vows. Went to Rome and was awarded dispensation from her vows, against the wishes of her parents. A judgement of the Parlement of Dijon decreed that she had to return to the monastery. She managed to evade the decree. She had published (under the name G.-S. Aristophile), at her own expense, *Traité de la morale et de la politique, divisé en trois parties, savoir: la liberté, la science et l'autorité où l'on voit que les personnes du Sexe, pour en être privées, ne laissent pas d'avoir une capacité naturelle qui les en peut rendre participantes. Avec un petit traité de la faiblesse, de la légèreté et de l'inconstance qu'on leur attribue mal à propos* (Lyon, 1693). In the three book-length parts devoted to 'liberty', 'science', and 'authority', she analyses these notions and argues that while women are in fact deprived of access to them, they are by nature suited for them. She displays a knowledge of the ancient Stoics, Cynics, Sceptics, and mediaeval scholastics. The work responds to the influential feminist treatise by the Cartesian François Poulain de la Barre, *De l'égalité des deux sexes* (Paris, 1673). An excerpt and review by M. le Président Cousin de Dijon appear in *Journal des Savants* (6 December 1694). There is a modern edition of the first part (Suchon, 1988). An extract of a second work, *Du célibat Volontaire, ou la Vie sans engagement, par Demoiselle Suchon* (Paris, 1700), and reviews appeared in *Nouvelles de la république des lettres* (May 1700) and *Journal des savants* (May 1700).

Secondary Sources: Papillon, P. (1745), *Bibliothèque des auteurs de Bourgogne*, Dijon: Philippe Marteret. Barbier, A. (1806–9), *Dictionnaire des ouvrages anonymes et pseudonymes composés, traduits ou publiés en français*, Paris; new release of the 1879 edition: (1963), Hildesheim: Olms. Richard, S. A. (1914), *Feminist Writers of the Seventeenth Century*, London. Ronzeaud, P. (1975), 'La Femme au pouvoir ou le monde à l'envers', *Revue XVIIe siècle*, no. 108. Albistur, M., and D. Armogathe (1977), *Histoire du féminisme français*, tome 1, Paris: Des femmes. Hoffman, P. (1978), 'Le féminisme spirituel de Gabrielle Suchon', *Revue XVIIe siècle*, no. 121. Ronzeaud, P. (1978), 'Note sur l'article de Paul Hoffman', *Revue XVIIe siècle*, no. 121. Fauré, C. (1985), *La Démocratie sans les femmes*, Paris: Presses Universitaires de France. Le Doeuff, M. (1989), *L'Etude et le rouet*, Paris: Les Editions du Seuil; English edition (1991), *Hipparchia's Choice*, trans. T. Selous, Oxford: Blackwell. [Eileen O'Neill]

THOMASIUS, CHRISTIAN (Thomas) b. Leipzig, 1655; d. Halle, 1728. Founding figure of German Enlightenment, 'eclectic' philosopher, natural lawyer, reformer in university and society. Son of philosopher Jakob Thomasius. Educated under prominent Pufendorf critic V. Alberti in Leipzig (magister in philosophy 1672) and Frankfurt an der Oder (doctorate in law 1679). Advocate in Leipzig 1679–86. Lectured on Grotius and Pufendorf at Leipzig 1682–90, initiating lectures in German (1687). Forced to leave Leipzig (Saxony) 1690; transferred to Halle (Brandenburg) and was instrumental in the founding of the Friederichs-Universität there (1694), a model for German Enlightenment universities. Direktor (president) of University for life from 1710. A huge *oeuvre* divides into three broad periods. In the 1680s, he worked to complete Pufendorf's programme, mainly in *Institutiones jurisprudentiae divinae* (Frankfurt a.d.O. and Leipzig, 1688; prefaced by important autobiographical account, 'Dissertatio prooemialis'; German trans. Halle, 1709). This was broadened to a comprehensive eclecticism, fully realised, both in theory and in institutional reform, in Halle; main works on this line: *Introductio ad philosophiam aulicam* (Halle, 1688; German trans. *Einleitung zur Hof-Philosophie,* Frankfurt a.d.O. and Leipzig, 1710), *Freymüthige Lustige und Ernsthafte iedoch Vernunfft- und Gesetz-Mäßige Gedanken oder Monats-Gespräche [über allerhand fürnehmlich aber Neue Bücher durch alle zwölf Monate des 1688. und 1689. Jahres durchgeführet von Christian Thomasius]* (Halle, 1690), *Einleitung der Vernunft-Lehre* (Halle, 1691), *Ausübung der Vernunft-Lehre* (Halle, 1691), *Einleitung der Sitten-Lehre* (Halle, 1692). After *Ausübung der Sitten-lehre* (Halle, 1696) a pietistic crisis set in for several years. This was broken with *Fundamenta juris naturae et gentium ex sensu communi deducta* (Halle and Leipzig, 1705; German trans. Halle, 1709). Continued to publish prodigiously. Of philosophical interest are especially *Paulo plenior historia juris naturalis* (Halle, 1719) and several of his more than 100 dissertations and scores of essays dealing with issues in moral enlightenment and law reform (bigamy, witchcraft, torture, heresy, adultery, etc.). There is no standard modern edition of his work, but a facsimile reprint edition of selected works is in progress, the *Ausgewählte Werke* (Hildesheim: Olms, 1994–    ). Some of his correspondence can be found in Pufendorf (1893), 'Briefe von Pufendorf', ed. K. Varrentrapp, *Historische Zeitschrift* 70:1–51, 192–232, and Pufendorf (1897), 'Pufendorf briefe an Falaiseau, Friese und Weigel', ed. K. Varrentrapp, *Historische Zeitschrift* 73:59–67.

Secondary Sources: Bienert, W. (1934), *Der Anbruch der christlichen deutschen Neuzeit dargestellt an Wissenschaft und Glauben des Christian Thomasius,* Halle: Akademie Verlag. Lieberwirth, R. (1955), *Christian Thomasius. Sein wissenschaftliches Lebenswerk,* Weimar: Hermann Böhlaus Nachfolger. Bloch, E. (1968), *Christian Thomasius, ein deutscher Gelehrter ohne Misere,* Frankfurt: Suhrkamp. Rüping, H. (1968), *Die Naturrechtslehre des Christian Thomasius und ihre Fortbildung in der Thomasius-Schule,* Bonn: L. Rohrscheid. Barnard, F. M. (1971), 'The "Practical Philosophy" of Christian Thomasius', *Journal of the History of Ideas* 32:221–46. Schneiders, W. (1971), *Naturrecht und Liebesethik: Zur Geschichte der praktischen Philosophie im Hinblick auf Christian Thomasius,* Hildesheim: Olms. Cattaneo, M. (1976), *Delitto e pena nel pensiero di Christian Thomasius,* Milano: Giuffre. Schubart-Fikentscher, G. (1977), *Christian Thomasius: Seine Bedeutung als Hochschullehrer am Beginn der deutschen Aufklärung,* Berlin: Akademie Verlag. Battaglia, F. (1982; 1st ed. 1936), *Christiano Thomasio. Filosofo e giurista,* Bologna: CLUEB. Barnard, F. M. (1988), 'Fraternity and Citizenship: Two Ethics of Mutuality in Christian Thomasius', *Review of Politics* 50:582–602. Schneiders, W. (ed.) (1989), *Christian Thomasius 1655–1728. Interpretationen zu Werk und Wirkung: Mit einer Bibliographie der neueren Thomasius-Literatur,* Hamburg: Meiner. [Knud Haakonssen]

TOLETUS (Francisco de Toledo) b. Cordova, 1532; d. Rome, 1596. Jesuit philosopher and cardinal. Studied in Valencia and Salamanca (under Domingo de Soto). Entered the Company of Jesus (1558; followed in 1562 by his former student Juan de Maldonado). Professor of philosophy (1559–62) and theology (1562–9) in Rome. For twenty-four years, penitentiary and preacher at the Pontifical Court. Sent as a diplomat in Poland (1572), Germany, Belgium (in Louvain, against Baius in 1580) and France.

Made a Cardinal by Clement VIII (1593). Published several commentaries of Aristotle, all of them with multiple editions (*Introductio in dialecticam Aristotelis,* Rome, 1561; *Commentaria una cum quaestionibus in universam Aristotelis logicam,* Rome, 1572; *Commentaria una cum quaestionibus in VIII libros de physica auscultatione,* Cologne, 1574; *Commentaria una cum quaestionibus in II libros De generatione et corruptione,* Venice, 1573). Most famous is his *Commentaria una cum quaestionibus in III libros De anima,* Venice, 1574, 23 editions until 1590). These works were collected in *Omnia quae hucusque extant opera,* 4 vols. (Lyon, 1587–8; 2d ed., Lyon, 1592 and 1608). Wrote also several biblical commentaries, mainly on the *Gospel of John,* 2 vols. (Rome, 1588–92), and the *Epistle to the Romans* (Rome, 1602).

Secondary Sources: Stegmüller, F. (1934–5), 'Tolet et Cajetan', *Revue Thomiste* 17:358–71. Special issue *Archivio teologico granadino* 3 (1940). Rodriguez Molero, F. (1932–92), 'Toledo', in Marcel Viller et al. (eds.) (1932–95), *Dictionnaire de spiritualité ascetique et mystique* (17 tomes in 21 vols.), Paris: Beauchesne, t. 15, col. 1013–17. Wallace, W. (1984), *Galileo and His Sources: The Heritage of the Collegio Romano in Galileo's Science,* Princeton: Princeton University Press. [Jean-Robert Armogathe]

TORRICELLI, EVANGELISTA b. Faenza, 1608; d. Florence, 1647. Mathematician, natural philosopher. Studied at Jesuit school in Faenza 1625–6; entered University of Rome ca. 1627. Corresponded with Galileo from 1632, moved to Florence 1641 for closer collaboration with Galileo. After latter's death 1642, succeeded to his post of philosopher and mathematician to grand duke of Tuscany. Published collection of mathematical works, *Opera geometrica* (Florence, 1644), pushing method of indivisibles beyond Cavalieri's work. In same year modified experiments discussed by Baliani and G. Berti by using mercury in place of water to demonstrate 'Torricellian vacuum'. The standard edition of his works is Torricelli (1919–44), *Opere di Evangelista Torricelli,* ed. Gino Loria and Giuseppe Vassura (4 vols. in 5), vols. 1–3, Faenza: G. Montanari, 1919; vol.4, Faenza: Fratelli Lega, 1944; see also Torricelli (1956), *Lettere e documenti riguardanti Evangelista Torricelli,* ed. Giuseppe Rossini, Faenza: Fratelli Lega.

Secondary Sources: Waard, C. de (1936), *L'Expérience barométrique: Ses antecedents et ses explications,* Thouars: Imprimerie nouvelle, chap. 9. *Convegno di studi torricelliani in occasione del 350ᵉ anniversario della nascita di Evangelista Torricelli (19–20 ottobre 1958)* (1959), Faenza: Fratelli Lega. Middleton, W. E. K. (1964), *The History of the Barometer,* Baltimore: Johns Hopkins University Press, chap. 2. Gliozzi, M. (1976), 'Evangelista Torricelli', in *DSB.* [Peter Dear]

VAN HELMONT, FRANCISCUS MERCURIUS b. Vilvorde, Spanish Netherlands (Belgium)(?), 1614(?); d. Cöln a.d. Spree(?), 1698(?) Son of the eminent physician and natural philosopher Johannes Baptista Van Helmont, Franciscus Mercurius Van Helmont was distinguished as a physician and joined the circles of several aristocrats as resident physician and philosopher in England and on the Continent. For decades he served the house of Palatine as diplomat and medical adviser; these duties allowed him to be a conduit of exchange between intellectuals from the Netherlands, the Low Countries, Germany, and England. He carried books and letters between the English Neoplatonic philosophers Henry More and Ralph Cudworth and Christian Knorr von Rosenroth, the German orientalist and kabbalist. From 1671 to 1679 he resided at Ragley in Warwickshire as the physician to the sickly and learned Lady Anne Conway. Introduced by Lady Conway to William Penn, George Barclay, and other distinguished Quakers. Van Helmont adopted many Quaker beliefs and considered himself a member of the sect. Van Helmont departed England with the death of his patron in 1679. In 1694 he was invited by Leibniz and Sophie, Electress of Brunswick, to visit Hanover and to expound his philosophical system. Leibniz drew much from the younger Van Helmont's vitalism and his insistence on the monistic unity of body and spirit. His works mingle ideas from Platonic, kabbalistic, Paracelsian, Rosicrucian, and Hermetic sources. Like many of his contemporaries, he engaged in the search for a universal language and developed a language for the deaf and dumb. He served as posthumous editor of his father's works.

He expounded his cosmographical vision in *The Paradoxal Discourse . . . concerning the Macrocosm and Microcosm* (London, 1685). Like More, he was especially interested in the idea of the pre-existence of souls and the Christian doctrine of reincarnation. He addressed these in his *Seder Olam, or the Order, Series or Succession of All the Ages . . .* (London, 1684), *The Divine Being and Its Attributes Philosophically Demonstrated* (London, 1683) and *Two Hundred Queries Moderately Propounded concerning the Doctrine of the Revolution of Humane Souls and Its Conformity to the Truths of Christianity* (London, 1684). Frequent references to Van Helmont are found in the correspondence of Leibniz and Henry More. While his own theological works have fallen into oblivion, historians remember him better for his facilitating communication between Continental and English thinkers and for promoting the publications of his father, Lady Conway, and William Penn.

Secondary Sources: Gottesman, Alison Coudert (1972), *F. M. Van Helmont: His Life and Thought,* Ph.D. diss., University of London. Gottesman, Alison Coudert (1976), 'A Quaker-Kabbalist Controversy', *Journal of the Warburg and Courtauld Institutes* 39:171–89. Merchant, Carolyn (1979), 'The Vitalism of Francis Mercury Van Helmont: Its Influence on Leibniz', *Ambix* 26:170–83. Nicholson, M. H., and S. Hutton (1992), *The Conway Letters, The Correspondence of Anne, Viscountess Conway, Henry More, and Their Friends 1642–84,* Oxford: Oxford University Press, pp. 308–84. [Martha Baldwin]

VAN HELMONT, JOHANNES BAPTISTA (Joan) b. Brussels, 1579; d. Vilvoorde, Spanish Netherlands (Belgium), 1644. Van Helmont enjoyed little distinction as a medical practitioner during his lifetime; after an acerbic battle over the publication of his *Curationis magneticae, et unguenti armarii magica impostura, clare demonstrata* (*Magnetic Cure of Wounds*) (Luxemburg, 1621), Van Helmont suffered persecution by the Inquisition. Historians of medicine have generally studied Van Helmont as an expositor of Paracelsus. Like Paracelsus, Van Helmont constructed his own synthesis of religion, natural philosophy, cosmology, empirical science, and medical theory and railed against traditional Galenic and Aristotelian learning of the universities. Following Paracelsus's example, Van Helmont freely introduced new words to his medical discourse which had puzzling, but wide, non-technical meanings. But Van Helmont was no slavish imitator of the master. Far more than Paracelsus, Van Helmont believed that matter is endowed with spiritual qualities which account for its activity and direction to certain ends. While historians of science and medicine commonly point to Van Helmont's use of quantification and experiment as evidence of his modernity, it is important to note that he considered experiment primarily a key to deciphering the hieroglyphic script of nature. Inclined to religious mysticism, Van Helmont accepted astral forces as part of his explanation of disease. Most of Van Helmont's published works appeared posthumously. These were collected and edited under the title *Ortus medicinae* (Amsterdam, 1648); seven later editions had appeared by 1707. English, German, and French translations appeared in 1664, 1683, and 1670, respectively. There is a modern reprint of the German translation, Van Helmont (1971), *Aufgang der Artznney-Kunst,* ed. W. Pagel and F. Kemp (2 vols.), Munich: Kosel-Verlag.

Secondary Sources: The best biography of Van Helmont remains Pagel, Walter (1982), *Joan Baptista Van Helmont, Reformer of Science and Medicine,* Cambridge: Cambridge University Press. See also: Metzger, Helene (1936), 'La philosophie chimique de J.-B. van Helmont', *Annales Guibhard* 12: 140–55. Pagel, Walter (1944), *The Religious and Philosophical Aspects of Van Helmont's Science and Medicine,* Baltimore: Johns Hopkins University Press. Reti, Ladislao (1988), *Some Aspects of Seventeenth-Century Medicine and Science,* Berkeley: University of California Press. [Martha Baldwin]

VANINI, GIULIO CESARE (Lucilio) b. Taurisano, near Naples, 1585; d. Toulouse, 1619. Italian philosopher, theologian, and lawyer. Studied with the Carmelites at Naples (doctor of civil and canon law, 1606) and at Padua. Travelled widely. Went to France in 1614, where he spent some time at Lyon and at Paris, before his fatal trip to Toulouse, circa 1617. Published *Amphiteatrum aeternae providentiae*

(Lyon, 1615) and *De admirandis naturae reginae Deaque mortalium arcanis libri IV* (Paris, 1616). Convicted of the crimes of atheism, blasphemy, and impiety, he was executed in 1619. The standard edition of his works is Vanini (1990), *Opera,* ed. G. Papuli and F. P. Raimondi, Galatina: Congedo.

Secondary Source: Namer, E. (1980), *La vie et l'oeuvre de J. C. Vanini,* Paris: Vrin. [Roger Ariew]

WHITE, THOMAS (Thomas Blacklo, Blacklow, Blackloe, Thomas Albius, Anglus, Vitus) b. Hutton, Essex, 1593; d. London, 1676. Catholic priest, natural philosopher, theologian, political theorist. Founder of a counter-reforming movement among English Roman Catholics, regarded by the Holy Office as a heresiarch. Educated in Catholic colleges on the Continent (Saint Omer, Valladolid, Seville, Louvain, Lisbon, and Douai), ordained priest at Arras in 1617. Taught philosophy and theology at Douai College from 1617 until 1624, when he moved to Paris to study canon law. Representative of the English secular clergy at Rome, 1625–30. President of English College in Lisbon, 1631–3. Left Lisbon for England after controversy over his orthodoxy and became important figure among English secular clergy. Theological disputes with Lucius Cary, Viscount Falkland, and William Chillingworth. Brought Sir Kenelm Digby back to the Roman church. *De mundo dialogi tres* (Paris, 1642) elicited major critique from Hobbes. In 1645 and 1646, went on missions to Rome to entreat for papal aid for Charles I. In 1647, his followers (Blackloists) drew up list of 'Instructions' for English Catholics to achieve toleration of worship. Attempted to develop an Aristotelian mechanical philosophy in *Institutionum peripateticarum* (Lyon, 1646; English trans., London, 1656), and to claim its absolute truth on rational grounds in *Euclides physicus sive de principiis naturae* (London, 1657), and *Euclides metaphysicus sive de principiis sapientiae* (London, 1658). *The Grounds of Obedience and Government* (London, 1655), an attempt to ingratiate English Catholics with Cromwell which advocated government by social contract and defended the regicide, proved embarrassing after the Restoration. After publishing claims about the way to arrive at truth in religion, *Controversy-Logicke* (Paris, 1659) and *Religion and Reason Mutually Corresponding and Assisting Each Other* (Paris, 1660), he engaged in controversy with Joseph Glanvill about possibility of arriving at certain truth, *Scirri sive scepticis et scepticorum a jure disputationis* (London, 1663; English trans. London, 1665). He ceased to write new works after this, presumably dispirited by increasing condemnation by the Holy Office (1655, 1657, 1661, 1663), and vilification of *Grounds of Obedience and Government.*

Secondary Sources: Bradley, R. I. (1963), 'Blacklo: An Essay in Counter-Reform', Ph.D. Diss., Columbia University. Jones, H. W. (1975), 'Leibniz' Cosmology and Thomas White's *Euclides Physicus',* *Archives internationales d'histoire des sciences,* 25:277–303. Lewis, J. M. (1976), 'Hobbes and the Blackloists: A Study in the Eschatology of the English Revolution', Ph.D. Diss., Harvard University. Southgate, B. C. (1979), 'The Life and Work of Thomas White', Ph.D. Diss., University of London. Henry, J. (1982), 'Atomism and Eschatology: Catholicism and Natural Philosophy in the Interregnum', *British Journal for the History of Science* 15:211–39. Southgate, B. C. (1985), ' "That Damned Booke": *The Grounds of Obedience and Government* (1655), and the Downfall of Thomas White', *Recusant History* 17:238–53. Southgate, B. C. (1987), 'A Philosophical Divinity: Thomas White and an Aspect of Mid-Seventeenth-Century Science and Religion', *History of European Ideas* 8:45–59. Lupoli, A. (1987), 'La filosofia politica di Thomas White', in *Miscellanea Secentesca: Saggi su Descartes, Fabri, White,* Milan: Cisalpino-Goliardica, pp. 127–81. Southgate, B. C. (1993), *"Covetous of Truth": The Life and Work of Thomas White, 1593–1676,* Dordrecht: Kluwer. [John Henry]

# BIBLIOGRAPHY

## DANIEL GARBER

Aaron, Richard I. (1971). *John Locke.* 3d ed. Oxford: Oxford University Press.

Abel, Günter (1978). *Stoizismus und Frühe Neuzeit.* Berlin: de Gruyter.

Abercrombie, Nigel (1936). *The Origins of Jansenism.* Oxford: Oxford University Press.

Abra de Raconis, Charles François d' (1633) (1646) (1651). *Totius philosophiae, hoc est logicae, moralis, physicae, et metaphysicae.* 2 vols. Paris.

Abraham, W. E. (1975). 'Predication', *Studia Leibnitiana.* 7:1–20.

Ackroyd, P. R., and Evans, C. F. (eds.) (1970). *The Cambridge History of the Bible.* Cambridge: Cambridge University Press.

Adams, Marilyn McCord (1987). *William Ockham* (2 vols.). Notre Dame, Ind.: University of Notre Dame Press.

Adams, Robert Merrihew (1982). 'Leibniz's Theories of Contingency', in Michael Hooker (ed.), *Leibniz: Critical and Interpretive Essays.* Minneapolis: University of Minnesota Press.

Adams, Robert Merrihew (1983). 'Phenomenalism and Corporeal Substance in Leibniz', in Peter A. French, Theodore E. Uehling, Jr., and Howard K. Wettstein (eds.), *Contemporary Perspectives on the History of Philosophy* (Midwest Studies in Philosophy). Minneapolis: University of Minnesota Press.

Adams, Robert Merrihew (1994). *Leibniz: Determinist, Theist, Idealist.* Oxford: Oxford University Press.

Aegidius Romanus [Giles of Rome] (1944). *Errores philosophorum,* ed. Josef Koch, trans. John Riedl. Milwaukee: Marquette University Press.

Agrippa, Henry Cornelius (1533). *De Occulta Philosophia.* Cologne. (Repr. Graz: Akademische Druck- und Verlanganstalt, 1967.)

Agrippa, Henry Cornelius (1974). *Of the Vanitie and Uncertaintie of Artes and Sciences,* ed. Catherine Dunn. Northridge: California State University.

Aidius, Andreas (1614). *Clavis philosophiae moralis sive In Aristotelis Nicomacheia commentarius.* Oppenheim.

Aiton, E. J. (1972). *The Vortex Theory of Planetary Motions.* New York: American Elsevier.

Aiton, E. J. (1985). *Leibniz: A Biography.* Bristol: Hilger.

Åkerman, Susanna (1990). 'Queen Christina and Messianic Thought', in D. S. Katz and J. Israel (eds.), *Sceptics, Millenarians and Jews.* Leiden: Brill.

Åkerman, Susanna (1991). *Queen Christina of Sweden and her Circle* (Brill Studies in Intellectual History). Leiden: Brill.

Alberti, V. (1678). *Compendium juris naturae, orthodoxae theologiae conformatum.* Leipzig.

Alberti, V. (1687). *Eros Lipsicus.* Leipzig.

Aldrich, Henricus (1704). *Artis logicae compendium.* Oxford. (1st ed. 1691.)

Alexander, Peter (1981). 'The Case of the Lonely Corpuscle: Reductive Explanation and Primitive Expressions', in Richard Healey (ed.), *Reduction, Time and Reality.* Cambridge: Cambridge University Press.

Alexander, Peter (1985). *Ideas, Qualities and Corpuscles: Locke and Boyle on the External World*. Cambridge: Cambridge University Press.

Alhazen (Ibn al-Haytham) (1572). *Opticae thesaurus. Alhazeni Arabis libri septem, nuncprimum editi. Eiusdem liber De crepusculis et nubium ascensionibus. Item Vitellonis Thuringopoloni libri X*. Basel. (Repr. New York: Johnson Reprint, 1972.)

Alhazen (Ibn al-Haytham) (1989). *Optics, Books I–III: On Direct Vision*, trans. A. I. Sabra (2 vols.). London: Warburg Institute.

Allard, Albéric (1868). *Histoire de la justice criminelle au seizième siècle*. Ghent/Paris/Leipzig. (Repr. Darmstadt: Scientia, 1970.)

Allen, Diogenes (1983). *Mechanical Explanations and the Ultimate Origin of the Universe according to Leibniz* (Studia Leibnitiana, Sonderheft 11). Wiesbaden: Steiner.

Allen, Don Cameron (1964). *Doubt's Boundless Sea: Skepticism and Faith in the Renaissance*. Baltimore: Johns Hopkins University Press.

Allen, Michael J. B. (1984). *The Platonism of Marsilio Ficino: A Study of His Phaedrus Commentary, Its Sources and Genesis*. Berkeley: University of California Press.

Allen, Michael J. B. (1989). *Icastes: Marsilio Ficino's Interpretation of Plato's Sophist*. Berkeley: University of California Press.

Allison, Henry E. (1987). *Benedict de Spinoza: An Introduction*. Rev. ed. New Haven, Conn.: Yale University Press.

Alquié, Ferdinand (1950). *La découverte métaphysique de l'homme*. Paris: Presses Universitaires de France.

Alquié, Ferdinand (1974). *Le cartésianisme de Malebranche*. Paris: Vrin.

Alquié, Ferdinand (1981). *Le rationalisme de Spinoza*. Paris: Presses Universitaires de France.

Alsted, Johann Heinrich (1610a). *Theatrum scholasticum, in quo consiliarius philosophicus proponit et exponit*. Herborn.

Alsted, Johann Heinrich (1610b). *Panacea philosophica; id est, facilis, nova et accurata methodus docendi and discendi universam encyclopaediam*. Herborn.

Alsted, Johann Heinrich (1612). *Philosophia digne restituta*. Herborn.

Alsted, Johann Heinrich (1613). *Compendium logicae harmonicae*. Herborn.

Alsted, Johann Heinrich (1614). *Logicae systema harmonicum*. Herborn.

Alsted, Johann Heinrich (1620). *Cursus Philosophici Encyclopaedia libris XXVII*. Herborn.

Alsted, Johann Heinrich (1623). *Theologia naturalis exhibens augustissimam naturae scholam; in qua creaturae Dei communi sermone ad omnes pariter docendos utuntur: adversus Atheos, Epicureos, et Sophistas huius temporis, duobus libris pertractata*. . . . Hannover.

Alsted, Johann Heinrich. (1626). *Compendium lexici philosophici*. . . . Herborn. (The pagination of the copy consulted – Paris, Bibliothèque Nationale, cote R. 10478 – begins at p. 1777.)

Alsted, Johann Heinrich (1628). *Summa casuum conscientiae, nova methodo elaborata*. Frankfurt.

Alsted, Johann Heinrich (1630). *Encyclopaedia, septem tomis distincta* . . . (7 vols.). Herborn. (Repr. Stuttgart-Bad Cannstatt: Frommann, 1989.)

Alsted, Johann Heinrich (1649). *Encyclopaedia* . . . (4 vols.). Lyon.

Alston, William P., and Bennett, Jonathan (1988). 'Locke on People and Substances', *Philosophical Review*. 97: 25–46.

Alvarez, Diego (1610). *De auxiliis divinae gratiae et humani arbitrii viribus, et libertate, ac legitima eius cum efficacia eorundem auxiliorum concordia*. Rome.

*Ame matérielle, (L'ouvrage anonyme)* (1969). Ed. Alain Niderst (Publications de l'Université de Rouen, 6. Serie littéraire). Paris: Nizet.

Amerio, Romano (1972). *Il sistema teologico di Tommaso Campanella*. Milan: Ricciardi.

Ames, William (1639). *Conscience with the Power and Cases Thereof*. London. (Repr. Norwood, N.J.: Johnson and Amsterdam: Theatrum Orbis, 1975.)

Ames, William (1643). *Conscience with the Power and Cases Thereof.* London.

Ames, William (1648). *Medulla theologica.* Amsterdam.

Ammann, Peter J. (1967). 'The Musical Theory and Philosophy of Robert Fludd', *Journal of the Warburg and Courtauld Institutes.* 30: 198–227.

Andersen, K. (1985). 'Cavalieri's method of indivisibles', *Archive for History of Exact Sciences.* 31:291–367.

Andrés Martín, Melquiades (1976–7). *La teologia española en el siglo XVI* (2 vols.). Madrid: La Editorial Católica.

Andrews, F. E. (1983). 'Leibniz' Logic within his Philosophical System', *Dionysius* (Halifax). 7:73–127.

Angelelli, I. A. (1975). 'On Saccheri's Use of the "Consequentia Mirabilis" ', in *Akten des II. Internationalen Leibniz-Kongresses Hannover, 17–22 Juli 1972* (4 vols.) (Studia Leibnitiana, Supplementa). Stuttgart: Steiner.

Angelelli, I. A. (1980). 'On Individual Relations', in *Theoria cum Praxi. Akten des III. Internationalen Leibniz-Kongresses, Hannover, 12–17.11.1977, bd. III* (Studia Leibnitiana, Supplementa 21). Stuttgart: Steiner.

Annas, Julia (1990). 'Stoic Epistemology', in Everson 1990.

Annas, Julia, and Barnes, Jonathan (1985). *The Modes of Scepticism.* Cambridge: Cambridge University Press.

*Annual Abstract of Statistics* (1992). London: H.M.S.O.

Anon. (1688). *La morale de Confucius, philosophe de la Chine.* Amsterdam.

Anon. (1691). *The Morals of Confucius a Chinese Philosopher.* London.

Appleton, William W. (1951). *A Cycle of Cathay: The China Vogue in England during the Seventeenth and Eighteenth Centuries.* New York: Columbia University Press.

Arbuthnot, John (1710). 'An Argument for Divine Providence, Taken from the Constant Regularity Observ'd in the Births of Both Sexes', *Philosophical Transactions of the Royal Society of London.* 27:186–90.

Arckenholtz, J. (1751–60). *Mémoires concernant Christine, reine de Suède pour servir d'éclaircissement à l'histoire de son regne et principalment de sa vie privée, et aux evenements de son tems civile et literaire* (4 vols.). Leipzig and Amsterdam.

Aricò, Denise (1987). *Il Tesauro in Europa. Studi sulle traduzioni della 'Filosofia morale'.* Bologna: Editrice CLUEB.

Ariew, Roger (1987). 'The Infinite in Descartes' Conversation with Burman', *Archiv für Geschichte der Philosophie.* 69:140–63.

Ariew, Roger (1990). 'Christopher Clavius and the Classification of Sciences', *Synthese.* 83:293–300.

Ariew, Roger (1992). 'Descartes and Scholasticism: The Intellectual Background to Descartes' Thought', in J. Cottingham (ed.), *Cambridge Companion to Descartes.* Cambridge: Cambridge University Press, pp. 58–90.

Ariew, Roger, and Grene, Marjorie (1995). 'Ideas, in and before Descartes', *Journal of the History of Ideas.* 56:87–106.

Aristotle (1619). *Opera,* ed. Guillaume Du Val (2 vols.). Paris.

Aristotle (1660). *Ethicorum ad Nicomachum libri decem,* ed. Samuel Rachelius. Helmstedt.

Aristotle (1908–52). *The Works,* ed. and tr. W. D. Ross et al. (12 vols.). Oxford.

Aristotle (1936). *Metaphysics,* ed. and trans. H. Tredennick (2 vols.) (Loeb Classical Library). London: William Heinemann.

Aristotle (1975). *Posterior Analytics,* ed. and trans. J. Barnes. Oxford: Oxford University Press.

Aristotle (1980). Aristotle, *Minor works,* trans. W. S. Hett. (Loeb Classical Library). London: William Heinemann.

Aristotle (1984). *The Complete Works of Aristotle* [trans.], ed. Jonathan Barnes (2 vols). Princeton, N.J.: Princeton University Press.

Armogathe, Jean-Robert (1970). *Une secte fantôme au XVIIIème siècle: les égoïstes.* Unpublished *memoire de maîtrise.* Paris: Libraries of the Sorbonne and the Ecole Normale Supérieure.

Armogathe, Jean-Robert (1977). *Theologia Cartesiana. L'explication physique de l'Eucharistie chez Descartes et Dom Desgabets.* The Hague: Nijhoff.

Armogathe, J.-R., and Carraud, V. (1992). *Bibliographia cartesiana II.* Paris: Presses Universitaires de France.

Armstrong, A. H. (ed.) (1967). *The Cambridge History of Later Greek and Early Medieval Philosophy.* Cambridge: Cambridge University Press.

Arnauld, Antoine (1643). *De la fréquente communion.* Paris.

Arnauld, Antoine (1683). *Des vraies et des fausses idées.* Cologne.

Arnauld, Antoine (1684). *Défense de M. Arnauld contre la réponse au livre des vraies et des fausses idées.* Cologne.

Arnauld, Antoine (1685). *Réflexions philosophiques et théologiques sur le nouveau système de la nature et de la grâce.* Cologne.

Arnauld, Antoine (1775–83). *Oeuvres de Messire Antoine Arnauld, docteur de la maison et société de Sorbonne* (43 vols.). Paris. (Repr. Brussels: Culture et Civilisation, 1965–7.)

Arnauld, Antoine (1843). *Oeuvres philosophiques,* ed. C. Jourdain. Paris.

Arnauld, Antoine (1986). *Des vrayes et des fausses idées,* ed. C. Frémont. Paris: Fayard.

Arnauld, Antoine (1990). *On True and False Ideas,* trans. Stephen Gaukroger. Manchester: Manchester University Press.

Arnauld, Antoine, and Lancelot, Claude (1660). *Grammaire générale et raisonnée.* Paris.

Arnauld, Antoine, and Nicole, Pierre (1662). *La Logique, ou l'art de penser.* Paris.

Arnauld, Antoine, and Nicole, Pierre (1668). *La logique, ou L'art de penser: Contenant, outre les regles communes, plusieurs observations nouvelles propres à former le jugement* (3d ed.). Paris.

Arnauld, Antoine, and Nicole, Pierre (1964). *The Art of Thinking: Port-Royal Logic,* trans. James Dickoff and Patricia James. Indianapolis: Bobbs-Merrill.

Arnauld, Antoine, and Nicole, Pierre (1965). *La logique; ou L'art de penser,* ed. Pierre Clair et François Girbal. Paris: Presses Universitaires de France.

Arnauld, Antoine, and Nicole, Pierre (1965–7). *L'art de penser: La logique de Port-Royal,* ed. Bruno Baron von Freytag Löringhoff and Herbert Brekle (3 vols.). Stuttgart: Frommann.

Arnauld, Antoine, and Nicole, Pierre (1970). *La logique; ou, L'art de penser,* ed. Louis Marin. Paris: Flammarion.

Arndt, Hans Werner (1971). *Methodo scientifica pertractatum. Mos geometricus und Kalkülbegriff in der philosophischen Theorienbildung des 17 und 18. Jahrhunderts.* Berlin: de Gruyter.

Arnold, Paul (1960). 'Descartes et les Rose-Croix', *Mercure de France.* 340: 266–84.

Arnold, Paul (1970). *La Rose-Croix et ses rapports avec la franc-maçonnerie: Essai de synthèse historique.* Paris: G.-P. Maisonneuve et Larose.

Arrais, Duarte Madeira (1650). *Novae philosophiae et medicinae de qualitatibus occultis a nemine unquam excultae pars prima philosophis, et medicis, pernecessaria, theologis vero apprime utilis* (2 vols.). Lisbon.

Arriaga, Rodericus de (1632). *Cursus philosophicus.* Antwerp.

Arthur, R. T. W. (1988). 'Continuous Creation, Continuous Time: A Refutation of the Alleged Discontinuity of Cartesian Time', *Journal of the History of Philosophy.* 26:349–75.

Ashcraft, R. (1969). 'Faith and Knowledge in Locke's Philosophy', in J. W. Yolton (ed.), *John Locke: Problems and Perspectives.* Cambridge: Cambridge University Press, pp. 194–223.

Ashcraft, R., Kroll, R., and Zagorin, P. (eds.), *Philosophy, Science, and Religion, 1640–1700.* Cambridge: Cambridge University Press.

Ashworth, E. Jennifer (1967). 'Joachim Jungius (1587–1657) and the Logic of Relations', *Archiv für Geschichte der Philosophie*. 49:72–85.

Ashworth, E. Jennifer (1968). 'Propositional Logic in the Sixteenth and Early Seventeenth Centuries', *Notre Dame Journal of Formal Logic*. 9:179–92.

Ashworth, E. Jennifer (1969). 'The Doctrine of Supposition in the Sixteenth and Seventeenth Centuries', *Archiv für Geschichte der Philosophie*. 51:260–85.

Ashworth, E. Jennifer (1974). *Language and Logic in the Post-Medieval Period*. Dordrecht: Reidel.

Ashworth, E. Jennifer (1978). *The Tradition of Medieval Logic and Speculative Grammar. From Anselm to the End of the Seventeenth Century. A Bibliography from 1836 Onwards* (Subsidia Mediaevalia). Toronto: Pontifical Institute of Mediaeval Studies.

Ashworth, E. Jennifer (1985). 'Introduction', in Robert Sanderson, *Logicae artis compendium* (Instrumenta rationis, Sources for the History of Modern Logic). Bologna: Editrice CLUEB.

Ashworth, E. Jennifer (1988). 'Traditional Logic', in Schmitt, Skinner, and Kessler 1988, pp. 143–72.

Aspelin, Gunnar (1943). 'Ralph Cudworth's Interpretation of Greek Philosophy', *Göteborgs Högskolas Årsskrift*. 49:3–47.

Assenmacher, Johannes (1926). *Die Geschichte des Individuationsprinzips in der Scholastik*. Leipzig: Meiner.

Atherton, Margaret (1983). 'Locke's Theory of Personal Identity', *Midwest Studies in Philosophy*. 8:273–93.

Atherton, Margaret (1990). *Berkeley's Revolution in Vision*. Ithaca, N.Y.: Cornell University Press.

Atherton, Margaret (1993). 'Cartesian Reason and Gendered Reason', in Louise M. Antony and Charlotte Witt (eds.), *A Mind of One's Own*. Boulder, Colo.: Westview, pp. 19–34.

Attfield, Robin (1977). 'Clarke, Collins and Compounds', *Journal of the History of Philosophy*. 15:45–54.

Attfield, Robin (1978). *God and the Secular: A Philosophical Assessment of Secular Reasoning from Bacon to Kant*. Cardiff: University College Cardiff Press.

Aubenque, Pierre (1978). 'Les origines de la doctrine de l'analogie de l'être. Sur l'histoire d'un contresens', *Les études philosophiques*. 1/1978:3–12.

Aubenque, Pierre (1987). 'Zur Enstehung der pseudo-aristotelischen Lehre von der Analogie des Seins', in J. Wiesner (ed.), *Aristoteles Werk und Wirkung. Paul Moraux gewidment* (2 vols.). Berlin: de Gruyter.

Aubert de Versé, Noel (1684). *L'impie convaincu, ou dissertation contre Spinoza*. Amsterdam.

Aubignac, François Hédelin, abbé d' (1664). *Macarise, ou la reine des isles fortunées. Histoire allegorique contenant la philosophie morale des Stoïques sous le voile de plusieurs aventures agreables en forme de roman* (2 vols.). Paris.

Aubrey, John (1972). *Brief Lives*, ed. Oliver Lawson Dick. Harmondsworth: Penguin.

Auger, Léon (1962). *Gilles Personne de Roberval (1602–1675)*. Paris: Blanchard.

Augustine (1972). *The City of God*. Harmondsworth: Penguin.

Averroes (Ibn Rushd) (1562–74). *Aristotelis opera cum Averrois commentariis* (12 vols.). Venice.

Averroes (Ibn Rushd) (1954). *Tahāfut al-Tahāfut* (The incoherence of the incoherence), trans. Simon Van den Bergh. London: Luzac.

Averroes (Ibn Rushd) (1984). *Ibn Rushd's Metaphysics*, trans. C. Genequand. Leiden: Brill.

Ayer, A. J. (1967). ' "I think, therefore I am" ', in Willis Doney (ed.), *Descartes: A Collection of Critical Essays*. Garden City, N.Y.: Doubleday.

Ayers, Michael R. (1981a). 'Locke versus Aristotle on Natural Kinds', *Journal of Philosophy*. 78:247–72.

Ayers, Michael R. (1981b). 'Mechanism, Superaddition, and the Proof of God's Existence in Locke's *Essay*', *Philosophical Review*. 90:210–51.

Ayers, Michael R. (1984). 'Berkeley and Hume: A Question of Influence', in R. Rorty, J. B. Schneewind, and Q. Skinner (eds.), *Philosophy in History: Essay on the Historiography of Philosophy*. Cambridge: Cambridge University Press.

Ayers, Michael [R.] (1985). ' "The End of Metaphysics" and the Historiography of Philosophy', in A. J. Holland (ed.), *Philosophy, Its History and Historiography*. Dordrecht: Reidel.

Ayers, Michael [R.] (1986). 'Are Locke's Ideas Images, Intentional Objects or Natural Signs?' *Locke Newsletter*. 17:3–36.

Ayers, Michael R. (1987). 'Divine Ideas and Berkeley's Proof of God's Existence', in Sosa 1987, pp. 115–28.

Ayers, Michael R. (1991). *Locke* (2 vols.). London: Routledge.

Ayers, Michael R. (1994). 'The Foundations of Knowledge and the Logic of Substance: The Structure of Locke's General Philosophy', in G. A. J. Rogers (ed.), *Locke's Philosophy: Content and Context*. Oxford: Oxford University Press.

Ayers, Michael R. (1996). 'Was Berkeley an Empiricist or a Rationalist'?, in K. Winkler (ed.), *The Cambridge Companion to Berkeley*. Cambridge: Cambridge University Press.

Azevedo, J. Lucio d' (1947). *A evolução do Sebastinismo*. 2d. ed. Lisbon: Teizeira.

Bachelard, Gaston (1967). *La Formation de l'esprit scientifique: Contribution à une psychanalyse de la connaissance objective*. 5th ed. Paris: Vrin.

Bacon, Francis (1605). *The Advancement of Learning*. London.

Bacon, Francis (1609). *De sapientia veterum*. London.

Bacon, Francis (1620). *Instauratio magna multi pertransibunt & augebitur scientia* [incl. *Novum organum*]. London.

Bacon, Francis (1623). *De dignitate et augmentis scientarum*. London.

Bacon, Francis (1627a). *New Atlantis*. London.

Bacon, Francis (1626b). *Sylva sylvarum*. London.

Bacon, Francis (1857–74). *The Works of Francis Bacon*, ed. J. Spedding, R. L. Ellis, D. D. Heath (14 vols.). London: Longmans. (Vols. 8–14 have the title page: *The Letters and the Life of Francis Bacon. . . .*) (Repr. London: Longmans, 1887–92; repr. Stuttgart: Frommann, 1989.)

Bacon, Francis (1860–4). *The Works of Francis Bacon*, ed. and trans. J. Spedding, R. L. Ellis, D. D. Heath (15 vols.). Boston: Houghton Mifflin. (This edition includes only the material in vols. 1–7 of Bacon 1857–74.)

Bacon, Francis (1878). *Novum Organum*, ed. Th. Fowler. Oxford: Oxford University Press.

Bacon, Francis (1960). *The New Organon and Related Writings*, ed. F. H. Anderson. Indianapolis: Bobbs-Merrill.

Bacon, Francis (1974). *The Advancement of Learning and New Atlantis*, ed. Arthur Johnston. Oxford: Oxford University Press.

Bacon, Francis (1984). *Francis Bacon's Natural Philosophy: A New Source. A Transcription of Manuscript Hardwick 72A*, trans. and commentary by Graham Rees, assisted by Christopher Upton (The British Society for the History of Science Monographs, 5). Chalfont Saint Giles, Bucks.: British Society for the History of Science.

Bacon, Francis (1985). *Sir Francis Bacon: The Essays or Counsels, Civill and Morall*, ed. M. Kirnan, Oxford: Oxford University Press.

Bacon, Roger (1900). *The Opus Majus of Roger Bacon*, ed. J. H. Bridges (3 vols.). London: Williams and Norgate.

Bacon, Roger (1983). *Roger Bacon's Philosophy of Nature: A Critical Edition, English Translation, Introduction, and Notes, of "De multiplicatione specierum" and "De speculis comburentibus"*, ed. and trans. David C. Lindberg. Oxford: Oxford University Press.

Badaloni, Nicola (1965). *Tommaso Campanella*. Milan: Feltrinelli.

Baillet, Adrien (1691). *La Vie de M. Descartes* (2 vols.). Paris.

Baillet, Adrien (1946). *Vie de Monsieur Descartes* [abr. vers. of 1693]. Paris: Table Ronde.

Baillie, James (1993). 'Recent Work on Personal Identity', *Philosophical Books*. 34:193–206.

Balfour, Robert (1620). *Commentarium in libros Aristotelis de philosophia.* Bordeaux.

Ballard, George (1752). *Memoirs of Several Ladies of Great Britain, Who Have Been Celebrated for Their Writings or Skill, in the Learned Languages, Arts and Sciences.* Oxford.

Balz, Albert G. A. (1951). *Cartesian Studies.* New York: Columbia University Press.

Báñez, Domingo (1942–8). *Tractatus de vera et legitima concordia liberi arbitrii creati cum auxiliis gratiae Dei efficaciter moventis humanam voluntatem,* in *Comentarios ineditos a la prima secundae de santo Tomas,* ed. Vicente Beltrán de Heredia (3 vols.). Salamanca: Instituto 'Francesco Suárez', vol. 3.

Barad, Judith (1986). 'Aquinas on Faith and the Consent/Assent Distinction', *Journal of the History of Philosophy.* 24:311–21.

Barbay, Pierre (1676). *Commentarius in Aristotelis physicam . . .* (2d ed.). Paris.

Barbay, Pierre (1680). *Commentarius in Aristotelis moralem . . .* (3d ed.). Paris.

Barber, Kenneth, and Gracia, Jorge J. E. (eds.) (1994). *Individuation and Identity in Early Modern Philosophy.* Albany, N.Y.: SUNY Press.

Barbeyrac, Jean (1749). 'Historical and Critical Account of the Science of Morality', in Samuel von Pufendorf, *The Law of Nature and Nations,* ed. J. Barbeyrac, trans. B. Kennet. London, pp. 1–75.

Barbour, Julian B. (1989). *Absolute or Relative Motion? A Study from a Machian Point of View of the Discovery and the Structure of Dynamical Theories* (2 vols. in progress): vol. 1, *The Discovery of Dynamics.* Cambridge: Cambridge University Press.

Barker, Peter (1985). 'Jean Pena (1528–58) and Stoic Physics in the Sixteenth Century', *Southern Journal of Philosophy.* 23(supp.):93–107.

Barker, Peter (1991). 'Stoic Contributions to Early Modern Science', in M. J. Osler (ed.), *Atoms, Pneuma and Tranquility: Epicurean and Stoic Themes in European Thought.* Cambridge: Cambridge University Press, pp. 135–54.

Barker, Peter, and Goldstein, Bernard R. (1984). 'Is Seventeenth-century Physics Indebted to the Stoics?' *Centaurus.* 27:148–64.

Barnard, F. M. (1966). 'Christian Thomasius: Enlightenment and Bureaucracy', *American Political Science Review.* 59:430–8.

Barnard, F. M. (1971). 'The "Practical Philosophy" of Christian Thomasius', *Journal of the History of Ideas.* 32:221–46.

Barnouw, Jeffrey (1980). 'Hobbes's Causal Account of Sensation', *Journal of the History of Philosophy.* 18:115–30.

Barrow, Isaac (1669). *Lectiones opticae.* London.

Barrow, Isaac (1670). *Lectiones geometricae: In quibus (praesertim) generalia curvarum linearum symptomata declarantur.* London.

Barrow, Isaac (1683). *Lectiones mathematicae XXIII.* London.

Barrow, Isaac (1734). *The Usefulness of Mathematical Learning Explained and Demonstrated . . .* trans. John Kirkby. London.

Barrow, Isaac (1859). *The Theological Works of Isaac Barrow,* ed. A. Napier (9 vols.). Cambridge: Cambridge University Press.

Barrow, Isaac (1860). *The Mathematical Works of Isaac Barrow,* ed. William Whewell. Cambridge: Cambridge University Press.

Bartas, Guillaume Saluste du (1611). *Les oeuvres de G. du Saluste Sⁱ du Bartas . . .* (2 vols.). Paris.

Barth, Else M. (1974). *The Logic of the Articles in Traditional Philosophy. A Contribution to the Study of Conceptual Structures.* Dordrecht: Reidel.

Bartha, Paul (1993). 'Substantial Form and the Nature of Individual Substance', *Studia Leibnitiana.* 25:43–54.

Bartholinus, Caspar (1665). *Enchiridion ethicum seu Epitome philosophiae moralis.* Oxford.

Barzilay, I. (1974). *Yoseph Schlomo Delmedigo, Yashar of Candia: His Life, Works, and Times.* Leiden: Brill.

Basnage, Jacques (1716). *Histoire des Juifs.* The Hague.

Basso, Sebastian (1621). *Philosophia naturalis adversus Aristotelem libri XII, in quibus abstrusa veterum physiologia restauratur . . . Aristotelis errores solidis rationibus refelluntur.* Geneva.

Basso, Sebastian (1649). *Philosophia naturalis adversus Aristotelem libri XII, in quibus abstrusa veterum physiologia restauratur . . . Aristotelis errores solidis rationibus refelluntur.* Amsterdam.

Battaglia, Felice (1982). *Cristiano Thomasio. Filosofo e giurista.* Bologna: CLUEB. (1st ed. 1936.)

Battail, Jean-François (1973). *L'avocat philosophe Géraud de Cordemoy.* The Hague: Nijhoff.

Bauer, Barbara (1987). 'Apathie des stoischen Weisen oder Ekstase der christlichen Braut? Jesuitische Stoakritik und Jacob Baldes *Jephtias*', in S. Neumeister and C. Wiedemann (eds.), *Res Publica Litteraria: Die Institutionen der Gelehrsamkeit in der frühen Neuzeit* (2 vols.). Wiesbaden: Otto Harrassowitz.

Baumgold, D. (1988). *Hobbes's Political Theory.* Cambridge: Cambridge University Press.

Bausola, A. (1969). 'Il perfezionamento dell'argomento ontologico nel carteggio Leibniz-Eckhard', in Bausola, *Indagini di storia della filosofia.* Milan: Vita e pensiero, pp. 3–28.

Baxter, Richard (1673). *A Christian Directory or a Summ of Practical Theology and Cases of Conscience Directing Christians How to Use Their Knowledge and Faith.* London.

Baxter, Richard (1682a). *Of the Immortality of Man's Soule, and the Nature of It and Other Spirits.* London.

Baxter, Richard (1682b). *Of the Nature of Spirits; Especially Mans Soul. In a Placid Collation with the Learned Dr. Henry More, In a Reply to his Answer to a Private Letter, Printed in His Second Edition of Mr. Glanviles Sadducismus Triumphatus,* in *Of the Immortality of Man's Soule, and the Nature of It and Other Spirits.* London.

Bayes, Thomas (1763). 'An Essay towards Solving a Problem in the Doctrine of Chances', *Philosophical Transactions of the Royal Society of London.* 53:370–418.

Bayle, Pierre (1682). *Lettre sur la comète.* Rotterdam.

Bayle, Pierre (1683). *Pensées diverses sur la comète.* Rotterdam.

Bayle, Pierre (ed.) (1684). *Recueil de quelques pièces curieuses concernant la philosophie de M. Descartes.* Amsterdam.

Bayle, Pierre (1686). *Commentaire philosophique sur les paroles de Jésus-Crist . . .* Canterbury.

Bayle, Pierre (1692). *Projet et fragmens d'un Dictionnaire critique.* Rotterdam.

Bayle, Pierre (1697). *Dictionnaire historique et critique.* Rotterdam.

Bayle, Pierre (1702). *Dictionnaire historique et critique.* 2d ed. Rotterdam.

Bayle, Pierre (1713). *Commentaire philosophique sur les paroles de Jésus-Christ . . . ou traité de la tolérance universelle.* Rotterdam.

Bayle, Pierre (1720). *Dictionnaire historique et critique.* 4th ed. Rotterdam.

Bayle, Pierre (1727). *Oeuvres diverses* (4 vols.). The Hague. (Repr. Hildesheim: Olms, 1964–8.)

Bayle, Pierre (1730). *Dictionnaire historique et critique* (4th ed. Prosper Marchand) (4 vols.). Amsterdam and Leiden.

Bayle, Pierre (1734–8). *Historical and Critical Dictionary.* 2d. ed. London (1st ed., 1710). (Repr. New York: Garland, 1984.)

Bayle, Pierre (1740). *Dictionnaire historique et critique.* 5th ed. (4 vols.). Amsterdam, Leiden, The Hague, and Utrecht. (This is represented as the 5th ed. by the editors, but it is actually the 8th.)

Bayle, Pierre (1911). *Pensées diverses sur la comète,* ed. A. Prat (2 vols.). Paris: Société Nouvelle de Librarie et d'Edition.

Bayle, Pierre (1965). *Historical and Critical Dictionary,* trans. R. Popkin. Indianapolis: Bobbs-Merrill.

Bayle, Pierre (1984). *Pensées diverses sur la comète,* eds. A. Prat and P. Rétat (2 vols.). Paris: Nizet.

Bazzoli, M. (1979). 'Giambattista Almici e la diffusione di Pufendorf nel settecento Italiano', *Critica storica.* 16:3–100.

Beaude, J. (1979). 'Cartésianisme et anticartésianisme de Desgabets', *Studia Cartesiana.* 1:1–24.

Becco, Anne (1978). 'Leibniz et François-Mercure Van Helmont: Bagatelle pour des monades', in *Magia Naturalis 1978.*

Becconsall, Thomas (1698). *The Grounds and Foundation of Natural Religion.* London.

Bechler, Zev (1974). 'Newton's 1672 Optical Controversies: A Study in the Grammar of Scientific Dissent', in Yehuda Elkana (ed.), *The Interaction between Science and Philosophy.* Atlantic Highlands, N.J.: Humanities Press.

Beck, L. J. (1952). *The Method of Descartes: A Study of the Regulae.* Oxford: Oxford University Press.

Beck, L. J. (1965). *The Metaphysics of Descartes: A Study of the Meditations.* Oxford: Oxford University Press.

Beck, Lewis White (1969). *Early German Philosophy: Kant and his Predecessors.* Cambridge, Mass.: Harvard University Press.

Bedini, Silvio A. (1991). *The Pulse of Time: Galileo Galilei, The Determination of Longitude, and the Pendulum Clock.* Florence: Leo S. Olschki.

Beeckman, Isaac (1644). *D. Isaaci Beeckmanni medici et rectoris apud Dordracenos mathematico-physicarum meditationum, quaestionum, solutionum centuria.* Utrecht.

Beeckman, Isaac (1939–53). *Journal tenu par Isaac Beeckman de 1604 à 1634,* ed. Cornelis de Waard (4 vols.). The Hague: Nijhoff.

Belaval, Yvon (1960). *Leibniz critique de Descartes.* Paris: Gallimard.

Belaval, Yvon (1964). 'Premières animadversions de Leibniz sur les Principes de Descartes', in *Mélanges Alexandre Koyré,* intro. Fernand Braudel (2 vols.) (Histoire de la Pensée, No. 13), vol. 2 (*L'aventure de l'esprit*). Paris: Herman, pp. 29–56.

Benedetti, Giovanni Battista (1585). *Diversarum speculationum mathematicarum, et physicarum liber.* Turin. (Also Venice, 1586 and 1599.)

Benesch, Otto (1969). *Artistic and Intellectual Trends from Rubens to Daumier as Shown in Book Illustration.* New York: Walker and Company and Cambridge, Mass.: Department of Printing and Graphic Arts, Harvard College Library.

Bénichou, Paul (1948). *Morales du grand siècle.* Paris: Gallimard.

Benítez, Miguel (1988). 'Matériaux pour un inventaire des manuscrits philosophiques clandestins des XVIIe et XVIIIe siècles', *Rivista di Storia della Filosofia.* NS43:503–31.

Benn, S. I. (1972). 'Hobbes on Power', in M. Cranston and R. Peters (eds.), *Hobbes and Rousseau: A Collection of Critical Essays.* Garden City, N.Y.: Doubleday, pp. 184–212.

Bennett, J. A. (1975). 'Hooke and Wren and the System of the World: Some Points towards an Historical Account', *British Journal for the History of Science.* 8:32–61.

Bennett, J. A. (1981). 'Cosmology and the Magnetical Philosophy, 1640–1680', *Journal of the History of Astronomy.* 12:165–77.

Bennett, J. A. (1989). 'Magnetical Philosophy and Astronomy from Wilkins to Hooke', in René Taton and Curtis Wilson (eds.), *The General History of Astronomy:* vol. 2, *Planetary Astronomy from the Renaissance to the Rise of Astrophysics. Part A: Tycho Brahe to Newton.* Cambridge: Cambridge University Press, pp. 222–30.

Bennett, Jonathan (1968). 'Berkeley and God', in C. B. Martin and D. M. Armstrong (eds.), *Locke and Berkeley: A Collection of Critical Essays.* Garden City, N.Y.: Doubleday, pp. 380–99.

Bennett, Jonathan (1971). *Locke, Berkeley, Hume: Central Themes.* Oxford: Oxford University Press.

Bennett, Jonathan (1984). *A Study of Spinoza's Ethics.* Cambridge: Cambridge University Press.

Bennett, Jonathan (1994). 'Locke's Philosophy of Mind', in Chappell 1994a.

Bennett, Jonathan, and Remnant, Peter (1978). 'How Matter Might First Be Made', *Canadian Journal of Philosophy.* Sup. IV:1–11.

Bentley, Richard (1692). *The Folly and Unreasonableness of Atheism . . . In Eight Sermons preached at the Lecture founded by the Honourable Robert Boyle. . . .* London.

Bentley, Richard (1693). *The Folly and Unreasonableness of Atheism . . . In Eight Sermons preached at the Lecture founded by the Honourable Robert Boyle. . . .* London. (Each sermon has a separate title page, some of which date 1692.)

Bentley, Richard (1699). *The Folly and Unreasonableness of Atheism*. . . . 4th ed. London.

Berckelius, Henricus (1623). *Theses ethicae de summo hominis bono civili . . . praeside . . . Francone Burgersdicio*. . . . Leiden.

Berkel, Klaas van (1983a). 'Beeckman, Descartes, et la philosophie physico-mathématique', *Archives de Philosophie*. 46:620–6.

Berkel, Klaas van (1983b). *Isaac Beeckman (1588–1637) en de Mechanisering van het Wereldbeeld (with a summary in English)*. Amsterdam: Rodopi.

Berkeley, George (1709). *An Essay towards a New Theory of Vision*. Dublin.

Berkeley, George (1710). *A Treatise concerning the Principles of Human Knowledge*. Dublin. (Rev. ed. London, 1734.)

Berkeley, George (1713). *Three Dialogues between Hylas and Philonous*. London. (Rev. ed. London, 1734.)

Berkeley, George (1721). *De Motu*. London.

Berkeley, George (1732). *Alciphron: Or the Minute Philosopher*. London.

Berkeley, George (1733). *The Theory of Vision, or Visual Language Vindicated and Explained*. London.

Berkeley, George (1734). *The Analyst*. London.

Berkeley, George (1945). *Philosophical Commentaries, Generally Called the Commonplace Book*, ed. A. A. Luce. London: T. Nelson.

Berkeley, George (1948–57). *The Works of George Berkeley*, ed. A. A. Luce and T. E. Jessop (9 vols.). Edinburgh, London: T. Nelson.

Berkeley, George (1975). *Philosophical Works*, ed. M. R. Ayers. London: J. M. Dent.

Berman, David (1988). *The History of Atheism in England: From Hobbes to Russell*. London: Crown Helm.

Bernier, François (1678). *Abrégé de la philosophie de Gassendi* (7 vols.). Lyon.

Bernier, François (1682). *Doutes de M. Bernier sur quelques uns des principaux chapitres de son Abrégé de Gassendi*. Paris.

Bernier, François (1684). *Abrégé de la philosophie de Gassendi*. 2d ed. (7 vols.). Lyon.

Bernier, François (1992). *Abrégé de la philosophie de Gassendi* (3 vols.). Paris: Fayard.

Bernoulli, Jakob (1713). *Ars conjectandi*. Basel.

Bernoulli, Jakob (1966). *Translations from Jakob Bernoulli*, trans. Bing Sung. Cambridge, Mass.: Harvard University Department of Statistics Technical Report no. 2 (12 February 1966).

Bernoulli, Jakob (1969–89). *Die Werke von Jakob Bernoulli* (3 vols.). Basel: Birkhäuser.

Bernoulli, Nicholas (1709). *De usu artis conjectandi in jure*. Basel. (Repr. in J. Bernoulli 1969–89, vol. 3, pp. 287–326.)

Bernstein, Howard (1984). 'Leibniz and Huygens on the "Relativity" of Motion', in Albert Heinekamp (ed.), *Leibniz' Dynamica* (Studia Leibnitiana, Sonderheft). Stuttgart: Steiner, pp. 85–102.

Berr, Henri (1960). *Du Scepticisme de Gassendi*, trans. B. Rochot. Paris: Albin Michel.

Berriot, François (1984). *Athéismes et athéistes au XVIe siècle en France* (2 vols.) (Series: Theses-Cerf). Paris: Cerf.

Bertelli, S. (ed.) (1980). *Il libertinismo in Europa*. Milan: Riccardi.

Berti, Sylvia; Charles-Daubert, Françoise; and Popkin, Richard (eds.) (1996). *Heterodoxy, Spinozism, and Free Thought in Early-Eighteenth-Century Europe: Studies on the* Traité des trois imposteurs. Dordrecht: Kluwer.

Bertoloni Meli, Domenico (1988). 'Leibniz on the Censorship of the Copernican System', *Studia Leibnitiana*. 20:19–42.

Bertoloni Meli, Domenico (1993). *Equivalence and Priority: Newton versus Leibniz*. Oxford: Oxford University Press.

Bérulle, Pierre de (1846). *Oeuvres complètes*, ed. J. P. Migne. Paris.

Betts, C. J. (1984). *The Early Deism in France*. The Hague: Nijhoff.

Beyssade, Jean-Marie (1979). *La Philosophie première de Descartes.* Paris: Flammarion.

Beyssade, Jean-Marie (1981). 'Création des vérités éternelles et doute métaphysique'. *Studia Cartesiana.* 2:86–105.

Beyssade, Jean-Marie (1983). 'La classification cartésienne des passions', *Revue Internationale de Philosophie.* 146:278–87.

Beyssade, Jean-Marie (1988). 'Descartes on the Freedom of the Will', *Graduate Faculty Philosophy Journal.* 13:81–96.

Beyssade, Jean-Marie (1992). 'Descartes on Material Falsity', in Cummins and Zoeller 1992.

Bianchi, Massimo Luigi (1982). 'Occulto e manifesto nella medicina del Rinascimento: Jean Fernel e Pietro Severino', *Atti e memorie dell'Accademia toscana de scienze e lettere, la Colombaria.* 47, n.s. 33:185–248.

Bianchi, Massimo Luigi (1983). 'Sapiente e Popolo nel *Theophrastus Redivivus*'. *Studi storici* 24:137–64.

Bianchi, Massimo Luigi (1987). *Signatura Rerum: Segni, magia e conoscenza da Paracelso a Leibniz* (Lessico Intellettuale Europeo, 43). Rome: Edizioni dell'Ateneo.

Biermann, Kurt-Reinhard (1955). 'Eine Untersuchung von G. W. Leibniz über die jährliche Sterblichkeitsrate', *Forschungen and Fortschritte.* 29:205–8.

Biermann, Kurt-Reinhard (1967). 'Uberblick über die Studien von G. W. Leibniz zur Wahrscheinlichkeitsrechnung', *Sudhoffs Archiv.* 51:79–85.

Biermann, Kurt-Reinhard, and Margot Faak (1957). 'G. W. Leibniz "De incerti aestimatione" ', *Forschungen und Fortschritte.* 31:45–50.

Birch, Andrea Croce (1991). 'The Problem of Method in Newton's Natural Philosophy', in Daniel O. Dahlstrom (ed.), *Nature and Scientific Method* (Studies in the History of Philosophy, vol. 22). Washington D.C.: Catholic University of America Press.

Blackwell, Richard J. (1966). 'Descartes' Laws of Motion'. *Isis.* 57: 220–34.

Blair, Ann (1990). 'Restaging Jean Bodin'. Ph.D. diss., Princeton University.

Blair, Heather (1995). 'Anti-Aristotelianism, the Soul, and the Mechanical Philosophy in Descartes and Hobbes'. Ph.D. diss., University of Chicago.

Blanché, R. (1970). *La logique et son histoire, d'Aristote à Russell.* Paris: Armand Colin.

Blanchet, Léon (1920a). *Les Antécédents historiques du 'Je pense, donc je suis'.* Paris: Presses Universitaires de France.

Blanchet, Léon (1920b). *Campanella.* Paris: Presses Universitaires de France.

Blau, Joseph Leon (1944). *The Christian Interpretation of the Cabala in the Renaissance.* New York: Columbia University Press.

Blay, Michel (1992). *La naissance de la mécanique analytique: La science du mouvement au tournant des XVIIe et XVIIIe siècles.* Paris: Presses Universitaires de France.

Bloch, E. (1968). *Christian Thomasius, ein deutscher Gelehrter ohne Misere.* Frankfurt: Suhrkamp.

Bloch, Marc (1989). *The Royal Touch,* trans. J. E. Anderson. New York: Dorset Press.

Bloch, Olivier René (1971). *La philosophie de Gassendi: Nominalisme, matérialisme et métaphysique* (International Archives of the History of Ideas). The Hague: Nijhoff.

Bloch, Olivier René (1978). 'Sur les premières apparitions du mot matérialiste', *Raison Présente.* 47:3–16.

Bloch, Olivier René (1985). *Le matérialisme* (Que sais-je?). Paris: Presses Universitaires de France.

Blom, H. W. (1993). '*Felix qui potuit rerum cognoscere causas.* Burgersdijk's Moral and Political Thought', in E. P. Bos and H. A. Krop (eds.), *Franco Burgersdijk (1590–1635): Neo-Aristotelianism in Leiden.* Amsterdam: Rodopi, pp. 119–50.

Blount, Charles (1693). *Oracles of Reason.* London.

Blount, Charles (1695). *Miscellaneous Works.* London.

Blüher, K. A. (1969). *Seneca in Spanien: Untersuchung zur Geschichte der Seneca-Rezeption in Spanien vom 13. bis 17. Jahrhundert.* Munich: Francke.

Blumenfeld, David (1973). 'Leibniz's Theory of the Striving Possibles', *Studia Leibnitiana.* 5:163–77.

Blumenfeld, David (1984–5). 'Leibniz on Contingency and Infinite Analysis', *Philosophy and Phenomenological Research.* 45:483–514.

Blumenfeld, David (1988–9). 'Freedom, Contingency, and Things Possible in Themselves', *Philosophy and Phenomenological Research.* 49:81–101.

Boas, Marie (1952). 'The Establishment of the Mechanical Philosophy', *Osiris.* 10:412–541.

Boas, Marie (1958). *Robert Boyle and Seventeenth-Century Chemistry.* Cambridge: Cambridge University Press.

Boas Hall, Marie (1965). *Robert Boyle on Natural Philosophy: An Essay with Selections from His Writings.* Bloomington: Indiana University Press.

Boas Hall, Marie (1975). 'Newton's Voyage in the Strange Seas of Alchemy', in M. L. Rhigini Bonelli and William R. Shea (eds.), *Reason, Experiment and Mysticism in the Scientific Revolution.* New York: Science History Publications.

Boas Hall, Marie (1978). 'Matter in Seventeenth Century Science', in Ernan McMullin (ed.), *The Concept of Matter in Modern Philosophy.* Notre Dame, Ind.: University of Notre Dame Press.

Boas Hall, Marie (1981). *The Mechanical Philosophy.* New York: Arno Press.

Bobbio, N. (1993). *Thomas Hobbes and the Natural Law Tradition.* Chicago: University of Chicago Press.

Bobik, Joseph (1965). 'Matter and Individuation', in McMullin 1965, pp. 281–95.

Bochenski, I. M. (1961). *History of Formal Logic.* Notre Dame, Ind.: Notre Dame University Press.

Bodin, Jean (1590?). *Colloquium heptaplomeres.* Herzog August Bibliothek, Wolfenbüttel, Handschrift Extrav. 89.1 and 220.2. (Manuscript).

Bodin, Jean (1857). *Colloquium heptaplomeres,* ed. L. Noack. Paris and London.

Bodin, Jean (1975). *Colloquium of the Seven about Secrets of the Sublime,* trans. Marion Kuntz. Princeton, N.J.: Princeton University Press.

Boehm, Alfred (1962). *Le "Vinculum substantiale" chez Leibniz. Ses origines historiques.* Paris: Vrin.

Boehm, Alfred (1965). 'L'Aristotélisme d'Honoré Fabri (1607–1688)', *Revue des sciences religieuses.* 39:305–60.

Boethius (1973). *The Theological Tractates,* ed. and trans. H. F. Stewart, E. K. Rand, and S. J. Tester. Cambridge, Mass.: Harvard University Press.

Bohatec, J. (1912). *Die Cartesianische Scholastik in der Philosophie und Theologie der reformierten Dogmatik des 17. Jahrhunderts.* Leipzig: Deichert. (Repr. Hildesheim: Olms, 1966.)

Bold, Samuel (1705). *A Discourse concerning the Resurrection of the Same Body.* London.

Bolton, Martha Brandt (1987). 'Berkeley's Objection to Abstract Ideas and Unconceived Objects', in Ernest Sosa (ed.), *Essays on the Philosophy of George Berkeley.* Dordrecht: Reidel.

Bolton, Martha Brandt (1992). 'The Idea-Theoretic Basis of Locke's Antiessentialist Doctrine of Nominal Essence', in Phillip Cummins and Guenter Zoeller (eds.), *Minds, Ideas and Objects.* Atascedero, Calif.: Ridgeview.

Bolton, Martha Brandt (1994). 'The Real Molyneux Question and the Basis of Locke's Answer', in G. A. J. Rogers (ed.), *Locke's Philosophy: Content and Context.* Oxford: Oxford University Press.

Bonansea, Bernardino M. (1969). *Tommaso Campanella: Renaissance Pioneer of Modern Thought.* Washington, D.C.: Catholic University of America Press.

Bonansea, Bernardino M. (1983). *Man and His Approach to God in John Duns Scotus.* Lanham, Md.: University Press of America.

Bondi, E. (1966). 'Predication: A Study Based in the *Ars logica* of John of St. Thomas', *Thomist.* 30:260–94.

Bonno, Gabriel D. (1955). *Les relations intellectuelles de Locke avec la France.* Berkeley: University of California Press.

Bordo, Susan (1987). *The Flight to Objectivity. Essays on Cartesianism and Culture.* Albany: State University of New York Press.

Borkowski, S. von Dunin (1904). 'Zur Textgeschichte und Textkritik der altesten Lebensbeschreibung Benedikt Despinosas', *Archiv für Geschichte der Philosophie.* 18:1–34.

Borst, Clive (1992). 'Leibniz and the Compatibilist Account of Free Will', *Studia Leibnitiana.* 24:49–58.

Bos, H. J. M. (1972). 'Huygens', in Gillispie 1970–80, vol. 6, pp. 597–613.

Bos, H. J. M. (1974). 'Differentials, Higher-Order Differentials and the Derivative in the Leibnizian Calculus', *Archive for History of Exact Sciences.* 14:1–90.

Bos, H. J. M. (1988). 'Tractional Motion and the Legitimation of Transcendental Curves', *Centaurus.* 31:9–62.

Bossu, R. le (1674). *Parallèle des principes de la physique d'Aristote et de celle de Descartes.* Paris. (Repr. Paris: Vrin, 1981.)

Bossuet, Jacques-Bénigne (1879). *Oeuvres complètes,* ed. Guillaume (10 vols.). Lyon.

Bossuet, Jacques-Bénigne (1964). *Platon et Aristote: Notes de lectures,* ed. T. Goyet. Paris: Klincksieck.

Bouillier, Francisque (1868). *Histoire de la philosophie cartésienne.* 3d. ed. (2 vols.). Paris. (Repr. New York: Garland, 1987.)

Bouju, Théophraste (1614). *Corps de toute la philosophie.* Paris.

Bourke, Vernon (1937). 'An Illustration of the Attitude of the Early French Jesuits towards Cartesianism', in *Cartesio nel terzo centenario nel' Discorso del Metodo,* in *Rivista di filosofia neo-scolastica.* 20(supp):129–37.

Bourne, H. R. Fox (1876). *The Life of John Locke* (2 vols.). London: H. S. King.

Boutroux, E. (1927). *Des vérités éternelles chez Descartes,* trans. [French] G. Canguilhem. Paris: Alcan.

Bouvet, Joachim (1989). *Eine Wissenschaftliche Akademie für China,* ed. Claudia von Collani (Studia Leibnitiana, Sonderheft 18). Stuttgart: Steiner.

Boyce Gibson, A. (1929–30). 'The Eternal Verities and the Will of God in the Philosophy of Descartes', *Proceedings of the Aristotelian Society.* N.s. 30:31–54.

Boylan, Michael (1980). 'Henry More's Space and the Spirit of Nature', *Journal of the History of Philosophy.* 18:395–405.

Boyle, Robert (1660). *New Experiments Physico-Mechanicall, Touching the Spring of the Air.* Oxford. (2d ed. Oxford, 1662.)

Boyle, Robert (1661). *The Sceptical Chymist.* London.

Boyle, Robert (1666). *The Origine of Formes and Qualities, (According to the Corpuscular Philosophy), Illustrated by Considerations and Experiments, (Written by way of Notes upon an Essay about Nitre).* Oxford.

Boyle, Robert (1674). *The Excellency of Theology, Compared with Natural Philosophy, (as both are objects of men's study). Discours'd of in a Letter to a Friend . . . To which are annex'd Some Occasional Thoughts about the Excellency and Grounds of the Mechanical Hypothesis . . .* (2 parts paginated separately). London.

Boyle, Robert (1675). *Some Considerations about the Reconcileableness of Reason and Religion.* London.

Boyle, Robert (1685/6). *A Free Enquiry into the Vulgarly Receiv'd Notion of Nature.* London.

Boyle, Robert (1688). *Disquisitions concerning the Final Causes of Natural Things.* London.

Boyle, Robert (1690). *The Christian Virtuoso.* London.

Boyle, Robert (1744). *The Works of the Honourable Robert Boyle,* ed. Thomas Birch (5 vols.). London.

Boyle, Robert (1772). *The Works of the Honourable Robert Boyle,* ed. Thomas Birch (6 vols.). London. (Repr. Hildesheim: Olms, 1965.)

Boyle, Robert (1911). *The Sceptical Chymist.* London: Dent.

Boyle, Robert (1965). *Robert Boyle on Natural Philosophy,* ed. Marie Boas Hall. Bloomington: Indiana University Press.

Boyle, Robert (1979). *Selected Philosophical Papers of Robert Boyle,* ed. M. A. Stewart. Manchester: Manchester University Press.

Boyle, Robert (1991). *The Early Essays and Ethics of Robert Boyle,* ed. J. T. Harwood. Carbondale and Edwardsville: Southern Illinois University Press.

Bracken, Harry (1974). *Berkeley.* London: Macmillan.

Bradley, R. I. (1966). 'Blacklo and the Counter-Reformation: An Inquiry into the Strange Death of Catholic England', in C. H. Carter (ed.), *From the Renaissance to the Counter-Reformation: Essays in Honour of Garrett Mattingly.* London: Cape, pp. 348–70.

Bradwardine, Thomas (1505). *Tractatus de proportionibus.* Venice.

Brändli, Rodolfo (1964). *Virgilio Malvezzi politico e moralista.* Basel: Tipografia dell'USC.

Brandt, F. (1928). *Thomas Hobbes' Mechanical Conception of Nature.* Copenhagen: Levin and Munksgaard.

Brandt, Reinhard (1991). 'Locke und Kant', in M. P. Thompson (ed), *John Locke und Immanuel Kant. Historische Rezeption und Gegenwärtige Relevanz.* Berlin: Duncker und Humblot, pp. 87–108.

Brann, Noel L. (1979–80). 'The Conflict between Reason and Magic in Seventeenth-Century England: A Case Study of the Vaughan-More Debate', *Huntington Library Quarterly.* 43:103–26.

Brauen, Fred (1982). 'Athanasius Kircher (1602–1680)', *Journal of the History of Ideas.* 43:129–34.

Breger, Herbert (1990). 'Know-how in der Mathematik. Mit einer Nutzanwendung auf die unendlichkleinen Größen', in *Rechnen mit dem Unendlichen: Beiträge zur Entwicklung eines kontroversen Gegenstandes.* Basel: Birkhäuser, pp. 43–57.

Bréhier, E. (1937). 'La création des vérités éternelles dans le système de Descartes', *Revue Philosophique.* 103:15–29.

Bréhier, E. (1967). 'The Creation of the Eternal Truths in Descartes's System', in Willis Doney (ed.), *Descartes: A Collection of Critical Essays.* Garden City, N.Y.: Doubleday.

Bremond, Henri (1967). *Histoire Littéraire du Sentiment Religieux en France.* Paris: Armand Colin.

Brerewood, Edward (1640). *Tractatus ethici sive Commentarii in aliquot Aristotelis libros ad Nicomachum de moribus.* Oxford.

Brickman, Benjamin (1941). *An Introduction to Francesco Patrizi's Nova de Universis Philosophia.* New York: Columbia University Press.

Brizzi, Gian Paolo (1976). *La formazione della classe dirigente nel Sei-Settecento.* Bologna: Il Mulino.

Broad, C. D. (1975). *Leibniz: An Introduction.* Cambridge: Cambridge University Press.

Brockliss, L. W. B. (1981). 'Aristotle, Descartes, and the New Science: Natural Philosophy at the University of Paris, 1600–1740', *Annals of Science.* 38:33–69.

Brockliss, L. W. B. (1987). *French Higher Education in the Seventeenth and Eighteenth Centuries: A Cultural History.* Oxford: Oxford University Press.

Broughton, Janet, and Mattern, Ruth (1978). 'Reinterpreting Descartes on the Notion of the Union of Mind and Body', *Journal of the History of Philosophy.* 16:23–32.

Brown, Clifford (1990). *Leibniz and Strawson: A New Essay in Descriptive Metaphysics.* Munich and Vienna: Philosophia.

Brown, Harcourt (1934). *Scientific Organizations in Seventeenth-Century France (1620–1680).* Baltimore: Williams and Wilkins.

Brown, K. C. (1962). 'Hobbes's Grounds for Belief in a Deity', *Philosophy.* 37:336–44.

Brown, K. C. (ed.) (1965). *Hobbes Studies.* Oxford: Blackwell.

Brown, Stuart (1984). *Leibniz (Philosophers in Context).* Minneapolis: University of Minnesota Press.

Browne, Sir Thomas (1977). *Religio Medici (1643),* in *Sir Thomas Browne. The Major Works,* ed. C. A. Patrides. Harmondsworth: Penguin, pp. 59–161.

Broydé, Isaac (1905). 'Spaeth, Johann Peter', in Isidore Singer et al. (eds.), *The Jewish Encyclopedia* (12 vols.). New York: Funk and Wagnalls.

Brucker, Johann Jakob (1742–4). *Historia critica philosophiae* (5 vols.). Leipzig.

Brundell, Barry (1987). *Pierre Gassendi. From Aristotelianism to a New Natural Philosophy.* Dordrecht: Reidel.

Brunet, Jean (1686). *Journal de Medicine.* Paris.

Brunet, Pierre (1931). *L'introduction des théories de Newton en France au xviiie siècle.* Paris: Blanchard.

Brunner, Fernand (1951). *Etudes sur la signification historique de la philosophie de Leibniz.* Paris: Vrin.

Bruno, Giordano (1584a). *La cena de le ceneri.* London.

Bruno, Giordano (1584b). *De la causa, principio et uno.* London.

Bruno, Giordano (1584c). *De l'infinito universo e mondi.* London.

Bruno, Giordano (1584d). *Lo spaccio de la bestia trionfante.* London.

Bruno, Giordano (1585). *De gli eroici furori.* London.

Bruno, Giordano (1879–91). *Opere latine,* ed. F. Fiorentino et al. Naples and Florence: Morano. (Repr. Stuttgart: Frommann, 1969.)

Bruno, Giordano (1957). *Dialoghi italiani,* ed. G. Gentile and G. Aquilecchia. Florence: Sanson.

Bruno, Giordano (1964). *The Expulsion of the Triumphant Beast,* trans. Arthur D. Imerti. New Brunswick, N.J.: Rutgers University Press.

Bruno, Giordano (1973). *De la causa, principio et uno,* ed. G. Aquilecchia. Turin: Einaudi.

Bruno, Giordano (1976). *Cause, Principle, and Unity,* trans. J. Lindsay. Westport, Conn.: Greenwood Press.

Brunschvicg, L. (1945). *Descartes et Pascal lecteurs de Montaigne.* Neuchâtel: La Baconnière.

Brush, Craig (1966). *Montaigne and Bayle. Variations on the Theme of Scepticism.* The Hague: Nijhoff.

Bruyère, Nelly (1984). *Méthode et dialectique dans l'oeuvre de La Ramée: Renaissance et âge classique.* Paris: Vrin.

Brykman, Geneviève (1984). *Berkeley. Philosophie et apologétique.* Paris: Vrin.

Buchdahl, Gerd (1969). *Metaphysics and the Philosophy of Science: The Classical Origins, Descartes to Kant.* Oxford: Blackwell.

Buchdahl, Gerd (1970). 'Gravity' in Robert E. Butts and John W. Davis (eds.), *The Methodological Heritage of Newton.* Toronto: University of Toronto Press.

Buckle, S. (1991). *Natural Law and the Theory of Property. Grotius to Hume.* Oxford: Oxford University Press.

Buckley, Michael (1987). *At the Origin of Modern Atheism.* New Haven, Conn.: Yale University Press.

Buickerood, J. G. (1985). 'The Natural History of the Understanding: Locke and the Rise of Facultative Logic in the Eighteenth Century', *History and Philosophy of Logic.* 6:157–90.

Bullokar, John (1616). *An English Expositor, Teaching the Interpretation of the Hardest Words Used in Our Language. . . .* London.

Buonamici, Francesco (1591). *De Motu.* Florence.

Burgersdijck, Franco (1622). *Idea philosophiae naturalis.* Leiden.

Burgersdijck, Franco (1623). *Idea philosophiae moralis.* Leiden.

Burgersdijck, Franco (1626). *Institutionum logicarum, libri duo.* Leiden.

Burgersdijck, Franco (1629). *Idea philosophiae moralis.* Leiden.

Burgersdijck, Franco (1631). *Idea philosophiae tum naturalis tum moralis sive epitome compendiosa utriusque ex Aristotele excerpta et methodice disposita, . . . editio tertia prioribus emendatior.* Oxford.

Burgersdijck, Franco (1632). *Collegium physicum in quo tota philosophia naturalis aliquot disputationibus perspicue et compendiose explicatur.* Leiden.

Burgersdijck, Franco (1640). *Institutionum metaphysicarum libri duo.* Leiden.

Burgersdijck, Franco (1644). *Institutiones logicae.* Cambridge. (1st ed. Leiden, 1626.)

Burgersdijck, Franco (1654). *Idea philosophiae, tum moralis tum naturalis.* Oxford.

Burgersdijck, Franco (1675). *Institutiones Metaphysicae.* Oxford.

Buridan, J. (1509). *Questiones super octo physicorum libros Aristotelis.* Paris. (Repr. Frankfurt: Minerva, 1964.)

Buridan, Jean (1985). *Logic. The Treatise on Supposition. The Treatise on Consequences,* trans. Peter King. Dordrecht: Reidel.

Burke, Edmund (1989). *The Writings and Speeches of Edmund Burke,* ed. P. Langford. Vol. 8, ed. L. G. Mitchell and W. B. Todd. Oxford: Oxford University Press.

Burkhardt, H. (1980a). *Logik und Semiotik in der Philosophie von Leibniz* (Analytica. Untersuchungen zu Logik, Ontologie und Sprachphilosophie). Munich: Philosophia Verlag.

Burkhardt, H. (1980b). 'Skizze der Leibnizschen Theorie der Prädikation', in *Theoria cum Praxi. Akten des III. Internationalen Leibniz-Kongresses, Hannover, 12–17.11.1977, bd. III* (Studia Leibnitiana, Supplementa 21). Stuttgart: Steiner.

Burkhardt, H. (1983a). 'Die Leibnizsche Logik. Forschungsbericht', *Information Philosophie*. 1:4–17.

Burkhardt, H. (1983b). 'Modaltheorie und Modallogik in der Scholastik und bei Leibniz', *Anuario filosofico*. 16:273–91.

Burnet, Richard (1699). *An Exposition of the Thirty-Nine Articles of the Church of England*. London.

Burnet, Thomas (1681). *Telluris Theoria Sacra*. London.

Burnet, Thomas (1689). *Telluris Theoria Sacra*. 2d ed. London.

Burnet, Thomas (1692). *Archaeologiae Philosophicae*. London.

Burnet, Thomas (1697a). *Remarks upon an Essay concerning Human Understanding*. London.

Burnet, Thomas (1697b). *Second Remarks upon an Essay concerning Humane Understanding*. London.

Burnet, Thomas (1699). *Third Remarks upon an Essay concerning Humane Understanding*. London.

Burnham, Frederic B. (1974). 'The More-Vaughan Controversy: The Revolt against Philosophical Enthusiasm', *Journal of the History of Ideas*. 35:33–49.

Burns, Norman (1972). *Christian Mortalism from Tyndale to Milton*. Cambridge, Mass.: Harvard University Press.

Burnyeat, Myles (1982). 'Idealism and Greek Philosophy: What Descartes Saw and Berkeley Missed', *Philosophical Review*. 91:3–40. (Also in Godfrey Vesey (ed.), *Idealism Past and Present*. Cambridge: Cambridge University Press, 1982.)

Burnyeat, Myles (1984). 'The Sceptic in His Place and Time', in Richard Rorty et al. (eds.), *Philosophy in History*. Cambridge: Cambridge University Press.

Burthogge, Richard (1670). Ταγαϑον, *or Divine Goodness Explicated and Vindicated from the Exceptions of the Atheist*. London.

Burthogge, Richard (1678). *Organum vetus et novum; or a Discourse of Reason and Truth*. London.

Burthogge, Richard (1687). *Prudential Reasons for Repealing the Penal Laws against All Recusants, and for a General Toleration*. London.

Burthogge, Richard (1690). *The Nature of Church-Government, Freely Discussed and Set Out*. London?

Burthogge, Richard (1694). *An Essay upon Reason, and the Nature of Spirits*. London. (Repr. New York: Garland, 1976.)

Burthogge, Richard (1699). *Of the Soul of the World, and of Particular Souls. In a Letter to Mr. Lock*. London.

Burthogge, Richard (1702). *Christianity a Revealed Mystery*. London.

Burthogge, Richard (1921). *The Philosophical Writings of Richard Burthogge*, ed. M. W. Landes. Chicago: Open Court.

Burton, Robert (1989–94). *The Anatomy of Melancholy*, ed. T. C. Faulkner, Nicolas K. Kiessling, and Rhonda L. Blair (3 vols.). Oxford: Oxford University Press.

Burtt, E. A. (1932). *The Metaphysical Foundations of Modern Physical Science*. London: Routledge. (2d ed. New York: Humanities Press, 1980.)

Bury, Arthur (1690). *The Naked Gospel*. London.

Busenbaum, Hermann (1688). *Medulla theologiae moralis, facili ac perspicua methodo resolvens casus conscientiae. . . .* Cologne.

Busson, Henri (1933). *La pensée religieuse française de Charron à Pascal*. Paris: Vrin.

Butler, Joseph (1736). *The Analogy of Religion*. London.

Butts, Robert E. (1980). 'Leibniz' Monads: A Heritage of Gnosticism and a Source of Rational Science', *Canadian Journal of Philosophy*. 10:47–62.

Butts, Robert E., and Pitt, Joseph C. (eds.) (1978). *New Perspectives on Galileo. Papers Deriving from and Related to a Workshop on Galileo Held at Virginia Polytechnic Institute and State University, 1975*. Dordrecht: Reidel.

Byrne, Edward F. (1968). *Probability and Opinion. A Study in the Medieval Presuppositions of Post-Medieval Theories of Probability.* The Hague: Martinus-Nijhoff.

Cafiero, Luca (1964–5). 'Robert Fludd e la polemica con Gassendi', *Rivista critica di storia della filosofia.* 19:367–410; 20:3–15.

Cajetan, Thomas de Vio [Cardinal] (1598). *Commentaria de Anima.* Palermo.

*Calendar of State Papers, Domestic series, of the Reign of Charles II* (28 vols.) (1860–1939). London: Longmans.

Calvin, Jean (1559). *Institutio christianae religionis* (1536), ed. Petrus Barth and Guilelmus Niesel. Geneva.

Calvin, Jean (1961). *Institutes of the Christian Religion,* trans. Ford L. Battles and ed. John T. McNeill (2 vols.) (Library of Christian Classics). London: S.C.M. Press.

Campanella, Tommaso (1617). *Prodromus philosophiae instauratae, id est, dissertationis de natura rerum compendium secundum vera principia ex scriptis Thomae Campanellae praemissum.* Frankfurt.

Campanella, Tommaso (1620). *De sensu rerum et magia.* Frankfurt.

Campanella, Tommaso (1622). *Apologia pro Galileo.* Frankfurt.

Campanella, Tommaso (1635). *Medicinalium iuxta propria principia libri septem.* Lyon.

Campanella, Tommaso (1638a). *Universalis Philosphiae, seu Metaphysicarum Rerum Iuxta Propria Dogmata Partes Tres. libri XVIII.* Paris.

Campanella, Tommaso (1638b). *Philosophia Rationalis Partes Quinque.* Paris.

Campanella, Tommaso (1647). *Atheismus triumphatus.* Paris.

Campanella, Tommaso (1925). *Del senso delle cose e della magia: Teso inedito italiano,* ed. A. Bruers. Bari: Laterza.

Campanella, Tommaso (1939). *Epilogo magna (Fisiologia italiana): Testo italiano inedito,* ed. C. Ottaviano. Rome: Reale Accademia d'Italia.

Campanella, Tommaso (1951). *Opusculi inediti,* ed. L. Firpo. Florence: Olschki.

Campanella, Tommaso (1954). *Tutte le opere di Tommaso Campanella,* ed. L. Firpo. Milan: Mondadori.

Campanella, Tommaso (1957). *Magia e grazia: inediti; theologicorum liber XIX,* ed. R. Amerio. Rome: Istituto di Studi Filosofici.

Campanella, Tommaso (1974). *La filosofia che i sensi ci additano (Philosophia sensibus demonstrata),* ed. Luigi De Franco. Naples: Libreria Scientifica Editrice.

Campanella, Tommaso (1975). *Opera Latini, Francofurti impressa annis 1617–1630,* ed. L. Firpo (2 vols.). Turin: Bottega d'Erasmo.

Camus, Jean Pierre (1614). *Traite des Passions de L'Ame* in *Les Diversitez,* vol. 9. Paris.

Canfeld, Benoît de (1982). *Règle de Perfection,* ed. J. Orchibal. Paris: Presses Universitaires de France.

Canguilhem, G. (1955). *La formation du concept de réflexe au XVII<sup>e</sup> et XVIII<sup>e</sup> siècles.* Paris: Presses Universitaires de France. (2d ed. Paris: Vrin, 1977.)

Capp, Bernard S. (1972). *The Fifth Monarchy Men.* Totowa, N.J.: Rowman and Littlefield.

Capp, Bernard (1979). *English Almanacs, 1500–1800: Astrology and the Popular Press.* Ithaca, N.Y.: Cornell University Press.

Cardano, Girolamo (1663). *Opera omnia* (10 vols.). Lyon. (Repr. Stuttgart: Frommann, 1966.)

Cardano, Girolamo (1961). *The Book on Games of Chance,* trans. Sydney Henry Gould. New York: Holt, Rinehart & Winston.

Carlsen, Olaf (1938). *Hugo Grotius og Sorø En Kritisk Studie.* Taastrup: Handelstrykkeriet.

Carmona, Michel (1988). *Les diables de Loudun: sorcellerie et politique sous Richelieu.* Paris: Fayard.

Carpenter, Nathanael (1621). *Philosophia libera duplici exercitationum decade proposita: In qua paradoxa quaedam ad exercenda juvenum ingenia adversus vulgates huius temporis philosophos suscipiuntur, validisque rationibus confirmantur. Authore N. C. Cosmopolitano. Cui praeit paradoxon, ignorantem docto praeferendum esse.* Frankfurt. (Also Oxford 1622 and 1636.)

Carraud, V. (1987). 'Le refus pascalien des preuves métaphysiques', *Actes du Colloque Pascal et Descartes.*

Descartes and Tours: Ville de Descartes and Université de Tours. (Also published in *Revue des sciences philosophiques et théologiques.* 1991 (1):19–45.)

Carraud, V. (1992). *Pascal et la philosophie.* Paris: Presses Universitaires de France.

Carriero, John (1986). 'The Second Meditation and the Essence of the Mind', in Rorty 1986a, pp. 199–221.

Carriero, John (1987). 'The First Meditation', *Pacific Philosophical Quarterly.* 68:222–48.

Carroll, Robert Todd (1975). *The Common-Sense Philosophy of Religion of Bishop Edward Stillingfleet 1635–1699.* The Hague: Nijhoff.

Carter, Richard B. (1983). *Descartes' Medical Philosophy: The Organic Solution to the Mind–Body Problem.* Baltimore: Johns Hopkins University Press.

Carugo, Adriano, and Crombie, Alistair C. (1983). 'The Jesuits and Galileo's Ideas of Science and of Nature', *Annali dell'Istituto e Museo di Storia della Scienza di Firenze.* 8 (fasc. 2):3–68.

Caruso, Esther (1987). 'Honoré Fabri gesuita e scienziato', in *Miscellanea secentesca: Saggi su Descartes, Fabri, White* (Università degli Studi di Milano, Facoltà di Lettere e Filosofia: Quaderni di Acme, 8). Milan: Cisalpino-Goliardica, pp. 85–126.

Cary, Lucius, Lord Falkland (1651). *Discourse of Infallibility, with an Answer to It.* London.

Casaubon, Meric (1655). *A Treatise concerning Enthusiasme.* London.

Casaubon, Meric (1659). *A True & Faithful Relation of What Passed for Many Yeers between Dr. John Dee . . . and Some Spirits.* London.

Casaubon, Meric (1668). *Of Credulity and Incredulity in Things Natural, Civil, and Divine: Wherein, among Other Things, the Sadducism of These Times, in Denying Spirits, Witches, and Supernatural Operations, by Pregnant Instances and Evidences, Is Fully Confuted.* London.

Casaubon, Meric (1669). *Letter . . . to Peter du Moulin concerning Natural Experimental Philosophie.* Cambridge.

Casaubon, Meric (1670). *Of Credulity and Incredulity in Things Divine & Spiritual: Wherein (among Other Things) a True and Faithful Account Is Given of the Platonick Philosophy, as It Hath Reference to Christianity. . . . : as also the business of witches and witchcraft, against a late writer, fully argued and disputed.* London.

Casaubon, Meric (1980). *Letter . . . to Peter du Moulin concerning Natural Experimental Philosophie,* in Spiller 1980.

Casper, Bernhard (1968–9). 'Der Gottesbegriff *ens causa sui* ', *Philosophisches Jahrbuch.* 76:315–31.

Cassirer, Ernst (1906–57). *Das Erkenntnisproblem in der Philosophie und Wissenschaft der neueren Zeit* (4 vols.). Berlin: B. Cassirer.

Cassirer, Ernst (1927). *Individuum und Cosmos in der Philosophie der Renaissance.* Leipzig: B. G. Teubner.

Cassirer, Ernst (1932). *Die Platonische Renaissance in England und die Schule von Cambridge* (Studien der Bibliothek Warburg 24). Leipzig: Teubner.

Cassirer, Ernst (1953). *The Platonic Renaissance in England,* trans. J. P. Pettegrove. Austin: University of Texas Press.

Cassirer, Ernst, Kristeller, P. O., and Randall, J. H. (eds.) (1948). *The Renaissance Philosophy of Man.* Chicago: University of Chicago Press.

Castro, Americo (1954). *The Structure of Spanish History.* Princeton, N.J.: Princeton University Press.

Caussin, Nicolas (1624). *La cour sainte ou l'institution chrétienne des grands.* Paris.

Caussin, Nicolas (1630). *La cour sainte.* Paris, 1630. (Translated into English by Sir Thomas Hawkins. London, 1663.)

Cavalieri, Bonaventura (1635). *Geometria indivisibilibus continuorum nova quadam ratione promota.* Bologna.

Cavalieri, Bonaventura (1646). *Trattato della ruota planetaria perpetua e dell'uso di quella.* Bologna. (Under the pseudonym Silvio Filomantio.)

Cavalieri, Bonaventura (1647). *Exercitationes geometricae sex.* Bologna.

Cavalieri, Bonaventura (1653). *Nova geometria indivisibilibus promota.* Bologna.

Cavalieri, Bonaventura (1985). '*Opere inedite*. A cura di Sandra Giuntini, Enrico Giusti, Elisabetta Ulivi', *Bollettino di Storia delle Scienze Matematiche*. 5(1/2):1–352.

Cavalieri, Bonaventura (1987). *Carteggio*, ed. Giovanna Baroncelli (Archivio della corrispondenza degli scienziati italiani, 3). Florence: Olschki.

Cavendish, Margaret (1655). *Philosophical and Physical Opinions*. London.

Cavendish, Margaret (1664). *Philosophical Letters: Or, Modest Reflections upon Some Opinions in Natural Philosophy*. London.

Cavendish, Margaret (1666). *Observations upon Experimental Philosophy*. London.

Cavendish, Margaret (1668). *Grounds of Natural Philosophy*. London.

Ceñal, R. (1970). 'El argumento ontologico de la existencia de Dios en la escolastica de los siglos 17 y 18', in Sociedad de Estudios y Publicaciones (eds.), *Homenaje a Xavier Zubiri*. Madrid: Editorial Moneda y Crédito, pp. 247–325.

Ceñal, R. (1972). 'La historia de la lógica en España y Portugal de 1500 a 1800', *Pensamiento*. 28:277–319.

Ceriziers, René de (1643). *Le philosophe français*. Paris.

Chadwick, Henry (1967). 'Clement of Alexandria', in Armstrong 1967.

Chadwick, Henry (1981). *Boethius: The Consolations of Music, Logic, Theology, and Philosophy*. Oxford: Oxford University Press.

*Chaldean Oracles, The: Text, Translation and Commentary* (1989). Ed. and trans. Ruth Majercik. Leiden: Brill.

Chambers, Ephraim (1728). *Cyclopaedia: Or, an Universal Dictionary of Arts and Sciences* (2 vols.). London.

Channevelle, Jacques (1666). *Ethica seu Philosophia moralis juxta principia Aristotelis* (2 vols.). Paris.

Chapman, George (1941). *The Poems*, ed. P. B. Bartlett. New York: Oxford University Press.

Chappell, Vere (1986). 'The Theory of Ideas', in Rorty 1986a.

Chappell, Vere (1989). 'Locke and Relative Identity', *History of Philosophy Quarterly*. 6:69–83.

Chappell, Vere (ed.) (1994a). *The Cambridge Companion to Locke*. Cambridge: Cambridge University Press.

Chappell, Vere (ed.) (1994b). 'Locke's Theory of Ideas', in Chappell 1994a.

Chappell, Vere, and Doney, Willis (eds.) (1987). *Twenty-five Years of Descartes Scholarship 1960–1984: A Bibliography*. New York: Garland.

Charbonnel, J.-Roger (1919). *La Pensée italienne au XVIe siècle et le courant libertin*. Paris: Champion.

Charles-Daubert, Françoise (1985). 'Le libertinage et la recherche contemporaine'. *XVIIe siècle* no. 149:409–32.

Charleton, Walter (1652). *The Darkness of Atheism Dispelled by the Light of Nature*. London.

Charleton, Walter (1654). *Physiologia Epicuro-Gassendo-Charltoniana: Or a Fabrick of Science Natural, upon the Hypothesis of Atoms, Founded by Epicurus, Repaired by Petrus Gassendus, Augmented by Walter Charleton*. London. (Repr. New York and London: Johnson, 1966.)

Charleton, Walter (1656). *Epicurus's Morals*. London.

Charleton, Walter (1657). *The Immortality of the Soul*. London.

Charleton, Walter (1670). *Epicurus's Morals*. London.

Charleton, Walter (1674). *A Natural History of the Passions*. London.

Charleton, Walter (1680). *Enquiries into Human Nature*. London.

Charleton, William (1981). 'Spinoza's Monism', *Philosophical Review*. 90:503–29.

Charron, Pierre (1593). *Les Trois Véritez contre les athées, idolâtres, juifs, mahométans, hérétiques et schismatiques*. Paris.

Charron, Pierre (1601). *De la sagesse*. Bordeaux.

Charron, Pierre (1606). *Of Wisdome Three Books*, trans. Samson Lennard. London.

Charron, Pierre (1635). *Toutes les oeuvres* (new ed.) (2 vols.). Paris. (Repr. Geneva: Slatkine, 1970.)

Charron, Pierre (1986). *De la Sagesse,* ed. Barbara de Negroni. Paris: Fayard.

Chasteigner de la Rochepozay, Henri Louis (1619). *Celebriorum distinctionum tum philosophicarum tum theologicarum synopsis: Authore Henrico-Ludovico Castanaeo de la Rochepozay Pictavorum Episcopo. Editio altera multo locupletior cum selectorum axiomatum additamento.* Poitiers. (1st ed.: Poitier, 1612. At least a dozen editions appeared between 1612 and 1667, including Chasteigner de la Rochepozay 1658.)

Chasteigner de la Rochepozay, Henri Louis (1658). *Celebriorum distinctionum tum philosophicarum tum theologicarum synopsis . . . cum Samuelis Maresii notis perpetuis, quibus singularum distinctionum usus vel abusus in rebus theologicis, breviter ostenditur.* Groningen.

Chauvin, Stephanus (1713). *Lexicon philosophicum.* 2d ed. (1st ed. 1692.) Leeuwarden. (Repr. Düsseldorf: Stern-Verlag Janssen & Co., 1967.)

Cherel, Albert (1918). 'Ramsay et la tolérance de Fénélon', *Revue du dix-huitième siècle.* 5:17–32.

Cherpack, Clifton (1983). *Logos in Mythos: Ideas and Early French Narrative.* Lexington, Ky.: French Forum.

Chevreul, Jacques Du (1625–6, 1628–9, 1633–5). 'Philosophia'. Bibliothèque Municipale de Cherbourg, MS 22–5.

Chew, Audrey (1988). *Stoicism in Renaissance English Literature: An Introduction.* New York: Peter Lang.

Chichon, Nicolas (1620). *L'athéisme des prétendus réformés.* Poitiers.

Chillingworth, William (1638). *Religion of the Protestants a Safe Way to Salvation.* Oxford and London.

Chillingworth, William (1685). *Religion of the Protestants a Safe Way to Salvation.* London.

Chillingworth, William (1687). *Religion of the Protestants a Safe Way to Salvation.* London.

Chillingworth, William (1727). *The Works of William Chillingworth.* London.

Christina, Queen of Sweden (1959). *Drottning Kristina Maximer – Les Sentiments Héroiques,* ed. Sven Stolpe (Acta Academiae Catholicae Suecanae). Stockholm: Bonniers.

Chroust, A.-H. (1943). 'Hugo Grotius and the Scholastic Natural Law Tradition', *New Scholasticism.* 17:101–33.

Chroust, A.-H. (1979). 'Some Critical Remarks about Samuel Pufendorf and His Contributions to Jurisprudence', *American Journal of Jurisprudence.* 24:72–85.

Cicero, Marcus Tullius (1931). *De finibus bonorum et malorum,* trans. H. Rackham (Loeb Classical Library). Cambridge, Mass.: Harvard University Press. London: Heinemann.

Cicero, Marcus Tullius (1960). *De inventione. De optimo genere oratorum. Topica,* trans. H. M. Hubbell (Loeb Classical Library). Cambridge, Mass.: Harvard University Press.

Cioffari, Vincenzo (1973). 'Fortune, Fate, and Chance', in Philip P. Wiener (ed.), *Dictionary of the History of Ideas* (5 vols.). New York: Charles Scribner's Sons.

Clagett, Marshall (1959). *The Science of Mechanics in the Middle Ages.* Madison: University of Wisconsin Press.

Clagett, Marshall (1968). *Nicole Oresme and the Medieval Geometry of Qualities and Motions.* Madison, University of Wisconsin Press.

Clair, Colin (1960). *Christopher Plantin.* London: Cassell.

Clair, Pierre (1976). 'Louis de la Forge et les origines de l'occasionalisme', *Recherches sur le XVII^e siècle.* 1:63–72.

Clark, Stuart (1984). 'The Scientific Status of Demonology', in Brian Vickers (ed.), *Occult and Scientific Mentalities in the Renaissance.* Cambridge: Cambridge University Press.

Clarke, Desmond M. (1980). 'Pierre-Sylvain Régis: A Paradigm of Cartesian Methodology', *Archiv für Geschichte der Philosophie.* 62:289–310.

Clarke, Desmond M. (1981). 'Descartes' Critique of Logic', in George Henry R. Parkinson (ed.), *Truth, Knowledge and Reality. Inquiries into the Foundations of Seventeenth Century Rationalism* (Studia Leibnitiana, Sonderheft). Stuttgart: Steiner.

Clarke, Desmond M. (1982). *Descartes' Philosophy of Science*. Manchester: Manchester University Press.

Clarke, Desmond M. (1985). 'Cartesian Science in France, 1660–1700', in A. J. Holland (ed.), *Philosophy, Its History and Historiography*. Dordrecht: Reidel.

Clarke, Desmond M. (1989). *Occult Powers and Hypotheses: Cartesian Natural Philosophy under Louis XIV*. Oxford: Oxford University Press.

Clarke, Samuel (1705). *A Demonstration of the Being and Attributes of God: More Particularly in Answer to Mr Hobbs, Spinoza, and Their Followers. Wherein the Notion of Liberty Is Stated, and the Possibility and Certainty of It Proved.* . . . London.

Clarke, Samuel (1706a). *A Discourse concerning the Unchangeable Obligations of Natural Religion and the Truth and Certainty of the Christian Revelation.* . . . London.

Clarke, Samuel (1706b). *A Discourse concerning the Being and Attributes of God, the Obligations of Natural Religion, and the Truth and Certainty of the Christian Religion*. London. (This includes Clarke 1705 and Clarke 1706a.)

Clarke, Samuel (1738). *The Works of Samuel Clarke* (4 vols.). London.

Clarke, Samuel, and Leibniz, G. W. See: Leibniz, G. W., and Clarke, Samuel.

Clatterbaugh, K. (1973). *Leibniz's Doctrine of Individual Accidents* (Studia Leibnitiana sonderheft 4). Stuttgart: Steiner.

Clauberg, Johann (1647). *Elementa philosophiae sive ontosophia*. Gronigen.

Clauberg, Johann (1652). *Defensio Cartesiana*. Amsterdam.

Clauberg, Johann (1654). *Logica vetus et nova*. Amsterdam.

Clauberg, Johann (1655). *Initiatio philosophi, seu dubitatio Cartesiana*. Duisburg.

Clauberg, Johann (1656). *De cognitione Dei et nostri*. Duisburg.

Clauberg, Johann (1658). *Paraphrasis in R. Des Cartes Meditationes de prima philosophia*. Duisburg.

Clauberg, Johann (1664a). *Physica, quibus rerum corporearum vis & natura, Mentis ad Corpus relatae proprietates, denique Corporis ac Mentis arcta & admirabilis in Homine conjunctio explicantur*. Amsterdam.

Clauberg, Johann (1664b). *Metaphysica de ente quae rectius ontosophia*. Amsterdam.

Clauberg, Johann (1691). *Opera omnia philosophica*, ed. J. T. Schalbruch (2 vols.). Amsterdam (Repr. Hildesheim: Olms, 1968.)

Clavelin, Maurice (1974). *The Natural Philosophy of Galileo*. Cambridge, Mass.: MIT Press.

Clericuzio, Antonio (1990). 'A Redefinition of Boyle's Chemistry and Corpuscular Philosophy', *Annals of Science*. 47:561–89.

Clerselier, Claude (1667a). 'Lettre de M^r Clerselier, (qui fut luë dans l'assemblée de M. de Montmor le treiziéme Iuillet 1658 sous le nom de Monsieur Descartes, & comme si c'eust esté luy qui l'eust autrefois écrite à quelqu'un de ses Amis) servant de réponse aux difficultez que Monsieur de Roberval y avoit proposées en son absence, touchant le mouvement dans le plein', in Descartes 1657–67, vol. 3, Lettre 97, pp. 538–51.

Clerselier, Claude (1667b). 'A Monsieur de la Forge, Medecin à Saumur. Observations de Monsieur Clerselier, touchant l'action de l'Ame sur le Corps. A Paris le 4 Decembre 1660', in Descartes 1657–67, vol. 3, Lettre 125, pp. 640–6.

Clucas, Stephen (1994). 'The Atomism of the Cavendish Circle: A Reappraisal', *The Seventeenth Century* 9:247–73.

Clulee, Nicholas (1988). *John Dee's Natural Philosophy: Between Science and Religion*. London: Routledge.

Cocceji, Samuel von (1699). *Disputatio inauguralis de Principio juris naturalis unico, vero et adaequato*, . . . Frankfort a.d.O.

Cocceji, Samuel von (1702). *Tractatus juris gentium de principio juris naturalis unico, vero et adæquato*. Frankfort a.d.O.

Cockburn, Catharine Trotter (1702). *A Defence of the Essay of Human Understanding, written by M^r Locke*. London.

Cockburn, Catherine [Trotter] (1751). *The Works of Mrs. Catharine Cockburn, Theological, Moral, Dramatic and Poetical*, ed. Thomas Birch (2 vols.). London.

Coëffeteau, Nicolas (1630). *Tableau des Passions Humaines, de leurs causes et leurs effets.* Paris.

Cognet, L. (1966). *La spiritualité moderne* (Histoire de la Spiritualité chrétienne, vol. 3, pt. 2). Paris: Aubier.

Cohen, I Bernard (1964a). ' "Quantum in se est": Newton's Concept of Inertia in Relation to Descartes and Lucretius', *Notes and Records of the Royal Society.* 19:131–55.

Cohen, I Bernard (1964b). 'Isaac Newton, Hans Sloane, and the Académie Royale des Sciences', in *Mélanges Alexandre Koyré, publiés à l'occasion de son soixante-dixième anniversaire*, intro. Fernand Braudel (2 vols.) (Histoire de la Pensée, No. 13) (*L'aventure de la science*). Paris: Hermann, vol. 1, pp. 61–116.

Cohen, I Bernard (1968). 'The French Translation of Isaac Newton's *Philosophiae Naturalis Principia Mathematica* (1751, 1759, 1966)', *Archives Internationales d'Histoire des Sciences.* 21:261–90.

Cohen, I Bernard (1971). *Introduction to Newton's 'Principia'.* Cambridge, Mass.: Harvard University Press.

Cohen, I Bernard (1980). *The Newtonian Revolution. With Illustrations of the Transformation of Scientific Ideas.* Cambridge: Cambridge University Press.

Cohen, I Bernard (1985). *The Birth of a New Physics.* Rev. ed. New York: W. W. Norton.

Cohen de Herrera, Abraham (1974). *Pforte des Himmels*, trans. Friedrich Häussermann. Frankfurt: Suhrkamp Verlag.

Cohen de Herrera, Abraham (1987). *Puerta del cielo*, ed. Kenneth Krabbenhoft. Madrid: Fundacion Universitaria Espanola.

Coke, Sir Edward (1684). *The First Part of the Institutes of the Laws of England. Or, a Commentary upon Littleton.* 9th ed. London.

Cole, John R. (1992). *The Olympian Dreams and Youthful Rebellion of René Descartes.* Urbana and Chicago: University of Illinois Press.

Coleman, Janet (1994). 'The Christian Platonism of Saint Augustine', in Anna Baldwin and Sarah Hutton (eds.). *Platonism and the English Imagination.* Cambridge: Cambridge University Press, pp. 27–37.

Colie, Rosalie L. (1957). *Light and Enlightenment: A Study of the Cambridge Platonists and Dutch Arminians.* Cambridge: Cambridge University Press.

Colie, Rosalie L. (1963). 'Spinoza in England, 1665–1730', *Proceedings of the American Philosophical Society.* 107:183–219.

Colish, Marcia L. (1992). 'Stoicism and the New Testament: An Essay in Historiography', in Wolgang Haase (ed.), *Aufstieg und Niedergang der römischen Welt.* Berlin: de Gruyter, Teil 2, vol. 26.1, pp. 334–79.

Collas, Georges (1912). *Jean Chapelain, 1595–1674.* Paris: Perrin.

*Collegium Complutense philosophicum hoc est artium cursus sive disputationes in Aristotelis dialecticam et philosophiam naturalem* (1624). Complutum (Alcalá de Henares, Spain).

*Collegium Conimbricense* (1592). *In octo libros physicorum Aristotelis.* Coimbra.

*Collegium Conimbricense* (1598). *In tres libros de anima Aristotelis.* Coimbra.

*Collegium Conimbricense* (1600). *In tres libros de anima Aristotelis.* Lyon.

*Collegium Conimbricense* (1602). *In octo libros physicorum Aristotelis.* Coimbra.

*Collegium Conimbricense* (1603). *In quatuor libros de coelo, meteorologicos et parva naturalia Aristotelis Stagiritae.* Cologne.

*Collegium Conimbricense* (1606a). *In universam dialecticam Aristotelis.* Coimbra.

*Collegium Conimbricense* (1606b). *In libros de generatione et corruptione Aristotelis Stagiritae.* Mainz.

*Collegium Conimbricense* (1607). *In universam dialecticam Aristotelis.* Lyon.

*Collegium Conimbricense* (1609a). *In octo libros physicorum Aristotelis Stagiritae, prima pars.* Cologne.
*Collegium Conimbricense* (1609b). *In octo libros physicorum Aristotelis Stagiritae, secunda pars.* Frankfurt.
*Collegium Conimbricense* (1625). *In octo libros physicorum Aristotelis.* Lyon.
*Collegium Conimbricense* (1957). *Moral a Nicómaco, de Aristóteles,* ed. A. A. de Andrade. Lisbon: Istituto de alta cultura.
Collier, Arthur (1713). *Clavis Universalis; Or, A New Inquiry after Truth. Being a Demonstration of the Non-Existence or Impossibility of an External World.* London. (Repr. New York: Garland, 1978.)
Collins, Anthony (1707). *Reflections on Mr. Clark's Second Defence of his Letter to Mr. Dodwell.* London.
Collins, Anthony (1708). *An Answer to Mr. Clark's Third Defence of His Letter to Mr. Dodwell.* London.
Collins, James (1960). *God in Modern Philosophy.* London: Routledge.
Collins, James (1984). *Spinoza on Nature.* Carbondale: Southern Illinois University Press.
Colman, John (1983). *John Locke's Moral Philosophy.* Edinburgh: Edinburgh University Press.
Comenius, Johann Amos (1942). *The Labyrinth of the World and the Paradise of the Heart,* trans. Matthew Spinka. Chicago: National Union of Czechoslovak Protestants in America.
Comenius, Johann Amos (1969–    ). *Dílo Jana Amose Komenského (Opera Omnia),* ed. Antonio Skarka et al. Prague: Academia scientiarum Bohemoslovaca.
Company of Parish-Clerks of London (1665). *London's Dreadful Visitation: Or, A Collection of All the Bills of Mortality for This Present Year.* London.
Connell, D. (1967). *The Vision in God. Malebranche's Scholastic Sources.* Louvain-Paris: Nauwelaerts.
Connolly, T. K. (1967–89a). 'Molinos', in *New Catholic Encyclopedia* (18 vols.). New York: McGraw-Hill.
Connolly, T. K. (1967–89b). 'Quietism', in *New Catholic Encyclopedia* (18 vols.). New York: McGraw-Hill.
Conway, Anne (1690). *Principia Philosophiae Antiquissimae et Recentissimae: de Deo, Christo et Creatura; Id est, de Spiritu et Materia in genere.* Amsterdam.
Conway, Anne (1692). *The Principles of the Most Ancient and Modern Philosophy, concerning God, Christ, and the Creatures, viz. of Spirit and Matter in General. . . .* London.
Conway, Anne (1982). *Principles of the Most Ancient and Modern Philosophy,* ed. Peter Loptson. (International Archives of the History of Ideas, No. 101). The Hague: Nijhoff. (This reprints the text of the 1690 Latin edition (Amsterdam) and of the 1692 English translation (London).)
Cooke, Monte (1974). 'Arnauld's Alleged Representationalism', *Journal of the History of Philosophy.* 12:53–64.
Cope, Jackson (1956). *Joseph Glanvill: Anglican Apologist.* St. Louis: Washington University Press.
Copenhaver, Brian P. (1978). *Symphorien Champier and the Reception of the Occultist Tradition in Renaissance France.* The Hague: Mouton.
Copenhaver, Brian (1980). 'Jewish Theologies of Space in the Scientific Revolution: Henry More, Joseph Raphson, Isaac Newton and Their Predecessors', *Annals of Science.* 37:489–548.
Copenhaver, Brian (1984). 'Scholastic Philosophy and Renaissance Magic in the *De vita* of Marsilio Ficino', *Renaissance Quarterly.* 37:523–54.
Copenhaver, Brian (1986). 'Renaissance Magic and Neoplatonic Philosophy: "Ennead" 4.3.5 in Ficino's "De vita coelitus comparanda"', in G. C. Garfagnini, ed., *Marsilio Ficino e il ritorno di Platone.* Florence: Olschki.
Copenhaver, Brian (1988a). 'Astrology and Magic', in C. B. Schmitt et al. (eds.), *The Cambridge History of Renaissance Philosophy.* Cambridge: Cambridge University Press.
Copenhaver, Brian (1988b). 'Hermes Trismegistus, Proclus, and the Question of a Philosophy of Magic in the Renaissance', in I. Merkel and A. G. Debus (eds.), *Hermeticism and the Renaissance: Intellectual History and the Occult in Early Modern Europe.* Washington, D.C.: Folger Shakespeare Library.

Copenhaver, Brian (1990). 'Natural Magic, Hermetism, and Occultism in Early Modern Science', in *Reappraisals of the Scientific Revolution,* ed. D. C. Lindberg and R. S. Westman. Cambridge: Cambridge University Press.

Copenhaver, Brian (1991). 'A Tale of Two Fishes: Magical Objects in Natural History from Antiquity through the Scientific Revolution', *Journal of the History of Ideas.* 52:373–98.

Copenhaver, Brian (1992a). 'Did Science Have a Renaissance?' *Isis.* 83:387–407.

Copenhaver, Brian (1992b). 'The Power of Magic and the Poverty of Erudition: Magic in the Universal Library', in Peter Ganz (ed.), *Das Buch als magisches und als Repräsentationsobjekt: 26 Wolfenbütteler Symposion vom 11 bis 15 September 1989 in der Herzog August Bibliothek.* Wiesbaden: Harrassowitz.

Copenhaver, Brian (1992c). *Hermetica: The Greek Corpus Hermeticum and the Latin Asclepius in a New English Translation with Notes and Introduction.* Cambridge: Cambridge University Press.

Copenhaver, Brian, and Schmitt, Charles B. (1992). *A History of Western Philosophy:* vol. 3, *Renaissance Philosophy.* Oxford: Oxford University Press.

Copleston, Frederick (1958). *A History of Philosophy* (7 vols.). Paramus, N.J.: Newman Press.

Copleston, Frederick (1972). *A History of Mediaeval Philosophy.* London: Methuen.

Cordemoy, Gérauld de (1666). *Discernement du corps et de l'âme.* Paris.

Cordemoy, Gérauld de (1668a). *Discours physique de la Parole.* Paris.

Cordemoy, Gérauld de (1668b). *Lettre Ecrite à un sçavant Religieux.* Paris.

Cordemoy, Gérauld de (1691). *Divers Traitez de Metaphysique, d'Histoire, et de Politique.* Paris.

Cordemoy, Gérauld de (1704). *Les Oeuvres de Feu Monsieur de Cordemoy.* Paris.

Cordemoy, Gérauld de (1968). *Oeuvres Philosophiques,* ed. P. Clair and F. Girbal (Le mouvement des idées au XVIIe siècle). Paris: Presses Universitaires de France.

Cornwallis, William (1600). *Essayes.* London.

Cornwallis, William (1601). *Discourses upon Seneca the Tragedian.* London.

Corsano, Antonio (1961). *Tommaso Campanella.* Bari: Laterza.

Corsano, Antonio (1965). 'Campanella e Galileo', *Giornale critico della filosofia italiana.* 3d ser., 19:313–32.

Costa, M. J. (1983). 'What Cartesian Ideas Are Not', *Journal of the History of Philosophy.* 12:53–64.

Costabel, Pierre (1956). 'La "loi admirable" de Christiaan Huygens', *Revue d'Histoire des Sciences.* 9:208–20.

Costabel, Pierre (1957). 'La *septième règle du choc élastique* de Christiaan Huygens', *Revue d'Histoire des Sciences.* 10:120–31.

Costabel, Pierre (1960). *Leibniz et la dynamique: les textes de 1692.* Paris: Hermann.

Costabel, Pierre (1973). *Leibniz and Dynamics: The Texts of 1692,* trans. R. E. W. Maddison. London: Methuen.

Costabel, Pierre (1986). 'Mariotte et les règles du mouvement', in [Michel Blay] (ed.), *Mariotte (†1684): analyse d'une renommée savant et philosophe.* Paris: Vrin, pp. 75–89.

Costello, William T. (1958). *The Scholastic Curriculum at Early Seventeenth-Century Cambridge.* Cambridge, Mass.: Harvard University Press.

Cottier, A. (1943). *Der Gottesbeweis in der modernen Aufklärungsphilosophie. Descartes, Spinoza, Leibniz, Wolff, Kant.* Bern: H. Luthy.

Cottingham, John G. (1986). *Descartes.* Oxford: Blackwell.

Cottingham, John G. (1988). 'The Intellect, the Will and the Passions: Spinoza's Critique of Descartes'. *Journal of the History of Philosophy.* 26:239–57.

Cottingham, John G., (ed.) (1994). *Reason, Will, and Sensation.* Oxford: Oxford University Press.

Coudert, Allison (1975). 'A Cambridge Platonist's Kabbalist Nightmare', *Journal of the History of Ideas.* 36:633–52.

Coudert, Allison (1978). 'Some Theories of a Natural Language from the Renaissance to the Seventeenth Century,' in *Magia Naturalis* 1978.

Coudert, Allison (1995). *Leibniz and the Kabbalah* (International Archives of the History of Ideas). Dordrecht: Kluwer.

Coumet, Ernest (1970). 'La théorie du hasard est-elle née par hasard?' *Annales: Economies, Sociétés, Civilisations.* 25:574–98.

Couplet, Philippe, S. J., et al. (1687). *Confucius Sinarum Phiilosophus.* Paris.

Courcelle, P. (1981). *L'entretien de Pascal et Sacy. Ses sources et ses énigmes.* 2d ed. Paris: Vrin.

Courtine, J.-F. (1979). 'Le projet suarézien de la métaphysique', *Archives de Philosophie.* 42:235–74.

Courtine, J.-F. (1980). 'Le statut ontologique du possible selon Suarez', *Cuadernos Salmatinos de Filosofia.* VII:247–67.

Courtine, J.-F. (1990). *Suarez et le système de la métaphysique.* Paris: Presses Universitaires de France.

Cousin, V. (1845). *Fragments de philosophie cartésienne.* Paris. (2d ed. 1866.)

Couturat, L. (1901). *La logique de Leibniz d'après des documents inédits.* Paris: Alcan. (Repr. Hildesheim: Olms, 1961.)

Craig, Edward (1987). *The Mind of God and the Works of Man.* Oxford: Oxford University Press.

Craig, John (1699). *Theologiae christianae principia mathematica.* London.

Craig, John (1964). *Rules of Historical Evidence* (History and Theory). The Hague: Mouton.

Cranston, M., and Peters, R. S. (eds.) (1972). *Hobbes and Rousseau: A Collection of Critical Essays.* Garden City, N.Y.: Doubleday.

Cranston, Maurice (1957). *John Locke: A Biography.* London: Longmans, Green.

Cranz, Edward F. (1959). *An Essay on the Development of Luther's Thought on Justice, Law and Society.* Cambridge, Mass.: Harvard University Press.

Crapulli, Giovanni (1969). *Mathesis universalis: Genesi di un'idea nel XVI secolo.* Rome: Edizioni dell'Ateneo.

Crassot, J. (1618). *Physica.* Paris.

Craven, James B. (1902). *Doctor Robert Fludd, Robertus de Fluctibus, the English Rosicrucian: Life and Writings.* Kirkwall: Wm. Peace.

Crell, Johann (1663). *Ethica Aristotelica ad sacrarum literarum normam emendata . . . Ethica Christiana, seu Explicatio virtutum et vitiorum quorum in sacris literis fit mentio.* Lüneburg.

Cress, Donald (1973). 'Does Descartes' "Ontological Argument" Stand on Its Own?' *International Studies in Philosophy.* 5:127–36.

Cristofolini, Paolo (1974). *Cartesiani e sociniani.* Urbino: AGE.

Crocker, Robert (1990). 'Mysticism and Enthusiasm in Henry More', in Hutton 1990, pp. 137–55.

Crombie, Alistair C. (1953). *Robert Grosseteste and the Origins of Experimental Science. 1100–1700.* Oxford: Oxford University Press.

Crombie, Alistair C. (1959). *Medieval and Early Modern Science.* 2d ed. Garden City, N.Y.: Doubleday.

Crombie, Alistair C. (1975). 'Marin Mersenne and the Problem of Scientific Acceptability', *Physis.* 17:186–204.

Cronin, T. J. (1960). 'Eternal truths in the thought of Descartes and of His adversary', *Journal of the History of Ideas.* 21:553–9.

Cronin, T. J. (1966). *Objective Being in Descartes and Suarez.* Rome: Analecta Gregoriana.

Crowe, Michael B. (1977a). 'An Eccentric Seventeenth-century Witness to the Natural Law: John Selden (1584–1654)', *Natural Law Forum.* 12:184–95.

Crowe, Michael B. (1977b). *The Changing Profile of Natural Law.* The Hague: Nijhoff.

Crusius, Christian August (1745). *Entwurf der nothwendigen Vernunft-Wahrheiten.* Leipzig.

Cudworth, Ralph (1678). *The True Intellectual System of the Universe* (2 vols.). London. (Repr. Stuttgart: Frommann, 1964 and New York: Garland, 1978.)

Cudworth, Ralph (1731). *A Treatise concerning Eternal and Immutable Morality*. London. (Repr. New York: Garland, 1976.)

Cudworth, Ralph (1837–8). *The True Intellectual System of the Universe . . .; A Treatise on Immutable Morality, etc.*, ed. Thomas Birch (2 vols.). Andover, Mass.

Cudworth, Ralph (1838). *A Treatise of Free Will*. London.

Cudworth, Ralph (1845). *True Intellectual System of the Universe: Wherein All the Reason and Philosophy of Atheism Is Confuted, and Its Impossibility Demonstrated, with a Treatise concerning Eternal and Immutable Morality*, with notes by J. L. Mosheim, trans. J. Harrison (3 vols.). London: T. Tegg.

Culverwel, Nathaniel (1651). *Spiritual Opticks: Or a Glasse Discovering the Weakness and Imperfection of a Christians Knowledge in This Life*. Cambridge.

Culverwel, Nathaniel (1652). *An Elegant and Learned Discourse of the Light of Nature. . . .* London. (Repr. New York: Garland, 1978.)

Culverwel, Nathaniel (1857). *An Elegant and Learned Discourse of the Light of Nature*, ed. John Brown. Edinburgh: Constable.

Culverwel, Nathaniel (1971). *An Elegant and Learned Discourse of the Light of Nature*, ed. R. A. Green and H. MacCallum. Toronto: University of Toronto Press.

Cumberland, Richard (1672). *De legibus naturae. Disquisitio philosophica, in qua earum forma, summa capita, ordo, promulgatio & obligatio e rerum natura investigantur; quinetiam elementa philosophiae Hobbianae, cum moralis tum civilis, considerantur & refutantur*. London.

Cumberland, Richard (1727). *A Treatise of the Laws of Nature*. London.

Cumberland, Richard (1744). *Traité philosophique des loix naturelles*, trans. J. Barbeyrac. Amsterdam.

Cummins, J. S. (1993). *A Question of Rites: Friar Domingo Navarrete and the Jesuits in China*. Aldershot, Hants: Scolar Press.

Cummins, Phillip, and Zoeller, Guenter (eds.) (1992). *Minds, Ideas and Objects*. Atascedero, Calif.: Ridgeview.

Cunaeus, Petrus (1617). *De Republica Hebraeorum*. Leiden.

Cureau de la Chambre, Marin (1634). *Nouvelles pensées sur les causes de la lumière, du débordement du Nil et de l'amour d'inclination*. Paris.

Cureau de la Chambre, Marin (1640). *Les charactères des passions, volume I: amour, joie, rire, désir, espérance*. Paris.

Cureau de la Chambre, Marin (1645). *Les charactères des passions, volume II: des passions courageuses. . . .* Paris.

Cureau de la Chambre, Marin (1647). *Traité de la connoissance des animaux*. Paris.

Cureau de la Chambre, Marin (1648). *Les caractères des passions*. Paris.

Cureau de la Chambre, Marin (1650). *Nouvelles observations et conjectures sur l'iris*. Paris.

Cureau de la Chambre, Marin (1657). *La lumière*. Paris.

Cureau de la Chambre, Marin (1658). *Les caractères des passions* (vols. 1 and 2). Amsterdam.

Cureau de la Chambre, Marin (1659a). *Les charactères des passions, volumes III et IV: haine, doleur. . . .* Paris.

Cureau de la Chambre, Marin (1659b). *L'art de connoistre les hommes. Première partie où sont contenus les discours préliminaires. . . .* Paris.

Cureau de la Chambre, Marin (1662). *Les charactères des passions, volume V: larmes, crainte, désespoir*. Paris.

Cureau de la Chambre, Marin (1664). *Le Système de l'âme*. Paris.

Cureau de la Chambre, Marin (1666). *L'art de connoistre les hommes. Partie troisième qui contient la défense de l'extension des parties libres de l'âme*. Paris.

Cureau de la Chambre, Marin (1667). *Discours de l'amitié et de la haine qui se trouvent envers les animaux*. Paris.

Cureau de la Chambre, Marin (1989). *Traité de la connoissance des animaux,* ed. O. Le Guern. Paris: Fayard.

Curley, E. M. (1969). *Spinoza's Metaphysics: An Essay in Interpretation.* Cambridge, Mass.: Harvard University Press.

Curley, E. M. (1975). 'Descartes, Spinoza, and the Ethics of Belief', in M. Mandelbaum and E. Freeman (eds.), *Spinoza: Essays in Interpretation.* LaSalle Ill.: Open Court.

Curley, E. M. (1978). *Descartes against the Skeptics.* Cambridge, Mass.: Harvard University Press.

Curley, E. M. (1982). 'Leibniz on Locke on Personal Identity', in M. Hooker (ed.), *Leibniz: Critical and Interpretative Essays.* Minneapolis: University of Minnesota Press. pp. 302–26.

Curley, E. M. (1984). 'Descartes on the Creation of the Eternal Truths', *Philosophical Review.* 93:569–97.

Curley, E. M. (1986). 'Analysis in the *Meditations:* The Quest for Clear and Distinct Ideas', in Rorty 1986a.

Curley, E. M. (1988). *Behind the Geometrical Method. A Reading of Spinoza's Ethics.* Princeton, N.J.: Princeton University Press.

Curley, E. M., and Moreau, Pierre-François, eds. (1990). *Spinoza: Issues and Directions.* Leiden: Brill.

Curry, Patrick (1985). 'Revisions of Science and Magic', *History of Science.* 23:299–325.

Curry, Patrick (1989). *Prophecy and Power: Astrology in Early Modern England.* Princeton, N.J.: Princeton University Press.

Cuvillier, Armand (1954). *Essai sur la mystique de Malebranche.* Paris: Vrin.

D'Agostino, F. B. (1976). 'Leibniz on Compossibility and Relational Predicates', *The Philosophical Quarterly.* 26:125–38.

Dalgarno, George (1661). *Ars signorum, vulgo character universalis et lingua philosophica.* London.

Damrosch, Leopold (1979). 'Hobbes as Reformation Theologian: Implications of the Free-Will Controversy', *Journal of the History of Ideas.* 40:339–52.

Daniel, Gabriel (1690). *Voiage du Monde de Descartes.* Paris.

Daniel, Gabriel (1693). *Nouvelles difficultés proposées par un péripatéticien à l'auteur du Voyage du monde de Descartes.* Paris. (Repr. Amsterdam: Rodopi, 1970.)

Daniel, Gabriel (1694). *Entretiens de Cléandre et d'Eudoxe sur les Lettres provinciales de Pascal.* Cologne and Rouen.

Darmon, Albert (1985). *Les corps immatériels. Esprits et images dans l'oeuvre de Marin Cureau de la Chambre (1594–1669).* Paris: Vrin.

Darnton, Robert (1970). *Mesmerism and the End of the Enlightenment in France.* New York: Schocken.

Darwall, Stephen (forthcoming). 'Norm and normativity', in *The Cambridge History of Eighteenth-Century Philosophy,* ed. Knud Haakonssen. Cambridge: Cambridge University Press.

Dascal, M. (1980). 'Leibniz's Early View on Definition', in *Theoria cum Praxi. Akten des III. Internationalen Leibniz-Kongresses, Hannover, 12–17.11.1977, bd. III* (Studia Leibnitiana, Supplementa 21). Stuttgart: Steiner.

Daston, Lorraine (1988). *Classical Probability in the Enlightenment.* Princeton, N.J.: Princeton University Press.

Davies, B. (1985). *Thinking about God.* London: Chapman.

Davies, David (1954). *The World of the Elseviers: 1580–1712.* The Hague: Nijhoff.

Davion, Julien (1660). *La Philosophie de Socrate. Le Crayon du Christianisme en la philosophie de Socrate.* Paris.

De Angelis, Enrico (1964). *Il metodo geometrico nella filosofia del seicento.* Pisa: Istituto di filosofia.

Dear, Peter (1984). 'Marin Mersenne and the Probabilistic Roots of "Mitigated Scepticism' ", *Journal of History of Philosophy.* 22:173–205.

Dear, Peter R. (1988). *Mersenne and the Learning of the Schools.* Ithaca, N.Y.: Cornell University Press.

De Beer, G. R. (1950). 'Some Letters of Thomas Hobbes', *Notes and Records of the Royal Society.* 7:195–206.

Debus, Allen G. (1965). *The English Paracelsians.* London: Oldbourne.

Debus, Allen G., ed. (1972). *Science, Medicine and Society in the Renaissance* (2 vols.). New York: Science History Publications.

Debus, Allen G. (1977). *The Chemical Philosophy: Paracelsian Science and Medicine in the Sixteenth and Seventeenth Centuries* (2 vols.). New York: Science History Publications.

Debus, Allen G. (1987). *Chemistry, Alchemy and the New Philosophy, 1550–1700.* London: Variorum.

Debus, Allen G. (1991). *The French Paracelsians: The Chemical Challenge to Medical and Scientific Tradition in Early Modern France.* Cambridge: Cambridge University Press.

de Dainville, François (1978). *L'éducation des jésuites (XVI<sup>e</sup>-XVIII<sup>e</sup> siècles).* Paris: Les Editions de Minuit.

De Dijn, H. (1974). 'Historical Remarks on Spinoza's Theory of Definition', in J. G. van der Bend (ed.), *Spinoza on Knowing, Being and Freedom.* Assen: Van Gorcum.

De Dijn, H. (1986). 'Spinoza's Logic or Art of Perfect Thinking', *Studia Spinozana.* 2:15–24.

Deer Richardson, Linda (1985). 'The Generation of Disease: Occult Causes and Diseases of the Total Substance', in A. Wear, R. K. French, and I. M. Lonie (eds.), *The Medical Renaissance of the Sixteenth Century.* Cambridge: Cambridge University Press.

Deferrari, Roy J.; Barry, Sister M. Inviolata; and McGuiness, Ignatius (eds.) (1948). *A Lexicon of St. Thomas Aquinas based on The Summa Theologica and Selected Passages of His Other Works.* Washington, D.C.: Catholic University of America Press.

De Gandt, François (1986a). 'Les *Mécaniques* attribuées à Aristote et le renouveau de la science des machines au XVI<sup>e</sup> siècle', *Les études philosophiques.* 1986:391–405.

De Gandt, François (1986b). 'Le style mathématique des Principia de Newton', *Revue d'histoire des sciences.* 39:195–222.

De Launay, Gilles (1673). *Dialectique.* Paris.

Della Porta, Giambattista (1658). *Natural Magick.* London.

Della Rocca, Michael (1993). 'Spinoza's Argument for the Identity Theory', *The Philosophical Review.* 102:183–213.

Della Rocca, Michael (1996). 'Spinoza's Metaphysical Psychology', in Don Garrett (ed.), *The Cambridge Companion to Spinoza.* Cambridge: Cambridge University Press.

Della Rocca, Michael (forthcoming). 'Egoism and the Imitation of Affects in Spinoza', in Yirmiyahu Yovel (ed.), *Reason and the Free Man.* Leiden: E. J. Brill.

Del Noce, A. (1965). *Il problema dell'ateismo.* 2d. ed. Bologna: Il Mulino.

Del Torre, Maria Assunta 1968. *Studi su Cesare Cremonini. Cosmologia e logica nel aristotelismo padovano.* Padua: Antenore.

Deman, Thomas (1936). 'Probabilisme', in A. Vacant, E. Mangenot, and E. Amann, eds., *Dictionnaire de Théologie.* Paris: Librarie Letouzey et Ané.

De Mas, Enrico (1982). *L'attesa del secolo aureo (1603–1625): saggio di storia delle idee del secolo XVII.* Florence: L. S. Olschki.

Demé, Nelly (1985). 'La table des catégories chez Hobbes', *Archives de philosophie.* 48:251–75.

De Moivre, Abraham (1756). *The Doctrine of Chances.* 3d ed. London.

Denley, Peter (1981). 'Recent Studies on Italian Universities of the Middle Ages and Renaissance', *History of Universities.* 1:193–205.

Den Uyl, D., and Rice, L. (1990). 'Spinoza and Hume on Individuals', *Reason Papers.* 15:91–117.

Denzer, H. (1972). *Moralphilosophie und Naturrecht bei Samuel pufendorf. Eine geistes- und wissenschafts-geschichtliche Untersuchung zur Geburt des Naturrechts aus der praktischen Philosophie.* Munich: Beck.

Denzinger, Henricus (1963). *Enchiridion Symbolorum, Definitionum et declarationum de rebus fidei et morum.* 32d ed. A. Schonmetzer. Rome and Freiburg i.B.: Herder.

De Pauley, William C. (1937). *The Candle of the Lord; Studies in the Cambridge Platonists.* New York: Macmillan.

Deprun, Jean (1963). 'Jean Meslier et l'héritage cartésien', *Studies on Voltaire and the Eighteenth Century* 24:443–55.

Deprun, Jean (1988). 'Qu'est-ce qu'une passion de l'âme? Descartes et ses prédécesseurs', *Revue philosophique Français.* 178:407–18.

Derathé, R. (1988). *Jean-Jacques Rousseau et la science politique de son temps.* Paris: Vrin.

Derham, William (1716). *Physico-Theology, Or, A Demonstration of the Being and Attributes of God from His Works of Creation.* 4th ed. rev. London. (Repr. New York: Arno Press, 1977.)

Derrida, Jacques (1967). 'Le Cogito et l'histoire de la folie', in *L'Ecriture et la différence.* Paris: Seuil.

Descartes, René (1637). *Discours de la methode pour bien conduire sa raison & chercher la verité dans les sciences. Plus La dioptrique. Les meteores. Et La geometrie. Qui sont des essais de cete methode.* Leiden.

Descartes, René (1641). *Meditationes de prima philosophia, in qua Dei existentia, et animae immortalitas demonstratur.* Paris.

Descartes, René (1642). *Meditationes de prima philosophia, In quibus Dei existentia, et animae humanae à corpore distinctio, demonstratur.* Amsterdam.

Descartes, René (1644). *Principia philosophiae.* Paris.

Descartes, René (1647a). *Les principes de la philosophie.* Paris.

Descartes, René (1647b). *Les méditations métaphysiques de René Descartes touchant la premiere philosophie dans lesquelles l'esistence de Dieu, et la distinction réelle entre l'ame et le corps de l'homme, sont demonstrées.* Paris.

Descartes, René (1649). *Les passions de l'âme.* Paris.

Descartes, René (1657–67). *Lettres de Mr Descartes,* ed. C. Clerselier (3 vols.). Paris.

Descartes, René (1664). *L'Homme de René Descartes, et un Traité de la Formation du Foetus du mesme Autheur, Avec les Remarques de Louys de la Forge . . . sur le Traitte de l'Homme de René Descartes, et sur les Figures par luy inventées.* Paris.

Descartes, René (1677). *L'Homme de René Descartes, et la Formation du Foetus, avec les Remarques de Louis de la Forge. A quoy l'on a ajouté Le Monde, ou Traité de la Lumiere, du mesme Autheur.* Paris.

Descartes, René (1936–63). *Descartes: Correspondence publiée avec une introduction et des notes,* ed. C. Adam and G. Milhaud (8 vols.). Paris: Alcan and Presses Universitaires de France.

Descartes, René (1954). *The Geometry of René Descartes: With a Facsimile of the First Edition, 1637,* trans. David Eugene Smith and Marcia L. Latham. New York: Dover.

Descartes, René (1959). *Lettres à Regius et remarques sur l'explication de l'esprit humain,* ed. G. Rodis-Lewis. Paris: Vrin.

Descartes, René (1964–74). *Oeuvres de Descartes,* ed. Charles Adam and Paul Tannery. New ed. (11 vols.). Paris: CNRS/Vrin. (Original ed. Paris: Cerf, 1897–1913.)

Descartes, René (1967). *Discours de la méthode. Texte et commentaire par Etienne Gilson.* 4th ed. (Bibliothèque des Textes Philosophiques: Textes et Commentaires). Paris: Vrin. (1st ed. 1925.)

Descartes, René (1970a). *Philosophical Letters,* trans. A. Kenny. Oxford: Oxford University Press.

Descartes, René (1970b). *The World, or Treatise on Light.* (*Le monde, ou Traité de la lumière* (1632; Paris, 1664)), trans. M. S. Mahoney. New York. Abaris Books.

Descartes, René (1972). *Treatise of Man,* trans. T. S. Hall. Cambridge, Mass.: Harvard University Press.

Descartes, René (1976). *Conversation with Burman,* trans. J. Cottingham. Oxford: Oxford University Press.

Descartes, René (1977). *Règles utiles et claires pour la direction de l'esprit en la recherche de la vérité,* ed. and trans. Jean-Luc Marion. The Hague: Nijhoff.

Descartes, René (1979). *Le monde, ou Traité de la lumière; The World, or Treatise on Light,* trans. M. Mahoney. New York: Abaris Books.

Descartes, René (1981). *L'entretien avec Burman,* ed. J.-M. Beyssade. Paris: Presses Universitaires de France.

Descartes, René (1984–91). *The Philosophical Writings of Descartes,* ed. and trans. John Cottingham, Robert Stoothoff, Dugald Murdoch, and Anthony Kenny (3 vols.). Cambridge: Cambridge University Press.

Desgabets, Robert (1675). *Critique de la critique de la recherche de la vérité.* Paris.

Desgabets, Robert (1983). *Oeuvres Philosophiques inédites,* ed. J. Beaude. Amsterdam: Quadratures.

Detel, Wolfgang (1978). *Scientia Rerum Natura Occultarum. Methodologischen Studien zur Physik Pierre Gassendis.* Berlin: de Gruyter.

De Vries, Gerard (1718). *De catholicis rerum attributis determinationes ontologicae.* 6th ed. Edinburgh.

Dewhurst, Kenneth (1963). *John Locke (1632–1704), Physician and Philosopher: A Medical Biography with an Edition of the Medical Notes in his Journals.* London: Wellcome Historical Medical Library.

Dewhurst, Kenneth (1966). *Dr. Thomas Sydenham (1624–1689).* London: Wellcome Historical Medical Library.

De Witt, Johann (1671). *Waerdye van Lyf-Renten.* The Hague. (Repr. in J. Bernoulli 1969–89, vol. 3, pp. 327–50.)

De Witt, Johann (1856). *Waerdye van Lyf-Renten,* trans. F. Hendricks, in Robert G. Barnwell, *A Sketch of the Life and Times of John De Witt.* New York: Pudney and Russell.

Dibon, Paul (1950). 'Notes bibliographiques sur les cartésiens hollandais', in Dijksterhuis et al. 1950, pp. 261–300.

Dibon, Paul (1954). *La Philosophie néerlandaise au siècle d'or: Tome I, L'Enseignement philosophique dans les universités à l'époque précartésienne (1575–1650).* Paris: Elsevier.

Diesselhorst, Malte (1959). *Die Lehre des Hugo Grotius vom Versprechen.* Cologne and Graz: Böhlau.

Diesselhorst, Malte (1976). *Zum Vermögensrechtssystem Samuel Pufendorfs.* Göttingen: Schwartz.

Diethelm, Oskar (1971). *Medical Dissertations of Psychiatric Interest Printed Before 1750.* New York: S. Karger.

Digby, Sir Kenelm (1638). *A Conference with a Lady about Choyce of Religion.* Paris.

Digby, Sir Kenelm (1643). *Observations upon Religio Medici.* London.

Digby, Sir Kenelm (1644a). *Two Treatises. In the one of which, the Nature of Bodies; in the other, the Nature of Mans Soule; Is Looked into: In the Way of Discovery, of the Immortality of Reasonable Soules.* Paris. (Repr. New York: Garland, 1978.)

Digby, Sir Kenelm (1644b). *Observations upon Religio Medici . . . The second Edition Corrected and Amended.* London. (Repr. Menston: Scolar Press, 1973.)

Digby, Sir Kenelm (1645). *Two Treatises. . . .* London.

Digby, Sir Kenelm (1658a). *Discours fait en une célèbre assemblée, par le Chevalier Digby . . . touchant la guérison des playes par la poudre de sympathie.* Paris.

Digby, Sir Kenelm (1658b). *A Late Discourse Made in a Solemne Assembly of Nobles and Learned Men of Montpellier in France by Sr. Kenelme Digby, Knight, &c., Touching the Cure of Wounds by the Powder of Sympathy, with Instructions How to Make the Said Powder, Whereby Many Other Secrets of Nature Are Unfolded.* London.

Dijksterhuis, E. J. (1961). *The Mechanization of the World Picture,* trans. C. Dikshoorn. Oxford: Oxford University Press.

Dijksterhuis, E. J., et al. (1950). *Descartes et le cartésianisme hollandais. Etudes et documents.* Paris and Amsterdam: Presses Universitaires de France and Editions Françaises d'Amsterdam.

Di Napoli, Giovanni (1947). *Tommaso Campanella: Filosofo della restaurazione cattolica.* Padua.

Diogenes Laertius (1688). *The Lives, Opinions, and Remarkable Sayings of the Most Famous Ancient Philosophers.* London.

Diogenes Laertius (1925). *Lives of Eminent Philosophers,* trans. R. D. Hicks (2 vols., Loeb Classical Library). Cambridge, Mass.: Harvard University Press. London: Heinemann.

Dobbs, Betty Jo Teeter (1971). 'Studies in the Natural Philosophy of Sir Kenelm Digby, Part I', *Ambix.* 18:1–25.

Dobbs, Betty Jo Teeter (1973). 'Studies in the Natural Philosophy of Sir Kenelm Digby, Part II, Digby and Alchemy ', *Ambix.* 20:143–63.

Dobbs, Betty Jo Teeter (1974). 'Studies in the Natural Philosophy of Sir Kenelm Digby, Part III, Digby's Experimental Alchemy – the Book of Secrets ', *Ambix.* 21:1–28.

Dobbs, Betty Jo Teeter (1975). *The Foundations of Newton's Alchemy, or 'The Hunting of the Greene Lyon'.* Cambridge: Cambridge University Press.

Dobbs, Betty Jo Teeter (1982). 'Newton's Alchemy and His Theory of Matter', *Isis.* 73: 511–28.

Dobbs, Betty Jo Teeter (1985). 'Conceptual Problems in Newton's Early Chemistry: A Preliminary Study', in M. J. Osler and P. L. Farber (eds.), *Religion, Science, and Worldview.* Cambridge: Cambridge University Press.

Dobbs, Betty Jo Teeter (1988). 'Alchemy', in P. B. Scheurer and G. Debrock (eds.), *Newton's Scientific and Philosophical Legacy.* Dordrecht: Kluwer.

Dobbs, Betty Jo Teeter (1991). *The Janus Faces of Genius: The Role of Alchemy in Newton's Thought.* Cambridge: Cambridge University Press.

*Documents Relating to the Univeristy and Colleges of Cambridge* (3 vols.) (1852). London.

Dod, Bernard G. (1982). 'Aristoteles latinus', in Kretzmann, Pinborg, and Kenny 1982, pp. 80–98.

Domat, Jean (1691–7). *Les Loix civiles dans leur ordre naturel.* 2d ed. (3 vols.). Paris.

Dominicy, M. (1984). *La naissance de la grammaire moderne: Langage, logique et philosophie à Port-Royal.* Brussels: Mardaga.

Donagan, Alan (1973). 'Spinoza's Proof of Immortality', in M. Grene (ed.), *Spinoza: A Collection of Critical Essays.* Garden City, N.Y.: Doubleday.

Donagan, Alan (1982). 'Thomas Aquinas on Human Action', in Kretzmann, Kenny, and Pinborg 1982.

Donagan, Alan (1988). *Spinoza.* Chicago: University of Chicago Press.

Donaldson, Walter (1610). *Moralis disciplinae summa, ex decem libris Aristotelis ad Nicomachum desumpta, ac duodecim disputationibus in illustri Academia Sedanensi propositis . . . comprehensa.* Hanau.

Doney, Willis (1955). 'The Cartesian Circle', *Journal of the History of Ideas.* 16:324–38.

Donne, John (1952). *Essays in Divinity.* Oxford: Oxford University Press.

Doren, A. (1922–3). 'Fortuna im Mittelalter und in der Renaissance', *Vorträge der Bibliothek Warburg.* 2:71–151.

Döring, Detlef (1988). 'Samuel Pufendorf (1632–1694) und die Leipziger Gelehrtengesellschaften in der Mitte des 17. Jahrhunderts', *Lias.* 15:13–48.

Döring, Detlef (1992). *Pufendorf-Studien. Beiträge zur Biographie Samuel von Pufendorfs und seiner Entwicklung als Historiker und theologischer Schriftsteller.* Berlin: Duncker und Humblot.

Drake, Stillman (1975). 'Free Fall from Albert of Saxony to Honoré Fabri', *Studies in History and Philosophy of Science.* 5:347–66.

Drake, Stillman (1978). *Galileo at Work.* Chicago: University of Chicago Press.

Drake, Stillman, and Drabkin, I. E. (eds.) (1969). *Mechanics in Sixteenth-Century Italy. Selections from Tartaglia, Benedetti, Guido Ubaldo, & Galileo* (University of Wisconsin Publications in Medieval Science). Madison: University of Wisconsin Press.

Dryden, John (1900). *The Essays*, ed. W. P. Ker (2 vols.). Oxford: Oxford University Press.

Dryden, John (1958). *The Poems*, ed. James Kinsley (4 vols.). Oxford: Oxford University Press.

Dubarle, D. (1986). *Dieu avec l'être. De Parménide à Saint Thomas.* Paris: Beauchesne.

Duchesneau, François (1973). *L'empirisme de Locke* (International Archives of the History of Ideas, 57). The Hague: Nijhoff.

Duchesneau, François (1994). *La dynamique de Leibniz.* Paris: Vrin.

Dufour, Alfred (1976). *Le mariage dans l'école romande du droit naturel au XVIIIe siècle.* Geneva: Georg.

Dufour, Alfred (1986), 'Pufendorfs Ausstrahlung im französischen und im anglo-amerikanischen

Kulturraum', in K. Å. Modéer (ed.), *Samuel von Pufendorf 1632–1982.* Stockholm: Nordiska Bokhandeln, pp. 96–119.

Dugas, René (1957). *A history of mechanics,* trans. J. R. Maddox, pref. Louis de Broglie. London: Routledge and Kegan Paul.

Dugas, René (1958). *Mechanics in the Seventeenth Century,* trans. Freda Jacquot. Neuchâtel: Editions de Griffon.

Du Hamel, Jean (1692). *Reflexions critiques sur le système cartésien de la philosophie de Mr Regis.* Paris.

Du Hamel, Jean (1699). *Lettre de Monsieur Du Hamel, ancien professeur de philosophie de l'Université de Paris, pour servir de replique à Monsieur Régis.* Paris.

Du Hamel, Jean (1705). *Philosophia universalis, sive commentarius in universam Aristotelis philosophiam ad usum scholarum comparatam quaedam recentiorum philosophorum ac praesertim Cartesii propositiones damnatae ac prohibitae.* Paris.

Du Hamel, Jean-Baptiste (1663). *De consensu veteris et novae philosophiae.* Paris.

Du Hamel, Jean-Baptiste (1672). *De mente humana.* Paris.

Du Hamel, Jean-Baptiste (1678). *Philosophia vetus et nova ad usum scholae accomodata.* Paris.

Duhem, Pierre (1913–59). *Le système du monde: Histoire des doctrines cosmologiques de Platon au Copernic* (10 vols.). Paris: Hermann.

Duhem, Pierre (1985). *Medieval Cosmology: Theories of Infinity, Place, Time, Void and the Plurality of Worlds,* ed. and trans. Roger Ariew. Chicago: University of Chicago Press.

Duncan, David Allen (1993). 'Mersenne and Modern Learning: The Debate over Music', in Tom Sorrel (ed.), *The Rise of Modern Philosophy.* Oxford: Oxford University Press.

Dunn, John (1969). *The Political Thought of John Locke.* Cambridge: Cambridge University Press.

Dunn, John (1980). *Political Obligation in Its Historical Context.* Cambridge: Cambridge University Press.

Dunn, John (1984). *John Locke.* Oxford: Oxford University Press.

Dunne, George, S. J. (1962). *Generation of Giants: The Story of the Jesuits in China in the Last Decades of the Ming Dynasty.* Notre Dame, Ind.: University of Notre Dame Press.

Duns Scotus, John (1639). *Opera Omnia,* ed. L. Wadding (12 vols. in 16). Lyon. (Repr. Hildesheim: Olms, 1968.)

Duns Scotus, John (1891–95). *Opera omnia,* ed. L. Wadding (26 vols). Paris: Vives.

Duns Scotus, John (1950–     ). *Opera omnia.* Vatican City: Typis Polyglottis Vaticana.

Duns Scotus, John (1968). *Cuestiones Cuodlibetales,* ed. and trans. (Latin with Spanish trans.) F. Alluntis. Madrid: Biblioteca de Autores Cristianos.

Duns Scotus, John (1975). *God and Creatures. The Quodlibetal Questions,* ed. & trans. F. Alluntis and A. B. Wolter. Princeton, N.J.: Princeton University Press.

Duns Scotus, John (1987). *Philosophical Writings,* ed. and trans. Allan Wolter. Indianapolis, Ind.: Hackett.

Duns Scotus, John (1988). *Sur la connaissance de Dieu et l'univocité de l'étant.* ed. O. Boulnois. Paris: Presses Universitaires de France.

Dupaquier, Jacques (1973). 'Sur une table (prétendument) florentine d'espérance de vie', *Annales: Economies, Sociétés, Civilisations.* 23:1066–70.

Dupleix, Scipion (1606). *La curiosité naturelle redigée en questions, selon l'ordre alphabetique.* Paris.

Dupleix, Scipion (1610). *L'Ethique ou Philosophie morale.* Paris.

Dupleix, Scipion (1623). *Corps de philosophie, contenant la logique, l'ethique, La physique, et la metaphysique.* Geneva.

Dupleix, Scipion (1627). *Corps de philosophie, contenant la logique, l'ethique, La physique, et la metaphysique.* Geneva.

Dupleix, Scipion (1990). *La physique.* Paris: Fayard.

Dupleix, Scipion (1991). *La métaphysique.* Paris: Fayard.

Duplessis-Mornay, Philippe (1581). *De la vérité de la religion chrétienne.* Paris.

Durandus a Sancto Porciano (1571). *In Petri Lombardi Sententias theologicas commentariorum libri IIII.* Venice.

Durkheim, Emile (1968). *Les Formes élémentaires de la vie religieuse: Le Système totémique en Australie.* Paris: Presses Universitaires de France.

Du Rondel, Jacques (1679). *La Vie d'Epicure.* Paris.

Dury, John (1643). *A Copy of Mr. J.D.'s Letter Presented in Sweden to the . . . Lord Forbes . . .* London.

Dury, John (1649). *A Seasonable Discourse . . . on How Even in These Times of Distraction, the Work May Be Advanced by the Knowledge of Oriental Tongues and Jewish Mysteries.* London.

Dury, John (1650). *The Reformed Librarie-Keeper.* London. (Repr. intro. R. H. Popkin and Thomas Wright. Los Angeles: Clarke Library and University of California (Augustan Reprint Society).)

Du Trieu, Philippe (1826). *Manuductio ad logicam.* London. (1st ed. 1614.)

Du Vair, Guillaume (1946). *De la sainte philosophie. La Philosophie morale des stoïques,* ed. G. Michaut. Paris: J. Vrin.

Echarri, J. (1950). 'Uno influjo español desconcido en la formación del sistema cartesiano; dos textos paralelos de Toledo y Descartes sobre el espacio', *El Pensamiento.* 6:291–32.

Edwards, C. S. (1981). *Hugo Grotius. The Miracle of Holland. A Study in Political and Legal Thought.* Chicago: Nelson-Hall.

Edwards, John (1697). *The Socinian Creeds: Or a Brief Account of the Professed Tenets and Doctrines of the Foreign and English Socinians. . . .* London.

Edwards, Paul (ed.) (1967). *The Encyclopedia of Philosophy* (8 vols.). New York: Macmillan.

Edwards, Thomas (1646). *Gangraena: Or a Catalogue and Discovery of Many of the Errours, Heresies, Blasphemies, and Pernicious Practices of the Sectaries of This Time. . . .* London.

Edwards, William F. (1967). 'Randall on the Development of Scientific Method in the School of Padua – A Continuing Reappraisal', in John P. Anton (ed.), *Naturalism and Historical Understanding: Essays on the Philosophy of John Herman Randall, Jr.* Albany: State University of New York Press.

Edwards, William F. (1976). 'Niccolò Leoniceno and the Origins of Humanist Discussion of Method', in Edward P. Mahoney (ed.), *Philosophy and Humanism: Renaissance Essays in Honor of Paul Oskar Kristeller.* New York: Columbia University Press.

Edwards, William F. (1983). 'Paduan Aristotelianism and the Origins of Modern Theories of Method', in Luigi Olivieri (ed.), *Aristotelismo veneto e scienza moderna* (2 vols.). Padua: Editrice Antenore.

Eichel von Rautenkorn, Johannes (1654). *Programma quo ad publicam disputationem operis Nicomachici de moribus civilis sapientiae cultores invitat in illustri Academia Iulia . . . J. Erichelius.* Helmstedt.

Eisenberg, Paul (1990). 'On the Attributes and their Alleged Independence of One Another: A Commentary on Spinoza's *Ethics* IP10', in Curley and Moreau 1990, pp. 1–15.

Eisler, Rudolph (1910). *Wörterbuch der philosophischen Begriffe.* 3d ed. (3 vols.). Berlin: Mittler.

Elzinga, Aant (1972). *On a Research Program in Early Modern Physics.* Göteborg: Akademiförlaget.

Elzinga, Aant (1980). 'Christiaan Huygens' Theory of Research', *Janus.* 67:281–300.

Emerton, Norma E. (1984). *The Scientific Reinterpretation of Form.* Ithaca, N.Y.: Cornell University Press.

Englebretsen, G. (1982). 'Leibniz on Logical Syntax', *Studia Leibnitiana.* 14:119–26.

Epictetus (1610). *His Manual . . . ,* trans. John Healey. London.

Epictetus (1688). *Le Manuel . . . avec des réflexions tirées de la morale de l'Evangile,* ed. Nicolas Coquelin. Paris.

Erasmus, Desiderius (1969–   ). *Opera Omnia,* ed. J. H. Waszink et al. Amsterdam: North-Holland.

Erasmus, Desiderius (1974–   ). *Collected Works of Erasmus.* Toronto: University of Toronto Press.

Erasmus, Desiderius (1979). *The Praise of Folly,* trans. Clarence H. Miller. Princeton, N.J.: Princeton University Press.

Erle, Manfred (1952). *Die Ehe im Naturrecht des 17. Jahrhunderts.* Göttingen. diss. University of Göttingen.

Ermini, Giuseppe (1947). *Storia dell Universita di Perugia.* Bologna: N. Zachelli.

Esmein, A. (1882). *Histoire de la procédure criminelle en France.* Paris: Larose et Forcel.

Ettinghausen, Henry (1972). *Francisco de Quevedo and the Neostoic Movement.* Oxford: Oxford University Press.

Euchner, W. (1979). *Naturrecht und Politik bei John Locke.* Frankfurt a.M.: Suhrkamp Verlag.

Euler, Leonhard (1959). *Vollständige Anleitung zur Algebra* (St. Petersburg, 1770), ed. J. E. Hofmann. Stuttgart: Reclam-Verlag.

Eustachius a Sancto Paulo (1609). *Summa philosophiae quadripartita, de rebus Dialecticis, Ethicis, Physicis, & Metaphysicis.* Paris.

Eustachius a Sancto Paulo (1613–16). *Summa theologiae tripartita.* Paris.

Eustachius a Sancto Paulo (1629). *Summa philosophiae quadripartita, de rebus Dialecticis, Ethicis, Physicis, & Metaphysicis.* Cologne.

Eustachius a Sancto Paulo (1638). *Summa philosophiae quadripartita, de rebus Dialecticis, Ethicis, Physicis, & Metaphysicis.* Cologne and Geneva.

Eustachius a Sancto Paulo (1648). *Summa philosophiae quadripartita, de rebus Dialecticis, Ethicis, Physicis, & Metaphysicis.* Cambridge.

Eustachius a Sancto Paulo (1654). *Ethica sive Summa moralis disciplinae. . . .* Cambridge.

Eustratius (1892). *In Ethica Nicomachea commentaria,* ed. G. Heylbut. Berlin: G. Reimerus.

Evans, R. J. W. (1981). 'German Universities after the Thirty Years War', *History of Universities.* 1:169–90.

Evelyn, John (1656). *Essay on the First Book of T. Lucretius Carus, De rerum natura.* London.

Everson, S. (ed.) (1990). *Companions to Ancient Thought 1: Epistemology.* Cambridge: Cambridge University Press.

Ewin, R. E. (1991). *Virtues and Rights. The Moral Philosophy of Thomas Hobbes.* Boulder, Colo., San Francisco, Calif., Oxford: Westview Press.

Fabri, Honoré (1646a) [ed. Pierre Mousnier]. *Tractatus physicus de motu locali, in quo effectus omnes, qui ad impetum, motum naturalem, violentum, & mixtum pertinent, explicantur, & ex principiis physicis demonstrantur. Auctore Petro Mousnerio Doctore Medico; cuncta excerpta ex praelectionibus R. P. Honorati Fabry, Societatis Jesu.* Lyon.

Fabri, Honoré (1646b). *Philosophiae tomus primus.* Lyon.

Fabri, Honoré (1669–71). *Physica, id est, scientia rerum corporearum, in decem tractatus distributa.* Lyon.

Fabro, C. (1964). *Introduzione all'ateismo moderno.* 2d ed. Rome: Editrice Studium.

Fardella, Michelangelo (1691). *Universae philosophiae systema in quo nova quadam et extricata methodo naturalis scientiae et moralis fundamenta explanantur, tomus primus, rationalis et emendatae dialecticae specimen tradens, cui accedit appendix de triplici scholarum sophismate detecto et rejecto, opus in tironum gratiam elucubratum.* Venice.

Farr, James (1987). 'The Way of Hypotheses: Locke on Method', *Journal of the History of Ideas.* 48:51–72.

Farrington, Benjamin (1964). *The Philosophy of Francis Bacon: An Essay on Its Development from 1603 to 1609, with New Translations of Fundamental Texts.* Liverpool: Liverpool University Press.

Faye, E. (1986). 'Le corps de philosophie de Scipion Dupleix et l'arbre cartésien des sciences', *Corpus.* 2:7–15.

Febvre, Lucien (1982). *The Problem of Unbelief in the Sixteenth Century: The Religion of Rabelais,* trans. Beatrice Gottlieb. Cambridge, Mass.: Harvard University Press.

Feenstra, R. (1984). 'Quelques remarques sur les sources utilisées par Grotius dans ses travaux de droit naturel', in *The World of Hugo Grotius (1583–1645), Proceedings of the International Colloquium Organized* by the Grotius Committee of the Royal Netherlands Academy of Arts and Sciences, Rotterdam 6–9 April 1983. Amsterdam and Maarssen: APA-Holland University Press.

Feingold, Mordechai (1984a). *The Mathematicians' Apprenticeship: Science, Universities, and Society in England, 1560–1640.* Cambridge: Cambridge University Press.

Feingold, Mordechai (1984b). 'The Occult Tradition in the English Universities of the Renaissance: A Reassessment', in Brian Vickers (ed.), *Occult and Scientific Mentalities in the Renaissance.* Cambridge: Cambridge University Press, pp. 73–94.

Felgenhauer, Paul (1655). *Bonum Nuncium Israeli.* Amsterdam.

Femiano, Salvatore (1968). *La metafisica di Tommaso Campanella.* Milan: Marzorati.

Femiano, Salvatore (1969). 'L'antiaristotelismo essenziale di Tommaso Campanella', in *Tommaso Campanella nel IV centenario della sua nascita (1568–1968).* Naples: EDI-Sapienza.

Fénelon, François (1712). *Démonstration de l'existence de Dieu, Tirée de la conoissance de la Nature et proportionée à la faible intelligence des plus simples.* Paris.

Fénelon, François (1713). *Démonstration de l'existence de Dieu.* . . . Paris.

Fénelon, François (1718). *Démonstration de l'existence de Dieu.* . . . Paris.

Fénelon, François (1731). *Démonstration de l'existence de Dieu.* . . . Paris.

Fénelon, François (1820–30). *Oeuvres de Fénelon,* ed. J. E. M. Gosselin and A. Caron (35 vols.). Versailles.

Fénelon, François (1848–52). *Oeuvres complètes de Fénelon* (10 vols.). Paris: Leroux-Gaume.

Fénelon, François (1854). *Oeuvres de Fénelon,* ed. L. Vivès (8 vols.). Paris.

Fénelon, François (1972–     ). *Correspondance de Fénelon,* ed. J. Orcibal. Paris: Klincksieck.

Fénelon, François (1990). *Traité de l'existence de Dieu,* ed. J.-L. Dumas. Paris: Editions Universitaires.

Fermat, Pierre de (1679). *Varia opera mathematica.* Toulouse.

Fermat, Pierre de (1891–1922). *Oeuvres de Fermat,* ed. C. Henry and P. Tannery (4 vols.) with suppl. by C. de Waard (vol. 5). Paris: Gauthier-Villars.

Ferrier, F. (1978). *Un oratorien ami de Descartes: Guillaume Gibieuf.* Paris: Vrin.

Festugière, A. J. (1983). *La Révélation d'Hermès Trismégiste.* Paris: Les Belles Lettres.

Feyerabend, Paul K. (1970). 'Classical Empiricism', in Robert E. Butts and John W. Davis (eds.), *The Methodological Heritage of Newton.* Toronto: University of Toronto Press.

Fichant, Michel (1974). 'La "réforme" leibnizienne de la dynamique, d'après des textes inédits', in *Akten des II. Internationalen Leibniz-Kongresses, Hannover, 17–22 Juli 1972: Wissenschaftstheorie und Wissenschaftsgeschichte* (Studia Leibnitiana, Supplementa). Stuttgart: Steiner, vol. 2, pp. 195–214.

Fichant, Michel (1978). 'Les concepts fondamentaux de la mécanique selon Leibniz, en 1676', in *Leibniz à Paris (1672–1676),* Symposium de la G-W Leibniz-Gesellschaft (Hannover) et du Centre National de la Recherche Scientifique (Paris) à Chantilly (France) du 14 au 18 novembre 1976 (Studia Leibnitiana, Supplementa). Stuttgart: Steiner, vol. 1, pp. 219–32.

Fichant, Michel (1992). 'L'appropriation des preuves: le cas du *De corporum concursu* de Leibniz', in *Les procédures de preuve sous le regard de l'historien des sciences et des techniques.* Paris: Société Française d'Histoire des Sciences et des Techniques, pp. 123–36.

Fichant, Michel (1993). 'Leibniz lecteur de Mariotte', *Revue d'Histoire des Sciences.* 46:333–405.

Ficino, Marsilio (1576). *Opera Omnia* (2 vols.). Basil. (Repr. Torino: Bottego d'Erasmo, 1959.)

Ficino, Marsilio (1964). *Théologie platonicienne de l'immortalité des âmes,* ed. and trans. (French) Raymond Marcel (3 vols.). Paris: Les Belles Lettres.

Ficino, Marsilio (1975). *The Philebus Commentary,* ed. and trans. Michael J. B. Allen. Berkeley: University of California Press.

Ficino, Marsilio (1981). *Marsilio Ficino and the Phaedran Charioteer,* ed. and trans. M. J. B. Allen. Berkeley: University of California Press.

Ficino, Marsilio (1989). *Three Books on Life: A Critical Edition and Translation with Introduction and Notes,* ed. and trans. C. V. Kaske and J. R. Clark. Binghamton, N.Y.: MRTS.

Fiering, Norman (1981). *Moral Philosophy at Seventeenth-Century Harvard*. Chapel Hill: University of North Carolina Press.

Firpo, Luigi (1940). *Bibliografia degli Scritti di Tommaso Campanella*. Torino: Vincenzo Bona.

Firth, Katherine R. (1979). *The Apocalyptic Tradition in Reformation Britain 1530–1645*. Oxford: Oxford University Press.

Fischer, Kuno (1889). *Geschichte der neuern Philosophie* I. 3d ed. Munich-Heidelberg: Bassermann-Winter.

Fisher, Samuel (1679). *The Testimony of Truth Exalted*. London.

Fitzpatrick, Edward A. (ed.) (1933). *St. Ignatius and the Ratio Studiorum*. New York: McGraw-Hill.

Fitzpatrick, P. J. (1987). 'Some Seventeenth-Century Disagreements and Transubstantiation', in B. Davies (ed.), *Language, Meaning and God: Essays in Honour of Herbert McCabe O.P.* London: Chapman.

Fleischmann, Wolfgang Bernard (1964). *Lucretius and English Literature 1680–1740*. Paris: A. Nizet.

Fleitmann, Sabina (1986). *Walter Charleton (1620–1707), "Virtuoso": Leben und Werk*. Frankfurt am Main etc.: Peter Lang.

Flemyng, Malcolm (1751). *A New Critical Examination of an Important Passage in Mr. Locke's Essay on Human Understanding*. London.

Fletcher, Harris Francis (1956–61). *The Intellectual Development of John Milton* (2 vols.). Urbana, Ill.: University of Illinois Press.

Fletcher, J. M. (1981). 'Change and Resistance to Change: A Consideration of the Development of English and German Universities during the Sixteenth Century', *History of Universities*. 1:1–36.

Fletcher, J. M. (1986). 'The Faculty of Arts', in J. K. McConica (ed.), *History of the University of Oxford*: vol. 3, *The Collegiate University*. Oxford: Oxford University Press, pp. 157–99.

Flew, A. (1968). 'Locke and the Problem of Personal Identity', in C. B. Martin and D. M. Armstrong (eds.), *Locke and Berkeley: A Collection of Critical Essays*. Garden City, N.Y.: Doubleday, pp. 155–78.

Fludd, Robert (1617–21). *Utriusque cosmi mairoris scilicet minoris metaphysica, physica atque technica historia*. Oppenheim and Frankfurt.

Fludd, Robert (1621). *Veritatis proscaenium . . . seu demonstratio quaedam analytica*. Frankfurt.

Fludd, Robert (1629). *Sophiae cum moria certamen, in quo lapis Lydius a falso structore, Fr. Marino Mersenne monacho, reprobata celeberrima voluminis sui Babylonici (in Genesin) figmenta accurate examinat*. Frankfurt.

Fludd, Robert (1633). *Clavis philosophiae et alchymiae Fluddanae sive Roberti Fluddi . . . ad epistolicam Petri Gassendi theologi exercitationem responsum, in quo inanes Marini Mersenni monachi objectiones . . . examinantur*. Frankfurt.

Fludd, Robert (1638). *Philosophia Moysaica*. Gouda.

Fludd, Robert (1659). *Mosaicall Philosophy, Grounded upon the Essential Truth or Eternal Sapience, Written First in Latin and Afterwards Thus Rendered into English [by the author]*. London.

Fonblanque, E. de (1887). *Annals of the House of Percy from the Conquest to the Opening of the Nineteenth Century* (2 vols.). London.

Fonseca, Pedro da (1615). *Commentarium in metaphysicorum Aristotelis Stagiritae libros tomi quatuor*. Cologne. (Repr. Hildesheim: Olms, 1964.)

Fontenelle, Bernard de le Bovier de (1683–4). *Nouveaux dialogues des morts*. Paris.

Fontenelle, Bernard de le Bovier de (1686). *Entretiens sur la pluralité des mondes*. Paris and Lyon.

Fontenelle, Bernard de le Bovier de (1725). *Histoire de l'Académie Royale des Sciences [1700]*. Paris.

Fontenelle, Bernard de le Bovier de (1727). *Eléments de la géométrie de l'infini*. Paris.

Fontenelle, Bernard de le Bovier de (1746). 'Eloge de M. Bernoulli', in *Histoire de l'Académie royale des Sciences, 1705*. Amsterdam.

Fontenelle, Bernard [de] le Bovier de (1825). *Oeuvres de Fontenelle*, ed. G. Depping (5 vols.). Paris.

Fontenelle, Bernard de le Bovier de (1955). *Entretiens sur la pluralité des mondes* ed. R. Shackleton. Oxford: Oxford University Press.

Fontialis, J. (1740). *Opera Posthuma*. Namur. (Repr. Hildesheim 1989.)

Forbes, D. (1975). *Hume's Philosophical Politics*. Cambridge: Cambridge University Press.

Forbes, D. (1982). 'Natural law and the Scottish Enlightenment', in R. H. Campbell and A. S. Skinner (eds.), *The Origins and Nature of the Scottish Enlightenment*. Edinburgh: J. Donald.

Force, James E. (1985). *William Whiston, Honest Newtonian*. Cambridge: Cambridge University Press.

Foss, Kåre (1934). *Ludvig Holbergs Naturrett på Idéhistorisk Bakgrunn*. Oslo: Gyldendal Norsk Forlag.

Foucault, Michel (1966). *Les mots et les choses: Une archéologie des sciences humaines*. Paris: Gallimard.

Foucault, Michel (1972). *L'Histoire de la folie*. Paris: Gallimard.

Foucher, Simon (1675). *Critique de la Recherche de la vérité, où l'on examine en même-tems une partie des principes de Mr Descartes. Lettre, par un academicien*. Paris. (Repr. New York: Johnson, 1969.)

Foucher, Simon (1676). *Réponse pour la critique à la préface du second volume de la recherche de la vérité*. Paris.

Foucher, Simon (1679). *Nouvelle Dissertation sur la Recherche de la vérité, contenant la réponse à la critique de la critique de la Recherche de la Vérité, où l'on découvre les erreurs des dogmatistes, tant anciens que nouveaux, avec une discution particuliere du grand principe des cartésiens*. Paris.

Foucher de Careil, Alexandre-Louis (1861). *Leibniz, la philosophie juive et la Cabale*. Paris.

Fowden, Garth (1993). *The Egyptian Hermes: An Historical Approach to the Late Pagan Mind*. Princeton, N.J.: Princeton University Press.

Fox, Christopher (1988). *Locke and the Scriblerians. Identity and Consciousness in Early Eighteenth-Century Britain*. Berkeley: University of California Press.

Franco, Luigi de (1969). 'La *Philosophia Sensibus Demonstrata* di Tommaso Campanella e la dottrina di Bernardino Telesio', in *Tommaso Campanella (1568–1639): Miscellanea di studi nel 40 centenario della sua nascita*. Naples: Fausto Fiorentino.

François, Jean, S. J. (1655). *Traité de la quantité considerée absolument et en elle mesme, relativement et en ses rapports, materiellement et en ses plus nobles sujets. Pour servir d'introduction aux sciences et arts mathematiques, & aux disputes philosophiques de la quantité*. Rennes.

François de Sales, Saint (1613). *An Introduction to a Devoute Life*, trans. J. Yakesley. Douai.

François de Sales, Saint (1892–1964). *Oeuvres de Saint François de Sales*, ed. Mackey–Navratel (27 vols.). Annecy: J. Niérat.

François de Sales, Saint (1969). *Oeuvres*, ed. A. Ravier and R. Devos. Paris: Gallimard.

François de Sales, Saint (1971). *A Treatise on the Love of God*, trans. H. B. Mackey, vol. 2 of *Works of St. Francis de Sales*. Westport, Conn.: Greenwood.

Frankel, Lois (1981). 'Leibniz's Principle of Identity of Indiscernibles', *Studia Leibnitiana*. 13:192–211.

Frankfurt, Harry (1962). 'Memory and the Cartesian Circle', *Philosophical Review*. 71:505–11.

Frankfurt, Harry (1966). 'Descartes' Discussion of His Existence in the Second Meditation', *Philosophical Review*. 75:329–356.

Frankfurt, Harry (1967). 'Descartes' Validation of Reason' in W. Doney (ed.), *Descartes: A Collection of Critical Essays*. Garden City, N.Y.: Doubleday.

Frankfurt, Harry (1970). *Demons, Dreamers and Madmen: The Defense of Reason in Descartes' Meditations*. Indianapolis: Bobbs-Merrill.

Frankfurt, Harry (1977). 'Descartes on the Creation of Eternal Truths', *Philosophical Review*. 86:36–57.

Frankfurt, Harry (1978). 'Descartes on the Consistency of Reason', in Michael Hooker (ed.), *Descartes: Critical and Interpretive Essays*. Baltimore: Johns Hopkins University Press.

Frassen, Claude (1686). *Philosophia academica, quam ex selectissimis Aristotelis et Doctoris subtilis Scoti rationibus ac sententiis . . .* 3d ed. (4 vols. in 2). Toulouse.

Frede, Michael (1987). 'The Sceptic's Beliefs', in *Essays in Ancient Philosophy*. Minneapolis: University of Minnesota Press.

Frede, Michael (1990). 'An Empiricist View of Knowledge', in Everson 1990.

Freedman, Joseph S. (1982). *The Life, Significance, and Philosophy of Clemens Timpler (1563/4–1624)*. Ph.D. diss., University of Wisconsin-Madison.

Freedman, Joseph S. (1985). *Deutsche Schulphilosophie im Reformationszeitalter (1500–1650)* (Arbeiten zur Klassifikation). Münster: MAKS Publikationen.

Freedman, Joseph S. (1988). *European Academic Philosophy in the Late Sixteenth and Early Seventeenth Centuries: The Life, Significance, and Philosophy of Clemens Timpler (1563/4–1624)* (2 vols.). Hildesheim: Olms.

Fremont, Christiane (1981). *L'être et la relation*. Paris: Vrin.

Freudenthal, Gad (1983). 'Theory of Matter and Cosmology in William Gilbert's *De magnete*', *Isis*. 74:22–37.

Frey, J.-C. (1633). *Universae philosophiae compendium*. Paris.

Friedensburg, Walter (1926–7). *Urkundenbuch der Universität Wittenberg* (2 vols.). Magdeburg: Historische Kommission für die Provinz Sachsen.

Friedman, Joel (1977). 'Spinoza's Denial of Free Will in Man and God', in Jon Wetlesen (ed.), *Spinoza's Philosophy of Man*. Oslo: Universitetsforlaget, pp. 51–84.

Fuhrmann, Manfred (1979). 'Persona, ein Römischer Rollenbegriff', in Odo Marquard and Karlheinz Stierle (eds.), *Identität*. Munich: Wilhelm Fink, pp. 83–106.

Funkenstein, A. (1980). 'Descartes, Eternal Truths and Divine Omnipotence', in Stephen Gaukroger (ed.), *Descartes: Philosophy, Mathematics and Physics*. Brighton: Harvester Press.

Funkenstein, Amos (1986). *Theology and the Scientific Imagination from the Middle Ages to the Seventeenth Century*. Princeton, N.J.: Princeton University Press.

Furlan, A. (1974). 'Logic according to Spinoza', in J. G. van der Bend (ed.), *Spinoza on Knowing, Being and Freedom*. Assen: Van Gorcum.

Gabbey, Alan (1970). 'Les trois genres de découverte selon Descartes', in *Actes du XIIe Congrès International d'Histoire des Sciences, Paris 1968*. Paris, vol. 2, pp. 45–9.

Gabbey, Alan (1973). Review of W. L. Scott, *The Conflict between Atomism and Conservation Theory 1644–1860* (1970), *Studies in History and Philosophy of Science*. 4:373–85.

Gabbey, Alan (1977). 'Anne Conway et Henry More, Lettres sur Descartes', *Archives de philosophie*. 40:379–404.

Gabbey, Alan (1980a). 'Force and Inertia in the Seventeenth Century: Descartes and Newton', in Gaukroger 1980, pp. 230–320.

Gabbey, Alan (1980b). 'Huygens and Mechanics', in H. J. M. Bos et al. (eds.), *Studies on Christiaan Huygens. Invited papers from the Symposium on the life and work of Christiaan Huygens, Amsterdam, 22–5 August 1979*. Lisse, Netherlands: Swets & Zeitlinger, pp. 166–99.

Gabbey, Alan (1982). 'Philosophia Cartesiana Triumphata: Henry More (1646–1671)', in T. M. Lennon, J. M. Nicholas, and J. W. Davis (eds.), *Problems of Cartesianism*. Kingston and Montreal: McGill-Queens University Press, pp. 171–250.

Gabbey, Alan (1985). 'The Mechanical Philosophy and Its Problems: Mechanical Explanations, Impenetrability, and Perpetual Motion', in J. C. Pitt (ed.), *Change and Progress in Modern Science*. Dordrecht: Reidel, pp. 9–84.

Gabbey, Alan (1990a). 'Newton and natural philosophy', in R. C. Olby, G. N. Cantor, J. R. R. Christie, and M. J. S. Hodge (eds.), *Companion to the History of Modern Science*. London: Routledge, pp. 243–63.

Gabbey, Alan (1990b). 'Henry More and the Limits of Mechanism', in S. Hutton (ed.), *Henry More*. Dordrecht: Kluwer, pp. 19–35.

Gabbey, Alan (1990c). 'Explanatory Structures and Mode in Descartes's Physics', in G. Belgioioso et al. (eds.), *Descartes: Il metodo e i saggi*. Rome: Istituto della Enciclopedia Italiana, vol. I, pp. 273–86.

Gabbey, Alan (1990d). 'The Case of Mechanics: One Revolution or Many?', in *Reappraisals of the Scientific Revolution*, ed. David C. Lindberg and Robert S. Westman. Cambridge: Cambridge University Press, chap. 13.

Gabbey, Alan (1992). 'Newton's "Mathematical Principles of Natural Philosophy": A Treatise on "Mechanics"?', in *The Investigation of Difficult Things,* ed. P. M. Harman and Alan Shapiro. Cambridge: Cambridge University Press, pp. 305–22.

Gabbey, Alan (1996). 'Spinoza's Natural Science and Methology', in D. Garrett, ed., *The Cambridge Companion to Spinoza.* Cambridge: Cambridge University Press, pp. 142–91.

Gale, George (1973). 'Leibniz's Dynamical Metaphysics and the Origins of the *Vis Viva* Controversy', *Systematics.* 11:184–207.

Galen (1979). *On the Natural Faculties,* trans. Arthur John Brock (Loeb Classical Library). Cambridge, Mass.: Harvard University Press.

Galilei, Galileo (1623). *Il Saggiatore.* Rome.

Galilei, Galileo (1632). *Dialogo sopra i due massimi sistemi del mondo.* Florence.

Galilei, Galileo (1638). *Discorsi e dimostrazioni matematiche intorno à due nuove scienze.* Leiden.

Galilei, Galileo (1890–1909). *Opere,* ed. A. Favaro (20 vols.). Florence: Barbera. (Reissued 1929–39, 1965.)

Galilei, Galileo (1957). *The Discoveries and Opinions of Galileo,* ed. S. Drake. Garden City, N.Y.: Doubleday.

Galilei, Galileo (1960a). *The Controversy on the Comets of 1618: Galileo Galilei, Horatio Grassi, Mario Guiducci, Johann Kepler.* Trans. S. Drake and C. D. O'Malley. Philadelphia: University of Pennsylvania Press.

Galilei, Galileo (1960b). *On Motion and On Mechanics,* trans. I. E. Drabkin and S. Drake. Madison: University of Wisconsin Press.

Galilei, Galileo (1967). *Dialogue concerning the Two Chief World Systems,* trans. Stillman Drake. 2d ed. Berkeley: University of California Press.

Galilei, Galileo (1969). *Opere,* ed. Arrigo Pachi (2 vols.). Napoli: Fulvio Rossi.

Galilei, Galileo (1974). *Two New Sciences. Including Centers of Gravity & Force of Percussion,* trans. with introduction and notes by Stillman Drake. Madison: University of Wisconsin Press.

Gallagher, David (1991). 'Thomas Aquinas on the Will as Rational Appetite', *Journal of the History of Philosophy.* 29:559–84.

Gallie, Roger (1987). 'The Same Self', *Locke Newsletter.* 18:45–62.

Gallie, Roger (1989). *Thomas Reid and 'The Way of Ideas'.* Dordrecht: Kluwer.

Galluzzi, Paolo (1973). 'Il "Platonismo" del tardo Cinquecento e la filosofia di Galileo', in Paola Zambelli (ed.), *Ricerche sulla cultura dell'Italia moderna.* Bari: Editore Laterza.

Galluzzi, Paolo (1979). *Momento: Studi galileiani* (Lessico Intellettuale Europeo, no. 19). Rome: Edizioni dell'Ateneo & Bizzarri.

Galluzzi, Tarquinio (1632–45). *In Aristotelis libros . . . moralium ad Nicomachum nova interpretatio, commentaria, quaestiones* (2 vols.). Paris.

Garasse, François (1623). *La doctrine curieuse des beaux esprits de ce temps ou prétendus tels.* Paris.

Garber, Daniel (1982). 'Motion and Metaphysics in the Young Leibniz', in Michael Hooker (ed.), *Leibniz: Critical and Interpretative Essays,* pp. 160–84. Minneapolis: University of Minnesota Press.

Garber, Daniel (1983a). 'Understanding Interaction: What Descartes Should Have Told Elisabeth', *Southern Journal of Philosophy.* 21 supp.:15–32.

Garber, Daniel (1983b). 'Mind, Body, and the Laws of Nature in Descartes and Leibniz', *Midwest Studies in Philosophy.* 8:105–33.

Garber, Daniel (1985). 'Leibniz and the Foundations of Physics: The Middle Years', in K. Okruhlik and J. R. Brown (eds.), *The Natural Philosophy of Leibniz.* Dordrecht: Reidel, pp. 27–130.

Garber, Daniel (1986). '*Semel in vita:* The Scientific Background to Descartes' *Meditations*', in Rorty 1986a, pp. 81–116.

Garber, Daniel (1987a). 'How God Causes Motion: Descartes, Divine Sustenance, and Occasionalism', *Journal of Philosophy.* 84:567–80.

Garber, Daniel (1987b). 'La méthode du *Discours*', in Jean-Luc Marion and Nicolas Grimaldi (eds.), *Le Discours et sa méthode*. Paris: Presses Universitaires de France.

Garber, Daniel (1992a). *Descartes' Metaphysical Physics*. Chicago: University of Chicago Press.

Garber, Daniel (1992b). 'Descartes' physics', in J. Cottingham, ed., *The Cambridge Companion to Descartes*. Cambridge: Cambridge University Press, pp. 286–334.

Garber, Daniel (1993a). 'Descartes and Occasionalism', in S. Nadler (ed.), *Causation in Early Modern Philosophy*. University Park, Pa.: Pennsylvania State University Press, pp. 9–26.

Garber, Daniel (1993b). 'Descartes and Experiment in the *Discourse* and *Essays*', in Voss 1993, pp. 288–310.

Garber, Daniel (1995). 'Leibniz: Physics and Philosophy', in N. Jolley (ed.), *The Cambridge Companion to Leibniz*. Cambridge: Cambridge University Press, pp. 270–352.

Garber, Daniel, and Sandy Zabell (1979). 'On the Emergence of Probability', *Archive for History of Exact Sciences*. 21:33–53.

Gardeil, H. D. (1956). *Introduction to the Philosophy of St. Thomas Aquinas,* trans. J. A. Otto (4 vols.). St. Louis: B. Herder.

Gargani, Aldo G. (1971). *Hobbes e la scienza*. Turin: Einaudi.

Garin, Eugenio (1937). *Giovanni Pico della Mirandola: Vita e dottrina*. Florence: Le Monnier.

Garin, Eugenio (1954). *Medioevo e rinascimento*. Bari: Laterza.

Garin, Eugenio (1983). *Astrology in the Renaissance: The Zodiac of Life,* trans. C. Jackson, J. Allen, and C. Robertson. London: Routledge.

Garin, P. (1932). *Thèses cartésiennes et thèses thomistes*. Bruges: Desclée, De Brouwer.

Garrett, Brian (1990). 'Persons and Human Beings', *Logos. Philosophic Issues in Christian Perspective*. 11:47–56.

Garrett, Don (1991). 'Spinoza's Necessitarianism', in Yirmiyahu Yovel (ed.), *God and Nature: Spinoza's Metaphysics*. Leiden: Brill, pp. 191–218.

Garrigou-LaGrange, Reginald (1946). *God: His Existence and His Nature,* trans. Dom Bede Rose from the 5th French ed. (2 vols.). St Louis: Herder.

Gaskell, Philip (1972). *A New Introduction to Bibliography*. Oxford: Oxford University Press.

Gassendi, Pierre (1624). *Exercitationes paradoxicae adversus Aristoteleos* (part I). Grenoble.

Gassendi, Pierre (1642a). *De motu impresso a motore translato epistolae duae*. Paris.

Gassendi, Pierre (1642b). *De Deo et rectore mundi*. Unpublished ms. Ashburnham 1239, ff. 501r–75r. Florence: Biblioteca Lorenziana.

Gassendi, Pierre (1644). *Disquisitio metaphysica*. Amsterdam.

Gassendi, Pierre (1647). *De vita et moribus Epicuri libri octo*. Lyon.

Gassendi, Pierre (1649). *Animadversiones in decimum librum Diogenis Laertii* (2 vols.). Lyon. (Repr. New York: Garland, 1987.)

Gassendi, Pierre (1658). *Opera omnia* (6 vols.). Lyon. (Repr. Stuttgart: Frommann, 1964.)

Gassendi, Pierre (1727). *Opera omnia in sex tomos divisa*. Florence.

Gassendi, Pierre (1959). *Exercitationes Paradoxicae adversus Aristoteleos,* ed. and trans. [French] Bernard Rochot. Paris: Vrin.

Gassendi, Pierre (1962). *Disquisitio Metaphysica,* ed. and trans. [French] B. Rochot. Paris: Vrin.

Gassendi, Pierre (1972). *Selected Works,* ed. and trans. C. B. Brush. New York: Johnson Reprint.

Gassendi, Pierre (1981). *Pierre Gassendi's Institutio logica (1658),* ed. and trans. Howard Jones. Assen: Van Gorcum.

Gastaldi, Sylvia (1987). '*Pathe* and *Polis*: Aristotle's Theory of Passions in the *Rhetoric* and the *Ethics*', *Topoi*. 6:105–10.

Gaukroger, Stephen (1978). *Explanatory Structures: A Study of concepts of Explanation in Early Physics and Philosophy*. Hassocks, Sussex: Harvester.

Gaukroger, Stephen. (ed.) (1980a). *Descartes: Philosophy, Mathematics and Physics*. Sussex: Harvester Press.

Gaukroger, Stephen (1980b). 'Descartes' Project for a Mathematical Physics', in Gaukroger 1980a.

Gaukroger, Stephen (1989). *Cartesian Logic. An Essay on Descartes's Conception of Inference.* Oxford: Oxford University Press.

Gaukroger, Stephen (ed.) (1991). *The Uses of Antiquity.* Dordrecht: Kluwer.

Gaukroger, Stephen (1995). *Descartes: An Intellectual Biography.* Oxford: Oxford University Press.

Gaultruche, Pierre (1665). *Philosophiae ac mathematicae totius clara, brevis, et accurata institutio* (6 vols.). Caen.

Gauthier, David P. (1969). *The Logic of Leviathan.* Oxford: Oxford University Press.

Gauthier, David P. (1977). 'Why Ought One to Obey God? Reflections on Hobbes and Locke', *Canadian Journal of Philosophy.* 7:425–46.

Gauthier, René Antoine (1970). *Aristote: L'Ethique à Nicomaque. Introduction.* Louvain and Paris: Publications universitaires and Béatrice-Nauwelaerts.

Geier, Johannes Christianus (1683). *Dissertatio ethica de mediocritate virtutis moralis, . . . praeside . . . Jacobo Thomasio. . . .* Leipzig.

Gerdil, H. S. (1747). *L'Immaterialité de l'âme demontrée contre M. Locke, par les mêmes Principes, par lesquels ce Philosophe démontre l'Existence et l'Immatérialité de Dieu, et de l'âme.* Turin.

Gerrish, B. A. (1962). *Grace and Reason. A Study in the Theology of Luther.* Oxford. Oxford University Press.

Geulincx, Arnold (1662). *Logica fundamentis suis, a quibus hactenus collapsa fuerat, restituta.* Leiden.

Geulincx, Arnold (1663). *Methodus inveniendi argumenta quae solertia quibusdam dicitur.* Leiden.

Geulincx, Arnold (1665). *De virtute et primis ejus proprietatibus tractatus ethicus primus.* Leiden.

Geulincx, Arnold (1675). *Ethica.* Leiden.

Geulincx, Arnold (1891–3). *Opera philosophica*, ed. J. P. N. Land. (3 vols.). The Hague: Nijhoff. (Repr. Stuttgart: Frommann, 1965.)

al-Ghazālī (1953). 'Deliverance from Error', in W. M. Watt, ed. and trans., *The Faith and Practice of al-Ghazali.* London: Allen and Unwin.

Gibieuf, Guillaume (1630). *De libertate Dei et creaturae.* Paris.

Gibson, James (1917). *Locke's Theory of Knowledge and Its Historical Relations.* Cambridge: Cambridge University Press.

Gibson, Strickland (ed.) (1931). *Statuta Antiqua Universitatis Oxoniensis.* Oxford: Oxford University Press.

Gierke, Otto Friedrich von (1958). *Natural Law and the Theory of Society 1500 to 1800,* trans. Ernest Barker. Cambridge: University Press.

Gigante, Marcello (1988). 'Ambrogio Traversari interprete di Diogene Laerzio', in G. C. Garfagnini (ed.), *Ambrogio Traversari nel VI centenario della nascita. Convegno internazionale di studi (Camaldoli-Firenze . . . 1986).* Florence: Olschki.

Gilbert, Neal W. (1961). *Renaissance Concepts of Method.* New York: Columbia University Press.

Gilbert, Neal W. (1963). 'Galileo and the School of Padua', *Journal of the History of Philosophy.* 1:223–31.

Gilbert, William (1600). *De magnete, magnetisque corporibus, et de magno magnete tellure: Physiologia nova plurimis et argumentis et experimentis demonstrata.* London. (Repr. Berlin: Mayer and Müller, 1892; Brussels: Culture et Civilisation, 1967.)

Gilbert, William (1651). *De mondo nostro sublunari nova philosophia.* Amsterdam. (Repr. Amsterdam: Menno Hertzberger, 1965.)

Gilbert, William (1958). *De magnete,* trans. P. Fleury Mottelay. New York: Dover.

Gilead, Amihud (1983). 'Spinoza's *Principium Individuationis* and Personal Identity', *International Studies in Philosophy.* 15:41–57.

Gilen, L. (1957). 'Über die Beziehung Descartes' zur zeitgenössischen Scholastik', *Scholastik.* 22:41–66.

Gilissen, John (1965). 'La Preuve en Europe du XVIe au début du XIXe siècle. Rapport de synthèse', in *La Preuve. Deuxième Partie: Moyen Age et Temps Modernes, Recueils de la Société Jean Bodin pour l'Histoire Comparative des Institutions.* 17:755–833.

Gill, Christopher (1988). 'Personhood and Personality: The Four-*Personae* Theory in Cicero, *De Officiis* I', *Oxford Studies in Ancient Philosophy.* 6:169–99.

Gillispie, Charles Coulston (ed.) (1970–80). *Dictionary of Scientific Biography* (16 vols.). New York: Charles Scribner's Sons.

Gilson, Etienne (1913). *La liberté chez Descartes et la théologie.* Paris: Alcan. (Repr., Paris: Vrin, 1982, with a foreword by J.-L. Marion.)

Gilson, Etienne (1925). *Discours de la méthode: texte et commentaire.* Paris.

Gilson, Etienne (1930). *Etudes sur le rôle de la pensée médiévale dans la formation du système cartésien.* Paris: Vrin.

Gilson, Etienne (1941). *God and Philosophy.* New Haven, Conn.: Yale University Press.

Gilson, Etienne (1945). *Le Thomisme.* 5th ed. Paris: Vrin.

Gilson, Etienne (1947). *L'être et l'essence.* Paris: Vrin.

Gilson, Etienne (1956). *The Christian Philosophy of St. Thomas Aquinas,* trans. L. K. Shook. New York: Random House.

Gilson, Etienne (1962). *Being and Some Philosophers.* Toronto: Pontifical Institute of Mediaeval Studies.

Gilson, Etienne (1966). 'Postface', in Gilson 1979, pp. 358–70.

Gilson, Etienne (1967a). *Etudes sur le rôle de la pensée médiévale dans la formation du système cartésien.* 3d ed. Paris: Vrin.

Gilson, Etienne (1967b). *Les tribulations de Sophie.* Paris: Vrin.

Gilson, Etienne (1979). *Index scolastico-cartésien.* 2d ed. Paris: Vrin. (1st. ed., 1913.)

Gilson, Etienne (1982). *La liberté chez Descartes et la théologie.* 2d ed. Paris: Alcan.

Giusberti, F. (1982). *Materials for a Study of Twelfth Century Scholasticism.* Naples: Bibliopolis.

Gjertsen, Derek (1986). *The Newton Handbook.* London: Routledge.

Glanvill, Joseph (1661). *The Vanity of Dogmatizing; Or, Confidence in Opinions.* London. (Repr. Hildesheim: Olms, 1970.)

Glanvill, Joseph (1662). *Lux Orientalis.* London.

Glanvill, Joseph (1665). *Scepsis Scientifica.* London. (Repr. New York: Garland, 1978; repr. Hildesheim: Olms, 1985.)

Glanvill, Joseph (1666). *Philosophical Considerations Touching Witches and Witchcraft.* London.

Glanvill, Joseph (1668). *Plus Ultra; Or, The Progress and Advancement of Knowledge since the Days of Aristotle.* London. (Repr. Gainesville: Scholars' Facsimiles and Reprints.)

Glanvill, Joseph (1670). *A Discourse concerning the Difficulties of the Way to Happiness, Whence They Arise and How They May Be Overcome.* London.

Glanvill, Joseph (1676). *Essays on Several Important Subjects in Philosophy and Religion.* London. (Repr. New York: Johnson, 1970.)

Glanvill, Joseph (1681). *Saducismus triumphatus, Or, Full and Plain Evidence concerning Witches and Apparitions,* ed. Henry More. London. (2d ed., London: 1682.)

Glanvill, Joseph (1682). *Two Choice and Useful Treatises: The One Lux Orientalis; Or an Enquiry into the Opinion of the Eastern Sages concerning the Praeexistence of Souls. Being a Key to Unlock the Grand Mysteries of Providence. In Relation to Mans Sin and Misery. The Other, A Discourse of Truth, By the late Reverend Dr. Rust, Lord Bishop of Dromore in Ireland. With Annotations on Them Both [by Henry More].* London. (Repr. New York: Garland, 1978.)

Glanvill, Joseph (1689). *Saducismus Triumphatus.* 3d ed. London. (Repr. Gainesville, Florida: Scholars' Facsimiles and Reprints, 1966.)

Glanvill, Joseph (1970). *The Vanity of Dogmatizing,* ed. S. Medcalf. Sussex: Harvester Press.

Glisson, Francis (1672). *Tractatus de natura substantiae energetica, seu de vita naturae, eiusque tribus primis facultatibus, I, perceptiva naturalibus, II, appetitiva naturalibus, III, motiva naturalibus &c.* London.

Glover, W. B. (1965). 'God and Thomas Hobbes' in K. C. Brown (ed.), *Hobbes Studies*. Oxford: Blackwell.

Goclenius, Rudolf (1597). *Problemata logica*. Marburg. (Repr. Frankfurt: Minerva, 1967.)

Goclenius, Rudolf (1613). *Lexicon philosophicum*. Frankfurt. (Repr. Hildesheim: Olms, 1964.)

Godoy, Petrus de (1668). *Disputationes Theologicae* (3 vols.). Venice.

Godwin, Joscelyn (1979). *Robert Fludd: Hermetic Philosopher and Surveyor of Two Worlds*. Boulder, Colo.: Shambala.

Goldsmith, M. M. (1966). *Hobbes's Science of Politics*. New York: Columbia University Press.

Gonzalez de la Calle, Pedro Urbano, and Huarte y Echenique, Amalio (1925–6). 'Constituciones de la Universidad de Salamanca (1422)', *Revista de Archivos, Bibliotecas y Museos*. 47:217–28, 345–59, 402–19; 47:348–71, 467–501.

Goorle, David van (1620). *Exercitationes philosophicae quibus universa fere discutitur philosophia theoretica*. Leiden.

Goorle, David van (1651). *Idea physicae, cui adjuncta est Epistola cuiusdam anonymi de terrae motu*. Utrecht.

Gordon, Cosmo Alexander (1962). *A Bibliography of Lucretius* (Soho Bibliographies). London: Rupert Hart-Davis.

Gordon, Cosmo Alexander (1985). *A Bibliography of Lucretius*. Bury Saint Edmunds, Suffolk: St Paul's Bibliographies.

Gorland, A. (1907). *Der Gottesbegriff bei Leibniz*. Tübingen: Mohr.

Goshen-Gottstein, Moshe (1989). 'Bible et judaisme', in J.-R. Armogathe, (ed.), *Le Grand siècle et la Bible*. Paris: Beauchesne, pp. 33–8.

Goudin, Antoine (1864). *Philosophie suivant les principes de Saint Thomas*, trans. (French) T. Bourard. Paris. (1st Latin ed. 1668.)

Gouhier, Henri (1926a). *La vocation de Malebranche*. Paris: Vrin.

Gouhier, Henri (1926b). *La philosophie de Malebranche et son expérience religieuse*. Paris: Vrin. (2d ed. 1947.)

Gouhier, Henri (1937). *Essais sur Descartes*. Paris: Vrin.

Gouhier, Henri (1948). *La philosophie de Malebranche et son expérience religieuse*. 2d ed. Paris: Vrin.

Gouhier, Henri (1954a). 'Doute méthodique ou négation méthodique?', *Les Etudes Philosophiques*. 9:135–62.

Gouhier, Henri (1954b). 'La crise de la théologie au temps de Descartes', *Revue de Théologie et de Philosophie*. 3e ser. 4:45–7.

Gouhier, Henri (1958). *Les premières pensées de Descartes: Contribution à l'histoire de l'anti-Renaissance (De Pétrarque à Descartes)*. Paris: Vrin.

Gouhier, Henri (1962). *La pensée métaphysique de Descartes*. Paris: Vrin. (2d ed. 1969, 3d ed. 1978.)

Gouhier, Henri (1966). *Pascal. Commentaires*. Paris: Vrin. (3d ed. 1978.)

Gouhier, Henri (1972). *La pensée religieuse de Descartes*. 2d ed. Paris: Vrin.

Gouhier, Henri (1977). *Fénelon philosophe*. Paris: Vrin.

Gouhier, Henri (1978). *Cartésianisme et Augustinisme au XVIIe siècle*. Paris: Vrin.

Gouhier, Henri (1986). *Blaise Pascal. Conversation et Apologétique*. Paris: Vrin.

Goyard-Fabre, Simone (1994). *Pufendorf et le droit naturel*. Paris: Presses Universitaires de France.

Grabmann, Martin (1917). 'Die *Disputationes metaphysicae* des Francesco Suarez " ihrer methodischen Eigenart und Fortwirkung', in Grabmann 1926–56, vol. 1, pp. 525–60.

Grabmann, Martin (1926–56). *Mittelalterliches Geistesleben*. (3 vols.). Munich: M. Hueber.

Gracia, Jorge J. E. (1984). *Introduction to the Problem of Individuation in the Early Middle Ages (Analytica)*. Munich and Vienna: Philosophia.

Gracia, Jorge J. E. (1991). 'The Centrality of the Individual in the Philosophy of the Fourteenth Century', *History of Philosophy Quarterly*. 8:235–51.

Gracia, Jorge J. E. (1993). 'Christian Wolff on Individuation', *History of Philosophy Quarterly*. 10:147–64.

Gracia, Jorge J. E. (ed.) (1994). *Individuation in Scholasticism: The Later Middle Ages and the Counter-Reformation.* Albany, N.Y.: SUNY Press.

Graff, Harvey J. (1987). *The Legacies of Literacy: Continuities and Contradictions in Western Culture and Society.* Bloomington, Ind.: Indiana University Press.

Grant, Edward (1981). *Much Ado About Nothing: Theories of Space and Vacuum from the Middle Ages to the Scientific Revolution.* Cambridge: Cambridge University Press.

Grant, Robert M. (1952). *Miracle and Natural Law in Graeco-Roman and Early Christian Thought.* Amsterdam: North-Holland.

Graunt, John (1662). *Natural and Political Observations Mentioned in a Following Index and Made Upon the Bills of Mortality.* London.

Gravelle, François de (1601). *Abrégé de la philosophie.* Paris.

Grayling, A. C. (1986). *Berkeley: The Central Arguments.* La Salle, Ill.: Open Court.

Green, L. C., and Dickason, O. P. (1989). *The Law of Nations and the New World.* Edmonton: University of Alberta Press.

Greene, R. A., and MacCallum, H. (1971). 'Introduction', in Culverwel 1971, pp. ix–lvii.

Greenwood, Major (1970). 'Medical Statistics from Graunt to Farr', in E. S. Pearson and M. G. Kendall (eds.), *Studies in the History of Statistics and Probability.* Darien, Conn.: Hafner.

Gregory, James (1668). *Geometriae pars universalis.* Padua.

Gregory, Tullio (1961). *Scetticismo ed empirismo. Studio su Gassendi.* Bari: Laterza.

Gregory, Tullio (1964). 'Studi sull'atomismo del seicento. I. Sebastiano Basson', *Giornale critico della filosofia italiana.* 43:38–65.

Gregory, Tullio (1966). 'Studi sull'atomismo del seicento. II. David van Goorle e Daniel Sennert', *Giornale critico della filosofia italiana.* 45:44–63.

Gregory, Tullio (1967). 'Studi sull'atomismo del seicento. III. Cudworth e l'atomismo', *Giornale critico della filosofia italiana.* 46:528–41.

Gregory, Tullio (1974). 'Dio ingannatore e genio maligno. Nota in margine alla *Meditationes* di Descartes', *Giornale critico della filosofia italiana.* 53:477–516.

Gregory, Tullio (1982). 'La troperie divine', *Studia Medievali.* 23:517–27.

Gregory, Tullio (1986). *Etica e religione nella critica libertina.* Naples: Guida.

Gregory, Tullio, et al. (eds.) (1981). *Ricerche su letteratura libertina e letteratura clandestina nel Seicento.* Florence: Nuova Italia.

Gregory of Rimini [Gregorius Ariminensis] (1522). *Super primum et secundum sententiarum.* Venice.

Gregory of Rimini [Gregorius Ariminensis] (1978–87). *Lectura super primum et secundum sententiarum,* A. D. Trapp et al. (eds.) Berlin: de Gruyter.

Grene, Marjorie (1986). 'Die Einheit des Menschen: Descartes unter den Scholastikern', *Dialectica.* 40:309–22.

Gresh, Stephen (1986). *Middle Platonism and Neoplatonism: The Latin Tradition* (2 vols.). Notre Dame, Ind.: Notre Dame University Press.

Greshake, Gisbert (1981). 'Die theologische Herkunft des Personbegriffs', in G. Pöltner (ed.), *Personale Freiheit und Pluralistische Gesellschaft.* Vienna: Herder, pp. 75–86.

Griffin, Martin I. J. (1992). *Latitudinarianism in the Seventeenth-Century Church of England.* Leiden: Brill.

Griffin, Nicholas (1977). *Relative Identity.* Oxford: Oxford University Press.

Grimaldi, Nicolas and Marion, Jean-Luc, eds. (1987). *Le Discours et sa méthode: Colloque pour le 350e anniversaire du Discours de la méthode* (Epiméthée). Paris: Presses Universitaires de France.

Grisard, J. (1976). *François Viète, mathématicien de la fin du seizième siècle: Essai bio-bibliographique presenté en vue de l'obtention du doctorat de troisième cycle.* Paris: Ecole Pratique des Hautes Etudes, VIème section.

Groarke, Leo (1984). 'Descartes' First Meditation: Something Old, Something New, Something Borrowed', *Journal of the History of Philosophy.* 22:281–301.

Grosholz, Emily (1991). *Cartesian Method and the Problem of Reduction*. Oxford: Oxford University Press.

Grotius, Hugo (1609). *Mare liberum, sive de iure quod Batavis competit ad Indicana commercia, dissertatio*. Leiden.

Grotius, Hugo (1625). *De iure belli ac pacis*. Paris.

Grotius, Hugo (1627). *De veritate religionis christianae*. Leiden.

Grotius, Hugo (1643). *De origine gentium americanum dissertatio altera adversus obtrectatorem*. Paris.

Grotius, Hugo (1679). *De veritate religionis christianae*. In his *Opera theologica*. Amsterdam. Vol. 3, pp. 3–96.

Grotius, Hugo (1724). *Le droit de la guerre et de la paix*, trans. J. Barbeyrac (2 vols.). Amsterdam.

Grotius, Hugo (1735). *De iure belli ac pacis libri tres* [1625], ed. J. F. Gronovius and J. Barbeyrac. Amsterdam.

Grotius, Hugo (1738). *The Rights of War and Peace, in three Books*, ed. J. Barbeyrac, trans. anonymous. London.

Grotius, Hugo (1805). *Truth of the Christian Religion in Six Books* [1627], ed. J. Le Clerc, trans. J. Clarke. London.

Grotius, Hugo (1868). *De Jure Praedae Commentarius*, ed. G. Hamaker. The Hague: Nijhoff.

Grotius, Hugo (1916). *Mare liberum / The Freedom of the Seas* [1609], trans. J. Brown Scott. New York: Oxford University Press.

Grotius, Hugo (1925). *De Iure belli ac Pacis* (4 vols.), Latin and English edition, trans. F. W. Kelsey. Oxford: Oxford University Press.

Grotius, Hugo (1928–    ). *Briefwisseling*. The Hague: Nijhoff (vols. 1–11); Assen/Maastricht: van Gorcum (vol. 12); The Hague: Instituut voor Nederlandse Geschiedenis (vol. 13).

Grotius, Hugo (1950). *De jure praedae commentarius* [1604], trans. G. L. Williams and W. H. Zeydel (2 vols.). Oxford: Oxford University Press.

Grunwald, G. (1907). *Geschichte der Gottesbeweise im Mittelalter bis zum Ausgang der Hochscholastik* (Beiträge zur Geschichte der Philosophie des Mittelalters VI, 3). Münster: Aschendorfsche buchhandlung.

Guareschi, I. (1916). 'La teoria atomistica e Sebastiano Basso con notizie e considerazioni su William Higgins', *Memoria della Regale Accademia dei Lincei, Classe di Scienze Fisiche, Matematiche et Naturali*. 11:289–388.

Guerlac, Henry (1973). 'Newton and the Method of Analysis', in P. P. Wiener (ed.), *Dictionary of the History of Ideas* (5 vols.). New York: Charles Scribner's Sons.

Guerlac, Henry (1981). *Newton on the Continent*. Ithaca, N.Y.: Cornell University Press.

Gueroult, Martial (1953). *Descartes: Selon l'ordre des raisons*. Paris: Aubier.

Gueroult, Martial (1955). *Nouvelles réflexions sur la preuve ontologique*. Paris: Vrin.

Gueroult, Martial (1955–9). *Malebranche* (3 vols.). Paris: Aubier.

Gueroult, Martial (1956). *Berkeley. Quatre études sur la perception et sur Dieu*. Paris: Aubier.

Gueroult, Martial (1967). *Leibniz: Dynamique et métaphysique*. Paris: Aubier.

Gueroult, Martial (1968–74). *Spinoza* (2 vols.). Paris: Aubier.

Gueroult, Martial (1980). 'The Metaphysics and Physics of Force in Descartes', in Gaukroger 1980a, pp. 196–229.

Gueroult, Martial (1984). *Descartes' Philosophy Interpreted according to the Order of Reasons*, trans. Roger Ariew. (2 vols.). Minneapolis: University of Minnesota Press.

Guy, Basil (1963). *The French Image of China before and after Voltaire*. Geneva: Institut et Musée Voltaire.

Gysi, Lydia (1962). *Platonism and Cartesianism in the Philosophy of Ralph Cudworth*. Bern: Lang.

Haakonssen, Knud (1985). 'Hugo Grotius and the History of Political Thought', *Political Theory*. 13:239–65.

Haakonssen, Knud (1988). 'Moral Philosophy and Natural Law: From the Cambridge Platonists to the Scottish Enlightenment', *Political Science*. 40:97–110.

Haakonssen, Knud (1996). *Natural Law and Moral Philosophy: From Hugo Grotius to the Scottish Enlightenment*. Cambridge: Cambridge University Press.

Haakonssen, Knud (forthcoming a). 'The Character and Obligation of Natural Law according to Richard Cumberland', in M. A. Stewart (ed.), *Philosophy in the Age of Locke*. Oxford: Oxford University Press.

Haakonssen, Knud (forthcoming b). 'Natural Law and the German Tradition', in M. Goldie and R. Wokler (eds.), *The Cambridge History of Eighteenth-Century Political Thought*. Cambridge: Cambridge University Press.

Hacking, Ian (1971a). 'Equipossibility Theories of Probability', *British Journal for the Philosophy of Science*. 22:339–55.

Hacking, Ian (1971b). 'The Leibniz–Carnap Program for Inductive Logic', *Journal of Philosophy*. 68:597–610.

Hacking, Ian (1971c). 'Jacques Bernoulli's *Art of Conjecturing*', *British Journal for the Philosophy of Science*. 22:209–29.

Hacking, Ian (1972). 'Individual Substance', in H. G. Frankfurt (ed.), *Leibniz: A Collection of Critical Essays*. Garden City, N.Y.: Doubleday, pp. 137–53.

Hacking, Ian (1975a). *The Emergence of Probability: A Philosophical Study of Early Ideas about Probability, Induction and Statistical Inference*. Cambridge: Cambridge University Press.

Hacking, Ian (1975b). 'The Identity of Indiscernibles', *Journal of Philosophy*. 72:249–56.

Hacking, Ian (1975c). *Why Does Language Matter to Philosophy?* Cambridge: Cambridge University Press.

Hägerström, Axel (1965). *Recht, Pflicht und bindende Kraft des Vertrages nach römischer und naturrechtlicher Anschauung,* ed. K. Olivecrona (Acta Societatis Litterarum Humaniorum Regiae Upsaliensis 44:3). Stockholm: Almqvist and Wiksell and Wiesbaden: Harrassowitz.

Haggenmacher, Peter (1983). *Grotius et la doctrine de la guerre juste* (Publications de l'Institut Universitaire de Hautes Etudes Internationales Genève). Paris: Presses Universitaires de France.

Hahm, David E. (1977). *The Origins of Stoic Cosmology*. Columbus, Ohio: Ohio State University Press.

Hahm, David E. (1985). 'The Stoic Theory of Change', *Southern Journal of Philosophy*. 23 (Supplement: Spindel Conference 1984: Recovering the Stoics):39–56.

Hall, A. Rupert (1966). 'Mechanics and the Royal Society, 1668–1670', *British Journal for the History of Science*. 3:24–38.

Hall, A. Rupert (1975a). 'Newton in France: A New View', *History of Science*. 13:233–50.

Hall, A. Rupert (1975b). 'Magic, Metaphysics and Mysticism in the Scientific Revolution', in M. L. Rhigini Bonelli and William R. Shea (eds.), *Reason, Experiment and Mysticism in the Scientific Revolution*. New York: Science History Publications.

Hall, A. Rupert (1980). *Philosophers at War: The Quarrel between Newton and Leibniz*. Cambridge: Cambridge University Press.

Hall, A. Rupert (1990). *Henry More: Magic, Religion and Experiment* (Blackwell Science Biographies). Oxford: Blackwell.

Hall, Joseph (1948). *Heaven upon Earth and Characters of Vertues and Vices,* ed. R. Kirk. New Brunswick, N.J.: Rutgers University Press.

Hall, Marie Boas. See Boas Hall, Marie.

Hall, Thomas Steele (1969). *Ideas of Life and Matter: Studies in the History of General Physiology 600 B.C.–1900 A.D.* (2 vols.). Chicago: University of Chicago Press. (Editions published 1975 and later under the title *A General History of Physiology*.)

Halley, Edmund (1693). 'An Estimate of the Degrees of the Mortality of Mankind, Drawn from Curious Tables of the Births and Funerals at the City of Breslaw; With an Attempt to Ascertain the Price of Annuities upon Lives', *Philosophical Transactions of the Royal Society of London*. 17:596–610.

Hamblin, C. L. (1975). 'Saccherian Arguments and the Self-Application of Logic', *Australasian Journal of Philosophy*. 53:157–60.

Hamelin, Octave (1911). *Le système de Descartes.* Paris: Félix Alcan.

Hamilton, B. (1963). *Political Thought in Sixteenth-Century Spain: A Study of the Political Ideas of Vitoria, De Soto, Suárez, and Molina.* Oxford: Oxford University Press.

Hammerstein, Notker (1972). *Jus und Historie. Ein Beitrag zur Geschichte des historischen Denkens an deutschen Universitäten im späten 17. und im 18. Jahrhundert.* Göttingen: Vandenhoeck und Ruprecht.

Hammerstein, Notker (1986). 'Zum Fortwirken von Pufendorf's Naturrechtslehre an den Universitäten des Heiligen Römischen Reiches Deutscher Nation während des 18. Jahrhunderts', in *Samuel von Pufendorf 1632–1982,* ed. K. Å. Modéer. Stockholm: Nordiska Bokhandeln, pp. 31–51.

Hampshire, Stuart (1973). 'Spinoza and the Idea of Freedom', in Marjorie Grene (ed.), *Spinoza: A Collection of Critical Essays.* Garden City, N.Y.: Doubleday, pp. 297–317.

Hampton, Jean (1986). *Hobbes and the Social Contract Tradition.* Cambridge: Cambridge University Press.

Hankins, James (1990). *Plato in the Italian Renaissance* (2 vols.). Leiden: Brill.

Hankins, Thomas L. (1967). 'The Influence of Malebranche on the Science of Mechanics during the Eighteenth Century', *Journal of the History of Ideas.* 28:193–210.

Hannaway, Owen (1975). *The Chemists and the Word: The Didactic Origins of Chemistry.* Baltimore: Johns Hopkins University Press.

Hannequin, A. (1896). 'La preuve ontologique de Descartes défendue contre Leibniz', *Revue de métaphysique et de morale.* 4:433–58 (also in *Etudes d'Histoire des Sciences et d'Histoire de la Philosophie,* vol. 1, pp. 233–64. Paris: Alcan 1908).

Hannequin, A. (1908). 'La première philosophie de Leibnitz', in A. Hannequin, *Etudes d'histoire des sciences et d'histoire de la philosophie* (2 vols.). Paris: Alcan, vol. 2, pp. 17–224.

Hardin, C. L. (1978). 'Spinoza on Immortality and Time', in R. Shahan and J. Biro (eds.), *Spinoza: New Perspectives.* Norman: University of Oklahoma Press.

Hardouin, Jean (1733). *Athei detecti,* in *Opera Varia.* Amsterdam, pp. 1–258.

Harris, E. (1975). 'Spinoza's Theory of Immortality', in M. Mandelbaum and E. Freeman (eds.), *Spinoza: Essays in Interpretation.* LaSalle, Ill. Open Court.

Harris, Ian (1993). *The Mind of John Locke. A Study in Political Theory in Its Intellectual Setting.* Cambridge: Cambridge University Press.

Harris, John (1708–10). *Lexicon Technicum: Or, an Universal English Dictionary of Arts and Sciences Explaining Not Only the Terms of Art, but the Arts Themselves.* 2d ed. (2 vols). London. (1st ed. of vol. 1 alone, London 1704; the 1708–10 is the 2d ed. of vol. 1 and the 1st ed. of vol. 2.)

Harrison, Charles Trawick (1934). 'The Ancient Atomists and English Literature of the Seventeenth Century', *Harvard Studies in Classical Philology.* 45:1–79.

Harrison, Peter (1993). 'Newtonian Science, Miracles and the Laws of Nature (abstract)', in K. Haakonssen and U. Thiel (eds.), *Reason, Will and Nature: Voluntarism in Metaphysics and Morals from Ockham to Kant* (Yearbook of the Australasian Society for the History of Philosophy, vol. 1). Canberra: Australasian Society for the History of Philosophy, pp. 89–97.

Harth, E. (1992). *Cartesian Women: Versions and Subversions of Rational Discourse in the Old Regime.* Ithaca, N.Y.: Cornell University Press.

Hartley, David (1749). *Observations on Man, His Frame, His Duty, and His Expectations* (2 vols.). London.

Hatfield, Gary (1979). 'Force (God) in Descartes' Physics', *Studies in History and Philosophy of Science.* 10:113–40.

Hatfield, Gary (1985). 'First Philosophy and Natural Philosophy in Descartes', in A. J. Holland (ed.), *Philosophy: Its History and Historiography.* Dordrecht and Boston: Reidel.

Hatfield, Gary (1986). 'The Senses and the Fleshless Eye: The *Meditations* as Cognitive Exercises', in Rorty 1986a.

Hatfield, Gary (1989). 'Science, Certainty, and Descartes', in A. Fine and J. Leplin (eds.), *PSA 1988* (2 vols.), vol. 2. East Lansing, Mich.: Philosophy of Science Association.

Hatfield, Gary (1990). 'Metaphysics and the New Science', in D. Lindberg and R. Westman (eds.), *Reappraisals of the Scientific Revolution*. Cambridge: Cambridge University Press.

Hatfield, Gary (1992). 'Descartes' Physiology and Its Relation to His Psychology', in J. Cottingham (ed.), *Cambridge Companion to Descartes*. Cambridge: Cambridge University Press.

Hatfield, Gary (1993). 'Reason, Nature, and God in Descartes', in Voss 1993.

Hatfield, Gary, and Epstein, William (1979). 'The Sensory Core and the Medieval Foundations of Early Modern Perceptual Theory', *Isis*. 70:363–84.

Hawes, Joan L. (1968). 'Newton and the "Electrical Attraction Unexcited"', *Annals of Science*. 24: 121–30.

Hazard, Paul (1935). *La Crise de conscience européene, 1680–1715*. Paris: Boivin.

Hearne, Thomas (ed.) (1720). *A Collection of Curious Discourses*. Oxford.

Heereboord, Adrian (1643). *Parallelismus Aristotelicae et Cartesianae philosophiae naturalis*. Leiden.

Heereboord, Adrian (1648). *Sermo extemporaneus de recta philosophice disputandi ratione*. Leiden.

Heereboord, Adrian (1654a). *Meletemata philosophica in quibus pleraeque res metaphysicae ventilantur*. Leiden.

Heereboord, Adrian (1654b). *Philosophia rationalis, moralis et naturalis*. Leiden.

Heereboord, Adrian (1663). *Philosophia naturalis cum . . . novis commentariis partim e nob. D. Cartesio . . . aliisque praestantioribus hujus seculi philosophis petitis, partim ex propria opinione dictatis, explicata*. Leiden.

Heereboord, Adrian (1680). *Meletemata philosophica*. Amsterdam.

Hegel, G. W. F. (1969–79). *Werke*. ed. Eva Moldenhauer and Karl Markus Michel (20 vols.). Frankfurt: Suhrkamp.

Hegel, G. W. F. (1995). *Lectures on the History of Philosophy* (3 vols.). Lincoln: University of Nebraska Press.

Heidegger, Martin (1957a). *Identität und Differenz*. Pfullingen: G. Neske.

Heidegger, Martin (1957b). 'Die onto-theologische Verfassung der Metaphysik', in Heidegger 1957a.

Heider, Wolfgang (1629). *Philosophiae moralis systema seu Commentationes in universam Aristotelis ethicem*. Jena.

Heilbron, John L. (1979). *Electricity in the 17th and 18th Centuries: A Study of Early Modern Physics*. Berkeley, Los Angeles: University of California Press.

Heilbron, John L. (1982). *Elements of Early Modern Physics*. Berkeley: University of California Press.

Heilbron, John L. (1993). *Weighing Imponderables and Other Quantitative Science Around 1800* (suppl. to Vol. 24, Part 1, of *Historical Studies in the Physical and Biological Sciences*). Berkeley: University of California Press.

Heimsoeth, H. (1960). *Atom, Seele, Monade: Historische Ursprünge und Hintergründe von Kants Antinomie der Teilung* (Akad. d. Wiss. und Lit. Mainz, Abhandlungen der Geist.-Sozialwiss. Klasse). Stuttgart: Steiner.

Heinekamp, Albert (ed.) (1983). *Leibniz et la Renaissance* (Studia Leibnitiana Supplementa, 23). Stuttgart: Steiner.

Heinekamp, Albert (ed.) (1988). *Leibniz. Questions de logique*. (Studia Leibnitiana, Sonderheft). Stuttgart: Steiner.

Helbing, Mario Otto (1989). *La filosofia di Francesco Buonamici, professore di Galileo a Pisa*. Pisa: Nistri-Lischi.

Hemmingsen, Niels (1562). *De lege naturae apodictica methodus*. Wittenberg.

Henderson, G. D. (1952). *Chevalier Ramsay*. London: Thomas Nelson.

Henninger, Mark G. (1989). *Relations. Medieval Theories 1250–1325*. Oxford: Oxford University Press.

Henrich, D. (1960). *Der ontologische Gottesbeweis*. Tübingen: Mohr.

Henricides, Guilelmus (1627). *Decas . . . philosophica. . . .* Leiden.

Henry, John (1982a). 'Thomas Harriot and Atomism: A Reappraisal', *History of Science*. 20:267–96.

Henry, John (1982b). 'Atomism and Eschatology: Catholicism and Natural Philosophy in the Interregnum', *British Journal for the History of Science*. 15:211–39.

Henry, John (1986a). 'A Cambridge Platonist's Materialism: Henry More and the Concept of Soul', *Journal of the Warburg and Courtauld Institutes.* 49:172–95.

Henry, John (1986b). 'Occult Qualities and the Experimental Philosophy: Active Principles in pre-Newtonian Matter Theory', *History of Science.* 24:335–81.

Henry, John (1987). 'Medicine and Pneumatology: Henry More, Richard Baxter and Francis Glisson's *Treatise on the Energetic Nature of Substance*', *Medical History.* 31:15–40.

Henry, John (1988). 'Newton, Matter and Magic', in John Fauvel et al. (eds.), *Let Newton Be!* Oxford: Oxford University Press.

Henry, John (1989a). 'The Matter of Souls: Medical Theory and Theology in Seventeenth-Century England', in R. French and A. Wear, (eds.), *The Medical Revolution of the Seventeenth Century.* Cambridge: Cambridge University Press, pp. 87–113.

Henry, John (1989b). 'Robert Hooke, the Incongruous Mechanist', in Michael Hunter and Simon Schaffer (eds.), *Robert Hooke: New Studies.* Woodbridge: Boydell.

Henry, John (1990). 'Henry More versus Robert Boyle: The Spirit of Nature and the Nature of Providence', in Hutton 1990, pp. 55–76.

Henry, John (1993). 'Henry More and Newton's Gravity', *History of Science.* 31:83–97.

Henry, John (1994). ' "Pray Do Not Ascribe That Notion to Me": God and Newton's Gravity', in James Force and Richard Popkin (eds.), *The Books of Nature and Scripture:* Dordrecht: Kluwer, pp. 123–47.

Hepburn, R. W. (1972). 'Hobbes on the Knowledge of God', in Maurice Cranston and Richard S. Peters (ed.), *Hobbes and Rousseau: A Collection of Critical Essays.* Garden City, N.Y.: Doubleday.

Herbert of Cherbury, Edward, Lord (1624). *De veritate, prout distinguitur a revelatione, a verisimili, a possibili, et a falso.* Paris.

Herbert of Cherbury, Edward, Lord (1633). *De veritate, prout distinguitur a revelatione, a verisimili, a possibili, et a falso.* 2d ed. London.

Herbert of Cherbury, Edward, Lord (1645). *De veritate . . . cui operi additi sunt duo alii tractatus: Primus, de causis errorum: alter, de religione laici; una cum appendice ad sacerdotes de religione laici, et quibusdam Poematibus,* 3d ed. London. (Repr. Stuttgart: Friedrich Frommann, 1966.)

Herbert of Cherbury, Edward, Lord (1663). *De religione gentilium.* Amsterdam. (Repr. Stuttgart: Friedrich Frommann, 1967.)

Herbert of Cherbury, Edward, Lord (1768). *A Dialogue between a Tutor and His Pupil.* London. (Repr. Stuttgart: Friedrich Frommann, 1971.)

Herbert of Cherbury, Edward, Lord (1937). *De veritate,* trans. Meyrick H. Carré. Bristol: Arrowsmith.

Herbert of Cherbury, Edward, Lord (1944). *De religione laici,* trans. H. R. Hutchenson. New Haven, Conn.: Yale University Press.

Herivel, John W. (1965). *The Background to Newton's Principia.* Oxford: Oxford University Press.

Hermes Trismegistus, Pseudo- (1924). *Hermetica,* ed. and trans. Walter Scott. Oxford: Oxford University Press.

Hermes Trismegistus, Pseudo- (1945–54). *Corpus Hermeticum,* ed. Arthur D. Nock, trans. [French] A. J. Festugière (4 vols.). Paris: Les Belles Lettres.

Hervada, J. (1983). 'The Old and the New in the Hypothesis "Etiamsi Daremus" of Grotius', *Grotiana.* N.s. 4:3–20.

Hesse, Mary B. (1970). 'Hermeticism and Historiography: An Apology for the Internal History of Science', in Roger H. Stuewer (ed.), *Minnesota Studies in the Philosophy of Science:* vol. 5, *Historical and Philosophical Perspectives of Science.* Minneapolis: University of Minnesota Press.

Hesse, Mary B. (1978). 'Action at a Distance', in Ernan McMullin (ed.), *The Concept of Matter in Modern Philosophy.* Notre Dame, Ind.: University of Notre Dame Press.

Heyd, Michael (1979). 'From Rationalist Theology to Cartesian Voluntarism', *Journal of the History of Ideas.* 40:527–42.

Heyd, Michael (1981). 'The Reaction to Enthusiasm in the Seventeenth Century: Towards an Integrative Approach', *Journal of Modern History.* 53: 258–80.

Hick, J., and McGill, A. C. (eds.) (1967). *The Many-faced Argument. Recent Studies on the Ontological Argument for the Existence of God.* New York: Macmillan.

Hildesheimer, Françoise (1991). *Le Jansenisme en France au XVIIe et XVIII siècles.* Paris: Publisud.

Hill, J. E. Christopher (1971). *The Antichrist in 17th Century England.* Oxford: Oxford University Press.

Hill, J. E. Christopher (1972). *The World Turned Upside Down: Radical Ideas in the English Revolution.* London: Temple Smith.

Hill, J. E. Christopher (1975). *The World Turned Upside Down: Radical Ideas in the English Revolution.* Harmondsworth: Penguin.

Hill, J. E. Christopher (1977). *Milton and the English Revolution.* London: Faber and Faber.

Hill, J. E. Christopher (1988). 'Till the Conversion of the Jews', in R. H. Popkin (ed.), *Millenarianism and Messianism in English Literature and Thought 1650–1800.* Leiden: Brill.

Hill, Nicholas (1601). *Philosophia Epicurea, Democritiana, Theophrastica proposita simpliciter, non edocta. Per Nicolaum Hill Anglum, Londinensem.* Paris. (2d ed., Geneva and Cologne, 1619.)

Hillenaar, Henk (1967). *Fénelon et le Jésuites.* The Hague: Nijhoff.

Hintikka, Jaakko (1962). '*Cogito, ergo sum:* Inference or Performance?' *Philosophical Review.* 71:3–32. (Also in Willis Doney (ed.), *Descartes: A Collection of Critical Essays.* Garden City, N.Y.: Doubleday, 1967.)

Hintikka, Jaako (1978). 'A Discourse on Descartes's Method', in Michael Hooker (ed.), *Descartes: Critical and Interpretive Essays.* Baltimore: Johns Hopkins University Press.

Hintikka, Jaako, and Remes, Unto (1974). *The Method of Analysis: Its Geometrical Origin and Its General Significance* (Boston Studies in the Philosophy of Science). Dordrecht: Reidel.

Hippocrates (1981). *The Hippocratic Treatises: 'On Generation', 'On the Nature of the Child', 'Diseases IV'* (Ars Medica), ed. I. M. Lonie. Berlin: de Gruyter.

Hirsch, Emanuel (1949). *Geschichte der neueren evangelischen Theologie im Zusammenhang mit den allgemeinen Bewegungen des europäischen Denkens.* Gutersloh: C. Bertelsmann.

Hirschman, Albert O. (1977). *The Passions and the Interests. Political Arguments for Capitalism before Its Triumph.* Princeton, N.J.: Princeton University Press.

Hobbes, Thomas (1629). *Eight bookes of the Peloponnesian warre written by Thucydides.* London.

Hobbes, Thomas (1642). *Elementorum philosophiae sectio tertia De Cive.* Paris.

Hobbes, Thomas (1644). *Tractatus opticus,* in M. Mersenne, *Universae geometriae mixtaeque mathematicae synopsis.* Paris.

Hobbes, Thomas (1650a). *Human Nature: Or the Fundamental Elements of Policy.* London.

Hobbes, Thomas (1650b). *De Corpore Politico: Or the Elements of Law, Moral and Politic.* London.

Hobbes, Thomas (1651). *Leviathan, or the Matter, Forme, and Power of a Commonwealth Ecclesiasticall and Civill.* London.

Hobbes, Thomas (1655). *Elementorum philosophiae sectio prima De Corpore.* London.

Hobbes, Thomas (1658). *Elementorum philosophiae sectio secunda De Homine.* London.

Hobbes, Thomas (1668). *Thomæ Hobbes Malmesburiensis opera philosophica, quae Latine scripsit, omnia.* Amsterdam.

Hobbes, Thomas (1679). *A Dialogue between a Philosopher and a Student of the Common Laws of England.* London.

Hobbes, Thomas (1681). *Behemoth, or the Long Parliament.* London.

Hobbes, Thomas (1839–45a). *Opera philosophica quae Latine scripsit omnia,* ed. Sir William Molesworth (5 vols.). London. (Repr. Darmstadt: Scientia, 1966.)

Hobbes, Thomas (1839–45b). *The English Works of Thomas Hobbes of Malmesbury,* ed. Sir William Molesworth (11 vols.). London. (Repr. Darmstadt: Scientia, 1962.)

Hobbes, Thomas (1928). *The Elements of Law,* ed. Ferdinand Tönnies. Cambridge: Cambridge University Press.

Hobbes, Thomas (1957). *Leviathan,* ed. M. Oakeshott. Oxford: Blackwell.

Hobbes, Thomas (1963). '*Tractatus opticus*', ed. F. Alessio, *Rivista critica di storia della filosofia.* 18:147–228.

Hobbes, Thomas (1968). *Leviathan,* ed. C. B. MacPherson. Harmondsworth: Penguin Books.

Hobbes, Thomas (1969). *The Elements of Law,* ed. F. Tönnies (2d ed). New York: Barnes and Noble.

Hobbes, Thomas (1972). *Man and Citizen,* ed. Bernard Gert. Garden City, N.Y.: Doubleday.

Hobbes, Thomas (1973). *Critique du* De mundo *de Thomas White,* ed. J. Jacquot and H. W. Jones (L'Histoire des Sciences: Texte et Etudes). Paris: Vrin.

Hobbes, Thomas (1976). *Thomas White's* De mundo *Examined,* trans. H. W. Jones. London: Bradford University Press in association with Crosby Lockwood Staples.

Hobbes, Thomas (1981). *Computatio sive logica. Logic. (De corpore, part I)* trans. A. Martinich, ed. Isabel C. Hungerland and G. R. Vick. New York: Abaris Books.

Hobbes, Thomas (1983a). *De cive, The Latin Version,* ed. Howard Warrender. Oxford: Oxford University Press.

Hobbes, Thomas (1983b). *De cive, The English Version,* ed. Howard Warrender. Oxford: Oxford University Press.

Hobbes, Thomas (1988). *Court traité des premiers principes: Le* Short Tract on First Principles *de 1630–1631. La naissance de Thomas Hobbes à la pensée moderne,* ed., trans. and commentary by Jean Bernhardt (Epiméthée: Essais Philosophiques). Paris: Presses Universitaires de France.

Hobbes, Thomas (1991). *Leviathan,* ed. R. Tuck. Cambridge: Cambridge University Press.

Hobbes, Thomas (1994). *The Correspondence of Thomas Hobbes,* ed. Noel Malcolm (2 vols.). Oxford: Oxford University Press.

Hochstrasser, Timothy (1993). 'Conscience and Reason: The Natural Law Theory of Jean Barbeyrac', *Historical Journal.* 36:289–308.

Hochstrasser, Timothy (forthcoming). 'Beyond Pufendorf's *Socialitas:* Christian Thomasius and Practical Philosophy', in H.-E. Bödeker and I. Hont (eds.), *Unsocial Sociability. Natural Law and the Eighteenth-Century Discourse on Society.* London: Routledge.

Hody, Humphry (1694). *The Resurrection of the (Same) Body Asserted.* London.

Hoeres, W. (1965). 'Francis Suarez and the Teaching of John Duns Scotus on *univocatio entis*', in J. K. Ryan and B. Bonensea (eds.), *John Duns Scotus 1265–1965.* Washington, D.C.: Catholic University of America Press.

Hoffman, Paul (1986). 'The Unity of Descartes' Man', *Philosophical Review.* 95:342–9.

Hoffman, Paul (1990). 'Cartesian Passions and Cartesian Dualism', *Pacific Philosophical Quarterly.* 71:310–32.

Holland, A. J. (ed.) (1985). *Philosophy, Its History and Historiography.* Dordrecht: Reidel.

Höltgen, K. J. (1965). 'Synoptische Tabellen in der medizinischen Literatur und die Logik Agricolas und Ramus', *Sudhoffs Archiv für Geschichte der Medizin und der Naturwissenschaften.* 49:371–90.

Holzgrefe, J. L. (1989). 'The Origins of Modern International Relations Theory', *Review of International Studies.* 15:11–26.

Hont, I. (1987). 'The Language of Sociability and Commerce: Samuel Pufendorf and the Theoretical Foundations of the "Four stages Theory"', in A. R. D. Pagden (ed.), *The Languages of Political Theory in Early-Modern Europe.* Cambridge: Cambridge University Press.

Hood, F. C. (1964). *The Divine Politics of Thomas Hobbes.* Oxford: Oxford University Press.

Hooke, Robert (1665). *Micrographia.* London. (Repr. London: Science Heritage Ltd., 1987.)

Hooke, R. (1705). *Posthumous Works of Robert Hooke,* ed. R. Waller. London. (Repr. London: Cass, 1971.)

Hooke, R. (1726). *Philosophical Experiments and Observations of the Late Eminent Dr. Robert Hooke*, ed. W. Derham. London. (Repr. London: Cass, 1967.)

Hooker, Michael (1982). 'Berkeley's Argument from Design', in Turbayne 1982, pp. 261–70.

Hooper, George (1699). 'A Calculation of the Credibility of Human Testimony', *Philosophical Transactions of the Royal Society of London*. 21:359–65.

Hooper, George (1757). *The Works of the Right Reverend Father in God, George Hooper, D.D.* Oxford.

Hoormann, C. F. A. (1976). 'A Further Examination of Saccheri's Use of the Consequentia Mirabilis', *Notre Dame Journal of Formal Logic*. 17:239–47.

Hooykaas, R. (1947). 'Het ontstaan van de chemische atoomleer', *Tijdschrift voor Philosophie*. 9:63–135.

Hooykaas, R. (1949). 'Chemical Trichotomy before Paracelsus?', *Archives internationales d'histoires des sciences*. 28:1063–74.

Hooykaas, R. (1970). 'Isaac Beeckman', in Gillispie 1970–80, vol. 1, pp. 566–8.

Hooykaas, R. (1972). *Religion and the Rise of Modern Science*. Edinburgh and London: Scottish Academic Press.

Höpfl, H. (1985). *The Christian Polity of John Calvin*. Cambridge: Cambridge University Press.

Horne, T. A. (1990). *Property Rights and Poverty. Political Argument in Britain, 1605–1834*. Chapel Hill: University of North Carolina Press.

Horowitz, Maryanne Cline (1974). 'Natural Law as the Foundation for an Autonomous Ethics: Pierre Charron's *De la sagesse*', *Studies in the Renaissance*. 21:204–27.

Hostler, J. (1975). *Leibniz's Moral Philosophy*. New York: Barnes and Noble.

Houston, R.A. (1988). *Literacy in Early Modern Europe: Culture and Education 1500–1800*. London: Longmans.

Howell, W. S. (1956). *Logic and Rhetoric in England, 1500–1700*. New York: Russell & Russell.

Howell, W. S. (1971). *Eighteenth-Century British Logic and Rhetoric*. Princeton, N.J.: Princeton University Press.

Howells, B. (1984). 'Pascal's "Pari" ', *Modern Language Review*. 79:45–63.

Hoyles, John (1971). *The Waning of the Renaissance, 1640–1740: Studies in the Thought and Poetry of Henry More, John Norris and Isaac Watts*. The Hague: Nijhoff.

Hruschka, Joachim (1984). 'Ordentliche und ausserordentliche Zurechnung bei Pufendorf. Zur Geschichte und zur Bedeutung der Differenz von actio libera in se und actio libera in sua causa', *Zeitschrift für die gesamte Strafrechtswissenschaft*. 96:661–702.

Hruschka, Joachim (1986). *Das deontologische Sechseck bei Gottfried Achenwall im Jahre 1767. Zur Geschichte der deontischen Grundbegriffe in der Universaljurisprudenz zwischen Suárez und Kant*. Hamburg: Vandenhoeck and Ruprecht.

Hübener, Wolfgang (1983). 'Leibniz und der Renaissance-Lullismus', in Albert Heinekamp (ed.), *Leibniz et la Renaissance* (Studia Leibnitiana Supplementa, 23), Stuttgart: Steiner.

Hübner, J. (1975). *Die Theologie Johannes Keplers zwischen Orthodoxie und Naturwissenschaft*. Tübingen: Mohr.

Hudde, Johannes (1679). *Stads-finantie geredresfeert in den jaare 1679 . . . Balansen-enz. betreffende de lofen lijfrenten*. MS. G610, AMEV Library, Utrecht.

Huet, Pierre-Daniel (1689). *Censura Philosphiae Cartesianae*. Paris. (Repr. Hildesheim: Olms, 1971.)

Huet, Pierre-Daniel (1692). *Nouveaux Mémoires pour servir à l'histoire du cartésianisme* (n.p.).

Huet, Pierre-Daniel (1723). *Traité philosophique de la foiblesse de l'esprit humain*. Amsterdam.

Huffman, William H. (1988). *Robert Fludd and the End of the Renaissance*. London: Routledge.

Hume, David (1976). *Natural History of Religion*, ed. John Valdimir Price. Oxford: Oxford University Press.

Hume, David (1978). *A Treatise of Human Nature*, ed. L. A. Selby-Bigge, rev. P. H. Nidditch. Oxford: Oxford University Press.

Hungerland, Isabel C., and Vick, G. R. (1981). 'Hobbes' Theory of Language, Speech and Reasoning', in Hobbes 1981.

Hunter, Michael (1981). *Science and Society in Restoration England*. Cambridge: Cambridge University Press.

Hunter, Michael (1989). *Establishing the New Science: The Experience of the Early Royal Society*. Woodbridge, Suffolk: Boydell.

Huonder, Quirin (1968). *Die Gottesbeweise. Geschichte und Schicksal*. Stuttgart: W. Kohlhammer.

Hussey, Edward (1990). 'The Beginnings of Epistemology: From Homer to Philolaus', in Everson 1990.

Hutcheson, Francis (1728). *An Essay on the Nature and Conduct of the Passions*. London.

Hutchison, Keith (1982). 'What Happened to Occult Qualities in the Scientific Revolution?' *Isis*. 73:233–53.

Hutchison, Keith (1983). 'Supernaturalism and the Mechanical Philosophy', *History of Science*. 21:297–333.

Hutchison, Keith (1991). 'Dormitive Virtues, Scholastic Qualities, and the New Philosophies', *History of Science*. 29:245–78.

Hutin, S. (1966). *Henry More: Essai sur les doctreines théosophiques chez les Platoniciens de Cambridge*. Hildesheim: Olms.

Hutton, Sarah (ed.) (1990). *Henry More (1614–1687): Tercentenary Studies*, Biography and Bibliography by Robert Crocker (International Archives of the History of Ideas, 127). Dordrecht: Kluwer.

Huygens, Christiaan (1657). *Tractatus de rationciniis in aleae ludo*. Leiden.

Huygens, Christiaan (1659). *De motu corporum ex percussione* [1659], in Huygens 1888–1950, vol. 16.

Huygens, Christiaan (1690). *Traité de la lumière . . . avec un discours de la cause de la pesanteur*. Paris.

Huygens, Christiaan (1703). *Opuscula postuma*. Leiden.

Huygens, Christiaan (1888–1950). *Oeuvres complètes*, eds. D. Bierans de Haan, J. Bosscha, D. J. Kortweg, J. A. Vollgraff (22 vols.). The Hague: Société Hollandaise des Sciences and Nijhoff.

Huygens, Christiaan (1912). *Treatise on Light*, trans. Silvanus P. Thompson. London: Macmillan.

Huygens, Christiaan (1977). 'Christiaan Huygens' *The Motion of Colliding Bodies*', trans. Richard J. Blackwell, *Isis*. 68:574–97.

Hyman, Arthur, and Walsh, James J. (eds.) (1973). *Philosophy in the Middle Ages*. Indianapolis, Ind.: Hackett.

Hyman, Arthur, and Walsh, James J., eds. (1986). *Philosophy in the Middle Ages: The Christian, Islamic, and Jewish Traditions*. 2d ed. Indianapolis, Ind.: Hackett.

Idel, Moshe (1988). *Kabbalah: New Perspectives*. New Haven, Conn.: Yale University Press.

Ignatius of Loyola (1950). *The Spiritual Exercises*, trans. W. H. Longridge (4th ed.). London: Mowbray.

Ignatius of Loyola (1969). *Exercitia spiritualia* (Monumenta historica Societatis Iesu), ed. J. Calveras. Rome: Institutum historicum Societatis Iesu.

Ignatius of Loyola (1989). *The Spiritual Exercises of St. Ignatius Loyola*, trans. Halcyon Backhouse. London: Hodder and Stoughton.

Ilting, Karl-Heinz (1983). *Naturrecht und Sittlichkeit*. (Sprache und Geschichte). Stuttgart: Klett-Cotta.

Iltis, Carolyn (1971). 'Leibniz and the *Vis Viva* Controversy', *Isis*. 62:21–35.

Iltis, Carolyn (1973). 'The Leibnizian-Newtonian Debates: Natural Philosophy and Social Psychology', *British Journal for the History of Science*. 6:343–77.

Iltis, Carolyn (1974). 'Leibniz' Concept of Force: Physics and Metaphysics', in *Akten des II. Internationalen Leibniz-Kongresses Hannover, 17–22 Juli 1972* (4 vols.). (*Studia Leibnitiana, Supplementa*). Stuttgart: Steiner, vol. 2, pp. 143–9.

Ingegno, Alfonso (1988). 'The New Philosophy of Nature', in Schmitt, Skinner, and Kessler 1988, pp. 236–63.

Inwood, Brad (1985). *Ethics and Human Action in Early Stoicism*. Oxford: Oxford University Press.

Ishiguro, Hidé (1972). *Leibniz's Philosophy of Logic and Language*. Ithaca, N.Y.: Cornell University Press. (2d ed. 1990.)

Jacob, J. R. (1977). *Robert Boyle and the English Revolution: A Study in Social and Intellectual Change* (Studies in the History of Science). New York: Burt Franklin.

Jacquot, Jean (1952). 'Thomas Harriot's Reputation for Impiety', *Notes and Records of the Royal Society of London.* 9:164–87.

Jacquot, Jean (1974). 'Harriot, Hill, Warner and the New Philosophy', in Shirley 1974, pp. 107–28.

Jaeger, F. M. (1921). 'Goorle (David van) Junior'. *Nieuw Nederlandsch Biografisch Woordenboek*. Leiden: A.W. Sijthoff's Uitgevers-Maatschappij, vol. 5, p. 210.

Jaki, S. T. (1978). *The Road of Science and the Ways to God*. Edinburgh: Scottish University Press.

Jalabert, J. (1960). *Le Dieu de Leibniz*. Paris: Vrin.

James, Susan (1987). 'Certain and Less Certain Knowledge', *Proceedings of the Aristotelian Society.* 87:227–42.

James, Susan (1993). 'Spinoza the Stoic', in Tom Sorell (ed.), *The Rise of Modern Philosophy*. Oxford: Oxford University Press, pp. 289–316.

Janke, W. (1963). 'Das ontologische Argument in der Frühzeit des Leibnizschen Denkens (1676–1678)', *Kant-Studien.* 54:359–87.

Jansenius, Cornelius (1640). *Augustinus* (3 vols.). Louvain. (Repr. Frankfurt: Minerva, 1964.)

Jardine, Lisa (1974). *Francis Bacon: Discovery and the Art of Discourse*. Cambridge: Cambridge University Press.

Jardine, Lisa (1982). 'Humanism and the Teaching of Logic', in N. Kretzmann, A. Kenny, J. Pinborg (eds.), *The Cambridge History of Later Medieval Philosophy*, pp. 797–807. Cambridge: Cambridge University Press.

Jardine, Lisa (1985). '*Experientia literata* ou *Novum Organum?* Le dilemme de la méthode scientifique de Bacon', in Michel Malherbe and Jean-Marie Pousseur (eds.), *Francis Bacon: Science et méthode, Actes du Colloque de Nantes*. Paris: Vrin.

Jardine, Lisa (1988). 'Humanistic Logic', in Schmitt, Skinner, and Kessler 1988, pp. 173–98.

Jardine, Nicholas (1976). 'Galileo's Road to Truth and the Demonstrative Regress', *Studies in History and Philosophy of Science.* 7:277–318.

Jardine, Nicholas (1984). *The Birth of History and Philosophy of Science: Kepler's A Defense of Tycho against Ursus with Essays on Its Provenance and Significance*. Cambridge: Cambridge University Press.

Jardine, Nicholas (1988). 'Epistemology of the Sciences', in Schmitt, Skinner, and Kessler 1988, pp. 685–711.

Jesseph, Douglas M. (1989). 'Philosophical Theory and Mathematical Practice in the Seventeenth Century', *Studies in History and Philosophy of Science.* 20:215–44.

Jesseph, Douglas [M.] (1993). *Berkeley's Philosophy of Mathematics*. Chicago: University of Chicago Press.

John Damascene (1860). *Opera*, ed. J. P. Migne and P. Michael Lequien. (3 vols.). (Patrologia Graeca). Paris.

John of St. Thomas (1930–7). *Cursus Philosophicus Thomisticus*, ed. B. Reiser (3 vols.). Turin: Marietti.

John of the Cross (1645–7). *Oeuvres spirituelles du Bienheureux Père Jean de la Croix,* trans. [French] Père Cyprien de la Nativité (2 vols.). Paris.

John of the Cross (1974). *The Dark Night of the Soul,* trans. Benedict Zimmerman. Greenwood, S.C.: Attic Press.

Johnston, George A. (1923). *The Development of Berkeley's Philosophy*. London: Macmillan.

Jolley, Nicholas (1975). 'An Unpublished Leibniz MS on Metaphysics', *Studia Leibnitiana.* 7:161–89.

Jolley, Nicholas (1984). *Leibniz and Locke: A Study of the* New Essays on Human Understanding. Oxford: Oxford University Press.

Jolley, Nicholas (1986). 'Leibniz and Phenomenalism', *Studia Leibnitiana*. 18:38–51.

Jolley, Nicholas (1988). 'Leibniz and Malebranche on Innate Ideas', *Philosophical Review*. 97:71–91.

Jolley, Nicholas (1990). *The Light of the Soul: Theories of Ideas in Leibniz, Malebranche, and Descartes*. Oxford: Oxford University Press.

Jolley, Nicholas (ed.) (1995). *The Cambridge Companion to Leibniz*. Cambridge: Cambridge University Press.

Jones, Howard (1981). *Pierre Gassendi, 1592–1655. An Intellectual Biography*. Nieuwkoop: De Graaf.

Jones, Howard (1989). *The Epicurean Tradition*. London: Routledge.

Jones, Rufus (1954). *Spiritual Reformers of the Sixteenth and Seventeenth Centuries*. New York: Peter Smith.

Jonsen, Albert R., and Toulmin, Stephen (1988). *The Abuse of Casuistry: A History of Moral Reasoning*. Berkeley: University of California Press.

Jordan, Mark D. (1984). 'The Intelligibility of the World and the Divine Ideas in Aquinas', *Review of Metaphysics*. 38:17–32.

Joseph, H. W. B.(1949). *Lectures on the Philosophy of Leibniz*. Oxford: Oxford University Press.

Joy, Lynn (1987). *Gassendi the Atomist: Advocate of History in an Age of Science* (Ideas in Context). Cambridge: Cambridge University Press.

Joy, Lynn (1992). 'Epicureanism in Renaissance Moral and Natural Philosophy', *Journal of the History of Ideas*. 53:573–83.

Judovitz, Dalia (1988). *Subjectivity and Representation in Descartes: The Origins of Modernity*. Cambridge: Cambridge University Press.

Judovitz, Dalia (1993). 'Vision, Representation and Technology in Descartes', in David Michael Levin (ed.), *Modernity and the Hegemony of Vision*. Berkeley: University of California Press.

Julien Eymard d'Angers, Father (1951). 'Le Stoïcisme dans le traité "De l'usage des passions" de l'Oratorien J. F. Senault (1641)', *Revue des sciences religieuses*. 25:40–68.

Julien Eymard d'Angers, Father (1976). *Recherches sur le stoïcisme aux XVII<sup>e</sup> et XVIII<sup>e</sup> siècles*, ed. L. Antoine. Hildesheim: Olms.

Jungius, Joachim (1638). *Logica Hamburgensis*. Hamburg.

Jungius, Joachim (1957). *Logica Hamburgensis*, ed. R. W. Meyer (Veröffentlichungen der Joachim Jungius-Gesellschaft der Wissenshaften, Hamburg, 1). Hamburg: J. J. Augustin.

Jungius, Joachim (1977). *Joachimi Jungii Logicae Hamburgensis additamenta*, ed. W. Risse (Veröffentlichungen der Joachim Jungius-Gesellschaft der Wissenschaften, Hamburg, 29). Göttingen: Vandenhoeck and Ruprecht.

Jungius, Joachim (1982). *Joachim Jungius. Praelectiones physicae. Historisch-kritische Edition*, ed. C. Meinel (Veröffentlichungen der Joachim Jungius-Gesellschaft der Wissenschaften, 45). Göttingen: Vandenhoeck and Ruprecht.

Jungst, Walter (1912). *Das Verhältnis von Philosophie und Theologie bei den Cartesianern Malebranche, Poiret und Spinoza. Eine philosophiegeschichtliche Untersuchung*. Leipzig: Quelle & Meyer.

Jurieu, Pierre (1687). *The Accomplishment of Scripture Prophecies*. London.

Kabitz, Willy (1909). *Die Philosophie des jungen Leibniz*. Heidelberg: Carl Winter.

Kabitz, Willy (1932). 'Leibniz und Berkeley', *Sitzungsberichte der preussischen Akademie der Wissenschaften, Philosophische-historische Klasse*. 24:623–36.

Kagan, Richard L. (1974). *Students and Society in Early Modern Spain*. Baltimore: Johns Hopkins University Press.

Kahn, Charles (1966). 'Sensation and Consciousness in Aristotle's Psychology', *Archiv für Geschichte der Philosophie*. 48:34–81.

Kalinowski, G. (1977). 'La logique juridique de Leibniz. Conception et contenu', *Studia Leibnitiana*. 9:168–89.

Kalinowski, G., and Gardies, J.-L. (1974). 'Un logicien déontique avant la lettre: Gottfried Wilhelm Leibniz', *Archiv für Rechts- und Sozialphilosophie*. 60:79–112.

Kalmar, Martin (1977). 'Thomas Harriot's De Reflexione Corporum Rotundorum: An Early Solution to the Problem of Impact', *Archive for History of Exact Sciences*. 16:201–30.

Kangro, Hans (1975). 'Daniel Sennert', in Gillispie 1970–80, vol. 12, pp. 310–13.

Kant, Immanuel (1900–    ). *Kants gesammelte Schriften,* ed. Königlich Preussischen Akademie der Wissenschaften, later the Deutsche Akademie der Wissenschaften (27 vols. to date). Berlin: G. Reimer, later de Gruyter.

Kant, Immanuel (1933). *Critique of Pure Reason,* trans. Norman Kemp Smith. London: Macmillan Press.

Kaplan, Yosef (1989). *From Christianity to Judaism. The Life of Isaac Orobio de Castro.* Oxford: Oxford University Press.

Kargon, Robert H. (1965). 'William Petty's Mechanical Philosophy', *Isis.* 56:63–6.

Kargon, Robert H. (1966). *Atomism in England from Harriot to Newton.* Oxford: Oxford University Press.

Kassler, Jamie C. (1991). 'The Paradox of Power: Hobbes and Stoic Naturalism', in Stephen Gaukroger (ed.), *The Uses of Antiquity.* Dordrecht: Kluwer, pp. 53–78.

Katz, David S. (1982). *Philo-semitism and the Readmission of the Jews to England.* Oxford: Oxford University Press.

Katz, David S. (1988). *Sabbath and Sectarianism in Seventeenth-Century England.* Leiden: Brill.

Kaufmann, V. Milo (1966). *The Pilgrim's Progress and Traditions in Puritan Meditation.* New Haven, Conn.: Yale University Press.

Kavka, Gregory S. (1986). *Hobbesian Moral and Political Theory.* Princeton, N.J.: Princeton University Press.

Kearney, Hugh (1970). *Scholars and Gentlemen: Universities and Society in Pre-Industrial Britain 1500–1700.* London: Faber and Faber.

Keckermann, Bartholomaeus (1600). *Systema logicae.* Hanau.

Keckermann, Bartholomaeus (1606a). *Gymnasium logicum.* London.

Keckermann, Bartholomaeus (1606b). *Praecognitorum logicorum tractatus III.* Hanau.

Keckermann, Bartholomaeus (1607). *Systema ethicae. . . .* London.

Keckermann, Bartholomaeus (1609). *Scientiae metaphysicae compendiosum systema.* Hanau.

Keckermann, Bartholomaeus (1612). *Systema physicum.* Hanau.

Keckermann, Bartholomaeus (1613). *Systema systematum.* Hanau.

Keckermann, Bartholomaeus (1614). *Operum omnium quae extant tomus primus et secundus* (2 vols). Geneva.

Kelly, Suzanne (1965). *The De Mundo of William Gilbert.* Amsterdam: Menno Hertzberger.

Kelpius, Johannes, and Ericius, Johannes (1690). *Ethicus ethnicus ineptus Christianae juventutis hodegus. . . .* Altdorf.

Kemp, J. (1970). *Ethical Naturalism: Hobbes and Hume.* London: Macmillan and St. Martin's Press.

Kemp Smith, Norman (1902). *Studies in the Cartesian Philosophy.* London: Macmillan. (Repr., New York: Russell and Russell 1962.)

Kemp Smith, Norman (1941). *The Philosophy of David Hume.* London: Macmillan.

Kendall, M. G. (1956). 'The Beginnings of a Probability Calculus', *Biometrika.* 43:1–14. (Repr. in E. S. Pearson and M. G. Kendall (eds.), *Studies in the History of Statistics and Probability,* Darien, Conn.: Hafner, 1970.)

Kendall, M. G. (1977). 'Where Shall the History of Statistics Begin?', in R. L. Plackett and M. G. Kendall (eds.), *Studies in the History of Statistics and Probability.* London: Griffin.

Kendall, M. G., and Plackett, R. L. (eds.) (1977). *Studies in the History of Statistics and Probability.* London: Griffin.

Kennington, Richard (1971). 'Finitude of Descartes' Evil Genius', *Journal of the History of Ideas.* 32:441–6.

Kenny, Anthony (1968). *Descartes.* New York: Random House.

Kenny, Anthony (1970). 'The Cartesian Circle and the Eternal Truths', *Journal of Philosophy.* 57:685–700.

Kenny, Anthony (1972). 'Descartes on the Will', in R. J. Butler (ed.), *Cartesian Studies.* Oxford: Blackwell.

Keohane, Nannerl O. (1980). *Philosophy and the State in France: The Renaissance to the Enlightenment.* Princeton, N.J.: Princeton University Press.

Kepler, Johannes (1596). *Prodromus Dissertationum Cosmographicarum seu Mysterium Cosmographicum.* Tübingen.

Kepler, Johannes (1602). *De Fundamentis Astrologia Certioribus.* Prague.

Kepler, Johannes (1604). *Ad Vitellionem Paralipomena, quibus Astronomiae pars Optica traditur.* Frankfurt.

Kepler, Johannes (1609). *Astronomia Nova.* Prague.

Kepler, Johannes (1611). *Dioptrice.* Augsburg.

Kepler, Johannes (1618–21). *Epitome Astronomiae Copernicanae.* Linz and Frankfurt.

Kepler, Johannes (1619). *De Harmonice Mundi.* Augsburg.

Kepler, Johannes (1621). . . . *Mysterium Cosmographicum.* 2d ed. Frankfurt.

Kepler, Johannes (1937–    ). *Gesammelte Werke.* ed. W. von Dyck and M. Caspar (20 vols. to date). Munich: C. H. Beck.

Kern, W. (1964). 'Über den ontologischen Gottesbeweis in der Metaphysik des 17. Jhts. Anhang eines Buches von D. Henrich', *Scholastik.* 39:87–107.

Kessler, Eckhard (1988). 'The Intellective Soul', in Schmitt, Skinner, and Kessler 1988, pp. 485–534.

Keynes, John Maynard (1947). 'Newton, the Man', in *The Royal Society Newton Tercentenary Celebrations 15–19 July 1946.* Cambridge: Cambridge University Press.

Kilcullen, John (1988). *Sincerity and Truth: Essays on Arnauld, Bayle, and Toleration.* Oxford: Oxford University Press.

Kilcullen, John (1994). 'Natural Law and Will in Ockham', in K. Haakonssen and U. Thiel (eds.), *History of Philosophy Yearbook,* 1 (Reason, Will and Nature: Voluntarism in Metaphysics and Morals from Ockham to Kant). Canberra: Australasian Society for the History of Philosophy, pp. 1–34.

King, Peter, 7th Baron King (1830). *The Life of John Locke with Extracts from His Correspondence, Journals, and Commonplace Books* (2 vols.). London.

King, William (1781). *De origine mali* (1702), trans. Edmund Law. London, 1731; 5th ed. London.

Kircher, Athanasius, S.J. (1641). *Magnes, sive de Arte Magnetica.* Rome.

Kircher, Athanasius, S.J. (1665). *Mundus subterraneus.* Amsterdam.

Kircher, Athanasius, S.J. (1667). *China illustrata.* Amsterdam.

Kirk, G. S.; Raven, J. E.; and Schofield, M. (eds.) (1983). *The Presocratic Philosophers: A Critical History with a Selection of Texts.* 2d ed. Cambridge: Cambridge University Press.

Kirk, Linda (1987). *Richard Cumberland and Natural Law.* Cambridge: J. Clarke and Co.

Klaaren, E. M. (1977). *Religious Origins of Modern Science: Belief in Creation in Seventeenth-Century Thought.* Grand Rapids: William B. Erdmans.

Kline, A. David (1987). 'Berkeley's Divine Language Argument', in Sosa 1987, pp. 129–42.

Kneale, William, and Kneale, Martha (1962). *The Development of Logic.* Oxford: Oxford University Press.

Knecht, H. H. (1981). *La logique chez Leibniz. Essai sur le rationalisme baroque.* Lausanne: Editions l'âge de l'homme.

Knight, William Stanley Macbean (1925). *The Life and Works of Hugo Grotius.* London: Sweet and Maxwell.

Knorr, Wilbur R. (1993). *The Ancient Tradition of Geometric Problems.* New York: Dover. (Orig. ed. Boston: Birkhäuser Verlag, 1986.)

Knorr von Rosenroth, Christian (ed.) (1677). *Kabbala Denudata, seu Doctrina hebraeorum transcendentalis et metaphysica atque theologica* (2 vols.). Sulzbach.

Koester, Helmut (1968). 'Νομός Φύσεως: the Concept of Natural Law in Greek Thought', in Jacob Neusner (ed.), *Religions in Antiquity.* Leiden: Brill.

Kolakowski, Leszek (1987). *Chrétiens sans église,* trans. [French] Anna Posner (Bibliothèque de philosophie). Paris: Gallimard.

Kors, Alan Charles (1990). *Atheism in France 1650–1729. Vol. I: The Orthodox Sources of Disbelief.* Princeton, N.J.: Princeton University Press.

Koyré, Alexandre (1922). *Essai sur l'idée de Dieu et les preuves de son existence chez Descartes.* Paris: Leroux. (Revised German text: *Descartes und die Scholastik.* Bonn: F. Cohen, 1923.)

Koyré, Alexandre (1929). *La Philosophie de Jacob Boehme.* Paris.

Koyré, Alexandre (1957). *From the Closed World to the Infinite Universe.* New York: Harper.

Koyré, Alexandre (1959). 'Jean Baptiste Benedetti, critique d'Aristote', in *Mélanges offerts à Etienne Gilson.* Paris: Vrin, and Toronto: Pontifical Institute of Mediaeval Studies, pp. 351–72.

Koyré, Alexandre (1966). *Etudes galiléennes.* 2d ed. Paris: Hermann.

Koyré, Alexandre (1968a). *Newtonian Studies.* Chicago: University of Chicago Press.

Koyré, Alexandre (1968b). 'Concept and Experience in Newton's Scientific Thought', in Koyré 1968a, pp. 25–52.

Koyré, Alexandre (1968c). 'Newton's "Regulae Philosophandi"', in Koyré 1968a, pp. 261–72.

Koyré, Alexandre (1978). *Galileo Studies.* Atlantic Highlands: Humanities Press.

Krailsheimer, A. J. (1962). *Studies in Self-Interest. From Descartes to La Bruyère.* Oxford: Oxford University Press.

Krailsheimer, A. J. (1980). *Pascal.* Oxford: Oxford University Press.

Kraus, Pamela A. (1983). 'From Universal Mathematics to Universal Method: Descartes's "Turn" in Rule IV of the Regulae', *Journal of the History of Philosophy.* 21:159–74.

Kraus, Pamela A. (1986). '"Whole Method": The Thematic Unity of Descartes' *Regulae*', *Modern Schoolman.* 63:83–109.

Kraye, Jill (1988). 'Moral Philosophy', in Schmitt, Skinner, and Kessler 1988, pp. 303–86.

Kraye, Jill (1994). 'The Transformation of Platonic Love in the Italian Renaissance', in Anna Baldwin and Sarah Hutton (eds.), *Platonism and the English Imagination.* Cambridge: Cambridge University Press. pp. 76–85.

Kremer, K. (1969). *Gott und Welt in der klassischen Metaphysik.* Stuttgart: Kohlhammer.

Kretzmann, Norman (1993). 'Philosophy of Mind', in Norman Kretzmann and Eleanore Stump (eds.), *The Cambridge Companion to Aquinas.* Cambridge: Cambridge University Press.

Kretzmann, Norman; Kenny, Anthony; and Pinborg, Jan (eds.) (1982). *The Cambridge History of Later Medieval Philosophy.* Cambridge: Cambridge University Press.

Krieger, L. (1965). *The Politics of Discretion. Pufendorf and the Acceptance of Natural Law.* Chicago: University of Chicago Press.

Kristeller, Paul O. (1943). *The Philosophy of Marsilio Ficino.* New York: Columbia University Press.

Kristeller, Paul O. (1960). 'Ludovico Lazzarelli e Giovanni da Correggio, due ermetici del Quattrocento, e il manoscritto II.D.I.4 della Biblioteca degli Ardenti di Viterbo', in *Biblioteca degli Ardenti della Città di Viterbo: Studi e ricerche nel 150° della fondazione.* Viterbo: Agnesotti.

Kristeller, Paul O. (1968). 'The Myth of Renaissance Atheism and the French Tradition of Free Thought', *Journal of the History of Philosophy.* 6:233–43.

Kristeller, Paul O. (1984). 'Stoic and Neoplatonic Sources of Spinoza's *Ethics*', *History of European Ideas.* 5:1–15.

Krook, Dorothea (1993). *John Sergeant and His Circle: A Study of Three Seventeenth-Century Aristotelians,* ed. B. C. Southgate. Leiden: Brill.

Kuksewicz, Z. (1982a). 'The Potential and the Agent Intellect', in Kretzmann, Kenny, and Pinborg 1982, pp. 595–601.

Kuksewicz, Z. (1982b). 'Criticisms of Aristotelian Psychology and the Augustinian-Aristotelian Synthesis', in Kretzmann, Kenny, and Pinborg 1982, pp. 623–8.

Kulstad, M. A. (1980). 'A Closer Look at Leibniz's Alleged Reduction of Relations', *Southern Journal of Philosophy.* 18:417–32.

Kuntz, Marion Daniels (1981). *Guillaume Postel, the Prophet of the Restitution of All Things.* The Hague: Nijhoff.


Labrousse, Elisabeth (1963–4). *Pierre Bayle* (2 vols.). The Hague: Nijhoff.

Labrousse, Elisabeth (1983). *Bayle* (Past Masters). Oxford: Oxford University Press.

La Bruyère, Jean de (1951). *Oeuvres complètes,* ed. J. Benda. Paris: Gallimard.

La Bruyère, Jean de (1990). *Les caractères,* ed. R. Garapon. Paris, Garnier.

Lach, Donald (1953). 'The Sinophilism of Christian Wolff (1679–1754)', *Journal of the History of Ideas.* 14:561–74.

Lach, Donald (1965). *Asia in the Making of Europe:* vol. 1, *The Century of Discovery.* Chicago: University of Chicago Press.

Lach, Donald (1968). 'China in Western Thought and Culture', vol. 1 of Philip P. Wiener (ed.), *Dictionary of the History of Ideas,* pp. 361–3. New York: Scribner.

La Forge, Louis de (1666). *Traitté de l'esprit de l'homme et de ses facultez et fonctions, et de son union avec le corps. Suivant les principes de René Descartes.* Paris.

La Forge, Louis de (1974). *Oeuvres Philosophiques,* ed. P. Clair (Le mouvement des idées au XVIIe siècle). Paris: Presses Universitaires de France.

Lagarde, Bernardette (1973). 'Le *De Differentiis* de Pléthon d'après l'autographe de la Marcienne', *Byzantion.* 43:312–43.

Lagrée, Jacqueline (1994). *Juste Lipse et la restauration du stoicisme.* Paris: Vrin.

Lai, Yuen-ting (1985). 'The Linking of Spinoza to Chinese Thought by Bayle and Malebranche', *Journal of the History of Philosophy.* 23:151–78.

Laird, John (1920). *A Study in Realism.* Cambridge: Cambridge University Press.

Laird, John (1924). 'The Legend of Arnauld's Realism', *Mind.* 33:176–9.

Laird, John (1934). *Hobbes.* New York: Russell and Russell.

Lalande, A. (1911). 'Sur quelques textes de Bacon et de Descartes', *Revue de métaphysique et de morale.* 19:296–311.

Lambert, Johann Heinrich (1771). *Anlage zur Architectonic,* vol. 1. Riga.

La Mothe le Vayer, François (1630–3?). *Dialogues faites à l'imitation des anciens.* Paris?

La Mothe le Vayer, François (1636). *Discours de la contrariété d'humeurs qui se trouve entre certaines nations.* Paris.

La Mothe le Vayer, François (1642). *De la vertu des payens.* Paris.

La Mothe le Vayer, François (1643). *De la liberté et de la servitude.*

La Mothe le Vayer, François (1662). *Oeuvres* (2 vols). Paris.

La Mothe le Vayer, François (1669a). *Oeuvres . . . nouvelle édition augmentée de plusieurs nouveaux traittez* (15 vols.). Paris: L. Billaine.

La Mothe le Vayer, François (1669b). *Discours pour montrer que les doutes de la philosophie sceptique sont de grand usage dans les sciences,* in La Mothe le Vayer 1669a, vol. 15.

La Mothe le Vayer, François (1756–9). *Oeuvres . . . nouvelle édition* (14 vols.). Dresden.

La Mothe le Vayer, François (1988). *Dialogues faits à l'imitation des anciens,* ed. A. Pessel. Paris: Fayard.

Lamy, Bernard (1675). *L'art de parler.* Paris. (2d ed. Paris, 1676; 3d ed. Paris, 1688; 4th ed. Amsterdam, 1699, and Paris, 1701.)

Lamy, Bernard (1683). *Entretiens sur les sciences.* Grenoble and Paris. (2d ed. Lyon, 1694; 3d. ed. Lyon, 1706.)

Lamy, Bernard (1684). *Entretiens sur les sciences.* Brussels.

Lamy, Bernard (1966). *Entretiens sur les Sciences,* ed. F. Girbal and P. Clair. Paris: Presses Universitaires de France.

Lamy, Dom François (1694–8). *De la connoissance de soi-mesme.* Paris.

Lamy, Dom François (1696). *Le Nouvel athéisme renversé, ou Réfutation du sistème de Spinosa, tirée pour la plupart de la conoissance de la nature de l'homme.* Paris.

Lamy, Dom François (1703). *Lettres philosophiques sur divers sujets importans.* Paris.

Lamy, Dom François (1706). *Les premiers élémens des sciences, ou Entrée aux connoissances solides.* . . . Paris.

Lamy, Guillaume (1669). *De principiis rerum.* Paris.

Landucci, S. (1986). *La teodicea nell'eta cartesiana.* Naples: Bibliopolis.

Langbein, John H. (1976). *Torture and the Law of Proof.* Chicago: University of Chicago Press.

Lanion, Pierre [pseud. Wander, Guillaume] (1678). *Méditations sur la métaphysique.* Paris. (Repr. in Bayle 1684, pp. 267–333.)

La Peyrère, Isaac (1643). *Du rappel des Juifs.* Paris.

La Peyrère, Isaac (1655). *Prae Adamitae.* Amsterdam.

La Peyrère, Isaac (1656). *Men before Adam.* Amsterdam.

Laporte, J. (1950). *Le rationalisme de Descartes.* Paris: Presses Universitaires de France.

La Rochefoucauld, F. (1705). *Réflexions ou Sentences et Maximes morales de Monsieur de la Rochefoucauld, Maximes de Madame la marquise de Sablé. Pensées diverses de M. L.D. et les Maximes chrétiennes de M**** [Madame La Sablière].* Amsterdam.

La Rochefoucauld, F. (1967). *Maximes, suivés par des Reflexions diverses, du Portrait de la Rochefoucauld par lui-même et des Remarques de Christine de Suède sur les Maximes,* ed. J. Truchet. Paris: Garnier.

Larmore, Charles (1984). 'Descartes' Psychologistic Theory of Assent', *History of Philosophy Quarterly.* 1:61–74.

Larmore, Charles (1986). 'La critique newtonienne de la méthode cartésienne', *Dix-huitième siècle.* 18:269–79.

Larmore, Charles (1987a). 'L'Explication scientifique chez Descartes', in Grimaldi and Marion 1987, pp. 109–28.

Larmore, Charles (1987b). 'Newton's Critique of Cartesian Method'. *Graduate Faculty Philosophy Journal.* 12:81–109.

Larmore, Charles (1988). 'La notion de certitude chez Newton', *Revue d'histoire des sciences.* 41:377–84.

Larmore, Charles (1993). *Modernité et morale.* Paris: Presses Universitaires de France.

Lasswitz, Kurd (1890). *Geschichte der Atomistik vom Mittelalter bis Newton* (2 vols.). Hamburg and Leipzig: L. Voss.

Lattis, James M. (1994). *Between Copernicus and Galileo: Christoph Clavius and the Collapse of Ptolemaic Cosmology.* Chicago: University of Chicago Press.

Lattre, Alain de (1967). *L'occasionalisme d'Arnold Geulincx: Etude sur la constitution de la doctrine.* Paris: Editions de Minuit.

Laudan, Laurens (1966). 'The Clock Metaphor and Probabilism: The Impact of Descartes on English Methodological Thought, 1650–65', *Annals of Science.* 22:73–104.

Laurent, Pierre (1982). *Pufendorf et la loi naturelle.* Paris: Vrin.

Law, Edmund (1734). *An Essay on the Origin of Evil by Dr. William King, translated from the Latin with notes, etc.* (2 vols.). 2d ed. Cambridge.

Law, Edmund (1769). *A Defence of Mr. Locke's Opinion concerning Personal Identity*. Cambridge. (Repr. in Locke 1823, vol. 3, pp. 165–84.)

Layton, Henry (1698). *Observations upon a Short Treatise, Written by Timothy Manlove: Intituled, The Immortality of the Soul Asserted*. London.

Le Brun, Charles (1696). 'Conference sur l'Expression Generale et Particuliere', in Henri Testelin, *Sentiments des plus habiles peintres sur la practique de la peintures et sculptures mis en tables par Henri Testelin*. Paris. (Repr. Geneva: Minkoff, 1972.)

Leclerc, Ivor (1986). *The Philosophy of Nature* (Studies in Philosophy and the History of Philosophy, vol. 14). Washington, D.C.: Catholic University of America Press.

Le Clerc, Jean (1692). *Logica sive ars ratiocinandi*. Amsterdam.

Le Clerc, Jean (1695). *Physica sive de rebus corporeis*. Amsterdam.

Le Clerc, Jean (1696). *De l'incrédulité où l'on examine les motifs et les raisons générales qui portent les incrédules à rejeter la religion chrétienne*. Amsterdam.

Le Clerc, Jean (1698). *Opera philosophica* (4 vols.). Amsterdam.

Le Clerc, Jean (1709). *De eligenda inter Christianos dissentientes sententia*. Amsterdam. (This is appended to his edition of that year of Grotius, *De veritate religionis christianae*.)

Le Clerc, Jean (1724). *Contra indifferentiam religionum*. The Hague. (This is appended to his edition of that year of Grotius, *De veritate religionis christianae*.)

Le Comte, Louis, S.J. (1696). *Nouveaux mémoires sur l'etat présent de la Chine*. Paris.

Le Coq, Petrus (1626). *Disputatio philosophica, continens varias positiones morales, . . . praeside Francone Burgersdicio. . . .* Leiden.

Lee, Henry (1702). *Anti-Scepticism: Or, Notes upon Each Chapter of Mr. Lock's Essay concerning Humane Understanding*. London. (Repr. New York: Garland, 1984.)

Le Grand, Antoine (1662). *Le Sage des Stoiques ou l'Homme sans Passions. Selon les sentiments de Séneque*. The Hague.

Le Grand, Antoine (1665). *Les caractères de l'homme sans passions, selon les sentiments de Séneque*. Paris.

Le Grand, Antoine (1669). *L'Epicure spirituel, ou l'empire de la volupté sur les vertus*. Paris.

Le Grand, Antoine (1672). *Institutio philosophiae secundum principia R. Descartes. . . .* London.

Le Grand, Antoine (1675). *Man without Passion: Or the Wise Stoic according to the Sentiments of Seneca*, trans. G. R. London.

Le Grand, Antoine (1679a). *Apologia pro R. Des-Cartes contra S. Parkerum. . . .* London.

Le Grand, Antoine (1679b). *Institutio philosophiae secundum principia D. Renati Descartes. . . .* Nuremberg.

Le Grand, Antoine (1694). *An Entire Body of Philosophy according to the Principles of the Famous Renate Des Cartes,* trans. R. Blome. London.

Le Grand, H. E. (1978). 'Galileo's Matter Theory', in Robert E. Butts and Joseph C. Pitt (eds.), *New Perspectives on Galileo*. Dordrecht: Reidel.

Leibniz, Gottfried Wilhelm (1684). 'Nova methodus pro maximis et minimis, itemque tangentibus, quae nec fractas, nec irrationales quantitates moratur', *Acta Eruditorum*, pp. 466–73, in *Ger. Math.* V 220–6.

Leibniz, Gottfried Wilhelm (1686). 'De geometria recondita et analysi indivisibilium et infinitorum', *Acta eruditorum*. pp. 292–300, in *Ger. Math.* V 226–33.

Leibniz, Gottfried Wilhelm (1694a). 'Considérations sur la différence qu'il y a entre l'analyse ordinaire et le nouveau calcul des transcendentes', *Journal des sçavans*; in *Ger. Math.* V 306–8.

Leibniz, Gottfried Wilhelm (1694b). 'Nova calculi differentialis applicatio & usus, ad multiplicem linearum constructionem, ex data tangentium conditione', *Acta eruditorum*, pp. 311–16; repr. in *Ger. Math.* V 301–6.

Leibniz, Gottfried Wilhelm (1718). 'Jugement d'un anonyme sur l'original de cet abrégé [*De officio*]: Avec des reflexions du Traducteur [Barbeyrac] . . .' in S. Pufendorf, *Les devoirs de l'homme, et du citoien,* ed. J. Barbeyrac. Amsterdam, pp. 429–95.

Leibniz, Gottfried Wilhelm (1765). *Nouveaux essais sur l'entendement humain,* in R. E. Raspe (ed.), *Oeuvres philosophiques latines & francoises de feu Mr. de Leibnitz; Tirées de ses manuscrits qui se conservent dans la bibliotheque royale a Hanovre.* Amsterdam, and Leipzig.

Leibniz, Gottfried Wilhelm (1768). *Leibnitii opera omnia,* ed. L. Dutens (6 vols.). Geneva.

Leibniz, Gottfried Wilhelm (1840). *Opera Philosophica quae extant Latina Gallica Germanica Omnia,* ed. J. E. Erdmann. Berlin.

Leibniz, Gottfried Wilhelm (1849–63). *Mathematische Schriften.* ed. C. I. Gerhardt (7 vols.). Berlin and Halle: A. Asher et comp. and H. W. Schmidt. (Repr. Hildesheim: Olms, 1962.)

Leibniz, Gottfried Wilhelm (1854). *Réfutation inédite de Spinoza,* ed. A. Foucher de Careil. Paris.

Leibniz, Gottfried Wilhelm (1855). 'Analysis tetragonistica ex centrobarycis' [October, 1675], in C. I. Gerhardt, *Die Entdeckung der höheren Analysis* (= *Die Geschichte der höheren Analysis*). Halle.

Leibniz, Gottfried Wilhelm (1857). *Nouvelles lettres et opuscules inédits de Leibniz,* ed. A. Foucher de Careil. Paris.

Leibniz, Gottfried Wilhelm (1860). *Theologisches System,* ed. and trans. (German) Carl Haas. Tübingen. (Repr. Hildesheim: Olms, 1966.)

Leibniz, Gottfried Wilhelm (1867). 'Réponse à la Critique de la Critique de la Recherche de la vérité', in F. Rabbe, *Etude philosophique sur l'Abbé Simon Foucher.* Paris: Didier.

Leibniz, Gottfried Wilhelm (1874). *Correspondance de Leibniz avec l'électrice Sophie de Brunswick-Lunebourg,* ed. O. Klopp (3 vols.). Hanover: Kindworth.

Leibniz, Gottfried Wilhelm (1875–90). *Die philosophischen Schriften,* ed. C. I. Gerhardt (7 vols.). Berlin: Weidmannsche Buchhandlung. (Repr. Hildesheim: Olms, 1978.)

Leibniz, Gottfried Wilhelm (1885). *Rechtsphilosophisches aus Leibnizens ungedruckten Schriften,* ed. G. Mollat. Leipzig: Cassel.

Leibniz, Gottfried Wilhelm (1903). *Opuscules et fragments inédits,* ed. L. Couturat. Paris: Alcan. (Repr. Hildesheim: Olms, 1966.)

Leibniz, Gottfried Wilhelm (1906). *Leibnizens nachgelassene Schriften physikalischen, mechanischen, und technischen Inhalts,* ed. E. Gerland. Leipzig: Teubner.

Leibniz, Gottfried Wilhelm (1920). *The Early Mathematical Manuscripts of Leibniz,* ed. and trans. J. M. Child. Chicago: Open Court.

Leibniz, Gottfried Wilhelm (1923– ). *Sämtliche Schriften und Briefe,* ed. Deutsche [before 1945, Preussische] Akademie der Wissenschaften. Berlin: Akademie Verlag.

Leibniz, Gottfried Wilhelm (1948). *Textes inédits d'après les manuscrits de la bibliothèque provinciale de Hanovre,* ed. G. Grua (2 vols.). Paris: Presses Universitaires de France.

Leibniz, Gottfried Wilhelm (1951). *Theodicy,* trans. E. M. Huggard. London: Routledge.

Leibniz, Gottfried Wilhelm (1957). *The Preface to Leibniz' Novissima Sinica,* ed., trans., comm. Donald Lach. Honolulu: University of Hawaii Press.

Leibniz, Gottfried Wilhelm (1960). *Fragmente zur Logik,* ed. F. Schmidt. Berlin: Akademie-Verlag.

Leibniz, Gottfried Wilhelm (1966). *Logical Papers,* ed. and trans. G. H. R. Parkinson. Oxford: Oxford University Press.

Leibniz, Gottfried Wilhelm (1967). *The Leibniz-Arnauld Correspondence,* ed. and trans. H. T. Mason. Manchester: Manchester University Press.

Leibniz, Gottfried Wilhelm (1968). *Zwei Briefe über das binäre Zahlensystem und die chinesische Philosophie,* trans. (German) Renate Loosen and Franz Vonessen. Stuttgart: Belser-Presse.

Leibniz, Gottfried Wilhelm (1969). *Philosophical Papers and Letters,* ed. and trans. L. E. Loemker. Dordrecht: Reidel.

Leibniz, Gottfried Wilhelm (1972). *The Political Writings of Leibniz,* ed. and trans. Patrick Riley. Cambridge: Cambridge University Press.

Leibniz, Gottfried Wilhelm (1973). *Philosophical Writings,* ed. G. H. R. Parkinson, trans. M. Morris and G. H. R. Parkinson. London: Dent.

Leibniz, Gottfried Wilhelm (1977). *Discourse on the Natural Theology of the Chinese*, trans. Daniel J. Cook and Henry Rosemont, Jr. Honolulu: University of Hawaii Press.

Leibniz, Gottfried Wilhelm (1979a). *Analysis particularum*, in *Die intensionale Logik bei Leibniz und in der Gegenwart*, ed. Albert Heinekamp and F. Schupp (Studia Leibnitiana, Sonderheft). Stuttgart: Steiner.

Leibniz, Gottfried Wilhelm (1979b). *Das Neueste von China (1697) – Novissima Sinica*, ed. and trans. (German) Heinz-Günther Nesselrath and Hermann Reinbothe. Cologne: Deutsche-China Gesellschaft.

Leibniz, Gottfried Wilhelm (1981). *New Essays on Human Understanding*, trans. P. Remnant and J. Bennett. Cambridge: Cambridge University Press.

Leibniz, Gottfried Wilhelm (1982a). *Generales inquisitiones de analysi notionum et veritatum*, ed. and trans. F. Schupp. Hamburg: Meiner.

Leibniz, Gottfried Wilhelm (1982b). *Specimen Dynamicum*, ed. and trans. (German) by H. G. Dosch, G. W. Most, and E. Rudolph. Hamburg: Meiner.

Leibniz, Gottfried Wilhelm (1982–91). *Vorausedition zur Reihe VI – philosophische Schriften – in der Ausgabe der Akademie [der Wissenschaften] der DDR [Berlin]* (10 vols.). Münster: Leibniz-Forschungssteller der Universität Münster.

Leibniz, Gottfried Wilhelm (1985). *Theodicy: Essays on the Goodness of God, the Freedom of Man and the Origin of Evil*, ed. A. Farrer, trans. E. M. Huggard. La Salle, Ill.: Open Court.

Leibniz, Gottfried Wilhelm (1988). *Discourse on Metaphysics and Related Writings*, ed. and trans. R. N. D. Martin and S. Brown. Manchester: Manchester University Press.

Leibniz, Gottfried Wilhelm (1989). *Leibniz: Philosophical Essays*, ed. and trans. R. Ariew and D. Garber. Indianapolis, Ind.: Hackett.

Leibniz, Gottfried Wilhelm (1990). *Leibniz korrespondiert mit China: Der Briefwechsel mit den Jesuiten Missionaren (1689–1714)*, ed. Rita Widmaier. Frankfurt: Klostermann.

Leibniz, Gottfried Wilhelm (1993). *Leibniz-Thomasius corresondance 1663–1672*, ed. and trans. (French) Richard Bodéüs. Paris: Vrin.

Leibniz, Gottfried Wilhelm (1994). *La réforme de la dynamique: De corporum concursu (1678) et autres textes inédits*, ed. and commentary Michel Fichant. Paris: Vrin.

Leibniz, Gottfried Wilhelm (forthcoming). *The Leibniz-Arnauld Correspondence*, ed. R. Finster, trans. S. Voss (The Yale Leibniz). New Haven, Conn.: Yale University Press.

Leibniz, G. W., and Clarke, Samuel (1717). *A Collection of Papers, Which Passed between the Late Learned Mr. Leibnitz and Dr. Clarke in the Years 1715 and 1716*. London.

Leibniz, G. W., and Clarke, Samuel (1956). *The Leibniz-Clarke Correspondence*, ed. H. G. Alexander. Manchester: Manchester University Press.

Leibniz, G. W., and Clarke, Samuel (1957). *Correspondance Leibniz-Clarke*, ed. André Robinet. Paris: Presses Universitaires de France.

[Lejeune, Père Antoine de Saint-Pierre] (1646). *La vie du R. P. Dom Eustache de S. Paul Asseline, Docteur de Sorbonne & Religieux de la Congregation de Nre Dame de Fueillens* [sic]. *Ensemble quelques opuscules spirituels utils, aux ames pieuses & religieuses. Le tout recueilly par un Religieux de la mesme Congregation*. Paris. (There is a copy of this rare work in the Bibliothèque Nationale, Paris, pressmark 8° Ln$^{27}$ 690.)

Lelevel, H. (1694). *La vraye et la fausse metaphysique, ou l'on refute les sentimens de M. Regis sur cette affaire*. Rotterdam.

Lemaire, P. (1901). *Le cartésianisme chez les bénédictins. Dom Robert Desgabets, son système, son influence et son école*. Paris: Alcan.

Le Moyne, Pierre (1640–3). *Les Peintures morales, où les passions sont représentées par tableaux . . .* (3 vols.). Paris.

Le Moyne, Pierre (1668). *La gallerie des femmes fortes*, 6th edn. Paris.

Lenders, W. (1980). 'Die Theorie der Argumentation bei Leibniz', in *Theoria cum Praxi. Akten des III.*

*Internationalen Leibniz-Kongresses, Hannover, 12–17.11.1977*, bd. III (Studia Leibnitiana, Supplementa). Stuttgart: Steiner.

Lennon, Thomas M. (1974a). 'Occasionalism and the Cartesian Metaphysic of Motion'. *Canadian Journal of Philosophy*. supp. 1:29–40.

Lennon, Thomas M. (1974b). 'The Inherence Pattern and Descartes' Ideas', *Journal of the History of Philosophy*. 12:43–52.

Lennon, Thomas M. (1977). 'Jansenism and the *Crise Pyrrhonienne*', *Journal of the History of Ideas*. 38:297–306.

Lennon, Thomas M. (1983a). 'Locke's Atomism', *Philosophy Research Archives*. 9:1–28.

Lennon, Thomas M. (1983b). 'The Leibnizian Picture of Descartes', in William R. Shea (ed.), *Nature Mathematized*. Dordrecht: Reidel, pp. 215–26.

Lennon, Thomas M. (1985). '*Veritas Filia Temporis:* Hume on Time and Causation', *History of Philosophy Quarterly*. 2:275–90.

Lennon, Thomas M. (1993). *The Battle of the Gods and Giants: The Legacies of Descartes and Gassendi, 1655–1715*. Princeton, N.J.: Princeton University Press.

Lennon, Thomas M.; Nicholas, John; and Davis, John (eds.) (1982). *Problems of Cartesianism*. Kingston and Montreal: McGill-Queen's University Press.

Lenoble, Robert (1971). *Mersenne ou la naissance du mécanisme*. 2d ed. Paris: Vrin. (First published in 1943.)

Lenzen, Wolfgang (1990). *Das System der Leibnizschen Logik* (Grundlagen der Kommunikation und Kognition). Berlin: de Gruyter.

Le Rees, François (1642). *Cursus philosophicus* (3 vols.). Paris.

Lerner, Ralph, and Mahdi, Muhsin, eds. (1972). *Medieval Political Philosophy: A Sourcebook*. Ithaca, N.Y.: Cornell University Press.

Leslie, Charles (1721). *Theological Works*. London.

Lessius, L. (1640). *Quinquaginta nomina Dei*. Brussels.

Letwin, S. R. (1976). 'Hobbes and Christianity', *Daedalus* (Cambridge, Mass.). 105:1–21.

Levi, Anthony (1964). *French Moralists: The Theory of the Passions 1585 to 1649*. Oxford: Oxford University Press.

Lévinas, E. (1983). 'Sur l'idée de l'infini en nous', in *La passion de la raison. Hommage à F. Alquié*, Paris: Presses Universitaires de France.

Lévy, Jean-Philippe (1939). *La Hiérarchie de preuves dans le droit savant du Moyen-Age. Depuis la Renaissance du droit romain jusqu'à la fin du XIVe siècle* (Annales de l'Université de Lyon). Paris: Société Anonyme.

Lewalter, E. (1967). *Spanisch-jesuitische und deutsch-lutherische Metaphysik des 17. Jahrhunderts*. 2d ed. Darmstadt: Wissenschaftliche Buchgesellschaft.

Leyden, W. von (1948). 'Locke and Nicole: Their Proofs of the Existence of God and Their Attitude towards Descartes', *Sophia* (Padova). 16:41–55.

Leyden, W. von (1956). 'John Locke and Natural Law', *Philosophy*. 31:23–35.

Leyden, W. von (1968). *Seventeenth-Century Metaphysics. An Examination of Some Main Concepts and Theories*. London: Duckworth.

Lezius, Friedrich (1900). *Der Toleranzbegriff Lockes und Pufendorfs. Ein Beitrag zur Geschichte der Gewissensfreiheit*. Leipzig: Dieterich (Repr. Darmstadt: Scientia, 1987.)

Lichtenstein, Aharon, (1962). *Henry More. The Rational Theology of a Cambridge Platonist*. Cambridge, Mass.: Harvard University Press.

Liddell, Henry G., and Scott, Robert (eds.) (1968). *A Greek-English Lexicon. . . .* 9th ed., ed. H. S Jones. Oxford: Oxford University Press.

Lieberwirth, R. (1955). *Christian Thomasius. Sein wissenschaftliches Lebenswerk. Eine Bibliographie*. Weimar: H. Böhlaus Nachfolger.

Lievers, Menno (1992). 'The Molyneux Problem', *Journal of the History of Philosophy*. 30:399–416.

Limborch, Philip van (1686). *Theologia Christiana*. Amsterdam.

Lindberg, Bo (1976). *Naturrätten i Uppsala 1655–1720*. Stockholm: Almqvist and Wiksell.

Lindberg, David C. (1967). 'Alhazen's Theory of Vision and Its Reception in the West', *Isis*. 58:321–41.

Lindberg, David C. (1970). *John Pecham and the Science of Optics: Perspectiva communis*. Madison: University of Wisconsin Press.

Lindberg, David C. (1976). *Theories of Vision from al-Kindi to Kepler*. Chicago: University of Chicago Press.

Lindberg, David C. (ed.) (1978). *Science in the Middle Ages* (The Chicago History of Science and Medicine). Chicago: University of Chicago Press.

Lindberg, David C. (1986). 'The Genesis of Kepler's Theory of Light: Light Metaphysics from Plotinus to Kepler', *Osiris*. 2d ser. 2:5–42.

Lindeboom, G. A. (1979). *Descartes and Medicine*. Amsterdam: Rodopi.

Lipsius, Justus (1586). *Epistolarum Centuria Prima*. London.

Lipsius, Justus (1589). *Politicorum sive civilis doctrinae libri sex*. Lyon.

Lipsius, Justus (1591). *Epistolarum Centuria Secunda*. London.

Lipsius, Justus (1601). *Epistolarum Centuria Tertia*. Antwerp.

Lipsius, Justus (1604a). *Manuductio ad Stoicam Philosophiam*. Antwerp.

Lipsius, Justus (1604b). *Physiologia Stoicorum*. Antwerp.

Lipsius, Justus (1604c). *Centuria Singularis ad Italos et Hispanos*. Antwerp.

Lipsius, Justus (1605a). *Centuria Singularis ad Germanos et Gallos*. Antwerp.

Lipsius, Justus (1605b). *Centuria Singularis ad Belgos*. Antwerp.

Lipsius, Justus (1607). *Epistolarum Centuria Quarta*. Antwerp.

Lipsius, Justus (1978–    ). *Epistolae*, ed. A. Gerlo et al. Brussels: Koninklijke Academie voor Wetenschappen.

Livet, P. (1978). 'Le Traitement de l'information dans le *Traité des Passions*'. *Revue philosophique française*. 168:3–35.

Livi-Bacci, Massimo (1992). *A Concise History of World Population,* trans. Carl Ipsen. Oxford: Blackwell.

Lloyd, A. C. (1972). 'On Augustine's Concept of a Person', in R. A. Markus (ed.), *Augustine: A Collection of Critical Essays*. Garden City, N.Y.: Doubleday, pp. 191–205.

Lloyd, A. C. (1990). *The Anatomy of Neoplatonism*. Oxford: Oxford University Press.

Lloyd, Genevieve (1984). *The Man of Reason: 'Male' and 'Female' in Western Philosophy*. Minneapolis: University of Minnesota Press.

Lloyd, S. A. (1992). *Ideals and Interests in Hobbes'* Leviathan. Cambridge: Cambridge University Press.

Locke, John (1683). *Identity of persons,* Bodleian Library MS Locke f. 7, p. 107.

Locke, John (1685). *An Essay concerning Humane Understanding* ('Draft C'). Unpublished ms., Pierpont Morgan Library.

Locke, John (1689). *Epistola de tolerantia*. Gouda.

Locke, John (1690a). *An Essay concerning Humane Understanding*. London.

Locke, John (1690b). *Two Treatises of Government*. London.

Locke, John (1690c). *A Second Letter concerning Toleration*. London.

Locke, John (1692). *A Third Letter for Toleration*. London.

Locke, John (1693). *Some Thoughts concerning Education*. London.

Locke, John (1695). *The Reasonableness of Christianity*. London.

Locke, John (1697a). *A Letter to the Right Rev. Edward Ld. Bishop of Worcester . . .* London.

Locke, John (1697b). *Mr. Locke's Reply to the Right Rev. the Lord Bishop of Worcester's Answer to His Letter*. London.

Locke, John (1699). *Mr. Locke's Reply to the Right Rev. the Lord Bishop of Worcester's Answer to His Second Letter*. London.

Locke, John (1708). *Some Familiar Letters between Mr. Locke, and Several of His Friends.* London.

Locke, John (1731). *An Abridgment of Mr. Locke's Essay Concerning Human Understanding,* abridged by John Wynne. 4th ed. London.

Locke, John (1755). *Essai Philosophique Concernant L'Entendement Humain,* trans. (French) Pierre Coste. 5th ed. Amsterdam and Leipzig. (Repr. ed. Emilienne Naert, Paris: Vrin, 1972.)

Locke, John (1812). *The Works,* 11th ed. (10 vols.). London.

Locke, John (1823). *The Works* (10 vols.). London. (Repr. Darmstadt: Scientia, 1963.)

Locke, John (1824). *The Reasonableness of Christianity, as Delivered in the Scriptures,* in *The Works of John Locke* (9 vols.), vol. 6. London.

Locke, John (1936). *An Early Draft of Locke's Essay, together with Excerpts from His Journals,* ed. R. I. Aaron and J. Gibb. Oxford: Oxford University Press.

Locke, John (1953). *Locke's Travels in France 1675–1679,* ed. John Lough. Cambridge: Cambridge University Press.

Locke, John (1954). *Essays on the Law of Nature,* ed. Wolfgang von Leyden. Oxford: Oxford University Press.

Locke, John (1961). *Scritti editi e inediti sulla tolleranza,* ed. C. A. Viano. Turin: Taylor.

Locke, John (1967a). *Two Treatises of Government* [1689], 2d ed., ed. P. Laslett. Cambridge: Cambridge University Press.

Locke, John (1967b). *Two Tracts on Government,* ed. P. Abrams. Cambridge: Cambridge University Press.

Locke, John (1968). *Some Thoughts concerning Education,* ed. James L. Axtell. Cambridge: Cambridge University Press.

Locke, John (1975). *An Essay concerning Human Understanding,* ed. Peter H. Nidditch. Oxford: Oxford University Press.

Locke, John (1976). *The Correspondence,* ed. E. S. de Beer (9 vols.). Oxford: Oxford University Press.

Locke, John (1987). *A Paraphrase and Notes on the Epistles of St. Paul to the Galatians, 1 and 2 Corinthians, Romans, Ephesians,* ed. A. W. Wainwright (2 vols.). Oxford: Oxford University Press.

Locke, John (1989). *Some Thoughts concerning Education,* ed. J. W. Yolton and J. S. Yolton. Oxford: Oxford University Press.

Locke, John (1990a). *Questions concerning the Law of Nature,* ed. and trans. R. Horwitz, Jenny Strauss Clay, and Diskin Clay. Ithaca, N.Y.: Cornell University Press.

Locke, John (1990b). *Drafts for the Essay concerning Human Understanding, and other Philosophical Writings,* ed. P. H. Nidditch and G. A. J. Rogers. Oxford: Oxford University Press.

Loeb, Louis (1981). *From Descartes to Hume.* Ithaca, N.Y.: Cornell University Press.

Loeb, Louis (1992). 'The Cartesian Circle', in J. Cottingham (ed.), *The Cambridge Companion to Descartes.* Cambridge: Cambridge University Press.

Loemker, Leroy E. (1955). 'Boyle and Leibniz', *Journal of the History of Ideas.* 16:22–43.

Loemker, Leroy E. (1972). *Struggle for Synthesis: The Seventeenth Century Background of Leibniz's Synthesis of Order and Freedom.* Cambridge, Mass.: Harvard University Press.

Lohr, Charles H. (1974). 'Renaissance Latin Aristotle Commentaries: Authors A-B', *Studies in the Renaissance.* 21:228–89.

Lohr, Charles H. (1975). 'Renaissance Latin Aristotle Commentaries: Authors C', *Renaissance Quarterly.* 28:689–741.

Lohr, Charles H. (1976). 'Renaissance Latin Aristotle Commentaries: Authors D-F', *Renaissance Quarterly.* 29:714–45.

Lohr, Charles H. (1977). 'Renaissance Latin Aristotle Commentaries: Authors G-K', *Renaissance Quarterly.* 30:681–741.

Lohr, Charles H. (1978). 'Renaissance Latin Aristotle Commentaries: Authors L-M', *Renaissance Quarterly.* 31:532–603.

Lohr, Charles H. (1979). 'Renaissance Latin Aristotle Commentaries: Authors N-Ph', *Renaissance Quarterly.* 32:529–80.

Lohr, Charles H. (1980). 'Renaissance Latin Aristotle Commentaries: Authors Pi-Sm', *Renaissance Quarterly.* 33:623–734.

Lohr, Charles H. (1982). 'Renaissance Latin Aristotle Commentaries: Authors So-Z', *Renaissance Quarterly.* 35:164–256.

Lohr, Charles [H.] (1986). 'The Pseudo-Aristotelian *Liber de causis* and Latin Theories of Science in the Twelfth Century', in J. Kraye et al. (eds.), *Pseudo-Aristotle in the Middle Ages: The 'Theology' and Other Texts.* London: Warburg Institute.

Lohr, Charles [H.] (1988). 'Metaphysics', in Schmitt, Skinner, and Kessler 1988, pp. 537–638.

Long, A. A. (1986). *Hellenistic Philosophy,* 2d ed. Berkeley: University of California Press.

Long, A. A., and Sedley, D. N. (1987). *The Hellenistic Philosophers.* Vol. 1. Cambridge: Cambridge University Press.

Lounela, J. (1978). *Die Logik im XVII. Jahrhundert in Finland* (Annales Academiae Scientiarum Fennicae, Dissertationes Humanarum Litterarum). Helsinki: Suamalainen Tiedeakatemia.

Lovejoy, A. O. (1908). 'Kant and the English Platonists', in *Essays Philosophical and Psychological in Honor of William James.* New York: Longmans, Green.

Lovejoy, A. O. (1923). 'Representative Ideas in Malebranche and Arnauld', *Mind.* 32:449–61.

Lovejoy, A. O. (1924). 'Reply to Professor Laird', *Mind.* 33:180–1.

Lovejoy, A. O. (1960). *The Great Chain of Being.* New York: Harper & Row.

Luce, A. A. (1934). *Berkeley and Malebranche.* Oxford: Oxford University Press. (2d ed., Oxford: Oxford University Press, 1967.)

Luce, A. A. (1968). 'Berkeley's Existence in the Mind', in C. B. Martin and D. M. Armstrong, *Locke and Berkeley: A Collection of Critical Essays.* Garden City, N.Y.: Doubleday.

Lucretius (1659). *De la nature des choses,* trans. Michel de Marolles. Paris.

Lucretius (1682a). *Les Oeuvres,* trans. Jacques Parrain (2 vols.). Paris.

Lucretius (1682b). *His Six Books De natura rerum,* trans. Thomas Creech. Oxford.

Luig, K. (1972). 'Zur Verbreitung des Naturrechts in Europa', *Tijdschrift voor Rechtsgeschedenis/Revue d'historie du droit.* 40:539–57.

Lukács, Ladislaus, S.J. (ed.). (1986). *Ratio atque institutio studiorum societatis Iesu (1586, 1591, 1599)* (Monumenta Paedagogica Societatis Iesu, vol. 5; Monumenta Historica Societatis Iesu, vol. 129). Rome: Institutum Historicum Societatis Iesu.

Lukens, David C. (1979). *An Aristotelian Response to Galileo: Honoré Fabri, S. J. (1608–1688), on the Causal Analysis of Motion.* Ph.D. diss., University of Toronto, 1979. Diss. Abst. Int. 1980, 40:6369-A.

Luther, Martin (1955–86). *Works,* ed. J. Pelikan et al. (55 vols.). St. Louis: Concordia, and Philadelphia: Fortress.

McCann, Edwin (1985). 'Lockean Mechanism', in Holland, A. J. (ed.), *Philosophy, Its History and Historiography.* Dordrecht: Reidel.

McCann, Edwin (1987). 'Locke on Identity: Matter, Life, and Consciousness', *Archiv für Geschichte der Philosophie.* 69:54–77.

McClaughlin, Trevor (1979). 'Censorship and Defenders of the Cartesian Faith in Mid-Seventeenth Century France', *Journal of the History of Ideas.* 40:563–81.

McColley, Grant (1939). 'Nicholas Hill and the *Philosophia Epicurea*', *Annals of Science.* 4:390–405.

McCracken, Charles J. (1983). *Malebranche and British Philosophy.* Oxford: Oxford University Press.

McCracken, Charles J. (1986), 'Stages on a Cartesian Road to Immaterialism', *Journal of the History of Philosophy.* 24:19–40.

McCullough, Laurence B. (1977). 'Leibniz on the Identity of Relations', *Southwestern Journal of Philosophy.* 8:31–40.

McCullough, Laurence B. (1978). 'Leibniz and Traditional Philosophy', *Studia Leibnitiana*. 10:254–70.

McCullough, Laurence B. (1988). 'Leibniz on Individuals and Individuation: How the Mature Philosophy Resolves Problems of the Earliest Philosophy', in A. Heinekamp (ed.), *Leibniz. Tradition und Aktualität. V. Internationaler Leibniz-Kongress. Vorträge.* Hannover: Gottfried-Wilhelm-Leibniz-Gesellschafte, pp. 542–6.

Macdonald, Hugh, and Hargreaves, Mary (1952). *Thomas Hobbes: A Bibliography.* London: The Bibliographical Society.

McEvoy, James (1982). *The Philosophy of Robert Grosseteste.* Oxford: Oxford University Press.

McGrath, A. E. (1985). *Luther's Theology of the Cross: Martin Luther's Theological Breakthrough.* Oxford: Blackwell.

McGrath, A. E. (1986). *Iustitia Dei. A History of the Christian Doctrine of Justification* (2 vols.). Cambridge: Cambridge University Press.

McGuire, J. E. (1967). 'Transmutation and Immutability: Newton's Doctrine of Physical Qualities', *Ambix.* 14:69–95.

McGuire, J. E. (1968). 'Force, Active Principles and Newton's Invisible Realm', *Ambix.* 15:154–208.

McGuire, J. E. (1970). 'Atoms and the "Analogy of Nature": Newton's Third Rule of Philosophizing', *Studies in the History and Philosophy of Science.* 1:3–58.

McGuire, J. E. (1972). 'Boyle's Conception of Nature', *Journal of the History of Ideas.* 33:523–42.

McGuire, J. E. (1977). 'Neoplatonism and Active Principles: Newton and the *Corpus Hermeticum*', in Westman and McGuire 1977, pp. 95–142.

McGuire, J. E. (1978a). 'Existence, Actuality and Necessity: Newton on Space and Time', *Annals of Science.* 35:463–508.

McGuire, J. E. (1978b). 'Newton on Place, Time, and God: An Unpublished Source', *British Journal for the History of Science.* 11:114–29.

McGuire, J. E., and Rattansi, P. M. (1966). 'Newton and the "Pipes of Pan"', *Notes and Records of the Royal Society.* 21:108–43.

Machiavelli, Niccolò. (1560). *The Art of War,* trans. Peter Whitehorne. London. (Repr. New York: AMS Press, 1967.)

Machiavelli, Niccolò (1640). *The Prince,* trans. Edward Dacres. (Repr. New York: AMS Press, 1967.)

MacIntyre, Alasdair (1984). *A Short History of Ethics.* London etc.: Routledge.

McKeon, Michael (1976). 'Sabbatai Zevi in England', *Association for Jewish Studies Review.* 1:131–69.

Mackie, J. L. (1976). *Problems from Locke.* Oxford: Oxford University Press.

McLachlan, H. J. (1951). *Socinianism in Seventeenth-Century England.* Oxford: Oxford University Press.

McLaughlin, Peter (1993). 'Descartes on Mind–Body Interaction and the Conservation of Motion', *Philosophical Review.* 102:155–82.

Maclean, Ian (1977). *Woman Triumphant: Feminism in French Literature 1610–1652.* Oxford: Oxford University Press.

Maclean, J. (1959). *De historische Outwikkeling van Stootwetten van Aristoteles tot Huygens.* Rotterdam: Van Sijn.

MacLean, Kenneth (1962). *John Locke and English Literature of the Eighteenth Century.* New York: Russell & Russell.

McMullin, Ernan (ed.) (1965). *The Concept of Matter in Greek and Medieval Philosophy.* Notre Dame, Ind.: University of Notre Dame Press.

McMullin, Ernan (1978a). *Newton on Matter and Activity.* Notre Dame, Ind.: University of Notre Dame Press.

McMullin, Ernan (1978b). 'The Conception of Science in Galileo's Work', in Robert E. Butts and Joseph C. Pitt (eds.), *New Perspectives on Galileo.* Dordrecht: Reidel, pp. 209–57.

McMullin, Ernan (1978c). *The Concept of Matter in Modern Philosophy.* Notre Dame, Ind.: University of Notre Dame Press.

McMurrich, J. P. (1913). 'The Legend of the "Resurrection Bone"', *Transactions of the Royal Canadian Institute.* 9:45–51.

McNeill, J. T. (1946). 'Natural Law in the Teaching of the Reformers', *Journal of Religion.* 26:168–83.

McNeilly, F. S. (1968). *The Anatomy of Leviathan.* London: Macmillan.

Macpherson, C. B. (1962). *The Political Theory of Possessive Individualism. Hobbes to Locke.* Oxford: Oxford University Press.

McRae, Robert (1965). '"Idea" as a Philosophical Term in the Seventeenth Century', *Journal of the History of Ideas.* 26:175–90.

McRae, Robert (1972). 'Innate Ideas', in R. J. Butler (ed.) *Cartesian Studies.* Oxford: Blackwell.

McRae, Robert (1976). *Perception, Apperception, and Thought.* Toronto: University of Toronto Press.

McRae, Robert (1985). 'Miracles and Laws', in K. Okruhlik and J. Brown (eds.), *The Natural Philosophy of Leibniz.* Dordrecht: Reidel.

Madden, Edward H. (1957). 'Aristotle's Treatment of Probability and Signs', *Philosophy of Science.* 24:167–72.

Madden, Edward H. (ed.) (1960). *Theories of Scientific Method: The Renaissance Through the Nineteenth Century.* Seattle: University of Washington Press.

Maddison, R. E. W. (1969). *The Life of the Honourable Robert Boyle, F.R.S.* London: Taylor and Francis.

Madeira Arrais, Duarte (1650). *Novae philosophiae et medicinae de qualitatibus occultis.* Lisbon.

Magaillans (Magalhaes), Gabriel de, S.J. (1670). *Nouvelle relation de la Chine.* Paris.

*Magia Naturalis und die Entstehung der modernen Naturwissenschaften* (1978). (Studia Leibnitiana, Sonderheft 7). Wiesbaden: Steiner.

Magirus, Johannes (1642). *Johannis Magiri Physiologiae Peripateticae libri sex, cum commentariis: additis insuper notis quibusdam marginalibus, in posterioribus editionibus omissis: unà cum definitionibus, divisionibus, axiomatis, Graecè, ex Aristotele petitis. Quibus accessit Caspari Bartholini Malmogii Dani Metaphysica major, scholiis insignibus illustrata, & ab ipso autore edita. Accessit denique Johannis Magiri De memoria artificiosa liber singularis, in quatuor tractatus divisus . . .* Cambridge. (1st ed. Frankfurt 1597.)

Magnen, Jean Chrysostom (1646). *Democritus reviviscens sive de atomis . . . addita est Democriti vita cum indicibus necessariis.* Pavia.

Mahnerus, Adam (1623). *Disputatio IV. problematum philosophorum, in Academia Wittenbergensi proposita, praeside Iacobo Martini. . . .* Wittenberg.

Mahoney, Edward P. (1982). 'Sense, Intellect, and Imagination in Albert, Thomas, and Siger', in Kretzmann, Kenny, and Pinborg 1982, pp. 602–22.

Mahoney, Michael S. (1968). 'Another Look at Greek Geometrical Analysis', *Archive for History of Exact Sciences.* 5:318–48.

Mahoney, Michael S. (1980). 'Christiaan Huygens, The Measurement of Time and Longitude at Sea', in H. J. M. Bos et al. (eds.), *Studies on Christiaan Huygens.* Lisse: Swets, pp. 234–70.

Mahoney, Michael S. (1990). 'Barrow's Mathematics: Between Ancients and Moderns', in M. Feingold (ed.), *Before Newton: The Life and Times of Isaac Barrow.* Cambridge: Cambridge University Press, chap. 3.

Mahoney, Michael S. (1993). 'Algebraic vs. Geometric Techniques in Newton's Determination of Planetary Orbits', in Paul Theerman and Adele F. Seeff (eds.), *Action and Reaction: Proceedings of a Symposium to Commemorate the Tercentenary of Newton's* Principia. Newark: University of Delaware Press; London and Toronto: Associated University Presses, pp. 183–205.

Mahoney, Michael S. (1994). *The Mathematical Career of Pierre de Fermat,* 2d rev. ed. Princeton, N.J.: Princeton University Press. (1st ed., Princeton, 1973.)

Maier, Anneliese (1955). 'Die naturphilosophische Bedeutung der scholastischen Impetustheorie', *Scholastik.* 30:321–43.

Maier, Anneliese (1968). *Zwei Grundprobleme der scholastischen Naturphilosophie* (3d ed.). Rome: Storia e Letteratura.

Maistrov, L. E. (1974). *Probability Theory. A Historical Sketch,* trans. Samuel Kotz. New York: Academic.

Malagola, Carlo, ed. (1888). *Statuti delle universita a dei collegi dello studio Bolognese.* Bologna: N. Zanichelli.

Malebranche, Nicolas (1674–5). *De la recherche de la verité: ou l'on traitte de la nature de l'esprit de l'homme, & de l'usage qu'il en doit faire pour éviter l'erreur dans les sciences* (2 vols). Paris.

Malebranche, Nicolas (1680). *Traité de la nature et de la grâce.* Amsterdam.

Malebranche, Nicolas (1683). *Traité de Morale.* Cologne.

Malebranche, Nicolas (1688). *Entretiens sur la métaphysique.* Rotterdam.

Malebranche, Nicolas (1708). *Entretien d'un philosophe crétien et d'un philosophe chinois sur l'existence et la nature de Dieu.* Paris.

Malebranche, Nicolas (1715). *Réflexions sur la prémotion physique.* Paris.

Malebranche, Nicolas (1948). *Entretiens sur la métaphysique.* Paris: Vrin.

Malebranche, Nicolas (1958–84). *Oeuvres complètes.* ed. André Robinet (20 vols.). Paris: Vrin.

Malebranche, Nicolas (1980a). *The Search after Truth,* trans. T. M. Lennon and P. J. Olscamp. Columbus: Ohio State University Press.

Malebranche, Nicolas (1980b). *Dialogues on Metaphysics,* trans. W. Doney. New York: Abaris Books.

Malebranche, Nicolas (1980c). *Dialogue between a Christian Philosopher and a Chinese Philosopher on the Existence and Nature of God,* trans. Dominick A. Iorio. Washington, D.C.: Catholic University Press of America.

Malebranche, Nicolas (1992a). *Philosophical Selections. . . ,* trans. T. M. Lennon, P. J. Olscamp et al., ed. Steven Nadler. Indianapolis, Ind., and Cambridge, Mass.: Hackett.

Malebranche, Nicolas (1992b). *Treatise on Nature and Grace,* trans. Patrick Riley. Oxford: Oxford University Press.

Malherbe, Michel (1984). *Thomas Hobbes ou l'oeuvre de la raison.* Paris: Vrin.

Mallet, Charles Edward (1968). *A History of the University of Oxford* (3 vols.). New York and London: Barnes and Noble and Methuen.

Malvezzi, Virgilio (1632). *Il Tarquinio superbo.* Bologna.

Malvezzi, Virgilio (1634). *Davide perseguitato.* Bologna.

Malvezzi, Virgilio (1648). *Considerazioni con occasione d'alcuni luoghi delle vite d'Alcibiade e di Coriolano.* Bologna.

Mandonnet, Pierre Félix. (1908–11). *Siger de Brabant et l'averroisme latin au XIIIe siècle* (2 vols.). Louvain: Institut Supérieur de Philosophie de l'Université de Louvain.

Mandrou, Robert (1980). *Magistrats et sorciers en France au XVIIe siècle: Une Analyse de psychologie historique.* Paris: Seuil.

Manlove, Timothy (1697). *The Immortality of the Soul Asserted, and Practically Improved.* London.

Manuel, Frank (1963). *Isaac Newton, Historian.* Cambridge, Mass.: Harvard University Press.

Manuel, Frank (1974). *The Religion of Isaac Newton.* Oxford: Oxford University Press.

Marana, G. P. (1753). *Letters Writ by a Turkish Spy* (8 vols.). London.

Marandé, Léonard (1642). *Abrégé curieux de toute la philosophie.* Paris.

Marci von Kronland, Joannis Marcus (1639). *De proportione motus, seu Regula sphygmica ad celeritatem et tarditatem pulsuum ex illius motu ponderibus geometricis librato absque errore metiendam. Authore Ioanne Marco Marci Phil^{ae} et Medic^{ae} Doctore et ordinario Professore eiusdam Medic. facultatis in Universitate Pragensi, Physico Reg. Boh.* Prague. (Repr. in *Acta historiae rerum naturalium necnon technicarum: Czechoslovak Studies in the History of Science,* No. 3 (Special Issue, 1967): 131–258.)

Marci von Kronland, Joannis Marcus (1683). *Otho-sophia, seu Philosophia impulsus universalis Joannis Marci Marci à Kronland, Boëmi Landskronensis . . . opus posthumum nuperrimè in ejusdem authoris liturgia mentis promissum . . . nunc primum cum aenis figuris in lucem editum à Jacobo Joanne Wenceslao Dobrzensky de Nigro Ponte. . . .* Prague.

Marías-Aguilera, Julian (1954). 'San Anselmo y el Insensato', in J. Marías-Aguilera (ed.), *San Anselmo y el insensato: y otros estudios de filosofía*, 2d ed., Madrid: Revista de Occidente, pp. 5–32.

Marion, J.-L. (1975). *Sur l'ontologie grise de Descartes*. Paris: Vrin. (2d ed. 1981.)

Marion, J.-L. (1977). *L'idole et la distance*. Paris: Grasset.

Marion, J.-L. (1981). *Sur la théologie blanche de Descartes*. Paris: Presses Universitaires de France.

Marion, J.-L. (1982). *Dieu sans l'être*. Paris: Fayard.

Marion, J.-L. (1985). 'De la création des vérités éternelles au principe de raison suffisante. Remarques sur l'anti-cartésianisme de Spinoza, Malebranche et Leibniz', *XVIIe siècle*. 147:143–64.

Marion, J.-L. (1986a). *Sur le prisme métaphysique de Descartes. Constitution et limites de l'onto-théo-logie dans la pensée cartésienne*. Paris: Presses Universitaires de France.

Marion, J.-L. (1986b). 'The Essential Incoherence of Descartes' Definition of Divinity', in Rorty 1986a.

Marion, J.-L. (1987). 'Le statut métaphysique du *Discours de la Méthode*', in Jean-Luc Marion and Nicolas Grimaldi (eds.), *Le Discours et sa méthode*. Paris: Presses Universitaires de France.

Marion, J.-L. (1991a). *Questions Cartésiennes*. Paris: Presses Universitaires de France.

Marion, J.-L. (1991b). 'The Coherence of Spinoza's Definitions of God in *Ethics* I, Proposition 11', in Y. Yovel (ed.), *God and Nature: Spinoza's Metaphysics*. Leiden: Brill.

Marion, J.-L. (1991c). *God without Being*. Chicago: University of Chicago Press. (Trans. of Marion 1982.)

Marion, J.-L. (1992). 'Is the Ontological Argument Ontological?', *Journal of the History of Philosophy*. 30:201–18.

Marion, J.-L. (1994). "Entre analogie et principe de raison – la *causa sui*', in J.-M. Beyssade and J.-L. Marion, eds., *Descartes. Méditer, objecter, répondre*. Paris: Presses Universitaires de France.

Mark, T. C. (1977). 'The Spinozistic Attributes', *Philosophia*. 7:55–82.

Markie, Peter (1992). 'The Cogito and Its Importance', in J. Cottingham (ed.), *Cambridge Companion to Descartes*. Cambridge: Cambridge University Press.

Marks, Carol L. (1966). 'Thomas Traherne and Cambridge Platonism', *Publications of the Modern Language Association*. 81:521–34.

Markus, R. A. (1967). 'Augustine: Biographical Introduction: Christianity and Philosophy', in Armstrong 1967, pp. 341–53.

Marlin, Randal (1985). 'Cartesian Freedom and the Problem of the Mesland Letters', in Georges J. D. Moyal and Stanley Tweyman (eds.), *Early Modern Philosophy: Metaphysics, Epistemology, and Politics: Essays in Honour of Robert F. McRae*. Delmar N.Y.: Caravan.

Marshall, John (1994). *John Locke. Resistance, Religion, and Responsibility*. Cambridge: Cambridge University Press.

Martin, Gottfried (1964). *Leibniz, Logic and Metaphysics*, trans. K. J. Northcott and P. G. Lucas. Manchester: Manchester University Press.

Martin, H.-J. (1969). *Livre, Pouvoirs et Société à Paris au XVIIe siècle (1598–1701)* (2 vols.). Geneva: Droz.

Martin, Julian (1992). *Francis Bacon, the State, and the Reform of Natural Philosophy*. Cambridge: Cambridge University Press.

Martini, Martino, S.J. (1658). *Sinicae historiae decas prima*. Munich.

Martinich, A. P. (1992). *The Two Gods of* Leviathan: *Thomas Hobbes on Religion and Politics*. Cambridge: Cambridge University Press.

Mas, Diego (1599). *Commentarii in universam philosophiam Aristotelis* (2 vols.). Valencia.

Masères, Francis (1795). *The Doctrine of Permutations and Combinations*. London.

Massa, Daniel (1977). 'Giordano Bruno's Ideas in Seventeenth-Century England', *Journal of the History of Ideas*. 38:227–42.

Massault, J. P. (1961). 'Thomisme et Augustinisme dans l'apologétique du 17ème siècle', *Revue des Sciences Philosophiques et Théologiques*. 44:617–38.

Mates, Benson (1980). 'Nominalism and Evander's Sword', in *Theoria cum Praxi. Akten des III. Internationalen Leibniz-Kongresses, Hannover, 12–17.11.1977, bd. III* (Studia Leibnitiana, Supplementa 21). Stuttgart: Steiner.

Mates, Benson (1986). *The Philosophy of Leibniz: Metaphysics and Language.* Oxford: Oxford University Press.

Matheron, Alexandre (1969). *Individu et communauté chez Spinoza.* Paris: Minuit.

Matheron, Alexandre (1971). *Le Christ et le salut des ignorants chez Spinoza.* Paris: Aubier.

Mattern, Ruth (1980a). 'Moral Science and the Concept of Person in Locke', *Philosophical Review.* 89:24–45.

Mattern, R[uth]. M. (1980b). 'Locke on Active Power and the Obscure Idea of Active Power from Bodies', *Studies in the History and Philosophy of Science.* 11:39–77.

Mauss, Marcel (1972). *A General Theory of Magic.* London: Routledge.

Mauss, Marcel (1985). 'A Category of the Human Mind: The Notion of Person; the Notion of Self', trans. W. D. Halls, in M. Carrithers, S. Collins, S. Lukes (eds.), *The Category of the Person: Anthropology, Philosophy, History.* Cambridge: Cambridge University Press, pp. 1–25.

Mautner, Thomas (1986). 'Pufendorf and Eighteenth-Century Scottish Philosophy', in *Samuel von Pufendorf 1632–1982,* ed. K. Å. Modéer. Stockholm: Nordiska Bokhandeln, pp. 120–31.

Mautner, Thomas (1989). 'Pufendorf and the Correlativity Thesis of Rights', in S. Lindström and W. Rabinowics (eds.), *In So Many Words. Philosophical Essays dedicated to Sven Danielson on the Occasion of His Fiftieth Birthday.* Uppsala: Philosophical Studies Published by the Philosophical Society and the Department of Philosophy, University of Uppsala, no. 42, pp. 37–59.

May, William E. (1962). 'The God of Leibniz', *New Scholasticism.* 36:506–28.

Mayo, Thomas Franklin (1934). *Epicurus in England (1650–1725).* Dallas: Southwest Press.

Méchoulan, Henry (1987). 'Introduction' to Menasseh ben Israel, *The Hope of Israel.* Oxford: Oxford University Press.

Méchoulan, Henry (1989). 'Menasseh ben Israel and the World of the Non-Jew', in Y. Kaplan, H. Méchoulan, and R. Popkin (eds.), *Menasseh ben Israel and His World.* Leiden: Brill.

Mede, Joseph (1651). *Clavis Apocalyptica, or a Prophetical Key.* London. (First published in Latin, Cambridge, 1627.)

Medick, H. (1973). *Naturzustand und Naturgeschichte der bürgerlichen Gesellschaft. Die Ursprünge der bürgerlichen Socialtheorie als Geschichtsphilosophie und Sozialwissenschaft bei Samuel Pufendorf, John Locke und Adam Smith.* Göttingen: Vandenhoeck und Ruprecht.

Mehta, Uday Singh (1992). *The Anxiety of Freedom. Imagination and Individuality in Locke's Political Thought.* Ithaca, N.Y.: Cornell University Press.

Meinel, Christoph (1988a). 'Early Seventeenth-century Atomism: Theory, Epistemology and the Insufficiency of Experiment', *Isis.* 79:68–103.

Meinel, Christoph (1988b). '"Das letzte Blatt im Buch der Natur": Die Wirklichkeit der Atome und die Antinomie der Anschauung in den Korpuskulartheorien der frühen Neuzeit', *Studia Leibnitiana.* 20:1–18.

Meinel, Christoph (1988c). 'Empirical Support for the Corpuscular Theory in the Seventeenth Century', in Diderik Batens and Jean Paul van Bendegem (eds.), *Theory and Experiment.* Dordrecht: Reidel, pp. 77–92.

Melanchthon, Philipp (1834–60). *Opera quae supersunt omnia,* ed. C. G. Bretschneider (28 vols.). Halle: Schwetschke.

Melles, Etienne de (1669a). *Novum totius philosophiae syntagma . . . Pars de moribus.* Paris.

Melles, Etienne de (1669b). *Selecta opuscula isagogica ad novum ejusdem syntagma.* Paris.

Melsen, Andrew G. van (1960). *From Atomos to Atom: The History of the Concept Atom.* New York: Harper and Brothers. (Earlier eds., 1949, 1952.)

Ménage, Gilles (1690). *Historia mulierum philosopharum.* Lyon.

Menasseh ben Israel (1636). *De Resurrectione Mortuorum*. Amsterdam.

Menasseh ben Israel (1656). *Vindicae Judaeorum* (London).

Menasseh ben Israel (1987). *The Hope of Israel*, ed. Méchoulan and Nahon, trans. Moses Wall. Oxford: Oxford University Press.

Mendoza, Juan Gonzalez de (1585). *Historia de la cosas, ritos, y costumbres, del gran Reyno de la China*. Rome. (Rev. ed. Rome, 1586.)

Menjot-d'Elbenne, S., Vicomte (1923). *Mme de la Sablière, ses pensées chrétiennes et ses lettres a l'abbé de Rancéd*. Paris: Plon-Nourrit.

Menn, Stephen (1989). 'Descartes and Augustine'. Ph.D. diss., University of Chicago.

Menzel, Johanna (1956). 'The Sinophilism of J. H. G. Justi', *Journal of the History of Ideas*. 17:300–10.

Mercer, Christia (1989). 'The Origins of Leibniz's Metaphysics and the Development of his Conception of Substance'. Ph.D. diss., Department of Philosophy, Princeton University.

Mercer, Christia (1990). 'The Seventeenth-Century Debate between the Moderns and the Aristotelians: Leibniz and the Philosophia Reformata', in I. Marchlewitz and A. Heinekamp (eds.), *Leibniz' Auseinandersetzung mit Vorgängern und Zeitgenossen* (Studia Leibniziana Supplementa, 27). Stuttgart: Steiner.

Mercer, Christia (1993). 'The Vitality and Importance of Early Modern Aristotelianism', in Tom Sorell (ed.), *The Rise of Modern Philosophy*. Oxford: Oxford University Press.

Mercer, Christia (forthcoming). *Leibniz's Metaphysics: Its Origins and Development*. Cambridge: Cambridge University Press.

Merchant, Carolyn (1979). 'The Vitalism of Anne Conway: Its Impact on Leibniz's Concept of the Monad', *Journal of the History of Philosophy*. 17:255–70.

Merchant, Carolyn (1980). *The Death of Nature: Women, Ecology, and the Scientific Revolution*. San Francisco: Harper & Row.

Mersenne, Marin (1623). *Quaestiones celeberimae in Genesim*. Paris.

Mersenne, Marin (1624). *L'impiété des déistes, athées et libertins de ce temps, combatue et renversée* (2 vols.). Paris. (Repr. (vol. 1) Stuttgart: Frommann, 1975.)

Mersenne, Marin (1625). *La verité des sciences*. Paris. (Repr. Stuttgart: Frommann, 1969.)

Mersenne, Marin (1634). *Questions théologiques; Les méchaniques de Galilée; Les préludes de l'harmonie universelle*. Paris.

Mersenne, Marin (1636–7). *Harmonie universelle contenant la theorie et la pratique de la musique*. Paris.

Mersenne, Marin (1644a). *Cogitata physico-mathematica*. Paris.

Mersenne, Marin (1644b). *Universae geometriae mixtaeque mathematicae synopsis*. Paris.

Mersenne, Marin (1932–88). *Correspondance du P. Marin Mersenne, religieux minime*, ed. C. de Waard et al. (17 vols.). Paris: Beauchesne (vol. 1), Presses Universitaires de France (vols. 2–4), CNRS (vols. 5–17).

Mersenne, Marin (1985). *Questions Inouyes*, ed. André Pessel. Paris: Fayard.

Meslier, J. (1972). 'Anti-Fénelon' (J. Deprun, ed.), in *Oeuvres complètes*, ed. J. Deprun, R. Desné, and A. Soboul (3 vols.), vol. 3. Paris: Anthropos.

Mesnard, Pierre (1936). *Essai sur la morale de Descartes*. Paris: Boivin & Cie.

Metzger, Hélène (1938). *Attraction universelle et religion naturelle chez quelques commentateurs anglais de Newton*. Paris: Hermann.

Metzger, Hélène (1969). *Les Doctrines chimiques en France du début du XVII$^e$ à la fin du XVIII$^e$ siècle*. Paris: Blanchard.

Meuvret, Jean (1971). 'Les données démographiques et statistiques en histoire moderne et contemporaine', in Jean Meuvret, *Etudes d'histoire économique*. Paris: Librairie Armand Colin, pp. 313–40.

Meyer, Louis [Meijer, Lodewijk] (1666). *Philosophia S. Scripturae interpres*. 'Eleutheropolis'. Amsterdam.

Meyer, Louis [Meijer, Lodewijk] (1988). *La Philosophie interprète de l'Ecriture Sainte*, trans. (French) J. Lagrée and P. Moreau. Paris: Intertextes éditeur.

Meyer, Michael (1991). *Le Philosophie et les Passions*. Paris: Librairie Générale Française.

Meylan, P. (1937). *Jean Barbeyrac (1674–1744)*. Lausanne: F. Rouge.

Michael, Reuven (1971). 'Spaeth, Johann Peter', in *Encyclopaedia Judaica* (16 vols.). New York: Macmillan.

Michel, P.- H. (1973). *The Cosmology of Giordano Bruno*. Ithaca, N.Y.: Cornell University Press.

Micraelius, Johann (1653). *Lexicon Philosophicum*. Jena.

Micraelius, Johann (1662). *Lexicon Philosophicum*, 2d ed. Stettin.

Mijuskovic, Ben Lazare (1974). *The Achilles of Rationalist Arguments* (International Archives of the History of Ideas). The Hague: Nijhoff.

Milano, Andrea (1969). 'Magia e teologia in Tommaso Campanella', in *Tommaso Campanella nel IV centenario della sua nascita. (1568–1968)*. Naples: EDI-Sapienza.

Millen, Ron (1985). 'The Manifestation of Occult Qualities in the Scientific Revolution', in Margaret J. Osler and P. L. Farber (eds.), *Religion, Science and Worldview*, Cambridge: Cambridge University Press.

Milton, J. R. (1981a). 'The Origin and Development of the Concept of the "Laws of Nature" ', *Archives européene de sociologie*. 22:173–95.

Milton, J. R. (1981b). 'John Locke and the Nominalist Tradition', in R. Brandt (ed.), *John Locke. Symposium Wolfenbüttel 1979*. Berlin: de Gruyter, pp. 128–145.

Milton, J. R. (1985). 'Lockean Mechanism: A Comment', in A. J. Holland (ed.), *Philosophy, Its History and Historiography*, Dordrecht: Reidel.

Milton, John (1931–8). *The Works of John Milton*, ed. Frank Allen Patterson et al. (18 vols.). New York: Columbia University Press.

Mintz, Samuel I. (1962). *The Hunting of Leviathan: Seventeenth-Century Reactions to the Materialism and Moral Philosophy of Thomas Hobbes*. Cambridge: Cambridge University Press.

Mittelstrass, Jürgen (1981). 'Substance and Its Concept in Leibniz', in G. H. R. Parkinson (ed.), *Truth, Knowledge and Reality, Inquiries into the Foundations of Seventeenth Century Rationalism* (Studia Leibnitiana, Sonderheft 9). Wiesbaden: Steiner.

Modéer, K. Å. (ed.) (1986). *Samuel von Pufendorf 1632–1982* (Skrifter Utgivna av Institutet för Rättshistorisk Forskning, Ser. II: Rättshistoriska Studier 12). Stockholm: Nordiska Bokhandeln.

Molina, Luis de (1953). *Liberi arbitrii cum gratiae donis, divina praescientia, providentia, praedestinatione et reprobatione concordia* (Lisbon, 1588; 2d ed. Antwerp, 1595), ed. Johann Rabeneck S.J. Oña: Collegium maximum S.I. and Madrid: Soc. edit. 'Sapientia'.

Molina, Luis de (1988). *On Divine Foreknowledge*, trans. Alfred Freddoso. Ithaca, N.Y.: Cornell University Press.

Molinos, Miguel de (1909). *The Spiritual Guide*, ed. Kathleen Lyttleton. London: Methuen.

Moll, Konrad (1978). *Der junge Leibniz* (2 vols.). Stuttgart-Bad Cannstatt: Frommann-Holzboog.

Molland, A.G. (1982). 'The Atomisation of Motion: A Facet of the Scientific Revolution', *Studies in History and Philosophy of Science*. 13:31–54.

Mondadori, Fabrizio (1990). Review of *The Philosophy of Leibniz*, by Benson Mates, *Philosophical Review*. 99:613–29.

Monod, Albert (1916). *De Pascal à Chateaubriand: Les défenseurs français du christianisme de 1670 à 1802*. Paris: Alcan.

Monsarrat, Gilles D. (1984). *Light from the Porch: Stoicism and English Literature*. Paris: Didier-Erudition.

Montagnes, B. (1963). *La doctrine de l'analogie de l'être d'après saint Thomas d'Aquin*. Paris and Louvain: Publications Universitaires de Louvain.

Montaigne, Michel de (1922). *Les Essais de Michel de Montaigne*, ed. Pierre Villey. Paris: Alcan.

Montaigne, Michel de (1962a). *Essais*, ed. M. Rat (2 vols.). Paris: Garnier.

Montaigne, Michel de (1962b). *Oeuvres complètes*. ed. Albert Thibaudet and Maurice Rat. Paris: Gallimard.

Montaigne, Michel de (1965). *Complete Essays,* trans. Donald Frame. Stanford, Calif.: Stanford University Press.

Montaigne, M. [de] (1967). *Oeuvres complètes,* ed. R. Barral and P. Michel. Paris: Seuil.

Montmort, Pierre (1713). *Essay d'analyse sur les jeux de hazard.* 2d ed. Paris.

Moore, J. (1988). 'Natural Law and the Pyrrhonian Controversy', in P. Jones (ed.), *Philosophy and Science in the Scottish Enlightenment.* Edinburgh: John Donald Publishers, pp. 20–38.

Moore, J. (1991). 'Theological Politics: A Study of the Reception of Locke's *Two Treatises of Government* in England and Scotland in the Early Eighteenth Century, in M. Thompson, ed., *Locke and Kant.* Berlin: Duncker and Humblot.

Moore, J., and Silverthorne, M. (1983). 'Gershom Carmichael and the Natural Jurisprudence Tradition in Eighteenth-century Scotland', in I. Hont and M. Ignatieff (eds.), *Wealth and Virtue. The Shaping of Political Economy in the Scottish Enlightenment.* Cambridge: Cambridge University Press, pp. 73–87.

Moore, J. and Silverthorne, M. (1984). 'Natural Sociability and Natural Rights in the Moral Philosophy of Gerschom Carmichael', in V. Hope (ed.), *Philosophers of the Scottish Enlightenment.* Edinburgh: Edinburgh University Press, pp. 1–12.

More, Henry (1646). *Democritus Platonissans: Or, An essay upon the Infinity of Worlds out of Platonick Principles.* Cambridge.

More, Henry (1653). *An Antidote against Atheisme, or an Appeal to the Natural Faculties of the Minde of Man, Whether There Be Not a God.* London.

More, Henry (1656). *Enthusiasmus triumphatus.* London and Cambridge.

More, Henry (1659). *The Immortality of the Soule, So Farre Forth As It Is Demonstrable from the Knowledge of Nature and the Light of Reason.* London.

More, Henry (1662a). *A Collection of Several Philosophical Writings of Dr Henry More. . . .* London (Repr. New York: Garland, 1978.)

More, Henry (1662b). *Henrici Mori Epistolae ad Renatum Descartes.* London. In More 1662a.

More, Henry (1662c). *An Antidote against Atheism, or An Appeal to the Natural Faculties of the Mind of Man, Whether there be not a God.* 3d ed. London. In More 1662a.

More, Henry (1662d). *The Immortality of the Soul.* London. In More 1662a.

More, Henry (1662e). *Enthusiasmus Triumphatus, or, A Brief Discourse of the Nature, Causes, Kinds, and Cure of Enthusiasm.* London. In More 1662a.

More, Henry (1664). *The Apology of Dr Henry More . . .* London.

More, Henry (1668). *Divine Dialogues, Containing Sundry Disquisitions and Instructions concerning the Attributes and Providence of God. The Three First Dialogues Treating of the Attributes of God, and His Providence at Large. Collected and Compiled by the Care and Industry of F. P. [Franciscus Palaeopolitanus]* (2 vols.). London.

More, Henry (1671). *Enchiridion metaphysicum: sive, de rebus incorporeis succincta & luculenta dissertatio. Pars prima: de exsistentia & natura rerum incorporearum in genere. In qua quamplurima mundi phaenomena ad leges Cartesii mechanicas obiter expenduntur, illiúsque philosophiae, & aliorum omnino omnium qui mundana phaenomena in causas purè mechanicas solvi posse supponunt, vanitas falsitásque detegitur.* London.

More, Henry (1675–9). *Opera omnia* (3 vols.). London.

More, Henry (1677a). *Fundamenta Philosophiae sive Cabbalae Aëto-Paedomelissaeae,* in Knorr von Rosenroth 1677, 'Apparatus in Librum Sohar, pars secunda', pp. 293–312.

More, Henry (1677b). 'Ad Clarrissimum . . . Virum, N. N. De Rebus in amica sua responsione contentis ulterior disquisitio', in Knorr von Rosenroth 1677.

More, Henry (1679a). *Opera philosophica* (2 vols.). London. (= More 1975–9, vols. 2–3.)

More, Henry (1679b). *Enchiridion ethicum, praecipua moralis philosophiae rudimenta complectens.* Amsterdam.

More, Henry (1680). *Apocalysis Apocalypseos; Or, the Revelation of St. John the Divine Unveiled.* London.

More, Henry (1681). *A Plain and Continued Exposition of the Several Prophecies or Divine Visions of the Prophet Daniel.* London.

More, Henry (1690). *An Account of Virtue or Dr More's Abridgment of Morals Put into English*, trans. E. Southwell. London.

More, Henry (1713). *Divine Dialogues, containing Sundry Disquisitions and Instructions concerning the Attributes and Providence of God. Collected and Compiled by the Care and Industry of Franciscus Palaeopolitanus [Henry More]. . . .* London. (First ed., London, 1668.)

More, Henry (1980). *The Immortality of the Soul*, ed. A. Jacob. The Hague: Martinus Nijhof.

More, Louis Trenchard (1944). *The Life and Works of the Honourable Robert Boyle*. London: Oxford University Press.

Moreau, Joseph (1967). *Pour ou contre l'insensé? Essais sur la preuve anselmienne*. Paris: Vrin.

Morford, Mark (1991). *Stoics and Neostoics: Rubens and the Circle of Lipsius*. Princeton, N.J.: Princeton University Press.

Moriconi, E. (1980). 'Sul concetto di relazione di Leibniz', *Annali della Scuola normale superiore di Pisa*. 10:577–638.

Morin, Jean-Baptiste (1635). *Quod Deus sit*. Paris.

Morisanus, Bernardus (1625). *In Aristotelis logicam, physicam, ethicam apotelesma. . . .* Frankfurt.

Mormino, Gianfranco (1990). 'La relatività del movimento negli scritti sull'urto di Christiaan Huygens', in *De motu: studi di storia del pensiero su Galileo, Hegel, Huygens e Gilbert* (Università degli Studi di Milano, Facoltà di Lettere e Filosofia. Quaderni di Acme 12). Milan: Cisalpino, Istituto Editoriale Universitario, pp. 107–38.

Mormino, Gianfranco (1993). *Penetralia motus. La fondazione relativistica della meccanica in Christiaan Huygens, con l'edizione del "Codex Hugeniorum 7A"* (Pubblicazioni della Facoltà di Lettere et Filosofia dell'Università di Milano, CLIII. Sezione a cura del Dipartimento di Filosofia, 21). Florence: La Nuova Italia.

Morpurgo-Tagliabue, Guido (1963). *I processi di Galileo e l'epistemologia*. Milan: Edizioni di Comunità.

Morse, JoAnn S. (1981). 'The Reception of Diophantus' Arithmetic in the Renaissance'. Ph.D. diss., Princeton University.

Moscato, A. (1968). 'Il libertinismo', in *Il pensiero moderno (Secoli 17–18)*, vol. 12 of *Grande Antologia Filosofica*. Milan: Carlo Mazorati, pp. 787–890.

Mossner, E. C. (1948). 'Hume's Early Memoranda 1729–1740', *Journal of the History of Ideas*. 9:492–518.

Mossner, E. C. (1954). *The Life of David Hume*. Austin, Texas: University of Texas Press.

Mossner, E. C. (1959). "Did Hume Ever Read Berkeley?": A Rejoinder to Professor Popkin', *Journal of Philosophy*. 56:992–5.

Moulin, Pierre Du (1644). *La philosophie, mise en francois, et divisee en trois parties, scavoir, elements de la logique, la physique ou science naturelle, l'ethyque ou science morale*. Paris.

Mouy, Paul (1934). *Le développement de la physique cartésienne 1646–1712*. Paris: Vrin.

Moyal, Georges J.D. (1987). 'The Unity of Descartes' Conception of Freedom', *International Studies in Philosophy*. 19:33–51.

Mugnai, M. (1978). 'Bemerkungen zu Leibniz' Theorie der Relationen', *Studia Leibnitiana*. 10:2–21.

Mugnai, M. (1979). 'Intensionale Kontexte und *termini reduplicativi* in der *Grammatica rationis* von Leibniz', in *Die intensionale Logik bei Leibniz und in der Gegenwart*, ed. Albert Heinekamp and F. Schupp (Studia Leibnitiana, Sonderheft). Stuttgart: Steiner.

Mugnai, M. (ed.) (1990). 'Leibniz's Logic'. *Topoi*. 9:1–90.

Mugnai, M. (1992). *Leibniz's Theory of Relations* (Studia Leibniziana, Supplementa). Stuttgart: Steiner.

Muirhead, John H. (1931). *The Platonic Tradition in Anglo-Saxon Philosophy*. London: Allen and Unwin.

Müller-Jahncke, Wolf-Dieter (1985). *Astrologisch-magische Theorie und Praxis in der Heilkunde der frühen Neuzeit*. Wiesbaden: Steiner.

Multhauf, Robert P. (1966). *The Origins of Chemistry* (Oldbourne History of Science Library). London: Oldbourne.

Mulvaney, R. J. (1968). 'The Early Development of Leibniz's concept of Justice', *Journal of the History of Ideas.* 29:53–72.

Mungello, D. E. (1977). *Leibniz and Confucianism: The Search for Accord.* Honolulu: University of Hawaii Press.

Mungello, D. E. (1980). 'Malebranche and Chinese Philosophy', *Journal of the History of Ideas.* 41:551–78.

Mungello, D. E. (1985). *Curious Land: Jesuit Accommodation and the Origins of Sinology.* Stuttgart: Steiner.

Mungello, D. E. (1987). 'Aus den Anfängen der Chinakunde in Europa 1687–1770', in Harmut Walravens (ed.), *China illustrata; Das europäische Chinaverständnis im Spiegel des 16. bis 18. Jahrhundert.* Weinheim: Acta Humaniora, VCH Verlagsgesellschaft.

Munitz, Milton K. (ed.) (1957). *Theories of the Universe: from Babylonian Myth to Modern Science.* New York: Free Press.

Muñoz Delgado, V. (1982). 'Lógica hispano-portuguesa e iberoamericana en el siglo XVII. Introdución doctrinal. Bibliografía. Fuentes impresas y manuscritas', *Cuadernos Salmantinos de filosofía.* 9:279–390.

Munz, P. (1952). *The Place of Hooker in the History of Thought.* London: Routledge and Paul.

Murdoch, John E., and Sylla, Edith D. (1978). 'The Science of Motion', in Lindberg 1978, pp. 206–64.

Nadler, Steven (1988a). 'Arnauld, Descartes, and Transubstantiation: Reconciling Cartesian Metaphysics and Real Presence', *Journal of the History of Ideas.* 49:229–46.

Nadler, Steven (1988b). 'Cartesianism and Port-Royal', *Monist.* 71:573–84.

Nadler, Steven (1989). *Arnauld and the Cartesian Philosophy of Ideas.* Princeton, N.J.: Princeton University Press.

Nadler, Steven (1990). 'Deduction, Confirmation, and the Laws of Nature in Descartes's *Principia Philosophiae*', *Journal of the History of Philosophy.* 28:359–83.

Nadler, Steven (1992). *Malebranche and Ideas.* Oxford: Oxford University Press.

Nadler, Steven (1993a). 'Occasionalism and General Will in Malebranche', *Journal of the History of Philosophy.* 31:31–48.

Nadler, Steven (ed.) (1993b). *Causation in Early Modern Philosophy.* University Park: Pennsylvania State University Press.

Nadler, Steven (1993c). 'The Occasionalism of Louis de la Forge', in Nadler 1993b, pp. 57–73.

Nadler, Steven (1994). 'Descartes and Occasional Causation', *British Journal for the History of Philosophy.* 2:35–54.

Nadler, Steven (forthcoming). 'Occasionalism and the Mind–Body Problem', in M. A. Stewart (ed.), *Oxford Studies in the History of Philosophy 2.* Oxford: Oxford University Press.

Nagel, Ernst (1955). *Principles of the Theory of Probability* (International Encyclopedia of Unified Science). Chicago: University of Chicago Press.

Nagel, T. (1959). 'Hobbes's Concept of Obligation', *Philosophical Review.* 68:68–83.

Naify, James (1975). 'Arabic and European Occasionalism'. Ph.D. diss., University of California, San Diego.

Namer, Emile (1980). *La Vie et l'oeuvre de J.C. Vanini, Prince des libertins, mort à Toulouse sur le bûcher en 1619.* Paris: Vrin.

Napoli, A. and Canziani, G., eds. (1990). *Hobbes oggi* (Atti del convegno 1988). Milan: Franco Angeli.

Nardi, Bruno (1965). *Studi su Pietro Pomponazzi.* Florence: Le Monnier.

Naudé, Gabriel (1623). *Instruction a la France sur la verité de l'histoire des freres de la roze-croix.* Paris.

Naudé, Gabriel (1625). *Apologie pour tous les grands personnages qui ont esté faussement soupçonnez de magie.* Paris.

Naudé, Gabriel (1627). *Advis pour dresser une bibliothèque.* Paris.

Naudé, Gabriel (1649). *Iugement de tout ce qui esté imprimé contre le Cardinal Mazarin, depuis le sixiéme Ianvier iusques à la declaration du premier Avril mil six cens quarante-neuf.* n.p.

Naudé, Gabriel (1701). *Naudeana et Patiniana ou Singularitez remaquables prises des conversations des mess. Naudé et Patin.* Paris.

Naudé, Gabriel (1950). *Advice on Publishing a Library,* ed. Archer Taylor. Berkeley: University of California Press.

Nauert, Charles G. (1965). *Agrippa and the Crisis of Renaissance Thought.* Urbana: University of Illinois Press.

Nauta, Doede (1935). *Samuel Maresius.* Ph.D. diss., Vrije Universiteit, Amsterdam.

Needham, Joseph (1951). 'Human Laws and the Laws of Nature in China and the West', *Journal of the History of Ideas.* 12:3–32, 194–231.

Needham, Joseph (1959). *Science and Civilization in China.* Vol. 3. Cambridge: Cambridge University Press.

Newman, William R. (1991). *The* Summa Perfectionis *of Pseudo-Geber: A Critical Edition, Translation and Study.* Collection des Travaux de l'Académie Internationale d'Histoire des Sciences, t. 35. Leiden: Brill.

Newman, William R. (1993). 'The Corpuscular Theory of J. B. Van Helmont and Its Medieval Sources', *Vivarium.* 31:161–91.

Newton, Isaac (1672). 'A Serie's of *Quere's* Propounded by Mr. *Isaac Newton,* to Be Determin'd by Experiment, Positively and Directly Concluding His New Theory of Light and Colours; and Here Recommended to the Industry of the Lovers of Experimental Philosophy', *Philosophical Transactions of the Royal Society of London.* 7:5004–7.

Newton, Isaac (1687). *Philosophiae naturalis principia mathematica.* London. (2d ed. London 1713; 3d. ed. London 1726.)

Newton, Isaac (1704). *Opticks.* London.

Newton, Isaac (1714–15). 'An Account of the Book entituled *Commercium Epistolicum*', *Philosophical Transactions of the Royal Society.* 29:173–224.

Newton, Isaac (1730). *Opticks, or a Treatise of the Reflections, Refractions, Inflections & Colours of Light.* 4th ed. London.

Newton, Isaac (1733). *Observations on Daniel and the Apocalypse of St. John.* London.

Newton, Isaac (1779–85). *Isaaci Newtoni opera quae exstant omnia* (5 vols.). London.

Newton, Isaac (1934). *Mathematical Principles of Natural Philosophy,* trans. Andrew Motte, rev. Florian Cajori. Berkeley: University of California Press.

Newton, Isaac (1952). *Opticks, or A Treatise of the Reflections, Refractions, Inflections & Colours of Light* (based on the 4th ed., London, 1730), foreword Albert Einstein, intro. Edmund Whittaker, pref. I Bernard Cohen, Analytical Table of Contents prep. Duane H. D. Roller. New York: Dover.

Newton, Isaac (1958). *Isaac Newton's Papers and Letters on Natural Philosophy and Related Document,* ed. I B. Cohen and R. E. Schofield. Cambridge, Mass.: Harvard University Press.

Newton, Isaac (1959–77). *The Correspondence of Isaac Newton,* ed. H. W. Turnbull, J. F. Scott, A. R. Hall, Laura Tilling (7 vols.). Cambridge: Cambridge University Press.

Newton, Isaac (1962). *Unpublished Scientific Papers of Isaac Newton,* ed. C. R. Hall and M. B. Hall. Cambridge: Cambridge University Press.

Newton, Isaac (1967–81). *The Mathematical Papers of Isaac Newton,* ed. D. T. Whiteside (8 vols.). Cambridge: Cambridge University Press.

Newton, Isaac (1972). *Isaac Newton's Philosophia Naturalis Principia Mathematica: The Third Edition with Variant Readings,* ed. Alexandre Koyré, I Bernard Cohen, and Anne Whitman (2 vols.). Cambridge, Mass.: Harvard University Press.

Newton, Isaac (1978). *Papers and Letters on Natural Philosophy,* ed. I Bernard Cohen. 2d ed. Cambridge, Mass.: Harvard University Press.

Newton, Isaac (1983). *Certain Philosophical Questions: Newton's Trinity Notebook,* ed. J. E. McGuire and Martin Tamny. Cambridge: Cambridge University Press.

Newton, Isaac (1984–      ). *Optical Papers of Isaac Newton,* ed. A. E. Shapiro. Cambridge: Cambridge University Press.

Nicholas, John (1978). 'Newton's Extremal Second Law', *Centaurus.* 22:108–30.

Nicholas of Amiens (1855). *De arte seu articulis fidei catholicae,* in J.-P. Migne (ed.), *Patrologia latina.* Paris, vol. 210, pp. 594–618.

Nicolaus of Autrecourt (1964). 'The First Letter to Bernard of Arezzo', trans. E. A. Moody, in Herman Shapiro (ed.), *Medieval Philosophy: Selected Readings from Augustine to Buridan.* New York: Modern Library.

Nicole, Pierre (1679). *Essais de morale* (2d ed.). Paris.

Nicole, Pierre (1684). *Les prétendus reformez convaincus de schisme.* Brussels.

Nicole, Pierre (1730). *Essais de morale* (13 vols.). Paris.

Nicole, Pierre (1755). *Oeuvres de controverse de M. Nicole* (6 vols.). Paris.

Nicolson, M. H. (1930). *The Conway Letters: The Correspondence of Anne, Viscountess Conway, Henry More, and their Friends, 1642–1684.* New Haven, Conn.: Yale University Press.

Nicolson, M. H., and Hutton, S. (1992). *The Conway Letters: the Correspondence of Anne, Viscountess Conway, Henry More, and Their Friends, 1642–1684.* Rev. ed. Oxford: Oxford University Press.

Nielsen, Lauge Olaf (1988). 'A Seventeenth Century Physician on God and Atoms: Sebastian Basso', in N. Kretzmann (ed.), *Meaning and Inference in Medieval Philosophy.* Dordrecht: Kluwer, pp. 297–369.

Niewöhner, Friedrich (1989). *Veritas sive Varietas. Lessings Toleranzparabel und das Buch von den drei Betrügern.* Heidelberg: Lambert Schneider.

Nizolio, Mario (1956). *De Veris principiis et vera ratione philosophandi contra pseudophilosophos,* ed. Quirinus Breen. Rome: Fratelli Bocca. [First ed. 1553; ed. G. W. Leibniz, 1671]

Noonan, John T., Jr. (1957). *The Scholastic Analysis of Usury.* Cambridge, Mass: Harvard University Press.

Normore, Calvin (1982). 'Future Contingents', in Kretzmann, Kenny, and Pinborg 1982, pp. 358–81.

Normore, Calvin (1986). 'Objective Being: Descartes and His Sources', in Rorty 1986a.

Norris, John (1694). *The Theory and Regulation of Love. A Moral Essay.* London.

Norris, John (1701–4). *An Essay towards the Theory of the Ideal or Intelligible World* (2 vols.). London. (Repr. New York: Garland, 1978.)

Novotný, František (1977). *The Posthumous Life of Plato.* The Hague: Nijhoff.

Nuchelmans, G. (1980). *Late-Scholastic and Humanist Theories of the Proposition.* Amsterdam: North-Holland.

Nuchelmans, G. (1983). *Judgment and Proposition. From Descartes to Kant.* Amsterdam: North-Holland.

Nuchelmans, G. (1986). 'The Historical Background to Locke's Account of Particles (*Essay,* III, 7)', *Logique et Analyse.* 29:53–71.

Nuchelmans, G. (1988). 'Geulincx' Containment Theory of Logic', *Mededelingen van de Koninklijke Nederlandse Akademie van Wetenschappen, Afdeling Letterkunde.* N.s., 51:265–317.

Nuchelmans, G. (1992). 'A 17th-Century Debate on the *Consequentia mirabilis*', *History and Philosophy of Logic.* 13:43–58.

Nutkiewicz, M. (1983). 'Samuel Pufendorf: Obligation as the Basis of the State', *Journal of the History of Philosophy.* 21:15–29.

Oakeshott, M. (1975). *Hobbes on Civil Association.* Oxford: Blackwell.

Oakley, Francis (1961). 'Christian Theology and the Newtonian Science: The Rise of the Concept of the Laws of Nature', *Church History.* 30:433–57. (Reprinted in *Creation: The Impact of an Idea,* ed. D. O'Connor and F. Oakley (1969). New York: Charles Scribner's Sons.)

re, John (1986). 'Locke and the Ethics of Belief', in A. Kenny (ed.), *Empiricism, Rationalism and* ...*ism*. Oxford: Oxford University Press.

, Constantinos Apostolos, ed. (1969). *The Cambridge Platonists*. Cambridge, Mass.: Harvard ...ersity Press.

Francesco (1581). *Discussiones Peripateticae*. Basle.

Francesco (1591). *Nova de Universis Philosophia*. Ferrara (2d ed., Venice, 1593). (Repr. with ...(Serbo-Croat), ed. Vladimir Filipović and Kruno Krstić, trans. Tomislav Ladan and Serafin ...Sveučilišna Naklada Liber: Zagreb, 1979.)

Laurentius (1616). *ANTIPRAKTIKON . . . Scholae ethicae, seu animadversiones piae. . . .* Ros-

...nston (1992). 'Leibniz and the Miracle of Freedom', *Nous*. 26:218–35.

...ancesco (1633). *Summa ethicae. . . .* Oxford.

...gon, and Maurice Kendall, eds. (1970). *Studies in the History of Statistics and Probability*. ...Conn.: Hafner.

...nn (1659). *An Exposition of the Creed*. London.

...rl (1925). 'James Bernoulli's Theorem', *Biometrika*. 17:201–210.

...d (1978). *The History of Statistics in the Seventeenth and Eighteenth Centuries*. London: Griffin.

...n (1970). *John Pecham and the Science of Optics, Perspectiva Communis*, ed. D. C. Lindberg. ...University of Wisconsin Press.

...rsti Møller (1980). 'Techniques of the Calculus, 1630–1660', in Ivor Grattan-Guinness ...*the Calculus to Set Theory, 1630–1910*. London: Duckworth.

...A. (1927–30). *Studies of the Spanish Mystics* (2 vols.). London: Shedlor.

...1934). *St. Thomas and the Problem of the Soul in the Thirteenth Century* (St. Michael's ...dies). Toronto: Saint Michael's College.

...Antonio (1988). *Francis Bacon's Idea of Science and the Maker's Knowledge Tradition*. Oxford: ...ersity Press.

...n (1966). *A Discourse of Conscience*, in Thomas F. Merrill (ed.), *William Perkins 1558–* ...*Puritanist*. Nieuwkoop: de Graaf.

...(1987). *Death and Immortality*. Dordrecht: Nijhoff.

...972). *Tractatus*, ed. L. M. De Rijk. Assen: Van Gorcum.

...7). *Greek Philosophical Terms: A Historical Lexicon*. New York and London: New York ...s and University of London Press.

...956). *Hobbes*. Harmondsworth: Penguin.

...967). *Hobbes*. 2d ed. London: Peregrine.

...21). *Geschichte der aristotelischen Philosophie im protestantischen Deutschland*. Leipzig: ...Stuttgart: Frommann, 1962.)

...T. (1956). *Sir Kenelm Digby: The Ornament of England, 1603–1665*. Cambridge, Mass.: ...ty Press.

...(1975). *Opere Latine*, ed. and trans. (Italian) Antonietta Bufano et al. (2 vols.). ...pografico-Editrice Torinese.

...92). *Descartes' Theory of the Will*. Durango, Colo.: Hollowbrook.

...*Discourse Made before the Royal Society, the 26 of November 1674. Concerning the Use* ...*ion in Sundry Important Particulars: Together with a New Hypothesis of Springing or* ...ondon.

...*Political Arithmetick*. London.

...*Les devins, ou commentaire des principales sortes de devinations: distingué en quinze* ...& *impostures de Satan sont descouvertes, solidement refutees, & separees d'avec les* ...*d'avec les predictions naturalles. Escrit en Latin par M. Gaspar Peucer, tresdocte*

Oakley, Francis (1984). *Omnipotence, Covenant and Order: An Excursion in the History of Ideas from Abelard to Leibniz*. Ithaca, N.Y.: Cornell University Press.

Oberman, Heiko (1981). *Forerunners of the Reformation*. Philadelphia: Fortress Press.

Ockham, William [of] (1967). *Philosophical Writings,* ed. and trans. P. Boehner. London and Edinburgh: Nelson.

Ockham, William [of] (1974–9). *Opera philosophica,* ed. P. Boehner, G. Gál, and S. Brown (3 vols.). Saint Bonaventure: Franciscan Institute.

O'Daly, G. (1987). *Augustine's Philosophy of Mind*. London: Duckworth.

Odonis, Gerardus (1500). *Sententia et expositio cum questionibus super libros Ethicorum Aristotelis. . . .* Venice.

Oestreich, Gerhard (1982). *Neostoicism and the Early Modern State*. Cambridge: Cambridge University Press.

Office of Population, Censuses and Surveys (Great Britain) (1982). *Census 1981: Historical Tables, 1801– 1981: England and Wales*. London: HMSO.

Okruhlik, K. (1985). 'The Status of Scientific Laws in the Leibnizian System', in K. Okruhlik and J. Brown (eds.), *The Natural Philosophy of Leibniz*. Dordrecht: D. Reidel.

Oldenburg, Henry (1965–86). *The Correspondence of Henry Oldenburg,* ed. A. Rupert Hall, Marie Boas Hall (13 vols.). Vols. 1–9 Madison: University of Wisconsin Press; vols. 10–11 London: Mansell; vols. 12–13 London: Taylor and Francis.

Oldrini, Guido (1985). 'Le particularità del ramismo inglese', *Rinascimento*. 25:19–80.

Oldrini, Guido (1987). 'L'etica "ramista" di William Temple', *Rinascimento*. 27:75–94.

Olivecrona, Knut Hans Karl (1971). *Law as Fact*. 2d ed. London: Stevens and Sons.

Olivecrona, Knut Hans Karl (1973). 'Das Meinige nach der Naturrechtslehre', *Archiv für Rechts- und Sozialphilosophie*. 59:197–205.

Olivecrona, Knut Hans Karl (1977). 'Die zwei Schichten im naturrechtlichen Denken', *Archiv für Rechts- und Sozialphilosophie*. 63:79–103.

O'Neill, Eileen (1987). 'Mind–Body Interaction and Metaphysical Consistency: A Defense of Descartes', *Journal of the History of Philosophy*. 25:227–45.

O'Neill, Eileen (1993). 'Influxus Physicus', in S. Nadler, (ed.), *Causation in Early Modern Philosophy*. University Park: Pennsylvania State University Press, pp. 27–55.

Ong, Walter J. (1958). *Ramus, Method, and the Decay of Dialogue: From the Art of Discourse to the Art of Reason*. Cambridge, Mass.: Harvard University Press.

*Oracles Chaldaïques* (1971). Ed. and trans. [French] Edouard Des Places. Paris: Les Belles Lettres.

Orcibal, Jean (1959). *La rencontre du Carmel thérésien avec les mystiques du Nord*. Paris: Presses Universitaires de France.

Orcibal, Jean (1965). *Le cardinal de Bérulle, évolution d'une spiritualité*. Paris: Cerf.

Oresme, Nicole (1968). *Le Livre du Ciel et du Monde,* ed. and trans. Albert Menut. Madison: University of Wisconsin Press.

Orobio de Castro, Isaac (1770). *Israel vengé, ou exposition naturelle des prophéties hébraiques que les chrétiens appliquent à Jésus, leur prétendu Messie*. London.

Orr, R. R. (1967). *Reason and Authority: The Thought of William Chillingworth*. Oxford: Oxford University Press.

Osler, Margaret J. (1983). 'Providence and Divine Will in Gassendi's Views on Scientific Knowledge', *Journal of the History of Ideas*. 44:549–560.

Osler, Margaret J. (1985a). 'Baptizing Epicurean Atomism: Pierre Gassendi on the Immortality of the Soul', in M. J. Osler and P. L. Farber (eds.), *Religion, Science, and Worldview*. Cambridge: Cambridge University Press, pp. 163–83.

Osler, Margaret J. (1985b). 'Eternal Truths and the Laws of Nature: The Theological Foundations of Descartes' Philosophy of Nature', *Journal of the History of Ideas*. 46:349–62.

Osler, Margaret J. (1991). 'Fortune, Fate and Divination: Gassendi's Voluntarist Theology and the Baptism of Epicurus', in Margaret J. Osler (ed.), *Atoms, Pneuma, and Tranquillity: Epicurean and Stoic Themes in European Thought*. Cambridge: Cambridge University Press, pp. 155–74.

Osler, Margaret J. (1993). 'Ancients, Moderns, and the History of Philosophy: Gassendi's Epicurean Project', in Tom Sorell (ed.), *The Rise of Modern Philosophy: The Tension between the New and Traditional Philosophies from Machiavelli to Leibniz*. Oxford: Oxford University Press, pp. 129–43.

Osler, Margaret J. (1994). *Divine Will and the Mechanical Philosophy: Gassendi and Descartes on Contingency and Necessity in the Created World*. Cambridge: Cambridge University Press.

Osterhorn, E.-D. (1962). *Die Naturrechtslehre Valentin Albertis*. diss., Albert-Ludwig-Universität, Freiburg i. B.

Othmer, Sieglinde C. (1970). *Berlin und die Verbreitung des Naturrechts in Europa. Kultur- und Sozialgeschichtliche Studien zu Jean Barbeyracs Pufendorf-Übersetzungen und eine Analyse seiner Leserschaft*. Berlin and New York: de Gruyter.

Overton, Richard (1644). *Mans Mortallitie*. Amsterdam. (Repr. English Reprints Series, Liverpool: Liverpool University Press, 1968.)

Owens, Joseph, C. SS. R. (1982). 'Faith, Ideas, Illumination, and Experience', in Kretzmann, Kenny, and Pinborg 1982, pp. 440–59.

Pacchi, Arrigo (1965). 'Ruggero Bacone e Roberto Grossatesta in un inedito Hobbesiano del 1634', *Rivista Critica di Storia della Filosofia*. 20:498–503.

Pacchi, Arrigo (1987). 'Hobbes and the Passions', *Topoi*. 6:111–19.

Pace, Anna de (1987). 'Descartes critico di Descartes: il concetto di quiete nelle leggi del moto da *Il Mondo* ai *Principi*', in *Miscellanea secentesca: saggi su Descartes, Fabri, White* (Università degli Studi di Milano, Facoltà di Lettere e Filosofia: Quaderni di Acme, 8). Milan: Cisalpino-Goliardica, pp. 9–49.

Pacho, E. (1980). 'Molinos', in Marcel Viller et al. (eds.) (1932–95), *Dictionnaire de spiritualité ascétique et mystique* (17 tomes in 21 vols.), t. 10, cols. 1486–1514. Paris: Beauchesne.

Pachtler, G. M. (ed.) (1887–94). *Ratio studiorum et Institutiones scholasticae Societatis Jesu, per Germaniam olim vigentes . . .* (Monumenta Germaniae Paedagogica, Band V)( 4 vols.). Berlin: A. Hoffmann & Comp.

Pagden, A. R. D. (1981). 'The "School of Salamanca" and the Affair of the Indies', *History of Universities*. 1:71–112.

Pagden, A. R. D. (1982). *The Fall of Natural Man: The American Indian and the Origins of Comparative Ethnology*. Cambridge: Cambridge University Press.

Pagden, A. R. D. (1987). 'Dispossessing the Barbarian: The Language of Spanish Thomism and the Debate over the Property Rights of the American Indians', in A. R. D. Pagden (ed.), *The Languages of Political Theory in Early-Modern Europe*. Cambridge: Cambridge University Press.

Pagel, Walter (1982). *Joan Baptista Van Helmont: Reformer of Science and Medicine*. Cambridge: Cambridge University Press.

Pagel, Walter (1984). *The Smiling Spleen: Paracelsianism in Storm and Stress*. Basel: Karger.

Palladini, F. (1978). *Discussioni seicentesche su Samuel Pufendorf. Scritti latini: 1663–1700* (Pubblicazioni del Centro di Studio per la Storia della Storiografia Filosophica 6). Bologna: Il Mulino.

Palladini, F. (1984). 'Le due lettere di Pufendorf al Barone di Boineburg: Quella nota e quella "perduta"', *Nouvelles de la république des lettres* (Naples). 1:119–44.

Palladini, F. (1990). *Pufendorf discepolo di Hobbes*. Bologna: Il Mulino.

Palladini, F. (forthcoming). 'Is the "Socialitas" of Pufendorf Really Anti-Hobbesian?' in H.-E. Bödeker and I. Hont (eds.), *Unsocial Sociability. Natural Law and the Eighteenth-Century Discourse on Society*. London: Routledge.

Pallavicino, Sforza (1644). *Del bene libri quattro*. Rome.

Pardies, Ignace-Gaston (1672). *Discours de la connoissance des bestes*. Paris. ( 1972.)

Pardies, Ignace-Gaston (1691). *Oeuvres de mathématiques*. The Hague.

Pardies, Ignace-Gaston (1696). *Oeuvres du R.P. Ignace-Gaston Pardies*. Lyor

Parfit, Derek (1985). *Reasons and Persons*. Oxford: Oxford University Pre

Parinetto, Luciano (1974). *Magia e ragione: Una polemica sulle streghe in It* Nuova Italia.

Park, Katharine (1981). 'Albert's Influence on Late Medieval Psych *Albertus Magnus and the Sciences*. Toronto: Pontifical Institute of Me

Park, Katherine (1988). 'The Organic Soul', in Schmitt, Skinner, an

Park, Katherine, and Kessler, Eckhard (1988). 'The Concept of Psy Kessler 1988, pp. 455–63.

Parker, Samuel (1666a). *An Account of the Nature and Extent of the Refer to the Origenian Hypothesis concerning the Preexistence of Soul Vanity and Groundlessness of the Hypothesis It Self*. London.

Parker, Samuel (1666b). *A Free and Impartial Censure of the Plat* York: AMS Press.)

Parkinson, G. H. R. (1969). 'Science and Metaphysics in *Akten des internationalen Leibniz-Kongresses, Hannover, 14–1 Naturwissenschaften* (Studia Leibnitiana Supplementa 2). Wi

Parkinson, G. H. R. (1982). 'The "Intellectualization of Ap Sensation and Thought' in Michael Hooker (ed.), *Leibni* lis: University of Minnesota Press.

Parkinson, G. H. R. (1993). 'Spinoza: Metaphysics and K *Renaissance and Seventeenth-Century Rationalism*, vol. ƒ Routledge, pp. 273–312.

Parr, S. (ed.) (1837). *Metaphysical Tracts by English Philoso* Hildesheim: Olms, 1974.)

Parrain, Jacques (1695). *La Morale d'Epicure avec des réfl*

Partington, J. R. (1961–70). *A History of Chemistry* (4

Pascal, Blaise (1670). *Pensées de M. Pascal sur la religion sa mort parmi ses papiers*. Paris.

Pascal, Blaise (1904–14). *Oeuvres*, ed. L. Brunschv Kraus, 1965.)

Pascal, Blaise (1951). *Pensées sur la Religion et sur q* Luxembourg.

Pascal, Blaise (1962). *Pensées*, ed. Louis Lafuma. ƒ

Pascal, Blaise (1963). *Oeuvres complètes*, ed. Louí

Pascal, Blaise (1964). *Lettres provinciales*, ed. Clé

Pascal, Blaise (1964– ). *Oeuvres complètes*, Brouwer.

Pascal (1966). *Pensées*, trans. A. J. Krailsheime

Pascal, Blaise (1967). *Pensées et Opuscules*, ed

Pascal, Blaise (1992). *Discours sur la religion* A. Colin.

Passmore, John (1951). *Ralph Cudworth:* (Repr. Bristol: Thoemmes, 1990.)

Passmore, John (1953). 'Descartes, the P 62:545–53.

Passm
  *Idea*
Patride
  Univ
Patrizi,
Patrizi,
  trans.
  Hrkač
Paulinus,
  tock.
Paull, Cra
Pavone, F
Pearson, E
  Darien,
Pearson, Jo
Pearson, Ka
Pearson, Ka
Pecham, Joh
  Madison:
Pedersen, Ki
  (ed.), *From*
Peers, Edgar ƒ
Pegis, A. C.
  Medieval St
Pérez-Ramos,
  Oxford Univ
Perkins, William
  *1602. English*
Perrett, Roy W.
Peter of Spain (
Peters, F. E. (196
  University Pre
Peters, Richard (
Peters, Richard (
Petersen, Peter (
  Meiner. (Repr.
Petersson, Robert
  Harvard Univers
Petrarca, Francesco
  Turin: Unione T
Petrik, James M. (19
Petty, William (1674)
  *of Duplicate Propor*
  *Elastique Motions*. L
Petty, William (1690).
Peucer, Caspar (1584)
  *livres, esquels les ru*
  *sainctes propheties &*

*philosophe, mathematicien & medecin de nostre temps: nouvellement tourné en françois par S.G.S. . . .* Antwerp.

Phillips, Edward (1658). *The New World of English Words.* London. (Repr. Menston, Yorks: Scolar, 1969.)

Pico della Mirandola, Gianfrancesco (1972). *Opera Omnia* (Monumenta Politica Philosophica Humanistica Rariora). Turin: Bottega d'Erasmo.

Pico della Mirandola, Giovanni (1942). *De hominis dignitate; heptaplus; de ente et uno,* ed. E. Garin. Florence: Vallecchi Editore.

Pico della Mirandola, Giovanni (1965). *On the Dignity of Man, On Being and the One,* and *Heptaplus.* trans. C. G. Wallis, P. J. W. Miller, and D. Carmichael. Indianapolis: Bobbs-Merrill.

Pico della Mirandola, Giovanni (1971). *Opera Omnia* (2 vols.) (Monumenta Politica Philosophica Humanistica Rariora). Turin: Bottega d'Erasmo.

Pico della Mirandola, Giovanni (1973). *Conclusiones sive Theses DCCCC Romae anno 1486 publice disputandae, sed non admissae,* ed. Bohdan Kieszkowski. Geneva: Droz.

Pico della Mirandola, Giovanni (1993). *Oeuvres philosophiques,* ed. and trans. (Latin with French trans.) O. Boulnois and G. Tognon. Paris: Presses Universitaires de France.

Pine, Martin (1986). *Pietro Pomponazzi: Radical Philosopher of the Renaissance.* Padua: Antenore.

Pinot, Virgile (1932). *La Chine et la formation de l'esprit philosophique en France (1640–1740).* Paris: Paul Geuthner.

Pintard, René (1943). *Le Libertinage érudit dans la première moitié du XVIIe siècle.* Paris: Boivin. (Repr. Geneva: Slatkine, 1983.)

Pithoys, Claude (1621). *La descouverture des faux possedez.* Chalons.

Placette, Jean La (1696). *De insanabili romanae Ecclesiae scepticismo.* Amsterdam.

Plantinga, A. (ed.) (1968). *The Ontological Argument.* London: Macmillan.

Plethon, George Gemistus (1858). *Traité des Lois,* ed. C. Alexandre, trans. (French) A. Pellissier: Paris.

Plutarch (1959). *Plutarch's Lives,* vol. 1, ed. & trans. B. Perrin. London: William Heinemann; Cambridge, Mass.: Harvard University Press.

Plutarch (1967). *Non posse suaviter vivi secundum Epicurum* and *Adversus Colotem,* trans. Benedict Einarson and Phillip H. de Lacy, in *Plutarch's Moralia* (17 vols., Loeb Classical Library). Cambridge, Mass.: Harvard University Press. London: Heinemann, vol. 14, pp. 1–315.

Pocock, J. G. A. (1972). 'Time, History and Eschatology in the Thought of Thomas Hobbes', in *Politics, Language and Time.* London: Methuen.

Poiret, Pierre. (1677). *Cogitationum rationalium de Deo, anima et malo libri quattuor.* Amsterdam.

Poiret, Pierre (1685). *Cogitationum rationalium de Deo, anima, et malo.* Amsterdam.

Poiret, Pierre (1687). *L'oeconomie divine, ou système universel et démontré des oeuvres et des desseins de Dieu envers les hommes.* Amsterdam.

Poiret, Pierre (1707). *De Eruditione triplici, solida, superficiam et falsa.* Amsterdam.

Poiret, Pierre (1713). *The Divine Oeconomy; or, An Universal System of the Works and Purposes of God towards Man, Demonstrated* (6 vols.). London.

Poisson, Nicolas-Joseph. (1670). *Commentaire ou remarques sur la methode de René Descartes où on établit plusieurs principes generaux, necessaires pour entendre toutes ses Oeuvres.* Vendôme.

Polin, R. (1960). *La politique morale de John Locke.* Paris: Presses Universitaires de France.

Polin, R. (1981). *Hobbes, Dieu, et les hommes.* Paris: Presses Universitaires de France.

Politella, J. (1938). 'Platonism, Aristotelianism, and Cabalism in the Philosophy of Leibniz'. Ph.D. diss., University of Pennsylvania.

Pomponazzi, Pietro (1516). *Tractatus de immortalitate animae.* Bologna.

Pomponazzi, Pietro (1567). *De naturalium effectuum causis sive de Incantationibus.* Basel. (Repr. Hildesheim: Olms, 1970.)

Pomponazzi, Pietro (1938). *Tractatus de Immortalitate Animae,* trans. William Henry Hay II, followed by a facsimile of the editio princeps. Haverford: Haverford College.

Pomponazzi, Pietro (1948). 'On the Immortality of the Soul', trans. W. H. Hay II, rev. J. H. Randall, Jr., in E. Cassirer, P. O. Kristeller, and J. H. Randall, Jr. (eds.), *Renaissance Philosophy of Man.* Chicago: University of Chicago Press.

Pomponazzi, Pietro (1957). *Libri quinque De Fato, De Libero Arbitrio, et De Praedestinatione.* ed. Richard Lemay. Lugano: Thesaurus Mundi.

Pomponazzi, Pietro (1966). *Super Libello De Substantia Orbis et Quaestiones Quattuor,* ed. Antonino Poppi (Corsi Inediti dell' Insegnamento Padovano). Padua: Editrice Antenore.

Pona, Francesco (1627). *Discorsi sopra le Morali di Aristotele à Nicomaco . . . .* Venice.

Poncius, Johannes (1649). *Integer philosophiae cursus ad mentem Scoti.* Paris. (1st ed. 1643.)

Popkin, Richard H. (1959a). 'Pierre Bayle's Place in 17th Century Scepticism', in P. Dibon (ed.), *Pierre Bayle: Le Philosophe de Rotterdam.* Amsterdam: Elzevier.

Popkin, Richard H. (1959b). 'Did Hume Ever Read Berkeley?' *Journal of Philosophy.* 56:57–71.

Popkin, Richard H. (1960). 'Skepticism and the Counter-Reformation in France', *Archiv für Reformations-geschichte.* 51:58–87.

Popkin, Richard H. (1963). 'Scepticism in the Enlightenment', *Studies in Voltaire and the Eighteenth Century.* 26:1321–45.

Popkin, Richard H. (1964). *The History of Scepticism from Erasmus to Descartes.* Rev. ed. New York: Harper and Row.

Popkin, Richard H. (1971). 'The Philosophy of Bishop Stillingfleet', *Journal of the History of Philosophy.* 9:303–31.

Popkin, Richard H. (1972). 'Kierkegaard and Scepticism', in Josiah Thompson (ed.), *Kierkegaard: A Collection of Critical Essays.* Garden City, N.Y.: Doubleday.

Popkin, Richard H. (1974). 'Menasseh ben Israel and Isaac La Peyrère', *Studia Rosenthaliana.* 8:59–63.

Popkin, Richard H. (1976). 'The Pre-Adamite Theory in the Renaissance', in Edward P. Mahoney (ed.), *Philosophy and Humanism: Renaissance Essays in Honor of Paul Oskar Kristeller.* Leiden: Brill.

Popkin, Richard H. (1978). 'Pre-Adamism in 19th Century American Thought: Speculative Biology and Racism', *Philosophia.* 8:205–39.

Popkin, Richard H. (1979). *The History of Skepticism from Erasmus to Spinoza,* 4th ed. Berkeley: University of California Press.

Popkin, Richard H. (1980a). 'David Hume and the Pyrrhonian Controversy', in R. H. Popkin (ed.), *The High Road to Pyrrhonism.* San Diego: Austin Hill.

Popkin, Richard H. (1980b). 'The Philosophical Basis of Modern Racism', in R. H. Popkin (ed.), *The Highroad to Pyrrhonism,* San Diego: Austin Hill.

Popkin, Richard H. (1980c). 'Jewish Messianism and Christian Millenarianism', in Perez Zagorin (ed.), *Culture and Politics from Puritanism to the Enlightenment.* Berkeley: University of California Press, pp. 67–90.

Popkin, Richard [H.] (1980d). *The High Road to Pyrrhonism,* ed. R. A. Watson and J. E. Force. San Diego: Austin Hill Press.

Popkin, Richard H. (1983). 'The Third Force in Seventeenth Century Philosophy: Scepticism, Biblical Prophecy and Science', *Nouvelles de la Republique des Lettres.* 3:35–63.

Popkin, Richard H. (1984a). 'The First College of Jewish Studies', *Revue des études juives.* 143:351–64.

Popkin, Richard H. (1984b). 'Menasseh ben Israel and Isaac La Peyrère II', *Studia Rosenthaliana.* 18:12–20.

Popkin, Richard H. (1984c). 'Nathan Shapira's Visit to Amsterdam in 1657', in Joseph Michman (ed.), *Dutch Jewish History.* Jerusalem: Hebrew University.

Popkin, Richard H. (1984d). 'Spinoza's Relations with the Quakers in Amsterdam', *Quaker History.* 70:351–64.

Popkin, Richard H. (1985a). 'Un autre Spinoza', *Archives de Philosophie*. 48:37–57.

Popkin, Richard H. (1985b). 'Samuel Fisher and Spinoza', *Philosophia*. 15:219–36.

Popkin, Richard H. (1986a). 'The Third Force in Seventeenth-Century Thought: Skepticism, Science and Millenarianism', in E. Ullmann-Margalit (ed.), *The Prism of Science*. Dordrecht: D. Reidel.

Popkin, Richard H. (1986b). 'The Lost Tribes, the Caraites and the English Millenarians', *Journal of Jewish Studies*. 37:213–27.

Popkin, Richard H. (1986c). 'Could Spinoza Have Known Bodin's *Colloquium Heptaplomeres?*' *Philosophia*. 16:307–14.

Popkin, Richard H. (1987a). 'A Note on Moses Wall', in Menasseh ben Israel, *The Hope of Israel*, ed. Méchoulan and Nahon. Oxford: Oxford University Press.

Popkin, Richard H. (1987b). *Isaac La Peyrère: His Life, Work and Influence*. Leiden: Brill.

Popkin, Richard H. (1987c). 'Jacques Basnage's *Histoire des Juifs* and the *Biblioteca Sarraziana*', *Studia Rosenthaliana*. 21:154–62.

Popkin, Richard H. (1987d). 'A Late 17th Century Attempt to Convert the Jews to Reformed Judaism', in Shmuel Almog et al. (eds.), *Israel and the Nations: Essays Presented in Honor of Shmuel Ettinger*. Jerusalem: History Society of Israel.

Popkin, Richard H. (1987e). 'Introduction' to R. H. Popkin and M. J. Signer (eds.), *Spinoza's Earliest Publication?* Assen: Van Gorcum.

Popkin, Richard H. (1987f). 'The Religious Background of Seventeenth-Century Philosophy', *Journal of the History of Philosophy*. 25:35–50.

Popkin, Richard H. (1988a). 'Introduction' to *Pascal, Selections*. New York: Macmillan.

Popkin, Richard H. (1988b). 'Some Aspects of Jewish-Christian Theological Interchanges in Holland and England 1640–1700', in J. van den Berg and Ernestine G. E. van der Wall (eds.), *Jewish-Christian Relations in the Seventeenth Century*. Dordrecht: Kluwer.

Popkin, Richard H. (1988c). 'Newton's Biblical Theology and his Theological Physics', in P. B. Scheurer and G. Debrock (eds.), *Newton's Scientific and Philosophical Legacy*. Dordrecht: Kluwer.

Popkin, Richard H. (1988d). 'The Dispersion of Bodin's *Dialogues* in England, Holland and Germany', *Journal of the History of Ideas*. 49:157–60.

Popkin, Richard H. (1988e). 'Theories of Knowledge', in Schmitt, Skinner, and Kessler 1988.

Popkin, Richard H. (1989a). *The History of Scepticism from Erasmus to Spinoza*. Berkeley: University of California.

Popkin, Richard H. (1989b). 'The Rise and Fall of the Jewish Indian Theory', in Y. Kaplan, H. Méchoulan, and R. Popkin, (eds.), *Menasseh ben Israel and His World*. Leiden: Brill.

Popkin, Richard H. (1989c). 'A Jewish Merchant of Venice', *Shakespeare Quarterly*. 40:329–31.

Popkin, Richard H. (1989d). 'Spinoza's Earliest Philosophical Years', *Studia Spinoziana*. 4:37–55.

Popkin, Richard H. (1989e). 'Two Unused Sources about Sabbatai Zevi', in J. Michman (ed.), *Dutch Jewish History*. Jerusalem: Hebrew University.

Popkin, Richard H. (1990a). 'Spinoza and the Three Impostors', in Curley and Moreau 1990, pp. 347–58.

Popkin, Richard H. (1990b). 'The Crisis of Polytheism and the Answers of Vossius, Cudworth and Newton', in J. E. Force and R. H. Popkin (eds.), *Essays on the Context, Nature, and Influence of Isaac Newton's Theology*. Dordrecht: Kluwer.

Popkin, Richard H. (1990c). 'Polytheism, Deism, and Newton', in J. E. Force and R. H. Popkin (eds.), *Essays on the Context, Nature, and Influence of Isaac Newton's Theology*. Dordrecht: Kluwer.

Popkin, Richard H. (1990d). *The Third Force in 17th Century Philosophy*. Leiden: Brill.

Popkin, Richard H. (1990e). 'Newton and Maimonides II.', J. E. Force and R. H. Popkin (eds.), *Essays on the Context, Nature, and Influence of Isaac Newton's Theology*. Dordrecht: Kluwer.

Popkin, Richard H. (1990f). 'Newton as a Bible Scholar', in J. E. Force and R. H. Popkin (eds.), *Essays on the Context, Nature, and Influence of Isaac Newton's Theology*. Dordrecht: Kluwer.

Popkin, Richard H. (1990g). 'The Role of Jewish anti-Christian Arguments in the Rise of Scepticism', in John Henry and Sarah Hutton (eds.), *New Perspectives on Renaissance Thought*. London: Duckworth.

Popkin, Richard H. (1992a). 'Jewish Anti-Christian Arguments as a Source of Irreligion from the Seventeenth to the Early Nineteenth Century', in Michael Hunter and David Wootton (eds.), *Atheism from the Reformation to the Enlightenment*. Oxford: Oxford University Press, pp. 159–81.

Popkin, Richard H. (1992b). 'Spinoza, Neo-Platonic Kabbalist?', in Lenn E. Goodman (ed.), *Neoplatonism and Jewish Thought*. Albany: State University of New York Press.

Popkin, Richard H. (1992c). 'Fideism, Quietism and Unbelief: Scepticism for and against Religion in the Seventeenth and Eighteenth Centuries', in Marcus Hester (ed.), *Faith, Reason, and Skepticism*. Philadelphia: Temple University Press, pp. 121–54 and 169–74.

Popkin, Richard H. (forthcoming) 'Queen Christina and Isaac La Peyrère', to be published in a collection by the French Embassy in Stockholm.

Popkin, Richard H., and Weiner, Gordon (eds.) (1994). *Jewish Christians and Christian Jews in the Seventeenth and Eighteenth Centuries*. Dordrecht: Kluwer.

Popper, Karl (1982). *Unended Quest: An Intellectural Autobiography*. Glasgow: Fontana/Collins.

Poppi, Antonino (1972). *La dottrina della scienza in Giacomo Zabarella*. Padua: Antenore.

Poser, H. (1969). *Zur Theorie der Modalbegriffe bei G. W. Leibniz* (Studia Leibnitiana, Supplementa). Stuttgart: Steiner.

Postel, Guillaume (1543). *Sacrarum apodixeon, seu Euclidis christiani libri II*. Paris.

Postel, Guillaume (1969). *Le thrésor des prophetiés de l'univers*, ed. F. Secret. The Hague: Nijhoff.

Postel, Guillaume (1971). *Le candelabre de Moses*, ed. F. Secret. Nieuwkoop: B. de Graaf.

Poulain de la Barre, François (1673). *De l'égalité des deux sexes*. Paris.

Pousseur, Jean-Marie (1984). 'La distinction de la *ratio* et de la *methodus* dans le *Novum organum* et ses prolongements dans le rationalisme cartésien', in Marta Fattori (ed.), *Francis Bacon: Terminologia e fortuna nel XVII secolo (Seminario internazionale, Roma 11–13 marzo 1984)*. Rome: Edizione dell'Ateneo.

Pousseur, Jean-Marie (1985). 'Méthode et dialectique', in Michel Malherbe and Jean-Marie Pousseur (eds.), *Francis Bacon: Science et méthode, Actes du Colloque de Nantes*. Paris: Vrin.

Pousseur, Jean-Marie (1988). *Bacon 1561–1626: Inventer la science*. Paris: Belin.

Powell, E. E. (1899). *Spinozas Gottesbegriff*. Halle: Niemeyer.

Powicke, F. J. (1926). *The Cambridge Platonists*. London: Dent.

Pozzi, L. (1981). *Da Ramus a Kant. Il dibattito sulla sillogistica. Con appendice su Lewis Carroll* (Pubblicazioni dell' Istituto di Filosofia dell' Università di Parma, Studi). Milano: Franco Angeli.

Prendergast, Thomas L. (1972–3). 'Descartes and the Relativity of Motion', *Modern Schoolman*. 50:64–72.

Prendergast, Thomas L. (1975). 'Motion, Action, and Tendency in Descartes' Physics', *Journal of the History of Philosophy*. 13:453–62.

Prior, A. N. (1967). 'Logic, Traditional', in P. Edwards (ed.), *The Encyclopedia of Philosophy* (8 vols.). London: Collier-Macmillan, vol. 5, pp. 34–45.

Prost, J. (1907). *Essai sur l'atomisme et l'occasionalisme dans la philosophie cartésienne*. Paris: Paulin.

Pseudo-Dionysius (1608). *Les oeuvres du divin Denys l'Aréopagite*. Paris.

Ptolemy, Claudius (1989). *L'Optique de Claude Ptolémée dans la version latine d'après l'arabe de l'émir Eugène de Sicile*, ed. and trans. A. Lejeune. Leiden: Brill.

Pufendorf, Samuel von (1672). *De jure naturae et gentium*. Lund.

Pufendorf, Samuel von (1673). *De officio hominis et civis juxta legam naturalem*. Lund.

Pufendorf, Samuel von (1686). *Eris Scandia, quae adversus libros de jurae naturae et gentium objecta diluuntur*. Frankfurt.

Pufendorf, Samuel von (1706a). *Les devoirs de l'homme et du citoyen, tels qu'ils lui sont prescrits par la loi naturelle*, trans. J. Barbeyrac. Amsterdam.

Pufendorf, Samuel von (1706b). *Eris Scandica*. Frankfurt.

Pufendorf, Samuel von (1707). *Le droit de la nature et des gens, ou système général des principes les plus importants de la morale, de la jurisprudence, et de la politique*, trans J. Barbeyrac (2 vols.). Amsterdam.

Pufendorf, Samuel von (1717). *Of the Law of Nature and Nations*, trans. Basil Kennet. 3d ed. London.

Pufendorf, Samuel von (1749). *The Law of Nature and Nations*, ed. J. Barbeyrac, trans. B. Kennet. London.

Pufendorf, Samuel von (1893). 'Briefe von Pufendorf', ed. K. Varrentrapp, *Historische Zeitschrift*. 70:1–51, 192–232.

Pufendorf, Samuel von (1894). '*Briefe Pufendorf's* an Falaiseau, Friese und Weigel', ed. K. Varrentrapp, *Historische Zeitschrift*. 73:59–67.

Pufendorf, Samuel von (1897). *Briefe Samuel Pufendorfs an Christian Thomasius (1687–1693)*, ed. E. Gigas (Historische Bibliothek, 2). Munich and Leipzig: R. Oldenbourg.

Pufendorf, Samuel von (1927). *De officio hominis et civis juxta legem naturalem libri duo*, bilingual ed. trans. F. G. Moore (2 vols.). Oxford: Oxford University Press.

Pufendorf, Samuel von (1931). *Elementorum jurisprudentiae universalis libri duo*, bilingual ed. trans. W. A. Oldfather (2 vols.). Oxford: Oxford University Press.

Pufendorf, Samuel von (1967). *De iure naturae et gentium libri octo*, ed. J. N. Hertius, J. Barbeyrac, and G. Mascovius (2 vols.). Frankfurt: Minerva.

Pufendorf, Samuel von (1990). *On the Natural State of Men* [1678], trans. and ed. M. Seidler. Lewiston, N.Y.; Queenston, Ontario; and Lampeter, England: Edward Melden Press.

Pufendorf, Samuel von (1991). *On the Duty of Man and Citizen according to Natural Law*, trans. M. Silverthorne, ed. J. Tully. Cambridge: Cambridge University Press.

Purchotius, Edmundus (1751). *Institutiones philosophicae*. Padua.


Quevedo, Francisco de (1945–60). *Obras completas*, ed. L. Astrana Marin (2 vols.). Madrid: M. Aguilar.

Quevedo, Francisco de (1986). *Defensa de Epicuro contra la común opinión*, ed. E. Acosta Méndez. Madrid: Editorial Tecnos.


Rabbe, F. (1867). *Etude philosophique sur l'Abbé Simon Foucher*. Paris: Didier.

Rabe, H. (1958). *Naturrecht und Kirche bei Samuel von Pufendorf*. Tübingen: Fabianverlag.

Rabinovitch, Nachum L. (1973). *Probability and Statistical Inference in Ancient and Medieval Jewish Literature*. Toronto: University of Toronto Press.

Rademaker, C. S. M. (1981). *Life and Works of Gerardus Joannnes Vossius, (1577–1649)*. Assen: Van Gorcum.

Radner, Daisie (1978). *Malebranche: A Study of a Cartesian System*. Assen: Van Gorcum.

Raey, Johannes de (1651–52). *Disputationes physicae ad problemata Aristotelis*. Leiden.

Raey, Johannes de (1654). *Clavis philosophiae naturalis, seu introductio ad contemplationem naturae Aristotelico-Cartesiana*. Leiden.

Raey, Johannes de (1677). *Clavis philosophiae naturalis aristotelico-cartesiana*. Amsterdam.

Ramsay, Andrew Michael (1727). *Les voyages de Cyrus*. Paris.

Ramus, Peter (1569). *Scholae in Liberales Artes*. Basel. (Repr. Hildesheim: Olms, 1970.)

Randall, John Herman, Jr. (1940). 'The Development of Scientific Method in the School of Padua', *Journal of the History of Ideas*. 1:177–206.

Randall, John Herman, Jr. (1961). *The School of Padua and the Emergence of Modern Science*. Padua: Editrice Antenore.

Raphael, D. D. (1962). 'Obligations and rights in Hobbes', *Philosophy*. 37(1962):345–57.

Raphael, D. D. (1977). *Hobbes. Morals and Politics*. London: George Allen and Unwin.

Rashdall, Hastings (1936). *The Universities of Europe in the Middle Ages,* ed. F. M. Powicke and A. B. Emden. 2d ed. (3 vols.). Oxford: Oxford University Press.

Rashed, Roshdi (1984). *Entre arithmétique et algèbre: Recherches sur l'histoire des mathématiques arabes.* Paris: Les Belles Lettres.

Rathery, E.-J.-P., and Boutron (1873). *Mademoiselle de Scudéry: Sa vie et sa correspondance avec un choix de ses poésies.* Paris: Techener.

Rattansi, P. M. (1963). 'Paracelsus and the Puritan Revolution', *Ambix.* 11:24–32.

Rattansi, P. M. (1972). 'Newton's Alchemical Studies', in Debus 1972, vol. 1, pp. 167–82.

Raymond, Pierre (1975). *De la combinatoire aux probabilités.* Paris: François Massero.

Real, Hermann Josef (1970). *Untersuchungen zur Lukrez-Übersetzung von Thomas Creech.* Bad Homburg v.d.H.: Gehlen.

Redwood, John (1976). *Reason, Ridicule and Religion: The Age of Enlightenment in England, 1660–1750.* Cambridge, Mass.: Harvard University Press.

Reeb, Georg, S.J. (1636). *Axiomata philosophica frequentius iactari solita in Dilingana Academia anno M.DC.XXV. explicata . . .* Duaci.

Rees, Graham (1975). 'Francis Bacon's Semi-Paracelsian Cosmology', *Ambix.* 22:81–101.

Rees, Graham (1977a). 'The Fate of Bacon's Cosmology in the Seventeenth Century', *Ambix.* 24:27–38.

Rees, Graham (1977b). 'Matter Theory: A Unifying Factor in Bacon's Natural Philosophy?' *Ambix.* 24:110–25.

Rees, Graham (1980). 'Atomism and "Subtlety" in Francis Bacon's Philosophy', *Annals of Science.* 37:549–71.

Rees, Graham (1984a). 'Bacon's Philosophy: Some New Sources with Special Reference to the *Abecedarium novum naturae',* in Marta Fattori (ed.), *Francis Bacon: Terminologia e fortuna nel XVII secolo (Seminario internazionale, Roma 11–13 marzo 1984).* Rome: Edizione dell'Ateneo.

Rees, Graham (1984b). 'Francis Bacon's Biological Ideas: A New Manuscript Source', in Brian Vickers (ed.), *Occult and Scientific Mentalities in the Renaissance.* Cambridge: Cambridge University Press.

Reesink, Henrika Johanna (1931). *L'Angleterre et la littérature anglaise dans les trois plus anciens périodiques francais de Hollande de 1684 à 1709.* Paris: Champion.

Reeves, Marjorie (1969). *The Influence of Prophecy in the Late Middle Ages.* Oxford: Oxford University Press.

Régis, Pierre-Sylvain (1690). *Système de philosophie contenant la logique, la métaphysique, la physique et la morale* (3 vols.). Paris.

Régis, Pierre-Sylvain (1691a). *Cours entier de philosophie, ou système général selon les principes de M. Descartes* (3 vols.). Amsterdam. (Repr. New York: Johnson Reprint, 1970.)

Régis, Pierre-Sylvain (1691b). *Système de philosophie . . .* (7 vols.). Lyon.

Régis, Pierre-Sylvain (1692). *Réponse aux Reflexions critiques de M. Du Hamel.* Paris.

Régis, Pierre-Sylvain (1704). *L'usage de la raison et de la foi, ou l'accord de la foi et la raison.* Paris.

Regius, Henricus (1646). *Fundamenta Physices.* Amsterdam.

Regius, Henricus (1647). *Explicatio mentis humana.* Utrecht.

Regius, Henricus (1648). *Brevis explicatio mentis humana sive animae rationalis.* Utrecht.

Regius, Henricus (1650). *De affectibus animi dissertatio.* Utrecht.

Regius, Henricus (1654). *Philosophia naturalis. Editio secunda, priore multo locupletior et emendatior.* Amsterdam. (2d ed. of Regius 1646.)

Regius, Henricus (1661). *Philosophia Naturalis.* (Revision of 1654 ed., Amsterdam.)

Regnerus, Cyprianus (1986). *Demonstratio logicae verae iuridica,* ed. G. Kalinowski (Instrumenta rationis. Sources for the history of modern logic). Bologna: Editrice CLUEB.

Reibstein, E. (1953–4). 'Deutsche Grotius-Kommentatoren bis zu Christian Wolff', *Zeitschrift für ausländisches öffentliches Recht und Völkerrecht.* 15:76–102.

Reid, Thomas (1969). *Essays on the Intellectual Powers of Man.* Cambridge, Mass.: MIT Press.

Reid, Thomas (1975). *Inquiry and Essays.* Indianapolis: Bobbs-Merrill.

Reif, P. (1962). 'Natural Philosophy in Some Early Seventeenth Century Scholastic Textbooks'. Ph.D. diss., Saint Louis University.

Reif, P. (1969). 'The Textbook Tradition in Natural Philosophy, 1600–1650', *Journal of the History of Ideas.* 30:17–32.

Reiter, J. (1972). *System und Praxis. Zur kritische Analyse der Denkformen neuzeitlicher Metaphysik im Werk von Malebranche.* Freiburg-Munich: Alber.

Remec, Peter Paul (1960). *The Position of the Individual in International Law according to Grotius and Vattel.* The Hague: Nijhoff.

Remnant, Peter (1979). 'Descartes: Body and Soul', *Canadian Journal of Philosophy.* 9:377–86.

Rescher, Nicholas (1966). *Galen and the Syllogism.* Pittsburgh: University of Pittsburgh Press.

Rescher, Nicholas (1967). *The Philosophy of Leibniz.* Englewood Cliffs, N.J.: Prentice-Hall.

Rescher, Nicholas (1979). *Leibniz: An Introduction to His Philosophy.* Oxford: Blackwell.

Rescher, Nicholas (1981). 'Leibniz on Intermonadic Relations', in *Truth, Knowledge and Reality. Inquiries into the Foundations of Seventeenth Century Rationalism,* ed. George Henry R. Parkinson (Studia Leibnitiana, Sonderheft). Stuttgart: Steiner.

*Returns from Universities and University Colleges in Receipt of Treasury Grant 1922–23* (1924). London: HMSO.

Reventlow, H. Graf (1984). *The Authority of the Bible and the Rise of the Modern World.* London: SCM Press.

Revius, J. (1643). *Suarez Repurgatus.* Leiden.

Reynolds, Edward (1658). *A Treatise of the Passions and Faculties of the Soule of Man. . . .* London.

Reynolds, Rebecca L. (1993). 'Samuel Cocceji and the Tradition of Natural Jurisprudence', M. Phil. diss., University of Cambridge.

Rheinfelder, Hans (1928). *Das Wort 'Persona'. Geschichte seiner Bedeutungen mit besonderer Berücksichtigung des Französischen und Italienischen Mittelalters* (Beihefte zur Zeitschrift für Romanische Philologie, Heft 77). Halle: Max Niemeier.

Rhigini Bonelli, M. L., and Shea, William R. (eds.) (1975). *Reason, Experiment and Mysticism in the Scientific Revolution.* New York: Science History Publications.

Ricci, Matteo, and Trigault, Nicolas (1615). *De Christiana expeditione apud Sinas.* Augsburg.

Ricci, Matteo, and Trigault, Nicolas (1953). *China in the Sixteenth Century: The Journals of Matthew Ricci 1583–1610,* trans. Louis J. Gallagher, S.J. New York: Random House.

Rice, James V. (1939). *Gabriel Naudé, 1600–1653* (Johns Hopkins Studies in Romance Literatures and Languages, 35). Baltimore: Johns Hopkins University Press.

Rice, Lee C. (1975). 'Spinoza on Individuation', in M. Mandelbaum and E. Freeman (eds.), *Spinoza: Essays in Interpretation.* La Salle, Ill.: Open Court, pp. 195–214.

Richardson, Linda Deer (1985). 'The Generation of Disease: Occult Causes and Diseases of the Total Substance', in A. Wear, R. K. French, and I. M. Lonie (eds.), *The Medical Renaissance of the Sixteenth Century.* Cambridge: Cambridge University Press.

Richardson, Robert (1982). 'The "Scandal" of Cartesian Interaction', *Mind.* 92:20–37.

Riley, Patrick (1986). *The General Will before Rousseau.* Princeton, N.J.: Princeton University Press.

Risse, Wilhelm (1964–70). *Die Logik der Neuzeit* (2 vols.). Stuttgart: Frommann.

Risse, Wilhelm (1965). *Bibliographia logica. Verzeichnis der Druckschriften zur Logik mit Angabe ihrer Fundorte* (Studien und Materialien zur Geschichte der Philosophie). Hildesheim: Olms.

Risse, Wilhelm. (1983). 'Zaberellas Methodenlehre', in Luigi Olivieri (ed.), *Aristotelismo veneto e scienza moderna* (2 vols.). Padua: Editrice Antenore.

Ritter, Joachim (ed.) (1971). *Historisches Wörterbuch der Philosophie* (2 vols.). Basel-Stuttgart: Schwabe.

Roberval, Gilles Personne de (1644). *Aristarchi Samii de mundi systemate partibus et motibus eiusdem libellus.* Paris.

Roberval, Gilles Personne de (1693). *Traité des indivisibles*, in *Divers ouvrages de mathematique et de physique. Par Messieurs de l'Academie Royale des Sciences.* Paris, pp. 190–245. (Reprinted in *Divers ouvrages de M. de Roberva = Mémoires de l'Académie Royale des Sciences depuis 1666 à 1699*, vol. 6, Paris, 1730).

Robinet, André (1955). *Malebranche et Leibniz: Relations personnelles.* Paris: Vrin.

Robinet, André (1965). *Système et Existence dans l'oeuvre de Malebranche.* Paris: Vrin.

Robinet, André (1980). 'Suarez dans l'oeuvre de Leibniz', *Cuadernos Salmantinos de Filosofia (Salamanca).* 8:191–209.

Robinet, André (1981). 'Suarez im Werk von Leibniz', *Studia Leibnitiana.* 13:76–96.

Robinet, André (1983). 'Leibniz: Lecteur du *Treatise* de Berkeley', *Les études philosophiques.* 2/1983:217–23.

Robinet, André (1986). *Architectonique disjonctive, automates systémiques et idéalité transcendentale dans l'oeuvre de G. W. Leibniz.* Paris: Vrin.

Robinson, Lewis (1913). 'Un solipsiste au XVIIIe siècle', *Année philosophique.* 24:15–30.

Robles, Laureano (1979). *El estudio de la "Etica" en España (del siglo XIII al XX).* Salamanca: Calatrava.

Rochemonteix, C. de (1889). *Un collège des jésuites aux XVII$^e$ et XVIII$^e$ siècles: Le Collège Henri IV de la Flèche* (4 vols). Le Mans: Leguicheux.

Rochot, Bernard (1944). *Les travaux de Gassendi sur Epicure et sur l'atomisme. 1619–1658.* Paris: Vrin.

Rochot, Bernard (1952). 'Beeckman, Gassendi et le principe d'inertie', *Archives Internationales d'Histoire des Sciences.* 20-1:282–9.

Röd, Wolfgang (1969). 'Weigels Lehre von den entia moralia', *Archiv für Geschichte der Philosophie.* 51:58–84.

Röd, Wolfgang (1970). *Geometrischer Geist und Naturrecht. Methodengeschichtliche Untersuchungen zur Staatsphilosophie im 17. und 18. Jahrhundert.* Munich: Beck.

[Rodis-]Lewis, Geneviève (1950a). *Le problème de l'inconscient et le cartésianisme.* Paris: Presses Universitaires de France.

[Rodis-]Lewis, Geneviève (1950b). *L'individualité selon Descartes.* Paris: Vrin.

Rodis-Lewis, Geneviève (1957). *La Morale de Descartes.* Paris: Presses Universitaires de France.

Rodis-Lewis, Geneviève (1963). *Nicolas Malebranche.* Paris: Presses Universitaires de France.

Rodis-Lewis, Geneviève (1971). *L'oeuvre de Descartes* (2 vols.). Paris: Vrin.

Rodis-Lewis, Geneviève (1979). 'Quelques échos de la thèse de Desgabets sur l'indéfectibilité des substances', *Studia Cartesiana.* 1:121–8.

Rodis-Lewis, G[eneviève]. (1980). 'Quelques compléments sur la création des vérités éternelles', in *Etienne Gilson et nous: La philosophie et son histoire.* Paris: Vrin. (Repr. in Rodis-Lewis 1985.)

Rodis-Lewis, Geneviève (1981). 'Polémiques sur la création des possibles et sur l'impossible sans l'école cartésienne', *Studia Cartesiana.* 2:105–23. (Repr. in Rodis-Lewis 1985.)

Rodis-Lewis, Geneviève (1985). *Idées et vérités éternelles chez Descartes et ses successeurs.* Paris: Vrin.

Rodis-Lewis, Geneviève (1986). 'L'interprétation malebranchiste d'*Exode* 3, 14. L'être infini et universel', in E. Z. Brown (ed.), *Celui qui est – Interprétations juives et chrétiennes d'Exode 3, 14.* Paris: Cerf.

Rodis-Lewis, Geneviève (ed.) (1987a). *Méthode et métaphysique chez Descartes.* New York: Garland.

Rodis-Lewis, Geneviève (1987b). 'Le dernier fruit de la métaphysique cartésienne: La générosité', *Les études philosophiques.* 1/1987:43–4.

Rodis-Lewis, Geneviève (1990). 'Augustinisme et Cartésianisme', in G. Rodis-Lewis, *L'anthropologie cartésienne.* Paris: Presses Universitaires de France, pp. 101–26.

Rodriguez-San Pedro Bezares, Luis Enrique (1986). *La Universidad Salamantina del barroco periodo 1598–1625* (3 vols.) (Acta Salmaticensia, Historia de la Universidad 45). Salamanca: Ediciones Universidad de Salamonca.

Rogers, G. A. J. (1972). 'Descartes and the Method of English Science', *Annals of Science.* 29:237–55.

Rogers, G. A. J. (1978). 'Locke's *Essay* and Newton's *Principia*', *Journal of the History of Ideas.* 39: 217–32.

Rogers, G. A. J. (1988). 'Hobbes's Hidden Influences', in Rogers and Ryan 1988.

Rogers, G. A. J. (1990). 'Locke's *Essay* and Newton's *Principia*', in John Yolton (ed.), *Philosophy, Religion and Science in the Seventeenth and Eighteenth Centuries* (Library of the History of Ideas). Rochester, N.Y.: University of Rochester Press.

Rogers, G. A. J., and Ryan, A. (eds.) (1988). *Perspectives on Thomas Hobbes.* Oxford: Oxford University Press.

Rohan, Henri, Duc de (1638). *De l'interest des princes et des Estats de la Chrestienté.* Paris.

Rohault, Jacques (1671a). *Traité de physique.* Paris.

Rohault, Jacques (1671b). *Entretiens sur la philosophie.* Paris.

Rohault, Jacques (1682). *Oeuvres posthumes de Mr. Rohault,* ed. C. Clerselier. Paris.

Rohault, Jacques (1723). *A System of Natural Philosophy, Illustrated with Dr. Samuel Clarkes Notes . . . Done into English by John Clarke* (2 vols.). London. (Repr. New York: Johnson Reprint, 1969.)

Rohault, Jacques (1978). *Jacques Rohault: 1618–1672: bio-bibliographie, avec l'édition critique des Entretiens sur la philosophie,* ed. Pierre Clair. Paris: CNRS.

Röhr, Julius (1923). *Der okkulte Kraftbegriff im Altertum* (Philologus, Supplementband 17.1). Leipzig: Dieterich.

Rolf, B. (1983). 'The Port-Royal Theory of Definition', *Studia Leibnitiana.* 15:94–107.

Rome, Beatrice K. (1963). *The Philosophy of Malebranche.* Chicago: Regnery.

Rorty, Amélie O. (ed.) (1986a). *Essays on Descartes' Meditations.* Berkeley: University of California Press.

Rorty, Amélie O. (1986b). 'The Structure of Descartes' *Meditations*', in Rorty 1986a.

Rorty, Amélie O. (1986c). 'Cartesian Passions and the Union of Mind and Body', in Rorty 1986a.

Rorty, Amélie O. (1992). 'Descartes on Thinking with the Body', in J. Cottingham (ed.), *The Cambridge Companion to Descartes.* Cambridge: Cambridge University Press.

Rorty, Richard (1978). *Philosophy and the Mirror of Nature.* Princeton, N.J.: Princeton University Press.

Rose, Paul Lawrence, and Drake, Stillman (1971). 'The Pseudo-Aristotelian *Questions of Mechanics* in Renaissance Culture', *Studies in the Renaissance.* 18:65–104.

Rosenfield, Leonora Cohen (1957). 'Peripatetic Adversaries of Cartesianism in 17th Century France', *Review of Religion.* 22:14–40.

Rosenfield, Leonora Cohen (1968). *From Beast-Machine to Man-Machine: Animal Soul in French Letters from Descartes to La Mettrie.* 2d ed. New York: Octagon Books.

Ross, Alexander (1645). *Medicus Medicatus: Or the Physicians Religion Cured, by a Lenitive or Gentle Potion: With Some Animadversions upon Sir Kenelme Digbie's Observations on Religio Medici.* London.

Ross, G. MacDonald (1973). 'Rosicrucianism and the English Connection: On "The Rosicrucian Enlightenment" by Frances Yates', *Studia Leibnitiana.* 5:239–45.

Ross, G. MacDonald (1974). 'Leibniz and the Nuremberg Alchemical Society', *Studia Leibnitiana.* 6:22–48.

Ross, G. MacDonald (1978). 'Leibniz and Alchemy', in *Magia Naturalis* 1978.

Ross, G. MacDonald (1982). 'Alchemy and the Development of Leibniz's Metaphysics', *Theoria cum Praxi. Akten des III. Internationalen Leibniz-Kongresses, Hannover, 12–17.11.1977, bd. IV* (Studia Leibnitiana, Supplementa 22), pp. 40–5.

Ross, G. MacDonald (1983). 'Leibniz and Renaissance Neoplatonism', in Albert Heinekamp (ed.), *Leibniz et la Renaissance* (Studia Leibnitiana Supplementa, 23). Stuttgart: Steiner.

Ross, G. MacDonald (1984a). *Leibniz* (Past Masters). Oxford: Oxford University Press.

Ross, G. MacDonald (1984b). 'Leibniz's Phenomenalism and the Construction of Matter', in A. Heinekamp (ed.), *Leibniz' Dynamica* (Studia Leibnitiana Sonderheft, 13). Stuttgart: Steiner, pp. 26–36.

Ross, G. MacDonald (1985). 'Occultism and Philosophy in the Seventeenth Century', in A. J. Holland (ed.), *Philosophy, Its History and Historiography*. Dordrecht: Reidel.

Ross, Stephanie (1984). 'Painting the Passions: Charles le Brun's *Conference sur l'Expression*', *Journal of the History of Ideas*. 45:25–48.

Rossi, Paolo (1960). *Clavis universalis: Arti mnemoniche e logica combinatoria da Lullo a Leibniz*. Milan: Riccardo Ricciardi.

Rossi, Paolo (1968). *Francis Bacon: From Magic to Science*. London: Routledge.

Rossi, Paolo (1975). 'Hermeticism, Rationality and the Scientific Revolution', in M. L. Rhigini Bonelli and William R. Shea (eds.) *Reason, Experiment and Mysticism in the Scientific Revolution*. New York: Science History Publications.

Rossi, Paolo (1982). 'The Aristotelians and the Moderns: Hypothesis and Nature', *Annali dell'Istituto e Museo di Storia della Scienza di Firenze*. 7(fasc. 1):3–28.

Rossi, Paolo (1984). *The Dark Abyss of Time*. Chicago: University of Chicago Press.

Rossi, R. (1987). 'La critica di Locke alla logica Aristotelica', *Rivista Rosminiana di Filosofia e di Cultura*. 81:156–62.

Røstvig, Maren-Sofie (1962–71). *The Happy Man: Studies in the Metamorphoses of a Classical Ideal* (2 vols., Oslo Studies in English), 2d ed. Oslo: Norwegian Universities Press.

Roth, Cecil (1945). *A Life of Menasseh ben Israel*. Philadelphia: Jewish Publication Society.

Roth, Leon (1954). *Spinoza*. London: Allen and Unwin.

Rovane, Carol (1993). 'Self-Reference: the Radicalization of Locke', *Journal of Philosophy*. 90:73–97.

Rozemond, Marleen (1993). 'The Role of the Intellect in Descartes's Case for the Incorporeity of the Mind', in Voss 1993.

Rubius, Antonius (1620). *Commentarium in libros Aristotelis De anima*. Lyon.

Rubius, Antonius (1641). *In universam Aristotelis Dialecticam*. London.

Ruby, Jane E. (1986). 'The Origins of Scientific "Law"', *Journal of the History of Ideas*. 47:341–59.

Ruestow, Edward G. (1973). *Physics at Seventeenth and Eighteenth Century Leiden: Philosophy and the New Science in the University* (International Archives of the History of Ideas, 11). The Hague: Nijhoff.

Rüping, H. (1968). *Die Naturrechtslehre des Christian Thomasius und ihre Fortbildung in der Thomasius-Schule* (Bonner rechtswissenschaftliche Abhandlungen, 81). Bonn: L. Röhrscheid.

Rüping, H. (1970). 'Gottlieb Gerhard Titius und die Naturrechtslehre in Deutschland um die Wende vom 17. zum 18. Jahrhundert', *Zeitschrift der Savigny-Stiftung für Rechtsgeschichte*. Ger. Abt. 87:314–26.

Russell, Bertrand (1937). *A Critical Exposition of the Philosophy of Leibniz,* 2d ed. London: Allen and Unwin.

Rutherford, Donald (1993). 'Natures, Laws, and Miracles: The Roots of Leibniz's Critique of Occasionalism', in S. Nadler (ed.), *Causation in Early Modern Philosophy*. University Park: Pennsylvania State University Press, pp. 135–58.

Rutherford, Donald (1995). *Leibniz and the Rational Order of Nature*. Cambridge: Cambridge University Press.

Rutherford, Donald (forthcoming). 'Leibniz and the Problem of Monadic Aggregation', *Archiv für Geschichte der Philosophie*.

Sablé, Madeleine de Souvré, Marquise de (1865). *Les Amis de la Marquise de Sablé: Recueil de Lettres des principaux habitués de son salon,* ed. E. de Barthélemy. Paris: Dentu.

Sabra, A. I. (1981). *Theories of Light from Descartes to Newton*. Cambridge: Cambridge University Press. (1st ed., London: Oldbourne, 1967.)

Saccherius, Hieronymus (1697). *Logica demonstrativa*. Turin.

Sáenz de Aguirre, José (1677). *De virtutibus et vitiis disputationes ethicae. . . .* Salamanca.

Sáenz de Aguirre, José (1698). *Philosophia moralis, ab Aristotele tradita decem libris Ethicorum ad Nicomachum. . .* (2 vols.). Rome.

Sailor, Danton B. (1964). 'Moses and atomism', *Journal of the History of Ideas.* 25:3–16.

Saint-Evremond, Charles Marguetel de Saint Denis, seigneur de (1930). *The Letters,* ed. John Hayward. London: Routledge.

Sainte-Beuve, C. A. (1928). *Port-Royal* (7 vols.). Paris: La Connaissance.

Sakellariadis, Spyros (1982). 'Descartes's Use of Empirical Data to Test Hypotheses', *Isis.* 73:68–76.

Salmon, J. H. M. (1989). 'Stoicism and Roman Example: Seneca and Tacitus in Jacobean England', *Journal of the History of Ideas.* 50:199–225.

Sams, H. W. (1944). 'Anti-Stoicism in Seventeenth- and Early Eighteenth-Century England', *Studies in Philology.* 41:65–78.

Sanchez, Francisco (1581). *Quod nihil scitur.* Lyon.

Sanchez, Francisco (1618). *Quod nihil scitur.* Frankfurt am Main.

Sanchez, Francisco. (1984). *Quod Nihil Scitur,* ed. A. Comparot. Paris: Klincksieck.

Sanchez, Francisco (1988). *That Nothing Is Known; Quod nihil scitur,* trans. D. F. S. Thomson. Cambridge: Cambridge University Press.

Sanderson, Robertus (1985). *Logicae artis compendium,* ed. E. J. Ashworth (Instrumenta rationis. Sources for the history of modern logic). Bologna: Editrice CLUEB.

Sandys, J. E. (1906–8). *A History of Classical Scholarship* (3 vols.). 2d ed. Cambridge: Cambridge University Press.

Santillana, G. de (1955). *The Crime of Galileo.* Chicago: University of Chicago Press.

Santinello, Giovanni (ed.) (1981). *Storia delle Storie Generali della Filosofia* (3 vols.). Brescia: La Scuola.

Saraiva, A. J. (1972). 'Antonia Vieira, Menasseh ben Israel et le Cinquième Empire', *Studia Rosenthaliana.* 6:25–56.

Sarasohn, L. T. (1982). 'The Ethical and Political Philosophy of Pierre Gassendi', *Journal of the History of Philosophy.* 20:239–60.

Sarasohn, L. T. (1985). 'Motion and Morality: Pierre Gassendi, Thomas Hobbes and the Mechanical World-View', *Journal of the History of Ideas.* 46:363–79.

Sarasohn, L. T. (1991). 'Epicureanism and the Creation of a Privatist Ethic in Early Seventeenth-Century France', in Margaret J. Osler (ed.), *Atoms, Pneuma, and Tranquillity: Epicurean and Stoic Themes in European Thought.* Cambridge: Cambridge University Press, pp. 175–95.

Sargent, Rose-Mary (1986). 'Robert Boyle's Baconian Inheritance: A Response to Laudan's Cartesian Thesis', *Studies in History and Philosophy of Science.* 17:469–86.

Sargentich, T. (1974). 'Locke and Ethical Theory: Two Ms. Pieces', *The Locke Newsletter.* 5:24–31.

Sasaki, Chikara (1988). 'Descartes's Mathematical Thought'. Ph.D. diss., Princeton University.

Savonarola, Girolamo (1955–    ). *Edizione Nazionale delle opere di Girolamo Savonarola,* ed. Mario Ferrara. Rome: A. Belardetti.

Saw, Ruth (1969). 'Personal Identity in Spinoza', *Inquiry.* 12:1–14.

Saxby, T. J. (1987). *The Quest for the New Jerusalem, Jean de Labadie and the Labadists, 1610–1744.* Dordrecht: Nijhoff.

Schaffer, Simon (1985). 'Occultism and Reason', in A. J. Holland (ed.), *Philosophy, Its History and Historiography.* Dordrecht: Reidel.

Schankula, H. A. S. (1980). 'Locke, Descartes, and the Science of Nature', *Journal of the History of Ideas.* 41:459–77.

Scharf, Johannes (1643). *Metaphysica Exemplaris, seu Prima Philosophia.* 4th ed. Wittenberg.

Scheffler, Samuel (1976). 'Leibniz on Personal Identity and Moral Personality', in *Studia Leibnitiana.* 8:219–40.

Scheibler, Christoph (1636). *Metaphysica.* Geneva.

Schepers, H. (1966). 'Leibniz' Arbeiten zu einer Reformation der Kategorien', *Zeitschrift für philosophische Forschung.* 20:539–67.

Schepers, H. (1969). 'Begriffsanalyse und Kategorialsynthese. Zur Verflechtung von Logik und Metaphysik bei Leibniz', in *Akten des Internationalen Leibniz-Kongresses Hannover, 14–19 November 1966* (5 vols.) (Studia Leibnitiana, Supplementa). Stuttgart: Steiner.

Schepers, H. (1975). 'Leibniz' Disputationen *De conditionibus:* Ansätze zu einer juristischen Aussangenlogik', in *Akten des II. Internationalen Leibniz-Kongresses Hannover, 17–22 Juli 1972* (4 vols.) (Studia Leibnitiana, Supplementa). Stuttgart: Steiner, vol. 4, pp. 1–17.

Schmaltz, Tad M. (1992). 'Sensation, Occasionalism, and Descartes', in Cummins and Zoeller 1992.

Schmaus, M. (1927). *Die Psychologische Trinitätslehre des Hl. Augustinus.* Münster: Aschendorffsche Verlagsbuchhandlung.

Schmidt-Biggemann, Wilhelm (1983). *Topica universalis: Eine Modellgeschichte humanistischer und barocker Wissenschaft.* Hamburg: Meiner.

Schmitt, Charles B. (1965). 'Aristotle as a Cuttlefish: The Origin and Development of a Renaissance Image', *Studies in the Renaissance.* 12:60–72.

Schmitt, Charles B. (1967). *Gianfrancesco Pico della Mirandola (1469–1533) and His Critique of Aristotle.* The Hague: Nijhoff.

Schmitt, Charles B. (1972). *Cicero Scepticus.* The Hague: Nijhoff.

Schmitt, Charles B. (1978). 'Reappraisals in Renaissance Science', *History of Science.* 16:200–214.

Schmitt, Charles B. (1981). *Studies in Renaissance Philosophy and Science.* London: Variorum Reprints.

Schmitt, Charles B. (1983a). *Aristotle and the Renaissance.* Cambridge, Mass.: Harvard University Press.

Schmitt, Charles B. (1983b). *John Case and Aristotelianism in Renaissance England* (McGill-Queen's Studies in the History of Ideas 5). Kingston-Montreal: McGill-Queen's University Press.

Schmitt, Charles B. (1983c). 'Aristotelianism in the Veneto and the Origins of Modern Science: Some Considerations on the Problem of Continuity', in Luigi Olivieri (ed.), *Aristotelismo veneto e scienza moderna* (2 vols.). Padua: Editrice Antenore.

Schmitt, Charles B. (1983d). 'The Rediscovery of Ancient Skepticism in Modern Times', in M. Burnyeat (ed.), *The Skeptical Tradition.* Berkeley: University of California Press.

Schmitt, Charles B. (1984a). 'William Harvey and Renaissance Aristotelianism: A Consideration of the Praefatio to *De generatione animalium* (1651)', in Rudolf Schmitz and Gundolf Keil (eds.), *Humanismus und Medizin.* Weinheim: Acta Humaniora.

Schmitt, Charles B. (1984b). 'Galileo and the Seventeenth-Century Text-Book Tradition', in P. Galluzzi (ed.), *Novità celesti e crisi del sapere. Atti del convegno internazionale di studi galileiani.* Florence: Barbera, pp. 217–28.

Schmitt, Charles B. (1988). 'The Rise of the Philosophical Textbook', in Schmitt, Skinner, and Kessler 1988, pp. 792–804.

Schmitt, Charles B.; Skinner, Quentin; and Kessler, Eckhard (eds.) (1988). *The Cambridge History of Renaissance Philosophy.* Cambridge: Cambridge University Press.

Schmitt-Lermann, Hans (1954). *Der Versicherungsgedanke in deutschen Geistesleben des Barock und der Aufklärung* Munich: J. Jehle.

Schneewind, J. B. (1987). 'Pufendorf's Place in the History of Ethics', *Synthese.* 72:123–55.

Schneewind, J. B. (ed.) (1990). *Moral Philosophy from Montaigne to Kant: An Anthology* (2 vols.). Cambridge: Cambridge University Press.

Schneider, G. (1970). *Der Libertin. Zur Geistes und Sozialgeschichte des Bürgertums in 16. und 17. Jht.* Stuttgart: J. B. Melzler.

Schneider, H.-P. (1967). *Justitia Universalis. Quellenstudien zur Geschichte des 'Christlichen Naturrechts' bei Gottfried Wilhelm Leibniz.* Frankfurt: Klosterman.

Schneider, H.-P. (1979). 'Die wissenschaftliche Beziehungen zwischen Leibniz und den beiden Cocceji

(Heinrich und Samuel)', in *Humanismus und Naturrecht in Berlin, Brandenburg, Preussen*, ed. H. Thieme. Berlin and New York: de Gruyter, pp. 90–102.

Schneider, Ivo (1968–69). 'Der Mathematiker Abraham De Moivre (1667–1754)', *Archive for History of Exact Sciences*. 5:177–317.

Schneider, Ivo (1980). 'Why Do We Find the Origin of a Calculus of Probabilities in the Seventeenth Century?' in J. Hintikka, D. Gruender, and E. Agazzi (eds.), *Pisa Conference on the History and Philosophy of Science (1978)*. *Proceedings* (2 vols.). Dordrecht and Boston: Reidel.

Schneider, Ivo (1981). 'Leibniz on the Probable', in Joseph W. Dauben (ed.), *Mathematical Perspectives: Essays on Mathematics and Its Historical Development Presented to Professor Dr. Kurt-Reinhard Biermann on the Occasion of His Sixtieth Birthday*. New York: Academic Press.

Schneiders, W. (1966). 'Naturrecht und Gerechtigkeit bei Leibniz', *Zeitschrift für philosophische Forschung*. 20:607–650.

Schneiders, W. (1971). *Naturrecht und Liebesethik. Zur Geschichte der praktischen Philosophie im Hinblick auf Christian Thomasius*. Hildesheim: Olms.

Schneiders, W. (ed.) (1989). *Christian Thomasius 1655–1728. Interpretationen zu Werk und Wirkung. Mit einer Bibliographie der neueren Thomasius-Literatur*. Hamburg: Meiner.

Schofield, Robert E. (1970). *Mechanism and Materialism: British Natural Philosophy in an Age of Reason*. Princeton, N.J.: Princeton University Press.

Scholem, Gershom (1961). *Major Trends in Jewish Mysticism*. New York: Schocken.

Scholem, Gershom (1971). 'Doenmeh', in *Encyclopaedia Judaica* (16 vols.). New York: Macmillan, vol. 6, colls. 148–52.

Scholem, Gershom (1973). *Sabbatai Sevi: the Mystical Messiah (1626–1676)*, trans. R. J. Zwi Werblowsky. Princeton, N.J.: Princeton University Press.

Scholem, Gershom (1974). *Kabbalah*. Jerusalem: Keter.

Scholem, Gershom (1978). *Kabbalah*. New York: New American Library.

Schouls, Peter A. (1980). *The Imposition of Method: A Study of Locke and Descartes*. Oxford: Oxford University Press.

Schouls, Peter A. (1992). *Reasoned Freedom. John Locke and the Enlightenment*. Ithaca, N.Y.: Cornell University Press.

Schubart-Fikentscher, G. (1977). *Christian Thomasius. Seine Bedeutung als Hochschullehrer am Beginn der deutschen Aufklärung* (Sitzungsberichte der Sächsischen Akademie der Wissenschaften zu Leipzig. Philologische-historische Klasse Bd. 119, Heft 4). Berlin: Akademie Verlag.

Schuhmann, Karl (1992). 'Le vocabulaire de l'espace', in Yves-Charles Zarka (ed.), *Hobbes et son vocabulaire*. Paris: Vrin, pp. 61–82.

Schüling, Hermann (1967). *Bibliographie der psychologischen Literatur des 16. Jahrhunderts*. Hildesheim: Olms.

Schüling, Hermann (1969). *Die Geschichte der axiomatischen Methode im 16. und beginnenden 17 Jahrhundert*. Hildesheim: Georg Olms.

Schurman, Anna Maria van (1638). *Amica dissertatio inter Annam Mariam Schurmanniam et Andr. Rivetum de capacitate ingenii muliebris ad scientias*. Paris.

Schurman, Anna Maria van (1641). *Dissertatio logica de ingenii muliebris ad doctrinam et meliores litteras aptitudine, cui accedunt epistolae aliquot (Schurmanniae ipsius et Riveti) ejusdem argumenti*. Leiden.

Schurman, Anna Maria van (1648). *Nobiliss Virginis Annae Mariae à Schurman, Opuscula. Hebraea, Graeca, Latina, Gallica, prosaica et metrica*. Leiden. (Repr. 1650, 1652, 1794.)

Schurman, Anna Maria van (1673). *Euchlepia seu Melioris partis electio . . .* Altona.

Schuster, John A. (1977). 'Descartes and the Scientific Revolution, 1618–1644: An Interpretation'. Ph.D. diss., Princeton University.

Schuster, John A. (1980). 'Descartes' *Mathesis universalis*, 1619–28', in Stephen Gaukroger (ed.), *Descartes: Philosophy, Mathematics and Physics*. Brighton: Harvester Press.

Schuster, John A. (1984). 'Methodologies as Mythic Structures: A Preface to the Future Historiography of Method', *Metascience: Annual Review of the Australasian Association for the History, Philosophy and Social Studies of Science*. 1/2:15–36.

Schuster, John A. (1986). 'Cartesian Method as Mythic Speech: A Diachronic and Structural Analysis', in John A. Schuster and Richard R. Yeo (eds.), *The Politics and Rhetoric of Scientific Method: Historical Studies*. Dordrecht: Reidel.

Schuster, John A. (1993). 'Whatever Should We Do with Cartesian Method? Reclaiming Descartes for the History of Science', in Voss 1993.

Scott, J. F. (1952). *The Scientific Work of René Descartes (1596–1650)*. London: Taylor and Francis.

Scott, James Brown (ed.) (1934). *The Spanish Origins of International Law*. Oxford: Oxford University Press.

Screech, M. A. (1983). *Montaigne and Melancholy. The Wisdom of the Essay*. London: Duckworth.

Scudéry, Madeleine de (1806). *Lettres de Mesdames de Scudéry, de Salvan de Saliez, et de Mademoiselle Descartes*. Paris: Collin.

Sebba, G. (1964). *Bibliographia Cartesiana. A Critical Guide to the Descartes Literature 1800–1960*. The Hague: Martinus Nijhof.

Secada, J. E. K. (1990). 'Descartes on Time and Causality', *Philosophical Review*. 99:45–72.

Sedgwick, Alexander (1977). *Jansenism in Seventeenth Century France: Voices from the Wilderness*. Charlottesville: University Press of Virginia.

Seigel, Jerrold E. (1968). *Rhetoric and Philosophy in Renaissance Humanism*. Princeton, N.J.: Princeton University Press.

Seiler, J. (1936). *Der Zweck in der Philosophie des Franz Suarez*. Innsbrück: F. Rauch.

Selden, John (1640). *De iure naturali et gentium juxta disciplinam ebraeorum*. London.

Selden, John (1663). *Mare clausum: The Right and Dominion of the Sea in Two Books,* trans. J. H. London.

Selden, John (1726). *Opera omnia*, ed. D. Wilkins (3 vols.). London. (There is also a 1725 London ed.)

Sellier, Philippe (1970). *Pascal et Saint Augustin*. Paris: Colin.

Semedo, Alvaro, S.J. (1642). *Imperio de la China*. Madrid.

Senault, Jean-François (1649). *The Use of the Passions,* trans. Henry, Earl of Monmouth. London.

Senault, Jean-François (1987). *De l'usage des passions*. Paris: Fayard.

Seneca (1614). *The Works both Moral and Natural . . . ,* trans. Thomas Lodge. London.

Senlis, Sébastien de (1637). *Les Entretiens du sage*. Paris.

Senlis, Sébastien de (1638). *Les Maximes du sage*. Paris.

Senlis, Sébastien de (1642). *Le Flambeau du juste pour la conduite des esprits supérieurs*. Paris.

Sennert, Daniel (1618). *Epitome naturalis scientiae*. Wittenberg.

Sennert, Daniel (1619). *De chymicorum cum Aristotelicis et Galenicis consensu ac dissensu liber I*. Wittenberg. Also in Sennert 1641, vol. 1.

Sennert, Daniel (1636). *Hypomnemata physica*. Frankfurt-am-Main.

Sennert, Daniel (1637). *Hypomnemata physica*. 2d. ed. Lyon.

Sennert, Daniel (1641). *Opera omnia* (3 vols.). Venice. (1676 ed. repr. Hildesheim: Olms, 1987.)

Sepich, J. R. (1949). 'Naturaleza de la filosofia primera o metafisica en Francesco Suarez', *Philosophia* (Mendoza). 11–12:107–17.

Serene, Eileen (1982). 'Demonstrative Science', in N. Kretzmann, A. Kenny, and J. Pinborg (eds.), *The Cambridge History of Later Medieval Philosophy*. Cambridge: Cambridge University Press, pp. 496–517.

Sergeant, John (1665). *Sure-Footing in Christianity, or Rational Discourses on the Rule of Faith*. London.

Sergeant, John (1696). *The Method to Science*. London.

Sergeant, John (1697). *Solid Philosophy Asserted, against the Fancies of the Ideists: Or, The Method to Science Farther illustrated. With Reflections on Mr. Locke's Essay. . . .* London. (Repr. New York: Garland, 1984.)

Sergeant, John (1698). *Non Ultra: Or, A Letter to a Learned Cartesian.* London. (Repr. *Monist* (1929), 39:593–628.)

Sergeant, John (1700). *Transnatural Philosophy, or Metaphysics.* London.

Serveto, Miguel (1531). *De trinitatis erroribus libri septem.* Hagenau. (Repr. Frankfurt: Minerva G.M.B.H., 1965.)

Serveto, Miguel (1932). *Two Treatises of Servetus on the Trinity,* trans. E. M. Wilbur (Harvard Theological Studies XVI). Cambridge, Mass.: Harvard University Press.

Sève, René (1989). *Leibniz et l'école moderne du droit naturel.* Paris: Presses Universitaire de France.

Sextus Empiricus (1933). *Outlines of Pyrrhonism,* in *Sextus Empiricus,* trans. R. G. Bury (4 vols., Loeb Classical Library), vol. 1. Cambridge, Mass.: Harvard University Press. London: Heinemann.

Sextus Empiricus (1935). *Against the Logicians,* in *Sextus Empiricus,* trans. R. G. Bury (4 vols., Loeb Classical Library), vol. 2. Cambridge, Mass.: Harvard University Press. London: Heinemann.

Sextus Empiricus (1936). *Against the Physicists,* and *Against the Ethicists,* in *Sextus Empiricus,* trans. R. G. Bury (4 vols., Loeb Classical Library), vol. 3. Cambridge, Mass.: Harvard University Press. London: Heinemann.

Sextus Empiricus (1949). *Against the Professors,* in *Sextus Empiricus,* trans. R. G. Bury (4 vols., Loeb Classical Library), vol. 4. Cambridge, Mass.: Harvard University Press. London: Heinemann.

Shafer, Glenn (1978). 'Non-additive Probabilities in the Work of Bernoulli and Lambert', *Archive for History of Exact Sciences.* 19:309–70.

Shaftesbury, Anthony Ashley Cooper, Earl of (1900). *Characteristics,* ed. J. M. Robertson (2 vols.). London: Grant Richards.

Shapin, Steven (1984). 'Pump and Circumstance: Robert Boyle's Literary Technology', *Social Studies of Science.* 14:481–520.

Shapin, Steven, and Schaffer, Simon (1985). *Leviathan and the Air-Pump.* Princeton, N.J.: Princeton University Press.

Shapiro, Barbara J. (1969). *John Wilkins.* Berkeley: University of California Press.

Shapiro, Barbara J. (1983). *Probability and Certainty in Seventeenth-Century England; A Study of the Relationships between Natural Science, Religion, History, Law, and Literature.* Princeton, N.J.: Princeton University Press.

Sharrock, Robert (1660). ʽΥπόθεσισ ἠθική [*Hupothesis ethike*] *de officiis secundum naturae jus.* Oxford.

Shea, William R. (1970). 'Galileo's Atomic Hypothesis', *Ambix.* 17:13–27.

Shea, William R. (1972). *Galileo's Intellectual Revolution.* London: Macmillan.

Shea, William R. (1991). *The Magic of Numbers and Motion: The Scientific Career of René Descartes.* Canton, Mass.: Science History Publications.

Sherlock, William (1690). *A Vindication of the Doctrine of the Holy and Ever Blessed Trinity.* London.

Sherlock, William (1694). *A Defence of Dr. Sherlock's Notion of a Trinity in Unity.* London.

Sheynin, O. B. (1968). 'On the Early History of the Law of Large Numbers', *Biometrika.* 55:459–67. (Repr. in E. S. Pearson and M. G. Kendall, eds., *Studies in the History of Statistics and Probability.* Darien, Conn.: Hafner, 1970.)

Sheynin, O. B. (1970–1). 'Newton and the Classical Theory of Probability', *Archive for History of Exact Sciences.* 7:217–43.

Sheynin, O. B. (1974). 'On the Prehistory of the Theory of Probability', *Archive for History of Exact Sciences.* 12:97–141.

Shirley, John W. (ed.) (1974). *Thomas Harriot, Renaissance Scientist.* Oxford: Oxford University Press.

Shirley, John W. (1983). *Thomas Harriot, A Biography.* Oxford: Oxford University Press.

Silhon, Jean de (1624). *Les deux vérités de Silhon: l'une de Dieu, et de sa providence, l'autre de l'immortalité de l'ame.* Paris.

Silhon, Jean de (1634). *De l'immortalité de l'ame.* Paris.

Silhon, Jean de (1991). *Les deux vérités de Silhon – l'une de Dieu, et de sa providence, l'autre de l'immortalité de l'ame,* ed. J.-R. Armogathe. Paris: Fayard.

Sillem, Edward A. (1957). *George Berkeley and the Proofs for the Existence of God*. London: Longmans Green.

Simmons, Alison (1994). 'Explaining Sense Perception: A Scholastic Challenge', *Philosophical Studies*. 73:257–75.

Simon, G. (1981). 'Les vérités éternelles de Descartes, évidences ontologiques', *Studia Cartesiana*. 2:124–35.

Simon, Gérard (1979). *Kepler, astronome, astrologue*. Paris: Gallimard.

Simon, Richard (1680). *Critical History of the Old Testament*. London.

Simon, Richard (1702). *Lettres choisies*. Rotterdam.

Sinapius, Daniel (1645). *Dissertationes ethicae*. Leiden.

Sirven, J. (1930). *Les années d'apprentissage de Descartes (1596–1628)*. Paris: Vrin. (Also Albi: Imprimerie Coopérative du Sud-Ouest, 1928.) (Repr. New York: Garland, 1987.)

Skinner, Quentin (1978). *The Foundations of Modern Political Thought* (2 vols.). Cambridge: Cambridge University Press.

Skinner, Quentin (1994). 'Moral Ambiguity and the Renaissance Art of Eloquence', *Essays in Criticism*. 44:267–92.

Skinner, Quentin (1996). *Reason and Rhetoric in the Philosophy of Hobbes*. Cambridge: Cambridge University Press.

Slaughter, Mary M. (1982). *Universal Languages and Scientific Taxonomy in the Seventeenth Century*. Cambridge: Cambridge University Press.

Sleigh, R. C. (1990a). *Leibniz & Arnauld. A Commentary on Their Correspondence*. New Haven, Conn.: Yale University Press.

Sleigh, R. C. (1990b). 'Leibniz on Malebranche on Causality', in J. A. Cover and Mark Kuhlstad (eds.), *Central Themes in Early Modern Philosophy*. Indianapolis, Ind.: Hackett.

Sleigh, Robert (1982). 'Truth and Sufficient Reason in the Philosophy of Leibniz', in Michael Hooker (ed.), *Leibniz: Critical and Interpretive Essays*. Minneapolis: University of Minnesota Press.

Smiglecius, Martinus (1638). *Logica* [first ed. 1618]. Oxford.

Smiglecius, Martinus (1658). *Logica* [first ed. 1618]. Oxford.

Smith, A. Mark (1976). 'Galileo's Theory of Indivisibles: Revolution or Compromise', *Journal of the History of Ideas*. 27:571–88.

Smith, John (1660). *Select Discourses*. London.

Smith, John (1821). *Select Discourses*. 3d ed. London.

Smith, John (1969). *The True Way or Method of Attaining to Divine Knowledge,* in C. A. Patrides (ed.), *The Cambridge Platonists*. Cambridge: Cambridge University Press, pp. 128–44.

Smith, Matthew (1695). *A Philosophical Discourse of the Nature of Rational and Irrational Souls*. London.

Smith, Wesley D. (1979). *The Hippocratic Tradition*. Ithaca, N.Y.: Cornell University Press.

Snow, A. J. (1975). *Matter and Gravity in Newton's Physical Philosophy*. New York: Arno Press.

Snowdon, P. F. (1990). 'Persons, Animals, and Ourselves', in C. Gill (ed.), *The Person and the Human Mind*. Oxford: Oxford University Press, pp. 83–107.

Société Générale Néerlandaise d'Assurances sur la vie et de Rentes Viagères (1898). *Mémoires pour servir à l'historie des assurances sur la vie et des rentes viagères au Pays-Bas*. Amsterdam.

Solomon, Howard M. (1972). *Public Welfare, Science, and Propaganda in Seventeenth-Century France; The Innovations of Théophraste Renaudot*. Princeton, N.J.: Princeton University Press.

Sommerville, Johann P. (1984). 'John Selden, the Law of Nature, and the Origins of Government', *Historical Journal*. 27:437–47.

Sommerville, Johann P. (1986). *Politics and Ideology in England, 1603–1640*. London: Longman.

Sommerville, Johann P. (1992). *Thomas Hobbes: Political Ideas in Historical Context*. New York: St. Martin's.

Sommervogel, C., et al. (1890–1932), *Bibliothèque de la Compagnie de Jésus* (11 vols.). Brussels: Schepens.

Sophie, Electress of Hanover (1927). *Briefwechsel der Kurfürstin Sophie von Hanover.* Berlin: K. J. Koehler.

Sorabji, Richard (1980). *Necessity, Cause and Blame: Perspectives on Aristotle's Theory.* Ithaca, N.Y.: Cornell University Press.

Sorabji, Richard (1983). *Time, Creation and the Continuum.* Ithaca, N.Y.: Cornell University Press.

Sorbière, Samuel (1660). *Lettres et discours de M. de Sorbière sur diverses matières curieuses.* Paris.

Sorell, Tom (1986). *Hobbes.* London: Routledge.

Sorell, Tom (1993). 'Morals and Modernity in Descartes', in Tom Sorell (ed.), *The Rise of Modern Philosophy: The Tension between the New and Traditional Philosophies from Machiavelli to Leibniz.* Oxford: Oxford University Press, pp. 273–88.

Sørensen, K. E. (1976). 'A Study of the De proportione motus by Marcus Marci de Kronland: Part I', *Centaurus.* 20: 50–76.

Sortais, Gaston (1928–9). *Le cartésianisme chez les Jésuites français au 17ᵉ et 18ᵉ siècles (Archives de philosophie,* vol. 6, no. 3). Paris: Beauchesne.

Sosa, Ernest (ed.) (1987). *Essays on the Philosophy of George Berkeley.* Dordrecht: Reidel.

South, Robert (1693). *Animadversions upon Dr. Sherlock's Book, Entituled A Vindication of the Holy and Ever Blessed Trinity.* London.

South, Robert (1695). *Tritheism Charged upon Dr. Sherlock's New Notion of the Trinity.* London.

Southgate, B. C. (1981). 'Thomas White, 1593–1676: A Reputation and Its Decline', *Essex Recusant.* 23:29–36.

Southgate, B. C. (1993). *"Covetous of Truth": The Life and Work of Thomas White, 1593–1676.* Dordrecht: Kluwer.

Spanneut, Michel (1973). *Permanence du Stoïcisme: de Zénon à Malraux.* Gembloux: J. Duculot.

Specht, Rainer (1966). *Commercium mentis et corporis: über Kausalvorstellungen im Cartesianismus.* Stuttgart-Bad Cannstatt: Friedrich Frommann Verlag.

Spellman, W. M. (1988). *John Locke and the Problem of Depravity.* Oxford: Oxford University Press.

Spence, Jonathan (1984). *The Memory Palace of Matteo Ricci.* New York: Viking.

Sperling, Johann (1664). *Institutiones physicae Johannis Sperlings Profess. Publ. Editio quinta, auctior & correctior* . . . Frankfurt, Wittemberg.

Spiller, Michael R. G. (1980). *'Concerning Natural Experimental Philsophie': Meric Casaubon and the Royal Society.* The Hague: Nijhoff.

Spink, J. S. (1960). *French Free-Thought from Gassendi to Voltaire.* London: Athlone Press.

Spinoza, Benedictus de (1663). *Renati des Cartes principiorum philosophiae . . . more geometrico demonstratae per Benedictum de Spinoza . . . accesserunt ejusdem cogitata metaphysica. . . .* Amsterdam.

Spinoza, Benedictus de (1670). *Tractatus Theologico-Politicus.* Amsterdam. (The title page has the name of a false publisher in Hamburg.)

Spinoza, Benedictus de (1677). *Opera posthuma.* Amsterdam.

Spinoza, Benedictus de (1683). *Miracles no Violation of the laws of Nature,* trans. Charles Blount. London.

Spinoza, Benedictus de (1689). *A Treatise Partly Theological and Partly Political . . . Translated out of the Latin.* London.

Spinoza, Benedictus de (1910). *Short Treatise on God, Man, and His Well-Being,* ed. and trans. A. Wolf. London: Adam and Charles Black.

Spinoza, Benedictus de (1925). *Opera,* ed. Carl Gebhardt (4 vols.). Heidelberg: C. Winter.

Spinoza, Benedictus de (1928). *The Correspondence of Spinoza,* ed. and trans. A. Wolf. London: Allen and Unwin.

Spinoza, Benedictus de (1985). *Collected Works,* vol. 1, ed. and trans. E. M. Curley. Princeton, N.J.: Princeton University Press.

Spinoza, Benedictus de (1986). *Korte Verhandeling van God de Mensch en deszelfs Welstand,* ed. and trans. (Italian) F. Magnini. L'Aquila: Japadre.

Spragens, Thomas A. (1973). *The Politics of Motion: The World of Thomas Hobbes.* Lexington: University Press of Kentucky.

Sprat, Thomas (1667). _The History of the Royal Society_. London. (Repr. ed. Jackson I. Cope and Harold Whitmore Jones. St. Louis, Mo.: Washington University Press, 1958.)

Stahl, Georg Ernst (1723). _Fundamenta chymiae dogmaticae & experimentalis, & quidem tum communioris physicae mechanicae pharmaceuticae ac medicae tum sublimioris sic dictae hermeticae atque alchymicae. Olim in privatos auditorum usus posita, jam vero indultu autoris publicae luci exposita_. . . . Nuremberg.

Stahl, Georg Ernst (1730). _Philosophical Principles of Universal Chemistry: Or, the Foundation of a Scientifical Manner of Inquiring into and Preparing the Natural and Artificial Bodies for the Uses of Life_ . . . _Design'd as a General Introduction to the Knowledge and Practice of Artificial Philosophy: Or, Genuine Chemistry in all Its Branches_, trans. Peter Shaw. London: Osborn and Longman.

Standaert, N., S.J. (1991). 'Inculturation and Chinese-Christian Contacts in the Late Ming and Early Qing', _Ching Feng_. 34:1–16.

Stanley, Thomas (1655–62). _The History of Philosophy_ (3 vols.). London.

Stanley, Thomas (1701). _The History of Philosophy_. 3d ed. London.

Starobinski, Jean (1982). _Montaigne en mouvement_. Paris: Gallimard.

Starobinski, Jean (1985). _Montaigne in Motion_. Chicago: University of Chicago Press.

_Statuta Almae Universitatis D.D. Philosophorum, & Medicorum_ (1607). Padua.

Stein, Howard (1977). 'Some Philosophical Prehistory of General Relativity', in J. Earman, C. Glymour, J. Stachel (eds.), _Foundations of Space-Time Theories_ (Minnesota Studies in the Philosophy of Science, no. 8). Minneapolis: University of Minnesota Press, pp. 3–49.

Steneck, Nicholas (1974). 'Albert the Great on the Classification of Internal Senses', _Isis_. 65:193–211.

Steneck, Nicholas (1982). 'Greatrakes the Stroker: The Interpretation of Historians', _Isis_. 73:161–77.

Stephens, W. P. (1986). _The Theology of Huldryck Zwingli_. Oxford: Oxford University Press.

Stevin, Simon (1586). _De Beghinselen der Weeghconst_. Leiden. (Repr. with trans. in Ernst Crone et al. (eds.), _Principal Works_ (5 vols. in 6). Amsterdam: C. V. Swets & Zeitlinger, 1955–66), vol. 1.)

Stewart, Roy A. (1961). _Rabbinic Theology_. Edinburgh, London: Oliver and Boyd.

Stierius, Johannes (1647). _Praecepta doctrinae_ . . . _ethicae_ . . . _brevibus tabellis compacta_. Cambridge.

Stigler, Stephen M. (1986a). _The History of Statistics. The Measurement of Uncertainty before 1900_. Cambridge, Mass.: Harvard University Press.

Stigler, Stephen M. (1986b). 'John Craig and the Probability of History: From the Death of Christ to the Birth of Laplace', _Journal of the American Statistical Association_. 81:879–87.

Stillingfleet, Edward (1659). _Irenicum: A Weapon-Salve for the Churches Wounds_ . . . : _Whereby a Foundation Is Laid for the Churches Peace, and the Accommodation of Our Present Differences_. . . . London.

Stillingfleet, Edward (1662). _Origines Sacrae_. London.

Stillingfleet, Edward (1664). _A Rational Account of the Grounds of Protestant Religion_. London.

Stillingfleet, Edward (1687). _The Doctrine of the Trinity and Transubstantiation Compared: The Second Part_. London.

Stillingfleet, Edward (1697a). _A Discourse in Vindication of the Doctrine of the Trinity: With an Answer to the Late Socinian Objections against It from Scripture, Antiquity and Reason_. London.

Stillingfleet, Edward (1697b). _An Answer to Mr. Locke's Letter, concerning Some Passages Relating to His Essay of Humane Understanding_. London.

Stillingfleet, Edward (1698). _An Answer to Mr. Locke's Second Letter; Wherein His Notion of IDEAS Is Prov'd to be Inconsistent with It Self, and with the ARTICLES of the CHRISTIAN FAITH_. London.

Stillingfleet, Edward (1710). _The Works of that Eminent and Most Learned Prelate, Dr. Edw. Stillingfleet, Late Lord Bishop of Worcester_ (6 vols.). London.

Stolleis, M. (1988). _Geschichte des öffentlichen Rechts in Deutschland_. Munich: Beck.

Stolpe, Sven (1966). _Christina of Sweden_. New York: Macmillan.

Stone, Lawrence (1964). 'The Educational Revolution in England 1560–1640', _Past and Present_. 28:41–80.

Strauss, Leo (1952). *Persecution and the Art of Writing*. Glencoe, Ill.: Free Press.

Strauss, Leo (1963). *Political Philosophy of Hobbes. Its Basis and Genesis*. 2d ed. Chicago: University of Chicago Press. (1st ed. Oxford: Oxford University Press, 1936.)

Strier, Richard (1983). *Love Known. Theology and Experience in George Herbert's Poetry*. Chicago: University of Chicago Press.

Suárez, Francisco (1619). *Metaphysicarum disputationum, in quibus, & universa naturalis theologia ordinatè traditur, & quaestiones ad omnes duodecim Aristotelis libros pertinentes, accuratè disputantur, tomi duo.* . . . Venice. (First ed. Salamanca, 1597.)

Suárez, Francisco (1856–78). *Opera Omnia*, ed. D. M. André (28 vols.). Paris. (*Disputationes Metaphysicae* (vols. 25–6) repr. Hildesheim: Olms, 1965.)

Suárez, Francisco (1944). *Selections from Three Works* (2 vols.). Oxford: Oxford University Press.

Suárez, Francisco, (1960–6). *Disputaciones metafisicas*, ed. and trans. (Latin with Spanish trans.) S. Rábade Romeo, S. Caballero Sánchez, and A. Puigcerver Zanón (7 vols.). Madrid: Editorial Gredos.

Suárez, Francisco, (1964). *On Formal and Universal Unity, De unitate formali et universali*, trans. J. F. Ross. Milwaukee: Marquette University Press.

Suárez, Francisco (1971–81). *Tractatus de legibus, ac Deo legislatore*, bilingual ed. trans. (Spanish) L. Pereña et al. (8 vols.). Madrid: Consijo Superior de Investigaciones Científicas, Instituto Francisco de Vitoria.

Suárez, Francisco (1976). *De Unitate Individuali eiusque Principio / Über die Individualität und das Individuationsprinzip*, ed. and trans. (German) R. Specht (2 vols.). Hamburg: Meiner.

Suárez, Francisco (1978–81). *De anima: commentaria una cum quaestionibus in libros Aristotelis De anima / comentarios a los libros de Aristoteles Sobre el alma*, ed. and trans. (Spanish) Salvador Castellote. Madrid: Sociedad de Estudios y Publicaciones.

Suárez, Francisco (1982). *Suarez on Individuation. Metaphysical Disputation V: Individual Unity and Its Principle*, ed. and trans. J. J. E. Gracia. Milwaukee, Wisc.: Marquette University Press.

Suárez, Francisco (1983). *On the Essence of Finite Being, etc.*, trans. Norman Wells. Milwaukee, Wisc.: Marquette University Press.

Suchon, Gabrielle (1988). *Traité de la morale et de la politique: La liberté*, ed. Séverine Auffret. Paris: Des femmes.

Süssmilch, Johann (1775). *Die göttliche Ordnung in den veränderungen des menschlichen Geschlechts*. 3d ed. Berlin.

Sylla, Edith (1982). 'The Oxford Calculators', in Kretzmann, Kenny, and Pinborg 1982, pp. 540–63.

Sylvius, Iacobus (1626). *Disputatio philosophica continens quaestionum decadem*, . . . *praeside Francone Burgersdicio*. . . . Leiden.


Tachau, Katherine H. (1988). *Vision and Certitude in the Age of Ockham: Optics, Epistemology and the Foundations of Semantics, 1250–1345*. Leiden: Brill.

Tack, Reiner (1974). *Untersuchungen zum Philosophie- und Wissenschaftsbegriff bei Pierre Gassendi (1592–1655)*. Meisenheim am Glan: Verlag Anton Hain.

Talaska, Richard A. (1988). 'Analytic and Synthetic Method according to Hobbes', *Journal of the History of Philosophy*. 26:207–37.

Talmor, Sascha (1981). *Glanvill: The Uses and Abuses of Scepticism*. Oxford: Pergamon.

Tamm, Ditlev (1986). 'Pufendorf und Dänemark', in *Samuel von Pufendorf 1632–1982*, ed. K. Å. Modéer. Stockholm: Nordiska Bokhandeln, pp. 81–9.

Tatakis, Basile (1949). *La philosophie Byzantine*, second supplementary fascicle to Brehier, Emile, *Histoire de la Philosophie*. Paris: Presses Universitaires de France.

Taton, René (1965). *Les origines de l'Académie royale des sciences* (Palais de la Découverte, D 105). Paris: Palais de la Découverte.

Taylor, A. E. (1908). *Hobbes*. London: Constable.

Taylor, A. E. (1965). 'The Ethical Doctrine of Hobbes', in K. C. Brown (ed.), *Hobbes Studies.* Oxford: Blackwell, pp. 35–55.

Taylor, Charles (1983). 'Réponse à Jean-Marie Beyssade', *Revue internationale de philosophie.* 146:288–92.

Taylor, Jeremy (1660). *Ductor dubitantium, or The Rule of Conscience. . . .* London.

Teichman, Jenny (1985). 'The Definition of *Person*', *Philosophy.* 60:175–85.

Telesio, Bernardino (1965–76). *De Rerum Natura Juxta Propria Principia,* ed. and trans. (Italian) Luigi de Franco (3 vols.). Consenza 1965, Consenza 1974, and Florence: La Nuova Italia, 1976.

Temple, William (1814). *Works* (4 vols.). London.

Temple, William (1908). *Upon the Garden of Epicurus,* ed. A. F. Sieveking. London: Gollancz.

Temple, William (1963). *Five Miscellaneous Essays,* ed. S. H. Monk. Ann Arbor: University of Michigan Press.

Tennant, R. C. (1982). 'The Anglican Response to Locke's Theory of Personal Identity', *Journal of the History of Ideas.* 43:73–90.

ter Meulen, Jacob, and Diermanse, P. J. J. (1950). *Bibliographie des écrits imprimés de Hugo Grotius.* The Hague: Nijhoff.

Tesauro, Emanuele (1670). *La filosofia morale derivata dall'alto fonte del grande Aristotele Stagirita.* Turin.

Testu de Mauroy, abbé Jean (1666). *Les Doctrines de la raison, ou l'honnesteté des moeurs selon les maximes de Sénèque.* Paris.

Thackray, Arnold (1970). *Atoms and Powers: An Essay on Newtonian Matter – Theory and the Development of Chemistry* (Harvard Monographs in the History of Science). Cambridge, Mass.: Harvard University Press.

*Theophrastus redivivus,* edizione prima e critica (1981–82). Eds. G. Canziani and G. Paganini. Florence: La Nuova Italia.

Thiel, Udo (1981). 'Locke's Concept of Person', in R. Brandt (ed.), *John Locke. Symposium Wolfenbüttel 1979.* Berlin: de Gruyter, pp. 181–92.

Thiel, Udo (1983). *Lockes Theorie der personalen Identität.* Bonn: Bouvier.

Thiel, Udo (1990). *John Locke.* Reinbek bei Hamburg: Rowohlt Taschenbuch Verlag.

Thiel, Udo (1991). 'Cudworth and Seventeenth-Century Theories of Consciousness', in S. Gaukroger (ed.), *The Uses of Antiquity.* Dordrecht: Kluwer, pp. 79–99.

Thiel, Udo (1994). 'Hume's Notions of Consciousness and Reflection in Context', *British Journal for the History of Philosophy* 2:75–115.

Thieme, H. (ed.) (1979). *Humanismus und Naturrecht in Berlin, Brandenburg, Preussen.* Berlin: de Gruyter.

Thijssen-Schoute, C. Louise (1950). 'Le cartésianisme au Pays-Bas', in Dijksterhuis et al. 1950, pp. 183–260.

Thijssen-Schoute, C. Louise (1954). *Nederlands Cartesianisme.* Amsterdam: North-Holland.

Thomas, I. (1964). 'Medieval Aftermath: Oxford Logic and Logicians of the Seventeenth Century', in *Oxford Studies Presented to Daniel Callus* (Oxford Historical Society). Oxford: Oxford University Press.

Thomas, I. (1967). 'Logic, History of: Interregnum and Precursors of Modern Logic', in P. Edwards (ed.), *The Encyclopedia of Philosophy* (8 vols.). London: Collier-Macmillan.

Thomas, Keith (1971). *Religion and the Decline of Magic.* New York: Scribner.

Thomas Aquinas, Saint (1882–   ). *Opera omnia,* ed. Leonis XIII. Rome: Typographia Polyglotta.

Thomas Aquinas, Saint (1927). *Opuscula omnia,* ed. P. Mandonnet (5 vols.). Paris: Lethielleux.

Thomas Aquinas, Saint (1946). *De ente et essentia,* ed. C. Boyer. Rome: Aedes Universitatis Gregorianae.

Thomas Aquinas, Saint (1950). *In duodecim libros metaphysicorum Aristotelis expositio,* ed. M.-R. Cathala and R. M. Spiazzi. Turin and Rome: Marietti.

Thomas Aquinas, Saint (1952–4). *Truth,* trans. R. W. Mulligan (3 vols). Chicago: Regnery.

Thomas Aquinas, Saint (1953). *De physico auditu sive physicorum Aristotelis*, ed. Angelus M. Pirota. Naples: M. D'Auria.

Thomas Aquinas, Saint (1954). *De natura loci*, opusculum 52 of *Opuscula Philosophica*, ed. M. Spiazzi. Turin: Marietti.

Thomas Aquinas, Saint (1961). *Commentary on the Metaphysics of Aristotle*, ed. and trans. J. P. Rowan (2 vols). Chicago: Henry Regnery.

Thomas Aquinas, Saint (1963). *Commentary on the Physics of Aristotle*, trans. Richard J. Blackwell, Richard J. Spath, and W. Edmund Thirlkel, intro. Vernon J. Bourke. London: Routledge.

Thomas Aquinas, Saint (1964–80). *Summa theologiae*, ed. and trans. by Thomas Gilby et al. (61 vols). London: Blackfriars' Eyne and Spottiswoode.

Thomas Aquinas, Saint (1965). *Selected Writings of St. Thomas Aquinas: The Principles of Nature, On Being and Essence, On the Virtues in General, On Free Choice*, trans. Robert P. Goodwin. Indianapolis: Bobbs-Merrill.

Thomas Aquinas, Saint (1968a). *On the Unity of the Intellect against the Averroists*, trans. B. H. Zedler. Milwaukee, Wisc.: Marquette University Press.

Thomas Aquinas, Saint (1968b). *Questiones de anima*, ed. J. H. Robb. Toronto: Pontifical Institute of Mediaeval Studies.

Thomas Aquinas, Saint (1968c). *On Being and Essence*, ed. and trans. A. Maurer. Toronto: Pontifical Institute of Medieval Studies.

Thomas Aquinas, Saint (1984). *Questions on the Soul*, trans. J. H. Robb. Milwaukee, Wisc.: Marquette University Press.

Thomasius, Christian (1688). *Institutiones jurisprudentiae divinae*. Frankfurt a.d.O., Leipzig.

Thomasius, Christian (1705). *Fundamenta juris naturæ et gentium ex sensu communi deducta*. Halle and Leipzig.

Thomasius, Christian (1720). *Institutionum jurisprudentiae divinae libri tres*. Halle.

Thomasius, Jacob (1658). *Breviarium ethicorum Aristotelis ad Nicomachum*. Leipzig.

Thorndike, Lynn (1923–58). *A History of Magic and Experimental Science* (8 vols.). New York: Columbia University Press.

Thornton, Mark (1991). 'Same Human Being, Same Person?' *Philosophy*. 66:115–18.

Tierney, B. (1987). 'Villey, Ockham and the Origin of Individual Rights', in John Witte, Jr., and Frank S. Alexander (eds.), *The Weightier Matters of the Law . . . A Tribute to Harold Berman*. Atlanta: Scholar's Press.

Tierney, B. (1988). 'Conciliarism, Corporatism, and Individualism: The Doctrine of Individual Rights in Gerson', *Cristianesimo nella storia*. 9:81–111.

Tierney, B. (1989). 'Origins of Natural Rights Language: Texts and Contexts, 1150–1250', *History of Political Thought*. 10:615–46.

Tierney, B. (1991). 'Marsilius on Rights', *Journal of the History of Ideas*. 52:3–17.

Tillotson, John (1728). *The Works of the Most Reverend Dr. John Tillotson* (3 vols.). London.

Tillotson, John (1748). *The Works of the Most Reverend Dr. John Tillotson* (10 vols.). Edinburgh.

Timpler, Clemens (1604). *Metaphysicae systema methodicum*. Steinfurt.

Timpler, Clemens (1605). *Physica, seu philosophiae naturalis systema methodicum, in tres partes digestum . . . pars prima; complectens empsychologiam*. Hannover.

Timpler, Clemens (1607). *Philosophiae practicae systema methodicum . . . pars prima complectens ethicam generalem. . . .* Hanau.

Tipton, I. C. (1974). *Berkeley, the Philosophy of Immaterialism*. London: Methuen.

Tipton, I. C. (ed.) (1977). *Locke on Human Understanding. Selected Essays*. Oxford: Oxford University Press.

Todhunter, Isaac (1865). *A History of the Mathematical Theory of Probability*. London: Macmillan.

Toland, John (1696). *Christianity Not Mysterious.* London.

Toletus, Franciscus (1573). *Commentaria una cum quaestionibus in octo libros de Physica auscultatione.* Venice.

Toletus, Franciscus (1589). *Commentaria una cum quaestionibus in octo libros de Physica auscultatione.* Venice.

Toletus, Franciscus (1594). *Commentaria una cum quaestionibus in tres libros Aristotelis de anima.* Cologne.

Toletus, Franciscus (1596). *Commentaria una cum quaestionibus universam in Aristotelis Logicam.* Cologne.

Tonelli, Giorgio (1958). 'La tradizione delle categorie aristoteliche nella filosofia moderna sino a Kant', *Studi Urbinati.* 32-B:121–43.

Tonelli, Giorgio (1959). 'La nécessité des lois de la nature au XVIIIᵉ siècle et chez Kant en 1762', *Revue d'histoire des sciences.* 12:225–41.

Tönnies, F. (1925). *Thomas Hobbes. Leben und Lehre.* 3d ed. Stuttgart: Frommann. (1st ed. 1896.)

Topliss, Patricia (1966). *The Rhetoric of Pascal: A Study of His Art of Persuasion in the 'Provinciales' and the Pensées.* Leicester: Leicester University Press.

Torricelli, Evangelista (1644). *De dimensione parabolae, solidique hyperbolici problemata duo.* Florence. In Torricelli 1919–44, vol. 1, pt. I.

Torricelli, Evangelista (1919–44). *Opere di Evangelista Torricelli,* ed. Gino Loria and Giuseppe Vassura (4 vols. in 5). Vols. 1–3, Faenza: G. Montanari, 1919; vol.4, Faenza: Fratelli Lega, 1944.

Torricelli, Evangelista (1956). *Lettere e documenti riguardanti Evangelista Torricelli,* ed. Giuseppe Rossini. Faenza: Fratelli Lega.

Tournemine, René-Joseph de (1703). 'Conjectures sur l'union de l'âme et du corps', and 'Suite des conjectures . . .', *Mémoires pour l'histoire des sciences et des beaux arts (Mémoires de Trévoux)* May 1703:864–75, and June 1703:1063–85.

Traherne, Thomas (1675). *Christian Ethicks.* London.

Traherne, Thomas (1962). *Christian Ethicks* (1675). Published as *The Way to Blessedness,* ed. Margaret Bottrall. London: Faith Press.

Traherne, Thomas (1968). *Christian Ethicks,* ed. C. L. Marks and G. R. Guffey. Ithaca, N.Y.: Cornell University Press.

*Traité des trois imposteurs* (1973), ed. Piere Rétat. Saint-Etienne: Universités de la Région Rhône-Alpes.

*Trattato dei tre impostori. La vita e lo spirito del Signor Benedetto de Spinoza* (1994). French and Italian texts, ed. Silvia Berti. Turin: Einuadi.

Trendelenburg, Adolf (1908).'Zur Geschichte des Wortes Person', *Kant-Studien.* 13:1–17.

Trentman, John A. (1976). 'The Study of Logic and Language in England in the Early Seventeenth Century', *Historiographia Linguistica.* 3:179–201.

Trentman, John A. (1982). 'Scholasticism in the Seventeenth Century', in Kretzmann, Kenny, and Pinborg 1982, pp. 818–37.

Trevor-Roper, Hugh (1967). 'Three Foreigners: The Philosophers of the Puritan Revolution', in *Religion, the Reformation and Social Change.* London: Macmillan.

Trevor-Roper, Hugh (1987a). *Catholics, Anglicans and Puritans. Seventeenth-Century Essays.* Chicago: University of Chicago Press.

Trevor-Roper, Hugh (1987b). 'Nicholas Hill, the English Atomist', in Trevor-Roper 1987a, pp. 1–39.

Trexler, Richard C. (1971). 'Une table florentine d'espérance de vie', *Annales: Economies, Sociétés, Civilisations.* 26:137–9.

*Tribus impostoribus, de* (1960), trans. Rolf Walther, ed. Gerhard Bartsch. Berlin: Akademie Verlag.

Tuck, Richard (1979). *Natural Rights Theories. Their Origin and Development.* Cambridge: Cambridge University Press.

Tuck, Richard (1982). '"The Ancient Law of Freedom": John Selden and the Civil War', in J. Morrill (ed.), *Reactions to the English Civil War 1642–1649,* New York: St. Martin's.

Tuck, Richard (1983). 'Grotius, Carneades, and Hobbes', *Grotiana.* N.s. 4:43–62. (Published by the Grotius Committee of the Royal Netherlands Academy of Arts and Sciences.)

Tuck, Richard (1987a). 'The "Modern" Theory of Natural Law', in Anthony Pagden (ed.), *The Languages of Political Theory in Early-Modern Europe*. Cambridge: Cambridge University Press.

Tuck, Richard (1987b). 'Optics and Sceptics: The Philosophical Foundations of Hobbes' Political Thought', in Edmund Leites (ed.), *Conscience and Casuistry in Early Modern Europe*. Cambridge: Cambridge University Press.

Tuck, Richard (1988). 'Hobbes and Descartes', in G. A. J. Rogers and A. Ryan (eds.), *Perspectives on Thomas Hobbes*. Oxford: Oxford University Press.

Tuck, Richard (1989). *Hobbes*. Oxford: Oxford University Press.

Tuck, Richard (1993). *Philosophy and Government 1572–1651*. Cambridge: Cambridge University Press.

Tuck, Richard (forthcoming). 'Grotius and Pufendorf', in H. E. Bödeker and I. Hont (eds.), *Unsocial Sociability. Natural Law and the Eighteenth-Century Discourse on Society*. London: Routledge.

Tulloch, John (1872). *Rational Theology and Christian Philosophy in England in the Seventeenth Century* (2 vols.). Edinburgh: William Blackwood.

Tully, James (1980). *A Discourse on Property. John Locke and His Adversaries*. Cambridge: Cambridge University Press.

Tully, J[ames] (1988). 'Governing Conduct', in Edmund Leites (ed.), *Conscience and Casuistry in Early Modern Europe*. Cambridge: Cambridge University Press.

Tully, James (1993). *An Approach to Political Philosophy: Locke in Contexts*. Cambridge: Cambridge University Press.

Turbayne, Colin M. (ed.) (1982). *Berkeley: Critical and Interpretive Essays*. Minneapolis: University of Minnesota Press.

Turnbull, G. H. (1947). *Dury, Hartlib, Comenius*. London: University Press of Liverpool.

Turner, John (1685). *A Discourse concerning the Messias . . . To Which is Prefixed a Large Preface, Asserting and Explaining the Doctrine of the Blessed Trinity, against the Late Writer of the Intellectual System*. London.

Turrettini, Jean-Alphonse (1692). *Pyrrhonismus pontificus*. Leiden.

Tuveson, Ernest (1955). 'Locke and the Dissolution of the Ego', *Modern Philology*. 52:155–74.

Tuveson, Ernest (1960). *The Imagination as a Means of Grace: Locke and the Aesthetics of Romanticism*. Berkeley: University of California Press.

Tyrrell, James (1701). *A Brief Disquisition of the Law of Nature, according to the Principles and Method Laid Down in the Reverend Dr. Cumberland's . . . Latin Treatise on that Subject. . . .* Rev. ed. London. (Original ed., London, 1692.)

Urbach, Peter (1987). *Francis Bacon's Philosophy of Science: An Account and a Reappraisal*. La Salle, Ill.: Open Court.

Urmson, J. O. (1967). 'Ideas', in P. Edwards (ed.), *The Encyclopedia of Philosophy*. New York: Macmillan.

Ussher, James (1650–4). *Annales veteris et novi Testamenti*. London.

Uzgalis, William L. (1990). 'Relative Identity and Locke's Principle of Individuation', *History of Philosophy Quarterly*. 7:283–97.

Vailati, Ezio (1985). 'Leibniz's Theory of Personal Identity in the *New Essays*', *Studia Leibnitiana*. 17:36–43.

Vailati, Ezio (1986). 'Leibniz on Necessary and Contingent Predication', *Studia Leibnitiana*. 18:195–210.

Valente, José Angel (1974). *Ensayo sobre Miguel de Molinos*. Barcelona: Barral Editores.

Valla, Lorenzo (1688). *De Linguae Latinae Elegantiae*. Cambridge.

van den Berg, Jan (1989). 'Menasseh ben Israel, Henry More and Johannes Hoornbeeck on the Pre-existence of the Soul', in Y. Kaplan, H. Méchoulan, and R. Popkin, (eds.), *Menasseh ben Israel and His World*. Leiden: Brill.

van der Wall, Ernestine (1987). *De mystieke chiliast Petrus Serrarius (1600–1669) en zijn wereld.* Dordrecht: ICG Printing.

van der Wall, Ernestine (1989). 'Petrus Serrarius and Menasseh ben Israel: Christian Millenarianism and Jewish Messianism in Seventeenth-Century Amsterdam', in Y. Kaplan, H. Méchoulan, and R. Popkin, (eds.), *Menasseh ben Israel and His World.* Leiden: Brill.

Van Egmond, Warren (1985). 'A Catalog of François Viète's Printed and Manuscript Works', in Menso Folkerts und Uta Lindgren (eds.), *Mathemata: Festschrift fur Helmuth Gericke.* Stuttgart: Steiner, pp. 359–96.

Van Helmont, F. M. (1677). *Ad Fundamenta cabbalae aëto-paedo-melissaeae,* in Knorr von Rosenroth 1677.

Van Helmont, F. M. (1682). *A Cabbalistical Dialogue in Answer to the Opinion of a Learned Doctor in Philosophy and Theology,* trans. D. Foote. London.

Van Helmont, F. M. (1685). *The Paradoxal Discourse . . . concerning the Macrocosm and Microcosm.* London.

Vanini, Giulio Cesare (1615). *Amphiteatrum aeternae providentiae.* Lyon.

Vanini, Giulio Cesare (1616). *De admirandis naturae reginae Deaque mortalium arcanis libri IV.* Paris.

Vanini, Giulio Cesare (1990). *Opera,* ed. G. Papuli and F. P. Raimondi (4 vols.). Galatina: Congedo.

Van Leeuwen, Henry G. (1963). *The Problem of Certainty in English Thought 1630–1690.* The Hague: Nijhoff.

Vasoli, Cesare (1968). *La dialettica e la retorica dell'Umanesimo: 'Invenzione' e 'Metodo' nella cultura del XV e XVI secolo.* Milan: Feltrinelli.

Vasoli, Cesare (1974). *Profezia e ragione: Studi sulla cultura del Cinquencento e del Seicento.* Naples: Morano.

Vasquez, Gabriel (1598). *Commentarium ac Disputationum in Iam Partem D. Thomae.* Compluti.

Vasquez, G[abriel] (1598–1617). *Opera Omnia.* Alcalà.

Vasquez, Gabriel (1609). *Commentariorum ac disputationum in Primam Partem S. Thomae tomus primus (secundus), Disputatio CIV* (2 vols.). Ingoldstadt.

Vasquez, G[abriel] (1620). *Commentariorum ac disputationum in Primam Partem s. Thomae tomus primus, Disputatio CIV.* Lyon.

Vaughan, Thomas (1984). *Works,* ed. Alan Rudrum. Oxford: Oxford University Press.

Vaughn, K. I. (1980). *John Locke, Economist and Social Scientist.* Chicago: University of Chicago Press.

Velsten, Heinrich (1620). *Centuria quaestionum ethicarum.* Giessen.

Verbeek, Theo (1988). *La querelle d'Utrecht.* Paris: Les impressions nouvelles.

Verbeek, Theo (1992a). *Descartes and the Dutch: Early Reactions to Cartesianism (1637–1650)* (Journal of the History of Philosophy Monograph Series). Carbondale: Southern Illinois University Press.

Verbeek, Theo (1992b), '"Ens per Accidens": Le origini della Querelle di Utrecht', *Giornale Critico della Filosofia Italiana.* 71:276–88.

Verbeek, Theo (ed.) (1993). *Descartes et Regius: Autour de l'Eplication de l'esprit.* Amsterdam: Rodopi.

Verbeek, Theo (1994). 'Regius's *Fundamenta Physices', Journal of the History of Ideas.* 55:533–51.

Verga, Leonardo (1964). *La filosofia morale di Malebranche.* Milan: Società editrice vita e pensiero.

Vernière, P. (1982). *Spinoza et la pensée française avant la Révolution.* 2d ed. Paris: Presses Universitaires de France.

Vickers, Brian (1979). 'Frances Yates and the Writing of History', *Journal of Modern History.* 51:287–316.

Vickers, Brian (ed.) (1984). *Occult and Scientific Mentalities in the Renaissance.* Cambridge: Cambridge University Press.

Vickers, Brian (1991). 'On the Goal of the Occult Sciences in the Renaissance', in Georg Kauffmann (ed.), *Die Renaissance im Blick der Nationen Europas.* Wiesbaden: Harrassowitz.

Vickers, Brian (1992). 'Critical Reactions to the Occult Sciences during the Renaissance', in E. Ullmann-Margalit (ed.), *The Scientific Enterprise* (Boston Studies in the Philosophy of Science, 146). Dordrecht: Kluwer.

Vidgrain, J. (1923). *Le Christianisme dans la philosophie de Malebranche.* Paris: Alcan.

Viète, François (1600). *Apollonius Gallus.* Paris.

Viète, François (1615). *De aequationum recognitione et emendatione tractatus duo.* Paris.

Viète, François (1646). *Francisci Vietae Opera mathematica,* ed. Frans van Schooten Leiden. (Repr. Hildesheim: Olms, 1970.)

Vilain, Christiane (1993). *Huygens et le mouvement relatif.* Paris. Thesis, Université de Paris VII.

Villey, M. (1975). *La formation de la pensée juridique moderne.* Paris: Montchretien.

Villey, Pierre (1908). *Les sources et l'évolution des Essais de Montaigne.* Paris: Hachette.

Villey, Pierre (1972). *Les Essais de Montaigne.* Paris: Nizet.

Vincent, Le P. Jean (1658–71). *Cursus philosophicus* (5 vols.). Toulouse.

Vincent, Le P. Jean (1660). *Cursus philosophicus.* Toulouse.

Viret, Pierre (1564). *Instruction crestienne en la doctrine de la loy de l'evangile.* . . . Geneva.

Viret, Pierre (1565). *L'interim fait par dialogues.* Lyon.

Vives, Juan Luis (1979). *Against the Pseudodialecticians,* ed. and trans. Rita Guerlac. Dordrecht: Reidel.

Vives, Juan Luis (1990). *The Passions of the Soul. The Third Book of De Anima et Vita,* trans. Carlos G. Norena. Lewiston, N.Y.: Mellen.

Vlastos, Gregory (1975). *Plato's Universe.* Seattle: University of Washington Press.

Vleeschauwer, H. J. de (1937). 'Descartes et Comenius', in *Congrès Descartes: Travaux du IXe Congrès International de Philosophie.* Paris, vol. 2, pp. 109–14.

Vleeschauwer, H. J. de (1938). 'Les Antinomies kantiennes de la Clavis Universalis', *Mind.* 47:303–20.

Vleeschauwer, H. J. de (1953–4). 'Les Antécédents du Transcendentalisme Kantien: Geulincx et Kant', *Kant Studien.* 45:245–73.

Voet, Leon (1969–72). *The Golden Compasses: A History and Evaluation of the Printing and Publishing Activities of the Officiana Plantiniana at Antwerp* (2 vols.). Amsterdam: Van Gend.

Vogel, C. J. de (1963). 'The Concept of Personality in Greek and Christian Thought', *Studies in Philosophy and the History of Philosophy.* 2:20–60.

Vogelsang, Ioannes (1624). *Quaestionum philosophicarum decas una . . . praeside . . . Francone Burgersdicio.* . . . Leiden.

Vollrath, E. (1962). 'Die Gliederung der Metaphysik in eine *Metaphysica generalis* und eine *Metaphysica specialis*', *Zeitschrift für philosophische Forschung.* 16:258–84.

Voltaire, François Marie Arouet de (1785). *Essai sur les probabilités en fait de justice,* in *Oeuvres complètes de Voltaire* (70 vols.). Paris: Société Littéraire-Typographique, vol. 30, pp. 415–49.

Voss, Stephen (ed.) (1993). *Essays on the Philosophy and Science of René Descartes.* New York: Oxford University Press.

Vossius, Dionysius (1641). *R. Mosis Maimonidae De idolatria liber, cum interpretatione Latine et notis Dionysii Vossii.* Amsterdam.

Vossius, Gerardus Joannes (1641). *De theologia gentili et physiologia Christiana, sive de origine ac progressu idolatriae.* Amsterdam.


Waard, Cornelis de (1936). *L'Expérience barométrique: Ses antécédents et ses explications.* Thouars: Imprimerie nouvelle.

Waard, Cornelis de (1953). 'Un Entretien avec Descartes en 1634 ou 1635', *Archives internationales d'Histoire des Sciences.* 6:14–16.

Wachter, Johann Georg (1699). *Der Spinozismus im Jüdenthumb, oder die von dem heutigen Jüdentumb und dessen Geheimen Kabbala vergötterte Welt.* Amsterdam.

Wade, Ira O. (1938). *The Clandestine Organization and Diffusion of Philosophic Ideas in France from 1710–1750.* Princeton, N.J.: Princeton University Press.

Waithe, M. E. (ed.) (1989). *Medieval, Renaissance, and Enlightenment Women Philosophers, a.d. 500–1600* (A History of Women Philosophers). Dordrecht: Kluwer.

Waithe, M. E. (ed.) (1991). *Modern Women Philosophers, 1600–1900* (A History of Women Philosophers). Dordrecht: Kluwer.

Walaeus, Antonius (1620). *Compendium ethicae Aristotelicae ad normam veritatis Christianiae revocatum.* Leiden.

Waldman, Theodore (1959). 'Origins of the Legal Doctrine of Reasonable Doubt', *Journal of the History of Ideas.* 20:299–316.

Walker, Daniel Pickering (1958). *Spiritual and Demonic Magic from Ficino to Campanella.* London: Warburg Institute.

Walker, Daniel Pickering (1964). *The Decline of Hell: Seventeenth-Century Discussion of Eternal Torment.* Chicago: University of Chicago Press.

Walker, Daniel Pickering (1972). *The Ancient Theology: Studies in Christian Platonism from the Fifteenth to the Eighteenth Century.* London: Duckworth.

Walker, Daniel Pickering (1981). *Unclean Spirits: Possession and Exorcism in France and England in the Late Sixteenth and Early Seventeenth Centuries.* Philadelphia: University of Pennsylvania Press.

Walker, Daniel Pickering (1984a). 'Medical Spirits and God and the Soul', in M. Fattori and M. Bianchi (eds.), *Spiritus* (Lessico Intellettuale Europeo: IV° Colloquio Internazionale, Roma, 7–9 gennaio 1983). Rome: Ateneo.

Walker, Daniel Pickering (1984b). 'Valentine Greatrakes, the Irish Stroker and the Question of Miracles', in P.-G. Castex (ed.), *Mélanges sur la littérature de la Renaissance à la mémoire de V. L. Saulnier.* Geneva: Droz.

Walker, Daniel Pickering (1986). *Il concetto di spirito o anima in Henry More e Ralph Cudworth.* Naples: Bibliopolis.

Walker, Nigel (1968). *Crime and Insanity in England.* Vol. 1. Edinburgh: Edinburgh University Press.

Walker, Ralph (1983). 'Gassendi and Scepticism', in Myles Burnyeat (ed.), *The Sceptical Tradition.* Berkeley: University of California Press.

Walkington, Thomas (1639). *The Optick Glass of Humours.* London.

Wallace, William A. (1959). *The Scientific Methodology of Theodoric of Freiburg.* Fribourg: University of Fribourg Press.

Wallace, William A. (1972–4). *Causality and Scientific Explanation* (2 vols.). Ann Arbor: University of Michigan Press.

Wallace, William A. (1981). *Prelude to Galileo: Essays on Medieval and Sixteenth-Century Sources of Galileo's Thought* (Boston Studies in the Philosophy of Science, vol. 62). Dordrecht: Reidel.

Wallace, William A. (1984). *Galileo and His Sources: The Heritage of the Collegio Romano in Galileo's Science.* Princeton, N.J.: Princeton University Press.

Wallace, William A. (1988a). 'Randall *Redivivus*: Galileo and the Paduan Aristotelians', *Journal of the History of Ideas.* 49:133–49.

Wallace, William A. (1988b). 'Traditional Natural Philosophy', in Schmitt, Skinner, and Kessler 1988, pp. 201–35.

Wallace, William A. (1992). *Galileo's Logic of Discovery and Proof: The Background, Content, and Use of His Appropriated Treatises on Aristotle's 'Posterior Analytics'.* Dordrecht: Kluwer.

Wallis, John (1670). *Mechanica, sive de Motu.* London.

Wallis, John (1693–9). *Johannis Wallis S. T.D. . . . Opera Mathematica* (3 vols.). Oxford. (Repr. Hildesheim: Olms, 1972.)

Wallis, John (1729). *Institutio logicae.* Oxford. (1st ed. 1687.)

Walton, Craig (1972). *De la recherche du bien: A Study of Malebranche's Science of Ethics.* The Hague: Nijhoff.

Ward, Richard (1911). *The Life of the Learned and Pious Dr. Henry More.* London: The Theosophical Society.

Ward, Seth (1652). *A Philosophical Essay towards an Eviction of the Being and Attributes of God. The Immortality of the Soule. The Truth and Authority of Scripture.* Oxford.

Warren, Edward (1667). *No Praeexistence. Or a Brief Dissertation against the Hypothesis of Humane Souls, Living in a State Antecedaneous to This.* London.

Warrender, Howard (1957). *The Political Philosophy of Hobbes.* Oxford: Oxford University Press.

Warrender, Howard (1960). 'The Place of God in Hobbes's Philosophy: A Reply to Mr. Plamenatz', *Political Studies.* 8:48–57.

Watkins, J. W. N. (1965). *Hobbes's System of Ideas: A Study in the Political Significance of Philosophical Theories.* London: Hutchinson. (2d ed. 1973.)

Watson, Richard A. (1964). 'A Note on the Probabilistic Physics of Régis', *Archives Internationales d'Histoire des Sciences.* 17:33–6.

Watson, Richard A. (1966). *The Downfall of Cartesianism 1673–1712* (International Archives of the History of Ideas, 2). The Hague: Nijhoff.

Watson, Richard A. (1982). 'Transubstantiation among the Cartesians', in T. M. Lennon, J. M. Nicholas, and J. W. Davis (eds.), *Problems of Cartesianism.* Kingston and Montreal: McGill-Queen's University Press, pp. 127–48.

Watson, Richard A. (1987). *The Breakdown of Cartesian Metaphysics.* Atlantic Highlands, N.J.: Humanities Press.

Watt, Ian (1957). *The Rise of the Novel.* Berkeley: University of California Press.

Watts, Isaac (1726). *Logick: Or, The Right Use of Reason.* 2d ed. London. (Repr. New York: Garland, 1984.)

Wear, Andrew (1985). 'Explorations in Renaissance Writings on the Practice of Medicine', in A. Wear, R. K. French, and I. M. Lonie (eds.), *The Medical Renaissance of the Sixteenth Century.* Cambridge: Cambridge University Press.

Webb, John (1669). *An Historical Essay Endeavoring a Probability That the Language of the Empire of China Is the Primitive Language.* London.

Weber, Jean-Paul (1964). *La constitution du texte des Regulae.* Paris: Société d'édition d'enseignement supérieur.

Weber, Jean-Paul (1972). 'La Méthode de Descartes d'après les Regulae', *Archives de Philosophie.* 35:51–60.

Webster, Charles (1970). *Samuel Hartlib and the Advancement of Learning.* Cambridge: Cambridge University Press.

Webster, Charles (1975). *The Great Instauration: Science, Medicine and Reform, 1626–1660.* London: Duckworth.

Webster, Charles (1983). *From Paracelsus to Newton: Magic and the Making of Modern Science.* Cambridge: Cambridge University Press.

Webster, Charles (1986). 'The Great Instauration: Science, Medicine and Reform 1626–1660', in E. Ullmann-Margalit (ed.), *The Prism of Science.* Dordrecht: Reidel.

Wedeking, Gary (1990). 'Locke on Personal Identity and the Trinity Controversy of the 1690s', *Dialogue.* 29:163–88.

Weeks, Andrew (1991). *Boehme: An Intellectual Biography of the Seventeenth-Century Philosopher and Mystic.* Albany, N.Y.: State University of New York Press.

Weier, Winfried (1981). 'Der Okkasionalismus des Johannes Clauberg und sein Verhältnis zu Descartes, Geulincx, Malebranche', *Studia Cartesiana.* 2:43–62.

Weimann, Karl-Heinz (1978). 'Leibniz und die medizinischen Strömungen seiner Zeit', in *Magia Naturalis 1978.*

Weinberg, Julius R. (1965). 'The Concept of Relation: Some Observations on Its History', in J. R. Weinberg, *Abstraction, Relation, and Induction. Three Essays in the History of Thought*. Madison: University of Wisconsin Press, pp. 61–119.

Weisheipl, James A. (1965a). 'The Concept of Matter in Fourteenth-century Science', in McMullin 1965, pp. 147–69.

Weisheipl, James A. (1965b). 'The Principle *Omne quod movetur ab alio movetur* in Medieval Physics', *Isis*. 56:26–45.

Weisheipl, James A. (1982). 'The Interpretation of Aristotle's Physics and the Science of Motion', in Kretzmann, Kenny, and Pinborg 1982, pp. 521–36.

Wells, N. J. (1981). 'Suarez on the Eternal Truths', *The Modern Schoolman*. 58:73–104, 159–74.

Wells, N. J. (1982). 'Descartes' Uncreated Truths', *The New Scholasticism*. 56:185–99.

Welzel, H. (1958). *Die Naturrechtslehre Samuel Pufendorfs*. Berlin: de Gruyter.

Wenn, H. (1956). *Das Schuldrecht Pufendorfs*. diss., Georg-August-Universität Göttingen.

Werner, Karl (1883). 'Die Cartesisch-Malebranche'sche Philosophie in Italien: M. A. Fardella', *Sitzungsberichte der philosophisch-historischen Klasse der Kaiserlichen Akademie de Wissenschaften*. 102:75–141.

Wernham, A. G. (1965). 'Liberty and Obligation in Hobbes', in K. C. Brown (ed.), *Hobbes Studies*. Oxford: Blackwell.

Wertz, Spencer, and Linda (1975). 'Some Correlations between Swift's Gulliver and Locke on Personal Identity', *Journal of Thought*. 10:262–70.

Westfall, Richard S. (1956). 'Unpublished Boyle Papers Relating to Scientific Method', *Annals of Science*. 12:63–73, 103–17.

Westfall, Richard S. (1958). *Science and Religion in Seventeenth-Century England*. New Haven: Yale University Press.

Westfall, Richard S. (1962). 'The Foundations of Newton's Philosophy of Nature', *British Journal for the History of Science*. 1:171–83.

Westfall, Richard S. (1971a). *The Construction of Modern Science: Mechanisms and Mechanics*. New York: John Wiley.

Westfall, Richard S.(1971b). *Force in Newton's Physics: The Science of Dynamics in the Seventeenth Century*. London: Macdonald.

Westfall, Richard S. (1972). 'Newton and the Hermetic Tradition', in Debus 1972, vol. 1, pp. 183–98.

Westfall, Richard S. (1975). 'The Role of Alchemy in Newton's Career', in M. L. Rhigini Bonelli and William R. Shea (eds.), *Reason, Experiment and Mysticism in the Scientific Revolution*. New York: Science History Publications.

Westfall, Richard S. (1980). *Never at Rest, A Biography of Isaac Newton*. Cambridge: Cambridge University Press.

Westfall, Richard S. (1984). 'Newton and Alchemy', in Vickers 1984, pp. 315–35.

Westman, R. S. (1984). 'Nature, Art and Psyche: Jung, Pauli, and the Kepler-Fludd Polemic', in Vickers 1984.

Westman, Robert S., and McGuire, J. E. (1977). *Hermeticism and the Scientific Revolution. Papers read at a Clark Library Seminar, March 9 1974*. Los Angeles: William Andrews Clark Memorial Library, University of California at Los Angeles.

Whewell, William (1862). *Lectures on the History of Moral Philosophy*. Cambridge and London.

Whichcote, Thomas (1969). *The Use of Reason in Matters of Religion*, in C. A. Patrides (ed.), *The Cambridge Platonists*. Cambridge: Cambridge University Press.

Whitby, Daniel (1684). *Ethices compendium in usum academicae juventutis*. Oxford.

White, Thomas (1642). *De mundo dialogi tres, quibus materia, hoc est, quantitas, numerus, figura, partes, partium qualitas & genera: forma, hoc est, magnorum corporum motus, & motuum intentata hactenus*

*philosophis origo: caussae, hoc est, movens, efficiens, gubernans, caussa finalis, durationis quoque principium &*
*terminus: et tandem definitio, rationibus purè à natura depromptis aperiuntur, concluduntur.* Paris.

White, Thomas (1646). *Institutionum peripateticarum ad mentem . . . Kenelmi equitis Digbaei pars theorica*
. . . Lyon. (Eng. trans, 1656.)

White, Thomas (1651). *An Answer to the Lord Faulklands Discourse of Infallibility,* in Cary (1651).

White, Thomas (1656). *Peripateticall Institutions in the Way of . . . Sir Kenelm Digby: The Theoricall Part.*
London.

White, Thomas (1657). *Euclides physicus, sive de principiis naturae stoecheida. . . .* London.

White, Thomas (1658). *Euclides metaphysicus, sive de principiis sapientiae. . . .* London.

Whiteside, Derek T. (1977). 'From His Claw the Greene Lyon', *Isis.* 68:116–21.

Whitmore, P. J. S. (1967). *The Order of the Minims in Seventeenth-Century France* (International Archives
of the History of Ideas). The Hague: Nijhoff.

Whitmore, P. J. S. (1972). *A Seventeenth-Century Exposure of Superstition: Select Texts of Claude Pithoys*
*(1587–1676)* (International Archives of the History of Ideas). The Hague: Nijhoff.

Widmaier, Rita (1983). *Die Rolle der chinesischen Schrift in Leibniz' Zeichentheorie* (Studia Leibnitiana,
Supplementa 24). Wiesbaden: Steiner.

Wiggins, David (1980). *Sameness and Substance.* Oxford: Blackwell.

Wilenius, Reijo (1963). *The Social and Political Theory of Francisco Suárez.* Helsinki: Societas Philosophicae Fennica.

Wilkins, John (1688). *Essay toward a Real Character and Philosophical Language.* London.

Wilkins, John (1699). *Of the Principles and Duties of Natural Religion.* 4th ed. London.

Willems, Alphonse (1880). *Les Elzevier. Histoire et annales typographiques.* Brussels: G. A. van Trigt.

William of Ockham (1967–86). *Opera theologica* (10 vols.). Saint Bonaventure, N.Y.: Saint Bonaventure
University.

William of Ockham (1990). *Philosophical Writings,* trans. with intro. and notes by Philotheus Boehner;
Latin texts and English trans. revised and new foreword and bibliography by Stephen F. Brown.
Indianapolis, Ind.: Hackett.

William of Sherwood (1968). *Treatise on Syncategorematic Words,* trans. N. Kretzmann. Minneapolis:
University of Minnesota Press.

Williams, Bernard (1973). *Problems of the Self.* Cambridge: Cambridge University Press.

Williams, Bernard (1978). *Descartes: The Project of Pure Enquiry.* Hassock, Sussex: Harvester.

Williams, Bernard (1983). 'Descartes' Use of Scepticism', in Myles Burnyeat (ed.), *The Sceptical*
*Tradition.* Berkeley: University of California Press.

Williams, George H. (1962). *The Radical Reformation.* Philadelphia: Westminster.

Williams, Michael (1986). 'Descartes and the Metaphysics of Doubt', in Rorty 1986a.

Williams, Penry (1986). 'Elizabethan Oxford: State, Church, and University', in J. K. McConica (ed.),
*History of the University of Oxford, vol. 3: The Collegiate University.* Oxford: Oxford University Press,
pp. 397–440.

Williamson, Arthur H. (1979). *Scottish National Consciousness in the Age of James VI: The Apocalypse, the*
*Union and the Shaping of Scotland's National Culture.* Edinburgh: John Donald.

Williamson, Arthur H. (1989). 'The Jewish Dimension of the Scottish Apocalypse: Climate, Covenant
and World Renewal', in Y. Kaplan, H. Méchoulan, and R. Popkin (eds.), *Menasseh ben Israel and His*
*World.* Leiden: Brill.

Wilson, Catherine (1989). *Leibniz's Metaphysics: A Historical and Comparative Study.* Princeton, N.J.:
Princeton University Press.

Wilson, Catherine (1990). 'Visual Surface and Visual Symbol: The Microscope and the Occult in Early
Modern Science', in John Yolton (ed.), *Philosophy, Religion and Science in the Seventeenth and Eighteenth*
*Centuries* (Library of the History of Ideas). Rochester, N.Y.: University of Rochester Press.

Wilson, Margaret (1971). 'Possibility, Propensity, and Chance: Some Doubts about the Hacking Thesis', *Journal of Philosophy*. 68:610–17.

Wilson, Margaret (1976a). 'Leibniz's Dynamics and Contingency in Nature', in P. K. Machamer and R. G. Turnbull (eds.), *Motion and Time, Space and Matter*. Columbus: Ohio State University Press.

Wilson, Margaret (1976b).'Leibniz: Self-Consciousness and Immortality in the Paris Notes and After', *Archiv für Geschichte der Philosophie*. 58:335–52.

Wilson, Margaret (1978). *Descartes* (Arguments of the Philosophers). London: Routledge.

Wilson, Margaret (1979). 'Superadded Properties: The Limits of Mechanism in Locke', *American Philosophical Quarterly*. 16:143–50.

Wilson, Margaret (1980). 'Objects, Ideas, and "Minds": Comments on Spinoza's Theory of Mind', in Richard Kennington (ed.), *The Philosophy of Baruch Spinoza* (Studies in Philosophy and History of Philosophy 7). Washington, D.C.: Catholic University of America.

Wilson, Margaret (1987). 'The Phenomenalism of Leibniz and Berkeley', in E. Sosa (ed.), *Essays on the Philosophy of Berkeley*. Dordrecht: Reidel.

Wilson, Margaret (1990). 'Descartes on the Representationality of Sensation', in J. A. Cover and Mark Kulstad (eds.), *Central Themes in Early Modern Philosophy*. Indianapolis, Ind.: Hackett.

Wilson, Margaret (1991). 'Descartes on the Origin of Sensation', *Philosophical Topics*. 19:293–323.

Winkler, Kenneth P. (1989). *Berkeley: An Interpretation*. Oxford: Oxford University Press.

Winkler, Kenneth P. (1991). 'Locke on Personal Identity', *Journal of the History of Philosophy*. 29:201–26.

Winter, Alois (1986). 'Selbstdenken – Antinomien – Schranken. Zum Einfluss des späten Locke auf die Philosophie Kants', *Aufklärung*. 1:27–66.

Wippel, John F. (1982). 'Essence and Existence', in Kretzmann, Kenny, and Pinborg 1982, pp. 385–410.

Wisan, Winifred L. (1978). 'Galileo's Scientific Method: A Re-examination', in Robert E. Butts and Joseph C. Pitt (eds.), *New Perspectives on Galileo*. Dordrecht: Reidel.

Witelo (1535). *Peri optikes, id est de natura, ratione, & proiectione radiorum uisus, luminum, colorum atque formarum, quam uulgo perspectivam vocant, libri X*. Nuremberg.

Wolf, E. (1963). *Grosse Rechtsdenker der deutschen Geistesgeschichte*. Tübingen: Mohr.

Wolff, Christian (1736). *Philosophia Prima, sive Ontologia. Editio Nova*. Frankfurt and Leipzig. (Repr. Hildesheim: Olms, 1962.)

Wolff, Christian (1751). *Vernünfftige Gedancken von Gott, der Welt und der Seele des Menschen, auch allen Dingen überhaupt*. Halle and Frankfurt. (Repr. Hildesheim: Olms, 1983.)

Wolff, Christian (1985). *Rede über die Praktische Philosophie der Chinesen (Oratio de Sinarum philosophia practica)*, ed. and trans. (German) Michael Albrecht. Hamburg: Meiner.

Wolfson, Harry A. (1929). *Crescas' Critique of Aristotle*. Cambridge, Mass.: Harvard University Press.

Wolfson, Harry A. (1934). *The Philosophy of Spinoza* (2 vols.). Cambridge, Mass.: Harvard University Press.

Wolter, Allan Bernard (1965). 'The Ockhamist Critique', in McMullin 1965, pp. 124–46.

Wolter, Allan Bernard (1990). *The Philosophical Theology of John Duns Scotus*. Ithaca, N.Y.: Cornell University Press.

Wong, D. (1980). 'Leibniz's Theory of Relations', *Philosophical Review*. 89:241–56.

Wood, Anthony (1813–20). *Athenae Oxonienses*, ed. P. Bliss (4 vols.). London.

Woodhouse, C. M. (1986). *George Gemistos Plethon*. Oxford: Oxford University Press.

Woodruff, Paul (1990). 'Plato's Early Theory of Knowledge', in Everson 1990.

Woolhouse, Roger S. (1971). *Locke's Philosophy of Science and Knowledge: A Consideration of Some Aspects of* An Essay concerning Human Understanding. Oxford: Blackwell.

Woolhouse, Roger S. (1982). 'The Nature of an Individual Substance', in Michael Hooker (ed.), *Leibniz: Critical and Interpretive Essays*. Minneapolis: University of Minnesota Press, pp. 45–64.

Woolhouse, Roger S. (1983). *Locke* (Philosophers in Context). Minneapolis: University of Minnesota Press.

Woolhouse, Roger S. (1988). *The Empiricists* (The History of Western Philosophy: 5). Oxford: Oxford University Press.

Woolhouse, Roger S. (1993). *Descartes, Spinoza, Leibniz. The Concept of Substance in Seventeenth-Century Metaphysics.* London. Routledge.

Wootton, D. (1990). 'John Locke: Socinian or Natural Law Theorist?' in J. E. Crimmins (ed.), *Religion, Secularization and Political Thought. Thomas Hobbes to J. S. Mill.* London: Routledge.

Worthington, John (1847–86). *The Diary and Correspondence of Dr. John Worthington,* ed. James Crossley (3 vols.), in *Remains Historical and Literary Connected with the Palatine Counties of Lancaster and Chester,* vols. 13, 36, 64. Manchester.

Wren, Christopher (1750). *Parentalia; Or Memoirs of the Family of the Wrens.* London.

Wright, John (1983). *The Sceptical Realism of David Hume.* Manchester: Manchester University Press.

Wright, Thomas (1604). *The Passions of the Minde in Generall.* London.

Wright, Thomas (1630). *The Passions of the Minde in Generall.* London. (Repr. ed. T. O. Sloan, Urbana: University of Illinois Press, 1971.)

Wrigley, E. A., and Schofield, R. S. (1981). *The Population History of England 1541–1871.* Cambridge, Mass.: Harvard University Press.

Wundt, Max (1939). *Die deutsche Schulmetaphysik des 17. Jahrhunderts.* Tübingen: J. C. B. Mohr.

Yates, Frances (1964). *Giordano Bruno and the Hermetic Tradition.* Chicago: University of Chicago Press.

Yates, Frances (1966). *The Art of Memory.* Chicago: University of Chicago Press.

Yates, Frances (1968). 'The Hermetic Tradition in Renaissance Science', in Charles S. Singleton (ed.), *Art, Science and History in the Renaissance.* Baltimore: Johns Hopkins University Press.

Yates, Frances (1975). *The Rosicrucian Enlightenment.* Frogmore: Paladin.

Yates, Frances (1979). *The Occult Philosophy in the Elizabethan Age.* London: Routledge.

Yolton, John W. (1951). 'Locke's Unpublished Marginal Replies to John Sergeant', *Journal of the History of Ideas.* 12:528–59.

Yolton, John W. (1956). *John Locke and the Way of Ideas.* Oxford: Oxford University Press.

Yolton, John W. (ed.) (1969). *John Locke. Problems and Perspectives. A Collection of New Essays.* Cambridge: Cambridge University Press.

Yolton, John W. (1970). *Locke and the Compass of Human Understanding.* Cambridge: Cambridge University Press.

Yolton, John W. (1971). *John Locke and Education.* New York: Random House.

Yolton, John W. (1975a). 'Ideas and Knowledge in Seventeenth-Century Philosophy', *Journal of the History of Philosophy.* 13:145–65.

Yolton, John W. (1975b). 'On Being Present to the Mind. A Sketch for the History of an Idea'. *Dialogue.* 14:373–88.

Yolton, John W. (1983). *Thinking Matter. Materialism in Eighteenth-Century Britain.* Minneapolis: University of Minnesota Press.

Yolton, John W. (1984). *Perceptual Acquaintance from Descartes to Reid.* Minneapolis: University of Minnesota Press.

Yolton, John W. (1985). *Locke: An Introduction.* Oxford: Blackwell.

Yolton, John W. (ed.) (1990). *Philosophy, Religion and Science in the Seventeenth and Eighteenth Centuries* (Library of the History of Ideas). Rochester, N.Y.: University of Rochester Press.

Yolton, John W. (1991). *Locke and French Materialism.* Oxford: Oxford University Press.

Yost, R. M. (1990). 'Locke's Rejection of Hypotheses about Sub-microscopic Events', in John Yolton (ed.), *Philosophy, Religion and Science in the Seventeenth and Eighteenth Centuries* (Library of the History of Ideas). Rochester, N.Y.: University of Rochester Press.

Young, Robert Fitzgibbon (1971). *Comenius in England.* New York: Arno Press.

Yovel, Y. (1989). *Spinoza and Other Heretics* (2 vols.). Princeton, N.J.: Princeton University Press.

Zabarella, Jacopo (1586). *De naturalis scientiae constitutione.* Venice.

Zabarella, Jacopo (1597). *Opera Logica.* Cologne. (Repr. Hildesheim: Olms, 1966.)

Zabarella, Jacopo (1606). *Commentarii in III. Aristotelis Libros de Anima.* Frankfurt am Main.

Zabarella, Jacopo (1985). *De methodis libri quatuor; Liber de regressu,* ed. Cesare Vasoli. Bologna: CLUEB.

Zagorin, Perez (1992). 'Cudworth and Hobbes on Is and Ought', in R. Kroll et al. (eds.), *Philosophy, Science, and Religion in England 1640–1700.* Cambridge: Cambridge University Press, pp. 128–45.

Zagorin, Perez (1993). 'Hobbes's Early Philosophical Development', *Journal of the History of Ideas.* 54:505–18.

Zambelli, Paola (1960). 'A proposito del *De vanitate scientiarum et artium* di Cornelio Agrippa', *Rivista critica di storia della filosofia.* 28:1271–96.

Zambelli, Paola (1973a). 'Il Problema della magia naturale nel Rinascimento', *Rivista critica di storia della filosofia.* 15:166–80.

Zambelli, Paola (1973b). 'Platone, Ficino e la magia', in E. Hora and E. Kessler (eds.), *Studia humanitatis: Ernesto Grassi zum 70. Geburtstag.* Munich: Fink.

Zambelli, Paola (1976). 'Magic and Radical Reformation in Agrippa of Nettesheim', *Journal of the Warburg and Courtauld Institutes.* 39:69–103.

Zambelli, Paola (1978). 'Aut diabolus aut Achillinus: Fisionomia, astrologia e demonologia nel metodo di un aristotelico', *Rinascimento.* 2d ser. 18:59–86.

Zambelli, Paola (1991). *L'Ambigua natura della magia: Filosofi, streghe, riti nel rinascimento.* Milan: Il Saggiatore.

Zanier, G. (1975). *Ricerche sulla diffusione e fortuna del 'De incantationibus' di Pomponazzi.* Florence: La Nuova Italia.

Zanier, G. (1977). *La medicina astrologica e la sua teoria: Marsilio Ficino e i suoi critici contemporanei.* Rome: Edizioni dell'Ateneo & Bizzarri.

Zarka, Yves-Charles (1988). 'La matière et la représentation: L'expérience dans la philosophie naturelle de Descartes', in Henry Méchoulan (ed.), *Problématique et réception du Discours de la méthode et des Essais.* Paris: Vrin, pp. 81–98.

Zeisold, Johannes (1661). *De Aristotelis . . . cum scriptura sacra consensu, ab eaque apparente dissensu tractatus.* Jena.

Zilsel, Edgar (1942). 'The Genesis of the Concept of Physical Law', *Philosophical Review.* 51:245–79.

Zimara, Marcantonio (1562). *Solutiones contradictionum in dictis Aristotelis, et Averrois super libros Physicorum,* in Averroes 1562–74, vol. 4, pp. 464v–508r.

Zurbuchen, Simone (1991). *Naturrecht und natürliche Religion. Zur Geschichte des Toleranzbegriffs von Samuel Pufendorf bis Jean-Jacques Rousseau.* Würzburg: Königshausen und Neumann.

# INDEX OF NAMES

# INDEX OF SUBJECTS

Aristotelian(ism) (*cont.*)

649–51; and natural philosophy, 425–9; on nature, 850; Oresme's criticisms of, 41; as paradigm of dogmatism, 1157–8; and passions, 1360; Petrarca's criticisms of, 41–2; and physics, 41; Pico's attack on, 44–5; Platonist anti-, 39–41; reactions against, 1007–8; on sensation and essences, 45; on soul, 759–64, 924; theory of passions in, 914, 916–17; varieties of anti-, 47

arithmetic, political, 1131, 1133

Arminianism, 1196, 1221, 1246, 1254–6; Dutch, 1225

*Ars conjectandi* (Jakob Bernoulli), 1109, 1126, 1133–4, 1138

Arsenal of Venice, 705

*Ars magna sciendi, sive combinatoria* (Kircher), 94

*Artis logicae compendium* (Aldrich), 104

*Art of Thinking, The* (Arnauld and Nicole), *see Logique* (Port-Royal)

assent, 1012, 1014, 1016, 1043; grounds of, 1027–8; *see also* affirmation; belief; judgement

assertion, 142–3; and assertive force, 118, 127–9; primary vs. secondary, 127–8

association, principle of, 1019–20

astrology, 65, 426, 455, 469, 486, 1109

astronomy, 665, 964, 1009, 1157; epicyclic, 684; as mixed science, 704

*ataraxia,* 1150, 1157

*Athei detecti* (Hardouin), 324

atheism, 318, 320, 325, 370, 465–6, 1013–14, 1178; classical arguments of, 306; conditions of, 305–8; as epistemological possibility, 305; as unbelief, 306–7

atomism, 58, 339, 341, 348, 428, 433, 456, 472, 484, 553–4, 699, 974–5, 1007, 1157, 1294–6; Aristotelian, 554–6; early conceptions of, 554–65; Epicurean, 569–73; in Gassendi, 569–73; geometrical, 561–3; Greek, 426; and identity, 233–44; *see also* corpuscularianism; mechanism

attribute(s), 186, 192; in Descartes, 658, 767, 803–4; divine, 265–93, in Hobbes, 319; indefinite, 284; in Leibniz, 813; negative, 284; in Spinoza, 228–9, 529, 879, 591–3, 637–8, 778–80, 843–4, 815–18, 1076–8; *see also* essence(s); God, properties of

Augustinianism, 282, 290, 325, 346, 370–3, 1011, 1014–16, 1241, 1288; in Descartes, 1011–14, 1063

*Augustinius* (Jansenius), 1205, 1383

authority: papal, 1036; political, 1037–8; reaction against, 1279; sovereign, 1037–8, 1279, 1319–20, 1333; *see also* faith; fideism

automata, automatism, 847, 928, 948

Averroism, 35, 49, 60, 762; and Averroist controversy, 47–53; on creation, 50

Babel, Tower of, 92–3

*Bartholomew Fair* (Jonson), 1289

*Basilica chymica* (Croll), 463

being, 112, 326; and non-being, 338; objective, 1064–9, 1081–4, 1091–8, *see also* idea(s); intentionality; objective potential, 1065; univocal concept of, 267–8; *see also* categories; entity; existence

belief, 641, 1006, 1024, 1027, 1129; and assent, 1173; common, 284; *doxa* vs. *episteme,* 1108, 1111; erroneous, 1041–9; intensity of, 1130; and passion, 1362; reasons for, 1120; religious, 1031–41; as statistical, 1114; suspension of, 1042–3, 1180; *see also* assent; faith; judgement; opinion; probability

Bernoulli's theorem, 1133–8

Bible, 365–8, 395, 397, 413, 414, 464, 465, 632–3, 775, 1033, 1039, 1287, 1376, 1383, 1390; and biblical criticism, 412–16; credibility of, 1126; interpretation of, 68, 1033–4, 1036–7; Spinoza on, 368–9, 1038–9; Ussher's chronology of, 91–2

*Bibliothèque universelle et historique* (Le Clerc), 30

biology, 536; in Descartes, 764–5; in Digby, 769–70

birthmarks, 476

blindness, 1093, 1096; Molyneux's problem of, 986–8, 1092

blood, 929; Harvey's discovery of circulation of, 72

body, bodies, 353; in Descartes, 224–7, 574–80, 625–37, 765–9, 873–4; existence of external, 624–44, 1146, 1153, 1165, 1177; and extension, 582, 592–602; impenetrability of, 435–6, 578–9, 809; interaction between, 531–6; in Leibniz, 594–602, 781–5, 638–40, 845; in Locke, 608–10, 1159–61; mechanist view of, 553–610; natural, 432–5; natural vs. artificial, 432–3; in Spinoza, 229–31, 591–4, 638, 879, 1077–80; types of, 433; *see also* matter; mechanism; soul (mind) and body

*Bonum nuncium Israeli* (Felgenhauer), 407

brain, 837–8, 980, 982, 983, 1078–9; and mind, 761, 1071–3

*Brevis demonstratio memorabilis erroris Cartesii* (Leibniz), 690

bucket experiment (Newton), 597–8

*Calculation of the Credibility of Human Testimony, A* (anon.), 1125–6

calculus, 698, 703–4, 723; of chances, 1128; conceptual origins of, 731–7; of expectations, 1125; in Leibniz, 141–2, 726, 737–9; of probabilities, 1116, 1122, 1133–4; of real addition, 141–2; in Varignon, 747–9

Calvinism, 318, 458, 1034, 1296, 1377, 1382–3

Cambridge Platonists, 68, 183, 376, 402, 406, 485–6, 776, 784, 796, 808–11, 878, 883, 982–5, 1008, 1291–3, 1343, 1385

*Caractères* (La Bruyère), 1361

Cartesian(ism), 287–80, 336, 346, 353–4, 372, 585–8, 805–11, 825–7, 840, 873–80, 888, 890; and Cartesian circle, 337; and causality, 1211–13; and determinism,

Eucharist, 214, 219, 226–7, 366, 370–1, 378, 436, 1035; *see also* transubstantiation

Europe: languages of, 9–10; population of, 9, 11; and eurocentrism, 98

evidence, 990, 1010, 1021, 1041, 1108, 1125, 1141; circumstantial, 1113; classifications of, 1113; and faith, 1035; hearsay, 1113; in Locke, 1128–9; probability of, 1125–6; and rumor, 1113; *see also* certainty; probability; reason

evil, 331, 858, 1258–9, 1337, 1341

*Examen vanitatis doctrinae gentium* (Pico della Mirandola), 1145

*Exercitationes paradoxicae adversus Aristoteleos* (Gassendi), 57, 457, 469, 963, 967, 1156, 1294

*Exercitia spiritualia* (Loyola), 1381

exhaustion, method of, 733

existence: as individuating, 233–4; and non-existence, 317–18; possible vs. necessary, 314, 316; real, 1160–1, 1174–6; *see also* being

*ex nihilo*, see creation

*ex nihilo nihil fit*, 333–4

Exodus, book of, 281, 284

expectation, 1127, 1133, 1141; in probability theory, 1123–5; as reasonableness, 1125; *see also* probability

explanation, 513–46; in Boyle, 526–8; and cause, 513–14; in Descartes, 522–5; and final causes, 529–31; and forces, 542–6; in later scholasticism, 516–18; mechanistic, 518–22; in natural law tradition, 681–3; and occasional causation, 536–42; Peripatetic, 514–16; problems of, in mechanistic accounts, 531–6; scientific forms of, 680–99; *see also* cause(s)

expression in Leibniz, 1087

extension, 199, 582, 635–6, 805–6, 809, 817, 1009; as attribute of God, 288–91; body and, 582, 592–602; in Descartes, 575, 577–9; as divisible, 290; excluded from mind, 767–9; and *extensio potentiae*, 767; in Gassendi, 572; in Hobbes, 581–4; intelligible, 348, 985–6; vs. intension, 110; in Leibniz, 594–602; material, 348; mathematical conception of, 290; in Spinoza, 591–4, 637–8; and thought, 843–4; three-dimensionality and, 433–5; *see also* body; divisibility; space

faculties (faculty), 767, 917–18, 939, 942, 988–90; appetitive, 962; apprehensive or imaginative, 962; in Aristotelianism, 760, 955–7; in Berkeley, 985; classifications of, 954, 962–3, 966, 971, 984–6; in Cudworth, 983–4; in Descartes, 969–72; in Gassendi, 975–7; in Hobbes, 973–5; intellectual, 962; in Locke, 984–5; in Malebranche, 980–2; in More, 983; in Platonism, 954–5; as powers of mind, 984; in rationalism, 977–82; and scepticism, 961–5; in scholasticism, 954–7; sensitive, 962; in Spinoza, 977–8; of thinking, 1160;

vegetative, 962; *see also* imagination; intellect; memory; senses

faith, 1008, 1010, 1146, 1177, 1180, 1387; and authority, 1036–7; divine, 1031; and reason, 1031–41, 1178, 1181; rule of, 397–8; in Thomas Aquinas, 1031–3; *see also* fideism

Fall, the, 373, 487, 857, 927, 1180, 1334, 1382, 1390; in Malebranche, 373–4

fatalism, 343

Faustus, Marlowe's, 476

feeling, 806

*femmes fortes,* 1378

fermentation, 601

fideism, 367, 397–8, 1117, 1150, 1153, 1180; Protestant, 1033–4

*Filosofia morale, La* (Tesauro), 1282

Flood, the, 91

flower of matter (*flos materiae*), 472, 771, 774, 839–40

fluxions, 723–6

force (*vis*), 652; as active principle, 559; of attraction and of repulsion, 603, 706; centrifugal, 668–9, 717–18, 720; in collision, 667, 670–3; in Descartes, 579–80; and impetus, 651–3, 661–2; laws of, 692; in Leibniz, 535–6, 814; and motion, 708; in Newton, 542–6, 605–6, 720–3; primitive, 783; uniform accelerative, 854; *vis inertiae*, 602–3, 660; *vis radiativa*, 559; *vis viva*, 690–1, 719; *see also* motion(s)

form(s), 179, 213–14, 218, 427, 710, 798; in Aristotelianism, 514–16; 955; in Aristotle, 1005; in Bacon, 154–5; in Hooker, 681–2; incorporeal, 820; Platonic, 955, 961, 1004; seminal, 810; substantial, 430–1, 456–60, 479, 500–2, 683–4, 686, 762–3, 765, 781, 799, 850, 855; substantial vs. accidental, 183; *see also* hylemorphism; matter

formal reality, *see* reality

fortune, 1115–16; good and bad, 1140

foundations of knowledge, 1003, 1012; in Descartes, 1166; and foundationalism, 337, 1041; scholastic, 1166; *see also* epistemology

Franciscanism, 35–6, 50

*Free and Impartial Censure of the Platonick Philosophie* (Parker), 1292

freedom, 883, 892, 1195–1270, 1337; and anticompatibilism, 1237–9; and compatibilism, 1206–7, 1215–16, 1266; defined, 1207, 1245; in Descartes, 1206–16; and free will, 1031, 1097–1201, 1318; in Hobbes, 1216–26; and *homo liber,* 1232; and incompatibilism, 1195–6; in Leibniz, 1256–69; and libertarianism, 1195–6, 1206, 1249, 1259; in Locke, 1244–56; in Malebranche, 1236–44; in Spinoza, 1226–36; in Thomism, 1196–9; *see also* determinism; fatalism; free will; will

free-thinkers, 466